ESSENTIALS OF

CONTEMPORARY

BUSINESS

LAW

HENRY R. CHEESEMAN

Clinical Professor of Business Law
Director of the Legal Studies Program
School of Business
University of Southern California

Prentice Hall, Upper Saddle River, New Jersey 07458

Acquisitions Editor: Donald J. Hull
Editorial Assistant: Paula D'Introno
Editor-in-Chief: Natalie Anderson
Marketing Manager: Tamara Wederbrand
Assistant Editor: Kristen Imperatore
Production Editor: Cindy Spreder
Managing Editor: Dee Josephson
Manufacturing Buyer: Diane Peirano
Manufacturing Supervisor: Arnold Vila
Manufacturing Manager: Vincent Scelta
Design Manager: Patricia Smythe
Interior Design: Robin Hoffman
Cover Design: Robin Hoffman
Composition: UG Production Services

Library of Congress Cataloging-in-Publication Data

Cheeseman, Henry R.
    Essentials of contemporary business law / Henry R. Cheeseman. —
1st ed.
     p.   cm.
    Includes bibliographical references and index.
    ISBN 0-13-080400-2
    1. Business law—United States—Cases.   I. Title.
KF888.C463   1998
346.7307—dc21   98-21985
                                                      CIP

Prentice-Hall International (UK) Limited, London
Prentice-Hall of Australia Pty. Limited, Sydney
Prentice-Hall Canada, Inc., Toronto
Prentice-Hall Hispanoamericana, S.A., Mexico
Prentice-Hall of India Private Limited, New Delhi
Prentice-Hall of Japan, Inc., Tokyo
Prentice-Hall Asia Pte. Ltd., Singapore
Editora Prentice-Hall do Brasil, Ltda., Rio de Janeiro

Printed in the United States of America

10 9 8 7

KANG SHOU-YI

When in love's embrace,

cry like drops of water
running down a window
during a spring rain,

shine with the brilliance
of the Northern Lights on a
dark summer night,

shake like the leaves
on a maple tree
in an autumn gale,

scream like the east wind
rushing to shore
during winter's grip,

and when the storm is over,
rest in my arms
like a newborn sand dune.

CONTENTS IN BRIEF

CONTENTS

CONTENTS

PREFACE

Essentials of Contemporary Business Law (Essentials) is the newest of my books published by Prentice Hall for the Legal Studies in Business market. Each title is designed for a specific market segment of students and professors. *Essentials* provides complete coverage of business law topics and addresses the legal environment in which business must operate. *Essentials* does this in a briefer format. Because the study of the legal environment of business is as much a study of history, ethics, social responsibility, policy, diversity, and economics as it is a study of the laws themselves, I have integrated these issues into my presentation of business law topics. Over 100 enrichment boxes throughout the book focus on contemporary, ethical, and international issues. Every case ends with questions about the ethical and business implications of the issue before the court. In addition, more space is devoted to the fundamental concepts of ethics, environmental, government regulation, and international topics than in other books, allowing this text to meet the AACSB's standards on ethics and globalization in the curriculum.

Sine Leges Nulla Libertas ("There is no freedom without law.")

Focuses of the Book

The Legal Environment of Business

This book first presents topics used in traditional business law courses. Unit one contains six chapters that introduce the student to the "legal environment of business." The first chapter discusses American legal heritage and constitutional law. Chapter 2 is a separate chapter on "Ethics and Social Responsibility of Business." Chapter 3 discusses the litigation process, and alternative dispute resolution.

Chapter 4 covers traditional tort law, including intentional torts, negligence, and strict liability. Chapter 5 covers intellectual property rights laws and telecommunications law. Chapter 6 covers crimes, including white collar and business crimes.

Unit two contains six chapters that cover the common law of contracts. This is traditional contract law, modernized with recent cases.

Unit three, "Commercial Transactions," includes eight chapters. The primary focus of this unit is the Uniform Commercial Code (UCC). Two chapters focus on sales and lease contracts, one on warranty and product liability law, and three on negotiable instruments, checks, and the banking system. The final two chapters of this unit discuss secured transactions, lender liability, credit, and bankruptcy.

Unit four, "Business Organizations," begins with a chapter on agency and employment law, then chapter 2 discusses sole proprietorships and franchises. The third chapter covers partnerships, both general and limited, and limited liability companies. The next four chapters cover the formation and financing of corporations, rights and liability of corporate officers and directors, mergers and acquisitions, and the issuance of securities by corporations and other businesses.

Unit five, "Property," is a three-chapter unit that includes chapters on personal property and bailments, real property and landlord-tenant relationships, and a chapter on insurance, wills, and trusts.

From these materials a professor can design a business law course that fits the needs of the school and students.

Ethics and Social Responsibility

Ethics is integrated throughout the book in three ways: (1) by discussing ethics frequently in the text itself, (2) by asking ethics questions after every case, and (3) by including special "Ethical Perspective" boxes in all chapters. Chapter 2 is devoted exclusively to ethics and social responsibility of business. Moral theories of Kant and other philosophers are discussed and applied to actual cases.

The ethics boxes set forth the facts of real court cases and ask the reader to consider the ethical issues raised in the case. This is the format of *applied ethics*—asking

xvii

probing ethics questions pertaining to real business situations, rather than using hypothetical cases. For example, in "Breast Implant Litigation" (p. 339), students are asked to apply their understanding of *equity* to a dispute over product liability. The answer requires students to consider the bounds of fairness in a particular situation.

Contemporary Business Law

One of the primary goals of this book is to review *contemporary* business law concepts and topics. This is done by presenting modern statutory and regulatory law and recent court decisions in (1) the cases and (2) the Contemporary Business Environment boxes. The choice of cases balances contemporary cases against more traditional cases usually taught to illustrate specific concepts. The Contemporary Business Environment boxes highlight modern legal issues faced by business and also indicate how the law evolves as new business-related issues arise. For example, "E-mail Messages Used as Evidence" (p. 62) describes how e-mail has become a source of evidence in both criminal and civil trials. There is at least one Contemporary Business Environment box in every chapter.

International Law

Because of the importance placed on international issues in today's business education, I thoroughly integrate international issues into the presentation in several ways.

First, the major legal systems of the world are discussed in chapter 1.

Second, chapter 3 introduces international law, courts, and organizations. This chapter also discusses the U.S. government's role in foreign affairs, sources of international law, and how international business disputes are resolved.

Third, every chapter has at least one International Perspective box. These boxes focus on specific international issues relevant to the chapter. For example, the intellectual property rights chapter—chapter 5—includes the International Perspective box "International Protection of Intellectual Property Rights" (p. 120).

Business Application

Many of today's Business Law and Legal Environment textbooks take a too "legalistic" approach to presenting legal topics to business students. This book recognizes that what is important to business students is the *application* of court decisions, statutes, and government regulation to business. I have included two features in this book that clearly demonstrate the application of law and government regulation to the business environment.

The first is a special Business Application box. In these boxes I have taken a modern business law topic and shown how it affects business and business managers and owners. For example, the box entitled "Dow Corning Files for Bankruptcy" (p. 482) discusses how excess liability exposure led a company to declare bankruptcy. Almost every chapter features a Business Application Box.

The second feature is the Business Checklist box that appears in each chapter. These boxes are designed to show business people the laws and regulations they should consider when making a business decision and the steps to take to comply with the law. For example, the box entitled "Why Operate a Business as a Limited Liability Company (LLC)?" (p. 568) discusses the benefits and detriments of using this new form of business entity.

These two features further enhance this book's underlying pedagogy of showing students how the law affects business and business decision-making.

Development of the Text

Our goal in developing this text has been to provide professors and students with the kind of text that gives the clearest, most relevant explanation of the fundamental principles of business law and legal environment of business. At the same time we have attempted to convey the fascinating interplay of ethical, social, environmental, and global issues with emerging trends in law.

To ensure that the text's 30 chapters are accurate and up to date, Prentice Hall arranged for reviewers to read the chapters in the manuscript stage. The reviewers made numerous helpful suggestions that I believe have improved the text substantially and enable *Essentials* to meet its educational goal.

Marsha Leest developed all of my previous books. Although Marsha's role was indirect in developing *Essentials*, her influence can be seen on all its pages.

Pedagogical Features

Cases

Cases are the examples in a business law course. They show how the abstractions of the law are actually applied to disputes. For students, cases must clearly illustrate points of law. For professors, cases can be the basis of student exercises that involve the student in the thought process behind the rules of law. In this book and in the supplements that accompany it, Prentice Hall and I have kept these two goals in mind. The 108 (approximately) cases clearly identify the issues under question, yet retain the voice of the court in the opinions. Each case provides (1) the facts, (2) the issue, (3) the decision, (4) the opinion, and (5) case questions that explore the critical legal thinking, ethical, and business implications of the case.

Exhibits

Because the law has its own forms and documents that are perhaps foreign to the student, this book includes many illustrations of these items. For example, on p. 673 there is a tombstone advertisement from when the Walt Disney Company sold its debt securities. Most of the exhibits are available to the instructor in the Transparency Masters supplement.

Chapter Summaries

At the end of each chapter, students will find a detailed, well-organized chapter summary that reviews the important topics covered in each chapter. The chapter summaries contain page references that refer students to the appropriate page in the text if they wish to review the topic in detail.

Student Annotations

Students will find the notes placed in the margins helpful as they study each chapter. These annotations encourage students to consider important aspects of the topics they are reading—to expand their understanding of the topic and to give study advice. The types of annotations include

- **Caution:** Notes that alert the reader to a possible misapplication or misperception of the law
- **Note:** Dates, places, and people important to business law
- **Business Brief:** Applications that are specific to the functioning of a business

In addition, a **running glossary** in the margins helps students learn key terms.

Critical Legal Thinking Cases

Each chapter presents approximately 10 **Critical Legal Thinking Cases** drawn from real-life cases whose facts and situations have been edited and written to test the application of the legal concepts and principles developed in the chapter. These questions can be used for class discussion or as homework assignments. The answers to these questions appear in the *Instructor's Resource Manual*.

Critical Legal Thinking Writing Assignments

Each chapter ends with a suggested **Critical Legal Thinking Writing Assignment** for the student. The name of the case and the questions the students are to address appear at the end of each chapter. The actual writing assignment cases themselves—which are in the court's language—appear in Appendix A and are numbered by chapter. For example, Case A.1 is the writing assignment case for chapter 1. These writing assignments are designed to teach the student to write better and to apply *critical legal thinking*. The student is to brief the case and answer the questions posed.

These writing assignments are optional and may be assigned at the discretion of individual professors. They can be used as homework assignments, group projects, additional cases to cover in class discussions, test questions, or otherwise.

Working the Web

The Internet has become an important and valuable tool in education. Applications have developed over the last few years in education that put more information in the hands of professors and students than at any other time in our history. *Essentials* includes Internet materials in the text itself and in the supplements package (more on that later in the preface). Each chapter of the text has a Working the Web section. Working the Web contains URLs and descriptive information about the Web sites. All of the Web sites selected are relevant to the particular chapter. Five or six exercises are also included so that students have the opportunity to apply some of what was learned by exploring the Web sites. These exercises can be used for in–class or homework assignments.

Supplements

In addition to the text itself, we have assembled a full and dynamic supplements package that is designed to streamline the course preparation and administrative process for instructors and enrich the student's experience and exposure to the ideas and implications of the law for business. The supplements include both traditional print and media components. Contact your Prentice Hall sales representative for examination or desk copies.

TotaLaw

One thing that you will notice right away is that there is a CD ROM automatically packaged with each copy of *Essentials*. Prentice Hall is the first college publisher to include a CD ROM with every copy of the text for a business law or legal environment of business text. TotaLaw is a comprehensive CD ROM that includes the complete text of 30 of the most important and relevant acts that have made an impact on the business world. A feature is built in that allows the user to search by keywords. Textbooks have traditionally included appendixes that contain the Constitution, the Uniform Commercial Code, and other important materials, but have always been limited by the amount of space (paper) that this information takes up. TotaLaw is a much deeper resource and will be more fun for the students to use. Perhaps best of all is that TotaLaw is free with each new copy purchased! TotaLaw is easy to load and to use, but feel free to contact your Prentice Hall sales representative for a personal demonstration.

Custom Video Series

Starting this fall Prentice Hall will be releasing customized videos that illustrate the important relationship between business, management, and law. The first five videos in a series of fifteen will be available to adopters of *Essentials*. These videos have been carefully planned and developed by a partnership including Prentice Hall Business Publishing's Senior Editor Don Hull, Peter Shedd of the University of Georgia and Prentice Hall's Consulting Editor in Legal Studies in Business, and DWJ-TV of Ridgewood, New Jersey. The goal of these videos is to illustrate business law/legal environment concepts in a realistic business setting. The entire series of videos revolves around the activities of a single company and its employees, suppliers, and other associates. Each video is about 10 minutes in length so that they can be easily incorporated in the classroom.

Prentice Hall Custom Video Series for Legal Studies in Business

1. Litigation Process & Alternative Dispute Resolution*

2. Constitutional Authority to Regulate Business

---

* Video available fall 1998.

3. Torts
4. Ethics in the Legal Environment of Business
5. Contracts: Offer & Acceptance*
6. Contracts: Third Party Rights
7. Sale of Goods
8. Product Liability*
9. Suretyship
10. Agency*
11. Formation/Dissolution of Business Partnership
12. Securities Regulation
13. Employment Discrimination*
14. Labor Relations
15. Anti–Trust/Price Discrimination

PHLIP—Web Site Support
www.phlip.marist.edu or *www.prenhall.com/phbusiness*

Prentice Hall's Learning on the Internet Partnership (PHLIP) 1999 is the only Internet resource you need. PHLIP supports both faculty and students with a variety of components such as Faculty Lounge, Talk to the Tutor, or current event articles formatted and linked to the book. Rick Kunkel of the University of St. Thomas serves as Prentice Hall's content expert for PHLIP.

Lexis

Prentice Hall has renewed its business relationship with Lexis-Nexis and will provide professors who adopt *Essentials* with 10 free hours of Lexis, the legal, on–line database service used by law professionals. This offer is valid each semester the text is in use and applies to adoptions where new books are purchased. You can get the ball rolling on your free Lexis account by contacting your local Prentice Hall sales representative.

Instructor's Manual

Nancy Neslund of Nazareth College in Rochester, New York has prepared this important supplement. The Instructor's Manual is designed to streamline and assist in class preparation time. It includes a substantial amount of material and ideas that full-time and adjunct professors will find useful.

Study Guide

Nan Ellis of Loyola College in Maryland has prepared the Study Guide. It contains sample multiple choice; fill-in and essay questions so the students can test their knowledge of the subject and better prepare for exams.

Test Bank and Prentice Hall Custom Test

Rhonda Carlson of The Last Word and Denver University Law School has written the test questions that appear in both the written test bank and the computer test bank, PH Custom Test. PH Custom Test is available for Windows in 3.5 disk format. A variety of questions are available so that professors can construct effective examinations.

PowerPoint Slides

Jimidene Murphey and Leila Lake of South Plains College, Texas, have prepared the PowerPoint presentation slides. There are approximately 10 slides per chapter. The graphics can be used as part of a classroom computer presentation or printed out to make traditional overhead transparencies.

Prentice Hall/*New York Times*—Themes of *The Times*

Once again Prentice Hall and *The New York Times* are providing exclusive newspaper supplements free to adopters and their students. This supplement contains articles from the business section of *The New York Times* specifically related to business law/legal environment of business. These newspapers are free and updated twice each year. Prentice Hall provides them free of charge for students enrolled in the course.

---

* Video available fall 1998.

College Newslink

Link up to world news everyday! Visit *www.ssnewslink.com* for a free trial. College Newslink is a service that provides information about business law/legal environment of business from over 80 newspapers a day. Illustrate the concepts of your course with fresh business examples each day. College Newslink is a unique educational service that brings today's news from the leading newspapers of the world to your computer via e-mail. Again, visit *www.ssnewslink.com* for an introduction and trial.

Surfing for Success in Legal Studies

This free book is a student's guide to the Internet. It includes general information about the Internet and specific information about the Internet and the field of legal studies in business. Alan C. Roline and Rajiv Vaidyanathan of the University of Minnesota-Duluth have once again expertly prepared this very popular guide. It is available free of charge packaged with new copies of *Essentials*.

Beginning Your Career Search

This booklet is also free of charge when packaged with new copies of *Essentials*. It is a basic introduction and student guide for preparing employment communication. *Beginning Your Career Search* has been prepared by James S. O'Rourke IV of the College of Business Administration, University of Notre Dame.

Acknowledgments

When I first began writing this book, I was a solitary figure researching cases in the law library and writing text at my desk. As time passed, others entered the scene, touched the project and made it better. Although my name appears on the cover of this book, it is no longer mine alone. I humbly thank the following persons for their contributions:

- The publishing professionals at Prentice Hall Business Publishing have proven again that they are by far the best in the business. I would like to thank and acknowledge each of the following for their contribution to this project.
- Don Hull, senior editor (Don has worked on every text that I have written at Prentice Hall); Sandy Steiner, president, Business Publishing Division; James Boyd, editorial director; Natalie Anderson, editor-in-chief; Steve Deitmer, director of development; Paula D'Introno, editorial assistant; Tami Wederbrand, marketing manager; Joanne Jay, AVP and director of production and manufacturing; Dee Josephson, managing editor; Cindy Spreder, production editor; Pat Smythe, design director; Vincent Scelta, manufacturing manager; Arnold Vila, manufacturing supervisor; and Diane Peirano, manufacturing buyer.
- The following reviewers, whose comments, suggestions, and criticisms are seen in the final product: Susan J. Mitchell, Des Moines Area Community College; John McGee, Southwest Texas State University; Trudi Manuel, Aims Community College; John Eichelberger, Hillsborough Community College; Claude W. Dotson, Northwest College.
- The following research assistants: Trent Anderson and Williana Chang, the University of Southern California Law Center.
- My family: Henry B., Florence, Gregory, and Marcia Cheeseman.
- And thanks to Spinner for his companionship during this time; and to Los Angeles, California, and Mackinac Island, Michigan, where most of this book was written.

While writing this preface, I have thought about the thousands of hours I have spent researching, writing, and preparing this manuscript. I loved every minute, and the knowledge gained has been sufficient reward for the endeavor.

With joy and sadness, emptiness and fullness, honor and humility,
I surrender the fruits of this labor.

Henry R. Cheeseman
Summer 1998

ESSENTIALS OF

CONTEMPORARY

BUSINESS

LAW

CHAPTER 1

CRITICAL LEGAL THINKING

AND THE U.S. CONSTITUTION

Chapter Objectives

*After studying this chapter,
you should be able to*

1. Define *law*
2. List and describe the functions of law
3. Explain the development of the U.S. legal system
4. List and describe the sources of law in the United States
5. Describe the concept of federalism and the doctrine of separation of powers
6. Define and apply the Supremacy Clause of the U.S. Constitution
7. Explain the federal government's authority to regulate interstate and foreign commerce under the Commerce Clause
8. Explain state and local governments' authority to regulate commerce under their "police power"
9. Describe how commercial speech may be regulated by proper time, place, and manner restrictions
10. Apply critical legal thinking in analyzing judicial decisions

Chapter Contents

"Let every American, every lover of liberty, every well-wisher to his posterity, swear by the blood of the Revolution never to violate in the least particular the laws of the country, and never to tolerate their violation by others."

Abraham Lincoln
Speech
January 27, 1837

Every society makes and enforces laws that govern the conduct of the individuals, businesses, and other organizations that function within it. In the words of Judge Learned Hand, "Without law we cannot live; only with it can we insure the future which by right is ours. The best of men's hopes are enmeshed in its success."[1]

Although the law of this country is primarily based on English common law, other legal systems, such as Spanish and French civil law, also influenced it. The sources of law in this country are the U.S. Constitution, state constitutions, federal and state statutes, ordinances, administrative agency rules and regulations, executive orders, and judicial decisions by federal and state courts.

The U.S. Constitution establishes the basic framework of the federal government and creates many of the rights we enjoy as citizens. The Constitution grants power to the federal government to regulate business. The states also have the power to regulate certain aspects of businesses. In addition, businesses are subject to the laws of other countries in which they operate.

This chapter discusses the history and sources of law in this country, constitutional rights and proscriptions, and the constitutional authority of government to regulate business.

WHAT IS LAW?

"Two things most people should never see made: sausages and laws."
An Old Saying

The law consists of rules that regulate the conduct of individuals, businesses, and other organizations within society. It is intended to protect persons and their property from unwanted interference from others. In other words, the law forbids persons from engaging in certain undesirable activities. Consider the following passages:[2]

> Hardly anyone living in a civilized society has not at some time been told to do something, or to refrain from doing something, because there is a law requiring it, or because it is against the law. What do we mean when we say such things? Most generally, how are we to under-stand statements of the form "*x* is law"? This is an ancient question. In his *Memorabilia* (I,ii), Xenophon reports a statement of the young Alcibiades, companion of Socrates, who in con-versation with the great Pericles remarked that "no one can really deserve praise unless he knows what a law is."
>
> At the end of the 18th century, Immanuel Kant wrote of the question "What is law?" that it "may be said to be about as embarrassing to the jurist as the well-known question 'What is truth?' is to the logician."

Definition of Law

law   "That which must be obeyed and followed by citizens subject to sanctions or legal consequences; a body of rules of action or conduct prescribed by controlling authority, and having binding legal force." (*Black's Law Dictionary*)

The concept of **law** is very broad. Although it is difficult to state a precise definition, *Black's Law Dictionary*[3] gives one that is sufficient for this text:

> Law, in its generic sense, is a body of rules of action or conduct prescribed by controlling au-thority, and having binding legal force. That which must be obeyed and followed by citizens subject to sanctions or legal consequences is a law.

Functions of the Law

The law is often described by the functions it serves within a society. The primary *functions* served by the law in this country are as follows:

1. Keeping the peace, which includes making certain activities crimes;
2. Shaping moral standards (e.g., enacting laws that discourage drug and alcohol abuse);

3. Promoting social justice (e.g., enacting statutes that prohibit discrimination in employment);
4. Maintaining the status quo (e.g., passing laws preventing the forceful overthrow of the government);
5. Facilitating orderly change (e.g., passing statutes only after considerable study, debate, and public input);
6. Facilitating planning (e.g., well-designed commercial laws allow businesses to plan their activities, allocate their productive resources, and assess the risks they take);
7. Providing a basis for compromise (approximately 90 percent of all lawsuits are settled prior to trial); and
8. Maximizing individual freedom (e.g., the rights of freedom of speech, religion, and association granted by the First Amendment to the U.S. Constitution).

Flexibility of the Law

One of the main attributes of American law is its *flexibility*—that is, its responsiveness to cultural, technological, economic, and social changes. For example, laws that are no longer viable—such as those that restricted the property rights of women—are often repealed.

Sometimes it takes years before the law reflects the norms of society. Other times, society is led by the law. The Supreme Court's landmark decision in *Brown v. Board of Education*[4] is an example of the law leading the people. The Court's decision overturned the old "separate but equal" doctrine that condoned separate schools for black children and white children.

U.S. law evolves and changes along with the norms of society, technology, and the growth and expansion of commerce in the United States and the world. The following quote discusses the value of the adaptability of law:

> The law always has been, is now, and will ever continue to be, largely vague and variable. And how could this be otherwise? The law deals with human relations in their most complicated aspects. The whole confused, shifting helter-skelter of life parades before it—more confused than ever, in our kaleidoscopic age.
>
> Men have never been able to construct a comprehensive, eternalized, set of rules anticipating all possible legal disputes and formulating in advance the rules which would apply to them. Situations are bound to occur which were never contemplated when the original rules were made. How much less is such a frozen legal system possible in modern times?
>
> The constant development of unprecedented problems requires a legal system capable of fluidity and pliancy. Our society would be straightjacketed were not the courts, with the able assistance of the lawyers, constantly overhauling the law and adapting it to the realities of ever-changing social, industrial, and political conditions; although changes cannot be made lightly, yet rules of law must be more or less impermanent, experimental and therefore not nicely calculable.
>
> Much of the uncertainty of law is not an unfortunate accident; it is of immense social value.[5]

Fairness of the Law

On the whole, the American legal system is one of the most comprehensive, fair, and democratic systems of law ever developed and enforced. Nevertheless, some misuses and oversights of our legal system—including abuses of discretion and mistakes by judges and juries, unequal applications of the law, and procedural mishaps—allow some guilty parties to go unpunished.

In *Standefer v. United States*,[6] the Supreme Court affirmed the criminal conviction of a Gulf Oil Corporation executive for aiding and abetting the bribery of an Internal Revenue Service agent. The agent had been acquitted in a separate trial. In writing the opinion of the Court, Chief Justice Burger stated, "This case does no more than manifest the simple, if discomforting, reality that different juries may reach different results under any criminal statute. That is one of the consequences we accept under our jury system."

"Where there is no law, there is no freedom."
John Locke
Second Treatise of Government, Sec. 57

"The Law, in its majestic equality, forbids the rich as well as the poor to sleep under bridges."
Anatole France

LANDMARK DECISION
In Brown v. Board of Education, *the U.S. Supreme Court overturned precedent and held that providing separate schools for black children and white children was unconstitutional.*

BUSINESS BRIEF
Laws cannot be written in advance to anticipate every dispute that could arise in the future. Therefore, general principles *are developed to be applied by courts and juries to individual disputes. This flexibility in the law leads to some uncertainty in predicting results of lawsuits.*

CAUTION
Sometimes the law, because of error or misuse, does not reach a fair result.

CONTEMPORARY BUSINESS ENVIRONMENT

Feminist Legal Theory

In the past, the law treated men and women unequally. For example, women were denied the right to vote, could not own property if they were married, were unable to have legal abortions, and could not hold the same jobs as men. The enactment of statutes, the interpretation of constitutional provisions, and the courts have changed all of these things. The Nineteenth Amendment gave women the right to vote. States have repealed constraints on the ability of women to own property. The famous U.S. Supreme Court decision in *Roe v. Wade*, 410 U.S. 959 (1973), gave women the constitutional right to an abortion.

Title VII of the Civil Rights Act of 1964 prohibits employment discrimination based on sex. In addition, the equal protection clause of the U.S. and state constitutions provides that women cannot be treated differently than men (and vice versa) by the government unless some imperative reason warrants different treatment.

But is it enough for women to be treated like men? Should the female perspective be taken into account when legislators and judges develop, interpret, and apply the law? A growing body of scholarship known as **feminist legal theory**, or **feminist ju-**risprudence, is being created around just such a theory.

The so-called "battered woman's syndrome" illustrates how this type of theory works. It has been introduced into evidence to prove self-defense in homicide cases in which a woman is accused of killing her husband or another male. This defense asserts that sustained domestic violence against a woman might justify such a murder. Although rejected by many courts, some courts have recognized the battered woman's syndrome as a justifiable defense.

Some other areas of the law where a woman's perspective might differ from a man's include male-only combat rules in the military, rights to privacy, family law, child custody, surrogate motherhood, job security for pregnant women, rape, sexual assault, abortion, and sexual harassment.

Even the traditional "reasonable man standard," so prevalent in American law, is being attacked as being gender-biased. The supporters of this theory argue that merely renaming it the "reasonable person theory" is not enough. They assert that women will be judged by the reasonable actions expected of men until this standard is redefined to take into account females' unique values.

This view seems to be gaining ground. For instance, in a recent sexual harassment case, the court recognized that a "reasonable woman standard" should be used to determine whether a male's conduct toward a female co-employee violated Title VII. The court stated, "We prefer to analyze harassment from the victim's perspective. A complete understanding of the victim's view requires, among other things, an analysis of the different perspectives of men and women. Conduct that many men consider unobjectionable may offend many women" [*Ellison v. Brady*, 924 F.2d 872 (9th Cir. 1991)].

One of the major disappointments to the feminist legal movement was the defeat of the Equal Rights Amendment in 1981. This proposed constitutional amendment, which would have forbidden the denial of rights based on sex, was not ratified by the number of states needed for approval.

Critics of feminist legal theory argue that existing laws adequately protect the equal rights of females in society. Feminist legal theorists counter that justice for women will remain elusive until the female perspective is recognized by the law.

SCHOOLS OF JURISPRUDENTIAL THOUGHT

jurisprudence The philosophy or science of law.

The study of law is referred to as **jurisprudence**. There are several different philosophies about how the law developed. They range from the classical natural theory to modern theories of law and economics and critical legal studies. Legal philosophers can generally be grouped into the major categories discussed in the sections that follow.

The Natural Law School

The **Natural Law School** of jurisprudence postulates that the law is based on what is "correct." Natural Law philosophers emphasize a **moral theory of law**—that is, law should be based on morality and ethics. Natural law is "discovered" by man through the use of reason and choosing between good and evil. Documents such as the U.S. Constitution, the Magna Carta, and the United Nations Charter reflect this theory.

The Historical School   The **Historical School** of jurisprudence believes that the law is an aggregate of social traditions and customs that have developed over the centuries. It believes that changes in the norms of society will gradually be reflected in the law. To these legal philosophers, the law is an evolutionary process. Thus, historical legal scholars look to past legal decisions (precedent) to solve contemporary problems.

The Analytical School   The **Analytical School** of jurisprudence maintains that the law is shaped by logic. Analytical philosophers believe results are reached by applying principles of logic to the specific facts of the case. The emphasis is on the logic of the result rather than on how the result is reached.

The Sociological School   The **Sociological School** of jurisprudence asserts that the law is a means of achieving and advancing certain sociological goals. The followers of this philosophy, who are known as *realists*, believe that the purpose of law is to shape social behavior. Sociological philosophers are unlikely to adhere to past law as precedent.

The Command School   The philosophers of the **Command School** of jurisprudence believe that the law is a set of rules developed, communicated, and enforced by the ruling party rather than a reflection of the society's morality, history, logic, or sociology. This school maintains that the law changes when the ruling class changes.

> *"Human beings do not ever make laws; it is the accidents and catastrophes of all kinds happening in every conceivable way, that make law for us."*
> Plato
> *Laws IV, 709*

> *"Law must be stable and yet it cannot stand still."*
> Roscoe Pound
> *Interpretations of Legal History* (1923)

CONTEMPORARY BUSINESS ENVIRONMENT

Two Modern Schools of Jurisprudential Thought

1. Law and Economics   Should free market principles, like the supply and demand and cost-benefit theories, determine the outcome of lawsuits and legislation? U.S. Court of Appeals Judge Richard Posner thinks so—and so do a growing number of other judges and legal theorists. These people are members of the **Law and Economics School** (or the "Chicago School") of jurisprudence, which had its roots at the University of Chicago.

According to the Law and Economics School, which is unofficially headed by Judge Posner, promoting market efficiency should be the central goal of legal decision making. In the area of

antitrust law, for example, Law and Economics theorists would not find corporate mergers and takeovers to be illegal simply because they resulted in market domination. Instead, they would find this practice to be illegal only if it rendered the overall market less efficient.

Focusing on cold economic categories like market efficiency might seem appropriate when making decisions in cases that involve businesses. However, proponents of Law and Economics theory use this type of analysis in cases involving everything from freedom of religion to civil rights.

Despite the naysayers who warn that the morality of certain

rights and liberties must be safeguarded even if it is unpopular or costly from an economic point of view, proponents of Law and Economics are gaining increased acceptance in law schools and increased appointments to the judiciary.

2. Critical Legal Studies   Unlike the Law of Economics School, the **Critical Legal Studies School** does not concern itself with creating a set of guidelines for judicial decision making or constitutional interpretation. It proposes that legal rules are unnecessary and are used as an obstacle by the powerful to maintain the status

continued

quo. Instead, Critical Legal theorists (the "Crits") seek to expose the real aim of the American legal system, which is to provide an air of legitimacy for our unjust society. In other words, they contend that the real purpose of our legal system is to make sure that the rich get richer and the poor stay where they are.

The Crits argue that legal disputes should be solved by applying arbitrary rules that are based on broad notions of what is "fair" in the circumstances. Under this theory, subjective decision making by judges would be permitted.

Critics of the Crits claim that they are long on criticism and short on positive ideas for change.

Others suggest that the Crits are really socialists, waving their flag under a new name.

Although no one expects Crits to rule the legal roost anytime soon, they have gained a foothold in many law schools and can be expected to continue to challenge the concepts and goals of traditional legal theory.

HISTORY OF AMERICAN LAW

When the American colonies were first settled, the English system of law was generally adopted as the system of jurisprudence. This was the foundation from which American judges developed a common law in America.

English Common Law

common law   Developed by judges who issued their opinions when deciding a case. The principles announced in these cases became precedent for later judges deciding similar cases. *. Not all courts. Only appealate . Courts*

English **common law** was law developed by judges who issued their opinions when deciding a case. The principles announced in these cases became **precedent** for later judges deciding similar cases. The English common law can be divided into cases decided by the law courts, equity courts, and merchant courts.

law court   A court that developed and administered a uniform set of laws decreed by the kings and queens after William the Conqueror; legal procedure was emphasized over merits at this time.

Law Courts   Prior to the Norman conquest of England in 1066, each locality in England was subject to local laws as established by the lord or chieftain in control of the local area. There was no countrywide system of law. After 1066, William the Conqueror and his successors to the throne of England began to replace the various local laws with one uniform system of law. To accomplish this, the king or queen appointed loyal followers as judges in all local areas. These judges were charged with administering the law in a uniform manner. These were called **law courts**. Law at this time tended to emphasize form (legal procedure) over the substance (merits) of the case. The only relief available at law courts was a monetary award for damages.

Court of Chancery   Court that granted relief based on fairness. Also called *equity court. English Court*

"A lawyer without history or literature is a mechanic, a mere working mason; if he possesses some knowledge of these, he may venture to call himself an architect."
Sir Walter Scott
Guy Mannering,
Ch. 37 (1815)

Chancery (Equity) Courts   Because of the unfair results and the limited remedy available in the law courts, a second set of courts—the **Court of Chancery** (or **equity court**)—was established. These courts were under the authority of the Lord Chancellor. Persons who believed that the decision of the law court was unfair or that the law court could not grant an appropriate remedy could seek relief in the Court of Chancery. The Chancery Court inquired into the merits of the case, rather than emphasizing legal procedure. The Chancellor's remedies were called **equitable remedies** because they were shaped to fit each situation. Equitable orders and remedies of the Court of Chancery took precedent over the legal decisions and remedies of the law courts.

Merchant Courts   As trade developed in the Middle Ages, the merchants who traveled about England and Europe developed certain rules to solve their commercial disputes. These rules, known as the "law of merchants" or the **Law Merchant**, were based on common trade practices and usage. Eventually, a separate set of courts was established to administer these rules. This court was called the **Merchant Court**. In the early 1900s, the Merchant Court was absorbed into the regular law court system of England.

Adoption of English Common Law in America

All the states except Louisiana base their legal systems primarily on the English *common law*. Because of its French heritage, Louisiana bases its law on the *civil law* (see discussion of international legal systems later in this chapter). Elements of California and Texas law, as well as other southwestern states, are rooted in civil law. In the United States, the law, equity, and merchant courts have been merged. Thus, most U.S. courts permit the aggrieved party to seek both law and equitable orders and remedies.

The importance of common law to the American legal system is described in the following excerpt from Justice Douglas's opinion in the 1841 case of *Penny v. Little*:[7]

> The common law is a beautiful system, containing the wisdom and experiences of ages. Like the people it ruled and protected, it was simple and crude in its infancy, and became enlarged, improved, and polished as the nation advanced in civilization, virtue, and intelligence. Adapting itself to the conditions and circumstances of the people and relying upon them for its administration, it necessarily improved as the condition of the people was elevated. The inhabitants of this country always claimed the common law as their birthright, and at an early period established it as the basis of their jurisprudence.

NOTE
The U.S. legal system is based primarily on English common law and secondarily on Roman civil law.

SOURCES OF LAW IN THE UNITED STATES

In the 200 years since the founding of this country and the adoption of the English common law, the lawmakers of this country have developed a substantial body of law. The *sources of modern law* in the United States are discussed in the sections that follow.

Constitutions

The **Constitution of the United States of America** is the *supreme law of the land*. This means that any law—whether federal, state, or local—that conflicts with the U.S. Constitution is unconstitutional and, therefore, unenforceable.

The principles enumerated in the Constitution are extremely broad because the Founders intended them to be applied to evolving social, technological, and economic conditions. The U.S. Constitution is often referred to as a "living document" because it is so adaptable.

The U.S. Constitution established the structure of the federal government. It created the following three branches of government and gave them the following powers:

- Legislative (Congress)—power to make (enact) the law;
- Executive (President)—power to enforce the law; and
- Judicial (courts)—power to interpret and determine the validity of the law.

Powers not given to the federal government by the Constitution are reserved to the states. States also have their own constitutions. These are often patterned after the U.S. Constitution, although many are more detailed. State constitutions establish the legislative, executive, and judicial branches of state government and establish the powers of each branch. Provisions of state constitutions are valid unless they conflict with the U.S. Constitution or any valid federal law.

Constitution of the United States of America The supreme law of the United States.

"The Constitution of the United States is not a mere lawyers' document: it is a vehicle of life, and its spirit is always the spirit of the age."
Woodrow Wilson
Constitutional Government in the United States 69 (1927)

Treaties

The U.S. Constitution provides that the president, with the advice and consent of the Senate, may enter into **treaties** with foreign governments. Treaties become part of the supreme law of the land. With increasing international economic relations among nations, treaties will become an even more important source of law that will affect business in the future.

treaty A compact made between two or more nations.

Codified Law

statute Written law enacted by the legislative branch of the federal and state governments that establishes certain courses of conduct that must be adhered to by covered parties.

Statutes are written laws that establish certain courses of conduct that must be adhered to by covered parties. The U.S. Congress is empowered by the Commerce Clause and other provisions of the U.S. Constitution to enact **federal statutes** to regulate foreign and interstate commerce. Federal statutes include antitrust laws, securities laws, bankruptcy laws, labor laws, equal employment opportunity laws, environmental protection laws, consumer protection laws, and such. State legislatures enact **state statutes**. State statutes include corporation laws, partnership laws, workers' compensation laws, the Uniform Commercial Code, and the like. The statutes enacted by the legislative branches of the federal and state governments are organized by topic into code books. This is often called **codified law**.

ordinances Laws enacted by local government bodies such as cities and municipalities, counties, school districts, and water districts.

State legislatures often delegate lawmaking authority to local government bodies, including cities and municipalities, counties, school districts, water districts, and such. These governmental units are empowered to adopt **ordinances**. Examples of ordinances are traffic laws, local building codes, and zoning laws. Ordinances are also codified.

Executive Orders

executive order An order issued by a member of the executive branch of the government.

The executive branch of government—which includes the President of the United States and state governors—is empowered to issue **executive orders**. This power is derived from express delegation from the legislative branch and is implied from the U.S. Constitution and state constitutions. For example, in 1993, President Clinton issued an executive order that lifted the so-called "gag" rule forbidding abortion counseling in federally funded family planning clinics.

Judicial Decisions

judicial decision A decision about an individual lawsuit issued by federal and state courts.

When deciding individual lawsuits, federal and state courts issue **judicial decisions**. In these written opinions, the judge or justice usually explains the legal reasoning used to decide the case. These opinions often include interpretations of statutes, ordinances, administrative regulations, and the announcement of legal principles used to decide the case. Many court decisions are printed (reported) in books that are available in law libraries.

precedent A rule of law established in a court decision. Lower courts must follow the precedent established by higher courts.

The Doctrine of *Stare Decisis* Based on the common law tradition, past court decisions become **precedent** for deciding future cases. Lower courts must follow the precedent established by higher courts. That is why all federal and state courts in the United States must follow the precedents established by U.S. Supreme Court decisions.

The courts of one jurisdiction are not bound by the precedent established by the courts of another jurisdiction, although they may look to each other for guidance. For example, state courts of one state are not required to follow the legal precedent established by the courts of another state.

stare decisis Latin: "to stand by the decision." Adherence to precedent.

Adherence to precedent is called ***stare decisis*** ("to stand by the decision"). The doctrine of *stare decisis* promotes uniformity of law within a jurisdiction, makes the court system more efficient, and makes the law more predictable for individuals and businesses. A court may later change or reverse its legal reasoning if a new case is presented to it and change is warranted. The doctrine of *stare decisis* is discussed in the following excerpt from Justice Musmanno's decision in *Flagiello v. Pennsylvania*:[8]

> Without *stare decisis*, there would be no stability in our system of jurisprudence. *Stare decisis* channels the law. It erects lighthouses and flies the signals of safety. The ships of jurisprudence must follow that well-defined channel which, over the years, has been proved to be secure and worthy.

BUSINESS APPLICATION

Regulations and Orders of Administrative Agencies

The legislative and executive branches of federal and state governments are empowered to establish **administrative agencies** to enforce and interpret statutes enacted by Congress and state legislatures. Many of these agencies regulate business. For example, Congress has created the Securities and Exchange Commission (SEC) and the Federal Trade Commission (FTC), among others.

Congress or the state legislatures usually empower these agencies to adopt **administrative rules and regulations** to interpret the statutes that the agency is authorized to enforce. These rules and regulations have the force of law. Administrative agencies usually have the power to hear and decide disputes. Their decisions are called *orders*. Because of their power, administrative agencies are often informally referred to as the "fourth branch" of government.

Priority of Law in the United States

As mentioned previously, the U.S. Constitution and treaties take precedence over all other laws. Federal statutes take precedence over federal regulations. Valid federal law takes precedence over any conflicting state or local law. State constitutions rank as the highest state law. State statutes take precedence over state regulations. Valid state law takes precedence over local laws.

INTERNATIONAL PERSPECTIVE

Legal Systems of the World

Several other major legal systems have been developed in the world in addition to the *Anglo-American common law system*. These are the Romano-Germanic, Sino-Soviet, Hindu, and Islamic legal systems. Other minor forms of law have also been developed, including tribal laws in Africa and hybrid systems. The major legal systems of the world follow.

Romano-Germanic Civil Law System
The *Romano-Germanic civil law system*, which is commonly called the *civil law*, dates to 450 B.C. when Rome adopted the Twelve Tables, a code of laws applicable to the Romans. A compilation of Roman law, called the *Corpus Juris Civilis* (the Body of Civil Law), was completed in 534. Later, two national codes—the

French Civil Code of 1804 (the Napoleonic Code) and the German Civil Code of 1896—became models for countries that adopted civil codes.

In contrast to the Anglo-American common law, in which laws are created by the judicial system as well as by congressional legislation, the Civil Code and parliamentary statutes that expand and interpret it are the sole sources of the law in most civil law countries. Thus, the adjudication of a case is simply the application of the Code or the statutes to a particular set of facts. In some civil law countries, court decisions do not have the force of law.

Today, Austria, Belgium, Greece, Indochina, Indonesia, Japan, Latin America, the Netherlands, Poland, Portugal, South Korea, Spain, Sub-Saharan

Africa, Switzerland, and Turkey follow the civil law.

Sino-Soviet Law System
The youngest of the major legal families is the *Sino-Soviet socialist law system*, which applies to more than 30 percent of the people of the world. The Sino-Soviet theory of law is based on the philosophy of Karl Marx, which advocated the eradication of capitalism and the elimination of the private ownership of property. After the creation of the Soviet state following the Russian Revolution of 1917, Lenin replaced the old court system with a system of law meted out by workers, peasants, and the military. This legal nihilism (or absence of law) did not last long, and a formal legal system was restored pursuant to

continued

new criminal and civil law codes that promoted the socialist ideal. With its emphasis on codes, the Sino-Soviet legal system is a variant of the civil law.

Because private property in most respects is not permitted under Sino-Soviet law, the legal system is composed mostly of public law. Therefore, property law, contract law, and business organization law (e.g., corporation and partnership law), which are prevalent in common law and civil law countries, are not important in Sino-Soviet law. Sino-Soviet public law preserves the authority of the state over property and the means of production.

Today, socialist law forms the basis of the legal systems of Angola, Bulgaria, Cambodia, China, Cuba, Ethiopia, Guinea, Guyana, Laos, Libya, Mozambique, North Korea, Somalia, and Vietnam. As the republics of the now dismantled Soviet Union and Eastern bloc countries adopt free market economies, Sino-Soviet public law will be replaced by laws establishing and protecting private property rights.

Hindu Law System
More than 20 percent of the world's population is Hindu. Most live in India, where they make up 80 percent of the population. Others live in Burma, Kenya, Malaysia, Pakistan, Singapore, Tanzania, and Uganda. *Hindu law* is a religious law. As such, individual Hindus apply this law to

themselves regardless of their nationality or place of domicile.

Classical Hindu law rests neither on civil codes nor on court decisions, but on the works of private scholars that were passed along for centuries by oral tradition and eventually were recorded in the *smitris* (law books). Hindu law—called *dharmasastra* in Sanskrit; that is, the doctrine of proper behavior—is linked to the divine revelation of Veda (the holy collection of Indian religious songs, prayers, hymns, and sayings written between 2000 and 1000 B.C.). Most Hindu law is concerned with family matters and the law of succession.

After India became a British colony, British judges applied a combination of Hindu law and common law in solving cases. This Anglo-Hindu law, as it was called, was ousted when India gained its independence. In the mid-1950s, India codified Hindu law by enacting the Hindu Marriage Act, the Hindu Minority and Guardianship Act, the Hindu Succession Act, and the Hindu Adoptions and Maintenance Act. Outside of India, Anglo-Hindu law applies in most other countries populated by Hindus.

Islamic Law System
Approximately 20 percent of the world's population is Muslim. Islam is the principal religion of Afghanistan, Algeria, Bangladesh, Egypt, Indonesia, Iran, Iraq, Jordan, Kuwait, Libya, Malaysia, Mali,

Mauritania, Morocco, Niger, North Yemen, Oman, Pakistan, Qatar, Saudi Arabia, Somalia, South Yemen, Sudan, Syria, Tunisia, Turkey, and the United Arab Emirates. *Islamic law* (or *Shari'a*) is the only law in Saudi Arabia. In other Islamic countries, the *Shari'a* forms the basis of family law but coexists with other laws.

The Islamic law system is derived from the Koran, the Sunnah (decisions and sayings of the Prophet Muhammad), and reasoning by Islamic scholars. By the tenth century A.D., Islamic scholars decided that no further improvement of the divine law could be made, closed the door of *ijtihad* (independent reasoning), and froze the evolution of Islamic law at that point. Islamic law prohibits *riba*, or the making of unearned or unjustified profit. Making a profit from the sale of goods or the provision of services is permitted. The most notable consequence of *riba* is that the payment of interest on loans is forbidden. To circumvent this result, the party with the money is permitted to purchase the item and resell it to the other party at a profit, or to advance the money and become a trading partner who shares in the profits of the enterprise.

Today, Islamic law is primarily used in the areas of marriage, divorce, and inheritance, and to a limited degree in criminal law. To resolve the tension between *Shari'a* and the practice of modern commercial law, the *Shari'a* is often ignored in commercial transactions.

THE CONSTITUTION AND BUSINESS

"The American Constitution is, so far as I can see, the most wonderful work ever struck off at a given time by the brain and purpose of man."
W. E. Gladstone
Kin Beyond Sea
(1878)

In 1776, the 13 original colonies declared independence from England and the American Revolution began. In 1778, the Continental Congress formed a *federal government* and adopted the **Articles of Confederation**. The Articles of Confederation was a particularly weak document that gave limited power to the newly created federal government. The **Constitutional Convention** was convened in Philadelphia in May 1787. After substantial debate, the delegates agreed to a new

U.S. Constitution. The Constitution was reported to Congress in September 1787. State ratification was completed in 1788. Many amendments, including the **Bill of Rights**, have been added to the Constitution since that time.

Each of the Constitution's seven **Articles**, as well as various amendments, contain numerous provisions that are important to business.

U.S. Constitution The fundamental law of the United States of America. It was ratified by the states in 1788.

The Doctrine of Separation of Powers

The U.S. Constitution creates the three branches of the federal government and allocates powers to these branches:

1. **Article I** of the Constitution establishes the **legislative branch** of government. This branch is bicameral; that is, it consists of the Senate and the House of Representatives. Collectively, they are referred to as *Congress*.[9] Each state has two senators. The number of representatives to the House of Representatives is determined according to the population of each state. The current number of representatives is determined from the 1990 census.

2. **Article II** of the Constitution establishes the **executive branch** of government by providing for the election of the president and vice president. The president is not elected by popular vote but instead is selected by the *Electoral College*, whose representatives are appointed by state delegations.[10]

3. **Article III** establishes the **judicial branch** of the government by establishing the Supreme Court and providing for the creation of other federal courts by Congress.[11]

legislative branch The part of the government that consists of Congress (the Senate and the House of Representatives).

executive branch The part of the government that consists of the President and Vice President.

judicial branch The part of the government that consists of the Supreme Court and other federal courts.

The federal government is based on the doctrine of **separation of powers**. The legislative branch makes the laws; the executive branch enforces the laws; and the judicial branch interprets the laws. There is some overlap to these functions.

Certain **"checks and balances"** are built into the Constitution to ensure that no one branch of the federal government becomes too powerful. Some of the checks and balances in our system of government follow:

1. The judicial branch has authority to examine the acts of the other two branches of government and determine whether these acts are constitutional.[12]

2. The executive branch can enter into treaties with foreign governments only with the advice and consent of the Senate.

3. The legislative branch is authorized to create federal courts and determine their jurisdiction and to enact statutes that change judicially made law.

NOTE
Checks and balances are the way the U.S. Constitution prevents any one of the three branches of the government from becoming too powerful.

Federalism and Delegated Powers

Our country's form of government is referred to as **federalism**. That means that the federal government and the 50 state governments share powers.

When the states ratified the Constitution, they *delegated* certain powers to the federal government, called **enumerated powers**. The federal government is authorized to deal with national and international affairs. Any powers that are not specifically delegated to the federal government by the Constitution are reserved to the state governments. State governments are empowered to deal with local affairs.

federalism The United States' form of government; the federal government and the 50 state governments share powers.

enumerated powers Certain powers delegated to the federal government by the states.

THE SUPREMACY CLAUSE

The **Supremacy Clause** establishes that the federal Constitution, treaties, federal laws, and federal regulations are the supreme law of the land.[13] State and local laws that conflict with valid federal law are unconstitutional. The concept of federal law taking precedent over state or local law is commonly called the **preemption doctrine**.

Congress may expressly provide that a particular federal statute *exclusively* regulates a specific area or activity. No state or local law regulating the area of activity is valid if there

Supremacy Clause A clause of the U.S. Constitution that establishes that the federal Constitution, treaties, federal laws, and federal regulations are the supreme law of the land.

preemption doctrine The concept that federal law takes precedent over state or local law.

is such a statute. More often, though, federal statutes do not expressly provide for exclusive jurisdiction. In these instances, state and local governments have *concurrent jurisdiction* to regulate the area or activity. However, any state or local law that "directly and substantially" conflicts with valid federal law is preempted under the Supremacy Clause.

In the following case, the U.S. Supreme Court held that a state law was unconstitutional because it conflicted with a valid federal statute.

CASE 1.1

Capital Cities Cable, Inc. v. Crisp, Director, Oklahoma Alcoholic Beverage Control Board

467 U.S. 691, 104 S.Ct. 2694, 81 L.Ed.2d.580 (1984) United States Supreme Court

Facts The Federal Communications Act (Act) authorizes the Federal Communications Commission (FCC) to regulate television and radio broadcasts in this country. The FCC adopted a regulation that requires cable television operators to transmit all signals "in full, without deletion or alteration of any portion," including commercials. A provision in the Oklahoma state constitution prohibited the advertising of alcoholic beverages within the state. Many out-of-state cable broadcasts contain alcoholic beverage commercials. When the director of the Oklahoma Alcoholic Beverage Control Board (Board) threatened to criminally prosecute cable operators that televised out-of-state alcoholic beverages commercials in the state, Capital Cities Cable, Inc., and other cable operators sued the Board, alleging that the Oklahoma law was preempted by federal law. The U.S. district court held for the cable operators, but the U.S. court of appeals reversed. The cable operators appealed to the U.S. Supreme Court.

Issue Is the provision in the Oklahoma constitution that prohibits the advertising of alcoholic beverage commercials by cable operators preempted by federal law?

Decision Yes. In a unanimous opinion, the U.S. Supreme Court held that the provision in the Oklahoma constitution directly and substantially conflicted with a valid federal regulation and was therefore unconstitutional under the Supremacy Clause of the U.S. Constitution.

Reason The Supremacy Clause of the U.S. Constitution provides that valid federal law takes precedence over any conflicting state or local law. Federal regulations adopted by federal administrative agencies have the same preemptive effect as federal statutes. Therefore, the enforcement of state law is preempted by federal law when compliance with both state and federal law is impossible. Because the Oklahoma advertising ban plainly conflicted with a specific federal regulation, the Court held that the federal regulation prevailed and the Oklahoma law was preempted under the Supremacy Clause. Thus, the provision in the Oklahoma constitution prohibiting the advertising of alcoholic beverage commercials in the state by cable operators is unconstitutional.

CASE QUESTIONS

Critical Legal Thinking Should federal law preempt state and local law? Why or why not? What would be the effect if the Supremacy Clause were not part of the U.S. Constitution?

Ethics Should a state, through its laws, try to impose ethical standards on its residents like Oklahoma tried to do in this case?

Business Implication What would have been the economic consequences to cable operators if the Oklahoma law in this case had been upheld?

THE COMMERCE CLAUSE

Commerce Clause A clause of the U.S. Constitution that grants Congress the power "to regulate commerce with foreign nations, and among the several states, and with Indian tribes."

The **Commerce Clause** of the U.S. Constitution grants Congress the power "to regulate commerce with foreign nations, and among the several states, and with Indian tribes."[14] Because this clause authorizes the federal government to regulate commerce, it has a greater impact on business than any other provision in the Constitution. Among other things, this clause is intended to foster the development of a national market and free trade among the states.

Federal Regulation of Foreign Commerce

The Commerce Clause gives the federal government the exclusive power to regulate commerce with foreign nations. Direct and indirect regulation of **foreign commerce** by state or local governments is a violation of this clause. For example, the federal government could prohibit the sale of music and video CDs from the People's Republic of China because of that country's lax enforcement of intellectual property laws (e.g., copyright law), but the state of California could not take the same actions.

Federal Regulation of Interstate Commerce

The Commerce Clause gives the federal government the authority to regulate **interstate commerce**. Originally, the courts interpreted this clause to mean that the federal government could regulate only commerce that moved *in* interstate commerce. The modern rule, however, allows the federal government to regulate activities that *affect* interstate commerce.

Under the **effects on interstate commerce test**, the regulated activity does not itself have to be in interstate commerce. Thus, any local (intrastate) activity that has an effect on interstate commerce is subject to federal regulation. Theoretically, this test subjects a substantial amount of business activity in the United States to federal regulation.

For example, in the famous case of *Wickard, Secretary of Agriculture v. Filburn,*[15] a federal statute limited the amount of wheat that a farmer could plant and harvest for home consumption. Filburn, a farmer, violated the law. The U.S. Supreme Court upheld the statute on the grounds that it prevented nationwide surpluses and shortages of wheat. The Court reasoned that wheat grown for home consumption would affect the supply of wheat available in interstate commerce.

In the following case, the U.S. Supreme Court had to decide whether the challenged activity had an effect on interstate commerce.

> **BUSINESS BRIEF**
> *The Commerce Clause gives the federal government the exclusive power to regulate commerce with foreign nations.*

> **interstate commerce**
> Commerce that moves between states or that affects commerce between states.

> **BUSINESS BRIEF**
> *The federal government may regulate*
> 1. Interstate *commerce that crosses state borders.*
> 2. Intrastate *commerce that affects interstate commerce.*

CASE 1.2

United States v. Lopez
115 S.Ct. 1624 (1995) United States Supreme Court

Facts In 1990, the Congress enacted the Gun-Free School Zone Act (Act), a federal statute that made it a crime "for any individual knowingly to possess a firearm at a place that the individual knows, or has reasonable cause to believe, is a school zone." On March 10, 1992, Alfonso Lopez, Jr., a 12th-grade student at Edison High School in San Antonio, Texas, arrived at school carrying a concealed .38 caliber handgun and five bullets. After being caught and arrested, he was charged with violating the Act. The trial court found the defendant guilty and sentenced him to six months' imprisonment. The court of appeals reversed, holding that the Act did not recognize "interstate commerce" and was therefore an unconstitutional exercise of the federal government's power under the Commerce Clause of the Constitution. The U.S. Supreme Court agreed to hear an appeal.

Issue Is the possession of a gun in a local school zone a commercial activity that substantially affects interstate commerce?

Decision No. The U.S. Supreme Court held that the Act neither regulates commercial activity nor requires that the possession of a firearm be connected in any way to interstate commerce.

Reason Although in the past the Supreme Court has permitted expanded congressional power under the Commerce Clause, in this case the Court held that the federal government had exceeded the outer limits of this power. The Supreme Court noted that under the Commerce Clause the federal government can regulate the channels and instrumentalities of interstate commerce and activities having a substantial effect on interstate commerce. The Supreme Court
continued

found that the activity of carrying a gun in a local school zone does not involve a channel or instrumentality of interstate commerce or have a substantial effect on interstate commerce. The Court concluded that the Act was invalid as beyond the power of Congress under the Commerce Clause.

CASE QUESTIONS

Critical Legal Thinking Should the "affects" test be applied in determining the scope of the federal government's power to regulate interstate commerce under the Commerce Clause? Why or why not?

Ethics Was it ethical for the defendant to challenge the applicability of the Act to his action rather than to face the merits of the case?

Business Implication Do you think the framers of the Constitution envisioned the broad federal regulation of business today? Explain.

State and Local Government Regulation of Business-State "Police Power"

police power The power of states to regulate private and business activity within their borders.

The states did not delegate all power to regulate business to the federal government. They retained the power to regulate *intrastate* and much interstate business activity that occurs within their borders. This is commonly referred to as states' **police power**.

BUSINESS BRIEF

States may enact laws that protect or promote the public health, safety, morals, and general welfare as long as the law does not unduly burden interstate commerce.

Police power permits states (and, by delegation, local governments) to enact laws to protect or promote the *public health, safety, morals, and general welfare*. This includes the authority to enact laws that regulate the conduct of business. Zoning ordinances, state environmental laws, corporation and partnership laws, and property laws are enacted under this power.

State and local laws cannot **unduly burden interstate commerce**. If they do, they are unconstitutional because they violate the Commerce Clause. For example, if the federal government has chosen not to regulate the area that it has the power to regulate (*dormant Commerce Clause*), but the state does regulate it, the state law cannot unduly burden interstate commerce.

In the following case, the Court had to determine whether an action by a local government constituted an undue burden on interstate commerce in violation of the Commerce Clause.

CASE 1.3

Fort Gratiot Sanitary Landfill, Inc. v. Michigan Department of Natural Resources
112 S.Ct. 2019, 119 L.Ed.2d 139 (1992) United States Supreme Court

Facts In 1988, the state of Michigan added the Waste Import Restrictions to its Solid Waste Management Act. These restrictions prohibited privately owned landfills in the state from accepting solid wastes (e.g., garbage, rubbish, sludges, and industrial waste) from any source outside the county in which the landfill was located unless the county expressly permitted it. Fort Gratiot Sanitary Landfill, Inc. (Fort Gratiot) submitted an application to the county government to allow it to accept up to 1,750 tons per day of out-of-state solid waste. The county rejected the application. Fort Gratiot sued the county and state, alleging that

the Waste Import Restrictions violated the Commerce Clause of the U.S. Constitution. The U.S. district court concluded that the restrictions did not discriminate against interstate commerce. The U.S. court of appeals agreed. The U.S. Supreme Court granted certiorari.

Issue Do Michigan's Waste Import Restrictions violate the Commerce Clause?

Decision Yes. The Supreme Court held that the Waste Import Restrictions discriminated against interstate commerce in violation of the Commerce Clause of the U.S. Constitution.

Reason The defendants argued that the Commerce Clause did not apply because no interstate commerce was involved. The Supreme Court rejected this argument. It stated, "Solid waste, even if it has no value, is an article of interstate commerce." The Court next noted that the case involved the "dormant" Commerce Clause because no federal law regulated the same subject matter as the state law in question. The Court held that Michigan's Waste Import Restrictions caused an undue burden on, and discriminated against, interstate commerce. The Court stated, "The restrictions enacted by Michigan authorize each of its 83 counties to isolate itself from the national economy. The Court has consistently found parochial legislation of this kind to be constitutionally invalid."

CASE QUESTIONS

Critical Legal Thinking Do you think some states will "export" their wastes to other states rather than provide landfills within their own boundaries?

Ethics Is it ethical for a state to prohibit wastes from other states to be dumped within its boundaries? Was the state of Michigan acting in "good faith"?

Business Implication What effect will the Supreme Court's ruling have on landfill operators? Would your answer be different if the restriction was found constitutional?

THE BILL OF RIGHTS AND BUSINESS

In 1791, the 10 amendments that are commonly referred to as the **Bill of Rights** were approved by the states and became part of the U.S. Constitution. The Bill of Rights guarantees certain fundamental rights to natural persons and protects these rights from intrusive government action. Most of these rights have also been found applicable to so-called artificial persons (i.e., corporations).

In addition to the Bill of Rights, 16 other amendments have been added to the Constitution. These amendments cover a variety of things. For instance, they have abolished slavery, prohibited discrimination, authorized a federal income tax, given women the right to vote, and specifically recognized that persons 18 years of age and older have the right to vote.

> **NOTE**
> *The first 10 amendments to the Constitution are called the Bill of Rights. They were added to the U.S. Constitution in 1791.*

Freedom of Speech

One of the most honored freedoms guaranteed by the Bill of Rights is the **freedom of speech** of the First Amendment. Many other constitutional freedoms would be meaningless without it. The First Amendment's Freedom of Speech Clause protects speech only, not conduct. The U.S. Supreme Court places speech into three categories: (1) *fully protected* (2) *limited protected* and (3) *unprotected speech.*

> **freedom of speech** The right to oral, written, and symbolic speech protected by the First Amendment.

Fully Protected Speech Fully protected speech is speech that the government cannot prohibit or regulate. Political speech is an example of such speech. For example, the government could not enact a law that forbids citizens from criticizing the current administration. The First Amendment protects oral, written, and symbolic speech.

> **fully protected speech** Speech that the government cannot prohibit or regulate.

Limited Protected Speech The Supreme Court has held that certain types of speech have only *limited protection* under the First Amendment. The government cannot forbid this type of speech, but it can subject this speech to **time, place, and manner restrictions**.

Offensive speech is speech that offends many members of society. The Supreme Court has held that offensive speech may be restricted by the government under time, place, and manner restrictions. For example, the Federal Communications Commission (FCC) can regulate the use of offensive language on television by limiting such language to time periods when children would be unlikely to be watching (e.g., late at night).

> **limited protected speech** Speech that cannot be forbidden by the government, but that is subject to *time, place, and manner restrictions.*

Note that offensive speech is different from obscene speech. Obscene speech is discussed under the next heading.

unprotected speech
Speech that is not protected by the First Amendment and may be forbidden by the government.

Unprotected Speech　The Supreme Court has held that the following types of speech are not protected by the First Amendment and may be totally forbidden by the government:

- Dangerous speech (including such things as yelling "fire" in a crowded theater when there is no fire)
- Fighting words that are likely to provoke a hostile or violent response from an average person[16]
- Speech that incites the violent or revolutionary overthrow of the government; the mere abstract teaching of the morality and consequences of such action is protected[17]
- Defamatory language[18]
- Child pornography[19]
- Obscene speech.[20]

"I disapprove of what you say, but I will defend to the death your right to say it."
　　　　　　Voltaire

The definition of **obscene speech** is quite subjective.

Commercial Speech

commercial speech
Speech used by businesses, such as advertising. It is subject to time, place, and manner restrictions.

Commercial speech, such as advertising, was once considered unprotected by the First Amendment. The Supreme Court's landmark decision in *Virginia State Board of Pharmacy v. Virginia Citizens Consumer Council, Inc.*,[21] changed this rule. In that case, the Supreme Court held that a state statute prohibiting a pharmacist from advertising the price of prescription drugs was unconstitutional because it violated the Free Speech Clause. However, the Supreme Court held that commercial speech is subject to proper time, place, and manner restrictions.

In the following case, the Supreme Court found that a federal statute violated a corporation's commercial free speech rights.

CASE 1.4

Rubin v. Coors Brewing Company
115 S.Ct. 1585 (1995) United States Supreme Court

Facts　The Coors Brewing Company (Coors) is a brewer that produces and sells beer under various brand names. Coors applied to the Bureau of Alcohol, Tobacco and Firearms (ATF), the federal administrative agency that regulates the sale of alcoholic beverages in the United States, for permission to disclose the alcohol content of its beer on the labels on its beer cans and bottles. The ATF rejected the application, citing the fact that the Federal Alcohol Administration Act (Act) prohibited the disclosure of alcohol content of beer on labels. Coors sued in federal court for injunctive relief, alleging that the restriction violated its commercial speech rights. The federal government defended the Act, arguing that the prohibition on disclosing alcohol content on beer labels prevented the threat of "strength wars" among brewers who would seek to compete in the marketplace based on the potency of their beer. The district court held in favor of Coors and the court of appeals affirmed. The federal government appealed to the U.S. Supreme Court.

Issue　Is the ban on the disclosure of alcohol content on beer labels a valid restriction on commercial speech?

Decision　No. The U.S. Supreme Court held that the ban on the disclosure of alcohol content on beer labels violated Coor's commercial speech rights.

Reason The Supreme Court noted that commercial speech is protected by the Free Speech Clause of the U.S. Constitution but that it is subject to reasonable time, place, and manner restrictions imposed by the government. The Court held that the government's ban on the disclosure of alcohol content on beer labels was an unreasonable restraint on commercial speech. The Court held that the government failed to present any credible evidence showing that the disclosure of alcohol content would promote strength wars. The Court also found that the disclosure of alcohol content was not misleading and that the ban did not advance any substantial government interest.

CASE QUESTIONS

Critical Legal Thinking Should commercial speech be accorded the same protection as noncommercial speech? Why or why not?

Ethics Was the federal government's reason for the ban justified? Why do you think Coors wanted to disclose this information?

Business Implication Do you think the Supreme Court's decision would have been the same if the federal government enacted a statute that prohibited beer commercials on television? Explain.

CRITICAL LEGAL THINKING

Judges apply *legal reasoning* in reaching a decision in a case. That is, the judge must specify the issue presented by the case, identify the key facts in the case and the applicable law, and then apply the law to the facts to come to a conclusion that answers the issue presented. This process is called **critical legal thinking**. Skills of analysis and interpretation are important in deciding legal cases.

(Process)

critical legal thinking
The process of specifying the issue presented by a case, identifying the key facts in the case and applicable law, and then applying the law to the facts to come to a conclusion that answers the issue presented.

Key Terms

Before you embark upon the study of law, you should know the following key legal terms:

- *Plaintiff*—The "plaintiff" is the party who originally brought the lawsuit.
- *Defendant*—The "defendant" is the party against whom the lawsuit has been brought.
- *Petitioner or Appellant*—The "petitioner," often referred to as the "appellant," is the party who has appealed the decision of the trial court or lower court. The petitioner can be either the plaintiff or defendant, depending on who lost the case at the trial court or lower court level.
- *Respondent or Appellee*—The "respondent," often referred to as the "appellee," is the party who must answer the petitioner's appeal. The respondent can be either the plaintiff or defendant, depending upon which party is the petitioner. In some cases, both the plaintiff *and* the defendant disagree with the trial court's or lower court's decision, and both parties could appeal the decision.

"Commerce never really flourishes so much, as when it is delivered from the guardianship of legislators and ministers."
William Godwin
Enquiry Concerning Political Justice
(1798)

Briefing a Case

It is often helpful for a student to "brief" a case in order to clarify the legal issues involved and to gain a better understanding of the case.

The procedure for briefing a case is as follows. The student must summarize, or brief, the court's decision in no more than 400 words. (Some professors may shorten or lengthen this limit.) The assignment's format is highly structured, consisting of five parts, each of which is numbered and labeled:

case brief A summary of each of the following items of a case:

1. Case name and citation
2. Key facts
3. Issue presented
4. Holding of the court
5. Court's reasoning.

PART	MAXIMUM WORDS
1. Case name and citation	25
2. A summary of the key facts in the case	125
3. The issue presented by the case, stated as a one-sentence question answerable only by "yes" or "no"	25
4. The court's resolution of the issue (the "holding")	25
5. A summary of the court's reasoning justifying the holding	200
Total words	400

Briefing a case consists of making a summary of each of the following items of the case.

1. Case Name and Citation

The name of the case should be placed at the beginning of each briefed case. The case name usually contains the names of the parties to the lawsuit. However, where there are multiple plaintiffs or defendants, some of the names of the parties may be omitted from the case name. Abbreviations are also often used in case names.

The case *citation* consists of a number such as "126 L.Ed.2d 295 (1993)" and, along with the year in which the case was decided, is set forth below the case name. The case citation identifies the book in the law library in which the case can be found. For example, the case in the previous citation can be found in Volume 126 of the *Supreme Court Reporter Lawyers' Edition (Second)*, page 295. The name of the court that decided the case should be set forth below the case name for the case.

2. Summary of the Key Facts in the Case

The important facts of a case should be stated briefly. Extraneous facts and facts of minor importance should be omitted from the brief. The facts of the case can usually be found at the beginning of the case, but not necessarily. Important facts might be found throughout the case.

3. Issue Presented by the Case

It is crucial in the briefing of a case to identify the *issue* presented to the court to decide. The issue on appeal is most often a legal question, although questions of fact are sometimes the subject of an appeal. The issue presented in each case is usually quite specific, and should be asked in a one-sentence question that is answerable only by a "yes" or "no." For example, the issue statement, "Is Mary liable?" is too broad. A more proper statement of the issue would be, "Is Mary liable to Joe for breach of the contract made between them based on her refusal to make the payment due on September 30?"

"The main part of intellectual education is not the acquisition of facts, but learning how to make the facts live."
Oliver Wendell Holmes
Oration before Harvard Law School Association (1886), *Speeches* 29 (1913) 29; *Coll. Leg. Pap.* 37.

4. Holding

The "holding" is the decision reached by the present court. It should be "yes" or "no." The holding should also state which party won.

5. Summary of the Court's Reasoning

When an appellate court or supreme court issues a decision, which is often called an "opinion," the court will normally state the reasoning it used in reaching its decision. The rationale for the decision may be based on the specific facts of the case, public policy, prior law, and other matters. In stating the reasoning of the court, the student should reword the court's language into the student's own language. This summary of the court's reasoning should pick out the meat of the opinions and weed out the nonessentials.

Following is a U.S. Supreme Court opinion for briefing. The case is presented in the language of the United States Supreme Court.

CASE FOR BRIEFING

Reno v. American Civil Liberties Union
1997 WL 348012 (1997)
United States Supreme Court

Case Name, Citation, and Court

Opinion, Stevens, Justice.

Opinion of the Court/Facts

The Internet is an international network of interconnected computers. The Internet has experienced extraordinary growth. The number of "host" computers—those that store information and relay communications—increased from about 300 in 1981 to approximately 9.4 million by the time of the trial in 1996. Roughly 60 percent of these hosts are located in the United States. About 40 million people used the Internet at the time of trial, a number that is expected to mushroom to 200 million by 1999. Individuals can obtain access to the Internet from many different sources, generally hosts themselves or entities with a host affiliation. Most colleges and universities provide access for their students and faculty; many corporations provide their employees with access through an office network. Several major national on-line services such as America Online, CompuServe, the Microsoft Network, and Prodigy offer access to their own extensive proprietary networks as well as a link to the much larger resources of the Internet.

Anyone with access to the Internet may take advantage of a wide variety of communication and information retrieval methods. These methods are constantly evolving and difficult to categorize precisely. But, as presently constituted, those most relevant to this case are electronic mail (e-mail), automatic mailing list services (mail exploders, sometimes referred to as listservs), newsgroups, chat rooms, and the World Wide Web. All of these methods can be used to transmit text; most can transmit sound, pictures, and moving video images. Taken together, these tools constitute a unique medium—known to its users as cyberspace—located in no particular geographical location but available to anyone, anywhere in the world, with access to the Internet.

The best known category of communication over the Internet is the World Wide Web, which allows users to search for and retrieve information stored in remote computers, as well as, in some cases, to communicate back to designated sites. In concrete terms, the Web consists of a vast number of documents stored in different computers all over the world. Some of these documents are simply files containing information. However, more elaborate documents, commonly known as Web pages, are also prevalent. Navigating the Web is relatively straightforward. A user can either type the address of a known page or enter keywords into a commercial "search engine" in an effort to locate sites on a subject of interest. Users generally explore a given Web page, or move to another, by clicking a computer "mouse" on one of the page's icons or links. Sexually explicit material on the Internet includes text, pictures, and chat and extends from the modestly titillating to the hardest-core. Some of the communications over the Internet that originate in foreign countries are also sexually explicit.

The Telecommunications Act of 1996, Pub.L. 104–104, 110 Stat. 56, was an unusually important legislative enactment. Title V—known as the "Communications Decency Act of 1996" (CDA)—contains provisions that were added either in executive committee after Congressional hearings were concluded or as amendments offered during floor debate on the legislation. An amendment offered in the Senate was the source of the two statutory provisions challenged in this case. They are informally described as the "indecent transmission" provision and the "patently offensive display" provision. The first, 47 U.S.C.A. Section 223(a), prohibits the knowing transmission of obscene or indecent messages to any recipient under 18 years of age. The second provision, Section 223(d), prohibits the knowing sending or displaying of patently offensive messages in a manner that is available to a person under 18 years of age.

Statute Being Interpreted

**Lower Court's
Opinion**

On February 8, 1996, immediately after the President signed the statute, 20 plaintiffs filed suit against the Attorney General of the United States and the Department of Justice challenging the constitutionality of Sections 223(a) and 223(d). A second suit was then filed by 27 additional plaintiffs, the two cases were consolidated, and a three-judge District Court was convened pursuant to Section 561 of the Act. After an evidentiary hearing, that Court entered a preliminary injunction against enforcement of both of the challenged provisions.

Issue

At issue is the constitutionality of two statutory provisions enacted to protect minors from "indecent" and "patently offensive" communications on the Internet.

**U.S. Supreme
Court's Reasoning**

Each medium of expression may present its own problems. Thus, some of our cases have recognized special justifications for regulation of the broadcast media that are not applicable to other speakers. In these cases, the Court relied on the history of extensive government regulation of the broadcast medium, the scarcity of available frequencies at its inception, and its "invasive" nature. Those factors are not present in cyberspace. Neither before nor after the enactment of the CDA have the vast democratic fora of the Internet been subject to the type of government supervision and regulation that has attended the broadcast industry. Moreover, the Internet is not as "invasive" as radio or television. The District Court specifically found that "communications over the Internet do not invade an individual's home or appear on one's computer screen unbidden. Users seldom encounter content by accident." It also found that "almost all sexually explicit images are preceded by warnings as to the content," and cited testimony that "odds are slim that a user would come across a sexually explicit sight by accident."

Unlike the conditions that prevailed when Congress first authorized regulation of the broadcast spectrum, the Internet can hardly be considered a "scarce" expressive commodity. It provides relatively unlimited, low-cost capacity for communication of all kinds. This dynamic, multifaceted category of communication includes not only traditional print and news services, but also audio, video, and still images, as well as interactive, real-time dialogue. Through the use of chat rooms, any person with a phone line can become a town crier with a voice that resonates farther than it could from any soapbox. Through the use of Web pages, mail exploders, and news groups, the same individual can become a pamphleteer. As the District Court found, "the content on the Internet is as diverse as human thought."

The vagueness of the CDA is a matter of special concern for two reasons. First, the CDA is a consent-based regulation of speech. The vagueness of such a regulation raises special First Amendment concerns because of its obvious chilling effect on free speech. Second, the CDA is a criminal statute. In addition to the opprobrium and stigma of a criminal conviction, the CDA threatens violators with penalties including up to two years in prison for each act of violation. The severity of criminal sanctions may well cause speakers to remain silent rather than communicate even arguably unlawful words, ideas, and images. Given the vague contours of the coverage of the statute, it unquestionably silences some speakers whose messages would be entitled to constitutional protection.

Systems have been developed to help parents control the material that may be available on a home computer with Internet access. A system can either limit a computer's access to an approved list of sources that have been identified as containing no adult material, it might block designated inappropriate sites, or it might attempt to block messages containing identifiable objectionable features. Although parental control software currently can screen for certain suggestive words or for known sexually explicit sites, it cannot now screen for sexually explicit images. Nevertheless, the evidence indicates that a reasonably effective method by which parents can prevent their children from accessing sexually explicit and other material that parents might believe is inappropriate for their children will soon be available.

We are persuaded that the CDA lacks the precision that the First Amendment requires when a statute regulates the content of speech. In order to deny minors access to potentially harmful speech, the CDA effectively suppresses a large amount of speech that adults have a constitutional right to receive and to address to one another. In evaluating the free speech rights of adults, we have made it perfectly clear that "sexual expression which is indecent but not obscene is protected by the First Amendment" [Sable Communications of Cal., Inc. v. FCC, 492 U.S. 115 (1989)]. The Government may not reduce the adult population to only what is fit for children. The CDA, casting a far darker shadow over free speech, threatens to torch a large segment of the Internet community.

Notwithstanding the legitimacy and importance of the congressional goal of protecting children from harmful materials, we agree with the three-judge District Court that the statute abridges "the freedom of speech" protected by the First Amendment. For the foregoing reasons, the judgment of the district court is affirmed. It is so ordered.

Holding

Exhibit 1.1
Brief of the Case

1. **Case Name, Citation, and Court**

   RENO V. AMERICAN CIVIL LIBERTIES UNION
   1997 WL 348012 (1997)
   United States Supreme Court

2. **Summary of the Key Facts**

   A. The Internet is an international network of interconnected computers, including the World Wide Web.
   B. Text, sound, pictures, and moving video images are transmitted over the Internet. This includes sexually explicit material.
   C. The federal government erected the "Communications Decency Act of 1996" (Act) that prohibits the knowing translation of "indecent" and "patently offensive" messages over the Internet to persons under 18 years of age.
   D. Plaintiffs, comprised of Internet users and providers, sued, alleging that the Act violated their First Amendment free speech rights.
   E. The U.S. District Court held that the challenged provisions were unconstitutional and issued a preliminary injunction against enforcement of the provisions.
   F. The U.S. Supreme Court agreed to hear the government's appeal.

3. **The Issue**

   Does the "indecent" and patently offensive" provisions of the Act violate free speech rights guaranteed by the First Amendment to the U.S. Constitution?

4. **The Holding**

   Yes. The Supreme Court held that the challenged provisions violated the plaintiffs' free speech rights.

5. **Summary of the Court's Reasoning**

   The Supreme Court held that the Internet differs from heavily regulated broadcast media (radio and television) in that sexually explicit communications over the Internet do not "invade" an individual's home or appear on a computer screen unbidden, and usually contain a warning as to its content. The Court held that any person can become a "town crier" or "pamphleteer" using the Internet and that this mode of expression should therefore be accorded the highest First Amendment free speech protection. The Court struck down the "indecent" and "patently offensive" language of the Act as being vague and overbroad and noted that the vagueness and criminal penalties of the Act would silence some speakers where the message would be entitled to Constitutional protection.

   The Court placed the burden on parents to regulate their childrens' use of the Internet and noted that software is currently being developed to help parents control children's access to sexually explicit material over the Internet. The Supreme Court stated that "the government may not reduce the adult population to only what is fit for children" and held that the challenged provisions would "torch a large segment of the Internet community" if enforced.

WORKING THE WEB

The Great American Web Site "The U.S. Government is the largest source of information anywhere in the world—and it belongs to you!! The mission of the Great American Web Site is to highlight the best, newest and most useful information in the government's domain and to help you navigate the maze of government agencies. This site has something for everyone."

Visit at http://www.uncle-sam.com/

The White House Beginning with the Clinton administration, the government made a serious commitment to providing access to government information via the Internet. Through this site, you can find out about the President and Vice President and their families and send them electronic mail, find out what is happening at the White House, take a tour of the White House, search White House documents—even listen to speeches and view photos (with the right computer equipment).

Visit at http://www.whitehouse.gov

The U.S. House of Representatives Do you want to read the full text of bills introduced into the House of Representatives? Do you want to find out how each member voted pro and con? Do you want to find out how a bill becomes a law? Maybe you want to find out who your representative is (you can search by state and zip code), visit their Web page, and send them some electronic mail. You can do all this and much more on the House of Representatives' Web site. There are up to the hour committee hearing schedules as well as an annual congressional schedule.

Visit at http://www.house.gov/

The U.S. Senate Do you want to find out what is happening in the U.S. Senate? Then visit its Web site. You can get information on recent legislative actions, scheduled activities, committee information, senators and Senate leadership, Senate history, procedures, terminology, and links to other information. This site is less comprehensive than its House counterpart.

Visit at http://www.senate.gov/

Thomas The Library of Congress began the Thomas Web site, in the spirit of Thomas Jefferson, in 1995. It is a collection of legislative information on the Internet. You can find out about floor activities of the House and Senate; bills (by topic, short title, bill number, and so on), bill summaries and status, and public laws; text of the *Congressional Record*, committee information, historical documents, and links to other U.S. government Internet resources.

Visit at http://www.thomas.loc.gov

Critical Thinking Community This site is a resource center that provides the latest information on critical thinking; a bookstore that informs users of materials that are available on-line; a conference center that gives detailed information about upcoming events of interest to the critical thinking community; and a library that holds a growing collection of articles and reference materials on critical thinking.

Visit at http://www.sonoma.edu/cthink/

CYBER EXERCISES:

1. You are interested in a bill that was introduced into the U.S. House of Representatives last month. You want to read the full text of the bill and find out what has happened to it (its legislative history). Using the U.S. House of Representatives Web site, retrieve a current House bill and its legislative history. Print out your results.

2. You want to find out who your representative is in the House of Representatives. Using the U.S. House of Representatives' Web site, determine who your representative is. Print out the biographical material about him or her. Find out what his or her e-mail address is.

3. You want to find out what is on-line from the Internal Revenue Service. Using the Great American Web Site, navigate your way to the Internal Revenue Service and print out its home page.

4. Send a message to the President or Vice President on an issue of importance to you. Using the White House Web site, navigate to the page that lets you send e-mail to the President or Vice President. Print out that page.

5. You want to find out more about critical thinking. Using the Critical Thinking Community Web site, click on "college and university"; then click on "library." From the library, find the *Glossary of Critical Thinking Terms* and print or write out the definition for "dialogical thinking."

CHAPTER SUMMARY

WHAT IS LAW? P. 2

Law	*Law* is a body of rules or action or conduct that has binding legal force. Law must be obeyed by citizens subject to sanction or legal consequences.
Functions of the Law	1. Keep the peace 2. Shape moral standards 3. Promote social justice 4. Maintain the status quo 5. Facilitate orderly change 6. Facilitate planning 7. Provide a basis for compromise 8. Maximize individual freedom
Flexibility and Fairness of the Law	1. *Flexibility.* The law must be flexible to meet social, technological, and economic changes in the United States and the world. 2. *Fairness.* Although the American legal system is one of the fairest and most democratic systems of law, abuses of process and mistakes in the application of the law do occur.

SCHOOLS OF JURISPRUDENTIAL THOUGHT, P. 4

Schools of Jurisprudential Thought	1. *Natural Law School.* Postulates that law is based on what is "correct." It emphasizes a moral theory of law—that is, law should be based on morality and ethics. 2. *Historical School.* Believes that law is an aggregate of social traditions and customs. 3. *Analytical School.* Maintains that law is shaped by logic. 4. *Sociological School.* Asserts that the law is a means of achieving and advancing certain sociological goals. 5. *Command School.* Believes that the law is a set of rules developed, communicated, and enforced by the ruling party. 6. *Law and Economics School.* Believes that promoting market efficiency should be the central concern of legal decision making. 7. *Critical Legal Studies School* (the Crits). Maintains that legal rules are unnecessary and that legal disputes should be solved by applying arbitrary rules based on fairness.

HISTORY OF AMERICAN LAW, P. 6

Foundation of American Law	The English common law (judge-made law) forms the basis of the legal systems of most states in this country. Louisiana bases its law on the French civil code.

SOURCES OF LAW IN THE UNITED STATES, P. 7

Sources of Law in the United States	1. *Constitutions.* The U.S. Constitution establishes the federal government and enumerates its powers. Powers not given to the federal government are reserved to the states. State constitutions establish state governments and enumerate their powers. 2. *Treaties.* The President, with the advice and consent of the Senate, may enter into treaties with foreign countries. 3. *Codified law. Statutes* are enacted by the federal Congress and state legislatures. *Ordinances* are passed by municipalities and local government bodies. They establish courses of conduct that must be followed by covered parties.

4. *Administrative agency regulations and orders.* Administrative agencies are created by the legislative and executive branches of government. They may adopt administrative regulations and issue orders.

5. *Executive orders.* Issued by the President and governors of states. They regulate the conduct of covered parties.

6. *Judicial decisions.* Federal and state courts decide controversies. In doing so, they issue decisions that state the holding of the case and the reasoning used by the court in reaching its decision.

THE CONSTITUTION AND BUSINESS, P. 10	
The U.S. Constitution	The Constitution consists of seven articles and 26 amendments. It establishes the three branches of the federal government, enumerates their powers, and provides important guarantees of individual freedom. The Constitution was ratified by the states in 1788.
Basic Constitutional Concepts	1. *Federalism.* The Constitution created the federal government. The federal government and the 50 state governments share powers in this country.
	2. *Delegated powers.* When the states ratified the Constitution, they delegated certain powers to the federal government. These are called *enumerated powers.*
	3. *Reserved powers.* Those powers not granted to the federal government by the Constitution are reserved to the states.
	4. *Separation of powers.* Each branch of the federal government has separate powers: a. Legislative branch—power to make the law; b. Executive branch—power to enforce the law; c. Judicial branch—power to interpret the law.
	5. *Checks and balances.* Certain checks and balances are built into the Constitution to ensure that no one branch of the federal government becomes too powerful.
THE SUPREMACY CLAUSE, P. 11	
The Supremacy Clause	Stipulates that the U.S. Constitution, treaties, and federal law (statutes and regulations) are the *supreme law of the land.* State or local laws that conflict with valid federal law are unconstitutional. This is called the *preemption doctrine.*
THE COMMERCE CLAUSE, P. 12	
The Commerce Clause	1. *Commerce Clause.* Authorizes the federal government to regulate commerce with foreign nations, among the states, and with Indian tribes.
	2. *Interstate commerce.* Under the broad *effects test*, the federal government may regulate any activity (even intrastate commerce) that *affects* interstate commerce.
	3. *Undue burden on interstate commerce.* Any state or local law that causes an undue burden on interstate commerce is unconstitutional as a violation of the Commerce Clause.
THE BILL OF RIGHTS AND BUSINESS, P. 15	
The Bill of Rights	Consists of the first 10 amendments to the Constitution. They establish basic individual rights. The Bill of Rights was ratified in 1791.
Freedom of Speech	1. *Freedom of Speech Clause.* Clause of the First Amendment that guarantees that the government shall not infringe on a person's right to

speak. Protects oral, written, and symbolic speech. This right is not absolute—that is, some speech is not protected and other speech is granted only limited protection.

2. *Fully protected speech.* Speech that cannot be prohibited or regulated by the government.

3. *Limited protected speech.* The following types of speech are granted only limited protection under the Freedom of Speech Clause—that is, they are subject to governmental *time, place, and manner restrictions*:
   a. Offensive speech
   b. Commercial speech

4. *Unprotected speech.* The following speech is not protected by the Freedom of Speech Clause:
   a. Dangerous speech
   b. Fighting words
   c. Speech that advocates the violent overthrow of the government
   d. Defamatory language
   e. Child pornography
   f. Obscene speech

CRITICAL LEGAL THINKING CASES

1.1 Flexibility of the Law In 1909, the state legislature of Illinois enacted a statute called the "Woman's 10-Hour Law." The law prohibited women who were employed in factories and other manufacturing facilities from working more than 10 hours per day. The law did not apply to men. W.A. Ritchie & Co., an employer, brought a lawsuit that challenged the statute as being unconstitutional in violation of the Equal Protection Clause of the Illinois constitution. In upholding the statute, the Illinois Supreme Court stated,

> It is known to all men (and what we know as men we cannot profess to be ignorant of as judges) that woman's physical structure and the performance of maternal functions place her at a great disadvantage in the battle of life; that while a man can work for more than ten hours a day without injury to himself, a woman, especially when the burdens of motherhood are upon her, cannot; that while a man can work standing upon his feet for more than ten hours a day, day after day, without injury to himself, a woman cannot; and that to require a woman to stand upon her feet for more than ten hours in any one day and perform severe manual labor while thus standing, day after day, has the effect to impair her health, and that as weakly and sickly women cannot be mothers of vigorous children.
>
> We think the general consensus of opinion, not only in this country but in the civilized countries of Europe, is, that a working day of not more than ten hours for women is justified for the following reasons: (1) the physical organization of women; (2) her maternal function; (3) the rearing and education of children; (4) the maintenance of the home; and these conditions are, so far, matters of general knowledge that the courts will take judicial cognizance of their existence.
>
> Surrounded as women are by changing conditions of society, and the evolution of employment which environs them, we agree fully with what is said by the Supreme

Court of Washington in the *Buchanan* case: "Law is, or ought to be, a progressive science."

Is the statute fair? Would the statute be lawful today? Should the law be a "progressive science"? [*W.A. Ritchie & Co. v. Wayman, Attorney for Cook County, Illinois*, 91 N.E. 695 (Ill. 1910)]

1.2 Separation of Powers In 1951, a dispute arose between steel companies and their employees about the terms and conditions that should be included in a new labor contract. At the time, the United States was engaged in a military conflict in Korea that required substantial steel resources from which to make weapons and other military goods. On April 4, 1952, the steelworkers' union gave notice of a nationwide strike called to begin at 12:01 A.M. on April 9. The indispensability of steel as a component in weapons and other war materials led President Dwight D. Eisenhower to believe that the proposed strike would jeopardize the national defense and that governmental seizure of the steel mills was necessary in order to ensure the continued availability of steel. Therefore, a few hours before the strike was to begin, the President issued Executive Order 10340, which directed the secretary of commerce to take possession of most of the steel mills and keep them running. The steel companies obeyed the order under protest and brought proceedings against the President. Was the seizure of the steel mills constitutional? [*Youngstown Co. v. Sawyer, Secretary of Commerce*, 343 U.S. 579, 72 S.Ct. 863 (1952)]

1.3 Preemption Doctrine Article 1, section 8, clause 8 of the U.S. Constitution grants Congress the power to enact laws to give inventors the exclusive right to their discoveries. Pursuant to this power, Congress enacted federal patent laws that establish the requirements to obtain a patent. After a patent is granted, the patent holder has exclusive rights to use the patent. Bonito Boats, Inc. (Bonito) developed a hull design for a fiberglass recreational boat that it marketed under the trade name Bonito Boats Model 5VBR. The manufacturing process involved creating a hardwood model that was sprayed with fiberglass to create a mold. The mold then served to produce the finished fiberglass boats for sale. Bonito did not file a patent application to protect the utilitarian or design aspects of the hull or the manufacturing process. After the Bonito 5VBR was on the market for six years, the Florida legislature enacted a statute prohibiting the use of a direct molding process to duplicate unpatented boat hulls and forbid the knowing sale of hulls so duplicated. The protection afforded under the state statute was broader than that provided for under the federal patent statute. Subsequently, Thunder Craft Boats, Inc. (Thunder Craft) produced and sold boats made by the direct molding process. Bonito sued Thunder Craft under Florida law. Is the Florida statute valid? [*Bonito Boats, Inc. v. Thunder Craft Boats, Inc.*, 489 U.S. 141, 109 S.Ct. 971 (1989)]

1.4 Commerce Clause The Heart of Atlanta Motel, located in the state of Georgia, has 216 rooms available to guests. The motel is readily accessible to interstate highways 75 and 85 and to state highways 23 and 41. The motel solicits patronage from outside the state of Georgia through various national advertising media, including magazines of national circulation, and it maintains more than 50 billboards and highway signs within the state. Approximately 75 percent of the motel's registered guests are from out of state. Congress enacted the Civil Rights Act of 1964, which made it illegal for public accommodations to discriminate against guests based on their race. Prior to that, the Heart of Atlanta Motel had refused to rent rooms to blacks. After the Act was passed, it alleged that it intended to continue not to rent rooms to blacks. The owner of the motel brought an action to have the Civil Rights Act of 1964 declared unconstitutional, alleging that Congress, in passing the Act, had exceeded its powers to regulate commerce under the Commerce Clause of the U.S. Constitution. Who wins? [*Heart of Atlanta Motel v. United States*, 379 U.S. 241, 85 S.Ct. 348 (1964)]

1.5 Commerce Clause The state of Iowa imposes a business tax on corporations. Iowa taxes dividends that a corporation receives from foreign subsidiaries but does not tax dividends received from domestic (U.S.) subsidiaries. In 1981, Kraft General Foods, Inc. (Kraft) operated a business throughout the United States and in several foreign countries through the use of subsidiary corporations. Because part of its business was conducted in Iowa, it was subject to the Iowa business tax on corporations. Kraft deducted dividends it had received from six corporate subsidiaries located in foreign countries from its 1981 Iowa tax return. The Iowa Department of Revenue and Finance (Iowa) assessed a deficiency, which Kraft challenged in Iowa courts. The Iowa Supreme Court rejected Kraft's argument that the Iowa tax violated the Commerce Clause of the

U.S. Constitution. The U.S. Supreme Court granted review. Does the Iowa tax scheme violate the Commerce Clause of the U.S. Constitution? [*Kraft General Foods, Inc. v. Iowa Department of Revenue and Finance*, 112 S.Ct. 2365 (1992)]

1.6 Commerce and Supremacy Clauses In 1972, Congress enacted a federal statute, called the Ports and Waterways Safety Act, that established uniform standards for the operation of boats on inland waterways in the United States. The Act coordinated its provisions with those of foreign countries so that there was a uniform body of international rules that applied to vessels that traveled between countries. Pursuant to the Act, a federal rule was adopted that regulated the design, length, and size of oil tankers, some of which traveled the waters of the Puget Sound area in the state of Washington. Oil tankers from various places entered Puget Sound to bring crude oil to refineries located in Washington. In 1975, the state of Washington enacted a statute that established different designs, smaller lengths, and smaller sizes for oil tankers serving Puget Sound than allowed by the federal law. Oil tankers used by the Atlantic Richfield Company (ARCO) to bring oil into Puget Sound met the federal standards but not the state standards. ARCO sued to have the state statute declared unconstitutional. Who wins? [*Ray, Governor of Washington v. Atlantic Richfield Co.*, 435 U.S. 151, 98 S.Ct. 988 (1978)]

1.7 Undue Burden on Interstate Commerce Most trucking firms, including Consolidated Freightways Corporation (Consolidated), use 65-foot-long "double" trailer trucks to ship commodities on the highway system across the United States. Almost all states permit vehicles on their highways. The federal government does not regulate the length of trucks that can use the nation's highways. The state of Iowa enacted a statute that restricts the length of trucks that can use highways in the state to 55 feet. This means that if Consolidated wants to move goods through Iowa it must either use smaller trucks or detach the double trailers and shuttle them through the state separately. Its only other alternative is to divert its 65-foot doubles around Iowa. Consolidated filed suit against Iowa alleging that the state statute is unconstitutional. Is it? [*Kassel v. Consolidated Freightways Corporation*, 450 U.S. 662, 101 S.Ct. 1309 (1981)]

1.8 Commercial Speech The city of San Diego, California, enacted a city zoning ordinance that prohibited outdoor advertising display signs—including billboards. On-site signs at a business location were exempted from this rule. The city based the restrictions on traffic safety and esthetics. Metromedia, Inc., a company that is in the business of leasing commercial billboards to advertisers, sued the city of San Diego, alleging that the zoning ordinance is unconstitutional. Is it? [*Metromedia, Inc. v. City of San Diego*, 453 U.S. 490, 101 S.Ct. 2882 (1981)]

 ETHICS CASES

1.9 Ethical Perspective In 1975, after the war in Vietnam, the U.S. government discontinued draft registration for men in the United States. In 1980, after the Soviet Union invaded

Afghanistan, President Jimmy Carter asked Congress for funds to reactivate draft registration. President Carter suggested that both males and females be required to register. Congress allocated funds only for the registration of males. Several men who were subject to draft registration brought a lawsuit that challenged the law as being unconstitutional in violation of the Equal Protection Clause of the U.S. Constitution. The U.S. Supreme Court upheld the constitutionality of the draft registration law, reasoning as follows:

> The question of registering women for the draft not only received considerable national attention and was the subject of wide-ranging public debate, but also was extensively considered by Congress in hearings, floor debate, and in committee. The foregoing clearly establishes that the decision to exempt women from registration was not the "accidental by-product of a traditional way of thinking about women."
>
> "This is not a case of Congress arbitrarily choosing to burden one of two similarly situated groups, such as would be the case with an all-black or all-white, or an all-Catholic or all-Lutheran, or an all-Republican or all-Democratic registration. Men and women are simply not similarly situated for purposes of a draft or registration for a draft."

Justice Marshall dissented, stating that "The Court today places its imprimatur on one of the most potent remaining public expressions of 'ancient canards about the proper role of women.' It upholds a statute that requires males but not females to register for the draft, and which thereby categorically excludes women from a fundamental civic obligation. I dissent."

Was the decision fair? Has the law been a "progressive science" in this case? Is it ethical for males, but not females, to have to register for the draft? [*Rostker, Director of the Selective Service v. Goldberg*, 453 U.S. 57, 101 S.Ct. 2646 (1981)]

1.10 Ethical Perspective The Federal Communications Act (Act) authorizes the Federal Communications Commission (FCC) to regulate television and radio broadcasts in this country. The FCC adopted a regulation that requires cable television operators to transmit all signals "in full, without deletion or alteration of any portion," including commercials. A provision in the Oklahoma state constitution prohibited the advertising of alcoholic beverages within the state. Many out-of-state cable broadcasts contain alcoholic beverage commercials. When the director of the Oklahoma Alcoholic Beverage Control Board (Board) threatened to criminally prosecute cable operators that televised out-of-state alcoholic beverage commercials in the state. Capital Cities Cable, Inc. and other cable operators sued the Board, alleging that the Oklahoma law was preempted by federal law. The U.S. district court held for the cable operators, but the U.S. court of appeals reversed. The cable operators appealed to the U.S. Supreme Court.

Is the provision in the Oklahoma constitution that prohibits the advertising of alcoholic beverage commercials by cable operators preempted by federal law? Should a state, through its laws, try to impose ethical standards on its residents like Oklahoma tried to do in this case? [*Capital Cities Cable, Inc. v. Crisp, Director, Oklahoma Alcoholic Beverage Control Board*, 467 U.S. 691, 104 S.Ct. 2694 (1984)]

1.11 Ethical Perspective The Coors Brewing Company (Coors) is a brewer that produces and sells beer under various brand names. Coors applied to the Bureau of Alcohol, Tobacco and Firearms (ATF), the federal administrative agency that regulates the sale of alcoholic beverages in the United States, for permission to disclose the alcohol content of its beer on the labels on its beer cans and bottles. The ATF rejected the application, citing the fact that the Federal Alcohol Administration Act (Act) prohibited the disclosure of alcohol content of beer on labels. Coors sued in federal court for injunctive relief, alleging that the restriction violated its commercial speech rights. The federal government defended the Act, arguing that the prohibition on disclosing alcohol content on beer labels prevented the threat of "strength wars" among brewers who would seek to compete in the marketplace based on the potency of their beer. The district court held in favor of Coors and the court of appeals affirmed. The federal government appealed to the U.S. Supreme Court.

Is the ban on the disclosure of alcohol content on beer labels a valid restriction on commercial speech? Was the federal government's reason for the ban justified? Why do you think Coors wanted to disclose this information? [*Rubin v. Coors Brewing Company*, 115 S.Ct. 1585 (1995)]

 CRITICAL LEGAL THINKING WRITING ASSIGNMENT

Read Case A.1 in the Case Appendix [*Lee v. Weisman*]. This case is excerpted from the U.S. Supreme Court's opinion. Review and brief the case. In your brief, be sure to answer the following questions:

1. Who are the plaintiff and defendant?
2. What does the Establishment Clause provide?

3. Was the fact that the prayer was nonsectarian important to the Supreme Court's decision?
4. What argument did the dissenting opinion make in support of allowing prayer at high school graduation ceremonies?
5. How close was the vote by the justices in this case?

NOTES

1 *The Spirit of Liberty*, 3d ed (New York: Alfred A. Knopf, 1960).
2 Introduction, *The Nature of Law: Readings in Legal Philosophy*, ed. M.P. Golding (New York: Random House, 1966).

3 *Black's Law Dictionary*, 5th ed (St. Paul, Minn.: West Publishing Co., 1979).
4 347 U.S. 483, 74 S.Ct. 686, 98 L.Ed. 873 (1954).
5 Judge Jerome Frank, *Law and the Modern Mind* (New York: Brentano's, 1930).

[6] 447 U.S. 10, 100 S.Ct. 1999, 64 L.E.2d 689 (1980).

[7] 4 Ill. 301 (Ill. 1841).

[8] 208 A.2d 193 (Pa. 1965).

[9] To be elected to Congress, an individual must be a U.S. citizen, either naturally born or granted citizenship. To serve in the Senate, a person must be 30 years of age or older. To serve in the House of Representatives, a person must be 25 years of age or older.

[10] To be President, a person must be 35 years of age or older and a natural citizen of the United States. By amendment to the Constitution (Amendment XXII), a person can serve only two full terms as President.

[11] Federal court judges and justices are appointed by the President with the consent of the Senate.

[12] The principle that the U.S. Supreme Court is the final arbiter of the U.S. Constitution evolved from *Marbury v. Madison*, 1 Cranch 137 (1803). In that case, the Supreme Court held that a judiciary statute enacted by Congress was unconstitutional.

[13] Article VI, Section 2.

[14] Article I, Section 8, clause 3.

[15] 317 U.S. Ill. 63 S.Ct. 82, 87 L.Ed. 122 (1942).

[16] *Chaplinsky v. New Hampshire*, 315 U.S. 568, 62 S.Ct. 766, 86 L.Ed. 1031 (1942).

[17] *Brandenburg v. Ohio*, 395 U.S. 444, 89 S.Ct. 1827, 23 L.Ed. 430 (1969).

[18] *Beauharnais v. Illinois*, 343 U.S. 250, 72 S.Ct. 725, 96 L.Ed. 919 (1952).

[19] *New York v. Ferber*, 458 U.S. 747, 102 S.Ct. 3348, 73 L.Ed.2d 1113 (1982).

[20] *Roth v. United States*, 354 U.S. 476, 77 S.Ct. 1304, 1 L.Ed.2d 1498 (1957).

[21] 425 U.S. 748, 96 S.Ct. 1817, 48 L.Ed.2d 346 (1976).

CHAPTER 2

ETHICS AND SOCIAL

RESPONSIBILITY OF BUSINESS

Chapter Objectives

*After studying this chapter,
you should be able to*

1. Describe ethical fundamentalism
2. Describe utilitarianism as a moral theory
3. Describe Kantian ethics
4. Describe Rawls's social justice theory
5. Describe ethical relativism
6. Describe maximizing profits as a theory of social responsibility
7. Describe the moral minimum theory of social responsibility
8. Describe the stakeholder interest theory of social responsibility
9. Describe the corporate citizenship theory of social responsibility
10. Describe corporate social audits

Chapter Contents

- Law and Ethics
- Moral Theories and Business Ethics
  Ethical Perspective General Motors Skips Town
  Ethical Perspective Can Company Canned
  Ethical Perspective Sears's Auto Repair Centers: Who Got the Lube Job?
  Ethical Perspective Hypocrite or Hippocratic Oath: A Difficult Choice
- The Social Responsibility of Business
  International Perspective Ethical Issues in International Business: Payment of Bribes
  Ethical Perspective The Exxon Valdez: Did Business Run Aground on Environmental Protection?
  Ethical Perspective Constituency Statutes
  Ethical Perspective Where There's Smoke, *There's* . . .
  Business Checklist The Corporate Social Audit
  International Perspective Caux Round Table Principles for International Business
- Working the Web
- Chapter Summary
- Ethics Cases
- Critical Legal Thinking Writing Assignment

> *Ethical considerations can no more be excluded from the administration of justice, which is the end and purpose of all civil laws, than one can exclude the vital air from his room and live.*
>
> John F. Dillon
> *Laws and Jurisprudence of England and America*
> Lecture I (1894)

"Ethics precede laws as man precedes society."
Jason Alexander
Philosophy for Investors (1979)

Businesses organized in the United States are subject to its laws. They are also subject to the laws of other countries in which they operate. In addition, businesspersons owe a duty to act ethically in the conduct of their affairs, and businesses owe a social responsibility not to harm society.

Although much of the law is based on ethical standards, not all ethical standards have been enacted as law. The law establishes a minimum degree of conduct expected by persons and businesses in society. Ethics demands more. This chapter discusses business ethics and the social responsibility of business.

LAW AND ETHICS

ethics A set of moral principles or values that governs the conduct of an individual or a group.

Sometimes the rule of law and the golden rule of **ethics** demand the same response by the person confronted with a problem. For example, federal and state laws make bribery unlawful. Thus, a person violates the law if he or she bribes a judge for a favorable decision in a case. Ethics would also prohibit this conduct.

The law may permit something that would be ethically wrong.

"The notion that a business is clothed with a public interest and has been devoted to the public use is little more than a fiction intended to beautify what is disagreeable to the sufferers."
Justice Holmes
Tyson & Bro-United Theatre Ticket Officers v. Banton (1927)

CONSIDER THIS EXAMPLE: Occupational safety laws set standards for emissions of dust from toxic chemicals in the workplace. Suppose a company can reduce the emissions below the legal standard by spending additional money. The only benefit from the expenditure would be better employee health. Ethics would require the extra expenditure; the law would not.

Alternatively, the law may demand certain conduct that goes against a person's ethical standards.

CONSIDER THIS EXAMPLE: Federal law prohibits employers from hiring certain illegal alien workers. Suppose an employer advertises the availability of a job and receives no responses except from a person who cannot prove he is a citizen of this country or does not possess a required visa. He and his family are destitute. Should the employer hire him? The law says no, but ethics says yes (see Exhibit 2.1).

Exhibit 2.1
Law and Ethics

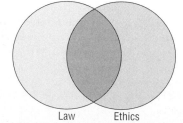

Law   Ethics

MORAL THEORIES AND BUSINESS ETHICS

"He who seeks equity must do equity."
Joseph Story
Equity Jurisprudence (1836)

How can ethics be measured? The answer is very personal: What is considered ethical by one person may be considered unethical by another. However, there seems to be some universal rules about what conduct is ethical and what conduct is not. The following discussion highlights five major theories of ethics.

Ethical Fundamentalism

Under **ethical fundamentalism**, a person looks to an *outside source* for ethical rules or commands. This may be a book (e.g., the Bible or the Koran) or a person (e.g., Karl Marx). Critics argue that ethical fundamentalism does not permit people to determine right and wrong for themselves. Taken to an extreme, the result could be considered unethical under most other moral theories. For example, a literal interpretation of the maxim "an eye for an eye" would permit retaliation.

Many companies have adopted **codes of ethics** that establish ethical principles for their employees.

ethical fundamentalism
When a person looks to an outside source for ethical rules or commands.

Utilitarianism

Utilitarianism is a moral theory with its origins in the works of Jeremy Bentham (1748–1832) and John Stuart Mill (1806–1873). This moral theory dictates that people must choose the action or follow the rule that provides the *greatest good to society*. This does not mean the greatest good for the greatest number of people. For instance, if one action would increase the good of 25 people one unit each, and an alternative action would increase the good of one person 26 units, the latter action should be taken.

utilitarianism A moral theory that dictates that people must choose the action or follow the rule that provides the greatest good to society.

CONSIDER THIS EXAMPLE: A company is trying to determine whether it should close an unprofitable plant located in a small community. Utilitarianism would require that the benefits to shareholders from closing the plant be compared to the benefits to employees, their families, and others in the community in keeping it open.

Utilitarianism has been criticized because it is difficult to estimate the "good" that will result from different actions, it is hard to apply in an imperfect world, and it treats morality as if it were an impersonal mathematical calculation.

"The ultimate justification of the law is to be found, and can only be found, in moral considerations."
Lord MacMillan
Law and Other Things (1937)

ETHICAL PERSPECTIVE

General Motors Skips Town

For decades, job-hungry communities have offered tax abatements, low-interest loans, and other financial inducements to lure companies to locate in their community. Some companies take these incentives but then leave town when they run out. Cities are fighting back, and many are bringing lawsuits.

Consider the case of Ypsilanti, Michigan. From 1984 to 1988, Ypsilanti gave General Motors Corporation (GM) $13 million in tax abatements to keep its Willow Run plant, which produced Chevrolet automobiles, in the city. In 1991, GM announced that it was going to close the Willow Run plant and move the work

being done there to its Arlington, Texas, plant. The closure meant the loss of thousands of jobs in a city already suffering severe unemployment and financial difficulties.

Ypsilanti sued GM for reneging on its implied promise to stay put in return for the tax breaks. The trial court judge invoked the doctrine of promissory estoppel and enjoined GM from closing its plant in Ypsilanti.

The trial court judge stated, "There would be a gross inequity and patent unfairness if General Motors, having lulled the people of the Ypsilanti area into giving up millions of tax dollars which they desperately need to educate

their children and provide basic governmental services, is allowed to simply decide it will desert 4,500 workers and their families because it thinks it can make these same cars cheaper somewhere else."

The Michigan court of appeals reversed, however. The appeals court held that GM made no promise to stay put in Ypsilanti as a quid pro quo for the tax abatements. The court held that any statements made by GM concerning maintaining continuous employment at the Willow Run plant were merely expressions of hope or expectation, but did not amount to a promise. The court's *continued* decision permits GM to transfer production from the Michigan plant to Texas. [*Charter Township of Ypsilanti, Michigan v. General Motors Corporation*, No. 161245 (Mich. App. 1993)]

1. Did GM act ethically by attempting to close its plant in Ypsilanti? Would your answer be different if GM were losing money at the plant?
2. Which court do you think was

correct, the trial court or the court of appeals?
3. Could Ypsilanti have protected itself from what happened in this case? Explain.

Kantian Ethics

Kantian or duty ethics A moral theory that says that people owe moral duties that are based on universal rules such as the categorical imperative "Do unto others as you would have them do unto you."

Immanuel Kant (1724–1804) is the best-known proponent of **duty ethics**, or **deontology** (from the Greek word *deon*, meaning duty). Kant believed that people owe moral duties that are based on *universal rules*. For example, keeping a promise to abide by a contract is a moral duty even if that contract turns out to be detrimental to the obligated party. Kant's philosophy is based on the premise that man can use reasoning to reach ethical decisions. His ethical theory would have people behave according to the *categorical imperative* "Do unto others as you would have them do unto you."

Deontology's universal rules are based on two important principles: (1) consistency, that is, all cases are treated alike with no exceptions; and (2) reversibility, that is, the actor must abide by the rule he or she uses to judge the morality of someone else's conduct. Thus, if you are going to make an exception for yourself, then that exception becomes a universal rule that applies to all others. For instance, if you rationalize that it is all right for you to engage in deceptive practices, then it is all right for competitors to do so also. A criticism of Kantian ethics is that it is hard to reach a consensus as to what the universal rules should be.

ETHICAL PERSPECTIVE

Can Company Canned

The Continental Can Company (Continental) manufactured and sold steel cans to food, beverage, and packaging companies. It had more than 50 plants located throughout the United States. In the late 1960s, Continental was the leading producer of metal cans in this country. Its workers were represented by the United Steel Workers Union.

Beginning in the 1960s, many users began self-manufacturing the cans they needed. In addition, aluminum cans were introduced and took over a large seg-

ment of the beverage can market. By 1980, more than 90 percent of the beverage business was in aluminum cans. As a result of self-manufacturing and aluminum cans, the demand for Continental's steel cans declined. Continental was left with obsolete factories and underutilized workers. Continental decided to reduce employment in its steel can business and enter new lines of business.

However, there was a problem with reducing the number of employees: Continental had entered

into a collective bargaining agreement with the United Steel Workers Union that required Continental to pay a special pension (the "Magic Number" pension) to workers who were discharged who met stipulated qualifications. A discharged worker qualified for this special pension if he or she had at least 15 years of regular continuous service with Continental and was 50 years of age or older. The pension liability was unfunded, however. Consequently, the monies to pay the pensions would have to be paid out of current income and assets at a cost of more than $100,000 per worker.

Continental's top management devised a secret plan, called the "Bell" system, to reduce its workforce while avoiding liability for the Magic Number pensions. Under the system, workers who had already qualified for the pension were not discharged. Instead, the company targeted employees who were close to qualifying.

Continental developed a sophisticated computer program that enabled management to identify which employees to target. These employees were then discharged.

In addition, a "red flag" program was instituted to keep track of laid-off employees in order to prevent their rehire anywhere in the company because that would resurrect their pension rights. The Bell and red flag systems

were kept secret from the affected employees.

In 1983, when the systems came to light, many discharged employees sued Continental for damages. They asserted that Continental violated Section 510 of the federal **Employee Retirement Income Security Act of 1974 (ERISA)** [29 U.S.C. § 1140]. This section provides, "It shall be unlawful for any person to discharge, fine, suspend, expel, discipline, or discriminate against a participant or beneficiary for exercising any right to which he is entitled under the provisions of an employee benefit plan, or for interfering with the attainment of any right to which such participant may become entitled under the plan."

After a lengthy trial, the court held in favor of the plaintiffs. The court stated, "The court has found that Continental violated ERISA and set upon a deliberate course of conduct aimed at de-

priving employees of eligibility for bargained-for pensions." The court added, "For a corporation of this magnitude to engage in a complex, secret and deliberate scheme to deny its workers bargained-for pension benefits raises questions of corporate morality, ethics and decency which far transcend the factual and legal issues posed in this matter."

Eventually, a settlement was reached and the affected workers received payment of their pension benefits. [*McLendon v. Continental Group, Inc.*, 749 F.Supp. 582 (D.N.J. 1989)]

1. Did the top management of Continental act unethically by instituting the Bell and red flag systems?
2. Did Continental act unethically in defending the lawsuits? Is it ever ethical to defend a lawsuit when the defendant knows that he or she is guilty?

Rawls's Social Justice Theory

John Locke (1632–1704) and Jean Jacques Rousseau (1712–1778) proposed a **social contract** theory of morality. Under this theory, each person is presumed to have entered into a *social contract* with all others in society to obey moral rules that are necessary for people to live in peace and harmony. This implied contract states, "I will keep the rules if everyone else does." These moral rules are then used to solve conflicting interests in society.

The leading proponent of the modern social justice theory is John Rawls, a contemporary philosopher at Harvard University. Under Rawls's **distributive justice theory**, fairness is considered the essence of justice. The principles of justice should be chosen by persons who do not yet know their station in society—thus, their "evil of ignorance" would permit the fairest possible principles to be selected. For instance, the principle of equal opportunity would be promulgated by people who would not yet know if they were in a favored class. As a caveat, Rawls also proposes that the least advantaged in society must receive special assistance to allow them to realize their potential.

Rawls's theory of distributive justice is criticized for two reasons. First, establishing the blind "original position" for choosing moral principles is impossible in the real world. Second, many persons in society would choose not to maximize the benefit to the least advantaged persons in society.

Rawls's social contract
A moral theory that says each person is presumed to have entered into a social contract with all others in society to obey moral rules that are necessary for people to live in peace and harmony.

"If we are to keep our democracy, there must be one commandment: Thou shalt not ration justice."
Learned Hand
Address (1951)

ETHICAL PERSPECTIVE

Sears's Auto Repair Centers: Who Got the Lube Job?

Sears Roebuck & Co. is a venerable retailer at which generations of Americans have shopped for clothes, tools, appliances, and other goods and services. For years, the company billed itself as the place "where Americans shop." Sears's auto repair centers, which generate more than $3 billion in annual sales, have been charged with being the place where Americans get robbed.

Spurred by a 50 percent increase in consumer complaints over a three-year period, several states conducted undercover investigations to determine the legitimacy of those complaints. The New Jersey Division of Consumer Affairs found that all six Sears Auto Centers visited by undercover agents recommended unnecessary repairs. The California Department of Consumer Affairs found that Sears—the largest provider of auto services in the state—had systematically overcharged an average of $223 for repairs and routinely billed for work that was not done. Forty-one other states lodged similar complaints.

The "bait and rip off" scheme worked as follows: Sears would send consumers coupons advertising discounts on brake jobs. When customers came in to redeem their coupons, the sales staff would convince them to authorize additional repairs. Sears also established quotas for repair services that their employees had to meet.

California officials got the company's attention when the state started proceedings to revoke Sears's auto repair license. Sears quickly agreed to settle all lawsuits against it. As part of the settlement, Sears agreed to distribute $50 worth of coupons to almost one million customers nationwide who obtained one of five specific repair services from Sears between August 1, 1990, and January 31, 1992. The coupons could be redeemed for merchandise and services at Sears stores. In addition, Sears agreed to pay $3.5 million to cover the costs of various government investigations, to contribute $1.5 million to community colleges to conduct auto mechanic training programs, and to abandon its repair service quotas. The settlement cost Sears $30 million.

California placed Sears on an embarrassing three-year probation. The state can revoke Sears's auto repair license if the retailer violates its probation by charging consumers for unneeded repairs.

In the meantime, undercover investigations will continue.

In agreeing to the settlement, Sears denied any wrongdoing, simply stating that "mistakes were made." It said that it agreed to the settlement to avoid the burden, expenses, and uncertainty of prolonged litigation.

Consumer advocates criticize the settlement as being too low. They also assert that the settlement should have been made in cash because it will boost sales of Sears's stores as consumers go there to redeem the coupons. Proponents of the settlement argue that Sears has been punished adequately. They also point to the fact that Sears's auto repair sales dropped 15 to 20 percent since the scandal broke.

1. Did Sears act ethically in this case? Should it have admitted culpability?
2. Why do you think Sears chose to settle the cases instead of defending itself in court?
3. Do you think Sears let the "profit motive" overshadow its ethics?
4. Is the settlement sufficient? Do you think Sears engaged in this conduct prior to the undercover investigation?

Ethical Relativism

ethical relativism A moral theory that holds that individuals must decide what is ethical based on their own feelings as to what is right or wrong.

Ethical relativism holds that individuals must decide what is ethical based on their *own feelings* as to what is right or wrong. Under this moral theory, if a person meets his own moral standard in making a decision, no one can criticize him or her for it. Thus, there are no universal ethical rules to guide a person's conduct. This theory has been criticized because action that is usually thought to be unethical (e.g., committing fraud) would not be unethical if the perpetrator thought it was in fact ethical. Few philosophers advocate ethical relativism as an acceptable moral theory.

ETHICAL PERSPECTIVE

Hypocrite or Hippocratic Oath: A Difficult Choice

Dr. Grace Pierce was a medical doctor employed as the director of medical research by the Ortho Pharmaceutical Corporation (Ortho), a company that produces drugs and health care products. In 1975, Dr. Pierce was assigned to a project to develop loperamide, a liquid drug administered for the treatment of diarrhea in infants, children, and elderly persons.

The proposed formulation of loperamide contained high levels of saccharin in amounts approximately 44 times greater than the level permitted by law in soft drinks. Saccharin had been shown to cause cancer in laboratory animals when taken in excessive quantities. Ortho filed a new drug application with the federal Food and Drug Administration (FDA) to test loperamide on human beings. Evidence showed that Ortho acted lawfully in conducting all research relating to loperamide and in seeking approval of the FDA to test it on humans.

Dr. Pierce voiced disappointment with Ortho's decision to test the drug on human beings because she believed the high level of saccharin would pose a danger to the subjects. She told her supervisor that her continued work on the project violated her interpretation of the Hippocratic oath and her

personal ethical principles. The Hippocratic oath is taken by physicians and other health-care professionals. In it they promise to save human lives. The part of the oath cited by Dr. Pierce states: "I will prescribe regimen for the good of my patients according to my ability and my judgment and never do harm to anyone."

Ortho informed Dr. Pierce that she would no longer be assigned to the loperamide project and asked her to choose another project to which to be assigned. Dr. Pierce, who viewed this as a demotion, tendered her resignation. She then sued Ortho to recover damages for wrongful termination, alleging that Ortho effectively discharged her by forcing her to resign from her position. The trial court granted Ortho's motion for summary judgment and dismissed Dr. Pierce's complaint. The appellate court reversed and remanded the case for a full trial. Ortho appealed to the Supreme Court of New Jersey. The supreme court reversed the appellate court and reinstated the summary judgment in favor of Ortho.

The court found that Dr. Pierce was an employee "at will" who could be dismissed by Ortho for failing to perform her assigned and lawful duties. In upholding her dismissal by Ortho, the court stated,

"An employee does not have a right to continued employment when he or she refuses to conduct research simply because it would contravene his or her personal morals. An employee at will who refuses to work for an employer in answer to a call of conscience should recognize that other employees and their employer might heed a different call." The court noted, "Chaos would result if a single doctor engaged in research were allowed to determine, according to his or her individual conscience, whether a project should continue. To hold otherwise would seriously impair the ability of drug manufacturers to develop new drugs according to their best judgment." The state supreme court ordered Dr. Pierce's case against Ortho dismissed. [*Pierce v. Ortho Pharmaceutical Corporation*, 417 A.2d 505 (N.J. 1980)]

1. Did Ortho violate the law by dismissing Dr. Pierce from the loperamide project? Did it act unethically in doing so?
2. Should Dr. Pierce be admired for letting her ethical principles guide her decision not to work on the loperamide project? What would you have done in her situation?
3. Did Dr. Pierce act ethically in suing Ortho?

CONCEPT SUMMARY	THEORIES OF ETHICS
Theory	**Description**
Ethical fundamentalism	Persons look to an outside source (e.g., Bible or Koran) or central figure for ethical guidelines.
Utilitarianism	Persons choose the alternative that would provide the greatest good to society.
Kantian ethics	A set of universal rules establishes ethical duties. The rules are based on reasoning, and require (1) consistency in application and (2) reversibility.
Rawls's social justice theory	Moral duties are based on an implied social contract. Fairness is justice. The rules are established from an original position of a "veil of ignorance."
Ethical relativism	Individuals decide what is ethical based on their own feelings as to what is right or wrong.

THE SOCIAL RESPONSIBILITY OF BUSINESS

social responsibility Duty owed by businesses to act socially responsible in producing and selling goods and services.

Business does not operate in a vacuum. Decisions made by businesses have far-reaching effects on society. In the past, many business decisions were made solely on a cost-benefit analysis and how it affected the "bottom line." Such decisions, however, may cause negative externalities for others. For example, the dumping of hazardous wastes from a manufacturing plant into a river affects homeowners, farmers, and others who use the river's waters. Thus, corporations are considered to owe some degree of **social responsibility** for their actions. Four theories of the social responsibility of business are discussed in the following sections.

Maximizing Profits

maximize profits A theory of social responsibility that says a corporation owes a duty to take actions that maximize profits for shareholders.

The traditional view of the social responsibility of business is that business should **maximize profits** for shareholders. This view, which dominated business and the law during the 19th century, holds that the interests of other constituencies (e.g., employees, suppliers, residents of the communities in which businesses are located) are not important in and of themselves.

In the famous case of *Dodge v. Ford Motor Company*,[1] a shareholder sued the car company when Henry Ford introduced a plan to reduce the price of cars so that more people would be put to work and more people could own cars. The shareholders alleged that such a plan would not increase dividends. Mr. Ford testified, "My ambition is to employ still more men, to spread the benefits of this industrial system to the greatest number, to help them build up their lives and their homes." The court sided with the shareholders and stated that "[Mr. Ford's] testimony creates the impression that he thinks the Ford Motor Company has made too much money, has had too large profits and that, although large profits, might still be earned, a sharing of them with the public, by reducing the price of the output of the company, ought to be undertaken."

BUSINESS BRIEF

Patagonia, the Ventura, California–based outdoor apparel company, gives the greater of 10 percent of annual pretax profits or 1 percent of sales to environmental causes.

"Public policy: That principle of the law which holds that no subject can lawfully do that which has a tendency to be injurious to the public, or against the public good."
Lord Truro
Egerton v. Brownlow (1853)

There should be no confusion of the duties which Mr. Ford conceives that he and the stockholders owe to the general public and the duties that in law he and his codirectors owe to protesting, minority stockholders. A business corporation is organized and carried on primarily for the profit of the stockholders. The powers of the directors are to be employed for that end. The discretion of directors is to be exercised in the choice of means to attain that end and does not extend to a change in the end itself, to the reduction of profits, or to the nondistribution of profits among stockholders in order to devote them to other purposes. Milton Friedman, who won the Nobel Prize in economics when he taught at the University of Chicago, advocated this theory. Friedman asserted that in a free society "there is one and only one social responsibility of business—to use its resources and engage in activities designed to increase its profits as long as it stays within the rules of the game, which is to say, engages in open and free competition without deception and fraud."[2]

INTERNATIONAL PERSPECTIVE

Ethical Issues in International Business: Payment of Bribes

Universal ethical rules might exist within a country, but they definitely do not exist for the world as a whole. This is because the cultures and laws of countries are different. Thus, what might be unethical in one country might be considered ethical in another. A corporation that operates in many countries—a "transnational company"—is faced with a dilemma: Does it follow the ethical rule of its parent country or its host country?

The Lockheed Corporation (Lockheed), a *Fortune* 500 company that manufactures aircraft, faced this problem. In the 1970s, it manufactured the L-1011, or "TriStar," commercial airliner. It competed with McDonnell Douglas and Boeing, both U.S. corporations, as well as other competitors, to sell the aircraft to airline carriers in the United States and other countries.

In 1975, an investigation revealed that Lockheed had paid more than $12 million to the president of All Nippon Airlines (ANA) and several Japanese politicians and government officials in conjunction with its sale of L-1011s to the airline carrier. A. Carl Kotchian, the chairman of Lockheed, authorized the payments. Congressional hearings on the matter revealed that such payments were common in the aircraft industry.

Mr. Kotchian provided several justifications for his actions. First, he cited the fact that such payments by Lockheed in Japan did not at the time violate any U.S. laws. Second, he testified that the payments were "worthwhile from Lockheed's standpoint" because "they would provide Lockheed workers with jobs, and thus redound to the benefit of their dependents, their communities, and stockholders of the corporation."

Concerning one of the payments, Mr. Kotchian wrote:

> My initiation into the chill realities of extortion, Japanese style, began in 1972. In August of that year I flew to Tokyo to work for the sale to a Japanese airline of Lockheed's

wide-bodied TriStar passenger plane.

Soon after landing in Japan, I found myself deep in conversation with Toshiharu Okubo, an official of Marubeni, the trading company that was serving as Lockheed's representative and go-between in the already ongoing TriStar negotiations.

Beaming, Okubo reviewed Marubeni's efforts on behalf of TriStar, then gave me the good news that "tomorrow at seven-thirty A.M. we are seeing Prime Minister Tanaka" about the matter. I was quite impressed with and encouraged by the "power of Marubeni"—power that made it possible to make an appointment with the prime minister only 24 hours after I had asked Marubeni to set up such a meeting. Then came an unexpected development: When we began to discuss in detail how to bring about the sale of TriStar, Okubo suddenly suggested that I make a "pledge" to pay money for a major favor like this. Though the proposal did not appall and outrage me, I was nonetheless quite astonished that the question of money had been brought up so abruptly—especially since in broaching the idea Okubo mentioned the name of the prime minister's secretary, Toshio Enomoto.

"How much money do we have to pledge?" I asked.

"The going rate when asking for a major favor is usually five hundred million yen."

I was now faced with the problem of whether to make a payment to Japan's highest government office. Sensing my hesitation, Okubo reiterated, "If you wish to be successful in selling the aircraft, you would do well to pledge five hundred million yen."

Lockheed made this payment and similar payments and was successful in selling planes to the Japanese.

The Lockheed case and similar cases led Congress to enact the **Foreign Corrupt Practices Act of 1977** (15 U.S.C. § 78m). This act, as amended, makes it a crime for U.S. companies to bribe a foreign official, a foreign political party official, or a candidate for foreign political office. The payment of a bribe does not violate the act if the payment was lawful under the written laws of the foreign country in which it was paid, however.

1. Did Lockheed act morally in making the payments? Did it violate the ethical principles dominant in the United States or Japan?
2. Did the fact that U.S. law did not make the payments unlawful at that time they were made justify them?
3. Should economic factors (e.g., jobs) outweigh ethics? Explain.

Moral Minimum

Some proponents of corporate social responsibility argue that a corporation's duty is to *make a profit while avoiding causing harm to others*. This theory of social responsibility is called the **moral minimum**. Under this theory, as long as business avoids or corrects the social injury it causes, it has met its duty of social responsibility. For example, a corporation that pollutes the waters and then compensates those whom it injures has met its moral minimum duty of social responsibility.

The legislative and judicial branches of government have established laws that enforce the moral minimum of social responsibility on corporations. Occupational safety laws establish minimum safety standards for protecting employees from injuries in the workplace. Consumer protection laws establish safety requirements for products and make manufacturers and sellers liable for injuries caused by defective products. Other laws establish similar minimum standards of conduct for business in other areas.

moral minimum A theory of social responsibility that says a corporation's duty is to make a profit while avoiding harm to others.

BUSINESS BRIEF

Many people do not buy tuna because the tuna nets also catch dolphins. Is this socially responsible behavior? Should someone care about the tuna?

ETHICAL PERSPECTIVE

The *Exxon Valdez*: Did Business Run Aground on Environmental Protection?

On March 12, 1989, the *Exxon Valdez*, a supertanker carrying more than 11 million gallons of oil, left a terminal near Valdez, Alaska. The weather was calm as it moved through Prince William Sound toward the open waters of the Pacific Ocean and its final destination, an oil refinery located along the West Coast. The ship was under the command of Captain Hazelwood, who was alleged to have been drinking prior to leaving shore. He had a known history of alcohol abuse and had lost his driver's license for drunk driving. At about midnight, Captain Hazelwood left the bridge of the ship for his cabin, instructing third mate Gregory Cousins to steer clear of any ice in the water. What happened after that was a nightmare.

After passing the Busby Island light, Cousins steered the ship too far south until it was almost on Bligh Reef. When he realized the situation, he called for a hard-right rudder—but it was too late to prevent the ship from crashing into a submerged rock at 12 knots and going aground. The hull of the ship ripped open in eight places, sending millions of gallons of oil surging into the water of the sound.

Alyeska is a service company formed by the seven oil companies with North Slope interests that is primarily responsible for responding to such disasters. When Alyeska's ranking executive was called at home within half an hour of the grounding, he dispatched a subordinate to check things out and rolled over and went back to sleep. The plan that Alyeska had previously submitted to the Alaskan government stipulated that it could reach any disaster site with equipment to deal with the problem within five hours. In actuality, one Alyeska barge reached the site 14 hours after the spill. The millions of gallons of oil overwhelmed the handful of oil skimmers that Alyeska had brought. Over the next few days, a 100-square-mile oil slick formed and moved toward the Alaskan shore. Eventually, 1,100 miles of shoreline were soaked by the oil.

Exxon's inadequate and inefficient response to the disaster has been documented and severely criticized. Exxon proposed that dispersants—chemical sprays that pulverize an oil slick into droplets that dissipate into the water—be used. One of the things Exxon liked about dispersants was that they got the oil out of sight. However, out of sight is where the salmon and other fish swim. Because the effect of such dispersants on wildlife is not fully known, the U.S. Coast Guard allowed only limited use.

Eventually, Exxon mobilized and paid more than 12,000 people for the cleanup effort—many of them local residents who could no longer fish because of the spill. They bagged the dead animals, birds, and fish that lay strewn on the shore. They used booms and skimmers to try to contain the oil spill. They "treated"—the government would not let Exxon use the word *cleaned*—the 1,100 miles of Alaskan coastline affected by the spill. Roughly 230 otters were saved at a cost of about $40,000 each.

Approximately six months after the spring accident had occurred, Exxon departed Alaska just ahead of the autumn storms, proclaiming that it had met its social responsibility in addressing the disaster. Of the 11-million-gallon sea of petroleum, 2.6 million gallons were recovered and returned to Exxon. The *Exxon Valdez* was refloated, towed away, repaired, and renamed by Exxon.

The final toll of the disaster was 30,000 to 40,000 dead birds, more than 1,000 dead otters, and unknown numbers of dead fish and other wildlife. And the future? Only time will tell the ultimate effect that the oil spill has had on the ecological system of Prince William Sound and the birds, otters, fish, and other wildlife—and humans—who depend on it.

The wreck of the *Exxon Valdez* has been the greatest environmental disaster in American history to date, and the most expensive. Exxon spent more than $1.2 billion on cleanup efforts alone, of which $400 million will be reimbursed by insurance companies. (Exxon's net income for 1989 was more than $5.2 billion.) If Exxon expected thanks for its efforts, it got shredded credit cards and lawsuits. Exxon now faces hundreds of civil lawsuits by fishers and others seeking damages caused by the oil spill.

But the biggest hit was yet to come. In June 1994, an Alaskan jury found that Exxon and Mr. Hazelwood had acted recklessly in causing the accident. The jury awarded 15,000 fishers $287 million in compensatory damages and ordered Exxon to pay $5 billion in punitive damages to all plaintiffs in *Exxon Valdez* cases. The jury also assessed $5,000 in punitive damages against Mr. Hazelwood.

1. Who should be assigned the moral responsibility for the *Exxon Valdez* catastrophe?
2. Did Exxon meet its duty of social responsibility in this case?
3. Should corporations adopt and adhere to the *Valdez* Principles?

Exhibit 2.2
The *Valdez* Principles

INTRODUCTION. By adopting these principles, we publicly affirm our belief that corporations and their shareholders have a direct responsibility for the environment. We believe that corporations must conduct their business as responsible stewards of the environment and seek profits only in a manner that leaves the Earth healthy and safe. We believe that corporations must not compromise the ability of future generations to sustain their needs.

We recognize this to be a long-term commitment to update our practices continually in light of advances in technology and new understandings in health and environment science. We intend to make consistent, measurable progress in implementing these principles and to apply them wherever we operate throughout the world.

1. **Protection of the Biosphere.** We will minimize and strive to eliminate the release of any pollutant that may cause environmental damage to the air, water or earth or its inhabitants. We will safeguard habitats in rivers, lakes, wetlands, coastal zones, and oceans and will minimize contributing to the green house effect, depletion of the ozone layer, acid rain, or smog.

2. **Sustainable Use of Natural Resources.** We will make sustainable use of renewable natural resources, such as water, soils, and forests. We will conserve nonrenewable natural resources through efficient use and careful planning. We will protect wildlife habitats, open spaces, and wilderness, while preserving biodiversity.

3. **Reduction and Disposal of Waste.** We will minimize the creation of waste, especially hazardous waste, and whenever possible recycle materials. We will dispose of all wastes through safe and responsible methods.

4. **Wise Use of Energy.** We will make every effort to use environmentally safe and sustainable energy sources to meet our needs. We will invest in improved energy efficiency and conservation in our operations. We will maximize the energy efficiency of products we produce or sell.

5. **Risk Reduction.** We will minimize the environmental, health, and safety risks to our employees and the communities in which we operate by employing safe technologies and operating procedures and by being constantly prepared for emergencies.

6. **Marketing of Safe Products and Services.** We will sell products or services that minimize adverse environmental impacts and that are safe as consumers commonly use them. We will inform consumers of the environmental impacts of our products or services.

7. **Damage Compensation.** We will take responsibility for any harm we cause to the environment by making every effort to fully restore the environment and to compensate those persons who are adversely affected.

8. **Disclosure.** We will disclose to our employees and to the public incidents relating to our operations that cause environmental harm or pose health or safety hazards. We will discuss potential environmental, health or safety hazards posed by our operations, and we will not take any action against employees who report any condition that creates a danger to the environment or poses health and safety hazards.

9. **Environmental Directors and Managers.** At least one member of the board of directors will be a person qualified to represent environmental interests. We will commit management resources to implement these principles, including the funding of an office of vice president for environmental affairs or an equivalent executive position, reporting directly to the CEO, to monitor and report upon our implementation efforts.

10. **Assessment and Annual Audit.** We will conduct and make public an annual self-evaluation of our progress in implementing these principles and in complying with all applicable laws and regulations throughout our worldwide operations. We will work toward the timely creation of independent environmental audit procedures which we will complete annually and make available to the public.

Valdez **Principles** Recently, a group called the Coalition for Environmentally Responsible Economies (CERES)—which takes its acronym from the Roman goddess of agriculture—released a set of 10 commitments it calls the *Valdez* **Principles** to guide corporations regarding their social responsibility to protect the environment.

Stakeholder Interests

stakeholder interest
A theory of social responsibility that says a corporation must consider the effects its actions have on persons other than its stockholders.

Businesses have relationships with all sorts of people other than their stockholders, including employees, suppliers, customers, creditors, and the local community. Under the **stakeholder interest** theory of social responsibility, a corporation must consider the effects its actions have on these *other stakeholders*. For example, a corporation would violate the stakeholder interest theory if it viewed employees solely as a means of maximizing stockholder wealth.

This theory is criticized because it is difficult to harmonize the conflicting interests of stakeholders. For example, in deciding whether to close a plant, certain stakeholders might benefit (e.g., stockholders and creditors) while other stakeholders might not (e.g., current employees and the local community).

ETHICAL PERSPECTIVE

Constituency Statutes

Under the traditional business judgment rule, directors of a corporation owe a fiduciary duty to act on an informed basis, with reasonable care, and in good faith. Historically, this duty has been rigidly and exclusively owed to the corporation and its shareholders and to no others. Under this classical theory of the corporation, the rights of other constituents—such as employees, bondholders and creditors, suppliers, and customers—exist by contract, period.

This view prevailed during the 1980s, when leveraged buyouts and the greed of corporate raiders caused the demise of many venerable companies, dislodged workers, destroyed pension rights, and

ruined many local economies. In response, more than 30 states have enacted constituency statutes that allow directors to consider constituents other than shareholders when making decisions.

For example, Minnesota adopted the following statute:

> In discharging the duties of the position of director, a director may, in considering the best interests of the corporation, consider the interests of the corporation's employees, customers, suppliers, and creditors, the economy of the state and nation, community and societal considerations, and the long-term as well as short-term interests of the corporation and its shareholders, including the possibility that these interests

may be best served by the continued independence of the corporation. [Minn. Stat. § 302A.251(5)]

Most constituency statutes are permissive, not mandatory. That is, directors may take into account nonstockholder interests but are not required to do so.

Constituency statutes recognize the complex nature of the modern corporation and the modern view that shareholders are not the only "owners" of corporations. These statutes acknowledge the rights of a variety of participants, including lenders, employees, managers, suppliers, distributors, customers, and the local communities in which corporations are located.

Corporate Citizenship

corporate citizenship
A theory of social responsibility that says a business has a responsibility to do good.

The **corporate citizenship** theory of social responsibility argues that business has a responsibility to do good. That is, business is responsible for helping to solve social problems that it did little, if anything, to cause. For example, under this theory corporations owe a duty to subsidize schools and help educate children.

This theory contends that *corporations owe a duty to promote the same social goals as do individual members of society*. Proponents of the "do good" theory argue that corporations owe a debt to society to make it a better place, and that this duty arises because of the social power bestowed on them. That is, this social power is a gift from society and should be used to good ends.

A major criticism of this theory is that the duty of a corporation to do good cannot be expanded beyond certain limits. There is always some social problem that needs to be addressed, and corporate funds are limited. Further, if this theory were taken to its maximum limit, potential shareholders might be reluctant to invest in corporations.

ETHICAL PERSPECTIVE

Where There's Smoke, There's . . .

For several decades, cigarette smoking has been under attack by doctors, health professionals, non-smokers, and others. In 1964, the Surgeon General of the United States issued a report that identified the dangers of smoking. Current statistics estimate that more than 1,000 people die each day in the United States from the direct effects of cigarette smoking and more than 50,000 nonsmokers die annually from secondhand smoke.

Congress enacted the **Federal Cigarette Labeling and Advertising Act** in 1965. The original act required the following warning to be placed on cigarette packages: "Caution: Cigarette Smoking May Be Hazardous to Your Health." In 1969, Congress changed the warning to: "Warning: The Surgeon General Has Determined That Cigarette Smoking Is Dangerous to Your Health." In 1984, Congress again changed the warning. One of the following four warning labels (which must be rotated every quarter) must be placed on each cigarette package after the words "SURGEON GENERAL'S WARNING" [15 U.S.C. §§ 1331–1340]:

1. Smoking Causes Lung Cancer, Heart Disease, Emphysema, and May Complicate Pregnancy.
2. Cigarette Smoke Contains Carbon Monoxide.
3. Quitting Smoking Now Greatly Reduces Serious Risks to Your Health.
4. Smoking by Pregnant Women May Result in Fetal Injury, Premature Birth, and Low Birth Weight.

Rose Cipollone began smoking in 1942, when she was 17 years old. She continued to smoke between one and two packs per day until the early 1980s.

Here's her story: She smoked Chesterfield brand cigarettes manufactured by Liggett Group, Inc. (Liggett), until 1955. In her deposition, Mrs. Cipollone testified that she smoked the Chesterfield brand to be "glamorous," to "imitate" the "pretty girls and movie stars" depicted in Chesterfield advertisements, and because the advertisements stated that Chesterfield cigarettes were "mild." She stated that she understood the description of Chesterfield cigarettes as "mild" to mean that they were safe.

Among other things, Mrs. Cipollone testified that she was an avid reader of a variety of magazines, frequently listened to the radio, and often watched television during the years she smoked the Chesterfield brand. During that period, Chesterfield cigarettes were advertised as being manufactured with "electronic miracle" technology that makes "cigarettes . . . more better [sic] and safer for you."

In 1955, Mrs. Cipollone stopped smoking Chesterfield cigarettes, and began to smoke L&M filter cigarettes, also made by Liggett. When asked why she desired the filter tip, she testified that "it was the new thing and I figured, well, go along—it was better—the bad stuff would stay in the filter then." One series of advertisements that appeared on television and in magazines stated that L&M's "miracle tip" filters were "just what the doctor ordered!" She concluded, "through advertising, I was led to assume that they were safe and they wouldn't harm me."

In 1968, Mrs. Cipollone stopped smoking the L&M brand and started smoking the Virginia Slims brand, manufactured by Philip Morris, Inc. She stated she switched "because it was very glamorous and had very attractive ads and it was a nice looking cigarette that persuaded me." In the 1970s, Mrs. Cipollone switched to Parliament brand, also manufactured by Philip Morris. She testified that this brand was advertised as having a "recessed" filter and that she thought that this made it healthier. In 1974, she changed from Parliament to the True brand, a cigarette manufactured by Lorillard, Inc., and advertised as low in tar.

In 1981, Mrs. Cipollone was diagnosed as having lung cancer. Even though her doctors advised her to quit smoking, she was unable to do so. Mrs. Cipollone continued to smoke until June 1982 when her lung was removed. Even after that, she smoked occasionally in secret. She only stopped smoking in 1983, after she had become terminally ill with cancer.

On August 1, 1983, Mrs. Cipollone and her husband, Antonio, filed a complaint against the manufacturers of the cigarettes she had smoked. Mrs. Cipollone alleged that as a result of smoking the defendants' cigarettes for almost 40 years, she sustained personal injuries. Her husband sought compensation for loss of consortium. Mrs. Cipollone died on October 21, 1984, but her husband continued to prosecute the action, individually and as executor of his wife's estate. When he died, their son, executor of both estates, continued the action.

The defendants asserted that the federal warnings on the

continued

cigarette packages *preempted* Mrs. Cipollone's tort lawsuit against them for the period that the warnings were required. The U.S. district court ruled in the defendants' favor, holding that the plaintiffs' claims were preempted by the federal labeling laws. The U.S. court of appeals affirmed. The U.S. Supreme Court granted certiorari.

The Supreme Court reversed in part and affirmed in part. The Court held that claims based on a failure to warn of the dangers of cigarette smoking were preempted by the federal labeling laws. However, the Court ruled that the labeling acts do not bar lawsuits against cigarette compa-

nies for claims based on breach of express warranty, fraudulent misrepresentation, fraudulent concealment, or conspiracy among cigarette companies to misrepresent or conceal material facts. Nevertheless, in 1992, the Cipollone family and their attorneys withdrew the lawsuit.

Proponents of the *Cipollone* decision argue that the Supreme Court's ruling will open the floodgates for successful litigation against cigarette companies. Spokespersons for the cigarette industry contend that they will continue to be able to convince juries that plaintiffs should not collect damages for their injuries. [*Cipol-*

lone v. Liggett Group, Inc., 112 S.Ct. 2608, 120 L.Ed.2d 407 (1992)]

1. Did the cigarette companies meet their duty under any of the theories discussed earlier in this chapter?
2. Did the cigarette companies act socially responsible under any of the theories discussed earlier in this chapter?
3. Do you think that the statutory warnings adequately warn smokers against the dangerous and addictive propensity of smoking?
4. Based on your ethical standards, would you work for a cigarette company?

CONCEPT SUMMARY	THEORIES OF SOCIAL RESPONSIBILITY
Theory	**Social Responsibility**
Maximizing profits	To maximize profits for stockholders.
Moral minimum	To avoid causing harm and to compensate for harm caused.
Stakeholder interest	To consider the interests of all stakeholders, including stockholders, employees, customers, suppliers, creditors, and local community.
Corporate citizenship	To do good and solve social problems.

BUSINESS CHECKLIST

The Corporate Social Audit

BUSINESS BRIEF

Corporations that conduct social audits will be more apt to prevent unethical and illegal conduct by managers, employees, and agents.

It has been suggested that corporate audits should be extended to include not only audits of the financial health of a corporation but also of its moral health. Corporations that conduct social audits will be more apt to prevent unethical and illegal conduct by managers, employees, and agents. The audit would examine how well employees have adhered to the company's code of ethics and how well the corporation has met its duty of social responsibility. Such audits would focus on the corporation's efforts to promote employment opportunities for members of protected classes, worker safety, environmental protection, consumer protection, and the like. Social audits are not easy. First, it might be hard to conceptualize just what is being audited. Second, it might be difficult to measure results. Despite these factors, more companies are expected to undertake social audits.

Companies should institute the following procedures when conducting a social audit:

- An independent outside firm should be hired to conduct the audit. This will ensure autonomy and objectivity in conducting the audit.
- The company's personnel should cooperate fully with the auditing firm while the audit is being conducted.
- The auditing firm should report its findings directly to the company's board of directors.
- The results of the audit should be reviewed by the board of directors.
- The board of directors should determine how the company can better meet its duty of social responsibility and can use the audit to implement a program to correct any deficiencies it finds.

INTERNATIONAL PERSPECTIVE

Caux Round Table Principles for International Business

Ethics is a function of history, culture, religion, and other factors. It differs from culture to culture and person to person. The social responsibility of business also differs considerably, depending on the corporation's philosophy and the influence of the home country's mores.

To try to bring uniformity to this area, a group called the Caux Round Table—a collaboration of leaders from various multinational corporations—promulgated an international ethics code called the *Principles of Business*. These principles are unique because they are based on transnational values from the East and West: the Japanese concept of *kyosei* (living and working together for the common good) and the Western concept of the dignity of the human person. Since they were first introduced in 1994, the *Principles* have been adopted by many multinational corporations around the world.

The Caux Round Table *Principles for Business* are set forth as follows:

Section 1. Preamble
The mobility of employment, capital, products, and technology is making business increasingly global in its transactions and its effects.

Laws and market forces are necessary but insufficient guides for conduct.

Responsibility for the policies and actions of business and respect for the dignity and interests of its stakeholders are fundamental.

Shared values, including a commitment to shared prosperity, are as important for a global community as for communities of smaller scale.

For these reasons, and because business can be a powerful agent of positive social change, we offer the following principles as a foundation for dialogue and action by

business leaders in search of business responsibility. In so doing, we affirm the necessity for moral values in business decision making. Without them, stable business relationships and a sustainable world community are impossible.

Section 2. General Principles
- Principle 1. The Responsibilities of Businesses: Beyond Shareholders Toward Stakeholders

The value of a business to society is the wealth and employment it creates and the marketable products and services it provides to consumers of a reasonable price commensurate with quality. To create such value, a business must maintain its own economic health and viability, but survival is not a sufficient goal.

Businesses have a role to play in improving the lives of all their

continued

customers, employees, and shareholders by sharing with them the wealth they have created. Suppliers and competitors as well should expect businesses to honor their obligations in a spirit of honesty and fairness. As responsible citizens of the local, national, regional, and global communities in which they operate, businesses share a part in shaping the future of those communities.

- Principle 2. The Economic and Social Impact of Business: Toward Innovation, Justice, and World Community

Businesses established in foreign countries to develop, produce, or sell should also contribute to the social advancement of those countries by creating productive employment and helping to raise the purchasing power of their citizens. Businesses also should contribute to human rights, education, welfare, and vitalization of the countries in which they operate.

Businesses should contribute to economic and social development not only in the countries in which they operate, but also in the world community at large, through effective and prudent use of resources, free and fair competition, and emphasis upon methods, marketing, and communications.

- Principle 3. Business Behavior: Beyond the Letter of Law Toward a Spirit of Trust

While accepting the legitimacy of trade secrets, businesses should recognize that sincerity, candor, truthfulness, the keeping of promises, and transparency contribute not only to their own credibility and stability but also to the smoothness and efficiency of business transactions, particularly on the international level.

- Principle 4. Respect for Rules

To avoid trade frictions and to promote freer trade, equal conditions for competition, and fair and equitable treatment for all participants, businesses should respect international and domestic rules. In addition, they should recognize that some behavior, although legal, may still have adverse consequences.

- Principle 5. Support for Multilateral Trade

Businesses should support the multilateral trade systems of the GATT/World Trade Organization and similar international agreements. They should cooperate in efforts to promote the progressive and judicious liberalization of trade and to relax those domestic measures that unreasonably hinder global commerce, while giving due respect to national policy objectives.

- Principle 6. Respect for the Environment

A business should protect and, where possible, improve the environment, promote sustainable development, and prevent the wasteful use of natural resources.

- Principle 7. Avoidance of Illicit Operations

A business should not participate in or condone bribery, money laundering, or other corrupt policies: indeed, it should seek cooperation with others to eliminate them. It should not trade in arms or other materials used for terrorist activities, drug traffic, or other organized crime.

WORKING THE WEB

KPMG US—Business Ethics Practice
This site aims to provide a place where businesspeople can turn for guidance on ethical problems that threaten their progress as well as the prosperity of their organizations. Are you looking for ways to measure whether your organization is grounded in sound values such as integrity, respect, trust, and fairness? Try this site for an answer.

Visit at http://www.us.kpmg.com/ethics/

Students for Responsible Business
Students for Responsible Business (SRB) has es-

tablished a communications network that facilitates the exchange of ideas, information, and experiences both within SRB and beyond to the community at large. Do you want to find out about SRB's summer internship program, annual conference, career services, or membership information? Check out this site for this and other information.

Visit at http://www.srb.org/

Business for Social Responsibility
"Business for Social Responsibility (BSR) is an or-

ganization that believes that member companies can achieve long-term success by implementing policies and practices that honor high ethical standards and meet their responsibilities to all who are affected by their decisions." It publishes a simple, informative guidebook on social responsibility called the *BSR Social Responsibility Starter Kit.* Check out this site to find out what companies are members.

Visit at http://www.bsr.org

Business Ethics Resources on the World Wide Web This site provides information such as corporate and business association codes of ethics and articles and publications about business ethics. There are also links to other resources.

Visit at http://www.ethics.ubc.ca/resources/business.html

On-Line Journal of Ethics This site is an on-line journal of cutting edge research in the field of business and professional ethics published by the Institute for Business and Professional Ethics at DePaul University.

Visit at http://www.depaul.edu/ethics/ojbea.html

CYBER EXERCISES:

1. One part of the KPMG US—Business Ethics Practice site is "Business Ethics Resources." One resource is the Markula Center for Applied Ethics at Santa Clara University that publishes an electronic version of *Issues in Ethics* magazine. Print out the page that indicates who the editor of *Issues in Ethics* is.

2. In the "Resource Center" area of the Students for Responsible Business site, find a book called *The Promise of Diversity.* Print out the page that indicates which publisher published that book.

3. In the "About BSR" area of the Business for Social Responsibility site, find out if Wild Oats Market is a member of BSR. Print out the page that gives you that information.

4. Use the Business Ethics Resources on the World Wide Web site to find the corporate code of ethics for Texas Instruments. When was the Ethics Committee established at Texas Instruments? Print out the page that indicates the answer.

5. Randy Richards wrote an article in Volume 1, Issue 2 of the *On-Line Journal of Ethics* called "Cicero and the Ethics of Honest Business Dealings." Using the *On-Line Journal of Ethics* site, find out where Randy Richards teaches. Print out the page that gives you that information.

CHAPTER SUMMARY

MORAL THEORIES AND BUSINESS ETHICS, P. 30

Moral Theories	1. *Ethical fundamentalism.* Persons look to an outside source (e.g., Bible or Koran) or central figure to set ethical guidelines.
	2. *Utilitarianism.* Persons choose the alternative that would provide the greatest good to society.
	3. *Kantian ethics.* A set of universal rules establishes ethical duties. The rules are based on reasoning and require (1) consistency in application and (2) reversibility.
	4. *Rawls's social justice theory.* Moral duties are based on an implied social contract. Fairness is justice. The rules are established from an original position of a "veil of ignorance."
	5. *Ethical relativism.* Individuals decide what is ethical based on their own feelings as to what is right or wrong.

THE SOCIAL RESPONSIBILITY OF BUSINESS, P. 36

Theories of Social Responsibility	1. *Maximizing profits.* To maximize profits for shareholders.
	2. *Moral minimum.* To make a profit and avoid harm, and to compensate for harm caused.

> 3. *Stakeholder interests*. To consider the interests of all stakeholders, including stockholders, employees, customers, suppliers, creditors, and the local community.
> 4. *Corporate citizenship*. To do good and help solve social problems.

THE CORPORATE SOCIAL AUDIT, P. 42

Corporate Social Audit	Audit of a corporation by independent auditors that examines how well employees have adhered to the company's code of ethics and how well the company has met its duty of social responsibility.

ETHICS CASES

2.1 Ethical Perspective On July 5, 1884, an English yacht sank in a storm off the Cape of Good Hope. Four members of the crew—Dudley, Stephens, Brooks, and Parker—were cast adrift in a small lifeboat 1,600 miles from shore. After three days, they ran out of food and water. On the fourth day they caught a small turtle, on which they fed until the twelfth day. On the eighteenth day, after being without food for a week, Dudley and Stephens proposed that the four sailors draw lots to see who should be killed so that the others could eat his body and live. Brooks refused to draw lots.

Dudley and Stephens then suggested that they kill the boy Parker, who by then was lying at the bottom of the boat weak from hunger. Brooks dissented. Dudley and Stephens told Brooks to go to the other end of the boat, which he did. Dudley and Stephens offered a prayer, then slit the boy's throat with a knife. Dudley, Stephens, and Brooks fed on the boy until they were rescued four days later. England sued Dudley and Stephens, charging them with the crime of murder. Did Dudley and Stephens act ethically? What would you have done? Did Brooks act ethically in refusing to participate in the killing but then feeding on the boy? [*The Queen v. Dudley and Stephens*, 14 Q.B.D. 273 (1884)]

2.2 Ethical Perspective The A. H. Robbins Company manufactured the Dalkon Shield, an intrauterine device (IUD) used by more than 2 million women for contraception during the early 1970s. The device was defectively designed and caused women problems of infection, pelvic inflammatory disease, infertility, and spontaneous abortion, as well as health defects in their children. Thousands of product liability lawsuits were filed against the company by the women and children injured by the Dalkon Shield. The company and its insurers chose to fight these cases aggressively and spent multimillions of dollars in legal fees.

U.S. District Court Judge Miles Lord handled many of these cases. He called the Dalkon Shield an "instrument of death, mutilation, and disease" and chastised the executives of the company for violating "every ethical precept" of the Hippocratic oath, the medical profession's promise to save lives. Judge Lord stated,

> Your company in the face of overwhelming evidence denies its guilt and continues its monstrous mischief. You have taken the bottom line as your guiding beacon and the low road as your route. This is corporate irresponsibility at its meanest.

The company eventually filed for bankruptcy. The U.S. court of appeals censored Judge Lord for being too vocal. Is it ethical for a company to aggressively contest lawsuits that are filed against it even if it knows that it is responsible for the injury?

2.3 Ethical Perspective The Warner-Lambert Company (Warner-Lambert) has manufactured and distributed Listerine antiseptic mouthwash since 1879. Its formula has never changed. Ever since its introduction, the company has represented Listerine as being beneficial in preventing and curing colds and sore throats. Direct advertising of these claims to consumers began in 1921. In 1971 Warner-Lambert spent $10 million advertising these claims in print media and in television commercials.

In 1972, the Federal Trade Commission filed a complaint against Warner-Lambert alleging that the company engaged in false advertising in violation of federal law. Four months of hearings were held before an administrative law judge that produced an evidentiary record of more than 4,000 pages of documents from 46 witnesses. In 1975, after examining the evidence, the FTC issued an opinion that held that the company's representations that Listerine prevented and cured colds and sore throats were false. The U.S. court of appeals affirmed.

Did Warner-Lambert act ethically in making its claims for Listerine? What remedy should the court impose on the company? Would making Warner-Lambert cease such advertising be sufficient? [*Warner-Lambert Company v. Federal Trade Commission*, 562 F.2d 749 D. (C. Cir. 1977)]

2.4 Ethical Perspective Stanford University is one of the premier research universities in the country. Stanford has an operating budget of approximately $400 million a year and receives about $175 million a year in direct research funding from the federal government. In addition, the government reimburses the university for certain overhead and indirect costs associated with the research. This amounts to about $85 million a year.

In 1990, a Navy accountant took a close look at Stanford's books and alleged that the university may have overstated overhead and indirect costs associated with research by as much as $200 million during the 1980s. The university provides a house for its president, Donald Kennedy. Some of the expenses charged against overhead for research were (a) $3,000 for a cedar-lined closet at the president's home, (b) $4,000 for the president's 1987 wedding reception, (c) $7,000 in bed sheets and table linens, and (d) $184,000 in depreciation on a yacht donated to Stanford's sailing program. Did the administration of Stanford act ethically in charging these expenditures as overhead against research? What penalty should be assessed?

2.5 Social Responsibility The Johns-Manville Corporation was a profitable company that made a variety of building and other products. It was a major producer of asbestos, which was used for insulation in buildings and for a variety of other uses. It has been medically proven that excessive exposure to asbestos causes asbestosis, a fatal lung disease. Thousands of employees of the company and consumers who were exposed to asbestos and contracted this fatal disease sued the company for damages. In 1983, the lawsuits were being filed at the rate of more than 400 per week.

As a response, the company filed for reorganization bankruptcy. It argued that if it did not, an otherwise viable company that provided thousands of jobs and served a useful purpose in this country would be destroyed, and that without the declaration of bankruptcy a few of the plaintiffs who first filed their lawsuits would win awards of hundreds of millions of dollars, leaving nothing for the remainder of the plaintiffs. Under the bankruptcy court's protection, the company was restructured to survive. As part of the release from bankruptcy, the company contributed money to a fund to pay current and future claimants. The fund is not large enough to pay all injured persons the full amount of their claims.

Was it ethical for Johns-Manville to declare bankruptcy? Did it meet its duty of social responsibility in this case? If you were a member of the board of directors of the company, would you have voted to place the company in bankruptcy? Why or why not? [*In re Johns-Manville Corporation*, 36 B.R. 727 (B.C. S.D.N.Y. 1984)]

2.6 Social Responsibility In 1977, Reverend Leon H. Sullivan, a Baptist minister from Philadelphia who was also a member of the board of directors of General Motors Corporation, proposed a set of rules to guide American-owned companies doing business in the Republic of South Africa. The **Sullivan Principles**, as they became known, call for the nonsegregation of races in South Africa. They call for employers to (a) provide equal and fair employment practices for all employees and (b) improve the quality of employees' lives outside the work environment in such areas as housing, schooling, transportation, recreation, and health facilities. The principles also require signatory companies to report regularly and be graded on their conduct in South Africa.

Eventually, the Sullivan Principles were subscribed to by several hundred U.S. corporations with affiliates doing business in South Africa. Concerning the companies that have subscribed to the Sullivan Principles, which of the following theories of social responsibility are they following?

1. Maximizing profits
2. Moral minimum
3. Stakeholder interest
4. Corporate citizenship

To put additional pressure on the government of the Republic of South Africa to end apartheid, in 1987 Reverend Sullivan called for the complete withdrawal of all U.S. companies doing business in or with South Africa. Very few companies agreed to do so. Did companies owe a social duty to withdraw from South Africa?

2.7 Social Responsibility In 1974, Kaiser Aluminum & Chemical Corporation (Kaiser) entered into a collective bargaining agreement with the United Steelworkers of America (USWA), a union that represented employees at Kaiser's plants. The agreement contained an affirmative action program to increase the representation of minorities in craft jobs. To enable plants to meet these goals, on-the-job training programs were established to teach unskilled production workers the skills necessary to become craft workers. Assignment to the training program was based on seniority; however, the plan reserved 50 percent of the openings for black employees.

In 1974, 13 craft trainees were selected from Kaiser's Gramercy plant for the training program. Of these, seven were black and six white. The most senior black selected had less seniority than several white production workers who had applied for the positions but were rejected. Brian Webster, one of the rejected white employees, instituted a class action lawsuit alleging that the affirmative action plan violated Title VII of the Civil Rights Act of 1964, which made it "unlawful to discriminate because of race" in hiring and selecting apprentices for training programs. The U.S. Supreme Court upheld the affirmative action plan in this case. The decision stated,

> We therefore hold that Title VII's prohibition against racial discrimination does not condemn all private, voluntary, race-conscious affirmative action plans. At the same time, the plan does not unnecessarily trammel the interests of the white employees. Moreover, the plan is a temporary measure; it is not intended to maintain racial balance, but simply to eliminate a manifest racial imbalance.

Do companies owe a duty of social responsibility to provide affirmative action programs? [*Steelworkers v. Weber*, 443 U.S. 193, 99 S.Ct. 2721, 61 L.Ed.2d 480 (1979)]

2.8 Social Responsibility Iroquois Brands, Ltd. (Iroquois) is a Delaware corporation that had $78 million in assets, $141 million in sales, and $6 million in profits in 1984. As part of its business, Iroquois imports pâté de foie gras (goose pâté) from France and sells it in the United States. Iroquois derived only $79,000 in revenues from sales of such pâté. The French producer force-feeds the geese from which the pâté is made. Peter C. Lovenheim, who owns 200 shares of Iroquois common stock, proposed to include a shareholder proposal in Iroquois's annual proxy materials to be sent to shareholders. His proposal criticized the company because the force-feeding caused "undue stress, pain, and suffering" to the geese and requested that shareholders vote to have Iroquois discontinue importing and selling pâté produced by this method.

Iroquois refused to allow the information to be included in its proxy materials. Iroquois asserted that its refusal was based on the fact that Lovenheim's proposal was "not economically significant" and had only "ethical and social" significance. The company reasoned that because corporations are economic entities, only an economic test applied to its activities, and it was not subject to an ethical or social responsibility test. Is the company correct, that is, should only an economic test be applied in judging the activities of a corporation? Or should a corporation also be subject to an ethical or social responsibility test? [*Lovenheim v. Iroquois Brands, Ltd.*, 618 F.Supp. 554 (D.C. 1985)]

CRITICAL LEGAL THINKING WRITING ASSIGNMENT

Read Case A.2 in the Case Appendix [*Ramirez v. Plough, Inc.*]. This case is excerpted from the court of appeals opinion. Review and brief the case. In your brief, be sure to answer the following questions:

1. Did Plough, Inc., act ethically in participating in efforts to influence the government to reject mandatory warning labels?
2. Did the company act ethically in voluntarily providing the warning labels? How "voluntary" was its decision?

3. Does a company owe a duty of social responsibility to provide warning labels in foreign languages? If so, under what circumstances?
4. If a causal connection is shown between the use of aspirin and Reye's syndrome, would you find Plough liable for the death of the child? If so, what amount of damages would you award?

NOTES

[1]170 N.W. 668 (Mich. 1919).
[2]Milton Friedman, "The Social Responsibility of Business Is to Increase Its Profits," *The New York Times Magazine*, September 13, 1970.

CHAPTER 3

JUDICIAL, ALTERNATIVE,

AND INTERNATIONAL

DISPUTE RESOLUTION

Chapter Objectives

*After studying this chapter,
you should be able to*

1. Describe subject matter jurisdiction of courts and venue
2. Describe in personam jurisdiction of courts and service process
3. Describe the federal and state court systems
4. Explain the jurisdiction of federal courts and how a case reaches the U.S. Supreme Court
5. Explain how a justice is chosen for the U.S. Supreme Court
6. Describe the pretrial litigation process, including pleadings, discovery, dismissals and pretrial judgments, and settlement conferences
7. Describe how a case proceeds through trial and how a trial court decision is appealed
8. Describe administrative agency functions and procedure
9. Explain the use of arbitration and other nonjudicial methods of alternative dispute resolutions
10. Describe the use of arbitration to settle international disputes

Chapter Contents

> *I was never ruined but twice; once when I lost a lawsuit, and once when I won one.*
>
> Voltaire

"The law, wherein, as in a magic mirror, we see reflected, not only our own lives, but the lives of all men that have been! When I think on this majestic theme, my eyes dazzle."
Oliver Wendell Holmes
The Law, Speeches 17 (1913)

There are two major court systems in the United States: (1) the federal court system and (2) the court systems of the 50 states and the District of Columbia. Each of these systems has jurisdiction to hear different types of lawsuits. The process of bringing, maintaining, and defending a lawsuit is called **litigation**. Litigation is a difficult, time-consuming, and costly process that must comply with complex procedural rules. Although it is not required, most parties employ a lawyer to represent them when they are involved in a lawsuit.

In response to the expense and difficulty of bringing a lawsuit, several forms of nonjudicial dispute resolution have developed. These methods, collectively called **alternative dispute resolution**, are being used increasingly often to resolve commercial disputes.

This chapter discusses the various court systems, the jurisdiction of courts to hear and decide cases, the litigation process, alternative dispute resolution, and international dispute resolution.

THE STATE COURT SYSTEMS

Each state, and the District of Columbia, has a separate court system. Most state court systems include the following: limited-jurisdiction trial courts, general-jurisdiction trial courts, appellate courts, and a supreme court.

Limited-Jurisdiction Trial Court

limited-jurisdiction trial court A court that hears civil cases involving small dollar amounts.

State **limited-jurisdiction trial courts**, which are sometimes referred to as **inferior trial courts**, hear matters of a specialized or limited nature. In many states, traffic courts, juvenile courts, justice-of-the-peace courts, probate courts, family law courts, and courts that hear misdemeanor criminal law cases and civil cases involving lawsuits under a certain dollar amount are examples of such courts. Because these courts are trial courts, evidence can be introduced and testimony given. Most limited-jurisdiction courts keep a record of their proceedings. Their decisions usually can be appealed to a general-jurisdiction court or an appellate court.

small claims court A court that hears civil cases involving small dollar amounts.

Many states also have **small claims court**. These courts hear civil cases involving small dollar amounts (e.g., $5,000). Generally, the parties must appear individually and cannot have a lawyer represent them. Often, the decision of small claims courts are appealable to general-jurisdiction trial courts or appellate courts.

General-Jurisdiction Trial Court

general-jurisdiction trial court A court that hears cases of a general nature that are not within the jurisdiction of limited-jurisdiction trial courts. Testimony and evidence at trial are recorded and stored for future reference.

Every state has a **general-jurisdiction trial court**. These courts can be referred to as **courts of record** because the testimony and evidence at trial are recorded and stored for future reference. They hear cases that are not within the jurisdiction of limited-jurisdiction trial courts (e.g., felonies, civil cases over a certain dollar amount). Some states divide their general-jurisdiction courts into two divisions, one for criminal cases and another for civil cases. Evidence and testimony are given at general-jurisdiction trial courts. The decisions handed down by these courts are appealable to an intermediate appellate court or the state supreme court, depending on the circumstances.

Intermediate Appellate Court

intermediate appellate court An intermediate court that hears appeals from trial courts.

In many states, **intermediate appellate courts** (also called **appellate courts** or **courts of appeal**) hear appeals from trial courts. They review the trial court record to determine if there have been any errors at trial that would require reversal or modification of the trial court's decision. In making a determination, the appellate court may review either pertinent parts or the whole trial court record from the lower court. No new evidence or testimony is permitted. The parties usually file legal briefs with the appellate court stating the law and facts that support their positions. Appellate courts usually grant a brief oral hearing to the parties. Appellate court decisions are appealable to the state's highest court. In states that do not have an intermediate appellate court, trial court decisions are appealable directly to the state's highest court.

Highest State Court

Each state court system has a highest court. Most states call their highest court the **supreme court**. The function of a state supreme court is to hear appeals from intermediate state courts and certain trial courts. No new evidence or testimony is heard. The parties usually submit pertinent parts of or the entire lower court record for review. The parties also submit legal briefs to the court and are usually granted a brief oral hearing. Decisions of state supreme courts are final, unless a question of law is involved that is appealable to the U.S. Supreme Court.

Exhibit 3.1 portrays a typical state court system.

state supreme court   The highest court in a state court system; it hears appeals from intermediate state courts and certain trial courts.

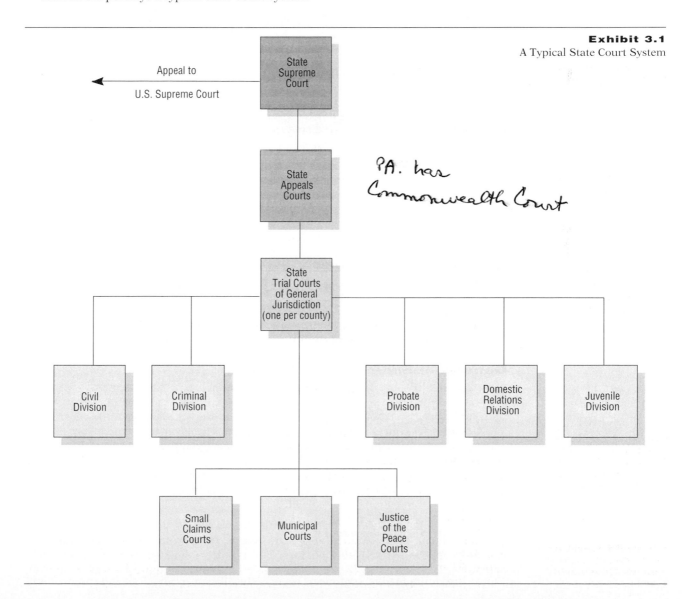

Exhibit 3.1
A Typical State Court System

BUSINESS APPLICATION

Specialized Courts Hear Commercial Disputes

In most states, business and commercial disputes are heard by the same judges who hear and decide criminal, landlord–tenant, matrimonial, medical malpractice, and other non–business-related cases. The one major exception to this standard has been the state of Delaware, where a special Chancery Court hears and decides business litigation. The court, which mainly deals with cases involving corporate–government disputes, has earned a reputation for its expertise in handling and deciding corporate matters. Perhaps the existence of this special court and a corporation code that tends to favor corporate management are the primary reasons that more than 60 percent of the corporations listed on the New York Stock Exchange are incorporated in Delaware.

New York has followed Delaware's lead in this area. New York has designated four courts within its general court system to hear commercial disputes. These courts, which began operating in 1993, hear contracts, sales, insurance, unfair competition, libel and slander, shareholder, business-related tort, and other commercial cases. Other states are expected to establish courts that specialize in commercial matters in the near future.

Businesses tend to favor special commercial courts because the judges presiding over them are expected to have the expertise to handle complex commercial lawsuits. Also, the courts are expected to be more efficient in deciding business-related cases, thus saving time and money for the parties.

THE FEDERAL COURT SYSTEM

"Pieces of evidence, each by itself insufficient, may together constitute a significant whole, and justify by their combined effect a conclusion."
Lord Wright
Grant v. Australian Knitting Mills, Ltd.
(1936)

special federal courts
Federal courts that hear matters of specialized or limited jurisdiction.

Article III of the United States Constitution provides that the federal government's judicial power is vested in one "Supreme Court." This is the **U.S. Supreme Court**. The Constitution also authorizes Congress to establish "inferior" federal courts. Pursuant to this power, Congress has established special federal courts, the U.S. district courts, and the U.S. courts of appeal. Federal judges are appointed for life by the President with the advice and consent of the Senate (except bankruptcy court judges, who are appointed for 14-year terms).

Special Federal Courts

The **special federal courts** established by Congress have limited jurisdiction. They include the following courts:

- **U.S. tax court**—Hears cases involving federal tax laws
- **U.S. claims court**—Hears cases brought against the United States
- **U.S. Court of International Trade**—Hears cases involving tariffs and international commercial disputes
- **U.S. bankruptcy courts**—Hear cases involving federal bankruptcy laws.

U.S. District Courts

U.S. district courts   The federal court system's trial courts of general jurisdiction.

The **U.S. district courts** are the federal court system's trial courts of general jurisdiction. There is at least one federal district court in each state and the District of Columbia, although more populated states have more than one district court. The geographical area served by each court is referred to as a *district*. Presently, there are 96 federal district courts. The federal district courts are empowered to impanel juries, receive evidence, hear testimony, and decide cases. Most federal cases originate in federal district courts.

U.S. Courts of Appeals

U.S. courts of appeals
The federal court system's intermediate appellate courts.

The **U.S. courts of appeals** are the federal court system's intermediate appellate courts. There are 13 circuits in the federal court system. The first 12 are geographical. Eleven are designated by a number, such as the "First Circuit," "Second Circuit," and so on. The geographical area served by each court is referred to as a circuit. The twelfth circuit court is located in Washington, D.C., and is called the "District of Columbia Circuit."

As appellate courts, these circuit courts hear appeals from the district courts located in their circuit as well as from certain special courts and federal administrative agencies. The courts review the record of the lower court or administrative agency proceedings to determine if there has been any error that would warrant reversal or modification of the lower court decision. No new evidence or testimony is heard. The parties file legal briefs with the court and are given a short oral hearing. Appeals are usually heard by a three-judge panel. After a decision is rendered by the three-judge panel, a petitioner can request a review *en banc* by the full court.

The 13th court of appeals was created by Congress in 1982. It is called the **Court of Appeals for the Federal Circuit** and is located in Washington, D.C.[1] This court has special appellate jurisdiction to review the decisions of the Claims Court, the Patent and Trademark Office, and the Court of International Trade. This court was created to provide uniformity in the application of federal law in certain areas, particularly patent law.

Exhibit 3.2 shows the 13 federal circuit courts of appeals.

Court of Appeals for the Federal Circuit A court of appeals in Washington, D.C., that has special appellate jurisdiction to review the decisions of the Claims Court, the Patent and Trademark Office, and the Court of International Trade.

Exhibit 3.2
The 13 Federal Judicial Circuits

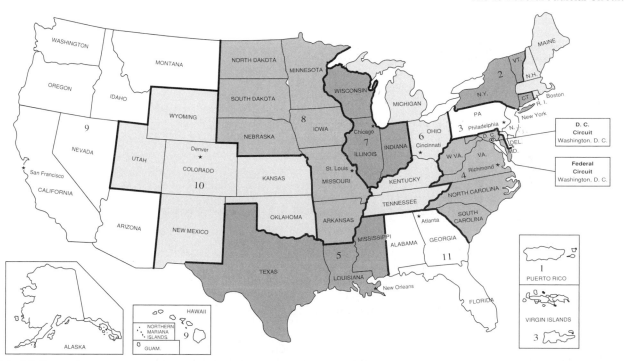

U.S. Supreme Court

The highest court in the land is the **Supreme Court of the United States**, located in Washington, D.C. The Court is composed of nine justices who are nominated by the President and confirmed by the Senate. The President appoints one justice as chief justice. The other eight justices are associate justices. The chief justice is responsible for the administration of the Supreme Court.

The Supreme Court, which is an appellate court, hears appeals from federal circuit courts of appeals and, under certain circumstances, from federal district courts, special federal courts, and the highest state courts. No evidence or testimony is heard. As

U.S. Supreme Court The highest court in the land. It is located in Washington, D.C.

"We're the jury, dread our fury!"

William S. Gilbert
Trial by Jury

with other appellate courts, the lower court record is reviewed to determine whether there has been an error that warrants a reversal or modification of the decision. Legal briefs are filed, and the parties are granted a brief oral hearing. The Supreme Court's decision is final. The federal court system is illustrated in Exhibit 3.3.

Exhibit 3.3
The Federal Court System

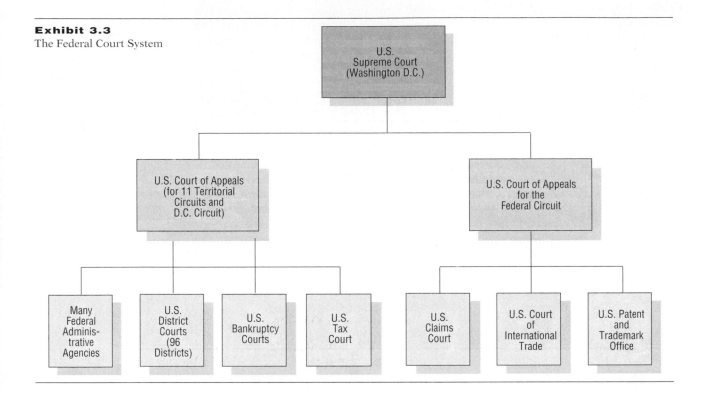

Decisions by the U.S. Supreme Court

"Sancho: But if this is hell, why do we see no lawyers?"
"Clarindo: They won't receive them, lest they bring lawsuits here."
"Sancho: If there are no lawsuits here, hell's not so bad."

Lope de Vega
The Star of Seville,
Act 3, scene 2

The U.S. Constitution gives Congress the authority to establish rules for the appellate review of cases by the Supreme Court. Except in the rare case where mandatory review is required, Congress has given the Supreme Court discretion to decide what cases it will hear.[2]

A petitioner must file a **petition for certiorari** asking the Supreme Court to hear the case. If the Court decides to review a case, it will issue a **writ of certiorari**. Because the Court issues only about 150 to 200 opinions each year, writs are usually granted only in cases involving constitutional and other important issues.

Each justice of the Supreme Court, including the chief justice, has an equal vote. The Supreme Court can issue the following types of decisions:

- *Unanimous decision.* If all of the justices voting agree as to the outcome and reasoning used to decide the case, it is a unanimous opinion. Unanimous decisions are precedent for later cases.
- *Majority decision.* If a majority of the justices agrees to outcome and reasoning used to decide the case, it is a majority opinion. Majority decisions are precedent for later cases.
- *Plurality decision.* If a majority of the justices agrees to the outcome of the case, but not as to the reasoning for reaching the outcome, it is a plurality opinion. A plurality decision settles the case but is not precedent for later cases.

• *Tie decision.* Sometimes the Supreme Court sits without all nine justices being present. This could happen because of illness, conflict of interest, or a justice has not been confirmed to fill a vacant seat on the Court. If there is a tie vote, the lower court decision is affirmed. Such votes are not precedent for later cases.

A justice who agrees with the outcome of a case, but not the reason proffered by other justices, can issue a **concurring opinion** that sets forth his or her reasons for deciding the case. A justice who does not agree with a decision can file a **dissenting opinion** that sets forth the reasons for his or her dissent.

BUSINESS CHECKLIST

Cost-Benefit Analysis of a Lawsuit

In most civil lawsuits each party is responsible for paying its own attorney's fees, whether the party wins or loses. This is called the "American rule." The court can award attorney's fees to the winning party if a statute so provides, the parties have so agreed (e.g., in a contract), or the losing party has acted maliciously or pursued a frivolous case. Accused parties in criminal cases are responsible for paying their own attorney fees if they can afford to do so. If the accused is indigent, the government will provide an attorney (e.g., a public defender) free of charge.

An attorney in a civil lawsuit can represent the plaintiff on an hourly, project, or contingency fee basis. Hourly fees usually range from $75 to $500 per hour, depending on the type of case, the expertise of the lawyer, and the locality of the lawsuit. Under a *contingent fee arrangement*, the lawyer receives a percentage of the amount recovered for the plaintiff upon winning or settling the case. Contingency fees normally range from 20 percent to 50 percent of the award or settlement, with the average being about 35 percent. Lawyers for defendants in lawsuits are normally paid on an hourly basis.

The choice of whether to bring or defend a lawsuit should be analyzed like any other business decision. This includes performing a **cost-benefit analysis** of the lawsuit. For the plaintiff, it might be wise not to sue. For the defendant, it might be wise to settle. The following factors should be considered in deciding whether to bring or settle a lawsuit:

- The probability of winning or losing
- The amount of money to be won or lost
- Lawyer's fees and other costs of litigation
- Loss of time by managers and other personnel
- The long-term effects on the relationship and reputations of the parties
- The amount of prejudgment interest provided by law
- The aggravation and psychological costs associated with a lawsuit
- The unpredictability of the legal system and the possibility of error
- Other factors peculiar to the parties and lawsuit.

Focus on this from a business perspective.

THE JURISDICTION OF COURTS

Not every court has the authority to hear all types of cases. To bring a lawsuit in a court, the plaintiff must have *standing to sue*. In addition, the court must have *jurisdiction* to hear the case, and the case must be brought in the proper *venue*.

Standing to Sue

standing to sue The plaintiff must have some stake in the outcome of the lawsuit.

To bring a lawsuit, a plaintiff must have **standing to sue**. This means that the plaintiff must have some stake in the outcome of the lawsuit.

CONSIDER THIS EXAMPLE: Linda's friend Jon is injured in an accident caused by Emily. Jon refuses to sue. Linda cannot sue Emily on Jon's behalf because she does not have an interest in the result of the case.

A few states now permit investors to invest money in a lawsuit for a percentage return of any award or judgment. Courts hear and decide actual disputes involving specific controversies. Hypothetical questions will not be heard and trivial lawsuits will be dismissed.

Subject Matter Jurisdiction of Federal and State Courts

subject matter jurisdiction Jurisdiction over the subject matter of a lawsuit.

To hear and decide a case, a court must have **subject matter jurisdiction** over the case. Some courts can only decide cases involving specific types of disputes. Such courts have only *limited jurisdiction*.

Federal courts have jurisdiction to hear only certain types of cases (discussed subsequently). Certain state courts, such as probate courts and small claims courts, can hear only designated types of cases. If a court does not have subject matter jurisdiction, it cannot hear the case. For example, a bankruptcy court cannot decide an antitrust case.

federal question A case arising under the U.S. Constitution, treaties, and federal statutes and regulations.

Jurisdiction of Federal Courts Article III, section 2 of the U.S. Constitution sets forth the jurisdiction of federal courts. Federal courts have *limited jurisdiction* to hear cases involving **federal questions**. These cases arise under the U.S. Constitution, treaties, and federal statutes and regulations. There is no dollar-amount limit on federal question cases that can be brought in federal court.[3]

diversity of citizenship A case between (1) citizens of different states, (2) a citizen of a state and a citizen or subject of a foreign country, and (3) a citizen of a state and a foreign country where a foreign country is the plaintiff.

The Supreme Court also has limited jurisdiction to hear cases involving **diversity of citizenship**. These cases arise between (1) citizens who live in different states and (2) a citizen of a state and a citizen or subject of a foreign country. The reason for providing diversity of citizenship jurisdiction was to prevent state court bias against nonresidents. The federal court must apply the appropriate state law in deciding the case. The dollar amount of the controversy must exceed $75,000. If this requirement is not met, the action must be brought in the appropriate state court.[4]

Federal courts have exclusive jurisdiction to hear cases involving federal crimes, antitrust, bankruptcy; patent and copyright cases; suits against the United States; and most admiralty cases. State courts cannot hear these cases.

State and federal courts have concurrent jurisdiction to hear cases involving diversity of citizenship and federal questions over which federal courts do not have exclusive jurisdiction (e.g., cases involving federal securities laws). If a case involving concurrent jurisdiction is brought by a plaintiff in state court, the defendant can remove the case to federal court. If a case does not qualify to be brought in federal court, it must be brought in the appropriate state court.

Exhibit 3.4 illustrates the jurisdiction of federal and state courts.

In Personam, in Rem, and Quasi in Rem Jurisdiction

in personam jurisdiction Jurisdiction over the parties to a lawsuit.

service of process A summons is served on the defendant to obtain personal jurisdiction over him or her.

Jurisdiction over the person is called **in personam jurisdiction**, or **personal jurisdiction**. A plaintiff, by filing a lawsuit with a court, gives the court in personam jurisdiction over himself or herself. The court must also have in personam jurisdiction over the defendant, which is usually obtained by having that person served a summons within the territorial boundaries of the state (i.e., **service of process**). Service of process usually is accomplished by personal service of the summons and complaint on

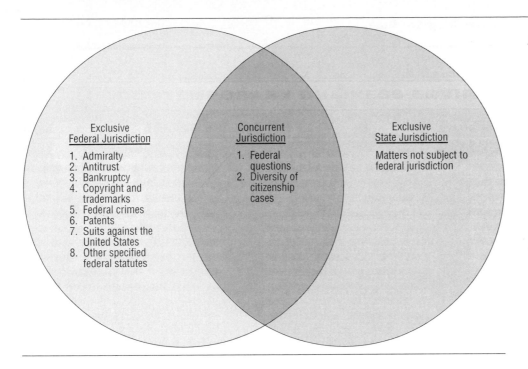

Exhibit 3.4
Jurisdiction of Federal and
State Courts

Exclusive
Federal Jurisdiction

1. Admiralty
2. Antitrust
3. Bankruptcy
4. Copyright and
   trademarks
5. Federal crimes
6. Patents
7. Suits against the
   United States
8. Other specified
   federal statutes

Concurrent
Jurisdiction

1. Federal
   questions
2. Diversity of
   citizenship
   cases

Exclusive
State Jurisdiction

Matters not subject to
federal jurisdiction

the defendant. If this is not possible, alternative forms of notice such as mailing of the summons or publication of a notice in a newspaper may be permitted.

A corporation is subject to personal jurisdiction in the state in which it is incorporated, has its principal office, and is doing business. A party who disputes the jurisdiction of a court can make a special appearance in that court to argue against the imposition of jurisdiction. Service of process is not permitted during such an appearance.

A court may have jurisdiction to hear and decide a case because it has jurisdiction over the property of the lawsuit. This is called **in rem jurisdiction** ("jurisdiction over the thing"). For example, a state court would have jurisdiction to hear a dispute over the ownership of a piece of real estate located within the state. This is so even if one or more of the disputing parties live in another state or states.

Sometimes a plaintiff who obtains a judgment against a defendant in one state will try to collect the judgment by attaching property of the defendant that is located in another state. This is permitted under **quasi in rem**, or **attachment jurisdiction**.[5]

Long-Arm Statutes

In most states, a state court can obtain jurisdiction over persons and businesses located in another state or country through the state's **long-arm statute**. These statutes extend a state's jurisdiction to nonresidents who were not served a summons within the state. The nonresident must have had some minimum contact with the state. In addition, the maintenance of the suit must uphold the traditional notions of fair play and substantial justice.[6]

The exercise of long-arm jurisdiction is generally permitted over nonresidents who have (1) committed torts within the state (e.g., caused an automobile accident in the state); (2) entered into a contract in the state or that affects the state (and allegedly breached the contract); or (3) transacted other business in the state that allegedly caused injury to another person.

Parties to a contract may include a **forum-selection clause** that designates a certain court to hear any dispute concerning nonperformance of the contract. In the following case, the U.S. Supreme Court upheld a forum-selection clause in a contract.

in rem jurisdiction
Jurisdiction to hear a case because of jurisdiction over the property of the lawsuit.

quasi in rem jurisdiction
Jurisdiction allowed a plaintiff who obtains a judgment in one state to try to collect the judgment by attaching property of the defendant located in another state.

long-arm statute A statute that extends a state's jurisdiction to nonresidents who were not served a summons within the state.

forum-selection clause
Contract provision that designates a certain court to hear any dispute concerning nonperformance of the contract.

CASE 3.1

Carnival Cruise Lines, Inc. v. Shute
499 U.S. 585, 111 S.Ct. 1522, 113 L.Ed.2d 622 (1991) United States Supreme Court

Facts Mr. and Mrs. Shute, residents of the state of Washington, purchased passage for a seven-day cruise on the *Tropicale*, a cruise ship operated by the Carnival Cruise Lines, Inc. (Carnival). They paid the fare to the travel agent, who forwarded the payment to Carnival's headquarters in Miami, Florida. Carnival prepared the tickets and sent them to the Shutes. Each ticket consisted of five pages, including contract terms. The ticket contained a forum-selection clause that designated the state of Florida as the forum for any lawsuits arising under or in connection with the ticket and cruise. The Shutes boarded the *Tropicale* in Los Angeles, which set sail for Puerto Vallarta, Mexico. While the ship was on its return voyage and in international waters off the Mexican coast, Mrs. Shute was injured when she slipped on a deck mat during a guided tour of the ship's galley. Upon return to Washington, she filed a negligence lawsuit against Carnival in U.S. district court in Washington seeking damages.

Carnival filed a motion for summary judgment contending that the suit could be brought only in a court located in the state of Florida. The district court granted Carnival's motion. The court of appeals reversed, holding that Mrs. Shute could sue Carnival in Washington. Carnival appealed to the U.S. Supreme Court.

Issue Is the forum-selection clause in Carnival Cruise Lines' ticket enforceable?

Decision The U.S. Supreme Court held that the forum-selected clause in Carnival's ticket is fair and reasonable and therefore enforceable against Mrs.

Shute. If she wishes to sue Carnival, she must do so in a court in the state of Florida, not in a court in the state of Washington.

Reason The Supreme Court stated that including a reasonable forum clause in form contract may well be permissible for several reasons. "First, a cruise line has a special interest in limiting the fora in which it potentially could be subject to suit. Because a cruise ship typically carries passengers from many locales, it is not unlikely that a mishap on a cruise could subject the cruise line to litigation in several different fora. Additionally, a clause establishing the forum for dispute resolution has the salutary effect of dispelling any confusion where suits arising from the contract must be brought and defended, sparing litigants the time and expense of pretrial motions to determine the correct forum, and conserving judicial resources that otherwise would be devoted to deciding those motions. Finally, it stands to reason that passengers who purchase tickets containing a forum clause like that at issue in this case benefit in the form of reduced fares reflecting the savings that the cruise line enjoys by limiting the fora in which it may be sued."

CASE QUESTIONS

Critical Legal Thinking Should forum-selection clauses be enforced? Why or why not?

Ethics Did Carnival Cruise Lines act ethically by placing the forum-selection clause in their tickets?

Business Implication Do forum-selection clauses serve any legitimate purpose? Explain.

Venue

venue A concept that requires lawsuits to be heard by the court with jurisdiction that is nearest the location in which the incident occurred or where the parties reside.

Venue requires lawsuits to be heard by the court with jurisdiction nearest the location in which the incident occurred or where the parties reside.

CONSIDER THIS EXAMPLE: Harry, a Georgia resident, commits a felony crime in Los Angeles County, California. The California Superior Court located in Los Angeles is the proper venue because the crime was committed there, the witnesses are probably from the area, and so on.

Occasionally, pretrial publicity might prejudice jurors located in the proper venue. In such cases, a change of venue may be requested so that a more impartial jury can be found. The courts generally frown upon forum shopping (i.e., looking) for a favorable court without a valid reason.

INTERNATIONAL PERSPECTIVE

Comparison of the Japanese and American Legal Systems

Businesses often complain that there are too many lawyers and too much litigation in the United States. There are currently more than 800,000 lawyers and more than 20 million lawsuits per year in this country. On the other hand, in Japan, a country with about half the population, there are only 15,000 lawyers and little litigation. Why the difference?

Much of the difference is cultural: Japan nurtures the attitude that confrontation should be avoided. Litigious persons in Japan are looked down upon. Therefore, companies rarely do battle in court. Instead, they opt for private arbitration of most of their disputes.

Other differences are built into the legal system itself. For example, there is only one place to go

to become a *bengoshi*, or lawyer, in Japan—the government-operated National Institute for Legal Training. Only 2 percent of 35,000 applicants are accepted annually, and only 400 new *bengoshi* are admitted to Japan's exclusive legal club per year.

There are other obstacles, too. For example, no class actions or contingency fee arrangements are allowed. Plaintiffs must pay their lawyers a front fee of up to 8 percent of the damages sought, plus a nonrefundable filing fee to the court of one-half of 1 percent of the damages. To make matters even more difficult, no discovery is permitted. Thus, plaintiffs are denied access before trial to an opponent's potential evidence. And, even if the plaintiff wins the lawsuit, damage awards are low.

Some experts argue that Japan

has more legal practitioners than the statistics reveal. For example, there are about 5,000 non-*bengoshi* patent specialists that perform services similar to U.S. patent attorneys. Another 50,000 licensed tax practitioners offer services similar to U.S. tax attorneys. Many non-*bengoshi* legal experts handle tasks such as contract negotiation and drafting. In addition, sales personnel and front-line managers often act as problem solvers.

The Japanese bias against courtroom solutions remains strong. The current system is designed to save time, money, and to preserve long-term relationships. The belief that disputes can be solved amicably without litigation is a concept American businesses are starting to embrace.

THE PRETRIAL LITIGATION PROCESS

As stated at the beginning of this chapter, the bringing, maintaining, and defense of a lawsuit is generally referred to as the **litigation process**, or **litigation**. The pretrial litigation process can be divided into the following major phases: pleadings, discovery, settlement conference, and dismissals and pretrial judgments. Each of these phases is discussed in the sections that follow.

> **litigation**   The process of bringing, maintaining, and defending a lawsuit.

The Pleadings

The paperwork that is filed with the court to initiate and respond to a lawsuit is referred to as the **pleadings**. The major pleadings are the *complaint, answer, cross-complaint*, and *reply*.

> **pleadings**   The paperwork that is filed with the court to initiate and respond to a lawsuit.

Complaint and Summons   To initiate a lawsuit, the party who is suing (the **plaintiff**) must file a **complaint** with the proper court. The complaint must name the parties to the lawsuit, allege the ultimate facts and law violated, and contain a "prayer for relief" for a remedy to be awarded by the court. The complaint can be as long as necessary, depending on the case's complexity. A sample complaint appears in Exhibit 3.5.

> **plaintiff**   The party who files the lawsuit.
>
> **complaint**
> The document the plaintiff files with the court and serves on the defendant to initiate a lawsuit.

Exhibit 3.5
A Sample Complaint

IN THE UNITED STATES DISTRICT COURT
FOR THE DISTRICT OF IDAHO

John Doe   Civil No. 2-1001
   Plaintiff

    v.   COMPLAINT

Jane Roe
   Defendant

The plaintiff, by and through his attorney, alleges:

1. The plaintiff is a resident of the State of Idaho, the defendant is a resident of the State of Washington, and there is diversity of citizenship between the parties.

2. The amount in controversy exceeds the sum of $50,000, exclusive of interest and costs.

3. On January 10, 1999, plaintiff was exercising reasonable care while walking across the intersection of Sun Valley Road and Main Street, Ketchum, Idaho when defendant negligently drove his car through a red light at the intersection and struck plaintiff.

4. As a result of the defendant's negligence, plaintiff has incurred medical expenses of $54,000 and suffered severe physical injury and mental distress.

WHEREFORE, plaintiff claims judgment in the amount of $1,000,000 interest at the maximum legal rate, and costs of this action.

By _____
    Edward Lawson
    Attorney for Plaintiff
    100 Main Street
    Ketchum, Idaho

---

summons A court order directing the defendant to appear in court and answer the complaint.

CAUTION
Some complaints in complicated cases exceed 100 pages.

answer The defendant's written response to the plaintiff's complaint that is filed with the court and served on the plaintiff.

After a complaint has been filed with the court, the court issues a **summons**. A summons is a court order directing the defendant to appear in court and answer the complaint. The complaint and summons are served on the defendant by a sheriff, other government official, or a private process server.

Answer The defendant must file an **answer** to the plaintiff's complaint. The defendant's answer is filed with the court and served on the plaintiff. In the answer, the defendant admits or denies the allegations contained in the plaintiff's complaint. A judgment will be entered against a defendant who admits all of the allegations in the complaint. The case will proceed if the defendant denies all or some of the allegations. If the defendant does not answer the complaint, a default judgment is entered against him. A default judgment establishes the defendant's liability. The plaintiff then has only to prove damages.

In addition to answering the complaint, a defendant's answer can assert affirmative defenses. For example, if a complaint alleges that the plaintiff was personally injured by the defendant, the defendant's answer could state that he or she acted in self-defense. Another affirmative defense would be an assertion that the plaintiff's lawsuit is barred because the statute of limitations (time within which to bring a lawsuit) has run out.

Cross-Complaint and Reply A defendant who believes that he or she has been injured by the plaintiff can file a **cross-complaint** against the plaintiff in addition to an answer. In the cross-complaint, the defendant (now the cross-complainant) sues the plaintiff (now the cross-defendant) for damages or some other remedy. The original plaintiff must file a **reply** (answer) to the cross-complaint. The reply, which can include affirmative defenses, must be filed with the court and served on the original defendant.

cross-complaint Filed by the defendant against the plaintiff to seek damages or some other remedy.

reply Filed by the original plaintiff to answer the defendant's cross-complaint.

Intervention and Consolidation If other persons have an interest in a lawsuit, they may **intervene** and become parties to the lawsuit. For example, a bank that has made a secured loan on a piece of real estate can intervene in a lawsuit between parties who are litigating ownership of the property.

If several plaintiffs have filed separate lawsuits stemming from the same fact situation against the same defendant, the court can **consolidate** the cases into one case if it would not cause undue prejudice to the parties. Suppose, for example, that a commercial airplane crashes, killing and injuring many people. The court could consolidate all of the lawsuits against the defendant airplane company.

intervention The act of others to join as parties to an existing lawsuit.

consolidation The act of a court to combine two or more separate lawsuits into one lawsuit.

Discovery

The legal process provides for a detailed pretrial procedure called **discovery**. During discovery, both parties engage in various activities to discover facts of the case from the other party and witnesses prior to trial. Discovery serves several functions, including preventing surprise, allowing parties to thoroughly prepare for trial, preserving evidence, saving court time, and promoting the settlement of cases. The major forms of discovery follow.

discovery A legal process during which parties engage in various activities to discover facts of the case from the other party and witnesses prior to trial.

Depositions A **deposition** is the oral testimony given by a party or witness prior to trial. The person giving the deposition is called the **deponent**. The parties to the lawsuit must give their deposition if called upon by the other party to do so. The deposition of a witness can be given voluntarily or pursuant to a subpoena (court order). The deponent can be required to bring documents to the deposition. Most depositions are taken at the office of one of the attorneys. The deponent is placed under oath and then asked oral questions by one or both of the attorneys. The questions and answers are recorded in written form by a court reporter. Depositions can also be videotaped. The deponent is given an opportunity to correct his or her answers prior to signing the deposition. Depositions are used to preserve evidence (e.g., if the deponent is deceased, ill, or is not otherwise available at trial) and impeach testimony given by witnesses at trial.

deposition Oral testimony given by a party or witness prior to trial. The testimony is given under oath and is transcribed.

deponent Party who gives his or her deposition.

Interrogatories **Interrogatories** are written questions submitted by one party to a lawsuit to another party. The questions can be very detailed. In addition, it might be necessary to attach certain documents to the answers. A party is required to answer the interrogatories in writing within a specified time period (e.g., 60 to 90 days). An attorney usually helps with the preparation of the answers. The answers are signed under oath.

interrogatories Written questions submitted by one party to another party. The questions must be answered in writing within a stipulated time.

Production of Documents Often, particularly in complex business cases, a substantial portion of the lawsuit might be based on information contained in documents (e.g., memoranda, correspondence, company records). One party to a lawsuit may request that the other party produce all documents that are relevant to the case prior to trial. This is called a **production of documents**. If the documents sought are too voluminous to be moved, are in permanent storage, or would disrupt the ongoing business of the party who is to produce them, the requesting party might be required to examine the documents at the other party's premises.

production of documents Request by one party to another party to produce all documents relevant to the case prior to trial.

physical or mental examination   Upon request of a party, the court may order another party to submit to a physical or mental examination prior to trial.

Physical or Mental Examination   In cases that concern the physical or mental condition of a party, a court can order the party to submit to certain **physical or mental examinations** to determine the extent of the alleged injuries. This would occur, for example, where the plaintiff has been injured in an accident and is seeking damages for physical injury and mental distress.

CONTEMPORARY BUSINESS ENVIRONMENT

E-Mail Messages Used as Evidence

E-mail has made it faster and easier to communicate with others, whether for business or personal reasons. E-mail messages have also become a source of evidence to be used at both criminal and civil trials. Consider the following case.

Karen Strauss worked for Microsoft Corporation as an assistant editor for the *Microsoft Systems Journal*. When she was passed over for a promotion and then subsequently dismissed from her job, she brought a sex discrimination case against Microsoft. She alleged that her supervisor, Jon Lazarus, sexually harassed her by making certain remarks and sending messages to her by e-mail. She alleged that Lazarus referred to another woman in the office as "Spandex Queen," told another woman that he would pay her $500 if he could call her "Sweet

Georgia Brown," and referred to himself as the "president of the Amateur Gynecology Club." Strauss also wanted to introduce e-mail evidence that Lazarus followed these remarks with e-mail messages to Strauss containing a satirical essay titled "Alice in UNIX Land," an advertisement for the replacement of "Mouse Balls," and a parody on a play titled "A Girl's Guide to Condoms."

The e-mail messages had been erased, but the plaintiff retrieved them from backup tapes automatically made by the company's computer network.

Microsoft made a motion to the court to preclude this evidence, including the e-mail messages, from being introduced at trial. The district court denied Microsoft's motion. The court stated that the e-mail messages, when

viewed in light of Strauss's other evidence, could lead a reasonable jury to conclude that Microsoft engaged in the challenged conduct. The court noted that although the e-mail messages might be embarrassing to Microsoft, such evidence is admissible. The court stated, "The Federal Rules of Evidence favor placing even the nastier side of human nature before the jury if to do so would aid its search for the truth." The court permitted Strauss to sue Microsoft for sexual harassment using the e-mail messages as evidence.

As e-mail continues to increase in use, it will become a greater— and very tangible—source of evidence at criminal and civil trials. [*Strauss v. Microsoft Corporation*, 68 Fair Empl. Prac. Cases (BNA) 1576 (S.D.N.Y. 1995)]

Settlement Conference

pretrial hearing   A hearing before the trial in order to facilitate the settlement of a case. Also called a *settlement conference*.

Federal court rules and most state court rules permit the court to direct the attorneys or parties to appear before the court for a **pretrial hearing**, or **settlement conference**. One of the major purposes of such hearings is to facilitate the settlement of the case. Pretrial conferences are often held informally in the judge's chambers. If no settlement is reached, the pretrial hearing is used to identify the major trial issues and other relevant factors. More than 90 percent of all cases are settled before they go to trial.

Dismissals and Pretrial Judgments

There are several **pretrial motions** that parties to a lawsuit can make to try to dispose of all or part of a lawsuit prior to trial. The two major pretrial motions are explained in the following sections.

motion for judgment on the pleadings   Motion that alleges that if all the facts presented in the pleadings are taken as true, the moving party would win the lawsuit when the proper law is applied to these asserted facts.

Motion for Judgment on the Pleadings   A motion for judgment
on the pleadings can be made by either party when the pleadings are complete. This motion alleges that if all of the facts presented in the pleadings are true, the moving

party would win the lawsuit when the proper law is applied to these facts. In deciding this motion, the judge cannot consider any facts outside the pleadings.

Motion for Summary Judgment   The trier of fact (i.e., the jury, or, if there is no jury, then the judge) determines factual issues. A **motion for summary judgment** asserts that there are no factual disputes to be decided by the jury and that the judge should apply the relevant law to the undisputed facts to decide the case. Motions for summary judgment, which can be made by either party, are supported by evidence outside the pleadings. Affidavits from the parties and witnesses, documents (e.g., a written contract between the parties), depositions, and such are common forms of evidence. If, after examining the evidence, the court finds no factual dispute, it can decide the issue or issues raised in the summary judgment motion. This could dispense with the entire case or with part of the case. If the judge finds that a factual dispute exists, the motion will be denied and the case will go to trial.

> **motion for summary judgment**   Motion that asserts that there are no factual disputes to be decided by the jury; if so, the judge can apply the proper law to the undisputed facts and decide the case without a jury. These motions are supported by affidavits, documents, and deposition testimony.

THE TRIAL

Pursuant to the Seventh Amendment to the U.S. Constitution, a party to an action at law is guaranteed the right to a jury trial in cases at law in federal court.[7] Most state constitutions contain a similar guarantee for state court actions. If either party requests a jury, the trial will be by jury. If both parties waive their right to a jury, the trial will be without a jury. The judge sits as the **trier of fact** in nonjury trials. At the time of trial, the parties usually submit **trial briefs** to the judge that contain legal support for their side of the case.

Trials are usually divided into the following phases:

> **trier of fact**   The jury in a jury trial; the judge where there is not a jury trial.
>
> **trial briefs**   Documents submitted by the parties' attorneys to the judge that contain legal support for their side of the case.

1. Jury Selection   The pool of potential jurors is usually selected from voter or automobile registration lists. Individuals are selected to hear specific cases through a process called *voir dire* ("to speak the truth"). Lawyers for each party and the judge can ask prospective jurors questions to determine if they would be biased in their decision. Biased jurors can be prevented from sitting on a particular case. When the appropriate number of jurors are selected (usually 6–12 jurors), they are impaneled to hear the case and are sworn in. The trial is ready to begin. A jury can be sequestered (i.e., separated from family and so on) in important cases. Jurors are paid minimum fees for their service.

> *voir dire*   Process whereby prospective jurors are asked questions by the judge and attorneys to determine if they would be biased in their decision.

2. Opening Statements   Each party's attorney is allowed to make an **opening statement** to the jury. In the opening statement, the attorney usually summarizes the main factual and legal issues of the case and describes why he or she believes his or her client's position is valid. The information given in this statement is not considered as evidence.

> **opening statements**   Statements made by the attorneys to the jury in which they summarize the factual and legal issues of the case.

3. The Plaintiff's Case   The plaintiff bears the **burden of proof** to persuade the trier of fact of the merits of his case. This is called the **plaintiff's case**. The plaintiff's attorney will call witnesses to give testimony. After a witness has been sworn in, the plaintiff's attorney examines (i.e., questions) the witness. This is called *direct examination*. Documents and other evidence can be introduced through each witness. After the plaintiff's attorney has completed his questions, the defendant's attorney can question the witness. This is called cross-examination. The defendant's attorney can ask questions only about the subjects that were brought up during the direct examination. After the defendant's attorney completes his or her questions, the plaintiff's attorney can again ask questions of the witness. This is called *redirect examination*. The defendant's attorney can then again ask questions of the witness. This is called *recross examination*.

> **burden of proof**   The plaintiff bears the burden of proving the allegations made in his complaint.
>
> **plaintiff's case**   Process by which the plaintiff introduces evidence to prove the allegations contained in the complaint.

defendant's case Process by which the defendant (1) rebuts the plaintiff's evidence, (2) proves affirmative defenses, and (3) proves allegations made in a cross-complaint.

4. The Defendant's Case

The **defendant's case** proceeds after the plaintiff has concluded his case. The defendant's case must (1) rebut the plaintiff's evidence, (2) prove any affirmative defenses asserted by the defendant, and (3) prove any allegations contained in the defendant's cross-complaint. The defendant's witnesses are examined in much the same way as the plaintiff's witnesses. First, the defendant's attorney directly examines his or her witnesses. Then, the plaintiff's attorney cross-examines the witness. This is followed by redirect and recross examination.

5. Rebuttal and Rejoinder

After the defendant's attorney has completed calling witnesses, the plaintiff's attorney can call witnesses and put forth evidence to rebut the defendant's case. This is called a *rebuttal*. The defendant's attorney can call additional witnesses and introduce other evidence to counter the rebuttal. This is called the *rejoinder*.

closing arguments Statements made by the attorneys to the jury at the end of the trial to try to convince the jury to render a verdict for their client.

6. Closing Arguments

At the conclusion of the evidence, each party's attorney is allowed to make a **closing argument** to the jury. Each attorney tries to convince the jury to render a verdict for his or her client by pointing out the strengths in the client's case and the weaknesses in the other side's case. Information given by the attorneys in their closing statements is not evidence.

jury instruction Instructions given by the judge to the jury that inform them of the law to be applied in the case.

7. Jury Instructions

After the closing arguments are completed, the judge reads **jury instructions** (or **charges**) to the jury. These instructions inform the jury about what law to apply when they decide the case. For example, in a criminal trial the judge will read the jury the statutory definition of the crime charged. In an accident case, the judge will read the jury the legal definition of negligence.

8. Jury Deliberation

The jury then retires to the jury room to deliberate its findings. This can take from a few minutes to many weeks. After deliberation, the jury will announce its **verdict**. In a civil case, the jury also assesses damages. The judge assesses penalties in criminal cases.

verdict Decision reached by the jury.

judgment The official decision of the court.

judgment notwithstanding the verdict In a civil case, the judge may overturn the jury's verdict if he or she finds bias or jury misconduct.

9. Entry of Judgment

After the jury has returned its verdict, in most cases the judge will enter **judgment** to the successful party based on the verdict. This is the official decision of the court. The court, however, can overturn the verdict if it finds bias or jury misconduct. This is called a **judgment notwithstanding the verdict** or **judgment n.o.v.** or **j.n.o.v.** In a civil case, the judge may reduce the amount of monetary damages awarded by the jury if he or she finds the jury to have been biased, emotional, or inflamed. This is called *remittitur*. The trial court usually issues a written memorandum setting forth the reasons for the judgment. This memorandum, together with the trial transcript and evidence introduced at trial, constitutes the permanent record of the trial court proceeding.

In the following case, the court was asked to grant a judgment notwithstanding the verdict.

CASE 3.2

Ferlito v. Johnson & Johnson Products, Inc.

771 F.Supp. 196 (1991) United States District Court, E.D. Michigan

Facts Susan and Frank Ferlito were invited to a Halloween party. They decided to attend as Mary (Mrs. Ferlito) and her little lamb (Mr. Ferlito). Mrs. Ferlito constructed a lamb costume for her husband by gluing cotton batting manufactured by Johnson & Johnson Products, Inc. (JJP) to a suit of long underwear. She used the same cotton batting to fashion a headpiece, complete with ears. The costume covered Mr. Ferlito from his head to his ankles, except for his face and hands, which were blackened with paint. At the party, Mr. Ferlito attempted to light a cigarette with a butane lighter. The flame passed close to his left arm, and the cotton batting ignited. He suffered burns over one-third of his body. The Ferlitos sued JJP to recover damages, alleging that JJP failed to warn them of the ignitability of cotton batting. The jury returned a verdict for Mr. Ferlito in the amount of $555,000 and for Mrs. Ferlito in the amount of $70,000. JJP filed a motion for judgment notwithstanding the verdict (j.n.o.v.).

Issue Should defendant JJP's motion for j.n.o.v. be granted?

Decision The trial court granted defendant JJP's motion for j.n.o.v. By doing so, the court vacated the verdict entered by the jury in favor of Mr. and Mrs. Ferlito.

Reason If, after reviewing the evidence, the court is of the opinion that reasonable minds could not come to the result reached by the jury, then the motion for j.n.o.v. should be granted. At trial, both plaintiffs testified that they knew that cotton batting burns when exposed to flame. The court stated, "Because both plaintiffs were already aware of the danger, a warning by JJP would have been superfluous." Mrs. Ferlito testified that the idea for the costume was hers alone. As described on the product's package, its intended uses are for cleansing, applying medications, and infant care. The court concluded, "Plaintiffs' showing that the product may be used on occasions in classrooms for decorative purposes failed to demonstrate the foreseeability of an adult male encapsulating himself from head to toe in cotton batting and then lighting up a cigarette."

CASE QUESTIONS

Critical Legal Thinking Should trial courts have the authority to enter a j.n.o.v., or should jury verdicts always be allowed to stand? Explain your answer.

Ethics Did the Ferlitos act ethically in suing JJP in this case? Were they responsible for their own injuries?

Business Implication What would have been the business implications had JJP been found liable?

THE APPEAL

In a civil case, either party can **appeal** the trial court's decision after a final judgment is entered. Only the defendant can appeal in a criminal case. The appeal is made to the appropriate appellate court. A notice of appeal must be filed within a prescribed time after judgment is entered (usually within 60 or 90 days). The appealing party is called the **appellant**, or **petitioner**. The responding party is called the **appellee**, or **respondent**. The appellant is often required to post a bond (e.g., one and one-half times the judgment) on appeal.

The parties may designate all or relevant portions of the trial record to be submitted to the appellate court for review. The appellant's attorney may file an opening brief with the court that sets forth legal research and other information to support his contentions on appeal. The appellee can file a responding brief answering the appellant's contentions. Appellate courts usually permit a brief oral argument at which each party's attorney is heard.

An appellate court will reverse a lower court decision if it finds an **error of law** in the record. An error of law occurs if the jury was improperly instructed by the trial court judge, prejudicial evidence was admitted at trial when it should have been excluded, prejudicial evidence was obtained through an unconstitutional search and seizure, and the like. An appellate court will not reverse a finding of fact unless such finding is unsupported by the evidence or is contradicted by the evidence.

appellant The appealing party in an appeal. Also known as *petitioner*.

appellee The responding party in an appeal. Also known as *respondent*.

NOTE
Trial court decisions are overturned on appeal only if there has been an error of law or the decision is not supported by the evidence.

JUDICIAL RESTRICTIONS ON THE RESOLUTION OF INTERNATIONAL DISPUTES

The majority of cases involving international law disputes are heard by the **national courts** of individual nations. This is primarily the case for commercial disputes between private litigants that do not qualify to be heard by an international court. Some

national courts The courts of individual nations.

countries have specialized courts that hear international commercial disputes. Other countries permit such disputes to proceed through their regular court system. In the United States, commercial disputes between U.S. companies and foreign governments or parties may be brought in federal district court.

Most often, cases involving international disputes are brought in the national court of the host country or the plaintiff's home country. Jurisdiction is often a highly contested issue.

In hearing international disputes, national courts, including those in the United States, might have difficulty securing jurisdiction over the parties and discovering evidence. In addition, national courts are limited by two principles of judicial restraint—the act of state doctrine and the doctrine of sovereign immunity.

Act of State Doctrine

A general principle of international law is that a country has absolute authority over what transpires within its own territory. In furtherance of this principle, the **act of state doctrine** states that judges of one country cannot question the validity of an act committed by another country within that other country's own borders. In *United States v. Belmont*,[8] the U.S. Supreme Court declared, "Every sovereign state must recognize the independence of every other sovereign state; and the courts of one will not sit in judgment upon the acts of the government of another, done within its own territory." This restraint on the judiciary is justified under the doctrine of separation of powers and permits the executive branch of the federal government to arrange affairs with foreign governments.

act of state doctrine States that judges of one country cannot question the validity of an act committed by another country within that other country's own borders. It is based on the principle that a country has absolute authority over what transpires within its own territory.

The Doctrine of Sovereign Immunity

One of the oldest principles of international law is the **doctrine of sovereign immunity**. Under this doctrine, countries are granted immunity from suits in courts in other countries. For example, if a U.S. citizen wanted to sue the government of China in a U.S. court, he or she could not (subject to the exceptions discussed subsequently).

Originally, the United States granted absolute immunity to foreign governments from suits in U.S. courts. In 1952, the United States switched to the principle of qualified or restricted immunity, which was eventually codified in the **Foreign Sovereign Immunities Act of 1976 (FSIA)**.[9] This act now exclusively governs suits against foreign nations in the United States, whether in a federal or state court. Most Western nations have adopted the principle of restricted immunity. Other countries still follow the doctrine of absolute immunity.

doctrine of sovereign immunity States that countries are granted immunity from suits in courts of other countries (subject to certain exceptions).

Exceptions   The FSIA provides that a foreign country is not immune from lawsuits in U.S. courts in the following two situations:

1. The foreign country has waived its immunity, either explicitly or by implication.
2. The action is based on a commercial activity carried on in the United States by the foreign country or carried on outside the United States but causing a direct effect in the United States.

What constitutes "commercial activity" is the most litigated aspect of the FSIA. If it is commercial activity, the foreign sovereign is subject to suit in the United States; if it is not, the foreign sovereign is immune from suit in this country.

In the following case, the Supreme Court had to decide whether a foreign sovereign had engaged in commercial activity that would subject it to suit in the United States.

CASE 3.3

Republic of Argentina v. Weltover, Inc.
112 S.Ct. 2160, 119 L.Ed.2d 394 (1992) United States Supreme Court

Facts In an attempt to stabilize its currency, Argentina and its central bank, Banco Central (collectively Argentina), issued bonds called "Bonods." The bonds, which were sold to investors worldwide, provided for repayment in U.S. dollars through transfers on the London, Frankfurt, Zurich, and New York markets at the bondholder's election. Argentina lacked sufficient foreign exchange to retire the bonds when they matured. Argentina unilaterally extended the time for payment and offered bondholders substitute instruments as a means of rescheduling the debts. Two Panamanian corporations and a Swiss bank refused the rescheduling and insisted that full payment be made in New York. When Argentina did not pay, they brought a breach of contract action against Argentina in U.S. district court in New York. Argentina moved to dismiss, alleging that it was not subject to suit in U.S. courts under the federal Foreign Sovereign Immunities Act. The plaintiffs asserted that the "commercial activity" exception to the act applied, subjecting Argentina to suit in U.S. court. The district court denied Argentina's motion for dismissal and the court of appeals affirmed. Argentina appealed to the U.S. Supreme Court.

Issue Does the doctrine of sovereign immunity prevent the plaintiffs from suing Argentina in a U.S. court?

Decision No. The Supreme Court held that Argentina's issuance of the bonds was a commercial activity that had a direct effect in the United States. Therefore, the commercial activity exception to the sovereign immunities act applied, which allowed the plaintiffs to sue Argentina in a U.S. court.

Reason The U.S. Supreme Court noted that when a foreign government acts, not as a regulator of a market, but in the manner of a private player within it, the foreign sovereign's actions are commercial in nature. The Court found that the issuance of the Bonods by Argentina was a commercial activity. The Court noted, "The commercial character of the Bonods is confirmed by the fact that they are in almost all respects garden-variety debt instruments: they may be held by private parties; they are negotiable and may be traded on the international market; and they promise a future stream of income." The Court also found that Argentina's issuance, nonpayment, and rescheduling of the bonds had a direct effect in the United States: Money that was supposed to have been delivered to a New York bank for deposit was not forthcoming. The Court concluded that the plaintiffs, who were foreign corporations, could sue Argentina in U.S. district court based on the commercial activity exception to the Foreign Sovereign Immunities Act.

CASE QUESTIONS

Critical Legal Thinking Should the United States recognize the doctrine of absolute sovereign immunity or qualified immunity? Explain.

Ethics Did the government of Argentina act ethically in not paying the bonds when due and unilaterally rescheduling the debt?

Business Implication Is there more risk for investors who invest in obligations of foreign countries than in obligations of the U.S. government?

INTERNATIONAL PERSPECTIVE

International Dispute Resolution: The World Trade Organization

In 1995, the **World Trade Organization (WTO)** was created as part of the Uruguay Round of trade negotiations on the *General Agreement on Tariffs and Trade*

(GATT). GATT is a multilateral treaty that establishes trade agreements and limits tariffs and trade restrictions among its over 100 member nations.

The WTO, which is located in Geneva, Switzerland, is a new international organization. One of its primary functions is to hear

continued

and decide trade disputes between member nations. Prior to the creation of the WTO, GATT governed trade disputes between signatory nations. This system was inadequate because any member nation that was found to have violated any GATT trade agreement could itself veto any sanctions imposed by GATT's governing body. The WTO solved this problem by adopting a "judicial" mode of dispute resolution to replace GATT's more politically based one.

WTO members have entered into many trade agreements among themselves, including international agreements on investments, sale of goods, provision of services, intellectual property, licensing, tariffs, subsidies, and the removal of trade barriers. A member nation that believes that another member nation has breached one of these agreements can initiate a proceeding to have the WTO hear and decide the dispute.

The dispute is first heard by a three-member **panel** of the WTO. The panel issues a "panel report," which contains the panel's decision, its findings of fact and law, and the remedy ordered if a violation has been found. The report is then referred to the WTO's newly created **Dispute Settlement Body**. This body is required to adopt the panel report unless, by consensus, it agrees not to adopt it. Because each member nation has a representative on this settlement body, it can be presumed that panel reports will automatically be adopted because the winning nation to the dispute will almost assuredly vote to adopt it. This is a radical change from the former GATT settlement procedure. Under GATT, unanimity was required to enforce a panel report, and the losing party usually voted to "block" the implementation of a panel's findings against it. One of the most important features of the WTO is the elimination of the blocking power of member nations.

The WTO creates an **Appellate Body** to which a party can appeal a decision of the Dispute Settlement Body. This appeals court is composed of seven professional justices selected from member nations. Appeals are heard by panels composed of three members of the Appellate Body. Appeals are limited to issues of law, not fact. The entire dispute proceeding is completed within 9 months when a panel report is not appealed, and in 12 months when there is an appeal. A shortened period is available if the parties agree or if there is an urgent matter that must be decided quickly.

If a violation of a trade agreement is found, the general report and appellate decision can order the offending nation to cease from engaging in the violating practice and to pay damages to the other party. If the offending nation refuses to abide by the order, the WTO can order retaliatory trade sanctions (e.g., tariffs) by other member nations against the non-complying nation.

The WTO, which has been referred to as the "Supreme Court of Trade," is destined to become the globe's most important trade organization. The WTO has jurisdiction to enforce the most important and comprehensive trade agreements in the world among its more than 100 member nations. Some critics argue that the WTO has been granted too much power and will impinge upon the sovereignty of individual nations. Others herald the WTO as a much needed world court that can peaceably solve trade disputes among nations.

ALTERNATIVE DISPUTE RESOLUTION

alternative dispute resolution (ADR) Methods of resolving disputes other than litigation.

The use of the court system to resolve business and other disputes can take years and cost thousands, if not millions, of dollars in legal fees and expenses. In commercial litigation, the normal business operations of the parties are often disrupted. To avoid or lessen these problems, businesses are increasingly turning to methods of **alternative dispute resolution (ADR)** and other aids to resolving disputes. The most common form of ADR is arbitration. Other forms of ADR consist of mediation, conciliation, minitrial, fact-finding, and a judicial referee.

arbitration A form of ADR in which the parties choose an impartial third party to hear and decide the dispute.

Arbitration

In **arbitration**, the parties choose an impartial third party to hear and decide the dispute. This neutral party is called the **arbitrator**. Abritrators are usually selected from members of the American Arbitration Association (AAA) or another arbitration association. Labor union agreements, franchise agreements, leases, and other commercial contracts often contain **arbitration clauses** that require disputes arising out of the contract to be submitted to arbitration. If there is no arbitration clause, the parties

arbitration clause A clause in contracts that requires disputes arising out of the contract to be submitted to arbitration.

can enter into a submission agreement whereby they agree to submit a dispute to arbitration after the dispute arises.

Evidence and testimony are presented to the arbitrator at a hearing held for this purpose. Less formal evidentiary rules are usually applied in arbitration hearings than at court. After the hearing, the arbitrator reaches a decision and enters an **award**. The parties often agree in advance to be bound by the arbitrator's decision and award. If the parties have not so agreed, the arbitrator's award can be appealed to court. The courts give great deference to the arbitrator's decision.

Congress enacted the **Federal Arbitration Act** to promote the arbitration of disputes.[10] About half of the states have adopted the **Uniform Arbitration Act**. This act promotes the arbitration of disputes at the state level. Many federal and state courts have instituted programs to refer legal disputes to arbitration or another form of alternative dispute resolution.

CONTEMPORARY BUSINESS ENVIRONMENT

The Federal Arbitration Act

The **Federal Arbitration Act (FAA)** was originally enacted in 1925 to reverse the longstanding judicial hostility to arbitration agreements that had existed at English common law and had been adopted by American courts. The act provides that arbitration agreements involving commerce are valid, irrevocable, and enforceable contracts, unless some grounds exist at law or equity (e.g., fraud, duress) to revoke them. The FAA permits one party to obtain a court order to compel arbitration if the other party has failed, neglected, or refused to comply with an arbitration agreement.

Since the FAA's enactment, the courts have wrestled with the problem of which types of disputes should be arbitrated. Breach of contract cases, tort claims, and such are clearly candidates for arbitration if there is a valid arbitration agreement. In addition, the U.S. Supreme Court has enforced arbitration agreements that call for the resolution of disputes arising under federal statutes. For example, in *Shearson/American Express, Inc. v. McMahon*, 482 U.S. 220 (1987), and *Rodriguez de Quijas v. Shearson/American Express, Inc.*,

490 U.S. 4777 (1990), the Court held that certain civil claims arising under federal securities laws and the Racketeer Influenced and Corrupt Organizations Act (RICO) were arbitrative. In these cases, the Court enforced arbitration clauses contained in customer agreements with the securities firm.

In another case, *Gilmer v. Interstate/Johnson Lane Corporation*, Ill. S.Ct. 1647 (1991), the Supreme Court upheld an arbitration clause in an employment contract. In that case, a 62-year-old employee who was dismissed from his job sued his employer for alleged age discrimination in violation of the federal Age Discrimination in Employment Act (ADEA). The employer countered with a motion to compel arbitration. The Supreme Court upheld the motion and stated, "By agreeing to arbitrate a statutory claim, a party does not forgo the substantive rights afforded by the statute, it only submits to their resolution in an orbital, rather than a judicial, forum."

The Court did not agree with the employee's complaint that he would be penalized by the more limited discovery allowed in arbitration. The Court found that the

discovery process in arbitration, which allows for documented production, information requests, depositions, and subpoenas, was sufficient to allow ADEA claimants a fair opportunity to investigate and present their claims.

Another argument advanced by the employee is that there is unequal bargaining power between employers and employees. The Court responded that inequality of bargaining power is not a sufficient reason to hold that arbitration agreements are never enforceable in an employment contract.

The Court did not find any reason to revoke the contract. There was no indication that the employee was coerced or defrauded into agreeing to the arbitration clause at issue in the case.

Because the Supreme Court has placed its imprimatur on the use of arbitration to solve employment disputes, it is likely that such clauses will appear in more employment contracts. Critics contend that this gives the advantage to employees. Proponents argue that arbitration is the only way to combat skyrocketing jury verdicts.

The statement "See you in court" might have less clout.

Mediation and Conciliation

mediation A form of ADR in which the parties choose a *neutral* third party to act as the mediator of the dispute.

In **mediation**, the parties choose a neutral third party to act as the **mediator** of the dispute. Unlike an arbitrator, a mediator does not make a decision or award. Instead, the mediator acts as a conveyor of information between the parties and assists them in trying to reach a settlement of the dispute. A mediator often meets separately with each of the parties. A settlement agreement is reached if the mediator is successful. If not, the case proceeds to trial. In a **conciliation**, the parties choose an interested third party, the **conciliator**, to act as the mediator.

conciliation A form of mediation in which the parties choose an *interested* third party to act as the mediator.

Minitrial

A **minitrial** is a session, usually lasting a day or less, in which the lawyers for each side present their cases to representatives of each party who have authority to settle the dispute. In many cases, the parties hire a neutral person (e.g., a retired judge) to preside over the minitrial. Following the presentations, the parties meet to try to negotiate a settlement.

Fact-finding

Fact-finding is a process whereby the parties hire a neutral person to investigate the dispute. The **fact-finder** reports his or her findings to the adversaries and may recommend a basis for settlement.

Judicial Referee

If the parties agree, the court may appoint a **judicial referee** to conduct a private trial and render a judgment. The referee, who is often a retired judge, has most of the powers of a trial judge, and his or her decision stands as a judgment of the court. The parties usually reserve their right to appeal.

INTERNATIONAL PERSPECTIVE

Arbitration of International Business Disputes

Many international commercial contracts contain arbitration clauses. Sometimes the lawfulness of these clauses is challenged in court. Consider the following case.

Mitsubishi Motors Corporation (Mitsubishi) is a Japanese corporation that manufactures automobiles and has its principal place of business in Tokyo, Japan. Soler Chrysler-Plymouth, Inc. (Soler) is a Puerto Rican corporation with its principal place of business in Puerto Rico. On October 31, 1979, Soler entered into a sales and distributor agreement that gave Soler the right to sell Mitsubishi-manufactured automobiles within a

designated area, including metropolitan San Juan. The agreement included an arbitration clause that stipulated, "All disputes, controversies, or differences which may arise between the parties out of this Agreement or for the breach thereof, shall be finally settled by arbitration in Japan in accordance with the rules and regulations of the Japan Commercial Arbitration Association." Initially, Soler did a brisk business in Mitsubishi-manufactured vehicles. In early 1981, the new-car market slackened, and Soler ran into serious difficulties in meeting the agreed-upon minimum sales volume. Soler repudiated its agree-

ment with Mitsubishi. Mitsubishi requested arbitration before the Japan Commercial Arbitration Association and brought an action in U.S. district court in Puerto Rico for an order compelling arbitration. Soler filed a cross-complaint alleging that Mitsubishi violated U.S. antitrust laws. The district court held that all claims were subject to arbitration. The court of appeals reversed as to the antitrust claims. Mitsubishi appealed to the U.S. Supreme Court, arguing that issues involving U.S. antitrust laws are subject to arbitration by an arbitration panel located in a foreign country.

The U.S. Supreme Court agreed with Mitsubishi and held that issues involving U.S. antitrust laws may be arbitrated by a foreign arbitration panel and ordered the arbitration agreement between Soler and Mitsubishi enforced. The Supreme Court noted that by agreeing to arbitrate a statutory claim, a party does not forgo the substantive rights afforded by the statute; it only submits to their resolution in an arbitral, rather than a judicial, forum. It trades the procedures and opportunity for review of the courtroom for the simplicity, informality, and expedition of arbitration. In upholding international arbitration of the antitrust claims, the Supreme Court noted, "The expansion of American business and industry will hardly be encouraged if, notwithstanding solemn contracts, we insist on a parochial concept that all disputes must be resolved under our laws and in our courts. We cannot have trade and commerce in world markets and international waters exclusively on our terms, governed by our laws, and resolved in our courts. We conclude that concerns of international comity, respect for the capacities of foreign and transnational tribunals, and sensitivity to the need of the international commercial system for predictability in the resolution of disputes require that we enforce the parties' arbitration agreement." [*Mitsubishi Motors Corporation v. Soler Chrysler-Plymouth, Inc.*, 473 U.S. 614, 105 S.Ct. 3346 (1985)]

WORKING THE WEB

U.S. Supreme Court The U.S. Supreme Court does not have its own self-generated Web site at this time. Cornell University maintains a site that features recent decisions and selected historic decisions of the U.S. Supreme Court. You can search for decisions by date, by party, and by subject.

Visit at http://supct.law.cornell.edu/supct/index/html

U.S. Court of Appeals The U.S. Courts of Appeals do not have their own self-generated Web sites at this time. The Villanova Center for Information Law and Policy is your gateway to various circuit courts whose Web sites are located at different universities. Most include a syllabus and summaries of decisions for recent cases and one or more ways to search for the decisions.

Visit at http://www.vcilp.org/Fed-Ct/fedcourt.html

U.S. District Courts Some U.S. District Courts publish their opinions on the Internet. The Villanova Center for Information Law and Policy is also a gateway to those decisions.

Visit at http://www.vcilp.org/Fed-Ct/fedcourt.html

State courts State courts are far ahead of the federal government when it comes to creating and maintaining their own Web sites. There are a number of places with links to state court information. Many state courts have their own Web pages.

Visit at http://www.law.vill.edu/State-Ct/

Note: Although many sites are adding retrospective cases all the time, most cases that can be found on the Internet are *current decisions*. To find older decisions, you will have to use traditional research methods, i.e. books, or computer assisted legal research databases such as LEXIS and WESTLAW.

Many lower state court decisions and municipal court decisions are not reported anywhere including the Internet. Some information about these decisions on "hot" topics can be found in news archives on the Internet and by using news based databases such as NEXIS.

American Arbitration Association Information on alternative dispute resolutions can be found on the American Arbitration Association Web site. This site contains information on labor relations, employment, commerce, and international disputes. It includes rules, forms, and articles about alternative dispute resolution.

Visit at http://www.adr.org

CYBER EXERCISES:

1. Using the Cornell Web site, click on the "gallery of current justices." Print out the biography of Justice Ginsburg.

continued

2. Using the Villanova gateway, find the U.S. Court of Appeals for the circuit in which your state is located. Find and print out a recent decision.
3. Using the Villanova gateway, find out if any U.S. District Courts for your state publish opinions on the Internet. List the courts and dates of coverage for each court.
4. Find the home page for courts in your state. Which courts in your state are reporting cases on the Internet? What are the dates of coverage for each court in your state?
5. Using the American Arbitration Association Web site, click on "Customer Service." Print out a form for "Submission to Dispute Resolution."

CHAPTER SUMMARY

THE STATE COURT SYSTEMS, P. 50

State Court Systems	
	1. *Limited-jurisdiction trial court.* State courts that hear matters of a specialized or limited nature (e.g., misdemeanor criminal matters, traffic tickets, civil matters under a certain dollar amount). Many states have created small claims courts that hear small-dollar-amount civil cases (e.g., under $3,000) where the parties cannot be represented by lawyers.
	2. *General-jurisdiction trial court.* State courts that hear cases of a general nature that are not within the jurisdiction of limited-jurisdiction trial courts.
	3. *Intermediate appellate court.* State courts that hear appeals from state trial courts. The appellate court reviews the trial court record in making its decision; no new evidence is introduced at this level.
	4. *Highest state court.* Each state has a highest court in its court system. This court hears appeals from appellate courts, and where appropriate, trial courts. This court reviews the record in making its decision; no new evidence is introduced at this level. Most states call this court the supreme court.

THE FEDERAL COURT SYSTEM, P. 52

Federal Court System	
	1. *Special federal courts.* Federal courts that have specialized or limited jurisdiction. They include:
	a. *U.S. tax court.* Hears cases involving federal tax laws.
	b. *U.S. claims court.* Hears cases brought against the United States.
	c. *U.S. Court of International Trade.* Hears cases involving tariffs and international commercial disputes.
	d. *U.S. bankruptcy courts.* Hear cases involving federal bankruptcy law.
	2. *U.S. district courts.* Federal trial courts of general jurisdiction that hear cases not within the jurisdiction of specialized courts. There is at least one U.S. district court per state; more populated states have several district courts. The area covered by one of these courts is called a *district*.
	3. *U.S. courts of appeals.* Intermediate federal appellate courts that hear appeals from district courts located in their circuit, and in certain instances from special federal courts and federal administrative agencies. There are 12 geographical *circuits* in this country. Eleven serve areas that are comprised of several states, while another is located in Washington, D.C. A thirteenth circuit court—the *Court of Appeals for the Federal Circuit*—is located in Washington, D.C., and reviews patent, trademark, and international trade cases.

4. *U.S. Supreme Court.* Highest court of the federal court system. It hears appeals from the circuit courts, and in some instances from special courts and U.S. district courts. The Court, which is located in Washington, D.C., is composed of nine justices, one of whom is named chief justice.

5. *Decisions by the U.S. Supreme Court.*
   a. *Writ of certiorari.* To have a case heard by the U.S. Supreme Court, a petitioner must file a *petition for certiorari* with the Court. If the Court decides to hear the case, it will issue a *writ of certiorari.*
   b. Voting by the U.S. Supreme Court:
      i. *Unanimous decision.* All of the justices agree as to the outcome and reasoning used to decide the case. The decision becomes precedent.
      ii. *Majority decision.* A majority of the justices agrees as to the outcome and reasoning used to decide the case. The decision is precedent.
      iii. *Plurality decision.* A majority of the justices agrees to the outcome but not to the reasoning. The decision is not precedent.
      iv. *Tie decision.* If there is a tie vote, the lower court's decision stands. The decision is not precedent.
      v. *Concurring opinion.* A justice who agrees as to the outcome of the case but not the reasoning used by other justices may write a concurring opinion setting forth his or her reasoning.
      vi. *Dissenting opinion.* A justice who disagrees with the outcome of a case may write a dissenting opinion setting forth his or her reasoning for dissenting.

Jurisdiction of Federal and State Courts	1. *Jurisdiction of federal courts.* Federal courts may hear the following cases:
	  a. *Federal question.* Cases arising under the U.S. Constitution, treaties, and federal statutes and regulations. There is no dollar amount limit in federal question cases.
	  b. *Diversity of citizenship.* Cases between (i) citizens of different states and (ii) citizens of a state and a citizen or subject of a foreign country. Federal courts must apply the appropriate state law in such cases. The controversy must exceed $75,000 for the federal court to hear the case.
	2. *Jurisdiction of state courts.* State courts hear some cases that may be heard by federal courts.
	  a. *Exclusive jurisdiction.* Federal courts have exclusive jurisdiction to hear cases involving federal crimes, antitrust, and bankruptcy; patent and copyright cases; suits against the United States; and most admiralty cases. State courts may not hear these matters.
	  b. *Concurrent jurisdiction.* State courts have concurrent jurisdiction to hear cases involving diversity of citizenship cases and federal question cases over which the federal courts do not have exclusive jurisdiction. The defendant may have the case removed to federal court.

THE JURISDICTION OF COURTS, P. 55

Standing to Sue, Jurisdiction, and Venue	1. *Standing to sue.* To bring a lawsuit, the plaintiff must have some stake in the outcome of the lawsuit. 2. *Subject matter jurisdiction.* The court must have jurisdiction over the subject matter of the lawsuit. Each court has limited jurisdiction to hear only certain types of cases.

3. *In personam jurisdiction* (or *personal jurisdiction*). The court must have jurisdiction over the parties to a lawsuit. The plaintiff submits to the jurisdiction of the court by filing the lawsuit there. Personal jurisdiction is obtained over the defendant by serving that person *service of process*.

4. *In rem jurisdiction*. A court may have jurisdiction to hear and decide a case because it has jurisdiction over the property at issue in the lawsuit (e.g., real property located in the state).

5. *Quasi in rem jurisdiction* (or *attachment jurisdiction*). A plaintiff who obtains a judgment against a defendant in one state may utilize the court system of another state to attach property of the defendant's located in the second state.

6. *Long-arm statutes*. Permit a state to obtain personal jurisdiction over an out-of-state defendant as long as the defendant had the requisite minimum contact with the state. The out-of-state defendant may be served process outside the state in which the lawsuit has been brought.

7. *Venue*. A case must be heard by the court that has jurisdiction nearest to where the incident at issue occurred or where the parties reside. A *change of venue* will be granted if prejudice would occur because of pretrial publicity or another reason.

8. *Forum-selection clause*. A clause in a contract that designates the court that will hear any dispute that arises out of the contract.

THE PRETRIAL LITIGATION PROCESS, P. 59

Pleadings	Paperwork that indicates and responds to a lawsuit. Pleadings include: 1. *Complaint*. Filed by the plaintiff with the court and served with a *summons* on the defendant. It sets forth the basis of the lawsuit. 2. *Answer*. Filed by the defendant with the court and served on the plaintiff. It usually denies most allegations of the complaint. 3. *Cross-complaint*. Filed and served by the defendant if he or she countersues the plaintiff. The defendant is the *cross-complainant* and the plaintiff is the *cross-defendant*. The cross-defendant must file and serve a *reply* (answer). 4. *Intervention*. A person who has an interest in a lawsuit may intervene and become a party to the lawsuit. 5. *Consolidation*. Separate cases against the same defendant arising from the same incident may be consolidated by the court into one case if it would not cause prejudice to the parties.
Discovery	The pretrial process for discovering facts of the case from the other party and witnesses. Discovery consists of: 1. *Depositions*. Oral testimony given by a *deponent*, either a party or witness. Depositions are transcribed. 2. *Interrogatories*. Written questions submitted by one party to the other party. They must be answered within a specified period of time. 3. *Production of documents*. A party to a lawsuit may obtain copies of all relevant documents from the other party. 4. *Physical and mental examination*. These examinations of a party are permitted upon order of the court where injuries are alleged that could be verified or disputed by such examination.
Dismissals and Pretrial Judgments	1. *Motion for judgment on the pleadings*. Alleges that if all facts as pleaded are true, the moving party would win the lawsuit. No facts outside the pleadings may be considered.

	2. *Motion for summary judgment*. Alleges that there are no factual damages, so the judge may apply the law and decide the case without a jury. Evidence outside the pleadings may be considered (e.g., affidavits, documents, depositions).
Settlement Conference	Conference prior to trial between the parties in front of the judge to facilitate the settlement of the case. Also called *pretrial hearing*. If a settlement is not reached, the case proceeds to trial.

THE TRIAL, P. 63

Phases of a Trial	1. *Jury selection*. Done through a process called *voir dire*. Biased jurors are dismissed and replaced.
	2. *Opening statements*. Made by the parties' lawyers. Are not evidence.
	3. *The plaintiff's case*. The plaintiff bears the burden of proof. It calls witnesses and introduces evidence to try to prove its case.
	4. *The defendant's case*. The defendant calls witnesses and introduces evidence to rebut the plaintiff's case and to prove affirmative defenses and cross-complaints.
	5. *Rebuttal and rejoinder*. The plaintiff and defendant may call additional witnesses and introduce additional evidence.
	6. *Closing arguments*. Made by the parties' lawyers. Are not evidence.
	7. *Jury instructions*. Judge reads instructions to the jury as to what law they are to apply to the case.
	8. *Jury deliberation*. Jury retires to the jury room and deliberates until it reaches a *verdict*.
	9. *Entry of judgment*. The judge may:
	a. Enter the verdict reached by the jury as the court's *judgment*.
	b. Grant a motion for *judgment n.o.v.* if the judge finds the jury was biased. This means that the jury's verdict does not stand.
	c. Order *remittitur* (reduction) of any damages awarded if the judge finds the jury to have been biased or emotional.

THE APPEAL, P. 65

Appeal	Both parties in a civil suit and the defendant in a criminal trial may appeal the decision of the trial court. *Notice of appeal* must be filed within a specified period of time. The appeal must be made to the appropriate appellate court.

JUDICIAL RESTRICTIONS ON THE RESOLUTION OF INTERNATIONAL DISPUTES, P. 65

Principles of Judicial Restraint	National courts are limited by the following two principles of judicial restraint:
	1. *Act of state doctrine*. States that judges of one country cannot question the validity of an act committed by another country *within* that other country's borders.
	2. *Doctrine of sovereign immunity*. States that countries are granted immunity from suits in courts in other countries. Some countries provide for *absolute immunity* while other countries (such as the United States) provide *qualified* or *restricted immunity*.
	Exceptions. The United States provides that a foreign country is not immune from lawsuits in U.S. courts if:
	a. The foreign country has waived its immunity.
	b. The foreign country has engaged in commercial activity in the United States or outside the United States that causes a direct effect in the United States.

ALTERNATIVE DISPUTE RESOLUTION, P. 68	
Alternative Dispute Resolution (ADR)	*Nonjudicial* means of solving legal disputes. ADR usually saves time and money of costly litigation.

Types of ADR	1. *Arbitration*. An impartial third party, called the arbitrator, hears and decides the dispute. The arbitrator makes an award. The award is appealable to a court if the parties have not given up this right. Arbitration is designated by the parties pursuant to:
	  a. Arbitration clause. Agreement contained in a contract stipulating that any dispute arising out of the contract will be arbitrated.
	  b. Submission agreement. Agreement to submit a dispute to arbitration after the dispute arises.
	2. *Mediation*. A neutral third party, called a *mediator*, assists the parties in trying to reach a settlement of their dispute. The mediator does not make an award.
	3. *Conciliation*. An interested third party, called a *conciliator*, assists the parties in trying to reach a settlement of their dispute. The conciliator does not make an award.
	4. *Minitrial*. A short session in which the lawyers for each side present their cases to representatives of each party who have the authority to settle the dispute.
	5. *Fact-finding*. The parties hire a neutral third person, called a *fact-finder*, to investigate the dispute and report his or her findings to the adversaries.
	6. *Judicial referee*. With the consent of the parties, the court appoints a judicial referee (usually a retired judge or lawyer) to conduct a private trial and render a judgment. The judgment stands as the judgment of the court and may be appealed to the appropriate appellate court.

CRITICAL LEGAL THINKING CASES

3.1 Federal Question Nutrilab, Inc. (Nutrilab), manufactures and markets a product known as "Starch Blockers." The purpose of the product is to block the human body's digestion of starch as an aid in controlling weight. On July 1, 1982, the U.S. Food and Drug Administration (FDA) classified Starch Blockers as a drug and requested that they be removed from the market until the FDA approved of their use. The FDA claimed that it had the right to classify new products as drugs and prevent their distribution until their safety is determined. Nutrilab disputes the FDA's decision and wants to bring suit to halt the FDA's actions. Do the federal courts have jurisdiction to hear this case? [*Nutrilab, Inc. v. Schweiker*, 713 F.2d 335 (7th Cir. 1983)]

3.2 Diversity of Citizenship James Clayton Allison, a resident of the state of Mississippi, was employed by the Tru-Amp Corporation as a circuit breaker tester. As part of his employment, Allison was sent to inspect, clean, and test a switch gear located at the South Central Bell Telephone Facility in Brentwood, Tennessee. On August 26, 1988, he attempted to remove

a circuit breaker manufactured by ITE Corporation (ITE) from a bank of breakers, when a portion of the breaker fell off. The broken piece fell behind a switching bank and, according to Allison, caused an electrical fire and explosion. Allison was severely burned in the accident. Allison brought suit against ITE in a Mississippi state court, claiming more than $50,000 in damages. Can this suit be removed to federal court? [*Allison v. ITE Imperial Corp.*, 729 F.Supp. 45 (S.D. Miss. 1990)]

3.3 In Personam Jurisdiction Saul and Elaine Mozuck borrowed money from the Peoples Trust Company of Bergen County (Peoples Trust) and cosigned a promissory note promising to repay the money. When Peoples Trust contacted the Mozucks about payment, they denied liability on the ground that the bank improperly filled in the due date on the note. Peoples Trust filed suit against Mozucks in a New Jersey state court. A process server went to the Mozuck's home in New Jersey to serve the summons. The process server rang the bell at the home and a woman appeared at the upstairs window. The process server asked her if she was Mrs. Mozuck, and the woman replied in the affirmative. When the process server identified himself, the woman denied that she was Mrs. Mozuck and refused to come out of the house. The process server told the woman that he would leave the papers in the mailbox if she refused to open the door. When the woman did not reappear, the process server placed the summons in the mailbox and left.

Is the service of process good? [*Peoples Trust Co. v. Mozuck*, 236 A.2d 630 (N.J.Super. 1967)]

3.4 Long-Arm Statute Sean O'Grady, a professional boxer, was managed by his father, Pat. Sean was a contender for the world featherweight title. On January 30, 1978, Pat entered into a contract with Magna Verde Corporation (Magna Verde), a Los Angeles-based business, to copromote a fight between Sean and the current featherweight champion. The fight was scheduled to take place on February 5, 1978, in Oklahoma City, Oklahoma. To promote the fight, Pat O'Grady scheduled a press conference for January 20, 1978. At the conference, Pat was involved in a confrontation with a sportswriter named Brooks. He allegedly struck Brooks in the face. Brooks brought suit against Pat O'Grady and Magna Verde Corporation in an Oklahoma state court. Court records showed that the only contact Magna Verde had with Oklahoma was that a few of its employees had taken several trips to Oklahoma in January 1978 to plan the title fight. The fight was never held. Oklahoma has a long-arm statute. Magna Verde was served by mail and made a special appearance in Oklahoma state court to argue that Oklahoma does not have personal jurisdiction over it. Does Oklahoma have jurisdiction over Magna Verde Corporation? [*Brooks v. Magna Verde Corp.*, 619 P.2d 1271 (Okla.App. 1980)]

3.5 Minimum Contacts The National Enquirer, Inc., is a Florida corporation with its principal place of business in Florida. It publishes the *National Enquirer*, a national weekly newspaper with a total circulation of more than 5 million copies. About 600,000 copies, almost twice the level of the next highest state, are sold in California. On October 9, 1979, the *Enquirer* published an article about Shirley Jones, an entertainer. Jones, a California resident, filed a lawsuit in California state court against the *Enquirer* and its president, who was a resident of Florida. The suit sought damages for alleged defamation, invasion of privacy, and intentional infliction of emotional distress. Are the defendants subject to suit in California? [*Calder v. Jones*, 465 U.S. 783, 104 S.Ct. 1482, 79 L.Ed.2d 804 (1984)]

3.6 Service of Process On May 9, 1983, attorneys for Ronald Schiavone filed a lawsuit against *Fortune* magazine in U.S. district court in New Jersey. The complaint claimed that *Fortune* had defamed Schiavone in a cover story titled "The Charges against Reagan's Labor Secretary," which appeared in the May 31, 1982, issue of the magazine. The complaint named *Fortune* as the defendant. *Fortune*, however, is only a trademark owned by Time, Incorporated, a New York corporation. Time, Incorporated, refused to accept service of the complaint because it had not been named as a defendant. Has there been proper service of process? [*Schiavone v. Fortune*, 477 U.S. 21, 106 S.Ct. 2379, 91 L.Ed.2d 18 (1986)]

3.7 Summary Judgment Captain Conrad was a pilot for Delta Airlines. In 1970, Conrad was forced to resign by the airline.

He sued, alleging that he was discharged due to his prounion activities and not because of poor job performance, as claimed by Delta. During discovery, a report written by a Delta flight operations manager was produced that stated: "More than a few crew members claimed that Conrad professed to being a leftist-activist. His overactivity with the local pilots' union, coupled with inquiries regarding company files to our secretary, lead to the conclusion that potential trouble will be avoided by acceptance of his resignation." Conrad claims that the report is evidence of the antiunion motivation for his discharge. Delta made a summary judgment motion to the trial court. Should its summary judgment motion be granted? [*Conrad v. Delta Airlines, Inc.*, 494 F.2d 914 (7th Cir. 1974)]

3.8 Judgment N.O.V. On November 9, 1965, Mr. Simblest was driving a car that collided with a fire engine at an intersection in Burlington, Vermont. The accident occurred on the night on which a power blackout left most of the state without lights. Mr. Simblest, who was injured in the accident, sued the driver of the fire truck for damages. During the trial, Simblest testified that when he entered the intersection, the traffic light was green in his favor. All of the other witnesses testified that the traffic light had gone dark at least 10 minutes before the accident. Simblest testified that the accident was caused by the fire truck's failure to use any warning lights or sirens. Simblest's testimony was contradicted by four witnesses who testified that the fire truck had used both its lights and sirens. The jury found that the driver of the fire truck had been negligent and rendered a verdict for Simblest. The defense made a motion for judgment n.o.v. Who wins? [*Simblest v. Maynard*, 427 F.2d 1 (2d Cir. 1970)]

3.9 Arbitration AMF Incorporated and Brunswick Corporation both manufacture electric and automatic bowling center equipment. In 1983 the two companies became involved in a dispute over whether Brunswick had advertised certain automatic scoring devices in a false and deceptive manner. The two parties settled the dispute by signing an agreement that any future problems between them involving advertising claims would be submitted to the National Advertising Council for arbitration. In March 1985, Brunswick advertised a new product, Armor Plate 3000, a synthetic laminated material used to make bowling lanes. Armor Plate 3000 competed with wooden lanes produced by AMF. Brunswick's advertisements claimed that bowling centers could save up to $500 per lane per year in maintenance and repair costs if they switched to Armor Plate 3000 from wooden lanes. AMF disputed this claim and requested arbitration. Is the arbitration agreement enforceable? [*AMF Incorporated v. Brunswick Corp.*, 621 F.Supp. 456 (E.D.N.Y. 1985)]

3.10 Delegation Doctrine The Federal Communications Commission (FCC) is a federal administrative agency that is empowered to enforce the federal Communication Act of 1934. This act, as amended, gives the FCC power to regulate broadcasting on radio and television. In *United States v. Midwest Video Corporation*, 406 U.S. 649 (1972), the U.S. Supreme Court held that the FCC also has the power to regulate cable television. In May 1976, the FCC promulgated rules requiring cable television operators that have 3,500 or more subscribers to (1) develop a 20-channel capacity; (2) make four channels available for use by public, educational, local, government, and leased-access users; (3) make equipment available for those utilizing these public-access channels; and (4) limit the fees cable operators could charge for their services. Do these rules exceed the statutory authority of the FCC? [*Federal Communications Commission v. Midwest Video Corporation*, 440 U.S. 689, 99 S.Ct. 1435, 59 L.Ed.2d 692 (1979)]

3.11 Act of State Doctrine Prior to 1918, the Petrograd Metal Works, a Russian corporation, deposited a large sum of money with August Belmont, a private banker doing business in New York City under the name of August Belmont & Co. (Belmont). In 1918, the Soviet government nationalized the corporation and appropriated all of its property and assets wherever situated, including the deposit account with Belmont. As a result, the deposit became the property of the Soviet government. In 1933, the Soviet government and the United States entered into an agreement to settle claims and counterclaims between them. As part of the settlement, it was agreed that the Soviet government would take no steps to enforce claims against American nationals (including Belmont), and assigned all such claims to the United States. The United States brought this action against the executors of Belmont's estate to recover the money originally deposited with Belmont by Petrograd Metal Works. Who owns the money? [*United States v. Belmont*, 301 U.S. 324, 57 S.Ct. 758 (1937)]

3.12 Act of State Doctrine Banco Nacional de Costa Rica (Bank) is a bank wholly owned by the government of Costa Rica. It is subject to the rules and regulations adopted by the Minister of Finance and Central Bank of Costa Rica. In December 1980, the Bank borrowed $40 million from a consortium of private banks located in the United Kingdom and the United States. The Bank signed promissory notes agreeing to repay the principal plus interest on the loan in four equal installments due on July 30, August 30, September 30, and October 30, 1981. The money was to be used to provide export financing of sugar and sugar products from Costa Rica. The loan agreements and promissory notes were signed in New York City, and the loan proceeds were tendered to the Bank there.

On July 30, 1981, the Bank paid the first installment on the loan. The Bank did not, however, make the other three installment payments and defaulted on the loan. The lending banks sued the Bank in U.S. district court in New York to recover the unpaid principal and interest. The Bank alleged in defense that on August 27, 1981, the Minister of Finance and the Central Bank of Costa Rica issued a decree forbidding the repayment of loans by the Bank to private lenders, including the lending banks in this case. The action was taken because Costa Rica was having trouble servicing debts to foreign creditors. The Bank alleged the act of state doctrine prevented the plaintiffs from recovering on their loans to the Bank. Who wins? [*Libra Bank Limited v. Banco Nacional de Costa Rica*, 570 F.Supp. 870 (S.D.N.Y. 1983)]

3.13 Forum-Selection Clause Zapata Off-Shore Company (Zapata) is a Houston, Texas–based American corporation that engages in drilling oil wells throughout the world. Unterweser Reederei, GMBH (Unterweser) is a German corporation that provides ocean shipping and towing services. In November 1967, Zapata requested bids from companies to tow its self-elevating drilling rig "Chaparral" from Louisiana to a point off Ravenna, Italy, in the Adriatic Sea, where Zapata had agreed to drill certain wells. Unterweser submitted the lowest bid and was requested to submit a proposed contract to Zapata, which it did. The contract submitted by Unterweser contained the following provision: "Any dispute arising must be treated before the London Court of Justice." Zapata executed the contract without deleting or modifying this provision.

On January 5, 1968, Unterweser's deep sea tug *Bremen* departed Venice, Louisiana, with the Chaparral in tow, bound for Italy. On January 9, while the flotilla was in international waters in the middle of the Gulf of Mexico, a severe storm arose. The sharp roll of the Chaparral in Gulf waters caused portions of it to break off and fall into the sea, seriously damaging the Chaparral. Zapata instructed the *Bremen* to tow the Chaparral to Tampa, Florida, the nearest port of refuge, which it did.

On January 12, Zapata filed suit against Unterweser and the *Bremen* in U.S. district court in Florida, alleging negligent towing and breach of contract. The defendants assert that suit can be brought only in the London Court of Justice. Who is correct? [*M/S Bremen and Unterweser Reederei, GMBH v. Zapata Off-Shore Company*, 407 U.S. 1, 92 S.Ct. 1907, 32 L.Ed.2d 513 (1972)]

3.14 International Arbitration Alberto-Culver Company (Alberto-Culver) is an American company incorporated in Delaware with its principal office in Illinois. It manufactures and distributes toiletries and hair products in the United States and other countries. Fritz Scherk owned three interrelated businesses organized under the laws of Germany and Liechtenstein that were engaged in the manufacture of toiletries. After substantial negotiations, in February 1969, Alberto-Culver entered into a contract with Scherk to purchase his three companies along with all rights held by these companies to trademarks in cosmetic goods. The contract contained a number of express warranties whereby Scherk guaranteed the sole and unencumbered ownership of these trademarks. The contract also contained a clause that provided that "any controversy or claim that shall arise out of this agreement or breach thereof" was to be referred to arbitration before the International Chamber of Commerce in Paris, France. The transaction closed in June 1969 in Geneva, Switzerland.

Nearly one year later, Alberto-Culver allegedly discovered that the trademark rights purchased under the contract were subject to substantial encumbrances that threatened to give other parties superior rights to the trademarks and to restrict or preclude Alberto-Culver's use of them. Alberto-Culver sued Scherk in U.S. district court in Illinois, alleging fraudulent misrepresentation in violation of Section 10(b) of the federal Securities Exchange Act of 1934. Scherk asserts in defense that the case is subject to mandatory arbitration in Paris. Who is correct? [*Scherk v. Alberto-Culver Co.*, 417 U.S. 506, 94 S.Ct. 2249, 41 L.Ed.2d 270 (1974)]

ETHICS CASES

3.15 Ethical Perspective One day Joshua Gnaizda, a three-year-old, received what he (or his mother) thought was a tantalizing offer in the mail from Time, Inc. (Time). The front of the envelope contained a see-through window that revealed the following statement: "Joshua Gnaizda, I'll give you this versatile new calculator watch free just for opening this envelope before Feb. 15, 1985." Beneath the offer was a picture of the calculator watch itself. When Joshua's mother opened the envelope, she realized that the see-through window had not revealed the full text of Time's offer. Not viewable through the see-through window were the following words: "And mailing this Certificate today." The certificate required Joshua to purchase a subscription to *Fortune* magazine in order to receive the free calculator watch. Joshua (through his father, a lawyer) sued Time in a class action, seeking compensatory damages in an amount equal to the value of the calculator watch and $15 million in punitive damages. The trial court dismissed the lawsuit as being too trivial for the court to hear. Joshua appealed. Should Joshua be permitted to maintain his lawsuit against Time, Inc.? Did Time act ethically? Should Joshua's father have sued for $15 million? [*Harris v. Time, Inc.*, 191 C.A.3d 449, 237 Cal. Rptr. 584 (Cal. App. 1987)]

3.16 Ethical Perspective Dennis and Francis Burnham were married in 1976 in West Virginia. In 1977, the couple moved to New Jersey, where their two children were born. In July 1987, the Burnhams decided to separate. Mrs. Burnham, who intended to move to California, was to have custody of the children. Mr. Burnham agreed to file for divorce on grounds of "irreconcilable differences." In October 1987, Mr. Burnham threatened to file for divorce in New Jersey on grounds of "desertion." After unsuccessfully demanding that Mr. Burnham adhere to the prior agreement, Mrs. Burnham brought suit for divorce in California state court in early January 1988. In late January, Mr. Burnham visited California on a business trip. He then visited his children in the San Francisco Bay area, where his wife resided. He took the older child to San Francisco for the weekend. Upon returning the child to Mrs. Burnham's home, he was served with a California court summons and a copy of Mrs. Burnham's divorce petition. He then returned to New Jersey. Mr. Burnham made a special appearance in the California court and moved to quash the service of process. Did Mr. Burnham act ethically in trying to quash the service of process? Did Mrs. Burnham act ethically in having Mr. Burnham served on his visit to California? Is the service of process good? [*Burnham v. Superior Court of California*, 495 U.S. 604, 110 S.Ct. 2105, 109 L.Ed.2d 631 (1990)]

CRITICAL LEGAL THINKING WRITING ASSIGNMENT

Read Case A.3 in the Case Appendix [*Gnazzo v. G. D. Searle & Co.*]. This case is excerpted from the court of appeals opinion. Review and brief the case. In your brief, be sure to answer the following questions:

1. What is a statute of limitations? What purposes are served by such a statute?

2. What was the Connecticut statute of limitations for the injury alleged by the plaintiff?
3. What is summary judgment? When will it be granted?
4. What was the decision of the trial court? Of the court of appeals?
5. Was the decision fair? Should the plaintiff have been granted her day in court against the defendant?

NOTES

1 Federal Courts Improvement Act of 1982. Pub. L. 97-164, 96 Stat. 25, 28 U.S.C. § 1292 and § 1295.
2 Effective September 25, 1988, mandatory appeals were all but eliminated except for reapportionment cases and cases brought under the Civil Rights and Voting Rights Acts, antitrust laws, and the Presidential Election Campaign Fund Act.
3 Prior to 1980, there was a minimum dollar-amount controversy requirement of $10,000 to bring a federal question action in federal court. This minimum amount was eliminated by the Federal Question Jurisdictional Amendment Act of 1980, Public Law 96-486.
4 Effective May 18, 1989, the amount was raised from

$50,000 to $75,000, by the 1996 Federal Courts Improvement Act.
5 Under the Full Faith and Credit Clause of the U.S. Constitution, a judgment of a court in one state must be given "full faith and credit" by the courts of another state. Article IV, Section 1.
6 *International Shoe Co. v. Washington*, 326 U.S. 310, 66 S.Ct. 154, 90 L.Ed. 95 (1945).
7 There is no right to a jury trial for actions in equity (e.g., injunctions, specific performance).
8 301 U.S. 324, 57 S.Ct. 758 (1937).
9 28 U.S.C. §§ 1602-1611.
10 9 U.S.C. §§ 1 et seq.

CHAPTER 4

INTENTIONAL TORTS,

NEGLIGENCE, AND STRICT

LIABILITY

Chapter Objectives

*After studying this chapter,
you should be able to*

1. List and describe intentional torts against persons and against property
2. Define the tort of false imprisonment and apply merchant protection statutes
3. List and explain the elements necessary to prove negligence
4. Determine when there has been professional malpractice
5. Define and distinguish between the torts of intentional and negligent infliction of emotional distress
6. List and describe defenses to tort liability
7. Apply special negligence doctrines of *res ipsa loquitur* and negligence per se
8. Describe and list the elements to prove the tort of fraud
9. Define racketeering under the civil RICO statute and the remedies that are awarded to successful plaintiffs
10. Describe and apply the doctrine of strict liability

Chapter Contents

- Intentional Torts against Persons
  Case 4.1 *Colonial Stores, Inc. v. Fishel (GA)*
  Business Checklist Bringing a Malicious Prosecution Case
- Intentional Torts against Property
- Unintentional Torts (Negligence)
  Contemporary Business Environment Ouch! The Coffee's Too Hot!
  Case 4.2 *Fischer v. Pepsi Cola Bottling Company of Omaha, Inc. (8th Cir.)*
  Ethical Perspective Is a Singer Liable When Someone Acts upon His Lyrics?
  Contemporary Business Environment Accountants' Liability
- Special Negligence Doctrines
  Case 4.3 *Estrada v. Aeronaves de Mexico, S.A. (9th Cir.)*
- Defenses against Negligence
  Case 4.4 *Knight v. Jewett (CA)*
- Business Torts
- Strict Liability
- Torts Associated with Contracts
  Case 4.5 *Klein v. Pyrodyne Corporation (WA)*
  International Perspective Israeli Tort Law
- Working the Web
- Chapter Summary
- Critical Legal Thinking Cases
- Ethics Cases
- Critical Legal Thinking Writing Assignment

In our complex society the accountant's certificate and the lawyer's opinion can be instruments for inflicting pecuniary loss more potent than the chisel or the crowbar.

Justice Brennan
Dissenting Opinion
Ernst & Ernst v. Hochfelder
425 U.S. 185 (1976)

Tort is the French word for a "wrong." Tort law protects a variety of injuries and provides remedies for them. Under tort law, an injured party can bring a civil lawsuit to seek compensation for a wrong done to the party or to the party's property. Many torts have their origin in common law. The courts and legislatures have extended tort law to reflect changes in modern society.

Tort damages are monetary damages that are sought from the offending party. They are intended to compensate the injured party for the injury suffered. They can consist of past and future medical expenses, loss of wages, pain and suffering, mental distress, and other damages caused by the defendant's tortious conduct. If the victim of a tort dies, his or her beneficiaries can bring a wrongful death action to recover damages from the defendant. Punitive damages, which are awarded to punish the defendant, may be recovered in intentional tort and strict liability cases. Other remedies, such as injunctions, may be available, too.

This chapter discusses various tort laws, including intentional torts, negligence, and strict liability.

tort A wrong. There are three categories: (1) intentional torts, (2) unintentional torts (negligence), and (3) strict liability.

"Thoughts much too deep for tears subdue the Court When I assumpsit bring, and godlike waive a tort."
J. L. Adolphus
The Circuiteers
(1885)

INTENTIONAL TORTS AGAINST PERSONS

The law protects a person from unauthorized touching, restraint, or other contact. In addition, the law protects a person's reputation and privacy. Violations of these rights are actionable as torts. Torts against the person are discussed in the sections that follow.

intentional tort A category of torts that requires that the defendant possessed the intent to do the act that caused the plaintiff's injuries.

Assault

Assault is (1) the threat of immediate harm or offensive contact or (2) any action that arouses reasonable apprehension of imminent harm. Actual physical contact is not necessary. Threats of future harm are not actionable. For example, suppose a 6-foot-5-inch, 250-pound male makes a fist and threatens to punch a 5-foot, 100-pound woman. If the woman is afraid that the man will physically harm her, she can sue him for assault. If she is a black-belt karate champion and laughs at the threat, there is no assault because the threat does not cause any apprehension.

assault (1) The threat of immediate harm or offensive contact or (2) any action that arouses reasonable apprehension of imminent harm. Actual physical contact is unnecessary.

Battery

Battery is unauthorized and harmful or offensive physical contact with another person. Basically, the interest protected here is each person's reasonable sense of dignity and safety. For example, intentionally hitting someone is considered battery because it is harmful. Note that there does not have to be direct physical contact between the victim and the perpetrator. If an injury results, throwing a rock, shooting an arrow or a bullet, knocking off a hat, pulling a chair out from under someone, and poisoning a drink are all instances of actionable battery. The victim need not be aware of the harmful or offensive contact (e.g., it may take place while the victim is asleep). Assault and battery often occur together, although they do not have to (e.g., the perpetrator hits the victim on the back of the head without any warning).

battery Unauthorized and harmful or offensive physical contact with another person. Direct physical contact is not necessary.

BUSINESS BRIEF
Tort law imposes a duty on persons and business agents not to intentionally or negligently injure others in society. Civil lawsuits allow injured victims to recover dollar damages from the responsible parties.

Transferred Intent Doctrine Sometimes a person acts with the intent to injure one person but actually injures another. The doctrine of transferred intent applies to these situations. Under this doctrine, the law transfers the perpetrator's intent from the target to the actual victim of the act. The victim can then sue the defendant.

False Imprisonment

false imprisonment The intentional confinement or restraint of another person without authority or justification and without that person's consent.

The intentional confinement or restraint of another person without authority or justification and without that person's consent constitutes **false imprisonment**. The victim may be restrained or confined by physical force, barriers, threats of physical harm, or the perpetrator's false assertion of legal authority (i.e., **false arrest**). A threat of future harm or moral pressure is not considered false imprisonment. The false imprisonment must be complete. For example, merely locking one door to a building when other exits are not locked is not false imprisonment. A person is not obliged to risk danger or an affront to his or her dignity by attempting to escape.

merchant protection statutes A statute that allows merchants to stop, detain, and investigate suspected shoplifters without being held liable for false imprisonment if (1) there are reasonable grounds for the suspicion, (2) suspects are detained for only a reasonable time, and (3) investigations are conducted in a reasonable manner.

Merchant Protection Statutes Shoplifting causes substantial losses to merchants each year. Almost all states have enacted **merchant protection statutes**, also known as the **shopkeeper's privilege**. These statutes allow merchants to stop, detain, and investigate suspected shoplifters without being held liable for false imprisonment if:

- There are reasonable grounds for the suspicion,
- Suspects are detained for only a reasonable time, and
- Investigations are conducted in a reasonable manner.

In the following case, the court had to decide whether a shopkeeper who detained a suspected shoplifter was protected by the merchant protection statute.

CASE 4.1

Colonial Stores, Inc. v. Fishel

288 S.E.2d 21 (1981) Court of Appeals of Georgia

Facts Hank Fishel was stopped by an armed guard while he was shopping at the Big Star Supermarket in Savannah, Georgia. The store is owned by Colonial Stores, Inc. (Colonial Stores). The security guard accused Fishel of stealing a bottle of aspirin that Fishel had in the top pocket of his sweater. The guard detained Fishel and called the store manager. Fishel informed the store manager and the guard that he had purchased the aspirin at a drugstore prior to coming into the Big Star Supermarket and that he was looking at the aspirin in Colonial's store to compare prices. Fishel suggested that if the manager would count the aspirins in the bottle he would find that Fishel had already taken two of the aspirin. Fishel also suggested that if they would go to the drugstore where Fishel had purchased the aspirin, they would find the empty aspirin box in the trash receptacle in front of the drugstore. The manager and the guard ignored both requests. The manager and the security guard took Fishel to the stockroom, where they searched him and then handcuffed him to a large metal container. The store manager called the police. When the police arrived, the manager filed a criminal complaint against Fishel. The store had a policy of prosecuting almost everyone the guard apprehended for shoplifting. At the criminal hearing, the charge against Fishel was dismissed because the guard failed to appear as a witness. Fishel brought this action against Colonial Stores to recover damages. The jury returned a verdict in favor of Fishel and awarded him $400 actual damages and $175,000 punitive damages. Colonial Stores appealed.

Issue Is Colonial Stores, Inc., liable for the intentional tort of false imprisonment?

Decision Yes. The appellate court found no error in the trial court's finding that the defendant, Colonial Stores, Inc., committed the intentional tort of false imprisonment.

Reason The Georgia merchant protection statute extends to merchants and their agents a privilege to detain any person reasonably suspected to be shoplifting. However, the merchant or agent could be liable for failing to conduct an investigation if a "reasonable man" would have investigated before beginning a criminal proceeding. The evidence showed that the store manager knew that Fishel's story could be verified simply by telephoning the drugstore or by sending someone there. Also, the store manager could have looked in his own store for the empty aspirin box that Fishel supposedly "ditched," before having Fishel arrested. The court found that Colonial Stores had not complied with the merchant protection statute and was therefore liable to plaintiff Fishel for the intentional tort of false imprisonment.

CASE QUESTIONS

Critical Legal Thinking Should a store owner be able to stop and search a patron suspected of shoplifting? Is the present law adequate to protect the interests of both parties?

Ethics Did Colonial Stores act ethically in prosecuting Hank Fishel in this case?

Business Implication Are merchant protection statutes easy for businesses to follow? Was the award of $175,000 punitive damages warranted in this case?

Intentional Infliction of Emotional Distress

In some situations, a victim might suffer mental or emotional distress without first being physically harmed. The Restatement (Second) of Torts provides that a person whose *extreme and outrageous conduct* intentionally or recklessly causes severe emotional distress to another is liable for that emotional distress.[1] This is called the tort of **intentional infliction of emotional distress**, or the **tort of outrage**. The plaintiff must prove that the defendant's conduct was "so outrageous in character and so extreme in degree as to go beyond all possible bounds of decency, and to be regarded as atrocious and utterly intolerable in a civilized society."[2] An indignity, an annoyance, rough language, or an occasional inconsiderate or unkind act does not constitute outrageous behavior. However, repeated annoyances or harassment coupled with threats are considered "outrageous."

The tort does not require any publication to a third party or physical contact between the plaintiff and defendant. For example, a credit collection agency making harassing telephone calls to a debtor every morning between 1:00 A.M. and 5:00 A.M. is outrageous conduct.

The mental distress suffered by the plaintiff must be severe. Many states require that this mental distress be manifested by some form of physical injury, discomfort, or illness, such as nausea, ulcers, headaches, or miscarriage. This requirement is intended to prevent false claims. Some states have abandoned this requirement. The courts have held that shame, humiliation, embarrassment, anger, fear, and worry constitute severe mental distress.

> **intentional infliction of emotional distress** A tort that says a person whose extreme and outrageous conduct intentionally or recklessly causes severe emotional distress to another person is liable for that emotional distress. Also known as the *tort of outrage*.

> *"Negligence is the omission to do something which a reasonable man would do, or doing something which a prudent and reasonable man would not do."*
> B. Alderson
> *Blyth v. Birmingham Waterworks Co.* (1856)

BUSINESS CHECKLIST

Bringing a Malicious Prosecution Case

Sometimes a defendant in a lawsuit believes that the plaintiff has wrongly sued and wants to get back at the plaintiff. If certain requirements are met, our legal system allows the defendant to do so through a lawsuit for **malicious prosecution**. In a lawsuit for malicious prosecution, the defendant sues the plaintiff. Thus, in this lawsuit, the original defendant becomes the plaintiff, and the original plaintiff becomes the defendant.

The courts do not look favorably on malicious prosecution lawsuits because they feel they inhibit the original plaintiff's incentive to sue. Therefore, to succeed in a malicious prosecution lawsuit, the courts require the plaintiff prove the following:

- The plaintiff in the original lawsuit (now the defendant) instituted or was responsible for instituting the original lawsuit;
- There was no *probable cause* for the first lawsuit (that is, it was a frivolous lawsuit);

continued

- The plaintiff in the original action brought it with *malice* (Caution: this is a very difficult element to prove);
- The original lawsuit was terminated in favor of the original defendant (now the plaintiff); and
- The current plaintiff suffered injury as a result of the original lawsuit.

INTENTIONAL TORTS AGAINST PROPERTY

"Every unjust decision is a reproach to the law or the judge who administers it. If the law should be in danger of doing injustice, then equity should be called in to remedy it. Equity was introduced to mitigate the rigour of the law."

Lord Denning,
M. R.
Re Vandervell's Trusts (1974)

trespass to land   A tort that interferes with an owner's right to exclusive possession of land.

There are two general categories of property: real property and personal property. Real property consists of land and anything permanently attached to that land. Personal property consists of things that are movable, such as automobiles, books, clothes, pets, and such. The law recognizes certain torts against real and personal property. These torts are discussed in the sections that follow.

Trespass to Land

Interference with an owner's right to exclusive possession of land constitutes the tort of **trespass to land**. There does not have to be any interference with the owner's use or enjoyment of the land; the ownership itself is what counts. Thus, unauthorized use of another person's land is trespass even if the owner is not using the land. Actual harm to the property is not necessary.

Examples of trespass to land include entering another person's land without permission, remaining on the land of another after permission to do so has expired (e.g., a guest refuses to leave), or causing something or someone to enter another's land (e.g., one person builds a dam that causes another person's land to flood). A person who is pushed onto another's land or enters that land with good reason is not liable for trespass. For example, a person may enter onto another person's land to save a child or a pet from harm.

trespass to personal property   A tort that occurs whenever one person injures another person's personal property or interferes with that person's enjoyment of his or her personal property.

conversion of personal property   A tort that deprives a true owner of the use and enjoyment of his or her personal property by taking over such property and exercising ownership rights over it.

Trespass to and Conversion of Personal Property

The tort of **trespass to personal property** occurs whenever one person injures another person's personal property or interferes with that person's enjoyment of his or her personal property. The injured party can sue for damages. For example, breaking another's car window is trespass to personal property.

Depriving a true owner of the use and enjoyment of his or her personal property by taking over such property and exercising ownership rights over it constitutes the tort of **conversion of personal property**. Conversion also occurs when someone who originally is given possession of personal property fails to return it (e.g., fails to return a borrowed car). The rightful owner can sue to recover the property. If the property was lost or destroyed, the owner can sue to recover the value of the property.

punitive + compensatory damages

UNINTENTIONAL TORTS (NEGLIGENCE)

unintentional tort or **negligence**   A doctrine that says a person is liable for harm that is the foreseeable consequence of his or her actions.

Under the doctrine of **unintentional tort**, commonly referred to as **negligence**, a person is liable for harm that is the **foreseeable consequence** of his or her actions. Negligence is defined as "the omission to do something which a reasonable man would do, or doing something which a prudent and reasonable man would not do."[3]

CONSIDER THIS EXAMPLE: A driver who causes an automobile accident because he fell asleep at the wheel is liable for any resulting injuries caused by his negligence.

Elements of Negligence

To be successful in a negligence lawsuit, the plaintiff must prove that (1) the defendant owed a duty of care to the plaintiff, (2) the defendant breached this duty of care, (3) the plaintiff suffered injury, and (4) the defendant's negligent act caused the plaintiff's injury. Each of these elements is discussed in the sections that follow.

Duty of Care To determine whether a defendant is liable for negligence, it must first be ascertained whether the defendant owed a **duty of care** to the plaintiff. Duty of care refers to the obligation we all owe each other—that is, the duty not to cause any unreasonable harm or risk of harm. For example, each person owes a duty to drive his or her car carefully, not to push or shove on escalators, not to leave skateboards on the sidewalk, and the like. Businesses owe a duty to make safe products, not to cause accidents, and so on.

The courts decide whether a duty of care is owed in specific cases by applying a reasonable person standard. Under this test, the courts attempt to determine how an objective, careful, and conscientious person would have acted in the same circumstances and then measure the defendant's conduct against this standard. The defendant's subjective intent ("I did not mean to do it") is immaterial in assessing liability. Certain impairments do not affect the reasonable person standard. For instance, there is no reasonable alcoholic's standard.

Defendants with a particular expertise or competence are measured against a reasonable professional standard. This standard is applied in much the same way as the reasonable person standard. For example, a brain surgeon is measured against a reasonable brain surgeon standard, rather than a lower reasonable doctor standard. Children are generally required to act as a reasonable child of similar age and experience would act.

Breach of Duty When a court finds that the defendant actually owed the plaintiff a duty of care, it must determine whether the defendant breached this duty. A **breach of the duty of care** is the failure to exercise care. In other words, it is the failure to act as a reasonable person would act. A breach of this duty may consist of either an action (e.g., throwing a lit match on the ground in a forest and causing a fire) or a failure to act when there is a duty to act (e.g., a firefighter who refuses to put out a fire). Generally, passersby are not expected to rescue others gratuitously to save them from harm.

duty of care The obligation we all owe each other not to cause any unreasonable harm or risk of harm.

BUSINESS BRIEF

Domino's Pizza canceled its 30-minute delivery guarantee after juries concluded in several cases that Domino's drivers, trying to meet this deadline, negligently caused accidents.

"No court has ever given, nor do we think ever can give, a definition of what constitutes a reasonable or an average man."
Lord Goddard C. J.
R. v. McCarthy
(1954)

breach of the duty of care A failure to exercise care or to act as a reasonable person would act.

CONTEMPORARY BUSINESS ENVIRONMENT

Ouch! The Coffee's Too Hot!

Studies have shown that people care less about how good their coffee tastes than if it is hot. So restaurants, coffee shops, and other sellers make their coffee hot. McDonald's, however, discovered that it was in hot water for making its coffee *too* hot. Consider this case.

Stella Liebeck, an 81-year-old resident of Albuquerque, New Mexico, visited a "drive-through" window of a McDonald's restaurant with her grandson. Her grandson, the driver of the vehicle, placed the order. When it came, he handed a hot cup of coffee to Liebeck. As her grandson drove away from the drive-through window, Liebeck took the lid off the coffee cup she held in her lap. The coffee spilled all over Liebeck, who suffered third-degree burns on her legs, groin, and buttocks. She required medical treatment, was hospitalized, and suffers permanent scars from the incident.

Liebeck sued McDonald's for selling coffee that was too hot and for failing to warn her of the danger of the hot coffee it served.
continued

McDonald's rejected Liebeck's pretrial offer to settle the case for $300,000. At trial, McDonald's denied that it had been negligent and asserted that Liebeck's own negligence—opening a hot coffee cup on her lap—caused her injuries. The jury heard evidence that McDonald's enforces a quality-control rule that requires its restaurants and franchises to serve coffee at 180 to 190 degrees Fahrenheit. Evidence showed that this was 10 to 30 degrees hotter than coffee served by competing restaurant chains, and approximately 40 to 50 degrees hotter than normal house-brewed coffee.

Based on this evidence, the jury concluded that McDonald's acted recklessly and awarded Liebeck $200,000 compensatory damages (reduced by $40,000 for her own negligence), and $2.7 million punitive damages. After the trial court judge reduced the amount of punitive damages to $480,000, the parties reached an out-of-court settlement for an undisclosed amount. Because of this case, McDonald's and other purveyors of coffee have reduced the temperature at which they sell coffee and have placed warnings on their coffee cups.

Injury to Plaintiff   Even though a defendant's act might have breached a duty of care owed to the plaintiff, this breach is not actionable unless the plaintiff suffers **injury**. For example, a business's negligence causes an explosion and fire to occur at its factory at night. No one is injured and there is no damage to the neighbors' property. The negligence is not actionable.

injury   The plaintiff must suffer personal injury or damage to his or her property in order to recover monetary damages for the defendant's negligence.

The damages recoverable depend on the effect of the injury on the plaintiff's life or profession. Suppose two men injure their hands when a train door malfunctions. The first man is a professional basketball player. The second is a college professor. The first man can recover greater damages.

In the following case, the court held the defendant liable for the injuries caused to the plaintiff.

CASE 4.2

Fischer v. Pepsi Cola Bottling Company of Omaha, Inc.

972 F.2d 906 (1992) United States Court of Appeals, Eighth Circuit

Facts   On March 4, 1987, Robert J. Fischer was in Omaha, Nebraska, attending a seminar, and was a guest at the Red Lion Inn. At the end of the seminar's first day, Fischer took a swim in the inn's pool. Following his swim, Fischer stopped to purchase a pop from a vending machine on the inn's eleventh floor. The machine was owned and operated by Pepsi Cola Bottling Company of Omaha, Inc. (Pepsi). Fischer was still wearing his wet swimming trunks and was barefoot. As he inserted his money into the vending machine, an electrical current passed through his body.

After Fischer reported the accident, a service technician inspected the machine and found that the power cord connecting the rear of the machine to the electrical socket was resting underneath the machine's metal cabinet. He noticed that the power cord's metal conducting wires were exposed and came into contact with the machine's cabinet. After the accident, Fischer suffered pain while having sexual relations with his wife and became impotent. According to expert testimony, Fischer's impotence resulted from the electrical shock. He sued Pepsi for damages for alleged negligence in not inspecting and correcting the problem with the vending machine. The trial court found in favor of Fischer and awarded him $324,000. Pepsi appealed.

Issue   Is Pepsi liable for negligence?

Decision   Yes. The court of appeals held that Pepsi had been negligent for failing to inspect the vending machine and correct the problem associated with electrical shocks caused by the machine. Affirmed.

Reason Evidence showed that the machine in question was part of a group of approximately 10,000 machines owned and operated by Pepsi. Pepsi received one or two complaints a month that a vending machine was causing electrical shocks. The court of appeals held that Pepsi owed a duty to inspect its vending machines for the defect that electrocuted customers and breached that duty by failing to do so. The court stated, "For a supplier to be liable for failing to exercise reasonable care, it is not necessary for the supplier to know that a particular chattel is dangerous. Where the chattel supplied is part of a lot, it is sufficient that the supplier knows some of the chattels in the lot are dangerous."

CASE QUESTIONS

Critical Legal Thinking Should the law recognize the type of injury claimed in this case? Is it hard to prove (or disprove) the injury alleged?

Ethics Was it ethical for Pepsi to deny liability in this case?

Business Implication How could Pepsi have protected itself from liability in this case?

Causation A person who commits a negligent act is not liable unless this act was the **cause** of the plaintiff's injuries. Courts have divided causation into two categories—causation in fact and proximate cause—and require each to be shown before the plaintiff may recover damages:

1. **Causation in Fact**. The defendant's negligent act must be the **causation in fact** (or **actual cause**) of the plaintiff's injuries. For example, suppose a corporation negligently pollutes the plaintiff's drinking water. The plaintiff dies of a heart attack unrelated to the polluted water. Although the corporation has acted negligently, it is not liable for the plaintiff's death. There was a negligent act and an injury, but there was no cause-and-effect relationship between them. If instead, the plaintiff had died from the pollution, there would have been causation in fact and the polluting corporation would have been liable. If two (or more) persons are liable for negligently causing the plaintiff's injuries, both (or all) can be held liable to the plaintiff if each of their acts is a substantial factor in causing the plaintiff's injuries.

2. **Proximate Cause**. Under the law, a negligent party is not necessarily liable for all damages set in motion by his or her negligent act. Based on public policy, the law establishes a point along the damage chain after which the negligent party is no longer responsible for the consequences of his or her actions. This limitation on liability is referred to as **proximate cause** (or **legal cause**). The general test of proximate cause is foreseeability. A negligent party who is found to be the actual cause—but not the proximate cause—of the plaintiff's injuries is not liable to the plaintiff. Situations are examined on a case-by-case basis.

> **causation in fact or actual cause** The actual cause of negligence. A person who commits a negligent act is not liable unless causation in fact can be proven.

> **proximate cause or legal cause** A point along a chain of events caused by a negligent party after which this party is no longer legally responsible for the consequences of his or her actions.

The landmark case establishing the doctrine of proximate cause is *Palsgraf v. Long Island Railroad Company*.[4] Helen Palsgraf was standing on a platform waiting for a passenger train. The Long Island Railroad Company owned and operated the trains and employed the station guards. As a man carrying a package wrapped in a newspaper tried to board the moving train, railroad guards tried to help him. In doing so, the package was dislodged from the man's arm, fell to the railroad tracks, and exploded. The package contained hidden fireworks. The explosion shook the railroad platform, causing a scale located on the platform to fall on Palsgraf, injuring her. She sued the railroad for negligence. Justice Cardoza denied her recovery, finding that the railroad was not the proximate cause of her injuries.

> *"Negligence is not actionable unless it involves the invasion of a legally protected interest, the violation of a right. Proof of negligence in the air, so to speak, will not do."*
>
> C. J. Cardozo
> *Palsgraf v. Long Island Railroad Co.* (1928)

ETHICAL PERSPECTIVE

Is a Singer Liable When Someone Acts upon His Lyrics?

Many people, particularly youths, are influenced by singers, musicians, sports figures, movie stars, and other celebrities. Some listeners, readers, or watchers will be moved to love; others to tears; some to creativity, spirituality, or fear. But what happens when a person is so moved by a song, movie, or book that he or she commits a crime or engages in other dangerous conduct? Is the songwriter, singer, author, scriptwriter, or movie company liable for this conduct? This question was posed to the court in *McCollum v. CBS, Inc., and Osbourne.*

John "Ozzie" Osbourne is a well-known singer of rock and roll music and has become a cult figure. The words and music of his songs demonstrate a preoccupation with unusual, antisocial, and even bizarre attitudes and beliefs, often emphasizing such things as satanic worship, the mocking of religious beliefs, death, and suicide. CBS Records (CBS) produced and distributed Osbourne's albums.

On Friday night, October 26, 1984, John Daniel McCollum (John) listened over and over again to certain music recorded by Osbourne. He was a 19-year-old youth who had a problem with alcohol abuse as well as serious emotional problems. John was in his bedroom using headphones to listen to the final side of Osbourne's two-record album, *Speak to the Devil*, when he placed a .22 caliber handgun next to his right temple and took his own life.

One of the songs that John had been listening to was called "Suicide Solution," which preached that suicide is the only way out for a person involved in excessive drinking. Three of the verses of the song stated:

> Wine is fine but whiskey's quicker
> Suicide is slow with liquor
> Take a bottle drown your sorrows
> Then it floods away tomorrows
> Made your bed, rest your head
> But you lie there and moan
> Suicide is the only way out
> Don't you know what it's really about
> Ah know people
> You really know where it's at
> You got it
> Why try, why try
> Get the gun and try it
> Shoot, shoot, shoot

John's relative, Jack McCollum, and John's estate sued Ozzie Osbourne and CBS for negligence, alleging that the lyrics of Osbourne's music incited John to commit suicide. When the trial court dismissed the action, the plaintiffs appealed. The appellate court held that although Osbourne's lyrics might have been an actual cause of John's suicide, they were not the proximate cause of the suicide.

The court stated, "John's tragic self-destruction, while listening to Osbourne's music, was not a reasonably foreseeable risk or consequence of defendant's remote artistic activities."

In reaching its conclusion, the court further stated, "John's suicide, an admittedly irrational response to Osbourne's music, was not something that any of the defendants intended, planned, or had any reason to anticipate. Finally, and perhaps most significantly, it is simply not acceptable to a free and democratic society to impose a duty upon performing artists to limit and restrict their creativity in order to avoid the dissemination of ideas in artistic speech that may adversely affect emotionally troubled individuals. Such a burden would quickly have the effect of reducing and limiting artistic expression to only the broadest standard of taste and acceptance and the lowest level of offense, provocation, and controversy. No case has ever gone so far. We find no basis in law or public policy for doing so here."

The appellate court concluded that the defendants, as a matter of law, were not the proximate cause of John's suicide. [*McCollum v. CBS, Inc., and Osbourne*, 202 Cal.App.3d 989, 249 Cal.Rptr. 187 (Cal.App. 1988)]

---

professional malpractice
The liability of a professional who breaches his or her duty of ordinary care.

NOTE
A professional—such as a doctor—who breaches his or her duty of ordinary care is guilty of professional malpractice.

Professional Malpractice

Professionals, such as doctors, lawyers, architects, accountants, and others, owe a duty of ordinary care in providing their services. This duty is known as the **reasonable professional standard**. A professional who breaches this duty of care is liable for the injury his or her negligence causes. This liability is commonly referred to as **professional malpractice**. For example, a doctor who amputates a wrong leg is liable for **medical malpractice**. A lawyer who fails to file a document with the court on time, causing the client's case to be dismissed, is liable for **legal malpractice**. An accountant who fails to use reasonable care, knowledge, skill, and judgment when providing auditing and other accounting services to a client is liable for **accounting malpractice**.

Professionals who breach this duty are liable to their patients or clients. They may also be liable to some third parties.

CONTEMPORARY BUSINESS ENVIRONMENT

Accountants' Liability

Accountants owe a duty to use **reasonable care, knowledge, skill, and judgment** when providing auditing and other accounting services to a client. In other words, an accountant's actions are measured against those of a *reasonable accountant* in similar circumstances. The development of **generally accepted accounting principles (GAAPs) and generally accepted auditing standards (GAASs)** has generally made this a national standard. An accountant who fails to meet this standard may be sued for negligence (also called *accountant malpractice*).

Clients may sue their own accountants for malpractice. Third parties, such as shareholders or creditors of the audited company, may be able to sue accountants if state law permits it. There are three major rules of liability that a state may adopt in determining whether an accountant is liable in negligence to *third parties*:

- **The Ultramares Doctrine** provides that an accountant is not liable for negligence to third parties unless the plaintiff was either in *privity of contract* or a

privity-like relationship with the accountant [*Ultramares Corp. v. Touche*, 174 N.E. 441 (N.Y. App. 1931)]. Privity of contract would occur if a client employed an accountant to prepare financial statements to be used by an identified third party for a specific purpose that the accountant was made aware of (e.g., to secure a bank loan from a specific bank).

- **Section 552 of the Restatement (Second) of Torts** is a broader standard. It provides that an accountant is liable for his or her negligence to any member of a *limited class of intended users*, including the client for whose benefit he or she has prepared the financial statements, and those to whom he or she knows copies will be distributed. The accountant does not have to know the specific identity of the third party.

- **The foreseeability standard**, which is the broadest standard for finding accountants' liability to third parties, has been adopted by a few states. Under this standard, an accountant is liable to any foreseeable user of the client's financial state-

ments. The accountant's liability does not depend on his or her knowledge of the identity of either the user or the intended class of users. This standard is the traditional means for assessing tort liability in nonaccounting contexts. Thus, other than this standard, accountants are provided more limited liability than most other professionals.

Accountants often settle cases against them. For example, in 1992, Ernst & Young, a giant accounting firm, paid a record $400 million to federal bank regulators to settle the government's claims that the firm improperly audited federally insured banks and savings institutions that later failed. The settlement—under which the firm did not acknowledge any wrongdoing—avoided years of costly litigation. Insurance companies paid about $300 million of the settlement. The remainder was paid by the accounting partnership.

Accountants will remain targets for lawsuits because of their "deep pockets" and the liability insurance they carry.

SPECIAL NEGLIGENCE DOCTRINES

The courts have developed many special negligence doctrines. The most important of these are discussed in the sections that follow.

Negligent Infliction of Emotional Distress

Some jurisdictions have extended the tort of emotional distress to include the **negligent infliction of emotional distress**. The most common examples of this involve bystanders who witness the injury or death of a loved one that is caused by another's

negligent infliction of emotional distress A tort that permits a person to recover for emotional distress caused by the defendant's negligent conduct.

negligent conduct. The bystander, even though not personally physically injured, can sue the negligent party for his or her own mental suffering under this tort.

Generally, to be successful in this type of case, the plaintiff must prove that (1) a close relative or significant other was killed or injured by the defendant, (2) the plaintiff suffered severe emotional distress, and (3) the plaintiff's mental distress resulted from a sensory and contemporaneous observance of the accident. Some states require that the plaintiff's mental distress be manifested by some physical injury; other states have eliminated this requirement.

In the following case, a plaintiff recovered damages for negligent infliction of emotional distress.

NOTE

Damages for negligent infliction of emotional distress are usually recovered by those who see close relatives injured or killed by the negligent conduct of the defendant.

CASE 4.3

Estrada v. Aeronaves de Mexico, S.A.
967 F.2d 1421 (1992) United States Court of Appeals, Ninth Circuit

Facts On the morning of August 31, 1986, Theresa Estrada left her home near Cerritos, California, to go shopping at a nearby grocery store. She left her husband at home reading the newspaper, and her three children were still in bed. Returning from the store, Estrada saw, heard, and felt a big explosion. Within minutes, she maneuvered her way through burning homes, cars, and debris to find her home engulfed in flames. Her husband and children died in the house. Although she did not know it at the time, an Aeromexico passenger airplane had crashed into her home after colliding with a privately owned plane. Estrada suffered severe emotional distress from the incident. She sued for the wrongful death of her family. Aeromexico was found not responsible for the accident. The jury found the private pilot 50 percent liable, and the United States 50 percent liable because air traffic controllers had failed to detect the private plane's intrusion into commercial airspace and to give a traffic advisory to the Aeromexico flight. The jury awarded Estrada $5.5 million for the death of her family and $1 million for negligent infliction of emotional distress. The U.S. government appealed the $500,000 judgment against it for negligent infliction of emotional distress.

Issue Was Estrada entitled under the law to recover damages for negligent infliction of emotional distress?

Decision Yes. The court of appeals held that Estrada had established the elements necessary to recover damages for the negligent infliction of emotional distress.

Reason The court of appeals held that Estrada satisfied the elements necessary to recover for negligent infliction of emotional distress. First, she was a close family member. Second, she was present at the scene of the injury-producing event. Third, she suffered severe emotional distress. The U.S. government argued that Estrada was not present when the airplane crashed into her home. The court rejected this argument, stating that the plaintiff need not visibly perceive the injury while it is being inflicted.

CASE QUESTIONS

Critical Legal Thinking Should the law recognize the doctrine of negligent infliction of emotional distress? Should the elements be expanded so that they are easier to meet?

Ethics Did the U.S. government act ethically in arguing against paying Mrs. Estrada the award assessed by the jury?

Business Implication What economic effects does the doctrine of negligent infliction of emotional distress have on businesses?

Negligence Per Se

negligence per se Tort where the violation of a statute or ordinance constitutes the breach of the duty of care.

Statutes often establish duties owed by one person to another. The violation of a statute that proximately causes an injury is **negligence per se**. The plaintiff in such an action must prove that (1) a statute existed, (2) the statute was enacted to prevent the type of injury suffered, and (3) the plaintiff was within a class of persons meant to be protected by the statute. For example, most cities have an ordinance that places the responsibility for fixing public sidewalks in residential areas on the homeowners whose homes front the sidewalk. A homeowner is liable if he or she fails to repair a damaged sidewalk in front of his or her home and a pedestrian trips and is injured because of the damage. The injured party does not have to prove that the homeowner owed the duty, because the statute establishes that.

Res Ipsa Loquitur

Doctrine of

If a defendant has superior knowledge of the circumstances surrounding an injury and it is in the defendant's best interests not to disclose these circumstances, the plaintiff might have difficulty proving negligence. One traditional example of such cases involves surgical instruments left in a patient's body during surgery. A patient–plaintiff who was under anesthesia would be hard pressed to identify the doctor or nurse who left the instrument in his or her body. In such a situation the law applies the doctrine of *res ipsa loquitur* (Latin for "the thing speaks for itself"). This doctrine raises an inference or presumption of negligence and places the burden on the defendant to prove that he or she was *not* negligent. *Res ipsa loquitur* applies in cases where (1) the defendant had exclusive control of the instrumentality or situation that caused the injury and (2) the injury would not have ordinarily occurred "but for" someone's negligence (e.g., surgical instruments are not ordinarily left in patients' bodies). Other typical *res ipsa loquitur* cases involve commercial airplane crashes, falling elevators, and the like.

res ipsa loquitur Tort where the presumption of negligence arises because (1) the defendant was in exclusive control of the situation and (2) the plaintiff would not have suffered injury but for someone's negligence. The burden switches to the defendant(s) to prove they were not negligent.

Dram Shop Acts

Many states have enacted **dram shop acts**, which make a tavern and bartender civilly liable for injuries caused to or by patrons who are served too much alcohol. The alcohol must be either served in sufficient quantity to make the patron intoxicated or served to an already intoxicated person. Both the tavern and the bartender are liable to third persons injured by the patron and for injuries suffered by the patron. They are also liable for injuries caused by or to minors served by the tavern, regardless of whether the minor is intoxicated.

dram shop act Statute that makes taverns and bartenders liable for injuries caused to or by patrons who are served too much alcohol.

Social Host Liability

Several states have adopted the **social host liability** rule. This rule provides that a social host is liable for injuries caused by guests who are served alcohol at a social function (e.g., a birthday party, a wedding reception) and later cause injury because they are intoxicated. The injury may be to a third person or to the guest him- or herself. The alcohol served at the social function must be the cause of the injury. A few states have adopted statutes that relieve social hosts from such liability.[5]

social host liability Rule that provides that social hosts are liable for injuries caused by guests who become intoxicated at a social function. States vary as to whether they have this rule in effect.

Guest Statutes

Many states have enacted **guest statutes** that provide that if a driver voluntarily and without compensation gives a ride in a vehicle to another person (e.g., a hitchhiker), the driver is not liable to the passenger for injuries caused by the driver's ordinary negligence. However, if the passenger pays compensation to the driver, the driver owes a duty of ordinary care to the passenger and will be held liable. The driver is always liable to the passenger for wanton and gross negligence, for example, injuries caused because of excessive speed.

guest statutes Statute that provides that if a driver of a vehicle voluntarily and without compensation gives a ride to another person, the driver is not liable to the passenger for injuries caused by the driver's ordinary negligence.

Good Samaritan Laws

In the past, liability exposure made many doctors and other medical professionals reluctant to stop and render aid to victims in emergency situations, such as highway accidents. Almost all states have enacted **Good Samaritan laws**, which relieve medical professionals from liability for ordinary negligence in such circumstances. Good Samaritan laws do not protect medical professionals from liability for gross negligence or intentional misconduct.

Good Samaritan laws Statutes that relieve medical professionals from liability for ordinary negligence when they stop and render aid to victims in emergency situations.

Fireman's Rule

Under the **fireman's rule**, a firefighter who is injured while putting out a fire may not sue the party whose negligence caused the fire. This rule has been extended to police officers and other government workers. The bases for this rule are as follows: (1) people might not call for help if they could be held liable, (2) firefighters, police officers, and other such workers receive special training for their jobs, and (3) these workers have special medical and retirement programs paid for by the public.

"Danger Invites Rescue" Doctrine

The law recognizes a **"danger invites rescue" doctrine**. Under this doctrine, a rescuer who is injured while going to someone's rescue can sue the person who caused the dangerous situation. For example, a passerby who is injured while trying to rescue children from a fire set by an arsonist can bring a civil suit against the arsonist.

Liability of Common Carriers and Innkeepers

The common law holds common carriers and innkeepers to a higher standard of care than most other businesses. Common carriers and innkeepers owe a **duty of utmost care**—rather than a duty of ordinary care—to their passengers and patrons. For example, innkeepers must provide security for their guests. The concept of utmost care is applied on a case-by-case basis. Obviously, a large hotel must provide greater security to guests than a "mom-and-pop" motel. Some states and cities have adopted specific statutes and ordinances relating to this duty.

Liability of Landowners

Owners and renters of real property owe certain duties to protect visitors from injury while on the property. A landowner's and tenant's liability generally depends on the status of the visitor. Visitors fall into the following categories:

1. **Invitees and Licensees**. An **invitee** is a person who has been expressly or implicitly invited onto the owner's premises for the *mutual benefit* of both parties (e.g., guests invited for dinner, the mail carrier, customers of a business). A **licensee** is a person who, *for his or her own benefit*, enters onto the premises with the express or implied consent of the owner (e.g., the Avon representative, encyclopedia salesperson, Seventh-Day Adventists). An owner owes a **duty of ordinary care** to invitees and licensees. An owner is liable if he or she negligently causes injury to an invitee or licensee. For example, a homeowner is liable if she leaves a garden hose across the walkway on which an invitee or a licensee trips and is injured.

2. **Trespassers**. A **trespasser** is a person who has no invitation, permission, or right to be on another's property. Burglars are a common type of trespasser. Generally, an owner does not owe a duty of ordinary care to a trespasser. For example, if a trespasser trips and injures himself on a bicycle the owner negligently left out, the owner is not liable. An owner does owe a **duty not to willfully or wantonly injure** a trespasser. Thus, an owner cannot set traps to injure trespassers.

A few states have eliminated the invitee-licensee-trespasser distinction. These states hold that owners and renters owe a duty of ordinary care to all persons who enter upon the property.

DEFENSES AGAINST NEGLIGENCE

A defendant in a negligence lawsuit may raise several defenses to the imposition of liability. These defenses are discussed in the following sections.

Superseding or Intervening Event

Under negligence, a person is liable only for foreseeable events. Therefore, an original negligent party can raise a **superseding** (or **intervening**) **event** as a defense to liability. For example, assume that an avid golfer negligently hits a spectator with a golf ball, knocking the spectator unconscious. While lying on the ground waiting for an ambulance to come, the spectator is struck by a bolt of lightning and killed. The golfer is liable for the injuries caused by the golf ball. She is not liable for the death of the spectator, however, because the lightning bolt was an unforeseen intervening event.

superseding event
A defendant is not liable for injuries caused by a superseding or intervening event for which he or she is not responsible.

Assumption of the Risk

If a plaintiff knows of and voluntarily enters into or participates in a risky activity that results in injury, the law recognizes that the plaintiff assumed, or took on, the risk involved. Thus, the defendant can raise the defense of **assumption of the risk** against the plaintiff. This defense assumes that the plaintiff (1) had knowledge of the specific risk and (2) voluntarily assumed that risk. For example, under this theory, a race car driver assumes the risk of being injured or killed in a crash.

Assumption of the risk is raised as a defense in the following case.

assumption of the risk
A defense a defendant can use against a plaintiff who knowingly and voluntarily enters into or participates in a risky activity that results in injury.

CASE 4.4

Knight v. Jewett
3 Cal.4th 296, 11 Cal.Rptr.2d 2 (1992) Supreme Court of California

Facts On January 25, 1987, the day of the 1987 Super Bowl football game, Kendra Knight and Michael Jewett, together with a number of other social acquaintances, attended a Super Bowl party at the house of a mutual friend. During halftime, several guests decided to play an informal game of touch football on an adjoining vacant lot, using a "peewee" football. Each team included four or five women and men. Knight and Jewett were on different teams. Five minutes into the game, Jewett ran into Knight during a play. She told him to be more careful. On the next play, Jewett tried to intercept a pass to Knight, and in doing so collided with her, knocking her down. When Jewett landed, he stepped backward onto Knight's hand. Because of the injury, Knight had to have her little finger amputated. Knight sued Jewett for damages. The trial court applied the doctrine of assumption of the risk and granted defendant Jewett's motion for summary judgment. The court of appeals affirmed. Knight appealed.

Issue Does the doctrine of assumption of the risk bar recovery?

Decision Yes. The state supreme court, in a divided decision, held that, under the doctrine of assumption of the risk, summary judgment was properly entered barring recovery in this case. Affirmed.

Reason The supreme court held that when a person voluntarily participates in an activity like touch football, that person implicitly agrees to reduce the duty of care owed to her by others. The court stated, "A participant in an active sport breaches a legal duty of care to other participants . . . only if the participant intentionally injures another player or engages in conduct that is so reckless as to be totally outside the range of the ordinary activity involved in the sport." The court concluded that the facts established that there was no liability because the defendant did not intend to injure the plaintiff and that his conduct was not reckless.

CASE QUESTIONS

Critical Legal Thinking Do you think the law should recognize the doctrine of assumption of the risk? Why or why not?

Ethics Did Jewett act properly in playing hard during the touch football game? Should Knight have sued him?

Business Implication Should the doctrine of assumption of the risk be applied when spectators are injured at professional sports events?

Contributory Negligence

contributory negligence
A doctrine that says a plaintiff who is partially at fault for his or her own injury cannot recover against the negligent defendant.

Under the common law doctrine of **contributory negligence**, a plaintiff who is partially at fault for his or her own injury cannot recover against the negligent defendant. For example, suppose a driver who is driving over the speed limit negligently hits and injures a pedestrian who is jaywalking. Suppose the jury finds that the driver is 80 percent responsible for the accident and the jaywalker is 20 percent responsible. The pedestrian suffered $100,000 in injuries. Under the doctrine of contributory negligence, the pedestrian cannot recover any damages from the driver.

There is one major exception to the doctrine of contributory negligence: The defendant has a duty under the law to avoid the accident if at all possible. This rule is known as the *last clear chance rule*. For example, a driver who sees a pedestrian walking across the street against a "Don't Walk" sign must avoid hitting him if possible. When deciding cases involving this rule, the courts consider the attentiveness of the parties and the amount of time each has to respond to the situation.

Comparative Negligence

comparative negligence
A doctrine under which damages are apportioned according to fault.

As seen, the application of the doctrine of contributory negligence could reach an unfair result when a party only slightly at fault for his or her injuries could not recover from an otherwise negligent defendant. Many states have replaced the doctrine of contributory negligence with the doctrine of **comparative negligence**. Under this doctrine, damages are apportioned according to fault. When the comparative negligence rule is applied to the previous example, the result is much fairer. The plaintiff–pedestrian can recover 80 percent of his damages (or $80,000) from the defendant–driver.

This is an example of *pure comparative negligence*. Several states have adopted *partial comparative negligence*, which provides that a plaintiff must be less than 50 percent responsible for causing his or her own injuries to recover under comparative negligence; otherwise, contributory negligence applies.

BUSINESS TORTS

Many of the torts previously discussed are committed by or against businesses. Certain other torts that commonly involve businesses are discussed in the following sections.

Entering Certain Businesses and Professions without a License

BUSINESS BRIEF
A license must be obtained from the government to enter certain industries, such as banking and broadcasting, and to practice certain professions, such as law and medicine.

There are government restrictions and prohibitions on the freedom of entry into certain businesses and professions. These restrictions are intended to protect the public from unqualified practitioners and to promote the efficient operation of the economy.

For instance, a person cannot simply erect a television or radio transmitter and start broadcasting: The Federal Communications Commission grants television and radio station licenses for assigned frequencies. In addition, many occupations, such as lawyers, physicians, dentists, real estate brokers, and hairdressers, require state licenses. In some states, even palm readers and astrologists must be licensed. To obtain the necessary license, an applicant must (1) meet certain educational requirements and (2) demonstrate a certain level of proficiency in the subject matter through examination, experience, or both. Entry into these industries or professions without permission subjects the violator to various civil and criminal penalties. In many states, a licensed professional can bring an action to prevent an unlicensed person from practicing.

Intentional Misrepresentation (Fraud)

intentional misrepresentation
Intentionally defrauding another person out of money, property, or something else of value.

One of the most pervasive business torts is **intentional misrepresentation**. This tort is also known as **fraud** or **deceit**. It occurs when a wrongdoer deceives another person out of money, property, or something else of value. A person who has been injured by an intentional misrepresentation can recover damages from the wrongdoer. The elements required to find fraud are as follows:

1. The wrongdoer made a false representation of material fact
2. The wrongdoer had knowledge that the representation was false and intended to deceive the innocent party
3. The innocent party justifiably relied on the misrepresentation
4. The innocent party was injured.

"There are some frauds so well conducted, that it would be stupidity not to be deceived by them."
C. C. Colton
Lacon, Vol. I (1820)

Item 2, called **scienter**, includes situations in which the wrongdoer recklessly disregards the truth in making a representation that is false. Intent or recklessness can be inferred from the circumstances.

Civil RICO

In an effort to combat organized crime, Congress enacted the **Racketeer Influenced and Corrupt Organizations Act (RICO)**.[6] The act outlaws a pattern of "racketeering activity," including arson, counterfeiting, gambling, dealing in narcotics, bribery, embezzlement, mail and wire fraud, securities fraud, and other enumerated criminal activities. (For a discussion of criminal RICO, see chapter 6.)

Persons injured by a RICO violation can bring a private civil action against the violator. RICO permits recovery only for injury to business or property. Recovery for personal injury is not permitted under RICO. The plaintiff can sue to recover **treble damages** (three times actual loss), plus attorney fees.[7] A defendant in a civil RICO case does not have to be first found guilty of criminal RICO.[8]

Because by definition commercial and securities fraud is a racketeering activity, many fraud cases are now being brought as RICO cases. Thus, securities dealers, insurance companies, banks, and other businesses are being sued in RICO treble damage actions.

Racketeer Influenced and Corrupt Organizations Act (RICO)   Federal statute that authorizes civil lawsuits against defendants for engaging in a pattern of racketeering activities.

treble damages   Civil damages three times actual damages may be awarded to persons whose business or property is injured by a RICO violation.

STRICT LIABILITY

Strict liability is another category of torts. Strict liability is liability without fault. That is, a participant in a covered activity will be held liable for any injuries caused by the activity even if he or she was not negligent. This doctrine holds that (1) there are certain activities that can place the public at risk of injury even if reasonable care is taken and (2) the public should have some means of compensation if such injury occurs.

Strict liability was first imposed for **abnormally dangerous activities**, such as crop dusting, blasting, fumigation, burning fields, storage of explosives, and keeping wild animals as pets.

In the following case, the court applied the doctrine of strict liability to a dangerous activity.

strict liability   Liability without fault.

CASE 4.5

Klein v. Pyrodyne Corporation
810 P.2d 917 (1991) Supreme Court of Washington

Facts Pyrodyne Corporation (Pyrodyne) is a licensed fireworks-display company that contracted to display fireworks at the Western Washington State Fairgrounds in Puyallup, Washington, on July 4, 1987. During the fireworks display, one of the mortar launchers discharged a rocket on a horizontal trajec-

tory parallel to the earth. The rocket exploded near a crowd of onlookers, including Danny Klein. Klein's clothing was set on fire, and he suffered facial burns and serious injury to his eyes. Klein sued Pyrodyne for strict liability to recover for his injuries. Pyrodyne

continued

asserted that the Chinese manufacturer of the fireworks was negligent in producing the rocket, and therefore Pyrodyne should not be held liable. The trial court applied the doctrine of strict liability and held in favor of Klein. Pyrodyne appealed.

Issue Is the conducting of public fireworks displays an abnormally dangerous activity that justifies the imposition of strict liability?

Decision Yes. The Washington supreme court held that the public display of fireworks is an abnormally dangerous activity that warrants the imposition of strict liability. Affirmed.

Reason Section 519 of the Restatement (Second) of Torts provides that any party carrying on an "abnormally dangerous activity" is strictly liable for ensuing damages. The public display of fireworks fits this definition. The court stated, "Any time a person ignites rockets with the intention of sending them aloft to explode in the presence of large crowds of people, a high risk of serious personal injury or property damage is created. That risk arises because of the possibility that a rocket will malfunction or be misdirected." Pyrodyne argued that its liability was cut off by the Chinese manufacturer's negligence. The court rejected this argument, stating, "Even if negligence may properly be regarded as an intervening cause, it cannot function to relieve Pyrodyne from strict liability."

CASE QUESTIONS

Critical Legal Thinking Should the law recognize the doctrine of strict liability? What is the public policy underlying the imposition of liability without fault?

Ethics Did Pyrodyne act ethically in denying liability in this case?

Business Implication Does the doctrine of strict liability increase the cost of doing business? Explain.

INTERNATIONAL PERSPECTIVE

Israeli Tort Law

David Ben Gurion proclaimed the establishment of the State of Israel on May 14, 1948. Historically, the Jewish people have been governed by biblical law. With the advent of a national state, secular laws were developed and coexist with religious law. One of the laws developed by the State of Israel is tort law. Israeli tort law is based on the theory that monetary compensation is awarded to promote justice and to ensure fair compensation when a tort occurs.

American tort law allows juries almost unlimited discretion to evaluate injuries and award damages. Under Israeli tort law, there is no right to trial by jury. Instead, all actions are tried by a panel of three judges or three lay people who decide both questions of fact and law. In essence, they are closer to arbitrators than judges.

Under Israeli tort law, all damages awarded must be assessed under one of these categories of damages:

1. **Medical expenses *(ripui)*** actually incurred and those expected to be incurred in order to cure the victim or return him or her as close as possible to preinjury state.
2. **Loss of earnings *(shevet)*** incurred during the time of the victim's injury and recovery.
3. **Loss of income *(nezek)*** for the long-term decrease in the victim's market value as a worker and skills he or she will never recover.
4. **Pain and suffering *(tza'ar)*** for short-term pain and suffering incurred at the time of the injury and their immediate consequences.
5. **Embarrassment *(boshet)*** for long-term pain and suffering caused from such things as permanent disfigurement, emotional distress, and such.

Israeli law limits the assessment of noneconomic damages (categories 4 and 5) to cases of willful, intentional, or grossly negligent infliction of harm.

Medical malpractice is one area of tort law where American and Israeli systems differ. Under American law, doctors are liable for their negligent conduct unless a Good Samaritan law relieves them of liability. Israeli law goes one step further. It excuses doctors from liability for their negligence in most situations. This is based on the public policy that the fear of such liability would otherwise discourage people from going into the medical profession.

WORKING THE WEB

American Bar Association The American Bar Association maintains a Web site, ABANetwork, as a service to its members and the Internet community. It has news about legal issues, ABA entities, ABA meetings, and technology. Here you can buy books and other publications, join a discussion group, or link to other legal sites.

Visit at http://www.abanet.org

ABA Tort and Insurance Practice Section (TIPS) This 30,000 member American Bar Association section brings together plaintiffs attorneys, defense attorneys, and insurance company counsel for the exchange of information and ideas in a unique nonadversarial setting. TIPS members can interact on a personal basis with nationally renown experts in tort and insurance matters.

Visit at http://www.abanet.org/tips/home.html

Law Journal Extra Torts Page Law Journal Extra Torts Page contains a table of contents, practice areas, news, resources, and links to law firms. This is a great place to get information on current torts cases of national interest.

Visit at http://www.ljextra.com/practice/negligence/index.html

Georgetown University Torts Page Georgetown University has a torts page that links to primary legal materials, associations and organizations, journals and newsletters, and specific subjects.

Visit at http://www.ll.georgetown.edu/lr/rs/torts.html

Academy of Legal Studies in Business The Academy of Legal Studies in Business is the leading national organization for college and university business law teachers. Here you can find information about regional and national meetings, job placement, and the *Journal of Legal Studies Education.*

Visit at http://miavxl.acs.muohio.edu/~herrondj/

CYBER EXERCISES:

1. Visit ABANet and see what it has to offer. Then click on "Lawmart." What kind of Internet services are advertised in this area? Print out a description of one such service.
2. Visit the home page of the ABA Tort and Insurance Practice Section. Click on "Publications and Videos." Then click on "Ethics and Professionalism." What is the price of a publication called *Making Rain: Business Development and Professionalism—Commercial Torts*?
3. Visit the Academy of Legal Studies in Business home page. Print out information about the next annual meeting.
4. Using the Law Journal Extra Torts Page, read the most current issue of the Personal Injury Newsletter.
5. From the Georgetown University Torts Page, find and read the Consumer Law Page.

CHAPTER SUMMARY

INTENTIONAL TORTS AGAINST PERSONS, P. 81

Intentional Torts against Persons	1. *Assault.* Threat of immediate harm or offensive contact, or any action that arouses reasonable apprehension of imminent harm.
	2. *Battery.* The unauthorized and harmful or offensive physical content with another person.
	a. *Transferred intent doctrine.* If a person intends to injure one person but actually harms another person, the law transfers the perpetrator's intent from the target to the actual victim.
	3. *False imprisonment.* Intentional confinement or restraint of another person without authority or justification and without that person's consent.
	a. *Merchant protection statutes.* Permit businesses to stop, detain, and investigate suspected shoplifters (and not be held liable for false imprisonment) if the following requirements are met:

>   i. There are reasonable grounds for the suspicion.
>   ii. Suspects are detained for only a reasonable time.
>   iii. Investigations are conducted in a reasonable manner.
> 4. *Intentional infliction of emotional distress.* Extreme and outrageous conduct intentionally or recklessly done that causes severe emotional distress. Some states require that the mental distress be manifested by physical injury. Also known as the *tort of outrage.*
> 5. *Malicious prosecution.* A successful defendant in a prior lawsuit can sue the plaintiff if the first lawsuit was frivolous.

INTENTIONAL TORTS AGAINST PROPERTY, P. 84

Intentional Torts against Property	1. *Trespass to land.* Interference with a landowner's right to exclusive possession of his or her land. 2. *Trespass to personal property.* A person injures another person's personal property or interferes with that person's enjoyment of his or her property. 3. *Conversion of personal property.* Taking over another person's personal property and depriving him or her of the use and enjoyment of the property.

UNINTENTIONAL TORTS (NEGLIGENCE), P. 84

Negligence	"The omission to do something which a reasonable man would do, or doing something which a prudent and reasonable man would not do."

Elements of Negligence	To establish negligence, the plaintiff must prove:
	1. The defendant owed a *duty of care* to the plaintiff.
	2. The defendant *breached this duty.*
	3. The plaintiff suffered *injury.*
	4. The defendant's negligent act *caused* the plaintiff's injury. Two types of causation must be shown:
	  a. *Causation in fact (or actual cause).* The defendant's negligent act was the actual cause of the plaintiff's injury.
	  b. *Proximate cause (or legal cause).* The defendant is liable only for the *foreseeable* consequences of his negligent act.

Professional Malpractice	Doctors, lawyers, architects, accountants, and other professionals owe a duty of ordinary care in providing their services. They are judged by a *reasonable professional standard.* Professionals who breach this duty are liable to clients and some third parties for *professional malpractice.*

Negligent Infliction of Emotional Distress	A person who witnesses a close relative's injury or death may sue the negligent party who caused the accident to recover damages for any emotional distress suffered by the bystander.
	   To recover for *negligent infliction of emotional distress*, the plaintiff must prove:
	  a. A relative was killed or injured by the defendant.
	  b. The plaintiff suffered severe emotional distress.
	  c. The plaintiff's mental distress resulted from a sensory and contemporaneous observance of the accident.
	Some states require that the mental distress be manifested by physical injury.

SPECIAL NEGLIGENCE DOCTRINES, P. 89

Special Negligence Doctrines	1. *Negligence per se.* A **statute** or ordinance establishes the duty of care. A violation of the statute or ordinance constitutes a breach of this duty of care.

2. *Res ipsa loquitur.* A presumption of negligence is established if the defendant had exclusive control of the instrumentality or situation that caused the plaintiff's injury and the injury would not have ordinarily occurred but for someone's negligence. The defendants may rebut this presumption.

3. *Dram shop acts.* State statutes that make taverns and bartenders liable for injuries caused to or by patrons who are served too much alcohol and cause injury to themselves or others.

4. *Social host liability.* Some states make social hosts liable for injuries caused by guests who are served alcohol at a social function and later cause injury because they are intoxicated.

5. *Guest statutes.* Provide that a driver of a vehicle is not liable for ordinary negligence to passengers he or she gratuitously transports. The driver is liable for gross negligence.

6. *Good Samaritan laws.* Relieve doctors and other medical professionals from liability for ordinary negligence when rendering medical aid in emergency situations.

7. *Fireman's rule.* Firefighters, police officers, and other government employees who are injured in the performance of their duties cannot sue the person who negligently caused the dangerous situation that caused the injury.

8. *"Danger invites rescue" doctrine.* A person who is injured while going to someone's rescue may sue the person who caused the dangerous situation.

9. *Common carriers and innkeepers.* Owe a duty of *utmost care,* rather than the duty of ordinary care, to protect their passengers and patrons from injury.

10. *Landowners.* Landowners (and tenants) owe the following duties to persons who come upon their property:
    a. *Invitees:* Duty of ordinary care
    b. *Licensees:* Duty of ordinary care
    c. *Trespassers:* Duty not to willfully and wantonly injure trespassers.

DEFENSES AGAINST NEGLIGENCE, P. 92

Defenses against Negligence	1. *Superseding event.* An intervening event caused by another person that caused the plaintiff's injuries that relieves the defendant from liability.
	2. *Assumption of the risk.* A defendant is not liable for the plaintiff's injuries if the plaintiff had knowledge of a specific risk and voluntarily assumed that risk.
	3. *Plaintiff partially at fault.* States have adopted one of the following two rules that affect a defendant's liability if the plaintiff has been partially at fault for causing his or her own injuries: a. *Contributory negligence.* A plaintiff cannot recover anything from the defendant. b. *Comparative negligence.* Damages are apportioned according to the parties' fault. Also called *comparative fault.*

BUSINESS TORTS, P. 94

Business Torts	1. *Entering business without a license.* The law requires that persons obtain a license from the government prior to entering certain businesses or professions.
	2. *Intentional misrepresentation.* A wrongdoer defrauds another person out of money, property, or something else of value. Also known as *fraud* or *deceit.* The following elements must be shown:

a. The wrongdoer made a false representation of material fact
b. The wrongdoer had knowledge that the representation was false and intended to deceive the innocent party
c. The innocent party justifiably relied on the misrepresentation
d. The innocent party was injured.
3. *Civil RICO*. Federal law that outlaws engaging in a pattern of racketeering activity such as arson, bribery, embezzlement, fraud, and other enumerated crimes. A private plaintiff who is injured in his or her business or property may recover *treble damages* from the wrongdoer in a civil lawsuit.

STRICT LIABILITY, P. 95

Strict Liability	Liability is assessed on defendants without regard to fault. Applies to *abnormally dangerous activities* and certain products.

CRITICAL LEGAL THINKING CASES

4.1 Intentional Tort On September 16, 1975, the Baltimore Orioles professional baseball team was at Boston's Fenway Park to play the Boston Red Sox. Ross Grimsley was a pitcher for the visiting Baltimore club. During one period of the game, Grimsley was warming up in the bullpen, throwing pitches to a catcher. During this warmup, Boston spectators in the stands heckled Grimsley. After Grimsley had completed warming up and the catcher had left from behind the plate in the bullpen, Grimsley wound up as if he were going to throw the ball in his hand at the plate, then turned and threw the ball at one of the hecklers in the stand. The ball traveled at about 80 miles an hour, passed through a wire fence protecting the spectators, missed the heckler whom Grimsley was aiming at, and hit another spectator, David Manning, Jr., causing injury. Manning sued Grimsley and the Baltimore Orioles. Are the defendants liable? [*Manning v. Grimsley*, 643 F.2d 20 (1st Cir. 1981)]

4.2 Merchant Protection Statute At about 7:30 P.M. on September 8, 1976, Deborah A. Johnson entered a Kmart store located in Madison, Wisconsin, to purchase some diapers and several cans of motor oil. She took her small child along to enable her to purchase the correct size diapers, carrying the child in an infant seat, which she had purchased at Kmart two or three weeks previously. A large Kmart price tag was still attached to the infant seat. Johnson purchased the diapers and oil and some children's clothes. She was in a hurry to leave because it was 8:00 P.M., her child's feeding time, and she hurried through the checkout lane. She paid for the diapers, the oil, and the clothing. Just after leaving the store she heard someone ask her to stop. She turned around and saw a Kmart security officer. He showed her a badge and asked her to come back into the store, which she did. The man stated, "I have reason to believe that you have stolen this car seat." Johnson explained that she had purchased the seat previously. She demanded to see the manager, who was called to the scene. When Johnson pointed out that the seat had cat hairs, food crumbs, and milk stains on it, the man said, "I'm really sorry, there's been a terri-

ble mistake. You can go." Johnson looked at the clock when she left, which read 8:20 P.M. Johnson sued Kmart for false imprisonment. Is Kmart liable? [*Johnson v. Kmart Enterprises, Inc.*, 297 N.W.2d 74 (Wis.App. 1980)]

4.3 Trespass A.C. Wade operated a liquor store in Cordele, Georgia. Because the store had been burglarized on several occasions and money had been stolen from a cigarette vending machine, Wade booby-trapped the machine with dynamite with the intent to scare away thieves when they tried to steal money from the vending machine. Robert McKinsey, a 16-year-old, was killed when the dynamite attached to the vending machine exploded when McKinsey was burglarizing the liquor store. Mrs. Ella McKinsey, Robert's mother, although admitting her son was committing a crime at the time he was killed, brought action for damages against Wade for the wrongful death of her son. Who wins? [*McKinsey v. Wade*, 220 S.E.2d 30 (Ga. 1975)]

4.4 Negligence In January 1984, George Yanase was a paying guest at the Royal Lodge-Downtown Motel (Royal) in San Diego, California. Yanase was a member of the Automobile Club of Southern California (Auto Club). The Auto Club publishes a "Tourbook" in which it lists hotels and motels and rates the quality of their services, including the cleanliness of rooms, quality of the restaurant, level of personal service, and the like. Yanase had selected the Royal from the Tourbook. On the night of his stay at the Royal, Yanase was shot in the parking lot adjacent to the motel and died as a result of his injuries. Yanase's widow sued Auto Club for negligence. Is the Auto Club liable? [*Yanase v. Automobile Club of Southern California*, 212 Cal.App.3d 468, 260 Cal.Rptr. 513 (Cal.App. 1989)]

4.5 Causation In February 1973, W. L. Brown purchased a new large Chevrolet truck from Days Chevrolet (Days). The truck had been manufactured by General Motors Corporation (General Motors). On March 1, 1973, an employee of Brown's was operating the truck when it ceased to function in rush-hour traffic on Interstate Highway 75 in the Atlanta suburbs. A defect within the alternator caused a complete failure of the truck's electrical system. The defect was caused by General Motors' negligence in manufacturing the truck. When the alternator failed to operate, the truck came to rest in the right-hand lane of two northbound lanes of freeway traffic. Because of the electrical failure, no blinking lights could be used to warn traffic of the danger. The driver, however, tried to motion traffic around the truck. Some time later when the freeway traffic had returned to normal, the large Chevrolet truck was still motionless on the freeway. At approximately 6:00 P.M. a panel truck approached the stalled truck in the right-hand lane of traffic at freeway speed. Immediately behind the panel truck, Mr. Davis, driving a Volkswagen fastback, was unable to see the stalled truck. At the last moment the driver of the panel truck saw the stalled truck and swerved into another lane to avoid it. Mr. Davis drove his Volkswagen into the stalled truck at freeway speed, causing his death. Mr. Davis' wife brought a wrongful death action based on negligence against General Motors. Was there causation linking the negligence of the defendant to the fatal accident? [*General Motors Corporation v. Davis*, 233 S.E.2d 835 (Ga.App. 1977)]

4.6 Negligence Per Se On March 21, 1980, Julius Ebanks set out from his home in East Elmhurst, Queens, New York, en route to his employment in the downtown district of Manhattan. When Ebanks reached the Bowling Green subway station, he boarded an escalator owned and operated by the New York City Transit Authority (Transit Authority). While the escalator was ascending, Ebanks' left foot became caught in a two-inch gap between the escalator step on which he was standing and the side wall of the escalator. Ebanks was unable to free himself. When he reached the top of the escalator he was thrown to the ground, fracturing his hip and suffering other serious injuries. The two-inch gap exceeded the three-eighths-inch standard required by the city's building code. Ebanks sued the Transit Authority to recover damages for his injuries. Who wins? [*Ebanks v. New York City Transit Authority*, 70 N.Y.2d 621, 518 N.Y.S.2d 776 (N.Y.App. 1986)]

4.7 Res Ipsa Loquitur Elsie Mack was admitted as a patient to the Lydia E. Hall Hospital for a surgical procedure for the treatment of rectal cancer. Dr. Joseph Jahr was the surgeon in charge of the operation. An anesthesiologist, nurses, and other hospital personnel assisted with the operation. An electrical instrument called an electrocosgulator was used during the surgery to coagulate Mack's blood vessels and stop the bleeding. A component part of the electrocosgulator known as a grounding pad was placed on Mack's left thigh and remained there throughout the surgery. While under anesthesia, Mack sustained third-degree burns on the side of her left thigh during the course of surgery. This was because the pad came in full contact with Mack's skin tissue. When the grounding pad was removed at the conclusion of the operation, a burn more than one-half inch deep and over two inches in diameter was discovered where the pad had been. The burn was excised along with the nerves and a two and three-fourths-inch scar remains. Mack sued the hospital, Dr. Jahr, and other medical personnel to recover damages caused by their negligence. Does the doctrine of *res ipsa loquitur* apply to this lawsuit? [*Mack v. Lydia E. Hall Hospital*, 503 N.Y.S.2d 131 (N.Y.Sup.Ct. 1986)]

4.8 Liability of Landowners George and Beverly Wagner own a 1.6-acre parcel of land upon which they operate "Bowag Kennels," which caters to training, boarding, and caring for show dogs. The property is entirely surrounded by land owned by Reuben Shiling and W. Dale Hess. In August 1964, Shiling and Hess granted the Wagners an easement right-of-way over their land that connected the kennel to Singer Road, a rural, unlit two-lane public road running through a wooded area. The right-of-way is an unpaved, unlit narrow road that crosses an uninhabited wooded area leading to the Bowag Kennels. On numerous occasions, unauthorized motorcyclists drove upon the right-of-way. On several occasions, the bikers had loud parties along the right-of-way. In September 1982, the Wagners stretched a large metal chain between two poles at the entrance of the right-of-way. The Wagners testified that they marked the chain with reflectors and signs. Just before midnight on October 2, 1982, William E. Doehring, Jr., and his passenger, Kelvin Henderson, drove their motorcycle off Singer Road and turned onto the right-of-way. The motorcycle they were riding was not equipped with a headlight and the riders were not wearing helmets. Doehring and Henderson had not been granted permission by the Wagners or Shiling or Hess to use the right-of-way. The motorcycle struck the chain and the riders were thrown off. Doehring died several hours later at a hospital. Doehring's father filed a wrongful death and survival action against the Wagners. Who wins? [*Wagner v. Doehring*, 553 A.2d 684 (Md.App. 1989)]

4.9 Social Host Liability David Andres was a 19-year-old student at Northeast Missouri State University. He was a member of Alpha Kappa Lambda Fraternity and lived in the fraternity house. During the evening of December 11, 1979, and the early morning hours of December 12, 1979, the fraternity sponsored a mixer at its house with the Delta Zeta Sorority at which alcoholic beverages were furnished without restriction as to age. Missouri's lawful age for drinking alcoholic beverages was 21. Andres was observed drinking before, during, and following the mixer. During the early morning hours of December 12, he was sitting at the bar in the fraternity house, matching straight shots of whiskey with a fraternity brother. After watching them for some time, another fraternity brother took the bottle from them. Several fraternity brothers helped Andres into the television room, where a pillow and blanket were obtained for him. He was left to "sleep it off" on the television room floor. At about 10:00 A.M. on December 12, when Andres could not be awakened, he was taken to a local hospital but could not be revived. The autopsy showed Andres' blood level measured 0.43 percent, and the cause of death was acute alcohol intoxication with aspiration. Andres' parents brought a wrongful death action against the fraternity. Who wins? [*Andres v. Alpha Kappa Lambda Fraternity*, 730 S.W.2d 547 (Mo. 1987)]

4.10 Liability of Common Carrier The Southern California Rapid Transit District (RTD) is a public common carrier that operates public buses throughout the Los Angeles area. Carmen and Carla Lopez were fare-paying passengers on an RTD bus when a group of juveniles began harassing them and other passengers. When the bus driver was notified of this problem, he failed to take any precautionary measures and continued to operate the bus. The juveniles eventually physically assaulted

Carmen and Carla, who were injured. The RTD was aware of a history of violent attacks on its bus line. Carmen and Carla sued the RTD to recover damages for their injuries. Who wins? [*Lopez v. Southern California Rapid Transit District*, 40 Cal.3d 780, 221 Cal.Rptr. 840 (Cal. 1985)]

4.11 Emotional Distress Virginia Rulon-Miller began working for International Business Machines Corporation (IBM) in 1967. Over the course of several years she was promoted to a marketing-representative position, selling typewriters and office equipment in San Francisco's financial district. She became one of the most successful salespersons in the office and received money prizes and awards for her work. She also received the highest merit rating an employee could receive under the IBM rating system. In 1976, Rulon-Miller met Matt Blum, who was an account manager for IBM. They began dating shortly thereafter and became involved in a romantic relationship. This fact was widely known at IBM. In 1977, Blum left IBM to work at QXY, a competitor of IBM. Rulon-Miller and Blum continued their relationship. About one year later, Phillip Callahan, who was Rulon-Miller's immediate manager, called her into his office. He told her that her dating Blum constituted a "conflict of interest," told her to stop dating Blum, and told her he would give her a "couple of days to a week" to think about it. The next day, however, Callahan called Rulon-Miller in again and told her he had "made up her mind for her" and dismissed her. Rulon-Miller suffered severe emotional distress because of this incident. She sued IBM for intentional infliction of emotional distress. Who wins? [*Rulon-Miller v. International Business Machines Corporation*, 162 Cal.App.3d 241, 208 Cal.Rptr. 524 (Cal.App. 1985)]

4.12 Emotional Distress On August 10, 1983, Gregory and Demetria James, brother and sister, were riding their bicycles north on 50th Street in Omaha, Nebraska. Spaulding Street intersects 50th Street. A garbage truck owned by Watts Trucking Service, Inc. (Watts), and driven by its employee, John Milton Lieb (Lieb), was backing up into the intersection of 50th and Spaulding streets. The truck backed into the intersection of 50th and Spaulding streets, through a stop sign, and hit and ran over Demetria, killing her. Gregory helplessly watched the entire accident but was not in danger himself. As a result of watching his sister's peril, Gregory suffered severe emotional distress. Gregory sued Watts and Lieb to recover damages for his emotional distress. Who wins? [*James v. Watts Trucking Service, Inc.*, 375 N.W.2d 109 (Neb. 1985)]

4.13 Defense On the night of June 13, 1975, the New York Yankees professional baseball team played the Chicago White Sox at Yankee Stadium, New York. Elliot Maddox played center field for the Yankees that night. It had rained the day before, and the previous night's game had been canceled because of bad weather. On the evening of June 13 the playing field was still wet, and Maddox commented on this fact several times to the club's manager but continued to play. In the ninth inning, when Maddox was attempting to field a ball in center field, he slipped on a wet spot, fell, and injured his right knee. Maddox sued the City of New York that owned the Stadium, the Metropolitan Baseball Club, Inc., as lessee, the architect, the consulting engineer, and the American League. Maddox alleged that the parties were negligent in causing the field to be wet, and that the injury ended his professional career. Who wins? [*Maddox v. City of New York*, 496 N.Y.S.2d 726 (N.Y.App. 1985)]

 ETHICS CASES

4.14 Ethical Perspective Radio station KHJ was a successful Los Angeles broadcaster of rock music that commanded a 48 percent market share of the teenage audience in the Los Angeles area. KHJ was owned and operated by RKO General, Inc. (RKO General). In July 1973, KHJ inaugurated a promotion titled "The Super Summer Spectacular." As part of this promotion, KHJ had a disc jockey known as "The Real Don Steele" (Steele) ride around the Los Angeles area in a conspicuous red automobile. Periodically KHJ would announce to its radio audience Steele's location. The first listener to thereafter locate Steele and answer a question received a cash prize and participated in a brief interview on the air with Steele. On July 16, 1973, one KHJ broadcast identified Steele's next destination as Canoga Park. Robert Sentner, 17 years old, heard the broadcast and immediately drove to Canoga Park. Marsha Baime, 19 years old, also heard the broadcast and drove to Canoga Park. By the time Sentner and Baime located Steele, someone else had already claimed the prize. Without the knowledge of the other, Sentner and Baime each decided to follow Steele to the next destination and to be first to "find" him.

Steele proceeded onto the freeway. For the next few miles Sentner and Baime tried to jockey for position closest to the Steele vehicle, reaching speeds of up to 80 miles per hour. There is no evidence that the Steele vehicle exceeded the speed limit. When Steele left the freeway at the Westlake off ramp, Sentner and Baime tried to follow. In their attempts to do so, they knocked another vehicle driven by Mr. Weirum into the center divider of the freeway, where it overturned. Mr. Weirum died in the accident. Baime stopped to report the accident. Sentner, after pausing momentarily to relate the tragedy to a passing police officer, got back into his car, pursued and successfully located Steele, and collected the cash prize. The wife and children of Mr. Weirum brought a wrongful death negligence action against Sentner, Baime, and RKO General. Who wins? Did RKO General, Inc., act responsibly in this case? [*Weirum v. RKO General, Inc.*, 15 Cal.3d 40, 123 Cal.Rptr. 468 (Cal. 1975)]

4.15 Ethical Perspective Guy Portee, a seven-year-old, resided with his mother in an apartment building in Newark, New Jersey. Edith and Nathan Jaffee owned and operated the building. On the afternoon of May 22, 1976, Guy became trapped in the building's elevator between its outer door and the wall of the elevator shaft. When someone activated the elevator, the boy was dragged up to the third floor. Another child who saw the accident ran to seek help. Soon afterward, Renee Portee, the boy's mother, and officers of the Newark Police Department arrived. The officers worked for four and one-half hours trying to release the boy, during which time the mother watched as her son moaned, cried out, and flailed his arms. The police contacted the Atlantic Elevator Company (Atlantic), which was responsible for the installation and maintenance of the elevator, and requested the company to send a mechanic to assist in the effort to free the boy. Apparently no one came. The boy suffered multiple bone fractures and massive internal hemorrhaging. He died while still trapped, his mother a helpless observer.

After her son's death, Renee became severely distressed and seriously self-destructive. On March 24, 1979, she attempted to take her own life. She survived and the wound was repaired by surgery, but she has since required considerable physical therapy. She had received extensive counseling and psychotherapy to help overcome the mental and emotional problems associated with her son's death. Renee sued the Jaffees and Atlantic to recover damages for her emotional distress. Who wins? Did either of the defendants act unethically in this case? [*Portee v. Jaffee*, 417 A.2d 521 (N.J. 1980)]

4.16 Ethical Perspective Rosina Crisci owned an apartment building in which Mrs. DiMare was a tenant. One day while Mrs. DiMare was descending a wooden staircase on the outside of the apartment building, she fell through the staircase and was left hanging 15 feet above the ground until she was saved. Crisci had a $10,000 liability insurance policy on the building from the Security Insurance Company (Security) of New Haven, Connecticut. Mrs. DiMare sued Crisci and Security for $400,000 for physical injuries and psychosis suffered from the fall. Prior to trial, Mrs. DiMare agreed to take $10,000 in settlement of the case. Security refused this settlement offer. Mrs. DiMare reduced her settlement offer to $9,000, of which Crisci offered to pay $2,500. Security again refused to settle the case. The case proceeded to trial and the jury awarded Mrs. DiMare and her husband $110,000. Security paid $10,000 pursuant to the insurance contract, and Crisci had to pay the difference. Crisci, a 70-year-old widow, had to sell her assets, became dependent on her relatives, declined in physical health, and suffered from hysteria and suicide attempts. Crisci sued Security for tort damages for breach of the implied covenant of good faith and fair dealing. Who wins? Did Security Insurance Company act ethically in this case? [*Crisci v. Security Insurance Company of New Haven, Connecticut*, 426 P.2d 173, 66 Cal.App.2d 425, 58 Cal.Rptr. 13 (Cal. App. 1967)]

CRITICAL LEGAL THINKING WRITING ASSIGNMENT

Read Case A.4 in the Case Appendix [*Braun v. Soldier of Fortune Magazine, Inc.*]. This case is excerpted from the court of appeals opinion. Review and brief the case. In your brief, be sure to answer the following questions:

1. Who are the plaintiffs? What are they suing for?

2. When does a magazine owe a duty to refrain from publishing an advertisement?
3. Was the advertisement the proximate cause of the plaintiff's injuries?
4. Should the award of punitive damages have been reduced?

NOTES

1. *Restatement (Second) of Torts*, Section 46.
2. *Restatement (Second) of Torts*, Section 46, comment d.
3. Justice B. Anderson, *Blyth v. Birmingham Waterworks Co.*, 11 Exch. 781, 784 (1856).
4. 248 N.Y. 339, 162 N.E. 99 (1928).

5. For example, see Cal. Civil Code, Section 1714(c).
6. 18 U.S.C. §§ 1961–1968.
7. 18 U.S.C. § 1964(C).
8. *Sedima, S.P.R.L. v. Imrex Co., Inc.*, 473 U.S. 479, 105 S.Ct. 3275, 87 L.Ed.2d 346 (1985).

CHAPTER 5

INTELLECTUAL PROPERTY

RIGHTS

Chapter Objectives

*After studying this chapter,
you should be able to*

1. Define unfair competition and describe the business torts of palming off and misappropriating trade secrets
2. Describe the business torts of disparagement and misappropriating the right to publicity
3. Describe the torts of defamation of character and invasion of privacy
4. Describe how an invention can be patented under federal patent laws
5. Apply the public use doctrine and describe the penalties for patent infringement
6. List what writings can be copyrighted and describe the terms of protection provided by federal copyright law
7. Apply the fair use doctrine and describe the penalties for copyright infringement
8. Describe the legal rights that computer and software designers have in their works
9. Define trademarks and service marks and describe how these are registered
10. Apply the generic name doctrine and describe the penalties for trademark infringement

Chapter Contents

> *In all well-tempered governments there is nothing which should be more jealously maintained than the spirit of obedience to law, more especially in small matters; for transgression creeps in unperceived and at last ruins the state, just as the constant recurrence of small expenses in time eat up a fortune.*
>
> Aristotle
> *Politics, Bk. 5, Ch. 8*
> (Jowett trans.)

The American economy is based on a principle of freedom of competition under which persons and businesses compete openly to produce and distribute goods and services. This system gives entrepreneurs the opportunity to start new businesses and ensures that consumers have a range of products and services to choose from. There are limits on how the progress and efficiency engendered by the system are achieved, however. Certain injurious actions by businesses and business executives constitute **business torts**.

business tort A tort based on common law and on statutory law that affects business.

Reputation and goodwill might be the most important assets a business or individual has. The law protects a business's and an individual's reputation, right to publicity, and right to privacy. In business, violation of these rights is referred to as *unfair competition*. A business also has a right to protect its trade secrets. If any of these rights are violated, the injured business or individual can recover damages from the responsible party.

BUSINESS BRIEF

According to International Trade Commission estimates, American companies lose $40 billion to $50 billion annually—or 30 percent to 40 percent of the U.S. trade deficit—because their technology and intellectual property are misappropriated by foreign manufacturers.

In addition, federal law provides certain protections for intellectual property, such as patents, copyrights, and trademarks. The holders of these rights are given exclusive control over their use. Anyone who infringes on these rights may be stopped from doing so and is liable for damages. Computers and computer software are accorded special protection from infringement.

This chapter discusses unfair competition, infringement of intellectual property rights, and computer law.

UNFAIR COMPETITION

In most situations, competitors are free to compete vigorously, even if that means that someone is driven out of business or sustains severe losses. However, competitors may not engage in illegal **unfair competition** or **predatory practices**. The most common forms of unfair competition are discussed in the sections that follow.

unfair competition Competition that violates the law.

Palming Off

The common law tort of **palming off** is one of the oldest forms of unfair competition. This tort usually occurs when a small company tries to "palm off" its products as those of a rival. For example, if a company implied that it was affiliated with International Business Machines (IBM) by selling computers under the IBM label, it would be liable for the business tort of palming off.

palming off Unfair competition that occurs when a company tries to pass off one of its products as that of a rival.

To prove the tort of palming off, the plaintiff must prove that (1) the defendant used the plaintiff's logo, symbol, mark, and so on and (2) there is a likelihood of confusion as to the source of the product. Actual consumer confusion need not be shown. The key element is whether consumers are likely to be confused as to the origin of the copied product. This doctrine is not used often because many products and services are now patented, copyrighted, or trademarked, and the plaintiff can bring an infringement lawsuit under federal law.

ETHICAL PERSPECTIVE

Hallmark Greeted by an Unfair Competition Lawsuit

Imitation may be a form of flattery. In a business setting, however, it may constitute unfair competition. Consider the following case.

Susan Polis Schutz and Stephen Schutz own Hartford House, Ltd., which does business under the trade name Blue Mountain Art (Blue Mountain). Blue Mountain is in the greeting card business. In 1981 and 1983, Blue Mountain introduced two lines of cards titled "AireBrush Feelings" and "WaterColor Feelings," respectively. The cards contained non-occasion emotional messages concerning love and personal relationships superimposed on soft airbrush and watercolor artwork. The cards were printed on high-quality, uncoated textured art paper and contained lengthy free-verse poetry with many letters and words printed in hand-lettered calligraphy. The cards were a commercial success.

Hallmark Cards, Inc. (Hallmark), which has produced and marketed greeting cards for 75 years, is the giant of the greeting card industry. In 1986, Hallmark introduced a line of cards called "Personal Touch." Like Blue Mountain's cards, the cards were done in soft watercolors that convey emotional messages about personal relationships in free-verse poetry. Hallmark mounted an intense effort to capture the emotionally expressive non-occasion greeting card market and designed and marketed its Personal Touch cards to appeal to the same type of consumer who purchases Blue Mountain's cards.

Blue Mountain sued Hallmark for the tort of unfair competition. It alleged that Hallmark's Personal Touch line of greeting cards was deceptively and confusingly similar to Blue Mountain's and infringed upon the trade dress of Blue Mountain's AireBrush Feelings and WaterColor Feelings lines.

The U.S. district court issued an injunction that prohibited Hallmark from selling or distributing its Personal Touch cards. The court held that Hallmark had engaged in unfair competition by infringing upon Blue Mountain's distinctive trade dress of its lines of cards. The court determined that there was a likelihood of confusion among card purchasers as to the source of Blue Mountain's two lines and Hallmark's Personal Touch line. The court of appeals affirmed. The court stated, "It is Blue Mountain's specific artistic expression, in combination with other features to produce an overall Blue Mountain look, that is being protected." [*Hartford House, Ltd. v. Hallmark Cards, Incorporated*, 846 F.2d 1268 (10th Cir. 1988)]

1. Did Hallmark act ethically in this case?
2. Should trade dress be protected? Why or why not?
3. Do you think Hallmark engaged in unfair competition in this case?

Misappropriation of Trade Secrets

trade secrets A product formula, pattern, design, compilation of data, customer list, or other business secrets.

Many businesses are successful because their **trade secrets** set them apart from their competitors. Trade secrets can be product formulas, patterns, designs, compilations of data, customer lists, or other business secrets. Many trade secrets either do not qualify to be—or simply are not—patented, copyrighted, or trademarked. Many states have adopted the **Uniform Trade Secrets Act** to give statutory protection to trade secrets.

State unfair competition laws allow the owner of a trade secret to bring a lawsuit for misappropriation against anyone who steals a trade secret. To be actionable, the defendant (often an employee of the owner or a competitor) must have obtained the trade secret through unlawful means such as theft, bribery, or industrial espionage. No tort has occurred if there is no misappropriation. For example, a competitor can lawfully discover a trade secret by performing reverse engineering (i.e., taking apart and examining a rival's product).

BUSINESS BRIEF
Businesses should take all necessary precautions to protect their trade secrets from unwanted discovery.

The owner of a trade secret is obliged to take all reasonable precautions to prevent those secrets from being discovered by others. Such precautions include fencing in buildings, placing locks on doors, hiring security guards, and the like. If the owner fails to take such actions, the secret is no longer subject to protection under state unfair competition laws.

Generally, a successful plaintiff in a trade secret action can (1) recover the profits made by the offender from the use of the trade secret, (2) recover for damages, and (3) obtain an injunction prohibiting the offender from divulging or using the trade secret.

Defamation of Character

A person's reputation is a valuable asset. Therefore, every person is protected from false statements made by others during his or her lifetime. This protection ends upon a person's death. The tort of **defamation of character** requires a plaintiff to prove that (1) the defendant made an untrue statement of fact about the plaintiff and (2) the statement was intentionally or accidentally published to a third party. In this context, publication simply means that a third person heard or saw the untrue statement. It does not just mean appearance in newspapers, magazines, or books.

The name for an oral defamatory statement is **slander**. A false statement that appears in a letter, newspaper, magazine, book, photograph, movie, video, and the like is called **libel**. Most courts hold that defamatory statements in radio and television broadcasts are considered libel because of the permanency of the media.

The publication of an untrue statement of fact is not the same as the publication of an opinion. The publication of opinions is usually not actionable. "My lawyer is lousy" is an opinion. Because defamation is defined as an untrue statement of fact, truth is an absolute defense to a charge of defamation.

Public Figures as Plaintiffs In *New York Times Co. v. Sullivan*,[1] the U.S. Supreme Court held that *public officials* cannot recover for defamation unless they can prove that the defendant acted with "actual malice." Actual malice means that the defendant made the false statement knowingly or with reckless disregard of its falsity. This requirement has since been extended to public figure plaintiffs such as movie stars, sports personalities, and other celebrities.

Disparagement

Business firms rely on their reputation and the quality of their products and services to attract and keep customers. That is why state unfair competition laws protect businesses from disparaging statements made by competitors or others. A disparaging statement is an untrue statement made by one person or business about the products, services, property, or reputation of another business.

To prove **disparagement**, which is also called **product disparagement**, **trade libel**, or **slander of title**, the plaintiff must show that the defendant (1) made an untrue statement about the plaintiff's products, services, property, or business reputation, (2) published this untrue statement to a third party, (3) knew the statement was not true, and (4) made the statement maliciously (i.e., with intent to injure the plaintiff).

Section 43(a) of the Lanham Act Section 43(a) of the Lanham Act, a federal statute, prohibits false and misleading advertising.[2] Under this act, private parties may obtain injunctions and recover damages from competitors who make disparaging or false or misleading statements about the plaintiff's products. For example, companies often engage in comparative advertising in which they compare the qualities of their products to those of competitors. Truthful comparative advertising is lawful. However, untruthful comparative advertising constitutes disparagement of product and false and misleading advertising in violation of Section 43(a) of the Lanham Act.

In the following case, the court issued an injunction against false and misleading comparative advertising.

---

defamation of character False statement(s) made by one person about another. In court, the plaintiff must prove that (1) the defendant made an untrue statement of fact about the plaintiff and (2) the statement was intentionally or accidentally published to a third party.

slander Oral defamation of character.

libel A false statement that appears in a letter, newspaper, magazine, book, photograph, movie, video, and so on.

product disparagement False statements about a competitor's products, services, property, or business reputation.

BUSINESS BRIEF
Companies that engage in comparative advertising must be able to substantiate their claims of superiority over a rival's products or services.

CASE 5.1

McNeil-P.C.C., Inc. v. Bristol-Myers Squibb Co.
938 F.2d 1544 (1991) United States Court of Appeals, Second Circuit

Facts McNeil-P.C.C., Inc. (McNeil), the leading manufacturer of over-the-counter analgesic pain remedies, markets Extra-Strength Tylenol (Tylenol). A two-tablet dose of Tylenol contains 1,000 milligrams of acetaminophen. In the spring of 1990, Bristol-Myers Squibb Company (Bristol-Myers) began marketing a competing analgesic pain remedy called Aspirin-Free Excedrin (Excedrin). A two-tablet dose of Excedrin contains 1,000 milligrams of acetaminophen plus 130 milligrams of caffeine. To market its new pain reliever, Bristol-Myers sent promotional literature to drug retailers and began a television advertising campaign that claimed that Excedrin "works better" than Tylenol. The claim was based on a "cross-over" study conducted by Bristol-Myers. A cross-over study has the patients take one drug in period 1 and another drug in period 2 and then evaluate the performance of both drugs. Because McNeil believed that the Bristol-Myers "works better" claim was false, it sued Bristol-Myers for violating Section 43(a) of the Lanham Act. The district court held in favor of McNeil and permanently enjoined Bristol-Myers from making such a claim. Bristol-Myers appealed.

Issue Did defendant Bristol-Myers make false advertising claims about the superiority of its product in violation of the Lanham Act?

Decision Yes. The court of appeals held that Bristol-Myers had made false advertising claims and therefore violated the Lanham Act.

Reason The evidence showed that the period 1 tests showed no statistical difference between the performance of Excedrin and Tylenol. The court found that although period 2 tests showed a slight difference, the results were tainted because they were distorted by psychological effects. Consequently, the court determined that the Bristol-Myers tests did not prove the superiority of its product. McNeil proved that the Bristol-Myers "works better" claim was false.

CASE QUESTIONS

Critical Legal Thinking Should false advertising constitute a tort?

Ethics Did Bristol-Myers act ethically in making its "works better" claim?

Business Implication Should companies be permitted to engage in comparative advertising? If so, when?

Invasion of the Right to Privacy

invasion of the right to privacy A tort that constitutes the violation of a person's right to live his or her life without being subjected to unwarranted and undesired publicity.

The law recognizes each person's right to live his or her life without being subjected to unwarranted and undesired publicity. A violation of this right constitutes the tort of **invasion of the right to privacy**. Examples of this tort include reading someone else's mail, wiretapping, and such. Publication to a third person is necessary. In contrast to defamation, the fact does not have to be untrue. Therefore, truth is not a defense to a charge of invasion of privacy. If the fact is public information, there is no claim of privacy. However, a fact that was once public (e.g., the commission of a crime) may become private after the passage of time.

Placing someone in a false light constitutes an invasion of privacy. For example, sending an objectionable telegram to a third party and signing another's name would place the purported sender in a false light in the eyes of the receiver. Falsely attributing beliefs or acts to another can also form the basis of a lawsuit.

In the following case, the court found invasion of privacy.

CASE 5.2

Mitchell v. Globe International Publishing, Inc.
978 F.2d 1065 (1992) United States Court of Appeals, Eighth Circuit

Facts Globe International, Inc. (Globe) publishes several supermarket tabloids, including the *National Examiner* and the *Sun*. In 1980, the *National Examiner* published an article about Nellie Mitchell, a 96-year-old Arkansas woman, a single parent who had raised her family on what she earned from delivering newspapers. A photograph of Mitchell accompanied the article. On October 2, 1990, the *Sun* published a front-page headline story "Pregnancy Forces Granny to Quit Work at Age 101." The story purported to be about a woman named Audrey Wiles from Stirling, Australia. Supposedly, Audrey delivered newspapers for 94 years before she became pregnant by a reclusive millionaire she met on her route. The previously published photograph of Mitchell was published on the *Sun's* cover as being that of Audrey Wiles. When the *Sun* was published, Mitchell, who was then 106, suffered severe humiliation and embarrassment. She sued Globe for false light invasion of privacy. The jury returned a verdict awarding her $650,000 in compensatory damages and $850,000 in punitive damages. Globe appealed.

Issue Was Globe International, Inc., liable for the tort of false light invasion of privacy?

Decision Yes. The appellate court held that Globe had committed the tort of false light invasion of privacy by publishing the photograph of Nellie Mitchell as that of a pregnant centenarian. The appellate court upheld the award of punitive damages

but remanded the case to the trial court with instructions to reduce the award of compensatory damages.

Reason The appellate court held that the plaintiff proved that (1) the false light in which she was placed by the publicity would be highly offensive to a reasonable person, and (2) the defendant acted with actual malice in publishing the article. Globe asserted that the story was "pure fiction" and that no reasonable reader could have believed it. The court rejected this argument, noting that the format and style of the newspaper suggest that its contents are based on fact. The court held that Globe acted maliciously. It cited evidence that the editor of the pregnancy story was the same editor who had written the original story about Nellie Mitchell and that he intentionally used her picture for the second story because he thought she was dead.

CASE QUESTIONS

Critical Legal Thinking Should the courts recognize the tort of invasion of privacy? Why or why not? .

Ethics Did Globe act ethically in this case? Do you think many stories in supermarket tabloids are fictitious?

Business Implication Did the facts of this case warrant the imposition of punitive damages?

Misappropriation of the Right to Publicity

Each person has the exclusive legal right to control and profit from the commercial use of his or her name and personality during his or her lifetime. This is a valuable right, particularly to well-known persons such as sports figures and movie stars. Any attempt by another person to appropriate a living person's name or identity for commercial purposes is actionable. The wrongdoer is liable for the **tort of misappropriation of the right to publicity** (also called the **tort of appropriation**). In such cases, the plaintiff can (1) recover the unauthorized profits made by the offending party and (2) obtain an injunction against further unauthorized use of his or her name or identity. Many states provide that the right to publicity survives a person's death and may be enforced by the deceased's heirs.

In the following case, the court permitted a celebrity to pursue her case against the defendants for alleged misappropriation of the right to publicity.

tort of misappropriation of the right to publicity An attempt by another person to appropriate a living person's name or identity for commercial purposes.

CASE 5.3

White v. Samsung Electronics America, Inc.
971 F.2d 1395 (1992) United States Court of Appeals, Ninth Circuit

Facts Vanna White is the hostess of *The Wheel of Fortune*, one of the most popular game shows in television history. An estimated 40 million people watch the program daily. Capitalizing on her fame, White markets her identity to various advertisers. Samsung Electronics America, Inc. (Samsung), distributes various electronics products in the United States. Samsung and its advertising agency, David Deutsch Associates, Inc. (Deutsch), devised a series of advertisements that followed the same theme. Each depicted a current item of popular culture and a Samsung electronics product. The advertisements were set in the 21st century in order to convey the message that the Samsung product would still be in use at that time.

The advertisement that prompted the current dispute was for Samsung's videocassette recorders (VCRs). The ad depicted a robot that was outfitted to resemble White. The set in which the robot was posed was instantly recognizable as *The Wheel of Fortune* game show set, and the robot's stance was one for which White is famous. The caption of the ad read: "Longest-running game show, 2012 A.D." Defendants referred to the ad as the "Vanna White" ad. White did not consent to the ads and was not paid. White sued Samsung and Deutsch to recover damages for alleged misappropriation of her right to publicity. The district court granted defendants' motions for summary judgment. White appealed.

Issue Did White properly plead the claim of misappropriation of the right to publicity?

Decision Yes. The court of appeals held that the law of misappropriation of the right of publicity had been properly pleaded by White under the facts of this case. The court reversed and remanded the case. The case went to trial, and in January 1994 the jury awarded Vanna White $403,000 in damages.

Reason The individual aspects of the advertisement in the present case say little. Viewed together, though, they leave little doubt about whom the celebrity is that the ad is meant to depict. Although the female-shaped robot was dressed exactly like Vanna White dresses at times, so do many other women. The look-alike robot is in the process of turning a block letter on a gameboard, but similarly attired Scrabble-playing women may do this as well. But the robot is standing on what looks to be *The Wheel of Fortune* game show set—and Vanna White is the only one who dresses like this and turns letters on *The Wheel of Fortune* game show. Indeed, the defendants themselves referred to their ad as the "Vanna White" ad. Television exposure created Vanna White's marketable celebrity value. The court stated, "The law protects the celebrity's sole right to exploit this value whether the celebrity has achieved her fame out of rare ability, dumb luck or a combination thereof."

CASE QUESTIONS

Critical Legal Thinking Should the right to publicity be a protected right? Why or why not?

Ethics Did Samsung act ethically in using Vanna White's celebrity status without getting her permission or paying her?

Business Implication Sometimes the worth of a celebrity's publicity goes up in value after his or her death. Can you think of any examples?

CONTEMPORARY BUSINESS ENVIRONMENT

Sound-Alikes

Tom Waits is a professional singer, songwriter, and actor of some renown. He has a raspy, gravelly singing voice, described by one fan as "like how you'd sound if you drank a quart of bourbon, smoked a pack of cigarettes, and swallowed a pack of razor blades." Waits has recorded more than 17 albums and has played to sold-out audiences throughout the United States, Canada, Europe, Japan, and Australia. Waits follows a strict personal policy against doing commercials.

When Frito-Lay, Inc., which is in the business of manufacturing, distributing, and selling prepared and packaged food products, decided to introduce a new product, SalsaRio Doritos corn chips, it hired Tracy-Locke, Inc., an advertising agency, to help develop a marketing campaign. Tracy-Locke found inspiration in a 1976 Waits song, "Step Right Up." The agency wrote a commercial that echoed the rhyming wordplay of the Waits song. Only one problem remained: Waits refused to do commercials, so who would sing the song in the commercial?

Tracy-Locke auditioned many singers, but none could imitate Waits's gravelly style. Finally, the agency found Stephen Carter, a professional musician who did Tom Waits imitations. Carter had performed Waits's songs as part of his band's repertoire for more than 10 years, and he had perfected an imitation of Waits's voice.

The commercial, which was recorded with Frito-Lay's authorization, was broadcast on more than 250 radio stations located in 61 markets nationwide. After Waits heard the commercial during an appearance on a Los Angeles radio station, he sued Frito-Lay and Tracy-Locke. Waits claimed misappropriation of the right to publicity. The jury found in Waits's favor and awarded him $375,000 compensatory damages and $2 million punitive damages. The defendants appealed.

The court of appeals affirmed the judgment, holding that voice misappropriation is a form of the tort of misappropriation of the right to publicity. The court stated, "We recognize that when voice is a sufficient indicia of a celebrity's identity, the right to publicity protects against its imitation for commercial purposes without the celebrity's consent." The court found that the award of punitive damages was warranted because the defendants acted with malice and conscious disregard toward Waits by recording and broadcasting the commercial that pirated his voice.

Waits's victory is expected to make advertisers and their agencies think twice before producing "sound-alike" commercials that misappropriate a celebrity's vocal style. [*Waits v. Frito-Lay, Inc.*, 978 F.2d 1093 (9th Cir. 1992)]

INTELLECTUAL PROPERTY

Intellectual property such as inventions, writings, trademarks, and the like are often a business's most valuable asset. A comprehensive federal statutory scheme protects the following three types of intellectual property: (1) patents, (2) copyrights, and (3) trademarks and other marks. They are discussed in the sections that follow.

intellectual property
Objects such as inventions, writings, trademarks, and so on, which are often a business's most valuable asset.

PATENTS

Pursuant to the express authority granted in the U.S. Constitution,[3] Congress enacted the **Federal Patent Statute of 1952**.[4] This law is intended to provide an incentive for inventors to invent and make their inventions public and to protect patented inventions from infringement. Federal patent law is exclusive; there are no state patent laws. The *United States Court of Appeals for the Federal Circuit* in Washington, D.C., was created in 1982 to hear patent appeals. The court was established to promote uniformity in patent law.

Federal Patent Statute of 1952 Federal statute that establishes the requirements for obtaining a patent and protects patented inventions from infringement.

Patenting an Invention

To be patented, the invention must be *novel, useful,* and *nonobvious*. In addition, only certain subject matters can be patented. Patentable subject matter includes (1) machines; (2) processes; (3) compositions of matter; (4) improvements to existing machines, processes, or compositions of matter; (5) designs for an article of manufacture; (6) asexually reproduced plants; and (7) living material invented by man.[5] Abstractions and scientific principle cannot be patented unless they are part of the tangible environment. For example, Einstein's Theory of Relativity ($e = mc^2$) cannot be patented.

Patent applicants must file a patent application containing a written description of the invention with the **United States Patent and Trademark Office** in Washington,

BUSINESS BRIEF
Patent applications are complicated. An inventor should hire a patent attorney to assist in obtaining a patent for the invention.

"The patent system added the fuel of interest to the fire of genius."

Abraham Lincoln
Lectures on Discoveries, Inventions, and Improvements (1859)

D.C. If a patent is granted, the invention is assigned a patent number. Patent holders usually affix the word *Patent* or *Pat.* and the patent number to the patented article. If a patent application is filed but a patent has not yet been issued, the applicant usually places the words *patent pending* on the article. Any party can challenge either the issuance of a patent or the validity of an existing patent.

INTERNATIONAL PERSPECTIVE

Changes in Patent Law Mandated by GATT

In 1994, the **General Agreement on Tariffs and Trade (GATT)** established the **World Trade Organization (WTO)**, an international trade organization of which the United States is a member. GATT's intellectual property provisions, and implementing legislation passed by Congress, made the following important changes in U.S. patent law:

1. Patents are valid for *20 years*, instead of the previous term of 17 years.
2. The patent term begins to run from the date the patent application is *filed*, instead of when the patent is issued as was previously the case.

These changes, which became effective June 8, 1995, brought the U.S. patent system in harmony with the majority of other developed nations. The United States still follows the first to invent rule, rather than the first to file rule followed by some other countries.

Public Use Doctrine

public use doctrine
A doctrine that says a patent may not be granted if the invention was used by the public for more than one year prior to the filing of the patent application.

Under the **public use doctrine**, a patent may not be granted if the invention was used by the public for more than one year prior to the filing of the patent application. This doctrine forces inventors to file their patent applications at the proper time. Consider this example: Suppose a person invents a new invention on January 1. He allows the public to use his invention and does not file a patent application until February of the following year. The inventor has lost the right to patent his invention.

Patent Infringement

patent infringement
Unauthorized use of another's patent. A patent holder may recover damages and other remedies against a patent infringer.

Patent holders own exclusive rights to use and exploit their patent. **Patent infringement** occurs when someone makes unauthorized use of another's patent. In a suit for patent infringement, a successful plaintiff can recover (1) money damages equal to a reasonable royalty rate on the sale of the infringed articles, (2) other damages caused by the infringement (such as loss of customers), (3) an order requiring the destruction of the infringing articles, and (4) an injunction preventing the infringer from such action in the future. The court has the discretion to award up to treble damages if the infringement was intentional.

ETHICAL PERSPECTIVE

Inventor Wipes Ford's and Chrysler's Windshields Clean

In 1967, Robert Kearns, a professor at Wayne State University in Detroit, Michigan, patented his design for the electronic intermit-tent windshield wiper for automobiles and other vehicles. He shopped his invention around to many automobile manufacturers but never reached a licensing deal with any of them. In 1969, automobile manufacturers began producing cars with Kearns' invention. Virtually all cars sold in the United States today now have these wipers as standard equipment.

Kearns filed patent infringement lawsuits against Ford in 1978 and Chrysler in 1982. He later filed patent infringement cases against virtually all automobile manufacturers. The Ford case went to trial first. Kearns sought $325 million in damages from Ford. Ford alleged that Kearns's patents were not valid because of obviousness and prior art. The jury disagreed with Ford and decided that Kearns's patents were valid. The jury ordered Ford to pay $5.2 million, plus interest. In 1990, Ford settled by paying Kearns $10.2 million and agreeing to drop all appeals. This represented 50¢ per Ford vehicle that used the wiper system.

Kearns sought $468 million in damages from Chrysler. In that case, Kearns fired his lawyers and represented himself. This was at least the fourth law firm hired and fired in the course of Kearns's patent infringement lawsuits. Kearns won a second victory: In 1991, the jury found that Chrysler had infringed Kearns's patents and awarded him $11.3 million. The court denied Kearns injunctive relief because his 17-year patents had expired years ago. The court of appeals affirmed the judgment and the Supreme Court refused to hear Kearns's appeal. Kearns received more than $21 million from Chrysler, which amounted to 90¢ for every vehicle sold by Chrysler with the wiper system.

In 1993 and 1994, courts dismissed Kearns's lawsuits against 23 automobile manufacturers, including General Motors, Porsche, Nissan, Toyota, Honda, and Rolls Royce, among others, because Kearns failed to comply with court orders to disclose documents relevant to the cases. The district court then ordered Kearns to pay his fired lawyers $5.4 million in contingency fees. Thus ended Kearns's more than 30-year saga and legal battle with the automobile industry. In an interview Kearns stated, "The patent system is a fraud pure and simple."

1. Did the automobile manufacturers act unethically in these cases? Other than Ford and Chrysler, did the other auto manufacturers get off too easily?
2. Do you think Kearns could have won more money? Explain.

CONTEMPORARY BUSINESS ENVIRONMENT

Say Cheese! Camera Companies Lose Patent Infringement Case

U.S. companies often complain that they spend huge amounts of money on research and development only to find that foreign companies make profits by selling goods that contain the misappropriated technology. The following case demonstrates that the courts may be a good place to begin tackling this problem.

In the early 1970s, researchers at Honeywell, Inc., which is based in Minneapolis, invented autofocus technology for cameras. This technology, which uses computer chips to focus camera lenses automatically, takes over a task previously done manually by photographers. Between 1975 and 1977,

Honeywell obtained four patents for the technology, but it left the camera business without ever using the technology. Instead, it tried to market the technology to other manufacturers, most of them in Japan.

The companies Honeywell approached chose not to purchase or license Honeywell's technology. Instead, they developed their own autofocus technology. One such company was Minolta, which introduced the Maxxum camera with autofocus technology in 1985. The Maxxum was a hit with consumers. It sent Minolta into its current position as the leading camera maker in the United States, with annual

sales of more than $400 million and 30 percent of the market.

There was only one hitch: Honeywell thought Minolta had infringed on its patented autofocus technology. Honeywell sued Minolta, as well as 14 other camera makers from the Far East, alleging patent infringement.

In 1992, after a four-month trial, a federal jury of nine persons found that Minolta had infringed two of Honeywell's four patents. The jury ordered Minolta to pay Honeywell $96 million in back royalties. Within months, Minolta paid Honeywell $124 million in a settlement in which

continued

Honeywell agreed not to seek a ban on the sale of Minolta cameras in the United States. The two patents found to have been infringed expired in late 1992.

Since the jury verdict against Minolta was announced, 14 other camera makers have settled infringement suits with Honeywell. These companies include Canon, Nikon, Pentax, Olympus, Ricoh, Chinon, and Vivitar. The settlements put more than $300 million in Honeywell's coffer.

The Minolta decision and the other settlements should mean that foreign companies will be more apt to license technology from U.S. patent holders legally. Pirating the technology will not be as attractive an option as it once appeared.

1. Did Minolta act ethically in this case?
2. Do you think patents should be granted by the federal government? Why or why not? Is the patent period of 20 years long enough?

COPYRIGHTS

Copyright Revision Act of 1976 Federal statute that (1) establishes the requirements for obtaining a copyright and (2) protects copyrighted works from infringement.

Berne Convention An international copyright treaty. The United States and many other nations are signatories to this treaty.

"The law in respect to literature ought to remain upon the same footing as that which regards the profits of mechanical inventions and chemical discoveries."
William Wordsworth
Letter (1838)

CAUTION
The expression of an idea is copyrightable. The idea itself is not.

"Whatever a man publishes he publishes at his peril."
Lord Mansfield
C. J. R. v. Woodfall (1774)

Congress enacted a federal copyright law pursuant to an express grant of authority in the U.S. Constitution.[6] This law protects the work of authors and other creative persons from the unauthorized use of their copyrighted materials and provides a financial incentive for authors to write, thereby increasing the number of creative works available in society. The **Copyright Revision Act of 1976** governs copyright law.[7] Effective March 1, 1989, the United States became a member of the **Berne Convention,** an international copyright treaty. Federal copyright law is exclusive; there are no state copyright laws.

Registration of Copyrights

Only tangible writings—that is, writings that can be physically seen—are subject to copyright registration and protection. The term *writing* has been broadly defined to include books, periodicals, and newspapers; lectures, sermons, and addresses; musical compositions; plays, motion pictures, and radio and television productions; maps; works of art, including paintings, drawings, sculpture, jewelry, glassware, tapestry, and lithographs; architectural drawings and models; photographs, including prints, slides, and filmstrips; greeting cards and picture postcards; motion pictures and photoplays, including feature films, cartoons, newsreels, travelogues, and training films; and sound recordings published in the form of tapes, cassettes, compact discs, and phonograph albums.

To be protected under federal copyright law, the work must be the original work of the author. Published and unpublished works may be copyrighted and registered with the **United States Copyright Office** in Washington, D.C. Registration is permissive and voluntary and can be effected at any time during the term of the copyright. Registration itself does not create the copyright. Individuals are given statutory protection for the life of the author plus 50 years. If a corporation or business registers the copyright, the copyright is protected for the shorter of either 100 years from the date of creation of the work or 75 years from the date of publication.[8]

Prior to March 1, 1989, to protect a published work, the copyright holder must place the following copyright notice on the work: (1) his or her name, (2) a "(c)" or "©" or "Copyright" or "copr.," and (3) the year the material is copyrighted. Failure to provide the appropriate notice on works could cause the loss of copyright. Under the Berne Convention, notice is not required on works entering the public domain on or after March 1, 1989. Although notice is now permissive, it is recommended that notice be placed on copyrighted works to defeat a defendant's claim of innocent infringement.

BUSINESS CHECKLIST

Artists' "Moral Rights" in Creative Works Protected under Federal Statute

Today, an artist who produces a painting, sculpture, photograph, or other work of art holds a copyright in the work. Prior to 1990, when the artist sold the work, the buyer usually obtained the copyright unless the artist and buyer contracted otherwise.

Things changed when Congress passed the **Visual Artists Rights Act** in 1990. The act gives artists **"moral rights"** in their creations that continue even after the sale of the artwork. Although long recognized in European countries, the notion of "moral rights" is new in this country.

The rights granted to artists under the Act include the following:

- The artist is given moral right in his or her work that transcends the sale of the artwork and the transfer of the copyright to it.
- Before an owner of the artist's work can change, modify, or tamper with the artwork, reproduce it in any other medium (e.g., produce prints from a painting), or remove certain artwork (e.g., remove a mural from a building wall), the owner must notify the artist.
- The artist has 90 days after notice to respond to the owner. If the artist and owner do not settle the issue, the artist may file a lawsuit that seeks an injunction to prevent the owner from taking the proposed action.
- If the case goes to litigation, the court must decide whether the artist's moral rights have been violated and whether to grant injunctive relief.
- When purchasing a piece of artwork, the buyer can seek a waiver of moral rights from the artist so that the buyer is not restricted in the future use of the artwork.

Copyright Infringement

Copyright infringement occurs when a party copies a substantial and material part of the plaintiff's copyrighted work without permission. The copying does not have to be either word for word or the entire work. A successful plaintiff can recover (1) the profit made by the infringer from the copyright infringement, (2) damages suffered by the plaintiff, (3) an order requiring the impoundment and destruction of the infringing works, and (4) an injunction preventing the infringer from doing so in the future. The court, in its discretion, can award statutory damages ranging from $200 for innocent infringement up to $100,000 for willful infringement in lieu of actual damages.

copyright infringement
When a party copies a substantial and material part of the plaintiff's copyrighted work without permission. A copyright holder may recover damages and other remedies against the infringer.

The Fair Use Doctrine

The copyright holder's rights in the work are not absolute. The law permits certain limited unauthorized use of copyrighted materials under the **fair use doctrine**. The following uses are protected under this doctrine: (1) quotation of the copyrighted work for review or criticism, or in a scholarly or technical work, (2) use in a parody or satire, (3) brief quotation in a news report, (4) reproduction by a teacher or student of a small part of the work to illustrate a lesson, (5) incidental reproduction of a work in a newsreel or broadcast of an event being reported, and (6) reproduction of a work in a legislative or judicial proceeding. The copyright holder cannot recover for copyright infringement where fair use is found.

fair use doctrine
A doctrine that permits certain limited use of a copyright by someone other than the copyright holder without the permission of the copyright holder.

BUSINESS APPLICATION

Supreme Court Raps Roy Orbison's "Oh, Pretty Woman" Recording

Fair use permits one party to use another party's copyrighted work in a limited way without having to obtain permission to do so and without having to pay for the use. But when is fair use fair? Consider the following case.

In 1964, Roy Orbison collaborated with another song writer and wrote a rock ballad called "Oh, Pretty Woman." The song was copyrighted under federal copyright law. Roy Orbison recorded the song, which became a memorable classic from the 1960s. The writers assigned their rights in the song to Acuff-Rose Music, Inc. (Acuff-Rose).

2 Live Crew is a popular rap music group led by Luther R. Campbell. In 1989, Campbell wrote a song called "Pretty Woman" which was a parody of Roy Orbison's original recording. The lyrics of Campbell's version differed from Roy Orbison's version, except for the first line, which was verbatim from the original. 2 Live Crew wrote Acuff-Rose and asked permission to record their rap version of the song and stated that they were willing to pay a fee for the right

to do so. When Acuff-Rose refused the permission, 2 Live Crew recorded the song anyway and put it on their rap album "As Clean as They Wanna Be," which sold more than 250,000 copies. The rap version of "Pretty Woman" used the same rhythm as the original, although the rap version included additional sounds such as scraper noises, overlays of different keys, and altered drum beats.

Acuff-Rose sued 2 Live Crew and their record company, Luke Skywalker Records, for copyright infringement. The defendants asserted the affirmative defense of fair use based on parody. The district court found fair use, but the court of appeals reversed. The U.S. Supreme Court agreed to hear the case to decide the issue it had not previously addressed: whether commercial parody could be fair use.

The Supreme Court came down on the side of parody, stating that it could constitute fair use in the proper circumstances. The Supreme Court rejected the court of appeals ruling that presumed that all commercial use of

a copyrighted work—even a parody—is illegal. Instead, the Court said that there is no bright line test for determining fair use and that this determination requires a court to examine each situation on a case-by-case basis. The Court noted that there is a strong public interest in protecting humor, parody, and comic satire in the publication of secondary works based on original copyrighted works. Basically, the Supreme Court gave a "green light" to commercial parody, but cautioned that if too much of the original work is appropriated, then the secondary work loses its fair use protection.

Where does this decision leave us? As a question of law, the Supreme Court has held that commercial parody could qualify for fair use, but as a question of fact commercial parody might or might not qualify as fair use depending on the facts of each situation. The Court remanded the case for this determination. Do you think there was fair use in this case? (See the lyrics that follow.) [*Campbell v. Acuff-Rose Music, Inc.*, 114 S.Ct. 1164, 127 L.Ed.2d 500 (1994)]

Roy Orbison's Version of "Oh, Pretty Woman"

Pretty Woman, walking down the street,
Pretty Woman, the kind I like to meet,
Pretty Woman, I don't believe you, you're not the truth,
No one could look as good as you
Mercy
Pretty Woman, won't you pardon me,
Pretty Woman, I couldn't help but see,
Pretty Woman, that you look lovely as can be
Are you lonely just like me?
Pretty Woman, stop a while,
Pretty Woman, talk a while,
Pretty Woman, give your smile to me
Pretty Woman, yeah, yeah, yeah
Pretty Woman, look my way,
Pretty Woman, say you'll stay with me
Cause I need you, I'll treat you right

2 Live Crew's Version of "Pretty Woman"

Pretty woman walkin' down the street
Pretty woman girl you look so sweet
Pretty woman you bring me down to that knee
Pretty woman you make me wanna beg please
Oh, pretty woman
Big hairy woman you need to shave that stuff
Big hairy woman you know I bet it's tough
Big hairy woman all that hair it ain't legit
Cause you look like 'Cousin It' Big hairy woman
Bald headed woman girl your hair won't grow
Bald headed woman you got a teeny weeny afro
Bald headed woman you know your hair could look nice
Bald headed woman first you got to roll it with rice
Bald headed woman here, let me get this hunk of biz for ya

Come to me baby, be mine tonight
Pretty Woman, don't walk on by,
Pretty Woman, don't make me cry,
Pretty Woman, don't walk away,
Hey, O.K.
If that's the way it must be, O.K.
I guess I'll go on home, it's late
There'll be tomorrow night, but wait!
What do I see
Is she walking back to me?
Yeah, she's walking back to me!
Oh, Pretty Woman.

Ya know what I'm saying you look better than
   rice a roni
Oh bald headed woman
Big hairy woman come on in
And don't forget your bald headed friend
Hey pretty woman let the boys jump in
Two timin' woman girl you know you ain't right
Two timin' woman you's out with my boy last night
Two timin' woman that takes a load off my mind
Two timin' woman now I know the baby ain't mine
Oh, two timin' woman
Oh pretty woman

CONTEMPORARY BUSINESS ENVIRONMENT

Copyrighting Software

The advent of new technology challenges the ability of laws to protect it. For example, the invention of computers and the writing of software programs caused problems for existing copyright laws. These laws had to be changed to afford protection to software.

In 1980, Congress enacted the **Computer Software Copyright Act**, which amended the Copyright Act of 1976. The 1980 amendments included computer programs in the list of tangible items protected by copyright law. The amendments define *computer program* broadly as "a set of statements or instructions to be used directly or indirectly in a computer in order to bring about a certain result" [17 U.S.C. § 101].

A computer program is written first in programming language, which is called a "source code." It is then translated into another language, called an "object code," which is understood by the computer. In an important decision, *Apple Computer, Inc. v. Franklin Computer Corp.*, 714 F.2d 1240 (3d Cir. 1983), the court held that object codes could be copyrighted.

As with other works, the creator of a copyrightable software program obtains automatic copyright protection. The **Judicial Improvement Act of 1990** authorizes the Register of Copyright to accept and record any document pertaining to computer software and to issue a **certificate of recordation** to the recorder [P.L. 101–650].

Congress passed the **Semiconductor Chip Protection Act of 1984** to provide greater protection of the hardware components of a computer. This law protects masks that are used to create computer chips. A *mask* is an original layout of software programs that is used to create a semiconductor chip. This act is sometimes referred to as the "Mask Work Act." Notice on the work is optional but when used must contain (1) the words *Mask Work* or the symbol *M* or (M) and (2) the name of the owner [17 U.S.C. §§ 901–914].

The extent of the protection afforded to computer software and semiconductor chips by these new laws is not yet certain. These laws will be applied on a case-by-case basis.

TRADEMARKS

Trademark law is intended to (1) protect the owner's investment and goodwill in a **mark** and (2) prevent consumers from being confused as to the origin of goods and services. In 1946, Congress enacted the **Lanham Trademark Act** to provide federal protection to trademarks, service marks, and other marks.[9] Congress passed the **Trademark Law Revision Act of 1988**, which amended trademark law in several

Lanham Trademark Act
An act enacted in 1946 that provides for the registration of trademarks and service marks with the Federal Patent Office in Washington, D.C.

respects.[10] The amendments made it easier to register a trademark but harder to maintain it. States may also enact trademark laws.

Registration of Trademarks

Trademarks are registered with the **United States Patent and Trademark Office** in Washington, D.C. The original registration of a mark is valid for 10 years and can be renewed for an unlimited number of 10-year periods.[11] The registration of a trademark, which is given nationwide effect, serves as constructive notice that the mark is the registrant's personal property. The registrant is entitled to use the registered trademark symbol ® in connection with a registered trademark or service mark. Use of the symbol is not mandatory. Note that the frequently used notations "TM" and "SM" have no legal significance.

An applicant can register a mark if (1) it was in use in commerce (e.g., actually used in the sale of goods or services) or (2) the applicant verifies a bona fide intention to use the mark in commerce and actually does so within six months of its registration. Failure to do so during this period causes loss of the mark to the registrant. A party other than the registrant can submit an opposition to a proposed registration of a mark or the cancellation of a previously registered mark.

distinctive   A brand name that is unique and fabricated.

secondary meaning When an ordinary term has become a brand name.

To qualify for federal protection, a mark must be **distinctive** or have acquired a "**secondary meaning**." For example, marks such as *Acura, Dr. Pepper, Roto-Rooter*, and *Apple Computer* are distinctive. A term such as *English Leather*, which literally means leather processed in England, has taken on a "secondary meaning" as a trademark for an aftershave lotion. Words that are descriptive but have no secondary meaning cannot be trademarked. For example, the word *cola* alone could not be trademarked.

Marks That Can Be Trademarked

mark   The collective name for trademarks, service marks, certification marks, and collective marks that all can be trademarked.

trademark   A distinctive mark, symbol, name, word, motto, or device that identifies the goods of a particular business.

service mark   A mark that distinguishes the services of the holder from those of its competitors.

The following types of marks can be trademarked. Collectively, these marks are referred to as **marks**:

- **Trademarks**. A **trademark** is a distinctive mark, symbol, name, word, motto, or device that identifies the goods of a particular business. For example, the words *Xerox, Coca-Cola*, and *IBM* are trademarks.
- **Service marks**. A **service mark** is used to distinguish the services of the holder from those of its competitors. The trade names *United Airlines, Marriott Hotels*, and *Weight Watchers* are examples of service marks.
- **Certification marks**. A **certification mark** is a mark that is used to certify that goods and services are of a certain quality or originate from particular geographical areas, for example, wines from the "Napa Valley" of California or "Florida" oranges. The owner of the mark is usually a nonprofit corporation that licenses producers that meet certain standards or conditions to use the mark.
- **Collective marks**. A **collective mark** is a mark used by cooperatives, associations, and fraternal organizations. "Boy Scouts of America" is an example of a collective mark.

Certain marks cannot be registered. They include (1) the flag or coat of arms of the United States, any state, municipality, or foreign nation, (2) marks that are immoral or scandalous, (3) geographical names standing alone (e.g., "South"), (4) surnames standing alone (note that a surname can be registered if it is accompanied by a picture or fanciful name, such as "Smith Brothers' Cough Drops"; even then, exclusive use of surnames is prohibited), and (5) any mark that resembles a mark already registered with the federal Patent and Trademark Office.

CONTEMPORARY BUSINESS ENVIRONMENT

Color May Be Trademarked

The issue of whether color could be trademarked confused the courts of appeal for years: Some said it could, while others said it could not. In 1995, the U.S. Supreme Court ended this division and decided the issue in the following case.

Since the 1950s, Qualitex Company has manufactured and sold dry cleaning pads with a special shade of green-gold color. These pads are used on cleaning presses at dry cleaning firms. Qualitex registered the special green-gold

color of its pads with the Patent and Trademark Office as a trademark.

In 1989, Jacobson Products, a Qualitex rival, began to sell its own press pads to dry cleaning firms, and it colored these pads a similar green-gold. Qualitex sued Jacobson for trademark infringement. Qualitex won the lawsuit in the district court, but the court of appeals reversed. Qualitex appealed to the U.S. Supreme Court.

The Supreme Court, in a unanimous decision, held that color

qualifies for registration as a trademark when it is associated with a particular good where the color has obtained a secondary meaning that identifies a particular brand and manufacturer as its source. The Court held that Qualitex's special green-gold color on its press pads met this requirement and could be registered and protected as a trademark. [*Qualitex Company v. Jacobson Products Company, Inc.*, 115 S.Ct. 1300, 131 L.Ed.2d 248 (1995)]

Trademark Infringement

The owner of a mark can sue a third party for the unauthorized use of a mark. To succeed in a **trademark infringement** case, the owner must prove that (1) the defendant infringed the plaintiff's mark by using it in an unauthorized manner and (2) such use is likely to cause confusion, mistake, or deception of the public as to the origin of the goods or services. A successful plaintiff can recover (1) the profits made by the infringer by the unauthorized use of the mark, (2) damages caused to the plaintiff's business and reputation, (3) an order requiring the defendant to destroy all goods containing the unauthorized mark, and (4) an injunction preventing the defendant from such infringement in the future. The court has discretion to award up to treble (triple) damages where intentional infringement is found.

trademark infringement
Unauthorized use of another's mark. The holder may recover damages and other remedies from the infringer.

ETHICAL PERSPECTIVE

It Is a Violation of the Lanham Act to Wear Another's Trade Dress

Certain designs, such as a restaurant's decor, do not usually qualify for formal trademark registration. The design can be a valuable company asset, however. To address this problem, Congress drafted Section 43(a) of the Lanham Act, which protects unregistered "trade dress" from misappropriation as long as it is distinctive. Consider the following case.

In 1978, Taco Cabana, Inc. opened its first fast-food "Taco Cabana" Mexican restaurant in San Antonio, Texas. It quickly opened other restaurants across Texas. Taco Cabana's Mexican-style trade dress consisted of a festive eating atmosphere having interior dining and patio areas decorated with artifacts, bright colors, paintings, murals, awnings, and umbrellas, and stepped building exteriors

decorated in a vivid color scheme using border paint and neon stripes. In 1985, Two Pesos, Inc., a rival, opened a Mexican restaurant in Houston that adopted a motif similar to Taco Cabana's. Both restaurant chains expanded until they began serving many of the same markets.

Taco Cabana sued Two Pesos for violating Section 43(a). The
continued

district court and court of appeals held that Two Pesos had brazenly and deliberately infringed on Taco Cabana's trade dress and that this created the likelihood of confusion on the part of customers. The court awarded damages to Taco Cabana. Two Pesos appealed the case to the U.S. Supreme Court, which decided to hear the case.

The Supreme Court held that trade dress is the total image and overall appearance of a business, including the shape and general appearance of the exterior of the restaurant, the identifying sign, the interior, the decor, the menu, the equipment used to serve the food, the servers' uniforms, and other features. The Court held that Taco Cabana's trade dress was inherently distinctive and therefore protectable from misappropriation by Two Pesos under Section 43(a). The Supreme Court affirmed the lower courts' ruling in favor of Taco Cabana. [*Two Pesos, Inc. v. Taco Cabana, Inc.*, 112 S.Ct. 2753, 120 L.Ed.2d 615 (1992)]

1. Did Two Pesos act ethically in copying Taco Cabana's trade dress? Why do you think it did this?
2. Should trade dress be protected from copying? Why or why not?

Generic Names

Most companies promote their trademarks and service marks to increase the public's awareness of the availability and quality of their products and services. At some point in time, however, the public might begin to treat the mark as a common name to denote the type of product or service being sold, rather than as the trademark or trade name of an individual seller. A trademark that becomes a common term for a product line or type of service is called a **generic name**. When that happens, the term loses its protection under federal trademark law because it has become *descriptive* rather than *distinctive* (see Exhibit 5.1).

generic name   A term for a mark that has become a common term for a product line or type of service and therefore has lost its trademark protection.

State Antidilution Statutes

States recognize common law trademarks. In addition, many states have enacted their own trademark statutes. These state laws, which allow persons and companies to register trademarks and service marks, are often called **antidilution statutes**. They prevent others from infringing on and diluting a registrant's mark. Companies that do business only locally sometimes register under these laws.

INTERNATIONAL PERSPECTIVE

International Protection of Intellectual Property Rights

To provide protection to intellectual property across national borders, many countries have entered into international treaties and conventions. The major international treaties and conventions protecting patent, copyright, and trademark rights around the world, and to which the United States is a signatory, are discussed here.

The major convention that provides international protection to patents is the **1883 Convention of the Union of Paris (Paris Convention)**. The Convention's major purpose is to allow the nationals of each member country to file for patents in all other member nations. The Convention does not, however, eliminate the need to file separate patent applications in each member nation in which the applicant desires protection. The Convention gives an applicant who has filed for a patent in one member country 12 months to submit applications in other member countries.

The major copyright treaty is the **Berne Convention of 1886**, as revised, to which the United States became a signatory in 1989. The Convention provides for the recognition of a copyright in all member nations. The Convention establishes a minimum copyright term of the life of the author plus 50

continued

Exhibit 5.1
Reprinted with permission
of Xerox Corporation

XEROX

Once a trademark,
not always a trademark.

They were once proud trademarks, now they're just names. They failed to take precautions that would have helped them have a long and prosperous life.

We need your help to stay out of there. Whenever you use our name, please use it as a proper adjective in conjunction with our products and services: e.g., Xerox

copiers or Xerox financial services. And never as a verb: "to Xerox" in place of "to copy," or as a noun: "Xeroxes" in place of "copies."

With your help and a precaution or two on our part, it's "Once the Xerox trademark, always the Xerox trademark."

Team Xerox. We document the world.

XEROX® is a registered trademark of XEROX CORPORATION.

BUSINESS BRIEF

Nestlé Company, Inc., lost its trademark on the term "Toll House" for its chocolate chip cookies when a court ruled that the term had become generic because the public had come to associate the name Toll House with chocolate chip cookies in general, not only those sold by Nestlé [Nestlé Company, Inc. v. Chester's Market, Inc., 571 F.Supp. 763 (D.Conn. 1983)].

years and eliminates the requirement to put a © on copyrighted works.

The **Paris Convention** also allows nationals of each member nation to file for trademarks and service marks in all other member nations on an individual, nondiscriminatory basis, even if the applicant does not own the mark in the country of origin. The applicant has six months after his or her original registration to submit applications to other member countries.

In 1994, the Uruguay Round of the General Agreement on Tariffs and Trade (GATT) created the **World Trade Organization (WTO)**. More than 100 nations have become members of the WTO. Most WTO member countries have also signed a separate agreement with GATT titled the agreement on **Trade Related Aspects of Intellectual Property Rights**, or **TRIPs**. The TRIPs agreement requires each signatory country to adhere to the substantive provisions of the world's most important intellectual property conventions, such as the Paris Convention on patents and trademarks and the Berne Convention on copyrights. Intellectual property infringement cases against WTO member countries can be brought in the newly created WTO court (see chapter 7).

WORKING THE WEB

U.S. Library of Congress The Library of Congress Web site contains a database of copyright records from 1978 to the present.

Visit at http://lcweb.loc.gov/

U.S. Patent and Trademark Office The U.S. Patent and Trademark Office has a Web site where you can download forms, order copies, link to legal materials, and find statistical information.

Visit at http://www.uspto.gov/

U.S. Federal Communications Commission The U.S. Federal Communications Commission Web site links to economic information, industry statistics, consumer information, and a host of other resources.

Visit at http://www.fcc.gov

U.S. Copyright Office Information about copyright basics, copyright law, copyright forms, copyright records, and other copyright materials can be found at this Web site.

Visit at http://www.loc.gov/copyright

International Trademark Association The International Trademark Association is an association of trademark owners and advisors worldwide. It is dedicated to the support and advancement of trademarks and related intellectual property concepts as essential elements of effective national and international commerce.

Visit at http://www.inta.org/

CYBER EXERCISES:

1. Using the Library of Congress Web site, find the home page for the U.S. Copyright Office Records and print it out.
2. Using the Patent and Trademark Office Web site, find out about jobs at the U.S. Patent and Trademark Office.
3. Use the U.S. Federal Communications Web site to find information about the v-chip. Print out the first page of that document.
4. Using the U.S. Copyright Office Web site, print out the materials on copyright registration.
5. Using the International Trademark Association Web site, visit the Brand Names Education Foundation.

CHAPTER SUMMARY

UNFAIR COMPETITION, P. 105

Unfair Competition	Conducting business by using wrongful conduct such as fraud, intimidation, coercion, espionage, and the like. Unfair competition is a *business tort* actionable under federal and state laws.

Types of Unfair Competition	1. *Palming off*. A company passes off its products or services as those of another company.
	2. *Misappropriation of a trade secret*. A *trade secret* is a product formula, pattern, design, compilation of data, customer list, or other business secret that makes a business successful. Obtaining another's trade secret through unlawful means such as theft, bribery, or espionage is a tort. The owner of a trade secret must take reasonable precautions to prevent its trade secret from being discovered by others.
	3. *Defamation of character*. The defendant makes an untrue statement of fact about the plaintiff that is published to a third party. Truth is an absolute defense.
	a. Types of defamation:
	i. *Slander*. Oral defamation
	ii. *Libel*. Written defamation
	b. *Public figure plaintiffs*. Must prove the additional element of *malice*.
	4. *Disparagement*. An untrue statement about the products, services, property, or reputation of a business. Also called *product disparagement, trade libel*, or *slander of title*.
	5. *Misleading advertising*. Section 43(a) of the Lanham Act, a federal law, prohibits false and misleading advertising. State laws also prohibit false and misleading advertising.
	6. *Invasion of privacy*. Unwarranted and undesired publicity of a private fact about a person. The fact does not have to be untrue. Truth is not a defense.
	7. *Misappropriation of the right to publicity*. Appropriating another person's name or identity for commercial purposes without that person's consent. Also called the *tort of appropriation*.

INTELLECTUAL PROPERTY, P. 111

Intellectual Property	Inventions, writings, and trade names and symbols.

PATENTS, P. 111

Patents	Patent law is exclusively federal law; there are no state patent laws.
	1. *Patent*. Patentable subject matter includes inventions such as machines; processes; composition of matter; improvements to existing machines, processes, or compositions of matter; designs for articles of manufacture; asexually reproduced plants; and living matter invented by man.
	To be patented, an invention must be:
	a. Novel
	b. Useful
	c. Nonobvious.
	2. *Patent appeals*. Are heard by the *United States Court of Appeals for the Federal Circuit* in Washington, D.C.
	3. *Patent application*. An application containing a written description of the invention must be filed with the *United States Patent and Trademark Office* in Washington, D.C.
	4. *Term*. Patents are valid for 20 years.
	5. *Public use doctrine*. A patent may not be granted if the invention was used by the public for more than one year prior to the filing of the patent application.
	6. *Patent infringement*. The unauthorized use of another's patent. The patent holder may recover damages and other remedies against the infringer.

COPYRIGHTS, P. 114

Copyrights	Copyright law is exclusively federal law; there are no state copyright laws.

1. *Copyright.* Only tangible writings can be copyrighted. These include books, newspapers, addresses, musical compositions, motion pictures, works of art, architectural plans, greeting cards, photographs, sound recordings, computer programs, and mask works fixed in semiconductor chips.
2. *Requirements for copyright.* The writing must be the original work of the author.
3. *Copyright registration.* Copyright registration is permissive and voluntary. Published and unpublished works may be registered with the *United States Copyright Office* in Washington, D.C. Registration itself does not create the copyright.
4. *Term.* Copyrights are for the following terms.
   a. Individual registrant. Life of the author plus 50 years.
   b. Business registrant. Either (1) 100 years from the date of creation or (2) 75 years from the date of publication, whichever is less.
5. *Copyright infringement.* The copying of a substantial and material part of a copyrighted work without the holder's permission. The copyright holder may recover damages and other remedies against the infringer.
6. *Fair use doctrine.* Permits use of copyrighted material without the consent of the copyright holder for limited use (e.g., scholarly work, parody or satire, and brief quotation in news reports).

TRADEMARKS, P. 117

Trademarks and Service Marks	

1. *Mark.* Trade name, symbol, word, logo, design, or device that distinguishes the owner's goods or services. Marks are often referred to collectively as *trademarks.* Types of marks are as follows:
   a. *Trademark.* Identifies goods of a particular business
   b. *Service mark.* Identifies services of a particular business
   c. *Certification mark.* Certifies that goods or services are of a certain quality or origin
   d. *Collective mark.* Used by cooperatives, associations, and fraternal organizations.
2. *Requirement for a trademark.* The mark must either (a) be *distinctive* or (b) have acquired a *secondary meaning.* The mark must have been used in commerce or the holder intends to use the mark in commerce and actually does so within six months after registering the mark.
3. *Trademark registration.* Marks are registered with the *United States Patent and Trademark Office* in Washington, D.C.
4. *Term.* The original registration of a mark is valid for 10 years and can be renewed for an unlimited number of 10-year periods.
5. *Trademark infringement.* The unauthorized use of another's registered trademark. The mark holder may recover damages and other remedies from the infringer.
6. *Generic name.* A mark that becomes a common term for a product line or type of service loses its protection under federal trademark law.

CRITICAL LEGAL THINKING CASES

5.1 Palming Off Stiffel Company (Stiffel) designed a pole lamp (a vertical tube that can stand upright between the floor and ceiling of a room with several lamp fixtures along the outside of it). Pole lamps proved to be a decided commercial success. Soon after Stiffel brought them on the market, Sears, Roebuck & Company (Sears) put a substantially identical pole lamp on the market. The Sears retail price was about the same as Stiffel's wholesale price. Sears used its own name on the lamps it sold. Stiffel sued Sears for unfair competition, alleging that Sears had engaged in the tort of palming off. Is Sears liable for palming off? [*Sears, Roebuck & Co. v. Stiffel Co.*, 376 U.S. 225, 84 S.Ct. 1131, 12 L.Ed.2d 87 (1964)]

5.2 Defamation Dorchen Leidholdt is a New Yorker who is a vigorous opponent of pornography. She is a founding member of the organization Women Against Pornography, has given public speeches against pornography, and has debated opponents in the national media. Larry Flynt Publications is a California corporation that owns *Hustler* magazine (*Hustler*). *Hustler* regularly includes a monthly column in which some personage whose activities *Hustler* opposes is vilified in graphic terms. *Hustler's* June 1985 issue featured Leidholdt in the column. The article criticizes Leidholdt and her fellow antipornographers in scatological terms, employing such phrases as a "pus bloated walking sphincter," "sexually repressed," "hating men, hating sex, and hating themselves," and "this frustrated group of sexual fascists." The article was accompanied by a small photograph of Leidholdt's face superimposed over the buttocks of a bent-over naked man. Leidholdt sued *Hustler* for defamation. Who wins? [*Leidholdt v. Larry Flynt Publications*, 860 F.2d 890 (9th Cir. 1988)]

5.3 Right to Privacy On December 15, 1956, Marvin Briscoe and another man hijacked a truck in Danville, Kentucky. They were caught and convicted, and Briscoe served a term in prison. After release from prison, Briscoe established a life of respectability. In 1967, *Reader's Digest* published an article titled "The Big Business of Hijacking," stating that the looting of trucks had reached a rate of more than $100 million per year. Without indicating that the Briscoe hijacking had occurred 11 years earlier, the article contained the following sentence: "Typical of many beginners, Marvin Briscoe and another man stole a 'valuable-looking' truck in Danville, Ky., and then fought a gun battle with the local police, only to learn that they had hijacked four bowling pin spotters." After publication of the article, Briscoe brought an action for damages against Reader's Digest Association, Inc., for the intentional tort of invasion of the right of privacy. The complaint alleged that as a result of the *Reader's Digest* publication, the plaintiff's 11-year-old daughter, as well as the plaintiff's friends, learned of his criminal record for the first time, and thereafter scorned and abandoned him. Did Briscoe's complaint state a cause of action for invasion of the right to privacy? [*Briscoe v. Reader's Digest Association, Inc.*, 4 Cal.2d 529, 93 Cal.Rptr. 866 (Cal. 1971)]

5.4 Trade Secret CRA-MAR Video Center, Inc. (CRA-MAR), sells electronic equipment and videocassettes, as does its competitor, Koach's Sales Corporation (Koach's). Both CRA-MAR and Koach's purchased computers from Radio Shack. CRA-MAR used the computer to store customer lists, movie lists, personnel files, and financial records. Because the computer was new to CRA-MAR, Randall Youts, Radio Shack's salesman and programmer, agreed to modify CRA-MAR's programs when needed, including the customer list program. At one point, CRA-MAR decided to send a mailing to everyone on its customer list. The computer was unable to perform the function, so Youts took the disks containing the customer lists to the Radio Shack store to work on the program. Somehow Koach's came into possession of CRA-MAR's customer lists and did advertising mailings to the parties on the lists. When CRA-MAR discovered this fact, it sued Koach's, seeking an injunction against any further use of its customer lists. Is a customer list a trade secret that can be protected from misappropriation? [*Koach's Sales Corp. v. CRA-MAR Video Center, Inc.*, 478 N.E.2d 110 (Ind. App. 1985)]

5.5 Trade Secret Acuson Corporation (Acuson), a Delaware corporation, and Aloka Co., Ltd. (Aloka), a Japanese company, are competitors who both manufacture ultrasonic imaging equipment, a widely used medical diagnostic tool. The device uses sound waves to produce moving images of the inside of a patient's body, which a computer processes into an image that is displayed on a video monitor. Acuson's unit provides finer resolution than Aloka's unit. Both companies have sold many units to hospitals and medical centers. In November 1985, Aloka decided to purchase an Acuson unit. Aloka had another company make the actual purchase because it was concerned that Acuson would not sell the unit to a competitor. After the unit was shipped to Tokyo, Aloka's engineers partially dismantled the Acuson unit. They recorded their observations in notebooks. When Acuson discovered that Aloka had purchased one of its units, it sued Aloka, seeking an injunction and return of the unit. Is Aloka liable for misappropriation of a trade secret? [*Acuson Corp. v. Aloka Co., Ltd.*, 10 U.S.P.Q.2d 1814, 257 Cal.Rptr. 368 (Cal.App. 1989)]

5.6 Disparagement Robin Williams, a comedian, did a comedy performance at the Great American Music Hall, a San Francisco nightclub. During the performance he told a joke that contained the following words: "Whoa—White Wine. This is a little wine here. If it's not wine it's been through somebody already. Oh—There are White wines, there are Red wines, but why are there no Black wines like: Rege? It goes with fish, meat, any damn thing it wants to. I like my wine like I like my women, ready to pass out." Audio versions of the performance were distributed by Polygram Records, Inc. (Polygram), and a video version was shown on Home Box Office (HBO). David H. Rege, who sells and distributes assorted varieties of "Rege" brand wines from his San Francisco store, Rege Cellars, sued Williams, Polygram, and HBO for disparagement of his products and business (trade libel). Are the defendants liable for disparagement? [*Polygram Records, Inc. v. Superior Court*, 170 Cal.App.3d 543, 216 Cal.Rptr. 252 (Cal. App. 1985)]

5.7 Right to Publicity In the mid-1960s, the Beatles, a rock group from Liverpool, England, became one of the most famous and successful singing and recording groups in history. The Beatles produced and sold millions of records and albums. Two members of the group, John Lennon and Paul McCartney, wrote most of the music and lyrics for the Beatles. The two other members of the group were George Harrison and Ringo Starr. The Beatles disbanded as a group in the early 1970s and assigned their right to publicity to Apple Corps Limited, a corporation. In the mid-1970s, Steven Leber, David Krebs, and Beatlemania, Ltd., produced a multimedia stage production called *Beatlemania*. Imitators of the Beatles, wearing clothes and haircuts in the style of the Beatles from the 1960s, performed live on stage. During each 90-minute live performance, these imitators sang Beatles songs, with slides, movie clips, and pictures of events from the 1960s being shown on a screen in the background. The New York company of *Beatlemania* alone performed eight concerts a week for more than three years. In addition, two national touring companies and a road group performed *Beatlemania* concerts across the country. Millions of people saw *Beatlemania* in 7,000 live performances, which grossed more than $45 million. Apple Corps and the Beatles objected to these performances. Apple Corps brought this action against Leber, Krebs, and Beatlemania, Ltd., to recover damages. Did the defendants misappropriate the Beatles' (and Apple Corps') right to publicity? [*Apple Corps Ltd. v. Leber*, No. C 299149 (Los Angeles Superior Ct. Cal. 1986)]

5.8 Patent Infringement In 1968, Patent No. 3,397,928 (928) was issued to Edward M. Galle, an executive of Hughes Tool Company (Hughes). Galle assigned the patent, and other related patents, to Hughes. The patent was for an O-ring rubber seal that was used to seal bearings in the cone of a rock bit that rotated to drill holes in rocks. Rock bits were used to drill oil wells. Hughes did not license its 928 patent, which was a substantial commercial success. Smith International, Inc. (Smith), was Hughes's major competitor in this industry. Between 1971 and 1984, Smith made more than 460,000 rock bits (reaping sales of about $1.3 billion) that contained rubber seals that infringed on Hughes's patents. Hughes sued Smith for patent infringement and requested $1.2 billion in lost royalties and interest. Smith offered $20 million to $60 million in settlement. The case went to trial, and the court found Smith liable for patent infringement. How much in damages should Hughes be awarded? [*Smith Internat'l, Inc. v. Hughes Tool Co.*, 229 U.S.P.Q. 81 (Fed. Cir. 1986)]

5.9 Copyright When Spiro Agnew resigned as Vice President of the United States, President Richard M. Nixon appointed Gerald R. Ford as Vice President. In 1974, amid growing controversy surrounding the Watergate scandal, President Nixon resigned and Vice President Ford acceded to the presidency. As President, Ford pardoned Nixon for any wrongdoing regarding the Watergate affair and related matters. Ford served as President until he was defeated by Jimmy Carter in the 1976 presidential election. In 1973, Ford entered into a contract with Harper & Row, Publishers, Inc. (Harper & Row), to publish his memoirs in book form. The memoirs were to contain significant unpublished materials concerning the Watergate affair and Ford's personal reflections on that time in history. The publisher instituted security measures to protect the confidentiality of the manuscript. Several weeks before the book was to be released, an unidentified person secretly brought a copy of the manuscript to Victor Navasky, editor of *The Nation*, a weekly political commentary magazine. Navasky, knowing that his possession of the purloined manuscript was not authorized, produced a 2,250-word piece entitled "The Ford Memoirs" and published it in the April 3, 1979, issue of *The Nation*. Verbatim quotes of between 300 and 400 words from Ford's manuscript, including some of the most important parts, appeared in the article. Harper & Row sued the publishers of *The Nation* for copyright infringement. Who wins? [*Harper & Row, Publishers, Inc. v. Nation Enterprises*, 471 U.S. 539, 105 S.Ct. 2218, 85 L.Ed.2d 588 (1985)]

5.10 Copyright The Sony Corporation of America (Sony) manufactures videocassette recorders (VCRs) that can be used to videotape programs and films that are shown on television and cable stations. VCRs are used by consumers and others to videotape both copyrighted and uncopyrighted works. The primary use for VCRs is by consumers for "time shifting"—that is, taping a television program for viewing at a more convenient time. Universal City Studios, Inc. (Universal), and Walt Disney Productions (Disney) hold copyrights on a substantial number of motion-picture and audiovisual works that are shown on television and cable stations, which pay them a fee to do so. Some of Universal's and Disney's copyrighted works have been copied by consumers using Sony's VCRs. Universal and Disney sued Sony, seeking an injunction against the sale of VCRs by Sony. Is Sony liable for contributory copyright infringement? [*Sony Corp. of Am. v. Universal City Studios, Inc.*, 464 U.S. 417, 104 S.Ct. 774, 78 L.Ed.2d 574 (1984)]

5.11 Fair Use Doctrine In the dark days of 1977, when the City of New York teetered on the brink of bankruptcy, on the television screens of America there appeared an image of a top-hatted Broadway showgirl, backed by an advancing phalanx of dancers, chanting: "I-I-I-I-I-I Love New Yo-o-o-o-o-rk." As an ad campaign for an ailing city, it was an unparalleled success. Crucial to the campaign was a brief but exhilarating musical theme written by Steve Karmin called "I Love New York." Elsmere Music, Inc., owned the copyright to the music. The success of the campaign did not go unnoticed. On May 20, 1978, the popular weekly variety program "Saturday Night Live" (SNL) performed a comedy sketch over National Broadcasting Company's network (NBC). In the sketch the cast of SNL, portraying the mayor and members of the chamber of commerce of the biblical city of Sodom, were seen discussing Sodom's poor public image with out-of-towners and its effect on the tourist trade. In an attempt to recast Sodom's image in a more positive light, a new advertising campaign was revealed, with the highlight of the campaign being a song "I Love Sodom" sung a cappella by a chorus line of SNL regulars to the tune of "I Love New York." Elsmere Music did not see the humor of the sketch and sued NBC for copyright infringement. Who wins? [*Elsmere Music, Inc. v. National Broadcasting Co., Inc.*, 623 F.2d 252 (2d Cir. 1980)]

5.12 Trademark Clairol Incorporated manufactures and distributes hair tinting, dyeing, and coloring preparations. In 1956, Clairol embarked on an extensive advertising campaign to promote the sale of its "Miss Clairol" hair-color preparations that included advertisements in national magazines, on outdoor billboards, on radio and television, in mailing pieces, and on point-of-sale display materials to be used by retailers and beauty salons. The advertisements prominently displayed the slogans "Hair Color So Natural Only Her Hairdresser Knows for Sure" and "Does She or Doesn't She?" Clairol registered these slogans as trademarks. During the next decade Clairol spent more than $22 million for advertising materials resulting in more than a billion separate audio and visual impressions using the slogans. Roux Laboratories, Inc., a manufacturer of hair-coloring products and a competitor of Clairol's, filed an opposition to Clairol's registration of the slogans as trademarks. Do the slogans qualify for trademark protection? [*Roux Laboratories, Inc. v. Clairol Inc.*, 427 F.2d 823 (Cust.Pat.App. 1970)]

5.13 Trademark In 1967, two friends from California designed a sailing surfboard that combined the sports of sailing and surfing. Originally they called it a "sailboard." They filed for and were granted a patent on the sailboard, which was assigned to the company Windsurfing International, Inc. (WSI). In 1968, WSI's Seattle dealer coined the term *windsurfing.* WSI applied for and was granted trademarks for terms using the word *Windsurfer.* Between 1969 and 1976, WSI produced a particular type of board called the Windsurfer. At that time, WSI controlled more than 95 percent of the market. In the early years, there was no generic word for the sport or craft. To promote sales, WSI and its employees continually referred to the sport as windsurfing and individual sportspeople as windsurfers. WSI also engaged in an extensive advertising campaign using the terms *windsurfing* to describe the sport and *windsurfer* to describe individual sportspersons. People who participated in the sport, trade magazines, and the general public used the word *windsurfing* to describe the sport. In 1977, WSI started to police the use of its trademarked term. However, its efforts remained rather futile, as evidence showed that the general public used the terms *windsurfing* and *windsurfer* in a general, common sense to mean the sport and its participants. AMF Incorporated (AMF) seeks cancellation of

WSI's trademarks containing the term *Windsurfer.* Should the trademark be canceled? [*AMF Inc. v. Windsurfing Internat'l, Inc.*, 613 F.Supp. (D.C.N.Y. 1985)]

5.14 Trademark Since 1972, Mead Data Central, Inc. (Mead), has provided computer-assisted legal research services to lawyers and others under the trademark "LEXIS." LEXIS is based on *lex*, the Latin word for law, and *IS*, for information systems. Through extensive sales and advertising, Mead has made LEXIS a strong mark in the computerized legal research field, particularly among lawyers. However, LEXIS is recognized by only one percent of the general population, with almost half of this one percent being attorneys. Toyota Motor Corporation has for many years manufactured automobiles, which it markets in the United States through its subsidiary Toyota Motor Sales, U.S.A., Inc. (Toyota). On August 24, 1987, Toyota announced a new line of luxury automobiles to be called LEXUS. Toyota planned on spending almost $20 million for marketing and advertising LEXUS during the first nine months of 1989. Mead filed suit against Toyota, alleging that Toyota's use of the name LEXUS violated New York's antidilution statute and would cause injury to the business reputation of Mead and a dilution of the distinctive quality of the LEXIS mark. Who wins? [*Mead Data Central, Inc. v. Toyota Motor Sales, U.S.A., Inc.*, 875 F.2d 1026 (2d Cir. 1989)]

5.15 Generic Name The Miller Brewing Company (Miller), a national brewer, produces a reduced-calorie beer called "Miller Lite." Miller began selling beer under this name in the 1970s and has spent millions of dollars promoting the Miller Lite brand name on television, print, and other forms of advertising. Since July 11, 1980, Falstaff Brewing Corporation (Falstaff) has been brewing and distributing a reduced-calorie beer called "Falstaff Lite." Miller brought suit under the Lanham Trademark Act seeking an injunction to prevent Falstaff from using the term *Lite.* Is the term *Lite* a generic name that does not qualify for trademark protection? [*Miller Brewing Co. v. Falstaff Brewing Corp.*, 655 F.2d 5 (1st Cir. 1981)]

ETHICS CASES

5.16 Ethical Perspective Integrated Cash Management Services, Inc. (ICM) designs and develops computer software programs and systems for banks and corporate financial departments. ICM's computer programs and systems are not copyrighted, but they are secret. After Alfred Sims Newlin and Behrouz Vafa completed graduate school, they were employed by ICM as computer programmers. They worked at ICM for several years writing computer programs. In March 1987, they left ICM to work for Digital Transactions, Inc. (DTI). Before leaving ICM, however, they copied certain ICM files onto personal diskettes. Within two weeks of starting to work at DTI, they created prototype computer programs that operated in substantially the same manner as comparable ICM programs and were designed to compete directly with ICM's programs. ICM sued Newlin, Vafa, and DTI for misappropriation of trade secrets. Are the defendants liable? Did the defendants act ethi-

cally in this case? [*Integrated Cash Management Services, Inc. v. Digital Transactions, Inc.*, 920 F.2d 171 (2d Cir. 1990)]

5.17 Ethical Perspective John W. Carson (Carson) was the host and star of *The Tonight Show*, a well-known nightly television talk show broadcast by the National Broadcasting Company (NBC) until he retired in 1992. Carson also appears as an entertainer in theaters and night clubs around the country. From the time that he began hosting *The Tonight Show* in 1962, he had been introduced on the show each night with the phrase "Here's Johnny." The phrase "Here's Johnny" was generally associated with Carson by a substantial segment of the television viewing public. Carson had licensed the use of the phrase to a chain of restaurants, a line of toiletries, and other business ventures. Johnny Carson Apparel, Inc. (Apparel), founded in 1970, manufactures and markets men's clothing to retail stores. Carson, president of Apparel and owner of 20 percent of its stock, had licensed Apparel to use the phrase "Here's Johnny" on labels for clothing and in advertising campaigns. The phrase had never been registered by Carson or Apparel as a trademark or service mark.

Earl Broxton was the owner and president of Here's Johnny Portable Toilets, Inc. (Toilets), a Michigan corporation that engages in the business of renting and selling "Here's Johnny" portable toilets. Broxton was aware when he formed the corporation that the phrase "Here's Johnny" was the introductory slogan for Carson on *The Tonight Show*. Broxton indicated that he coupled the phrase "Here's Johnny" with a second one, "The World's Foremost Commodian," to make a good play on the phrase. Shortly after Toilets went into business in 1976, Carson and Apparel sued Toilets, seeking an injunction prohibiting the further use of the phrase "Here's Johnny" as a corporate name for or in connection with the sale or rental of its portable toilets. Who wins? Did Broxton act ethically by appropriating the phrase "Here's Johnny" to promote the sale and rental of portable toilets? [*Carson v. Here's Johnny Portable Toilets, Inc.*, 698 F.2d 831 (6th Cir. 1983)]

5.18 Ethical Perspective Master Distributors, Inc. (MDI) manufactures and sells "Blue Max," a blue leader splicing tape which is used to attach undeveloped film to a leader cord for photoprocessing through a minilab machine that develops the film and prints the photographs. Leader tape can be created in any color, and MDI dyed its Blue Max tape aquamarine blue. Blue Max is well known and enjoys a reputation as the industry standard. Both distributors and customers often order Blue Max by asking for "the blue tape" or simply for "blue." When MDI learned that Pakor, Inc. (Pakor) was manufacturing and selling a brand of aquamarine blue leader splicing tape, "Pakor Blue," it brought suit for trademark infringement. Did Pakor act morally in copying MDI's color for its splicing tape? Why do you think Pakor did this? Was there trademark infringement? [*Master Distributors, Inc. v. Pakor Corp., Inc.*, 956 F.2d 219 (8th Cir. 1993)]

CRITICAL LEGAL THINKING WRITING ASSIGNMENT

Read Case A.5 in the Case Appendix [*Feist Publications, Inc. v. Rural Telephone Service Company, Inc.*]. This case is excerpted from the U.S. Supreme Court opinion. Review and brief the case. In your brief, be sure to answer the following questions:

1. Who was the plaintiff? Who was the defendant?
2. What had the defendant done that caused the plaintiff to sue?
3. What is the issue in this case?
4. What was the decision of the U.S. Supreme Court?

NOTES

1 376 U.S. 254, 84 S.Ct. 710 (1964).
2 15 U.S.C. § 1125(a).
3 Article I, section 8, clause 8 of the U.S. Constitution provides:

   The Congress shall have the power . . . To promote the Progress of Science and useful Arts, by securing for limited Times to Authors and Inventors the exclusive Right to their respective Writings and Discoveries.

4 35 U.S.C. §§ 10 et seq.
5 *Diamond v. Chakrabarty*, 447 U.S. 303, 100 S.Ct. 2204, 65 L.Ed.2d 144 (1980). The U.S. Supreme Court held that genetically engineered bacterium that was capable of breaking up oil spills was patentable subject matter.
6 Article I, section 8, clause 8 of the U.S. Constitution.
7 17 U.S.C. §§ 101 et seq.
8 Prior to the 1976 Act, copyrights were valid for 28 years and could be renewed for another 28 years.
9 15 U.S.C. §§ 1114 et seq.
10 Senate Bill 1883, effective November 16, 1989.
11 Prior to the 1988 amendments, original registration of a mark was valid for 20 years and could be renewed for an unlimited number of 20-year periods.

CHAPTER 6

CRIMINAL LAW

AND BUSINESS CRIMES

Chapter Objectives

*After studying this chapter,
you should be able to*

1. Define and list the essential elements of a crime
2. Distinguish between felonies and misdemeanors
3. Describe criminal procedure, including arrest, indictment, arraignment, and the criminal trial
4. List and describe crimes against persons and property
5. Define major white-collar crimes, such as mail fraud, embezzlement, and bribery
6. Explain the elements necessary to find criminal fraud
7. List and describe computer crimes
8. Describe the scope of the Racketeer Influenced and Corrupt Organizations Act (RICO)
9. Explain the constitutional safeguards provided by the Fourth, Fifth, Sixth, and Eighth Amendments to the U.S. Constitution
10. Explain the scope of the Foreign Corrupt Practices Act

Chapter Contents

- Definition of a Crime
- Criminal Procedure
  Ethical Perspective Should Crime Pay?
- Crimes Affecting Business
  Case 6.1 *Evans v. United States (U.S.)*
- White-Collar Crimes
  Ethical Perspective Criminal Fraud: ZZZZ Best
  International Perspective The Foreign Corrupt Practices Act
  Case 6.2 *Russello v. United States (U.S.)*
- Computer Crime
  Contemporary Business Environment The Modern Washing Machine: Money Laundering
- Corporate Criminal Liability
  Case 6.3 *United States v. Hughes Aircraft Co., Inc. (9th Cir.)*
- Inchoate Crimes
- Constitutional Safeguards
  Contemporary Business Environment Warrantless Searches of Regulated Industries
  Business Checklist The Miranda Rights
- Working the Web
- Chapter Summary
- Critical Legal Thinking Cases
- Ethics Cases
- Critical Legal Thinking Writing Assignment

> *It is better that ten guilty persons escape, than that one innocent suffer.*
>
> Sir William Blackstone
> *Commentaries on the Laws of England* (1809)

criminal law   A crime is a violation of a statute for which the government imposes a punishment.

For members of society to peacefully coexist and commerce to flourish, people and their property must be protected from injury by other members of society. Federal, state, and local governments' **criminal laws** are intended to accomplish this by providing an incentive for persons to act reasonably in society and imposing penalties on persons who violate them.

The United States has one of the most advanced and humane criminal law systems in the world. It differs from many other criminal law systems in several respects. A person charged with a crime in the United States is presumed innocent until proven guilty. The burden of proof is on the government to prove that the accused is guilty of the crime charged. Further, the accused must be found guilty "beyond a reasonable doubt." Under many other legal systems, a person accused of a crime is presumed guilty unless the person can prove he or she is not. In the United States, a person charged with a crime is also provided with substantial constitutional safeguards during the criminal justice process.

NOTE

In the United States, a person accused of a crime is presumed innocent until proven guilty. The government has the burden of proving that the accused is guilty of the crime charged.

This chapter discusses the definition of a crime, criminal procedure, crimes affecting business, white-collar crime, inchoate crime, criminal penalties, and constitutional safeguards afforded criminal defendants.

DEFINITION OF A CRIME

crime   An act done by an individual in violation of those duties that he or she owes to society and for the breach of which the law provides that the wrongdoer shall make amends to the public.

A **crime** is defined as any act done by an individual in violation of those duties that he or she owes to society and for the breach of which the law provides that the wrongdoer shall make amends to the public. Many activities have been considered crimes through the ages, and other crimes are of recent origin.

Penal Codes and Regulatory Statutes

penal codes   A collection of criminal statutes.

Statutes are the primary source of criminal law. Most states have adopted comprehensive **penal codes** that define in detail the activities considered to be crimes within their jurisdiction and the penalties that will be imposed for their commission. A comprehensive federal criminal code defines federal crimes.[1] In addition, state and federal regulatory statutes often provide for criminal violations and penalties. The state and federal legislatures are continually adding to the list of crimes.

The penalty for committing a crime can consist of the imposition of a fine, imprisonment, or both, or some other form of punishment (e.g., probation or community service). Generally, imprisonment is imposed to (1) incapacitate the criminal so he or she will not harm others in society; (2) provide a means to rehabilitate the criminal; (3) deter others from similar conduct; and (4) inhibit personal retribution by the victim.

Parties to a Criminal Action

NOTE

The plaintiff in a criminal trial is the government.

In a criminal lawsuit, the government (not a private party) is the plaintiff. The government is represented by a lawyer called the *prosecutor*. The accused is the defendant. The accused is represented by a defense attorney. If the accused cannot afford a defense lawyer, the government will provide one free of charge.

Classification of Crimes

All crimes fall into one of the categories described in the following sections.

Felonies Felonies are the most serious kinds of crimes. Felonies include crimes that are *mala in se*, that is, inherently evil. Most crimes against the person (e.g., murder, rape, and the like) and certain business-related crimes (e.g., embezzlement and bribery) are felonies in most jurisdictions. Felonies are usually punishable by imprisonment. In some jurisdictions, certain felonies (e.g., first-degree murder) are punishable by death. Federal law[2] and some state laws require mandatory sentencing for specified crimes. Many statutes define different degrees of crimes (e.g., first-, second-, and third-degree murder). Each degree earns different penalties.

felony The most serious type of crime; inherently evil crime. Most crimes against the person and some business-related crimes are felonies.

Misdemeanors Misdemeanors are less serious than felonies. They are crimes *mala prohibita*; that is, they are not inherently evil but are prohibited by society. Many crimes against property, such as robbery, burglary, and violations of regulatory statutes, are included in this category. Misdemeanors carry lesser penalties than felonies. They are usually punishable by fine and/or imprisonment for one year or less.

misdemeanor A less serious crime; not inherently evil but prohibited by society. Many crimes against property are misdemeanors.

Violations Crimes such as traffic violations, jaywalking, and such are neither felonies nor misdemeanors. These crimes, which are called **violations**, are generally punishable by a fine. Occasionally, a few days of imprisonment are imposed.

violation A crime that is neither a felony nor a misdemeanor that is usually punishable by a fine.

Essential Elements of a Crime

The following two elements must be proven for a person to be found guilty of most crimes:

1. Criminal Act The defendant must have actually performed the prohibited act. The actual performance of the criminal act is called the **actus reus** (guilty act). Killing someone without legal justification is an example of actus reus. Sometimes, the omission of an act constitutes the requisite actus reus. For example, a crime has been committed if a taxpayer who is under a legal duty to file a tax return fails to do so. However, merely thinking about committing a crime is not a crime because no action has been taken.

actus reus "Guilty act"—the actual performance of the criminal act.

2. Criminal Intent To be found guilty of a crime, the accused must be found to have possessed the requisite state of mind (i.e., specific or general intent) when the act was performed. This is called the **mens rea** (evil intent). Specific intent is found where the accused purposefully, intentionally, or with knowledge commits a prohibited act. General intent is found where there is a showing of recklessness or a lesser degree of mental culpability. The individual criminal statutes state whether the crime requires a showing of specific or general intent. Juries may infer an accused's intent from the facts and circumstances of the case. There is no crime if the requisite mens rea cannot be proven. Thus, no crime is committed if one person accidentally injures another person.

mens rea "Evil intent"—the possession of the requisite state of mind to commit a prohibited act.

Some statutes impose criminal liability based on **strict or absolute liability**. That is, a finding of mens rea is not required. Criminal liability is imposed if the prohibited act is committed. Absolute liability is often imposed by regulatory statutes, such as environmental laws.

strict or absolute liability Standard for imposing criminal liability without a finding of mens rea (intent).

Criminal Acts as the Basis for Tort Actions

An injured party may bring a civil tort action against a wrongdoer who has caused the party injury during the commission of a criminal act. Civil lawsuits are separate from the government's criminal action against the wrongdoer. In many cases, a person injured by a criminal act will not sue the criminal to recover civil damages. This is because the criminal is often judgment proof—that is, the criminal does not have the money to pay a civil judgment.

NOTE
The same act may be the basis for both a criminal lawsuit and a civil lawsuit.

The most famous modern criminal trial is the trial of ex-football star O. J. Simpson for the alleged double murder of his wife, Nicole Brown, and her friend, Ronald Goldman. The criminal trial, which lasted almost one year in a Los Angeles courtroom, resulted in a verdict of acquittal after two hours of jury deliberation. However, in a subsequent civil action alleging wrongful death, the heirs of Brown and Goldman won a $35 million judgment against Simpson.

CONCEPT SUMMARY	CIVIL AND CRIMINAL LAW COMPARED	
Issue	**Civil Law**	**Criminal Law**
Party Who Brings the Action	The plaintiff	The government
Trial by Jury	Yes, except actions for equity	Yes
Burden of Proof	Preponderance of the evidence	Beyond a reasonable doubt
Jury Vote	Judgment for plaintiff requires specific jury vote (e.g., 9 of 12 jurors)	Conviction requires unanimous jury vote
Sanctions and Penalties	Monetary damages and equitable remedies (e.g., injunction, specific performance)	Imprisonment, capital punishment, fine, probation

CRIMINAL PROCEDURE

The court procedure for initiating and maintaining a criminal action is quite detailed. It includes both pretrial procedures and the actual trial.

Pretrial Criminal Procedure

Pretrial criminal procedure consists of several distinct stages, including arrest, indictment or information, arraignment, and plea bargaining.

arrest warrant   A document for a person's detainment based upon a showing of probable cause that the person committed the crime.

Arrest   Before the police can arrest a person for the commission of a crime, they usually must obtain an **arrest warrant** based upon a showing of "probable cause." *Probable cause* is defined as the substantial likelihood that the person either committed or is about to commit a crime.

If there is no time for the police to obtain a warrant (e.g., if the police arrive during the commission of a crime, when a person is fleeing from the scene of the crime, or when it is likely that evidence will be destroyed), the police may arrest the suspect without a warrant. Warrantless arrests are judged by the probable cause standard.

After a person is arrested, he or she is taken to the police station to be "booked." Booking is the administrative proceeding for recording the arrest, fingerprinting, and so on.

Indictment or Information   Accused persons must be formally charged with a crime before they can be brought to trial. This is usually done by the issuance of a grand jury indictment or a magistrate's information statement.

Evidence of serious crimes, such as murder, is usually presented to a **grand jury**. Most grand juries are composed of between 6 and 24 citizens who are charged with evaluating the evidence presented by the government. Grand jurors sit for a fixed period of time, such as one year. If the grand jury determines that there is sufficient evidence to hold the accused for trial, it issues an **indictment**. Note that the grand jury does not determine guilt. If an indictment is issued, the accused will be held for later trial.

For lesser crimes (e.g., burglary, shoplifting, and such), the accused will be brought before a **magistrate** (judge). A magistrate who finds that there is enough evidence to hold the accused for trial will issue an **information**.

The case against the accused is dismissed if neither an indictment nor an information is issued.

indictment   The charge of having committed a crime (usually a felony), based on the judgment of a grand jury.

information   The charge of having committed a crime (usually a misdemeanor), based on the judgment of a judge (magistrate).

Arraignment   If an indictment or information is issued, the accused is brought before a court for an **arraignment** proceeding during which the accused is (1) informed of the charges against him or her and (2) asked to enter a **plea**. The accused may plead guilty, not guilty, or *nolo contendere*. A plea of nolo contendere means that the accused agrees to the imposition of a penalty but does not admit guilt. A nolo contendere plea cannot be used as evidence of liability against the accused at a subsequent civil trial. Corporate defendants often enter this plea. The government has the option of accepting a nolo contendere plea or requiring the defendant to plead guilty or not guilty.

arraignment   A hearing during which the accused is brought before a court and is (1) informed of the charges against him or her and (2) asked to enter a plea.

plea   A statement the accused makes about the crime he or she has or has not committed. The accused may plead (1) guilty, (2) not guilty, or (3) nolo contendere.

Plea Bargaining   Sometimes the accused and the government enter into a plea bargaining agreement. The government engages in plea bargaining to save costs, avoid the risks of a trial, and prevent further overcrowding of the prisons. This type of arrangement allows the accused to admit to a lesser crime than charged. In return, the government agrees to impose a lesser penalty or sentence than might have been obtained had the case gone to trial.

The Criminal Trial

At a criminal trial, all jurors must unanimously agree before the accused is found guilty of the crime charged. If even one juror disagrees (i.e., has reasonable doubt) about the guilt of the accused, then the accused is not guilty of the crime charged. If all of the jurors agree that the accused did not commit the crime, then the accused is not guilty of the crime charged. After trial, the following rules apply:

- If the defendant is found guilty, he or she may appeal.
- If the defendant is found not guilty, the government cannot appeal.
- If the jury cannot come to a unanimous decision about the defendant's guilt, the jury is considered a **hung jury**. The government may choose to retry the case before a new judge and jury.

hung jury   A jury that cannot come to a unanimous decision about the defendant's guilt. The government may choose to retry the case.

ETHICAL PERSPECTIVE

Should Crime Pay?

To satisfy the public's seemingly endless thirst for tales of crime, publishers have eagerly paid large sums of money to acquire criminal defendants' rights to tell their sensational stories. Convicted murderers have reaped substan-

tial profits from selling the publication rights to their stories.

However, the public's distaste at rewarding crime fueled the passage by state legislatures of laws that prevented enterprising criminals from pocketing megabucks

from selling their stories. Many of these laws, which were passed by 40 states, were patterned on New York's statute. New York's law was enacted in 1977 while New York City's "Son of Sam" killer *continued* held the population hostage by continuing a highly publicized killing spree despite one of the most intense manhunts in the city's history.

To preclude the Son of Sam and other criminals from cashing in on crime, the New York law required publishers and movie companies to deposit any profits earned by criminals with the state's victim's compensation agency. If there was a conviction, the money went to the victim or the victim's heirs. If the accused was acquitted, the money was used to pay the defense attorney's bills and any remainder was paid to the defendant.

The enactment of these statutes quieted the public's out-

cry. However, they were challenged by criminals and publishers as an unconstitutional abridgment of free speech rights. In 1991, the U.S. Supreme Court agreed that the Son of Sam laws were unconstitutional. In a case brought by publisher Simon & Schuster, which had published a book by a convicted criminal, the Supreme Court held that New York's law violated the Freedom of Speech Clause of the U.S. Constitution.

Opponents of this decision argue that the potential of lucrative book and movie contracts will provide an incentive for people to commit heinous crimes. They also continue to argue that "crime

should not pay." Proponents of the U.S. Supreme Court's decision assert that even criminals should be accorded full free-speech rights guaranteed by the Constitution. [*Simon & Schuster, Inc. v. Members of the New York State Crime Victim's Board*, 112 S.Ct. 501, 116 L.Ed.2d 476 (1991)]

1. Should a person who commits a crime be permitted to profit from that crime?
2. Will the U.S. Supreme Court's decision lead to more or fewer crimes? Explain.
3. Is it ethical for publishers, movie companies, and other entertainment firms to pay criminals for their stories?

CRIMES AFFECTING BUSINESS

Many crimes are committed against business property. These crimes often involve the theft, misappropriation, or fraudulent taking of property. Many of the most important crimes against business property are discussed in the following sections.

Robbery

robbery Taking personal property from another person by use of fear or force.

At common law, **robbery** is defined as the taking of personal property from another person by the use of fear or force. For example, if a robber threatens to physically harm a storekeeper unless the victim surrenders the contents of the cash register, it is robbery. If a criminal pickpockets somebody's wallet, it is not robbery because there has been no use of force or fear. Robbery with a deadly weapon is generally considered aggravated robbery (or armed robbery) and carries a harsher penalty.

Burglary

burglary Taking personal property from another's home, office, commercial, or other type of building.

At common law, **burglary** is defined as "breaking and entering a dwelling at night" with the intent to commit a felony. Modern penal codes have broadened this definition to include daytime thefts and thefts from offices and commercial and other buildings. In addition, the "breaking-in" element has been abandoned by most modern definitions of burglary. Thus, unauthorized entering of a building through an unlocked door is sufficient. Aggravated burglary (or armed burglary) carries stiffer penalties.

Larceny

larceny Taking another's personal property other than from his or her person or building.

At common law, **larceny** is defined as the wrongful and fraudulent taking of another person's personal property. Most personal property—including tangible property, trade secrets, computer programs, and other business property—is subject to larceny. The stealing of automobiles and car stereos, pickpocketing, and such are larceny. Neither the use of force nor the entry of a building is required.

Some states distinguish between grand larceny and petit larceny. This distinction depends on the value of the property taken.

Theft

Some states have dropped the distinction among the crimes of robbery, burglary, and larceny. Instead, these states group these crimes under the general crime of **theft**. Most of these states distinguish between *grand theft* and *petit theft*. The distinction depends upon the value of the property taken.

Receiving Stolen Property

It is a crime for a person to (1) knowingly receive stolen property and (2) intend to deprive the rightful owner of that property. Knowledge and intent can be inferred from the circumstances. The stolen property can be any tangible property (e.g., personal property, money, negotiable instruments, stock certificates).

receiving stolen property A person (1) knowingly receives stolen property and (2) intends to deprive the rightful owner of that property.

Arson

At common law, **arson** is defined as the malicious or willful burning of the dwelling of another person. Modern penal codes expanded this definition to include the burning of all types of private, commercial, and public buildings. Thus, in most states, an owner who burns his own building to collect insurance proceeds can be found liable for arson. If arson is found, the insurance company does not have to pay proceeds of any insurance policy on the burned property.

arson Willfully or maliciously burning another's building.

Forgery

The crime of **forgery** occurs if a written document is fraudulently made or altered and that change affects the legal liability of another person. Counterfeiting, falsifying public records, and the material altering of legal documents are examples of forgery. One of the most common forms of forgery is the signing of another person's signature to a check or changing the amount of a check. Note that signing another person's signature without intent to defraud is not forgery. For instance, forgery has not been committed if one spouse signs the other spouse's payroll check for deposit in a joint checking or savings account.

forgery Fraudulently making or altering a written document that affects the legal liability of another person.

Extortion

The crime of **extortion** means the obtaining of property from another, with his or her consent, induced by wrongful use of actual or threatened force, violence, or fear. For example, extortion occurs when a person threatens to expose something about another person unless that other person gives money or property. The truth or falsity of the information is immaterial. Extortion of private persons is commonly referred to as **blackmail**. Extortion of public officials is called extortion "under color of official right."

In the following case, the U.S. Supreme Court addressed the issue of when extortion under color of official right occurs.

extortion Threat to expose something about another person unless that other person gives money or property. Often referred to as "blackmail."

CASE 6.1

Evans v. United States
112 S.Ct. 1881, 119 L.Ed.2d 57 (1992) United States Supreme Court

Facts John H. Evans, Jr., was an elected member of the Board of Commissioners of DeKalb County, Georgia. During 1986, the Federal Bureau of Investigation (FBI) investigated allegations of public corruption in the Atlanta area. An FBI agent posing as a real estate developer talked on the telephone and met with Evans on a number of occasions. In the *continued* conversations, the agent sought Evans's assistance in an effort to rezone a 25-acre tract of land for high-density residential use. The conversations were recorded on audio- or videotape. On July 25, 1986, the agent handed Evans $7,000 cash. Evans took the money. Evans was later indicted for the crime of extortion under color of official right in violation of the federal Hobbs Act [26 U.S.C. § 7206(1)]. He was convicted by a jury. Evans appealed, alleging that he could not be found guilty of extortion unless the government could prove that he had demanded the payment.

Issue Is an affirmative act of inducement by a public official required to support a conviction for extortion under the color of official right?

Decision No. To be guilty of the crime of extortion, the U.S. Supreme Court held that it is sufficient to prove that the official knows that he is being offered the payment in exchange for a specific exercise of his official powers. Affirmed.

Reason The jury found that Evans accepted the cash knowing that it was intended to ensure that he would vote in favor of the rezoning application and that he would try to persuade his fellow commissioners to do likewise. The Supreme Court accepted this finding, stating, "Although petitioner did not initiate the transaction, his acceptance of the money constituted an implicit promise to use his official position to serve the interests of the giver." Passive acceptance of a benefit by a public official is sufficient to form the basis of a Hobbs Act violation if the official knows that he or she is being offered the payment in exchange for a specific requested exercise of his or her official power.

CASE QUESTIONS

Critical Legal Thinking How does lobbying differ from illegal bribery and extortion?

Ethics Did Evans act ethically in accepting the payment?

Business Implication Do you think many public officials demand to be paid "under the table" for favorable decisions? Should businesses pay these payments?

Credit Card Crimes

"The magnitude of a crime is proportionate to the magnitude of the injustice which prompts it. Hence, the smallest crimes may be actually the greatest."
Aristotle
The Rhetoric,
Bk. 1, Ch. XIV

A substantial number of purchases in this country are made with credit cards. This poses a problem if someone steals and uses another person's credit cards. Many states have enacted statutes that make the misappropriation and use of credit cards a separate crime. In other states, credit card crimes are prosecuted under the forgery statute.

Bad Check Legislation

Many states have enacted **bad check legislation** that makes it a crime for a person to make, draw, or deliver a check at a time when that person knows that there are insufficient funds in the account to cover the amount of the check. Some states require proof that the accused intended to defraud the payee of the check.

WHITE-COLLAR CRIMES

white-collar crimes
Crimes usually involving cunning and deceit rather than physical force.

Certain types of crime are prone to be committed by businesspersons. These crimes are often referred to as **white-collar crimes**. These crimes usually involve cunning and deceit rather than physical force. Many of the most important white-collar crimes are discussed in the sections that follow.

Criminal Fraud

criminal fraud Obtaining title to property through deception or trickery.

Obtaining title to property through deception or trickery constitutes the crime of **false pretenses**. This crime is commonly referred to as **criminal fraud** or **deceit**.

CONSIDER THIS EXAMPLE: Bob Anderson, a stockbroker, promises Mary Greenberg, a prospective investor, that he will use any money she invests to purchase interests in oil wells. Based on this promise, Ms. Greenberg decides to make the investment. Mr. Anderson never intended to invest the money. Instead, he used the money for his personal needs. This is criminal fraud.

Mail and Wire Fraud Federal law prohibits the use of mails or wires (e.g., telegraph or telephone) to defraud another person. These crimes are called *mail fraud*[3] and *wire fraud*,[4] respectively. The government often prosecutes a suspect under these statutes if there is insufficient evidence to prove the real crime that the criminal was attempting to commit or did commit.

mail fraud The use of mail to defraud another person.

wire fraud The use of telephone or telegraph to defraud another person.

ETHICAL PERSPECTIVE

Criminal Fraud: ZZZZ Best

A southern California gym was the unlikely setting for what eventually became one of the largest, and most bizarre, criminal frauds in history. There, Barry Minkow, at 16, grew to admire Tom Padgett, a Vietnam vet who could bench-press more than 300 pounds. Padgett, who was bored with his job as an insurance adjuster, was itching for something more exciting and lucrative to do. Minkow convinced Padgett to get a bank loan and lend him $4,500 to start a carpet cleaning company called "ZZZZ Best." With the money, Minkow started with a couple of vans and began charging $39.95 a pop to clean two rooms.

Not satisfied with making money from cleaning carpets, Minkow and Padgett decided to run a scam and instead take investors, bankers, and accountants to the cleaners. Minkow started "cooking the books" by recording fake carpet cleaning contracts on ZZZZ Best's financial statements. Most of this work was listed as restoring fire- and flood-damaged buildings. This would make it seem that ZZZZ Best was extremely successful and thereby enable the company to get bank loans and sell stock to the public.

There was only one problem: how to fool the auditors who had to certify ZZZZ Best's financial statements. Many of the false contracts listed on ZZZZ Best's books were not questioned by the auditors. Several were, however. But Minkow and Padgett devised schemes to hide the fraud from the accountants.

In 1986, Larry Gray, an accountant for Ernst & Whinney, noticed that one of the contracts listed by ZZZZ Best on its financial statements was a $7 million job to restore a damaged building in Sacramento. The accounting firm was auditing the financial statements because ZZZZ Best intended to make a public offering of stock. To verify the contract, Gray asked to see the job site. There was only one problem: There was no job site because the contract was phony.

So, Minkow's two henchmen, Padgett and Mark Roddy, went into action and flew to Sacramento. Once there, they discovered that there was only one building big enough to have suffered $7 million worth of fire damage—the 300 Capital Mall building. Padgett and Roddy told the building manager that they represented investors who were interested in leasing a considerable amount of space in the building, but that the investors were so busy they could see the building only on the weekend. The building manager gave them the keys.

On Sunday morning, November 23, 1986, Padgett and Roddy posted ZZZZ Best signs wherever they could in the building. Before leaving Los Angeles, Gray signed a document promising not to disclose the location of the site to anyone because it was "secret." Gray flew to Sacramento and arrived at the building around 1:00 P.M. He was shown six floors of the building, and later wrote in his file, "ZZZZ Best's work is substantially complete and has passed final inspection. The tour was beneficial in gaining insight as to the scope of the damage that had occurred and the type of work that the company can do." Minkow and Padgett ran similar routs whenever the accountants wanted to see other buildings, which were the subject of fake carpet-restoration contracts.

ZZZZ Best's financial statements were certified and the stock offering was made, which raised $11.5 million for the company. In addition, ZZZZ Best was given a $7-million line of credit by Union Bank and other bank loans. All the action surrounding ZZZZ Best sent its stock soaring. By the time he was 21, Minkow's ZZZZ Best reported annual sales of $50 million and had a stock value of $200 million in the over-the-counter market. Minkow began negotiations to buy the Seattle baseball team. Things were looking good, really good, or so it seemed.

Eventually, like all Ponzi schemes, ZZZZ Best collapsed. Acting on a tip that ZZZZ Best had invented accounts, Ernst & Whinney hired a team of investigators to check it out. The authorities *continued* were not far behind, as the fraud unraveled.

Criminal charges were brought against Minkow, Padgett, and other associates with ZZZZ Best. Minkow, Padgett, and 10 other associates were convicted of charges ranging from criminal fraud to conspiracy. Minkow, who claimed throughout the trial that mobsters had forced him to perpetrate the scam, was sentenced to 25 years in prison and forced to pay $25 million in restitution. Padgett got 8 years. The duo also faces a panoply of civil suits from bamboozled investors and lenders who lost more than $100 million. Ernst & Whinney and its insurance carriers paid millions of dollars to settle lawsuits arising from the ZZZZ Best audit.

1. Did Minkow deserve his sentence?
2. Did the accountants act ethically in this case?

Embezzlement

embezzlement The fraudulent conversion of property by a person to whom that property was entrusted.

Although it is unknown at common law, the crime of **embezzlement** is now a statutory crime. Embezzlement is the fraudulent conversion of property by a person to whom that property was entrusted. Typically, embezzlement is committed by an employer's employees, agents, or representatives (e.g., accountants, lawyers, trust officers, treasurers). Embezzlers often try to cover their tracks by preparing false books, records, or entries.

The key element here is that the stolen property was entrusted to the embezzler. This differs from robbery, burglary, and larceny, where property is taken by someone not entrusted with the property.

BUSINESS BRIEF

The property must have been entrusted to the defendant for the crime of embezzlement to be found.

CONSIDER THIS EXAMPLE: Embezzlement has been committed if a bank teller absconds with money that was deposited by depositors. The employer (the bank) entrusted the teller to take deposits from its customers.

Bribery

bribery When one person gives another person money, property, favors, or anything else of value for a favor in return. Often referred to as a paying "kickback."

Bribery is one of the most prevalent forms of white-collar crime. A bribe can be money, property, favors, or anything else of value. The crime of commercial bribery prohibits the payment of bribes to private persons and businesses. This type of bribe is often referred to as a **kickback** or **payoff**. Intent is a necessary element of this crime. The offeror of a bribe commits the crime of bribery when the bribe is tendered. The offeree is guilty of the crime of bribery when he or she accepts the bribe. The offeror can be found liable for the crime of bribery even if the person to whom the bribe is offered rejects the bribe.

BUSINESS BRIEF

Bribery is probably the most prevalent form of business crime.

CONSIDER THIS EXAMPLE: Harriet Landers is the purchasing agent for the ABC Corporation and is in charge of purchasing equipment to be used by the corporation. Neal Brown, the sales representative of a company that makes equipment that can be used by the ABC Corporation, offers to pay her a 10 percent kickback if she buys equipment from him. She accepts the bribe and orders the equipment. Both parties are guilty of bribery.

At common law, the crime of bribery is defined as the giving or receiving of anything of value in corrupt payment for an "official act" by a public official. Public officials include legislators, judges, jurors, witnesses at trial, administrative agency personnel, and other government officials. Modern penal codes also make it a crime to bribe public officials. For example, a developer who is constructing an apartment building cannot pay the building inspector to overlook a building code violation.

"There can be no equal justice where the kind of trial a man gets depends on the amount of money he has."

J. Black
Griffin v. Illinois
(1956)

CONSIDER THIS EXAMPLE: In 1995, two former top executives of American Honda Motor Co. were found guilty of criminal conspiracy for taking bribes from automobile dealers in exchange for allocating Honda cars that were in high demand to these dealers. This was the largest criminal bribery case in U.S. history, involving bribes of cash and goods worth $15 million.

INTERNATIONAL PERSPECTIVE

The Foreign Corrupt Practices Act

During the 1970s, several scandals were uncovered in which American companies were found to have bribed foreign government officials to obtain lucrative contracts. Congressional investigations discovered that the making of such payments—or bribes—was pervasive in conducting international business. To prevent American companies from engaging in this type of conduct, the U.S. Congress enacted the **Foreign Corrupt Practices Act of 1977 (FCPA)** [15 U.S.C. § 78m]. Congress amended the FCPA as part of the Omnibus Trade and Competitiveness Act of 1988.

The FCPA attacks the problem in two ways. First, it requires firms to keep accurate books and records of all foreign transactions and install internal accounting controls to ensure transactions and payments are authorized. Inadvertent or technical errors in maintaining books and records do not violate the FCPA.

Second, the FCPA makes it illegal for American companies, or their officers, directors, agents, or employees, to bribe a foreign official, a foreign political party official, or a candidate for foreign political office. A bribe is illegal only where it is meant to influence the awarding of new business or the retention of a continuing business activity. Payments to secure ministerial, clerical, or routine government action (such as scheduling inspections, signing customs documents, unloading and loading of cargo, and the like) do not violate the FCPA.

The FCPA imposes criminal liability only in circumstances in which a person knowingly fails to maintain the proper system of accounting, pays the illegal bribe himself, or supplies a payment to a third party or agent knowing that it will be used as a bribe. A firm can be fined up to $2 million and an individual can be fined up to $100,000 and imprisoned for up to five years for violations of the FCPA.

In 1995, the Lockheed Corporation pleaded guilty to a criminal charge of violating the Foreign Corrupt Practices Act by paying a member of the Egyptian Parliament a $1 million bribe to gain her influence in helping Lockheed sell three transport planes to Egypt. Lockheed was fined for the violation.

The 1988 amendments created two defenses. One excuses a firm or person charged with bribery under the FCPA if the firm or person can show that the payment was lawful under the written laws of that country. The other allows a defendant to show that a payment was a reasonable and bona fide expenditure related to the furtherance or execution of a contract.

Some people argue that the FCPA is too soft and permits American firms to engage in the payment of bribes internationally that would otherwise be illegal in this country. Others argue that the FCPA is difficult to interpret and apply and that American companies are placed at a disadvantage in international markets where commercial bribery is commonplace and firms from other countries are not hindered by laws similar to the FCPA.

Racketeer Influenced and Corrupt Organizations Act (RICO)

Organized crime has a pervasive influence on many parts of the American economy. In 1980, Congress enacted the Organized Crime Control Act. The **Racketeer Influenced and Corrupt Organizations Act (RICO)** is part of this act.[5] Originally, RICO was intended to apply only to organized crime. However, the broad language of the RICO statute has been used against nonorganized crime defendants as well. RICO, which provides for both criminal and civil penalties, is one of the most important laws affecting business today. (For a discussion of civil RICO, see chapter 4.)

RICO makes it a federal crime to acquire or maintain an interest in, use income from, or conduct or participate in the affairs of an "enterprise" through a "pattern" of "racketeering activity." An "enterprise" is defined as a corporation, a partnership, a sole proprietorship, another business or organization, and the government. Racketeering activity consists of a number of specifically enumerated federal and state crimes, including such activities as gambling, arson, robbery, counterfeiting, dealing in narcotics, and such.[6] Business-related crimes, such as bribery, embezzlement, mail fraud, wire fraud, securities fraud, and the like are also considered racketeering.

Racketeer Influenced and Corrupt Organizations Act (RICO) An act that provides for both criminal and civil penalties for "racketeering."

NOTE
In 1992, mob boss John Gotti was sentenced to life in prison after being convicted of criminal racketeering and murder charges.

BUSINESS BRIEF
Property or business interests acquired by funds obtained by RICO violations are forfeitable to the government.

To prove a pattern of racketeering, at least two predicate acts must be committed by the defendant within a 10-year period. For example, committing two different frauds would be considered a pattern. Individual defendants found criminally liable for RICO violations can be fined up to $25,000 per violation, imprisoned for up to 20 years, or both. In addition, RICO provides for the forfeiture of any property or business interests (even interests in a legitimate business) that were gained because of RICO violations. This provision allows the government to recover investments made with monies derived from racketeering activities. The government may also seek civil penalties for RICO violations. These include injunctions, orders of dissolution, reorganization of businesses, and the divestiture of the defendant's interest in an enterprise.

Whether a criminal RICO violation occurred is the issue addressed in the following case.

CASE 6.2

Russello v. United States
464 U.S. 16, 104 S.Ct. 296, 78 L.Ed.2d 17 (1983) United States Supreme Court

Facts Joseph C. Russello was a member of an arson ring that operated in Florida. The group consisted of property owners, arsonists, and insurance adjusters. A member of the group would buy a building, the arsonists would burn it, and the insurance adjusters would help the owner recover inflated insurance awards. Members of the group would share in the proceeds. The ring burned numerous buildings between July 1973 and April 1976. Russello owned the Capital Professional Building in Tampa. He arranged for the ring's arsonists to burn the building, which they did. Russello submitted an inflated claim to the insurance company. Joseph Carter, another member of the ring, was the adjuster on the insurance claim and helped Russello obtain the highest payment possible—$340,043. From the proceeds, Carter was paid $30,000 for his assistance. Russello took the remaining money out of the illegitimate enterprise and invested in other things. The federal government brought criminal RICO charges against Russello. The U.S. court of appeals affirmed. Russello appealed to the U.S. Supreme Court, which granted certiorari.

Issue Are the insurance proceeds obtained by Russello subject to forfeiture under the criminal RICO statute?

Decision Yes. The U.S. Supreme Court held that the insurance proceeds obtained by Russello were an "interest" that was gained because of a RICO violation. Affirmed.

Reason The criminal RICO statute provides that a person convicted under the statute shall forfeit to the United States "any interest he has acquired or maintained" because of the violation. The Supreme Court held that the term *interest* encompassed the insurance proceeds received by Russello. Russello argued that after the proceeds were invested outside the criminal enterprise, they were no longer subject to forfeiture under the RICO statute. In rejecting this argument, the Court stated, "Construing RICO to reach only interests in an illegitimate enterprise would blunt the effectiveness of the forfeiture provision in combating illegitimate enterprises, and would mean that whole areas of organized criminal activity would be placed beyond the reach of the statute." The Court concluded, "Congress emphasized the need to fashion new remedies in order to achieve its far-reaching objectives. From all this, the intent to authorize forfeiture of racketeering profits seems obvious."

CASE QUESTIONS

Critical Legal Thinking Is RICO needed to help attack the criminal activities of organized crime in this country? Do you think RICO is effective?

Ethics Is it ethical to burn buildings to collect insurance proceeds? Is it ethical for normal insureds to inflate insurance claims?

Business Implication Are legitimate businesses ever taken over by organized crime? Will RICO help prevent this?

COMPUTER CRIME

Many business transactions are initiated, processed, and completed through the use of computers. Computers can keep a company's financial records; issue its payroll checks; and store its trade secrets, engineering drawings, databases, and other proprietary information. The potential for the misuse of computers is enormous. Federal and state governments have enacted several laws that address computer crimes. The most important computer crime laws are discussed in the sections that follow.

"Law cannot persuade, where it cannot punish."
Thomas Fuller
Gnomolgia (1732)

Counterfeit Access Device and Computer Fraud and Abuse Act

The **Counterfeit Access Device and Computer Fraud and Abuse Act of 1984** makes it a federal crime to access a computer knowingly to obtain (1) restricted federal government information, (2) financial records of financial institutions, and (3) consumer reports of consumer reporting agencies. The act also makes it a crime to use counterfeit or unauthorized access devices, such as cards or code numbers, to obtain things of value or transfer funds or to traffic in such devices.[7]

Electronic Funds Transfer Act

This act regulates the payment and deposits of funds using electronic funds transfers, such as direct deposit of payroll and Social Security checks in financial institutions, transactions using automated teller machines (ATMs), and such. The act makes it a federal crime to use, furnish, sell, or transport a counterfeit, stolen, lost, or fraudulently obtained ATM card, code number, or other device used to conduct electronic funds transfers. The act imposes criminal penalties of up to 10 years' imprisonment and fines up to $10,000.[8]

State Laws

Often, larceny statutes cover only the theft of tangible property. Because computer software, programs, and data are intangible property, they are not covered by some existing state criminal statutes. To compensate for this, many states have either modernized existing laws to include computer crime or amended existing penal codes to make certain abuses of computers a criminal offense. Computer trespass, the unauthorized use of computers, tampering with computers, and the unauthorized duplication of computer-related materials are usually forbidden by these acts.[9]

Our growing reliance on computers has made us more aware of the risks associated with losing the data stored on them. As a result, it is likely that the safety of the nation's ever-expanding computer networks will be legislated even more in the future.

Counterfeit Access Device and Computer Fraud and Abuse Act of 1984 Makes it a federal crime to access a computer knowingly to obtain (1) restricted federal government information, (2) financial records of financial institutions, and (3) consumer reports of consumer reporting agencies.

Electronic Funds Transfer Act Makes it a federal crime to use, furnish, sell, or transport a counterfeit, stolen, lost, or fraudulently obtained ATM card, code number, or other device used to conduct electronic funds transfers.

BUSINESS BRIEF

The use of computers to commit business crimes is increasing. Businesses must implement safeguards to prevent computer crimes.

CONTEMPORARY BUSINESS ENVIRONMENT

The Modern Washing Machine: Money Laundering

Concerned about how the use of cash promotes and facilitates criminal activity, Congress enacted two types of laws: (1) currency reporting statutes and (2) money laundering statutes. These laws are designed to uncover narcotics trafficking, illegal business activity, and violations of tax laws.

Currency Reporting
Federal currency reporting laws require financial institutions and other entities (e.g., retailers, car and boat dealers, antique dealers, jewelers, travel agencies, real estate brokers, and other businesses) to file a **Currency Transaction Report (CTR)** with the
continued

Internal Revenue Service (IRS) reporting the following:

- The receipt in a single transaction or a series of related transactions of cash in an amount greater than $10,000. "Cash" is not limited to currency, but includes cashier's checks, bank drafts, traveler's checks, and money orders (but not ordinary checks) [26 U.S.C. § 60501].
- Suspected criminal activity by bank customers involving a financial transaction of $1,000 or more in funds [12 C.F.R. § 21.11(b)(3)].

The law also stipulates that it is a crime to structure or assist in structuring any transaction for the purpose of evading these reporting requirements [31 U.S.C. § 5324]. Financial institutions and entities may be fined for negligent violations of the currency reporting requirements. A $50,000 fine may be levied for a pattern of negligent violations. Willful failure to file reports may subject the violator to civil money penalties, charges of aiding and abetting the criminal activity, and prosecution for violating the money laundering statutes.

Money Laundering

The term *money laundering* is used to refer to the process by which criminals convert tainted proceeds into apparently legitimate funds or property. It applies equally to an international wire transfer of hundreds of millions of dollars in drug proceeds and the purchase of an automobile with funds robbed from a bank.

Money laundering is a federal crime. The following activities are among those that were criminalized by the Money Laundering Control Act:

- Knowingly engaging in a financial transaction involving the proceeds of some form of specified unlawful activity. Transactions covered include the sale of real property, personal property, intangible assets, and anything of value [18 U.S.C. § 1956].
- Knowingly engaging in a monetary transaction by, through, or to a financial institution involving property of a value greater than $10,000, which is derived from specified unlawful activity. Money transaction is defined as a deposit, withdrawal, transfer between accounts, and use of a monetary instrument [18 U.S.C. § 1957].

"Specified unlawful activity" includes narcotics activities and virtually any white-collar crime.

Money laundering statutes have been used to go after entities and persons involved in illegal check-cashing schemes, bribery, insurance fraud, Medicaid fraud, bankruptcy fraud, bank fraud, fraudulent transfer of property, criminal conspiracy, environmental crime, and other types of illegal activities.

Conviction for money laundering carries stiff penalties. Persons can be fined up to $500,000 or twice the value of the property involved, whichever is greater, and sentenced to up to 20 years in federal prison. In addition, violation subjects the defendant to provisions that mandate forfeiture to the government of any property involved in or traceable to the offense [18 U.S.C. §§ 981–982]. Any financial institution convicted of money laundering can have its charter revoked or its insurance of deposit accounts terminated.

To avoid running afoul of these increasingly complex statutes, banks and businesses must develop and implement policies and procedures to detect criminal activity and report money laundering by customers to the federal government.

CORPORATE CRIMINAL LIABILITY

BUSINESS BRIEF
Corporations may be held criminally liable for actions of their officers, employees, or agents.

NOTE
Corporate directors, officers, and employees are personally liable for the crimes they commit while acting on behalf of the corporation.

A corporation is a fictitious legal person that is granted legal existence by the state only after certain requirements are met. A corporation cannot act on its own behalf. Instead, it must act through agents such as managers, representatives, and employees.

The question of whether a corporation can be held criminally liable has intrigued legal scholars for some time. Originally, under the common law, it was generally held that corporations lacked the criminal mind (mens rea) to be held criminally liable. Modern courts, however, are more pragmatic. These courts have held that corporations are criminally liable for the acts of their managers, agents, and employees. In any event, because corporations cannot be put in prison, they are usually sanctioned with fines, loss of a license or franchise, and the like.

Corporate directors, officers, and employees are individually liable for crimes that they personally commit, whether for personal benefit or on behalf of the corporation. In addition, under certain circumstances a corporate manager can be held criminally liable for the criminal activities of his or her subordinates. To be held criminally liable, the manager must have failed to supervise the subordinate appropriately. This is an evolving area of the law.

In the following case, the court held that a corporation was guilty of criminal conspiracy.

CASE 6.3

United States v. Hughes Aircraft Co., Inc.
20 F.3d 974 (1994) United States Court of Appeals, Ninth Circuit

Facts Hughes Aircraft Co., Inc. (Hughes), an aircraft manufacturer, contracted with the United States government to manufacture microelectronic circuits, known as "hybrids," which are used as components in weapons defense systems. The contract required Hughes to perform tests on each hybrid. A Hughes employee, Donald LaRue, was the supervisor responsible for ensuring the accuracy of the hybrid testing process. LaRue falsely reported that all tests had been performed and that each hybrid had passed the test. When LaRue's subordinates called his actions to the attention of LaRue's supervisors, they did nothing about it. Instead, they responded that LaRue's decisions were his own and were not to be questioned. The United States sued Hughes and LaRue, charging criminal conspiracy to defraud the government. At trial, LaRue was acquitted, but Hughes was convicted of criminal conspiracy and fined $3.5 million. Hughes appealed its conviction, asserting that it should not be convicted of criminal conspiracy if its alleged co-conspirator, LaRue, was acquitted.

Issue Should Hughes be acquitted as a matter of law because the same jury that convicted Hughes acquitted its alleged co-conspirator of the charge of criminal conspiracy?

Decision No. The court of appeals held that Hughes may be found guilty of criminal conspiracy even though its co-conspirator had been acquitted of the same crime. Affirmed.

Reason The court of appeals, as a matter of law, held that the inconsistency of the jury verdicts of two defendants charged with criminal conspiracy does not mean that the convicted defendant should also be acquitted. The court noted that the jury may have been more lenient with defendant LaRue, an individual, than they were with Hughes, the corporate defendant. Moreover, the court stated that the jury could have found Hughes guilty of the required act of conspiracy based on evidence provided at trial by other Hughes employees that were called as witnesses.

CASE QUESTIONS

Critical Legal Thinking What are the elements of criminal conspiracy? Do you agree with the decision of the court of appeals? Why or why not?

Ethics Did LaRue act ethically in falsifying the test data? Did Hughes act ethically in ignoring the information about the fraud provided by LaRue's subordinates?

Business Implication Do you think that the corporate defendant, Hughes, was treated more harshly than the individual defendant, LaRue? Explain.

INCHOATE CRIMES

In addition to the substantive crimes previously discussed, a person can be held criminally liable for committing an inchoate crime. Inchoate crimes include incomplete crimes and crimes committed by nonparticipants. The most important inchoate crimes are discussed in the following sections.

Criminal Conspiracy

A **criminal conspiracy** occurs when two or more persons enter into an agreement to commit a crime. To be liable for a criminal conspiracy, an overt act must be taken to further the crime. The crime itself does not have to be committed, however.

criminal conspiracy
When two or more persons enter into an agreement to commit a crime and an overt act is taken to further the crime.

CONSIDER THIS EXAMPLE: Two securities brokers agree over the telephone to commit a securities fraud. They also obtain a list of potential victims and prepare false financial statements necessary for the fraud. Because they entered into an agreement to commit a crime and took overt action, the brokers are guilty of the crime of criminal conspiracy even if they never carry out the securities fraud. The government usually brings criminal conspiracy charges if (1) the defendants have been thwarted in their efforts to commit the substantive crime or (2) there is insufficient evidence to prove the substantive crime.

Attempt to Commit a Crime

attempt to commit a crime
When a crime is attempted but not completed.

The **attempt to commit a crime** is itself a crime. For example, suppose a person wants to kill his neighbor. He shoots at him but misses. The perpetrator is not liable for the crime of murder. He is, however, liable for the crime of attempted murder.

Aiding and Abetting the Commission of a Crime

aiding and abetting the commission of a crime
Rendering support, assistance, or encouragement to the commission of a crime; harboring a criminal after he or she has committed a crime.

Sometimes persons assist others in the commission of a crime. The act of **aiding and abetting the commission of a crime** is a crime. This concept, which is very broad, includes rendering support, assistance, or encouragement to the commission of a crime. Harboring a criminal after he or she has committed a crime is considered aiding and abetting.

CONSTITUTIONAL SAFEGUARDS

"The criminal is to go free because the constable has blundered."
J. Cardozo
People v. Defore
(1926)

When our forefathers drafted the U.S. Constitution, they included provisions that protect persons from unreasonable government intrusion and provide safeguards for those accused of crimes. Although these safeguards originally applied only to federal cases, the Fourteenth Amendment's Due Process Clause made them applicable to state criminal law cases as well. The most important of these constitutional safeguards are discussed in the following sections.

Fourth Amendment Protection against Unreasonable Searches and Seizures

unreasonable search and seizure   Any search and seizure by the government that violates the Fourth Amendment.

search warrant   A warrant issued by a court that authorizes the police to search a designated place for specified contraband, articles, items, or documents. The search warrant must be based on probable cause.

exclusionary rule   A rule that says evidence obtained from an unreasonable search and seizure can generally be prohibited from introduction at a trial or administrative proceeding against the person searched.

The Fourth Amendment to the U.S. Constitution protects persons and corporations from overzealous investigative activities by the government. It protects the rights of the people from **unreasonable search and seizure** by the government. It permits people to be secure in their persons, houses, papers, and effects.

"Reasonable" search and seizure by the government is lawful. **Search warrants** based on probable cause are necessary in most cases. Such warrants specifically state the place and scope of the authorized search. General searches beyond the specified area are forbidden. Warrantless searches are permitted (1) incident to arrest, (2) where evidence is in "plain view," or (3) where it is likely that evidence will be destroyed. Warrantless searches are also judged by the probable cause standard.

Certain hazardous and regulated industries—such as sellers of firearms and liquor, coal miners, automobile junkyards, and the like—are subject to warrantless searches by government authorities.

Evidence obtained from an unreasonable search and seizure is considered tainted evidence ("fruit of a tainted tree"). Under the **exclusionary rule**, such evidence generally can be prohibited from introduction at a trial or administrative proceeding against the person searched. However, this evidence is freely admissible against other persons. The U.S. Supreme Court created a good faith exception to the exclusionary rule.[10] This exception allows evidence otherwise obtained illegally to be introduced as evidence against the accused if the police officers who conducted the unreasonable search reasonably believed that they were acting pursuant to a lawful search warrant.

CONTEMPORARY BUSINESS ENVIRONMENT

Warrantless Searches of Regulated Industries

Generally, the government does not have the right to search business premises without a search warrant. Certain hazardous and regulated industries—such as sellers of firearms and liquor, coal mines, and the like—are subject to warrantless searches if proper statutory procedures are met. Consider the following case.

Joseph Burger is the owner of a junkyard in Brooklyn, New York. His business consists, in part, of dismantling automobiles and selling their parts. The state of New York enacted a statute that requires automobile junkyards to keep certain records. The statute authorizes warrantless searches of vehicle dismantlers and automobile junkyards without prior notice. At approximately noon on November 17, 1982, five plainclothes officers of the Auto Crimes Division of the New York City Police Department entered Burger's junkyard to conduct a surprise inspection. Burger did not have either a license to conduct the business or records of the automobiles and vehicle parts on his premises as required by state law. After conducting an inspection of the premises, the officers determined that Burger was in possession of stolen

vehicles and parts. He was arrested and charged with criminal possession of stolen property. Burger moved to suppress the evidence. The New York Supreme Court and appellate division held the search to be constitutional. When the New York court of appeals reversed, New York appealed.

The U.S. Supreme Court held that the New York statute that authorizes warrantless searches of vehicle dismantling businesses and automobile junkyards does not constitute an unreasonable search in violation of the Fourth Amendment to the U.S. Constitution. The Supreme Court reversed the judgment of the New York court of appeals and remanded the case for further proceedings consistent with its decision.

The U.S. Supreme Court stated that the Fourth Amendment's prohibition on unreasonable searches and seizures is applicable to commercial premises as well as homes, but that such expectation of privacy is attenuated in commercial premises employed in "closely regulated" industries. The Court held that a warrantless inspection of such premises is deemed reasonable if the following three criteria are met: (1)

There must be a substantial government interest that supports the regulatory scheme pursuant to which the inspection is made, (2) the warrantless inspections must be necessary to further the regulatory scheme, and (3) the statute's inspection program, in terms of the certainty and regularity of its application, must provide a constitutionally adequate substitute for a warrant.

In the case at hand, the Court found that the three criteria had been met. First, the state has a substantial interest in regulating the vehicle dismantling and automobile junkyard industry because of the high level of motor vehicle theft and the industry's part in the trafficking of such stolen parts. Second, warrantless inspection of the industry is necessary to further the state's interest in eradicating automobile theft by controlling the receiver of, or market for, stolen property. Third, the state statute provides a constitutionally adequate substitute for a warrant. The statute informs the operator of a vehicle dismantling business that inspection will be made on a regular basis. [*New York v. Burger*, 482 U.S. 691, 107 S.Ct. 2636, 96 L.Ed.2d 601(1987)]

Fifth Amendment Privilege against Self-Incrimination

The Fifth Amendment to the U.S. Constitution provides that no person "shall be compelled in any criminal case to be a witness against himself." Thus, a person cannot be compelled to give testimony against himself, although nontestimonial evidence (e.g., fingerprints, body fluids, and the like) may be required. A person who asserts this right is described as having "taken the Fifth." This protection applies to federal cases and is extended to state and local criminal cases through the Due Process Clause of the Fourteenth Amendment.

The protection against **self-incrimination** applies only to natural persons who are accused of crimes. Therefore, artificial persons (such as corporations and partnerships) cannot raise this protection against incriminating testimony.[11] Thus, business records of corporations and partnerships are not generally protected from disclosure,

self-incrimination The Fifth Amendment states that no person shall be compelled in any criminal case to be a witness against him- or herself.

even if they incriminate individuals who work for the business. However, certain "private papers" of businesspersons (such as personal diaries) are protected from disclosure.

BUSINESS CHECKLIST

The Miranda Rights

The Fifth Amendment privilege against self-incrimination is not useful unless a criminal suspect has knowledge of this right. In the landmark case, *Miranda v. Arizona* [384 U.S. 436, 86 S.Ct. 1602 (1966)] the Supreme Court held that criminal suspects must be informed of certain rights before they can be interrogated by the police or other government officials. Generally, any confession obtained from the suspect prior to being read his or her *Miranda* rights can be excluded from evidence. The following rights, which are called the **Miranda rights**, must be read to a criminal suspect:

- You have the right to remain silent
- Anything you say can and will be used against you
- You have the right to consult with a lawyer and to have a lawyer present with you during interrogation
- If you cannot afford a lawyer, a lawyer will be appointed (free of charge) to represent you. The accused does not have the right to the appointment of a lawyer in criminal cases of a minor nature (such as traffic violations).

immunity from prosecution The government agrees not to use any evidence given by a person granted immunity against that person.

attorney–client privilege
A rule that says a client can tell his or her lawyer anything about the case without fear that the attorney will be called as a witness against the client.

Immunity from Prosecution On occasion, the government may want to obtain information from a suspect who has asserted his or her Fifth Amendment privilege against self-incrimination. The government can often achieve this by offering the suspect **immunity from prosecution**. Immunity from prosecution means that the government agrees not to use any evidence given by a person granted immunity against that person. When immunity is granted, the suspect loses the right to assert his or her Fifth Amendment privilege. Grants of immunity are often given when the government wants the suspect to give information that will lead to the prosecution of other, more important criminal suspects. Partial grants of immunity are also available. For example, a suspect may be granted immunity from prosecution for a serious crime, but not a lesser crime, in exchange for information. The suspect must agree to a partial grant of immunity.

The Attorney–Client Privilege and Other Privileges

To obtain a proper defense, the accused person must be able to tell his or her attorney facts about the case without fear that the attorney will be called as a witness against the accused. The **attorney–client privilege** is protected by the Fifth Amendment. Either the client or the attorney can raise this privilege. For the privilege to apply, the information must be told to the attorney in his or her capacity as an attorney, and not as a friend or neighbor or such.

The following privileges have also been recognized under the Fifth Amendment: (1) **psychiatrist/psychologist–patient privilege**; (2) **priest/minister/rabbi–penitent privilege**; (3) **spouse–spouse privilege**; and (4) **parent–child privilege**. There are some exceptions. For example, a spouse or child who is beaten by a spouse or parent may testify against the accused. An **accountant–client privilege** has not been recognized under the Fifth Amendment. Several states have, however, enacted statutes that create an accountant–client privilege for state law criminal matters.

Fifth Amendment Protection against Double Jeopardy

The **double jeopardy clause** of the Fifth Amendment protects persons from being tried twice for the same crime. For example, if the state tries a suspect for the crime of murder and the suspect is found innocent, the state cannot bring another trial against the accused for the same crime. However, if the same criminal act involves several different crimes, the accused may be tried for each of the crimes without violating the double jeopardy clause. For example, suppose the accused kills two people during a robbery. The accused may be tried for two murders and the robbery.

If the same act violates the laws of two or more jurisdictions, each jurisdiction may try the accused. For instance, if an accused kidnaps a person in one state and brings the victim across a state border into another state, the act violates the laws of two states and the federal government. Thus, three jurisdictions can prosecute the accused without violating the double jeopardy clause.

double jeopardy clause
A clause of the Fifth Amendment that protects persons from being tried twice for the same crime.

Sixth Amendment Right to a Public Jury Trial

The Sixth Amendment guarantees certain rights to criminal defendants. These rights are (1) to be tried by an impartial jury of the state or district in which the accused crime was committed; (2) to confront (cross-examine) the witnesses against the accused; (3) to have the assistance of a lawyer; and (4) to have a speedy trial.[12]

Eighth Amendment Protection against Cruel and Unusual Punishment

The Eighth Amendment protects criminal defendants from cruel and unusual punishment. For example, it prohibits the torture of criminals. However, this clause does not prohibit capital punishment.[13]

"At the present time in this country there is more danger that criminals will escape justice than that they will be subjected to tyranny."

J. Holmes,
Dissenting,
Kepner v. United States (1904)

WORKING THE WEB

U.S. Department of Justice You can locate all sorts of Department of Justice information from this home page. You can link to Department of Justice organizations, find press releases, and link to federal documents.

Visit at http://www.usdoj.gov/

U.S. Constitution There are many places to find the U.S. Constitution on the Internet. One such place is the Cornell University Web site.

Visit at http://www.law.cornell.edu/constitution/constitution.billofrights.html

U.S. House of Representatives Internet Law Library Home Page The U.S. House of Representatives Internet Law Library Home Page has a page of links to materials about search and seizure. Cases, documents, and other sources are linked.

Visit at http://law.house.gov

Capital Punishment on the World Wide Web Georgetown University maintains a page with links to information on capital punishment.

Visit at http://www.ll.georgetown.edu/lr/rs/capital.html

National Rifle Association The National Rifle Association is an example of a powerful organization with a large presence on the World Wide Web. From this page you can link to state firearm laws and state legislative updates.

Visit at http://www.nra.org/

CYBER EXERCISES:

1. From the Department of Justice Web site, find the Civil Rights Division of the Department of Justice. Can you find the report of the National Church Arson Task Force?
2. One of the constitutional amendments of interest to criminal law researchers is Amendment VI.

What does that Amendment cover? Using the Cornell University Web site, print out a copy of Amendment VI.

3. Using the U.S. House of Representatives Internet Law Library Home Page for search and seizure, find the summaries of the police dog search and seizure cases and print out the first page.

4. From Georgetown University's Capital Punishment page, find a gateway to a page called Capital Punishment on the World Wide Web. What television show produces this page?

5. From the National Rifle Association Web site, find a document called "What Is the NRA?" and print it out.

CHAPTER SUMMARY

DEFINITION OF A CRIME, P. 130

Specifics of a Criminal Trial	1. The accused is *presumed innocent until proven guilty*. 2. The plaintiff (the government) bears the *burden of proof*. 3. The government must prove *beyond a reasonable doubt* that the accused is guilty of the crime charged. 4. The accused does not have to testify against him- or herself.

Definition of a Crime	1. *Crime*. Any act done by a person in violation of those duties that he or she owed to society and for the breach of which the law provides a penalty.
	2. *Penal codes*. State and federal statutes that define many crimes. Criminal conduct is also defined in many *regulatory statutes*.
	3. Parties to a criminal lawsuit:
	  a. *Plaintiff*. The government, which is represented by the *prosecuting attorney (or prosecutor)*.
	  b. *Defendant*. The person or business accused of the crime, who is represented by a *defense attorney*.

Classification of Crimes	1. *Felonies*. The most serious kinds of crimes. Mala in se (inherently evil). Usually punishable by imprisonment. 2. *Misdemeanors*. Less serious crimes. *Mala prohibita* (prohibited by society). Usually punishable by fine and/or imprisonment for less than one year. 3. *Violations*. Not a felony nor a misdemeanor. Generally punishable by a fine.
Elements of a Crime	Most crimes require that the following two elements be proven: 1. *Actus reus*: Guilty act 2. *Mens rea*: Evil intent

CRIMINAL PROCEDURE, P. 132

Pretrial Criminal Procedure	1. *Arrest*. Made pursuant to an *arrest warrant* based upon a showing of "probable cause," or, where permitted, by a *warrantless* arrest. 2. *Indictment or information*. Grand juries issue *indictments*; magistrates (judges) issue *informations*. These formally charge the accused with specific crimes. 3. *Arraignment*. The accused is informed of the charges against him or her and enters a *plea* in court; the plea may be *not guilty, guilty,* or *nolo contendere*. 4. *Plea bargaining*. The government and the accused may negotiate a settlement agreement wherein the accused agrees to admit to a lesser crime than charged.

Criminal Trial and Appeal	1. Criminal trial
	   a. *Conviction*. Requires unanimous vote of the jury
	   b. *Not guilty*. Requires unanimous vote of the jury
	   c. *Hung jury*. Nonunanimous vote of the jury. The government may prosecute the case again.
	2. Appeal
	   a. *Defendant*. May appeal his or her conviction
	   b. *Plaintiff (government)*. May not appeal a verdict of not guilty.

CRIMES AFFECTING BUSINESS, P. 134

Crimes Affecting Business	1. *Robbery*. The taking of personal property from another by fear or force. 2. *Burglary*. The unauthorized entering of a building to commit a felony. 3. *Larceny*. The wrongful taking of another's property other than from his person or building. 4. *Theft*. The wrongful taking of another's property, whether by robbery, burglary, or larceny. 5. *Receiving stolen property*. A person knowingly receives stolen property with the intent to deprive the rightful owner of that property. 6. *Arson*. The malicious and willful burning of another's building. 7. *Forgery*. Fraudulently making or altering a written document that affects the legal liability of another person. 8. *Extortion*. Threat to expose something about another person unless that person gives up money or property. 9. *Credit card crimes*. The misappropriation or use of another person's credit card. 10. *Bad check legislation*. The making, drawing, or delivery of a check by a person when that person knows that there are insufficient funds in the account to cover the check.

WHITE-COLLAR CRIMES, P. 136

White-Collar Crimes	*White-collar crimes*. Crimes that are prone to be committed by businesspersons that involve cunning and trickery rather than physical force.
	1. *Criminal fraud*. Obtaining title to another's property through deception or trickery. Also called *false pretenses* or *deceit*.
	2. *Mail fraud*. The use of mail to defraud another person.
	3. *Wire fraud*. The use of wire (telephone or telegraph) to defraud another person.
	4. *Embezzlement*. The fraudulent conversion of property by a person to whom the property was *entrusted*.
	5. *Bribery*. The offer of payment of money or property or something else of value in return for an unwarranted favor. The payor of a bribe is also guilty of the crime of bribery.
	   a. *Commercial bribery* is the offer of a payment of a bribe to private persons and businesses. This is often referred to as a *kickback* or *payoff*.
	   b. Bribery of public officials for an "official act" is a crime.
	6. *Computer crimes*. The use of computers to commit crimes. Various federal and state statutes define computer crimes.
	7. *Racketeer Influenced and Corrupt Organizations Act (RICO)*. Makes it a federal crime to acquire or maintain an interest in, use income from, or conduct or participate in the affairs of an "enterprise" through a "pattern" of "racketeering activity." Criminal penalties include the

	forfeiture of any property or business interests gained by a RICO violation.
CORPORATE CRIMINAL LIABILITY, P. 142	
Corporate Criminal Liability	1. Corporate directors, officers, and employees are criminally liable for crimes they commit for personal benefit or on behalf of the corporation. 2. A corporation is criminally liable for crimes committed by directors, officers, and employees while acting on behalf of the corporation.
INCHOATE CRIMES, P. 143	
Inchoate Crimes	*Inchoate crimes*. Crimes that are incomplete or that are committed by nonparticipants. 1. *Criminal conspiracy*. When two or more persons enter into an *agreement* to commit a crime and take some *overt act* to further the crime. 2. *Attempt to commit a crime*. The attempt to commit a crime is a crime even if the commissions of the intended crime is unsuccessful. 3. *Aiding and abetting the commission of a crime*. Rendering support, assistance, or encouragement to the commission of a crime, or knowingly harboring a criminal after he or she has committed a crime.
CONSTITUTIONAL SAFEGUARDS, P. 144	

Fourth Amendment Protection against Unreasonable Searches and Seizures	Protects persons and corporations from *unreasonable searches and seizures*.
	1. *Reasonable search and seizures* based on *probable cause* are lawful:
	  a. *Search warrant*. Stipulates the place and scope of the search
	  b. *Warranties search*. Permitted only:
	    i. Incident to an arrest
	    ii. Where evidence is in plain view
	    iii. Where it is likely that evidence will be destroyed.
	2. *Exclusionary rule*. Evidence obtained from an unreasonable search and seizure is *tainted evidence* that may not be introduced at a government proceeding against the person searched.
	3. *Business premises*. Protected by the Fourth Amendment, except that certain *regulated industries* may be subject to warrantless searches authorized by statute.

Fifth Amendment Privilege against Self-Incrimination	*Privilege against self-incrimination*. Provides that no person "shall be compelled in any criminal case to be a witness against himself." A person asserting this privilege is said to have taken the Fifth. 1. *Nontestimonial evidence*. This evidence (e.g., fingerprints, body fluids) is not protected. 2. *Businesses*. The privilege applies only to natural persons; businesses cannot assert the privilege. 3. *Miranda rights*. A criminal suspect must be informed of his or her Fifth Amendment rights before the suspect can be interrogated by the police or government officials. 4. *Immunity from prosecution*. Granted by the government to obtain otherwise privileged evidence. The government agrees not to use the evidence given against the person who gave it. 5. *Attorney–client privilege*. An accused's lawyer cannot be called as a witness against the accused.

	6. *Other privileges*. The following privileges have been recognized, with some limitations: a. Psychiatrist/psychologist–patient b. Priest/minister/rabbi–penitent c. Spouse–child d. Parent–child 7. *Accountant–client privilege*. None recognized at the federal level. Some states recognize this privilege in state law actions.
Fifth Amendment Protection against Double Jeopardy	Protects persons from being tried twice by the same jurisdiction for the same crime. If the act violates the laws of two or more jurisdictions, each jurisdiction may try the accused.
Sixth Amendment Right to a Public Jury Trial	Guarantees criminal defendants the following rights: 1. To be tried by an impartial jury 2. To confront the witness 3. To have the assistance of a lawyer 4. To have a speedy trial
Eighth Amendment Protection against Cruel and Unusual Punishment	Protects criminal defendants from cruel and unusual punishment. Capital punishment is permitted.

CRITICAL LEGAL THINKING CASES

6.1 Criminal Liability of Corporations Representatives of hotels, restaurants, hotel and restaurant supply companies, and other businesses located in Portland, Oregon, organized an association to attract conventions to their city. Members were asked to make contributions equal to one percent of their sales to finance the association. To aid collections, hotel members, including Hilton Hotels Corporation (Hilton Hotels), agreed to give preferential treatment to suppliers who paid their assessments and to curtail purchases from those who did not. This agreement violated federal antitrust laws. The United States sued the members of the association, including Hilton Hotels, for the crime of violating federal antitrust laws. Can a corporation be held criminally liable for the acts of its representatives? If so, what criminal penalties can be assessed against the corporation? [*United States v. Hilton Hotels Corp.*, 467 F.2d 1000 (9th Cir. 1973)]

6.2 Criminal Liability for Acts of Subordinates Acme Markets, Inc. (Acme) is a national retail food chain with approximately 36,000 employees working in 874 retail stores and 16 warehouses. Mr. Park is the president and chief executive officer of the corporation. In April 1970, the federal Food and Drug Administration (FDA) inspected Acme's Philadelphia warehouse and found unsanitary conditions, including rodent infestation. The FDA advised Mr. Park by letter of these conditions and demanded that they be corrected. In 1971, the FDA found that similar conditions existed at the warehouse. It again notified Park to correct the situation. An FDA inspection in March 1972 still showed unsanitary conditions and rodent infestation at the warehouse. Evidence showed that corporate

employees did not take appropriate action to correct this situation. The federal Food, Drug, and Cosmetic Act makes individuals, as well as corporations, criminally liable for violations of the act. The United States brought a criminal action against Mr. Park for the violations. Can a corporate officer such as Mr. Park be held criminally liable for actions of his subordinates? [*United States v. Park*, 421 U.S. 658, 95 S.Ct. 658 (1974)]

6.3 Receiving Stolen Property In December 1982, Whitehead bought a stereo from his friend, Walter Gibbs, for between $10 and $40. When Whitehead first saw the stereo, it was one of three in Gibbs's home. Whitehead knew that the stereo was new and was worth between $169 and $189. The stereo system, identified as one stolen in late 1982 from the J. C. Penny Warehouse, was found by police officers in Whitehead's bedroom on January 27, 1983. The serial number on the stereo had been scratched out. Is Whitehead guilty of any crime? Explain. [*Whitehead v. State of Georgia*, 313 S.E.2d 775 (Ga.App. 1984)]

6.4 Forgery Evidence showed that there was a burglary in which a checkbook belonging to Mary J. Harris, doing business as The Report Department, and a check encoder machine were stolen. Two of the checks from that checkbook were cashed at the Citizens & Southern National Bank branch office in Riverdale, Georgia, by Joseph Leon Foster, who was accompanied by a woman identified as Angela Foxworth. The bank teller who cashed the checks testified that the same man and woman cashed the checks on two different occasions at her drive-up window at the bank and that on both occasions they were in the same car. Each time the teller wrote the license tag number of the car on the back of the check. The teller testified that both times the checks and the driver's license used to identify the woman were passed to her by the man driving, and that the man received the money from her. What crime has been committed? [*Foster v. State of Georgia*, 387 S.E.2d 637 (Ga.App. 1989)]

6.5 Extortion On February 3, 1987, the victim (Mr. X) went to the premises at 42 Taylor Terrace in New Milford, Connecticut, where his daughter and her husband lived. Lisa Percoco, who was Gregory Erhardt's girlfriend, was at the residence. Mr. X and Percoco were in the bedroom, partially dressed, engaging in sexual activity, when Erhardt entered the room and photographed them. He then informed Mr. X that unless he procured $5,000 and placed it in a mailbox at a designated address by 8 P.M. that night, Erhardt would show the photographs to Mr. X's wife. Mr. X proceeded to make telephone arrangements for the procurement and placement of the money according to Erhardt's instructions. If the money were paid, what crime would have been committed? [*State of Connecticut v. Erhardt*, 553 A.2d 188 (Conn. App. 1989)]

6.6 Credit Card Fraud Remi Olu Abod, a Nigerian national, obtained a VISA credit card from a supplier, which bore the name "Norman Skinner." Abod purchased a counterfeit international driving permit bearing the name Norman Skinner at a passport photo shop in California. On June 27, 1984, Abod traveled from Los Angeles, California, to Corpus Christi, Texas. He first used the credit card to obtain $2,400 cash from each of two banks. He next appeared at the jewelry counter at Dillard's Department Store and tried to purchase $2,335 of jewelry with the credit card. When the store employee telephoned the VISA credit authorization center for approval, he was informed that the card was counterfeit. Corpus Christi police were summoned to the store, where they arrested Abod. What crime did Abod commit? [*United States v. Abod*, 770 F.2d 1293 (5th Cir. 1985)]

6.7 Criminal Fraud In 1978, Miriam Marlowe's husband purchased a life insurance policy on his own life, naming her as the beneficiary. After Marlowe's husband died in a swimming accident in July 1981, she received payment on the policy. Marlowe later met John Walton, a friend of a friend. He convinced her and her representative that he had a friend who worked for the State Department and had access to gold in Brazil, and that the gold could be purchased in Brazil for $100 an ounce and sold in the United States for $300 an ounce. Walton convinced Miriam to invest $25,000. Instead of investing the money in gold in Brazil, Walton opened an account at Tracy Collins Bank in the name of Jeffrey McIntyre Roberts and deposited Miriam's money in that account. He later withdrew the money in cash. What crime is Walton guilty of? [*State of Utah v. Roberts*, 711 P.2d 235 (Utah 1985)]

6.8 Embezzlement Marty W. ORR was employed as a deputy treasurer and bookkeeper in the treasurer's office of Washington County, Virginia. She was responsible for computing each day's revenue and depositing funds received on a daily basis. During the course of her work, she took cash totaling several thousand dollars. What crime has she committed? [*Orr v. Commonwealth of Virginia*, 344 S.E.2d 627 (Va.App. 1986)]

6.9 Bribery In 1979, the city of Peoria, Illinois, received federal funds from the Department of Housing and Urban Development (HUD) to be used for housing rehabilitation assistance. The city of Peoria designated United Neighborhoods, Inc. (UNI), a corporation, to administer the funds. Arthur Dixon was UNI's executive director and James Lee Hinton was its housing rehabilitation coordinator. In these capacities, they were responsible for contracting with suppliers and tradespeople to provide the necessary goods and services to rehabilitate the houses. Evidence showed that Dixon and Hinton used their positions to extract 10 percent payments back on all contracts they awarded. What crime have they committed? [*Dixon and Hinton v. United States*, 465 U.S. 482, 104 S.Ct. 1172, 79 L.Ed.2d 458 (1984)]

6.10 Attempt to Commit a Crime Mary G. Smith's MasterCard credit card was in her purse when it was stolen in June 1985. On June 28, 1985, Beulah Houston entered a Ventura store located in Griffith, Indiana, and indicated to the manager of the jewelry department that she wished to purchase a man's watch. After making a selection, Houston handed the manager a MasterCard bearing the name Mary G. Smith. Upon contacting the bank for authorization, the manager was told to hold the card. Houston then left the store and was later arrested. Can Houston be convicted of attempting to commit credit-card fraud? [*Houston v. State of Indiana*, 528 N.E.2d 818 (Ind.App. 1988)]

6.11 Administrative Search Lee Stuart Paulson owns the liquor license for "My House," a bar in San Francisco. The California Department of Alcoholic Beverage Control (Department) is the administrative agency that regulates bars in that state. The California Business and Professions Code, which the Department administers, prohibits "any kind of illegal activity on licensed premises." On February 11, 1988, an anonymous informer tipped the Department that narcotics sales were occurring on the premises of "My House" and that the narcotics were kept in a safe behind the bar on the premises. A special Department investigator entered the bar during its hours of operation, identified himself, and informed Paulson that he was conducting an inspection. The investigator, who did not have a search warrant, opened the safe without seeking Paulson's consent. Twenty-two bundles of cocaine, totaling 5.5 grams, were found in the safe. Paulson was arrested. At his criminal trial, Paulson challenged the lawfulness of the search. Was the warrantless search of the safe a lawful search? [*People v. Paulson*, 216 Cal.App.3d 1480, 265 Cal.Rptr. 579 (Cal. App. 1990)]

6.12 Search Warrant The Center Art Galleries-Hawaii (Center) sells artwork. Approximately 20 percent of its business involves art by Salvador Dali. The federal government, which suspected the Center of fraudulently selling forged Dali artwork, obtained identical search warrants for six locations controlled by the Center. The warrants commanded the executing officer to seize items that were "evidence of violations of federal criminal law." The warrants did not describe the specific crimes suspected and did not stipulate that only items pertaining to the sale of Dali's work could be seized. There was no evidence of any criminal activity unrelated to that artist. Is the search warrant valid? [*Center Art Galleries-Hawaii, Inc. v. United States*, 875 F.2d 747 (9th Cir. 1989)]

6.13 Fifth Amendment's Privilege against Self-incrimination John Doe is the owner of several sole proprietorship businesses. In 1980, during the course of an investigation of corruption in awarding county and municipal contracts, a federal grand jury served several subpoenas on John Doe demanding the production of certain business records. The subpoenas demanded the production of the following records: (1) general ledgers and journals, (2) invoices, (3) bank statements and canceled checks, (4) financial statements, (5) telephone company records, (6) safe-deposit box records, and (7) copies of tax returns. John Doe filed a motion in federal court seeking to quash the subpoenas, alleging that producing these business records would violate his Fifth Amendment privilege of not testifying against himself. Do the records have to be disclosed? [*United States v. John Doe*, 465 U.S. 605, 104 S.Ct. 1237, 79 L.Ed.2d 552 (1984)]

ETHICS CASES

6.14 Ethical Perspective R. Foster Winans was a reporter for *The Wall Street Journal* from 1981 through 1984, during which time he wrote a column called "Heard on the Street." In the column, Winans would discuss the future prospects of companies and their securities. Evidence showed that positive comments would make the company's stock increase in value; negative comments would have the opposite result. Winans systematically leaked the contents of his future "Heard" columns prior to publication to Peter Brant, a stockbroker, in exchange for a share of the profits made by Brant. Upon discovery, Winans was convicted of wire and mail fraud, which are federal crimes. The crimes were committed within the state of New York. In September 1985, Winans entered into a book publishing contract with St. Martin's Press and in 1988 St. Martin's published Winans's book *Trading Secrets*. The book details Winans's own actions that resulted in his federal conviction for insider trading. New York had previously adopted a "Son of Sam" law. The New York State Crimes Victims Board moved for an order directing St. Martin's to turn over the royalties due Winans, which would be deposited in an escrow account and held for the benefit of and payable to any victims of Winans's crimes. Who legally is entitled to the royalties? Is it ethical for a convicted criminal to make money by selling the media rights to the story about the crime? [*St. Martin's Press v. Zweibel*, N.Y. Law Journal, 2/26/90 (N.Y.Sup.Ct. 1990)]

6.15 Ethical Perspective In 1979, Leo Shaw, an attorney, entered into a partnership agreement with three other persons to build and operate an office building. From the outset, it was agreed that Shaw's role was to manage the operation of the building. Management of the property was Shaw's contribution to the partnership; the other three partners contributed the necessary capital. In January 1989, the other partners discovered that the loan on the building was in default and that foreclosure proceedings were imminent. Upon investigation, they discovered that Shaw had taken approximately $80,000 from the partnership's checking account. After heated discussions, Shaw repaid $13,000. In May 1989, when no further payment was forthcoming, a partner filed a civil suit against Shaw and notified the police. The state filed a criminal complaint against Shaw on March 15, 1990. On April 3, 1990, Shaw repaid the remaining funds as part of a civil settlement. At his criminal trial in November 1990, Shaw argued that the repayment of the money was a defense to the crime of embezzlement. Did Shaw act ethically in this case? Would your answer be different if he had really only "borrowed" the money and had intended to return it? [*People v. Shaw*, 10 Cal.App.4th 969, 12 Cal.Rptr.2d 665 (Cal.App. 1992)]

CRITICAL LEGAL THINKING WRITING ASSIGNMENT

Read Case A.6 in the Case Appendix [*Schalk v. Texas*]. This case is excerpted from the appellate court opinion. Review and brief the case. In your brief, be sure to answer the following questions:

1. What activities had the defendants engaged in?
2. What crime were the defendants accused of?
3. What was the decision of the appellate court?

NOTES

1. Title 18 of the United States Code contains the federal criminal code.
2. Sentencing Reform Act of 1984, 18 U.S.C. § 3551 et. seq. The sentencing guidelines for federal crimes, which were promulgated by the U.S. Sentencing Commission, became effective on November 1, 1987.
3. 18 U.S.C. § 1341.
4. 18 U.S.C. § 1343.
5. 18 U.S.C. §§ 1961–1968.
6. 18 U.S.C. § 1962.
7. Public Law 98–473, Title II.
8. 15 U.S.C. § 1693.
9. For example, see New York Session Laws, 1986, Chapter 514.
10. *United States v. Leon*, 468 U.S. 897, 104 S.Ct. 3405, 82 L.Ed.2d 677 (1984).
11. *Bellis v. United States*, 417 U.S. 85, 94 S.Ct. 2179, 40 L.Ed.2d 678 (1974).
12. The Speedy Trial Act requires that a criminal defendant be brought to trial within 70 days after indictment [18 U.S.C. § 3161(c)(1)]. Continuances may be granted by the court to serve the "ends of justice."
13. *Baldwin v. Alabama*, 472 U.S. 372, 105 S.Ct. 2727, 86 L.Ed.2d 300 (1985).

CHAPTER 7

NATURE AND CLASSIFICATION

OF CONTRACTS

Chapter Objectives

*After studying this chapter,
you should be able to*

1. List the elements necessary to form a valid contract
2. List and describe the sources of contract law
3. Distinguish between bilateral and unilateral contracts
4. Describe and distinguish between express and implied-in-fact contracts
5. Define and describe the objective theory of contracts
6. Define and describe quasi contracts
7. Distinguish between formal and informal contracts
8. Define and distinguish between executed and executory contracts
9. Describe and distinguish between valid, void, voidable, and unenforceable contracts
10. Apply the concept of equity to contracts

Chapter Contents

- Definition of a Contract
- Requirements of a Contract
- Sources of Contract Law
  Contemporary Business Environment The Evolution of the Modern Law of Contracts
- Classifications of Contracts
  Business Checklist The Different Performance Obligations for Bilateral and Unilateral Contracts
  Business Application Owner of Scrabble Spelled "L-O-S-E-R"
- Quasi Contracts (Implied-in-Law Contracts)
  Case 7.1 *Dines v. Liberty Mutual Insurance Company (MA)*
- Equity and the Law of Contracts
  Ethical Perspective Equity to the Rescue
- Working the Web
- Chapter Summary
- Critical Legal Thinking Cases
- Ethics Cases
- Critical Legal Thinking Writing Assignment

> *The movement of the progressive societies has hitherto been a movement from status to contract.*
>
> Sir Henry Maine
> *Ancient Law*, Ch. 5

Contracts are the basis of many of our daily activities. They provide the means for individuals and businesses to sell and otherwise transfer property, services, and other rights. The purchase of goods, such as books and automobiles, is based on sales contracts; the hiring of employees is based on service contracts; the lease of an apartment is based on a rental contract. The list is almost endless. Without enforceable contracts, commerce would collapse.

"A man must come into a court of equity with clean hands."

C. B. Eyre
Dering v. Earl of Winchelsea (1787)

Contracts are voluntarily entered into by parties. The terms of the contract become *private law* between the parties. One court has stated that "the contract between parties is the law between them and the courts are obliged to give legal effect to such contracts according to the true interests of the parties."[1]

Nevertheless, most contracts are performed without the aid of the court system. This usually is because the parties feel a moral duty to perform as promised. Most contracts are **legally enforceable**,[2] although illegal contracts, such as contracts to commit a crime, are not. If a party to a legal contract fails to perform as promised, the other party may call upon the courts to enforce the contract.

legally enforceable contract If one party fails to perform as promised, the other party can use the court system to enforce the contract and recover damages or other remedy.

This chapter introduces you to the study of contract law. Such topics as the definition of a contract, requirements for forming a contract, sources of contract law, and the various classifications of contracts are discussed.

DEFINITION OF A CONTRACT

A contract is an agreement that is enforceable by a court of law or equity. A simple and widely recognized definition of a contract is provided by the Restatement (Second) of Contracts: "A contract is a promise or a set of promises for the breach of which the law gives a remedy or the performance of which the law in some way recognizes a duty."[3]

Parties to a Contract

Every contract involves at least two parties. The **offeror** is the party who makes an offer to enter into a contract. The **offeree** is the party to whom the offer is made (see Exhibit 7.1). In making an offer, the offeror promises to do—or to refrain from doing—something. The offeree then has the power to create a contract by accepting the offeror's offer. A contract is created if the offer is accepted. No contract is created if the offer is not accepted.

offeror The party who makes an offer to enter into a contract.

offeree The party to whom an offer to enter into a contract is made.

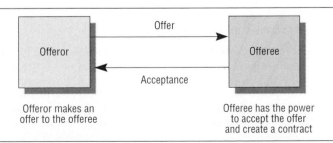

Offer

Offeror → **Offeree**

Acceptance

Offeror makes an offer to the offeree

Offeree has the power to accept the offer and create a contract

Exhibit 7.1
Parties to a Contract

REQUIREMENTS OF A CONTRACT

Elements of a Contract

To be an enforceable contract, the following four basic requirements must be met:

1. **Agreement**   To have an enforceable contract, the partners must have reached a mutual agreement. This requires an *offer* by the offeror and an *acceptance* of the offer by the offeree (chapter 8).
2. **Consideration**   The promise must be supported by a bargained-for consideration that is legally sufficient. Often, gift promises and moral obligations are not considered supported by valid consideration (chapter 8).
3. **Contractual Capacity**   The parties to a contract must have contractual capacity. Certain parties, such as persons adjudged insane, do not have contractual capacity (chapter 9).
4. **Lawful Object**   The object of the contract must be lawful. Contracts to accomplish illegal objects or contracts that are against public policy are void (chapter 9).

"Contracts must not be the sports of an idle hour, mere matters of pleasantry and badinage, never intended by the parties to have any serious effect whatever."

Lord Stowell
Dalrymple v. Dalrymple (1811)

Defenses to the Enforcement of a Contract

There are two *defenses* that can be raised to the enforcement of contracts:

1. **Genuineness of Assent**   The consent of the parties to create a contract must be genuine. If the consent is obtained by duress, undue influence, or fraud, there is no real consent.
2. **Writing and Form**   The law requires that certain contracts be in writing or in a certain form. Failure of these contracts to be in writing or to be in proper form can be raised against the enforcement of the contract.

These defenses are discussed more fully in chapter 10.

SOURCES OF CONTRACT LAW

There are several sources of contract law in the United States, including the *common law of contracts*, the *Uniform Commercial Code*, and the *Restatement (Second) of Contracts*. The following sections explain these sources in more detail.

The Common Law of Contracts

common law of contracts
Contract law developed primarily by state courts.

A major source of contract law is the **common law of contracts**. The common law of contracts developed from early court decisions that became precedent for later decisions. There is a limited federal common law of contracts that applies to contracts made by the federal government. A larger and more prevalent body of common law has been developed from state court decisions. Thus, while the general principles remain the same throughout the country, there is some variation from state to state (chapters 7–12).

The Uniform Commercial Code

Uniform Commercial Code
Comprehensive statutory scheme that includes laws that cover aspects of commercial transactions.

The **Uniform Commercial Code (UCC)** is another major source of contract law. The UCC, which was first drafted by the National Conference of Commissioners on Uniform State Law in 1952, has been amended several times. Its goal is to create a uniform system of commercial law among the 50 states. The provisions of the UCC normally take precedence over the common law of contracts (chapters 13–26).

The UCC is divided into nine main articles. Every state has adopted at least part of the UCC.

The Restatement of the Law of Contracts

In 1932, the American Law Institute completed the **Restatement of the Law of Contracts**. The Restatement is a compilation of contract law principles as agreed upon by the drafters. The Restatement, which is currently in its second edition, is cited in this book as **Restatement (Second) of Contracts**.

Note that the Restatement is not law. However, lawyers and judges often refer to it for guidance in contract disputes because of its stature.

> **Restatement of the Law of Contracts** A compilation of model contract law principles drafted by legal scholars. The Restatement is not law.

CONTEMPORARY BUSINESS ENVIRONMENT

The Evolution of the Modern Law of Contracts

The use of contracts originally developed in ancient times. The common law of contracts developed in England around the 15th century. American contract law evolved from the English common law.

At first, the United States adopted a *laissez-faire* approach to the law of contracts. The central theme of this theory was *freedom of contract*. The parties (such as consumers, shopkeepers, farmers, and traders) generally dealt with one another face-to-face, had equal knowledge and bargaining power, and had the opportunity to inspect the goods prior to sale. Contract terms were openly negotiated. There was little, if any, government regulation of the right to contract. This "pure" or **classical law of contracts** produced objective rules, which in turn produced certainty and predictability in the enforcement of contracts. It made sense until the Industrial Revolution.

The Industrial Revolution changed many of the underlying assumptions of pure contract law. For example, as large corporations developed and gained control of crucial resources, the traditional balance of parties' bargaining power shifted: Large corporations now had the most power. The chain of distribution for goods also changed because (1) buyers did not have to deal face-to-face with sellers, and (2) there was not always an opportunity to inspect the goods prior to sale.

Eventually, sellers began using *form contracts* that offered their goods to buyers on a take-it-or-leave-it basis. The majority of contracts in this country today are form contracts. Automobile contracts, mortgage contracts, and sales contracts for consumer goods, are examples of form contracts.

Both federal and state governments enacted statutes intended to protect consumers, creditors, and others from unfair contracts. In addition, the courts began to develop certain common law legal theories that allowed some oppressive or otherwise unjust contracts to be avoided. Today, under this **modern law of contracts**, there is substantial government regulation of the right to contract.

CLASSIFICATIONS OF CONTRACTS

There are several types of contracts. Each differs somewhat in formation, enforcement, performance, and discharge. The different types of contracts are discussed in the following sections.

> *"Law cannot stand aside from the social changes around it."*
> William J. Brennan, Jr.

Bilateral and Unilateral Contracts

Contracts are either *bilateral* or *unilateral*, depending upon what the offeree must do to accept the offeror's offer. The contract is **bilateral** if the offeror's promise is answered with the offeree's promise of acceptance. In other words, a bilateral contract is a "promise for a promise." This exchange of promises creates an enforceable contract. No act of performance is necessary to create a bilateral contract.

A contract is **unilateral** if the offeror's offer can be accepted only by the performance of an act by the offeree. There is no contract until the offeree performs the requested act. An offer to create a unilateral contract cannot be accepted by a promise to perform. It is a promise for an act.

> **bilateral contract** A contract entered into by way of exchange of promises of the parties; a "promise for a promise."
>
> **unilateral contract** A contract in which the offeror's offer can be accepted only by the performance of an act by the offeree; a "promise for an act."

The language of the offeror's promise must be carefully scrutinized to determine whether it is an offer to create a bilateral or a unilateral contract. If there is any ambiguity as to which it is, it is presumed to be a bilateral contract.

CONSIDER THE FOLLOWING EXAMPLES: Suppose Mary Douglas, the owner of the Chic Dress Shop, says to Peter Jones, a painter, "If you promise to paint my store by July 1, I will pay you $2,000." Peter promises to do so. A bilateral contract was created at the moment Peter promised to paint the dress shop (a promise for a promise). If Peter fails to paint the store, he can be sued for whatever damages result from his breach of contract. Similarly, Peter can sue Mary if she refuses to pay him after he has performed as promised.

However, if Mary had said, "If you paint my shop by July 1, I will pay you $2,000," the offer would have created a unilateral contract. The offer can be accepted only by the painter's performance of the requested act. If Peter does not paint the shop by July 1, there has been no acceptance and the painter cannot be sued for damages.

CAUTION

Distinguish bilateral from unilateral contracts according to the number of promises involved. Bilateral is "promise for promise." Unilateral is "promise for act."

Incomplete or Partial Performance Problems can arise if the offeror of a unilateral contract attempts to revoke an offer after the offeree has begun performance. Generally, an offer to create a unilateral contract can be revoked by the offeror anytime prior to the offeree's performance of the requested act. However, the offer cannot be revoked if the offeree has begun or has substantially completed performance. Suppose Alan Matthews tells Sherry Levine that he will pay her $5,000 if she finishes the Boston Marathon. Alan cannot revoke the offer after Sherry starts running the marathon.

BUSINESS CHECKLIST

The Different Performance Obligations for Bilateral and Unilateral Contracts

The parties to a *unilateral contract* have different obligations than the parties to a *bilateral contract*. That is why the parties to a contract should be careful to understand whether the language of the contract creates a bilateral or unilateral contract. Consider the following distinctions:

- A **bilateral contract** is created by an exchange of promises—in other words, a promise for a promise (e.g., the offeror states, "I will pay you $10,000 if you promise to repair my garage by August 1"; the offeree replies, "I agree"). A contract is created at the moment the offeree accepts the offer. If the offeree does not perform, the contract is breached and the offeror can sue the offeree for damages. The offeree can sue the offeror if the offeror fails to pay for the work performed.

- A **unilateral contract** is created by a promise for an act (e.g., the offeror states, "I will pay you $10,000 if you repair my garage by August 1"). In this case, the offeree is not obligated to perform, and no contract comes into existence until the offeree actually performs the requested act. Caution: If the offeree does not perform, there is no breach of contract. The offeree can sue the offeror if the offeror fails to pay for the work performed.

Express and Implied Contracts

An *actual contract* (as distinguished from a quasi-contract, which is discussed later in this chapter) can be either *express* or *implied in fact*.

Express contracts are stated in oral or written words. Examples of such contracts include an oral agreement to purchase a neighbor's bicycle and a written agreement to buy an automobile from a dealership.

express contract   An agreement that is expressed in written or oral words.

 Implied-in-fact contracts are implied from the conduct of the parties. Implied-in-fact contracts leave more room for questions. The following elements must be established to create an implied-in-fact contract:

implied-in-fact contract   A contract in which agreement between parties has been inferred from their conduct.

1. The plaintiff provided property or services to the defendant.
2. The plaintiff expected to be paid by the defendant for the property or services and did not provide the property or services gratuitously.
3. The defendant was given an opportunity to reject the property or services provided by the plaintiff but failed to do so.

BUSINESS APPLICATION

Owner of Scrabble Spelled "L-O-S-E-R"

Implied-in-fact contracts are implied from the conduct of the parties. Consider the following case.

Selchow & Richter (S&R) owns the trademark to the famous board game *Scrabble*. Mark Landsberg wrote a book on strategy for winning at Scrabble and contacted S&R to request permission to use the Scrabble trademark. In response, S&R requested a copy of Landsberg's manuscript, which he provided. After prolonged negotiations between the parties regarding the possibility of S&R's publication of the manuscript broke off, S&R brought out its own Scrabble strategy book. No express contract was ever entered into between Landsberg and S&R. Landsberg sued S&R and its subsidiary, Scrabble Crossword

Game Players, Inc., for damages for breach of an implied contract.

Was there an implied-in-fact contract between the parties?

The district court and appellate court held that an implied-in-fact contract had been formed between the parties and that the contract was breached by the defendants. The court noted that the law allows for recovery for the breach of an implied-in-fact contract when the recipient of a valuable idea accepts and uses the information without paying for it even though he or she knows that compensation is expected. Here, the court found that (1) Landsberg's disclosure of his manuscript was confidential and for the limited purpose of obtaining approval for the use of the Scrabble mark, and (2) given Landsberg's

express intention to exploit his manuscript commercially, the defendants' use of any portion of it was conditioned on payment. Landsberg was awarded $440,300 damages.

CASE QUESTIONS

Critical Legal Thinking Should the law recognize implied-in-fact contracts? Or should only express contracts be enforced?

Ethics Do you think Selchow & Richter acted ethically in this case?

Business Implication How can businesses, such as movie production companies and book publishers, protect themselves against false claims that they stole someone's idea for a screenplay or book?

Formal and Informal Contracts

Formal Contracts Contracts can be classified as either *formal* or *informal*. **Formal contracts** are contracts that require a special form or method of creation. The Restatement (Second) of Contracts identifies the following types of formal contracts:[4]

formal contract   A contract that requires a special form or method of creation.

- **Contracts Under Seal**. This type of contract is one to which a seal (usually a wax seal) is attached. Although no state currently requires contracts to be under seal, a few states provide that no consideration is necessary if a contract is made under seal.

NOTE
Originally, only contracts under seal were recognized as valid contracts in England. Around 1600, the common law courts of England began to enforce simple contracts that were not made under seal.

- **Recognizances**. In a recognizance, a party acknowledges in court that he or she will pay a specified sum of money if a certain event occurs. A bail bond is an example of a recognizance.
- **Negotiable Instruments**. Negotiable instruments, which include checks, drafts, notes, and certificates of deposit, are special forms of contracts recognized by the UCC. They require a special form and language for their creation and must meet certain requirements for their transfer. Negotiable instruments are discussed in detail in chapters 16–18.
- **Letters of Credit**. A letter of credit is an agreement by the issuer of the letter to pay a sum of money upon the receipt of an invoice and bill of lading. Letters of credit, which are governed by the UCC, are discussed in chapter 13.

informal contract
A contract that is not formal. Valid informal contracts are fully enforceable and may be sued upon if breached.

Informal Contracts All contracts that do not qualify as formal contracts are called **informal contracts** (or **simple contracts**). The term is a misnomer. Valid informal contracts (e.g., leases, sales contracts, service contracts) are fully enforceable and may be sued upon if breached. They are called informal contracts only because no special form or method is required for their creation.

Executed and Executory Contracts

executed contract
A contract that has been fully performed on both sides; a completed contract.

executory contract
A contract that has not been fully performed by either or both sides.

A completed contract, that is, one that has been fully performed on both sides, is called an **executed contract**. A contract that has not been performed by both sides is called an **executory contract**. Contracts that have been fully performed by one side but not by the other are classified as executory contracts.

CONSIDER THESE EXAMPLES: (1) Suppose Elizabeth Andrews signs a contract to purchase a new Jaguar automobile from Ace Motors. She has not yet paid for the car, and Ace Motors has not yet delivered it. This is an executory contract. (2) Assume that the car was paid for but Ace Motors has not yet delivered the car. Here, the contract is executed by Elizabeth but is executory as to Ace Motors. This is an executory contract. (3) Assume that Ace Motors now delivers the car to Elizabeth. The contract has been fully performed by both parties. It is an executed contract.

Valid, Void, Voidable, and Unenforceable Contracts

valid contract A contract that meets all of the essential elements to establish a contract; a contract that is enforceable by at least one of the parties.

void contract A contract that has no legal effect; a nullity.

voidable contract
A contract in which one or both parties have the option to avoid their contractual obligations. If a contract is avoided, both parties are released from their contractual obligations.

unenforceable contract
A contract in which the essential elements to create a valid contract are met, but there is some legal defense to the enforcement of the contract.

A **valid contract** is one that meets all the essential elements to establish a contract. In other words, it must (1) consist of an agreement between the parties, (2) be supported by legally sufficient consideration, (3) be between parties with contractual capacity, and (4) accomplish a lawful object. Valid contracts are enforceable by at least one of the parties.

A **void contract** is one that has no legal effect. It is as if no contract had ever been created. For example, a contract to commit a crime is void. If a contract is void, neither party is obligated to perform and neither party can enforce the contract.

A **voidable contract** is one in which at least one party has the *option* to avoid his or her contractual obligations. If the contract is avoided, both parties are released from their obligations under the contract. If the party with the option chooses to ratify (i.e., execute) the contract, both parties must fully perform their obligations. With certain exceptions, contracts may be voided by minors; insane persons; intoxicated persons; persons acting under duress, undue influence, or fraud; and cases involving mutual mistake.

An **unenforceable contract** is one in which there is some legal defense to the enforcement of the contract. For example, suppose a contract is not in writing even though the Statute of Frauds requires it to be written. The contract is unenforceable. The parties may voluntarily perform an unenforceable contract.

QUASI CONTRACTS (IMPLIED-IN-LAW CONTRACTS)

The equitable doctrine of **quasi contract**, also called **implied-in-law contract**, provides that the court may award monetary damages to a plaintiff for providing work or services to a defendant even though no actual contract existed between the parties. This doctrine, which is intended to prevent *unjust enrichment* and *unjust detriment*, does not apply where there is an enforceable contract between the parties. In addition, recovery is generally based on the reasonable value of the services received by the defendant.

A quasi contract is imposed where (1) one person confers a benefit on another who retains the benefit and (2) it would be unjust not to require that person to pay for the benefit received.

quasi or implied-in-law contract An equitable doctrine whereby a court may award monetary damages to a plaintiff for providing work or services to a defendant even though no actual contract existed. The doctrine is intended to prevent unjust enrichment and unjust detriment.

CONSIDER THIS EXAMPLE: After an automobile accident a person is rendered unconscious and injured alongside the highway. If a medical doctor stops and renders aid that saves the person, that person owes the medical doctor the reasonable value for the services rendered. The medical doctor can recover this amount under the doctrine of quasi contract.

The following case illustrates the doctrine of quasi contract.

CASE 7.1

Dines v. Liberty Mutual Insurance Company
548 N.E. 2d 1268 (1990) Appeals Court of Massachusetts

Facts Roger J. Dines is engaged in the business of towing and storing vehicles. On October 15, 1985, the state police recovered a stolen trailer and ordered it stored at Dines's facility. The rightful owner of the trailer, the Liberty Mutual Insurance Company (Liberty), learned that it was stored at Dines's facility on January 7, 1986, but it did nothing to recover its property. Dines discovered that Liberty owned the trailer on March 11, 1986. On March 14, 1986, Dines gave written notice to Liberty that its trailer was at his storage facility. He enclosed an invoice for storage fees computed at $20 per day. Liberty refused to pay the charges. On March 11, 1987, Liberty sued to replevy the trailer. Dines released the trailer to Liberty on March 18, 1987, but sued Liberty to recover $10,400 in storage fees. The trial court found an implied-in-law contract and awarded Dines $5,000, which represented the value of the trailer. Both parties appealed.

Issue Do the facts and circumstances justify the imposition of an implied-in-law contract?

Decision Yes. The appeals court held that the facts and circumstances of the case justified the imposition of an implied-in-law contract. Affirmed.

Reason A quasi contract is an obligation created by law for reasons of justice. The underlying basis for awarding quasi contract damages is unjust enrichment of one party and unjust detriment to the other party. Here, the property was stored in a safe facility preventing vandalism. Therefore, Liberty benefited from the storage of its property. The court noted that quasi contract damages are limited to the amount of benefit bestowed on the defendant. If Dines were permitted to recover the full amount he had billed, he would have recovered more than the benefit conferred on Liberty.

CASE QUESTIONS

Critical Legal Thinking What public policy underlies the doctrine of implied-in-law contract?

Ethics When should Liberty have notified Dines that he was holding its property? Was it ethical for Liberty to refuse to pay the storage charges?

Business Implication Should a business be made to pay contract damages when it has not entered into an express contract with the plaintiff?

EQUITY AND THE LAW OF CONTRACTS

equity A doctrine that permits judges to make decisions based on fairness, equality, moral rights, and natural law.

Recall that two separate courts developed in England, a court of law and a chancery court (or court of equity). The equity courts developed a set of maxims based on fairness, equality, moral rights, and natural law that were applied in settling disputes. **Equity** was resorted to when (1) an award of money damages "at law" would not be the proper remedy or (2) fairness required the application of equitable principles. Today, in most states of the United States, the courts of law and equity have been merged into one court. In an action "in equity" the judge decides the equitable issue; there is no right to a jury trial in an equitable action. The doctrine of equity is sometimes applied in contract cases.

ETHICAL PERSPECTIVE

Equity to the Rescue

The courts usually interpret a valid contract as a solemn promise to perform. This view of the sanctity of a contract can cause an ethical conflict. Consider the following case.

In 1975, a landlord leased a motel he owned to lessees for a 10-year period. The lessees had an option to extend the lease for an additional 10 years, commencing on March 1, 1985. To do so, they had to give written notice to the landlord on or before December 1, 1984. The lease provided for forfeiture of all furniture, fixtures, and equipment installed by the lessees, free of any liens, upon termination of the lease.

From 1975 to 1985, the lessees devoted most of their assets and a great deal of their energy building up the business. During this time, they transformed a disheveled, unrated motel into a AAA three-star operation. With the landlord's

knowledge, the lessees made extensive long-term improvements that greatly increased the value of both the property and the business. The landlord knew that the lessees had obtained long-term financing for the improvements that would extend well beyond the first 10-year term of the lease. The landlord also knew that the only source of income the lessees had to pay for these improvements was the income generated from the motel business. The lessees told the landlord in a conversation that they intended to extend the lease.

The lessees had instructed their accountant to exercise the option by December 1, 1984. Despite reminders from the lessees, the accountant failed to give the written notice by December 1, 1984. On December 13, 1984, as soon as they discovered the mistake, the lessees personally delivered written notice of renewal of the option to

the landlord, who rejected it as late and instituted a lawsuit for unlawful detainer to evict the lessees.

The trial and appellate courts held in favor of the lessees. They rejected the landlord's argument for the strict adherence to the deadline for giving notice of renewal of the lease. Instead, the courts granted **equitable relief** and permitted the late renewal notice. The court reasoned that "there is only minimal delay in giving notice, the harm to the lessor is slight, and the hardship to the lessee is severe." [*Romasanta v. Mitton*, 234 Cal.Rptr. 729 (Cal.App. 1987)]

1. Did the landlord act ethically in this case?
2. Should the court have applied equity and saved the lessees from their mistake? Or should they have been held to the terms of the lease?

WORKING THE WEB

Outlines Do you want to find some free outlines to help you study contracts? Then you might want to check out the LAWSCHOOL.ORG home-

page. Here you will find course and bar outlines galore.

Visit at http://www.lawschool.org/

USALAW USALAW, sponsored by a Florida law firm, has been providing legal information over the Internet for several years. It has many interesting features, including articles about contract law.

Visit at http://www.usalaw.com/

FindLaw FindLaw is a search engine that will help you find lots of legal information, including information on contracts. In it, you can find documents like the UCC and articles from journals about contract law. Cases, opinions, statutes, codes, law schools, law firms, consultants, experts, government resources, forms, software, law reviews, and legal associations are accessible from this site.

Visit at http://www.findlaw.com/

Cornell Law School Legal Information Institute Cornell Law School Legal Information Institute maintains a site that provides links to federal and state materials and other key Internet sites on contracts.

Visit at http://www.law.cornell.edu

Institute of International Commercial Law "Pace University School of Law maintains a database on the United Nations Convention on Contracts for the International Sale of Goods (CISG), the uniform international sales law of countries that account for two-thirds of all world trade."

Visit at http://cisgw3.law.pace.edu/

CYBER EXERCISES:
1. Use the LAWSCHOOL.ORG home page to find a contracts outline.
2. Using the USALAW Web site, find an article by Morris Silberman called "Avoiding Contract Lawsuits" and print it out.
3. Using the FindLaw search engine, find a publication called a Work for Hire Agreement. Print it out. What law firm contributed this publication to FindLaw?
4. Using the Cornell Law School Legal Information Institute Web site, find out if your state has adopted the UCC.
5. Using the Institute of International Commercial Law Web site, find out who the general editor of the database is.

CHAPTER SUMMARY

DEFINITION OF A CONTRACT, P. 155

Definition of a Contract	"A promise or set of promises for the breach of which the law gives a remedy or the performance of which the law in some way recognizes a duty."
Parties to a Contract	1. *Offeror.* Party who makes an offer to enter into a contract. 2. *Offeree.* Party to whom the offer is made.

REQUIREMENTS OF A CONTRACT, P. 156

Elements of a Contract	1. Agreement 2. Consideration 3. Contractual capacity 4. Lawful object
Defenses to the Enforcement of a Contract	1. Genuineness of assent 2. Writing and form

SOURCES OF CONTRACT LAW, P. 156

Sources of Contract Law	1. Common law of contracts (law). 2. Uniform Commercial Code (law). 3. Restatement (Second) of Contracts (advisory only, not law).
Theories of Contract Law	1. *Classical law of contracts.* Parties were free to negotiate contract terms without government interference.

2. *Modern law of contracts.* Parties may negotiate contract terms subject to government regulations.

CLASSIFICATIONS OF CONTRACTS, P. 157	
Formation	1. *Bilateral contract.* A promise for a promise. 2. *Unilateral contract.* A promise for an act. 3. *Express contract.* A contract expressed in oral or written words. 4. *Implied-in-fact contract.* A contract implied from the conduct of the parties. 5. *Formal contract.* A contract that requires a special form or method for creation. 6. *Informal contract.* A contract that requires no special form or method for creation.
Performance	1. *Executed contract.* A contract that is fully performed on both sides. 2. *Executory contract.* A contract that is not fully performed by one or both parties.
Enforceability	1. *Valid contract.* Meets all of the elements to establish a contract. 2. *Void contract.* No contract exists. 3. *Voidable contract.* A contract that one or both parties have the option of avoiding or enforcing. 4. *Unenforceable contract.* A contract that cannot be enforced because of a legal defense.

QUASI CONTRACTS, P. 161	
Quasi Contract	A contract implied by law to prevent unjust enrichment and unjust detriment.

EQUITY, P. 162	
Equity	A doctrine that permits judges to make decisions based on fairness, equality, moral rights, and natural law.

CRITICAL LEGAL THINKING CASES

7.1 Bilateral or Unilateral Contract On January 23, 1974, G. S. Adams, Jr., vice president of the Washington Bank & Trust Co., met with Bruce Bickham. An agreement was reached whereby Bickham agreed to do his personal and corporate banking business with the bank, and the bank agreed to loan Bickham money at 7½ percent interest per annum. Bickham would have 10 years to repay the loans. From January 1974 to September 1976, the bank made several loans to Bickham at 7½ percent interest. In September 1976, Adams resigned from the bank. The bank then notified Bickham that general economic changes made it necessary to charge a higher rate of interest on both outstanding and new loans. Bickham sued the bank for breach of contract. Was the contract a bilateral or a unilateral contract? Does Bickham win? [*Bickham v. Washington Bank & Trust Company*, 515 So.2d 457 (La.App. 1987)]

7.2 Implied-in-Fact Contract From October 1964 through May 1970, Lee Marvin, an actor, lived with Michelle Marvin. They were not married. In May 1970, Lee Marvin compelled Michelle Marvin to leave his household. He continued to support her until November 1971, but thereafter refused to provide further support. During their time together, Lee Marvin earned substantial income and acquired property, including motion-picture rights worth more than $1 million. Michelle Marvin brought an action against Lee Marvin, alleging that an implied-in-fact contract existed between them and that she was entitled to half of the property they had acquired while living together. She claimed that she had given up a lucrative career as an entertainer and singer to be a full-time companion, homemaker, housekeeper, and cook. Can an implied-in-fact contract result from conduct of unmarried persons who live together? [*Marvin v. Marvin*, 557 P.2d 106 (Cal. 1976)]

ETHICS CASES

7.3 Ethical Perspective On October 6, 1974, the Lewiston Lodge of Elks sponsored a golf tournament at the Fairlawn Country Club in Poland, Maine. For promotional purposes, Marcel Motors, an automobile dealership, agreed to give any golfer who shot a hole in one a new 1974 Dodge Colt. Fliers advertising the tournament were posted in the Elks Club and sent to potential participants. On the day of the tournament, the 1974 Dodge Colt was parked near the clubhouse with one of the posters conspicuously displayed on the vehicle. Alphee Chenard, Jr., who had seen the promotional literature regarding the hole in one offer, registered for the tournament and paid the requisite entrance fee. While playing the 13th hole of the golf course, Chenard shot a hole in one. When Marcel Motors refused to tender the automobile, Chenard sued for breach of contract. Was the contract a bilateral or a unilateral contract? Does Chenard win? Was it ethical for Marcel Motors to refuse to give the automobile to Chenard? [*Chenard v. Marcel Motors*, 387 A.2d 596 (Maine 1978)]

7.4 Ethical Perspective Loren Vranich, a doctor practicing under the corporate name Family Health Care, P.C., entered into a written employment contract to hire Dennis Winkel. The contract provided for an annual salary, insurance benefits, and other employment benefits. Another doctor, Dr. Quan, also practiced with Dr. Vranich. About nine months later, when Dr. Quan left the practice, Vranich and Winkel entered into an oral modification of their written contract whereby Winkel was to receive a higher salary and a profit-sharing bonus. During the next year Winkel received the increased salary. However, a disagreement arose, and Winkel sued to recover the profit-sharing bonus. Under Montana law, a written contract can be altered only in writing or by an executed oral agreement. Dr. Vranich argued that the contract could not be enforced because it was not in writing. Does Winkel receive the profit-sharing bonus? Did Dr. Vranich act ethically in raising the defense that the contract was not in writing? [*Winkel v. Family Health Care, P.C.*, 668 P.2d 208 (Mont. 1983)]

CRITICAL LEGAL THINKING WRITING ASSIGNMENT

Read Case A.7 in the Case Appendix [*Mark Realty, Inc. v. Rogness*]. This case is excerpted from the appellate court's opinion. Review and brief the case. In your brief, be sure to answer the following questions:

1. Who is the plaintiff? Who is the defendant?
2. Why did it make a difference if the court found the contract to be unilateral or bilateral? Who would win in each situation?

3. Which party did the appellate court find in favor of? What evidence did the court cite in reaching its conclusion?
4. How might an owner of property protect him- or herself from paying a broker's commission if the owner sold the property him- or herself?

NOTES

[1] *Rebstock v. Birthright Oil & Gas Co.*, 406 So.2d 636 (La.App. 1981).
[2] Restatement (Second) of Contracts, § 1.
[3] Restatement (Second) of Contracts, § 1.
[4] Restatement (Second) of Contracts, § 6.

CHAPTER 8

AGREEMENT AND

CONSIDERATION

Chapter Objectives

*After studying this chapter,
you should be able to*

1. Define an offer and an acceptance
2. Describe what terms can be implied in a contract
3. Describe how offers are terminated by action of the parties
4. Define a counteroffer and describe its effects
5. Describe how offers are terminated by operation of law
6. Define consideration
7. Identify when there is inadequacy of consideration
8. Analyze whether contracts are lacking in consideration
9. Describe the settlement of claims
10. Apply the doctrine of promissory estoppel

Chapter Contents

- Agreement
- Requirements of an Offer
  Case 8.1 *Mesaros v. United States (Fed. Cir.)*
- Termination of the Offer
  Case 8.2 *Logan Ranch, Karg Partnership v. Farm Credit Bank of Omaha (NE)*
  Business Application Option Contracts
- Acceptance
  Business Checklist Silence as Acceptance
  Case 8.3 *Soldau v. Organon, Inc. (9th Cir.)*
- Consideration
  Case 8.4 *Paterek v. Liberty Park of America (MI)*
  Business Checklist The Use of Output and Requirements Contracts in Business
- Contracts Lacking Consideration
  Ethical Perspective When Is Consideration Inadequate?
- Settlement of Claims
- Promissory Estoppel
- Working the Web
- Chapter Summary
- Critical Legal Thinking Cases
- Ethics Cases
- Critical Legal Thinking Writing Assignment

> "When I use a word," Humpty Dumpty said, in rather a scornful tone, "it means just what I choose it to mean—neither more nor less."
>
> "The question is," said Alice, "whether you can make words mean so many different things."
>
> "The question is," said Humpty Dumpty, "which is to be master—that's all."
>
> Lewis Carroll
Alice's Adventures in Wonderland (1865)

Contracts are voluntary agreements between the parties. One party makes an offer, the other accepts it. Without mutual assent, there is no contract. Assent may be expressly evidenced by the words of the parties or implied from their conduct.

> *"A contract is a mutual promise."*
> William Paley
> *The Principles of Moral and Political Philosophy* (1784)

To be enforceable, a contract must be supported by "consideration." Consideration is broadly defined as something of legal value. It can consist of money, property, the provision of services, the forbearance of a right, or anything else of value. Most contracts that are not supported by consideration are not enforceable. However, the parties may voluntarily perform a contract that is lacking in consideration.

This chapter discusses the primary elements of a contract: agreement (i.e., offer and acceptance) and consideration.

AGREEMENT

Agreement is the manifestation by two or more persons of the substance of a contract. It requires an *offer* and an *acceptance*. The process of reaching an agreement usually proceeds as follows: Prior to entering into a contract, the parties may engage in preliminary negotiations about price, time of performance, and such. At some point during these negotiations, one party makes an **offer**. The person who makes the offer is called the **offeror**, and the person to whom the offer is made is called the **offeree**. The offer sets forth the terms under which the offeror is willing to enter into the contract. The offeree has the power to create an agreement by accepting the offer.

agreement
The manifestation by two or more persons of the substance of a contract.

offeror The party who makes an offer.

offeree The party to whom an offer has been made.

REQUIREMENTS OF AN OFFER

Section 24 of the Restatement (Second) of Contracts defines an **offer** as "The manifestation of willingness to enter into a bargain, so made as to justify another person in understanding that his assent to that bargain is invited and will conclude it." The following three elements are required for an offer to be effective.

1. The offeror must *objectively intend* to be bound by the offer
2. The terms of the offer must be definite or reasonably *certain*
3. The offer must be *communicated* to the offeree.

offer "The manifestation of willingness to enter into a bargain, so made as to justify another person in understanding that his assent to that bargain is invited and will conclude it." (Section 24 of Restatement (Second) of Contracts)

Objective Intent

The intent to enter into a contract is determined using the **objective theory of contracts**, that is, whether a reasonable person viewing the circumstances would conclude that the parties intended to be legally bound. Subjective intent is irrelevant. Therefore, no valid contract results from preliminary negotiations; offers made in jest, anger, or undue excitement; or offers that are an expression of opinion.

objective theory of contracts A theory that says the intent to contract is judged by the reasonable person standard and not by the subjective intent of the parties.

Preliminary Negotiations A question such as "Are you interested in selling your building for $2 million?" is not an offer. It is an invitation to make an offer or an invitation to negotiate. However, the statement "I will buy your building for $2 million" is a valid offer because it indicates the offeror's present intent to contract.

BUSINESS BRIEF

It is always best to expressly state all the essential terms in the contract. This practice will prevent many lawsuits.

implied term A term in a contract which can reasonably be supplied by the courts.

BUSINESS BRIEF

A contract is a voluntary agreement between the parties. The parties must mutually agree as to the terms of the contract—in other words, there must be a "meeting of the minds."

advertisement A general advertisement is an invitation to make an offer. A specific advertisement is an offer.

Offers That Are Made in Jest, Anger, or Undue Excitement Suppose the owner of Company A has lunch with the owner of Company B. In the course of their conversation, Company A's owner exclaims in frustration, "For $2 I'd sell the whole computer division!" An offer such as that cannot result in a valid contract.

Offers That Are an Expression of Opinion A lawyer who tells her client that she thinks the lawsuit will result in an award of $100,000 cannot be sued for the difference if the trial jury awards only $50,000. The lawyer's statement is not an enforceable promise.

Definiteness of Terms

The terms of an offer must be clear enough for the offeree to be able to decide whether to accept or reject the terms of the offer. If the terms are indefinite, the courts cannot enforce the contract or determine an appropriate remedy for its breach.

To be considered definite, an offer (and contract) generally must contain the following terms: (1) identification of the parties, (2) identification of the subject matter and quantity, (3) consideration to be paid, and (4) time of performance. Complex contracts usually state additional terms.

Implied Terms The common law of contracts required an exact specification of contract terms. If one essential term was omitted, the courts would hold that no contract had been made. This rule was inflexible.

The modern law of contracts is more lenient. The Restatement (Second) of Contracts merely requires that the terms of the offer be "reasonably certain."[1] Accordingly, the court can supply a missing term if a reasonable term can be implied.[2] The definition of *reasonable* depends on the circumstances. Terms that are supplied in this way are called **implied terms**.

Generally, time of performance can be implied. Price can be implied if there is a market or source from which to determine the price of the item or service (e.g., "blue book" for an automobile price, New York Stock Exchange for a stock price). The parties or subject matter of the contract usually cannot be implied if an item or service is unique or personal—such as the construction of a house or the performance of a professional sports contract.

Communication

An offer cannot be accepted if it is not communicated to the offeree by the offeror or a representative or agent of the offeror. For example, suppose Mr. Jones, the chief executive officer (CEO) of Ace Corporation, decides to sell a manufacturing division to Baker Corporation. He puts the offer in writing, but he does not send it. Assume Mr. Griswald, the chief financial officer (CFO) of Baker Corporation, visits Mr. Jones and sees the written offer lying on Jones' desk. Griswald tells his CEO about the offer. Because Mr. Jones never communicated the offer to the CEO of Baker Corporation, there is no offer to be accepted.

Special Offer Situations

There are several special situations where there is a question whether an offer has been made. Advertisements, auctions, and rewards are examples of such situations.

Advertisements **Advertisements** for the sale of goods, even at specific prices, generally are treated as *invitations to make an offer*. Catalogs, price lists, quotation sheets, offering circulars, and other sales materials are viewed in the same way. This rule is intended to protect advertiser–sellers from the unwarranted breach of contract suits for nonperformance that would otherwise arise if the seller ran out of the advertised goods.

There is one exception to this rule: An advertisement is considered an offer if it is so definite or specific that it is apparent that the advertiser has the present intent to bind him- or herself to the terms of the advertisement. For example, an automobile dealer's advertisement to sell a "previously owned red 1994 Chrysler LeBaron, serial no. 3210674, $15,000" is an offer. Because the advertisement identifies the exact automobile for sale, the first person to accept the offer owns the automobile.

In the following case, the court had to decide whether an advertisement was a solicitation of an offer or an offer.

CASE 8.1

Mesaros v. United States
845 F.2d 1576 (1988) United States Court of Appeals, Federal Circuit

Facts In July 1985, the U.S. Congress directed the Secretary of the Treasury to mint and sell a stated number of specially minted commemorative coins to raise funds to restore and renovate the Statue of Liberty. In November and December 1985, the United States Mint mailed advertising materials to persons, including Mary and Anthony C. Mesaros, husband and wife, that described the various types of coins that were to be issued. Payment could be made by check, money order, or credit card. The materials included an order form. Directly above the space provided on this form for the customer's signature was the following: "YES, Please accept my order for the U.S. Liberty Coins I have indicated." On November 26, 1985, Mary Mesaros forwarded to the Mint a credit-card order of $1,675 for certain coins, including the $5 gold coin. All credit-card orders were forwarded by the Mint to Mellon Bank in Pittsburgh, Pennsylvania, for verification. This took a period of time. Meanwhile, cash orders were filled immediately, and orders by check were filled as the checks cleared. The issuance of 500,000 gold coins was exhausted before Mesaros' credit-card order could be filled. The Mint sent a letter to the Mesaroses notifying them of this fact. The gold coin increased in value by 200 percent within the first few months of 1986. On May 23, 1986, Mary and Anthony C. Mesaros filed a class action lawsuit against the United States seeking in the alternative either damages for breach of contract or a decree of mandamus ordering the Mint to deliver the gold coins to the plaintiffs. The district court held for the Mint. The Mesaroses appealed.

Issue Was the Mint's advertisement a solicitation of an offer or an offer?

Decision The court of appeals held that the advertising materials sent out by the Mint were a solicitation to make an offer and not an offer. Therefore, the Mint wins.

Reason It is well established that materials such as those mailed to prospective customers by the Mint are no more than advertisements or invitations to deal. They are mere solicitations of offers that create no power of acceptance in the recipient. The court stated: "Generally, it is considered unreasonable for a person to believe that advertisements and solicitations are offers that bind the advertiser. Otherwise, the advertiser could be bound by an excessive number of contracts requiring delivery of goods far in excess of amounts available. That is particularly true in the instant case where the gold coins were limited to 500,000 by the Act of Congress. We conclude that a thorough reading, construction, and interpretation of the materials sent to the plaintiffs by the Mint makes clear that the contention of the plaintiffs that they reasonably believed the materials were intended as an offer is unreasonable as a matter of law."

CASE QUESTIONS

Critical Legal Thinking Should an advertisement be treated as an offer instead of an invitation to make an offer? Why or why not?

Ethics Do you think the Mesaroses acted unethically by suing the Mint?

Business Implication Would it cause any problems for businesses if advertisements were considered offers? Explain.

auction with reserve
Unless expressly stated otherwise, an auction is an auction with reserve; that is, the seller retains the right to refuse the highest bid and withdraw the goods from sale.

auction without reserve
An auction in which the seller expressly gives up his or her right to withdraw the goods from sale and must accept the highest bid.

reward To collect a reward, the offeree must (1) have knowledge of the reward offer prior to completing the requested act and (2) perform the requested act.

Auctions At an auction, the seller offers goods for sale through an auctioneer. Unless otherwise expressly stated, an auction is considered an **auction with reserve**, that is, an invitation to make an offer. The seller retains the right to refuse the highest bid and withdraw the goods from sale. A contract is formed only when the auctioneer strikes the gavel down or indicates acceptance by some other means. The bidder may withdraw his or her bid at any time before the gavel is struck down.

If an auction is expressly announced to be an **auction without reserve**, the participants reverse their roles: The seller is the offeror and the bidders are the offerees. The seller must accept the highest bid and cannot withdraw the goods from sale. If the seller sets minimum bid, he or she has to sell the item only if the highest bid is equal to or greater than the minimum bid.

Rewards An offer to pay a **reward** (e.g., for the return of lost property or for the capture of a criminal) is an offer to form a unilateral contract. To be entitled to collect the reward, the offeree must (1) have knowledge of the reward offer prior to completing the requested act and (2) perform the requested act.

CONSIDER THIS EXAMPLE: John Anderson accidentally leaves a briefcase containing $500,000 in negotiable bonds on a subway train. He places newspaper ads stating "$5,000 reward for return of briefcase left on a train in Manhattan on January 10, 1993, at approximately 10 A.M. Call 212-555-6789." Helen Smith, who is unaware of the offer, finds the briefcase. She reads the luggage tag containing Mr. Anderson's name, address, and telephone number, and returns the briefcase to him. She is not entitled to the reward money because she did not know about it when she performed the requested act.

TERMINATION OF THE OFFER

A valid offer gives the offeree the power to accept the offer and thereby create a contract. This power, however, does not continue indefinitely. An offer can be terminated by the *action of the parties* or by *operation of law*.

Termination by Action of the Parties

An offer may be terminated by the following actions of the parties.

revocation Withdrawal of an offer by the offeror terminates the offer.

CAUTION
Generally, an offeror can revoke an offer at any time prior to its acceptance by the offeree.

Revocation of the Offer by the Offeror Under the common law, an offeror may **revoke** (i.e., withdraw) an offer anytime prior to its acceptance by the offeree. Generally, this is so even if the offeror promised to keep the offer open for a longer period of time. The revocation may be communicated to the offeree by either the offeror or a third party and made by (1) the offeror's express statement (e.g., "I hereby withdraw my offer") or (2) an act of the offeror that is inconsistent with the offer (e.g., selling the goods to another party). Most states provide that the revocation is not effective until it is actually received by the offeree or the offeree's agent.

Offers made to the public may be revoked by communicating the revocation by the same means used to make the offer. For example, if a reward offer for a lost watch was published in two local newspapers each week for four weeks, notice of revocation must be published in the same newspapers for the same length of time. The revocation is effective against all offerees, even those who saw the reward offer but not the notice of revocation.

rejection Express words or conduct by the offeree that rejects an offer. Rejection terminates the offer.

Rejection of Offer by the Offeree An offer is terminated if the offeree **rejects** it. Any subsequent attempt by the offeree to accept the offer is ineffective and is construed as a new offer that the original offeror (now the offeree) is free to accept or reject. A rejection may be evidenced by the offeree's express words (oral or written) or conduct. Generally, a rejection is not effective until it is actually received by the offeror.

CONSIDER THIS EXAMPLE: Harriet Jackson, sales manager of IBM Corporation, offers to sell 1,000 computers to Ted Green, purchasing manager of General Motors Corporation, for $250,000. The offer is made on August 1. Mr. Green telephones Ms. Jackson to say that he is not interested. This rejection terminates the offer. If Mr. Green later decides that he wants to purchase the computers, an entirely new contract must be formed.

Counteroffer by the Offeree A **counteroffer** by the offeree simultaneously terminates the offeror's offer and creates a new offer. For example, suppose in the prior example, Mr. Green says, "I think $250,000 is too high for the computers. I will pay you $200,000." He has made a counteroffer. The original offer is terminated; the counteroffer is a new offer that Ms. Jackson is free to accept or reject.

The following case illustrates the effect of counteroffers.

counteroffer A response by an offeree that contains terms and conditions different from or in addition to those of the offer. A counteroffer terminates an offer.

CASE 8.2

Logan Ranch, Karg Partnership v. Farm Credit Bank of Omaha
472 N.W.2d 704 (1991) Supreme Court of Nebraska

Facts Logan Ranch, Karg Partnership (Logan), is a partnership that owned farmland. The Farm Credit Bank of Omaha (FCB) made a loan to Logan and took back a mortgage on the farm land to secure the loan. When Logan ran into financial difficulty in 1984, it deeded the land to FCB in lieu of foreclosure. In 1988, Gene Welsh offered to purchase the land from FCB. Pursuant to the federal Agricultural Credit Act, FCB had to offer the previous owner, Logan, the opportunity to purchase the land first. On March 15, 1988, FCB made an offer to sell the land to Logan for $988,500. The balance of the purchase price (less the deposit) was to be paid when the deed was delivered, and closing was to occur on or before April 15, 1988.

On April 15, 1988, Logan returned FCB's offer, which it had altered by adding the following terms and conditions: (1) a balance of $150,000 to be paid when the deed is delivered, (2) conditional upon Logan's ability to obtain a loan in the amount of at least $739,650 from NorWest Trust, and (3) the loan to be obtained within 60 days. FCB rejected these terms and made arrangements to sell the land to Welsh. Logan sued for specific performance, alleging that it had accepted FCB's offer. The trial court granted summary judgment to FCB. Logan appealed.

Issue Had Logan accepted FCB's original offer, or had it made a counteroffer?

Decision The state supreme court upheld the trial court's decision. It held that the additional terms and conditions submitted by Logan constituted a counteroffer. Thus, no contract had been formed between Logan and FCB.

Reason Under the common law "mirror image" rule, the acceptance of an offer must be unconditional, or there is no contract. If the purported acceptance differs from the original offer in any way, it is a counteroffer and not an acceptance. A counteroffer acts as a rejection of the original offer. The supreme court held that the new terms and conditions added by Logan to FCB's offer were in essence a counteroffer and that no contract was created between Logan and FCB.

CASE QUESTIONS

Critical Legal Thinking Should a counteroffer be considered a rejection of the original offer? Why or why not?

Ethics Did Logan act ethically in suing FCB in this case?

Business Implication Businesses often engage in protracted negotiations before entering into a contract. Is it sometimes difficult to determine what the terms of an offer are?

Termination by Operation of Law

Offers can be terminated by operation of law in the following situations.

Destruction of the Subject Matter

The offer terminates if the subject matter of the offer is destroyed through no fault of either party prior to its acceptance. For example, if a fire destroys an office building that has been listed for sale, the offer automatically terminates.

Death or Incompetency of the Offeror or the Offeree

The death or incompetency of either the offeror or the offeree terminates the offer. Notice of the other party's death or incompetence is not a requirement. For example, suppose on June 1 Shari Hunter offers to sell her house to Damian Coe for $100,000, providing he decides on or before June 15. Ms. Hunter dies on June 7 before Mr. Coe has made up his mind. There is no contract prior to her death, so the offer automatically terminates on June 7.

Supervening Illegality

If the object of an offer is made illegal prior to the acceptance of an offer, the offer terminates. This usually occurs when a statute is enacted or a court case is announced that makes the object of the offer illegal. This is called a **supervening illegality**. For example, suppose City Bank offers to loan ABC Corporation $5 million at 18 percent interest rate. Prior to ABC's acceptance of the offer, the state legislature enacts a statute that sets a usury interest rate of 12 percent. City Bank's offer to ABC Corporation automatically terminated when the usury statute became effective.

supervening illegality The enactment of a statute or regulation or court decision that makes the object of an offer illegal. This terminates the offer.

Lapse of Time

The offer may state that it is effective only until a certain date. Unless otherwise stated, the time period begins to run when the offer is actually received by the offeree and terminates when the stated time period expires. Statements such as "This offer is good for 10 days" or "This offer must be accepted by January 1, 1997" are examples of such notices. If no time is stated in the offer, the offer terminates after a "reasonable time" dictated by the circumstances. Thus, a reasonable time to accept an offer to purchase stock traded on a national stock exchange may be a few moments, but a reasonable time to accept an offer to purchase a house may be a few days. Unless otherwise stated, an offer made face-to-face or during a telephone call usually expires after the conversation.

lapse of time An offer terminates when a stated time period expires. If no time is stated, an offer terminates after a reasonable time.

BUSINESS APPLICATION

Option Contracts

An offeree can prevent the offeror from revoking his or her offer by paying the offeror compensation to keep the offer open for an agreed-upon period of time. This is called an **option contract**. In other words, the offeror agrees not to sell the property to anyone but the offeree during the option period. The death or incompetency of either party does not terminate an option contract unless it is for the performance of a personal service.

CONSIDER THIS EXAMPLE: Anne Mason offers to sell a piece of real estate to Harold Greenberg for $1 million. Mr. Greenberg wants time to make a decision, so he pays Ms. Mason $20,000 to keep her offer open to him for six months. At any time during the option period, Mr. Greenberg may exercise his option and pay Ms. Mason the $1 million purchase price. If he lets the option expire, however, Ms. Mason may keep the $20,000 and sell the property to someone else.

ACCEPTANCE

Acceptance is a manifestation of assent by the offeree to the terms of the offer in a manner invited or required by the offer as measured by the objective theory of contracts.[3] Recall that generally (1) unilateral contracts can be accepted only by the offeree's performance of the required act and (2) a bilateral contract can be accepted by an offeree who promises to perform (or where permitted, by performance of) the requested act.

acceptance
A manifestation of assent by the offeree to the terms of the offer in a manner invited or required by the offer as measured by the objective theory of contracts.

Who Can Accept the Offer?

Only the offeree has the legal power to accept an offer and create a contract. Third persons do not usually have the power to accept an offer. If an offer is made individually to two or more persons, each has the power to accept the offer. When an offeree accepts the offer, though, it terminates as to the other offerees. An offer that is made to two or more persons jointly must be accepted jointly.

Unequivocal Acceptance

The offeree's acceptance must be *unequivocal*. The **mirror image rule** requires the offeree to accept the offeror's terms. Generally, a "grumbling acceptance" is a legal acceptance. For example, a response such as "Okay, I'll take the car, but I sure wish you would make me a better deal" creates an enforceable contract. An acceptance is equivocal if certain conditions are added to the acceptance. For example, suppose the offeree had responded, "I accept, but only if you repaint the car red." There is no acceptance in this case.

mirror image rule   States that in order for there to be an acceptance, the offeree must accept the terms as stated in the offer.

Proper Dispatch Rule

The acceptance must be **properly dispatched**. According to § 66 of the Restatement (Second) of Contracts, the acceptance must be properly addressed, be packaged in an appropriate envelope or container, and have prepaid postage or delivery charges. Under common law, if an acceptance is not properly dispatched, it is not effective until it is actually received by the offeror.

Section 67 of the Restatement (Second) of Contracts provides an exception to this rule: An acceptance is effective upon dispatch even if it is sent by an unauthorized means of communication or is improperly dispatched if (1) it is timely sent and (2) the offeror receives the communication within the same time period that a properly transmitted acceptance would have arrived.

proper dispatch   An acceptance must be properly addressed, packaged, and posted to fall within the mailbox rule.

✔ BUSINESS CHECKLIST

Silence as Acceptance

Generally, silence is not considered acceptance even if the offeror states that it is. This rule is intended to protect offerees from being legally bound to offers because they failed to respond.

Nevertheless, silence *does* constitute acceptance in these situations:

1. The offeree has indicated that silence means assent. (For example, "If you do not hear from me by Friday, ship the order.")
2. The offeree signed an agreement indicating continuing acceptance of delivery until further notification. CD-of-the-month club memberships are examples of such acceptances.

continued

3. Prior dealings between the parties indicate that silence means acceptance. For example, a fish wholesaler who delivers 30 pounds of fish to a restaurant each Friday for several years and is paid for the fish can continue the deliveries with expectation of payment until notified otherwise by the restaurant.

4. The offeree takes the benefit of goods or services provided by the offeror even though he or she (a) has an opportunity to reject the goods or services but fails to do so and (b) knows the offeror expects to be compensated. For example, a homeowner who stands idly by and watches a painter whom she has not hired mistakenly paint her house owes the painter for the work.

Mode of Acceptance

"The law has outgrown its primitive stage of formalism when the precise word was the sovereign talisman, and every slip was fatal. It takes a broader view today. A promise may be lacking, and yet the whole writing may be 'instinct with an obligation,' imperfectly expressed."
J. Cardozo
*Wood v.
Duff-Gordon* (1917)

Generally, an offeree must accept an offer by an authorized means of communication. The offer can stipulate that acceptance must be by a specified means of communication (e.g., registered mail, telegram). This is called *express authorization*. If the offeree uses an unauthorized means of communication to transmit the acceptance, the acceptance is not effective even if it is received by the offeror within the allowed time period. This is because the means of communication was a condition of acceptance.

Most offers do not expressly specify the means of communication required for acceptance. The common law recognizes certain implied means of communication. The authorized means of communication may be implied from what is customary in similar transactions, usage of trade, or prior dealings between the parties. This is called *implied authorization*. Section 30 of the Restatement (Second) of Contracts permits implied authorization "by any medium reasonable in the circumstances."

Time of Acceptance

mailbox rule   A rule that states that an acceptance is effective when it is dispatched, even if it is lost in transmission.

Under the common law of contracts, acceptance of a bilateral contract occurs at the time the offeree *dispatches* the acceptance by an authorized means of communication. This is called the **acceptance-upon-dispatch rule** or, more commonly, the **mailbox rule**. Under this rule, the acceptance is effective when it is dispatched even if it is lost in transmission. If an offeree first dispatches a rejection and then sends an acceptance, the mailbox rule does not apply to the acceptance.[4]

The problem of lost acceptances can be minimized by expressly altering the mailbox rule. The offeror can do this by stating in the offer that acceptance is effective only upon actual receipt of the acceptance.

In the following case, the court enforced the mailbox rule.

CASE 8.3

Soldau v. Organon, Inc.
860 F.2d 355 (1988) United States Court of Appeals, Ninth Circuit

Facts John Soldau was discharged by his employer, Organon, Inc. (Organon). He received a letter from Organon offering to pay him double the normal severance pay in exchange for a release by Soldau of all claims against Organon regarding the discharge. Soldau signed and dated the release and deposited it in a mailbox outside of a post office. When he returned home, he had received a check from Organon for the increased severance pay. Soldau returned to the post office, persuaded a postal employee to open the mailbox, and retrieved the release. He cashed the severance paycheck and brought this action against Organon, alleging a violation of the federal Age Discrimination in Employment Act. The district court granted summary judgment for Organon. Soldau appealed.

Issue Did Soldau accept the release contract?

Decision Yes. The court of appeals applied the "mailbox rule" and found that the acceptance was effective when Soldau first deposited it in the mailbox outside the post office. His later retrieval of the release did not undo his acceptance.

Reason The court of appeals stated: "Under federal as well as California law, Soldau's acceptance was effective when it was mailed. The so-called 'mailbox' or 'effective when mailed' rule was adopted and followed as federal common law by the Supreme Court prior to *Erie R.R. Co. v. Tomkins,* 304 U.S. 64 (1938). We could not change the rule, and there is no reason to believe the Supreme Court would be inclined to do so. It is almost universally accepted in the common law world. It is enshrined in the Restatement (Second) of Contracts, Section 63(a), and endorsed by the major contract treatises. Commentators are also virtually unanimous in approving the rule, pointing to the long history of the rule; its importance in creating certainty for contracting parties; and its essential soundness, on balance, as a means of allocating the risk during the period between the making of the offer and the communication of the acceptance or rejection to the offeror."

CASE QUESTIONS

Critical Legal Thinking Should the mailbox rule be changed to place the risk of loss of lost letters on the sender? Or is the present rule the best rule?

Ethics Did Soldau act ethically in this case?

Business Implication How can businesses that make offers protect themselves from the risk of loss associated with the mailbox rule?

CONSIDERATION

Consideration must be given before a contract can exist. **Consideration** is defined as something of legal value given in exchange for a promise. Consideration can come in many forms. The most common types consist of either a tangible payment (e.g., money or property) or the performance of an act (e.g., providing legal services). Less usual forms of consideration include the forbearance of a legal right (e.g., accepting an out-of-court settlement in exchange for dropping a lawsuit) and noneconomic forms of consideration (e.g., refraining from "drinking, using tobacco, swearing, or playing cards or billiards for money" for a specified time period).[5]

Written contracts are presumed to be supported by consideration. This is a rebuttable presumption that may be overcome by sufficient evidence. A few states provide that contracts made under seal cannot be challenged for lack of consideration.

consideration Something of legal value given in exchange for a promise.

Requirements of Consideration

Consideration consists of two elements: (1) Something of legal value must be given (e.g., either a legal benefit must be received or legal detriment suffered), and (2) there must be a bargained-for exchange. Each of these is discussed in the sections that follow.

Legal Value Under the modern law of contracts, a contract is considered supported by **legal value** if (1) the promise suffers a *legal detriment* or (2) the promisor receives a *legal benefit.*

CONSIDER THIS EXAMPLE: Suppose the Dallas Cowboys contract with a tailor to have the tailor make uniforms for the team. The tailor completes the uniforms, but the

NOTE
The more formal approach to finding consideration has been replaced by a modern definition that considers a contract supported by consideration if either (1) the promisee suffers a legal detriment or (2) the promisor receives a legal benefit.

team manager thinks the color is wrong and refuses to allow the team to wear them. Here, there has been no legal benefit to either the manager or the players. However, the tailor has suffered a legal detriment (time spent making the uniforms). Under the modern rule of contracts, there is sufficiency of consideration and the contract is enforceable.

Bargained-for Exchange To be enforceable, a contract must arise from a **bargained-for exchange**. In most business contracts, the parties engage in such exchanges. The commercial setting in which business contracts are formed lead to this conclusion.

    Gift promises, also called **gratuitous promises**, are unenforceable because they lack consideration. To change a gift promise into an enforceable promise, the promisee must offer to do something in exchange—that is, consideration—for the promise. For instance, suppose Mrs. Colby promised to give her son $10,000 and then rescinded the promise. The son would have no recourse because it was a gift promise that lacked consideration. However, if Mrs. Colby promised her son $10,000 for getting an "A" in his business law course and the son performed as required, the contract would be enforceable. A completed gift promise cannot be rescinded for lack of consideration.

    In the following case, the court had to determine whether a contract was supported by consideration.

bargained-for exchange Exchange that parties engage in that leads to an enforceable contract.

gift promise An unenforceable promise because it lacks consideration.

CASE 8.4

Paterek v. Liberty Park of America
465 N.W.2d 342 (1990) Court of Appeals of Michigan

Facts Daniel Paterek was a member of an amateur softball team. Before the start of the 1986 softball season, he signed a document titled "1986 Official Team Roster and Contract" with Liberty Park of America (Liberty), the owner of the softball field where the games were to be played. In the contract, the players acknowledged that softball was a hazardous and dangerous activity and agreed to personally assume all risks of injury. Paterek injured his knee while running to catch a fly ball during one of the games on the field. He sued Liberty for damages, claiming that the field was improperly maintained. Paterek argued that the release agreement was not valid because it was not supported by consideration. The trial court judge granted Liberty's motion for summary judgment. Paterek appealed.

Issue Were the contract and release agreement supported by adequate consideration?

Decision The appellate court held that the contract and release agreement were supported by consideration and were therefore enforceable. Affirmed.

Reason The appellate court found no merit in plaintiff's argument that the release was invalid for lack of consideration. The court held that the defendant's agreement to allow Daniel Paterek to play softball on its field was adequate consideration because it was (1) a legal detriment (2) which induced plaintiff's promise to release defendant from liability, and (3) plaintiff's promise to release defendant from liability induced defendant to suffer the detriment.

CASE QUESTIONS

Critical Legal Thinking Should contracts be required to be supported by consideration? Why or why not?

Ethics Was it ethical for Paterek to sign the release agreement and then sue Liberty?

Business Implication Should release agreements be enforced? Do they serve any useful business purpose?

BUSINESS CHECKLIST

The Use of Output and Requirements Contracts in Business

Generally, the courts tolerate a greater degree of uncertainty in business contracts than in personal contracts under the premise that sophisticated parties know how to protect themselves when negotiating contracts. The law imposes an obligation of good faith on the performance of the parties to requirements and output contracts.

The following are special types of business contracts that specifically allow a greater degree of uncertainty concerning consideration:

- **Output Contracts** In an **output contract**, the seller agrees to sell all of its production to a single buyer. Output contracts serve the legitimate business purposes of (1) assuring the seller of a purchaser for all its output and (2) assuring the buyer of a source of supply for the goods it needs.
- **Requirements Contracts** A **requirements contract** is one where a buyer contracts to purchase all of the requirements for an item from one seller. Such contracts serve the legitimate business purposes of (1) assuring the buyer of a uniform source of supply and (2) providing the seller with reduced selling costs.

CONTRACTS LACKING CONSIDERATION

Some contracts seem as though they are supported by consideration even though they are not. The following types of contracts fall into this category.

Illusory Promises

If parties enter into a contract, but one or both of the parties can choose not to perform their contractual obligations, the contract lacks consideration. Such promises, which are known as **illusory promises** (or **illusory contracts**), are unenforceable. For example, a contract that provides that one of the parties only has to perform if he or she chooses to do so is an illusory contract.

Moral Obligations

Promises made out of a sense of *moral obligation* or honor are generally unenforceable on the ground that they lack consideration. In other words, moral consideration is not treated as legal consideration. Contracts based on love and affection and deathbed promises are examples of such promises. A minority of states hold that moral obligations are enforceable.

Preexisting Duty

A promise lacks consideration if a person promises to perform an act or do something he or she is already under an obligation to do. This is called a **preexisting duty**. The promise is unenforceable because no new consideration has been given. For example, many states have adopted statutes that prohibit police officers from accepting rewards for apprehending criminals.

In the private sector, the preexisting duty rule often arises when one of the parties to an existing contract seeks to change the terms of the contract during the course of

illusory promise
A contract into which parties enter, but one or both of the parties can choose not to perform their contractual obligations. Thus, the contract lacks consideration.

CAUTION
Promises made out of a sense of moral obligation lack consideration. Such promises are unenforceable in most states.

preexisting duty
A promise lacks consideration if a person promises to perform an act or do something he or she is already under an obligation to do.

its performance. Such midstream changes are unenforceable: The parties have a pre-existing duty to perform according to the original terms of the contract.

Sometimes a party to a contract runs into substantial *unforeseen difficulties* while performing his or her contractual duties. If the parties modify their contract to accommodate these unforeseen difficulties, the modification will be enforced even though it is not supported by new consideration.

CONSIDER THIS EXAMPLE: Suppose a landowner enters into a contract with a contractor who agrees to excavate the hole for the foundation of a major office building. When the excavation is partially completed, toxic wastes are unexpectedly found at the site. Removal of toxic wastes is highly regulated by law and would substantially increase the cost of the excavation. If the landowner agrees to pay the contractor increased compensation to remove the toxic wastes, this modification of the contract is enforceable even though it is unsupported by new consideration.

Past Consideration

past consideration A prior act or performance. Past consideration (e.g., prior acts) will not support a new contract. New consideration must be given.

In a business setting, problems of **past consideration** often arise when a party to a contract promises to pay additional compensation for work done in the past.

CONSIDER THIS EXAMPLE: Felipe Chavez, who has worked for the Acme Corporation for 30 years, is retiring. The president of Acme says, "Because you were such a loyal employee, Acme will pay you a bonus of $25,000." The corporation refuses to pay the $25,000. Unfortunately for Mr. Chavez, the contract is unenforceable because it is based on past consideration.

ILLEGAL CONSIDERATION

illegal consideration
A promise to refrain from doing an illegal act. Such a promise will not support a contract.

A contract cannot be supported by a promise to refrain from doing an illegal act because that is **illegal consideration**. Contracts based on illegal consideration are void. For example, statements such as, "I will burn your house down unless you agree to pay me $10,000," cannot become enforceable contracts. Even if the threatened party agrees to make the payment, the contract is unenforceable and void because it is supported by illegal consideration (arson is unlawful).

ETHICAL PERSPECTIVE

When Is Consideration Inadequate?

The courts usually do not inquire into the **adequacy of consideration**. Generally, parties are free to agree on the consideration they are willing to pay or receive under a contract. This rule is based on the court's reluctance to inquire into the motives of a party for entering into a contract or to save a party from a "bad deal."

Some states recognize an exception to the general rule that the courts will not examine the sufficiency of consideration. These states permit a party to escape from a contract if the inadequacy of consideration "**shocks the conscience of the court**." This standard, which is applied on a case-by-case basis, considers the value of the item or service contracted for, the amount of consideration paid, the relationship of the parties, and other facts and circumstances of the case.

Consider this situation: Mr. and Mrs. James Paul DeLaney were married in January 1953. A few years later they acquired a painting, allegedly the work of Peter Paul Rubens titled *Hunting of the Caledonian Boar*. In 1966, the DeLaneys moved into an apartment building and became friends with Mr. and Mrs. Nicholas T. O'Neill.

Mr. DeLaney and Mr. O'Neill became close friends. On August 18, 1970, Mr. DeLaney purportedly sold the Rubens painting to Mr. O'Neill for $10 and "other good and valuable consideration." A written contract embodying the terms of the agreement was prepared and signed by Mr. DeLaney and Mr. O'Neill. Mrs. DeLaney was not informed of the sale. At the time of the sale, Mr. DeLaney told Mr. O'Neill that the painting was worth at least $100,000. The painting, however, remained with DeLaney and was in storage at the time of this lawsuit. In 1974, Mrs. DeLaney instituted a divorce action against Mr. DeLaney. At that time she learned of the purported sale of the painting to O'Neill. In the divorce action, Mrs. DeLaney claimed an interest in the painting as marital property. Mr. O'Neill instituted this action seeking a declaratory judgment regarding title to the painting.

The trial court held in favor of Mrs. DeLaney and voided the sales contract between Mr. DeLaney and Mr. O'Neill. The appellate court affirmed. The courts held that the consideration paid by Mr. O'Neill for the painting "shocked the conscience" of the court, and thereby rendered the transfer void. The appellate court stated: "Plaintiff expressly testified that 'other goods and valuable consideration' meant the love and affection plaintiff and James Paul DeLaney had for one another. In Illinois, love and affection does not constitute legal consideration. Thus, the only remaining valid consideration for the transaction was the tender of $10. A purchase price of $10 for such a valuable work of art is so grossly inadequate consideration as to shock the conscience of this court, as it did the trial court's. To find $10 valid consideration for this painting would be to reduce the re-quirement of consideration to a mere formality. This we will not do."

Critics of this case argue that the parties should be free to contract based upon what they feel is adequate consideration in the circumstances. Proponents of this case argue that courts should be allowed to examine the adequacy of consideration underlying a contract to prevent unfair contracts. [*O'Neill v. DeLaney*, 415 N.E.2d 1260 (Ill.App. 1980)]

1. Was it ethical for Mr. O'Neill to accept the painting without paying adequate consideration?
2. Should the courts be allowed to examine the adequacy of consideration underlying a contract, or should the parties be free to contract based upon what they feel is adequate consideration in the circumstances?

SETTLEMENT OF CLAIMS

The law promotes the voluntary settlement of disputed claims. Settlement saves judicial resources and serves the interests of the parties entering into the settlement. The most common forms of settlement agreements are discussed in the paragraphs that follow.

In some situations, one of the parties to a contract believes that he or she did not receive what he or she was due. This party may attempt to reach a compromise with the other party (e.g., by paying less consideration than was provided for in the contract). The compromise agreement is called an **accord**. If the accord is performed, it is called the **satisfaction**. This type of settlement is called an **accord and satisfaction** (or a **compromise**). If the accord is not satisfied, the other party can sue to enforce either the accord or the original contract. The issue of whether an accord and satisfaction require additional consideration to be enforceable depends on whether the debt is liquidated or unliquidated.

accord An agreement whereby the parties agree to accept something different in satisfaction of the original contract.

satisfaction The performance of an accord.

CONSIDER THIS EXAMPLE: Suppose that a contract stipulated that the cost of a computer system that keeps track of inventory, accounts receivable, and so on is $100,000. After it is installed, the computer system does not perform as promised. To settle the dispute, the parties agree that $70,000 is to be paid in full and final payment for the computer. This accord is enforceable even though no new consideration is given because reasonable persons would differ as to the worth of the computer system that actually was installed.

BUSINESS BRIEF
Businesses should consider settling potential legal disputes. The law promotes the settlement of disputes because it saves judicial time and resources.

PROMISSORY ESTOPPEL

promissory estoppel   An equitable doctrine that prevents the withdrawal of a promise by a promisor if it will adversely affect a promisee who has adjusted his or her position in justifiable reliance on the promise.

The courts have developed the doctrine of **promissory estoppel** (or **detrimental reliance**) to avoid injustice. This is a broad policy-based doctrine. It is used to provide a remedy to a person who has relied on another person's promise, but that person withdraws his or her promise and is not subject to a breach of contract action because one of the two elements discussed in this chapter (i.e., agreement or consideration) is lacking. The doctrine of promissory estoppel *estops* (prevents) the promisor from revoking his or her promise. Therefore, the person who has detrimentally relied on the promise for performance may sue the promisor for performance or other remedy the court feels is fair to award in the circumstances.

For the doctrine of promissory estoppel to be applied, the following elements must be shown:

1. The promisor made a promise

"Now equity is no part of the law, but a moral virtue, which qualifies, moderates, and reforms the rigour, hardness, and edge of the law, and is a universal truth."
Lord Cowper
Dudley v. Dudley
(1705)

2. The promisor should have reasonably expected to induce the promisee to rely on the promise.
3. The promisee actually relied on the promise and engaged in an action or forbearance of a right of a definite and substantial nature.
4. Injustice would be caused if the promise were not enforced.

CONSIDER THIS EXAMPLE: XYZ Construction Co., a general contractor, requests bids from subcontractors for work to be done on a hospital building that XYZ plans to submit a bid to build. Bert Plumbing Co. submits the lowest bid for the plumbing work, and XYZ incorporates Bert's low bid in its own bid for the general contract. In this example, the doctrine of promissory estoppel prevents Bert from withdrawing its bid. If XYZ is awarded the contract to build the hospital, it could enforce Bert's promise to perform.

WORKING THE WEB

CataLaw   "CataLaw is a catalog of catalogs of law on the Internet. It speeds research by arranging all legal and government indexes on the Internet into a single, simple, intuitive metaindex."
   Visit at http://www.catalaw.com/

FindLaw and LawCrawler   FindLaw has links to many legal resources. The LawCrawler search engine narrows searches to sites with legal information and within specific domains.
   Visit at http://www.lawcrawler.com/

Internet Legal Resource Guide   "The Internet Legal Resource Guide is a categorized index of 3,100 selected Web sites in 238 nations, islands, and territories. In addition, it contains more than 850 locally stored Web pages and files. This site serves as a comprehensive resource of the information available on the Internet concerning law and the

legal profession, with emphasis on the United States."
   Visit at http://www.ilrg.com/

Intralaw   Intralaw is a fee-based desktop interface that accesses legal information directly related to a jurisdiction of practice area.
   Visit at http://www.intralaw.com/

The Law Engine   The law engine links to many "on-line law sources from a well-organized, single-page format."
   Visit at http://www.fastsearch.com/law/

CYBER EXERCISES:
1-5. Select a recent U.S. Supreme Court case such as *Baker v. GMC*, __ U. S. __ , 118 S. Ct. 657, 139 L.Ed.2d 580 (1998). Select at least two of the search engines or indexes listed here and try to find the full text of the case.

CHAPTER SUMMARY

AGREEMENT, P. 167

Offer	1. *Offer.* Manifestation by one party of a willingness to enter into a contract. 2. *Offeror.* Party who makes an offer. 3. *Offeree.* Party to whom an offer is made. This party has the power to create an agreement by accepting the terms of the offer.

REQUIREMENTS OF AN OFFER, P. 167

Requirements of an Offer	1. *Objective intent.* The intent to enter into a contract is determined by the *objective theory of contracts*, that is, whether a reasonable person viewing the circumstances would conclude that the parties intended to be legally bound. 2. *Definite terms.* The terms of the offer must be definite so that the agreement between the parties can be determined. Reasonable terms (e.g., price, time for performance) may be *implied*. 3. *Communication.* The offer must be communicated to the offeree by the offeror.
Special Offer Situations	1. *Advertisement:* a. *General rule.* An invitation to make an offer. b. *Exception.* An offer if it is so definite and specific as to show the advertiser's intent to be bound to the terms of the advertisement. 2. *Reward.* An offer to create a unilateral contract. 3. *Auction:* a. *Auction with reserve.* An invitation to make an offer. The seller retains the right to refuse the highest bid and withdraw the goods from sale. b. *Auction without reserve.* An offer. The seller must accept the highest bid (above the minimum bid). This type of auction must be stipulated.

TERMINATION OF THE OFFER, P. 170

Termination of an Offer by Action of the Parties	1. *Revocation.* The offeror may *revoke* (withdraw) an offer any time prior to its acceptance by the offeree. 2. *Rejection.* An offer is terminated if the offeree rejects the offer by his or her words or conduct. 3. *Counteroffer.* A counteroffer by the offeree terminates the offeror's offer (and creates a new offer).
Termination of an Offer by Operation of Law	1. *Lapse of time.* An offer terminates upon the expiration of a stated time in the offer. If no time is stated, the offer terminates after a "reasonable time." 2. *Destruction of the subject matter.* An offer terminates if the subject matter of the offer is destroyed prior to acceptance through no fault of either party. 3. *Death or incompetency.* The death or incompetency of either the offeror or the offeree prior to acceptance terminates the offer. 4. *Supervening illegality.* If prior to the acceptance of an offer the object of the offer is made illegal by statute, regulation, court decision, or other law, the offer terminates.
Option Contract	If an offeree pays the offeror compensation to keep an offer open for an agreed upon period of time, an *optional contract* is created. The offeror cannot sell the property to anyone else during the option period.

ACCEPTANCE, P. 173

Acceptance	*Acceptance.* Manifestation of assent by the offeree to the terms of the offer. Acceptance of the offer by the offeree creates a contract. 1. *Mirror image rule.* Under the common law of contracts, the offeror must accept the terms offered by the offeror to create a contract. Any change in terms by the offeree constitutes a counteroffer, not an acceptance. 2. *Acceptance-upon-dispatch rule.* Unless otherwise provided in the offer, acceptance is effective when it is dispatched by the offeree. This is often called the *mailbox rule.* 3. *Proper dispatch rule.* An acceptance must be properly addressed and packaged and have prepaid postage or delivery charges to be effective when dispatched. Generally, improperly dispatched acceptances are not effective until actually received by the offeror. 4. *Mode of acceptance.* Acceptance must be by the express means of communication stipulated in the offer or, if no means is stipulated, then by reasonable means in the circumstances.

CONSIDERATION, P. 175

Consideration	Thing of value given in exchange for a promise. May be tangible or intangible property, performance of a service, forbearance of a legal right, or another thing of value.
Requirements of Consideration	1. *Legal value.* Something of legal value must be given. Either (a) the promisee suffers a *legal detriment* or (b) the promisor receives a *legal benefit.* 2. *Bargained-for exchange.* A contract must arise from a bargained-for exchange. *Gift promises* (or *gratuitous promises*) are unenforceable because they lack consideration.
Adequacy of Consideration	1. *Adequacy of consideration.* Courts usually do not inquire into the adequacy of consideration. Thus, *nominal consideration* (e.g., $1) is usually sufficient. 2. *Inadequacy of consideration.* Some states permit a party to escape from a contract if the consideration received is so inadequate as to *"shock the conscience of the court."*

CONTRACTS LACKING CONSIDERATION, P. 177

Contracts Lacking Consideration	The following contracts are unenforceable because they lack consideration: 1. *Illusory promise.* If one or both parties to a contract can choose not to perform their contractual duties. 2. *Moral obligation.* Promise made out of a sense of moral obligation, honor, or love and affection. 3. *Past consideration.* Promise that is based on a party's past consideration. 4. *Preexisting duty.* Promise to perform an act or do something that a person is already under an obligation to do. 5. *Illegal consideration.* Promise to refrain from doing an illegal act.

SETTLEMENT OF CLAIMS, P. 179

Settlement of Claims	1. *Accord and satisfaction.* Compromise agreement in which the parties agree to settle a contract dispute and do so. a. *Unliquidated debt.* One in which reasonable persons would differ as to the amount owed. Can be compromised without the payment of new consideration.

	b. *Liquidated debt*. One that is due and certain. Cannot be compromised unless new consideration is paid.

PROMISSORY ESTOPPEL, P. 180

Promissory Estoppel	*Promissory estoppel*. Policy-based equitable doctrine that prevents a promisor from revoking his or her promise even though the promise lacks consideration. The requirements are: 1. The promisor made a promise. 2. The promisor should have reasonably expected to induce the promisee to rely on the promise. 3. The promisee actually relied on the promise and engaged in an action or forbearance of a right of a definite and substantial nature. 4. Injustice would be caused if the promise were not enforced.

CRITICAL LEGAL THINKING CASES

8.1 Objective Theory While A.H. and Ida Zehmer, husband and wife, were drinking with W.O. Lucy, Mr. Zehmer made a written offer to sell a 471-acre farm the Zehmers owned to Lucy for $50,000. Zehmer contends that his offer was made in jest and that he only wanted to bluff Lucy into admitting that he did not have $50,000. Instead, Lucy appeared to take the offer seriously, offered $5 to bind the deal, and had Mrs. Zehmer sign it. When the Zehmers refused to perform the contract, Lucy brought this action to compel specific performance of the contract. Is the contract enforceable? [*Lucy v. Zehmer*, 84 S.E.2d 516 (Va.App. 1954)]

8.2 Objective Theory On July 24, 1973, Warren Treece appeared before the Washington State Gambling Commission to testify on an application for a license to distribute punchboards. During his testimony, Treece made the following statement: "I'll put a hundred thousand dollars to anyone to find a crooked board. If they find it, I'll pay it." The next day, Vernon Barnes watched a television news report of the proceeding and heard Treece's statement. He also read a newspaper report of the hearings that quoted Treece's statement. A number of years earlier, while employed as a bartender, Barnes had obtained two fraudulent punchboards. When Barnes presented the two crooked punchboards to Treece and demanded payment of the $100,000, Treece refused to pay. Did Treece's statement form the basis for an enforceable contract? [*Barnes v. Treece*, 549 P.2d 1152 (Wash.App. 1976)]

8.3 Essential Terms Ben Hunt and others operated a farm under the name S. B. H. Farms. Hunt went to McIlroy Bank and Trust and requested a loan to build hog houses, buy livestock, and expand farming operations. The bank agreed to loan S. B. H. Farms $175,000, for which short-term promissory notes were signed by Hunt and the other owners of S. B. H. Farms. At that time, oral discussions were held with the bank officer regarding long-term financing of S. B. H.'s farming operations; no dollar amount, interest rate, or repayment terms were discussed. When the owners of S. B. H. Farms defaulted

on the promissory notes, the bank filed for foreclosure on the farm and other collateral. S. B. H. Farms counterclaimed for $750,000 damages, alleging that the bank breached its oral contract to provide long-term financing. Was there an oral contract for long-term financing? [*Hunt v. McIlroy Bank and Trust*, 616 S.W.2d 759 (Ark.App. 1981)]

8.4 Implied Terms MacDonald Group, Ltd. (MacDonald) is the managing general partner of Fresno Fashion Square, a regional shopping mall in Fresno, California. The mall has several major anchor tenants and numerous smaller stores and shops, including Edmond's of Fresno, a jeweler. In 1969, Edmond's signed a lease with MacDonald that provided that "there shall not be more than two jewelry stores" located in the mall. In 1978, MacDonald sent Edmond's notice that it intended to expand the mall and lease space to other jewelers. The lease was silent as to the coverage of additional mall space. Edmond's sued MacDonald, arguing that the lease applied to mall additions. Who wins? [*Edmond's of Fresno v. MacDonald Group, Ltd.*, 171 Cal.App.3d 598, 217 Cal.Rptr. 375 (Cal. App. 1985)]

8.5 Reward Offer Rudy Turilli operated the "Jesse James Museum" in Stanton, Missouri. He contends the man who was shot, killed, and buried as the notorious desperado Jesse James in 1882 was an impostor and that Jesse James lived for many years thereafter under the alias J. Frank Dalton and last lived with Turilli at his museum until the 1950s. On February 27, 1967, Turilli appeared before a nationwide television audience and stated that he would pay $10,000 to anyone who could prove that his statements were wrong. After hearing this offer, Stella James, a relative of Jesse James, produced affidavits of persons related to and acquainted with the Jesse James family constituting evidence that Jesse James was killed as alleged in song and legend on April 3, 1882. When Turilli refused to pay the reward, James sued for breach of contract. Who wins? [*James v. Turilli*, 473 S.W.2d 757 (Mo. App. 1972)]

8.6 Counteroffer Glende Motor Company (Glende), an automobile dealership that sold new cars, leased premises from certain landlords. In October 1979, fire destroyed part of the leased premises, and Glende restored the leasehold premises. The landlords received payment of insurance proceeds for the fire. Glende sued the landlords to recover the insurance proceeds. On May 7, 1982, 10 days before the trial was to begin, the defendants jointly served on Glende a document titled "Offer to Compromise Before Trial," which was a settlement offer of $190,000. On May 16, Glende agreed to the amount of the settlement but made it contingent upon the execution of a new lease. On May 17, the defendants notified Glende that they were revoking the settlement offer. Glende thereafter tried to accept the original settlement offer. Has there been a settlement of the lawsuit? [*Glende Motor Company v. Superior Court,* 159 Cal.App.3d 389, 205 Cal.Rptr. 682 (Cal. App. 1984)]

8.7 Acceptance General Motors Corporation requested bids from contractors to construct a central air-conditioning unit at its Mesa, Arizona, proving grounds. Burr & Sons Construction Co. (Burr) decided to submit a bid to be the general contractor, and itself requested bids from subcontractors to do some of the work. Corbin-Dykes Electric Company submitted a bid to Burr to do the electrical work on the project. Burr incorporated Corbin-Dykes's bid in its own bid to General Motors. When Burr was awarded the General Motors' contract, it hired another subcontractor—not Corbin-Dykes—to do the electrical work. Corbin-Dykes sued Burr for breach of contract. Was a contract formed between Corbin-Dykes and Burr? [*Corbin-Dykes Electric Company v. Burr,* 500 P.2d 632 (Ariz. App. 1972)]

8.8 Silence Peter Andrus owned an apartment building that he had insured under a fire insurance policy sold by J. C. Durick Insurance (Durick). Two months prior to the expiration of the policy, Durick notified Andrus that the building should be insured for $48,000 (or 80 percent of the building's value) required by the insurance company. Andrus replied that (1) he wanted insurance to match the amount of the outstanding mortgage on the building (i.e., $24,000) and (2) if Durick could not sell this insurance he would go elsewhere. Durick sent a new insurance policy in the face amount of $48,000 with the notation that the policy was automatically accepted unless Andrus notified him to the contrary. Andrus did not reply. However, he did not pay the premiums on the policy. Durick sued Andrus to recover these premiums. Who wins? [*J. C. Durick Insurance v. Andrus,* 424 A.2d 249 (Vt. 1980)]

8.9 Time for Acceptance Economic Research Properties (ERP), a partnership, owned a tract of land in Florida. Donald R. Sullivan, who became interested in purchasing the property, mailed a written offer and deposit to Dwayne R. Klein, the managing partner of ERP, to purchase the property. The offer stated that it must be accepted by ERP by February 4, 1980, after which time the deposit was to be returned to Sullivan. ERP made several changes to the offer, including changing the time for acceptance from February 4 to February 14 so as to allow sufficient time for its counteroffer to reach Sullivan, and signed it.

Sullivan received the counteroffer several days before February 14. On February 18, 1980, Sullivan signed the counteroffer and mailed it to ERP. On February 19, Klein, having neither received the contract nor been notified of its acceptance, telephoned Sullivan and advised him that the negotiations were terminated. ERP later sold the property to another buyer. Sullivan sued ERP for breach of contract. Was a contract formed between ERP and Sullivan? [*Sullivan v. Economic Research Properties,* 455 So.2d 630 (Fla. App. 1984)]

8.10 The Mailbox Rule William Jenkins and Nathalie Monk owned a building in Sacramento, California. In 1979, they leased the building to Tuneup Masters for five years. The lease provided that Tuneup Masters could extend the lease for an additional five years if it gave written notice of its intention to do so by certified or registered mail at least six months prior to the expiration of the term of the lease, or August 1, 1983.

On July 29, 1983, Larry Selditz, vice president of Tuneup Masters, prepared a letter exercising the option, prepared and sealed an envelope with the letter in it, prepared U.S. Postal Service Form 3800 and affixed the certified mail sticker on the envelope, and had his secretary deliver the envelope to the Postal Service annex located on the ground floor of the office building. Postal personnel occupied the annex only between the hours of 9 and 10 A.M. At the end of each day, between 5 and 5:15 P.M., a postal employee picked up outgoing mail. The letter to the landlords was lost in the mail. The landlords thereafter refused to renew the lease and brought an unlawful detainer action against Tuneup Masters. Was the notice renewing the option effective? [*Jenkins v. Tuneup Masters,* 190 Cal.App.3d 1, 235 Cal.Rptr. 214 (Cal. App. 1987)]

8.11 Consideration Clyde and Betty Penley were married in 1949. In late 1967, Clyde operated an automotive tire business and Betty owned an interest in a Kentucky Fried Chicken (KFC) franchise. That year, when Betty became ill, she requested that Clyde begin spending additional time at the KFC franchise to ensure its continued operation. Subsequently, Betty agreed that if Clyde would devote full time to the KFC franchise, they would operate the business as a joint enterprise, share equally in the ownership of its assets, and divide its returns equally. Pursuant to this agreement, Clyde terminated his tire business and devoted his full time to the KFC franchise. On December 31, 1979, Betty abandoned Clyde and denied him any rights in the KFC franchise. Clyde sued to enforce the agreement with Betty. Is the agreement enforceable? [*Penley v. Penley,* 332 S.E.2d 51 (N.C. 1985)]

8.12 Forbearance to Sue When John W. Frasier died, he left a will that devised certain of his community and separate property to his wife, Lena, and their three children. These devises were more valuable to Lena than just her interest in the community property that she would otherwise have received without the will. The devise to her, however, was conditioned upon the filing of a waiver by Lena of her interest in the community property, and if she failed to file the waiver, she would then receive only her interest in the community property and nothing more. Lena hired her brother, D. L. Carter, an attorney, to represent her. Carter failed to file the waiver on Lena's behalf, thus preventing her from receiving her inheritance under the will. Instead, she received her interest in the community property, which was $19,358 less than she would have received under the will. Carter sent Lena the following letter:

This is to advise and confirm our agreement—that in the event the J. W. Frasier estate case now on appeal is not terminated so that you will receive settlement equal to your share of the estate as you would have done if your waiver had been filed in the estate in proper time, I will make up any balance to you in payments as suits my convenience and will pay interest on your loss at 6 percent.

The appeal was decided against Lena. When she tried to enforce the contract against Carter, he alleged that the contract was not enforceable because it was not supported by valid consideration. Who wins? [*Frasier v. Carter*, 437 P.2d 32 (Idaho 1968)]

8.13 Past Consideration A. J. Whitmire and R. Lee Whitmire were brothers. From 1923 to 1929, A. J. lived with his brother and his brother's wife, Lillie Mae. During this period, A. J. performed various services for his brother and sister-in-law. In 1925, R. Lee and Lillie Mae purchased some land. In 1944, in the presence of Lillie Mae, R. Lee told A. J., "When we're gone, this land is yours." A. J. had not done any work for R. Lee or Lillie Mae since 1929, and none was expected or provided in the future. On May 26, 1977, after both R. Lee and Lillie Mae had died, A. J. filed a claim with the estate of Lillie Mae seeking specific performance of the 1944 promise. Does A. J. get the property? [*Whitmire v. Watkins*, 267 So.2d 6 (Ga. 1980)]

8.14 Preexisting Duty Robert Chuckrow Construction Company (Chuckrow) was employed as the general contractor to build a Kinney Shoe Store. Chuckrow employed Ralph Gough to perform the carpentry work on the store. The contract with Gough stipulated that he was to provide all labor, materials, tools, equipment, scaffolding, and other items necessary to complete the carpentry work. On May 15, 1965, Gough's employees erected 38 trusses at the job site. The next day, 32 of the trusses fell off the building. The reason for the trusses' falling was unexplained, and evidence showed that it was not due to Chuckrow's fault or a deficiency in the building plans. Chuckrow told Gough that he would pay him to reerect the trusses and continue work. When the job was complete, Chuckrow paid Gough the original contract price but refused to pay him for the additional cost of reerecting the trusses. Gough sued Chuckrow for this expense. Can Gough recover? [*Robert Chuckrow Construction Company v. Gough*, 159 S.E.2d 469 (Ga. App. 1968)]

8.15 Charitable Pledge Milton Polinger pledged $200,000 as a charitable subscription to the United Jewish Appeal Federation of Greater Washington, Inc. (UJA). The pledge was not for a specific purpose and was not made in consideration of pledges by others, and UJA borrowed no money against this pledge. The pledge was to the UJA generally and to the Israel Emergency Fund. After paying $76,500 toward the pledge, Polinger died and the Maryland National Bank was appointed representative of the Polinger estate. The UJA filed a claim against the estate for the balance of $133,500. The bank, however, denied the claim, alleging that the promise was unenforceable for lack of consideration. Who wins? [*Maryland National Bank v. United Jewish Appeal Federation of Greater Washington, Inc.*, 407 A.2d 1130 (Md. App. 1979)]

ETHICS CASES

8.16 Ethical Perspective Kortney Dempsey took a cruise on a ship operated by Norwegian Cruise Line (Norwegian). In general, suits for personal injuries arising out of maritime torts are subject to a three-year statute of limitations. However, Congress permits this period to be reduced to one year by contract. The Norwegian passenger ticket limited the period to one year. Evidence showed that the cruise line ticket contained the notation "Important Notice" in a bright red box at the bottom right-hand corner of each of the first four pages of the ticket. The information in the box stated that certain pages of the ticket contain information that "affect[s] important legal rights." In addition, at the top of page 6 of the ticket, where the terms and conditions begin, it is stated in bold letters: "Passengers are advised to read the terms and conditions of the Passenger Ticket Contract set forth below." The clause at issue, which appears on page 8, clearly provides that suits must be brought within one year of injury.

More than one year after Dempsey had taken the cruise (but within three years), she filed suit against Norwegian seeking damages for an alleged injury suffered while on the cruise. Dempsey asserted that the one-year limitations period had not been reasonably communicated to her. Did Dempsey act ethically in suing when she did? Did Norwegian act ethically in re-

ducing the limitations period to one year? Who wins the lawsuit? [*Dempsey v. Norwegian Cruise Line*, 972 F.2d 998 (9th Cir. 1992)]

8.17 Ethical Perspective Al and Rosemary Mitchell owned a small secondhand store. On August 12, 1978, the Mitchells attended Alexander's Auction, where they frequently shopped to obtain merchandise for their business. While at the auction, they purchased a used safe for $50. They were told by the auctioneer that the inside compartment of the safe was locked and that no key could be found to unlock it. The safe was part of the Sumstad Estate. Several days after the auction, the Mitchells took the safe to a locksmith to have the locked compartment opened. When the locksmith opened the compartment he found $32,207 in cash. The locksmith called the City of Everett Police, who impounded the money. The City of Everett commenced an interpleader action against the Sumstad Estate and the Mitchells. The trial court entered summary judgment in favor of Sumstad Estate. The court of appeals affirmed. The Mitchells appealed. Who wins? Did the seller of the safe act ethically in alleging that no contract had been made with the Mitchells? [*City of Everett, Washington v. Mitchell*, 631 P.2d 366 (Wash. 1981)]

CRITICAL LEGAL THINKING WRITING ASSIGNMENT

Read Case A.8 in the Case Appendix [*Traco, Inc. v. Arrow Glass Co., Inc.*]. This case is excerpted from the appellate court opinion. Review and brief the case. In your brief, be sure to answer the following questions:

1. Who was the plaintiff? Who was the defendant?
2. Was there an express agreement between the parties?

3. What does the doctrine of promissory estoppel provide? Explain.
4. Did the court apply the doctrine of promissory estoppel in this case?

NOTES

[1] Restatement (Second) of Contracts, § 33(1).
[2] Ibid, § 204.
[3] Restatement (Second) of Contracts, § 50(1).

[4] Restatement (Second) of Contracts, § 40.
[5] *Hamer v. Sidway*, 124 N.Y. 538, 27 N.E. 256 (N.Y. 1891).

CAPACITY AND LEGALITY

> *An unconscionable contract is one which no man in his senses, not under delusion, would make, on the one hand, and which no fair and honest man would accept on the other.*
>
> *Hume v. United States,*
> 132 U.S. 406, 10 S.Ct. 134, 33 L.Ed. 393 (1889)

"The right of a minor to disaffirm his contract is based upon sound public policy to protect the minor from his own improvidence and the overreaching of adults."
Justice Sullivan
Star Chevrolet v. Green (1985)

Generally, the law presumes that the parties to a contract have the requisite **contractual capacity** to enter into the contract. However, certain persons do not have this capacity. They include minors, insane persons, and intoxicated persons. Both the common law of contracts and many state statutes protect persons who lack contractual capacity from having contracts enforced against them. The party asserting incapacity, his or her guardian, conservator, or other legal representative bears the burden of proof.

An essential element for the formation of a contract is that the object of the contract be lawful. A contract to perform an illegal act is called an **illegal contract**. Illegal contracts are void. That is, they cannot be enforced by either party to the contract. The term *illegal contract* is a misnomer, however, because no contract exists if the object of the contract is illegal. In addition, courts hold that **unconscionable contracts** are unenforceable. An unconscionable contract is one that is so oppressive or manifestly unfair that it would be unjust to enforce it.

Capacity to contract and the lawfulness of contracts are discussed in this chapter.

MINORS

minor   A person who has not reached the age of majority.

Minors do not always have the maturity, experience, or sophistication needed to enter into contracts with adults. The common law defines *minor* as females under the age of 18 and males under the age of 21. In addition, many states have enacted statutes that specify the **age of majority**. The most prevalent age of majority is 18 years of age for both males and females. Any age below the statutory age of majority is called the **period of minority**.

The Infancy Doctrine

infancy doctrine   A doctrine that allows minors to disaffirm (cancel) most contracts they have entered into with adults.

To protect minors, the law recognizes the **infancy doctrine**, which allows minors to **disaffirm** (or **cancel**) most contracts they have entered into with adults. This right is based on public policy, which reasons that minors should be protected from the unscrupulous behavior of adults. In most states, the infancy doctrine is an objective standard. If a person's age is below the age of majority, the court will inquire into his or her knowledge, experience, or sophistication. Generally, contracts for the necessaries of life, which we discuss later in this chapter, are exempted from the scope of this doctrine.

VOIDABLE By Minor

Under the infancy doctrine, a minor has the option of choosing whether to enforce the contract (i.e., the contract is **voidable** by a minor). The adult party is bound to the minor's decision. If both parties to the contract are minors, both parties have the right to disaffirm the contract.

If performance of the contract favors the minor, the minor will probably enforce the contract. Otherwise, the contract will probably be disaffirmed. A minor may not affirm one part of the contract and disaffirm another part.

disaffirmance   The act of a minor to rescind a contract under the infancy doctrine. Disaffirmance may be done orally, in writing, or by the minor's conduct.

Disaffirmance   A minor can expressly disaffirm a contract orally, in writing, or by his or her conduct. No special formalities are required. The contract may be disaffirmed at any time prior to reaching the age of majority plus a "reasonable time." The designation of a reasonable time is determined on a case-by-case basis.

Duties of Restitution and Restoration   If the minor's contract is executory and neither party has performed, the minor can simply disaffirm the contract.

There is nothing to recover because neither party has given the other party anything of value. However, if the parties have exchanged consideration and partially or fully performed the contract at the time the minor disaffirms the contract, the issue becomes one of what consideration or restitution must be made. The following rules apply:

- **Competent party's duty of restitution.** If the minor has transferred consideration—money, property, or other valuables—to the competent party before disaffirming the contract, that party must place the minor in status quo. That is, the minor must be restored to the same position he or she was in before the minor entered into the contract. This is usually done by returning the consideration to the minor. If the consideration has been sold or has depreciated in value, the competent party must pay the minor the cash equivalent. This is called the **competent party's duty of restitution**.
- **Minor's duty of restoration.** Generally, a minor is obligated only to return the goods or property he or she has received from the adult in the condition it is in at the time of disaffirmance (subject to several exceptions discussed later in this chapter). This is so even if the item has been consumed, lost, destroyed, or depreciated in value at the time of disaffirmance. This is called the **minor's duty of restoration**. This rule is based on the rationale that if a minor had to place the adult in status quo upon disaffirmance of a contract, there would be no incentive for an adult not to deal with a minor.
- **Minor's duty of restitution.** Most states provide that the minor must put the adult in status quo upon disaffirmance of the contract if the minor's intentional or grossly negligent conduct caused the loss of value to the adult's property. A few states have enacted statutes that require the minor to make restitution of the reasonable value of the item when disaffirming any contract. This is called the **minor's duty of restitution**.

Misrepresentation of Age On occasion, minors might misrepresent their age to an adult when entering into a contract. Under the common law, such a minor would still have the right to disaffirm the contract. Most states have changed this rule in recognition of its unfairness to adults. These states provide that minors who misrepresent their age must place the adult in status quo if they disaffirm the contract. In other words, a minor who has misrepresented his or her age when entering into a contract owes a duty of restoration and restitution when disaffirming it.

CONSIDER THIS EXAMPLE: Sherry McNamara, a minor, misrepresents that she is an adult and enters into a contract to purchase an automobile costing $20,000 from Bruce Ruffino, a competent adult. Mr. Ruffino delivers the automobile after he receives payment in full. The automobile later sustains $7,000 worth of damage in an accident that is not Ms. McNamara's fault. In order to disaffirm the contract, Ms. McNamara must return the damaged automobile plus $7,000 to Mr. Ruffino.

Ratification

If a minor does not disaffirm a contract either during the period of minority or within a reasonable time after reaching the age of majority, the contract is considered ratified (accepted). This means that the minor (who is now an adult) is bound by the contract: The right to disaffirm the contract has been lost. Note that any attempt by a minor to ratify a contract while still a minor can be disaffirmed just as the original contract can be disaffirmed.

The **ratification**, which relates back to the inception of the contract, can be by express oral or written words or implied from the minor's conduct (e.g., after reaching the age of majority the minor remains silent regarding the contract).

The following case presents the issue of whether a minor had ratified a contract when he reached the age of majority.

CASE 9.1

Jones v. Free Flight Sport Aviation, Inc.
623 P.2d 370 (1981) Supreme Court of Colorado

Facts On November 17, 1973, William Michael Jones, a 17-year-old minor, signed a contract with Free Flight Sport Aviation, Inc. (Free Flight), for the use of recreational sky-diving facilities. A covenant not to sue and an exculpatory clause exempting Free Flight from liability were included in the contract. On December 28, 1973, Jones attained the age of majority (18 years of age). Ten months later, while on a Free Flight sky-diving operation, the airplane crashed shortly after takeoff from Littleton Airport, causing severe personal injuries to Jones. Jones filed suit against Free Flight, alleging negligence and willful and wanton misconduct. The trial court granted summary judgment in favor of Free Flight. The Colorado court of appeals affirmed. Jones appealed.

Issue Did Jones ratify the contract?

Decision Yes. The supreme court held that Jones had ratified his contract with Free Flight by continuing, for 10 months after reaching the age of majority, to perform under the contract. Therefore, the covenant not to sue and the exculpatory clause exempting Free Flight from liability to Jones are enforceable.

Reason A minor may disaffirm a contract made during his minority within a reasonable time after at-

taining his majority, or he may, after becoming of legal age, by acts recognizing the contract, ratify it. The supreme court stated: "Affirmance is not merely a matter of intent. It may be determined by the actions of a minor who accepts the benefits of a contract after reaching the age of majority, or who is silent or acquiesces in the contract for a considerable length of time. We conclude that the trial court properly determined that Jones ratified the contract, as a matter of law, by accepting the benefits of the contract when he used Free Flight's facilities on October 19, 1974."

CASE QUESTIONS

Critical Legal Thinking Should children be allowed to disaffirm a minor's contract after reaching the age of majority? What is a reasonable length of time after reaching the age of majority to permit disaffirmance?

Ethics Did Jones act ethically by suing Free Flight Sport Aviation in this case?

Business Implication Should the covenant not to sue have been enforced here even though Jones was an adult?

Necessaries of Life

necessaries of life   A minor must pay the reasonable value of food, clothing, shelter, medical care, and other items considered necessary to the maintenance of life.

Minors are obligated to pay for the **necessaries of life** that they contract for. Otherwise, many adults would refuse to sell these items to them. There is no standard definition of what is a *necessary of life*, but items such as food, clothing, shelter, medical services, and the like are generally understood to fit this category. Goods and services such as automobiles, tools of trade, education, and vocational training have also been found to be necessaries of life in some situations. The minor's age, lifestyle, and status in life influence what is considered necessary. For example, necessaries for a married minor are greater than for an unmarried minor.

The seller's recovery is based on the equitable doctrine of **quasi contract** rather than on the contract itself. Under this theory, the minor is obligated only to pay the reasonable value of the goods or services received. Reasonable value is determined on a case-by-case basis.

BUSINESS CHECKLIST

Statutes That Make Minors Liable for Special Types of Contracts

The infancy doctrine of the common law of contracts allows minors to disaffirm many contracts they have entered into with adults. Based on public policy, many states have enacted statutes that make certain specified contracts enforceable against minors; that is, minors cannot assert the infancy doctrine against enforcement of these contracts. These usually include contracts for the following:

Medical, surgical, and pregnancy care
- Psychological counseling
- Health insurance
- Life insurance
- The performance of duties relating to stock and bond transfers, bank accounts, and the like
- Educational loan agreements
- Contracts to support children
- Contracts to enlist in the military
- Artistic, sports, and entertainment contracts that have been entered into with the approval of the court (many of these statutes require that a certain portion of the wages and fees earned by the minor be put in trust until the minor reaches the age of majority).

Parents' Liability for Their Children's Contracts

Generally, parents owe a legal duty to provide food, clothing, shelter, and other necessaries of life for their children. Parents are liable for their children's contracts for necessaries of life that they have not adequately provided.

The parental duty of support terminates if a minor becomes emancipated. **Emancipation** occurs when a minor voluntarily leaves home and lives apart from his or her parents. The courts consider factors such as getting married, setting up a separate household, joining the military service, and the like in determining whether a minor is emancipated. Each situation is examined on its merits.

emancipation When a minor voluntarily leaves home and lives apart from his or her parents.

CONTEMPORARY BUSINESS ENVIRONMENT

A Babe in the Woods?

Many businesses say that it is time for a change in the infancy doctrine. They cite the fact that young persons are demanding and assuming more responsibilities in their daily lives. In many respects, they are acting as adults. For instance, they are engaged in businesses, are charged with the responsibility for committing crimes, are being sued in tort claims for acts of negligence, are subject to military service, and are getting married and raising families. Businesses also argue that minors are using the infancy doctrine as a "sword rather than a shield" to get out of fair contracts.

Businesses are asking courts to reexamine the law pertaining to the contractual rights and duties of minors. Some courts are listening.

Consider the following case. In early April 1987, Joseph Eugene Dodson, then 16 years old, purchased a used 1984 pickup truck from Shrader's Auto Sales in Columbia, Tennessee. He paid

continued

$4,900. Shrader testified that Dodson looked 18 or 19 years of age.

Nine months after the purchase, the truck developed a mechanical problem. A mechanic diagnosed the problem as a burnt valve. Dodson did not have the money to make the repairs, so he drove the truck until its engine "blew up" and the truck became inoperable. He parked the truck in the front yard at his parents' home where he lived. While parked there, the truck was struck by a hit-and-run driver. Due to the engine damage and the collision, the truck's value plunged to $500.

Dodson asserted the infancy doctrine and sued to disaffirm the purchase agreement. The trial court permitted Dodson to rescind the contract and ordered Shrader, upon tender and delivery of the truck, to reimburse Dodson his $4,900 purchase price.

On appeal, the Tennessee supreme court reconsidered the fairness of this result. In an effort to balance more fairly the rights of minors against those of innocent merchants, the court adopted a new approach to the infancy doctrine. The court held that a minor's recovery of the full purchase price is subject to a deduction for his or her "use" of the consideration he or she received under the contract, or for the "depreciation" or "deterioration" of the consideration in his possession.

The court stated the following rule: "Where the minor has not been overreached in any way, and there has been no undue influence, and the contract is a fair and reasonable one, and the minor has actually paid money on the purchase price, and taken and used the article purchased, that he ought not to be permitted to recover the amount actually paid, without allowing the vendor of the goods reasonable compensation for the use of depreciation, and willful or negligent damage to the article purchased, while in his hands. If there has been any fraud or imposition on the part of the seller or if the contract is unfair, or any unfair advantage has been taken of the minor inducing him to make the purchase, then the rule does not apply."

Based on this new rule, the court remanded the case for a determination of damages.

The basic premise of the infancy doctrine is the same: An infant's contract is voidable and the infant has an absolute right to disaffirm. What has changed is the fact that the minor now owes a duty of restitution—rather than a duty of restoration—under the circumstances outlined by the Tennessee supreme court.

The court noted that this new standard is not a quantum leap in the evolution of the common law, only a practical recognition of the status of minors in our society. The court stated that the new rule will have a better moral influence on minors because the old rule lead to the "corruption of principles and encouraged young people in habits of trickery and dishonesty." The modern trend among states is to adopt this new standard for the infancy doctrine. [*Dodson v. Shrader's Auto Sales*, 824 S.W.2d 545 (Tenn. 1992)]

MENTALLY INCOMPETENT PERSONS

"Insanity vitiates all acts."
Sir John Nicholl
Countess of Portsmouth v. Earl of Portsmouth
(1828)

legal insanity A state of contractual incapacity as determined by law.

Mental incapacity can arise because of mental illness, brain damage, mental retardation, senility, and the like. The law protects people suffering from substantial mental incapacity from enforcement of contracts against them because such persons might not understand the consequences of their actions in entering into a contract.

To be relieved of his or her duties under a contract, the law requires a person to have been legally insane at the time of entering into the contract. This is called **legal insanity**. Most states use the *objective cognitive "understanding" test* to determine legal insanity. Under this test, the person's mental incapacity must render that person incapable of understanding or comprehending the nature of the transaction. Mere weakness of intellect, slight psychological or emotional problems, or delusions do not constitute legal insanity. The law has developed the following two standards concerning contracts of mentally incompetent persons.

Adjudged Insane

adjudged insane A person who has been adjudged insane by a proper court or administrative agency. A contract entered into by such person is *void*.

In certain cases, a relative, loved one, or other interested party may institute a legal action to have someone declared legally (i.e., adjudged) insane. If, after hearing the evidence at a formal judicial or administrative hearing, the person is **adjudged insane**, the court will make that person a ward of the court and appoint a guardian to act on that person's behalf. If a person has been adjudged insane, any contract entered into by that person is *void*. That is, no contract exists. The court-appointed guardian is the only one who has the legal authority to enter into contracts on behalf of the person.

Insane, but Not Adjudged Insane

If no formal ruling has been made, any contracts entered into by a person who suffers from a mental impairment that makes him or her legally insane are voidable by the insane person. Unless the other party does not have contractual capacity, he does not have the option to avoid the contract.

Some people have alternating periods of sanity and insanity. Any contracts made by such a person during a lucid interval are enforceable. Contracts made while the person was not legally sane can be disaffirmed.

A person who has dealt with an insane person must place that insane person in status quo if the contract is either void or voided by the insane person. Most states hold that a party who did not know he or she was dealing with an insane person must be placed in status quo upon avoidance of the contract. Insane persons are liable in *quasi-contract* to pay the reasonable value for necessaries of life they receive.

insane, but not adjudged insane A person who is insane but has not been adjudged insane by a court or administrative agency. A contract entered into by such person is generally *voidable*. Some states hold that such a contract is void.

INTOXICATED PERSONS

Most states provide that contracts entered into by **intoxicated persons** are voidable by that person. The intoxication can occur because of alcohol or drugs. The contract is not voidable by the other party if that party had contractual capacity.

Under the majority rule, the contract is voidable only if the person was so intoxicated when the contract was entered into that he or she was incapable of understanding or comprehending the nature of the transaction. In most states, this rule holds even if the intoxication was self-induced. Some states only allow the person to disaffirm the contract if the person was forced to become intoxicated or did so unknowingly.

The amount of alcohol or drugs that are necessary to be consumed by a person to be considered legally intoxicated to disaffirm contracts varies from case to case. The factors that are considered include the user's physical characteristics and his or her ability to "hold" intoxicants.

A person who disaffirms a contract based on intoxication generally must be returned to the status quo. In turn, the intoxicated person generally must return the consideration received under the contract to the other party and make restitution that returns the other party to status quo. After becoming sober, an intoxicated person can ratify the contracts he or she entered into while intoxicated. Intoxicated persons are liable in **quasi-contract** to pay the reasonable value for necessaries they receive.

In the following case, the court permitted a person to disaffirm the contract because she was intoxicated.

intoxicated person A person who is under contractual incapacity because of ingestion of alcohol or drugs to the point of incompetence.

"Men intoxicated are sometimes stunned into sobriety."

Lord Mansfield
R. v. Wilkes (1770)

CASE 9.2

Smith v. Williamson
429 So.2d 598 (1983) Court of Civil Appeals of Alabama

Facts Carolyn Ann Williamson entered into a contract to sell her house to Mr. and Mrs. Matthews at a time when her house was threatened with foreclosure. Evidence showed that Williamson was an alcoholic. Having read about the threatened foreclosure | in the newspaper, attorney Virgil M. Smith appeared at Williamson's home to discuss the matter with her. Williamson told Smith that she expected to receive $17,000 from the sale but had actually received

continued

$1,700. On the following day, after drinking a pint of 100-proof vodka, Williamson and her son went to Smith's office, where Smith prepared a lawsuit to have the sale of the house set aside based on Williamson's lack of capacity due to alcoholism. At that time, Smith loaned Williamson $500 and took back a note and mortgage on her house to secure repayment of this amount and his attorney fees. Evidence showed that Smith did not allow Williamson's son to read the mortgage. The sale to Mr. and Mrs. Matthews was set aside. Subsequently, Smith began foreclosure proceedings on Williamson's house to recover attorney's fees and advances. Williamson filed this lawsuit to enjoin the foreclosure. The trial court held that Smith's mortgage was void and permanently enjoined him from foreclosing on it. Smith appealed.

Issue Was Williamson's alcoholism a sufficient mental incapacity to void the mortgage?

Decision Yes. The appellate court held that Williamson was not bound to the contract and mortgage with attorney Smith because she was mentally incompetent by reason of intoxication at the time she signed the documents. Affirmed.

Reason In reaching its decision in favor of Williamson, the court stated: "To accept Smith's position would require us to ignore certain subtle ironies arising from the facts of this appeal. The

transaction between Ms. Williamson and the Matthewses was set aside. In overturning the contract and deed to the Matthewses, the court found that Ms. Williamson was incapable of understanding the nature of the transaction and also found that her intoxication, coupled with the gross inadequacy of consideration, supported this result. The record indicates that Ms. Williamson executed the note and mortgage on her home to Smith on October 12, 1978, the following morning. The record further shows that Ms. Williamson had consumed a pint of 100-proof vodka. To hold that Ms. Williamson was incapable of understanding the nature of the transaction with the Matthewses and then to hold that she was able to comprehend the nature of her dealings with Smith would be to reach illogical results, especially in light of the facts presented at trial."

CASE QUESTIONS

Critical Legal Thinking Should the law protect persons who voluntarily become intoxicated from their contracts?

Ethics Do you think that attorney Smith acted ethically in this case?

Business Implication Do you think many business deals are entered into after the parties have been drinking? Should these deals be allowed to be voided?

ILLEGALITY—CONTRACTS CONTRARY TO STATUTES

Both federal and state legislatures have enacted statutes that prohibit certain types of conduct. For example, penal codes make certain activities crimes, antitrust statutes prohibit certain types of agreements between competitors, and so on. Contracts to perform an activity that is prohibited by statute are illegal contracts.

Usury Laws

usury law A law that sets an upper limit on the interest rate that can be charged on certain types of loans.

State **usury laws** set an upper limit on the annual interest rate that can be charged on certain types of loans. The limits vary from state to state. Lenders who charge a higher rate than the state limit are guilty of usury. These laws are intended to protect unsophisticated borrowers from loan sharks and others who charge exorbitant rates of interest.

Most states provide criminal and civil penalties for making usurious loans. Some states require lenders to remit the difference between the interest rate charged on the loan and the usury rate to the borrower. Other states prohibit lenders from collecting any interest on the loan. Still other states provide that a usurious loan is a void contract, permitting the borrower not to have to pay the interest or the principal of the loan to the lender.

Most usury laws exempt certain types of lenders and loan transactions involving legitimate business transactions from the reach of the law. Often, these exemptions include loans made by banks and other financial institutions, loans above a certain dollar amount, loans made to corporations and other businesses, and such.

Gambling Statutes

All states either prohibit or regulate gambling, wagering, lotteries, and games of chance. States provide various criminal and civil penalties for illegal gambling. There is a distinction between lawful risk-shifting contracts and gambling contracts. For example, if property insurance is purchased on one's own car and the car is destroyed in an accident, the insurance company must pay the claim. This is a lawful risk-shifting contract because the purchaser had an "insurable interest" in the car. However, insurance purchased on a neighbor's car would be considered to be gambling. The purchaser does not have an insurable interest in the car and is betting only on its destruction.

There are many exceptions to wagering laws. For example, many states have enacted statutes that permit games of chance under a certain dollar amount, bingo games, lotteries conducted by religious and charitable organizations, and the like. Many states also permit and regulate horse racing, harness racing, dog racing, and state-operated lotteries.

gambling statutes
Statutes that make certain forms of gambling illegal.

Sabbath Laws

Certain states have enacted laws—called **Sabbath laws**, **Sunday laws**, or **blue laws**—that prohibit or limit the carrying on of certain secular activities on Sundays. Except for contracts for the necessaries of life, charitable donations, and such, these laws generally prohibit or invalidate executory contracts that are entered into on Sunday. Many states do not actively enforce these laws. In some states, they have even been found to be unconstitutional.

Sabbath law A law that prohibits or limits the carrying on of certain secular activities on Sundays.

Contracts to Commit a Crime

As mentioned previously, contracts to commit criminal acts are void. If the object of a contract became illegal after the contract was entered into because the government enacted a statute that made it unlawful, the parties are discharged from the contract. The contract is not an illegal contract unless the parties agree to go forward and complete it.

Licensing Statutes

All states require members of certain professions and occupations to be licensed by the state in which they practice. Lawyers, doctors, real estate agents, insurance agents, certified public accountants, teachers, contractors, and hairdressers are among them. In most instances, a **license** is granted to persons who demonstrate that they have the proper schooling, experience, and moral character required by the relevant statute. Sometimes, a written examination is also required.

Problems arise if an unlicensed person tries to collect payment for services provided to another under a contract. Some statutes expressly provide that unlicensed persons cannot enforce contracts to provide these services. If the statute is silent on the point, enforcement depends on whether it is a *regulatory statute* or a *revenue-raising statute*.

licensing statute Statute that requires a person or business to obtain a license from the government prior to engaging in a specified occupation or activity.

Regulatory Statutes Licensing statutes enacted to protect the public are called **regulatory statutes**. Generally, unlicensed persons cannot recover payment for services that a regulatory statute requires a licensed person to provide.

regulatory statute A licensing statute enacted to protect the public.

CONSIDER THIS EXAMPLE: State law provides that legal services can be provided only by lawyers who have graduated from law school and passed the appropriate bar exam. Nevertheless, Marie Sweiger, a first-year law student, agrees to draft a will for Randy McCabe for a $150 fee. Because Ms. Sweiger is not licensed to provide legal services, she has violated a regulatory statute. She cannot enforce the contract and recover payment from Mr. McCabe.

revenue-raising statute
A licensing statute with the primary purpose of raising revenue for the government.

Revenue-Raising Statutes Licensing statutes enacted to raise money for the government are called **revenue-raising statutes**. A person who provides services pursuant to a contract without the appropriate license required by such a statute can enforce the contract and recover payment for services rendered. For example: Suppose a state licensing statute requires licensed attorneys to pay an annual $200 license fee without requiring continuing education or other new qualifications. A licensed attorney who forgets to pay the fee can enforce contracts and recover payment for the legal services he or she renders. That is because the statute merely gathers revenue—protection of the public is not a factor.

BUSINESS APPLICATION

An Unlicensed Contractor Gets Dunked

The doctrine of illegality is designed to protect persons from certain types of contracts deemed unfair, unscrupulous, or unconscionable by society. The doctrine denies violators access to taxpayer-supported courts to enforce their illegal contracts. Should parties sometimes be allowed to enforce their otherwise illegal contract? Consider the following case.

Hydrotech Systems, Ltd. (Hydrotech) is a New York corporation that manufactures and installs patented equipment to simulate ocean waves. Oasis Waterpark (Oasis) is a California corporation that owns and operates a water-oriented amusement park in Palm Springs, California. Wessman Construction Company, Inc. (Wessman) is Oasis's general contractor at the park.

In July 1985, Wessman contracted with Hydrotech to design and construct a 29,000-square-foot "surfing pool" at the park using Hydrotech's wave equipment. The total contract price was

$850,000. Hydrotech was aware of a California law that requires a contractor to have a California contractor's license to provide construction services in California. The statute stipulates that an unlicensed contractor cannot sue in a California court to recover compensation for work requiring a California contractor's license [California Business and Professional Code § 7031].

Because it was concerned with the licensing problem, Hydrotech wished only to sell and deliver the equipment and to avoid involvement in the design or construction of the pool. However, Oasis insisted that Hydrotech's unique expertise in design and construction was essential. Oasis induced Hydrotech to provide these services by promising to pay Hydrotech even if the law provided otherwise.

In reliance on these promises, Hydrotech furnished equipment and services in full compliance with the contract. Hydrotech had been paid $740,000 during the

course of the contract. When it billed Oasis for the remaining $110,000, Oasis refused to pay. Hydrotech sued Oasis and Wessman for damages in California court for breach of contract and fraud. The defendants moved the court to dismiss the action because Hydrotech did not possess a California contractor's license as required by law.

The California Supreme Court agreed with the defendants and ordered Hydrotech's complaint dismissed. The court found that Hydrotech had violated the licensing statute. The supreme court stated, "The obvious statutory intent is to discourage persons who have failed to comply with the licensing law from offering or providing their unlicensed services for pay. Because of the strength and clarity of this policy, it is well settled that Section 7031 applies despite injustice to the unlicensed contractor." [*Hydrotech Systems, Ltd. v. Oasis Waterpark*, 52 Cal.3d 988, 277 Cal.Rptr. 517 (Cal. 1991)]

ILLEGALITY—CONTRACTS CONTRARY TO PUBLIC POLICY

contracts contrary to public policy Contracts that have a negative impact on society or interfere with the public's safety and welfare.

Certain contracts are illegal because they are **contrary to public policy**. Such contracts are void. Although *public policy* eludes a precise definition, the courts have held contracts to be contrary to public policy if they have a negative impact on society or interfere with the public's safety and welfare.

Immoral Contracts

Immoral contracts, that is, contracts whose objective is the commission of an act that is considered immoral by society, may be found to be against public policy. For example, a contract that is based on sexual favors has been held an immoral contract void as against public policy. Judges are not free to define morality based on their individual views. Instead, they must look to the practices and beliefs of society when defining immoral conduct.

The following case raises the issue of whether a contract violates public policy and is therefore illegal.

immoral contract A contract whose objective is the commission of an act that is considered immoral by society.

CASE 9.3

Flood v. Fidelity & Guaranty Life Insurance Co.
394 So.2d 1311 (1981) Court of Appeals of Louisiana

Facts Ellen and Richard Alvin Flood, who were married in 1965, lived in a house trailer in Louisiana. Richard worked as a maintenance man and Ellen was employed at an insurance agency. Evidence at trial showed that Ellen was unhappy with her marriage. Ellen took out a life insurance policy on the life of her husband and named herself as beneficiary. The policy was issued by Fidelity & Guaranty Life Insurance Co. (Fidelity). In June 1972, Richard became unexpectedly ill. He was taken to the hospital, where his condition improved. After a visit at the hospital from his wife, Richard died. Ellen was criminally charged with the murder of her husband by poisoning. Evidence showed that six medicine bottles at the couple's home, including Tylenol and paregoric bottles, contained arsenic. The court found that Ellen had fed Richard ice cubes laced with arsenic at the hospital. Ellen was tried and convicted of the murder of her husband. Ellen, as beneficiary of Richard's life insurance policy, requested Fidelity to pay her the benefits. Fidelity refused to pay the benefits and returned all premiums paid on the policy. This suit followed. The district court held in favor of Ellen Flood and awarded her the benefits of the life insurance policy. Fidelity appealed.

Issue Was the life insurance policy an illegal contract that is void?

Decision Yes. The appellate court held that the life insurance policy that Ellen Flood had taken out on the life of her husband was void based on public policy. Reversed.

Reason Louisiana follows the majority rule, which holds, as a matter of public policy, that a beneficiary named in a life insurance policy is not entitled to the proceeds of the insurance if the beneficiary feloniously kills the insured. Applying this rule, the appellate court held that Ellen Flood could not recover the life insurance benefits from the policy she had taken out on her husband's death. The court stated: "... life insurance policies are procured because life is, indeed, precarious and uncertain. Our law does not and cannot sanction any scheme that has as its purpose the certain infliction of death for, inter alia, financial gain through receipt of the proceeds of life insurance. To sanction this policy in any way would surely shackle the spirit, letter, and life of our laws."

CASE QUESTIONS

Critical Legal Thinking Should Ellen Flood have been allowed to retain the insurance proceeds in this case?

Ethics Did Ellen Flood act unethically in this case? Did she act illegally?

Business Implication What would be the economic consequences if persons could recover insurance proceeds for losses caused by their illegal activities (e.g., murder, arson)?

Contracts in Restraint of Trade

The general economic policy of this country favors competition. At common law, **contracts in restraint of trade**, that is, contracts that unreasonably restrain trade, were held to be unlawful. For example, it would be an illegal restraint of trade if all the

contract in restraint of trade A contract that unreasonably restrains trade.

bakers in a neighborhood agreed to fix the prices of the bread they sold. The bakers' contract would be void.

Covenants Not to Compete

The sale of a business often includes its "goodwill" or reputation. To protect this goodwill after the sale, the seller often enters into an agreement with the buyer not to engage in a similar business or occupation within a specified geographical area for a specified period of time following the sale. This agreement is called a **covenant not to compete**, or a **noncompete clause**. Employment contracts often contain noncompete clauses that prohibit an employee from competing with his or her employer for a certain time period after leaving the employment.

Covenants not to compete that are ancillary to a legitimate sale of a business or employment contract are lawful if they are reasonable in three aspects: (1) the line of business protected; (2) the geographical area protected; and (3) the duration of the restriction. A covenant that is found to be unreasonable is not enforceable as written. The reasonableness of covenants not to compete are examined on a case-by-case basis. If a covenant not to compete is unreasonable, the courts may either refuse to enforce it or change it so that it is reasonable. Usually, the courts choose the first option.

CONSIDER THIS EXAMPLE: Suppose Stacy Rogers is a certified public accountant (CPA) with a lucrative practice in San Diego, California. Her business includes a substantial amount of goodwill. When she sells her practice she agrees not to open another accounting practice in the state of California for a 50-year period. This covenant not to compete is reasonable in the line of business protected but is unreasonable in geographical scope and duration. It will not be enforced by the courts as written. The covenant not to compete would be reasonable and enforceable if it prohibited Ms. Rogers only from practicing as a CPA in the city of San Diego for five years.

A covenant not to compete that is not *ancillary* to a legitimate business transaction is void as against public policy because the noncompete clause is not protecting a legitimate business interest. For example, a contract in which one lawyer paid another lawyer not to open an office nearby would be void as against public policy because it is not ancillary to a legitimate business transaction.

Exculpatory Clauses

An **exculpatory clause** is a contractual provision that relieves one (or both) parties to the contract from tort liability. Exculpatory clauses can relieve a party of liability for ordinary negligence. They cannot be used in situations involving willful conduct, intentional torts, fraud, recklessness, or gross negligence. Exculpatory clauses are often found in leases, sales contracts, ticket stubs to sporting events, parking lot tickets, service contracts, and the like. Such clauses do not have to be reciprocal (i.e., one party may be relieved of tort liability while the other party is not).

Generally, the courts do not favor exculpatory clauses unless both parties have equal bargaining power. The courts are willing to permit competent parties of equal bargaining power to establish which of them bears the risk.

CONSIDER THIS EXAMPLE: Jim Jackson voluntarily enrolled in a parachute jump course and signed a contract containing an exculpatory clause that relieved the parachute center of liability. After receiving proper instruction, he jumped from an airplane. Unfortunately, Jim was injured when he could not steer his parachute toward the target area. He sued the parachute center for damages, but the court enforced the exculpatory clause, reasoning that parachute jumping did not involve an essential service and that there was no decisive advantage in bargaining power between the parties.

---

noncompete clause   An agreement whereby a person agrees not to engage in a specified business or occupation within a designated geographical area for a specified period of time following the sale.

"The law relating to public policy cannot remain immutable, it must change with the passage of time. The wind of change blows on it."
  L. J. Danckwerts
  Nagle v. Feilden
  (1966)

BUSINESS BRIEF
Noncompete clauses are often used in the sale of business contracts to preserve the "goodwill" of the business for the new owner. Without a noncompete clause, the seller could open next to the buyer and serve previous customers.

exculpatory clause
A contractual provision that relieves one (or both) parties to the contract from tort liability for ordinary negligence.

CAUTION
Exculpatory clauses are void as against public policy if they either (1) affect the public interest *or (2) result from the superior bargaining power of the party asserting the clause.*

Exculpatory clauses that either affect the *public interest* or result from superior bargaining power are usually found to be void as against public policy. Although the outcome varies with the circumstances of the case, the greater the degree that the party serves the general public, the greater the chance that the exculpatory clause will be struck down as illegal. The courts will consider such factors as the type of activity involved, the relative bargaining power, knowledge, experience, and sophistication of the parties as well as other relevant factors.

In the following case, the court had to decide the legality of an exculpatory clause.

CASE 9.4

Gardner v. Downtown Porsche Audi
180 Cal.App.3d 713, 225 Cal.Rptr. 757 (1986) Court of Appeals of California

Facts In late June 1978, Bruce Gardner took his 1976 Porsche 911 automobile to be repaired at Downtown Porsche Audi (Downtown), located in downtown Los Angeles, California. Evidence showed that Gardner signed Downtown's repair-order form contract, which contained the following exculpatory clause disclaiming Downtown from liability: "NOT RESPONSIBLE FOR LOSS OR DAMAGE TO CARS OR ARTICLES LEFT IN CARS IN CASE OF FIRE, THEFT OR ANY OTHER CAUSE BEYOND OUR CONTROL." Someone stole Gardner's Porsche while it was parked at Downtown's repair garage. Gardner sued Downtown for failing to redeliver the car to him. The trial court found in favor of Gardner and awarded him $16,000 plus costs against Downtown. Downtown appealed.

Issue Does the contract involve a "public interest" that would cause the exculpatory clause to be void?

Decision Yes. The appellate court held that the car repair contract involved the public's interest and the exculpatory clause was therefore void. Affirmed.

Reason This case raises an issue common in daily life: Can an automobile repair garage avoid liability for its negligence by having car owners sign a waiver form when they leave their cars with the garage? The

appellate court stated: "The modern citizen lives—and all too frequently dies—by the automobile. Members of the general public need cars not merely for discretionary recreational purposes but to get to and from their places of employment, to reach the stores where they can purchase the necessities—as well as the frivolities—of life. An out-of-repair automobile is an unreliable means of transportation. Moreover, it is a dangerous one as well—to pedestrians and other drivers, not just the owner. What is true of modern societies in general is doubly true in Southern California, the capital of the motor vehicle. It follows that clauses which exculpate repair firms for ordinary negligence in handling and securing vehicles under repair are invalid as contrary to public policy."

CASE QUESTIONS

Critical Legal Thinking Should exculpatory clauses that involve the public interest be struck down as void as against public policy? Would an exculpatory clause used by a doctor be valid?

Ethics Did Downtown Porsche Audi act ethically in denying liability in this case?

Business Implication Why do firms use exculpatory clauses?

EFFECT OF ILLEGALITY

Because illegal contracts are void, the parties cannot sue for nonperformance. Further, if an illegal contract is executed, the court will generally leave the parties where it finds them.

Exceptions to the General Rule

Certain situations are exempt from the general rule of the effect of finding an illegal contract. If an exception applies, the innocent party may use the court system to sue

CAUTION
As a general rule, the courts will refuse to enforce or rescind an illegal contract and will leave the parties where it finds them.

for damages or to recover consideration paid under the illegal contract. Persons who can assert an exception are the following:

1. Innocent persons who were justifiably ignorant of the law or fact that made the contract illegal. For example, a person who purchases insurance from an unlicensed insurance company may recover insurance benefits from the unlicensed company.

2. Persons who were induced to enter into an illegal contract by fraud, duress, or undue influence. For example, a shop owner who pays $5,000 "protection money" to a mobster so that his store will not be burned down by the mobster can recover the $5,000.

3. Persons who entered into an illegal contract withdrawn before the illegal act is performed. For example, if the president of New Toy Corporation pays $10,000 to an employee of Old Toy Corporation to steal a trade secret from his employer but reconsiders and tells the employee not to do it before he has done it, the New Toy Corporation may recover the $10,000.

4. Persons who were less at fault than the other party for entering into the illegal contract. At common law, parties to an illegal contract were considered *in pari delicto* (in equal fault). Some states have changed this rule and permit less-at-fault parties to recover restitution of the consideration they paid under an illegal contract from the more-at-fault party.

in pari delicto When both parties are equally at fault in an illegal contract.

In the following case, the court found an illegal contract and left the parties where it found them.

CASE 9.5

Ryno v. Tyra
752 S.W.2d 148 (1988) Court of Appeals of Texas

Facts R.D. Ryno, Jr., owned Bavarian Motors, an automobile dealership in Fort Worth, Texas. On March 5, 1981, Lee Tyra discussed purchasing a 1980 BMW M-1 from Ryno for $125,000. Ryno then suggested a double-or-nothing coin flip, to which Tyra agreed. When Tyra won the coin flip, Ryno said, "It's yours," and handed Tyra the keys and German title to the car. Tyra drove away in the car. This suit ensued as to the ownership of the car. The trial court held in favor of Tyra. Ryno appealed.

Issue Who owns the car?

Decision Tyra, the patron at the car dealership who won the coin toss, owns the car. The appellate court found that there was an illegal contract and left the parties where it found them—that is, with Tyra in possession of the car. Affirmed.

Reason The appellate court stated: "Ryno complains that the trial court erred in granting Tyra judgment because the judgment enforces a gambling contract. We find there was sufficient evidence to sustain

the jury finding that Ryno intended to transfer to Tyra his ownership interest in the BMW at the time he delivered the documents, keys, and possession of the automobile to Tyra. We agree with appellant Ryno that his wager with Tyra was unenforceable. The trial court could not have compelled Ryno to honor his wager by delivering the BMW to Tyra. However, Ryno did deliver the BMW to Tyra and the facts incident to that delivery are sufficient to establish a transfer by gift of the BMW from Ryno to Tyra."

CASE QUESTIONS

Critical Legal Thinking Should the court have lent its resources to help Ryno recover the car?

Ethics Did Ryno act ethically in this case?

Business Implication What is the moral of this story if you ever win anything in an illegal gambling contract?

UNCONSCIONABLE CONTRACTS

The general rule of freedom of contract holds that if (1) the object of a contract is lawful and (2) the other elements for the formation of a contract are met, the courts will enforce a contract according to its terms. Although it is generally presumed that parties are capable of protecting their own interests when contracting, it is a fact of life that dominant parties sometimes take advantage of weaker parties. As a result, some lawful contracts are so oppressive or manifestly unfair that they are unjust. To prevent the enforcement of such contracts, the courts developed the equitable **doctrine of unconscionability**, which is based on public policy. A contract found to be unconscionable under this doctrine is called an **unconscionable contract**, or a **contract of adhesion**.

> **unconscionability**
> A doctrine under which courts may deny enforcement of unfair or oppressive contracts.

The courts are given substantial discretion in determining whether a contract or contract clause is unconscionable. There is no single definition of *unconscionability*. The doctrine may not be used merely to save a contracting party from a bad bargain.

Elements of an Unconscionable Contract

The following elements must be shown to prove that a contract or clause in a contract is unconscionable:

1. The parties possessed severely unequal bargaining power.
2. The dominant party unreasonably used its unequal bargaining power to obtain oppressive or manifestly unfair contract terms.
3. The adhering party had no reasonable alternative.

In other words, the dominant party must *misuse* its greater power to obtain oppressive contract terms from the adhering party, and the adhering party must prove that it could not reasonably refuse to accept those terms. This is often proven by showing that the oppressive terms are contained in standard contracts used industrywide.

> *"An unconscionable contract is one which no man in his senses and not under delusion would make on the one hand, and as no honest and fair man would accept on the other."*
>
> Chief Justice Fuller
> *Hume v. United States* (1889)

Remedies for Unconscionability

If the court finds that a contract or a contract clause is unconscionable, it may (1) refuse to enforce the contract, (2) refuse to enforce the unconscionable clause but enforce the remainder of the contract, or (3) limit the applicability of any unconscionable clause so as to avoid any unconscionable result. The appropriate remedy depends on the facts and circumstances of each case. Note that because unconscionability is a matter of law, the judge may opt to decide the case without a jury trial.

> **CAUTION**
> *Unconscionability is extremely subjective. Just because the result seems unfair does not mean that it is unconscionable.*

ETHICAL PERSPECTIVE

Foreclosing on a Loan Shark

In ordinary circumstances, morality requires that persons honor their contracts. If people were free to break their contractual agreements, no contracts would be made. Can not living up to the terms of a contract ever be right? Consider the following case.

Jorge Arrospide, Sr., appointed George Arrospide, Jr., to act as his attorney in fact. Among other things, Jorge Sr. wanted to pay the medical expenses of his ailing parents.

Jorge Sr. needed to borrow the funds to pay these expenses. However, he had already borrowed $193,000 against his house, which was valued at $250,000.

On July 27, 1988, George Jr. signed a $4,000 note and deed of trust on behalf of his father in favor of Michael Carboni, a li-

continued

censed real estate broker. The note, which was secured by a fourth deed of trust on Jorge Sr.'s residence, carried an interest rate of 200 percent per annum and was due in three months. The loan was exempt from usury laws because it was made by a real estate broker. Carboni also advanced additional funds to Jorge Sr. By November 25, 1988, the principal amount of the note had ballooned to $99,346. The 200 percent interest rate was 10 times the interest rate then prevailing in the credit market for similar loans.

When Jorge Sr. failed to make any payments on the note after demand, Carboni filed a complaint for judicial foreclosure and deficiency judgment on June 21, 1989. At the time of trial in March

1990, the principal and accumulated interest amounted to nearly $390,000.

Jorge Sr. argued that the loan agreement was unconscionable. The trial court agreed as to the interest rate. Using its equity powers, the court reformed the contract to provide an interest rate of 24 percent per annum but allowed Carboni to foreclose on the property. Both parties appealed.

The court of appeals held that the shockingly high 200 percent interest rate was oppressive and unconscionable. To support its decision, the court noted that Jorge Sr. would have had difficulty obtaining credit elsewhere, there was inequality of bargaining power between the parties, and that Jorge Sr. was acting under

emotional distress when he was presented with Carboni's "take it or leave it" proposal. The court also stated that unconscionability "is an amorphous concept obviously designed to establish a broad business ethic." [*Carboni v. Arrospide*, 2 Cal.App.4th 76, 2 Cal.Rptr.2d 845 (Cal. App. 1991)]

1. Did Carboni act ethically in charging 200 percent interest on the loan? Did the risk warrant this interest rate?
2. Did Jorge Sr. act ethically in trying to get out from under the terms of the contract he had obligated himself to?
3. Should the equitable doctrine of unconscionability have saved Jorge Sr. from the contract in this case?

WORKING THE WEB

LawGuru.com LawGuru.com is a way to access more than 340 legal search engines and tools.
Visit at http://www.lawguru.com/

LawRunner LawRunner has advanced query parameters for legal researchers. It offers more than 1,100 advanced query templates to make locating legal information more efficient. It has a superior index of more than 30 million Web pages found on 476,000 servers.
Visit at http://www.lawrunner.com/

LibClient LibClient was developed by the University of North Carolina in conjunction with the American Association of Law Libraries. It is a very intelligent search tool for legal researchers.
Visit at http://www.ils.unc.edu/~≈vreer/libclient/

Meta-Index for U.S. Legal Research Meta-Index for U.S. Legal Research is a collection of primary federal law search engines from other sites and only covers U.S. materials.
Visit at http://gsulaw.gsu.edu/metaindex/

Yahoo-Law Yahoo-Law is a great index of links to many legal topics such as law schools, lawyer jokes, legal ethics, legal research, tax, and so on.
Visit at http://www.yahoo.com/Law/

CYBER EXERCISES:
1-5. Select a recent U.S. Court of Appeals case such as *Atkin v. Smith*, 1998 U.S. App. Lexis 3875 (1998). Select at least two of the search engines or indexes listed here and try to find the full text of the case.

CHAPTER SUMMARY

MINORS, P. 188

Minors	
	1. *Infancy doctrine.* Minors under the age of maturity may *disaffirm* (cancel) most contracts they have entered into with adults. The contract is *voidable* by the minor but not by the adult.
	2. *Disaffirmance.* Must occur before or within a reasonable time after the minor reaches the age of majority.
	3. *Competent party's duty of restitution.* If a minor disaffirms a contract, the adult must place the minor in status quo by returning the value of the consideration that the minor paid.
	4. *Minor's duty upon disaffirmance:*
	a. *Minor's duty of restoration.* Generally, upon disaffirmance of a contract, a minor owes a duty to return the consideration to the adult in whatever condition it is in at the time of disaffirmance.
	b. *Minor's duty of restitution.* A minor's duty to place the adult in status quo by returning the value of the consideration paid by the adult at the time of contracting if the minor (1) misrepresented his or her age or (2) intentionally or with gross negligence caused the loss to the adult's property.
	5. *Ratification.* If a minor does not disaffirm a contract during the period of minority or within a reasonable time after reaching the age of majority, the contract is *ratified* (accepted).
	6. *Necessaries of life.* Minors are obligated to pay the reasonable value for necessaries of life (e.g., food, clothing, shelter).
	7. *Special contracts.* Many states have enacted statutes that make minors liable on certain types of contracts, such as for medical care, health and life insurance, educational loan agreements, and the like.
	8. *Emancipation.* Occurs when a minor voluntarily leaves home and lives apart from his or her parents. The parent's duty to support the minor terminates upon emancipation.

MENTALLY INCOMPETENT PERSONS, P. 192

Mentally Incompetent Persons	
	1. *Adjudged insane.* Contracts by persons who have been adjudged insane are *void.* That is, the contract cannot be enforced by either the sane or insane party.
	2. *Insane, but not adjudged insane.* Contracts by persons who are insane but have not been adjudged insane are *voidable* by the insane person but not by the competent party to the contract.
	3. *Duty of restitution.* A person who has dealt with an insane person must place the insane person in status quo by returning the value of the consideration paid by the insane person at the time of contracting. Most states place the same duty on insane persons when they void a contract.
	4. *Necessaries of life.* Insane persons are obligated to pay the reasonable value for necessaries of life.

INTOXICATED PERSONS, P. 193

Intoxicated Persons	
	1. *Intoxicated persons.* Contracts by intoxicated persons are *voidable* by the intoxicated person but not by the competent party to the contract.
	2. *Duty of restitution.* Both parties owe a duty to place the other party in status quo by returning the value of the consideration paid by the other party at the time of contracting.

| | 3. *Necessaries of life*. Intoxicated persons are obliged to pay the reasonable value for necessaries of life. |

ILLEGALITY—CONTRACTS CONTRARY TO STATUTES, P. 194

Contracts Contrary to Statutes	Contracts that violate statutes are illegal, void, and unenforceable.
	1. *Usury laws*. Set the upper limit on the annual interest rate that can be charged on certain types of loans by certain lenders.
	2. *Gambling statutes*. Make certain types of gambling illegal.
	3. *Sabbath laws*. Prohibit or limit the carrying on of certain secular activities on Sundays. Also called *Sunday laws* or *blue laws*.
	4. *Criminal statutes*. Contracts to commit crimes are illegal.
	5. *Licensing statutes:*
	a. *Regulatory statutes*. Licensing statutes enacted to protect the public. Unlicensed persons cannot recover payment for providing services that a licensed person is required to provide.
	b. *Revenue-raising statutes*. Licensing statutes enacted to raise money for the government. Unlicensed persons can enforce contracts and recover for rendering services.

ILLEGALITY—CONTRACTS CONTRARY TO PUBLIC POLICY, P. 196

Contracts Contrary to Public Policy	Contracts that violate public policy are illegal, void, and unenforceable.
	1. *Immoral contracts*. Contracts whose objective is the commission of an act that is considered immoral by society are illegal.
	2. *Contracts in restraint of trade*. Contracts that unreasonably restrain trade are illegal contracts.
	3. *Covenants not to compete*. Contracts that provide that a seller of a business or an employee will not engage in a similar business or occupation within a specified geographical area for a specified time following the sale of the business or termination of employment. Also called *noncompete clauses*. They are illegal if they are *unreasonable* in scope, area, or time. Reasonable noncompete clauses are legal and enforceable.
	4. *Exculpatory clauses*. Contract clauses that relieve one or both of the parties to the contract from tort liability for ordinary negligence. Exculpatory clauses that affect public interests, that result from superior bargaining power, or that attempt to relieve one of liability for international torts, fraud, recklessness, or gross negligence are illegal. Reasonable exculpatory clauses between parties of equal bargaining power are legal.

EFFECT OF ILLEGALITY, P. 199

Effect of Illegality	1. *General rule*. An illegal contract is *void*. Therefore, the parties cannot sue for nonperformance. If the contract has been executed, the court will *leave the parties where it finds them*.
	2. *Exceptions to the general rule*. An innocent party can use the courts to recover consideration paid or damages under an illegal contract where the person
	a. Was justifiably ignorant of the law or fact that made the contract illegal
	b. Was induced to enter into the illegal contract by fraud, duress, or undue influence
	c. Withdrew from the illegal contract before it was performed
	d. Was less-at-fault than the other party to the illegal contract.

UNCONSCIONABLE CONTRACTS, P. 201

Unconscionable Contracts	*Unconscionable contracts.* Contracts that are oppressively unfair or unjust. Also called *contracts of adhesion.*
	1. *Elements of unconscionable contracts.*
	   a. The parties possessed severely unequal bargaining power
	   b. The dominant party unreasonably used its power to obtain oppressive or manifestly unfair contract terms
	   c. The adhering party had no reasonable alternative.
	2. *Remedies for unconscionability.* Where a contract or contract clause is found to be unconscionable, the court may do one of the following:
	   a. Refuse to enforce the contract
	   b. Refuse to enforce the unconscionable clause but enforce the remainder of the contract
	   c. Limit the applicability of any unconscionable clause so as to avoid any unconscionable result.

CRITICAL LEGAL THINKING CASES

9.1 Infancy Doctrine James Halbman, Jr., a minor, entered into a contract to purchase a 1968 Oldsmobile automobile from Michael Lemke. Halbman paid $1,000 cash and agreed to pay $25 per week until the full purchase price was paid. Five weeks later, a connecting rod on the vehicle's engine broke, and Halbman took the car to a garage, where it was repaired at a cost of $637.40. Halbman refused to pay for the repairs, disaffirmed the contract with Lemke, and notified Lemke where the car was located.

When Lemke refused to pick up the car and pay the repair bill, the garage legally satisfied its garageman's lien by removing the vehicle's engine. It then towed the car to Halbman's residence. Halbman notified Lemke to remove the car, but Lemke refused to do so. The car was subsequently vandalized, making it worthless and unsalvageable. Halbman sued to disaffirm the contract and recover the consideration from Lemke. Lemke argued that Halbman must make full restitution. Who is correct? [*Halbman v. Lemke*, 298 N.W.2d 562 (Wis. 1980)]

9.2 Disaffirmance of a Minor's Contract Steven M. Kiefer purchased an automobile from Fred Howe Motors, Inc. At the time of the purchase, Kiefer was a minor of 20 years of age, married, the father of a child, and emancipated from his parents. Kiefer then disaffirmed the contract, claiming his rights as a minor. Howe urged that emancipated minors are an exception to this rule and that emancipated minors are legally responsible for their contracts. Can Kiefer disaffirm the contract? [*Kiefer v. Fred Howe Motors, Inc.*, 158 N.W.2d 288 (Wis. 1968)]

9.3 Ratification of a Minor's Contract Charles Edwards Smith, a minor, purchased an automobile from Bobby Floars Toyota on August 15, 1973. Smith executed a security agreement to finance part of the balance due on the purchase price, agreeing to pay off the balance in 30 monthly installments. On September 25, 1973, Smith turned 18, which was the age of majority. Smith made 10 monthly payments after turning 18. He then decided to disaffirm the contract and stopped making the payments. Smith claimed that he could disaffirm the contract entered into when he was a minor. Toyota argued that Smith had ratified the contract since attaining the age of majority. Who is correct? [*Bobby Floars Toyota, Inc. v. Smith*, 269 S.E. 320 (N.C.App. 1980)]

9.4 Necessities of Life Bobby L. Rogers, a 19-year-old emancipated minor, had to quit engineering school and go to work in order to support his wife and expected baby. Rogers contracted with Gastonia Personnel Corporation, an employment agency, agreeing to pay Gastonia a $295 fee if it found him employment. Soon thereafter, Rogers was employed by a company referred to him by Gastonia. Rogers sought to disaffirm the contract to pay Gastonia the $295 fee. Gastonia sued for the fee, claiming that the contract was for necessaries. Who wins? [*Gastonia Personnel Corporation v. Rogers*, 172 S.E.2d 19 (N.C. 1970)]

9.5 Emancipation Dwaine Ebsen, an 18-year-old minor, lived with his widowed mother, Violet. After numerous arguments with his mother regarding the people he associated with, Dwaine and his mother agreed that he should move out and support himself. Dwaine took his personal belongings and moved to Orchard, Nebraska. After moving out, Dwaine received no further support from his mother. While living in Orchard, Dwaine was shot and was taken to a hospital for treatment. He remained in the hospital for two weeks. Thereafter, the hospital sought payment from Violet. When she refused to pay, the hospital turned the matter over to Accent Service Company, a collection agency, that brought this action against Violet. Is Violet liable for her son's medical expenses? [*Accent Service Company v. Ebsen*, 306 N.W.2d 575 (Neb. 1981)]

9.6 Adjudicated Insane Manzelle Johnson, who had been adjudicated insane, executed a quitclaim and warranty deed conveying real estate she owned to her guardian, Obbie Neal. Neal subsequently conveyed the real estate to James R. Beavers by warranty deed. Charles L. Weatherly, Miss Johnson's present guardian, brought this action seeking a decree of the court that title to the real estate be restored to Miss Johnson because of her inability to contract. Should Miss Johnson be allowed to void the contract? [*Beavers v. Weatherly*, 299 S.E.2d 730 (Ga. 1983)]

9.7 Intoxication Betty Galloway, an alcoholic, signed a settlement agreement upon her divorce from her husband, Henry Galloway. Henry, in Betty's absence in court, stated that she had lucid intervals from her alcoholism, had been sober for two months, and was lucid when she signed the settlement agreement on September 22, 1978. Betty moved only to vacate the settlement agreement on September 27, 1978, after she had retained present legal counsel. On January 23, 1979, Betty was declared incompetent to handle her person and her affairs, and a guardian and conservator was appointed. Betty, through her guardian, sued to have the settlement agreement voided. Who wins? [*Galloway v. Galloway*, 281 N.W.2d 804 (N.D. 1979)]

9.8 Contract to Commit a Crime In 1972, Jordanos', Inc., suspected and accused one of its employees, Arthur T. Allen, of theft. The union to which Allen belonged negotiated an oral contract with Jordanos' whereby Allen agreed to accept a permanent layoff if Jordanos' would not report the suspected theft to the state's unemployment agency so that Allen could collect unemployment benefits. Jordanos' agreed. It is a crime for an employer and employee to withhold relevant information from the state's unemployment agency. Jordanos' subsequently reported the suspected theft to the state's unemployment agency, and Allen was denied unemployment benefits. Allen sued Jordanos' for damages for breach of contract. Can Allen recover against Jordanos'? [*Allen v. Jordanos', Inc.*, 52 Cal.App.3d 160, 125 Cal. Rptr. 31 (Cal. App. 1975)]

9.9 Affect of an Illegal Contract James L. Strickland paid an unsolicited $2,500 bribe to Judge Sylvania W. Woods so that the judge would be lenient on a friend of Strickland's who had a case pending before Judge Woods. Paying a bribe to a government official is a crime. Judge Woods reported the incident and turned the money over to the state's attorney general. The state of Maryland indicted Strickland for bribery and sentenced him to four years in prison. Strickland filed a motion to recover the $2,500 from the state. Can Strickland recover the money? [*State of Maryland v. Strickland*, 400 A.2d 451 (Md. App. 1979)]

9.10 Licensing or Revenue-Raising Statute The state of Hawaii requires a person who wants to practice architecture to meet certain educational requirements and to pass a written examination before that person is granted a license to practice. After receiving the license, an architect must pay an annual license fee of $15. In 1967, Ben Lee Wilson satisfied the initial requirements and was granted an architecture license. He renewed his license by paying the annual fee up until April 1971, when he failed to pay the annual fee. In February 1972, Wilson contracted with Kealakekua Ranch, Ltd., and Gentry Hawaii (defendants) to provide architectural services for the Kealakekua Ranch Center Project. During the period February

1972 through May 1972, Wilson provided $33,994 of architectural services to the defendants. The defendants refused to pay this fee because Wilson did not have an architectural license. Wilson sued to collect his fees. Who wins? [*Wilson v. Kealakekua Ranch, Ltd., and Gentry Hawaii*, 551 P.2d 525 (Hawaii 1976)]

9.11 Public Policy American Home Enterprises, Inc., was a corporation that made jewelry and drug paraphernalia, such as roach clips and bongs to smoke marijuana and tobacco. Evidence showed that American Home predominantly produced drug paraphernalia and was not engaged significantly in jewelry production. In 1978, Robert Bovard and James T. Ralph contracted to purchase American Home and, as part of the purchase price, executed several promissory notes payable to the sellers. Although at the time of the sale the manufacture of drug paraphernalia was not itself illegal, the possession, use, and transfer of marijuana was illegal. When Bovard and Ralph defaulted on the promissory notes, the sellers sued to enforce the notes. Bovard and Ralph alleged that the contract was illegal and unenforceable as against public policy. Who wins? [*Bovard v. American Home Enterprises, Inc.*, 201 Cal.App.3d 832, 247 Cal.Rptr. 340 (Cal. App. 1988)]

✓**9.12 Covenant Not to Compete** Gerry Morris owned a silk screening and lettering shop in Tucson, Arizona. On April 11, 1974, Morris entered into a contract to sell the business to Alfred and Connie Gann. The contract contained the following covenant not to compete: "Seller agrees not to enter into silk screening or lettering shop business within Tucson and a 100-mile radius of Tucson, a period of ten (10) years from the date of this Agreement and will not compete in any manner whatsoever with buyers, and seller further agrees that he will refer all business contacts to buyers." Morris opened a silk screening and lettering business in competition with the Ganns and in violation of the noncompetition clause. The Ganns brought this action against Morris for breach of contract and to enforce the covenant not to compete. Is the covenant not to compete valid and enforceable in this case? [*Gann v. Morris*, 596 P.2d 43 (Ariz. App. 1979)]

9.13 Exculpatory Clause Grady Perkins owned the Raleigh Institute of Cosmetology, and Ray Monk and Rovetta Allen were employed as instructors at the Institute. The school trains students to do hairstyling and hair coloring, cosmetology, and other beauty services. The students receive practical training by providing services to members of the public under the supervision of the instructors. On March 28, 1985, Francis I. Alston went to the Institute to have her hair colored and styled by a student who was under the supervision of Monk and Allen. Before receiving any services, Alston signed a written release form that released the Institute and its employees from liability for their negligence. While coloring Alston's hair, the student negligently used a chemical that caused Alston's hair to fall out. Alston sued the Institute, Perkins, Monk, and Allen for damages. The defendants asserted that the release form signed by Alston barred her suit. Is the exculpatory clause valid? [*Alston v. Monk*, 373 S.E.2d 463 (N.C. App. 1988)]

9.14 Exculpatory Clause Wilbur Spaulding owned and operated the Jacksonville racetrack at the Morgan County Fairgrounds, where automobile races were held. Lawrence P. Koch was a flagman at the raceway. On May 28, 1982, when Koch arrived at the pit shack at the raceway, he was handed a clipboard upon which there was a track release and waiver of liability form that released the racetrack from liability for negligence. Koch signed the form and took up his position as flagman. During the first race, the last car on the track lost control and slid off the end of the track, striking Koch. Koch suffered a broken leg and other injuries and was unable to work for 14 months. Koch sued Spaulding for damages for negligence. Spaulding asserted that the release form signed by Koch barred his suit. Is the exculpatory clause valid against Koch? [*Koch v. Spaulding*, 529 N.E.2d 19 (Ill. App. 1988)]

9.15 Unconscionable Contract Bill Graham, an experienced promoter and producer of musical concerts, entered into a contract with Leon Russell, a rock singer who did business under the corporate name Scissor-Tail, Inc., whereby Graham would promote several concerts for Russell. Russell belonged to the American Federation of Musicians (AFM), a union that represented most big-name musicians. The contract between Graham and Russell was on a standard, preprinted form required to be used by all AFM members. The contract contained an arbitration clause that required any disputes regarding the contract to be heard and decided by the executive board of the AFM. When a monetary dispute arose between Graham and Russell regarding the division of proceeds from the concerts, Graham sued Russell in court. Russell filed a motion to compel arbitration. Graham asserted that the arbitration clause in the AFM contract is unconscionable. Is it? [*Graham v. Scissor-Tail, Inc.*, 28 Cal. App.3d 807, 171 Cal. Rptr. 604 (Cal. App. 1981)]

ETHICS CASES

9.16 Ethical Perspective Joe Plumlee owned and operated an ambulance company. He alleged that the law firm of Paddock, Loveless, and Roach agreed to pay him an up-front fee and a percentage of the law firm's fees generated from personal injury case referrals. When the law firm did not pay Plumlee, he sued to recover damages for breach of contract. Texas law prohibits lawyers from sharing fees with lay persons [Tex. Penal Code § 38.12; Supreme Court of Texas]. A disciplinary rule also forbids such activity [State Bar Rules Art. X, § 9]. The law firm asserted that the contract could not be enforced because it would be an illegal contract. Who wins? Did Plumlee act ethically in this case? If the contract existed, did the lawyers act ethically? [*Plumlee v. Paddock, Loveless, and Roach*, 832 S.W.2d 757 (Tex. App. 1992)]

9.17 Ethical Perspective Richard Zientara was friends with Chester and Bernice Kaszuba. All three were residents of Indiana. Bernice, who was employed in an Illinois tavern where Illinois state lottery tickets were sold, had previously obtained lottery tickets for Zientara because Indiana did not have a state lottery. In early April 1984, Zientara requested that Kaszuba purchase an Illinois lottery ticket for him. He gave Kaszuba the money for the ticket and the numbers 6–15–16–23–24–37. Kaszuba purchased the ticket, but when it turned out to be the winning combination worth $1,696,800, she refused to give the ticket to Zientara and unsuccessfully tried to collect the money. Zientara filed suit against Kaszuba in Indiana claiming the ticket and proceeds thereof. Was the contract legal? Did Kaszuba act ethically in this case? [*Kaszuba v. Zientara*, 506 N.E.2d 1 (Ind. 1987)]

9.18 Ethical Perspective On August 31, 1965, Clifton and Cora Jones, who were welfare recipients, received a visit from a salesman representing You Shop at Home Service, Inc. After a sales presentation, Jones signed a retail installment contract to purchase a home freezer unit for the sale price of $900.00. With the addition of time credit charges, credit life insurance, and credit property insurance, the contract price totaled $1,234.80. The freezer had a maximum retail value of $300.00. Evidence showed that the Joneses were unsophisticated and uneducated concerning contracts.

After paying $619.88, Jones brought an action to rescind the contract. Star Credit Corporation, which had come into possession of the credit contract, counterclaimed for $819.81, the amount remaining on the contract plus charges for missed payments. Is the contract unconscionable in the legal sense? If so, what remedy should be awarded? Was it ethical for the sales representative to prey upon ignorant and unsophisticated consumers? Was it ethical for the Joneses to attempt to get out of the contract they signed? [*Jones v. Star Credit Corp.*, 298 N.Y.S.2d 264 (N.Y. Sup. 1969)]

CRITICAL LEGAL THINKING WRITING ASSIGNMENT

Read Case A.9 in the Case Appendix [*Carnival Leisure Industries, Ltd. v. Aubin*]. This case is excerpted from the court of appeals opinion. Review and brief the case. In your brief, be sure to answer the following questions:
1. What were the plaintiff's contentions on appeal?
2. What law was applied by the court in this case, Bahamian law or Texas law? Why was that law applied?

3. What is the consequence of finding an illegal contract? Apply this rule to the facts of this case.
4. Did Aubin act ethically in avoiding an obligation that he knowingly made? Do you think he would have given back the money if he had won at gambling?

CHAPTER 10

DEFENSES

TO THE ENFORCEMENT

OF CONTRACTS

Chapter Objectives

*After studying this chapter,
you should be able to*

1. Explain genuineness of assent
2. Distinguish between unilateral and mutual mistakes of fact
3. Describe fraudulent misrepresentation
4. Define and describe undue influence
5. Describe physical and economic duress
6. List and describe the contracts that must be in writing under the Statute of Frauds
7. Describe the Statute of Frauds applicable to the sale of goods
8. Define and apply the doctrine of promissory estoppel
9. Apply the parol evidence rule
10. Define and describe the effects of an integration clause

Chapter Contents

- Mistakes
  Case 10.1 *Wells Fargo Credit Corp. v. Martin (FL)*
- Fraudulent Misrepresentation
  Business Checklist Elements of Fraud
  Case 10.2 *Wilson v. Western National Life Insurance Co. (CA)*
- Undue Influence
  Ethical Perspective The Doctrine of Undue Influence
- Duress
  Business Application Economic Duress
- Statute of Frauds—Writing Requirement
  Case 10.3 *Sutton v. Warner (CA)*
  International Perspective Writing Requirements for International Contracts
- Sufficiency of the Writing
  Case 10.4 *Malmstrom v. Kaiser Aluminum & Chemical Corp. (CA)*
  Business Checklist Standards of Interpretation for Contracts
- Working the Web
- Chapter Summary
- Critical Legal Thinking Cases
- Ethics Cases
- Critical Legal Thinking Writing Assignment

> *A verbal contract isn't worth the paper it's written on.*
>
> Samuel Goldwyn

A contract may sometimes not be enforced even if all of the required elements of a legal contract are met. This happens when the party against whom enforcement is sought raises certain defenses against its enforcement.

There are two primary defenses to the enforcement of a contract. The first is that the assent of one or both of the parties to the contract was not genuine or real. **Genuine assent** may be missing because a party entered into a contract based on mistake, fraudulent misrepresentation, duress, or undue influence. The second defense is that the contract did not meet the requirements of the Statute of Frauds. The Statute of Frauds requires certain contracts to be in writing or in a stipulated form.

Problems concerning genuineness of assent and writing are discussed in this chapter.

"Most of the disputes in the world arise from words."
Lord Mansfield, C.J.
Morgan v. Jones
(1773)

genuineness of assent
The requirement that a party's assent to a contract be genuine.

MISTAKES

A **mistake** occurs where one or both of the parties have an erroneous belief about the subject matter, value, or some other aspect of the contract. Mistakes can be either *unilateral* or *mutual*. The law permits **rescission** of some contracts made in mistake.

rescission An action to undo the contract.

Unilateral Mistakes

Unilateral mistakes occur when only one party is mistaken about a material fact regarding the subject matter of the contract. There are three types of situations in which the contract may not be enforced due to such a mistake:

1. One party makes a unilateral mistake of fact and the other party knew (or should have known) that a mistake was made.
2. A unilateral mistake occurs because of a clerical or mathematical error that is not the result of gross negligence.
3. The mistake is so serious that enforcing the contract would be unconscionable.[1]

In most cases, however, the mistaken party will not be permitted to rescind the contract. The contract will be enforced on its terms.

unilateral mistake When only one party is mistaken about a material fact regarding the subject matter of the contract.

"Words are chameleons, which reflect the color of their environment."
Justice L. Hand
Commissioner v. National Carbide Co. (1948)

CONSIDER THIS EXAMPLE: Suppose Trent Anderson wants to purchase a car from the showroom floor. He looks at several models. Although he decides to purchase a car with a sunroof, he does not tell the salesman about this preference. The model named in the contract he signs does not have this feature, although he believes it does. Mr. Anderson's unilateral mistake will not relieve him of his contractual obligation to purchase the car.

In the following case, the court had to decide whether to allow a party out of a contract because of the party's unilateral mistake.

CASE 10.1

Wells Fargo Credit Corp. v. Martin
650 So.2d 531 (1992) District Court of Appeals of Florida

Facts Wells Fargo Credit Corporation (Wells Fargo) obtained a judgment of foreclosure on a house owned by Mr. and Mrs. Clevenger. The total indebtedness stated in the judgment was $207,141. The foreclosure sale was scheduled for 11:00 A.M. on *continued*

July 12, 1991, at the west front door of the Hillsborough County Courthouse. Wells Fargo was represented by a paralegal, who had attended more than 1,000 similar sales. Wells Fargo's handwritten instruction sheet informed the paralegal to make one bid at $115,000, the tax-appraised value of the property. Because the first "1" in the number was close to the "$," the paralegal misread the bid instruction as $15,000 and opened the bidding at that amount. Harley Martin, who was attending his first judicial sale, bid $20,000. The county clerk gave ample time for another bid and then announced "$20,000 going once, $20,000 going twice, sold to Harley . . ." The paralegal screamed, "Stop, I'm sorry, I made a mistake!" The certificate of sale was issued to Martin. Wells Fargo filed suit to set aside the judicial sale based on its unilateral mistake. The trial court held for Martin. Wells Fargo appealed.

Issue Does Wells Fargo's unilateral mistake constitute grounds for setting aside the judicial sale?

Decision No. The appellate court held that Wells Fargo's unilateral mistake did not entitle it to relief from the judicial sale.

Reason The appellate court held that Martin's right to purchase the property vested at the moment the county clerk announced "sold." Generally, a unilateral mistake will not permit the mistaken party to rescind a contract. The appellate court held that the trial court had the discretion to place the risk of the mistake upon Wells Fargo.

CASE QUESTIONS

Critical Legal Thinking Should contracts be allowed to be rescinded because of unilateral mistakes? Why or why not?

Ethics Did Wells Fargo act ethically in trying to set aside the judicial sale?

Business Implication Do you think mistakes such as that made by Wells Fargo happen very often in business?

Mutual Mistakes

mutual mistake of fact
A mistake made by both parties concerning a material fact that is important to the subject matter of the contract.

"The meaning of words varies according to the circumstances of and concerning which they are used."

Justice Blackburn
Allgood v. Blake
(1873)

mutual mistake of value
A mistake that occurs if both parties know the object of the contract but are mistaken as to its value.

Either party may rescind the contract if there has been a **mutual mistake of a part or existing material fact**.[2] A material fact is one that is important to the subject matter of the contract. An ambiguity in a contract may constitute a mutual mistake of a material fact. An ambiguity occurs where a word or term of the contract is susceptible to more than one logical interpretation. If there has been a mutual mistake, the contract may be rescinded on the ground that no contract has been formed because there has been no "meeting of the minds" between the parties.

In the celebrated case of *Raffles v. Wichelhaus*,[3] which has become better known as the case of the good ship *Peerless*, the parties agreed on a sale of cotton, which was to be delivered from Bombay by the ship. However, there were two ships named *Peerless*, and each party, in agreeing to the sale, was referring to a different ship. Because the sailing time of the two ships was materially different, neither party was willing to agree to shipment by the other *Peerless*. The court ruled that there was no binding contract because each party had a different ship in mind when the contract was entered into.

The courts must distinguish between *mutual mistakes of fact* and *mutual mistakes of value*. A **mutual mistake of value** exists if both parties know the object of the contract but are mistaken as to its value. Here, the contract remains enforceable by either party because the identity of the subject matter of the contract is not at issue. If the rule were different, almost all contracts could later be rescinded by the party who got the "worst" of the deal.

CONSIDER THIS EXAMPLE: Suppose Phuong Kiet Le cleans her attic and finds a painting of tomato soup cans. She has no use for it, so she offers to sell it to Fred for $100. Fred, who likes the painting, accepts the offer and pays Phuong $100. It is later discovered that the painting is worth $200,000 because it was painted by Andy Warhol. Neither party knew this at the time of contracting. It is a mistake of value. Phuong cannot recover the painting.

FRAUDULENT MISREPRESENTATION

A **misrepresentation** occurs when an assertion is made that is not in accord with the facts.[4] An **intentional misrepresentation** occurs when one person consciously decides to induce another person to rely and act on a misrepresentation. Intentional misrepresentation is commonly referred to as **fraudulent misrepresentation**, or **fraud**. When a fraudulent misrepresentation is used to induce another to enter into a contract, the innocent party's assent to the contract is not genuine and the contract is voidable by the innocent party.[5] The innocent party can either rescind the contract and obtain restitution or enforce the contract and sue for contract damages.

misrepresentation An assertion that is made that is not in accord with the facts.

intentional misrepresentation Occurs when one person consciously decides to induce another person to rely and act on a misrepresentation. Also called *fraud*.

BUSINESS CHECKLIST

Elements of Fraud

To prove fraud, the following elements must be shown:

1. **Material misrepresentation of fact.** A misrepresentation can occur by words (oral or written) or by the conduct of the party to be actionable as fraud, the misrepresentation must be of a past or existing *material fact*. This means that the misrepresentation must have been a significant factor in inducing the innocent party to enter into the contract. It does not have to be the sole factor. Statements of opinion or predictions about the future generally do not form the basis of fraud.
2. **Intent to deceive.** To prove fraud, the person making the misrepresentation must have either had knowledge that the representation was false or made it without sufficient knowledge of the truth. This is called **scienter** ("guilty mind"). The misrepresentation must have been made with the intent to deceive the innocent party. Intent can be inferred from the circumstances.
3. **Reliance on the misrepresentation.** A misrepresentation is not actionable unless the innocent party to whom the misrepresentation was directed acted upon it. Further, an innocent party who acts in reliance on the misrepresentation must justify his or her reliance.[6] Justifiable reliance generally is found unless the innocent party knew that the misrepresentation was false or was so extravagant as to be obviously false. For example, reliance on a statement such as "This diamond ring is worth $10,000, but I'll sell it to you for $100" would not be justified.
4. **Injury to the innocent party.** To recover damages, the innocent party must prove that the fraud caused economic injury. The measure of damages is the difference between the value of the property as represented and the actual value of the property. This measure of damages gives the innocent party the "benefit of the bargain." In the alternative, the buyer can rescind the contract and recover the purchase price.

Types of Fraud

There are various types of fraud. Some of the most common ones follow.

Fraud in the Inception Fraud in the inception, or **fraud in the factum**, occurs if a person is deceived as to the nature of his or her act and does not know

fraud in the inception Occurs if a person is deceived as to the nature of his or her act and does not know what he or she is signing.

what he or she is signing. Such contracts are void rather than just voidable. For example, suppose Heather brings her professor a grade card to sign. The professor signs the front of the grade card. On the back, however, are contract terms that transfer all of the professor's property to Heather. Here there is fraud in the inception. The contract is void.

fraud in the inducement
Occurs when the party knows what he or she is signing but has been fraudulently induced to enter into the contract.

Fraud in the Inducement   A great many fraud cases concern **fraud in the inducement**. Here, the innocent party knows what he or she is signing but has been fraudulently induced to enter into the contract. Such contracts are voidable by the innocent party.

CONSIDER THIS EXAMPLE: Suppose Lyle Green tells Candice Young he is forming a partnership to invest in drilling for oil and invites her to invest in this venture. In reality, though, Lyle Green intends to use whatever money he receives for his personal expenses, and he absconds with Ms. Young's $30,000 investment. Here there has been fraud in the inducement. Ms. Young can rescind the contract and recover the money from Lyle Green—if he can be found.

fraud by concealment
Occurs when one party takes specific action to conceal a material fact from another party.

Fraud by Concealment   **Fraud by concealment** occurs when one party takes specific action to conceal a material fact from another party.[7] For example, suppose that ABC Blouses, Inc. contracts to buy a used sewing machine from Wear-Well Shirts, Inc. Wear-Well did not show ABC the repair invoices from the sewing machine, even though ABC asked to see them. Relying on the fact that the machine was in good condition and never had to be repaired, ABC bought the machine. If ABC discovers that a significant repair record has been concealed, it can sue Wear-Well for fraud.

Silence as Misrepresentation   Generally, neither party to a contract owes a duty to disclose all the facts to the other party. Ordinarily, such silence is not a misrepresentation unless (1) nondisclosure would cause bodily injury or death, (2) there is a fiduciary relationship (i.e., a relationship of trust and confidence) between the contracting parties, or (3) federal and state statutes require disclosure. The Restatement (Second) of Contracts specifies a broader duty of disclosure: Nondisclosure is a misrepresentation if it would constitute a failure to act in "good faith."[8]

Misrepresentation of Law   Usually, a misrepresentation of law is not actionable as fraud. The innocent party cannot generally rescind the contract. This is because each party to a contract is assumed to know the law that applies to the transaction either through his or her own investigation or by hiring a lawyer. There is one major exception to this rule: The misrepresentation will be allowed as a ground for rescission of the contract if one party to a contract is a professional who should know what the law is and intentionally misrepresents the law to a less sophisticated contracting party.[9]

Innocent Misrepresentation

innocent misrepresentation   Occurs when a person makes a statement of fact that he or she honestly and reasonably believes to be true, even though it is not.

An **innocent misrepresentation** occurs when a person makes a statement of fact that he or she honestly and reasonably believes to be true, even though it is not. Innocent misrepresentation is not fraud. If an innocent misrepresentation has been made, the aggrieved party may rescind the contract but may not sue for damages. Often, innocent misrepresentation is treated as a mutual mistake.

In the following case, the court allowed a contract to be rescinded.

CASE 10.2

Wilson v. Western National Life Insurance Co.
235 Cal.App. 3d 981, 1 Cal.Rptr.2d 157 (1991) California Court of Appeal

Facts Daniel and Doris Wilson were husband and wife. On August 13, 1985, Daniel fainted from a narcotics overdose and was rushed unconscious to the hospital. Doris accompanied him. Daniel responded to medication used to counteract a narcotics overdose and recovered. The emergency room physician noted that Daniel had probably suffered from a heroin overdose and that Daniel had multiple puncture sites on his arms.

On October 8, 1985, an agent for Western National Life Insurance Company (Western), met with the Wilsons in their home for the purpose of taking their application for life insurance. The agent asked questions and recorded the Wilsons' responses on a written application form. Daniel answered the following questions:

	Yes	No
13. In the past 10 years, have you been treated or joined an organization for alcoholism or drug addiction? If "Yes," explain on the reverse side.		X
17. In the past 5 years, have you consulted or been treated or examined by any physician or practitioner?		X

Both of the Wilsons signed the application form and paid the agent the first month's premium. Under insurance law and the application form, the life insurance policy took effect immediately. Daniel Wilson died from a drug overdose two days later. Western rescinded the policy and rejected Doris Wilson's claim to recover the policy's $50,000 death benefit for Daniel's death, alleging failure to disclose the August 13, 1985, incident. Doris sued to recover the death benefits. The trial court granted summary judgment for Western. Doris appealed.

Issue Was there a concealment of a material fact that justified Western's rescission of the life insurance policy?

Decision Yes. The appellate court held that there was a concealment by the Wilsons that warranted rescissions of the life insurance policy by Western.

Reason A material misrepresentation or concealment, whether intentional or innocent, entitles the injured party to rescind the contract. The court held that the Wilsons had made such a misrepresentation by concealment, that it was material, and that Western had relied on it and had been injured. The court found that Western would not have issued the life insurance policy to Daniel Wilson if it had been informed of his prior drug overdose.

CASE QUESTIONS

Critical Legal Thinking Should a contract be allowed to be rescinded because of an *innocent* misrepresentation? Why or why not?

Ethics Do you think the concealment was intentional or innocent?

Business Implication Do you think there is very much insurance fraud in this country? Explain.

UNDUE INFLUENCE

The courts may permit the rescission of a contract based on the equitable doctrine of **undue influence**. Undue influence occurs when one person (the dominant party) takes advantage of another person's mental, emotional, or physical weakness and unduly persuades that person (the servient party) to enter into a contract. The persuasion by the wrongdoer must overcome the free will of the innocent party. A contract that is entered into because of undue influence is voidable by the innocent party.[10] Wills often are challenged as having been made under undue influence.

undue influence Occurs where one person takes advantage of another person's mental, emotional, or physical weakness and unduly persuades that person to enter into a contract; the persuasion by the wrongdoer must overcome the free will of the innocent party.

The following elements must be shown to prove undue influence:

1. A fiduciary or confidential relationship must have existed between the parties.
2. The dominant party must have unduly used his or her influence to persuade the servient party to enter into a contract.

If there is a confidential relationship between persons—such as lawyer and client, doctor and patient, psychiatrist and patient—any contract made by the servient party that benefits the dominant party is presumed to be entered into under undue influence. This is a rebuttable presumption that can be overcome by proper evidence.

ETHICAL PERSPECTIVE

The Doctrine of Undue Influence

In 1966, Ralla Klepak, an attorney, met Virgil Robert Woodruff when she represented him in a criminal misdemeanor proceeding. Although their relationship began as attorney and client, it developed into one of friendship. They dined, attended operas, and vacationed together. Prior to his death, Woodruff retained Klepak in her capacity as an attorney to represent his interests in various legal and personal matters.

In October 1973, Woodruff purchased a condominium unit in the John Hancock Building on North Michigan Avenue in Chicago. Klepak represented Woodruff in the purchase of the condominium. At the same time, Klepak represented Woodruff in establishing a land trust that provided that the beneficial interest in the condominium would remain Woodruff's for his life and then pass to Klepak upon his death. The Lake Shore Bank was named as trustee of the trust. Klepak notarized the land trust agreement while they were at a restaurant. Woodruff died on May 29, 1984, at the age of 54. He was a bachelor, had never married, and had no living issue. His only heirs were two maternal aunts and a paternal cousin. Two days after Woodruff's death, Klepak delivered a certified copy of his death certificate to the Lake Shore

Bank. Klepak took possession of the condominium shortly after Woodruff's death and has had sole use and possession of the premises since that time. William L. Klaskin, who was named administrator of Woodruff's estate, brought this action to recover the condominium from Klepak. The trial court held in favor of the estate. The appellate court reversed. The estate appealed.

Did Ralla Klepak, as an attorney, rebut the presumption of undue influence that arose from this transaction?

Transactions between attorneys and clients are closely scrutinized. When an attorney engages in a transaction with a client and is benefited thereby, a presumption arises that the transaction proceeded from undue influence. When a presumption is raised, the burden shifts to the attorney to come forward with evidence that the transaction was fair, equitable, and just and that the benefit did not proceed from undue influence. Courts require clear and convincing evidence to rebut this presumption.

Some of the factors that the Supreme Court of Illinois deemed persuasive in determining whether the presumption of undue influence has been overcome include a showing by the attorney that (1) he or she made a

full and frank disclosure of all relevant information, (2) adequate consideration was given, and (3) the client had independent advice before completing the transaction. In this case, the court evaluated the evidence adduced at trial in light of these factors and concluded that Klepak failed to overcome the presumption of undue influence. The court held that Klepak never informed Woodruff of the legal consequences of naming her as beneficiary. The court also concluded that Klepak gave no consideration for being named as beneficiary and never advised Woodruff to seek independent legal advice after learning that she was named as beneficiary.

The state supreme court held that Ralla Klepak did not rebut the presumption of undue influence that arose from the transaction at issue in this case. The court reversed the judgment of the appellate court and affirmed the judgment of the trial court. [*Klaskin v. Klepak*, 534 N.E.2d 971 (Ill. 1989)]

1. Did Ralla Klepak act unethically in this case?
2. Should there be a presumption that transactions between an attorney and a client have been based on undue influence? Do you think there was actual undue influence in this case?

DURESS

Duress occurs where one party threatens to do some wrongful act unless the other party enters into a contract. If a party to a contract has been forced into making the contract, the assent is not voluntary. Such contracts are not enforceable against the innocent party.

The threat to commit physical harm or extortion unless someone enters into a contract constitutes duress. So does a threat to bring (or not drop) a criminal lawsuit. This is so even if the criminal lawsuit is well founded.[11] However, a threat to bring (or not drop) a civil lawsuit does not constitute duress unless such a suit is frivolous or brought in bad faith.

The courts have recognized another type of duress—**economic duress**. Economic duress usually occurs when one party to a contract refuses to perform his or her contractual duties unless the other party pays an increased price, enters into a second contract with the threatening party, or the like. The duressed party must prove that he or she had no choice but to give in to the threat.

duress Occurs when one party threatens to do a wrongful act unless the other party enters into a contract.

economic duress Occurs when one party to a contract refuses to perform his or her contractual duties unless the other party pays an increased price, enters into a second contract with the threatening party, or undertakes a similar action.

BUSINESS APPLICATION

Economic Duress

Economic duress is also called **business compulsion**, **business duress**, and **economic coercion**. The appropriateness of these terms becomes apparent when the facts of the following case are examined.

Ashton Development, Inc. (Ashton), hired Bob Britton, Inc. (Britton), a general contractor, to build a development for it. Britton signed a contract with a subcontractor, Rich & Whillock, Inc. (R & W), to provide grading and excavation work at the project. The contract stated that "any rock encountered will be considered an extra at current rates" and expressly excluded blasting work. The contract price was $112,990. In late March 1981, when R & W encountered rock at the project site, a meeting was held between the parties to discuss the problem. Britton directed R & W to go ahead with the rock work and agreed to pay for the additional

work. R & W proceeded with the excavation work and rock removal, which included blasting.

On June 17, 1981, after completing all of the required work and receiving $109,363 in payments to date, R & W submitted a final bill to Britton for $72,286. The total bill was $68,659 above the original contract price.

Ashton and Britton refused to pay this amount. R & W told Britton that it would go "broke" if payment was not received. On July 10, 1981, Britton presented R & W with an agreement whereby Britton would pay $25,000 upon the signing of the agreement and another $25,000 on August 10, 1981. When R & W complained of the financial bind it was in, Britton stated: "I have a check for you, and you just take it or leave it, this is all you get. If you don't take this, you have got to sue me." After claiming that it was "blackmail," R & W accepted the

$25,000 check. Britton did not pay the other $25,000 until August 20, 1981, after requiring R & W to sign a release of claims form.

In December 1981, R & W sued Ashton and Britton for breach of contract. The defendants argued that the settlement agreement and release signed by R & W prevented it from collecting. The trial and appellate courts held in favor of R & W, finding that Ashton and Britton's tactics amounted to economic duress. In applying the doctrine of economic duress to the case, the court stated: "The underlying concern of the economic duress doctrine is the enforcement in the marketplace of certain minimal standards of business ethics." The court ordered Ashton and Britton to pay the balance due on the contract to R & W. [*Rich & Whillock, Inc. v. Ashton Development, Inc.*, 157 Cal. App.3d 1154, 204 Cal. Rptr. 86 (Cal.App. 1984)]

STATUTE OF FRAUDS—WRITING REQUIREMENT

In 1677, the English Parliament enacted a statute called "An Act for the Prevention of Frauds and Perjuries." This Act required that certain types of contracts had to be in writing and signed by the party against whom enforcement was sought. Today, all states have enacted a **Statute of Frauds** that requires certain types of contracts to be in *writing*. This statute is intended to ensure that the terms of important contracts are not forgotten, misunderstood, or fabricated.

Although the statutes vary slightly from state to state, most states require the following types of contracts to be in writing:[12]

- Contracts involving interests in land *(purchase or rental)*
- Contracts that by their own terms <u>cannot possibly</u> be performed within one year
- Collateral contracts in which a person promises to answer for the debt or duty of another
- Promises made in consideration of marriage
- Contracts for the sale of goods for more than $500
- Real estate agents' contracts
- Agents' contracts where the underlying contract must be in writing
- Promises to write a will
- Contracts to pay debts barred by the statute of limitations or discharged in bankruptcy
- Contracts to pay compensation for services rendered in negotiating the purchase of a business
- Finder's fee contracts.

Generally, an *executory contract* that is not in writing even though the Statute of Frauds requires it to be is unenforceable by either party. (If the contract is valid in all other respects, however, it may be voluntarily performed by the parties.) The Statute of Frauds is usually raised by one party as a defense to the enforcement of the contract by the other party. If an oral contract that should have been in writing under the Statute of Frauds is already executed, neither party can seek to rescind the contract on the ground of noncompliance with the Statute of Frauds.

Contracts Involving Interests in Land

Any contract that transfers an ownership interest in **real property** must be in writing under the Statute of Frauds to be enforceable. Real property includes the land itself, buildings, trees, soil, minerals, timber, plants, crops, fixtures, and things permanently affixed to the land or buildings. Certain personal property that is permanently affixed to the real property—for example, built-in cabinets in a house—are **fixtures** that become part of the real property.

Other contracts that transfer an ownership interest in land must be in writing under the Statute of Frauds. These interests include the following:

- **Mortgages.** Borrowers often give a lender an interest in real property as security for the repayment of a loan. This must be done through the use of a written **mortgage** or **deed of trust**.
- **Leases.** A **lease** is the transfer of the right to use real property for a specified period of time. Most Statutes of Frauds require leases for a term over one year to be in writing.
- **Life Estates.** On some occasions, a person is given a **life estate** in real property. This means that the person has an interest in the land for the person's lifetime, and the interest will be transferred to another party on that person's death. A life estate is an ownership interest that must be in writing under the Statute of Frauds.
- **Easements.** An **easement** is a given or required right to use another person's land without owning or leasing it. Easements may be either express or implied. Express easements must be in writing to be enforceable, whereas implied easements need not be written.

Statute of Frauds State statute that requires certain types of contracts to be in writing.

"Statute of Frauds: That unfortunate statute, the misguided application of which has been the cause of so many frauds."
V.C. Bacon
Morgan v. Worthington (1878)

BUSINESS BRIEF
Although only certain contracts must be in writing under the Statute of Frauds, it is good practice to place other contracts in writing so there is no dispute as to the terms of the contract at a later date.

"To break an oral agreement which is not legally binding is morally wrong."
Talmud
Bava Metzi'a

real property The land itself as well as buildings, trees, soil, minerals, timber, plants, crops, and other things permanently affixed to the land.

fixtures Personal property that is permanently affixed to the real property, such as built-in cabinets in a house.

mortgage An interest in real property given to a lender as security for the repayment of a loan.

Part Performance Exception If an oral contract for the sale of land or transfer of another interest in real property has been partially performed, it might not be possible to return the parties to their status quo. To solve this problem, the courts have developed the equitable doctrine of **part performance**. This doctrine allows the court to order such an oral contract to be specifically performed if performance is necessary to avoid injustice. For this performance exception to apply, most courts require that the purchaser either pay part of the purchase price and take possession of the property or make valuable improvements on the land.

The following case applies the doctrine of part performance.

part performance A doctrine that allows the court to order an oral contract for the sale of land or transfer of another interest in real property to be specifically performed if it has been partially performed and performance is necessary to avoid injustice.

CASE 10.3

Sutton v. Warner

12 Cal.App.4th 415, 15 Cal.Rptr.2d 632 (1993) California Court of Appeal

Facts In 1983, Arlene and Donald Warner inherited a one-third interest in a home at 101 Molimo Street in San Francisco. The Warners bought out the other heirs and obtained a $170,000 loan on the property. Donald Warner and Kenneth Sutton were friends. In January 1984, Donald Warner proposed that Sutton and his wife purchase the residence. His proposal included a $15,000 down payment toward the purchase price of $185,000. The Suttons were to pay all mortgage payments and real estate taxes on the property for five years, and at any time during the five-year period they could purchase the house. All this was agreed to orally. The Suttons paid the down payment and cash payments equal to the monthly mortgage ($1,881) to the Warners. They paid the annual property taxes on the house. The Suttons also made improvement to the property. In July 1988, the Warners reneged on the sales/option agreement. At that time the house had risen in value to between $250,000 and $320,000. The Suttons sued for specific performance of the sales agreement. The Warners defended, alleging that the oral promise to sell real estate had to be in writing under the Statute of Frauds and was therefore unenforceable. The trial court applied the equitable doctrine of part performance and ordered specific performance. The Warners appealed.

Issue Does the equitable doctrine of part performance take this oral contract for the sale of real property out of the Statute of Frauds?

Decision Yes. The appellate court held that the doctrine of part performance applied and that the Statute of Frauds did not prevent the enforcement of the oral contract to sell real estate.

Reason Normally, a contract to purchase real property must be in writing to satisfy the Statute of Frauds. However, the court held that the part performance by the Suttons—making the down payment, paying the monthly mortgage payments and the annual property taxes, and making improvements to the property—sufficed to remove the bar of the Statute of Frauds. Therefore, the specific performance of the oral contract to sell real estate is equitable.

CASE QUESTIONS

Critical Legal Thinking What purposes are served by the Statute of Frauds? Explain.

Ethics Did the Warners act ethically in this case? Did the Statute of Frauds give them a justifiable reason not to go through with the deal?

Business Implication Should important business contracts be reduced to writing? Why or why not?

One-Year Rule

According to the Statute of Frauds, an executory contract that cannot be performed by its own terms within one year of its formation must be in writing.[13] This **one-year rule** is intended to prevent disputes about contract terms that might otherwise occur toward the end of a long-term contract. If the performance of the contract is possible within the one-year period, the contract may be oral (see Exhibit 10.1).

one-year rule An executory contract that cannot be performed by its own terms within one year of its formation must be in writing.

Exhibit 10.1
One-Year Rule

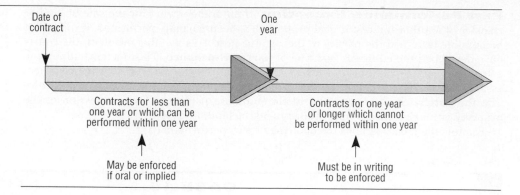

Date of contract

One year

Contracts for less than one year or which can be performed within one year

May be enforced if oral or implied

Contracts for one year or longer which cannot be performed within one year

Must be in writing to be enforced

The extension of an oral contract might cause the contract to violate the Statute of Frauds. For example, suppose the owner of a Burger King franchise hires Eugene Daly as a manager for six months. This contract may be oral. Assume that after three months, the owner and manager agree to extend the contract for an additional 11 months. At the time of the extension, the contract would be for 14 months (the three left on the contract plus 11 added by the extension). The modification would have to be in writing because it exceeds the one-year Statute of Frauds.

Collateral Promises

collateral contract
A promise in which one person agrees to answer for the debts or duties of another person.

A **collateral** or **guaranty contract** occurs when one person agrees to answer for the debts or duties of another person. Collateral promises are required to be in writing under the Statute of Frauds.[14]

guaranty contract   The contract between the guarantor and the original creditor.

In a guaranty situation, there are at least three parties and two contracts (see Exhibit 10.2). The *first contract*, which is known as the **original** or **primary contract**, is between the debtor and the creditor. It does not have to be in writing (unless another provision of the Statute of Frauds requires it to be). The *second contract*, called the **guaranty contract**, is between the person who agrees to pay the debt if the primary debtor does not (i.e., the **guarantor**) and the original creditor. The guarantor's liability is secondary because it does not arise unless the party primarily liable fails to perform.

guarantor   The person who agrees to pay the debt if the primary debtor does not.

Exhibit 10.2
Original and Guaranty
Contracts

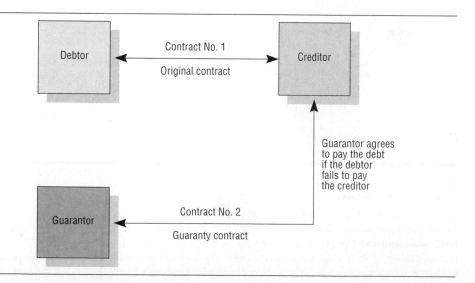

Debtor

Contract No. 1
Original contract

Creditor

Guarantor agrees to pay the debt if the debtor fails to pay the creditor

Guarantor

Contract No. 2
Guaranty contract

CONSIDER THIS EXAMPLE: Jay Hoberman, a recent college graduate, offers to purchase a new automobile on credit from a General Motors dealership. Because the purchaser does not have a credit history, the dealer will agree to sell the car only if there is a guarantor. Jay's mother signs the guaranty contract. She becomes responsible for any payments her son fails to make.

The "Main Purpose" Exception If the main purpose of a transaction and an oral collateral contract is to provide pecuniary (i.e., financial) benefit to the guarantor, the collateral contract is treated like an original contract and does not have to be in writing to be enforced.[15] This is called the **main purpose** or **leading object exception** to the Statute of Frauds. The exception is intended to ensure that the primary benefactor of the original contract (i.e., the guarantor) is answerable for the debt or duty.

CONSIDER THIS EXAMPLE: Suppose Ethel Brand is president and sole shareholder of Brand Computer Corporation, Inc. Assume that (1) the corporation borrows $100,000 from City Bank for working capital and (2) Ethel orally guarantees to repay the loan if the corporation fails to pay it. City Bank can enforce the oral guaranty contract against Ethel if the corporation does not meet its obligation because the main purpose of the loan was to benefit her as the sole shareholder of the corporation.

Promises Made in Consideration of Marriage

Under the Statute of Frauds, a unilateral promise to pay money or property in consideration for a promise to marry must be in writing. For example, a **prenuptial agreement**, which is a contract entered into by parties prior to marriage that defines their ownership rights in each other's property, must be in writing.

Contracts for the Sale of Goods

Section 201 of the **Uniform Commercial Code (UCC)** is the basic Statute of Frauds provision for sales contracts. It requires that contracts for the sale of goods costing *$500 or more* must be in writing to be enforceable.[16] If the contract price of an original sales contract is less than $500 and does not have to be in writing under the UCC Statute of Frauds, but a modification of the contract increases the sales price to $500 or more, the **modification** must be in writing to be enforceable.[17]

Agent's Contracts

Many state Statutes of Frauds require that *agent's contracts* to sell property covered by the Statute of Frauds must be in writing to be enforceable. This requirement is often referred to as the **equal dignity rule**.

CONSIDER THIS EXAMPLE: Suppose Barney Berkowitz hires Cynthia Lamont, a licensed Century 21 real estate agent, to sell his house. Because a contract to sell real estate must be in writing pursuant to the Statute of Frauds, the equal dignity rule requires the agent's contract to be in writing as well. Some state Statutes of Frauds expressly list the agent's contracts that must be in writing.

Promissory Estoppel

The doctrine of **promissory estoppel**, or **equitable estoppel**, is another equitable exception to the strict application of the Statute of Frauds. The Restatement (Second) of Contracts version of promissory estoppel provides that if parties enter into an oral contract that should be in writing under the Statute of Frauds, the oral promise is enforceable against the promisor if these three conditions are met: (1) The promise induces action or forbearance of action by another, (2) the reliance on the oral promise was foreseeable, and (3) injustice can be avoided only by enforcing the oral promise.[18]

---

main purpose or **leading object exception** If the main purpose of a transaction and an oral collateral contract is to provide pecuniary benefit to the guarantor, the collateral contract does not have to be in writing to be enforced.

prenuptial agreement A contract entered into by parties prior to marriage that defines their ownership rights in each other's property; must be in writing.

UCC Statute of Frauds Contracts for the sales of goods costing $500 or more must be in writing.

equal dignity rule A rule that says that agent's contracts to sell property covered by the Statute of Frauds must be in writing to be enforceable.

promissory estoppel An equitable doctrine that permits enforcement of oral contracts that should have been in writing. It is applied to avoid injustice.

Where this doctrine applies, the promisor is **estopped** (prevented) from raising the Statute of Frauds as a defense to the enforcement of the oral contract.

INTERNATIONAL PERSPECTIVE

Writing Requirement for International Contracts

Traditionally, many countries require certain contracts to be in writing. In civil law countries, this requirement generally does not apply to commercial transactions. In socialist countries, writings usually are required because of the need for certainty both in interpreting and enforcing foreign trade contracts.

Most of the delegates involved in the drafting of the United Nations Convention on Contracts for the International Sale of Goods

(CISG) decided that a writing requirement would be inconsistent with modern commercial practice, especially in market economies where speed and informality characterize so many transactions. Some delegates, however, insisted that a writing requirement is important for protecting their country's longtime pattern of making foreign trade contracts.

The result of this disagreement was a compromise. Article 11 of the Convention states: "A contract

of sale need not be concluded in or evidenced by writing and is not subject to any other requirement as to form. It may be proved by any means, including witnesses." The CISG's Article 96, however, authorizes a contracting nation that requires written sales contracts to stipulate at the time of ratification that Article 11 (and some other provisions of the Convention) does not apply if any party operates a business in that nation.

SUFFICIENCY OF THE WRITING

Both the common law of contracts and the UCC have adopted several rules regarding the legal sufficiency of written contracts. These rules are discussed in the following sections.

"Counsel Randle Jackson: In the book of nature, my lords, it is written—Lord Ellenborough: Will you have the goodness to mention the page, Sir, if you please."
Lord Campbell
Lives of the Chief Justices (1857)

Formality of the Writing

Some written commercial contracts are long, detailed documents that have been negotiated by the parties and drafted and reviewed by their lawyers. Others are preprinted forms with blanks that can be filled in to fit the facts of the particular situation.

However, a written contract does not have to be either drafted by a lawyer or formally typed to be legally binding. Generally, the law only requires a writing containing the essential terms of the parties' agreement. Any writing—including letters, telegrams, invoices, sales receipts, checks, handwritten agreements written on scraps of paper, and such—can be an enforceable contract under this rule.

Required Signature

The Statute of Frauds and the UCC require the written contract, whatever its form, to be signed *by the party against whom enforcement is sought.* The signature of the person who is enforcing the contract is not necessary. Thus, a written contract could be enforceable against one party but not the other party.

Generally, the signature may appear anywhere on the writing. In addition, it does not have to be a person's full legal name. The person's last name, first name, nickname, initials, seal, stamp, engraving, or other symbol or mark (e.g., an *X*) that indicates the person's intent can be binding. The signature may be affixed by an authorized agent.

Integration of Several Writings

Both the common law of contracts and the UCC permit several writings to be **integrated** to form a single written contract. That is, the entire writing does not have to appear in one document to be an enforceable contract.

Integration may be by an *express reference* in one document that refers to and incorporates another document within it. This is called **incorporation by reference**. Thus, what may often look like a simple one-page contract may actually be hundreds of pages long. For example, credit cards often incorporate by express reference such documents as the master document between the issuer and cardholders, subsequent amendments to the agreement, and such.

Several documents may be integrated to form a single written contract if they are somehow physically attached to each other to indicate a party's intent to show integration. For example, attaching several documents together by a staple, paper clip, or some other means may indicate integration. Placing several documents in the same container (e.g., an envelope) may also indicate integration. This is called *implied integration*.

The Parol Evidence Rule

By the time a contract is reduced to writing, the parties usually have engaged in prior or contemporaneous discussions and negotiations or exchanged prior writings. Any oral or written words outside of the *four corners* of the written contract are called **parol evidence**. *Parol* means "word."

The **parol evidence rule** was originally developed by courts as part of the common law of contracts. The UCC has adopted the parol evidence rule as part of the law of sales contracts.[19] The parol evidence rule states that if a written contract is a complete and final statement of the parties' agreement (i.e., a complete integration), any prior or contemporaneous oral or written statements that alter, contradict, or are in addition to the terms of the written contract are inadmissible in any court proceeding concerning the contract.[20] In other words, a completely integrated contract is viewed as the best evidence of the terms of the parties' agreement.

The parties to a written contract may include a clause stipulating that the contract is a complete integration and the exclusive expression of their agreement and that parol evidence may not be introduced to explain, alter, contradict, or add to the terms of the contract. This type of clause is called a **merger** or **integration clause**. It expressly reiterates the parol evidence rule.

Exceptions to the Parol Evidence Rule There are several major exceptions to the general rule excluding parol evidence. Parol evidence may be admitted in court in the following situations:

- It shows that a contract is void or voidable (e.g., evidence that the contract was induced by fraud, misrepresentation, duress, undue influence, or mistake)
- It explains ambiguous language
- It concerns a *prior course of dealing* or *course of performance* between the parties or a *usage of trade*[21]
- It *fills in the gaps* in the contract (e.g., if a price term or time of performance term is omitted from a written contract, the court can hear parol evidence in order to imply the reasonable price or time of performance under the contract)
- It corrects an obvious clerical or typographical error. The court can reform the contract to reflect the correction.

The following case illustrates the application of the parol evidence rule.

---

integration The combination of several writings to form a single contract.

incorporation by reference When integration is made by express reference in one document that refers to and incorporates another document within it.

parol evidence Any oral or written words outside the four corners of the written contract.

parol evidence rule A rule that says if a written contract is a complete and final statement of the parties' agreement, any prior or contemporaneous oral or written statements that alter, contradict, or are in addition to the terms of the written contract are inadmissible in court regarding a dispute over the contract.

merger clause A clause in a contract that stipulates that it is a complete integration and the exclusive expression of the parties' agreement. Parol evidence may not be introduced to explain, alter, contradict, or add to the terms of the contract.

BUSINESS BRIEF
It is good practice to include a merger clause in written contracts to avoid allegations of promises outside the contract.

CASE 10.4

Malmstrom v. Kaiser Aluminum & Chemical Corp.

187 Cal.App.3d 299, 231 Cal.Rptr. 820 (1986) California Court of Appeal

Facts On January 2, 1977, Carl M. Malmstrom applied for a job at Kaiser Aluminum & Chemical Corporation (Kaiser) in its aluminum can division. During the prehiring interviews with Kaiser, Malmstrom questioned his interviewers about the permanency of the position he was offered. Malmstrom testified that at the time he was hired, Mr. Johnson of Kaiser told him "as long as one does a commendable job up to Kaiser's expectations, that [he] had no fear of being laid off" and that "Kaiser never laid off anyone unless there was due cause obviously of some nature."

On January 3, 1977, Malmstrom was employed by Kaiser. He signed a one-page agreement with the company concerning his employment. Paragraph 1 provided: "Employer employs and shall continue to employ Employee at such compensation and for such a length of time as shall be mutually agreeable to Employer and Employee." Paragraph 6 of the employment contract was an integration clause that provided: "This agreement shall supersede all previous agreements by and between Employer and Employee and shall be retroactive to the date on which Employee commenced his employment."

In April 1981, because of a decrease in business, Kaiser began terminating many employees. On January 5, 1982, Malmstrom was told he was terminated as part of the staff reduction. In the two-year period following Malmstrom's layoff, the number of Kaiser employees declined from 27,000 to 18,000. Malmstrom sued Kaiser for breach of alleged oral contracts to provide permanent employment to him. The trial court granted summary judgment for Kaiser. Malmstrom appealed.

Issue Does the parol evidence rule make the evidence concerning the alleged oral contracts inadmissible?

Decision Yes. The appellate court held that the written employment agreement between Malmstrom and Kaiser was integrated and evidence of other alleged oral contracts between the parties is inadmissible under the parol evidence rule.

Reason California law presumes a written contract supersedes all prior or contemporaneous oral agreements. Parol evidence is admissible to establish the terms of the complete agreement of the parties only if the written agreement is not the complete and final embodiment of that agreement. The contract at issue in this case was integrated. The meaning of paragraph 6 was clear on its face. The alleged oral agreement occurred before Malmstrom signed the written agreement. The court stated, "We hold that the contract is a contract for employment terminable at will and that, since the contract is integrated and provides that it supersedes all prior agreements, evidence of an oral agreement which contradicts the terms of the written agreement is not admissible."

CASE QUESTIONS

Critical Legal Thinking Does the inadmissibility of parol evidence ever work an injustice?

Ethics Is it ethical to assert the parol evidence rule to prevent the introduction of evidence concerning other agreements between the parties?

Business Implication Do you think that businesses support or oppose the parol evidence rule? Explain.

BUSINESS CHECKLIST

Standards of Interpretation for Contracts

The parties to a contract may define the words and terms used in their contract. Many written contracts contain a detailed definitional section or glossary of terms. If the parties have not defined the words and terms of a contract, the courts apply the following **standards of interpretation**:

- *Ordinary words* are given their usual meaning according to the dictionary.
- *Technical words* are given their technical meaning, unless a different meaning is clearly intended. Testimony from expert witnesses is often necessary to determine the precise meaning of technical words.
- *Specific terms* are presumed to qualify *general terms*. For example, if a provision in a contract refers to the subject matter as "corn," but a later provision refers to the subject matter as "feed corn" for cattle, this specific term qualifies the general term.
- Where a preprinted form contract is used, *typed words* in a contract prevail over *preprinted words*. *Handwritten words* prevail over both preprinted and typed words.
- If there is an ambiguity in a contract, the ambiguity will be resolved against the party who drafted the contract.
- If both parties are members of the same trade or profession, words will be given their meaning as used in the trade (i.e., usage of trade). If the parties do not want trade usage to apply, the contract must indicate that.
- Words will be interpreted to promote the *principal object* of the contract. For example, if a word is subject to two or more definitions, the court will choose the definition that will advance the principal object of the contract.

WORKING THE WEB

Many business school libraries and law libraries have set up their own Web sites. These sites always contain information links about the school and campus but can also provide valuable links to legal and business resources. Some even have their library catalogs on-line. Here are some sites to visit:

Harvard Business School Library:
http://library.hbs.edu/

Babson College Library:
http://www.babson.edu/library/index.html

Harvard Law School Library:
http://www.law.harvard.edu/library

University of Colorado Law Library:
http://www.colorado.edu/Law/lawlib/

University of Denver Law Library:
http://www.law.du.edu/library

CYBER EXERCISES:

1. Find out if the business library at your business school has a Web site. If so, visit the site to see what information you can find there.
2. If your college or university has a law school, find out whether the law library has a Web site. If so, visit the site to see what information you can find there.
3. Visit the Harvard Business School Library Web site. Find a book in the Baker Online Catalog and print out your results.
4. Check out the research guides at the Babson College Library Web site.
5. Visit the University of Colorado Law Library Web site. Who is that library's director?

CHAPTER SUMMARY

MISTAKES, P. 209

Unilateral Mistakes	*Unilateral mistake.* Occurs when only one party is mistaken about a material fact regarding the subject matter of the contract. The legal consequences are:

	1. *General rule.* The mistaken party is not permitted to rescind the contract.
	2. *Exceptions.* The mistaken party can rescind the contract if:
	  a. The other party knew or should have known of the mistake and took advantage of it
	  b. The mistake occurred because of a clerical or mathematical error that was not the result of gross negligence
	  c. The mistake is so serious that enforcing the contract would be unconscionable.

Mutual Mistakes	1. *Mutual mistake of fact.* Both parties are mistaken about the essence or object of the contract. Either party may rescind the contract. 2. *Mutual mistake of value.* Both parties know the object of the contract but are mistaken as to its value. Neither party may rescind the contract.

FRAUDULENT MISREPRESENTATION, P. 211

Elements of Fraud	*Fraudulent misrepresentation.* When a person intentionally makes an assertion that is not in accord with the facts. Also called *fraud*.
	1. *Elements of fraud:*
	  a. The wrongdoer made a false representation of material fact
	  b. The wrongdoer intended to deceive the innocent party
	  c. The innocent party justifiably relied on the misrepresentation
	  d. The innocent party was injured.
	2. *Legal consequence if fraudulent misrepresentation is found.* The innocent party may:
	  a. Rescind the contract and obtain restitution, or
	  b. Enforce the contract and sue for damages.

Types of Fraud	1. *Common types of fraud:*
	  a. *Fraud in the inception.* An innocent person is deceived as to the nature of his or her act. Also called *fraud in the factum*
	  b. *Fraud in the inducement.* The wrongdoer fraudulently induces another party to enter into a contract
	  c. *Fraud by concealment.* The wrongdoer takes specific action to conceal a material fact from the other party
	  d. *Silence as misrepresentation.* The wrongdoer remains silent when he or she is under a legal obligation to disclose a material fact
	  e. *Misrepresentation of law.* A professional who should know what the law is intentionally misrepresents the law to a less sophisticated party.

Innocent Misrepresentation	When a person unintentionally makes an assertion that is not in accord with the facts. The innocent party may rescind the contract but cannot recover damages. Innocent misrepresentation is not fraud.

UNDUE INFLUENCE, P. 213

Undue Influence	Occurs when one person takes advantage of another person's mental, emotional, or physical weakness and unduly persuades that person to enter into a contract. A contract entered into under undue influence cannot be enforced.
	1. *Elements of undue influence:*
	  a. A fiduciary or confidential relationship existed between the dominant and servient parties
	  b. The dominant party unduly used his or her influence to persuade the servient party to enter into a contract

	2. *Presumption*. If there is a confidential relationship between persons, any contract by the servient party that benefits the dominant party is presumed to be entered into under undue influence. This is a *rebuttable presumption*.
DURESS, P. 215	

Duress	Occurs when one party threatens to do some wrongful act unless the other party enters into a contract. A contract entered into under duress cannot be enforced.
	1. *Types of duress:*
	  a. Physical duress
	  b. Extortion
	  c. Economic duress

STATUTE OF FRAUDS—WRITING REQUIREMENT, P. 216	

Writing Requirement	*Statute of Frauds*. A state statute that requires the following contracts to be in writing:
	1. *Contracts involving the transfer of interests in real property*. Includes contracts for the sale of land, buildings and items attached to land, mortgages, leases for a term of more than one year, and express easements.
	  a. *Part performance exception*. Permits the specific enforcement of oral contracts for the sale of land when they have been partially performed to avoid injustice.
	2. *Contracts that cannot be performed within one year of their formation.*
	3. *Collateral contracts*. Occur when one person promises to answer for the debts or duties of another person. Also called *guaranty contracts*.
	  a. *Main purpose exception*. Permits enforcement of oral collateral promises if main or leading purpose of collateral promise is to benefit the guarantor.
	4. *Promises made in consideration of marriage*, such as prenuptial agreements.
	5. *Contracts for the sale of goods costing $500 or more*. [UCC § 201]

Promissory Estoppel	Equitable doctrine that prevents the application of the Statute of Frauds. It permits the enforcement of oral contracts that should otherwise be in writing under the Statute of Frauds to prevent injustice or unjust enrichment.
SUFFICIENCY OF THE WRITING, P. 220	

Sufficiency of the Writing	1. *Formality of the writing*. A written contract does not have to be formal or drafted by a lawyer to be enforceable. Informal contracts, such as handwritten notes, letters, invoices, and the like, are enforceable contracts.
	2. *Required signature*. The party against whom enforcement of the contract is sought must have signed the contract. The signature may be the person's full legal name, last name, first name, nickname, initials, or other symbol or mark.
	3. *Integration of several writings*. Several writings may be integrated to form a contract. Integration may be by:
	  a. *Express reference*. One document expressly incorporates another document.
	  b. *Implied reference*. Documents are physically attached by staple, by paper clip, or are placed in the same envelope.

The Parol Evidence Rule	1. *Parol evidence.* Any oral or written words that are outside of the four corners of a written contract.
	2. *Parol evidence rule.* Provides that if a written contract is a complete integration, any prior or contemporaneous oral or written statements are inadmissible as evidence to alter or contradict the terms of the written contract.
	3. *Exceptions to the parol evidence rule.* Parol evidence may be admitted in court to:
	  a. Prove mistake, fraud, misrepresentation, undue influence, or duress
	  b. Explain ambiguous language
	  c. Explain a prior course of dealing or course of performance between the parties or a usage of trade
	  d. Fill in the gaps in a contract
	  e. Correct obvious clerical or typographical errors.

Interpretation of Contracts	The courts have developed the following rules for interpreting contracts: 1. *Ordinary words* are given their usual dictionary meaning. 2. *Technical words* are given their technical meaning, unless a different meaning is clearly intended. 3. *Specific terms* are presumed to qualify *general terms*. 4. *Typed words* prevail over *preprinted words*; *handwritten words* prevail over both preprinted and typed words. 5. Ambiguities in the contract are resolved against the party who drafted the contract. 6. Unless otherwise agreed, words will be given their usual meaning in the trade if both parties are members of the same trade. 7. Words will be interpreted to promote the *principal object* of the contract.

CRITICAL LEGAL THINKING CASES

10.1 Unilateral Mistake Mrs. Chaney died in 1985, leaving a house in Annapolis, Maryland. The representative of her estate listed the property for sale with a real estate broker, stating that the property was approximately 15,650 square feet. Drs. Steele and Faust made an offer of $300,000 for the property, which was accepted by the estate. A contract for the sale of the property was signed by all of the parties on July 3, 1985. When a subsequent survey done before the deed was transferred showed that the property had an area of 22,047 square feet, the estate requested the buyers to pay more money for the property. When the estate refused to transfer the property to the buyers, they sued for specific performance. Can the estate rescind the contract? [*Steele v. Goettee*, 542 A.2d 847 (Md. App. 1988)]

10.2 Mutual Mistake Ron Boskett, a part-time coin dealer, purchased a dime for nearly $450 that was purportedly minted in 1916 at the Denver Mint. The fact that the *D* on the coin signified Denver mintage made the coin rare and valuable. Boskett sold the coin to Beachcomber Coins, Inc. (Beachcomber), a retail coin dealer, for $500. A principal of Beach-

comber examined the coin for 15 to 45 minutes prior to its purchase. Soon thereafter, Beachcomber received an offer of $700 for the coin subject to certification of its genuineness by the American Numismatic Society. When this organization labeled the coin counterfeit, Beachcomber sued Boskett to rescind the purchase of the coin. Can Beachcomber rescind the contract? [*Beachcomber Coins, Inc. v. Boskett*, 400 A.2d 78 (N.J. 1979)]

10.3 Fraud Robert McClure owned a vehicle salvage and rebuilding business. He listed the business for sale and had a brochure printed that described the business and stated that during 1981 the business grossed $581,117 and netted $142,727. Fred H. Campbell saw the brochure and inquired about buying the business. Campbell hired a certified public accountant (CPA) to review McClure's business records and tax returns, but the CPA could not reconcile these with the income claimed for the business in the brochure. When Campbell asked McClure about the discrepancy, McClure stated that the business records did and tax returns did not accurately reflect the cash flow or profits of the business because it was such a high-cash operation with much of the cash not being reported to the Internal Revenue Service on tax returns. McClure signed a warranty that stated that the true income of the business was as represented in the brochure. Campbell bought the business based on these representations. However, the business, although operated in substantially the same manner as when owned by McClure, failed to yield a net income similar to that warranted by McClure. Evidence showed that McClure's representations were substantially overstated. Campbell sued McClure for damages of fraud. Who wins? [*Campbell v. McClure*, 182 Cal.App.3d 806, 227 Cal.Rptr. 450 (Cal. App. 1986)]

10.4 Fraud James L. "Skip" Deupree, a developer, was building a development of town houses called Point South in Destin, Florida. All of the town houses in the development were to have individual boat slips. Sam and Louise Butner, husband and wife, bought one of the town houses. The sales contract between Deupree and the Butners provided that a boat slip would be built and included in the price of the town house. The contract stated that permission from the Florida Department of Natural Resources (DNR) had to be obtained to build the boat slips. It is undisputed that a boat slip adds substantially to the value of the property and that the Butners relied on the fact that the town houses would have a boat slip. Prior to the sale of the town house to the Butners, the DNR had informed Deupree that it objected to the plan to build the boat slips and that permission to build them would probably not be forthcoming. Deupree did not tell the Butners this information but instead stated that there would be "no problem" in getting permission from the state to build the boat slips. When the DNR would not approve the building of the boat slips for the Butners town house, they sued for damages for fraud. Who wins? [*Deupree v. Butner*, 522 So.2d 242 (Ala. 1988)]

✓ **10.5 Economic Duress** Mr. Weller, who was in business in Coalinga, California, filed tax returns for 1943, 1944, and 1945 using the cash basis. Weller then hired Mr. Eyman, a CPA, to prepare his 1946 income tax return. While preparing the 1946 return using the accrual basis, Eyman examined the prior years' returns. Based on Eyman's suggestion, Eyman prepared revised tax returns for the prior years and Weller submitted these to the Internal Revenue Service (IRS) claiming an $1,800 refund. Instead of receiving the refund, however, the IRS assessed Weller $118,000 in unpaid taxes and fines. Eyman told Weller that the proposed assessment was asinine and it was a simple matter to clean up. Weller contracted with Eyman to do the necessary work for $1,000. After obtaining several extensions, the IRS notified Weller and Eyman that Monday, September 18, 1950, was the deadline for filing a protest to the proposed assessment. On Saturday, September 16, Eyman called Weller to his office to sign the protest. When Weller got there, Eyman produced a written contract purporting to be a fee arrangement whereby Eyman was to receive $1,000 plus 7½ percent of any monies saved of the assessment. When Weller refused to sign the new fee agreement, Eyman told him that the protest had to be in the mail that afternoon to reach the IRS on Monday, and that if it were not filed Weller would be liable for the $118,000 assessment. Weller signed the fee agreement and the protest was timely filed with the IRS. Weller filed a complaint to have the new fee agreement rescinded. Who wins? [*Thompson Crane & Trucking Co. v. Eyman*, 267 P.2d 1043, 123 Cal.App.2d 904 (Cal.App. 1954)]

10.6 Undue Influence Conrad Schaneman, Sr. had eight sons and five daughters. He owned four 80-acre farms in the Scottsbluff area of Nebraska. Conrad was born in Russia and could not read or write English. Prior to 1974, all of his children had frequent contact with Conrad and helped with his needs. In 1974, his eldest son, Lawrence, advised the other children that he would henceforth manage his father's business affairs. On March 18, 1975, after much urging by Lawrence, Conrad deeded the farm to Lawrence for $23,500. Evidence showed that at the time of the sale the reasonable fair market value of the farm was between $145,000 and $160,000. At the time of the conveyance, Conrad was more than 80 years of age; had deteriorated in health; suffered from heart problems, diabetes, and high and uncontrollable blood sugar levels; weighed almost 300 pounds; had difficulty breathing; could not walk more than 15 feet; and had to have a backhoist lift him in and out of the bathtub. He was for all purposes an invalid, relying on Lawrence for most of his personal needs, transportation, banking, and other business matters. After Conrad died, the conservators of the estate brought this action to cancel the deed transferring the farm to Lawrence. Can the conservators cancel the deed? [*Schaneman v. Schaneman*, 291 N.W.2d 412 (Neb. 1980)]

10.7 Undue Influence Margaret Delorey was a client of Joseph P. Plonsky, an attorney. In addition, they were friends of long standing. In September 1976, Delorey telephoned Plonsky's office and told him that she wanted him to draft a will for her naming him as executor and leaving everything she owned to him. Plonsky drafted the will and mailed it to her. She had the will executed and witnessed at a bank and mailed the will back to Plonsky. When Delorey died, Plonsky, as the sole legatee, attempted to take control under the will. At the time of her death, Delorey was survived by two nephews, two nieces, two grandnephews, and one grandniece, none of whom were named in the will. Does the doctrine of undue influence apply in this case? [*Matter of Delorey*, 529 N.Y.S.2d 153, 141 A.D.2d 540 (N.Y. App. 1988)]

10.8 Land Contract In 1976, Fritz Hoffman and Fritz Frey contacted the Sun Valley Company (Company) about purchasing a 1.64-acre piece of property known as the "Ruud Mountain Property," located in Sun Valley, Idaho, from the Company. Mr. Conger, a representative of the Company, was authorized to sell the property, subject to the approval of the executive committee of the Company. On January 21, 1977, Conger reached an agreement on the telephone with Hoffman and Frey whereby they would purchase the property for $90,000, payable at 30 percent down, with the balance to be payable quarterly at an annual interest rate of 9 3/4 percent. The next day Hoffman sent Conger a letter confirming the conversation. The executive committee of the Company approved the sale. Sun Valley Realty prepared the deed of trust, note, seller's closing statement, and other loan documents. However, before the documents were executed by either side, the Company sold all of its assets, including the Ruud Mountain Property, to another purchaser. When the new owner refused to sell the Ruud Mountain lot to Hoffman and Frey, they brought this action for specific performance of the oral contract. Do they win? [*Hoffman v. Sun Valley Company*, 628 P.2d 218 (Idaho 1981)]

10.9 Land Contract In 1955, Robert Briggs and his wife purchased a home located at 167 Lower Orchard Drive, Levittown, Pennsylvania. They made a $100 down payment and borrowed the balance of $11,600 on a 30-year mortgage. In late 1961, when the Briggs were behind on their mortgage payments, they entered into an oral contract to sell the house to Winfield and Emma Sackett if the Sacketts would pay the three months' arrearages on the loan and agree to make the future payments on the mortgage. Mrs. Briggs and Mrs. Sackett were sisters. The Sacketts paid the arrearages, moved into the house, and have lived there to date. In 1976, Robert Briggs filed an action to void the oral contract as in violation of the Statute of Frauds and evict the Sacketts from the house. Who wins? [*Briggs v. Sackett*, 418 A.2d 586 (Pa. App. 1980)]

10.10 One-Year Contract Robert S. Ohanian was vice president of sales for the West Region of Avis Rent a Car System, Inc. (Avis). Officers of Avis testified that Ohanian's performance in the West Region was excellent and, in a depressed economic period, Ohanian's West Region stood out as the one region that was growing and profitable. In the fall of 1980, when Avis's Northeast Region was doing badly, the president of Avis asked Ohanian to take over that region. Ohanian was reluctant to do so, because he and his family liked living in San Francisco, he had developed a good "team" in the West Region, was secure in his position, and feared the politics of the Northeast Region. Ohanian agreed to the transfer only after the general manager of Avis orally told him, "Unless you screw up badly, there is no way you are going to get fired—you will never get hurt here in this company." Ohanian did a commendable job in the Northeast Region. Approximately one year later, on July 27, 1982, at the age of 47, Ohanian was fired without cause by Avis. Ohanian sued Avis for breach of the oral lifetime contract. Avis asserted the Statute of Frauds against this claim. Who wins? [*Ohanian v. Avis Rent a Car System, Inc.*, 779 F.2d 101 (2nd Cir. 1985)]

10.11 Guaranty Contract On May 17, 1979, David Brown met with Stan Steele, a loan officer with the Bank of Idaho (now First Interstate Bank) to discuss borrowing $5,000 from the bank to start a new business. After learning that he did not qualify for the loan on the basis of his own financial strength, Brown told Steele that his former employers, James and Donna West of California, might be willing to guarantee the payment of the loan. On May 18, 1979, Steele talked to Mr. West, who orally stated on the telephone that he would personally guarantee the loan to Brown. Based on this guarantee, the bank loaned Brown $5,000. The bank sent a written guarantee to Mr. and Mrs. West for their signature, but it was never returned to the bank. When Brown defaulted on the loan, the bank filed suit against the Wests to recover on their guarantee contract. Are the Wests liable? [*First Interstate Bank of Idaho, N.A. v. West*, 693 P.2d 1053 (Idaho 1984)]

10.12 Guaranty Contract Six persons, including Benjamin Rosenbloom and Alfred Feiler, were members of the board of directors of the Togs Corporation. A bank agreed to loan the corporation $250,000 if the members of the board would personally guarantee the payment of the loan. Feiler objected to signing the guarantee to the bank because of other pending personal financial negotiations that the contingent liability of the guarantee might adversely affect. Feiler agreed with Rosenbloom and the other board members that if they were held personally liable on the guarantee, he would pay his one-sixth share of that amount to them directly. Rosenbloom and the other members of the board signed the personal guarantee with the bank, and the bank made the loan to the corporation. When the corporation defaulted on the loan, the five guarantors had to pay the loan amount to the bank. When they attempted to collect a one-sixth share from Feiler, he refused to pay, alleging that his oral promise had to be in writing under the Statute of Frauds. Does Feiler have to pay the one-sixth share to the other board members? [*Feiler v. Rosenbloom*, 416 A.2d 1345 (Md. App. 1980)]

10.13 Promissory Estoppel Natale and Carmela Castiglia were married in 1919 in Colorado. Carmela had a son from a previous marriage, Christie Lo Greco, who lived with them. Natale and Carmela moved to California where they invested their assets of $4,000 in agricultural property. Christie, then in his early teens, moved with them to California. In 1926, Christie, then 18 years old, decided to leave home and seek an independent living. Natale and Carmela, however, wanted him to stay with them and participate in the family venture. He received only his room and board and spending money. When Christie married, Natale told him that his wife should move in with the family and that Christie need not worry, for he would receive all the property when Natale and Carmela died. Natale and Carmela entered into identical wills leaving their property to Christie when they died. Natale died in the late 1940s. Shortly before his death, without the knowledge of Christie or Carmela, he had changed his will and left his share of the property to his grandson, Carmen Monarco. Christie sued to enforce Natale's oral promise. Does the doctrine of promissory estoppel prevent the application of the Statute of Frauds in this case? [*Monarco v. Lo Greco*, 220 P.2d 737, 35 Cal.2d 621 (Cal. 1950)]

10.14 Promissory Estoppel The Atlantic Wholesale Co. (Atlantic), which is located in Florence, South Carolina, is in the business of buying and selling gold and silver for customers' accounts. Gary A. Solondz, a New York resident, became a customer of Atlantic's in 1979 and thereafter made several purchases through Atlantic. On January 23, 1980, Solondz telephoned Atlantic and received a quotation on silver bullion. Solondz then bought 300 ounces of silver for a total price of $12,978. Atlantic immediately contacted United Precious Metals in Minneapolis and purchased the silver for Solondz. The silver was shipped to Atlantic, who paid for it. Atlantic placed the silver in its vault while it awaited payment from Solondz. When Atlantic telephoned Solondz about payment, he told Atlantic to continue to hold the silver in its vault until he decided whether to sell it. Meanwhile, the price of silver had fallen substantially and continued to fall. When Solondz refused to pay for the silver, Atlantic sold it for $4,650, sustaining a loss of $8,328. When Atlantic sued Solondz to recover this loss, Solondz asserted that the Statute of Frauds prevented enforcement of his oral promise to buy the silver. Does the doctrine of promissory estoppel prevent the application of the Statute of Frauds in this case? [*Atlantic Wholesale Co., Inc. v. Solondz*, 320 S.E.2d 720 (S.C. App. 1984)]

10.15 Sufficiency of a Writing Irving Levin and Harold Lipton owned the San Diego Clippers Basketball Club, a professional basketball franchise. On December 3, 1980, Levin and Lipton met with Philip Knight to discuss the sale of the Clippers to Knight. After the meeting, they both initialed a three-page handwritten memorandum that Levin had drafted during the meeting. The memorandum outlined the major terms of their discussion, including subject matter, price, and the parties to the agreement. On December 13, 1980, Levin and Lipton forwarded to Knight a letter and proposed sale agreement. Two days later, Knight informed Levin that he had decided not to purchase the Clippers. Levin and Lipton sued Knight for breach of contract. Knight argued in defense that the handwritten memorandum was not enforceable because it did not satisfy the Statute of Frauds. Is he correct? [*Levin v. Knight*, 865 F.2d 1271 (9th Cir. 1989)] *Yea*

ETHICS CASES

10.16 Ethical Perspective The First Baptist Church of Moultrie, Georgia, invited bids for the construction of a music, education, and recreation building. The bids, which were to be opened on May 15, 1986, were to be accompanied by a bid bond of 5 percent of the bid amount. Barber Contracting Company (Barber) submitted a bid in the amount of $1,860,000. A bid bond in the amount of 5 percent of the bid—$93,000—was issued by The American Insurance Company. The bids were opened by the church on May 15, 1986, as planned, and Barber's was the lowest bid.

On May 16, 1986, Albert W. Barber, the president of Barber Contracting Company, informed the church that its bid was in error and should have been $143,120 higher. The error was caused in totaling the material costs on Barber's estimate worksheets. The church had not been provided these worksheets. On May 20, 1986, Barber sent a letter to the church stating that it was withdrawing its bid. The next day the church sent a construction contract to Barber containing the original bid amount. When Barber refused to sign the contract and refused to do the work for the original contract price, the church signed a contract with the second lowest bidder, H & H Construction and Supply Company, Inc., to complete the work for $1,919,272. The church sued Barber Contracting Company and The American Insurance Company seeking to recover the amount of the bid bond. Who wins? Did Barber act ethically in trying to get out of the contract? Did the church act ethically in trying to enforce Barber's bid? [*First Baptist Church of Moultrie v. Barber Contracting Co.*, 377 S.E. 2d 717 (Ga.App. 1989)]

10.17 Ethical Perspective Adolfo Mozzetti, who owned a construction company, orally promised his son, Remo, that if Remo would manage the family business for their mutual benefit and would take care of him for the rest of his life, he would leave the family home to Remo. Section 2714 of the Delaware Code requires contracts for the transfer of land to be in writing. Section 2715 of the Delaware Code requires testamentary transfers of real property to be in writing. Remo performed as requested—he managed the family business and took care of his father until the father died. When the father died, his will devised the family home to his daughter, Lucia M. Shepard. Remo brought this action to enforce his father's oral promise that the home belonged to him. The daughter argued that the will should be upheld. Who wins? Did the daughter act ethically in trying to defeat the father's promise to leave the property to the son? Did the son act ethically in trying to defeat his father's will? [*Shepard v. Mozzetti*, 545 A.2d 621 (Del. 1988)]

CRITICAL LEGAL THINKING WRITING ASSIGNMENT

Read Case A.10 in the Case Appendix [*Continental Airlines, Inc. v. McDonnell Douglas Corporation*]. This case is excerpted from the appellate court opinion. Review and brief the case. In your brief, be sure to answer the following questions:

1. When did the action commence? When was the decision of the appellate court rendered?
2. Were the statements made by McDonnell Douglas opinions (i.e., puffing) or statements of fact?

3. Were the statements made by McDonnell Douglas material? What evidence supports your conclusion?
4. Did Continental rely on the statements of McDonnell Douglas? What evidence supports your conclusion?
5. Do false representations made recklessly and without regard to the truth constitute fraud?
6. What damages were awarded to Continental?

NOTES

[1] Restatement (Second) of Contracts, § 153.
[2] Restatement (Second) of Contracts, § 152.
[3] 159 Eng. Rep. 375 (1864).
[4] Restatement (Second) of Contracts, § 159.
[5] Restatement (Second) of Contracts, §§ 163 and 164.
[6] Restatement (Second) of Contracts, § 172.

[7] Restatement (Second) of Contracts, § 160.

[8] Restatement (Second) of Contracts, § 161.

[9] Restatement (Second) of Contracts, § 170.

[10] Restatement (Second) of Contracts, § 177.

[11] Restatement (Second) of Contracts, § 176.

[12] Restatement (Second) of Contracts, § 110.

[13] Restatement (Second) of Contracts, § 130.

[14] Restatement (Second) of Contracts, § 112.

[15] Restatement (Second) of Contracts, § 116.

[16] UCC § 2–201(1).

[17] UCC § 2–209(3).

[18] Restatement (Second) of Contracts, § 139.

[19] UCC § 2–202.

[20] Restatement (Second) of Contracts, § 213.

[21] UCC §§ 1–205, 2–202, and 2–208.

CHAPTER 11

THIRD-PARTY RIGHTS AND

DISCHARGE OF CONTRACTS

Chapter Objectives

After studying this chapter,
you should be able to

1. Describe assignment of contracts and what contract rights are assignable
2. Define anti-assignment and approval clauses and determine their lawfulness
3. Describe a delegation of duties and explain the liability of the parties to a delegation
4. Define an intended beneficiary and describe his or her rights under a contract
5. Define an incidental beneficiary
6. Define a covenant
7. Distinguish between conditions precedent, conditions subsequent, and concurrent conditions
8. Explain when the performance of a contract is excused because of objective impossibility
9. Define and apply the doctrine of commercial impracticability
10. Explain how contracts are discharged by operation of law

Chapter Contents

An honest man's word is as good as his bond.

Don Quixote

privity of contract   The state of two specified parties being in a contract.

"That what is agreed to be done, must be considered as done."
L. C. Lord Hardwicke
Guidot v. Guidot
(1745)

The parties to a contract are said to be in **privity of contract**. Contracting parties have a legal obligation to perform the duties specified in their contract. A party's duty of performance may be **discharged** by agreement of the parties or operation of law. If one party fails to perform as promised, the other party may enforce the contract and sue for breach.

With two exceptions, third parties do not acquire any rights under other people's contracts. The exceptions are (1) **assignees** to whom rights subsequently are transferred and (2) **intended third-party beneficiaries** to whom the contracting parties intended to give rights under the contract at the time of contracting.

This chapter discusses the rights of third parties under a contract, conditions to performance, and ways of discharging the duty of performance.

ASSIGNMENT OF RIGHTS

In many cases, the parties to a contract can transfer their rights under the contract to other parties. The transfer of contractual rights is called an **assignment of rights** or just an **assignment**.

assignment   The transfer of contractual rights by the obligee to another party.

Form of Assignment

The party who owes the duty of performance is called the *obligor*. The party owed a right under the contract is called the *obligee*. An obligee who transfers the right to receive performance is called an **assignor**. The party to whom the right has been transferred is called the **assignee**. The assignee can assign the right to yet another person (called a **subsequent assignee**, or **subassignee**). Exhibit 11.1 illustrates these relationships.

assignor   The obligee who transfers the right.

assignee   The party to whom the right has been transferred.

Exhibit 11.1
Assignment of a Right

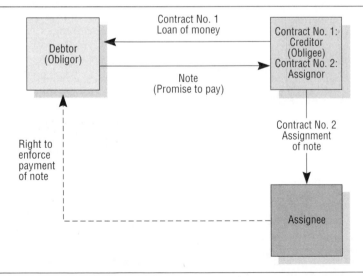

CONSIDER THIS EXAMPLE: Suppose the owner of a clothing store purchases $5,000 worth of goods on credit from a manufacturer. Payment is due in 120 days. Assume that the manufacturer needs cash before that period expires, so he sells his right to collect the money to a factor for $4,000. If the store owner is given proper notice of the assignment, he must pay $5,000 to the factor. The manufacturer is the assignor and the factor is the assignee.

Generally, no formalities are required for a valid assignment of rights. Although the assignor often uses the word *assign*, other words or terms, such as *sell*, *transfer*, *convey*, *give*, and the like, are sufficient to indicate an intent to transfer a contract right.

Rights That Can and Cannot Be Assigned

In the United States, public policy favors a free flow of commerce. That is why most contract rights are assignable, including sales contracts, contracts for the payment of money, and the like.

The types of contracts that present special problems for assignment are discussed in the following sections.

Personal Service Contracts Contracts for the provision of personal services are generally not assignable.[1] For example, if an artist contracts to paint someone's portrait, the artist cannot send a different artist to do the painting without the prior approval of the person to be painted. The parties may agree that a personal service contract may be assigned. For example, many professional athletes' contracts contain a clause permitting assignability of the contract.

Assignment of Future Rights Usually, a person cannot assign a currently nonexistent right that he or she expects to have in the future. For example, suppose a multimillionairess signs a will leaving all of her property to her grandson. The grandson cannot assign his expected right to receive his inheritance.

Contracts in Which Assignment Would Materially Alter the Risk A contract cannot be assigned if the assignment would materially alter the risks or duties of the obligor. For example, suppose Laura Peters, who has a safe driving record, purchases automobile insurance from an insurance company. Her rights to be insured cannot be assigned to another driver because the assignment would materially alter the risk and duties of the insurance company.

"If a man will improvidently bind himself up by a voluntary deed, and not reserve a liberty to himself by a power of revocation, this court will not loose the fetters he hath put upon himself, but he must lie down under his own folly."

L. C. Lord
Nottingham
Villers v. Beaumont
(1682)

Assignment of Legal Actions Legal actions involving personal rights cannot be assigned. For example, suppose Donald Matthews is severely injured by Alice Hollyfield in an automobile accident caused by her negligence. Mr. Matthews can sue Ms. Hollyfield to recover damages for his injuries. He may not assign his right to sue her to another person.

A legal right that arises out of a breach of contract may be assigned. For example, suppose Andrea borrows $10,000 from the bank. If she defaults on the loan, the bank may assign the legal right to collect the money to a collection agency.

In the following case, the court considered whether a contract was assignable.

CASE 11.1

Evening News Association, Inc. v. Peterson
477 F.Supp. 77 (1979) United States District Court, District of Columbia

Facts Post-Newsweek Stations, Inc. (Post-Newsweek), owned television station WTOP-TV (Channel 9) in the District of Columbia. From 1969 to 1978, Gordon Peterson was employed at the station as a newscaster-anchorman. On July 1, 1977, Pe-
continued

terson signed an employment contract with Post-Newsweek for a three-year term ending June 30, 1980. The contract could be extended for two additional one-year terms at the option of Post-Newsweek. In June 1978, Post-Newsweek sold the television station to the Evening News Association, Inc. (Evening News). In the contract of sale, all property and contracts owned by Post-Newsweek were transferred and assigned to the Evening News, including Peterson's employment contract. Peterson's work assignments and duties remained the same as they had been under the previous owner. After working for the new owner for one year, Peterson was offered a position at a competing television station. At that time, his original contract had one more year to run. When Peterson tendered his resignation, the Evening News sought an injunction against Peterson working at the other television station.

Issue Can Peterson's employment contract be assigned?

Decision Yes. The district court held that Peterson's employment contract was assignable. The court held that the assignment of the contract to the Evening News did not alter or vary Peterson's duties under the contract.

Reason The rule that contract rights are assignable subject to exception where the assignment would materially alter the duty of the obligor, increase the burden of risk imposed by the contract, or impair the obligor's chance of obtaining return performance. The court stated: "There has been no showing . . . that the services required of Peterson by the Post-Newsweek contract have changed in any material way since the Evening News entered the picture. . . . This Court cannot but conclude . . . that the defendant's contract was assignable."

CASE QUESTIONS

Critical Legal Thinking Should all contracts be assignable? Even personal service contracts?

Ethics Did Peterson act ethically in this case in trying to get out of the contract?

Business Implication Are many business contracts assignable? Give some examples.

Effect of an Assignment of Rights

CAUTION

Where there has been an assignment of a right, the assignee "stands in the shoes of the assignor" and is entitled to performance from the obligor.

Where there has been a valid assignment of rights, the assignee "stands in the shoes of the assignor." That is, the assignor is entitled to performance from the obligor. The unconditional assignment of a contract right extinguishes all of the assignor's rights, including the right to sue the obligor directly for nonperformance.[2]

An assignee takes no better rights under the contract than the assignor had. That is, if the assignor has a right to receive $10,000 from a debtor, the right to receive this $10,000 is all that the assignor can assign to the assignee. An obligor can assert any defenses he or she had against the assignor or the assignee. For example, an obligor can raise the fraud, duress, undue influence, minority, insanity, illegality of the contract, mutual mistake, or payment by worthless check by the assignor against enforcement of the contract by the assignee. The obligor can also raise any personal defenses (e.g., participation in the assignor's fraudulent scheme) he or she may have directly against the assignee.

Notice of Assignment

BUSINESS BRIEF

To protect his or her rights, an assignee should immediately notify the obligor that (1) the assignment has been made and (2) performance must be rendered to the assignee.

When an assignor makes an assignment of a right under a contract, the assignee is under a duty to notify the obligor that (1) the assignment has been made and (2) performance must be rendered to the assignee. If the assignee fails to notify the obligor of the assignment, the obligor may continue to render performance to the assignor, who no longer has a right to it. The assignee cannot sue the obligor to recover payment because the obligor has performed according to the original contract. The assignee's only course of action is to sue the assignor for damages.

The result changes if the obligor is notified of the assignment but continues to render performance to the assignor. In such situations, the assignee can sue the obligor and recover payment. The obligor will then have to pay twice—once wrongfully to the assignor and then rightfully to the assignee. The obligor's only recourse is to sue the assignor for damages.

Anti-Assignment and Approval Clauses

Some contracts contain **anti-assignment clauses** that prohibit the assignment of rights under the contract. Such clauses may be used if the obligor does not want to deal with or render performance to an unknown third party. Some contracts contain an **approval clause**. Such clauses require the obligor to approve any assignment. Many states prohibit the obligor from unreasonably withholding approval.

anti-assignment clause A clause that prohibits the assignment of rights under the contract.

approval clause A clause that permits the assignment of the contract only upon receipt of an obligor's approval.

BUSINESS CHECKLIST

Which Party Prevails When There Have Been Successive Assignments of the Same Right?

An obligee has the right to assign a contract right or benefit to another party. If the obligee makes successive assignments of the same right to a number of assignors, which assignor has the legal right to the assigned right? To answer this question, the following rules must be examined:

- **The American rule** (or New York rule) provides that the first assignment *in time* prevails, regardless of notice. Most states follow this rule.
- **The English rule** provides that the first assignee to *give notice* to the obligor prevails.
- **The possession of tangible token rule** provides that under either the American or English rule if the assignor makes successive assignments of a contract right that is represented by a tangible token, such as a stock certificate or a savings account passbook, the first assignee who receives delivery of the tangible token prevails over subsequent assignees. However, if the first assignee leaves the tangible token with the assignor, the subsequent assignee prevails. This is because the first assignee could have prevented the problem by having demanded delivery of the tangible token. In other words, physical possession of the tangible token is the pivotal issue.

DELEGATION OF DUTIES

Unless otherwise agreed, the parties to a contract generally can transfer the performance of their duties under the contract to other parties. This is called the **delegation of duties**, or just **delegation**.

The obligor who transferred his or her duty is the **delegator**. The party to whom the duty has been transferred is the **delegatee**. The party to whom the duty is owed is the *obligee*. Generally, no special words or formalities are required to create a delegation of duties. Exhibit 11.2 illustrates the parties to a delegation of a duty.

delegation of duties A transfer of contractual duties by the obligor to another party for performance.

delegator The obligor who transferred his or her duty.

delegatee The party to whom the duty has been transferred.

Duties That Can and Cannot Be Delegated

Often, contracts are entered into with companies or firms rather than with individuals. In such cases, the firm may designate any of its qualified employees to perform the contract. For example, if a client retains a firm of lawyers to represent them, the firm can delegate the duties under the contract to any qualified member of the firm. However, if the obligee has a substantial interest in having the obligor perform the acts required by the contract, duties may not be transferred.[3] This includes obligations under the following types of contracts:

1. **Personal service contracts calling for the exercise of personal skills, discretion, or expertise.** For example, if Michael Jackson is hired to give a concert on campus, Michael Jordan cannot appear in his place.
2. **Contracts whose performance would materially vary if the obligor's duties were delegated.** For example, if a person hires an experienced doctor to perform a complex surgery, a recent medical school graduate cannot be substituted in the operating room.

Exhibit 11.2
Delegation of a Duty

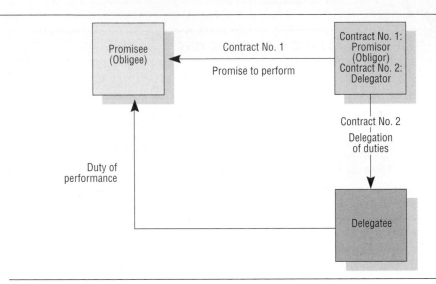

Effect of Delegation of Duties

"Freedom of contracts begins where equality of bargaining power begins."
Oliver Wendell Holmes, Jr. (1928)

assumption of duties
When a delegation of duties contains the term *assumption* or *I assume the duties* or other similar language, the delegatee is legally liable to the obligee for nonperformance.

declaration of duties   If the delegatee has not assumed the duties under a contract, the delegatee is not legally liable to the obligee for nonperformance.

anti-delegation clause   A clause that prohibits the delegation of duties under the contract.

assignment and delegation
Transfer of both rights and duties under the contract.

If the delegation is valid, the delegator remains legally liable for the performance of the contract. If the delegatee does not perform properly, the obligee can sue the obligor–delegator for any resulting damages.

The question of the delegatee's liability to the obligee depends on whether there has been an assumption of duties or a declaration of duties. Where a delegation of duties contains the term *assumption* or other similar language, there is an **assumption of duties** by the delegatee. The delegatee is liable to the obligee for nonperformance. The obligee can sue either the delegator or the delegatee.

If the delegatee has not assumed the duties under a contract, the delegation of duties is called a **declaration of duties**. Here, the delegatee is not legally liable to the obligee for nonperformance. The obligee's only recourse is to sue the delegator. A delegatee who fails to perform his or her duties is liable to the delegator for damages arising from this failure to perform.

Anti-Delegation Clauses

The parties to a contract can include an **anti-delegation clause** indicating that the duties cannot be delegated. Anti-delegation clauses are usually enforced. However, some courts have held that duties that are totally impersonal in nature—such as the payment of money—can be delegated despite such clauses.

An Assignment and Delegation

An **assignment and delegation** occurs when there is a transfer of both rights and duties under a contract. If the transfer of a contract to a third party contains only language of assignment, the modern view holds that there is a corresponding delegation of the duties of the contract.[4]

In the following case, the court held that a delegator was liable for the negligent conduct of the delegatee.

CASE 11.2

Loftus v. American Realty Company
334 N.W.2d 366 (1983) Court of Appeals of Iowa

Facts Raymond and Connie Loftus (Loftus) owned a house in Iowa. They entered into an exclusive listing agreement with American Realty Company to sell their house. Loftus moved out of the house and shut off all of the appliances with the exception of the furnace. Under the exclusive listing agreement, American Realty assumed the responsibility for performing any tasks necessary for the closing of the transaction, including turning on the utilities. An offer was made on the home, which Loftus accepted. Prior to closing, American Realty hired Mr. Fitzpatrick, an independent contractor, to light the gas water heater. In opening the gas valve to the water heater, Fitzpatrick also opened the gas line. As a result, the house exploded and burned, causing $22,500 in damages. Fitzpatrick was discharged in bankruptcy prior to trial in this matter. Loftus sued American Realty for damages for breach of contract. The trial court held in favor of American Realty. Loftus appealed.

Issue Is American Realty the delegator, liable for damages caused by the negligence of Fitzpatrick, the delegatee?

Decision Yes. The court of appeals held that the delegator, American Realty, was liable for the negligence of its delegatee, Fitzpatrick. The court of appeals reversed the judgment of the trial court and or-

dered judgment to be entered for the plaintiffs in the amount of $22,500.

Decision The court of appeals held that the trial court erred in refusing to impute Fitzpatrick's liability to American Realty. The general rule regarding obligations under a personal service contract is that they are not delegable. The performance of such delegated duties is regarded as performance by the obligor and liability remains with him or her. One who contracts to perform an undertaking is liable to his or her promise for the negligence of an independent contractor to whom he or she delegates performance. The fact that American Realty could delegate the duty to a third party, and did so delegate it, did not excuse it from liability for the faulty performance of the subcontractor.

CASE QUESTIONS

Critical Legal Thinking Should a delegator be held liable for the negligence of a delegatee? Why or why not?

Ethics Was it ethical for American Realty to deny liability in this case?

Business Implication Is there any economic consequence to a delegator when he or she delegates his or her duties? Explain.

THIRD-PARTY BENEFICIARIES

Third parties sometimes claim rights under others' contracts. Such third parties are either *intended* or *incidental beneficiaries*. Each of these designations is discussed here.

Intended Beneficiaries

When the parties enter into a contract, they can agree that one of the party's performances should be rendered to or directly benefit a third party. Under such circumstances, the third party is called an **intended third-party beneficiary**. An intended third-party beneficiary can enforce the contract against the party who promised to render performance.[5]

intended beneficiary
A third party who is not in privity of contract but who has rights under the contract and can enforce the contract against the obligor.

The beneficiary may be expressly named in the contract from which he or she is to benefit or may be identified by another means. For example, there is sufficient identification if the testator of a will leaves his estate to "all of my children, equally."

Intended third-party beneficiaries are classified as either *donee* or *creditor* beneficiaries. These terms are defined in the following sections. However, the Restatement (Second) of Contracts and many more state statutes have dropped this distinction and refer to both collectively as *intended beneficiaries.*[6]

Donee Beneficiaries   Where a person enters into a contract with the intent to confer a benefit or gift on an intended third party, the contract is called a **donee beneficiary contract**. A life insurance policy with a named beneficiary is an example of such a contract. The three persons involved in such a contract are as follows:

> **donee beneficiary contract**
> A contract entered into with the intent to confer a benefit or gift on an intended third party.

1. The **promisee** (the contracting party who directs that the benefit be conferred on another);
2. The **promisor** (the contracting party who agrees to confer performance for the benefit of the third person); and

> **donee beneficiary**   The third party on whom the benefit is to be conferred.

3. The **donee beneficiary** (the third person on whom the benefit is to be conferred).

If the promisor fails to perform the contract, the donee beneficiary can sue the promisor directly.

CONSIDER THIS EXAMPLE: Brian Peterson hires a lawyer to draft his will. He directs the lawyer to leave all of his property to his best friend, Jeffrey Silverman. Assume that (1) Mr. Peterson dies and (2) the lawyer's negligence in drafting the will causes it to be invalid. Consequently, Mr. Peterson's distant relatives receive the property under the state's inheritance statute. Mr. Silverman can sue the lawyer for damages because he was the intended donee beneficiary of the will (see Exhibit 11.3).

Exhibit 11.3
Donee Beneficiary Contract

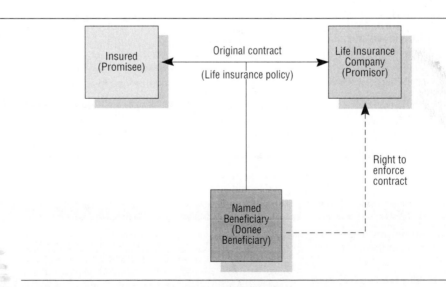

> **creditor beneficiary contract**   A contract that arises in the following situation: (1) A debtor borrows money, (2) the debtor signs an agreement to pay back the money plus interest, (3) the debtor sells the item to a third party before the loan is paid off, and (4) the third party promises the debtor that he or she will pay the remainder of the loan to the creditor.

Creditor Beneficiaries   The second type of intended beneficiary is the creditor beneficiary. A **creditor beneficiary contract** usually arises in the following fact situation:

1. A debtor borrows money from a creditor to purchase some item;
2. The debtor signs an agreement to pay the creditor the amount of the loan plus interest;
3. The debtor sells the item to another party before the loan is paid; and
4. The new buyer promises the debtor that he or she will pay the remainder of the loan amount to the creditor.

The creditor is the new intended creditor beneficiary to this second contract.[7] The parties to the second contract are the original debtor (the promisee), the new party (the promisor), and the original creditor (the **creditor beneficiary**) (see Exhibit 11.4).

creditor beneficiary
Original creditor who becomes a beneficiary under the debtor's new contract with another party.

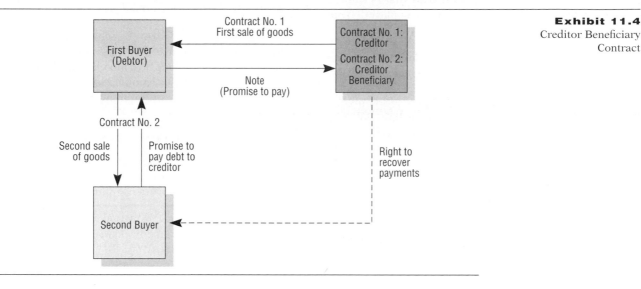

Exhibit 11.4
Creditor Beneficiary
Contract

If the promisor fails to perform according to the contract, the creditor beneficiary may either (1) enforce the original contract against the debtor–promisee or (2) enforce the new contract against the promisor. The creditor, however, can collect only once.

CONSIDER THIS EXAMPLE: Suppose Hilton Hotels, Inc., obtains a loan from City Bank to refurbish a hotel in Atlanta, Georgia. The parties sign a promissory note requiring the loan to be paid off in equal monthly installments over the next 10 years. Before the loan is paid, Hilton sells the hotel to ABC Hotels, another chain of hotels. ABC Hotels agrees with Hilton to complete the payments due on the City Bank loan. The bank has two options if ABC Hotels fails to pay: It can sue Hilton Hotels, Inc., on the promissory note to recover the unpaid loan amount, or it can use its status as a creditor beneficiary to sue ABC Hotels.

"If there's no meaning in it," said the King, "that saves a world of trouble, you know, we needn't try to find any."
Lewis Carroll
Alice in Wonderland
Ch. 12

Incidental Beneficiaries

In many instances, the parties to a contract unintentionally benefit a third party when the contract is performed. In such situations, the third party is referred to as an **incidental beneficiary**. An incidental beneficiary has no rights to enforce or sue under other people's contracts. Generally, the public and taxpayers are only incidental beneficiaries to contracts entered into by the government on their behalf. As such, they acquire no rights to enforce government contracts or to sue parties who breach these contracts.

Often, the courts are asked to decide whether a third party is an intended or an incidental beneficiary, as in the following case.

incidental beneficiary
A party who is unintentionally benefited by other people's contracts.

CASE 11.3

Bain v. Gillispie
357 N.W.2d 47 (1984) Court of Appeals of Iowa

Facts James C. Bain, a college basketball referee, had a contract with the Big 10 Basketball Conference (Big 10) to referee various basketball games. During a game that took place on March 6, 1982, Bain called a foul on a University of Iowa player that permitted free throws by a Purdue University player. That player scored the point that gave Purdue a last-minute victory and eliminated Iowa from the Big 10 championship. Some Iowa fans, including John and Karen Gillispie, asserted that the foul call was clearly in error. The Gillispies operated a novelty store in Iowa City that sold University of Iowa sports memorabilia. They filed a complaint against Bain, alleging that his negligent refereeing constituted a breach of his contract with the Big 10 and destroyed a potential market for their products. The Gillispies sought $175,000 compensatory damages plus exemplary damages. The trial court granted Bain's motion for summary judgment. The Gillispies appealed.

Issue Were the Gillispies intended beneficiaries of the contract between Bain and the Big 10 Basketball Conference?

Decision No. The appellate court held that the Gillispies were merely incidental beneficiaries of the contract between Bain and the Big 10 Basketball Conference. Therefore, they could not maintain their lawsuit for an alleged breach of that contract. Affirmed.

Reason The Gillispies claimed that they were direct donee beneficiaries. The real test is whether the contracting parties intended that a third person should receive a benefit that might be enforced in the courts. The court stated: "The Gillispies can be considered nothing more than incidental beneficiaries and as such are unable to maintain a cause of action."

CASE QUESTIONS

Critical Legal Thinking Should the law allow incidental beneficiaries to recover damages for the breach of other people's contracts? Why or why not?

Ethics Did the Gillispies bring a legitimate lawsuit in this case?

Business Implication Do third parties have rights under many business contracts? Give some examples.

PROMISES OF PERFORMANCE

In contracts, parties make certain promises to each other. These promises can be classified as *covenants* or *conditions*. The difference between each of these is discussed in the following sections.

Covenants

covenant An unconditional promise to perform.

A **covenant** is an unconditional promise to perform. Nonperformance of a covenant is a breach of contract that gives the other party the right to sue. For example, if Medcliff Corporation borrows $100,000 from a bank and signs a promissory note to repay this amount plus 10 percent interest in one year, this promise is a covenant. That is, it is an unconditional promise to perform.

Conditions of Performance

condition A qualification of a promise. There are three types of conditions: conditions precedent, conditions subsequent, and concurrent conditions.

A conditional promise (or qualified promise) is not as definite as a covenant. The promisor's duty to perform (or not perform) arises only if the **condition** does (or does not) occur.[8] However, it becomes a covenant if the condition is met.

Generally, contractual language such as *if, on condition that, provided that, when, after, as soon as,* and the like indicate a condition. A single contract may contain numerous conditions that trigger or excuse performance. There are three types of conditions: *conditions precedent*, *conditions subsequent*, and *concurrent conditions*.

Conditions Precedent

Conditions Precedent If the contract requires the occurrence (or nonoccurrence) of an event *before* a party is obligated to perform a contractual duty, there is a **condition precedent**. The happening (or nonhappening) of the event triggers the contract or duty of performance. If the event does not occur, no duty to perform arises because there is a failure of condition.

CONSIDER THIS EXAMPLE: Suppose E.I. duPont offers Joan Andrews a job as an industrial engineer upon her graduation from college. If Ms. Andrews graduates, the condition has been met. If the employer refuses to hire Ms. Andrews at that time, she can sue the employer for breach of contract. However, if Ms. Andrews does not graduate, duPont is not obligated to hire her because there has been a failure of condition.

condition precedent
A condition that requires the occurrence of an event before a party is obligated to perform a duty under a contract.

Conditions Based on Satisfaction

Conditions Based on Satisfaction Some contracts reserve the right to a party to pay for services provided by the other party only if the services meet the first party's "satisfaction." The courts have developed two tests—the *personal satisfaction test* and the *reasonable person test*—to examine whether this special form of condition precedent has been met.

The **personal satisfaction test** is a *subjective* test that applies if the performance involves personal taste and comfort (e.g., contracts for decorating, tailoring, etc.). The only requirement is that the person given the right to reject the contract acts in good faith.

condition based on satisfaction Clause in a contract that reserves the right of a party to pay for the item or services contracted for only if they meet his or her satisfaction.

personal satisfaction test
Subjective test that applies to contracts involving personal taste and comfort.

CONSIDER THIS EXAMPLE: Suppose Gretchen Davidson employs an artist to paint her daughter's portrait. Assume the contract provides that the client does not have to pay for the portrait unless she is satisfied with it. Accordingly, Ms. Davidson may reject the painting if she personally dislikes it, even though a reasonable person would be satisfied with it.

The **reasonable person test** is an *objective* test that is used to judge contracts involving mechanical fitness and most commercial contracts. Most contracts that require the work to meet a third person's satisfaction (e.g., an engineer or architect) are judged by this standard.

reasonable person test
Objective test that applies to commercial contracts and contracts involving mechanical fitness.

CONSIDER THIS EXAMPLE: Suppose Lillian Vernon, Inc., a large mail-order catalog business, hires someone to install a state-of-the-art computer system that will handle its order entry and record-keeping functions. The system is installed and operates to industry standards. According to the reasonable person test, the company cannot reject the contract as not meeting its satisfaction.

Time of Performance

Time of Performance Generally, there is a breach of contract if the contract is not performed when due. Nevertheless, if the other party is not jeopardized by the delay, most courts treat the delay as a minor breach and give the nonperforming party additional time to perform. Conversely, if the contract expressly provides that "**time is of the essence**" or similar language, performance by the stated time is an express condition. There is a breach of contract if the contracting party does not perform by the stated date.

CAUTION
If "time is of the essence" is stated in a contract, it is an express condition; failure to perform by the stated date is a material breach of contract.

Conditions Subsequent

Conditions Subsequent A **conditions subsequent** exists when a contract provides that the occurrence or nonoccurrence of a specific event automatically excuses the performance of an existing duty to perform. For example, many employment contracts include a clause that permits the employer to terminate the contract if the employee fails a drug test.

Note that the Restatement (Second) of Contracts eliminates the distinction between conditions precedent and conditions subsequent. Both are referred to as "conditions."[9]

conditions subsequent
A condition, if it occurs, that automatically excuses the performance of an existing contractual duty to perform.

concurrent condition
A condition that exists when the parties to a contract must render performance simultaneously; each party's absolute duty to perform is conditioned on the other party's absolute duty to perform.

Concurrent Conditions Concurrent conditions arise when the parties to a contract must render performance simultaneously—that is, when each party's absolute duty to perform is conditioned on the other party's absolute duty to perform.

CONSIDER THIS EXAMPLE: Suppose a contract to purchase goods provides that payment is due upon delivery. In other words, the buyer's duty to pay is conditioned on the seller's duty to deliver the goods, and vice versa. Recovery is available if one party fails to respond to the other party's performance.

implied-in-fact condition
A condition that can be implied from the circumstances surrounding a contract and the parties' conduct.

Implied Conditions Any of the previous types of conditions may be further classified as either an express or implied condition. An **express condition** exists if the parties expressly agree on it. An **implied-in-fact condition** is one that can be implied from the circumstances surrounding a contract and the parties' conduct. For example, a contract in which a buyer agrees to purchase grain from a farmer implies that there is proper street access to the delivery site, proper unloading facilities, and the like.

BUSINESS APPLICATION

Condition Precedents in Business Contracts

Businesses often include conditions precedent in their contracts that must be met before they have any duty to perform under the contract. Consider the following case.

Carley Capital Group (Carley) was the owner of a project in the city of Baltimore known as "Henderson's Wharf." The project was designed to convert warehouses into residential condominiums. On September 4, 1987, Carley hired Gilbane Building Company (Gilbane) to be the general contractor and construction manager for the project. Gilbane hired Ar-

chitectural Systems, Inc. (ASI), as the subcontractor to perform drywall and acoustical tile work on the project. The subcontract included the following clause: "It is specifically understood and agreed that the payment to the trade contractor is dependent, as a condition precedent, upon the construction manager receiving contract payments from the owner."

Gilbane received periodic payments from Carley and paid ASI as work progressed. By late 1988, ASI had satisfactorily performed all of its obligations under the subcontract and submitted a final

bill of $348,155 to Gilbane. Gilbane did not pay this bill because it had not received payment from Carley. On March 10, 1989, Carley filed for bankruptcy. ASI sued Gilbane seeking payment. Must Gilbane pay ASI?

The district court held that Gilbane was not obligated to pay ASI because the condition precedent to this payment—receipt of payment from Carley—had not occurred. The court granted summary judgment to Gilbane. [*Architectural Systems, Inc. v. Gilbane Building Co.*, 760 F.Supp. 79 (D.C.Md. 1991)]

DISCHARGE OF PERFORMANCE

A party's duty to perform under a contract may be discharged by *mutual agreement* of the parties, *impossibility of performance*, or *operation of law*. These methods of discharge are discussed in the sections that follow.

Discharge by Agreement

In many situations, the parties to a contract mutually decide to discharge their contractual duties. The different types of mutual agreements follow.

Mutual Rescission If a contract is wholly or partially executory on both sides, the parties can agree to rescind (i.e., cancel) the contract. **Mutual rescission** requires the parties to enter into a second agreement that expressly terminates the first one. Unilateral rescission of the contract by one of the parties without the other party's consent is not effective. Unilateral rescission of a contract constitutes a breach of that contract.

Substituted Contract The parties to a contract may enter into a new contract that revokes and discharges a prior contract. The new contract is called a **substituted contract**. If one of the parties fails to perform his or her duties under a substituted contract, the nonbreaching party can sue to enforce its terms against the breaching party. The prior contract cannot be enforced against the breaching party because it has been discharged.

Novation A **novation agreement** (commonly called **novation**) substitutes a third party for one of the original contracting parties. The new substituted party is obligated to perform the contract. All three parties must agree to the substitution. In a novation, the exiting party is relieved of liability on the contract.

novation An agreement that substitutes a new party for one of the original contracting parties and relieves the exiting party of liability on the contract.

Accord and Satisfaction The parties to a contract may agree to settle a contract dispute by an **accord and satisfaction**. The agreement whereby the parties agree to accept something different in satisfaction of the original contract is called an **accord**.[10] The performance of an accord is called a **satisfaction**.

An accord does not discharge the original contract. It only suspends it until the accord is performed. Satisfaction of the accord discharges both the original contract and the accord. If an accord is not satisfied when it is due, the aggrieved party may enforce either (1) the accord or (2) the original contract.

accord and satisfaction The settlement of a contract dispute.

Discharge by Impossibility

Under certain circumstances, the nonperformance of contractual duties are excused—discharged—because of *impossibility of performance*. The different doctrines of impossibility are discussed in the following sections.

Impossibility of Performance Impossibility of performance (or **objective impossibility**) occurs if the contract becomes impossible to perform.[11] The impossibility must be objective impossibility ("it cannot be done") rather than subjective impossibility ("I cannot do it"). The following types of objective impossibility excuse nonperformance:

impossibility of performance Nonperformance that is excused if the contract becomes impossible to perform; must be objective impossibility, not subjective.

1. The death or incapacity of the promisor prior to the performance of a personal service contract.[12] For example, if a professional athlete dies prior to or during a contract period, her contract with the team is discharged.
2. The destruction of the subject matter of a contract prior to performance.[13] For instance, if a building is destroyed by fire, the lessees are discharged from further performance unless otherwise provided in the lease.
3. A supervening illegality makes performance of the contract illegal.[14] For example, suppose an art dealer contracts to purchase native art found in a foreign country. The contract is discharged if the foreign country enacts a law forbidding native art from being exported from the country before the contract is performed.

In the following case, the court had to decide whether there was impossibility of performance.

CASE 11.4

Parker v. Arthur Murray, Inc.

295 N.E.2d 487 (1973) Appellate Court of Illinois

Facts In November 1959, Ryland S. Parker, a 37-year-old college-educated bachelor, went to the Arthur Murray Studios (Arthur Murray) in Oak Park, Illinois, to redeem a certificate entitling him to three free dancing lessons. At that time he lived alone in a one-room attic apartment. During the free lessons the instructor told Parker that he had "exceptional potential to be a fine and accomplished dancer." Parker thereupon signed a contract for more lessons. Parker attended lessons regularly and was praised and encouraged by his instructors despite his lack of progress. Contract extensions and new contracts for additional instructional hours were executed, which Parker prepaid. Each written contract contained the bold-type words, "NON-CANCELLABLE CONTRACT." On September 24, 1961, Parker was severely injured in an automobile accident, rendering him incapable of continuing his dancing lessons. At that time he had contracted for a total of 2,734 hours of dance lessons, for which he had prepaid $24,812. When Arthur Murray refused to refund any of the money, Parker sued to rescind the outstanding contracts. The trial court held in favor of Parker and ordered Arthur Murray to return the prepaid contract payments. Arthur Murray appealed.

Issue Does the doctrine of impossibility excuse Parker's performance of the personal service contracts?

Decision Yes. The appellate court held that the doctrine of impossibility of performance excused Parker's performance of the personal service contracts. Affirmed.

Reason In Illinois, impossibility of performance is recognized as a ground for rescission. Arthur Murray contended that the bold-type words "NON-CANCELLABLE CONTRACT" manifested the parties' mutual intent to waive their respective rights to invoke the doctrine of impossibility. The court replied, "This is a construction that we find unacceptable. We conclude that plaintiff never contemplated that by signing a contract that he was waiving a remedy expressly recognized by Illinois courts."

CASE QUESTIONS

Critical Legal Thinking Should the doctrine of impossibility excuse parties from performance of their contracts? Why or why not?

Ethics Did Arthur Murray act ethically in not returning Parker's money?

Business Implication Why do you think Arthur Murray fought this case?

---

commercial impracticability
Nonperformance that is excused if an extreme or unexpected development or expense makes it impractical for the promisor to perform.

Commercial Impracticability Many states recognize the doctrine of **commercial impracticability** as an excuse of nonperformance of contracts. Commercial impracticability excuses performance if an unforeseeable event makes it impractical for the promisor to perform. This doctrine has not yet been fully developed by the courts. It is examined on a case-by-case basis.

CONSIDER THIS EXAMPLE: A utility company enters into a contract to purchase uranium for its nuclear-powered generator from a uranium supplier at a fixed price of $1 million per year for five years. Suppose a new uranium cartel is formed worldwide and the supplier must pay $3 million for uranium to supply the utility with each year's supply. In this case, the court would likely allow the supplier to rescind its contract with the utility based on commercial impracticability. Note that it is not impossible for the supplier to supply the uranium.

CONTEMPORARY BUSINESS ENVIRONMENT

The Doctrine of Commercial Impracticability

Sometimes, unforeseen circumstances make the performance of a contract highly impracticable or very expensive. Modern contract law, including the Uniform Commercial Code (UCC), recognizes the doctrine of commercial impracticability as excusing nonperformance in certain situations. Consider the following case.

In July 1980, Alimenta (U.S.A.), Inc. (Alimenta), entered into a contract with Cargill, Incorporated (Cargill), under which Cargill agreed to deliver to Alimenta shelled, edible peanuts. The peanut crop had been planted in the fields at the time the contract was entered into. Cargill, which had contracts with other buyers as well, expected to make a $3 million profit from its peanut sales.

Unfortunately, there was a severe drought that year, and the crop yield was substantially reduced. This meant that Cargill could deliver to Alimenta only about 65 percent of the promised peanuts. Cargill delivered the same percentage to all of its customers. Alimenta filed suit against Cargill for breach of contract. Cargill asserted that further performance under the contract was excused by the doctrine of commercial impracticability. At trial the jury rendered a verdict for Cargill. Alimenta appealed.

Both the trial court and the court of appeals held that the drought in this case was unforeseen. The evidence showed that the shortage of peanuts in 1980 was unprecedented. In fact, there had been a surplus of domestic peanuts for the preceding 20 years.

The trial court found that it was not impossible for Cargill to perform the contract fully. Cargill could have gone into the market and purchased the peanuts, which were selling at a much higher price than contracted for, and delivered the peanuts to Alimenta. However, Cargill had already suffered a $47 million loss on its peanut contracts without doing this.

The court of appeals affirmed the trial court's ruling in favor of Cargill. The court held that Cargill was excused from further performance by the doctrine of commercial impracticability. The court stated that "the focus of impracticability analysis is upon the nature of the agreement and the expectations of the parties" and not on whether it is physically possible for the defendant to perform the contract. [*Alimenta (U.S.A.), Inc. v. Cargill, Incorporated*, 861 F.2d 650 (11th Cir. 1988)]

Frustration of Purpose The doctrine of **frustration of purpose** excuses the performance of contractual obligations if (1) the object or benefit of the contract is made worthless to a promisor, (2) both parties knew what the purpose was, and (3) the act that frustrated the purpose was reasonably unforeseeable.

CONSIDER THIS EXAMPLE: Suppose Eileen Ney leases a piece of property from a landowner for $1,000 to watch the Rose Bowl parade on January 1 in Pasadena, California. If the parade is unexpectedly canceled, Ms. Ney is excused from paying the rental fee. Note that the promisor is not prevented from performing, however. Ms. Ney could have used the leased land even though there was no parade.

frustration of purpose
A doctrine that excuses the performance of contractual obligations if (1) the object or benefit of a contract is made worthless to a promisor, (2) both parties knew what the purpose was, and (3) the act that frustrated the purpose was unforeseeable.

BUSINESS APPLICATION

Force Majeure Clauses

The parties may agree in their contract that certain events will excuse nonperformance of the contract. These clauses are called **force majeure clauses**.

Usually force majeure clauses excuse nonperformance caused by natural disasters such as floods, tornadoes, earthquakes, and such. Modern clauses often excuse performance due to labor strikes, shortages of raw materials, and the like.

Discharge by Operation of Law

Certain legal rules discharge parties from performing contractual duties. These rules are discussed in the following sections.

statute of limitations
Statute that establishes the time period during which a lawsuit must be brought; if the lawsuit is not brought within this period, the injured party loses the right to sue.

Begins ~~taken~~ from point or time of Knowledge.

Statutes of Limitations

Every state has a **statute of limitations** that applies to contract actions. While the time periods vary from state to state, the usual period for bringing a lawsuit based on breach of contract is one to five years. The UCC provides that a cause of action based on breach of a sales or lease contract must be brought within four years after the cause of action accrues [UCC 2-725, UCC 2A-506].

Bankruptcy

Bankruptcy, which is governed by federal law, is a means of allocating the debtor's nonexempt property to satisfy his or her debts. Debtors may also reorganize in bankruptcy. In most cases, the debtor's assets are insufficient to pay all of the creditors' claims. The debtor receives a **discharge** of the unpaid debts. This means that the debtor is relieved of legal liability to pay the discharged debts.

Alteration of the Contract

If a party to a contract intentionally alters the contract materially, the innocent party may opt either to discharge the contract or to enforce it. The contract may be enforced either on its original terms or on the altered terms. A material alteration is a change in price, quantity, or some other important term.

WORKING THE WEB

Internet research guides provide links to Internet resources and suggestions for finding legal information.

The Virtual Chase   *A Research Site for Legal Professionals*—"The Virtual Chase provides annotated hotlinked references to resources legal professionals and you might find useful in conducting research on the World Wide Web. The guide is arranged by type of information."

Visit at http://www.virtualchase.com/

Law on the Web, by Jim Milles   "Law on the Web provides links to information on United States law available on the Internet. A star next to an entry indicates a recommended site."

Visit at http://lawlib.slu.edu/misc/topical.htm

Legal Research Using the Internet, by Lyonette Louis-Jacques   This guide, written by a law librarian at the University of Chicago, explains why the Internet is useful for legal research. It describes some of the major resources available on the Internet for researching the law of the United States and other countries, comparative law, and international law.

Visit at http://www.lib.uchicago.edu/~llou/ mpoctalk.html

Finding Law-Related Internet Resources by Cindy L. Chick   At this site, legal information is divided by subject. Subjects such as company information, government information, court opinions, and services that rate Web sites can be found here.

Visit at http://www.llrx.com/sources.html

The Compleat Internet Researcher: Advanced Strategies and Techniques   Among other things, the Compleat Internet Researcher has rules (some intended to be broken) about Internet research and explains the odds about sure bets for Internet research.

Visit at http://www.aallnet.org/products/crab/

CYBER EXERCISES:

1. Using the Virtual Chase Web site, find a site called Internet Skills and Strategies for the Legal Researcher.
2. Can you link to the Thomas Web site using Law on the Web?
3. Go to Legal Research Using the Internet. Can you find a link on the first page dealing with women and the law?
4. Use Finding Law-Related Internet Resources to link to the Internet Law Library at the U.S. House of Representatives.
5. What is the origin of The Compleat Internet Researcher?

CHAPTER SUMMARY

ASSIGNMENT OF RIGHTS, P. 232

Form of Assignment	1. *Assignment.* Transfer of contractual rights by a party to a contract to a third person. 2. *Assignor.* Contract party who assigns the contractual rights. 3. *Assignee.* Third person to whom contract rights are assigned.
Effect of Assignment	The assignee "stands in the shoes of the assignor" and is entitled to performance of the contract by the obligor.
Notice of Assignment	1. *Duty to notify.* Assignee must notify the obligor that (1) the assignment has been made and (2) performance must be rendered to the assignee. 2. *Failure to give notice.* If the assignee fails to give proper notice to the obligee and the obligor renders performance to the assignor, the assignee's only course of action to recover is from the assignor.
Anti-assignment and Approval Clauses	1. *Anti-assignment clause.* Prohibits the assignment of rights under a contract. 2. *Approval clause.* Permits assignment of the contract only upon receipt of the obligor's approval.
Successive Assignments	If the obligee makes successive assignments of the same right, one of the following rules (depending on state law) applies: 1. *American rule.* First assignment in time prevails, regardless of notice. Also called the *New York rule.* 2. *English rule.* First assignee to give notice to the obligor prevails.

DELEGATION OF DUTIES, P. 235

Delegation of Duties	1. *Delegation.* Transfer of contractual duties by a party to a contract to a third person. 2. *Delegator.* Party who transfers his or her contractual duties. 3. *Delegatee.* Third person to whom contractual duties are delegated.
Effect of Delegation	Depends on whether there has been: 1. *Assumption of duties.* Delegatee is liable to obligee for nonperformance. Obligee may sue either the delegatee or the delegator. 2. *Declaration of duties.* Delegatee is not liable to the obligee for nonperformance. Obligee can sue only the delegator. The delegatee is liable to the delegator for any damages suffered by the delegator because of the delegatee's nonperformance.
Anti-delegation Clause	Prohibits the delegation of duties under a contract.

THIRD-PARTY BENEFICIARIES, P. 237	
Intended Beneficiaries	Third person who is owed performance under other parties' contract. There are two types: 1. *Donee beneficiary*. Person who is to be rendered performance gratuitously under a contract. For example, a beneficiary of a life insurance policy. Donee beneficiary may sue the promisor for nonperformance. 2. *Creditor beneficiary*. Creditor who becomes a beneficiary to a contract between the debtor and a third party who agrees to perform the debtor's obligation. If the debt is not paid, the creditor may sue either (1) the debtor under the original contract or (2) the third party as a creditor beneficiary.
Incidental Beneficiaries	A third person who incidentally receives some benefit under other parties' contract but who has no rights to enforce it or to sue for its nonperformance.

PROMISES OF PERFORMANCE, P. 240	
Covenants	Unconditional promises to perform. Nonperformance of a covenant is a breach of contract that gives the other party the right to sue.

Conditions of Performance	*Condition*. Promisor's duty to perform or not perform arises only if the *condition* does or does not occur. Also called a *qualified promise*. There are several types:
	1. *Condition precedent*. Requires the occurrence or nonoccurrence of an event before a party is obligated to perform. Conditions precedent based on "satisfaction" are measured by one of two standards:
	  a. *Personal satisfaction test*. The subjective intent of the decision maker applies if the performance involves personal taste or comfort
	  b. *Reasonable person test*. The objective intent of a reasonable person in the circumstances applies to contracts involving mechanical fitness or commercial contracts.
	2. *Condition subsequent*. Provides that the occurrence or nonoccurrence of a specific event automatically excuses performance under a contract.
	3. *Concurrent condition*. Arises when the parties to a contract must render performance spontaneously.
	4. *Implied-in-fact condition*. A condition that is implied from the circumstances surrounding a contract and the parties' conduct.

DISCHARGE OF PERFORMANCE, P. 242	
Discharge by Agreement	1. *Mutual rescission*. The parties mutually agree to rescind an executory contract. 2. *Substituted contract*. The parties enter into a new contract that revokes a prior contract. 3. *Novation*. The parties agree to the substitution of a third party for one of the original parties. The exiting party is relieved of liability and the entering party is obligated to perform the contract. 4. *Accord and satisfaction*. The parties agree to settle a contract dispute. The *satisfaction* of the *accord* discharges the original contract.
Discharge by Impossibility	1. *Impossibility of performance*. The contract is objectively impossible to perform because of an event. 2. *Commercial impracticability*. The contract is impractical for the promisor to perform because of an event.

	3. *Frustration of purpose.* The object of the contract, of which both parties have knowledge, becomes worthless because of an unforeseeable event. 4. *Force majeure clause.* The parties stipulate in the contract what events will excuse performance.
Discharge by Operation of Law	1. *Statute of limitations.* A contract action that is not brought within the stipulated limitations period discharges contractual duties. 2. *Bankruptcy.* Discharge in bankruptcy relieves the debtor of legal liability to pay the discharged debts. 3. *Alteration of a contract.* If a party to a contract intentionally alters it materially, the innocent party may opt either to discharge the contract or to enforce it on its original or altered terms.

CRITICAL LEGAL THINKING CASES

11.1 Third-Party Beneficiary Eugene H. Emmick hired L. S. Hamm, an attorney, to draft his will. The will named Robert Lucas and others (Lucas) as beneficiaries. When Emmick died, it was discovered that the will was improperly drafted, violated state law, and was therefore ineffective. Emmick's estate was transferred pursuant to the state's interstate laws. Lucas did not receive the $75,000 he would have otherwise received had the will been valid. Lucas sued Hamm for breach of the Emmick–Hamm contract to recover what he would have received under the will. Who wins? [*Lucas v. Hamm*, 364 P.2d 685, 56 Cal.2d 583, 15 Cal.Rptr. 821 (Cal. 1961)]

11.2 Third-Party Beneficiary Abrams and others sponsored a condominium project for a luxury condominium building on Manhattan's East Side. Abrams contracted with Lehrer/McGovern, Inc. (L/M), and other contracting companies to construct the building. After the building was completed and the individual condominium units sold, certain defects in construction appeared. Monarch Owners Committee, the condominium association, and individual condominium owners sued L/M and the other contracting companies for damages for breach of their contracts with Abrams. Can the condominium association and owners sue the contracting companies? [*Monarch Owners Committee v. Abrams*, 454 N.Y.S.2d 4 (N.Y.Sup. 1982)]

11.3 Third-Party Beneficiary Angelo Boussiacos hired Demetrios Sofias, a general contractor, to build a restaurant for him. Boussiacos entered into a loan agreement with the Bank of America (B of A) whereby the bank would provide construction financing to build the restaurant. As is normal with most construction loans, the loan agreement provided that loan funds would be periodically disbursed by the bank to Boussiacos at different stages of construction as requested by Boussiacos. Problems arose in the progress of the construction. When Boussiacos did not pay Sofias for certain work that had been done, Sofias sued B of A for breach of contract to collect payment directly from B of A. Can Sofias maintain the lawsuit against B of A? [*Sofias v. Bank of America*, 172 Cal.App.3d 583, 218 Cal.Rptr. 626 (Cal. App. 1985)]

11.4 Third-Party Beneficiary David Seeley owned an apartment building located at 15 East 21st Street in the Gramercy Park area of New York. Seeley contracted with Rem Discount Security Products, Inc. (Rem), to install security locks on the front door of the building. On June 7, 1981, when Lori Einhorn was visiting her fiancé at the building, she was accosted on the second-floor landing, dragged to her fiancé's apartment, and raped. Einhorn sued Seeley and Rem for breach of contract, alleging that the front-door lock to the building was negligently installed and could be opened by a firm push, even when the door was locked. Can Einhorn sue Rem for breach of contract? [*Einhorn v. Seeley and Rem Discount Security Products, Inc.*, 525 N.Y.S.2d 212 (N.Y.Sup. 1988)]

11.5 Assignment William John Cunningham, a professional basketball player, entered into a contract with Southern Sports Corporation (Southern Sports), which owned the Carolina Cougars, a professional basketball team. The contract provided that Cunningham was to play basketball for the Cougars for a three-year period commencing on October 2, 1971. The contract contained a provision that it could not be assigned to any other professional basketball franchise without Cunningham's approval. Subsequently, Southern Sports sold its assets, including its franchise and Cunningham's contract, to the Munchak Corporation (Munchak). There was no change in the Cougars' location after the purchase. When Cunningham refused to play for the new owners, Munchak sued to enforce Cunningham's contract. Is Cunningham's contract assignable to the new owner? [*Munchak Corporation v. Cunningham*, 457 F.2d 721 (4th Cir. 1972)]

11.6 Assignment In 1974, Berlinger Foods Corporation, pursuant to an oral contract, became a distributor for Häagen-Dazs ice cream. Over the next decade both parties flourished as the marketing of high-quality, high-priced ice cream took hold. Berlinger successfully promoted the sale of Häagen-Dazs to supermarket chains and other retailers in the Baltimore-Washington, D.C., area. In 1983, The Pillsbury Company acquired Häagen-Dazs. Pillsbury adhered to the oral distribution agreement and retained Berlinger as a distributor for Häagen-Dazs ice cream. In December 1985, Berlinger entered into a contract and sold its assets to Dreyers, a manufacturer of premium ice cream that competed with Häagen-Dazs. Dreyers ice cream had previously been sold primarily in the western part of the United States. Dreyers attempted to expand its market to the east by choosing to purchase Berlinger as a means to obtain distribution in the Mid-Atlantic region. When Pillsbury learned of the sale, it advised Berlinger that its distributorship for Häagen-Dazs was terminated. Berlinger, who wanted to remain a distributor for Häagen-Dazs, sued Pillsbury for breach of contract, alleging that the oral distribution agreement with Häagen-Dazs and Pillsbury was properly assigned to Dreyers. Who wins? [*Berlinger Foods Corporation v. The Pillsbury Company*, 633 F.Supp. 557 (D.Md. 1986)]

11.7 Right of an Assignee John Handy Jones paid Richard Sullivan, the chief of police of the Addison, Texas, Police Department, a $6,400 bribe in exchange for Sullivan's cooperation in allowing Jones and others to bring marijuana by airplane into the Addison airport without police intervention. Sullivan accepted the money but rather than perform the requested services, he arrested Jones and turned the money over to the Dallas County District Attorney's Office. The $6,400 was introduced as evidence at Jones's criminal trial, where he was convicted. Subsequent to his conviction, Jones assigned his interest in the money to Melvyn Carson Bruder. The City of Addison brought an action, claiming that the money belonged to the city. Bruder intervened in the suit and claimed that he was entitled to the money because of the assignment from Jones. Who wins? [*Bruder v. State of Texas*, 601 S.W.2d 102 (Tex.App. 1980)]

11.8 Approval Clause Lincoln Plaza Associates owned Lincoln Plaza (1900 Broadway at 64th Street) in New York. Chase Manhattan Bank (Chase) entered into a written lease whereby it leased premises in the building. The lease provided that Chase could not sublease or assign the premises without the landlord's prior approval. After occupying the premises for some time, Chase notified the landlord that it wished to sublease the premises to Bank Leumi, which was the 21st largest commercial bank in New York with 20 branches in New York City, assets of more than $3 billion, and a net worth of almost $150 million. The landlord refused to grant approval for the assignment. Chase sued the landlord for breach of contract. Who wins? [*The Chase Manhattan Bank, N.A. v. Lincoln Plaza Associates, N.Y. Law Journal*, 9 Jan. 1989 (N.Y.Sup. 1989)]

11.9 Anti-Assignment Clause In 1976, the city of Vancouver, Washington, contracted with B & B Contracting Corporation (B & B) to construct a well pump at a city-owned water station. The contract contained the following anti-assignment clause: "The Contractor shall not assign this contract or any part thereof, or any moneys due or to become due thereunder." The work was not completed on time, and the city withheld $6,510 as liquidated damages from the contract price. B & B assigned the claim to this money to Portland Electric and Plumbing Company (PEPCo). PEPCo, as the assignee, filed suit against the city of Vancouver, alleging that the city breached its contract with B & B by wrongfully refusing to pay $6,510 to B & B. Can PEPCo maintain the lawsuit against the city of Vancouver? [*Portland Electric and*

Plumbing Company v. city of Vancouver, 627 P.2d 1350 (Wash. App. 1981)]

11.10 Delegation of Duties C. W. Milford owned a registered quarterhorse named Hired Chico. In March 1969, Milford sold the horse to Norman Stewart. Recognizing that Hired Chico was a good stud, Milford included the following provision in the written contract that was signed by both parties: "I, C. W. Milford, reserve 2 breedings each year on Hired Chico registration #403692 for the life of this stud horse regardless of whom the horse may be sold to." The agreement was filed with the county court clerk of Shelby County, Texas. Stewart later sold Hired Chico to Sam McKinnie. Prior to purchasing the horse, McKinnie read the Milford-Stewart contract and testified that he understood the terms of the contract. When McKinnie refused to grant Milford the stud services of Hired Chico, Milford sued McKinnie for breach of contract. Who wins? [*McKinnie v. Milford*, 597 S.W.2d 953 (Tex. 1980)]

11.11 Condition Shumann Investments, Inc. (Shumann), hired Pace Construction Corporation (Pace), a general contractor, to build "Outlet World of Pasco County." In turn, Pace hired OBS Company, Inc. (OBS), a subcontractor, to perform the framing, drywall, insulation, and stucco work on the project. The contract between Pace and OBS stipulated: "Final payment shall not become due unless and until the following conditions precedent to final payment have been satisfied . . . (c) receipt of final payment for subcontractor's work by contractor from owner." When Shumann refused to pay Pace, Pace refused to pay OBS. OBS sued Pace to recover payment. Who wins? [*Pace Construction Corporation v. OBS Company, Inc.*, 531 So.2d 737 (Fla. App. 1988)]

11.12 Excuse of Condition In January 1976, Maco, Inc. (Maco), a roofing contractor, hired Brian Barrows as a salesperson. Barrows was assigned a geographical territory and was responsible for securing contracts for Maco within his territory. The employment contract provided that Barrows was to receive a 26 percent commission on the net profits from roofing contracts that he obtained. The contract contained the following provision: "To qualify for payment of the commission, the salesperson must sell and supervise the job; the job must be completed and paid for; and the salesperson must have been in the continuous employment of Maco, Inc., during the aforementioned period." In July 1977, Barrows obtained a $129,603 contract with the Board of Education of Cook County for Maco to make repairs to the roof of the Hoover School in Evanston, Illinois. During the course of the work, Barrows visited the site more than 60 times. In January 1978, before the work was completed, Maco fired Barrows.

Later Maco refused to pay Barrows the commission when the project was completed and paid for. Barrows sued Maco to recover the commission. Who wins? [*Barrows v. Maco, Inc.*, 419 N.E.2d 634 (Ill. App. 1981)]

11.13 Accord and Satisfaction Eugene and Irene Leonard owned a hardware business, including the building and land, in Humboldt, Iowa. The Leonards listed the business and property for sale with Merlyn J. Pollock, a licensed real estate broker. The asking price was $650,000, and Pollock was to receive a flat fee of $50,000 if he found a buyer. Pollock introduced the

Leonards to Vincent Kopacek. After substantial negotiations, the Leonards and Kopacek signed a contract for the sale of the hardware store. Thereafter, Mr. Leonard went to Pollock's office and tried to get him to lower his commission. After much discussion, Leonard told Pollock that if he would reduce his fee to $15,000, he would get two other hardware store owners to list their stores for sale with Pollock. Pollock agreed. Subsequently, the Leonards refused to sell their business to Kopacek, who sued and won a decree of specific performance. Can Pollock recover damages from the Leonards, and if so, how much? [*Sergeant, as Trustee for the Estate of Merlyn J. Pollock v. Leonard*, 312 N.W.2d 541 (Iowa 1981)]

11.14 Novation On July 21, 1981, Magnum Enterprises, Inc. (Magnum), executed an offer and agreement to purchase the Diamond Ring Ranch in Haakon County, South Dakota, from the Armstrong family for $10,800,000. Donald A. Haggar was the real estate broker on the transaction. The offer included a provision for a $500,000 earnest money deposit by a promissory note that was payable as follows: $50,000 due on August 10, 1981, $25,000 due on August 31, 1981, and $200,000 due on September 11, 1981. The closing date of the sale was set for November 2, 1981. The offer also contained a provision for liquidated damages of $500,000 if the buyer did not perform. Magnum paid the original $50,000 into Haggar's client trust account. On August 31, 1981, Magnum agreed to let Berja, a Montana investment group, purchase the ranch. Armstrong agreed to the substitution of Berja as the buyer, and Berja executed an offer and agreement to purchase the ranch on the same terms as Magnum. When Berja failed to close the sale, Haggar, as trustee, brought an action against Magnum to recover on the promissory note. Magnum counterclaimed to recover the $50,000 it paid into Haggar's client trust account. Who wins? [*Haggar v. Olfert*, 387 N.W.2d 45 (S.D. 1986)]

Magnum wins

ETHICS CASES

11.15 Ethical Perspective Pabagold, Inc. (Pabagold), a manufacturer and distributor of suntan lotions, hired Mediasmith, an advertising agency, to develop an advertising campaign for Pabagold's Hawaiian Gold Pabatan suntan lotion. In the contract, Pabagold authorized Mediasmith to enter into agreements with third parties to place Pabagold advertisements for the campaign and to make payments to these third parties for the Pabagold account. Pabagold agreed to pay Mediasmith for its services and to reimburse it for expenses incurred on behalf of Pabagold. The Pabagold-Mediasmith contract provided for arbitration of any dispute arising under the contract.

In April 1981, Mediasmith entered into a contract with Outdoor Services, Inc. (Outdoor Services), an outdoor advertising company, to place Pabagold ads on billboards owned by Outdoor Services. Outdoor Services provided the agreed-upon work and billed Mediasmith $8,545 for its services. Mediasmith requested payment of this amount from Pabagold so it could pay Outdoor Services. When Pabagold refused to pay, Outdoor Services filed a demand for arbitration as provided in the Pabagold–Mediasmith contract. Pabagold defended, asserting that Outdoor Services could not try to recover the money because it was not in privity of contract with Pabagold.

Did Pabagold act ethically in refusing to pay Outdoor Services? From a moral perspective, does it matter that Outdoor Services and Pabagold were not in privity of contract? Who wins? [*Outdoor Services, Inc. v. Pabagold, Inc.*, 185 Cal.App.3d 676, 230 Cal.Rptr. 73 (Cal.App. 1986)]

11.16 Ethical Perspective Indiana Tri-City Plaza Bowl (Tri-City) leases a building from Charles H. Glueck for use as a bowling alley. The lease provided that Glueck was to provide adequate paved parking for the building. The lease gave Tri-City the right to approve the plans for the construction and paving of the parking lot. When Glueck submitted paving plans to Tri-City, it rejected the plans and withheld its approval. Tri-City argues that the plans must meet its personal satisfaction before it has to approve them. Evidence showed that the plans were commercially reasonable in the circumstances. A lawsuit was filed between Tri-City and Glueck. Who wins? Was it ethical for Tri-City to reject the plans? [*Indiana Tri-City Plaza Bowl, Inc. v. Estate of Glueck*, 422 N.E.2d 670 (Ind. App. 1981)]

CRITICAL LEGAL THINKING WRITING ASSIGNMENT

Read Case A.11 in the Case Appendix [*Chase Precast Corp. v. John J. Paonessa Co., Inc.*]. This case is excerpted from the appellate court opinion. Review and brief the case. In your brief, be sure to answer the following questions:

1. Who were the contracting parties and what did their contract provide?

2. Why did the defendant not complete the contract?
3. What does the doctrine of frustration of purpose provide?
4. Did the doctrine of frustration of purpose excuse the defendant's nonperformance?

NOTES

[1] Restatement (Second) of Contracts, §§ 311 and 318.

[2] Restatement (Second) of Contracts, § 317.

[3] Restatement (Second) of Contracts, § 318(2).

[4] Restatement (Second) of Contracts, § 328.

[5] Restatement (Second) of Contracts, § 302.

[6] Restatement (Second) of Contracts, § 302(1)(b).

[7] Restatement (Second) of Contracts, § 302(1)(a).

[8] The Restatement (Second) of Contracts, § 224, defines a *condition* as "An event, not certain to occur, which must occur, unless its non-performance is excused, before performance under a contract is due."

[9] Restatement (Second) of Contracts, § 224.

[10] Restatement (Second) of Contracts, § 281.

[11] Restatement (Second) of Contracts, § 261.

[12] Restatement (Second) of Contracts, § 262.

[13] Restatement (Second) of Contracts, § 263.

[14] Restatement (Second) of Contracts, § 264.

CHAPTER 12

CONTRACT REMEDIES

AND TORTS ASSOCIATED

WITH CONTRACTS

Chapter Objectives

*After studying this chapter,
you should be able to*

1. Explain how complete performance discharges contractual duties
2. Identify substantial performance and describe the remedies available for minor breach
3. Identify inferior performance and the material breach of a contract
4. Describe compensatory, consequential, and nominal damages
5. Explain the duty of mitigation of damages
6. Describe liquidated damages and identify when they are a penalty
7. Describe the remedy of rescission of a contract
8. Define the equitable remedies of a specific performance, quasi-contract, and injunction
9. Describe torts associated with contracts
10. Define punitive damages

Chapter Contents

- Performance and Breach
  Case 12.1 *W. E. Erickson Construction, Inc. v. Congress-Kenilworth Corp. (IL)*
- Monetary Damages
  Case 12.2 *Super Valu Stores, Inc. v. Peterson (AL)*
  Case 12.3 *California and Hawaiian Sugar Co. v. Sun Ship, Inc. (9th Cir.)*
  Case 12.4 *Parker v. Twentieth Century-Fox Film Corp. (CA)*
- Rescission and Restitution
- Equitable Remedies
  Business Application Hard Dealing for the Hard Rock Cafe
  Business Application *Pennzoil v. Texaco:* An Expensive Handshake
- Torts Associated with Contracts
  Case 12.5 *Gourley v. State Farm Mutual Automobile Insurance Co. (CA)*
  Business Checklist Enforcement of Remedies: Attachment and Garnishment
- Working the Web
- Chapter Summary
- Critical Legal Thinking Cases
- Ethics Cases
- Critical Legal Thinking Writing Assignment

> *Contracts must not be sports of an idle hour, mere matters of pleasantry and badinage, never intended by the parties to have any serious effect whatsoever.*
>
> Lord Stowell
> *Dalrymple v. Dalrymple*, 2
> Hag.Con. 54, at 105 (1811)

Can be total or partial (handwritten)

breach of contract If a contracting party fails to perform an absolute duty owed under a contract.

"It is a vain thing to imagine a right without a remedy; for want of right and want of remedy are reciprocal."

Holt C. J.
Ashby v. White
(1703)

There are three levels of performance of a contract: complete, substantial, and inferior. Complete (or strict) performance by a party discharges that party's duties under the contract. Substantial performance constitutes a minor breach of the contract. Inferior performance constitutes a material breach that impairs or destroys the essence of the contract. Various remedies may be obtained by a nonbreaching party if a **breach of contract** occurs—that is, if a contracting party fails to perform an absolute duty owed under a contract.[1]

The most common remedy for a breach of contract is an award of **monetary damages**. This is often called the "law remedy." However, if a monetary award does not provide adequate relief, the court may order any one of several **equitable remedies**, including specific performance, reformation, quasi-contract, and injunction. Equitable remedies are based on the concept of fairness.

This chapter discusses breach of contracts and the remedies available to the nonbreaching party.

PERFORMANCE AND BREACH

"No cause of action arises from a bare promise."

Legal Maxim

Most common settlement: - monetary damages (handwritten)

If a contractual duty has not been discharged (i.e., terminated) or excused (i.e., relieved of legal liability), the contracting party owes an absolute duty (i.e., covenant) to perform the duty. As mentioned in the chapter introduction, there are three types of performance of a contract: (1) complete performance, (2) substantial performance (or minor breach), and (3) inferior performance (or material breach). These concepts are discussed in the following sections.

complete performance Occurs when a party to a contract renders performance exactly as required by the contract; discharges that party's obligations under the contract.

tender of performance Tender is an unconditional and absolute offer by a contracting party to perform his or her obligations under the contract.

substantial performance Performance by a contracting party that deviates only slightly from complete performance.

minor breach A breach that occurs when a party renders substantial performance of his or her contractual duties.

Complete Performance

Most contracts are discharged by the **complete** or **strict performance** of the contracting parties. Complete performance occurs when a party to a contract renders performance exactly as required by the contract. A fully performed contract is called an **executed contract**.

Note that **tender of performance** also discharges a party's contractual obligations. Tender is an unconditional and absolute offer by a contracting party to perform his or her obligations under the contract.

CONSIDER THIS EXAMPLE: Suppose Ashley's Dress Shops, Inc. contracts to purchase dresses from a dress manufacturer for $25,000. Ashley's has performed its obligation under the contract when it tenders the $25,000 to the manufacturer. If the manufacturer fails to deliver the dresses, Ashley's can sue it for breach of contract.

Substantial Performance: Minor Breach

Substantial performance occurs when there has been a **minor breach** of contract. In other words, it occurs when a party to a contract renders performance that deviates only slightly from complete performance. The nonbreaching party may either (1) convince the breaching party to elevate his or her performance to complete performance, (2) deduct the cost to repair the defect from the contract price and remit the balance to the breaching party, <u>or</u> (3) sue the breaching party to recover the cost to repair the defect if the breaching party has already been paid.

CONSIDER THIS EXAMPLE: Suppose Donald Trump contracts with Big Apple Construction Co. to have Big Apple construct an office building for $50 million. The architectural plans call for installation of three-ply windows in the building. Big Apple constructs the building exactly to plan except that it installs two-ply windows. There has been substantial performance. It would cost $300,000 to install the correct windows. If Big Apple agrees to replace the windows, its performance is elevated to complete performance, and Trump must remit the entire contract price. However, if Trump has to hire someone else to replace the windows, he may deduct this cost of repair from the contract price and remit the difference to Big Apple.

In the following case, the court found that there was a substantial performance of a contract.

"The very definition of a good award is, that it gives dissatisfaction to both parties."
M. R. Plumer
Goodman v. Sayers
(1820)

CASE 12.1

W. E. Erickson Construction, Inc.
v. Congress-Kenilworth Corp.
503 N.E.2d 233 (1986) Supreme Court of Illinois

Facts The Congress-Kenilworth Corporation (Congress) hired W. E. Erickson Construction, Inc. (Erickson), a general contractor, to construct "Thunder Mountain Rapids," a concrete water slide in Creswood, Illinois. The total cost of the slide was not to exceed $535,000. Construction of the water slide began on April 15, 1981, and the slide was completed on July 3, 1981, the day before the projected opening date. After construction, cracks appeared in the concrete flumes of the slide. The cracks did not interfere with the operation of the slide, but the defects did need to be repaired at a substantial cost. Erickson billed Congress $550,000 for full performance of the contract. At that point, Congress had paid Erickson $150,000. When Congress refused to pay Erickson for full performance, Erickson sued Congress for breach of contract to recover the full contract price. The trial court awarded Erickson $352,000, less the $150,000 already paid by Congress, for a judgment of $202,000. The appellate court affirmed. An appeal was taken.

Issue Did Erickson substantially perform the contract?

Decision Yes. The supreme court held that Erickson substantially performed the contract to build the water slide. The supreme court affirmed the judgment of the trial and appellate courts.

Reason The question of whether there has been substantial performance of the terms and conditions of a contract is always a question of fact. The supreme court stated: "We agree with the appellate court that the trial court did find that Erickson substantially performed under the contract.... The trial court found that the defects in the slide were not severe enough to support a finding that Erickson performed in a wholly unworkmanlike manner.... According to the record, the slide was completed on time and has served the purpose for which it was intended since its opening.... [I]t was clear from the evidence that the cracks have not interfered with the operation of the structure in its intended use. We therefore conclude that the trial court's finding of a substantial performance is not against the manifest weight of the evidence."

CASE QUESTIONS

Critical Legal Thinking Should the doctrine of substantial performance be recognized by the law, or should a party have to literally comply with and fully perform the contract before being paid anything?

Ethics Do you think either party acted unethically in this case?

Business Implication Do you think there was substantial performance in this case?

Inferior Performance: Material Breach

inferior performance
Occurs when a party fails to perform express or implied contractual obligations that impair or destroy the essence of the contract.

material breach A breach that occurs when a party renders inferior performance of his or her contractual duties.

A **material breach** of a contract occurs when a party fails to perform certain express or implied obligations that impair or destroy the essence of the contract. Because there is no clear line between a minor breach and a material breach, determination is made on a case-by-case basis.

Where there has been a material breach of a contract, the nonbreaching party has two choices:

1. The nonbreaching party may rescind the contract, seek restitution of any compensation paid under the contract to the breaching party, and be discharged from any further performance under the contract.[2]
2. The nonbreaching party may treat the contract as being in effect and sue the breaching party to recover damages.

"Men keep their agreements when it is an advantage to both parties not to break them."
Solon
(c. 600 B.C.)

CONSIDER THIS EXAMPLE: Suppose a university contracts with a general contractor to build a new three-story building with classroom space for 1,000 students. However, the completed building can support the weight of only 500 students because the contractor used inferior materials. The defect cannot be repaired without rebuilding the entire structure. Because this is a material breach, the university may rescind the contract and require removal of the building. The university is discharged of any obligations under the contract and is free to employ another contractor to rebuild the building. Alternatively, the university could accept the building and deduct damages caused by the defect from the contract price.

Anticipatory Breach

anticipatory breach A breach that occurs when one contracting party informs the other that he or she will not perform his or her contractual duties when due.

Anticipatory breach (or **anticipatory repudiation**) of contract occurs when the contracting party informs the other in advance that he or she will not perform his or her contractual duties when due. This type of material breach can be expressly stated or implied from the conduct of the repudiator. Where there is an anticipatory repudiation, the nonbreaching party's obligations under the contract are discharged immediately. The nonbreaching party also has the right to sue the repudiating party when the anticipatory breach occurs; there is no need to wait until performance is due.[3]

- This is subjective.
- Standard & proof are 2 separate things.   *loss is one thing, proving it is something else.*

MONETARY DAMAGES

Puts the buyer in the place of where they would have been if contract had been fulfilled.

A nonbreaching party may recover **monetary damages** from a breaching party. Monetary damages are available whether the breach was minor or material. Several types of monetary damages may be awarded, including compensatory, consequential, nominal, and liquidated damages.

Compensatory Damages

compensatory damages
A remedy intended to compensate a nonbreaching party for the loss of the bargain; they place the nonbreaching party in the same position as if the contract had been fully performed by restoring the "benefit of the bargain."

Compensatory damages are intended to compensate a nonbreaching party for the loss of the bargain. In other words, they place the nonbreaching party in the same position as if the contract had been fully performed by restoring the "benefit of the bargain."

CONSIDER THIS EXAMPLE: Suppose Lederle Laboratories enters into a written contract to employ a manager for three years at a salary of $6,000 per month. Before work is to start, the manager is informed that he will not be needed. This is a material breach of contract. Assume the manager finds another job, but it pays only $5,000 a month. The manager may recover $1,000 per month for 36 months (total $36,000) from Lederle Laboratories as compensatory damages. These damages place the manager in the same situation as if the contract with Lederle had been performed.

The amount of compensatory damages that will be awarded depends on the type of contract that was breached and which party failed to perform. Some special types of contracts are discussed in the following sections.

Sale of Goods The UCC governs compensatory damages for a breach of a sales contract involving goods. In such situations, the usual measure of damages is the difference between the contract price and the market price of the goods at the time and place the goods were to be delivered.[4]

"He who derives the advantage ought to sustain the burden."
Legal Maxim

CONSIDER THIS EXAMPLE: Suppose Revlon, Inc. contracted to buy a piece of equipment from Greenway Supply Co. for $20,000, but the equipment is not delivered. Revlon then purchases the equipment from another vendor but has to pay $25,000 because the current market price for the equipment has risen. Revlon can recover $5,000—the difference between the market price paid ($25,000) and the contract price ($20,000)—in compensatory damages.

Sale of Real Property Most states allow the same measure of compensatory damages for a breach of a contract to purchase or sell land as is permitted for the breach of a sales contract—that is, the difference between the contract price and the market price.

[handwritten: Court can force a person to sell house if owner reniges on agreement]

Construction Contracts A construction contract arises when the owner of real property contracts to have a contractor build a structure or do other construction work. The contractor may recover the profits he or she would have made if the owner breaches the contract before construction begins. The contractor can recover his or her lost profits plus the cost of construction to date if the owner decides not to go ahead with the new project after construction begins. If the builder breaches a construction contract, either before or during construction, the owner can recover the increased cost above the contract price that he or she has to pay to have the work completed by another contractor.

"Necessitous men are not, truly speaking, free men, but, to answer a present exigency, will submit to any terms that the crafty may impose upon them."
Lord Thomas Henley
Vernon v. Bethell (1762)

Employment Contracts An employee whose employer breaches an employment contract can recover lost wages or salary as compensatory damages. If the employee breaches the contract, the employer can recover the costs to hire a new employee plus any increase in salary paid to the replacement.

[handwritten: Not under employment at will only if written contract exists]

Consequential Damages

In addition to compensatory damages, a nonbreaching party sometimes can recover **special** or **consequential damages** from the breaching party. Consequential damages are *foreseeable* damages that arise from circumstances outside the contract. To be liable for consequential damages, the breaching party must know or have reason to know that the breach will cause special damages to the other party.

consequential damages Foreseeable damages that arise from circumstances outside the contract. In order to be liable for these damages, the breaching party must know or have reason to know that the breach will cause special damages to the other party.

CONSIDER THIS EXAMPLE: Suppose Soan-Allen Co., a wholesaler, enters into a contract to purchase 1,000 men's suits for $150 each from the Fabric Manufacturing Co., a manufacturer. Prior to contracting, the wholesaler tells the manufacturer that the suits will be resold to retailers for $225. The manufacturer breaches the contract by failing to manufacture the suits. The wholesaler cannot get the suits manufactured by anyone else in time to meet his contracts. He can recover $75,000 of lost profits on the resale contracts (1,000 suits × $75 profit) as consequential damages from the manufacturer because the manufacturer knew of this special damage to Soan-Allen Co. if it breached the contract.

In the following case, the court awarded consequential damages against a breaching party.

CASE 12.2

Super Valu Stores, Inc. v. Peterson

506 So.2d 317 (1987) Supreme Court of Alabama

Facts Super Valu Stores, Inc. (Super Valu), a wholesale operator of supermarkets, developed a new concept for a market called "County Market." The basic concept of the County Market was that it must be the lowest priced store in the marketplace and operate on a high-volume, low-profit margin structure. In 1981, Super Valu purchased a parcel of property in Oxford, Alabama, for the development of a County Market. It planned to lease the store to an independent retailer to operate. Thomas J. Peterson, who was an executive of Super Valu, applied for the operator's position at the proposed store. In January 1984, Peterson was approved as the retail operator of the proposed Oxford County Market. On February 24, 1984, Peterson retired from Super Valu so that he could operate the new store. When Super Valu failed to construct and lease the store to Peterson, he sued Super Valu for breach of contract. The trial court held in favor of Peterson and awarded him $5 million in lost profits that would have been derived by him from the store. Super Valu appealed.

Issue Are lost profits from an unestablished business recoverable as consequential damages even though it can be argued that they are inherently too speculative and conjectural?

Decision Yes. The supreme court held that lost profits from an unestablished business can be recovered as consequential damages if they can be determined with reasonable certainty. The court held that such damages were determined with reasonable cer-

tainty in this case and affirmed the trial court's judgment.

Reason Current Alabama law, like the law of other states, authorizes recovery of anticipated profits of an unestablished business, if proved with reasonable certainty. The supreme court states: "The fundamental basis for Peterson's evidence as to damages was Super Valu's own projections of profits, produced in its normal course of business long before this dispute arose. These projections were the product of an intense, exhaustive process involving many different Super Valu personnel. Super Valu's projections resulted from the application of a scientific methodology that for many years had accurately predicted the future performance of stores associated with Super Valu. These projections were also based upon the prior successful performances of the Super Valu business system, of which the Oxford County Market would have become a standardized part."

CASE QUESTIONS

Critical Legal Thinking Are lost profits too speculative to be awarded in breach of contract actions?

Ethics Did Super Valu act ethically by denying liability in this case?

Business Implication If unestablished businesses could not recover lost profits, would there be more or fewer breaches of contract with such businesses?

---

nominal damages
Damages awarded when the nonbreaching party sues the breaching party even though no financial loss has resulted from the breach; usually consists of $1 or some other small amount.

liquidated damages If the contract is breached, these are damages to which parties to a contract agree in advance.

Nominal Damages

The nonbreaching party can sue the breaching party even if no financial loss resulted from the breach. **Nominal damages** usually are awarded in a small amount such as $1. Cases involving nominal damages are usually brought on "principle."

Liquidated Damages

Under certain circumstances, the parties to a contract may agree in advance to the amount of damages payable upon a breach of contract. These are called **liquidated damages**. To be lawful, the actual damages must be difficult or impracticable to determine, and the liquidated amount must be reasonable in the circumstances.[5] An enforceable liquidated damage clause is an exclusive remedy even if actual damages are later determined to be different.

A liquidated damage clause is considered a **penalty** if actual damages are clearly determinable in advance or the liquidated damages are excessive or unconscionable. If a liquidated damage clause is found to be a penalty, it is unenforceable. The nonbreaching party may then recover actual damages.

In the following case, the court had to decide whether a liquidated damage clause was a penalty.

BUSINESS BRIEF

Many businesses include liquidated damage clauses in their commercial contracts. This helps to provide certainty, avoid lawsuits, and provide an incentive to enter into contracts.

CASE 12.3

California and Hawaiian Sugar Co. v. Sun Ship, Inc.

794 F.2d 1433 (1986) United States Court of Appeals, Ninth Circuit

Facts The California and Hawaiian Sugar Company (C&H), a California corporation, is an agricultural cooperative owned by 14 sugar plantations in Hawaii. It transports raw sugar to its refinery in Crockett, California. Sugar is a seasonal crop, with about 70 percent of the harvest occurring between April and October. C&H requires reliable seasonal shipping of the raw sugar from Hawaii to California. Sugar stored on the ground or left unharvested suffers a loss of sucrose and goes to waste.

After C&H was notified by its normal shipper that it would be withdrawing its services as of January 1981, C&H commissioned the design of a large hybrid vessel—a tug of a catamaran design consisting of a barge attached to the tug. After substantial negotiations, C&H contracted with Sun Ship, Inc. (Sun Ship), a Pennsylvania corporation, to build the vessel for $25,405,000. The contract, which was signed in the fall of 1979, provided a delivery date of June 30, 1981. The contract also contained a liquidated damage clause calling for a payment of $17,000 per day for each day that the vessel was not delivered to C&H after June 30, 1981. Sun Ship did not complete the vessel until March 16, 1982. The vessel was commissioned in mid-July 1982 and christened the *Moku Pahu.*

During the 1981 season, C&H was able to find other means of shipping the crop from Hawaii to its California refinery. Evidence established that actual damages suffered by C&H because of the nonavailability of the vessel from Sun Ship were $368,000. When Sun Ship refused to pay the liquidated damages, C&H filed suit to require payment of $4,413,000 in liquidated damages under the contract. The district court entered judgment in favor of C&H and awarded the corporation $4,413,000 plus interest. Sun Ship appealed.

Issue Is the liquidated damage clause enforceable, or is it a penalty clause that is not enforceable?

Decision The court of appeals held that the liquidated damage clause was not a penalty and was therefore enforceable. Affirmed.

Reason Contracts are contracts because they contain enforceable promises. Absent some overriding public policy, those promises are to be enforced. Parties who agree to pay damages of a fixed amount normally have a good sense of what damages can occur, and the courts are reluctant to override their judgment. In this case, the court of appeals stated, "Proof of this loss is difficult. . . . Whatever the loss, the parties had promised each other that $17,000 per day was a reasonable measure. . . . When sophisticated parties with bargaining parity have agreed what lack of this prize would mean, and it is now difficult to measure what the lack did mean, the court will uphold the parties' bargain."

CASE QUESTIONS

Critical Legal Thinking Should liquidated damage clauses be enforced or should nonbreaching parties be allowed to recover only actual damages caused by the breaching party?

Ethics Did either party act unethically in this case?

Business Implication Do you think many businesses use liquidated damage clauses? Can you give some examples?

Mitigation of Damages

mitigation A non-breaching party is under a legal duty to avoid or reduce damages caused by a breach of contract.

You can't let the damages run.

If a contract has been breached, the law places a duty on the innocent nonbreaching party to take reasonable efforts to **mitigate** (i.e., avoid and reduce) the resulting damages. The extent of mitigation required depends on the type of contract involved. For example, if an employer breaches an employment contract, the employee owes a duty to mitigate damages by trying to find substitute employment. The employee is only required to accept comparable employment. The courts consider such factors as compensation, rank, status, job description, and geographical location in determining the comparability of jobs.

In the following case, the court had to decide whether a job was comparable.

CASE 12.4

Parker v. Twentieth Century-Fox Film Corp.
3 Cal.3d 176, 89 Cal.Rptr. 737 (1970) California Supreme Court

Facts On August 6, 1965, Twentieth Century-Fox Film Corporation (Fox), a major film production studio, entered into an employment contract with Shirley MacLaine Parker (Parker), an actress. Under the contract, Parker was to play the leading female role in a musical production called *Bloomer Girl*, to be filmed in Los Angeles. In the movie, Parker would be able to use her talents as a dancer as well as an actress. The contract provided that Parker was to be paid guaranteed compensation of $53,571.42 per week for 14 weeks commencing on May 23, 1966, for a total of $750,000. On April 4, 1966, Fox sent Parker a letter notifying her that it was not going to film *Bloomer Girl*. The letter, however, offered Parker the leading female role in a film tentatively titled *Big Country*, which was to be a dramatic western to be filmed in Australia. The compensation Fox offered Parker was identical to that offered for *Bloomer Girl*. Fox gave Parker one week to accept. She did not and the offer expired. Parker sued Fox to recover the guaranteed compensation provided in the *Bloomer Girl* contract. The trial court granted summary judgment to Parker. Fox appealed.

Issue Was the job that Fox offered Parker in *Big Country* comparable employment that Parker was obligated to accept to mitigate damages?

Decision No. The supreme court held that the job that Fox offered to Parker in *Big Country* was not comparable to the role Fox had contracted Parker to play in *Bloomer Girl*. Therefore, Parker did not fail to mitigate damages by refusing to accept such employment. The supreme court affirmed the trial court's summary judgment.

Reason Before projected earnings from other employment opportunities not sought or accepted by the discharged employee can be applied in mitigation, the employer must show that the other employment was comparable, or substantially similar, to that of which the employee has been deprived. In finding that the offered employment was not comparable, the supreme court stated: "[I]t is clear that the trial court correctly ruled that plaintiff's failure to accept defendant's tendered substitute employment could not be applied in mitigation of damages because the offer of the *Big Country* lead was of employment both different and inferior. The mere circumstances that *Bloomer Girl* was to be a musical review, calling upon plaintiff's talents as a dancer as well as an actress, and was to be produced in the City of Los Angeles, whereas *Big Country* was a straight dramatic role in a Western-type story taking place in an opal mine in Australia, demonstrates the difference in kind between the two employments: The female lead as a dramatic actress in a Western-style motion picture can by no stretch of imagination be considered the equivalent of or substantially similar to the lead in a song-and-dance production."

CASE QUESTIONS

Critical Legal Thinking Should nonbreaching parties be under a duty to mitigate damages caused by the breaching party? Why or why not?

Ethics Did Fox act ethically in this case? Did Parker?

Business Implication Who is most likely to be able to mitigate damages when there is a breach of an employment contract: (1) the president of a large corporation (2) a middle manager or (3) a bank teller?

RESCISSION AND RESTITUTION

Rescission is an action to undo the contract. It is available when there has been a material breach of contract, fraud, duress, undue influence, or mistake. Generally, in order to rescind a contract, the parties must make **restitution** of the consideration they received under the contract.[6] Restitution consists of returning the goods, property, money, or other consideration received from the other party. If possible, the actual goods or property must be returned. If the goods or property have been consumed or are otherwise unavailable, restitution must be made by conveying a cash equivalent. The rescinding party must give adequate notice of the rescission to the breaching party. Rescission and restitution restore the parties to the position they occupied prior to the contract.

CONSIDER THIS EXAMPLE: Suppose Filene's Department Stores contracts to purchase $100,000 of goods from a sweater manufacturer. The store pays $10,000 as a down payment, and the first $20,000 of goods are delivered. The goods are materially defective, and the defect cannot be cured. This is a material breach. Filene's can rescind the contract. The store is entitled to receive its down payment back from the manufacturer, and the manufacturer is entitled to receive the goods back from the store.

> **rescission** An action to rescind (undo) the contract. Rescission is available if there has been a material breach of contract, fraud, duress, undue influence, or mistake.

> **restitution** Returning of goods or property received from the other party in order to rescind a contract; if the actual goods or property is not available, a cash equivalent must be made.

EQUITABLE REMEDIES

Equitable remedies are available if there has been a breach of contract that cannot be adequately compensated by a legal remedy. They are also available to prevent unjust enrichment. The most common equitable remedies are specific performance, reformation, quasi-contract, and injunction.

Specific Performance

An award of **specific performance** orders the breaching party to perform the acts promised in the contract. The courts have the discretion to award this remedy if the subject matter of the contract is unique.[7] This remedy is available to enforce land contracts because every piece of real property is considered to be unique. Works of art, antiques, items of sentimental value, rare coins, stamps, heirlooms, and such also fit the requirement for uniqueness. Most other personal property does not. Specific performance of personal service contracts is not granted because the courts would find it difficult or impracticable to supervise or monitor performance of the contract.

> *"Every unjust decision is a reproach to the law or the judge who administers it. If the law should be in danger of doing injustice, then equity should be called in to remedy it. Equity was introduced to mitigate the rigour of the law."*
> Lord Denning, M.R.
> *Re. Vandervelt's Trusts* (1974)

> **specific performance** A remedy that orders the breaching party to perform the acts promised in the contract; usually awarded in cases where the subject matter is unique, such as in contracts involving land, heirlooms, paintings, and the like.

BUSINESS APPLICATION

Hard Dealing for the Hard Rock Cafe

In the 1970s, Peter Morton operated a popular restaurant and tourist attraction in England known as the "Hard Rock Cafe." At that time, Milton Okun of the United States inquired about investing in the business. Morton declined Okun's offer but indicated that if he contemplated expanding the business to the United States, he would contact Okun. In December 1981, Morton located a site suitable for a Hard Rock Cafe in Los Angeles, California. Morton contacted Okun and offered him stock in the general partnership. An agreement was

continued

executed on March 2, 1982, whereby Okun contributed $100,000 in exchange for a 20 percent interest in the general partnership. Paragraph 9 of the agreement gave Okun the option to participate in future Hard Rock Cafes with the same 20 percent interest.

After raising funds from limited partners, the Hard Rock Cafe opened in the Beverly Center in Los Angeles and was a commercial success. As a result, Morton decided to exploit the San Francisco market. Per their agreement, Morton offered Okun a 20 percent interest, which Okun accepted.

In 1984, while Morton was finalizing plans for operating a Hard Rock Cafe in Chicago, Illinois, Morton and Okun had a disagreement. Morton advised Okun that he planned to exclude Okun from participating in the venture. Okun offered to participate on the terms of their 1982 agreement. Morton rejected that offer and proceeded with the development of restaurants in Houston, Honolulu, and Chicago without offering Okun a general partnership interest in these ventures. Okun sued Morton for breach of contract, seeking an order of specific performance of their 1982 agreement. The trial court held in favor

of Okun and ordered specific performance of the contract. Morton appealed.

Can the 1982 agreement between Morton and Okun be specifically performed?

The court of appeals noted that as a whole, the terms of the agreement were sufficient to establish from the outset the ways in which future ventures were to be financed, owned, and operated by the parties. The fundamental structure of all such undertakings was to be based on the 20/80 ratio established for the creation of the Los Angeles Hard Rock Cafe. The court stated that although the agreement admittedly does not deal in specifics, neither law nor equity requires that every term and condition be set forth in the contract. In light of the fact that neither defendant nor plaintiff could predict with any degree of certainty the success of the Los Angeles operation, it is not surprising that Paragraph 9 was drafted broadly enough to accommodate changing circumstances and unforeseen developments.

Defendant asserts, however, that specific performance should not have been granted because enforcement of the contract will require continuous and pro-

tracted judicial supervision. The courts of this state have generally followed this "archaic" rule. This case merely involves the offering of an opportunity to participate in a business venture and the concomitant payment of capital and expenses for that participation.

The court stated, "We are not here concerned with the day-to-day management of any particular Hard Rock Cafe or related enterprises that would require the close and ongoing cooperation of the parties or the court." The defendant retains the discretion under the terms of the judgment to structure each venture as he pleases so long as he maintains the 20/80 ratio and does nothing to interfere with or burden plaintiff's right to participate in the deal. Under these circumstances, the court concluded that the decree of specific performance is not unduly burdensome, nor does it require inordinate supervision by the trial court.

The appellate court held that the subject matter of the agreement between Morton and Okun was unique and therefore that the agreement can be specifically enforced. [*Okun v. Morton*, 203 Cal.App.3d, 250 Cal.Rptr. 220 (Cal.App. 1988)]

Reformation

reformation An equitable doctrine that permits the court to rewrite a contract to express the parties' true intentions.

can be done after the fact.

Reformation is an equitable doctrine that permits the court to rewrite a contract to express the parties' true intentions. For example, suppose that a clerical error is made during the typing of the contract and both parties sign the contract without discovering the error. If a dispute later arises, the court can reform the contract to correct the clerical error to read what the parties originally intended.

Quasi-Contract

quasi-contract An equitable doctrine that permits the recovery of compensation even though no enforceable contract exists between the parties.

A **quasi-contract** (also called **quantum meruit** or an **implied-in-law contract**) is an equitable doctrine that permits the recovery of compensation even though no enforceable contract exists between the parties because of lack of consideration, the Statute of Frauds has run out, or the like. Such contracts are imposed by law to prevent unjust enrichment. Under quasi-contract, a party can recover the reasonable value of the services or materials provided. For example, a physician who stops to render aid to an unconscious victim of an automobile accident may recover the reasonable value of his services from that person.

Injunction

An **injunction** is a court order that prohibits a person from doing a certain act. To obtain an injunction, the requesting party must show that he or she will suffer irreparable injury unless the injunction is issued.

injunction A court order that prohibits a person from doing a certain act.

CONSIDER THIS EXAMPLE: Suppose a professional football team enters into a five-year employment contract with a "superstar" quarterback. The quarterback breaches the contract and enters into a contract to play for a competing team. Here, the first team can seek an injunction to prevent the quarterback from playing for the other team.

BUSINESS APPLICATION

Pennzoil v. Texaco: An Expensive Handshake

There is substantial danger of being found liable for tortious conduct and being assessed punitive damages if one intentionally interferes with another's contract. Consider the celebrated case of *Texaco Inc. v. Pennzoil Company* [729 S.W.2d 768 (Tex.App. 1987)].

The saga began in 1983, when Pennzoil tried to buy up 20 percent of Getty Oil's outstanding stock for $100 per share. At that time, about 40 percent of Getty's outstanding stock was owned by the Sarah C. Getty Trust (Trust), 11.8 percent was owned by the J. Paul Getty Museum in Los Angeles (Museum), and the rest was held by other investors.

On January 1, 1984, the head of the Getty Trust met with representatives of Pennzoil. Pennzoil decided to make a play for total control of Getty Oil by offering investors a buy-out price of $110 per share. The Trust accepted a resolution approving Pennzoil's offer on January 3, 1984. Two days later, Getty, Pennzoil, the Trust, and the Museum, issued a joint press release announcing that the parties had "agreed in

principle" to a merger of Getty with Pennzoil. The parties shook hands and hoisted glasses of champagne to toast the deal. No writing had yet been signed by the parties, however.

Forty-eight hours later, the party was over. Texaco, Inc. (Texaco) had been tipped that Getty Oil was for sale. Representatives of Texaco met secretly with some trustees of the Trust and officials from the Museum about how Texaco could structure a takeover of Getty Oil. A written deal was reached whereby Texaco would purchase shares held by the Museum and the Trust for $125 per share and thereby acquire more than 50 percent of Getty's outstanding shares in a $10 billion deal. Texaco completed its takeover of Getty.

Not surprisingly, Pennzoil was not pleased with Texaco's maneuver. On February 8, 1985, Pennzoil filed suit in Texas alleging that Texaco had tortiously interfered with its agreement with Getty. Pennzoil argued that its handshake deal with Getty was a contract. It cited a Texas oil in-

dustry custom according to which handshakes were gentlemen's agreements that were to be honored. Texaco asserted that the argument would not get Pennzoil to first base because the contract had to be formalized in writing to be enforceable.

Before the trial even began, Texaco accused Pennzoil's lawyer of impropriety for having given a $10,000 campaign contribution to the state court judge who was presiding in the case. Another Texas judge found no reason for the trial court judge to withdraw.

After a hard-fought trial, the jury held that the handshake between the Getty and Pennzoil people did count as a contract and that a definitive written agreement was unnecessary to seal the deal. After finding that such an agreement had indeed been reached, the jury moved on to the question of whether the tactics Texaco used to reach its takeover agreement were tortious. The jury found that Texaco had intentionally interfered with Pennzoil's agreement with Getty.

continued

With the issue of liability resolved, the jury awarded a mind-boggling amount of money: $7.53 billion in actual damages. The jury heaped another $3 billion in punitive damages onto Pennzoil's award. This was the largest judgment in history. Texaco's appeals succeeded in getting the punitive damages reduced to $1 billion. Ultimately, to avoid the judgment, Texaco declared bankruptcy. Texaco emerged from bankruptcy one year later after the parties agreed to settle the entire matter for $3 billion. It is estimated that Pennzoil's lawyer, who had taken the case on contingency, earned a fee of approximately $600 million.

TORTS ASSOCIATED WITH CONTRACTS

"He that's cheated twice by the same man, is an accomplice with the cheater."
    Thomas Fuller
    Gnomologia
    (1732)

The recovery for breach of contract is usually limited to contract damages. However, a party who can prove a contract-related **tort** may also recover *tort damages*. Tort damages include compensation for personal injury, pain and suffering, emotional distress, and possibly punitive damages. The major torts associated with contracts are (1) intentional interference with contractual relations and (2) breach of the implied covenant of good faith and fair dealing.

Intentional Interference with Contractual Relations

intentional interference with contractual relations
A tort that arises when a third party induces a contracting party to breach the contract with another party.

A party to a contract may sue any third person who intentionally interferes with the contract and causes that party injury. The third party does not have to have acted with malice or bad faith. This tort, which is known as the tort of **intentional interference with contractual relations**, usually arises when a third party induces a contracting party to breach the contract with another party. The following elements must be shown:

1. A valid, enforceable contract between the contracting parties
2. Third-party knowledge of this contract
3. Third-party inducement to breach the contract.

A third party can contract with the breaching party without becoming liable for this tort if a contracting party has already breached the contract. This is because the third party cannot be held to have induced a preexisting breach.

Breach of the Implied Covenant of Good Faith and Fair Dealing

covenant of good faith and fair dealing   Under this implied covenant, the parties to a contract not only are held to the express terms of the contract but also are required to act in "good faith" and deal fairly in all respects in obtaining the objective of the contract.

Several states have held that a **covenant of good faith and fair dealing** is implied in certain types of contracts. Under this covenant, the parties to a contract not only are held to the express terms of the contract but also are required to act in "good faith" and deal fairly in all respects in obtaining the objective of the contract. A breach of this implied covenant is a tort for which tort damages are recoverable. This tort, which is sometimes referred to as the **tort of "bad faith,"** is an evolving area of the law. *equitable req't*

Punitive Damages

punitive damages
Damages that are awarded to punish the defendant, to deter the defendant from similar conduct in the future, and to set an example for others.

Generally, **punitive damages** are not recoverable for breach of contract. They are recoverable, however, for certain *tortious* conduct that may be associated with the nonperformance of a contract. This includes fraud, intentional conduct, or other egregious conduct. Punitive damages are in addition to actual damages and may be kept by the plaintiff. Punitive damages are awarded to punish the defendant, to deter the defendant from similar conduct in the future, and to set an example for others.

The court found a bad faith tort in the following case and awarded punitive demages.

CASE 12.5

Gourley v. State Farm Mutual Automobile Insurance Co.

227 Cal.App.3d 1099, 265 Cal.Rptr. 634 (1990) California Court of Appeals

Facts In late 1981, Julie Gourley was a passenger in an automobile that was struck by an out-of-control vehicle driven by an uninsured drunk driver. Gourley, who was not wearing a seat belt at the time of the accident, suffered a fractured right shoulder when she struck some portion of her vehicle's interior. Gourley made a claim under the uninsured motorist coverage in her automobile policy with State Farm Mutual Automobile Insurance Company (State Farm). Medical evidence showed that Gourley had some permanent disability and a limited range of motion, suffered residual pain, and might require surgery in the future. She demanded the policy limit of $100,000. In September 1982, State Farm's attorney, Barry Allen, advised Gourley that State Farm would contest the proximate cause of the injuries based upon Gourley's failure to wear her seat belt. Evidence showed that under California law the seat belt issue was not a defense. State Farm offered a settlement of $20,000. Gourley refused it. When Gourley reduced her demand to $60,000, State Farm responded with a counteroffer of $25,000. Because the parties could not reach a settlement, the case went to arbitration. In October 1984, the arbitrator awarded Gourley $88,137, which State Farm promptly paid. Gourley sued State Farm for breach of the implied covenant of good faith and fair dealing in handling the claim, and sought actual damages for emotional distress and punitive damages. The jury awarded her $15,765 in actual damages and $1,576,000 in punitive damages.

State Farm appealed.

Issue Did State Farm's conduct amount to a bad faith tort for which punitive damages could be awarded?

Decision Yes. The appellate court held that State Farm's actions in not settling the claim under the policy limits by asserting an illegal defense (failure of Gourley to wear a seat belt) constituted bad faith. Affirmed.

Reason There is an implied covenant in every insurance contract that the insurer will do nothing to impair the insured's right to receive the benefit of the contractual bargain. That is, the insurer is expected to promptly pay to the insured all sums due under the contract. A major motivation for the purchase of insurance is the peace of mind that claims will be paid promptly. Withholding benefits is unreasonable if it is without proper cause. In reaching its decision, the appellate court stated: "The jury could reasonably find 'intentional' bad faith. . . . State Farm . . . argues the evidence was insufficient as a matter of law to support the award of punitive damages. Not so. To support an award of punitive damages, the plaintiff must show 'oppression, fraud, or malice.' There was ample evidence to support an award of punitive damages."

CASE QUESTIONS

Critical Legal Thinking Should the law recognize the doctrine of bad faith tort? Why or why not?

Ethics Does an insurer act unethically whenever it refuses to settle a claim under the policy limits? Do you think State Farm acted unethically in this case?

Business Implication What effect will the recognition of bad faith torts associated with contracts have on businesses such as insurance companies? Explain.

BUSINESS CHECKLIST

Enforcement of Remedies: Attachment and Garnishment

If a nonbreaching party brings a successful lawsuit against a breaching party to a contract, the court will enter a *judgment* in his or her favor. This judgment must then be collected. If the breaching party refuses to pay the judgment, the court may do the following:

- *Issue a writ of attachment*—This writ orders the sheriff to seize property in the possession of the breaching party that he or she owns and to sell the property at auction to satisfy the judgment. In all states, certain property is exempt from attachment.
- *Issue a writ of garnishment*—This writ orders that wages, bank accounts, or other property of the breaching party that is in the hands of third parties be paid over to the nonbreaching party to satisfy the judgment. Federal and state laws limit the amount of the breaching party's wages or salary that can be garnished.

WORKING THE WEB

UNIDROIT Principles of International Commercial Contracts This site sets forth general United Nations rules for international commercial contracts.

Visit at http://www.unidroit.org/english/principles/pr-main.htms

Heiros Gamos The Comprehensive Legal Site—Heiros Gamos contains links to 12 directories, 200 practice areas, more than 300 discussion groups, current news (in audio if you have the right computer equipment), and many more research tools.

Visit at http://www.hg.org/

International Court of Arbitration The International Court of Arbitration promotes international trade, makes rules, and provides services to 63 countries and more than 7,000 companies.

Visit at http://www.iccwbo.org/

Canadian Contract Law Centre "This site contains a general summary of the common law and equity principles on contract law in Canada."

Visit at http://www.wwlia.org/ca-con1.htm

Professor Ray August's home page Professor August has written *International Business Law, 2d ed.* and *Public International Law*, both published by Prentice Hall. His home page contains a student guide to international business law and an international law dictionary as well as general reference materials and other useful links.

Visit at http://www.wsu.edu:8080/%7Eaugust/

CYBER EXERCISES:

1. From the UNIDROIT site, find a bibliography on the UNIDROIT Principles of International Commercial Contracts.
2. Using the Hieros Gamos site, can you find a treaty called the Convention on the Law Applicable to Contract Obligations?
3. Using the Hieros Gamos site, find the full text of NAFTA.
4. If your computer system is powerful enough and has sound capabilities, use the Heiros Gamos site to find audio of Preparing Your Clients to Commence Business Operations in the United States. Click on the audio icon to hear the tape.
5. Using the Canadian contract Law Centre site, print out information about contracts "under seal."

CHAPTER SUMMARY

PERFORMANCE AND BREACH, P. 254

Levels of Performance	1. *Complete performance.* A party renders performance exactly as required by the contract. That party's contractual duties are discharged. 2. *Substantial performance.* A party renders performance that deviates only slightly from complete performance. There is a *minor breach*. The nonbreaching party may recover damages caused by the breach. 3. *Inferior performance.* A party fails to perform express or implied contractual duties that impair or destroy the essence of the contract. There is a *material breach*. The nonbreaching party may either (1) rescind the contract and recover restitution or (2) affirm the contract and recover damages.
Anticipatory Breach	One contracting party informs the other party—by express words or by conduct—that he or she will not perform his or her contractual duties when due. Gives an immediate cause of action to the nonbreaching party to sue for breach of contract. Also called *anticipatory repudiation*.

MONETARY DAMAGES, P. 256

Monetary Damages	1. *Compensatory damages.* Damages that compensate a nonbreaching party for the loss of the contract. Restores the "benefit of the bargain" to the nonbreaching party as if the contract had been fully performed.
	2. *Consequential damages.* Foreseeable damages that arise from circumstances outside the contract and of which the breaching party either knew or had reason to know of. Also called *special damages*.
	3. *Nominal damages.* A small amount of damages awarded to a nonbreaching party who has suffered no financial loss because of the defendant's breach of contract. Usually awarded "on principle."
	4. *Liquidated damages.* Damages payable upon breach of contract that are agreed on in advance by the contracting parties. Liquidated damages substitute for actual damages. For a liquidated damage clause to be lawful, the following two conditions must be met:
	  a. The actual damages must be extremely difficult or impracticable to determine
	  b. The liquidated amount must be a reasonable estimate of the harm that would result from the breach.
	A liquidated damage clause is considered a *penalty* if actual damages are clearly determinable in advance or the liquidated damages are excessive or unconscionable. A penalty is unenforceable and the nonbreaching party may recover actual damages.

Mitigation of Damages	The duty the law places on a nonbreaching party to take reasonable efforts to avoid or reduce the resulting damages from a breach of contract. To mitigate a breach of an employment contract, the nonbreaching party must only accept "comparable" employment.

RESCISSION AND RESTITUTION, P. 261

	Rescission is an action by a nonbreaching party to undo the contract. Available upon the material breach of a contract. The parties must make *restitution* of the consideration they have received from the other party. *Rescission* and *restitution* restore the parties to the position they occupied prior to the contract.

EQUITABLE REMEDIES, P. 261

Equitable Remedies	*Equitable remedies* are available if the nonbreaching party cannot be adequately compensated by a legal remedy or to prevent unjust enrichment.

1. *Specific performance.* Court order that requires the breaching party to perform his or her contractual duties. Only available if the subject matter of the contract is *unique.*
2. *Reformation.* Permits the court to rewrite a contract to express the parties' true intention. Available to correct clerical and mathematical errors.
3. *Quasi-contract.* Permits the court to order recovery of compensation even though no enforceable contract exists between the parties. Used to prevent unjust enrichment. Also called an *implied-in-law contract* or *quantum meruit.*
4. *Injunction.* Court order that prohibits a person from doing a certain act. The requesting party must show that he or she will suffer irreparable injury if the injunction is not granted.

TORTS ASSOCIATED WITH CONTRACTS, P. 264

Types of Torts Associated with Contracts	1. *Intentional interference with contractual relations.* A third party intentionally interferes with another party's contract and induces the other party to that contract to breach it, causing the nonbreaching party injury.
	2. *Breach of the implied covenant of good faith and fair dealing.* A party to a contract does not act in good faith or fails to deal fairly in achieving the object of the contract. This duty is only implied in certain contracts (e.g., insurance contracts). Also called the *tort of bad faith.*
Tort Damages	1. *Actual damages.* Includes compensation for personal injury, pain and suffering, emotional distress, and other injuries caused by the defendant's tortious conduct.
	2. *Punitive damages.* Recoverable against a defendant for intentional or egregious conduct. Awarded to punish the defendant, to deter the defendant from similar conduct in the future, and to set an example for others. The plaintiff may keep these damages.

CRITICAL LEGAL THINKING CASES

12.1 Performance Louis Haeuser, who owned several small warehouses, contracted with Wallace C. Drennen, Inc. (Drennen), to construct a road to the warehouses. The contract price was $42,324. After Drennen completed the work, some cracks appeared in the road, causing improper drainage. In addition, "bird baths" appeared in the road, which accumulated water. When Haeuser refused to pay, Drennen sued to recover the full contract price. Haeuser filed a cross complaint to recover the cost of repairing the road. Who wins? [*Wallace C. Drennen, Inc. v. Haeuser*, 402 So.2d 771 (La. App. 1979)]

12.2 Anticipatory Repudiation In September 1976, Muhammad Ali (Ali) successfully defended his heavyweight boxing championship of the world by defeating Ken Norton. Shortly after the fight, Ali held a press conference and, as he had done on several occasions before, announced his retirement from boxing. At that time Ali had beaten every challenger except Duane Bobick, whom he had not yet fought. In November 1976, Madison Square Garden Boxing, Inc. (MSGB), a fight promoter, offered Ali $2.5 million if he would fight Bobick. Ali agreed, stating, "We are back in business again." MSGB and Ali signed a Fighters' Agreement and MSGB paid Ali $125,000 advance payment. The fight was to take place in Madison Square Garden on a date in February 1977. On November 30, 1976, Ali told MSGB that he was retiring from boxing and would not fight Bobick in February. Must MSGB wait until the date performance is due to sue Ali for breach of contract? [*Madison Square Garden Boxing, Inc. v. Muhammad Ali*, 430 F.Supp. 679 (N.D.Ill. 1977)]

12.3 Damages In 1978, Hawaiian Telephone Company (Hawaiian Telephone) entered into a contract with Microform Data Systems Inc. (Microform) for Microform to provide a computerized assistance system that would handle 15,000 calls per hour with a one-second response time and with a "nonstop" feature to allow automatic recovery from any component failure. The contract called for installation of the host computer no later than mid-February 1979. Microform was not able to meet the initial installation date, and at that time it was determined that Microform was at least nine months away from providing a system that met contract specifications. Hawaiian Telephone canceled the contract and sued Microform for damages. Did Microform materially breach the contract to allow recovery of damages? [*Hawaiian Telephone Co. v. Microform Data Systems, Inc.*, 829 F.2d 919 (9th Cir. 1987)]

12.4 Damages Raquel Welch was a movie actress who appeared in about 30 films between 1965 and 1980. She was considered a sex symbol, and her only serious dramatic role was a roller derby queen in *Kansas City Bomber*. In 1980, Michael Phillips and David Ward developed a film package based on the John Steinbeck novella, *Cannery Row*. In early 1981, Metro-Goldwyn-Mayer Film Co. (MGM) accepted to produce the project and entered into a contract with Welch to play the leading female character, a prostitute named Suzy. At 40 years old, Welch relished the chance to direct her career toward more serious roles. Welch was to receive $250,000 from MGM, with payment being divided into weekly increments during filming. Filming began on December 1, 1980. On December 22, 1980, MGM fired Welch and replaced her with another actress, Debra Winger. Welch sued MGM to recover the balance of $194,444 that remained unpaid under the contract. Who wins? [*Welch v. Metro-Goldwyn-Mayer Film Co.*, 207 Cal.App.3d 164, 254 Cal.Rptr. 645 (Cal. App. 1989)]

12.5 Damages On August 28, 1979, Ptarmigan Investment Company (Ptarmigan), a partnership, entered into a contract with Gundersons, Inc. (Gundersons), a South Dakota corporation in the business of golf course construction. The contract provided that Gundersons would construct a golf course for Ptarmigan for a contract price of $1,294,129. Gundersons immediately started work and completed about one-third of the work by late November 1979, when bad weather forced cessation of most work. Ptarmigan paid Gundersons for the work to that date. In the spring of 1980, Ptarmigan ran out of funds and was unable to pay for the completion of the golf course. Gundersons sued Ptarmigan and its individual partners to recover the lost profits that it would have made on the remaining two-thirds of the contract. Can Gundersons recover these lost profits as damages? [*Gundersons, Inc. v. Ptarmigan Investment Company*, 678 P.2d 1061 (Colo. App. 1983)]

12.6 Liquidated Damages In December 1974, H. S. Perlin Company, Inc. (Perlin), and Morse Signal Devices of San Diego (Morse) entered into a contract whereby Morse agreed to provide burglar and fire alarm service to Perlin's coin and stamp store. Perlin paid $50 per month for this service. The contract contained a liquidated damage clause limiting Morse's liability to $250 for any losses incurred by Perlin based on Morse's failure of service. During the evening of August 25, 1980, a burglary occurred at Perlin's store. Before entering the store, the burglars cut a telephone line that ran from the burglar system

in Perlin's store to Morse's central location. When the line was cut, a signal indicated the interruption of service at Morse's central station. Inexplicably, Morse took no further steps to investigate the interruption of service at Perlin's store. The burglars stole stamps and coins with a wholesale value of $958,000, and Perlin did not have insurance against this loss. Perlin sued Morse to recover damages. Is the liquidated damage clause enforceable? [*H. S. Perlin Company, Inc. v. Morse Signal Devices of San Diego*, 209 Cal.App.3d 1289, 258 Cal.Rptr. 1 (Cal. App. 1989)]

12.7 Liquidated Damages United Mechanical Contractors, Inc. (UMC), an employer, agreed to provide a pension plan for its unionized workers. UMC was to make monthly payments into a pension fund administered by the Idaho Plumbers and Pipefitters Health and Welfare Fund (Fund). Payments were due by the 15th of the month. The contract between UMC and the Fund contained a liquidated damage clause that provided if payments due from UMC were received later than the 20th of the month, liquidated damages of 20 percent of the required contribution would be assessed against UMC. In June 1985, the fund received UMC's payment on the 24th. The Fund sued UMC to recover $9,245.23 in liquidated damages. Is the liquidated damage clause enforceable? [*Idaho Plumbers and Pipefitters Health and Welfare Fund v. United Mechanical Contractors, Inc.*, 875 F.2d 212 (9th Cir. 1989)]

12.8 Nominal Damages In order to boost his career as an actor, John Ericson agreed with Playgirl, Inc. (Playgirl), that it could publish a picture of him posing naked at Lion Country Safari as the centerfold of the January 1974 issue of *Playgirl* magazine without compensation. The magazine was published with Ericson as the centerfold, but no immediate career boost to Ericson resulted from the publication. In April 1974, Playgirl wished to use Ericson's photograph in its annual edition titled *Best of Playgirl*. Playgirl and Ericson entered into a contract whereby Ericson's picture was to occupy a quarter of the front cover of the annual edition. Due to an editorial mixup, Ericson's picture did not appear on the cover of the *Best of Playgirl*. Ericson sued Playgirl, seeking damages for breach of contract. How much damages should Ericson recover for Playgirl's breach of contract? [*Ericson v. Playgirl, Inc.*, 73 Cal.App.3d 850, 140 Cal.Rptr. 921 (Cal. App. 1977)]

12.9 Specific Performance Liz Claiborne, Inc. (Claiborne) is a large maker of women's better sportswear in the United States and a well-known name in fashion, with sales of more than $1 billion a year. Claiborne distributes its products through 9,000 retail outlets in the United States. Avon Products, Inc. (Avon) is a major producer of fragrances, toiletries, and cosmetics, with annual sales of more than $3 billion a year. Claiborne, who desired to promote its well-known name on perfumes and cosmetics, entered into a joint venture with Avon whereby Claiborne would make available its names, trademarks, and marketing experience and Avon would engage in the procurement and manufacture of the fragrances, toiletries, and cosmetics. The parties would equally share the financial requirements of the joint venture. In 1986, its first year of operation, the joint venture had sales of more than $16 million. In the second year, sales increased to $26 million, making it one of the fastest-growing fragrance and cosmetic lines in the country. In 1987, Avon sought to "uncouple" the joint venture. Avon thereafter refused to procure and manufacture the line of fragrances and cosmetics for the joint venture. When Claiborne could not obtain the necessary fragrances and cosmetics from any other source for the fall/Christmas season, Claiborne sued Avon for breach of contract, seeking specific performance of the contract by Avon. Is specific performance an appropriate remedy in this case? [*Liz Claiborne, Inc. v. Avon Products, Inc.*, 530 N.Y.S.2d 425, 141 A.D.2d 329 (N.Y. Sup. App. 1988)]

12.10 Quasi-Contract Wood Dimension, Inc. (Wood) manufactured stereo speakers for resale to other companies. Fisher Corporation (Fisher), a major customer, accounted for 30–50 percent of Wood's business. In early 1982, Fisher stopped buying from Wood. In order to regain Fisher's business, the president of Wood solicited the help of L. Dale Watson, who had known the vice president of Fisher for many years. Wood agreed to pay Watson 5 percent of all Fisher's orders if he succeeded in persuading Fisher to buy at Wood again. They shook hands to seal the agreement. Due to Watson's efforts, Fisher again became a customer of Wood's. In May 1984, Wood terminated Watson's position. Between that time and July 1985, Fisher placed orders of almost $10 million with Wood. Although the oral contract between Wood and Watson was terminable at will, Watson sued Wood to recover commissions on Fisher's orders that were placed after he was discharged. Can Watson recover these damages under the theory of quasi-contract? [*Watson v. Wood Dimension, Inc.*, 209 Cal.App.3d 1359, 257 Cal.Rptr. 816 (Cal. App. 1989)]

12.11 Injunction In 1982, Anita Baker, a then-unknown singer, signed a multiyear recording contract with Beverly Glen Music, Inc. (Beverly Glen). Baker recorded a record album for Beverly Glen that was moderately successful. After having some difficulties with Beverly Glen, Baker was offered a considerably more lucrative contract by Warner Communications, Inc. (Warner). Baker accepted the Warner offer and informed Beverly Glen that she would not complete her contract because she had entered into an agreement with Warner. Beverly Glen sued Baker and Warner and sought an injunction to prevent Baker from performing as a singer for Warner. Is an injunction an appropriate remedy in this case? [*Beverly Glen Music, Inc. v. Warner Communications, Inc.*, 178 Cal.App.3d 1142, 224 Cal.Rptr. 260 (Cal. App. 1986)]

12.12 Intentional Interference with Contractual Relations In 1963, Pacific Gas and Electric Company (PG & E) entered into a contract with Placer County Water Agency (Agency) to purchase hydroelectric power generated by the Agency's Middle Fork American River Project. The contract was not terminable until 2013. As energy prices rose during the 1970s, the contract became extremely valuable to PG & E. The price PG & E paid for energy under the contract was much lower than the cost of energy from other sources. In 1982, Bear Stearns & Company (Bear Stearns), an investment bank and securities underwriting firm, learned of Agency's power contract with PG & E. Bear Stearns offered to assist the Agency in an effort to terminate the power contract with PG & E in exchange for a share of the Agency's subsequent profits and the right to underwrite any new securities issued by the Agency. Bear Stearns also agreed to pay the legal fees incurred by the Agency in litigation concerning their attempt to get out of the PG & E contract. Under what legal theory can PG & E sue Bear Stearns? [*Pacific Gas and Electric Company v. Bear Stearns & Company*, 50 Cal.3d 1118, 270 Cal.Rptr. 1 (Cal. App. 1990)]

ETHICS CASES

12.13 Ethical Perspective Walgreen Company (Walgreen) has operated a pharmacy in the Southgate Mall in Milwaukee since 1951, when the mall opened. Its current lease, signed in 1971 and carrying a 30-year term, contains an exclusivity clause in which the landlord, Sara Creek Property Company (Sara Creek), promises not to lease space in the mall to anyone else who wants to operate a pharmacy or a store containing a pharmacy. In 1990, after its anchor tenant went broke, Sara Creek informed Walgreen that it intended to lease the anchor tenant space to Phar-Mor Corporation (Phar-Mor). Phar-Mor, a "deep discount" chain, would occupy 100,000 square feet, of which 12,000 square feet would be occupied by a pharmacy the same size as Walgreen's. The entrances to the two stores would be within a few hundred feet of each other. Walgreen sued Sara Creek for breach of contract and sought a permanent injunction against Sara Creek's leasing the anchor premises to Phar-Mor. Do the facts of this case justify the issuance of a permanent injunction? Did Sara Creek act ethically in not living up to the contract? [*Walgreen Co. v. Sara Creek Property Co.*, 966 F.2d 273 (7th Cir. 1992)]

12.14 Ethical Perspective Rosina Crisci owned an apartment building in which Mrs. DiMare was a tenant. One day while DiMare was descending a wooden staircase on the outside of the apartment building, she fell through the staircase and was left hanging 15 feet above the ground until she was saved. Crisci had a $10,000 liability insurance policy on the building from the Security Insurance Company of New Haven, Connecticut (Security). DiMare sued Crisci and Security for $400,000 for physical injuries and psychosis suffered from the fall. Prior to trial, Mrs. DiMare agreed to take $10,000 in settlement of the case. Security refused this settlement offer. Mrs. DiMare reduced her settlement offer to $9,000, of which Crisci offered to pay $2,500. Security again refused to settle the case. The case proceeded to trial and the jury awarded DiMare and her husband $110,000. Security paid $10,000 pursuant to the insurance contract, and Crisci had to pay the difference. Crisci, a widow of 70 years of age, had to sell her assets, became dependent on her relatives, declined in physical health, and suffered from hysteria and suicide attempts. Crisci sued Security for tort damages for breach of the implied covenant of good faith and fair dealing. Did Security act in bad faith? [*Crisci v. Security Insurance Company of New Haven, Connecticut*, 426 P.2d 173, 66 Cal.App.2d 425, 58 Cal.Rptr. 13 (Cal. App. 1967)]

CRITICAL LEGAL THINKING WRITING ASSIGNMENT

Read case A.12 in the Case Appendix [*E. B. Harvey & Company, Inc. v. Protective Systems, Inc.*]. This case is excerpted from the appellate court opinion. Review and brief the case. In your brief, be sure to answer the following questions:

1. What were Protective System's duties under the contract?

2. What amount of damages was Protective Systems liable for under the express terms of the contract?
3. Was Protective Systems negligent in this case?
4. What policy considerations did the court cite in upholding the liquidated damage clause?

NOTES

[1] Restatement (Second) of Contracts, § 235(2).
[2] Restatement (Second) of Contracts, § 241.
[3] Restatement (Second) of Contracts, § 253; UCC § 2-610.
[4] UCC §§ 2-708 and 2-713.

[5] Restatement (Second) of Contracts, § 356(1).
[6] Restatement (Second) of Contracts, § 370.
[7] Restatement (Second) of Contracts, § 359.

CHAPTER 13

FORMATION OF SALES

AND LEASE CONTRACTS

Chapter Objectives

*After studying this chapter,
you should be able to*

1. Define sales contracts governed by Article 2 of the UCC
2. Define lease contracts governed by Article 2A of the UCC
3. Describe the formation of sales and lease contracts
4. Describe the UCC's firm offer rule and written confirmation rule
5. Describe the UCC's additional terms rule and apply it to solve the "battles of the forms"
6. Identify when title passes in sales contracts
7. Describe who bears the risk of loss when goods are lost, damaged, or destroyed
8. Identify who bears the risk of loss when goods are sold by nonowners such as thieves
9. Apply Article 6 of the UCC to bulk sales
10. Define letters of credit and describe how Article 5 of the UCC applies to them

Chapter Contents

Commercial law lies within a narrow compass, and is far purer and freer from defects than any other part of the system.

Henry Peter Brougham
House of Commons, February 7, 1828

Most tangible items—books, clothing, cars, and such—are considered **goods**. In medieval times, merchants gathered at fairs in Europe to exchange such goods. Over time, certain customs and rules evolved for enforcing contracts and resolving disputes. These customs and rules, which were referred to as the "Law Merchant," were enforced by "fair courts" established by the merchants. Eventually, the customs and rules of the Law Merchant were absorbed into the common law.

goods Tangible things that are movable at the time of their identification to the contract.

Toward the end of the 1800s, England enacted a statute (the Sales of Goods Act) that codified the common law rules of commercial transactions. In the United States, laws governing the sale of goods also developed. In 1906, the **Uniform Sales Act** was promulgated in the United States. This act was enacted in many states. It was quickly outdated, however, as mass production and distribution of goods developed in the 20th century.

In 1952, the Commissioners on Uniform State Laws promulgated a comprehensive statutory scheme called the **Uniform Commercial Code (the UCC)**. The UCC covers most aspects of commercial transactions.

Uniform Commercial Code Comprehensive statutory scheme that includes laws that cover most aspects of commercial transactions.

Article 2 (Sales) and Article 2A (Leases) of the UCC governs personal property leases. These articles are intended to provide clear, easy-to-apply rules that place the risk of loss of the goods on the party most able to either bear the risk or insure against it. The common law of contracts governs if either Article 2 or Article 2A is silent on an issue.

This chapter discusses sales and lease contracts. Other articles of the UCC are discussed in subsequent chapters.

SCOPE OF ARTICLE 2 (SALES)

All states except Louisiana have adopted some version of **Article 2 (Sales)** of the UCC. Article 2 is also applied by federal courts to sales contracts governed by federal law.

sale The passing of title from a seller to a buyer for a price.

What Is a Sale?

Article 2 applies to transactions in goods [UCC 2-102]. All states have held that Article 2 applies to the sale of goods. A "sale" consists of the passing of title from a seller to a buyer for a price [UCC 2-106(1)]. For example, the purchase of a book is a sale subject to Article 2. This is so whether the book was paid for by cash, check, credit card, or other form of consideration.

What Are "Goods"?

Goods are defined as tangible things that are movable at the time of their identification in the contract [UCC 2-105(1)]. Specially manufactured goods and the unborn young of animals are examples of goods. Certain items are not considered goods and are not subject to Article 2, including the following:

CAUTION
Article 2 applies only to transactions in goods. *Article 2 does not apply to transactions in items, real estate, or service.*

1. Money and intangible items, such as stocks, bonds, and patents, are not tangible goods.
2. Real estate is not a tangible good because it is not movable [UCC 2-105(1)]. Minerals, structures, growing crops, and other things that are severable from real estate may be classified as goods subject to Article 2, however. For example, the sale and removal of a chandelier in a house is a sale of goods subject to Article 2 because its

removal would not materially harm the realty. However, the sale and removal of the furnace would be a sale of real property because its removal would cause material harm [UCC 2-107(2)].

Goods Versus Services   Contracts for the provision of services—including legal services, medical services, dental services, and such—are not covered by Article 2. Sometimes, however, a sale involves both the provision of a service and a good in the same transaction. This is referred to as a **mixed sale**. Article 2 applies only to mixed sales if the goods are the predominant part of the transaction. The UCC provides no guidance for deciding cases based on mixed sales. Therefore, the courts decide these issues on a case-by-case basis.

mixed sale   A sale that involves the provision of a service and a good in the same transaction.

In the following case, the court had to decide whether a sale was of a good or a service.

CASE 13.1

Hector v. Cedars-Sinai Medical Center
180 Cal.App.3d 493, 225 Cal.Rptr. 595 (1986) California Court of Appeals

Facts   Frances Hector entered Cedars-Sinai Medical Center (Cedars-Sinai), Los Angeles, California, for a surgical operation on her heart. During the operation, a pacemaker was installed in Hector. The pacemaker, which was manufactured by American Technology, Inc., was installed at Cedars-Sinai by Hector's physician, Dr. Eugene Kompaniez. The pacemaker was defective, causing injury to Hector. Hector sued Cedars-Sinai under Article 2 of the UCC for breach of warranty. The trial court held that the sale was primarily a sale of a service and not of goods, and therefore the UCC did not apply. The court granted Cedars-Sinai's motion for summary judgment and dismissed Hector's lawsuit. Hector appealed.

Issue   Is the installation of a pacemaker by a hospital a sale of a good subject to Article 2 of the UCC?

Decision   No. The court of appeal held that Cedars-Sinai was a provider of medical services and not a seller of goods. Therefore, Cedars-Sinai was not liable for breach of warranty under the UCC because the UCC did not apply. Affirmed.

Reason   A hospital is not ordinarily engaged in the business of selling any of the products or equipment

it uses in providing such services. The essence of the relationship between a hospital and its patients does not relate essentially to any product or piece of equipment it uses but to the professional services it provides. Testimony indicated that Cedars-Sinai does not routinely stock pacemakers, nor is it in the business of selling, distributing, or testing pacemakers. The treatment provided by Cedars-Sinai in relation to implantation of pacemakers includes pre- and postoperative care, nursing care, a surgical operating room, and technicians. As a provider of services rather than a seller of a product, the hospital is not subject to liability for a defective product provided to the patient during the course of his or her treatment.

CASE QUESTIONS

Critical Legal Thinking   Should the UCC be extended to service providers?

Ethics   Was it ethical for the hospital to deny liability in this case?

Business Implication   Could American Technology, Inc. be held liable to the plaintiff in this case? Why do you think the plaintiff sued Cedars-Sinai in this case?

---

merchant   A person who (1) deals in the goods of the kind involved in the transaction, or (2) by his or her occupation holds him or herself out as having knowledge or skill peculiar to the goods involved in the transaction.

Who Is a Merchant?

Generally, Article 2 applies to all sales contracts, whether they involve merchants or not. However, Article 2 contains several provisions that either apply only to merchants or impose a greater duty on merchants. UCC 2-104(1) defines a **merchant** as (1) a person who deals in the goods of the kind involved in the transaction or (2) a person who by his or her occupation holds him or herself out as having knowledge or skill peculiar to the goods involved in the transaction. For example, a sporting goods dealer is a merchant with respect to sporting goods but is not if he sells his lawn mower to a neighbor. The courts disagree as to whether farmers are merchants within this definition.

SCOPE OF ARTICLE 2A (LEASES)

Personal property leases are a billion-dollar industry. Consumer rentals of automobiles or equipment and commercial leases of such items as aircraft and industrial machinery fall into this category. In the past, these transactions were governed by a combination of common law principles, real estate law, and reference to Article 2. Some of these legal rules and concepts do not quite fit a lease transaction.

Article 2A of the UCC was promulgated in 1987. This article, cited as the **Uniform Commercial Code—Leases**, directly addresses personal property leases [UCC 2A-101]. It establishes a comprehensive, uniform law covering the formation, performance, and default of leases in goods [UCC 2A-102, 2A-103(h)].

Article 2A is similar to Article 2. In fact, many Article 2 provisions were changed to reflect leasing terminology and practices and were carried over to Article 2A. Many states have adopted Article 2A, and many more are expected to do so in the future.

> **CAUTION**
> *Article 2A applies only to leases involving goods. Article 2A does not apply to real estate or other leases.*
>
> **Article 2A (leases)** Article of the UCC that governs lease of goods.

Definition of a Lease

A **lease** is a transfer of the right to the possession and use of the named goods for a set term in return for certain consideration [UCC 2A-103(1)(i)(x)]. The leased goods can be anything from a hand tool leased to an individual for a few hours to a complex line of industrial equipment leased to a multinational corporation for a number of years.

In an ordinary lease, the **lessor** is the person who transfers the right of possession and use of goods under the lease [UCC 2A-103(1)(p)]. The **lessee** is the person who acquires the right to possession and use of goods under a lease [UCC 2A-103(1)(n)].

> **lease** A transfer of the right to the possession and use of the named goods for a set term in return for certain consideration.
>
> **lessor** The person who transfers the right of possession and use of goods under the lease.
>
> **lessee** The person who acquires the right to possession and use of goods under a lease.

Special Forms of Leases

Certain provisions of Article 2A apply only to special forms of leases, such as consumer leases and finance leases. A **consumer lease** is one with a value of $25,000 or less between a lessor regularly engaged in the business of leasing or selling and a lessee who leases the goods primarily for a personal, family, or household purpose [UCC 2A-103(1)(e)].

A **finance lease** is a three-party transaction consisting of the lessor, the lessee, and the **supplier** (or vendor). The lessor does not select, manufacture, or supply the goods. Instead, the lessor acquires title to the goods or the right to their possession and use in connection with the terms of the lease [UCC 2A-103(1)(g)].

CONSIDER THIS EXAMPLE: The Dow Chemical Company decides to use robotics to manufacture most of its products. It persuades Ingersoll-Rand to design the robotic equipment that would meet its needs. To finance the purchase of the equipment, Dow Chemical goes to City Bank, which purchases the robotics equipment from Ingersoll-Rand and leases it to Dow Chemical. City Bank is the lessor, Dow Chemical is the lessee, and Ingersoll-Rand is the supplier.

> **consumer lease** A lease with a value of $25,000 or less between a lessor regularly engaged in the business of leasing or selling and a lessee who leases the goods primarily for a personal, family, or household purpose.
>
> **finance lease** A three-party transaction consisting of the lessor, the lessee, and the supplier.

CONTEMPORARY BUSINESS ENVIRONMENT

The Uniform Commercial Code (UCC)

One of the major frustrations of business persons conducting interstate business is that they are subject to the laws of each of the states in which they operate. To address this problem, in 1949 the National Conference of Commissioners on Uniform State Laws promulgated the **Uniform Commercial Code (UCC)**. The UCC is a **model act** that contains uniform rules that

continued

govern commercial transactions. In order to create this uniformity, individual states needed to enact the UCC as their commercial law statute. This is, in fact, what occurred, as every state (except Louisiana, which has adopted only parts of the UCC) enacted the UCC as a commercial statute.

The UCC is divided into Articles, with each article establishing uniform rules for a particular facet of commerce in this country. The articles of the UCC are as follows:

Article 1   General provisions
Article 2   Sales

Article 2A	Leases
Revised Article 3	Negotiable instruments
Article 4	Bank deposits and collections
Article 4A	Wire transfers
Article 5	Letters of credit
Article 6	Bulk transfers
Article 7	Documents of title
Article 8	Investment securities
Article 9	Secured transactions

Each of these articles is discussed in the chapters in this section of this book.

The UCC is continually being revised to reflect changes in modern commercial practices and technology. For example, Article 2A was drafted to govern leases of personal property, and Article 4A was added to regulate the use of wire transfers in the banking system. Articles 3 and 4, which cover the creation and transfer of negotiable instruments and the clearing of checks through the banking system, were substantially amended in 1990. Article 2, which covers the sale of goods, currently is in the initial stages of revision.

FORMATION OF SALES AND LEASE CONTRACTS

Like general contracts, the formation of sales and lease contracts requires an offer, an acceptance, consideration, and so on. The UCC-established rules for each of these elements often differ considerably from common law. Any rules established by Articles 2 and 2A take precedent over the common law of contracts.

Offer

CAUTION
Note that Article 2 and Article 2A of the UCC apply only to transactions involving goods. Contracts for real estate, services, or intangibles are subject to the common law of contracts.

A contract for the sale or lease of goods may be made in any manner sufficient to show agreement, including conduct by both parties that recognizes the existence of a contract [UCC 2-204(1), 2A-204(1)]. Under the UCC, an agreement sufficient to constitute a contract for the sale or lease of goods may be found even though the moment of its making is undetermined [UCC 2-204(2), 2A-204(2)].

Open Terms   Sometimes the parties to a sales or lease contract leave open a major term in the contract. The UCC is tolerant of open terms. According to UCC 2-204(3) and 2A-204(3), the contract does not fail for indefiniteness if (1) the parties intended to make a contract and (2) there is a reasonably certain basis for giving an appropriate remedy. In effect, certain **open terms** are permitted to be "read into" a sales or lease contract. These are commonly referred to as **gap-filling rules**.

gap-filling rule   A rule that says an open term can be "read into" a contract.

Some examples of terms that are commonly left open follow.

Open Price Term   If a sales contract does not contain a specific price **(open price term)**, a "reasonable price" is implied at the time of delivery. The contract may provide that a price is to be fixed by a market rate (e.g., a commodities market), as set or recorded by a third person or agency (e.g., a government agency), or by another standard either upon delivery or on a set date. If the agreed-upon standard is unavailable when the price is to be set, a reasonable price is implied at the time of delivery of the goods [UCC 2-305(1)].

A seller or buyer who reserves the right to fix a price must do so in good faith [UCC 2-305(2)]. When one of the parties fails to fix an open price term, the other party may opt either (1) to treat the contract as canceled or (2) to fix a reasonable price for the goods [UCC 2-305(3)].

Open Payment Term If the parties to a sales contract do not agree on payment terms, payment is due at the time and place at which the buyer is to receive the goods. If delivery is authorized and made by way of document of title, payment is due at the time and place at which the buyer is to receive the document of title, regardless of where the goods are to be received [UCC 2-310].

Open Delivery Term If the parties to a sales contract do not agree to the time, place, and manner of delivery of the goods, the place for delivery is the seller's place of business. If the seller does not have a place of business, delivery is to be made at the seller's residence. If identified goods are located at some other place and both parties know of this fact at the time of contracting, that place is the place of delivery [UCC 2-308].

Where goods are to be shipped, but the shipper is not named, the seller is obligated to make the shipping arrangements. Such arrangements must be made in good faith and within limits of commercial reasonableness [UCC 2-311(2)].

Open Time Term If the parties to the contract do not set a specific time of performance for any obligation under the contract, the contract must be performed within a reasonable time. If the sales contract provides for successive performances over an unspecified period of time, the contract is valid for a reasonable time [UCC 2-309].

Open Assortment Term If the assortment of goods to a sales contract is left open, the buyer is given the option of choosing those goods. For example, suppose Macy's contracts to purchase 1,000 dresses from Liz Claiborne, Inc. The contract is silent as to the assortment of colors of the dresses. The buyer may pick the assortment of colors for the dresses from the seller's stock. The buyer must make the selection in good faith and within limits set by commercial reasonableness [UCC 2-311(2)].

BUSINESS BRIEF
In recent years, the leasing of goods has increased dramatically in this country. Lease transactions include consumer leases of automobiles, as well as business leasing of equipment such as copying machines, computers, tractors, and the like. In 1987, Article 2A was added to the UCC to address personal property leases. Article 2A establishes uniform rules for the formation and enforcement of personal property leases.

✔ BUSINESS CHECKLIST

UCC Firm Offer Rule Changes the Common Law of Contracts

Recall that the common law of contracts allows the offeror to revoke the offer anytime prior to its acceptance. The only exception allowed by the common law is an *option contract* (i.e., where the offeree paid the offeror consideration to keep the offer open).

The UCC recognizes another exception, which is called the **firm offer rule**. This rule states that a merchant who (1) offers to buy, sell, or lease goods and (2) gives a written and signed assurance on a separate form that the offer will be held open cannot revoke the offer for the time stated or, if no time is stated, for a reasonable time. The maximum amount of time permitted under this rule is three months [UCC 2-205, 2A-205].

CONSIDER THIS EXAMPLE: On June 1, a merchant–seller offers to sell a Mercedes-Benz to a buyer for $50,000. She signs a written assurance to keep that offer open until August 30. On July 1, the merchant–seller sells the car to another buyer. On August 21, the original offeree tenders $50,000 for the car. The merchant–seller is liable to the original offeree for breach of contract.

Acceptance

Both the common law and the UCC provide that a contract is created when the offeree (i.e., the buyer or lessee) sends an acceptance to the offeror—not when the offeror receives the acceptance. For example, a contract is made when the acceptance letter is delivered to the post office. The contract remains valid even if the post office loses the letter.

Unless otherwise unambiguously indicated by language or circumstance, an offer to make a sales or lease contract may be accepted in any manner and by any reasonable medium of acceptance [UCC 2-206(1)(a), 2A-206(1)]. Applications of this rule are discussed in the following paragraphs.

"Law must be stable and yet it cannot stand still."
Roscoe Pound
Interpretations of Legal History (1923)

Methods of Acceptance
The UCC permits acceptance by any reasonable manner or method of communication.

CONSIDER THIS EXAMPLE: A seller sends a telegram to a proposed buyer offering to sell the buyer certain goods. The buyer responds by mailing a letter of acceptance to the seller. In most circumstances, mailing the letter of acceptance would be considered reasonable. However, if the goods were extremely perishable or the market for the goods was very volatile, a faster means of acceptance (such as a telegram) might be warranted.

If an order or other offer to buy goods requires prompt or current shipment, the offer is accepted if the seller (1) promptly promises to ship the goods or (2) promptly ships either conforming or nonconforming goods [UCC 2-206(1)(b)]. The shipment of conforming goods signals acceptance of the buyer's offer.

Acceptance of goods occurs after the buyer or lessee has a reasonable opportunity to inspect them and signifies that (1) the goods are conforming, (2) he or she will take or retain the goods in spite of their nonconformity, or (3) he or she fails to reject the goods within a reasonable time after tender or delivery [UCC 2-513(1), 2A-515(1)].

Accommodation Shipment
A shipment of nonconforming goods does not constitute an acceptance if the seller reasonably notifies the buyer that the shipment is offered only as an **accommodation** to the buyer [UCC 2-206(1)(b)]. For example, suppose a buyer offers to purchase 500 red candles from a seller. The seller is temporarily out of stock of red candles. He sends the buyer 500 green candles and notifies the buyer that these candles are being sent as an accommodation. The seller has not accepted (or breached) the contract. The accommodation is a counteroffer from the seller to the buyer. The buyer is free either to accept or to reject the counteroffer.

accommodation A shipment that is offered to the buyer as a replacement for the original shipment when the original shipment cannot be filled.

Additional Terms Permitted

Under the common law's *mirror-image rule*, the offeree's acceptance must be on the same terms as the offer. The inclusion of additional terms in the acceptance is considered a *counteroffer* rather than an acceptance. Thus, the offerors' original offer is extinguished.

UCC 2-207(1) is more liberal. It permits definite and timely expressions of acceptance or written confirmations to operate as an acceptance even though they contain terms that are additional to or different from the offered terms unless the acceptance is expressly conditional on assent to such terms. This rule differs for merchants and nonmerchants, as discussed in the following sections.

CAUTION
Under certain circumstances, the UCC permits an acceptance to contain terms in addition to or different from those in the offer.

One or Both Parties Are Nonmerchants
If one or both parties to the sales contract are nonmerchants, any additional terms are considered **proposed additions** to the contract. The proposed additions do not constitute a counteroffer or extinguish the original offer. If the offeree's proposed additions are accepted by the original offeror, they become part of the contract. If they are not accepted, the sales contract is formed on the basis of the terms of the original offer [UCC 2-207(2)].

"The foundation of justice is good faith."
Cicero (143-106 B.C.)
De Officiis, Bk. 1, Ch. VII

CONSIDER THIS EXAMPLE: A salesperson at a Lexus dealership offers to sell a top-of-the-line coupe to a buyer for $47,000. The buyer replies, "I accept your offer but I would like to have a compact disc (CD) player in the car." The CD player is a proposed addition to the contract. If the salesperson agrees, the contract between the parties consists of the terms of her original offer plus the additional term regarding the CD player. If the salesperson rejects the proposed addition, the sales contract consists of the terms of the original offer. This is because the buyer made a definite expression of acceptance.

BUSINESS APPLICATION

Who Wins the "Battle of the Forms"?

When merchants negotiate sales contracts, they often exchange preprinted forms. These "boilerplate" forms usually contain terms that favor the drafter. Thus, an offeror who sends a standard form contract as an offer to the offeree may receive an acceptance contract. This scenario—commonly called the **battle of the forms**—raises several questions: Is there a contract? If so, what are its terms? The UCC provides guidance in answering these questions.

Under UCC 2-207(2), if both parties are merchants, any additional terms contained in an acceptance become part of the sales contract unless (1) the offer expressly limits acceptance to the terms of the offer, (2) the additional terms materially alter the terms of the original contract, or (3) the offer notifies the offeree that he or she objects to the additional terms within a reasonable time after receiving the offeree's modified acceptance.

The most important point in the battle of the forms is that there is no contract if the additional terms so materially alter the terms of the original offer that the parties cannot agree on the contract. This is a fact-specific determination that is made on a case-by-case basis by the courts.

Consideration

The formation of sales and lease contracts require consideration. However, the UCC changes the common law rule that requires the modification of a contract to be supported by new consideration. An agreement modifying a sales or lease contract needs no consideration to be binding [UCC 2-209(1), 2A-208(1)].

Modification of a sales or lease contract must be made in good faith [UCC 1-203]. As in the common law of contracts, modifications are not binding if they are obtained through fraud, duress, extortion, and such.

Statute of Frauds

The UCC includes **Statute of Frauds** provisions that apply to all sales and lease contracts. All contracts for the sale of goods costing $500 or more and lease contracts involving payments of $1,000 or more must be in writing [UCC 2-201(1), 2A-201(1)]. The writing must be sufficient to indicate that a contract has been made between the parties. Except as discussed in the sections that follow, the writing must be signed by the party against whom enforcement is sought or by his or her authorized agent or broker. If a contract falling within these parameters is not written, it is unenforceable.

CONSIDER THIS EXAMPLE: A seller orally agrees to sell her computer to a buyer for $550. When the buyer tenders the purchase price, the seller asserts the Statute of Frauds and refuses to sell the computer to him. The seller is correct. The contract must be in writing to be enforceable because the contract price for the computer exceeds $499.99.

UCC Statute of Frauds
A rule that requires all contracts for the sale of goods costing $500 or more and lease contracts involving payments of $1,000 or more to be in writing.

**exceptions to the writing
requirements of the
Statute of Frauds**
(1) Specially manufactured
goods, (2) admissions in
pleadings or court, and
(3) part acceptance.

Exceptions to the Statute of Frauds   The three situations in which a sales or lease contract that would otherwise be required to be in writing is enforceable even if it is not in writing are discussed in the following paragraphs [UCC 2-201(3), UCC 2A-201(4)].

Specially Manufactured Goods. Buyers and lessees often order specially manufactured goods. If the contract to purchase or lease such goods is oral, the buyer or lessee may not assert the Statute of Frauds against the enforcement of the contract if (1) the goods are not suitable for sale or lease to others in the ordinary course of the seller's or lessor's business and (2) the seller or lessor has made either a substantial beginning of the manufacture of the goods or commitments for their procurement.

Admissions in Pleadings or Court. If the party against whom enforcement of an oral sales or lease contract is sought admits in pleadings, testimony, or otherwise in court that a contract for the sale or lease of goods was made, the oral contract is enforceable against that party. However, the contract is only enforceable as to the quantity of goods admitted.

Part Acceptance. An oral sales or lease contract that should otherwise be in writing is enforceable to the extent to which the goods have been received and accepted by the buyer or lessee.

CONSIDER THIS EXAMPLE: A lessor orally contracts to lease 100 personal computers to a lessee. The lessee accepts the first 20 computers tendered by the lessor. This is part acceptance. The lessee refuses to take delivery of the remaining 80 computers. Here the lessee must pay for the 20 computers she originally received and accepted. The lessee does not have to accept or pay for the remaining 80 computers.

BUSINESS APPLICATION

UCC Written Confirmation Rule

If both parties to an oral sales or lease contract are merchants, the Statute of Frauds requirement can be satisfied if (1) one of the parties to an oral agreement sends a written confirmation of the sale or lease to the other within a reasonable time after contracting and (2) the other merchant does not give written notice of an objection to the contract within 10 days after receiving the confirmation. This is so even though the party receiving the written confirmation has not signed it. The only stipulations are that the confirmation is sufficient and the party to whom it is sent has reason to know its contents [UCC 2-201(2)].

CONSIDER THIS EXAMPLE: A merchant–seller in Chicago orally contracts by telephone to sell goods to a merchant–buyer in Phoenix for $25,000. Within a reasonable time after contracting, the merchant–seller sends a sufficient written confirmation to the buyer. The buyer, who has reason to know the contents of the confirmation, fails to object to the contents of the confirmation in writing within 10 days after receiving it. The Statute of Frauds has been met and the buyer cannot thereafter raise it against enforcement of the contract.

When Written Modification Is Required

Oral modification of the contract is not enforceable if the parties agree that any modification of the sales or lease contract must be in a signed writing [UCC 2-209(2),

2A-208(2)]. In the absence of such an agreement, oral modifications to sales and lease contracts are binding if they do not violate the Statute of Frauds.

If the oral modification brings the contract within the Statute of Frauds, it must be in writing to be enforceable.

CONSIDER THIS EXAMPLE: A lessor and lessee enter into an oral lease contract for the lease of goods at a rent of $450. Subsequently, the contract is modified by raising the rent to $550. Because the modified contract rent is more than $500, the contract comes under the UCC Statute of Frauds, and the modification must be in writing to be enforceable.

Parol Evidence

The **parol evidence rule** states that when a sales or lease contract is evidenced by a writing that is intended to be a final expression of the parties' agreement or a confirmatory memorandum, the terms of the writing may not be contradicted by evidence of (1) a prior oral or written agreement or (2) a contemporaneous oral agreement (i.e., parol evidence) [UCC 2-202, 2A-202]. The rule is intended to ensure certainty in written sales and lease contracts.

Occasionally, the express terms of a written contract are not clear on their face and must be interpreted. In such cases, reference may be made to certain sources outside the contract. These sources are construed together when they are consistent with each other. If that is unreasonable, they are considered in descending order of priority [UCC 2-208(2), 2A-207(2)]:

1. **Course of performance.** The previous conduct of the parties regarding the contract in question
2. **Course of dealing.** The conduct of the parties in prior transactions and contracts
3. **Usage of trade.** Any practice or method of dealing that is regularly observed or adhered to in a place, a vocation, a trade, or an industry.

CONSIDER THIS EXAMPLE: A cattle rancher contracts to purchase corn from a farmer. The farmer delivers feed corn to the rancher. The rancher rejects this corn and demands delivery of corn that is fit for human consumption. Ordinarily, usage of trade would be the first source of interpretation of the word *corn*. If the parties had prior dealings, though, the usage of the term in their prior dealings would become the primary source of interpretation.

parol evidence rule
A rule that says if a written contract is a complete and final statement of the parties' agreement, any prior or contemporaneous oral or written statements that alter, contradict, or are in addition to the terms of the written contract are inadmissible in court regarding a dispute over the contract.

IDENTIFICATION AND PASSAGE OF TITLE

The **identification of goods** is rather simple. It simply means distinguishing the goods named in the contract from the seller's or lessor's other goods. The seller or lessor retains the risk of loss of the goods until he or she identifies them to a sales or lease contract. Further, UCC 2-401(1) and 2-501 prevent title to goods from passing from the seller to the buyer unless the goods are identified to the sales contract. In a lease transaction, title to the leased goods remains with the lessor or a third party. It does not pass to the lessee.

The identification of goods and the passage of title are discussed in the following sections.

identification of goods
Distinguishing the goods named in the contract from the seller's or lessor's other goods.

Identification

Identification of goods can be made at any time and in any manner explicitly agreed to by the parties to the contract. In the absence of such an agreement, the UCC mandates when identification occurs [UCC 2-501(1), 2A-217].

Already existing goods are identified when the contract is made and names the specific goods sold or leased. For example, a piece of farm machinery, a car, or a boat is identified when its serial number is listed on the sales or lease contract.

Goods that are part of a larger mass of goods are identified when the specific merchandise is designated. For example, if a food processor contracts to purchase 150 cases of oranges from a farmer who has 1,000 cases of oranges, the buyer's goods are identified when the seller explicitly separates or tags the 150 cases.

future goods Goods not yet in existence (ungrown crops, unborn stock animals).

Future goods are goods not yet in existence. Unborn young animals (such as unborn cattle) are identified when the young are conceived. Crops to be harvested are identified when the crops are planted or otherwise become growing crops. Future goods other than crops and unborn young are identified when the goods are shipped, marked, or otherwise designated by the seller or lessor as the goods to which the contract refers.

Passage of Title

When the goods exist and have been identified, title to the goods may be transferred from the seller to the buyer. Article 2 of the UCC establishes precise rules for determining the passage of title in sales contracts. (As mentioned earlier, lessees do not acquire title to the goods they lease.)

title Legal, tangible evidence of ownership of goods.

Under UCC 2-401(1), **title** to goods passes from the seller to the buyer in any manner and on any conditions explicitly agreed upon by the parties. If the parties do not agree to a specific time, title passes to the buyer when and where the seller's performance with reference to the physical delivery is completed. This point in time is determined by applying the rules discussed in the following sections [UCC 2-401(2)].

shipment contract A contract that requires the seller to ship the goods to the buyer via a common carrier.

Shipment and Destination Contracts A **shipment contract** requires the seller to ship the goods to the buyer via a common carrier. The seller is required to (1) make proper shipping arrangements and (2) deliver the goods into the carrier's hands. Title passes to the buyer at the time and place of shipment [UCC 2-401(2)(a)].

destination contract A contract that requires the seller to deliver the goods either to the buyer's place of business or to another destination specified in the sales contract.

A **destination contract** requires the seller to deliver the goods either to the buyer's place of business or to another destination specified in the sales contract. Title passes to the buyer when the seller tenders delivery of the goods at the specified destination [UCC 2-401(2)(b)].

document of title An actual piece of paper, such as a warehouse receipt or bill of lading, that is required in some transactions of pick up and delivery.

Delivery of Goods Without Moving Them Sometimes a sales contract authorizes the goods to be delivered without requiring the seller to move them. In other words, the buyer might be required to pick up the goods from the seller. In such situations, the time and place of the passage of title depends on whether the seller is to deliver a **document of title** (i.e., a warehouse receipt or bill of lading) to the buyer. If a document of title is required, title passes when and where the seller delivers the document to the buyer [UCC 2-401(3)(a)]. For example, if the goods named in the sales contract are located at a warehouse, title passes when the seller delivers a warehouse receipt representing the goods to the buyer.

If (1) no document of title is needed and (2) the goods are identified at the time of contracting, title passes at the time and place of contracting [UCC 2-401(3)(b)]. For example, if the buyer signs a sales contract to purchase bricks from the seller and the contract stipulates that the buyer will pick up the bricks at the seller's place of business, title passes when the contract is signed by both parties. This is true even if the bricks are not picked up until a later date.

CONTEMPORARY BUSINESS ENVIRONMENT

Bulk Sales Law Dumped

Article 6 (Bulk Sales) of the UCC establishes rules that were designed to prevent fraud when there is a bulk transfer of goods. A **bulk transfer** occurs when an owner transfers a major part of a business's material, merchandise, inventory, or equipment not in the ordinary course of business. This usually occurs upon the sale of the assets of a business.

If there is a bulk transfer of assets, Article 6 requires that (1) the seller furnish the buyer with a list of all of the creditors of the business and (2) the buyer notify all of the listed creditors at least 10 days before taking possession of or paying for the goods, whichever occurs first. The buyer is not responsible for or liable to unlisted creditors [UCC 6-105].

If all of the requirements of Article 6 are met, the buyer receives title to the goods free of all claims of the seller's creditors. If the requirements of Article 6 are not met, the goods in the buyer's possession are subject to the claims of the seller's creditors for six months after the date of possession [UCC 6-111].

In 1988, after much review, the National Conference of Commissioners on Uniform State Laws (NCCUSL) and the American Law Institute (ALI) reported that the regulation of bulk sales was no longer necessary. Consequently, they withdrew their support for Article 6 and encouraged states that had enacted the Article to repeal it.

The report criticized the bulk transfer law for adding costs—

without corresponding benefits— to business transactions. The report claimed that it was unfair to impose liability on an innocent buyer because a dishonest seller failed to pay its creditors. The committee then stated that changing laws and economics, as well as improved communications, made it more difficult for merchants to sell their merchandise and abscond with the proceeds. Further, the report noted that modern jurisdictional laws make it easier to obtain and enforce judgments against debtors who have left the state.

Recognizing that some state legislatures may wish to continue to regulate bulk transfers, the committee also promulgated a revised version of Article 6.

RISK OF LOSS—NO BREACH OF SALES CONTRACT

In the case of sales contracts, the common law placed the risk of loss to goods on the party who had title to the goods. Article 2 rejects this notion and allows the parties to a sales contract to agree among themselves who will bear the risk of loss if the goods subject to the contract are lost or destroyed. If the parties do not have a specific agreement concerning the assessment of the risk of loss, the UCC mandates who will bear the risk.

Carrier Cases—Movement of Goods

Unless otherwise agreed, goods that are shipped via carrier (e.g., railroad, ship, truck) are considered to be sent pursuant to a shipment contract or a destination contract. Absent any indication to the contrary, sales contracts are presumed to be shipment contracts rather than destination contracts.

Shipment Contracts A **shipment contract** requires the seller to ship goods conforming to the contract to a buyer via a carrier. The risk of loss passes to the buyer when the seller delivers the conforming goods to the carrier. The buyer bears the risk of loss of the goods during transportation [UCC 2-509(1)(a)].

Shipment contracts are created in two ways. The first requires the use of the term *shipment contract*. The second requires the use of one of the following delivery terms: F.O.B., F.A.S., C.I.F., or C. & F. (see Exhibit 13.1).

shipment contract The buyer bears the risk of loss during transportation.

Exhibit 13.1
Delivery Terms

F.O.B. (free on board) point of shipment (e.g., F.O.B. Anchorage, Alaska) requires the seller to arrange to ship the goods and put the goods in the carrier's possession. The seller bears the expense and risk of loss until this is done [UCC 2-319(1)(a)].

F.A.S. (free alongside) or **F.A.S. (vessel) port of shipment** (e.g., *The Gargoyle*, New Orleans) requires the seller to deliver and tender the goods alongside the named vessel or on the dock designated and provided by the buyer. The seller bears the expense and risk of loss until this is done [UCC 2-319(2)(a)].

C.I.F. (cost, insurance, and freight) and **C. & F. (C.F., cost and freight)** are pricing terms that indicate the cost for which the seller is responsible. These terms require the seller to bear the expense and the risk of loss of loading the goods on the carrier [UCC 2-320(1) and (3)].

F.O.B. place of destination (e.g., F.O.B. Miami, Florida) requires the seller to bear the expense and risk of loss until the goods are tendered to the buyer at the place of destination [UCC 2-319(1)(b)].

Ex-ship (from the carrying vessel) requires the seller to bear the expense and risk of loss until the goods are unloaded from the ship at its port of destination [UCC 2-322(1) and (2)(b)].

No-arrival, no-sale contracts require the seller to bear the expense and risk of loss of the goods during transportation. However, the seller is under no duty to deliver replacement goods to the buyer since there is no contractual stipulation that the goods will arrive at the appointed destination [UCC 2-324(a)(b)].

---

destination contract
A sales contract that requires the seller to deliver conforming goods to a specific destination. The seller bears the risk of loss during transportation.

Destination Contracts A sales contract that requires the seller to deliver conforming goods to a specific destination is a **destination contract**. Such contracts require the seller to bear the risk of loss to the goods during their transportation. Thus, with the exception of a no-arrival, no-sale contract, the seller is required to replace any goods lost in transit. The buyer does not have to pay for destroyed goods. The risk of loss does not pass until the goods are tendered to the buyer at the specified destination [UCC 2-509(1)(b)].

Unless otherwise agreed, destination contracts are created in two ways. The first method requires the use of the term destination contract. The alternative method requires use of the following delivery terms: F.O.B. place of destination, ex-ship, or no-arrival, no-sale contract (see Exhibit 13.1).

Noncarrier Cases—No Movement of Goods

Sometimes a sales contract stipulates that the buyer is to pick up the goods, either at the seller's place of business or another specified location. This type of arrangement raises a question: Who bears the risk of loss if the goods are destroyed or stolen after the contract date and before the buyer picks the goods up from the seller? The UCC provides two different rules for this situation. One applies to merchant–sellers and the other to nonmerchant–sellers [UCC 2-509(3)].

"The law is not a series of calculating machines where definitions and answers come tumbling out when the right levers are pushed."
William O. Douglas
The Dissent, a Safeguard of Democracy (1948)

Merchant–Seller If the seller is a merchant, the risk of loss does not pass to the buyer until the goods are received. In other words, a merchant–seller bears the risk of loss between the time of contracting and the time the buyer picks up the goods.

CONSIDER THIS EXAMPLE: On June 1, Tyus Motors, a merchant, contracts to sell a new automobile to a consumer. Tyus Motors keeps the car for a few days after contracting to prep it. During this period, the car is destroyed by fire. Under the UCC, Tyus Motors bears the risk of loss because of its merchant status.

Nonmerchant–Seller Nonmerchant–sellers pass the risk of loss to the buyer upon "tender of delivery" of the goods. Tender of delivery occurs when the seller (1) places or holds the goods available for the buyer to take delivery and (2) notifies the buyer of this fact.

CONSIDER THIS EXAMPLE: On June 1, a nonmerchant contracts to sell his automobile to his next-door neighbor. Delivery of the car is tendered on June 3 and the buyer is notified of this. The buyer tells the seller he will pick the car up "in a few days." The car is destroyed by fire before the buyer picks it up. In this situation, the buyer bears the risk of loss because (1) the seller is a nonmerchant and (2) delivery was tendered on June 3. If the car was destroyed on June 2—that is, before delivery was tendered—the seller would bear the risk.

Goods in the Possession of a Bailee Goods sold by a seller to a buyer are sometimes in the possession of a **bailee** (e.g., a warehouse). If such goods are to be delivered to the buyer without moving them, the risk of loss passes to the buyer when (1) the buyer receives a negotiable document of title (such as a warehouse receipt or bill of lading) covering the goods, (2) the bailee acknowledges the buyer's right to possession of the goods, or (3) the buyer receives a nonnegotiable document of title. or other written direction to deliver *and* has a reasonable time to present the document or direction to the bailee and demand the goods. If the bailee refuses to honor the document or direction, the risk of loss remains on the seller [UCC 2-509(2)].

bailee A holder of goods who is not a seller or a buyer (e.g., a warehouse).

RISK OF LOSS—CONDITIONAL SALES

Sellers often entrust possession of goods to buyers on a trial basis. These transactions are classified as sales on approval or sales on returns [UCC 2-326].

Sale on Approval

In a **sale on approval**, there is no sale unless and until the buyer accepts the goods. A sale on approval occurs when a merchant (e.g., a computer store) allows a customer to take the goods (e.g., an Apple computer) home for a specified period of time (e.g., three days) to see if it fits the customer's needs. The prospective buyer may use the goods to try them out during this time.

Acceptance of the goods occurs if the buyer (1) expressly indicates acceptance, (2) fails to notify the seller of rejection of the goods within the agreed-upon trial period (or, if no time is agreed upon, a reasonable time), or (3) uses the goods inconsistently with the purpose of the trial (e.g., the customer resells the computer to another person).

The goods are not subject to the claims of the buyer's creditors until the buyer accepts them. In a sale on approval, the risk of loss and title to the goods remain with the seller. They do not pass to the buyer until acceptance [UCC 2-327(1)].

sale on approval A type of sale in which there is no actual sale unless and until the buyer accepts the goods.

CAUTION
In a sale on approval, *the risk of loss and title remains with the seller.*

Sale or Return

In a **sale or return** contract, the seller delivers goods to a buyer with the understanding that the buyer may return them if they are not used or resold within a stated period of time (or a reasonable time if no specific time is stated). The sale is considered final if the buyer fails to return the goods within the specified time or reasonable time if no time is specified. The buyer has the option of returning all of the goods or any commercial unit of the goods.

CONSIDER THIS EXAMPLE: Suppose a fashion designer delivers ten dresses to a fashion boutique on a sale or return basis. The boutique pays $10,000 ($1,000 per dress). If the boutique does not resell the dresses within three months, it may return the unsold garments to the designer. At the end of three months, the boutique has sold four of the dresses. The remaining six dresses may be returned to the designer. The boutique can recover the compensation paid for the returned dresses.

In a sale or return contract, the risk of loss and title to the goods pass to the buyer when the buyer takes possession of the goods. In the previous example, if the dresses

sale or return A contract that says the seller delivers goods to a buyer with the understanding that the buyer may return them if they are not used or resold within a stated or reasonable period of time.

CAUTION
In a sale or return, *the risk of loss and title transfer to the buyer when he or she takes possession of the goods.*

were destroyed while they were at the boutique, the boutique owner would be responsible for paying the designer for them [UCC 2-327(2)]. Goods sold pursuant to a sales or return contract are subject to the claims of the buyer's creditors while the goods are in the buyer's possession.

Consignment

consignment An arrangement in which a seller (the **consignor**) delivers goods to a buyer (the **consignee**) for sale.

In a **consignment**, a seller (the **consignor**) delivers goods to a buyer (the **consignee**) to sell. The consignee is paid a fee if he or she sells the goods on behalf of the consignor. A consignment is treated as a sale or return under the UCC. Whether the goods are subject to the claims of the buyer's creditors usually depends on whether the seller filed a financing statement as required by Article 9 of the UCC. If the seller files a financing statement, the goods are subject to the claims of the seller's creditors. If the seller fails to file such statement, the goods are subject to the claims of the buyer's creditors [UCC 2-326(3)].

In the following case, the court had to assess risk of loss in a conditional sale situation.

CASE 13.2

Prewitt v. Numismatic Funding Corp.
745 F.2d 1175 (1984) United States Court of Appeals, Eighth Circuit

Facts Numismatic Funding Corporation (Numismatic), with its principal place of business in New York, sells rare and collector coins by mail throughout the United States. Frederick R. Prewitt, a resident of St. Louis, Missouri, responded to Numismatic's advertisement in *The Wall Street Journal*. Prewitt received several shipments of coins from Numismatic via the mails. These shipments were "on approval" for 14 days. Numismatic gave no instructions as to the method for returning unwanted coins. Prewitt kept and paid for several coins and returned the others to Numismatic fully insured via Federal Express. On February 10, 1982, Numismatic mailed Prewitt 28 gold and silver coins worth over $60,000 on a 14-day approval. On February 23, 1982, Prewitt returned all of the coins via certified mail and insured them for the maximum allowed, $400. Numismatic never received the coins. Prewitt brought this action seeking a declaratory judgment as to his nonliability. Numismatic filed a counterclaim. The trial court awarded Prewitt a declaratory judgment of nonliability. Numismatic appealed.

Issue Who bears the risk of loss, Prewitt or Numismatic Funding Corporation?

Decision The court of appeals held that the transaction in question was a sale on approval and that under UCC 2-327(1) Numismatic, the owner of the coins, bore the risk of their loss during the return shipment from Prewitt. Affirmed.

Reason The court determined that the delivery of coins between seller Numismatic and buyer Prewitt constituted a sale "on approval." Under the provisions of the UCC relating to risk of loss for sale on approval contracts, the risk of loss remains with the seller.

CASE QUESTIONS

Critical Legal Thinking Do you agree with how the UCC assesses risk of loss in sale on approval transaction?

Ethics Should Prewitt have fully insured the coins before sending them back to Numismatic?

Business Implication How could Numismatic have protected its interests in this case?

RISK OF LOSS—BREACH OF SALES CONTRACT

The risk of loss rules discussed in the previous section apply where there is no breach of contract. Separate risk of loss rules apply to situations involving breach of the sales contract [UCC 2-510].

Seller in Breach

A seller breaches a sales contract if he or she tenders or delivers nonconforming goods to the buyer. If the goods are so nonconforming that the buyer has the right to reject them, the risk of loss remains on the seller until (1) the defect or nonconformity is cured or (2) the buyer accepts the nonconforming goods.

CONSIDER THIS EXAMPLE: A buyer orders 1,000 talking dolls from a seller. The contract is a shipment contract, which normally places the risk of loss during transportation on the buyer. The seller ships nonconforming dolls that cannot talk. The goods are destroyed in transit. The seller bears the risk of loss because he breached the contract by shipping nonconforming goods.

"Laws are not masters but servants, and he rules them who obeys them."
Henry Ward Beecher
Proverbs from Plymouth Pulpit
(1887)

Buyer in Breach

Buyers breach a sales contract if they (1) refuse to take delivery of conforming goods, (2) repudiate the contract, or (3) otherwise breach the contract. A buyer who breaches a sales contract before the risk of loss would normally pass to him or her bears the risk of loss to any goods identified to the contract. The risk of loss only rests on the buyer for a commercially reasonable time. The buyer is only liable for any loss in excess of insurance recovered by the seller.

RISK OF LOSS IN LEASE CONTRACTS

The parties to a lease contract may agree as to who will bear the risk of loss of the goods if they are lost or destroyed. If the parties do not so agree, the UCC supplies the following risk of loss rules:

1. In the case of an ordinary lease, the risk of loss is retained by the lessor. If the lease is a finance lease, the risk of loss passes to the lessee [UCC 2A-219].
2. If a tender of delivery of goods fails to conform to the lease contract, the risk of loss remains with the lessor or supplier until cure or acceptance [UCC 2A-220(1)(a)].

SALES BY NONOWNERS

Sometimes, people sell goods even though they do not hold valid title to them. The UCC anticipated many of the problems this could cause and established rules concerning the title, if any, that could be transferred to the purchasers.

Void Title and Lease—Stolen Goods

In a case in which a buyer purchases goods or a lessee leases goods from a thief who has stolen them, the purchaser does not acquire title to the goods and the lessee does not acquire any leasehold interest in the goods. The real owner can reclaim the goods from the purchaser or lessee [UCC 2-403(1)].

This is called **void title**. It works this way: Suppose someone steals a truckload of Sony television sets that are owned by Sears. The thief resells the televisions to City-Mart, which does not know that the goods were stolen. If Sears finds out where the televisions are, it can reclaim them. Because the thief had no title in the goods, title was not transferred to City-Mart. City-Mart's only recourse is against the thief—if he or she can be found.

void title A thief acquires no title to the goods he or she steals.

voidable title Title that a purchaser has if the goods were obtained by (1) fraud, (2) a check that is later dishonored, or (3) impersonating another person.

Voidable Title—Sales or Lease of Goods to Good Faith Purchasers for Value

A seller or lessor has **voidable title** to goods if the goods were obtained by fraud, a check that is later dishonored, or impersonating another person. A person with voidable title to goods can transfer good title to a **good faith purchaser for value** or a

good faith purchaser for value A person to whom good title can be transferred from a person with voidable title. The real owner cannot reclaim goods from a good faith purchaser for value.

good faith subsequent lessee A person to whom a lease interest can be transferred from a person with voidable title. The real owner cannot reclaim the goods from the subsequent lessee until the lease expires.

good faith subsequent lessee. A good faith purchaser or lessee for value is someone who pays sufficient consideration or rent for the goods to the person he or she honestly believes has good title to those goods [UCC 2-201(1), 1-201(44)(d). The real owner cannot reclaim goods from such a purchaser [UCC 2-403(1)].

CONSIDER THIS EXAMPLE: Suppose a person buys a Rolex watch from his neighbor for near fair market value. It is later discovered that the seller obtained the watch from a jewelry store with a "bounced" check. The jewelry store cannot reclaim the watch because the second purchaser purchased the watch in good faith and for value.

Assume instead that the purchaser bought the watch from a stranger for far less than fair market value. It is later discovered that the seller obtained the watch from a jewelry store by fraud. The jewelry store can reclaim the watch because the second purchaser was not a good faith purchaser for value.

Entrustment Rule

buyer in the ordinary course of business
A person who in good faith and without knowledge that the sale violates the ownership or security interests of a third party buys the goods in the ordinary course of business from a person in the business of selling goods of that kind. A buyer in the ordinary course of business takes the goods free of any third-party security interest in the goods.

The rule found in UCC 2-403(2) holds that if an owner **entrusts** the possession of his or her goods to a merchant who deals in goods of that kind, the merchant has the power to transfer all rights (including title) in the goods to a **buyer in the ordinary course of business**. The real owner cannot reclaim the goods from this buyer.

CONSIDER THIS EXAMPLE: Kim Jones brings her computer into the Computer Store to be repaired. The Computer Store both sells and services computers. Jones leaves (entrusts) her computer at the store until it is repaired. The Computer Store sells her computer to Harold Green. Green, a buyer in the ordinary course of business, acquires title to the computer. Jones cannot reclaim the computer from Green. Her only recourse is against the Computer Store.

The entrustment rule also applies to leases. If a lessor entrusts the possession of his or her goods to a lessee who is a merchant who deals in goods of that kind, the merchant–lessee has the power to transfer all of the lessor's and lessee's rights in the goods to a buyer or sublease in the ordinary course of business [UCC 2A-305(2)].

The entrustment rule is raised in the following case.

CASE 13.3

Schluter v. United Farmers Elevator
479 N.W.2d 82 (1992) Court of Appeals of Minnesota

Facts Robert, David, and Hazel Schluter (Schluters) are grain farmers in Starbuck, Minnesota. They often hired a specific trucker to haul their grain to the public grain elevator, United Farmers Elevator, to whom they would sell their grain. On some occasions, the Schluters would sell their grain to the trucker, who would then resell the grain to the elevator or others. In the case at hand, the Schluters hired the trucker to haul their corn to the elevator. When the trucker got to the elevator, he represented that he owned the corn and sold it to the elevator for $288,000. The trucker absconded with the money. The Schluters sued the elevator to recover payment for their corn. The trial court applied the

entrustment rule and held that the elevator had title to the corn as a buyer in the ordinary course of business. The Schluters appealed.

Issue Who owns the corn, the Schluters or the elevator?

Decision The appellate court held that under the UCC entrustment rule the elevator owned the corn. Affirmed.

Reason The UCC provides that any entrusting of possession of goods to a merchant who deals in the goods of that kind gives him or her the power to transfer all rights of the entruster to a buyer in the ordinary course of business. The court held that the trucker was a merchant who ordinarily transported and purchased goods of the kind entrusted to him by the Schluters. The court found that the elevator was a buyer in the ordinary course of business who in good faith purchased the corn from the trucker. Under these facts, the Schluters, and not the elevator, must bear the loss.

CASE QUESTIONS

Critical Legal Thinking Do you agree with the UCC entrustment rule? Why or why not?

Ethics Did the Schluters act ethically in trying to shift the loss to the elevator?

Business Implication Would the Schluters have been better off if they had used a trucker who was employed by the grain elevator? Explain.

BUSINESS CHECKLIST

Insuring Against Loss in Sales and Lease Contracts

To protect against the financial loss that would occur if goods are damaged, destroyed, lost, or stolen, the parties to sales and lease contracts should purchase insurance against such loss. If the goods are then lost or damaged, the insured party receives reimbursement for the insurance company for the loss.

To purchase insurance, a party must have an *insurable interest* in the goods. A seller has an insurable interest in goods as long as he or she retains title or has a security interest in the goods. A lessor retains an insurable interest in the goods during the term of the lease. A buyer or lessee obtains an insurable interest in the goods when they are identified to the sales or lease contract. Both the buyer and seller, or lessee and lessor, can have an insurable interest in the goods at the same time [UCC 2-501 and 2A-218].

To obtain and maintain proper insurance coverage in goods, a contracting party should do the following:

- Determine the value of goods subject to the sales or lease contract

- Purchase insurance from a reputable insurance company covering the goods subject to the contract

- Maintain the insurance by paying the premiums when they are due

- If the goods are damaged, destroyed, lost, or stolen, immediately file the proper claim and supporting documentation with the insurance company

INTERNATIONAL PERSPECTIVE

Use of Letters of Credit in International Trade

The major risks in any business transaction involving the sale of goods are that the seller will not be paid after delivering the goods or that the buyer will not receive the goods after paying for them. These risks are even more acute in international transactions, in which the buyer and seller might not know each other, are dealing at long distance, and the judicial

continued

system of the parties' countries might not have jurisdiction to decide a dispute if one should arise. The irrevocable **letter of credit** has been developed to manage these risks in international sales. The function of a letter of credit is to substitute the credit of a recognized international bank for that of the buyer.

An irrevocable letter of credit works this way. Suppose a buyer in one country and a seller in another country enter into a contract for the sale of goods. The buyer goes to his bank and pays the bank a fee to issue a letter of credit in which the bank agrees to pay the amount of the letter (which is the amount of the purchase price of the goods) to the seller's bank if certain conditions are met. These conditions are usually the delivery of documents indicating that the seller has placed the goods in the hands of a shipper. The buyer is called the **account party**, the bank that issues the letter of credit is called the

lessing bank, and the seller is called the **beneficiary** of the letter of credit.

The issuing bank then forwards the letter of credit to a bank that the seller has designated in his country. This bank, which is called the **correspondent** or **confirming bank**, relays the letter of credit to the seller. Now that the seller sees that he is guaranteed payment, he makes arrangements to ship the goods and receives a bill of lading from the carrier proving so. The seller then delivers these documents to the confirming bank. The confirming bank will examine the documents and, if it finds them in order, will pay the seller and forward the documents to the issuing bank. By this time the buyer will usually have paid the amount of the purchase price to the issuing bank (unless an extension of credit has been arranged), and the issuing bank then charges the buyer's account. The issuing bank forwards the bill of lading and

other necessary documents to the buyer, who then picks up the goods from the shipper when they arrive.

If the documents (e.g., the bill of lading, proof of insurance) conform to the conditions specified in the letter of credit, the issuing bank must pay the letter of credit. If the account party does not pay the issuing bank, the bank's only recourse is to sue the account party to recover damages.

Article 5 (Letters of Credit) of the Uniform Commercial Code governs letters of credit unless otherwise agreed by the parties. The International Chamber of Congress has promulgated the **Uniform Customs and Practices for Documentary Credits (UCP)**, which contains rules governing the formation and performance of letters of credit. Although the UCP is neither a treaty nor a legislative enactment, most banks incorporate the terms of the UCP in letters of credit they issue.

WORKING THE WEB

Uniform Commercial Code Locator This site is maintained by the Legal Information Institute of Cornell Law School. It links to state statutes that correspond to articles of the Uniform Commercial Code.

Visit at http://www.law.cornell.edu/uniform.ucc.html

United States Code, Title 41, Public Contracts This site is maintained by the Legal Information Institute of Cornell Law School. It links you to all chapters of Title 41 of the U.S. Code.

Visit at http://www.law.cornell.edu/uscode/41/

United States Department of Commerce This government site links to many commercial sites on the World Wide Web. It also contains information about the Department of Commerce.

Visit at http://www.doc.gov/

Stat-USA Stat-USA is a one-stop Internet browsing site for business, trade, and economic information. Are you looking for information about doing business in foreign countries for your International Marketing class? Then this site is for you.

Visit at http://domino.stat-usa.gov/

The Business Law Site The Business Law Site is the home page of Methven & Associates, a law firm in California. It links to federal and state statutes, cases, agencies, legal research sites, business and high-tech law sites, and tax forms.

Visit at http://members.aol.com/bmethven/index.html

CYBER EXERCISES:

1. Using the Uniform Commercial Code Locator, find the text of Article 2 of the Uniform Commercial Code.

2. Using the Uniform Commercial Code Locator, find out whether your state has adopted Article 2 of the Uniform Commercial Code.

3. Use the U.S. Department of Commerce site to find the phone number for the director of the Bureau of Economic Analysis.

4. Use the U.S. Department of Commerce site to find the Commerce Strategic Plan.

5. Using the Business Law Site, find and print out a current California tax form.

CHAPTER SUMMARY

SCOPE OF ARTICLE 2 (SALES), P. 273

Article 2 (Sales)	Article of the UCC that applies to transactions in goods [UCC 2-102]. 1. *Goods*. Tangible things that are movable at the time of their identification to the sales contract [UCC 2-105(1)]. 2. *Scope of Article 2*. Article 2 applies to all sales contracts, whether they involve merchants or not.

SCOPE OF ARTICLE 2A (LEASES), P. 275

Article 2A (Leases)	Article of the UCC that applies to personal property leases of goods [UCC 2A-101].
	1. *Lease*. A transfer of the right to the possession and use of the named goods for a set term in return for certain consideration.
	2. *Parties to a lease:*
	  a. *Lessor*. Person who transfers the right of possession and use of goods [UCC 2A-103(1)(p)].
	  b. *Lessee*. Person who acquires the right to possession and use of the goods [UCC 2A-103(1)(n)].
	3. *Finance lease*. A three-party transaction of the lessor, the lessee, and the supplier of the leased goods. The parties to a finance lease are:
	  a. *Lessor*. Acquires title to the goods from the supplier and leases the goods to the lessee. The lessor is often a bank or other creditor
	  b. *Lessee*. Party who acquires the right to possession and use of the goods
	  c. *Supplier*. Third party who supplies the goods. The supplier usually sells the goods to the lessor.

FORMATION OF SALES AND LEASE CONTRACTS, P. 276

Offer	*Open terms*. If the parties leave open a major term in the sales or lease contract, the UCC permits the following terms to be read into the contract: 1. Price term 2. Payment term 3. Delivery term 4. Time term 5. Assortment term. These are commonly called *gap-filling rules* [UCC 2-204(3), 2A-204(3)].

Firm Offer Rule	A UCC rule that says that a merchant who (1) makes an offer to buy, sell, or lease goods and (2) assures the other party in a separate writing that the offer will be held open cannot revoke the offer for the time stated, or if no time is stated, for a reasonable time [UCC 2-205, 2A-205].
Acceptance	*Accommodation shipment.* A shipment that is offered to the buyer by the seller as a replacement for the original shipment when the original shipment cannot be filled. The buyer may either accept or reject this shipment [UCC 2-206(1)(b)].
Additional Terms Permitted	The UCC permits an acceptance of a sales contract to contain additional terms and still to act as an acceptance rather than a counteroffer in certain circumstances. The following UCC rules apply [UCC 2-207(2)]: 1. *One or both parties are nonmerchants.* The additional terms are considered proposed additions to the contract. If the offeree's proposed terms are accepted by the offeror, they become part of the contract. If they are not accepted, the sales contract is formed on the basis of the terms of the original offer. 2. *Both parties are merchants.* The additional terms contained in the acceptance become part of the sales contract *unless* (1) the offer expressly limits acceptance to the terms of the offer, (2) the additional terms materially alter the original contract, or (3) the offeror notifies the offeree that he or she objects to the additional terms within a reasonable time after receiving the offeree's modified acceptance. There is no contract if the additional terms so materially alter the terms of the original offer that the parties cannot agree on the contract.

Statute of Frauds	The UCC Statute of Frauds requires contracts for the sale of goods costing $500 or more and lease contracts involving payments of $1,000 or more to be in writing [UCC 2-201(1), 2A-201(1)].
	1. *Exceptions to the Statute of Frauds.* The UCC recognizes the following exceptions to the Statute of Frauds where a sales or lease contract that is required to be in writing is enforceable even though it is not in writing:
	  a. *Specially manufactured goods.* Contracts in which the goods are not suitable for sale or lease to others in the ordinary course of business and the seller or lessor has made either a substantial beginning of manufacture of the goods or commitments for their procurement.
	  b. *Admissions in pleadings or court.* A party admits in pleadings, testimony, or otherwise in court that he or she has entered into a contract.
	  c. *Part acceptance.* An oral sales or lease contract is enforceable to the extent to which the goods have been received and accepted by the buyer or lessee.

Written Confirmation Rule	If both parties to an oral sales or lease contract are merchants, the Statute of Frauds requirements are satisfied if (1) one of the parties sends a *written confirmation* of the sale to the other within a reasonable time after contracting and (2) the other merchant does not give written notice of an objection to the contract within 10 days after receiving the confirmation [UCC 2-201(2)].

IDENTIFICATION AND PASSAGE OF TITLE, P. 281	
Identification	Distinguishes the goods named in the contract from the seller's or lessor's other goods [UCC 2-501(1)].

Passage of Title	1. *Passage of title by agreement*. Title to goods of a sales contract passes from the seller to the buyer in any manner and on any conditions explicitly agreed upon by the parties.
	 2. *Passage of title where there is no agreement*. If the parties have no agreement as to the passage of title, title passes according to the following UCC rules [UCC 2-401(2)].
	   a. *Shipment contract*. Requires the seller to ship the goods to the buyer via a common carrier. Title passes to the buyer at the time and place of shipment
	   b. *Destination contract*. Requires the seller to deliver the goods to the buyer's place of business or other designated destination. Title passes to the buyer when the seller tenders delivery of the goods at the specified destination
	   c. *Goods that do not move*. If a sales contract authorizes the goods to be delivered without requiring the seller to move them, title passes at the time and place of contracting unless a document of title is required, in which case title passes when the seller delivers the document of title to the buyer.
	 3. *Passage of title in lease contracts*. Title to the leased goods remains with the lessor or a third party. Title does not pass to the lessee.

Article 6 (Bulk Sales)	1. *Bulk sales*. Occurs when an owner/debtor transfers a major part of a business's material, merchandise, inventory, or equipment not in the ordinary course of business. 2. *Article 6 (Bulk Sales)*. Establishes rules that require the buyer to notify the creditors of the seller of the proposed sale of assets. If such notice is given, the buyer receives title to the goods free of all claims of the seller's creditors. If the notice is not given, the goods in the buyer's possession are subject to the claims of the seller's creditors for six months after the date of possession. 3. *Amendment*. In 1988, the National Conference of Commissioners on Uniform State Laws (NC-CUSL) and the American Law Institute (ALI) recommended that states repeal Article 6. As an alternative, the NCCUSL issued a revised version of Article 6.
RISK OF LOSS—NO BREACH OF SALES CONTRACT, P. 283	
Risk of Loss—No Breach of Sales Contract	1. *Agreement*. The parties in a sales contract may agree among themselves as to who will bear the risk of loss of the goods if they are lost or destroyed. 2. *No agreement*. If the parties do not have a specific agreement concerning the assessment of risk of loss, the UCC mandates who will bear the risk [UCC 2-509].
Carrier Cases—Movement of Goods	1. *Shipment contract*. The risk of loss passes to the buyer when the seller delivers conforming goods to a carrier. The buyer bears the risk of loss during transportation. 2. *Destination contract*. The risk of loss does not pass to the buyer until the goods are tendered to the buyer at the designated destination. The seller bears the risk of loss during transportation.

Noncarrier Cases—No Movement of Goods	If the buyer is to pick the goods up from the seller's place of business or other specified location, the following UCC rules apply: 1. *Merchant–seller.* If the seller is a merchant, the risk of loss does not pass to the buyer until the goods are received by the buyer. The merchant–seller bears the risk of loss between the time of contracting and the time the buyer picks up the goods. 2. *Nonmerchant–seller.* If the seller is a nonmerchant, risk of loss passes to the buyer upon tender of delivery of the goods by the seller (i.e., the seller holds the goods available for the buyer to take delivery).

RISK OF LOSS—CONDITIONAL SALES, P. 285

Conditional Sales	The entrustment of goods by a seller to a buyer on a trial basis. The following UCC rules for risk of loss apply [UCC 2-327]: 1. *Sale on approval.* Occurs when a merchant allows a customer to take the goods for a specified period of time to try the goods. There is no sale unless and until the buyer accepts the goods. The risk of loss remains with the seller and does not transfer to the buyer until acceptance. 2. *Sale or return.* Occurs when a seller delivers goods to a buyer with the understanding that the buyer may return them if they are not used or resold during a stated period of time. The risk of loss passes to the buyer when the buyer takes possession of the goods. 3. *Consignment.* Occurs when a seller (*consignor*) delivers goods to a buyer (*consignee*) to sell. The risk of loss passes to the consignee when the consignee takes possession of the goods.

RISK OF LOSS—BREACH OF SALES CONTRACT, P. 286

Risk of Loss—Breach of Sales Contract	If there has been a *breach of the sales contract*, the UCC rules concerning risk of loss apply [UCC 2-510].
Seller in Breach	If a seller breaches the sales contract by tendering or delivering nonconforming goods, the risk of loss to the goods remains with the seller until (1) the defect or nonconformity is cured, or (2) the buyer accepts the nonconforming goods.
Buyer in Breach	If a buyer breaches a sales contract by refusing to take delivery of conforming goods or repudiating the contract before the risk of loss would normally transfer to him or her, the buyer bears the risk of loss to any goods identified to the contract for a reasonably commercial time.

RISK OF LOSS IN LEASE CONTRACTS, P. 287

Risk of Loss in Lease Contracts	1. *Agreement.* The parties to a lease contract may agree as to who will bear the risk of loss to the goods if they are lost or destroyed. 2. *No agreement.* If the parties do not have an agreement concerning the assessment of risk of loss, the following UCC rules for risk of loss apply [UCC 2A-219, 2A-220]: a. *Ordinary lease.* The risk of loss is retained by the lessor b. *Finance lease.* The risk of loss passes to the lessee c. *Breach of contract.* If a tender of delivery of goods fails to conform to the lease contract, the risk of loss remains with the lessor or supplier until acceptance or cure.

SALES BY NONOWNERS, P. 287	
Sales by Nonowners	If a person sells goods that he or she does not hold valid title to, the buyer acquires rights in the certain goods under the UCC [UCC 2-403].
Void Title and Lease—Stolen Goods	A thief acquires no title to goods he or she steals. A person who purchases stolen goods does not acquire title to the goods. This is called *void title*. The real owner can reclaim the goods from the purchaser. The purchaser's recourse is to recover from the thief.
Voidable Title—Sale or Lease of Goods to Good Faith Purchasers for Value	If goods are obtained by fraud, a check that is later dishonored, or by impersonating another person, the perpetrator acquires *voidable title* to the goods. If the perpetrator sells or leases the goods to a *good faith purchaser or lessee for value*—a person who pays sufficient consideration or rent for the goods and honestly believes that the seller or lessor has good title to the goods—the buyer or lessee acquires good title to the goods. The real owner's recourse is against the perpetrator who acquired the goods from him or her.
Entrustment Rule	If an owner entrusts possession of his or her goods to a merchant who deals in goods of that kind (e.g., for repair), and the merchant sells those goods to a *buyer in the ordinary course of business* (e.g., a customer of the merchant), the buyer acquires good title to the goods. The real owner's recourse is against the merchant who sold his or her goods. This is called the *entrustment rule*.
LETTERS OF CREDIT, P. 289	
Letters of Credit	A letter issued by a bank for a fee usually paid by a buyer of goods whereby the bank agrees to pay the seller of the goods the purchase price of the goods on behalf of the buyer. In essence, the credit of the bank is substituted for that of the buyer. 1. *Presentment*. When the letter of credit is presented to the seller, the seller ships the goods to the buyer. The seller delivers the required shipping and other documents to the bank for payment. 2. *Bank's obligations*. The issuing bank must pay the letter of credit if the proper documents are presented to it. If the buyer does not pay the issuing bank the purchase price for the letter of credit, the issuing bank cannot refuse to pay the letter of credit. The bank's recourse is against the buyer. 3. *Article 5 of the UCC (Letters of Credit)*. Governs letters of credit unless the parties agree otherwise. Banks usually stipulate that the *Uniform Customs and Practices for Documentary Credits (UCP)* governs letters of credit they issue.

CRITICAL LEGAL THINKING CASES

13.1 Good or Service? Gulash lived in Shelton, Connecticut. He wanted an above-ground swimming pool installed in his backyard. Gulash contacted Stylarama, Inc., a company specializing in the sale and construction of pools. The two parties entered into a contract that called for Stylarama to "furnish all labor and materials to construct a wavecrest brand pool, and furnish and install pool with vinyl liners." The total cost for materials and labor was $3,690. There was no break- down of costs between labor and materials. After the pool was installed, its sides began bowing out, the 2" × 4" wooden supports for the pool rotted and misaligned, and the entire pool became tilted. Gulash brought suit alleging that Stylarama had violated several provisions of Article 2 of the UCC. Is this transaction one involving "goods," making it subject to Article 2? [*Gulash v. Stylarama*, 364 A.2d 1221 (Conn. 1975)]

13.2 Open Terms Alvin Cagle was a potato farmer in Alabama who had had several business dealings with the H. C. Schmieding Produce Co. (Schmieding). Several months before harvest, Cagle entered into an oral sales contract with Schmieding. The contract called for Schmieding to pay the market price at harvest time for all the red potatoes that Cagle grew on his 30-acre farm. Schmieding asked that the potatoes be delivered during the normal harvest months. As Cagle began harvesting his red potatoes, he contacted Schmieding to arrange delivery. Schmieding told the farmer that no contract had been formed because the terms of the agreement were too indefinite. Cagle demanded that Schmieding buy his crop. When Schmieding refused, Cagle sued to have the contract enforced. Has a valid sales contract been formed? [*H. C. Schmieding Produce Co. v. Cagle*, 529 So.2d 243 (Ala. 1988)]

13.3 Statute of Frauds Cameron Lawrence lived in Marina Del Rey, California. Lawrence's next-door neighbor, Carey Heyward, owned a 35-foot sailboat. Because Heyward spent most of his time visiting in South America, he seldom used the boat. During one of his rare stays in California, Lawrence asked Heyward about the possibility of buying his sailboat. Heyward didn't want to sell but said he would lease the vessel for five years. Lawrence agreed to pay Heyward $2,000 every six months to lease the boat. No written contract was ever signed and the parties sealed their agreement with a handshake. Lawrence took possession of the boat on June 1 and sailed on it throughout the summer. On August 30, Lawrence decided he didn't want the boat anymore and refused to make the required payments. Heyward sued Lawrence. Lawrence claims the lease is unenforceable because it violates the Statute of Frauds. Who wins?

13.4 Firm Offer Gordon Construction Company (Gordon) was a general contractor in the New York City area. Gordon planned on bidding for the job of constructing two buildings for the Port Authority of New York. In anticipation of its own bid, Gordon sought bids from subcontractors. On April 22, 1963, E. A. Coronis Associates (Coronis), a fabricator of structured steel, sent a signed letter to Gordon. The letter quoted a price for work on the Port Authority Project and stated that the price could change, based upon the amount of steel used. The letter contained no information other than the price Coronis would charge for the job. On May 27, Gordon was awarded the Port Authority project. On June 1, Coronis sent Gordon a telegram withdrawing its offer. Gordon replied that it expected Coronis to honor the price quoted in its April 22 letter. When Coronis refused, Gordon sued. Gordon claimed that Coronis was attempting to withdraw a firm offer. Who wins? [*E. A. Coronis Associates v. M. Gordon Construction Co.*, 216 A.2d 246 (N.J.Super. 1966)]

13.5 Battle of the Forms Dan Miller was a commercial photographer who had taken a series of photographs that had appeared in *The New York Times*. *Newsweek* magazine wanted to use the photographs. When a *Newsweek* employee named Dwyer phoned Miller, he was told that 72 images were available. Dwyer said that he wanted to inspect the photographs and offered a certain sum of money for each photo *Newsweek* used. The photos were to remain Miller's property. Miller and Dwyer agreed to the price and the date for delivery. *Newsweek* sent a courier to pick up the photographs. Along with the pho-

tos, Miller gave the courier a "Delivery Memo" that set out various conditions for the use of the photographs. The memo included a clause that required *Newsweek* to pay $1,500 each if any of the photos were lost or destroyed. After *Newsweek* received the package, it decided it no longer needed Miller's work. When Miller called to have the photos returned, he was told that they all had been lost. Miller demands that *Newsweek* pay him $1,500 for each of the 72 lost photos. Assuming that the court finds Miller and *Newsweek* to be merchants, were the clauses in the delivery memo part of the sales contract? [*Miller v. Newsweek, Inc.*, 660 F.Supp. 852 (D.Del. 1987)]

13.6 Identification of Goods The Big Knob Volunteer Fire Company (Fire Co.) agreed to purchase a fire truck from Hamerly Custom Productions (Hamerly). Hamerly was in the business of assembling various component parts into fire trucks. Fire Co. paid Hamerly $10,000 toward the price two days after signing the contract. Two weeks later, it gave Hamerly $38,000 more toward the total purchase price of $53,000. Hamerly bought an engine chassis for the new fire truck on credit from Lowe and Meyer Co. After installing the chassis, Hamerly painted the Big Knob Fire Company's name on the side of the cab. Hamerly never paid for the engine chassis and the truck was repossessed by Lowe and Meyer. The Fire Co. seeks to recover the fire truck from Lowe and Meyer. Although the Fire Co. was the buyer of a fire truck, Louis and Meyer question whether any goods had ever been identified to the contract. Were they? [*Big Knob Volunteer Fire Co. v. Lowe and Meyer Garage*, 487 A.2d 953 (Pa.Super. 1985)]

13.7 Risk of Loss In June 1973 All America Export-Import Corp. (All America) placed an order for several thousand pounds of yarn with A. M. Knitwear Corporation (Knitwear). On June 4, All America sent Knitwear a purchase order. The purchase order stated the terms of the sale, including language that stated that the price was F.O.B. the seller's plant. On Friday, June 22, 1973, a truck hired by All America arrived at Knitwear's plant. On Monday, June 24, Knitwear turned the yarn over to the carrier and notified All America that the goods were now on the truck. The truck left Knitwear's plant and proceeded to a local warehouse. Sometime during the night of June 24, the truck was highjacked and all the yarn was stolen. All America had paid for the yarn by check but stopped payment on it when it learned that the goods had been stolen. Knitwear sued All America, claiming that it must pay for the stolen goods because it bore the risk of loss. Who wins? [*A. M. Knitwear v. All America, Etc.*, 390 N.Y.S.2d 832, 41 N.Y.2d 14 (N.Y. App. 1976)]

13.8 Risk of Loss Mitsubishi International Corporation (Mitsubishi) entered into a contract with the Crown Door Company (Crown). The contract called for Mitsubishi to sell 12 boxcar loads of plywood to Crown. According to the terms of the contract, Mitsubishi would import the wood from Taiwan and deliver it to Crown's plant in Atlanta. Mitsubishi had the wood shipped from Taiwan to Savannah, Georgia. At Savannah, the plywood was loaded onto trains and hauled to Atlanta. When the plywood arrived in Atlanta, it was discovered that the railroad had been negligent in loading the train. The negligent loading had caused the cargo to shift during the trip, and the shifting had caused extensive damage to the wood. Who bore the risk of loss? [*Georgia Ports Authority v. Mitsubishi International Corporation*, 274 S.E.2d 699 (Ga. App. 1980)]

13.9 Risk of Loss In 1982, Martin Silver ordered two rooms of furniture from Wycombe, Meyer and Co., Inc. (Wycombe), a manufacturer and seller of custom-made furniture. On February 23, 1982, Wycombe sent invoices to Silver advising him that the furniture was ready for shipment. Silver tendered payment in full for the goods and asked that one room of furniture be shipped immediately and that the other be held for shipment on a later date. Before any instructions were received as to the second room of furniture, it was destroyed in a fire. Silver and his insurance company attempt to recover the money he paid for the destroyed furniture. Wycombe refuses to return the payment, claiming that the risk of loss was upon Silver. Who wins? [*Silver v. Wycombe, Meyer & Co., Inc.*, 477 N.Y.S.2d 288 (N.Y.City Civ.Ct. 1984)]

13.10 Risk of Loss Cal-Ag Corporation (Cal-Ag) needed to lease a new box-sealing machine for its raisin packaging plant. Cal-Ag contacted the Uni-Box Co. (Uni-Box) and agreed to lease a Model 3000 Box Sealer from Uni-Box for 10 years. The parties signed a written lease agreement. The box sealer was supposed to be shipped within two weeks. The night before the machine was to be shipped, Uni-Box's employees selected a Model 3000, packaged it for shipping, and placed Cal-Ag's address on the carton. At four o'clock that morning, a fire destroyed the box sealer. Which party bears the risk of loss?

13.11 Stolen Goods John Torniero was employed by Michaels Jewelers, Inc. (Michaels). During the course of his employment Torniero stole pieces of jewelry, including several diamond rings, a sapphire ring, a gold pendant, and several loose diamonds. Over a period of several months, Torniero sold individual pieces of the stolen jewelry to G&W Watch and Jewelry Corporation (G&W). G&W had no knowledge of how Torniero obtained the jewels. Torniero was arrested when Michaels discovered the thefts. After Torniero admitted that he had sold the stolen jewelry to G&W, Michaels attempted to recover it from G&W. G&W claims title to the jewelry as a good faith purchaser for value. Michaels has challenged G&W's claim to title in court. Who wins? [*United States v. Michaels Jewelers, Inc.*, 42 U.C.C.Rep.Serv. 141 (D.C.Conn. 1985)]

13.12 Passage of Title J. A. Coghill owned a 1979 Rolls Royce Corniche, which he sold to a man claiming to be Daniel Bell-

man in 1984. Bellman gave Coghill a cashier's check for $94,500. When Coghill tried to cash the check, his bank informed him that the check had been forged. Coghill reported the vehicle as stolen. Early in September 1984, Barry Hyken responded to a newspaper ad listing a 1980 Rolls Royce Corniche for sale. Hyken went to meet the seller of the car, the man who claimed to be Bellman, in a parking lot. When Hyken asked why the car was advertised as a 1980 model when it was in fact a 1979, Bellman replied that it was a newspaper mistake. Hyken agreed to pay $62,000 for the car. When Hyken asked to see Bellman's identification, Bellman provided documents with two different addresses. Bellman explained that he was in the process of moving. Although there seemed to be some irregularities in the title documents to the car, Hyken took possession anyway. Three weeks later, the Rolls was seized by the police. Hyken sues to get it back. Who wins? [*Landshire Food Service, Inc. v. Coghill*, 709 S.W.2d 509 (Mo. App. 1986)]

13.13 Passage of Title On July 19, 1985 Cherry Creek Dodge (Cherry Creek) sold a 1985 Dodge Ramcharger to Executive Leasing of Colorado (Executive Leasing). Executive Leasing, which was in the business of buying and selling cars, paid for the Dodge with a draft. Cherry Creek maintained a security interest in the car until the draft cleared. The same day that Executive Leasing bought the Dodge, it sold the car to Bruce and Peggy Carter. The Carters paid in full for the Dodge with a cashier's check and the vehicle was delivered to them. The Carters had no knowledge of the financial arrangements between Executive Leasing and Cherry Creek. The draft that Executive Leasing gave Cherry Creek was worthless. Cherry Creek attempts to recover the vehicle from the Carters. Who wins? [*Cherry Creek Dodge, Inc. v. Carter*, 733 P.2d 1024 (Wyo. 1987)]

13.14 Insurable Interest On February 7, 1967 Donald Hayward signed a sales contract with Dry Land Marina, Inc. (Dry Land). The contract was for the purchase of a 30-foot Revel Craft Playmate Yacht for $10,000. The contract called for Dry Land to install a number of options on Hayward's yacht and then deliver it to him in April 1967. On March 1, 1967, before taking delivery of the yacht, Hayward signed a security agreement in favor of Dry Land and a promissory note. Several weeks later, a fire swept through Dry Land's showroom. Hayward's yacht was among the goods destroyed in the fire. Who had an insurable interest in the yacht? [*Hayward v. Potsma*, 188 N.W.2d 31 (Mich. App. 1971)]

ETHICS CASES

13.15 Ethical Perspective Kurt Perschke was a grain dealer in Indiana. In September 1972, he phoned Ken Sebasty, the owner of a large wheat farm, and offered to buy 14,000 bushels of wheat for $1.95 a bushel. Sebasty accepted the offer. Perschke said that he could send a truck for the wheat in March 1973. On the day of the phone call, Perschke's office manager sent a memorandum to Sebasty, stating the price and quantity of wheat that had been contracted for. In February 1973, Perschke called Sebasty to arrange for the loading of the wheat.

Sebasty stated that no contract had been made. When Perschke brought suit, Sebasty claimed that the contract was unenforceable because of the Statute of Frauds. Was it ethical for Sebasty to raise the Statute of Frauds as a defense? Assuming that both parties are merchants, who wins the suit? [*Sebasty v. Perschke*, 404 N.E.2d 1200 (Ind. App. 1980)]

13.16 Ethical Perspective In the summer and fall of 1982, Executive Financial Services, Inc. (EFS), purchased three tractors from Tri-County Farm Company (Tri-County), a John Deere dealership owned by Gene Mohr and James Loyd. The tractors cost $48,000, $19,000, and $38,000, respectively. EFS did not take possession of the tractors but instead left the tractors on Tri-County's lot. EFS leased the tractors to Mohr-Loyd Leasing (Mohr-Loyd), a partnership between Mohr and Loyd, with the understanding and representation by Mohr-Loyd that the tractors would be leased out to farmers. Instead of leasing the tractors, Tri-County sold them to three different farmers. EFS sued and obtained judgment against Tri-County, Mohr-Loyd, and Mohr and Loyd personally for breach of contract. Because that judgment remained unsatisfied, EFS sued the three farmers who bought the tractors to recover the tractors from them. Did Mohr and Loyd act ethically in this case? Who owns the tractors, EFS or the farmers? [*Executive Financial Services, Inc. v. Pagel*, 715 P.2d 181 (Kan. 1986)]

13.17 Ethical Perspective On March 11, 1985, Dugdale of Nebraska, Inc. (Dugdale), purchased a 1985 Ford LTD Crown Victoria automobile from Vannier Ford, an automobile dealership. Dugdale traded in a 1984 vehicle and paid cash for the remaining purchase price of the car. On the day that the vehicle was delivered, the president of Vannier Ford told the representative of Dugdale that the title papers to the vehicle had not yet been received but would be given to him as soon as they were received.

Approximately five days before selling the vehicle to Dugdale, Vannier Ford had pledged it as security for a loan from First State Bank, Gothenburg, Nebraska (First State Bank) and delivered the certificate of title to the bank. This fact was unknown by Dugdale. Vannier Ford did not transmit the proceeds of the sale to First State Bank. After the sale, Dugdale made numerous inquiries regarding the title papers, and each time was told by Vannier Ford that the papers had not yet arrived. Approximately two months later, after Vannier Ford defaulted on the loan, First State Bank contacted Dugdale and made demand for possession of the vehicle. Dugdale brought suit seeking a declaratory judgment as to its ownership rights. First State Bank filed a counterclaim. Did Vannier Ford act ethically in this case? Who owns title to the vehicle, Dugdale or First State Bank? [*Dugdale of Nebraska, Inc. v. First State Bank, Gothenburg, Nebraska*, 420 N.W.2d 273 (Neb. 1988)]

 CRITICAL LEGAL THINKING WRITING ASSIGNMENT

Read Case A.13 in the Case Appendix [*Burnett v. Purtell*]. This case is excerpted from the court of appeals opinion. Review and brief the case. In your brief, be sure to answer the following questions:

1. Who were the plaintiff and defendant? Were they merchants?

2. Describe the sales transaction.

3. Was there tender of delivery of the goods? Why is this issue important to the outcome of the case?

4. Who bore the risk of loss when the goods were destroyed?

CHAPTER 14

PERFORMANCE OF SALES

AND LEASE CONTRACTS

Chapter Objectives

*After studying this chapter,
you should be able to*

1. Describe the doctrines of good faith and reasonableness that govern the performance of sales and lease contracts
2. Define the perfect tender rule
3. Identify when the buyer or lessee has a right to reject nonconforming goods
4. Identify when the seller or lessor has a right to cure a nonconforming delivery of goods
5. Identify when the buyer or lessee has the right to revoke a prior acceptance
6. List and describe the seller's remedies for the buyer's breach of the sales contract
7. List and describe the buyer's remedies for the seller's breach of the sales contract
8. List and describe the lessor's remedies for the lessee's breach of the lease contract
9. List and describe the lessee's remedies for the lessor's breach of the lease contract
10. Identify limitations on remedies

Chapter Contents

> *Trade and commerce, if they were not made of India rubber, would never manage to bounce over the obstacles which legislators are continually putting in their way.*
>
> Henry D. Thoreau
> *Resistance to Civil Government* (1849)

obligation   An action a party to a sales or lease contract is required by law to carry out.

breach   Failure of a party to perform an obligation in a sales or lease contract.

Usually, the parties to a sales or lease **contract** owe a duty to perform the **obligations** specified in their agreement [UCC 2-301, 2A-301]. The seller's or lessor's general obligations is to transfer and deliver the goods to the buyer or lessee. The buyer's or lessee's general obligation is to accept and pay for the goods.

When one party **breaches** the sales or lease contract, the UCC provides the injured party with a variety of prelitigation and litigation remedies. These remedies are designed to place the injured party in as good a position as if the breaching party's contractual obligations were fully performed [UCC 1-106(1), 2A-401(1)]. The best remedy depends on the circumstances of the particular **case**.

The performance of obligations and **remedies** available for breach of sales and lease contracts are discussed in this chapter.

SELLER'S AND LESSOR'S OBLIGATIONS

tender of delivery   The obligation of the seller to transfer and deliver goods to the buyer in accordance with the sales contract.

Tender of delivery, or the transfer of delivery of goods to the buyer or lessee in accordance with the sales or lease contract is the seller's or lessor's basic obligation [UCC 2-301]. Tender of delivery requires the seller or lessor to (1) put and hold conforming goods at the buyer's or lessee's disposition and (2) give the buyer or lessee any notification reasonably necessary to enable delivery of the goods. The parties may agree as to the time, place, and manner of delivery. If there is no special agreement, tender must be made at a reasonable hour, and the goods must be kept available for a reasonable period of time. For example, the seller cannot telephone the buyer at 12:01 A.M. and tell him that he has 15 minutes to accept delivery [UCC 2-503(1), 2A-508(1)].

"The buyer needs a hundred eyes, the seller not one."
George Herbert
Jacula Prudentum
(1651)

Unless otherwise agreed or the circumstances permit either party to request delivery in lots, the goods named in the contract must be tendered in a single delivery. Payment of a sales contract is due upon tender of delivery unless an extension of credit between the parties has been arranged. If the goods are rightfully delivered in lots, the payment is apportioned for each lot [UCC 2-307]. Lease payments are due in accordance with the terms of the lease contract.

Place of Delivery

Many sales and lease contracts state where the goods are to be delivered. Often, the contract will say that the buyer or lessee must pick up the goods from the seller or lessor. If the contract does not expressly state where the delivery will take place, the UCC will stipulate place of delivery on the basis of whether a carrier is involved.

Noncarrier Cases   Unless otherwise agreed, the place of delivery is the seller's or lessor's place of business. If the seller or lessor has no place of business, the place of delivery is the seller's or lessor's residence. If the parties have knowledge at the time of contracting that identified goods are located in some other place, that place is the place of delivery. For example, if the parties contract regarding the sale of wheat located in a silo, then the silo is the place of delivery [UCC 2-308].

bailee   A holder of goods who is not a seller or a buyer (e.g., a warehouse).

Sometimes the goods are in the possession of a **bailee** (e.g., a warehouse) and are to be delivered without being moved. In such cases, tender of delivery occurs when the seller either (1) tenders to the buyer a negotiable document of title covering the goods or (2) procures acknowledgment from the bailee of the buyer's right to possession of the goods, or (3) tenders a nonnegotiable document of title or a written direction to the bailee to deliver the goods to a buyer. The seller must deliver all such documents in correct form [UCC 2-503(4) and (5)].

Carrier Cases Unless the parties have agreed otherwise, if delivery of the goods to the buyer is to be made by carrier, the UCC establishes different rules for shipment contracts and destination contracts. These rules are described in the following section.

Shipment Contracts Sales contracts that require the seller to send the goods to the buyer, but not to a specifically named destination, are called **shipment contracts**. Under such contracts, the seller must do all of the following:

1. Put the goods in the carrier's possession and contract for the proper and safe transportation of the goods
2. Obtain and promptly deliver or tender in correct form any documents (a) necessary to enable the buyer to obtain possession of the goods, (b) required by the sales contract, or (c) required by usage of trade
3. Promptly notify the buyer of the shipment [UCC 2-504].

The buyer may reject the goods if a material delay or loss is caused by the seller's failure to make a proper contract for the shipment of goods or properly notify the buyer of the shipment. For example, if a shipment contract involves perishable goods and the seller fails to ship the goods via a refrigerated carrier, the buyer may rightfully reject the goods if they spoil during transit.

Destination Contracts A sales contract that requires the seller to deliver the goods to the buyer's place of business or another specified destination is a **destination contract**. Unless otherwise agreed, destination contracts require delivery to be tendered at the buyer's place of business or other location specified in the sales contract. Delivery must be at a reasonable time and in a reasonable manner and with proper notice to the buyer. Appropriate documents of title must be provided by the seller to enable the buyer to obtain the goods from the carrier [UCC 2-503].

Perfect Tender Rule

The seller or lessor is under a duty to deliver conforming goods. If the goods or tender of delivery fails in any respect to conform to the contract, the buyer or lessee may opt either (1) to reject the whole shipment, (2) to accept the whole shipment, or (3) to reject part and accept part of the shipment. This is referred to as the **perfect tender rule** [UCC 2-601, 2A-509].

CONSIDER THIS EXAMPLE: A sales contract requires the seller to deliver 100 shirts to a buyer. When the buyer inspects the delivered goods, it is discovered that 99 shirts conform to the contract and one shirt does not conform. Pursuant to the perfect tender rule, the buyer may reject the entire shipment. If a buyer accepts nonconforming goods, the buyer may seek remedies against the seller.

Exceptions to the Perfect Tender Rule The UCC alters the perfect tender rule in the following situations.

Agreement of the Parties The parties to the sales or lease contract may agree to limit the effect of the perfect tender rule. For example, they may decide that (1) only the defective or nonconforming goods may be rejected, (2) the seller or lessor may replace nonconforming goods or repair defects, and (3) the buyer or lessee will accept nonconforming goods with appropriate compensation from the seller or lessor.

Substitution of Carriers The UCC requires the seller to use a commercially reasonable substitute if (1) the agreed-upon manner of delivery fails or (2) the agreed-upon type of carrier becomes unavailable [UCC 2-614(1)].

shipment contract A sales contract that requires the seller to send the goods to the buyer but not to a specifically named destination.

destination contract A sales contract that requires the seller to deliver the goods to the buyer's place of business or another specified destination.

perfect tender rule A rule that says if the goods or tender of a delivery fails in any respect to conform to the contract, the buyer may opt either (1) to reject the whole shipment, (2) to accept the whole shipment, or (3) to reject part and accept part of the shipment.

"Convenience is the basis of mercantile law."
Lord Mansfield
Medcalf v. Hall
(1782)

CONSIDER THIS EXAMPLE: A sales contract specifies delivery of goods by MacTrucks, Inc., a common carrier, but a labor strike prevents delivery by this carrier. The seller must use any commercially reasonable substitute (such as another truck line, the rails, or the like). The buyer cannot reject the delivery because there is a substitute carrier. Unless otherwise agreed, the seller bears any increased cost of the substitute performance.

cure An opportunity to repair or replace defective or nonconforming goods.

Cure The UCC gives a seller or lessor who delivers nonconforming goods an opportunity to **cure** the nonconformity. Although the term *cure* is not defined by the UCC, it generally means an opportunity to repair or replace defective or nonconforming goods [UCC 2-508, 2A-513].

A cure may be attempted if the time for performance has not expired and the seller or lessor notifies the buyer or lessee of his or her intention to make a conforming delivery within the contract time.

CONSIDER THIS EXAMPLE: A lessee contracts to lease a BMW 850i automobile from a lessor for delivery July 1. On June 15, the lessor delivers a BMW 740i to the lessee, which the lessee rejects as nonconforming. The lessor has until July 1 to cure the nonconformity by delivering the BMW 850i specified in the contract.

A cure may also be attempted if the seller or lessor had reasonable grounds to believe the delivery would be accepted. The seller or lessor may have a further reasonable time to substitute a conforming tender.

CONSIDER THIS EXAMPLE: A buyer contracts to purchase 100 red dresses from a seller for delivery July 1. On July 1 the seller delivers 100 blue dresses to the buyer. In the past, the buyer has accepted different-colored dresses than those ordered. This time, though, the buyer rejects the blue dresses as nonconforming. The seller has a reasonable time after July 1 to deliver conforming red dresses to the buyer.

In the following case, a seller attempted to cure a defective delivery.

CASE 14.1

Joc Oil USA, Inc. v. Consolidated Edison Co. of New York, Inc.

30 UCC Rep.Serv. 426 (1980) New York Supreme Court, New York County

Facts Joc Oil USA, Inc. (Joc Oil) contracted to purchase low-sulfur fuel oil from an Italian oil refinery. The Italian refinery issued a certificate to Joc Oil indicating that the sulfur content of the oil was 0.50 percent. Joc Oil entered into a sales contract to sell the oil to Consolidated Edison Co. of New York, Inc. (Con Ed). Con Ed agreed to pay $17.875 per barrel for oil not to exceed 0.50 percent sulfur. When the ship delivering the oil arrived, it discharged the oil into three Con Ed storage tanks. On February 20, 1974, a final report issued by Con Ed stated that the sulfur content of the oil was 0.92 percent. At a meeting that day, Joc Oil offered to reduce the price of the oil by $0.50 to $0.80 per barrel. Con Ed expressed a willingness to accept the oil at $13 per barrel (the market price of oil at that time). Joc Oil then made an offer to cure the defect by substituting a conform-

ing shipment of oil that was already on a ship that was to arrive within two weeks. Con Ed rejected Joc Oil's offer to cure. Joc Oil sued Con Ed for breach of contract.

Issue Did Joc Oil have a right to cure the defect in delivery?

Decision Yes. The court held that under the circumstances of this case Joc Oil had the right to cure the defect in delivery and that Con Ed breached the contract by refusing to permit this cure. The court entered judgment against Con Ed, and awarded Joc Oil $1,385,512 in damages plus interest and the cost of this action.

Reason The UCC statutory right to cure is an exception to the pre-Code "perfect tender rule." The

UCC cure provision was conceived to protect a seller from surprise rejection by the buyer. In this case, the court held that Joc Oil had reasonable grounds to believe that its original shipment would be acceptable to Con Ed. The court found that Joc Oil made its offer to cure by tendering a new conforming shipment that would arrive within two weeks, a reasonable time in the court's view. Under the circumstances, Joc Oil had the right to—and did—make a reasonable and timely offer to cure. Con Ed's rejection was improper.

CASE QUESTIONS

Critical Legal Thinking Should the law recognize the right to cure a defective tender of goods? Why or why not?

Ethics Did Con Ed act ethically in this case? Did Joc Oil?

Business Implication Why do you think Con Ed rejected Joc Oil's offer to cure the defect in delivery? Explain.

Installment Contracts An **installment contract** is one that requires or authorizes the goods to be delivered and accepted in separate lots. Such contracts must contain a clause that states "each delivery is a separate contract" or equivalent language. An example of an installment contract is one in which a buyer orders 100 shirts, to be delivered in four equal installments of 25 items.

The UCC alters the perfect tender rule with regard to installment contracts. The buyer or lessee may reject the entire contract only if the nonconformity or default with respect to any installment or installments substantially impairs the value of the entire contract. The buyer or lessee may reject any nonconforming installment if the value of the installment is impaired and the defect cannot be cured. Thus, in each case the court must determine whether the nonconforming installment impairs the value of the entire contract or only that installment [UCC 2-612, 2A-510].

> **installment contract**
> A contract that requires or authorizes the goods to be delivered and accepted in separate lots.

Destruction of Goods The UCC provides that if goods identified to a sales or lease contract are totally destroyed without the fault of either party before the risk of loss passes to the buyer or lessee, the contract is void. Both parties are then excused from performing the contract.

If the goods are only partially destroyed, the buyer or lessee may inspect the goods and then choose either to treat the contract as void or to accept the goods. If the buyer or lessee opts to accept the goods, the purchase price or rent will be reduced in compensation for the damage [UCC 2-613, 2A-221].

> *"This is the kind of order which makes the administration of justice stink in the nostrils of commercial men."*
> A.L. Smith, L.J.
> *Graham v. Sutton, Carden & Co.* (1897)

CONSIDER THIS EXAMPLE: A buyer contracts to purchase a sofa from a seller. The seller agrees to deliver the sofa to the buyer's home. The truck delivering the sofa is hit by an automobile and the sofa is totally destroyed. Because the risk of loss has not passed to the buyer, the contract is voided and the buyer does not have to pay for the sofa.

ETHICAL PERSPECTIVE

Good Faith and Reasonableness Govern the Performance of Sales and Lease Contracts

Generally, the common law of contracts only obligates the parties to perform according to the terms of their contract. There is no breach of contract unless the parties fail to meet these terms. It is as simple as that.

Recognizing that certain situations may develop that are not expressly provided for in the contract, or that strict adherence to the terms of the contract without doing more may not be sufficient to accomplish the contract's *continued* objective, the Uniform Commercial Code (UCC) adopts two broad principles that govern the performance of sales and lease contracts: *good faith* and *reasonableness*.

UCC 1-203 states that "Every contract or duty within this Act imposes an obligation of good faith in its performance or enforcement." Although both parties owe a duty of good faith in the performance of a sales or lease contract, merchants are held to a higher standard of good faith than nonmerchants. Nonmerchants are held to the subjective standard of honesty in fact while merchants are held to the objective standard of fair dealing in the trade [UCC 2-103(1)(b)].

The words *reasonable* and *reasonably* are used throughout the UCC to establish the duties of performance by the parties to sales and lease contracts. For example, unless otherwise specified, the parties must act within a "reasonable" time [UCC 1-204(1)(2)]. Another example is if the seller does not deliver the goods as contracted, the buyer may make "reasonable" purchases to cover (i.e., obtain substitute performance) [UCC 2-712(1)]. The term *commercial reasonableness* is used to establish the certain duties of merchants under the UCC. Articles 2 and 2A do not specifically define the terms *reasonable* or *commercial reasonableness*. Instead, these terms are defined by reference to the course of performance or the course of dealing between the parties, usage of trade, and such.

Note that the concepts of good faith and reasonableness extend to the "spirit" of the contract as well as the contract terms. The underlying theory is that the parties are more apt to perform properly if their conduct is to be judged against these principles. This is a major advance in the law of contracts. Some state courts have extended the UCC duties of good faith and reasonableness to common law contracts.

1. Do you think the UCC's mandate of "good faith" changes how contracting parties act in the performance of their contracts? Explain.
2. Should the "good faith" duty of the UCC be extended to all contracts? Why or why not?

BUYER'S AND LESSEE'S OBLIGATIONS

When the seller or lessor has properly tendered delivery, the buyer or lessee is obligated to accept and pay for the goods in accordance with the sales or lease contract. If there is no agreement, the provisions of the UCC control.

Right of Inspection

Unless otherwise agreed, the buyer or lessee has the right to inspect goods that are tendered, delivered, or identified to the sales contract prior to accepting or paying for them. If the goods are shipped, the inspection may take place after their arrival. If the inspected goods do not conform to the contract, the buyer or lessee may reject them without paying for them [UCC 2-513(1), 2A-515(1)].

The parties may agree as to the time, place, and manner of inspection. If there is not such agreement, the inspection must occur at a reasonable time, place, and manner. Reasonableness depends on the circumstances of the case, common usage of trade, prior course of dealing between the parties, and such. If the goods conform to the contract, the buyer pays for the inspection. If the goods are rejected for nonconformance, the cost of inspection can be recovered from the seller [UCC 2-513(2)].

C.O.D. shipment A type of shipment contract where the buyer agrees to pay the shipper cash upon the delivery of the goods.

Buyers who agree to **C.O.D. (cash on delivery)** deliveries are not entitled to inspect the goods before paying for them. In certain sales contracts (e.g., cost, insurance, and freight [or C.I.F.] contracts), payment is due from the buyer upon receipt of documents of title even if the goods have not yet been received. In such cases, the buyer is not entitled to inspect the goods before paying for them [UCC 2-513(3)].

Payment

Goods that are accepted must be paid for [UCC 2-607(1)]. Unless the parties agree otherwise, payment is due from a buyer when and where the goods are delivered even if the place of delivery is the same as the place of shipment. Buyers often purchase goods on credit extended by the seller. Unless the parties agree to other terms, the credit period begins to run from the time the goods are shipped [UCC 2-310]. A lessee must pay lease payments in accordance with the lease contract [UCC 2A-516(1)].

The goods can be paid for in any manner currently acceptable in the ordinary course of business (e.g., check, credit card, or the like) unless the seller demands payment in cash or the contract names a specific form of payment. If the seller requires cash payment, the buyer must be given an extension of time necessary to procure the cash. If the buyer pays by check, payment is conditional on the check being honored (paid) when it is presented to the bank for payment [UCC 2-511].

Acceptance

Acceptance occurs when the buyer or lessee takes any of the following actions after a reasonable opportunity to inspect the goods: (1) signifies to the seller or lessor in words or by conduct that the goods are conforming or that the buyer or lessee will take or retain the goods in spite of their nonconformity or (2) fails to effectively reject the goods within a reasonable time after their delivery or tender by the seller or lessor. Acceptance also occurs if a buyer acts inconsistently with the seller's ownership rights in the goods. For example, the buyer resells the goods delivered by the seller [UCC 2-606(1), 2A-515(1)].

Buyers and lessees may only accept delivery of a "commercial unit." A commercial unit is a unit of goods that commercial usage deems is a single whole for purpose of sale. Thus, it may be a single article (such as a machine), a set of articles (such as a suite of furniture or an assortment of sizes), a quantity (such as a bale, a gross, or a carload), or any other unit treated in use or in the relevant market as a single whole. Acceptance of a part of any commercial unit is acceptance of the entire unit [UCC 2-606(2), 2A-515(2)].

Revocation of Acceptance

A buyer or lessee who has accepted goods may subsequently revoke his or her acceptance if (1) the goods are nonconforming, (2) the nonconformity substantially impairs the value of the goods to the buyer or lessee, and (3) one of the following factors is shown: (a) the seller's or lessor's promise to seasonably cure the nonconformity is not met, (b) the goods were accepted before the nonconformity was discovered and the nonconformity was difficult to discover, or (c) the goods were accepted before the nonconformity was discovered and the seller or lessor assured the buyer or lessee that the goods were conforming.

Revocation is not effective until the seller or lessor is so notified. In addition, the revocation must occur within a reasonable time after the buyer or lessee discovers or should have discovered the grounds for the revocation. The revocation, which must be of a lot or commercial unit, must occur before there is any substantial change in the condition of the goods (e.g., before perishable goods spoil) [UCC 2-608(1), 2A-517(1)].

In the following case, the court had to decide whether to allow revocation of a sales contract.

acceptance Occurs when a buyer or lessee takes any of the following actions after a reasonable opportunity to inspect the goods: (1) signifies to the seller or lessor in words or by conduct that the goods are conforming or that the buyer or lessee will take or retain the goods in spite of their nonconformity; or (2) fails to effectively reject the goods within a reasonable time after their delivery or tender by the seller or lessor. Acceptance also occurs if a buyer acts inconsistently with the seller's ownership rights in the goods.

revocation Reversal of acceptance.

CASE 14.2

Fortin v. Ox-Bow Marina, Inc.
557 N.E.2d 1157 (1990) Supreme Judicial Court of Massachusetts

Facts In the spring of 1985, Robert and Marie Fortin ordered a 32-foot Bayliner Conquest power boat from Ox-Bow Marina, Inc. (Ox-Bow). In May, on the day of closing, the Fortins checked their boat and found that none of the preparation work had been done, none of the special equipment they had ordered had been installed, and several defects
continued

needed to be repaired or corrected, including a nonfunctioning hot water pump, a broken pedestal seat, a nonfunctioning flush mechanism in the marine toilet system, and chips in the wood trim. Ox-Bow's representative assured the Fortins that the problems would be corrected if they closed on the transaction. The Fortins agreed to close. In order to pay Ox-Bow, they traded in their old boat, paid $6,259 cash, and borrowed $51,500 from Horizon Financial.

In May and June, the Fortins requested Ox-Bow to correct the problems, which Ox-Bow did not do. When the Fortins set out on their maiden voyage on June 22, 1985, they discovered that the depth finder and marine radio did not work, the marine toilets were not functioning properly, and one of the two engines overheated and had to be shut down. Ox-Bow promised to fix these defects but again did not. The Fortins continued to request Ox-Bow to correct all of the defects. Although Ox-Bow always promised to comply, it never did.

Finally, on October 31, 1985, the Fortins notified Ox-Bow that they were revoking their acceptance of the Bayliner and sought a refund of their purchase price, plus damages. The judge ruled that the Fortins had effectively revoked acceptance of the boat and awarded them damages in the amount of $24,364, including sales tax and interest paid on the loan. Ox-Bow appealed.

Issue Was the Fortins' revocation of acceptance effective?

Decision Yes. The appellate court held that the Fortins' revocation of acceptance was effective. Affirmed.

Reason A buyer may subsequently revoke his or her acceptance of goods if the buyer can show that the nonconformity in the goods substantially impairs its value and that the buyer accepted the goods on the reasonable assumption that the nonconformity would be cured and it has not been reasonably cured. The court ruled that this was the situation in this case. The Fortins accepted the Bayliner on Ox-Bow's assurances that the defects would be cured. The Fortins had the legal right to revoke their acceptance because the defects were not cured and substantially impaired the value of the boat to them.

CASE QUESTIONS

Critical Legal Thinking Should a buyer be permitted to revoke his acceptance once it has been made? Why or why not?

Ethics Did Ox-Bow act ethically in this case?

Business Implication Why do you think Ox-Bow acted as it did in this case? Would it have been cheaper to have fixed the boat in the first place?

INTERNATIONAL PERSPECTIVE

The United Nations Convention on Contracts for the International Sale of Goods

Businesspersons who engage in international commerce face the daunting task of trying to comply with the laws of many nations. To ease this burden, more than 60 countries are signatories to the United Nations Convention on Contracts for the International Sale of Goods (CISG). This treaty, which took more than 50 years to negotiate, incorporates rules from all the major legal systems of the world.

The CISG establishes uniform rules for the formation and enforcement of contracts involving the international sale of goods. Many of its provisions are remarkably similar to the provisions of the American Uniform Commercial Code. The CISG applies if the buyer and seller have their places of business in different countries and both nations are parties to the convention. The contracting parties may agree to exclude (i.e., opt out of) the CISG and let other laws apply. The parties to any international contract can agree that the CISG controls even if one or both of their countries are not signatories to the convention.

ASSURANCE OF PERFORMANCE

Each party to a sales or lease contract expects that every other party will perform their contractual obligations. If one party to the contract has reasonable grounds to believe that the other party either will not or cannot perform his or her contractual obligations, an **adequate assurance of due performance** may be demanded in writing. If it is commercially reasonable, the party making the demand may suspend his or her performance until adequate assurance of due performance is received from the other party [UCC 2-609, 2A-401].

CONSIDER THIS EXAMPLE: A buyer contracts to purchase 1,000 bushels of wheat from a farmer. The contract requires delivery on September 1. In July, the buyer learns that floods have caused substantial crop loss in the area of the seller's farm. The farmer receives the buyer's written demand for adequate assurance on July 15. The farmer fails to give adequate assurance of performance. The buyer may suspend performance and treat the sales contract as repudiated.

> **adequate assurance of performance** A party to a sales or lease contract may demand an adequate assurance of performance from the other party if there is an indication that the contract will be breached by that party.

ANTICIPATORY REPUDIATION

Occasionally, a party to a sales or lease contract repudiates the contract before his or her performance is due under the contract. If the repudiation impairs the value of the contract to the aggrieved party, it is called **anticipatory repudiation**. Mere wavering on performance does not meet the test for anticipatory repudiation.

> **anticipatory repudiation** The repudiation of a sales or lease contract by one of the parties prior to the date set for performance.

If an anticipatory repudiation does occur, the aggrieved party can (1) await performance by the repudiating party for a commercially reasonable time (e.g., until the delivery date or shortly thereafter) or (2) treat the contract as breached at the time of the anticipatory repudiation, which gives the aggrieved party an immediate cause of action. In either case, the aggrieved party may suspend performance of his or her obligations under the contract [UCC 2-610, 2A-402].

An anticipatory repudiation may be retracted before the repudiating party's next performance is due if the aggrieved party has not (1) canceled the contract, (2) materially changed his or her position (e.g., purchased goods from another party), or (3) otherwise indicated that the repudiation is considered final. The retraction may be made by any method that clearly indicates the repudiating party's intent to perform the contract [UCC 2-611, 2A-403].

ETHICAL PERSPECTIVE

Unconscionable Sales and Lease Contracts

Can a contract term ever be so unfair as to be legally ignored by a party to the contract? After all, law and morality require that contracting parties adhere to the terms of their contract. The UCC's doctrine of unconscionability says that if a sales or lease contract (or any clause in it) is unconscionable, the court may either refuse to enforce the contract or limit the application of the unconscionable clause [UCC 2-302, 2A-108]. Consider the following case.

On August 31, 1975, Dynatron, Inc. (Dynatron), executed a lease agreement with Hertz Commercial Leasing Corporation (Hertz) to finance the lease of a Minolta copy machine that was supplied by A-Copy of Glastonbury, Connecticut (A-Copy). The lease agreement, which was prepared by Hertz, designated Dynatron as the lessee and Hertz as the lessor. The vendor was A-Copy. The lease was for a 60-month term, at a monthly rental of $3,720. Paragraph 11 of the lease is a liquidated damage clause that stipulates that in event of default, the lessee is obligated to pay the lessor any arrears of rentals, the entire balance of the rent, the lessor's expenses in retaking

continued

possession and removing the equipment, and up to 20 percent attorney's fees.

Dynatron claimed that almost immediately following delivery, the machine developed operational problems and that its reproduction qualities were defective. Dynatron wrote letters to Hertz and A-Copy demanding repair or replacement of the machine. The machine was not repaired or replaced. Dynatron made no payments on the lease. Finally, Dynatron requested that Hertz repossess the machine. Dynatron then purchased a Xerox copying machine. After the lapse of about one year, or about February 14, 1978, Hertz picked up the machine. In May 1978, Hertz sold the machine for $500. On August 30, 1980, Hertz sued Dynatron to recover a deficiency judgment.

Hertz pointed out that Paragraph 11 refers to the stated items of recoverable damages by the lessor as "liquidated damages and not as a penalty." The court held that this statement is not persuasive or binding on the court. The lessee, in spite of its default, may prove that the lease was the product of unconscionability. The court may refuse to enforce a liquidated damage clause on the ground that the lessor sustained no damages whatsoever from the particular breach of contract as a matter of law.

The court held that the terms and conditions of the finance lease agreement in this case were unconscionable and that the provisions of the lease are not enforceable against the lessee in any respect whatsoever. Judgment was therefore entered for Dynatron, Inc. [*Hertz Commercial Leasing Corporation v. Dynatron, Inc.* 472 A.2d 872 (Conn. 1980)]

1. Was it ethical for Hertz to include the liquidated damage clause in its form contract?
2. Did Dynatron act morally in signing the lease and then trying to get out from under its provision?
3. Is the doctrine of unconscionability easy to apply?

SELLER'S AND LESSOR'S REMEDIES

Various remedies are available to sellers and lessors if a buyer or lessee breaches the contract. These remedies are discussed in the paragraphs that follow.

Right to Withhold Delivery

withholding delivery The act of the seller or lessor purposefully refusing to deliver goods to the buyer or lessee upon breach of the sales or lease contract by the buyer or lessee or the insolvency of the buyer or lessee.

Delivery of goods may be withheld if the seller or lessor is in possession of them when the buyer or lessee breaches the contract. This remedy is available if the buyer or lessee wrongfully rejects or revokes acceptance of the goods, fails to make payment when due, or repudiates the contract. If part of the goods under a contract have been delivered when the buyer or lessee materially breaches the contract, the seller or lessor may withhold delivery of the remainder of the affected goods [UCC 2-703(a), 2A-523(1)(c)].

A seller or lessor who discovers that the buyer or lessee is insolvent before the goods are delivered may refuse to deliver as promised unless the buyer or lessee pays cash for the goods [UCC 2-702(1), 2A-525(1)]. Under the UCC, a person is insolvent when he (1) ceases to pay his debts in the ordinary course of business, (2) cannot pay his debts as they become due, or (3) is insolvent within the meaning of the federal bankruptcy law [UCC 1-201(23)].

Right to Stop Delivery of Goods in Transit

in transit A state in which goods are in the possession of a bailee or carrier and not in the hands of the buyer, seller, lessee, or lessor.

Often, sellers and lessors employ common carriers and other bailees (e.g., warehouses) to hold and deliver goods to buyers and lessees. The goods are considered to be **in transit** while they are in possession of these carriers or bailees. A seller or lessor that learns of the buyer's or lessee's insolvency while the goods are in transit may stop delivery of the goods irrespective of the size of the shipment.

Essentially the same remedy is available if the buyer or lessee repudiates the contract, fails to make payment when due, or otherwise gives the seller or lessor some other right to withhold or reclaim the goods. However, in these circumstances the delivery can be stopped only if it constitutes a carload, a truckload, a planeload, or larger express or freight shipment [UCC 2-705(1), 2A-526(1)].

The seller or lessor must give sufficient notice to allow the bailee, by reasonable diligence, to prevent delivery of the goods. After receipt of notice, the bailee must hold and deliver the goods according to the directions of the seller or lessor. The seller or lessor is responsible for all expenses borne by the bailee in stopping the goods [UCC 2-705(3), 2A-526(3)]. Goods may be stopped in transit until the buyer or lessee obtains possession of the goods or the carrier or other bailee acknowledges that it is holding the goods for the buyer or lessee [UCC 2-705(2), 2A-526(2)].

Right to Reclaim Goods

In certain situations, a seller or lessor may demand the return of the goods it sold or leased that are already in the possession of the buyer or lessee. In a sale transaction, **reclamation** is permitted in two situations. If the goods are delivered in a credit sale and the seller then discovers that the buyer was insolvent, the seller has 10 days within which to demand that the goods be returned [UCC 2-507(2)]. If the buyer misrepresented his or her solvency in writing within three months before delivery [UCC 2-702(2)] or paid for goods in a cash sale with a check that bounces [UCC 2-507(2)], the seller may reclaim the goods at any time. A lessor may reclaim goods in the possession of the lessee if the lessee is in default on the contract [UCC 2A-525(2)].

To exercise a right of reclamation, the seller or lessor must send the buyer or lessee a written notice demanding return of the goods. The seller or lessor may not use self-help to reclaim the goods if the buyer or lessee refuses to honor his or her demand. Instead, appropriate legal proceedings must be instituted.

Right to Dispose of Goods

If the buyer or lessee breaches or repudiates the sales or lease contract before the seller or lessor has delivered the goods, the seller or lessor may resell or release the goods and recover damages from the buyer or lessee [UCC 2-703(d), 2-706(1); UCC 2A-523(1)(e), 2A-527(1)]. This right also arises if the seller or lessor has reacquired the goods after stopping them in transit.

The disposition of the goods by the seller or lessor must be made in good faith and in a commercially reasonable manner. The goods may be disposed of as a unit or in parcels in a public or private transaction. The seller or lessor must give the buyer or lessee reasonable notification of his or her intention to dispose of the goods unless the goods threaten to quickly decline in value or are perishable. The party who buys or leases the goods in good faith for value takes the goods free of any rights of the original buyer or lessee [UCC 2-706(5), 2A-527(4)].

The seller or lessor may recover any damages incurred on the disposition of the goods. In the case of a sales contract, damages are defined as the difference between the disposition price and the original contract price. In the case of a lease contract, damages are the difference between the disposition price and the rent the original lessee would have paid.

The profit does not revert to the original buyer or lessee if the seller or lessor disposes of the goods at a higher price than the buyer or lessee contracted to pay. The seller or lessor may also recover any **incidental damages** (i.e., reasonable expenses incurred in stopping delivery, transportation charges, storage charges, sales commissions, and the like [UCC 2-710, 2A-530]) incurred on the disposition of the goods [UCC 2-706(1), 2A-527(2)].

CONSIDER THIS EXAMPLE: A buyer contracts to purchase a racehorse for $20,000. When the seller tenders delivery, the buyer refuses to accept the horse or pay for it. The seller, in good faith and in a commercially reasonable manner, resells the horse to

stopping delivery of goods in transit A seller or lessor may stop delivery of goods in transit if he or she learns of the buyer's or lessee's insolvency or the buyer or lessee repudiates the contract, fails to make payment when due, or gives the seller or lessor some other right to withhold the goods.

reclamation The right of a seller or lessor to demand the return of goods from the buyer or lessee under specified situations.

disposition of goods A seller or lessor that is in possession of goods at the time the buyer or lessee breaches or repudiate the contract may in good faith resell, release, or otherwise dispose of the goods in a commercially reasonable manner and recover damages, including incidental damages, from the buyer or lessee.

incidental damages When goods are resold or released, incidental damages are reasonable expenses incurred in stopping delivery, transportation charges, storage charges, sales commissions, and so on.

a third party for $17,000. Incidental expenses of $500 are incurred on the resale. The seller can recover $3,500 from the original buyer: the $3,000 difference between the resale price and the contract price and $500 for incidental expenses.

Unfinished Goods Sometimes the sales or lease contract is breached or repudiated before the goods are finished. In such cases, the seller or lessor may choose either (1) to cease manufacturing the goods and resell them for scrap or salvage value or (2) to complete the manufacture of the goods and resell, release, or otherwise dispose of them to another party [UCC 2-704(2), 2A-524(2)]. The seller or lessor may recover damages from the breaching buyer or lessee.

Right to Recover the Purchase Price or Rent

recovery of the purchase price or rent A seller or lessor may recover the contracted-for purchase price or rent from the buyer or lessee if the buyer or lessee (1) fails to pay for accepted goods, (2) breaches the contract and the seller or lessor cannot dispose of the goods, or if (3) the goods are damaged or lost after the risk of loss passes to the buyer or lessee.

In certain circumstances, the UCC provides that the seller or lessor may sue the buyer or lessee to recover the purchase price or rent stipulated in the sales or lease contract. This remedy is available in the following situations:

1. The buyer or lessee accepts the goods but fails to pay for them when the price or rent is due
2. The buyer or lessee breaches the contract after the goods have been identified to the contract and the seller or lessor cannot resell or dispose of them
3. The goods are damaged or lost after the risk of loss passes to the buyer or lessee [UCC 2-709(1), 2A-529(1)].

To recover the purchase price or rent, the seller or lessor must hold the goods for the buyer or lessee. However, if resale or other disposition of the goods becomes possible prior to the collection of the judgment, the seller or lessor may resell or dispose of them. In such situations, the net proceeds of any disposition must be credited against the judgment [UCC 2-709(2), 2A-529(2)(3)]. The seller or lessor may also recover incidental damages from the buyer or lessee.

Right to Recover Damages for Breach of Contract

recovery of damages A seller or lessor may recover damages measured as the difference between the contract price (or rent) and the market price (or rent) at the time and place the goods were to be delivered, plus incidental damages, from a buyer or lessee who repudiates the contract or wrongfully rejects tendered goods.

If a buyer or lessee repudiates a sales contract or wrongfully rejects tendered goods, the seller or lessor may sue to recover the damages caused by the buyer's or lessee's breach. Generally, the amount of damages is calculated as the difference between the contract price (or rent) and the market price (or rent) of the goods at the time and place the goods were to be delivered to the buyer or lessee, plus incidental damages [UCC 2-7081, 2A-528(1)].

recovery of lost profits If the recovery of damages would be inadequate to put the seller or lessor in as good a position as if the contract had been fully performed by the buyer or lessee, the seller or lessor may recover lost profits, plus an allowance for overhead and incidental damages, from the buyer or lessee.

If the preceding measure of damage will not put the seller or lessor in as good a position as performance of the contract would have, the seller or lessor can seek to recover any **lost profits** that would have resulted from the full performance of the contract, plus an allowance for reasonable overhead and incidental damages [UCC 2-708(2), 2A-528(2)].

Right to Cancel the Contract

cancellation A seller or lessor may cancel a sales or lease contract if the buyer or lessee rejects or revokes acceptance of the goods, fails to pay for the goods, or repudiates the contract in part or in whole.

The seller or lessor may cancel a sales or lease contract if the buyer or lessee breaches that contract by rejecting or revoking acceptance of the goods, failing to pay for the goods, or repudiating all or any part of the contract. The **cancellation** may refer only to the affected goods or to the entire contract if the breach is material [UCC 2-703(f), 2A-523(1)(a)].

A seller or lessor who rightfully cancels a sales or lease contract by notifying the buyer or lessee is discharged of any further obligations under that contract. The buyer's or lessee's duties are not discharged, however. The seller or lessor retains the right to seek damages for the breach [UCC 2-106(4), 2A-523(3)].

BUSINESS CHECKLIST

Lost Volume Seller

Should a seller be permitted to recover the profits it lost on a sale to a defaulting buyer if the seller sold the goods to another buyer? The answer is, it depends. If the seller had only one item or a limited number of items and could produce no more, then the seller cannot recover lost profits from the defaulting buyer. This is because the seller made those profits on the sale of the item to the new buyer. If, however, the seller could have produced more of the item, then the seller is a "lost volume seller." In this situation, the seller can make the profit from the sale of the item to the new buyer and sue the defaulting buyer to recover the profit it would have made from this sale.

BUYER'S AND LESSEE'S REMEDIES

The UCC provides a variety of remedies to a buyer or lessee upon the seller's or lessor's breach of a sales or lease contract. These remedies are discussed in the following paragraphs.

Right to Reject Nonconforming Goods or Improperly Tendered Goods

If the goods or the seller's or lessor's tender of delivery fails to conform to the sales or lease contract in any way, the buyer or lessee may (1) reject the whole, (2) accept the whole, or (3) accept any commercial unit and reject the rest. If the buyer or lessee chooses to reject the goods, he or she must identify defects that are ascertainable by reasonable inspection. Failure to do so prevents the buyer or lessee from relying on those defects to justify the rejection if the defect could have been cured by a seller or lessor who was notified in a timely manner [UCC 2-601, 2A-509].

Nonconforming or improperly tendered goods must be rejected within a reasonable time after their delivery or tender. The seller or lessor must be notified of the rejection. The buyer or lessee must hold any rightfully rejected goods with reasonable care for a reasonable time [UCC 2-602(2), 2A-512(1)].

If the buyer or lessee is a merchant, and the seller or lessor has no agent or place of business at the market where the goods are rejected, the merchant–buyer or merchant–lessee must follow any reasonable instructions received from the seller or lessor with respect to the rejected goods [UCC 2-603, 2A-511]. If the seller or lessor gives no instructions and the rejected goods are perishable or will quickly decline in value, the buyer or lessee may make reasonable efforts to sell them on the seller's or lessor's behalf [UCC 2-604, 2A-512].

Any buyer or lessee who rightfully rejects goods is entitled to reimbursement from the seller or lessor for reasonable expenses incurred in holding, storing, reselling, shipping, and otherwise caring for the rejected goods.

Right to Recover Goods from an Insolvent Seller or Lessor

If the buyer or lessee makes partial or full payment for the goods before they are received and the seller or lessor becomes insolvent within 10 days after receiving the first payment, then the buyer or lessee may recover the goods from the seller or lessor. To do so, the buyer or lessee must tender the unpaid portion of the purchase price or

rejection of nonconforming goods If the goods or the seller's or lessor's tender of delivery fails to conform to the contract, the buyer or lessee may (1) reject the whole, (2) accept the whole, or (3) accept any commercial unit and reject the rest.

recovery of goods from an insolvent seller or lessor A buyer or lessee who has wholly or partially paid for goods before they are received may recover the goods from a seller or lessor who becomes insolvent within 10 days after receiving the first payment; the buyer or lessee must tender the remaining purchase price or rent due under the contract.

rent due under the sales or lease contract. Only conforming goods that are identified to the contract may be recovered [UCC 2-502, 2A-522]. This remedy is often referred to as **capture**.

Right to Obtain Specific Performance

specific performance A decree of the court that orders a seller or lessor to perform his or her obligations under the contract; usually occurs when the goods in question are unique, such as art or antiques.

If the goods are unique or the remedy at law is inadequate, a buyer or lessee may obtain **specific performance** of the sales or lease contract. A decree of specific performance orders the seller or lessor to perform the contract. Specific performance is usually used to obtain possession of works of art, antiques, rare coins, and other unique items [UCC 2-716(1), 2A-521(1)].

CONSIDER THIS EXAMPLE: A buyer enters into a sales contract to purchase a specific Rembrandt painting from a seller for $10 million. When the buyer tenders payment, the seller refuses to sell the painting to the buyer. The buyer may bring an equity action to obtain a decree of specific performance from the court ordering the seller to sell the painting to the buyer.

Right to Cover

cover Right of a buyer or lessee to purchase or lease substitute goods if a seller or lessor fails to make delivery of the goods or repudiates the contract, or if the buyer or lessee rightfully rejects the goods or justifiably revokes their acceptance.

The buyer or lessee may **cover** by purchasing or renting substitute goods if the seller or lessor fails to make delivery of the goods or repudiates the contract, or the buyer or lessee rightfully rejects the goods or justifiably revokes their acceptance. The buyer's or lessee's cover must be made in good faith and without unreasonable delay. If the exact commodity is not available, the buyer or lessee may purchase or lease any commercially reasonable substitute.

A buyer or lessee who rightfully covers may sue the seller or lessor to recover as damages the difference between the cost of cover and the contract price or rent. The buyer or lessee may also recover incidental and consequential damages, less expenses saved (such as delivery costs) [UCC 2-712, 2A-518]. The UCC does not require a buyer or lessee to cover when a seller or lessor breaches a sales or lease contract. Failure of the buyer or lessee to cover does not bar the buyer from other remedies against the seller.

The issue of cover is addressed in the following case.

CASE 14.3

Red River Commodities, Inc. v. Eidsness
459 N.W.2d 811 (1990) Supreme Court of North Dakota

Facts In early 1988, George Eidsness, a North Dakota farmer, entered into a contract to grow and sell 229,000 pounds of confection sunflowers to Red River Commodities, Inc. (RRC), at a price of $0.1125 per pound. When Eidsness did not deliver any sunflowers to RRC from his 1988 crop, RRC purchased replacement sunflowers from other sellers at $0.26 per pound. In mid-December 1988, RRC learned that Eidsness was selling sunflowers to a competitor at $0.22 per pound. RRC sued Eidsness to recover damages. The trial court held in favor of RRC and awarded it the difference between the cost of cover at $0.26 per pound and the contract price of $0.1125 per pound. The award

amounted to $3,377,750 ($14.75 × 229,000). Eidsness appealed.

Issue Can RRC recover as damages the difference between the cost of cover and the original contract price?

Decision Yes. The appellate court held that RRC properly covered by purchasing replacement goods and was entitled to recover the increased cost of cover from Eidsness.

Reason The court held that Eidsness had breached the sales contract with RRC by failing to deliver sunflowers at the contract price. RRC had properly covered by purchasing replacement sunflowers from other sellers at $0.26 per pound. The $0.1475 per pound difference between the contract price and the cover price was recoverable.

CASE QUESTIONS

Critical Legal Thinking Should a buyer be permitted to cover by purchasing replacement goods

even if they are more expensive than the contract price? Why or why not?

Ethics Did Eidsness act ethically in this case?

Business Implication Does the cover and recovery of damages rule make an innocent buyer whole against the defaulting seller? Explain.

Right to Replevy Goods

A buyer or lessee may replevy (recover) goods from a seller or lessor who is wrongfully withholding them. The buyer or lessee must show that he or she was unable to cover or that attempts at cover will be unavailing. Thus, the goods must be scarce, but not unique. **Replevin** actions are available only as to goods identified to the sales or lease contract [UCC 2-716(3), 2A-521(3)].

replevin An action by a buyer or lessor to recover scarce goods wrongfully withheld by a seller or lessor.

CONSIDER THIS EXAMPLE: On January 1, IBM contracts to purchase monitors for computers from a seller for delivery on June 1. IBM intends to attach the monitors to a new computer that will be introduced on June 30. On June 1, the seller refuses to sell the monitors to IBM because it can get a higher price from another buyer. IBM tries to cover but cannot. IBM may successfully replevy the monitors from the seller.

Right to Cancel the Contract

If a seller or lessor fails to deliver conforming goods or repudiates the contract, or the buyer or lessee rightfully rejects the goods or justifiably revokes acceptance of the goods, the buyer or lessee may cancel the sales or lease contract. The contract may be canceled with respect to the affected goods or, if there is a material breach, the whole contract. A buyer or lessee who rightfully cancels a contract is discharged from any further obligations on the contract and retains his or her rights to other remedies against the seller or lessor [UCC 2-711(1), 2A-508(1)(a)].

cancellation A buyer or lessee may cancel a sales or lease contract if the seller or lessor fails to deliver conforming goods or repudiates the contract, or the buyer or lessee rightfully rejects the goods or justifiably revokes acceptance of the goods.

Right to Recover Damages for Nondelivery or Repudiation

If a seller or lessor fails to deliver the goods or repudiates the sales or lease contract, the buyer or lessee may recover damages. The measure of damages is the difference between the contract price (or original rent) and the market price (or rent) at the time the buyer or lessee learned of the breach. Incidental and consequential damages, less expenses saved, can also be recovered [UCC 2-713, 2A-519].

damages A buyer or lessee may recover damages from a seller or lessor who fails to deliver the goods or repudiates the contract; damages are measured as the difference between the contract price (or original rent) and the market price (or rent) at the time the buyer or lessee learned of the breach.

CONSIDER THIS EXAMPLE: Fresh Foods Company contracts to purchase 10,000 bushels of soybeans from Sunshine Farms for $5 per bushel. Delivery is to be on August 1. On August 1 the market price of soybeans is $7 per bushel. Sunshine Farms does not deliver the soybeans. Fresh Foods decides not to cover and to do without the soybeans. Fresh Foods sues Sunshine for market value minus the contract price damages. It can recover $20,000 ($7 market price minus $5 contract price multiplied by 10,000 bushels) plus incidental damages less expenses saved because of Sunshine's breach. Fresh Foods cannot recover consequential damages because it did not attempt to cover.

Right to Recover Damages for Accepted Nonconforming Goods

damages for accepted nonconforming goods
A buyer or lessee may accept the damages caused by the breach from the seller or lessor or deduct the damages from any part of the purchase price or rent still due under the contract.

A buyer or lessee may accept nonconforming goods from a seller or lessor. The acceptance does not prevent the buyer or lessee from suing the seller or lessor to recover as damages any loss resulting from the seller's or lessor's breach. Incidental and consequential damages may also be recovered. The buyer or lessee must notify the seller or lessor of the nonconformity within a reasonable time after the breach was or should have been discovered. Failure to do so bars the buyer or lessee from any recovery. If the buyer or lessee accepts nonconforming goods, he or she may deduct all or any part of the damages resulting from the breach from any part of the purchase price or rent still due under the contract [UCC 2-714(1), 2A-516(1)].

CONSIDER THIS EXAMPLE: A retail clothing store contracts to purchase 100 designer dresses for $100 per dress from a seller. The buyer pays for the dresses prior to delivery. After the dresses are delivered, the buyer discovers that 10 of the dresses have a flaw in them. The buyer may accept these nonconforming dresses and sue the seller for the reasonable damages resulting from the nonconformity.

STATUTE OF LIMITATIONS

UCC statute of limitations
A rule that provides that an action for breach of any written or oral sales or lease contract must commence within four years after the cause of action accrues. The parties may agree to reduce the limitations period to one year.

The **UCC statute of limitations** provides that an action for breach of any written or oral sales or lease contract must commence within four years after the cause of action accrues. The parties may agree to reduce the limitations period to one year, but they cannot extend it beyond four years.

A cause of action for breach of a sales contract accrues when the breach occurs, regardless of the aggrieved party's lack of knowledge of the breach. In the case of the default of a lease contract, a cause of action accrues either when the default occurs or when it is or should have been discovered by the aggrieved party, whichever is later. If a warranty explicitly extends to future performance, a cause of action does not accrue until the breach is or should have been discovered.

CONSIDER THIS EXAMPLE: A buyer purchases a snowmobile at a retailer's April "end of winter" sale. The buyer does not intend to use it until the following winter. In December, when the buyer first uses the snowmobile, it does not work properly. The statute of limitations begins to run in December.

The UCC statute of limitations does not apply if the action concerning the goods is based on a legal theory not provided in the UCC (e.g., strict liability, negligence). In such cases, the appropriate state's statute of limitations governs [UCC 2-725, 2A-506].

AGREEMENTS AFFECTING REMEDIES

"A proceeding may be perfectly legal and may yet be opposed to sound commercial principles."
L.J. Lindley
Verner v. General and Commercial Trust (1894)

The parties to a sales or lease contract may agree on remedies in addition to or in substitution for the remedies provided by the UCC. For example, the parties may limit the buyer's or lessee's remedies to repair and replacement of defective goods or parts or to the return of the goods and repayment (refund) of the purchase price or rent. The remedies agreed upon by the parties are in addition to the remedies provided by the UCC unless the parties expressly provide that they are exclusive. If an exclusive remedy fails of its essential purpose (e.g., there is an exclusive remedy of repair but there are no repair parts available), any remedy may be had as provided in the UCC.

Consequential damages for breach of a sales or lease contract may be limited or excluded unless the limitation or exclusion is unconscionable. With respect to consumer goods, a limitation of consequential damages for personal injuries is prima facie unconscionable. It is not unconscionable to limit consequential damages for a commercial loss [UCC 2-719, 2A-503].

The UCC permits parties to a sales or lease contract to establish in advance the damages that will be paid upon a breach of the contract. Such preestablished damages, called **liquidated damages**, substitute for actual damages. In a sales or lease contract, liquidated damages are valid if they are reasonable in light of the anticipated or actual harm caused by the breach, the difficulties of proof of loss, and the inconvenience or nonfeasibility of otherwise obtaining an adequate remedy [UCC 2-718(1), 2A-504].

liquidated damages
Damages that will be paid upon a breach of contract and that are established in advance.

INTERNATIONAL PERSPECTIVE

Nonconformity in International Sales Contracts

In the United States, the UCC lets a buyer reject goods if the goods or tender of delivery does not conform to the contract. When the goods are accepted, however, the buyer may refuse to keep the goods only if they have a substantial nonconformity that impairs their value to the buyer. The UCC rules are not widely copied in other countries, because they are generally perceived as unresponsive to commercial practice and the significant interests of the parties.

Outside the United States, sales laws try to encourage the seller to correct any defects while cautioning the buyer to be patient in awaiting the seller's performance. For example, under the French Civil Code a contracting party must seek a court order that releases him or her from his or her obligations to perform. In deciding whether to grant the request, the court considers a variety of factors, including the defendant's degree of fault and the seriousness of the breach.

In Germany, if a seller defaults, the buyer is required to give the breaching seller a reasonable time to correct the defect at the seller's expense. This is accompanied by the buyer's declaration that he or she will refuse to accept performance after the ex-

piration of the stated period. This declaration is known as a *Nachfrist* notice.

Many countries have adopted rules similar to this. The avoidance procedure adopted by the United Nations Convention on Contracts for the International Sale of Goods (CISG) is also based on the German rule.

Under the CISG, a buyer is allowed to avoid a contract (1) if the seller commits a fundamental breach or (2) if the seller either rejects the buyer's *Nachfrist* notice or does not perform within the period it specifies. Both the period and the obligation to perform must be clearly stated.

WORKING THE WEB

Zip Codes and Addresses The U.S. Post Office has a database of zip codes and addresses.
Visit at http://www.usps.gov/ncsc/

Toll-Free Internet Directory AT&T has a Toll-Free Internet Directory where you can find businesses by name or category.
Visit at http://www.tollfree.att.net/dir800/

Ultimate Yellow Pages The Ultimate Yellow Pages is a good place to find a business in another city even if you do not have the address. Check out this site, which allows you to search various databases by name, city, and category.
Visit at http://www.theultimates.com/yellow/

BISNIS Online "BISNIS Online is the Department of Commerce's Business Information Service for the Newly Independent States—a one-stop shop for doing business in Russia and the other states of the former Soviet Union."
Visit at http://www.iep.doc.gov/bisnis/bisnis.html

Country Commercial Guide List The Department of Commerce provides executive summaries on commerce in many countries.
Visit at http://www.ita.doc.gov/uscs/ccglist.html

CYBER EXERCISES:

1. Use the USPS site to find your parents' address and zip code.

2. Use the Toll-Free Internet Directory to find the toll-free number for a business.
3. Using BISNIS, find a country report on a country from the former Soviet Union.
4. Use the Country Commercial Guide List to find an executive summary for a South American country.
5. Use the Ultimate Yellow Pages to find a business in another state.

CHAPTER SUMMARY

SELLER'S AND LESSOR'S OBLIGATIONS, P. 300

Tender of Delivery	Requires the seller or lessor to (1) put and hold *conforming goods* at the buyer's or lessee's disposition and (2) give the buyer or lessee any notification reasonably necessary to enable the buyer or lessee to take delivery of the goods [UCC 2-503(1), 2A-508(1)].

Place of Delivery	1. *Agreement*. The parties may agree in the sales or lease contract as to the place of delivery.
	 2. *No agreement*. If there is no agreement in the contract as to the place of delivery, the following UCC rules apply:
	    a. *Noncarrier cases*. The place of delivery is the seller's or lessor's place of business, unless the seller or lessor has no place of business in which case the place of delivery is the seller's or lessor's residence.
	    b. *Carrier cases:*
	       i. *Shipment contracts*. A sales contract that requires the seller to send goods to the buyer by carrier. Delivery occurs when the seller puts the goods in the carrier's possession [UCC 2-504].
	       ii. *Destination contracts*. A sales contract that requires the seller to deliver the goods to the buyer's place of business or other destination. Delivery occurs when the goods reach this destination [UCC 2-503].

Perfect Tender Rule	The seller or lessor is under a duty to deliver *conforming goods* to the buyer or lessee. If the goods or tender of delivery fails in any respect to conform to the contract, the buyer or lessee may opt to (1) reject the whole shipment, (2) accept the whole shipment, or (3) reject part and accept part of the shipment [UCC 2-601, 2A-509]. *Exceptions to the perfect tender rule*: 1. *Agreement of the parties*. The parties may agree to limit the effect of the perfect tender rule. 2. *Substitution of carriers*. A seller must use a commercially reasonable substitute if the agreed-upon manner of delivery fails or the agreed-upon type of carrier becomes unavailable [UCC 2-614(1)]. 3. *Cure*. A seller or lessor who delivers nonconforming goods has the opportunity to *cure* the nonconformity by repairing or replacing defective or nonconforming goods if the time for performance has not expired and the seller or lessor notifies the buyer or lessee of his or her intention to make a conforming delivery within the contract time [UCC 2-508, 2A-513]. 4. *Installment contracts*. The buyer or lessee may reject any nonconforming installment if the value of the installment is impaired and the defect cannot be cured. The buyer or lessee may reject the entire contract upon the tender of a nonconforming installment only if the nonconformity substantially impairs the value of the entire contract [UCC 2-612, 2A-510].

	5. *Destruction of goods*. If goods identified to the contract are totally destroyed without fault of either party before the risk of loss passes to the buyer or lessee, the seller or lessor is excused from performance [UCC 2-613].
General Obligations	The UCC has adopted the following broad principles that govern the performance of sales and lease contracts: 1. *Good faith*. Parties to a sales or lease contract must perform their contract obligations in *good faith* [UCC 1-203]; 2. *Reasonableness*. Many UCC provisions required parties to take *reasonable* steps or to act *reasonably* in performing contract obligations; 3. *Commercial reasonableness*. Some provisions of the UCC require merchants to use *commercial reasonableness* in the performance of their contract obligations.

BUYER'S AND LESSEE'S OBLIGATIONS, P. 304

Right of Inspection	Unless otherwise agreed, the buyer or lessee has the right to inspect goods that are tendered, delivered, or identified to the sales contract prior to accepting or paying for them [UCC 2-513(1), 2A-515(1)].
Payment	*Duty to pay*. Goods that are accepted by the buyer must be paid for in accordance with the terms of the sales or lease contract. Unless otherwise agreed, payment or rent is due when and where the goods are delivered [UCC 2-310, 2A-516(1)].
Acceptance	Acceptance occurs when the buyer or lessee takes one of the following actions [UCC 2-606, 2A-515]: 1. Signifies in words or by conduct that the goods are conforming or that the goods will be taken or retained despite their nonconformity. 2. Fails to reject the goods within a reasonable time after their delivery by the seller or lessor. 3. When a buyer acts inconsistently with the seller's ownership rights in the goods. Buyers and lessees may only accept delivery of a *commercial unit*.

ASSURANCE OF PERFORMANCE, P. 307

Assurance of Performance	If one party to a sales or lease contract has reasonable grounds to believe that the other party either will not or cannot perform his or her contractual obligations, he or she may demand in writing an adequate assurance of performance from the other party. The party making the demand may suspend his or her performance until adequate assurance of performance is received [UCC 2-609, 2A-401].

ANTICIPATORY REPUDIATION, P. 307

Anticipatory Repudiation	Occurs when a party to a sales or lease contract repudiates the contract before his or her performance is due. The aggrieved party can (1) await performance when due or (2) treat the contract as breached at the time of the anticipatory repudiation [UCC 2-610, 2A-402].

SELLER'S AND LESSOR'S REMEDIES, P. 308

Right to Withhold Delivery	Delivery of goods may be withheld if the seller or lessor discovers that the buyer or lessee is insolvent before the goods are delivered [UCC 2-703(a), 2A-523(1)(c)].

	1. *Demand payment in cash.* If the seller or lessor discovers that the buyer or lessee is insolvent, he or she may refuse to deliver the goods except for payment of cash [UCC 2-702(1), 2A-525(1)].
Right to Stop Delivery of Goods in Transit	If the goods are in transit or in the bailee's possession, the seller or lessor may stop delivery (1) of a carload, a truckload, or a planeload of goods if the buyer or lessee repudiates the contract, fails to make a payment when due, or otherwise breaches the contract; or (2) of any size shipment if the buyer or lessee becomes insolvent [UCC 2-705(1), 2A-526(1)].
Right to Reclaim Goods	A seller or lessor may reclaim goods in the possession of the buyer or lessee if: 1. The goods are delivered in a credit sale and the seller then discovers that the buyer was insolvent [UCC 2-000]. 2. The buyer misrepresented his or her solvency in writing within three months before delivery or paid for goods in a cash sale with a check that bounces [UCC 2-702(2) and 507(2)].
Right to Dispose of Goods	If a buyer or lessee breaches or repudiates the sales or lease contract before the seller or lessor has delivered the goods, the seller or lessor may resell or release the goods and recover damages from the buyer or lessee. Damages are calculated as the difference between the disposition price or rent and the original contract price or rent [UCC 2-706(1), 2A-527(1)].
Right to Recover the Purchase Price or Rent	If the buyer or lessee accepts the goods but fails to pay for them when the contract price or rent is due, the seller or lessor may sue to recover the contracted-for purchase price or rent from the buyer or lessee [UCC 2-709(1), 2A-529(1)].
Right to Recover Damages for Breach of Contract	If a buyer or lessee repudiates a sales or lease contract, the seller or lessor may sue to recover the damages caused by the breach. Damages are calculated as the difference between the original contract price (or rent) and the market price (or rent) of the goods at the time and place the goods were to be delivered, or lost profits [UCC 2-708(1), 2-708(2), 2A-528(1), 2A-528(2)].
Right to Cancel the Contract	The seller or lessor may cancel the sales or lease contract if the buyer or lessee breaches the contract. The seller or lessor is discharged of any further obligations under the canceled contract [UCC 2-106(4), 2A-523(3)].

BUYER'S AND LESSEE'S REMEDIES, P. 311

Seller or Lessor Refuses to Deliver the Goods or Delivers Nonconforming Goods that the Buyer or Lessee Does Not Want	1. *Reject nonconforming goods.* If the goods or the seller's or lessor's tender of delivery fails to conform to the sales or lease contract in any way, the buyer or lessee may (1) reject the whole, (2) accept the whole, or (3) accept any commercial unit and reject the rest [UCC 2-601, 2A-509]. 2. *Revoke acceptance of nonconforming goods.* A buyer or lessee who has accepted goods may subsequently revoke his acceptance if (1) the goods are nonconforming, (2) the nonconformity substantially impairs the value of the goods to the buyer or lessee, and (3) one of the following factors is shown: (a) the seller's or lessor's promise is reasonably sure the nonconformity is not met, (b) the goods were accepted before the nonconformity was discovered and the nonconformity was difficult to discover, or (c) the goods were accepted

	before the nonconformity was discovered and the seller or lessor assured the buyer or lessee that the goods were nonconforming [UCC 2-608(1), 2A-517(1)]. 3. *Cover.* If the seller or lessor fails to make delivery of goods or repudiates a sales or lease contract, or the buyer or lessee rightfully rejects the goods or justifiably revokes their acceptance, the buyer or lessee may cover by purchasing or renting substitute goods from another party. The buyer or lessee may recover from the seller or lessor damages calculated as the difference between the cost of cover and the original contract price or rent [UCC 2-712, 2A-518]. 4. *Sue for breach of contract and recover damages.* If a seller or lessor fails to deliver the goods or repudiates the sales or lease contract, the buyer or lessee may recover damages from the seller or lessor. Damages are calculated as the difference between the contract price (or original rent) and the market price (or rent) at the time the buyer or lessee learned of the breach [UCC 2-713, 2A-519]. 5. *Cancel the contract.* A buyer or lessee may cancel a sales or lease contract if the seller or lessor fails to deliver conforming goods or repudiates the contract, or the buyer or lessee rightfully rejects the goods or justifiably revokes acceptance of the goods. The buyer or lessee is discharged from any further obligations under the canceled contract [UCC 2-711(1), 2A-508(1)(a)].
Seller or Lessor Tenders Nonconforming Goods and the Buyer or Lessee Accepts Them	1. *Sue for damages.* If a buyer or lessee accepts nonconforming goods from a seller or lessor, the buyer or lessee may recover as damages any loss resulting from the seller's or lessor's breach [UCC 2-714(1), 2A-516(1)]. 2. *Sue for breach of warranty.* If a seller or lessor breaches a warranty of quality made in association with the sale or lease of goods, the buyer or lessee may recover damages calculated as the difference between the value of the goods accepted and the value of the goods if they had been as warranted, unless special circumstances show proximate damages of a different amount [UCC 2-714(2), 2A-519(4)]. 3. *Deduct damages from unpaid purchase price or rent.* If a seller or lessor breaches the sales or lease contract and the buyer or lessee accepts nonconforming goods, the buyer or lessee may deduct all or any part of the damages resulting from the breach from any part of the price or rent still due under the sales or lease contract [UCC 2-717, 2A-519].
Seller or Lessor Refuses to Deliver the Goods and the Buyer or Lessee Wants Them	1. *Specific performance.* If the goods are unique, or the remedy at law is inadequate, a buyer or lessee may obtain a decree of specific performance that orders the seller or lessor to perform the sales or lease contract [UCC 2-716(1), 2A-521(1)]. 2. *Replevy the goods.* A buyer or lessee may replevy (recover) scarce goods from a seller or lessor who is wrongfully withholding them [UCC 2-716(3), 2A-521(3)]. 3. *Recover the goods from an insolvent seller or lessor.* If the buyer or lessee makes partial or full payment for the goods before they are received and the seller or lessor becomes insolvent within 10 days after receiving the first payment, then the buyer or lessee may recover the goods from the seller or lessor [UCC 2-502, 2A-522].
Unconscionable Sales and Lease Contracts	If a sales or lease contract or any clause in it is *unconscionable*, the court may either refuse to enforce the contract or limit the application of the unconscionable clause [UCC 2-302, 2A-108].

STATUTE OF LIMITATIONS, P. 314	
Statute of Limitations	The UCC provides that an action for breach of any written or oral sales or lease contract must commence within four years after the cause of action accrues. The parties may agree to reduce the limitations period to one year, but they cannot extend it beyond four years [UCC 2-725, 2A-506].

AGREEMENTS AFFECTING REMEDIES, P. 314	
Agreements Affecting Remedies	1. *Limitations on remedies*. The parties to a sales or lease contract may agree on remedies in addition to or in substitution for the remedies provided by Article 2 or 2A of the UCC [UCC 2-719(1), 2A-503(1)].
	2. *Unconscionable limitations*. Any agreement concerning the limitations or exclusion of damages that is found to be unconscionable is unenforceable. With respect to consumer goods, a limitation of consequential damages for personal injuries is prima facie unconscionable [UCC 2-719(3), 2A-503(3)].
	3. *Liquidated damages*. The parties to a sales or lease contract may establish in advance the damages that will be paid upon a breach of the contract [UCC 2-718(1), 2A-504].

CRITICAL LEGAL THINKING CASES

14.1 Good Faith Big Horn Coal Company (Coal Company) entered into a contract to supply coal for 20 years to Commonwealth Edison Company (Edison), a utility. The contract called for the two parties to determine each year how much coal was to be delivered during that period. The contract specified a minimum amount of coal that Edison was obliged to buy each year, but allowed Edison to purchase less than that amount if the coal could not be used due to environmental reasons. Several years after the contract was signed, Edison's business began to slump, and it was faced with an oversupply of coal. The utility began to reduce the amount of coal it purchased each year. Also, there was an accident at one of Edison's generating plants, which left the plant inoperative for six months. Faced with these problems, the utility ordered less than the minimum amount of coal for the following year. Edison asserted that an "environmental" problem caused it to order less than the minimum amount of coal. The coal company sued Edison. Who wins? [*Big Horn Coal Co. v. Commonwealth Edison Co.*, 852 F.2d 1259 (10th Cir. 1988)]

14.2 Commercial Reasonableness Allsopp Sand and Gravel (Allsopp) and Lincoln Sand and Gravel (Lincoln) both were in the business of supplying sand to construction companies. In March 1986, Lincoln's sand dredge became inoperable. In order to continue in business, Lincoln negotiated a contract with Allsopp to purchase sand over the course of a year. The contract called for the sand to be loaded on Lincoln's trucks during Allsopp's regular operating season (March through November). Loading at other times was to be done by "special arrangement." By November 1986, Lincoln had taken delivery of one quarter of the sand it had contracted for. At this point, Lincoln requested that several trucks of sand be loaded in

December. Allsopp informed Lincoln that it would have to pay extra for this special arrangement. Lincoln refused to pay extra, pointing out that the sand was already stockpiled at Allsopp's facilities. Allsopp also offered to supply an employee to supervise the loading. Negotiations between the parties broke down, and Lincoln informed Allsopp that it did not intend to honor the remainder of the contract. Allsopp sued Lincoln. Was it commercially reasonable for Lincoln to demand delivery of sand during December? [*Allsopp Sand and Gravel v. Lincoln Sand and Gravel*, 525 N.E.2d 1185 (Ill.App. 1988)]

14.3 Nonconforming Goods The Jacob Hartz Seed Company, Inc. (Hartz), bought soybeans for use as seed from E.R. Coleman. Coleman certified that the seed had an 80 percent germination rate. Hartz paid for the beans and picked them up from a warehouse in Card, Arkansas. After the seed was transported to Georgia, a sample was submitted for testing to the Georgia Department of Agriculture. When the department reported a germination level of only 67 percent, Coleman requested that the seed be retested. The second set of tests reported a germination rate of 65 percent. Hartz canceled the contract after the second test, and Coleman reclaimed the seed. Hartz sought a refund of the money it paid for the seed, claiming that the soybeans were nonconforming goods. Who wins? [*Jacob Hartz Seed Co., Inc. v. Coleman*, 612 S.W.2d 91 (Ark. 1981)]

14.4 Right to Cure On December 21, 1982, Connie R. Grady purchased a new Chevrolet Chevette from Al Thompson Chevrolet (Thompson). Grady gave Thompson a down payment on the car and financed the remainder of the purchase price through the General Motors Acceptance Corporation (GMAC). On December 22, 1982, Grady picked up the

Chevette. The next day the car broke down and had to be towed back to Thompson. Grady picked up the repaired car on December 24. The car's performance was still unsatisfactory in that the engine was hard to start, the transmission slipped, and the brakes had to be pushed to the floor to function. Grady again returned the Chevette for servicing on January 6, 1983. When she picked the car up that evening, the engine started, but the engine and brake warning lights came on. This pattern of malfunction and repair continued until March 3, 1983. On that day, Grady wrote a letter to Thompson revoking the sale. Thompson repossessed the Chevette. GMAC sued Grady to recover its money. Grady sued Thompson to recover her down payment. Thompson claimed that Grady's suit is barred because the company was not given adequate opportunity to cure. Who wins? [*General Motors Acceptance Corp. v. Grady*, 2 U.C.C.Rep.Ser.2d 887 (Ohio App. 1985)]

14.5 Revocation of Acceptance Roy E. Farrar Produce Co. (Farrar) was a packer and shipper of tomatoes in Rio Arribon County, New Mexico. Farrar contacted Wilson, an agent and salesman for International Paper Co. (International), and ordered 21,500 tomato boxes for $0.64 per box. The boxes each were to hold between 20 and 30 pounds of tomatoes for shipping. When the boxes arrived at Farrar's plant, 3,624 of them were immediately used to pack tomatoes. When the boxes were stacked, they began to collapse and crush the tomatoes contained within them. The produce company was forced to repackage the tomatoes and store the unused tomato boxes. Farrar contacted International and informed it that it no longer wanted the boxes because they could not perform as promised. International claims that Farrar had accepted the packages and must now pay for them. Who wins? [*International Paper Co. v. Farrar*, 700 P.2d 642 (N.M. 1985)]

14.6 Adequate Assurance Gal-Tex Oil Corporation owned and operated several oil rigs in the Gulf of Mexico. Gal-Tex provided living quarters for its workers on the oil rigs. These facilities included a small hospital ward. When Gal-Tex needed to lease some medical equipment for the hospital on its newest oil rig, it signed a five-year lease with International Medical Company (International). The contract called for International to provide five specific pieces of equipment. Two weeks after the contract was signed, Gal-Tex executives learned that International was insolvent. Gal-Tex's attorneys wrote to International requesting assurance that the lease would be complied with. International never replied to the letter. Forty-five days later, Gal-Tex enters into a new lease for hospital equipment with a different company. Does Gal-Tex still have any obligation under its lease with International?

14.7 Commercial Impracticability Charles C. Campbell was a farmer who farmed some 600 acres in the vicinity of Hanover, Pennsylvania. In May 1973, Campbell entered into a contract with Hostetter Farms, Inc. (Hostetter), a grain dealer with facilities in Hanover. The sales agreement called for Campbell to sell Hostetter 20,000 bushels of No. 2 yellow corn at $1.70 per bushel. Delivery was to be made in October 1973. Unfortunately, the summer of 1973 was an unusually rainy one, and Campbell could not plant part of his crop because of the wet ground. After the corn was planted, part of the crop failed due to the excessive rain. As a result, Campbell delivered

only 10,417 bushels. Hostetter sued Campbell for breach of contract. Campbell asserted the defense of commercial impracticability. Who wins? [*Campbell v. Hostetter Farms, Inc.*, 380 A.2d 463 (Penn. 1977)]

14.8 Seller's Right to Stop Goods in Transit Ramco Steel, Inc. (Ramco), was a steel manufacturer located in Buffalo, New York. Ramco made a sales agreement with Murdock Machine and Engineering Company (Murdock) to sell cold drawn steel to Murdock. The steel was sold to Murdock on credit. The contract called for the steel to be shipped from Ramco's plant in Buffalo to a warehouse in Indiana for reshipment to Murdock at Clearfield, Utah, the final destination. A shipment of steel bars left Ramco's plant on May 22, 1975. Murdock became insolvent on May 13, and Ramco learned of this fact on May 23. On that same day, Ramco stopped delivery of the steel that was being trucked to the warehouse in Indiana. Murdock had bought the steel to fulfill a government contract to build fins and nozzles for missiles. The government claimed that Ramco had no right to stop delivery of the steel. Did Ramco act properly in stopping delivery? [*In Re Murdock Machine & Engineering Company of Utah*, 620 F.2d 767 (10th Cir. 1980)]

14.9 Seller's Right to Reclaim Goods Archer Daniels Midland Company (Archer) sold ethanol for use in gasoline. Between April 11 and April 19, 1984, Archer sold 80,000 gallons of ethanol on credit to Charter International Oil Company (Charter). The ethanol was shipped to Charter's facility in Houston. Charter became insolvent sometime during that period. On April 21, Archer sent a written notice to Charter demanding the return of the ethanol. At the time Charter received the reclamation demand, it had only 12,000 gallons of ethanol remaining at its Houston facility. When Charter refused to return the unused ethanol, Archer sued to recover the ethanol. Who wins? [*Archer Daniels Midland v. Charter International Oil Company*, 60 B.R. 854 (M.D. Fla. 1986)]

14.10 Seller's Right to Resell Goods Meuser Material & Equipment Company (Meuser) was a dealer in construction equipment. On December 13, 1973, Meuser entered into an agreement with Joe McMillan for the sale of a bulldozer to McMillan. The agreement called for Meuser to deliver the bulldozer to McMillan's residence in Greeley, Colorado. McMillan paid Meuser with a check. On December 24, before taking delivery, McMillan stopped payment on the check. Meuser entered into negotiations with McMillan in an attempt to get McMillan to abide by the sales agreement. During this period, Meuser paid for the upkeep of the bulldozer. When it became apparent that further negotiations would be fruitless, Meuser began looking for a new buyer. Fourteen months after the original sale was supposed to have taken place, the bulldozer was resold for less than the original contract price. Meuser sued McMillan to recover the difference between the contract price and the resale price and the cost of upkeep on the bulldozer for 14 months. Who wins? [*McMillan v. Meuser Material & Equipment Company*, 541 S.W.2d 911 (Ark. 1976)]

14.11 Seller's Right to Recover the Purchase Price C.R. Daniels, Inc. (Daniels), entered into a contract for the design and sale of grass catcher bags for lawn mowers to Yazoo Manufacturing Co., Inc. (Yazoo). Daniels contracted to design grass catcher bags that would fit the "S" Series mower made by Yazoo. Yazoo provided Daniels with a lawn mower in order to design the bag. After Yazoo approved the design of the bags, it issued a purchase order for 20,000 bags. Daniels began to ship the bags. After accepting 8,000 bags, Yazoo requested that the shipment stop. Officials of Yazoo told Daniels that they would resume accepting shipments in a few months. Despite several attempts, Daniels could not get Yazoo to accept delivery of the remaining 12,000 bags. Daniels sued Yazoo to recover the purchase price of the grass bags still in their inventory. Who wins? [*C.R. Daniels, Inc. v. Yazoo Mfg. Co., Inc.*, 641 F.Supp. 205 (S.D.Miss. 1986)]

14.12 Seller's Right to Recover Lost Profits Saber Energy, Inc. (Saber), entered into a sale contract with Tri-State Petroleum Corporation (Tri-State). The contract called for Saber to sell Tri-State 110,000 barrels of gasoline per month from July to December 1981. Saber was to deliver the gasoline through the colonial pipeline in Pasadena, Texas. The first 110,000 barrels were delivered on time. On August 1, Saber was informed that Tri-State was canceling the contract. Saber sued Tri-State for breach of contract and sought to recover its lost profits as damages. Tri-State admitted its breach but claimed that lost profits is an inappropriate measure of damages. Who wins? [*Tri-State Petroleum Corporation v. Saber Energy, Inc.*, 845 F.2d 575 (5th Cir. 1988)]

14.13 Buyer's Right to Demand Specific Performance Dr. and Mrs. Sedmak (Sedmaks) were collectors of Chevrolet Corvettes. In July 1977, the Sedmaks saw an article in *Vette Vues* magazine concerning a new limited edition Corvette. The limited edition was designed to commemorate the selection of the Corvette as the official pace car of the Indianapolis 500. Chevrolet was manufacturing only 6,000 of these pace cars. The Sedmaks visited Charlie's Chevrolet, Inc. (Charlie's), a local Chevrolet dealer. Charlie's was to receive only one special edition car, which the sales manager agreed to sell to the Sedmaks for the sticker price of $15,000. When the Sedmaks went to pick up and pay for the car, they were told that because of the great demand for the special edition, it was going to be auctioned to the highest bidder. The Sedmaks sued the dealership for specific performance. Who wins? [*Sedmak v. Charlie's Chevrolet, Inc.*, 622 S.W.2d 694 (Mo.App. 1981)]

14.14 Buyer's Right to Cover and Recover Damages Kent Nowlin Construction, Inc. (Nowlin), was awarded a contract by the state of New Mexico to pave a number of roads. After Nowlin was awarded the contract, it entered into an agreement with Concrete Sales & Equipment Rental Company, Inc. (C&E). C&E was to supply 20,000 tons of paving material to Nowlin. Nowlin began paving the roads, anticipating C&E's delivery of materials. However, on the delivery date C&E shipped only 2,099 tons of paving materials. Because Nowlin had a deadline to meet, the company contracted with Gallup Sand and Gravel Company (Gallup) for substitute material. Nowlin sued C&E to recover the difference between the higher price it had to pay Gallup for materials and the contract price C&E had agreed to. C&E claims that it is not responsible for Nowlin's increased costs. Who wins? [*Concrete Sales & Equipment Rental Company, Inc. v. Kent Nowlin Construction, Inc.*, 746 P.2d 645 (N.M. 1987)]

14.15 Buyer's Right to Recover Damages Earl Miller is a well-known sailor and builder of sailboats. Miller operated his own company, Miller Marine, Inc., on Bainbridge Island, Washington. In 1981, Carole Badgley saw an advertisement for a sailboat built by Miller. The advertised sailboat was a light-weight, high-performance racing vessel named *The Bonnie*. Badgley entered into a contract with Miller for the purchase of *The Bonnie* at a price of $135,000. After she took possession of the sailboat, Badgley noticed a steady leak. Badgley had several naval engineers examine the vessel. The engineers attributed the leak to a design defect. Badgley paid $20,000 to have extensive repairs made to stop the leak. She then sued Miller to recover the $20,000. Who wins? [*Miller v. Badgley*, 753 P.2d 530 (Wash. App. 1988)]

14.16 Unconscionable Contract Jane Wilson leased a Toyota pickup truck from World Omni Leasing (Omni). Wilson had experience in business and had signed contracts before. In the past, Wilson had read the contracts before signing them. When signing the contract for the lease of the truck, however, Wilson did not take the opportunity to read the lease. She even signed a statement declaring that she had read and understood the lease. The lease contained a provision that made Wilson responsible for payments on the truck even if the truck was destroyed. Several months after leasing the truck, Wilson was involved in a two-vehicle collision. The pickup truck was destroyed. Omni demanded to be paid for the balance of the lease. Wilson refuses, claiming that the lease was unconscionable. Is the lease unconscionable? [*Wilson v. World Omni Leasing, Inc.*, 540 So.2d 713 (Ala. 1989)]

 ETHICS CASES

14.17 Ethical Perspective Ruby and Carmen Ybarra purchased a new double-wide mobile home from Modern Trailer Sales, Inc. (Modern). On March 11, 1974, Modern delivered the mobile home to the Ybarras. A few days after delivery, portions of the floor began to rise and bubble, creating an unsightly and troublesome situation for the Ybarras. The Ybarras complained to Modern about the floor as soon as the defects were discovered. Modern sent repairmen to cure the defective floor on at least three occasions, but each time they were unsuccessful. The Ybarras continued to complain about the defects. The Ybarras continued to rely on Modern's assurances that it was able and willing to repair the floor. After four years of complaints, the Ybarras sued to revoke their acceptance of the sales contract. Did the Ybarras properly revoke their acceptance of their sales contract? Did Modern act ethically in this case? Did the Ybarras? [*Ybarras v. Modern Trailer Sales, Inc.*, 609 P.2d 331 (N.M. 1980)]

14.18 Ethical Perspective In 1974, Alex Abatti was the sole owner of A&M Produce Company (A&M), a small farming company located in California's Imperial Valley. Although Abatti had never grown tomatoes, he decided to do so. He sought the advice of FMC Corporation (FMC), a large diversified manufacturer of farming and other equipment, as to what kind of equipment he would need to process the tomatoes. An FMC representative recommended a certain type of machine, which A&M purchased from FMC pursuant to a form sales contract provided by FMC. Within the fine print, the contract contained one clause that disclaimed any warranty liability by FMC and a second clause that stated that FMC would not be liable for consequential damages if the machine malfunctioned.

A&M paid $10,680 down toward the $32,041 purchase price, and FMC delivered and installed the machine. A&M immediately began experiencing problems with the machine. It did not process the tomatoes quickly enough. Tomatoes began piling up in front of the belt that separated the tomatoes for weight-sizing. Overflow tomatoes had to be sent through the machine at least twice, causing damage to them. Fungus spread through the damaged crop. Because of these problems,

the machine had to be continually started and stopped, which significantly reduced processing speed.

A&M tried on several occasions to get additional equipment from FMC, but on each occasion its request was rejected. Because of the problems with the machine, on June 17, 1974, A&M closed its tomato operation. A&M finally stated, "Let's call the whole thing off" and offered to return the machine if FMC would refund A&M's down payment. When FMC rejected this offer and demanded full payment of the balance due, A&M sued to recover its down payment and damages. It alleged breach of warranty caused by defect in the machine. In defense, FMC pointed to the fine print of the sales contract, stating that the buyer waived any rights to sue it for breach of warranty or to recover consequential damages from it.

Was it ethical for FMC to include waiver of liability and waiver of consequential damage clauses in its form contract? Did A&M act morally in signing the contract and then trying to get out from under its provisions? Legally, are the waiver clauses so unconscionable as to not be enforced? [*A&M Produce Company v. FMC Corporation*, 135 Cal.App.3d 473, 186 Cal.Rptr. 114 (Cal.App. 1982)]

CRITICAL LEGAL THINKING WRITING ASSIGNMENT

Read Case A.14 in the Case Appendix [*LNS Investment Company, Inc. v. Phillips 66 Company*]. This case is excerpted from the district court opinion. Review and brief the case. In your brief, be sure to answer the following questions:

1. What did the sales contract provide?
2. Was the contract performed?
3. What is the issue in this case?
4. In whose favor did the court rule?

CHAPTER 15

WARRANTIES

AND PRODUCT LIABILITY

Chapter Objectives

*After studying this chapter,
you should be able to*

1. Describe the warranties of good title, no security interests, no infringements, and no interference
2. Identify and describe express warranties
3. Describe the implied warranties of merchantability and fitness for a particular purpose
4. Identify warranty disclaimers and determine when they are unlawful
5. Describe how the Magnuson-Moss Warranty Act affects warranties regarding consumer goods
6. Define the doctrine of strict liability
7. Identify defects in manufacture, design, packaging, failure to warn, and failure to provide adequate instructions
8. List and describe the damages recoverable in a product liability action
9. Explain the doctrine of market share liability
10. List and describe the defenses to product liability lawsuits

Chapter Contents

> *A manufacturer is strictly liable in tort when an article he places on the market, knowing that it is to be used without inspection for defects, proves to have a defect that causes injury to a human being.*
>
> *Greenmun v. Yuba Power Products, Inc.*
> 59 Cal.2d 57, 27 Cal.Rptr. 697 (1963)

The doctrine of *caveat emptor*—let the buyer beware—governed the law of sales and leases for centuries. Finally, the law recognized that consumers and other purchasers and lessees of goods needed greater protection. Article 2 of the Uniform Commercial Code (UCC), which has been adopted in whole or part by all 50 states, establishes certain **warranties** that apply to the sale of goods. Article 2A of the UCC, which many states have adopted, establishes warranties that apply in lease transactions. Consumers and others can sue to recover damages caused by breach of warranty.

warranty A buyer's or lessee's assurance that the goods meet certain standards.

In addition, if a product defect causes injury to purchasers, lessees, users, or bystanders, the injured party may be able to recover for his or her injuries under certain tort theories, including negligence, misrepresentation, and the modern theory of strict liability. The liability of manufacturers, sellers, lessors, and others for injuries caused by defective products is commonly referred to as **products liability**.

products liability The liability of manufacturers, sellers, and others for the injuries caused by defective products.

The various warranty and tort principles that permit injured parties to recover damages caused by defective products are discussed in this chapter.

WARRANTIES OF TITLE AND NO INFRINGEMENTS

The UCC imposes the following warranties on sellers and lessors of goods.

Good Title

Unless properly disclaimed, sellers of goods warrant that they have valid title to the goods they are selling and that the transfer of title is rightful [UCC 2–312(1)(a)]. This is called the **warranty of good title**. Persons who transfer goods without proper title breach this warranty.

warranty of good title Sellers warrant that they have valid title to the goods they are selling and that the transfer of title is rightful.

CONSIDER THIS EXAMPLE: Ingersoll-Rand owns a heavy-duty crane. A thief steals the crane and sells it to Turner Corp. Turner does not know that the crane is stolen. If Ingersoll-Rand discovers that Turner has the equipment, it can reclaim it. Turner, in turn, can recover against the thief for breach of the warranty of title. This is because the thief implied (warranted) that he had good title to the equipment and that the transfer of title to Turner was rightful.

NOTE *Unfortunately, the probability of recovery against a thief is remote.*

No Security Interests

Under the UCC, sellers of goods automatically warrant that the goods they sell are delivered free from any third-party security interests, liens, or encumbrances that are not known to the buyer [UCC 2–312(1)(b)]. This is called the **warranty of no security interests**.

warranty of no security interests Sellers of goods warrant that the goods they sell are delivered free from any third-party security interests, liens, or encumbrances that are not known to the buyer.

CONSIDER THIS EXAMPLE: Albert Connors purchased a refrigerator on credit from PC Richards, an appliance store. The store took back a security interest in the refrigerator. Before completely paying off the refrigerator, Mr. Connors sells it to a friend for cash. The friend has no knowledge of the store's security interest. After Mr. Connors misses several payments, the appliance store repossesses the refrigerator. Mr. Connors' friend may recover against him based on his breach of warranty of no security interests in the goods [UCC 2–312(1)(b)].

The warranties of good title and no security interests may be excluded or modified by specific language [UCC 2–312(2)]. For example, specific language such as "seller hereby transfers only those rights, title, and interest as he has in the goods" is sufficient to disclaim these warranties. General language such as "as is" or "with all faults" is not specific enough to be a disclaimer to the warranties. The special nature of certain sales (e.g., sheriff's sales) tells the buyer that the seller is not giving title warranties with the sale of goods.

No Infringements

warranty against infringements A seller or lessor who is a merchant who regularly deals in goods of the kind sold or leased automatically warrants that the goods are delivered free of any third-party patent, trademark, or copyright claim.

Unless otherwise agreed, a seller or lessor who is a merchant regularly dealing in goods of the kind sold or leased automatically warrants that the goods are delivered free of any third-party patent, trademark, or copyright claim [UCC 2–312(3); UCC 2A-211(2)]. This is called the **warranty against infringements**.

CONSIDER THIS EXAMPLE: Adams & Co., a manufacturer of machines that make shoes, sells a machine to Smith & Franklin, a shoe manufacturer. Subsequently, Alice Jones claims that she has a patent on the machine. Jones proves her patent claim in court. Ms. Jones notifies Smith & Franklin that the machine can no longer be used without permission (and, perhaps, the payment of a fee). Smith & Franklin may rescind the contract with Adams & Co. based on the breach of the no infringement warranty.

No Interference

warranty against interference The lessor warrants that no person holds claim or interest in the goods that arose from an act or omission of the lessor that will interfere with the lessee's enjoyment of its leasehold interest.

When goods are leased, the lessor warrants that no person holds a claim or an interest in the goods that arose from an act or omission of the lessor that will interfere with the lessee's enjoyment of his or her leasehold interest [UCC 2A-211(1)]. This is referred to as the **warranty against interference** or the **warranty of quiet possession**.

CONSIDER THIS EXAMPLE: Suppose Occidental Petroleum leases a piece of heavy equipment from Aztec Drilling Co. Aztec later gives a security interest in the equipment to City Bank as collateral for a loan. If Aztec defaults on the loan and City Bank repossesses the equipment, Occidental can recover damages from Aztec for breach of the warranty of no interference.

WARRANTIES OF QUALITY

warranties of quality Seller's or lessor's assurance to buyer or lessee that the goods meet certain standards of quality. Warranties may be expressed or implied.

Warranties are the buyer's or lessee's assurance that the goods meet certain standards of quality. **Warranties of quality**, which are based on contract law, may be either expressly stated or implied by law. If the goods fail to meet a warranty, the buyer or lessee can sue the seller or lessor for breach of warranty. Warranties are discussed in the following sections.

Express Warranties

express warranty A warranty that is created when a seller or lessor makes an affirmation that the goods he or she is selling or leasing meet certain standards of quality, description, performance, or condition.

Express warranties, which are the oldest form of warranty, are created when a seller or lessor affirms that the goods he or she is selling or leasing meet certain standards of quality, description, performance, or condition [UCC 2–313(1); UCC 2A-210(1)]. Express warranties can be either written, oral, or inferred from the seller's contract.

It is not necessary to use formal words such as *warrant* or *guarantee* to create an express warranty. Express warranties can be made by mistake because the seller or lessor does not have to specifically intend to make the warranty [UCC 2–313(2); UCC 2A-210(2)].

Sellers and lessors are not required to make such warranties. Generally, they are made to entice consumers and others to buy or lease their products. That is why these warranties often are in the form of advertisements, brochures, catalogs, pictures, illustrations, diagrams, blueprints, and so on.

Express warranties are created when the seller or lessor indicates that the goods will conform to the following:

1. All **affirmations of fact or promise** made about them (e.g., statements such as "This car will go 100 miles per hour" or "This house paint will last at least five years");
2. Any **description** of them (e.g., terms such as *Idaho potatoes* and *Michigan cherries*);
3. Any **model** or **sample** of them (e.g., a model oil drilling rig or a sample of wheat taken from a silo).

Basis of the Bargain

Buyers and lessees can recover for breach of an express warranty if the warranty was a contributing factor—not necessarily the sole factor—that induced the buyer to purchase the product or the lessee to lease the product. This is known as the **basis of the bargain** [UCC 2–313(1); UCC 2A-210(1)]. The UCC does not define the term basis of the bargain, so this test is broadly applied by the courts. Generally, all statements by the seller or lessor prior to or at the time of contracting are presumed to be part of the basis of the bargain unless good reason is shown to the contrary. Post-sale statements that modify the contract are part of the basis of the bargain.

Generally, a retailer is liable for the express warranties made by manufacturers of goods it sells. Manufacturers are not liable for express warranties made by wholesalers and retailers unless the manufacturer authorizes or ratifies the warranty.

Puffery "BS" is not enforceable.

Statements of Opinion

Many express warranties arise during the course of negotiations between the buyer and the seller (or lessor and lessee). The seller's or **lessor's statements of opinion** (i.e., **puffing**) or commendation of the goods do not create an express warranty [UCC 2–313(2)]. Therefore, a used car salesperson's statement that "This is the best used car available in town" does not create an express warranty. However, a statement such as "This car has been driven only 20,000 miles" is an express warranty. It is often difficult to determine whether the seller's statement is an affirmation of fact (which creates an express warranty) or a statement of opinion (which does not create a warranty).

An affirmation of *value* of goods does not create an express warranty [UCC 2–313(2)]. For example, statements such as "This painting is worth a fortune" or "Others would gladly pay $20,000 for this car" do not create an express warranty.

In the following case, the court had to decide whether an express warranty had been created.

CASE 15.1

Daughtrey v. Ashe
413 S.E.2d 336 (1992) Supreme Court of Virginia

Facts In October 1985, W. Hayes Daughtrey consulted Sidney Ashe, a jeweler, about the purchase of a diamond bracelet as a Christmas present for his wife. Ashe showed Daughtrey a diamond bracelet that he had for sale for $15,000. When Daughtrey decided to purchase the bracelet, Ashe completed and signed an appraisal form that stated that the diamonds were "H color and v.v.s. quality." (v.v.s. is one of the highest ratings in a quality classification employed by jewelers.) After Daughtrey paid for the bracelet, Ashe put the bracelet and the appraisal form in a box. Daughtrey gave the bracelet to his wife as a Christmas present. In February 1987, when another jeweler looked at the bracelet, Daughtrey discovered that the diamonds were of substantially
continued

lower grade than v.v.s. Daughtrey filed a specific performance suit against Ashe to compel him to replace the bracelet with one mounted with v.v.s. diamonds or pay appropriate damages. The trial court denied relief for breach of warranty. Daughtrey appealed.

Issue Was an express warranty made by Ashe regarding the quality of the diamonds in the bracelet?

Decision Yes. The appellate court held that an express warranty had been created. The trial court's decision was reversed and the case was remanded for a determination of appropriate damages to be awarded to Daughtrey.

Reason Any description of the goods that is made a basis of the bargain creates an express warranty that the goods shall conform to the description. The appellate court found that Ashe's description of the

diamonds created an express warranty that became a part of the basis of the bargain between Ashe and Daughtrey. The court noted that it was not necessary for Ashe to have used the word *warrant* or *guarantee* to create an express warranty.

CASE QUESTIONS

Critical Legal Thinking What is the remedy when an express warranty has been breached? Is the remedy sufficient?

Ethics Did Ashe act ethically in denying that his statement created an express warranty?

Business Implication Do businesses have to make express warranties? Why do businesses make warranties about the quality of their products?

Implied Warranty of Merchantability

implied warranty of merchantability Unless properly disclosed, a warranty that is implied that sold or leased goods are fit for the ordinary purpose for which they are sold or leased.

If the seller or lessor of a good is a merchant with respect to goods of that kind, the sales contract contains an **implied warranty of merchantability** unless it is properly disclaimed. This requires the following standards to be met [UCC 2–314(2); UCC 2A-212(2)]:

- **The goods must be fit for the ordinary purposes for which they are used.** For example, a chair must be able to perform the function of a chair. Thus, if a normal-sized person sits in a chair that has not been tampered with and the chair collapses, there has been a breach of the implied warranty of merchantability. If, however, the same person is injured because he or she used the chair as a ladder and it tips over, there is no breach of implied warranty. This is because serving as a ladder is not the ordinary purpose of a chair
- **The goods be adequately contained, packaged, and labeled.** Thus, the implied warranty of merchantability applies to both the milk bottle as well as the milk inside the bottle
- **The goods must be of an even kind, quality, and quantity within each unit.** For example, all of the goods in a carton, package, or box must be consistent
- **The goods must conform to any promise or affirmation of fact made on the container or label.** For example, that the goods could be used safely in accordance with the instructions on the package or label
- **The quality of the goods must pass without objection in the trade.** That is, other users of the goods would not object to their quality
- **Fungible goods must meet a fair average or middle range of quality.** For example, to be classified as a certain grade, grain or ore must meet the average range of quality of that grade.

Note that the implied warranty of merchantability does not apply to sales or leases by nonmerchants or casual sales. For example, the implied warranty of merchantability applies to the sale of a lawn mower that is sold by a merchant who is in the business of selling lawn mowers. It does not apply when one neighbor sells a lawn mower to another neighbor.

The following case raised the issue of implied warranty of merchantability.

NOTE
The implied warranty of merchantability does not apply to sales or leases by nonmerchants or casual sales.

CASE 15.2

Denny v. Ford Motor Company
639 N.Y.S.2d 250, 87 N.Y.2d 248 (1995) Court of Appeals of New York

Facts Nancy Denny purchased a Bronco II, a small utility vehicle that was manufactured by Ford Motor Company. Denny purchased the Bronco II for use on paved city and suburban streets, and not for off-road use. On June 9, 1986, when Denny was driving the vehicle on a paved road, she slammed on the brakes in an effort to avoid a deer that had walked directly into her motor vehicle's path. The Bronco II rolled over and Denny was severely injured. Denny sued Ford Motor Company to recover damages for breach of the implied warranty of merchantability.

Denny alleged that the Bronco II presented a significantly higher risk of occurrence of rollover accidents than did ordinary passenger vehicles. Denny introduced evidence at trial that showed that the Bronco II had a low stability index because of its high center of gravity, narrow tracks, shorter wheel base, and the design of its suspension system. Ford countered that the Bronco II was intended as an off-road vehicle and was not designed to be used as a conventional passenger automobile on paved streets. The trial court found Ford liable and awarded Denny $1.2 million in damages. Ford appealed.

Issue Did Ford Motor Company breach the implied warranty of merchantability?

Decision The court of appeals held that Ford had breached the implied warranty of merchantability and upheld the jury award for the plaintiff.

Reason The plaintiff introduced a Ford marketing manual that predicted that many buyers would be attracted to the Bronco II because utility vehicles were suitable to "contemporary lifestyles" in some suburban areas. According to this manual, the sales presentation of the Bronco II should take into account the vehicle's "suitability for commuting and for suburban and city driving." In addition, the vehicle's ability to switch between two-wheel and four-wheel

drive would "be particularly appealing to women who may be concerned about driving in snow and ice with their children." Plaintiff testified that the perceived safety benefits of its four-wheel drive capacity was what attracted her to the Bronco II. She was not at all interested in its off-road use.

The law implies a warranty by a manufacturer that places its product on the market that the product is reasonably fit for the ordinary purpose for which it was intended. If it is, in fact, defective and not reasonably fit to be used for its intended purpose, the warranty is breached. Plaintiff's proof focused on the sale of the Bronco II for suburban driving and everyday road travel. Plaintiff also adduced proof that the Bronco II's design characteristics made it unusually susceptible to rollover accidents when used on paved roads. All of this evidence was useful in showing that routine highway and street driving was the "ordinary purpose" for which the Bronco II was sold and that it was not "fit"—or safe—for that purpose. The court concluded that under the evidence in this case, a rational fact finder could have concluded that the vehicle was not safe for the "ordinary purpose" of daily driving for which it was marketed and sold.

CASE QUESTIONS

Critical Legal Thinking Should the law impose an *implied* warranty of merchantability in the sale of goods? What is the public policy underlying this implied warranty?

Ethics Did Ford act ethically in defending that the Bronco II was sold only as an off-road vehicle? Was this argument persuasive?

Business Implication What are the business implications of this decision? Do you think that utility vehicles such as the Bronco II have a higher rollover danger than normal passenger automobiles?

Implied Warranty of Fitness for Human Consumption The common law implied a special warranty—the **implied warranty of fitness for human consumption**—to food products. The UCC incorporates this warranty, which applies to food and drink consumed on or off the premises, within the implied warranty of merchantability. Restaurants, grocery stores, fast-food outlets, and vending machine operators all are subject to this warranty.

Some states apply a foreign substance test to determine whether food products are unmerchantable. Under this test, a food product is unmerchantable if a foreign object

implied warranty of fitness for human consumption
A warranty that applies to food or drink consumed on or off the premises of restaurants, grocery stores, fast food outlets, and vending machines.

in that product causes injury to a person. For example, the warranty would be breached if an injury were caused by a nail in a cherry pie. If the same injury was caused by a cherry pit in the pie, the pie would not be unmerchantable.

The majority of states have adopted the modern consumer expectation test to determine the merchantability of food products. Under this implied warranty, if a person is injured by a chicken bone while eating fried chicken, the injury would not be actionable. However, the warranty would be breached if a person was injured by a chicken bone while eating a chicken salad sandwich. This is because a consumer would expect that the food preparer would have removed all bones from the chicken.

Implied Warranty of Fitness for a Particular Purpose

implied warranty of fitness for a particular purpose
A warranty that arises where a seller or lessor warrants that the goods will meet the buyer's or lessee's expressed needs.

The UCC contains an **implied warranty of fitness for a particular purpose**. This implied warranty is breached if the goods do not meet the buyer's or lessee's expressed needs. The warranty applies to both merchant and nonmerchant sellers and lessors.

The warranty of fitness for a particular purpose is implied at the time of contracting if the following are true:

1. The seller or lessor has reason to know the particular purpose for which the buyer is purchasing the goods or the lessee is leasing the goods.
2. The seller or lessor makes a statement that the goods will serve this purpose.
3. The buyer or lessee relies on the seller's or lessor's skill and judgment and purchases or leases the goods [UCC 2–315; UCC 2A-213].

CONSIDER THIS EXAMPLE: Susan Gonzalez wants to buy lumber to build a house, so she goes to Mr. Winter's lumberyard. Ms. Gonzalez describes the house she intends to build to Mr. Winter. She also tells Mr. Winter that she is relying on him to select the right lumber. Mr. Winter selects the lumber, and Ms. Gonzalez buys it and builds the house. Unfortunately, the house collapses because the timber was not strong enough to support it. Ms. Gonzalez can sue Mr. Winter for breach of the implied warranty of fitness for a particular purpose.

The following case raises the issue of implied warranty of fitness for a particular purpose.

CASE 15.3

Mack Massey Motors, Inc. v. Garnica
814 S.W.2d 167 (1991) Court of Appeals of Texas

Facts Felicitas Garnica sought to purchase a vehicle capable of towing a 23-foot Airstream trailer she had on order. She went to Mack Massey Motors, Inc. (Massey Motors), to inquire about purchasing a Jeep Cherokee that was manufactured by Jeep Eagle. After Garnica explained her requirements to the sales manager, he called the Airstream dealer concerning the specifications of the trailer Garnica was purchasing. The sales manager advised Garnica that the Jeep Cherokee could do the job of pulling the trailer. After purchasing the vehicle, Garnica claimed that it did not have sufficient power to pull the trailer. She brought the Jeep Cherokee back to Massey Motors several times for repairs for a slipping transmission.

Eventually, she was told to go to another dealer. The drive shaft on the Jeep Cherokee twisted apart at 7,229 miles. Garnica sued Massey Motors and Jeep Eagle for damages, alleging breach of the implied warranty of fitness for a particular purpose. The jury returned a verdict in favor of Garnica. Massey Motors and Jeep Eagle appealed.

Issue Did the defendants make and breach an implied warranty of fitness for a particular purpose?

Decision The appellate court held that Massey Motors had made and breached an implied warranty of fitness for a particular purpose, but that Jeep Eagle had not.

Reason The appellate court noted that the service provided by Massey Motors' sales staff included undertaking the responsibility of checking with the Airstream dealer and thereafter representing that the Jeep Cherokee, with an automatic transmission, was suitable for pulling the Airstream. Massey Motors' sales manager testified he knew the intended purpose for the appellee's use of the proposed vehicle and that he undertook to investigate the specifications of the Airstream. After having undertaken the inquiry, he recommended the Jeep Cherokee as being suitable for the purposes Mrs. Garnica was seeking—that of towing the Airstream trailer she had on order.

A claim of warranty of fitness requires that goods serve their particular purpose. The court concluded that the evidence supported the jury determination that the Jeep Cherokee simply was exceeding its towing capacity and that Massey Motors

had misrepresented the fact that this was the proper vehicle suitable for towing the Airstream trailer. In light of Massey Motors's superior knowledge and expertise concerning Mrs. Garnica's inquiry and reliance, the evidence was sufficient to support the jury's finding.

CASE QUESTIONS

Critical Legal Thinking Should the law recognize the implied warranty of fitness for a particular purpose? Or should buyers be held to know their own requirements?

Ethics Did Massey Motors act unethically in this case?

Business Implication Do you think damages should have been awarded in this case?

Implied Warranties of Course of Dealing and Usage of Trade

The UCC includes the **implied warranty arising from a course of dealing** or **usage of trade** that applies to both sales and lease transactions [UCC 2–314(3); UCC 2A-212(3)]. In effect, this is a two-part warranty because either course of dealing (i.e., prior dealing between the parties to the sales or lease contract) or usage of trade (customs of the industry or market) can be violated. Note that if the parties are knowledgeable members of the industry, the courts will infer that the parties intend trade usage to apply to their sales and lease contracts.

CONSIDER THIS EXAMPLE: Suppose it is customary for a seller to "prep" (e.g., oil, lubricate) new farm equipment prior to delivery. If a seller fails to prep a buyer's equipment prior to delivery, the buyer is injured by this failure. The seller may be sued for breach of the implied warranty arising from usage of trade. If prepping equipment is not a custom in the industry, but the seller has prepped the last few pieces of equipment sold to the buyer, failure to prep the equipment for sale this time would be a breach of the implied warranty arising from a course of dealing.

Overlapping and Inconsistent Warranties

Often, two or more warranties are present in the same sales or lease transaction. For example, a transaction may be subject to the seller's or lessor's express warranties with respect to the goods as well as the implied warranties of merchantability and fitness for a particular purpose. In such cases, the UCC provides that the warranties are cumulative if they are consistent with each other.

If the warranties are inconsistent, however, the intention of the parties determines which warranty is dominant. The following rules apply in determining intent [UCC 2-317; UCC 2A-215]:

1. Express warranties displace inconsistent implied warranties other than implied warranties of fitness for a particular purpose.
2. Exact or technical specifications displace inconsistent models or general language of description.
3. A sample from an existing bulk displaces inconsistent general language of description.

implied warranty arising from a course of dealing A warranty that is implied from a previous course of dealing between the parties.

implied warranty arising from usage of trade A warranty that is implied from customs of the industry or market.

Ref.: UCC - Common law where there's a history of dealings of parties, Court will insert the term. If no history the UCC uses the same test.

NOTE
If warranties are inconsistent, some warranties take precedent over other warranties.

Warranty Disclaimers

Subject to other state laws and the Magnuson-Moss Warranty Act (discussed later in this chapter), warranties can be disclaimed or limited. The rules for making such disclaimers follow:

NOTE
To disclaim the implied warranty of merchantability, the disclaimer must mention the word merchantability.

- If an express warranty is made, it can be limited if the disclaimer and the warranty can be reasonably construed with each other. The limitation is inoperative to the extent that such construction is unreasonable [UCC 2-316(1); UCC 2A-214(1)]. For example, if a seller or lessor makes an express warranty in one part of the contract and disclaims the warranty in another part, the courts consider the disclaimer unreasonable and thereby void.

- All implied warranties of quality may be disclaimed by expressions like *as is, with all faults*, or other such language that makes it clear to the buyer that there are no implied warranties [UCC 2-316(3)(a); UCC 2A-214(3)(a)]. This type of disclaimer, which is often included in sales contracts for used products, is effective whether it is oral or written.

NOTE
To disclaim the implied warranty of fitness for a particular purpose, the disclaimer must be in writing.

- If the preceding language is not used, disclaimers of the *implied warranty of merchantability* must specifically mention the term *merchantability*. The disclaimer may be oral or written [UCC 2-316(2); UCC 2A-214(2)].

- The *implied warranty of fitness for a particular purpose* may be disclaimed in general language without specific use of the term *fitness*. Language such as "There are no warranties which extend beyond the description on the face hereof" is sufficient to disclaim the fitness warranty. The disclaimer must be in writing [UCC 2-316(2); UCC 2A-214(3)].

BUSINESS BRIEF
Read all warrant notices carefully to see if any warranties have been disclaimed.

- When a buyer or lessee either (1) examines the goods (or the sample or model) as fully as he or she desires or (2) refuses to examine the goods after the seller or lessor demands him or her to do so, there are no implied warranties with regard to any defects that such an examination would have revealed [UCC 2-316(3)(b); UCC 2A-214(3)(b)]. Examination only includes obvious defects (e.g., a broken car windshield). Latent (nonobvious) defects (e.g., a problem in the transmission of the car) are not expected to be discovered during such an examination. Note that refusal only occurs if the seller or lessor demands the buyer or lessee to examine the goods and the buyer or lessee refuses to do so.

conspicuous
A requirement that warranty disclaimers be noticeable to the average person.

Conspicuous Display of Disclaimer Written disclaimers must be conspicuously displayed to be valid. The courts construe **conspicuous** as noticeable to a reasonable person. Thus, a heading printed in capitals or a typeface that is larger or in a different style than the rest of the body of a sales or lease contract will be construed to be conspicuous. Different-color type is also considered conspicuous [UCC 1-201(10); UCC 2A-214(4)].

unconscionable disclaimer
A disclaimer that is so oppressive or manifestly unfair that it will not be enforced by the court.

Unconscionable Disclaimers As a matter of law, a court may find a warranty disclaimer clause in a sales or lease contract to be **unconscionable**. In such cases, the court may avoid an unconscionable result by (1) refusing to enforce the clause, (2) refusing to enforce the entire contract, or (3) limiting the application of the clause [UCC 2-302(1); UCC 2A-108(1)]. In determining whether warranty disclaimers are unconscionable, the courts generally consider factors such as the sophistication, education, and bargaining power of the parties and whether the sales contract was offered on a take-it-or-leave-it basis.

compensatory damages
Damages that are generally equal to the difference between the value of the goods as warranted and the actual value of the goods accepted at the time and place of acceptance.

Damages Recoverable for Breach of Warranty

Where there has been a breach of warranty, the buyer or lessee may sue the seller or lessor to recover **compensatory damages**. The amount of recoverable compensatory damages is generally equal to the difference between (1) the value of the goods as warranted and (2) the actual value of the goods accepted at the time and place of acceptance [UCC 2-714(2); UCC 2A-508(4)].

CONSIDER THIS EXAMPLE: Suppose a used car salesperson warrants that a used car has been driven only 20,000 miles. If true, that would make the car worth $10,000. The salesperson gives the buyer a "good deal" and sells the car for $8,000. Unfortunately, the car was worth only $4,000 because it was actually driven 100,000 miles. The buyer discovers the breach of warranty and sues the salesperson for damages. The buyer can recover $6,000 ($10,000 warranted value minus $4,000 actual value). The contract price ($8,000) is irrelevant to this computation.

A purchaser or lessee can recover for personal injuries that are caused by a breach of warranty.

CONSIDER THIS EXAMPLE: Suppose Frances Gordon purchases new tires for her car and the manufacturer expressly warrants the tires against blowout for 50,000 miles. Suppose one of the tires blows out after being used only 20,000 miles, causing severe injury to Ms. Gordon. She can recover personal injury damages from the manufacturer because of the breach of warranty.

Unless legally excluded, modified, or otherwise limited by the parties, a buyer or lessee may also recover **consequential damages** from the seller or lessor for breach of warranty. The same is true of incidental damages [UCC 2-714(3); UCC 2A-519(4)]. Consequential damages may be limited or excluded unless the limitation is unconscionable. Limitation of consequential damages for personal injury with respect to consumer goods is prima facie unconscionable.

consequential damages Foreseeable damages that arise from circumstances outside the contract. In order to be liable for these damages, the breaching party must know or have reason to know that the breach will cause special damages to the other party.

Third-Party Beneficiaries of Warranties Third parties who are injured in their person or property by products may be able to recover from the sellers and lessors of the product for damages caused by breach of warranty. Generally, the common law of contracts only gives the parties to a contract (i.e., those in **privity of contract**) rights under the contract.[1]

In the landmark case *Henningsen v. Bloomfield Motors, Inc.,*[2] the court held that lack of privity did not prevent a third-party plaintiff from suing for breach of the implied warranty of merchantability. The UCC continued this evolutionary trend by limiting the doctrine of privity. The UCC gives each state the option of choosing between three alternative provisions for liability to third parties [UCC 2-318; UCC 2A-216].

Disclaimers and limitations of liability are not effective against third parties. This is because they do not have knowledge of and have not agreed to these terms.

privity of contract The state of two specified parties being in a contract.

LANDMARK CASE
In Henningsen v. Bloomfield Motors, Inc., *the court held that lack of privity of contract did not prevent a third-party plaintiff from suing for breach of warranty.*

Statute of Limitations The UCC contains a four-year **statute of limitations** that applies to both hidden and obvious defects. The parties may agree to reduce the period of limitation to not less than one year. However, they may not extend it beyond four years. The statute begins to run when the goods are tendered to the buyer or lessee. The only exception is if the warranty extends to the future performance of the goods (such as a "five years or 50,000 miles" warranty).

UCC statute of limitations The UCC provides for a four-year statute of limitations for breach of warranty actions. The parties may agree to reduce this period to not less than one year.

CONTEMPORARY BUSINESS ENVIRONMENT

Magnuson-Moss Warranty Act

In 1975, Congress enacted the **Magnuson-Moss Warranty Act** (the Act), which covers written warranties relating to *consumer* products. The Act is administered by the Federal Trade Commission (FTC) [15 U.S.C. §§2301-2312].

Commercial and industrial transactions are not governed by the Act. The Act does not require a seller or lessor to make express written warranties. However, persons who do make such warranties are subject to the provisions of the Act.

continued

Full and Limited Warranties If the cost of the good is more than $10 and the warrantor chooses to make an express warranty, the Magnuson-Moss Warranty Act requires that the warranty be labeled as either "full" or "limited."

To qualify as a **full warranty**, the warrantor must guarantee free repair or replacement of the defective product. The warrantor must indicate whether there is a time limit on the full warranty (e.g., "full 36-month warranty").

In a **limited warranty**, the warrantor limits the scope of a full warranty in some way (e.g., to return of the purchase price or re-placement or such). The fact that the warranty is full or limited must be conspicuously displayed. The disclosures must be in "understandable language."

A consumer may bring a civil action against a defendant for violating the provisions of the Act. A successful plaintiff can recover damages, attorney's fees, and other costs incurred in bringing the action. The Act authorizes warrantors to establish an informal dispute resolution procedure. The procedure must be conspicuously described in the written warranty. Aggrieved consumers must assert their claims through this procedure before they can take legal action.

Limitation on Disclaiming Implied Warranties The Act does not create any implied warranties. It does, however, modify the state law of implied warranties in one crucial respect: Sellers or lessors who make express written warranties are forbidden from disclaiming or modifying the implied warranties of merchantability and fitness for a particular purpose. A seller or lessor may set a time limit on implied warranties, but this time limit must correspond to the duration of any express warranty.

TORT LIABILITY BASED ON FAULT

Depending on the circumstances of the case, persons who are injured by defective products may be able to recover damages under the tort theories of misrepresentation and negligence. Both of these theories require the defendant to be at fault for causing the plaintiff's injuries. These theories are discussed in the sections that follow.

Misrepresentation

intentional misrepresentation When a seller or lessor fraudulently misrepresents the quality of a product and a buyer is injured thereby.

A buyer or lessee who is injured because a seller or lessor fraudulently misrepresented the quality of a product can sue the seller for the tort of **intentional misrepresentation** or **fraud**. Recovery is limited to persons who were injured because they relied on the misrepresentation.

Intentional misrepresentation occurs when a seller or lessor either (1) affirmatively misrepresents the quality of a product or (2) conceals a defect in it. Because most reputable manufacturers, sellers, and lessors do not intentionally misrepresent the quality of their products, fraud is not often used as the basis for product liability actions.

✔ BUSINESS CHECKLIST

Lemon Laws Protect Purchasers of Defective Automobiles

In the past, consumers who purchased automobiles and other vehicles that developed nagging mechanical problems had to try to convince the dealer or manufacturer to correct the problem. If the problem was not corrected, the consumer's only recourse was to seek redress through costly and time-consuming litigation. Today, most states have enacted **lemon laws**, which give consumers a new weapon in this battle.

Lemon laws provide a procedure for consumers to follow to correct reoccurring problems in vehicles. Lemon laws establish an administrative procedure that is less formal than a court proceeding. Most of these laws require that an arbitrator decide the dispute between a consumer and car dealer. Lemon laws stipulate that if the dealer or manufacturer does not correct a reoccurring defect in a vehicle within a specified number (e.g., four) of tries within a specified period of time (e.g., two years), the purchaser can rescind the purchase and recover a full refund of the vehicle's purchase price.

To properly invoke a state's lemon law, a consumer should take the following steps:

- Notify the car dealer immediately of any mechanical or other problems that develop in the vehicle
- Take the vehicle back to the dealer for the statutory number of times to give the dealer the opportunity to correct the defect
- If the defect is not corrected during the number of times and time period established by the state's lemon law, file a claim with the appropriate state agency seeking arbitration of the claim
- Attend the arbitration hearing and present evidence to substantiate the claim that the vehicle suffered from a defect that was not corrected by the dealer or manufacturer within the statutorily prescribed period.

Negligence

A person injured by a defective product may bring an action for **negligence** against the negligent party. To be successful, the plaintiff must prove that the defendant breached a duty of due care to the plaintiff that caused the plaintiff's injuries. Failure to exercise due care includes failing to assemble the product carefully, negligent product design, negligent inspection or testing of the product, negligent packaging, failure to warn of the dangerous propensities of the product, and such. It is important to note that in a negligence lawsuit only a party who was actually negligent is liable to the plaintiff.

The plaintiff and the defendant do not have to be in privity of contract.[3] For example, in the landmark case *MacPherson v. Buick Motor Co.*,[4] the court held that an injured consumer could recover damages from the manufacturer of a product even though the consumer was only in privity of contract with the retailer from whom he had purchased the product. The plaintiff generally bears the difficult burden of proving that the defendant was negligent.

CONSIDER THIS EXAMPLE: Assume that the purchaser of a motorcycle is injured in an accident. The accident occurred because a screw was missing from the motorcycle. How does the buyer prove who was negligent? Was it the manufacturer, who left the screw out during the assembly of the motorcycle? Was it the retailer, who negligently failed to discover the missing screw while preparing the motorcycle for sale? Was it the mechanic, who failed to replace the screw after repairing the motorcycle? Negligence remains a viable, yet difficult, theory upon which to base a product liability action.

In the following case, the court held a defendant manufacturer liable for negligence in a product liability lawsuit.

negligence A tort related to defective products in which the defendant has breached a duty of due care and caused harm to the plaintiff.

LANDMARK CASE
In MacPherson v. Buick Motor Co., *the court held that an injured consumer could recover damages from the manufacturer of a product even though he was only in privity of contract with the retailer from whom he had purchased the product.*

CASE 15.4

Benedi v. McNeil-P.P.C., Incorporated
66 F.3d 1378 (1995) United States Court of Appeals, Fourth Circuit

Facts Antonio Benedi consumed three to four glasses of wine a night during the week and sometimes more on the weekend. On February 5, 1993, Benedi began taking Extra-Strength Tylenol in normal doses for flu-like aches. On February 10, 1993, Benedi was admitted to the hospital in a coma and near death due to liver and kidney failure. On the night of February 12, 1993, Benedi underwent an emergency liver transplant. Because of the transplant, Benedi will have to undergo kidney dialysis in the future. Blood tests performed shortly after Benedi's admission to the hospital revealed that he suffered from acetaminophen (Tylenol) toxicity, which is caused by a combination of Tylenol and too much alcohol. The bottle from which Benedi took the Tylenol did not contain a warning of the dangers of the combination of Tylenol and excessive alcohol consumption. Benedi sued McNeil-P.P.C., Incorporated (McNeil), the manufacturer of Tylenol, for negligent failure to warn. The jury found McNeil negligent and awarded Benedi $7,850,000 in compensatory damages. McNeil appealed.

Issue Is McNeil liable for negligent failure to warn?

Decision The court of appeals affirmed the jury's verdict awarding plaintiff Benedi $7,850,000 against McNeil for negligent failure to warn.

Reason At trial, Benedi called two liver disease specialists who both testified that a warning of the possible danger to heavy drinkers from combining alcohol and acetaminophen should have been placed on the Tylenol label since the mid-1980s. These experts described exactly how the alcohol-acetaminophen mixture can become a toxin in the liver. They cited numerous treatises and articles published in medical journals prior to 1993 that describe the increased risk of liver injury when acetaminophen is combined with alcohol. One of the plaintiff's experts referred to 60 reports that McNeil had received by the end of 1992 documenting cases of liver injury associated with combining therapeutic doses of Tylenol with alcohol. The court of appeals stated that it was the jury's role to assess the weight and credibility of the evidence, and the jury found that Benedi proved causation. The court concluded that ample evidence existed from which a reasonable jury could find for Benedi.

Note In the summer of 1993 (after Benedi's injury), McNeil included a warning on Tylenol that persons who regularly consume three or more alcoholic drinks a day should consult a physician before using Tylenol.

CASE QUESTIONS

Critical Legal Thinking What elements are necessary to prove negligence? Do you think that Mc-Neil was negligent in this case? Do you think jurors are sophisticated enough to evaluate and judge scientific evidence?

Ethics Did McNeil act ethically in failing to put a warning on Tylenol? Do you think a warning was warranted?

Business Implication What will be the implication of this case to manufacturers of pain-killing drugs? Will consumers be better off because of this decision? Explain.

THE DOCTRINE OF STRICT LIABILITY

doctrine of strict liability in tort A tort doctrine that makes manufacturers, distributors, wholesalers, retailers, and others in the chain of distribution of a defective product liable for the damages caused by the defect *irrespective of fault*.

In the landmark case *Greenman v. Yuba Power Products, Inc.*,[5] the California supreme court adopted the **doctrine of strict liability in tort** as a basis for product liability actions. Most states have now adopted this doctrine as a basis for product liability actions. The doctrine of strict liability removes many of the difficulties for the plaintiff associated with other theories of product liability. The remainder of this chapter examines the scope of the strict liability doctrine.

The Restatement of Torts

The doctrine of strict liability is not part of the Uniform Commercial Code (UCC). The most widely recognized articulation of the doctrine is found in **Section 402A** of the **Restatement (Second) of Torts**, which provides the following:

1. One who sells any product in a defective condition unreasonably dangerous to the user or consumer or to his property is subject to liability for physical harm thereby caused to the ultimate user or consumer, or to his property, if
   a. the seller is engaged in the business of selling such a product, and
   b. it is expected to and does reach the user or consumer without substantial change in the condition in which it is sold.
2. The rule stated in Subsection (1) applies although
   a. the seller has exercised all possible care in the preparation and sale of his product, and
   b. the user or consumer has not bought the product from or entered into any contractual relation with the seller.

> **LANDMARK CASE**
> *In* Greenmun v. Yuba Power Products, Inc., *the California supreme court adopted the doctrine of strict liability in tort for product liability actions.*

Liability Without Fault

Unlike negligence, strict liability does not require the injured person to prove that the defendant breached a duty of care. *Strict liability is imposed irrespective of fault.* A seller can be found strictly liable even though he or she has exercised all possible care in the preparation and sale of his or her product.

The doctrine of strict liability applies to sellers and lessors of products who are engaged in the business of selling and leasing products. Casual sales and transactions by nonmerchants are not covered. Thus, a person who sells a defective product to a neighbor in a casual sale is not strictly liable if the product causes injury.

Strict liability applies only to products, not services. In hybrid transactions involving both services and products, the dominant element of the transaction dictates whether strict liability applies. For example, in a medical operation that requires a blood transfusion, the operation would be the dominant element and strict liability would not apply.[6] Strict liability may not be disclaimed.

Liability in the Chain of Distribution

All parties in the **chain of distribution** of a defective product are strictly liable for the injuries caused by that product. Thus, all manufacturers, distributors, wholesalers, retailers, lessors, and subcomponent manufacturers may be sued under this doctrine. This view is based on public policy. Lawmakers presume that sellers and lessors will insure against the risk of a strict liability lawsuit and spread the cost to their consumers by raising the price of products.

> **chain of distribution** All manufacturers, distributors, wholesalers, retailers, lessors, and subcomponent manufacturers involved in a transaction.

CONSIDER THIS EXAMPLE: Suppose a subcomponent manufacturer produces a defective tire and sells it to a truck manufacturer. The truck manufacturer places the defective tire on one of its new model trucks. The truck is distributed by a distributor to a retail dealer. Ultimately, the retail dealer sells the truck to a buyer. The defective tire causes an accident in which the buyer is injured. All of the parties in the tire's chain of distribution can be sued by the injured party. In this case, the liable parties are the subcomponent manufacturer, the truck manufacturer, the distributor, and the retailer.

A defendant who has not been negligent but who is made to pay a strict liability judgment can bring a separate action against the negligent party in the chain of distribution to recover its losses. In the preceding example, for instance, the retailer could sue the manufacturer to recover the strict liability judgment assessed against it.

Exhibit 15.1 compares the doctrines of negligence and strict liability.

Exhibit 15.1
Doctrines of Negligence and
Strict Liability Compared

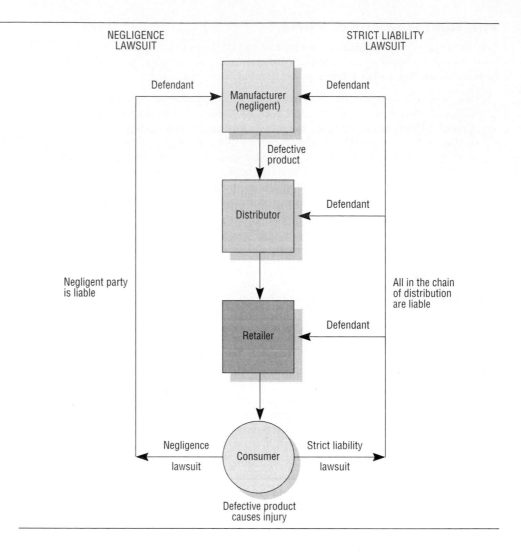

NEGLIGENCE
LAWSUIT

STRICT LIABILITY
LAWSUIT

Defendant → Manufacturer (negligent) ← Defendant

Defective product

Distributor ← Defendant

Negligent party
is liable

All in the chain
of distribution
are liable

Retailer ← Defendant

Negligence
lawsuit ← Consumer → Strict liability
lawsuit

Defective product
causes injury

Parties Who Can Recover for Strict Liability

Because strict liability is a tort doctrine, privity of contract between the plaintiff and the defendant is not required. In other words, the doctrine applies even if the injured party had no contractual relations with the defendant. Under strict liability, sellers and lessors are liable to the ultimate user or consumer. Users include the purchaser or lessee, family members, guests, employees, customers, and persons who passively enjoy the benefits of the product (e.g., passengers in automobiles).

Most jurisdictions have judicially or statutorily extended the protection of strict liability to bystanders. The courts have stated that bystanders should be entitled to even greater protection than a consumer or user. This is because consumers and users have the chance to inspect for defects and to limit their purchases to articles manufactured by reputable manufacturers and sold by reputable retailers, whereas bystanders do not have the same opportunity.[7]

Damages Recoverable for Strict Liability

The damages recoverable in a strict liability action vary by jurisdiction. Damages for personal injuries are recoverable in all jurisdictions that have adopted the doctrine of

BUSINESS BRIEF

Punitive damages are often awarded in strict liability lawsuits if the plaintiff proves that the defendant either intentionally injured him or her or acted with reckless disregard for his or her safety.

strict liability, although some jurisdictions limit the dollar amount of the award. Property damage is recoverable in most jurisdictions, but economic loss (e.g., lost income) is recoverable in only a few jurisdictions. **Punitive damages** are generally allowed if the plaintiff can prove that the defendant either intentionally injured him or her or acted with reckless disregard for his or her safety.

ETHICAL PERSPECTIVE

Breast Implant Litigation

During the past 25 years, more than two million women worldwide, half in the United States, have had silicone-gel breast implants inserted into their bodies. Twenty percent of these operations were done for women who had mastectomies, and the remainder were for cosmetic purposes. Dow Corning Corporation, a company headquartered in Midland, Michigan, sold more than half of these silicone-gel implants.

Dow Corning sold the implants for less than $200. The doctors who inserted them charged thousands of dollars for the surgical procedure. The implants made up a very small portion of Dow Corning's sales, and the company claims that it did not make any profits on the sale of the implants.

Many women who had these implants complained about various things. Some said the silicone-gel breast implants ruptured; others said they leaked. Women complained that the implants caused several forms of cancer, autoimmunal diseases, lupus, scleroderma, rheumatoid arthritis, tissue hardening, inflammation, aches and pains, fatigue, insomnia, memory loss, and headaches.

Beginning in about 1990, thousands of women filed lawsuits against Dow Corning and the other manufacturers of silicone-gel implants. The suits asserted that the defendants knew of these

dangers but failed to warn women of them. The defendants denied liability and pointed to the fact that there was no scientific evidence linking the alleged diseases to silicone-gel breast implants. Nonetheless, in 1992 the Federal Food and Drug Administration (FDA) requested manufacturers to discontinue selling silicone-gel breast implants. Dow Corning and the other manufacturers complied with this request.

Civil court juries examined the evidence using the preponderance of the evidence standard. They disagreed with Dow Corning and found the company liable in hundreds of lawsuits. Many multimillion-dollar judgments were rendered against Dow Corning. Eventually, several hundred thousand lawsuits were filed against Dow Corning and the other manufacturers. Because of the similarity of the claims, most of these lawsuits were consolidated in a class action lawsuit.

In 1994, the manufacturers of silicone-gel breast implants agreed to establish a global settlement fund of $4.5 billion. Dow Corning's share of the fund was $2 billion to be paid over a 30-year period, of which it expects to recover $600 million from insurers. Other manufacturers, including Bristol-Myers Squibb, Baxter International, and more than 50 smaller manufacturers, agreed to contribute the remaining funds.

More than 400,000 women have filed claims against the proposed fund.

On May 3, 1995, a federal judge stated that the settlement fund was inadequate and that claimants would be able to seek additional damages from Dow Corning and the other manufacturers. On May 16, 1995, Dow Corning filed for bankruptcy protection under Chapter 11 of the federal Bankruptcy Code. This bankruptcy filing froze the $2 billion that Dow Corning had originally agreed to contribute to the fund. The settlement agreement was set aside by the court, leaving it open for the lawsuits to proceed against the named defendants.

The women who have filed claims allege that the bankruptcy filing is unjust and is a legal maneuver by Dow Corning to avoid social and legal responsibility for the harm it has caused. Dow Corning asserts that its bankruptcy filing is necessary to consolidate the many implant claims it faces, stop frivolous claims, and avoid being found "guilty until proven innocent" by the civil court juries in this country.

1. Do you think Dow Corning's "guilty until proven innocent" charge is true? Could 400,000 female claimants be wrong?
2. Do you think Dow Corning acted socially responsibly by filing for bankruptcy? Explain.

THE CONCEPT OF DEFECT

defect Something wrong, inadequate, or improper in manufacture, design, packaging, warning, or safety measures of a product.

To recover for strict liability, the injured party must first show that the product that caused the injury was somehow **defective**. (Remember that the injured party does not have to prove who caused the product to become defective.) Plaintiffs can allege multiple product defects in one lawsuit. A product can be found to be defective in many ways.

The types of defects that are most commonly litigated are discussed in the following sections.

Defect in Manufacture

defect in manufacture A defect that occurs when the manufacturer fails to (1) properly assemble a product, (2) properly test a product, or (3) adequately check the quality of the product.

A **defect in manufacture** occurs when the manufacturer (1) fails to properly assemble a product, (2) fails to properly test a product, or (3) has inadequately checked the quality of the product.

CONSIDER THIS EXAMPLE: Acme Manufacturing Company manufactures ladders. Ruby, a consumer, purchases an Acme ladder. Unknown to Ruby, Acme failed to tighten a screw that holds the top step of the ladder in place. While she is painting her house, Ruby reaches the top step of the ladder, the loose screw falls out, and Ruby falls to the ground, severely injuring herself. Ruby can recover damages for her injuries from Acme for strict liability based on a defect in manufacture.

The following case is a classic example involving a defect in the manufacture.

CASE 15.5

Shoshone Coca-Cola Bottling Co. v. Dolinski
420 P.2d 855 (1967) Supreme Court of Nevada

Facts Leo Dolinski purchased a bottle of "Squirt," a soft drink, from a vending machine at a Sea and Ski plant, his place of employment. Dolinski opened the bottle and consumed part of its contents. He immediately became ill. Upon examination, it was found that the bottle contained the decomposed body of a mouse, mouse hair, and mouse feces. Dolinski visited a doctor and was given medicine to counteract nausea. Dolinski suffered physical and mental distress from consuming the decomposed mouse and developed an aversion to soft drinks. The Shoshone Coca-Cola Bottling Company (Shoshone) manufactured and distributed the Squirt bottle. Dolinski sued Shoshone, basing his lawsuit on the doctrine of strict liability. The state of Nevada had not previously recognized the doctrine of strict liability. However, the trial court adopted the doctrine of strict liability and the jury returned a verdict in favor of the plaintiff. Shoshone appealed.

Issue Should the state of Nevada judicially adopt the doctrine of strict liability? If so, was there a defect in the manufacture of the Squirt bottle that caused the plaintiff's injuries?

Decision Yes. The supreme court of Nevada adopted the doctrine of strict liability and held that the evidence supported the trial court's finding that there was a defect in manufacture. Affirmed.

Reason In adopting the doctrine of strict liability, the court stated, "Public policy demands that one who places upon the market a bottled beverage in a condition dangerous for use must be held strictly liable to the ultimate user for injuries resulting from such use, although the seller has exercised all reasonable care."

CASE QUESTIONS

Critical Legal Thinking Should the courts adopt the theory of strict liability? Why or why not?

Ethics Was it ethical for Shoshone to argue that it was not liable to Dolinski?

Business Implication Should all in the chain of distribution of a defective product—even those parties who are not responsible for the defect—be held liable under the doctrine of strict liability? Or should liability be based only on fault?

Defect in Design

A **defect in design** can support a strict liability action. Design defects that have supported strict liability awards include toys that are designed with removable parts that can be swallowed by children, machines and appliances designed without proper safeguards, and trucks and other vehicles designed without a warning device to let people know that the vehicle is backing up.

In evaluating the adequacy of a product's design, the courts apply a risk-utility analysis and consider the gravity of the danger posed by the design, the likelihood that injury will occur, the availability and cost of producing a safer alternative design, the social utility of the product, and other factors.

defect in design A defect that occurs when a product is improperly designed.

Crashworthiness Doctrine Often, when an automobile is involved in an accident, the driver or passengers are not injured by the blow itself. Instead, they are injured when their bodies strike something inside their own automobile (e.g., the dashboard or the steering wheel). This is commonly referred to as the "second collision." The courts have held that automobile manufacturers are under a duty to design automobiles to take into account the possibility of this second collision. This is called the **crashworthiness doctrine**. Failure to design an automobile to protect occupants from foreseeable dangers caused by a second collision subjects the manufacturer and dealer to strict liability.

crashworthiness doctrine A doctrine that says automobile manufacturers are under a duty to design automobiles so they take into account the possibility of harm from a person's body striking something inside the automobile in the case of a car accident.

ETHICAL PERSPECTIVE

Design Defect: Moseley v. General Motors

Manufacturers can often design products to be safer, but at a cost. The extra money or additional time necessary to do so is usually weighed against the benefits of creating a safer product. These cost-benefit decisions often present ethical dilemmas. Consider the following case.

Shortly after midnight on October 21, 1989, Shannon Moseley, age 17, was returning home after bringing his date to her house. He was driving a 1985 GMC Sierra pickup truck that his parents had bought him for his birthday. The truck was manufactured by General Motors Corporation (GM). As Shannon drove his truck through an intersection, David Ruprecht, a drunk driver, ran a red light and rammed into the driver's side of Shannon's truck. Shannon, whose truck immediately burst into flames, died in the accident.

Ruprecht, who was *judgment-proof* (i.e., did not have money to pay a jury award), served jail time for his offense. Shannon's parents also sued GM for product liability. They alleged that Shannon's pickup had dangerous side-saddle gas tanks mounted on the side of the vehicle outside the frame rail of the truck. Other manufacturers of pickup trucks placed their gas tanks inside the frame so that the vehicles could withstand collisions better. The Moseleys argued that GM's side-saddle gas tank was a design defect that caused Shannon's death.

The Moseleys' attorney, through the introduction of evidence, portrayed 20 years of corporate villainy by GM. This included evidence of clandestine crash testing, the results of which were never disclosed to the public, as well as document shredding. This evidence was designed to show not only poor product design but also GM's evil intent in

keeping dangerous vehicles on the road.

GM's counsel presented a very technical defense designed to show that the impact of Reprecht's vehicle—and not the design and placement of the fuel tank—killed Shannon instantly.

In the first phase of the trial, the jury returned a verdict of $4.24 million for Shannon's life plus $1 for pain and suffering. In the second phase, the jury returned a punitive damage verdict of *$101 million* against GM. GM appealed, and the appellate court overturned the decision. The case was later settled for an undisclosed sum of money. [*Moseley v. General Motors Corporation*, (1994)]

1. Did GM act ethically in this case?
2. Do you think an award of punitive damages would be justified in this case?

Defect in Packaging

defect in packaging
A defect that occurs when a product has been placed in packaging that is insufficiently tamper-proof.

Manufacturers owe a duty to design and provide safe packages for their products. This duty requires manufacturers to provide packages and containers that are tamper-proof or that clearly indicate if they have been tampered with. Certain manufacturers, such as drug manufacturers, owe a duty to place their products in containers that cannot be opened by children. A manufacturer's failure to meet this duty subjects the manufacturer and others in the chain of distribution of the product to strict liability.

In the following case, the court had to decide whether there was defective packaging.

CASE 15.6

Elsroth v. Johnson & Johnson
700 F.Supp. 151 (1988) United States District Court, Southern District New York

Facts On February 4, 1986, Harriet Notarnicola purchased a box of Extra-Strength Tylenol capsules from a Bronxville, New York, grocery store owned by The Great Atlantic & Pacific Tea Co. (A&P). The Tylenol was manufactured by McNeil Consumer Products Co., a division of McNeilab, Inc. (McNeil), under the name Johnson & Johnson. Diane Elsroth was visiting her boyfriend, Michael Notarnicola, for a week at the home of Michael's parents. Late on the night of February 7, Diane complained of a headache. Michael went to the kitchen, opened the box and plastic container of Extra-Strength Tylenol purchased by his mother at the A&P store and returned with two capsules and a glass of water for Diane. A short time after ingesting the capsules, Diane retired. Her dead body was found the next day. The medical examiner concluded that the Tylenol capsules ingested by Diane were contaminated by a lethal dose of potassium cyanide. The murder remains unsolved, but evidence shows that the Tylenol bottle had been tampered with after the product left the manufacturer's control. An unknown third party purchased the Tylenol, breached the packaging, substituted cyanide for some of the medicine contained in several of the gelatin capsules, somehow resealed the container and box in such a way that the tampering was not readily detectable and placed the contaminated box on the shelf of the A&P store. John Elsroth, administrator of Diane's estate, brought this strict liability action against McNeil and A&P seeking $1 million in compensatory damages and $92 million in punitive damages.

Issue Was there a defect in packaging that would support an action for strict liability?

Decision No. The court held that there was not a defect in packaging. The defendants are not therefore strictly liable for Ms. Elsroth's death.

Reason The makers of Tylenol have marketed the product in tamper-resistant packaging with the following features: (1) a foil seal glued to the mouth of the container or bottle, (2) a "shrink seal" around the neck and cap of the container, and (3) a sealed box (the end flaps of which are glued shut) in which the product and container are placed.

McNeil, through its research, knew that this packaging could be violated by a determined tamperer using sophisticated means and that no evidence of this kind of sophisticated tampering would be visible to the average consumer. As one McNeil official put it, tampering by "the Rembrandt kind of criminals" could not be prevented by this type of packaging. McNeil was also operating under the constraint, however, as recognized by the FDA that no packaging could prevent this kind of "exotic" tampering—tamperproof packaging is not possible.

The packaging alternative designed by McNeil employed not one, not two, but three of the tamper-resistant features listed as alternatives in the 1982 FDA regulations. When all of these factors are thrown into the mix, we find, as a matter of law, that under a risk-utility analysis this packaging was in a condition reasonably contemplated by the ultimate consumer and was not unreasonably dangerous for its intended use. Moreover, plaintiff had presented no evidence of what other steps might feasibly have been taken to ensure a higher degree of safety. If there are better tamper-resistant features available that would be feasible for use, plaintiff did not describe them. We return however, to the fundamental premise: no packaging can boast of being tamper-proof.

CASE QUESTIONS

Critical Legal Thinking Should manufacturers be forced to make tamper-proof packaging for their products? Is this possible? What would be the expense?

Ethics Did any of the parties in the case act unethically?

Business Implication Do you think the plaintiff's seeking $92 million in punitive damages was warranted?

Failure to Warn

Certain products are inherently dangerous and cannot be made any safer and still accomplish the task for which they are designed. For example, certain useful drugs cause side effects, allergies, and other injuries to some users. Many machines and appliances include dangerous moving parts that, if removed, would defeat the purpose of the machine or appliance. Manufacturers and sellers of such products are under a **duty to warn** users about the product's dangerous propensities. A proper and conspicuous warning placed on the product insulates the manufacturer and others in the chain of distribution from strict liability. **Failure to warn** of these dangerous propensities is a defect that will support a strict liability action.

The court found an inadequate warning in the following case.

failure to warn
A defect that occurs when a manufacturer does not place a warning on the packaging of products that could cause injury if the danger is unknown.

CASE 15.7

Nowak v. Faberge USA Inc.
32 F.3d 755 (1994) United States Court of Appeals, Third Circuit

Facts Faberge USA, Inc. (Faberge) manufactures Aqua Net, a hair spray that is sold in an aerosol can. In addition to the hair-holding spray, Aqua Net contains a mixture of butane or propane as the aerosol propellant and alcohol as a solvent. Alcohol, butane, and propane all are extremely flammable. Aerosol cans of Aqua Net carry a warning on the back stating, "Do not puncture" and "Do not use near fire or flame."

Alison Nowak, a 14-year-old girl, tried to spray her hair with a newly purchased can of Aqua Net. The spray valve would not work properly, so she cut open the can with a can opener. She thought she could then pour the contents into an empty aerosol bottle and use it. Nowak was standing in the kitchen near a gas stove when she punctured the can. A cloud of hair spray gushed from the can and the stove's pilot light ignited the spray into a ball of flame. She suffered severe, permanently disfiguring burns over 20 percent of her body.

Nowak sued Faberge for damages under strict liability, alleging that Faberge failed to warn her of the dangers of the flammability of Aqua Net. The jury held against Faberge and awarded Nowak $1.5 million. Faberge appealed.

Issue Did Faberge adequately warn the plaintiff of the flammability of Aqua Net?

Decision No. The court of appeals held that Faberge's warning was not adequate. Affirmed.

Reason A manufacturer owes a duty to adequately warn users of the dangerous propensities of their products. A product is defective if it is distributed without sufficient warnings to notify the ultimate user of the dangers inherent in the product. The trial court properly determined to send the case to the jury for this determination. The jury's verdict that Faberge's warning was inadequate is upheld.

CASE QUESTIONS

Critical Legal Thinking Should the law recognize a failure to warn as a basis for imposing strict liability on manufacturers and sellers of products? Why or why not?

Ethics Did Faberge violate its duty of social responsibility in this case? Explain.

Business Implication Do you think this case was decided properly? What else could Faberge have done to avoid liability?

Other Defects

failure to provide adequate instruction
A defect that occurs when a manufacturer does not provide detailed directions for safe assembly and use of a product.

Other defects can prove the basis for a strict liability action. **Failure to provide adequate instructions** for either the safe assembly or safe use of a product is a defect that subjects the manufacturer and others in the chain of distribution to strict liability.

Other defects include inadequate testing of products, inadequate selection of component parts or materials, and improper certification of the safety of a product. The concept of "defect" is an expanding area of the law.

DEFENSES TO PRODUCT LIABILITY

Defendants in strict liability or negligence actions may raise several **defenses** to the imposition of liability. These defenses are discussed in the sections that follow.

Supervening Event

supervening event   An alteration or modification of a product by a party in the chain of distribution that absolves all prior sellers from strict liability.

For a seller to be held strictly liable, the product it sells must reach the consumer or user "without substantial change" in its condition.[8] Under the doctrine of **supervening** or **intervening event**, the original seller is not liable if the product is materially altered or modified after it leaves the seller's possession and the alteration or modification causes an injury. A supervening event absolves all prior sellers in the chain of distribution from strict liability.

CONSIDER THIS EXAMPLE: A manufacturer produces a safe piece of equipment. It sells the equipment to a distributor, who removes a safety guard from the equipment. The distributor sells it to a retailer, who sells it to a buyer. The buyer is injured because of the removal of the safety guard. The manufacturer can raise the defense of supervening event against the imposition of liability. However, the distributor and retailer are strictly liable for the buyer's injuries.

Assumption of the Risk

Theoretically, the traditional doctrine of **assumption of the risk** is a defense to a product liability action. For this defense to apply, the defendant must prove that (1) the plaintiff knew and appreciated the risk and (2) the plaintiff voluntarily assumed the risk. In practice, the defense of assumption of the risk is narrowly applied by the courts.

Generally Known Dangers

generally known dangers
A defense that acknowledges that certain products are inherently dangerous and are known to the general population to be so.

Certain products are inherently dangerous and are known to the general population to be so. Sellers are not strictly liable for failing to warn of **generally known dangers**. For example, it is a known fact that guns shoot bullets. Manufacturers of guns do not have to place a warning on the barrel of a gun warning of this generally known danger. However, the manufacturer would be under a duty to place a safety lock on the gun.

Correction of a Defect

correction of a defect
A defense that permits a seller of a defective product to recall and repair the defect. The seller is not liable to purchasers who fail to have the defect corrected.

A manufacturer that produces a defective product and later discovers said defect must (1) notify purchasers and users of the defect and (2) correct the defect. Most manufacturers faced with this situation recall the defective product and either repair the defect or replace the product.

The seller must make reasonable efforts to notify purchasers and users of the defect and the procedure to correct it. Reasonable efforts normally consist of sending letters to known purchasers and users and placing notices in newspapers and magazines of general circulation. If a user ignores the notice and fails to have the defect corrected, the seller may raise this as a defense against further liability with respect to the defect. Many courts have held that reasonable notice is effective even against users who did not see the notice.

Government Contractor Defense

Many defense and other contractors manufacture products (e.g., rockets, airplanes) to government specifications. Most jurisdictions recognize a **government contractor defense** to product liability actions. To establish this defense, a government contractor must prove that (1) the precise specifications for the product were provided by the government, (2) the product conformed to those specifications, and (3) the contractor warned the government of any known defects or dangers of the product.

government contractor defense A defense that says a contractor who was provided specifications by the government is not liable for any defect in the product that occurs as a result of those specifications.

Misuse of the Product

Sometimes users are injured when they misuse a product. If they bring a product liability action, the defendant–seller may be able to assert the misuse as a defense. Whether the defense is effective depends on whether the misuse was foreseeable. The seller is relieved of product liability if the plaintiff has **abnormally misused** the product—that is, there has been an **unforeseeable misuse** of the product. However, the seller is liable if there has been a **foreseeable misuse** of the product. This reasoning is intended to provide an incentive for manufacturers to design and manufacture safer products.

In the following case, the court had to determine if there was a foreseeable or unforeseeable misuse of a product.

misuse A defense that relieves a seller of product liability if the user *abnormally* misused the product. Products must be designed to protect against *foreseeable* misuse.

CASE 15.8

Daniell v. Ford Motor Co., Inc.

581 F.Supp. 728 (1984) United States District Court, D. New Mexico

Facts In 1980, Connie Daniell felt "overburdened" and attempted to commit suicide by climbing into the trunk of a 1973 Ford LTD automobile and closing the trunk behind her. She remained locked inside for nine days until she was rescued. Daniell then sued Ford Motor Company, Inc. (Ford), the manufacturer of the LTD automobile, for strict liability to recover for psychological and physical injuries arising from the occurrence. She contended that the automobile had a design defect because the trunk lock or latch did not have an internal release or opening mechanism. She also maintained that Ford was liable for failing to warn her of this condition. Ford filed a motion for summary judgment.

Issue Was there an abnormal misuse of the automobile trunk that would relieve Ford Motor Company of strict liability?

Decision Yes. The court held that the plaintiff's use of the trunk of the Ford LTD automobile to attempt to commit suicide was an abnormal and unforeseeable misuse of the product and that the manufacturer had no duty to design the trunk with an internal release mechanism. The court also held that climbing into a trunk and closing the trunk lid behind you in an attempt to commit suicide is a known danger and the manufacturer owes no duty to warn against this danger. The court granted defendant Ford Motor Company's motion for summary judgment.

Reason A risk is not foreseeable by a manufacturer where a product is used in a manner that could not reasonably be anticipated by the manufacturer and that use is the cause of the plaintiff's injury. In this case, the court held that the "plaintiff's use of the trunk compartment as a means to attempt suicide was an unforeseeable use as a matter of law." The manufacturer had no duty to warn the plaintiff of the risk inherent in crawling into an automobile trunk and closing the trunk lid because such a risk is obvious.

continued

CASE QUESTIONS

Critical Legal Thinking Should any defenses be allowed against the application of strict liability? Do you think there was a foreseeable or abnormal misuse of the product in this case?

Ethics Was it ethical for the plaintiff to sue Ford Motor Company for her injuries?

Business Implication Do you think the doctrine of strict liability advances or harms the economic development of business in this country? Explain.

Statutes of Limitation and Statutes of Repose

statute of limitation
A statute that requires an injured person to bring an action within a certain number of years from the time that he or she was injured by the defective product.

Most states have **statutes of limitation** that require an injured person to bring an action within a certain number of years from the time that he or she was injured by the defective product. This limitation period varies from state to state. Failure to bring an action within the appropriate time relieves the defendant of liability.

In most jurisdictions, the statute of limitations does not begin to run until the plaintiff suffers an injury. This subjects sellers and lessors to exposure for an unspecified period of time because a defective product might not cause an injury for years, or even decades, after it was sold. Because this might be unfair to the seller, some states have enacted **statutes of repose**. Statutes of repose limit the seller's liability to a certain number of years from the date when the product was first sold. The period of repose varies from state to state.

statute of repose A statute that limits the seller's liability to a certain number of years from the date when the product was first sold.

Contributory and Comparative Negligence

contributory negligence
A defense that says a person who is injured by a defective product but has been negligent and has contributed to his or her own injuries cannot recover from the defendant.

comparative negligence
A doctrine that applies to strict liability actions that says a plaintiff who is contributorily negligent for his or her injuries is responsible for a proportional share of the damages.

Sometimes a person who is injured by a defective product is negligent and contributes to his or her own injuries. The defense of **contributory negligence** bars an injured plaintiff from recovering from the defendant in a negligence action. This doctrine generally does not bar recovery in strict liability actions, however.

Many states have held that the doctrine of **comparative negligence** (or **comparative** fault) applies to strict liability actions. Under this doctrine, a plaintiff who is contributorily negligent for his or her injuries is responsible for a proportional share of the damages. In other words, the damages are apportioned between the plaintiff and the defendant.

CONSIDER THIS EXAMPLE: Suppose an automobile manufacturer produces a car with a hidden defect and a consumer purchases the car from an automobile dealer. Assume that the consumer is injured in an automobile accident in which the defect is found to be 75 percent responsible for the accident and the consumer's own reckless driving is found to be 25 percent responsible. If the plaintiff suffers $1 million worth of injuries, the plaintiff may recover $750,000 from the defendant manufacturer and car dealer.

 INTERNATIONAL PERSPECTIVE

Product Liability Law in Japan

Japanese manufacturers sell many of the same products in Japan and the United States. In the United States, the products are subject to the same product liability laws as are American companies. In Japan, they enjoy near-immunity from product liability claims. For example, in almost 50 years, consumers have won only 150 product liability cases in Japan and recovered meager damages. In the same period, companies in the United States have lost tens of thousands of such suits and have paid out hundreds of millions of dollars in damages.

There are several reasons product liability claims are rare in Japan:

1. The plaintiff has the difficult burden of proving that the company was negligent. Japan has not adopted the U.S. doctrine of strict liability
2. Awards that are granted by courts are small (at least by U.S. standards), and punitive damages are not available.

The docile attitude of Japanese consumers is changing, and more injured consumers are suing to recover damages for their injuries. The Japanese government has adopted new consumer protection laws that make it easier to bring product liability lawsuits in Japan.

Critics argue that the Japanese system leaves injured consumers unrecompensed for injuries caused by defective products. Some argue that the near-immunity from product liability claims at home give Japanese manufacturers an edge in selling goods in international markets. Proponents of the Japanese system argue that it promotes the development and sale of products free from the oppressive liability costs that manufacturers face in the United States. They point to the fact that liability insurance costs are sometimes 20 times higher in the United States than in Japan.

WORKING THE WEB

U.S. Food and Drug Administration The U.S. Food and Drug Administration (FDA) links you to information about foods, human drugs, animal drugs, cosmetics, and many other subjects.

Visit at http://www. fda.gov/

Occupational Safety and Health Administration The U.S. Department of Labor has a Web site that links you to all the publications, programs, and services of the Occupational Safety and Health Administration (OSHA).

Visit at http://www.osha.gov/

American Medical Association The American Medical Association (AMA) links you to a plethora of medical information.

Visit at http://www.ama-assn.org/

Products Liability Law Page This Web page has all kinds of links to products liability information including information about asbestos, silicone breast implants, tobacco, medical malpractice, and more.

Visit at http://www.productslaw.com/

Tobacco Control Archives The Tobacco Control Archives is a project sponsored by the University of California San Francisco Library and Center for Knowledge Management. It collects materials relating to nonsmoking legislative initiatives and local ordinances.

Visit at http://galen.library.ucsf.edu/tobacco/

CYBER EXERCISES:

1. Use the FDA site to find information about the dietary supplement Herbal Fen-Phen.
2. Use the OSHA site to find a definition and description of ergonomics. Print out your results.
3. Use the AMA site to find AMA's Patient Bill of Rights.
4. Using the Products Liability Law page, find an article called *The Selling of Contraception* and print it out.
5. Use the Tobacco Control Archives site to find "The Cigarette Papers Online."

CHAPTER SUMMARY

WARRANTIES OF TITLE AND NO INFRINGEMENTS, P. 325

| Good Title, No Security Interests, No Infringements, and No Interference | 1. *Warranty of good title.* Sellers of goods warrant that they have good title to the goods they are selling.
2. *Warranty of no security interests.* Sellers of goods warrant that the goods are free from any third-party security interests, liens, or encumbrances that are not known to the buyer.
3. *Warranty against infringements.* Sellers and lessors who are merchants warrant that the goods are delivered free of any third-party patent, trademark, or copyright claim.
4. *Warranty against interference.* Lessors of goods warrant that no person holds a claim or interest in the goods that arose from an act or omission of the lessor that will interfere with the lessee's enjoyment of the leasehold interest. |

WARRANTIES OF QUALITY, P. 326

Express Warranty	Affirmation by a seller or lessor that the goods he or she is selling or leasing meet certain standards of quality, description, performance, or condition.

Implied Warranty of Merchantability	1. *Implied warranty of merchantability.* Warranty implied by law in sales and lease transactions that requires that the goods:
	  a. Be fit for the ordinary purposes for which they are used
	  b. Be adequately contained, packaged, and labeled
	  c. Be of an even kind, quality, and quantity within each unit
	  d. Conform to any promise or affirmation of fact made on the container or label
	  e. Pass without objection in the trade
	  f. Meet a fair or middle range of quality if the goods are fungible.
	2. *Implied warranty of fitness for human consumption.* Warranty implied by law that food products are fit for human consumption. States apply one of the two following tests:
	  a. *Foreign substance test.* A food is unmerchantable if a foreign object in the food caused plaintiff's injury.
	  b. *Consumer expectation test.* A food is unmerchantable if an object in the food that a consumer would not expect to be there caused the plaintiff's injury.
	The UCC incorporates this warranty within the implied warranty of merchantability.

Other Warranties	1. *Implied warranty of fitness for a particular purpose.* Warranty by a seller or lessor that the goods will meet the buyer's or lessee's expressed needs. 2. *Implied warranty arising from a course of dealing.* Warranty that arises from prior dealings between the parties to a sale or lease contract. 3. *Implied warranty arising from usage of trade.* Warranty that arises from customs of the industry or market.
Overlapping and Inconsistent Warranties	*Priority of inconsistent warranties:* 1. Implied warranty of fitness for a particular purpose 2. Express warranty 3. Implied warranty arising from a course of dealing 4. Implied warranty of custom or usage of trade 5. Implied warranty of merchantability.

| Warranty Disclaimers | 1. *Express warranties*. Can be limited if the warranty and disclaimer can be reasonably construed with each other.
2. *Implied warranties:*
 a. *Disclaimer*. Can be disclaimed by expressions like *as is, with all faults*, or such language. If such language is not used, implied warranties are disclaimed:
  i. *Implied warranty of merchantability*. Oral or written disclaimer that mentions the word merchantability.
  ii. *Implied warranty of fitness for a particular purpose*. Written disclaimer of general language.
 b. *Examination of goods*. The buyer or lessor fully examines the goods or refuses to do so. Applies only to obvious defects.
3. *Conspicuousness*. Written disclaimers must be conspicuously displayed to be enforceable. |
| Magnuson-Moss Warranty Act | Federal statute that covers written warranties that apply to *consumer* products.
Full and Limited Warranties If a good costs more than $10 and the warrantor makes an express warranty, the warranty must be labeled "full" or "limited."
1. *Full warranty*. Guarantees free repair or replacement of a defective product. A time limit may be placed on the warranty.
2. *Limited warranty*. Limits the scope of a full warranty in some way (e.g., to return of the purchase price).
Limitation on Disclaiming Implied Warranties If a seller or lessor makes an express warranty, he or she cannot disclaim or modify the implied warranties of merchantability and fitness for a particular purpose. A time limit may be placed on implied warranties but must correspond to the duration of the express warranty. |

TORT LIABILITY BASED ON FAULT, P. 334

| Negligence | Seller or lessor who breached his or her duty of due care by producing a defective product that causes injury to the plaintiff. Privity of contract between the seller or lessor and the plaintiff is not required. |
| Misrepresentation | Seller or lessor fraudulently misrepresents the quality of a product and the plaintiff relies on the misrepresentation and is injured thereby. |

THE DOCTRINE OF STRICT LIABILITY, P. 336

| Strict Liability in Tort | A manufacturer or seller who sells a defective product is liable to the ultimate user who is injured thereby. All in the chain of distribution are liable irrespective of fault. Sometimes called *vertical liability*. |

THE CONCEPT OF DEFECT, P. 340

| The Concept of Defect | 1. Defect in manufacture
2. Defect in design
3. Defect in packaging
4. Failure to warn
5. Failure to provide adequate instructions for assembly of a product
6. Other defects. |

DEFENSES TO PRODUCT LIABILITY, P. 344

| Defenses to Product Liability | A manufacturer or seller is not liable for damages caused by a product it manufactures or sells if one of the following defenses applies: |

1. *Supervening event*. The product was materially altered or modified after it left the seller's possession and the alteration or modification caused an injury. Also called intervening event.
2. *Assumption of the risk*. The plaintiff knew and appreciated the risk and voluntarily assumed the risk.
3. *Generally known dangers*. A seller is not liable for failing to warn about inherent dangers in products that are known to the general population.
4. *Correction of a defect*. A manufacturer or seller who learns about a defect in a product it has sold notifies purchasers and users of the defect and corrects the defect.
5. *Government contractor defense*. A manufacturer produces a product to government specifications and warns the government of any known defects in the specified design.
6. *Misuse of the product:*
   a. *Abnormal misuse*. The seller is not liable for injuries caused by the abnormal misuse of the product by the plaintiff. Also called unforeseeable misuse.
   b. *Foreseeable misuse*. The seller is liable for injuries caused by the foreseeable misuse of a product. The manufacturer must design products to be safe for foreseeable misuses.

Statutes of Limitation and Repose	1. *Statute of limitation*. Requires an injured person to bring a product liability lawsuit within a specified period of time after being injured by a defective product. 2. *Statute of repose*. Requires a person to bring a product liability lawsuit within a specified period of time after a defective product was first purchased or leased.
Contributory and Comparative Negligence	1. *Contributory negligence*. A person who is partially responsible for causing his or her own injuries may not recover anything from the manufacturer or seller of a defective product that caused the remainder of the person's injuries. 2. *Comparative negligence*. A person who is partially responsible for causing his or her own injuries is responsible for a proportional share of the damages. The manufacturer or seller of the defective product is responsible for the remainder of the plaintiff's damages. Also called *comparative fault*.

CRITICAL LEGAL THINKING CASES

15.1 Warranty of Title When James Redmond wanted to purchase an automobile, he spoke to a salesman at Bill Branch Chevrolet, Inc. The salesman offered to sell Redmond a blue Chevrolet Caprice for $6,200. The car was to be delivered to Redmond's residence. Redmond gave the salesman $1,000 cash and received a receipt in return. The next day, the salesman delivered the car to Redmond, and Redmond paid the remaining amount due. The salesman gave Redmond a printed sales contract that reflected the payments made with no balance due. One month later, Redmond called Bill Branch Chevrolet and asked for the title papers to the car. Redmond was told that the car had been reported stolen prior to the sale and that he could

not receive title until he contacted Bill Branch's insurance company. Redmond sued Bill Branch Chevrolet, Inc. Is Bill Branch liable? [*Bill Branch Chevrolet v. Redmond*, 378 So.2d 319 (Fla. App. 1980)]

15.2 Express Warranty The House of Zog manufactures and sells the "Golfing Gizmo," a training device designed to help golfers improve their swing. The device consists of a golf ball attached to one end of a cotton string, the other end of the string being tied to the middle of an elastic cord. The elastic cord is then stretched between two stakes placed in the ground forming a "T" configuration. This allows the ball to return automatically after it has been struck. The "Golfing Gizmo" is sold in a package that states "COMPLETELY SAFE—BALL WILL NOT HIT PLAYER." In 1966, Louise Hauter gave a Golfing Gizmo to her 13-year-old son, Fred, for Christmas. One afternoon, Fred decided to use the device, which had been set up in his front yard. Having used the Gizmo before, Fred felt no apprehension as he took his normal swing at the ball. The last thing he remembers is pain and dizziness. Fred had been hit in the head by the ball and had suffered serious injuries. Fred Hauter sues the House of Zog. Who wins? [*Hauter v. Zogarts*, 13 Cal.3d 104, 120 Cal.Rptr. 681 (Cal. 1975)]

15.3 Statement of Fact or Opinion? Jack Crothers went to Norm's Auto World (Norm's) to buy a used car. Maurice Boyd, a salesman at Norm's, showed Crothers a 1970 Dodge. While running the car's engine, Boyd told Crothers that the Dodge "had a rebuilt carburetor" and "was a good runner." After listening to the sales pitch, Crothers bought the car. As Crothers was driving the Dodge the next day, the car suddenly went out of control and crashed into a tree. Crothers was seriously injured. The cause of the crash was an obvious defect in the Dodge's accelerator linkage. Crothers sues Norm's Auto World. Who wins? [*Crothers v. Cohen*, 384 N.W.2d 562 (Minn. App. 1986)]

15.4 Implied Warranty of Merchantability Geraldine Maybank took a trip to New York City to visit her son and her two-year-old grandson. She borrowed her daughter's camera for the trip. Two days before leaving for New York, Maybank purchased a package of G.T.E. Sylvania Blue Dot flash cubes at a Kmart store. Kmart is owned by the S. S. Kresge Company. On the carton of the package were words to the effect that each bulb was safety coated. Upon arriving in New York, Maybank decided to take a picture of her grandson. She opened the carton of flash cubes and put one on the camera. When Maybank pushed down the lever to take a picture, the flash cube exploded. The explosion knocked her glasses off and caused cuts to her left eye. Maybank was hospitalized for eight days. Maybank sues S. S. Kresge company. Who wins? [*Maybank v. S. S. Kresge Company*, 266 S.E.2d 409 (N.C. App. 1980)]

15.5 Implied Warranty of Merchantability Gladys Flippo went to a ladies' clothing store in Baresville, Arkansas, known as Mode O'Day Frock Shops of Hollywood. Flippo tried on two pairs of pants that were shown to her by a saleswoman. The first pair proved to be too small. When Flippo put on the second pair, she suddenly felt a burning sensation on her thigh. Flippo immediately removed the pants, shook them, and a spider fell to the ground. An examination of her thigh revealed a reddened area, which grew progressively worse. Flippo was subsequently hospitalized for 30 days. According to her physician, the injury was caused by the bite of a brown recluse spider. Flippo sues Mode O'Day Frock Shops. Is Mode O'Day Frock Shops liable? [*Flippo v. Mode O'Day Frock Shops of Hollywood*, 449 S.W.2d 692 (Ark. 1970)]

15.6 Implied Warranty of Fitness for Human Consumption Tina Keperwes went to a Publix Supermarket in Florida and bought a can of Doxsee Brand Clam Chowder. Keperwes opened the can and prepared it at home. While eating the chowder, she bit down on a clam shell and injured one of her molars. Keperwes filed suit against Publix and Doxsee for breach of an implied warranty. In the lawsuit, Keperwes alleges that the clam chowder "was not fit for use as food, but was defective, unwholesome, and unfit for human consumption" and "was in such condition as to be dangerous to life and health." At the trial, Doxsee's General Manager testified as to the state-of-the-art methods Doxsee uses in preparing its chowder. Are Publix Supermarkets, Inc., and Doxsee liable for the injury to Keperwes's tooth? [*Keperwes v. Publix Supermarkets, Inc.*, 534 So.2d 872 (Fla. App. 1988)]

15.7 Implied Warranty of Fitness for a Particular Purpose Dennis Walker is the owner of several pizza parlors in Nebraska. The stores operate under the name of El Fredo Pizza Restaurants, Inc. Walker planned on opening a new restaurant in 1973. A business associate suggested that Walker purchase an oven from the Roto-Flex Oven Co. Walker contacted an agent of Roto-Flex and negotiated to buy a new oven. Walker told the agent the particular purpose for which he was buying the oven—to cook pizza—and that he was relying on the agent's skill and judgment in selecting a suitable oven. Based on the agent's suggestions, Walker entered into a contract to purchase a custom-built, Roto-Flex "Pizza Oven Special." The oven was installed in the new restaurant and problems immediately ensued. The oven failed to bake pizzas properly because of uneven heating. Constant monitoring of the oven was required, and delays occurred in serving customers. Roto-Flex was notified of the problem and attempted to fix the oven. The oven, however, continued to bake pizzas improperly. El Fredo Pizza, Inc., sues Roto-Flex Oven Company. Was a warranty of fitness for a particular purpose created in this case? [*El Fredo Pizza, Inc. v. Roto-Flex Oven Co.*, 291 N.W.2d 358 (Neb. 1978)]

15.8 Disclaimer of Warranties Cole Energy Company (Cole Energy) wanted to lease a gas compressor for use in its business of pumping and selling natural gas. Cole Energy began negotiating with the Ingersoll-Rand Company (Ingersoll-Rand). On December 5, 1983, the two parties entered into a lease agreement for a KOA gas compressor. The lease agreement contained a section labeled "WARRANTIES." Part of the section read "THERE ARE NO IMPLIED WARRANTIES OF MERCHANTABILITY OR FITNESS FOR A PARTICULAR PURPOSE CONTAINED HEREIN." The gas compressor that was installed failed to function properly. As a result, Cole Energy lost business. Cole Energy sued Ingersoll-Rand for the breach of an implied warranty of merchantability. Is Ingersoll-Rand liable? [*Cole Energy Development Company v. Ingersoll-Rand Company*, 678 F.Supp. 208 (C.D.Ill. 1988)]

15.9 Strict Liability Jeppesen and Company (Jeppesen) produces charts that graphically display approach procedures for airplanes landing at airports. These charts are drafted from tabular data supplied by the Federal Aviation Administration (FAA), a federal agency of the U.S. government. By law, Jeppesen cannot construct charts that include information different from that supplied by the FAA. On September 8, 1973, the pilot of an airplane owned by World Airways was on descent to land at the Cold Bay, Alaska, airport. The pilot was using an instrument approach procedure chart published by Jeppesen. The airplane crashed into a mountain near Cold Bay, killing all six crew members and destroying the aircraft. Evidence showed that the FAA data did not include the mountain. The heirs of the deceased crew members and World Airways brought a strict liability action against Jeppesen. Does the doctrine of strict liability apply to this case? Is Jeppesen liable? [*Brocklesby v. Jeppesen and Company*, 767 F.2d 1288 (9th Cir. 1985)]

is responsible

15.10 Defect The Emerson Electric Co. (Emerson) manufactures and sells a product called the Weed Eater Model XR-90. The Weed Eater is a multipurpose weed-trimming and brush-cutting device. It consists of a handheld gasoline-powered engine connected to a long drive shaft at the end of which can be attached various tools for cutting weeds and brush. One such attachment is a 10-inch circular saw blade capable of cutting through growth up to two inches in diameter. When this saw blade is attached to the Weed Eater, approximately 270 degrees of blade edge are exposed when in use. The owner's manual contained the following warning: "Keep children away. All people and pets should be kept at a safe distance from the work area, at least 30 feet, especially when using the blade." Donald Pearce, a 13-year-old boy, was helping his uncle clear an overgrown yard. The uncle was operating a Weed Eater XR-90 with the circular saw-blade attachment. When Pearce stooped to pick something up off the ground about 6 to 10 feet behind and slightly to the left of where his uncle was operating the Weed Eater, the saw blade on the Weed Eater struck something near the ground. The Weed Eater kicked back to the left and cut off Pearce's right arm to the elbow. Pearce, through his mother, Charlotte Karns, sued Emerson to recover damages under strict liability. Under ethical principles, should Emerson's warning have been clearer and stronger? Is Emerson liable? [*Karns v. Emerson Electric Co.*, 817 F.2d 1452 (1987)]

15.11 Crashworthiness Doctrine At 11 P.M. on April 10, 1968, Verne Prior, driving on U.S. 101 under the influence of alcohol and drugs at a speed of 65 to 85 miles per hour, crashed his 1963 Chrysler into the left rear of a 1962 Chevrolet station wagon stopped on the shoulder of the freeway for a flat tire. Christine Smith was sitting in the passenger seat of the parked car when the accident occurred. In the crash, the Chevrolet station wagon was knocked into a gully, where its fuel tank ruptured. The vehicle caught fire and Christine Smith suffered severe burn injuries. The Chevrolet station wagon was manufactured by General Motors Corporation (General Motors). Evidence showed that the fuel tank was located in a vulnerable position in the back of the station wagon outside of the crossbars of the frame. Evidence further showed that if the fuel tank had been located underneath the body of the station wagon between the crossbars of the frame, it would have been well protected in the collision. Smith sued General Motors for strict liability. Was the Chevrolet station wagon a defective product? [*Smith v. General Motors Corporation*, 42 C.A.3d 1, 116 Cal.Rptr. 575 (Cal. App. 1974)]

15.12 Defect Virginia Burke purchased a bottle of "Le Domaine" champagne that was manufactured by Almaden Vineyards, Inc. (Almaden). At home, she removed the wine seal from the top of the bottle but did not remove the plastic cork. She set the bottle on the counter, intending to serve it in a few minutes. Shortly thereafter, the plastic cork spontaneously ejected from the bottle, ricocheted off the wall, and struck Burke in the left lens of her eyeglasses, shattering the lens, and

driving pieces of glass into her eye. The champagne bottle did not contain any warning of this danger. Evidence showed that Almaden had previously been notified of the spontaneous ejection of the cork from its champagne bottles. Burke sued Almaden to recover damages for strict liability. Is Almaden liable? [*Burke v. Almaden Vineyards, Inc.*, 86 Cal.App.3d 768, 150 Cal.Rptr. 419 (Cal. App. 1978)]

15.13 Assumption of Risk Lillian Horn was driving her Chevrolet station wagon, which was designed and manufactured by General Motors Corporation (GM), down Laurel Canyon Boulevard in Los Angeles, California. Horn swerved to avoid a collision when a car coming toward her crossed the center line and was coming at her. In doing so, her hand knocked the horn cap off the steering wheel, which exposed the area underneath the horn cap, including three sharp prongs that had held the horn cap to the steering wheel. A few seconds later, when her car hit an embankment, Horn's face was impaled on the three sharp exposed prongs, causing her severe facial injuries. Horn sued GM for strict liability. GM asserted the defense of assumption of the risk against Horn. Who wins? [*Horn v. General Motors Corporation*, 17 C.3d 359, 131 Cal.Rptr. 78 (Cal. 1976)]

15.14 Misuse On the morning of February 25, 1980, Elizabeth Horton (name changed to Ellsworth) wore a lady's flannelette nightgown inside out. As a result, two pockets on the sides of the nightgown were protruding from the sides of the nightgown. Ellsworth turned on the left front burner of the electric stove to "high" and placed a tea kettle of water on the burner. The kettle only partially covered the burner. As Ellsworth reached above the stove to obtain coffee filters from one of the cupboards, the nightgown came in contact with the exposed portion of the burner and ignited. Ellsworth was severely burned and suffered permanent injuries. Ellsworth sued Sherme Lingerie, the seller of the nightgown, and Cone Mills Corporation, the manufacturer of the textile from which the nightgown was made, for strict liability. Is there a misuse of the product that would relieve the defendants of liability? [*Ellsworth v. Sherme Lingerie and Cone Mills Corporation*, 495 A.2d 348 (Md. App. 1985)]

15.15 Misuse The Wilcox-Crittendon Company manufactured harnesses, saddles, bridles, leads, and other items commonly used for horses, cattle, and other ranch and farm animals. One such item was a stallion or cattle tie, a five-inch-long iron hook with a one-inch ring at one end. The tongue on the ring opened outward to allow the hook to be attached to a rope or other object. In 1964, a purchasing agent for United Airlines, who was familiar with this type of hook because of earlier experiences on a farm, purchased one of these hooks from Keystone Brothers, a harness and saddlery wares outlet located in San Francisco, California. Four years later, on March 28, 1968, Edward Dosier, an employee of United Airlines, was working to install a new grinding machine at a United Airlines maintenance plant. As part of the installation process, Dosier attached the hook to a 1,700-pound counterweight and raised the counterweight into the air. While the counterweight was suspended in the air, Dosier reached under the counterweight to retrieve a missing bolt. The hook broke and the counterweight fell and crushed Dosier's arm. Dosier sued Wilcox-Crittendon for strict liability. Who wins? [*Dosier v. Wilcox-Crittendon Company*, 45 Cal.App.3d. 74, 119 Cal.Rptr. 135 (Cal. App. 1975)]

15.16 Market Share Liability From 1942 to 1975, Lee Copeland worked as a boilermaker. During his work, he was exposed to various asbestos-containing products, particularly the insulation used to make the boilers. The asbestos insulation Copeland handled was manufactured by Celotex and 15 other manufacturers. Each type of insulation was made from a different formulation of asbestos and other chemicals. During the early 1970s Copeland developed respiratory problems. These problems forced him to quit his job in 1975. He was diagnosed as having both asbestosis and cancer. Copeland has brought a strict liability lawsuit against all 16 insulation manufacturers. Copeland claimed that liability should be extended to each through application of the market share theory of liability. Is that theory applicable to this situation? [*Celotex Corporation v. Copeland*, 471 So.2d 533 (Fla. 1985)]

ETHICS CASES

15.17 Ethical Perspective During October 1978, Brian Keith, an actor, attended a boat show in Long Beach, California. At the boat show Keith obtained sales literature on a sailboat called the "Island Trader 41" from a sales representative of James Buchanan, a seller of sailboats. One sales brochure described the vessel as "a picture of sure-footed seaworthiness." Another brochure called the sailboat "a carefully well-equipped and very seaworthy live-aboard vessel." In November 1978, Keith purchased an Island Trader 41 sailboat from Buchanan for a total purchase price of $75,610. After delivery of the sailboat, a dispute arose in regards to the seaworthiness of the vessel. Keith sued Buchanan for breach of warranty. Buchanan defended, arguing that no warranty had been made. Was it ethical for Buchanan to try to avoid being held accountable for statements of quality about its product that were made in the sales brochure given Keith? Should sales "puffing" be considered to create an express warranty? Why or why not? Who wins this case? [*Keith v. Buchanan*, 173 Cal.App.3d 13, 220 Cal.Rptr. 392 (Cal.App. 1985)]

15.18 Ethical Perspective The Delano Growers' Cooperative Winery (Delano), a California winery, produces wine in bulk. Supreme Wine Co. Inc. (Supreme), operated a wine bottling plant in Boston. Since 1968, Supreme purchased finished wine in bulk from Delano and other wine producers, which it then bottled and sold to retailers under the "Supreme" label. Supreme purchased all its sweet wine from Delano, which was delivered to Supreme's bottling plant in tank cars. Supreme then pumped the wine into redwood vats in its building.

In 1973, Supreme began receiving widespread returns of sweet wine from its customers. All of the returned wine was produced by Delano. The wine was producing sediment, was cloudy, and contained a cottony or hairy substance. Supreme complained to Delano, who promised to correct the situation. Delano made other shipments of sweet wine to Supreme, but customers continued to return defective wine to Supreme. Evidence showed that the wine contained *lactobacillus trichodes*, also called "Fresno mold." More than 8,000 cases of wine were spoiled by the Fresno mold. When Supreme refused to pay an invoice of $25,825 for shipment of wine, Delano sued to collect this amount. Supreme filed a counterclaim to recover damages. Was it ethical for the seller to disavow liability in this case? Who wins? [*Delano Growers' Cooperative Winery v. Supreme Wine Co. Inc.*, 473 N.E.2d 1066 (Mass. 1985)]

15.19 Ethical Perspective Celestino Luque lived with his cousins Harry and Laura Dunn in Millbrae, California. The Dunns purchased a rotary lawn mower from Rhoads Hardware. The lawn mower was manufactured by Air Capital Manufacturing Company and was distributed by Garehime Corporation. On December 4, 1965, neighbors asked Luque to mow their lawn. While Luque was cutting the lawn, he noticed a small carton in the path of the lawn mower. Luque left the lawn mower in a stationary position with its motor running and walked around the side of the lawn mower to remove the carton. As he did so, he suddenly slipped on the wet grass and fell backward. Luque's left hand entered the unguarded hole of the lawn mower and was caught in its revolving blade, which turns at 175 miles per hour and 100 revolutions per second. Luque's hand was severely mangled and lacerated. The word *Caution* was printed above the unguarded hole on the lawn mower. Luque sued Rhoads Hardware, Air Capital, and Garehime Corporation for strict liability. The defendants argued that strict liability does not apply to *patent* (obvious) defects. Was it ethical for the defendants to argue that they were not liable for patent defects? Would patent defects ever be corrected if the defendants' contention was accepted by the court? Who wins? [*Luque v. McLean, Trustee*, 8 Cal.3d 136, 104 Cal.Rptr. 443 (Cal. 1972)]

CRITICAL LEGAL THINKING WRITING ASSIGNMENT

Read Case A.15 in the Case Appendix [*Johnson v. Chicago Pneumatic Tool Company*]. Review and brief this case. In your brief, be sure to answer the following questions:

1. Who was the plaintiff? Who was the defendant?

2. What law did the plaintiff assert was violated by the defendant?

3. What was the defendant's defense? Explain.

4. Was this defense effective in this case?

NOTES

[1] The two exceptions to the general rule are (1) valid assignments and (2) intended beneficiaries. These are discussed in Chapter 10.

[2] 161 A.2d 69 (N.J. 1960).

[3] Restatement (Second) of Torts, § 395.

[4] 111 N.E. 1050, 217 N.Y. 382 (N.Y. App. 1916).

[5] 59 Cal.2d 57, 27 Cal.Rptr. 697, 377 P.2d 897 (1963).

[6] Some states have enacted statutes that provide that the doctrine of strict liability does not apply to transactions involving the sale of blood or blood products.

[7] See, for example, *Elmore v. American Motors Corporation*, 70 Cal.2d 578, 76 Cal.Rptr. 652 (1969).

[8] Restatement (Second) of Torts, § 402A(1)(b).

CHAPTER 16

CREATION AND TRANSFER

OF NEGOTIABLE INSTRUMENTS

> *The great object of the law is to encourage commerce.*
>
> Judge Chambre
> *Beale v. Thompson* (1803)

negotiable instrument
A special form of contract that satisfies the requirements established by Article 3 of the UCC. Also called *commercial paper*.

Negotiable instruments (or **commercial paper**) are important for the conduct of business and personal affairs. In this country, modern commerce could not continue without them. Examples of negotiable instruments include checks (such as the one that may have been used to pay for this book) and promissory notes (such as the one executed by a borrower of money to pay for tuition).

To qualify as a negotiable instrument, the document must meet certain requirements established by Article 3 of the Uniform Commercial Code (UCC). If these requirements are met, a transferee who qualifies as a *holder in due course (HDC)* takes the instrument free of many defenses that can be asserted against the original payee. In addition, the document is considered an ordinary contract that is subject to contract law.

The concept of *negotiation* is important to the law of negotiable instruments. The primary benefit of a negotiable instrument is that it can be used as a substitute for money. As such, it must be freely transferable to subsequent parties. Technically, a negotiable instrument is negotiated when it is originally issued, however, the term **negotiation** is usually used to describe the transfer of negotiable instruments to subsequent transferees.

The types, creation, and transfer of negotiable instruments are discussed in this chapter.

█ BUSINESS BRIEF
If a document qualifies as a negotiable instrument, the terms of Article 3 of the UCC become as much a part of the instrument as if they were written on the instrument itself.

REVISED ARTICLE 3 (NEGOTIABLE INSTRUMENTS) OF THE UCC

Uniform Negotiable Instruments Law (NIL)
The predecessor of the UCC developed by the National Conference of Commissioners of Uniform Laws; used from 1886 until 1952.

Article 3 of the UCC
A code promulgated in 1952 that established rules for the creation of, transfer of, enforcement of, and liability on negotiable instruments.

Revised Article 3
A comprehensive revising of the UCC law of negotiable instruments, which was released in 1990, that reflects modern commercial practices.

Although negotiable instruments have been used in commerce since medieval times, the English law courts did not immediately recognize their validity. To compensate for this failure, the merchants developed rules governing their use. These rules, which were enforced by local private merchant courts, became part of what was called the **Law Merchant**. Eventually, in 1882, England enacted the Bills of Exchange Act, which codified the rules of the Law Merchant.

In 1886, the National Conference of Commissioners of Uniform Laws promulgated the **Uniform Negotiable Instruments Law (NIL)** in the United States. By 1920, all of the states had enacted the NIL as law, but the rapid development of commercial paper soon made the law obsolete.

Article 3 (Commercial Paper) of the Uniform Commercial Code, which was promulgated in 1952, established rules for the creation of, transfer of, enforcement of, and liability on negotiable instruments. All the states have replaced the NIL with Article 3.

In 1990, the American Law Institute and the National Conference of Commissioners on Uniform State Laws repealed Article 3 and replaced it with **Revised Article 3**. The new article, which is called "Negotiable Instruments" instead of "Commercial Paper," is a comprehensive revision of Article 3 that reflects modern commercial practices. Individual states are currently replacing Article 3 with Revised Article 3.

FUNCTIONS OF NEGOTIABLE INSTRUMENTS

Negotiable instruments serve the functions described in the following paragraphs.

Substitute for Money Merchants and consumers often do not carry cash for fear of loss or theft. Further, it would be almost impossible to carry enough cash for large purchases (e.g., a car or a house). Thus, certain forms of negotiable instruments—for example, checks—serve as a *substitute for money*.

Credit Device Some forms of negotiable instruments extend credit from one party to another. For instance, a seller may sell goods to a customer on the customer's promise to pay for the goods at a future time, or a bank may lend money to purchase goods to a buyer who signs a note promising to repay the money. Both these examples represent *extensions of credit*. Without negotiable instruments, the "credit economy" of the United States and other modern industrial countries would not be possible.

Record-keeping Device Negotiable instruments often serve as a *record-keeping device*. For example, banks usually return canceled checks to checking-account customers each month. These act as a record-keeping device for the preparation of financial statements, tax returns, and the like.

TYPES OF NEGOTIABLE INSTRUMENTS

The term **instrument** means negotiable instrument [UCC 3-104(b)]. These terms are often used interchangeably.

Revised Article 3 recognizes four kinds of instruments: (1) drafts, (2) checks, (3) promissory notes, and (4) certificates of deposit. Each of these is discussed in the following sections.

Drafts

A **draft**, which is a three-party instrument, is an unconditional written order by one party (the **drawer**) that orders a second party (the **drawee**) to pay money to a third party (the **payee**) [UCC 3-104(e)]. The drawee must be obligated to pay the drawer money before the drawer can order the drawee to pay this money to a third party (the payee).

For the drawee to be liable on a draft, the drawee must accept the drawer's written order to pay it. Acceptance is usually shown by the written word *accepted* on the face of the draft along with the drawee's signature and the date. The drawee is called the **acceptor** of the draft because it changes his or her obligation from that of having to pay the drawer to that of having to pay the payee. After the drawee accepts the draft, it is returned to the drawer or the payee. The drawer or the payee, in turn, can freely transfer it as a negotiable instrument to another party.

CONSIDER THIS EXAMPLE: Mary Owens owes Hector Martinez $1,000. Mr. Martinez writes out a draft that orders Ms. Owens to pay this $1,000 to Cindy Choy. Ms. Owens agrees to this change of obligation and accepts the draft. Mr. Martinez is the drawer, Ms. Owens is the drawee, and Ms. Choy is the payee.

A draft can be either a time draft or a sight draft. A **time draft** is payable at a designated future date. Language such as "pay on January 1, 1999" or "pay 120 days after date" creates a time draft (see Exhibit 16.1). A **sight draft** is payable on sight. A sight draft is also called a **demand draft**. Language such as "on demand pay" or "at sight pay" creates a sight draft. A draft can be both a time and a sight draft. Such a draft would provide that it is payable at a stated time after sight. For example, this type of draft is created by language such as "payable 90 days after sight."

A **trade acceptance** is a sight draft that arises when credit is extended with the sale of goods. In this type of draft, the seller is both the drawer and the payee. The buyer to whom credit is extended is the drawee. Even though only two actual parties are involved, it is considered a three-party instrument because three legal positions are involved.

instrument Term that means *negotiable instrument*.

draft A three-party instrument that is an unconditional written order by one party that orders the second party to pay money to a third party.

drawer of a draft The party who writes the order for a draft.

drawee of a draft The party who must pay the money stated in the draft. Also called the *acceptor* of a draft.

payee of a draft The party who receives the money from a draft.

time draft A draft payable at a designated future date.

sight draft A draft payable on sight. Also called a *demand draft*.

trade acceptance A sight draft that arises when credit is extended (by a seller to a buyer) with the sale of goods. The seller is both the drawer and the payee, and the buyer is the drawee.

Exhibit 16.1
A Time Draft

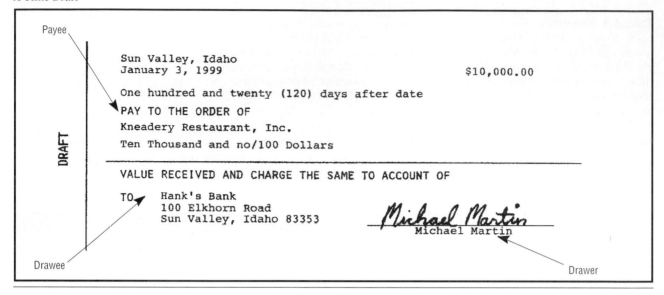

Checks

check   A distinct form of draft drawn on a financial institution and payable on demand.

A **check** is a distinct form of draft. It is unique in that it is drawn on a financial institution (the drawee) and is payable on demand [UCC 3-104(f)]. In other words, a check is an order to pay (see Exhibit 16.2). Most businesses and many people have checking accounts at financial institutions.

Exhibit 16.2
A Check

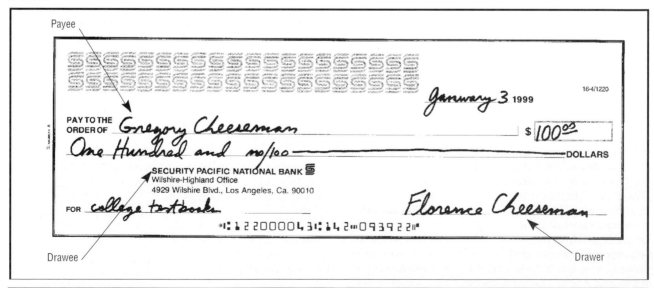

Like other drafts, a check is a three-party instrument. The customer who has the checking account and writes (draws) the check is the **drawer**. The financial institution upon whom the check is written is the **drawee**. And the party to whom the check is written is the **payee**.

In addition to traditional checks, there are several forms of special checks, including certified checks, cashier's checks, and traveler's checks. These special checks are discussed in Chapter 18.

Promissory Notes

A **promissory note** (or **note**) is an unconditional written promise by one party to pay money to another party [UCC 3-104(e)]. It is a two-party instrument (see Exhibit 16.3), not an order to pay. Promissory notes usually arise when one party borrows money from another. The note is evidence of (1) the extension of credit and (2) the borrower's promise to repay the debt.

drawer of a check The checking account holder and writer of the check.

drawee of a check The financial institution where the drawer has his or her account.

payee of a check The party to whom the check is written.

promissory note A two-party negotiable instrument that is an unconditional written promise by one party to pay money to another party.

Exhibit 16.3
A Promissory Note

Payee

PROMISSORY NOTE

$10,000.00   Missoula, Montana   January 3, **1999**

On or before 90 days after date, without grace, the undersigned promises to pay to the order of THE BIG SKY CORPORATION at its office in Missoula, Montana, the sum of Ten Thousand Dollars for value received, with interest from date at the rate of 10% per annum until paid. Principal and interest in lawful money of the United States.

_____
Paul Bunyan

Maker

The party who makes the promise to pay is the **maker** of the note (i.e., the borrower). The party to whom the promise to pay is made is the **payee** (i.e., the lender). A promissory note is a negotiable instrument that the payee can freely transfer to other parties.

The parties are free to design the terms of the note to fit their needs. For example, notes can be payable at a specific time (**time note**) or on demand (**demand note**). Notes can be made payable to a named payee or to "bearer." They can be payable in a single payment or in installments. The latter are called **installment notes**. Most notes require the borrower to pay interest on the principal.

Lenders sometimes require the maker of a note to post security for the repayment of the note. This security, which is called **collateral**, may be in the form of automobiles, houses, securities, or other property. If the maker fails to repay the note when it is due, the lender can foreclose and take the collateral as payment for the note. Notes are often named after the security that underlies the note. For example, notes that are secured by real estate are called **mortgage notes**, and notes that are secured by personal property are called **collateral notes**.

maker of a note The party who makes the promise to pay (borrower).

payee of a note The party to whom the promise to pay is made (lender).

time note A note payable at a specific time.

demand note A note payable on demand.

collateral Security against repayment of the note that lenders sometimes require; can be a car, a house, or other property.

BUSINESS APPLICATION

Promissory Notes as Negotiable Instruments

People and businesses borrow money from banks and other lenders to purchase automobiles, equipment, real estate, and other items. When people or businesses borrow money from lenders, they usually sign **promissory notes** promising to repay the borrowed money, plus interest, according to the terms of the note. The borrower is the **maker** of the note and the lender is the **payee**. The borrower is obligated to make payments (often monthly) until the principal amount borrowed, plus interest, is repaid.

A note that contains an unconditional written promise by one party to pay money to another party qualifies as a promissory note that is subject to the rules of **Revised Article 3** of the Uniform Commercial Code. This means that the promissory note can be negotiated to other parties who can enforce the note according to its terms against the borrower. In essence, the promissory note can be transferred like money, and its enforcement is subject to only a few defenses. (These defenses are discussed in chapter 18.)

---

certificate of deposit (CD)
A two-party negotiable instrument that is a special form of note created when a depositor deposits money at a financial institution in exchange for the institution's promise to pay back the amount of the deposit plus an agreed-upon rate of interest upon the expiration of a set time period agreed upon by the parties.

maker of a CD The bank (borrower).

payee of a CD The depositor (lender).

Certificates of Deposit

A **certificate of deposit (CD)** is a special form of note that is created when a depositor deposits money at a financial institution in exchange for the institution's promise to pay back the amount of the deposit plus an agreed-upon rate of interest upon the expiration of a set time period agreed upon by the parties [UCC 3-104(j)].

The financial institution is the borrower (the **maker**) and the depositor is the lender (the **payee**). A CD is a two-party instrument (see Exhibit 16.4). Note that a CD is a promise to pay, not an order to pay.

Unlike a regular passbook savings account, a CD is a negotiable instrument. CDs under $100,000 are commonly referred to as **small CDs**. CDs of $100,000 or more are usually called **jumbo CDs**.

Exhibit 16.4
A Certificate of Deposit

```
                                                                      Payee
 ——————————————— NEGOTIABLE CERTIFICATE OF DEPOSIT ———————————
 NO. 1000                    HANK'S BANK               January 3, 1999
                        MANCHESTER, NEW HAMPSHIRE           DATE

 THIS CERTIFIES THAT THERE HAS BEEN DEPOSITED IN THE UNDERSIGNED
 THE SUM OF $ 10,000.00

 Ten Thousand and no/100 —————————————————————————— DOLLARS

 WHICH IS PAYABLE TO THE ORDER OF  William O'Mara
 ON THE  3rd   DAY OF   January ,  2000 WITH INTEREST TO MATURITY
 AT THE RATE OF  10  % PER ANNUM UPON PRESENTATION AND SURRENDER OF
 THIS CERTIFICATE PROPERLY INDORSED.

 HANK'S BANK                          BY  Henry Hildabrand 2
                                          HENRY HILDABRAND II
                                          PRESIDENT
 Maker
```

CREATING A NEGOTIABLE INSTRUMENT

According to UCC 3-104(a), a **negotiable instrument** must

- Be in writing
- Be signed by the maker or drawer
- Be an unconditional promise or order to pay
- State a fixed amount of money
- Not require any undertaking in addition to the payment of money
- Be payable on demand or at a definite time
- Be payable to order or to bearer

These requirements must appear on the *face* of the instrument. If they do not, the instrument does not qualify as negotiable. Each of these requirements is discussed in the paragraphs that follow. A promise or order that conspicuously states that it is not negotiable or is not subject to Article 3 is not a negotiable instrument [UCC 3-104(d)].

A Writing

A negotiable instrument must be (1) in writing and (2) *permanent* and *portable*. Often, the requisite writing is on a preprinted form, but typewritten, handwritten, or other tangible agreements are also acceptable [UCC 1-201(46)]. In addition, the instrument can be a combination of different kinds of writing. For example, a check is often a preprinted form on which the drawer handwrites the amount of the check, the name of the payee, and the date of the check. Oral promises do not qualify as negotiable instruments because they are not clearly transferable in a manner that will prevent fraud. Tape recordings and videotapes are not negotiable instruments because they are not considered writings.

Most writings on paper meet the **permanency requirement**, although a writing on tissue paper does not because of its impermanence. The courts have held that writings on other objects (e.g., baseballs, shirts) meet this requirement. A promise or order to pay that is written in snow or sand is not permanent—and, therefore, is not a negotiable instrument. However, a photograph of such a writing that was signed by the maker or drawer would qualify as a negotiable instrument. The picture meets the requirement of permanence.

The **portability requirement** is intended to ensure free transfer of the instrument. For example, a promise to pay chiseled in a California redwood tree would not qualify as a negotiable instrument because the tree is not freely transferable in commerce. However, writing the same promise or order to pay on a small block of wood could qualify as a negotiable instrument.

The best practice is to place the written promise or order to pay on traditional paper. This ensures that the permanency and portability requirements are met so that transferees will readily accept the instrument.

Signed by the Maker or the Drawer

A negotiable instrument must be *signed* by the maker if it is a note or certificate of deposit and by the drawer if it is a check or draft. The maker or drawer is not liable on the instrument unless his or her signature appears on it. The signature can be placed on the instrument by the maker or drawer or by an authorized agent [UCC 3-401(a)]. Although the signature of the maker, drawer, or agent can be located anywhere on the face of the negotiable instrument, it is usually placed in the lower righthand corner.

The UCC broadly defines **signature** as any symbol executed or adopted by a party with a present intent to authenticate a writing [UCC 1-201(39)]. A signature is made by the use of any name, including a trade or assumed name, or by any word or mark used in lieu of a written signature [UCC 3-401(b)]. Thus, the requisite signature can be the maker's or drawer's formal name (Henry Richard Cheeseman), informal name (Hank Cheeseman), initials (HRC), or nickname (The Big Cheese). Any other symbol

negotiable instrument
Commercial paper that must meet these requirements: (1) be in writing, (2) be signed by the maker or drawer, (3) be an unconditional promise or order to pay, (4) state a fixed amount of money, (5) not require any undertaking in addition to the payment of money, (6) be payable on demand or at a definite time, and (7) be payable to order or to bearer.

CAUTION
A negotiable instrument must be in writing; oral promises or orders do not qualify as negotiable instruments. (They are enforceable, however, under ordinary contract law.)

permanency requirement
A requirement of negotiable instruments that says they must be in a permanent state, such as written on ordinary paper.

portability requirement
A requirement of negotiable instruments that says they must be able to be easily transported between areas.

signature requirement
A negotiable instrument must be signed by the drawer or maker. Any symbol executed or adopted by a party with a present intent to authenticate a writing qualifies as his or her signature.

BUSINESS BRIEF
Companies that are too large to have every check (e.g., payroll checks) individually signed by a corporate officer often use some form of mechanical or computer device to sign payroll checks.

or device (e.g., an *X* or a thumbprint) adopted by the signer as his or her signature also qualifies. The signer's intention to use the symbol as his or her signature is controlling. Typed, printed, lithographed, rubber-stamped, or other mechanical means of signing instruments are recognized as valid by the UCC.

Signature by an Authorized Representative As mentioned previously, a maker or drawer can appoint an *agent* to sign a negotiable instrument on his or her behalf. For example, corporations and other organizations use agents, usually corporate officers or employees, to sign the corporation's negotiable instruments. Individual persons can also appoint agents to sign their negotiable instruments.

A maker or drawer is liable on a negotiable instrument signed by an authorized agent. The agent is not personally liable on the negotiable instrument if his or her signature properly unambiguously discloses (1) his or her agency status and (2) the identity of the maker or drawer [UCC 3-402(b)] (see Exhibit 16.5). In the case of an organization, the agent's signature is proper if the organization's name is preceded or followed by the name and office of the authorized agent.

Exhibit 16.5
Negotiable Instrument
Properly Signed by an Agent

ENDORSE HERE

X *NorthShore, Inc. by Christine Mey President*

DO NOT WRITE, STAMP OR SIGN BELOW THIS LINE
RESERVED FOR FINANCIAL INSTITUTION USE

Unconditional Promise or Order to Pay

unconditional promise or order to pay requirement
A negotiable instrument must contain either an *unconditional promise to pay* (note or CD) or an *unconditional order to pay* (draft or check).

To be a negotiable instrument under the requirements of UCC 3-104(a), the writing must contain either an *unconditional* **promise to pay** (note or certificate of deposit) or an *unconditional* **order to pay** (draft or check). The term *unconditional*, which is discussed shortly, is key.

promise to pay A maker's (borrower's) unconditional and affirmative undertaking to repay a debt to a payee (lender).

Promise or Order To be negotiable, a **promise to pay** must be an unconditional and affirmative undertaking. The mere acknowledgment of a debt is not sufficient to constitute a negotiable instrument. In other words, an implied promise to pay is not negotiable, but an expressly stated promise to pay is negotiable. For example, the statement "I owe you $100" is merely an I.O.U. It acknowledges a debt, but it does not contain an express promise to repay the money. However, if the I.O.U. uses language such as "I promise to pay" or "the undersigned agrees to pay," a negotiable instrument would be created because the note would contain an affirmative obligation to pay.

order to pay A drawer's unconditional order for a drawee to pay a payee.

CDs are an exception to this rule. CDs do not require an express promise to pay because the bank's acknowledgment of the payee's bank deposit and other terms of the CD clearly indicate the bank's promise to repay the certificate holder. Nevertheless, most CDs contain an express promise to pay.

CAUTION
Notes and CDs contain promises *to pay; drafts and checks contain* orders *to pay.*

To be negotiable, a draft or check must contain the drawer's unconditional **order for the drawee to pay** a payee. An order is a direction to pay and must be more than an authorization or request to pay. The language of the order must be precise and contain the word *pay*. For example, the printed word *pay* on a check is a proper order that is sufficient to make the check negotiable. The order can be in a courteous form, such as "please pay" or "kindly pay." A mere request or acknowledgment, such as "I wish you would pay," is not sufficient because it lacks a direction to pay.

An order to pay a draft or check must identify the drawee who is directed to make the payment. The name of the drawee financial institution that is preprinted on a check is sufficient. The order can be directed to one or more parties jointly, such as "to A *and* B," or in the alternative, such as "to A *or* B." The order cannot, however, be in succession, such as "to A, and if she does not pay, then to B."

Unconditional Promise or Order To be negotiable, the promise or order must be **unconditional** [UCC 3-104(a)]. A promise or order that is **conditional** on another promise or event is not negotiable because the risk of the other promise or event not occurring would fall on the person who held the instrument. A conditional promise is subject to normal contract law.

CONSIDER THIS EXAMPLE: Suppose American Airlines buys a $10 million airplane from Boeing Aircraft. American signs a promissory note that promises to pay Boeing if it is "satisfied" with the airplane. This is a conditional promise. The condition—that American is satisfied with the airplane—destroys the negotiability of the note.

A promise or order is conditional and, therefore, not negotiable if it states (1) an express condition to payment, (2) that the promise or order is subject to or governed by another writing, or (3) the rights or obligations with respect to the promise or order are stated in another writing. The mere reference to another writing does not make the promise or order conditional [UCC 3-106(a)].

CONSIDER THIS EXAMPLE: Dow Chemical purchases equipment from Illinois Tool Works and signs a sales contract. Dow Chemical borrows the purchase price from Citibank and executes a promissory note evidencing this debt and promising to repay the borrowed money plus interest. The note contains the following reference: "sales contract—purchase of equipment." This reference does not affect the negotiability of the note. However, the note would not be negotiable if the reference stated, "This note hereby incorporates by this reference the terms of the sales contract between Dow Chemical and Illinois Tool Works of this date."

A promise or order remains unconditional even though it refers to another writing for rights to collateral, prepayment, or acceleration (e.g., "see collateral agreement dated January 15, 1999"). A promise or order may also stipulate that payment is limited to a particular fund or source (e.g., "payable out of the proceeds of the Tower Construction Contract") [UCC 3-106(b)].

Fixed Amount of Money

To be negotiable, an instrument must contain a promise or order to pay a **fixed amount of money** [UCC 3-104(a)]. This phrase can be analyzed as two promises or orders: (1) to pay a **fixed amount** and (2) to pay in **money**.

Fixed Amount The **fixed amount** requirement ensures that the value of the instrument can be determined with certainty. The principal amount of the instrument must appear on the *face* of the instrument.

An instrument does not have to be payable with interest, but if it is, the amount of interest being charged may be expressed as either a *fixed* or a *variable* rate. The amount or rate of interest may be stated or described in the instrument or may require reference to information not contained in the instrument. If an instrument provides for interest, but the amount of interest cannot be determined from the description, interest is payable at the judgment rate (legal rate) in effect at the place of payment of the instrument [UCC 3-112].

Thus, a note that contains a promise to pay $10,000 in one year at a stated rate of 10 percent interest is a negotiable instrument because the value of the note can be

---

unconditional Promises to pay and orders to pay must be unconditional in order for them to be negotiable.

CAUTION
A negotiable instrument may refer to another writing for rights as to collateral, prepayment, or acceleration.

"One cannot help regretting that where money is concerned it is so much the rule to overlook moral obligations."
Malins, V.C.
Ellis v. Houston
(1878)

fixed amount of money
A negotiable instrument must contain a promise or order to pay a fixed amount of money.

fixed amount
A requirement of a negotiable instrument that ensures that the value of the instrument can be determined with certainty.

determined at any time. A note that contains a promise to pay in goods or services is not a negotiable instrument because the value of the note would be difficult to determine at any given time.

Payable in Money UCC 3-104(a) provides that the fixed amount must be payable in "money." The UCC defines **money** as a "medium of exchange authorized or adopted by a domestic or foreign government as part of its currency" [UCC 1-201(24)]. For example, an instrument that is "payable in $10,000 U.S. currency" is a negotiable instrument.

Instruments that are fully or partially payable in a medium of exchange other than money are not negotiable. Thus, an instrument that is "payable in $10,000 U.S. gold" is not negotiable. Although the stated amount is a **fixed amount**, it is not payable in a medium of exchange of the U.S. government. Likewise, instruments that are payable in diamonds, commodities, goods, services, stocks, bonds, and such do not qualify as negotiable instruments.

money A "medium of exchange authorized or adopted by a domestic or foreign government" [UCC 1-201(24)].

CONTEMPORARY BUSINESS ENVIRONMENT

Are Variable Interest Rate Notes Negotiable Instruments?

Prior to the mid-1970s, most loans that were made in this country were fixed-rate loans; that is, they bore a stated interest rate (e.g., 8 percent) that did not change during the life of the loan. This type of loan was fine for the lender as long as market interest rates did not change considerably. However, since the mid-1970s, interest rates have become quite volatile.

To compensate for this volatility, many lending institutions began offering *variable interest rate loans*. These loans tied the interest rate to some set measure, such as a major bank's prime rate (e.g., Citibank's prime) or other well-known rate (e.g., Freddie Mac rate). A huge "secondary market" has developed in which these loans are bought and sold.

This raised one major question: Are variable interest rate notes negotiable instruments? If they are, they are governed by Article 3 of the UCC, which provides certain protection to the holder against third-party claims and defenses. If they are not, they are ordinary contracts that are not subject to the protection of Article 3.

The drafters of Revised Article 3 solved this dilemma. Prior to the revision of Article 3 in 1990, UCC 3-104(1)(b) stipulated that to be a qualified negotiable instrument, a promise or order to pay must state a "sum certain in money." The key legal issue was whether variable interest rate notes were promises to pay a "sum certain in money." The courts were divided on this issue.

The drafters of Revised Article 3 settled the matter by expressly providing that variable interest rate notes are negotiable instruments. UCC 3-112(b) provides: "Interest may be stated in an instrument as a fixed or variable amount of money or it may be expressed as a fixed or variable rate or rates." UCC 3-112(b) also provides that the amount or rate of interest may be determined by reference to information not contained in the instrument.

This change in Article 3, which recognizes variable interest rate notes as negotiable instruments, reflects modern commercial and banking practices.

Not Require any Undertaking in Addition to the Payment of Money

To qualify as a negotiable instrument, a promise or order to pay cannot state any other undertaking by the person promising or ordering payment to do any act in addition to the payment of money [UCC 3-104(a)(3)]. For example, if a note required the maker to pay a stated amount of money *and* perform some type of service, it would not be negotiable.

A promise or order may include authorization or power to protect collateral, dispose of collateral, waive any law intended to protect the obligee, and the like.

Payable on Demand or at a Definite Time

For an instrument to be negotiable, it is necessary to know when the maker, drawee, or acceptor is required to pay it. UCC 3-104(a)(2) requires the instrument to be payable either **on demand** or at a **definite time**, as noted on the face of the instrument.

Payable on Demand Instruments that are payable on demand are called **demand instruments**. Demand instruments are created by (1) language such as "payable on demand," "payable at sight," or "payable on presentment" or (2) silence regarding when payment is due [UCC 3-108(a)].

By definition, checks are payable on demand [UCC 3-104(f)]. Other instruments, such as notes, certificates of deposit, and drafts, can be, but are not always, payable on demand.

Payable at a Definite Time Instruments that are payable at a definite time are called **time instruments**. UCC 3-108(b) and (c) states that an instrument is payable at a definite time if it is payable:

1. At a fixed date (e.g., "payable on January 1, 1999").
2. On or before a stated date (e.g., "payable on or before January 1, 1999"). The maker or drawee has the option of paying the note before—but not after—the stated maturity date.
3. At a fixed period after sight (e.g., "payable 60 days after sight"). Drafts often contain this type of language. The holder must formally present this type of instrument for acceptance so that the date of sight can be established.
4. At a time readily ascertainable when the promise or order is issued (e.g., "payable 60 days after January 1, 1999").

Instruments that are payable upon an uncertain act or event are not negotiable. For example, suppose Sarah Smith's father executes a promissory note stating, "I promise to pay to the order of my daughter, Sarah, $100,000 on the date she marries Bobby Boggs." This note is nonnegotiable because the act and date of marriage are uncertain.

Prepayment, Acceleration, and Extension Clauses The inclusion of prepayment, acceleration, or extension clauses in an instrument does not affect its negotiability. Such clauses are commonly found in promissory notes.

A **prepayment clause** permits the maker to pay the amount due prior to the due date of the instrument.

An **acceleration clause** allows the payee or holder to accelerate payment of the principal amount of an instrument, plus accrued interest, upon the happening of an event (e.g., default).

An **extension clause** is the opposite of an acceleration clause. It allows the date of maturity of an instrument to be extended to some time in the future.

---

payable on demand or at a definite time requirement A negotiable instrument must be payable either *on demand* or *at a definite time*.

demand instrument An instrument payable on demand.

time instrument An instrument payable (1) at a fixed date, (2) on or before a stated date, (3) at a fixed period after sight, or (4) at a time readily ascertainable when the promise or order is issued.

"The great source of the flourishing state of this kingdom is its trade, and commerce, and paper currency, guarded by proper regulation and restrictions, is the life of commerce."

Ashhurst, J.
Jordaine v. Lashbrooke (1798)

✔ **BUSINESS CHECKLIST**

Negotiable Instruments Payable to Order or to Bearer

Because negotiable instruments are primarily intended to act as a substitute for money, they must be freely transferable to other persons or entities. The UCC requires that negotiable instruments be either **payable to order** or **payable to bearer** [UCC 3-104(a)(1)]. Promises or orders to pay that do not meet this requirement are not negotiable. They may, however, be assignable under contract law.

continued

Order Instruments

An instrument is an **order instrument** if it is payable (1) to the order of an identified person or (2) to an identified person or orders [(UCC 3-109(b)]. For example, an instrument that states "payable to the order of IBM" or "payable to IBM or order" is negotiable. It would not be negotiable if it stated either "payable to IBM" or "pay to IBM" because it is not payable to *order*.

An instrument can be payable to the order of the maker, the drawer, the drawee, the payee, two or more payees together, or, alternatively, to an office, an officer by his or her title, a corporation, a partnership, an unincorporated association, a trust, an estate, or another legal entity. A person to whom an instrument is payable may be identified in any way, including by name, identifying number, office, or account number. An instrument is payable to the person intended by the signer of the instrument even if that person is identified in the instrument by a name or other identification that is not that of the intended person [UCC 3-110].

For example, an instrument made "payable to the order of Lovey" is negotiable. The identification of "Lovey" may be determined by evidence. On the other hand, an instrument made "payable to the order of my loved ones" is not negotiable because the payees are not ascertainable with reasonable certainty.

Bearer Instruments

A **bearer instrument** is payable to anyone in physical possession of the instrument who presents it for payment when it is due. The person in possession of the instrument is called the **bearer**. Bearer paper results when the drawer or maker does not make the instrument payable to a specific payee.

An instrument is payable to bearer when any of the following language is used: "payable to the order of bearer," "payable to bearer," "payable to Xerox or bearer," "payable to cash," or "payable to the order of cash." In addition, any other indication that does not purport to designate a specific payee creates bearer paper [UCC 3-109(a)]. For example, an instrument "payable to my dog Fido" creates a bearer instrument.

NONNEGOTIABLE CONTRACTS

nonnegotiable contract
Fails to meet the requirements of a negotiable instrument and, therefore, is not subject to the provisions of UCC Article 3.

If a promise or order to pay does not meet one of the previously discussed requirements of negotiability, it is a **nonnegotiable contract**. As such, it is not subject to the provisions of UCC Article 3, however, this does not render the contract either nontransferable or nonenforceable. A nonnegotiable contract can be enforced under normal contract law. If the maker or drawer of a nonnegotiable contract fails to pay it, the holder of the contract can sue the nonperforming party for breach of contract.

INTERNATIONAL PERSPECTIVE

Negotiable Instruments Payable in Foreign Currency

The UCC expressly provides that an instrument may state that it is payable in foreign money [UCC 3-107]. For example, an instrument "payable in 10,000 yen in Japanese currency" is a negotiable instrument that is governed by Article 3 of the UCC.

Unless the instrument states otherwise, an instrument that is payable in foreign currency can be satisfied by the payment of the equivalent in U.S. dollars as determined on the due date. The conversion rate is the current bank-offered spot rate at the place of

payment on the due date. The instrument can expressly provide that it is payable only in the stated foreign currency. In this case, the instrument cannot be paid in U.S. dollars.

TRANSFER BY ASSIGNMENT OR NEGOTIATION

After they have been issued, negotiable instruments can be transferred to subsequent parties by *assignment* or by *negotiation*. The rights acquired by subsequent transferees differ according to the method of transfer. The different methods of transfer are discussed in the following paragraphs.

Transfer by Assignment

An **assignment** is the transfer of rights under a contract. It transfers the rights of the transferor (**assignor**) to the transferee (**assignee**). Because normal contract principles apply, the assignee acquires only the rights that the assignor possessed. Thus, any defenses to the enforcement of the contract that could have been raised against the assignor can also be raised against the assignee.

An assignment occurs when a nonnegotiable contract is transferred. In the case of a negotiable instrument, assignment occurs when the instrument is transferred but the transfer fails to qualify as a negotiation under Article 3. In this case, the transferee is an *assignee* rather than a *holder*.

assignment The transfer of rights under a contract.

assignor The transferor in an assignment situation.

assignee The transferee in an assignment situation.

Transfer by Negotiation

Negotiation is the transfer of a negotiable instrument by a person other than the issuer. The person to whom the instrument is transferred becomes the holder [UCC 3-201(a)]. The **holder** receives at least the rights of the transferor and may acquire even greater rights than the transferor if he or she qualifies as a holder in due course (HDC) [UCC 3-302]. An HDC has greater rights because he or she is not subject to some of the defenses that could otherwise have been raised against the transferor.

The proper method of negotiation depends on whether the instrument is order paper or bearer paper, as discussed next.

negotiation Transfer of a negotiable instrument by a person other than the issuer to a person who thereby becomes a *holder*.

holder What the transferee becomes if a negotiable instrument has been transferred by *negotiation*.

Negotiating Order Paper An instrument that is payable to a specific payee or indorsed to a specific indorsee is **order paper**. Order paper is negotiated by delivery with the necessary indorsement [UCC 3-201(b)]. Thus, for order paper to be negotiated there must be delivery and indorsement.

CONSIDER THIS EXAMPLE: Sam Bennett receives a weekly payroll check from his employer, Ace Plumbing Corporation. Mr. Bennett takes the check to a local store, signs the back of the check (indorsement), gives the check to the cashier (delivery), and receives cash for the check. Mr. Bennett has *negotiated* the check to the store. There has been delivery and indorsement.

order paper Order paper is negotiated by (1) *delivery* and (2) *indorsement*.

CAUTION
Bearer paper can be negotiated by delivery alone; indorsement is not required.

Negotiating Bearer Paper An instrument that is not payable to a specific payee or indorsee is **bearer paper**. Bearer paper is negotiated by *delivery;* indorsement is not necessary [UCC 3-201(b)]. Substantial risk is associated with the loss or theft of bearer paper.

CONSIDER THIS EXAMPLE: Suppose Mary draws a check "pay to cash" and gives it to Peter. There has been a negotiation because Mary delivered a bearer instrument (the check) to Peter. Subsequently, Carmen steals the check from Peter. There has not been a negotiation because the check was not voluntarily delivered. The fact that Carmen physically possesses the check is irrelevant. However, the negotiation is complete if Carmen delivers the check to an innocent third party. That party is a holder and may qualify as an HDC with all the rights in the check [UCC 3-302]. If the holder is an HDC, Peter's only recourse is to recover against Carmen.

bearer paper Bearer paper is negotiated by *delivery;* indorsement is not necessary.

CAUTION
There is substantial risk associated with the loss or theft of bearer paper.

Converting Order and Bearer Paper Instruments can be converted from order paper to bearer paper, and vice versa, many times until the instrument is paid [UCC 3-109(c)]. The deciding factor is the type of indorsement placed on the instrument at the time of each subsequent transfer.

CAUTION
Negotiable instruments can be converted from order paper to bearer paper, and vice versa, depending on the form of the indorsement.

indorsement The signature (and other directions) written by or on behalf of the holder somewhere on the instrument.

CONSIDER THIS EXAMPLE: Susan draws a check "pay to the order of Dan Jones." The check is order paper because it is made payable to a specific payee. If Dan indorses the back of the check without naming a specific indorsee, the check is converted to bearer paper. If he delivers the check to Constance and she indorses the back of the check "pay to Ferdinand Friendly," the bearer paper is converted to order paper.

INDORSEMENTS

indorser The person who indorses a negotiable instrument.

indorsee The person to whom a negotiable instrument is indorsed.

An **indorsement** is the signature of a signer (other than as a maker, a drawer, or an accepter) that is placed on an instrument to negotiate it to another person. The signature may (1) appear alone, (2) name an individual to whom the instrument is to be paid, or (3) be accompanied by other words [UCC 3-204(2)]. The person who indorses an instrument is called the **indorser**. If the indorsement names a payee, this person is called the **indorsee**.

Exhibit 16.6
Proper Placement of an
Indorsement

Indorsement should be placed at the top of the back of the check

Mary Neu

CONSIDER THIS EXAMPLE: Nikki Choy receives a $500 check for her birthday. She can transfer the check to anyone merely by signing her name on the back of the check. Suppose she indorses it "pay to Rob Dewey." Ms. Choy is the indorser, Rob Dewey is the indorsee.

Indorsements are usually placed on the reverse side of the instrument, such as on the back of a check (see Exhibit 16.6). If there is no room on the instrument, the indorsement may be written on a separate piece of paper called an **allonge**. The allonge must be affixed (e.g., stapled or taped) to the instrument [UCC 3-204(a)].

Indorsements are required to negotiate order paper. **Indorsements** are not required to negotiate bearer paper [UCC 3-201(b)]. However, for identification purposes and to impose liability on the transferor, the transferee often requires the transferor to indorse the bearer paper at negotiation.

allonge A separate piece of paper attached to the instrument on which the indorsement is written.

Types of Indorsements

Every indorsement is

1. Blank or special
2. Unqualified or qualified
3. Nonrestrictive or restrictive.

Three different types of indorsements are discussed in the following paragraphs.

CAUTION
An indorsement is necessary to negotiate order paper, but it is not required to negotiate bearer paper.

Blank Indorsements

A **blank indorsement** does not specify a particular indorsee. It may consist of a mere signature [UCC 3-205(b)]. For example, suppose Harold Green draws a check "pay to the order of Victoria Rudd" and delivers the check to Victoria. Victoria indorses the check in blank by writing her signature on the back of the check (see Exhibit 16.7).

blank indorsement An indorsement that does not specify a particular indorsee. It creates *bearer paper.*

Exhibit 16.7
A Blank Indorsement

Order paper that is indorsed in blank becomes bearer paper. As mentioned previously, bearer paper can be negotiated by delivery; indorsement is not required. So, if Victoria Rudd loses the check she indorsed in blank and Mary Smith finds it, Mary Smith can deliver it to another person without indorsing it. Thus, the lost check can be presented for payment or negotiated to another holder.

Special Indorsements

special indorsement An indorsement that contains the signature of the indorser and specifies the person (indorsee) to whom the indorser intends the instrument to be payable. Creates *order paper.*

A **special indorsement** contains the signature of the indorser and specifies the person (indorsee) to whom the indorser intends the instrument to be payable [UCC 3-205(a)]. Words of negotiation (e.g., pay to the order of . . .) are not required for a special indorsement. Words such as "pay Emily Ingman" are sufficient to form a special indorsement. For example, a special indorsement would be created if Betsy McKenny indorsed her check and then wrote "pay to Dan Jones" above her signature (see Exhibit 16.8). The check is negotiated when Betsy gives it to Dan. A special indorsement creates *order paper.* As mentioned earlier, order paper is negotiated by indorsement and delivery.

Exhibit 16.8
A Special Indorsement

Pay to Chelsea Eastin
Garner Witherspoon

CAUTION

Order paper can be negotiated only by indorsement and delivery; delivery alone is not sufficient to negotiate order paper.

To prevent the risk of loss from theft, a special indorsement (which creates order paper) is preferred over a blank indorsement (which creates bearer paper). A holder can convert a blank indorsement into a special indorsement by writing any contract consistent with the character of the indorsement over the signature of the indorser in blank [UCC 3-205(c)]. Words such as "pay to John Jones" written above the indorser's signature are enough to convert bearer paper to order paper.

In the following case, the court had to decide whether a negotiable instrument was order paper or bearer paper.

CASE 16.1

J. Gordon Neely Enterprises, Inc.
v. American National Bank of Huntsville
403 So.2d 887 (1981) Supreme Court of Alabama

Facts Mr. and Mrs. Neely owned and operated J. Gordon Neely Enterprises, Inc., dba Midas Muffler (Neely). The corporate bank account was maintained at First Alabama Bank of Huntsville, N.A. (First Alabama). In 1976, Neely employed B. Louise Bradshaw as a Kelly Girl temporary employee. Mrs. Neely became friendly with Bradshaw and hired her as a part-time bookkeeper for the company. Bradshaw talked the Neelys into opening another corporate bank account at American National Bank of Huntsville (American National), where Bradshaw had a personal bank account. Mr. and Mrs. Neely signed the bank signature card and corporate resolutions that stated that American National was authorized to pay out funds, on either bearer or order paper, to any of the signatories. The Neelys entrusted Bradshaw to return these documents to the bank. Before doing so, without knowledge of the Neelys, Bradshaw added her name to these documents and signed the signature card.

In transferring funds between the two bank accounts, on several occasions Bradshaw drew checks on First American made payable to American National. Mrs. Neely signed the checks and instructed Bradshaw to deposit the funds into Neely's corporate account at American National. Instead, Bradshaw cashed the checks at American National and either kept the cash or deposited the funds into her personal bank account at American National. Bradshaw picked up the monthly bank accounts and altered them with liquid erasure to conceal her fraudulent scheme. The Neelys hired a new accountant in the latter part of 1977 who discovered that Bradshaw's defalcation totaled $17,005. The Neelys sued American National to recover the funds. The trial court held that American National was not liable because the negotiable instruments it had paid on were bearer instruments. The Neelys appealed.

Issue Were the checks cashed by Bradshaw bearer paper that American National Bank of Hunstville properly paid to B. Louise Bradshaw upon negotiation by delivery?

Decision Yes. The state supreme court held that American National paid the proceeds out on properly negotiated bearer paper. Affirmed.

Reason In the banking profession, a check that is drawn payable to the order of a bank is recognized as equivalent to a check made payable to the order of cash. Legally, therefore, the instrument becomes bearer paper and is properly negotiated by delivery alone. Because these checks were bearer paper and were validly negotiated when Bradshaw delivered them for presentment, American National is not liable for paying to her the proceeds even though she was not named as payee. The Neelys' only recourse is against Bradshaw.

CASE QUESTIONS

Critical Legal Thinking Should the law recognize bearer paper? Or should all negotiable instruments be required to be made payable to a specific payee? Explain.

Ethics Was it ethical for the Neelys to sue American National in this case? Why or why not?

Business Implication How could the Neelys have protected themselves from this fraudulent scheme? Explain.

Unqualified and Qualified Indorsements

Generally, an indorsement is a promise by the indorser to pay the holder or any subsequent indorser the amount of the instrument if the maker, drawer, or acceptor defaults on it. This is called an **unqualified indorsement**. Unless otherwise agreed, the order and liability of the indorsers is presumed to be the order in which they indorse the instrument [UCC 3-415(a)].

CONSIDER THIS EXAMPLE: Cindy draws a check payable to the order of John. John (indorser) indorses the check and negotiates it to Steve (indorsee). When Steve presents the check for payment, there are insufficient funds in Cindy's account to pay the check. John, as an **unqualified indorser**, is liable on the check. John can recover from Cindy.

The UCC permits **qualified indorsements**, that is, indorsements that disclaim or limit liability on the instrument. A **qualified indorser** does not guarantee payment of the instrument if the maker, drawer, or acceptor defaults on it. A qualified indorsement is created by placing a notation such as "without recourse" or other similar language that disclaims liability as part of the indorsement [UCC 3-415(b)] (see Exhibit 16.9). A qualified indorsement protects only the indorser who wrote it on the instrument. Subsequent indorsers must also place a qualified indorsement on the instrument to be protected from liability. An instrument containing a qualified indorsement can be further negotiated.

unqualified indorsement An indorsement whereby the indorser promises to pay the holder or any subsequent indorser the amount of the instrument if the maker, drawer, or acceptor defaults on it.

unqualified indorser An indorser who signs an *unqualified indorsement* to an instrument.

qualified indorsement An indorsement that includes the notation "without recourse" or similar language that disclaims liability of the indorser.

qualified indorser An indorser who signs a *qualified indorsement* to an instrument.

Exhibit 16.9
A Qualified Indorsement

Pay to Ashley Eastin
without recourse
James Witherspoon

Qualified indorsements are often used by persons signing instruments in a representative capacity. For example, suppose an insurance company that is paying a claim makes out a check payable to the order of the attorney representing the payee. The attorney can indorse the check to his client (the payee) with the notation "without recourse." The notation ensures that the attorney is not liable as an indorser if the insurance company fails to pay the check.

A qualified indorsement can be either a special qualified indorsement or a blank qualified indorsement. A **special qualified indorsement** creates order paper that can be negotiated by indorsement and delivery. A **blank qualified indorsement** creates bearer paper that can be further negotiated by delivery without further indorsement.

In the following case, the court held that an indorser was liable on a promissory note because of her unqualified indorsement.

CASE 16.2

Alves v. Baldaia
470 N.E.2d 459 (1984) Court of Appeals of Ohio

Facts In January 1973, Keith R. Alves loaned $15,000 to Beatrice and William Baldaia. The Baldaias signed a promissory note payable to the order of Keith's wife, Joyce Ann Alves, who was the Baldaias' daughter. In February, Keith and Joyce (now Joyce Schaller) were divorced. As part of the settlement agreement, Joyce agreed to transfer her rights to the note to Keith. The separation agreement provided: "Wife agrees to assign to Husband any and all rights, title, and interest she may have in a certain note, executed by her parents, dated January 3, 1973, on or before the date of the final hearing." Joyce signed the promissory note, "Pay to the Order of Keith R. Alves, /s/ Joyce Ann Alves," and delivered the note to Keith.

Sometime later, Keith sought to collect payment on the note from the makers of the note, the Baldaias. They defaulted and refused to pay the note. Keith notified his former wife, Joyce Schaller, that the makers had dishonored the note. Keith sued the Baldaias as makers and his ex-wife Joyce as an indorser to recover payment on the note. The trial court entered judgment for Keith Alves. Joyce Shaller appealed.

Issue Did Joyce Schaller place an unqualified indorsement on the note and is therefore secondarily liable on it as an indorser?

Decision Yes. The court of appeals held that Joyce Schaller's signature on the promissory note operated as an unqualified indorsement. As such, she is secondarily liable on the note to plaintiff Keith Alves. Affirmed.

Reason The court held that, as a matter of law, Joyce Schaller's signature on the note operated as an unqualified indorsement. Unless the indorsement otherwise specifies, as by such words as *without recourse*, every indorser engages that upon dishonor and any necessary notice of dishonor and protest he or she will pay the instrument according to its tenor at the time of his or her indorsement to the holder or to any subsequent indorser who takes it up.

Thus, when Schaller signed the promissory note, she contracted to pay the instrument, according to its tenor, to the holder thereof if the maker dishonored the note at maturity. If Schaller had desired to pass title to the note (i.e., to formally negotiate it),

without creating any potential contract liability for herself, she had but to qualify her indorsement with the language "without recourse." However, not having done so, she acquired the full contractual liability of an indorser and was thereby obligated to pay the instrument following dishonor by the makers.

CASE QUESTIONS

Critical Legal Thinking Should indorsers be held secondarily liable on negotiable instruments when the makers (acceptors or drawers) default? Why or why not?

Ethics Did anyone act unethically in this case?

Business Implication What is the economic lesson of this case?

Nonrestrictive and Restrictive Indorsements

Most indorsements are **nonrestrictive**. Nonrestrictive indorsements do not have any instructions or conditions attached to the payment of the funds. For example, the indorsement is nonrestrictive if the indorsee merely signs his or her signature to the back of an instrument or includes a notation to pay a specific indorsee ("pay to Sam Smith").

Occasionally, an indorser includes some form of instruction in an indorsement. This is called a **restrictive indorsement**. A restrictive indorsement restricts the indorsee's rights in some manner. An indorsement that purports to prohibit further negotiation of an instrument does not destroy the negotiability of the instrument. For example, a check that is indorsed "pay to Sarah Stein only" can still be negotiated to other transferees. Because of its ineffectiveness, this type of restrictive indorsement is seldom used.

UCC 3-206 recognizes the following types of restrictive indorsements:

- **Conditional indorsement.** An indorser can condition the guarantee of payment of an instrument dependent on the happening or nonhappening of a specified event.

CONSIDER THIS EXAMPLE: Vincent White, a holder of a check, indorses the check "pay to John Jones if he completes construction of my house by January 1, 1994." This is a valid conditional indorsement. Neither Jones nor any subsequent holder can require Vincent White to pay the check until this condition is met.

- **Indorsement for deposit or collection.** An indorser can indorse an instrument so as to make the indorsee his collecting agent. This is often done when an indorser deposits a check or other instrument for collection at a bank. Words such as *for collection, for deposit only, pay any bank*, and the like create this type of indorsement. Banks use this type of indorsement in the collection process.
- **Indorsement in trust.** An indorsement can state that it is for the benefit or use of the indorser or another person. For example, checks are often indorsed to attorneys, executors of estates, real estate agents, and other fiduciaries in their representative capacity for the benefit of clients, heirs, or others. These are called **trust indorsements** or **agency indorsements** (see Exhibit 16.10). The indorser is not personally liable on the instrument if there is a proper trust or agency indorsement.

An indorsee who does not comply with the instructions of a restrictive indorsement is liable to the indorser for all losses that occur because of such noncompliance.

nonrestrictive indorsement An indorsement that has no instructions or conditions attached to the payment of the funds.

restrictive indorsement An indorsement that contains some sort of instruction from the indorser.

indorsement for deposit or collection An indorsement that makes the indorsee the indorser's collecting agent (e.g., "for deposit only").

Exhibit 16.10
A Trust Indorsement

Pay to Gloria Chau in trust for Elizabeth Chau and Samantha Chau
James Witherspoon

CONSIDER THIS EXAMPLE: Suppose a check is drawn "payable to Anne Spencer, Attorney, in trust for Joseph Watkins." If Ms. Spencer indorses the check to an automobile dealer in payment for a car that she purchases personally, the automobile dealer (indorsee) has not followed the instructions of the restrictive indorsement. He is liable to Joseph Watkins for any losses that arise because of his noncompliance with the restrictive indorsement.

Misspelled or Wrong Name

Where the name of a payee or indorsee is misspelled on a negotiable instrument, the payee or indorsee can indorse the instrument in the misspelled name, the correct name, or both. For example, if Susan Worth receives a check payable to "Susan Wirth," she can indorse the check "Susan Wirth" or "Susan Worth" or both. A person paying or taking the instrument for value or collection may require signature in both the misspelled and the correct name [UCC 3-204(d)].

FORGED INDORSEMENTS

forged document The forged signature of a *payee* or holder on a negotiable instrument.

Article 3 establishes certain rules for assessing liability when a negotiable instrument has been paid over a **forged indorsement**. With few exceptions, unauthorized indorsements are wholly inoperative as that of the person whose name is signed [UCC 3-401(a)]. Where an indorsement on an instrument has been forged or is unauthorized, the general rule is that the loss falls on the party who first takes the forged instrument after the forgery.

CONSIDER THIS EXAMPLE: Suppose Andy draws a check payable to the order of Mallory. Leslie steals the check from Mallory, forges Mallory's indorsement, and cashes the check at the liquor store. The liquor store is liable. Andy, the drawer, is not. The liquor store can recover from Leslie, the forger (if she can be found).

There are two exceptions to this rule where a drawer or maker bears the loss where an indorsement is forged. The rules governing these circumstances—the imposter rule and the fictitious payee rule—are discussed in the sections that follow.

The Imposter Rule

For purposes of the imposter rule, an **imposter** is one who impersonates a payee and induces the maker or drawer to issue an instrument in the payee's name and give the instrument to the imposter. If the imposter forges the indorsement of the named payee, the drawer or maker is liable on the instrument to any person who, in good faith, pays the instrument or takes it for value or for collection [UCC 3-404(a)]. This is called the **imposter rule**.

CONSIDER THIS EXAMPLE: Suppose Fred purchases goods by telephone from Cynthia. Fred has never met Cynthia. Beverly goes to Fred and pretends to be Cynthia. Fred draws a check payable to the order of Cynthia and gives the check to Beverly, believing her to be Cynthia. Beverly forges Cynthia's indorsement and cashes the check at the liquor store. Under the imposter rule, Fred is liable. The liquor store is not. This is because Fred was in the best position to have prevented the forged indorsement.

The imposter rule does not apply if the wrongdoer poses as the agent of the drawer or maker. For instance, suppose in the prior example that Beverly lied to Fred and said that she was Cynthia's agent. Believing this, Fred draws the check payable to the order of Cynthia and gives it to Beverly. Beverly forges Cynthia's indorsement and cashes the check at the liquor store. Here, the liquor store is liable because the imposter rule does not apply. The liquor store may recover from Beverly, if she can be found.

In the following case, the court applied the imposter rule.

"A trader is trusted upon his character, and visible commerce: that credit enables him to acquire wealth. If by secret liens, a few might swallow up all, it would greatly damp that credit."

Lord Mansfield
Worseley v. Demattos (1758)

imposter A person who impersonates a payee and induces a maker or drawer to issue an instrument in the payee's name and to give it to the imposter.

imposter rule A rule that says if an imposter forges the indorsement of the named payee, the drawer or maker is liable on the instrument and bears the loss.

CASE 16.3

Cornwell Quality Tool Co. v. Centran Bank
532 N.E.2d 772 (1987) Court of Appeals of Ohio

Facts Linda Zelner embezzled $57,000 from Akron Novelty Company while she was employed there as a bookkeeper. Her defalcation was discovered, and she was discharged on April 6, 1984. On April 30, 1984, Zelnar was employed as an accounts payable clerk at Cornwell Quality Tool Company (Cornwell). She filled an employment application listing Akron Novelty as her previous employer, but Cornwell did not make any inquiry as to this employment. Zelnar's duties at Cornwell included the preparation of checks to pay the company's creditors. Cornwell regularly did business with Model Industries, Inc., of Chicago. When mailing more than one check to a creditor, it was Cornwell's practice to make the first check in the group payable to the full name of the payee (e.g., Model Industries, Inc., of Chicago) and the remaining checks payable to an abbreviated name (e.g., "Model"). The first check would be inserted in the

window of the envelope, and the remaining checks would be placed behind this check.

Zelnar opened an account at Centran Bank in the name "Linda R. Zelnar, d.b.a. "Model." Over a three-month period, she prepared six checks payable to "Model," which were drawn on Cornwell's account at First National Bank. She presented the checks to her superiors at Cornwell for proper signatures and then took the checks, indorsed them "For Deposit Only, Model," and deposited them in her account at Centran. First National debited Cornwell's account when the checks were presented for payment. The checks exceeded $50,000. When Cornwell discovered the embezzlement, it sued Centran Bank, alleging that it had failed to exercise ordinary care in establishing Zelnar's account and collecting the "Model" checks. The trial court applied the imposter rule and found
continued

Cornwell liable on the checks. The court granted summary judgment to the bank. Cornwell appealed.

Issue Does the imposter rule prevent Cornwell from recovering from Centran Bank?

Decision Yes. The court of appeals held that the imposter rule made Cornwell, the drawer, liable on the checks. Affirmed.

Reason The court of appeals held that the requirements of the imposter rule were met. First, Zelnar supplied the name of the payee, "Model," to her employer, Cornwell. And second, Zelnar intended the payee, "Model," to have no interest in the checks. Having met the requirements of the imposter rule, the forged indorsement must be considered effective to pass good title on the instrument, and Cornwell must bear the loss. The court stated, "The policy behind this rule is explained in Official Comment 4: The principle followed is that the loss should fall upon the employer as a risk of his business enter-prise rather than upon the subsequent holder or drawee. The reasons are that the employer is normally in a better position to prevent such forgeries by reasonable care in the selection or supervision of his employees, or, if he is not, is at least in a better position to cover the loss by fidelity insurance, and that the cost of such insurance is properly an expense of his business rather than of the business of the holder or drawee."

CASE QUESTIONS

Critical Legal Thinking Should the law recognize the imposter rule? Or should holders and drawee/payor/collecting banks always be held liable for forged indorsements?

Ethics Did Ms. Zelnar act ethically in this case? Did Cornwell act ethically in suing the bank?

Business Implication As an employer, what is the moral of this case?

The Fictitious Payee Rule

fictitious payee rule
A rule that says a drawer or maker is liable on a forged or unauthorized indorsement of a fictitious payee.

A drawer or maker is liable on a forged or unauthorized indorsement under the **fictitious payee rule**. This rule applies when a person signing as or on behalf of a drawer or maker intends the named payee to have no interest in the instrument or the person identified as the payee is a fictitious person [UCC 3-404(b)].

CONSIDER THIS EXAMPLE: Marcia is the treasurer of the Weld Corporation. As treasurer, Marcia makes out and signs payroll checks for the company. Marcia draws a payroll check payable to the order of her neighbor, Harold Green, who does not work for the company. Marcia does not intend Harold to receive this money. She indorses Harold's name on the check and names herself as the indorsee. She cashes the check at the liquor store. Under the fictitious payee rule, Weld Corporation is liable because it was in a better position to have prevented the fraud.

The fictitious payee rule also applies if an agent or employee of the drawer or maker supplies the drawer or maker with the name of a fictitious payee [UCC 3-405(c)].

CONSIDER THIS EXAMPLE: Elizabeth is an accountant for the Baldridge Corporation. She is responsible for drawing up a list of employees who are to receive payroll checks. The treasurer of Baldridge Corporation actually signs the checks. Elizabeth places the name "Annabelle Armstrong" (a fictitious person) on the list. Baldridge Corporation issues a payroll check to this fictitious person. Elizabeth indorses the instrument "Annabelle Armstrong" and names herself as indorsee. She cashes the check at the liquor store. Under the fictitious payee rule, Baldridge Corporation is liable. The liquor store is not.

BUSINESS CHECKLIST

Multiple Payees or Indorsees

Drawers, makers, and indorsers often make checks, promissory notes, and other negotiable instruments payable to two or more payees or indorsees. The question then arises: Can the instrument be negotiated by the signature of one payee or indorsee, or are all of their signatures required to negotiate the instrument?

UCC 3-110(d) of Revised Article 3 and cases that have interpreted that section establish the following rules:

- If an instrument is *payable jointly* using the word *and* (e.g., pay to Shou-Yi Kang and Men-Weir Chen), then both persons' indorsements are necessary to negotiate the instrument.
- If the instrument is *payable in the alternative* using the word *or* (e.g., pay to Shou-Yi Kang or Men-Weir Chen), then either person's indorsement alone is sufficient to negotiate the instrument.
- If a *virgule*—a slash mark—is used, courts have held that the instrument is payable in the alternative. Thus, if a virgule is used (e.g., pay to Shou-Yi Kang/Men-Weir Chen), either person may individually indorse and negotiate the instrument. [*Mumma v. Rainer National Bank*, 808 P.2d 767 (Wash.App. 1991)]

WORKING THE WEB

Money and Payment Systems This Web site has lots of links to information about money.

Visit at http://www.gwdg.de/~ifbg/gild.html

U.S. Treasury Department Are you working on your income or other taxes? This is the place to find and download all the forms as well as lots of other information about the Treasury Department.

Visit at http://www.ustreas.gov/

American Stock Exchange Get current information about the American Stock Exchange at this Web site.

Visit at http://www.amex.com/

Chambers of Commerce Directory Here you can find information on chambers of commerce anywhere in the world.

Visit at http://clickcity.com/

Companies Online At this site, you can search for companies by name, city, and ticker symbol.

Visit at http://www.companiesonline.com/

CYBER EXERCISES:

1. Use the Money and Payment Systems Web site to find an article written by Benjamin Franklin called "A Modest Enquiry into the Nature and Necessity of Paper Currency." Print out that article.
2. Use the U.S. Treasury Department Web site to find and download a tax form. Print out your result.
3. Use the American Stock Exchange to get today's closing statistics.
4. Using the Chambers of Commerce Directory, find the chamber of commerce in your city.
5. Find a company in your city using Companies Online.

CHAPTER SUMMARY

REVISED ARTICLE 3 (NEGOTIABLE INSTRUMENTS) OF THE UCC, P. 356

Revised Article 3 (Negotiable Instruments) of the UCC	1. *Article 3 of the UCC.* Article of the Uniform Commercial Code promulgated in 1952 to govern the creation of, transfer of, enforcement of, and liability on negotiable instruments. 2. *Revised Article 3.* In 1990, the American Law Institute and the National Conference of Commissioners on Uniform State Laws approved new *Revised Article 3.* This new Article replaces Article 3. It made substantial changes to the law governing negotiable instruments.

FUNCTIONS OF NEGOTIABLE INSTRUMENTS, P. 356

Functions of Negotiable Instruments	1. Substitute for money 2. Credit device 3. Record-keeping device

TYPES OF NEGOTIABLE INSTRUMENTS, P. 357

Types of Negotiable Instruments	There are four types of negotiable instruments: 1. *Draft.* An order to pay. A three-party instrument. 2. *Check.* An order to pay. A three-party instrument. 3. *Promissory note.* A promise to pay. A two-party instrument. 4. *Certificate of deposit (CD).* A promise to pay. A two-party instrument.

Drafts	An unconditional written order by one party (the *drawer*) that orders a second party (the *drawee*) to pay money to a third party (the *payee*). The drawee must owe money to the drawer for the drawer to issue a draft ordering the money to be paid to the payee.
	1. *Drawer.* The party who writes the order for a draft.
	2. *Drawee.* The party who must pay the money stated in a draft. The drawee is also called the *acceptor.*
	3. *Payee.* The party who receives the money from a draft.
	4. *Types of drafts:*
	   a. *Time draft.* A draft payable at a designated future date
	   b. *Sight draft.* A draft payable on sight. Also called a *demand draft*
	   c. *Trade acceptance.* A sight draft that arises when credit is extended (by a seller to a buyer) with the sale of goods. The seller is both the drawer and the payee, and the buyer is the drawee

Checks	A form of draft drawn on a financial institution (the *drawee*) and payable on demand. The checking account holder (the *drawer*) orders the financial institution (the *drawee*) to pay money to a third party (the *payee*).
	1. *Drawer.* The checking account holder and writer of the check.
	2. *Drawee.* The financial institution where the drawer has his or her checking account and which pays the money to the payee.
	3. *Payee.* The party to whom the check is written.
	4. *Types of checks:*
	   a. Ordinary checks
	   b. Special checks
	      i. Certified checks
	      ii. Cashier's checks
	      iii. Traveler's checks

Promissory Notes	An unconditional written promise by one party (the *maker*) to pay money to another party (the *payee*). Promissory notes are also called *notes*.

	1. *Maker.* The party who makes the promise to pay (the borrower).
	2. *Payee.* The party to whom the promise to pay is made (the lender).
	3. *Types of promissory notes:*
	  a. *Time note.* A note payable at a specific time
	  b. *Demand note.* A note payable on demand
	  c. *Installment note.* A note that is paid in more than one installment
	  d. *Mortgage note.* A note secured by real estate
	  e. *Collateral note.* A note secured by personal property

Certificates of Deposit (CD)	A special form of note that is created when a depositor (the *payee*) deposits money at a financial institution (the *maker*) in exchange for the institution's promise to pay back the amount of the deposit plus an agreed-upon rate of interest upon the expiration of a set time period agreed upon by the parties.
	1. *Maker.* The financial institution (the borrower).
	2. *Payee.* The depository (the lender).
	3. *Types of CDs:*
	  a. *Small CD.* A CD under $100,000
	  b. *Jumbo CD.* A CD of $100,000 or more

CREATING A NEGOTIABLE INSTRUMENT, P. 361

Creating a Negotiable Instrument	A negotiable instrument must 1. Be in writing. 2. Be signed by the maker or drawer. 3. Be an unconditional promise or order to pay. 4. State a fixed amount of money. 5. Not require any undertaking in addition to the payment of money. 6. Be payable on demand or at a definite time 7. Be payable to order or to bearer.

A Writing	1. *Writing.* A negotiable instrument must be in writing; oral promises or orders do not qualify as negotiable instruments.
	2. *Requirements of the writing:*
	  a. *Permanency requirement.* The writing must be in a permanent state, such as written on ordinary paper
	  b. *Portability requirement.* The writing must be able to be easily transported between areas.

Signed by the Maker or the Drawer	1. *Signature.* A negotiable instrument must be signed by the *maker* if it is a note or CD and by the *drawer* if it is a draft or check.
	2. *Type of signature.* Any symbol executed or adopted by the maker or drawer with a present intent to authenticate a writing qualifies as his or her signature. This can be a formal name, an informal name, initials, a nickname, or any symbol or device.
	3. *Signature of an unauthorized agent.* A maker or drawer can appoint an *agent* to sign a negotiable instrument on his or her behalf. *Liability of the parties:*
	  a. *Maker or drawer.* Liable on a negotiable instrument signed by an authorized agent
	  b. *Agent.* An agent is not personally liable on the negotiable instrument if his or her signature discloses (1) his or her *agency status* and (ii) the *identity of the maker or drawer.* An agent who fails to meet these requirements is personally liable on the instrument.

Unconditional Promise or Order to Pay	1. *Promise or order.* A *maker's promise to pay* must be an unconditional and affirmative undertaking to repay the debt evidenced by the note or CD. A *drawer's order to pay* must be an unconditional order to a drawee to pay a payee.
	2. *Unconditional promise or order.* Promises to pay and orders to pay must be *unconditional* in order for them to be negotiable.
	3. *Conditional promise or order.* A promise or order that is *conditional* on another promise or event is not negotiable. A promise or order is conditional if it states:
	  a. An express condition to payment
	  b. That the promise or order is subject to or governed by another writing
	  c. The rights or obligations with respect to the promise or order are stated in another writing.
	A promise or order remains *unconditional* if it merely references another writing or refers to another writing for rights as to *collateral, prepayment,* or *acceleration.*

Fixed Amount of Money	1. *Fixed amount.* The value of the instrument must be able to be determined with certainty. An instrument does not have to provide for the payment of *interest,* but if it does, interest may be expressed as a *fixed* or *variable* amount or rate. The amount or rate of interest may be determined by reference to information not contained in the instrument (e.g., a bank's prime rate or a government index). 2. *Payable in money.* The fixed amount must be payable in *money,* which is any medium of exchange authorized or adopted by a domestic or foreign government. Instruments that are payable in gold, diamonds, commodities, goods, services, stocks, bonds, and such do not qualify as negotiable instruments.
Not Require Any Undertaking in Addition to the Payment of Money	The promise or order cannot require the person promising or ordering payment to do any act in addition to the payment of money. A note that would require such additional undertaking (e.g., the provision of a service) is not negotiable.

Payable on Demand or at a Definite Time	A negotiable instrument must be payable either on demand or at a definite time.
	1. *Payable on demand.* An instrument that is payable on demand, at sight, or on presentment, or that is silent regarding when payment is due. This is called a *demand instrument.*
	2. *Payable at a definite time.* An instrument is payable at a definite time if it is payable
	  a. At a fixed date
	  b. On or before a stated date
	  c. At a fixed period after sight
	  d. At a time readily ascertainable when the promise or order is issued
	3. *Prepayment, acceleration, and extension clauses.* The following clauses in an instrument do not affect its negotiability:
	  a. *Prepayment clause.* A clause that permits a maker or drawee to pay an instrument prior to its due date
	  b. *Acceleration clause.* A clause that allows the payee or holder to accelerate payment of an instrument upon the happening of an event
	  c. *Extension clause.* A clause that allows the maturity of an instrument to be extended to some time in the future.

Payable to Order or to Bearer	A negotiable instrument must be payable to order or to bearer. 1. *Order instruments.* An instrument payable to the order of an *identified person* or to an identified person or order. The term *order* must be included in the instrument; otherwise, it is not negotiable. For example, an instrument that states "payable to the order of IBM" or "payable to IBM or order" is negotiable; a writing that states "payable to IBM" or "pay to IBM" is not negotiable. 2. *Bearer instruments.* An instrument that is payable to *anyone in physical possession* of the instrument. An instrument is payable to bearer when any of the following language is used: "payable to bearer," "payable to the order of bearer," "payable to IBM or bearer," "payable to cash," or "payable to the order of cash." The person in possession of a bearer instrument is called the *bearer*.

NONNEGOTIABLE CONTRACTS, P. 366

Nonnegotiable Contracts	A writing that fails to qualify as a negotiable instrument is a *nonnegotiable contract*. Nonnegotiable contracts are subject to normal contract law rather than Revised Article 3 of the UCC.

TRANSFER BY ASSIGNMENT OR NEGOTIATION, P. 367

Transfer by Assignment or Negotiation	When issued, negotiable instruments can be transferred by *assignment* or *negotiation*. The rights acquired by transferees differ according to the method of transfer.
Transfer by Assignment	1. *Assignment.* Transfer of rights that the transferor (*assignor*) has in a contract to a transferee (*assignee*). Ordinary contracts, writings that do not qualify as negotiable instruments, and negotiable instruments that are not transferred by negotiation can be transferred by assignment. 2. *Assignor.* The transferor in an assignment situation. 3. *Assignee.* The transferee in an assignment situation. 4. *Rights acquired under an assignment.* The transferee acquires only the rights that the transferor had, and is subject to all of the defenses that can be raised against the transferor.
Transfer by Negotiation	1. *Negotiation.* A transfer of a negotiable instrument by a person other than the issuer to a person who becomes a *holder*. *Negotiation* is a term signifying that a negotiable instrument has met certain requirements in being transferred. 2. *Transferor.* Person who transfers a negotiable instrument by negotiation. 3. *Holder.* Person who receives a negotiable instrument by negotiation. 4. *Rights acquired under a negotiation.* The holder receives at least the rights of the transferor and may acquire even greater rights than the transferor if he or she qualifies as a *holder in due course (HDC)*. This includes not being subject to some of the defenses that can be raised against the transferor. 5. *Negotiating order paper.* Order paper (an instrument payable to a specific payee or indorsee) is negotiated by *delivery and indorsement*. That is, the transferor signs (indorses) the instrument, with or without other notation, and delivers the instrument to the holder. 6. *Negotiating bearer paper.* Bearer paper (an instrument that is not payable to a specific payee) is negotiated by *delivery* (indorsement is not required). There is substantial risk associated with the loss or theft of bearer paper.

7. *Converting order and bearer paper.* Negotiable instruments can be *converted from order paper to bearer paper* by the holder indorsing the instrument without naming a specific payee. An instrument can be *converted from bearer paper to order paper* by the holder indorsing the instrument and naming a specific payee.

INDORSEMENTS, P. 368

Indorsement	An *indorsement* is the signature of the signer (other than as a maker, a drawer, or an acceptor) that is placed on an instrument to negotiate it to another person, for example, a holder signing the back of a check. An indorsement may be a signature alone (creating bearer paper), be accompanied by the name of a specific payee (creating order paper), or be accompanied by other words (e.g., "without recourse"). 1. *Indorser.* The person who indorses a negotiable instrument. 2. *Indorsee.* The person to whom a negotiable instrument is indorsed. 3. *Allonge.* Indorsements are usually placed on the reverse side of the negotiable instrument. If there is no room on the instrument, the indorsement may be placed on a separate sheet of paper called an *allonge.* The allonge must be firmly affixed to the instrument. 4. *Instruments requiring indorsement.* Indorsements are required to negotiate *order paper* (indorsement and delivery required). Indorsements are not required to negotiate *bearer paper* (only delivery is required).
Types of Indorsements	Every indorsement is 1. Blank or special 2. Unqualified or qualified 3. Nonrestrictive or restrictive
Blank Indorsements	An indorsement that does not specify a particular indorsee. This occurs when an indorser merely signs the instrument without naming a payee. This indorsement creates *bearer paper.*
Special Indorsements	An indorsement that specifies a named payee. This occurs when the indorser signs the instrument and names a particular indorsee. This indorsement creates *order paper.*
Unqualified and Qualified Indorsements	1. *Unqualified indorsement.* An indorsement that does not disclaim or limit the liability of the indorser. An *unqualified indorser* is liable to pay any holder or subsequent indorser if the maker, drawer, or acceptor does not pay the instrument. 2. *Qualified indorsement.* An indorsement that disclaims or limits the liability of the indorser. A *qualified indorser* is not liable to pay any holder or subsequent indorser if the maker, drawer, or acceptor does not pay the instrument. This is done by adding the words *without recourse* or similar language that disclaims liability.
Nonrestrictive and Restrictive Indorsements	1. *Nonrestrictive indorsement.* An indorsement that has no instructions or conditions attached to the payment of the funds. This occurs when the indorser signs his or her signature to the instrument (either naming a specific payee or not), but does not add any specific condition or instruction concerning the payment of the money. 2. *Restrictive indorsement.* An indorsement that contains some sort of instruction from the indorser. The UCC recognizes the following restrictive indorsements:

	a. *Conditional indorsement*. An indorsement that conditions the payment of an instrument upon the happening or nonhappening of a specified event
	b. *Indorsement for deposit or collection*. An indorsement that makes the indorsee the indorser's collection agent (e.g., indorsement "for deposit only")
	c. *Indorsement in trust*. An indorsement that states that it is for the benefit or use of the indorser or another person.
	An indorsement that purports to prohibit further negotiation of a negotiable instrument (e.g., "pay to Sarah Smith only") is ineffective and does not destroy the negotiability of the instrument.
Misspelled or Wrong Name	If the name of the payee or indorsee is misspelled or is wrong, the payee or indorsee can indorse the instrument in the misspelled or wrong name, the correct name, or both.
Multiple Payees or Indorsees	1. *Payable jointly*. An instrument that is payable to two or more persons with *and* between their names. All of their indorsements are required to negotiate the instrument.
	2. *Payable in the alternative*. An instrument that is payable to two or more persons with *or* between their names. Only one of their indorsements is required to negotiate the instrument.
FORGED INDORSEMENTS, P. 374	
Forged Indorsements	1. *Forged indorsement*. The forged indorsement of a payee or holder on a negotiable instrument.
	2. *Liability on a forged indorsement*. Generally, the person who took the check from the forger is liable on a forged indorsement.
	3. *Exceptions*. There are two exceptions to the general rule: The imposter rule and the fictitious payee rule.
The Imposter Rule	1. *An imposter*. A person who impersonates a payee and induces a maker or drawer to issue an instrument in the payer's name and give it to the imposter.
	2. *The imposter rule*. States that if an imposter forges the indorsement of the named payee, the drawer or maker is liable on the instrument and bears the loss.
The Fictitious Payee Rule	A rule that says a drawer or maker is liable on a forged or unauthorized indorsement of a fictitious payee. This rule applies when a person signing as or on behalf of a drawer or maker intends the named payee to have no interest in the instrument or when the person identified as the payee is a fictitious person.

CRITICAL LEGAL THINKING CASES

16.1 Indorsement On November 15, 1979, Katherine Warnock purchased a cashier's check in the amount of $53,541, payable to her order and drawn on the Pueblo Bank and Trust Company (Pueblo Bank). At some time between November 15 and November 30, 1979, Warnock indorsed "Kathleen Warnock" on the reverse side of the check. Eventually, the check came into the hands of Warnock's attorney, Jerry Quick. Quick added the words *for deposit only* under her indorsement and then had the check deposited into his trust account at the La Junta State Bank. Warnock died on November 10, 1981. The executor of her estate suspected that Quick illegally converted Warnock's funds into his own account. The executor claimed that the cashier's check that Quick deposited should have been payable only to Warnock because it was made to a named payee. When the executor discovered that Quick's trust account had been liquidated, the executor sued the La Junta State Bank where the deposit had been made. Who wins? [*La Junta State Bank v. Travis*, 727 P.2d 48 (Col. 1986)]

16.2 Time or Demand Instrument Mullins Enterprises, Inc. (Mullins), was a business operating in the state of Kentucky. To raise capital, Mullins obtained loans from Corbin Deposit Bank & Trust Co. (Corbin Bank). Between 1971 and 1975, Corbin made eight loans to Mullins. Mullins executed a promissory note setting out the amount of the debt, the dates and times of installment payments, and the date of final payment and delivered it to the bank each time a loan was made. The notes were signed by an officer of Mullins'. In 1980, a dispute arose between Mullins and Corbin as to the proper interpretation of the language contained in the notes. The bank contended that the notes were demand notes. Mullins claimed that the notes were time instruments. Who wins? [*Corbin Deposit Bank & Trust Co. v. Mullins Enterprises, Inc.*, 34 UCC Rptr. Ser. 1201 (Ky. App. 1982)]

16.3 Note On August 17, 1979, Sandra McGuire and her husband entered into a contract to purchase the inventory, equipment, accounts receivable, and name of "Becca's Boutique" from Pascal and Rebecca Tursi. Becca's Boutique was a clothing store that was owned as a sole proprietorship by the Tursis. The McGuires agreed to purchase the store for $75,000, with a down payment of $10,000 and the balance to be paid by October 5, 1979. The promissory note signed by the McGuires read: "For value received, Thomas J. McGuire and Sandra A. McGuire, husband and wife, do promise to pay to the order of Pascal and Rebecca Tursi the sum of $65,000." Is the note an order to pay or a promise to pay? [*P P Inc. v. McGuire*, 509 F.Supp. 1079 (D.N.J. 1981)]

16.4 Bearer or Order Instrument Broadway Management Corporation (Broadway) owned and operated the American Nursing Center. Conan Briggs had received services from the center and had executed an instrument to pay for those services. The instrument reads in relevant part: "Ninety days after date, I, we, or either of us, promises to pay to the order of _____ $3,498.45." Briggs refused to pay on the note. Broadway claims that this note is "bearer paper" and as such is payable to the holder. Briggs claims that the note is "order paper" and is therefore payable only to a named payee. Can Broadway collect on this note as its bearer? [*Broadway Management Corporation v. Briggs*, 332 N.E.2d 131 (Ill. App. 1975)]

16.5 Formal Requirements Mr. Higgins operated a used-car dealership in the state of Alabama. In 1978, Higgins purchased a 1977 Chevrolet Corvette for $8,115. He paid for the car with a draft on his account at the First State Bank of Albertville. Soon after, Higgins resold the car to Mr. Holsonback for $8,225. To pay for the car, Holsonback signed a check that was printed on a standard-sized envelope. The reason the check was printed on the envelope is that this practice made it easier to transfer title and other documents from the seller to the buyer. The envelope on which the check was written contained a certificate of title, a mileage statement, and a bill of sale. Does a check printed on an envelope meet the formal requirements to be

classified as a negotiable instrument under the UCC? [*Holsonback v. First State Bank of Albertville*, 30 UCC Rep. Serv. (Ala. 1980)]

16.6 Unconditional Promise M. S. Horne executed a $100,000 note in favor of R. C. Clark. The note stipulated that it could not be transferred, pledged, or assigned without Horne's consent. Along with the note, Horne signed a letter authorizing Clark to use the note as collateral for a loan. Clark pledged the note as collateral for a $50,000 loan from First State Bank of Gallup (First State). First State telephoned Horne to confirm that Clark could pledge the note and Horne indicated that it was okay. Clark eventually defaulted on the loan. First State attempted to collect on the note, but Horne refused to pay. Did the restriction written on Horne's promissory note cause it to be nonnegotiable despite the letter of authorization? [*First State Bank of Gallup v. Clark and Horne*, 570 P.2d 1144 (N.M. 1977)]

16.7 Negotiable Instrument In 1982, William H. Bailey, M.D., executed a note payable to California Dreamstreet. Dreamstreet is a joint venture that solicits investments for a cattle breeding operation. Bailey's promissory note read: "Dr. William H. Bailey hereby promises to pay to the order of California Dreamstreet the sum of $329,800." In 1986, Dreamstreet negotiated the note to Cooperatieve Centrale Raiffeisen-Boerenleenbank B.A. (Cooperatieve), a foreign bank. A default occurred and Cooperatieve filed suit against Bailey to recover on the note. Was the note executed by Bailey a negotiable instrument? [*Cooperatieve Centrale Raiffeisen-Boerenleenbank B.A. v. Bailey*, 9 UCC Rep. Serv. 2d 145 (C.D.Cal. 1989)]

16.8 Reference to Another Agreement In 1972, Holly Hill Acres, Ltd. (Holly Hill) purchased land from Rogers and Blythe. As part of its consideration, Holly Hill gave Rogers and Blythe a promissory note and purchase money mortgage. The note, which was executed on April 28, 1972, read in part: "This note with interest is secured by a mortgage on real estate made by the maker in favor of said payee. The terms of said mortgage are by reference made a part hereof." Rogers and Blythe assigned this note and mortgage to Charter Bank of Gainesville (Charter Bank) as security in order to obtain a loan from the bank. Within a few months, Rogers and Blythe defaulted on their obligation to Charter Bank. Charter Bank sued to recover on Holly Hill's note and mortgage. Does the reference to the mortgage in the note cause it to be nonnegotiable? [*Holly Hill Acres, Ltd. v. Charter Bank of Gainesville*, 314 So.2d 209 (Fla. App. 1975)]

16.9 Demand Instrument In July 1977, Stewart P. Blanchard borrowed $50,000 from Progressive Bank & Trust Company (Progressive) to purchase a home. As part of the transaction, Blanchard signed a note secured by a mortgage. The note provided for a 10 percent annual interest rate. Under the terms of the note, payment was "due on demand, if no demand is made, then $600 monthly beginning 8/1/77." Blanchard testified that he believed Progressive could only demand immediate payment if he failed to make the monthly installments. After one year, Blanchard received notice that the rate of interest on the note would rise to 11 percent. Despite the notice, Blanchard continued to make $600 monthly payments. One year later, Progressive notified Blanchard that the interest rate on the loan would be increased to 12.75 percent. Progressive requested that Blanchard sign a form consenting to the interest rate adjustment. When Blanchard refused to sign the form, Progressive demanded immediate payment of the note balance. Progressive sued Blanchard to enforce the terms of the note. Was the note a demand instrument? [*Blanchard v. Progressive Bank & Trust Company*, 413 So.2d 589 (La. App. 1982)]

16.10 Extension Clause Robert and Sandra Evans were stockholders in Traditional Development, Inc. (Traditional). Traditional planned to build townhouses in Arizona. In 1972, the Evanses approached Security Mortgage Company (Security) to obtain financing for the project. Security agreed to make Traditional a $514,000 loan that would be secured by a note. On May 19, 1972, the note was executed, and the Evanses signed as guarantors. The note contained the following language: "The makers and endorsers expressly agree that this note, or any payment thereunder, may be extended from time to time without in any way affecting the liability of the makers and endorsers hereof."

The original maturity date of the note was January 14, 1973, or 245 days after origination. However, the project was delayed so the note's due date was extended to May 13, 1973, an additional 114 days. The guarantors consented to the extension in writing. Several months later, the note was extended to January 15, 1974. When Traditional realized it was unable to complete the project, it assigned its interest in the note to Union Construction Company, Inc. (Union). One final extension of the note was granted, making the maturity date of the loan January 15, 1975. Do the multiple extensions of the note render it nonnegotiable? [*Union Construction Company, Inc. v. Beneficial Standard Mortgage Investors*, 28 UCC Rep Serv. 711 (Ariz. App. 1980)]

16.11 Order or Bearer Paper Samuel C. Mazilly wrote a personal check that was drawn on Calcasieu-Marine Nation Bank of Lake Charles, Inc. (CMN Bank). The check was made payable to the order of Lee St. Mary and was delivered to him. St. Mary indorsed the check in blank and delivered it to Leland H. Coltharp, Sr., in payment for some livestock. Coltharp accepted the check and took it to the City Savings Bank & Trust Company (City Savings) to deposit it. He indorsed the check as follows: "Pay to the order of City Savings Bank & Trust Company, DeRidder, Louisiana." City Savings accepted the check and forwarded it to CMN Bank for payment. The check never arrived at CMN Bank. Some unknown person stole the check while it was in transit and presented it directly to CMN Bank for payment. The teller at CMN Bank cashed the check without indorsement of the person who presented it. At the time CMN Bank accepted the check, was it order or bearer paper? [*Coltharp v. Calcasieu-Marine National Bank of Lake Charles, Inc.*, 199 So.2d 568 (La. App. 1967)]

16.12 Multiple Payees Muaray Walter, Inc. (Walter, Inc.) was the general contractor for the construction of a waste treatment plant in New Hampshire. Walter, Inc. contracted with H. Johnson Electric, Inc. (Johnson Electric), to install the electrical system in the treatment plant. Johnson Electric purchased its supplies for the project from General Electric Supply (G.E. Supply). On May 1, 1980, Walter, Inc. issued a check payable to "Johnson Electric and G.E. Supply" in the amount of $54,900 drawn on its account at Marine Midland Bank (Marine Midland). Walter, Inc. made the check payable to both the subcontractor and its material supplier to be certain that the supplier was paid by Johnson Electric. Despite this precautionary measure, Johnson Electric negotiated the check without G.E. Supply's indorsement, and the check was paid by Marine Midland Bank. Johnson Electric negotiated the check without G.E. Supply's indorsement, and the check was paid by Marine Midland Bank. Johnson Electric never paid G.E. Supply. G.E. Supply then demanded payment from Walter, Inc. When Walter, Inc., learned that Marine Midland paid the check without G.E. Electric's indorsement, it demanded to be reimbursed. When Marine Midland refused, Walter, Inc. sued Marine Midland to recover for the check. Was Johnson Electric's indorsement sufficient to legally negotiate the check to Marine Midland Bank? [*Murray Walter, Inc. v. Marine Midland Bank*, 39 UCC Rep Serv 972 (N.Y.Sup.Ct. 1984)]

16.13 Imposter Rule Allan Q. Mowatt was employed as a bookkeeper at the law firm of McCarthy, Kenney & Reidy, P.C. The law firm maintained a primary checking account at the First National Bank of Boston (Bank of Boston) and two smaller accounts at other banks to pay operating expenses. The law firm's secondary account with the Union Bank of Lowell was under the name Clement McCarthy, the firm's senior partner. It was funded by checks drawn on the Bank of Boston account and payable to "Clement McCarthy." The checks used to fund the secondary accounts were signed by any of four attorneys with check-writing authority. When either of the two accounts was running low, Mowatt would make out a check payable to "Clement McCarthy" and have it signed by one of the authorized attorneys. In addition to drawing checks needed to fund the secondary accounts, Mowatt began making out extra checks on the Bank of Boston account payable to Clement McCarthy. Mowatt would explain that the extra checks were needed to maintain funds in the secondary accounts. Mowatt then forged the indorsement of Clement McCarthy to the extra checks and deposited them into his own bank account. Who is liable for the loss caused by this forgery? [*McCarthy, Kenney & Reidy, P.C. v. First National Bank of Boston*, 2 UCC Rep Serv 2d 977 (Ma.Sup.Ct. 1986)]

ETHICS CASES

16.14 Ethical Perspective Llobell was the president of Klem Ventures, Ltd. (Klem Ventures). Klem Ventures owed P.J. Panzeca, Inc. (Panzeca), a total of $57,000 for labor and materials used in a construction project. On February 1, 1972, Llo-

bell, acting in his capacity as president, executed two notes to pay the debt owed by Klem Ventures to Panzeca. One of the notes was in the amount of $18,000 and was payable 30 days from the date of making; the other note was for $29,000 and was payable 60 days from the date of making. Llobell signed both notes on the reverse side. His signature was the only thing written on the back of the notes. When Panzeca presented the notes for payment, they were both dishonored. On September 20, 1974, Panzeca sued Llobell, claiming that he was personally liable for the amount of the notes. Llobell argued he was not personally liable because he signed the notes as an agent for the corporation. Did Llobell act ethically in denying personal liability? [*P.J. Panzeca, Inc. v. Llobell*, 19 UCC Rep. Serv. 564 (N.Y.Sup.Ct. 1976)]

16.15 Ethical Perspective Samuel K. Yucht was an attorney practicing law in the state of New Jersey. Yucht specialized in personal injury cases. Over the course of a year, Yucht submitted numerous claims on behalf of his clients against the Allstate Insurance Company (Allstate). In each case, Yucht informed Allstate that his client was willing to settle the claim and submitted a signed release. All of the signatures on the releases were forged by Yucht. When Allstate issued settlement checks made payable to the client and Yucht as their attorney, Yucht again forged his clients' indorsements. He added his own indorsement and then deposited the checks into his personal account. Yucht never informed his clients of the settlements he had made on their behalf or of the money he had received in their names. Did Yucht act ethically in this case? Is Allstate liable for the losses caused by Yucht's actions under the imposter rule? [*Clients' Security Fund of the Bar of New Jersey v. Allstate Insurance Company*, 5 UCC Rep. Serv. 2d 127 (N.J.Sup.Ct. 1987)]

 ## CRITICAL LEGAL THINKING WRITING ASSIGNMENT

Read Case A.16 in the Case Appendix [*Federal Deposit Insurance Corporation v. Woodside Construction, Inc.*]. This case is excerpted from the court of appeals opinion. Review and brief the case. In your brief, be sure to answer the following questions:

1. Was Galt acting as an agent when he signed the negotiable instrument? If so, who was his principal?

2. What type of negotiable instrument did Galt sign? How did he sign it?

3. Was Galt's signature proper to notify a holder that his signature was made in a representative capacity?

4. Was Galt found personally liable on the negotiable instrument?

CHAPTER 17

HOLDER IN DUE COURSE,

LIABILITY, AND DEFENSES

Chapter Objectives

*After studying this chapter,
you should be able to*

1. Define a holder and a holder in due course
2. Identify and apply the requirements for becoming a holder in due course
3. Distinguish between primary and secondary liability on negotiable instruments
4. Describe the signature liability of makers, drawees, drawers, acceptors, and accommodation parties
5. List the transfer warranties and describe the liability of parties for breaching them
6. List the presentment warranties and describe the liability of parties for breaching them
7. Identify real defenses that can be asserted against a holder in due course
8. Identify personal defenses that cannot be asserted against a holder in due course
9. Describe the Federal Trade Commission rule that prohibits the holder in due course rule in consumer transactions
10. Describe how liability on a negotiable instrument is discharged

Chapter Contents

> *If one wants to know the real value of money, he needs but to borrow some from his friends.*
>
> Confucius
> Analects, c. 500 B.C.

"A negotiable bill or note is a courier without luggage."
Chief Justice Gibson
Overton v. Tyler
(1846)

If payment is not made on a negotiable instrument when it is due, the holder can use the court system to enforce the instrument. Various parties, including both signers and nonsigners, may be liable on it. Some parties are primarily liable on the instrument, whereas others are secondarily liable. Accommodation parties (i.e., guarantors) can also be held liable.

Recall that the primary purpose of commercial paper is to act as a substitute for money. For this to occur, the holder of a negotiable instrument must qualify as a holder in due course (HDC). Commercial paper held by an HDC is virtually as good as money because HDCs take an instrument free of all claims and most defenses that can be asserted by other parties.

This chapter discusses the liability of parties on negotiable instruments, the requirements that must be met to qualify as an HDC, the defenses that can be raised against the imposition of liability, and the discharge of liability.

HOLDER VERSUS HOLDER IN DUE COURSE

holder A person who is in possession of a negotiable instrument that is drawn, issued, or indorsed to him or her or his or her order, or to bearer, or in blank.

holder in due course (HDC) A holder who takes a negotiable instrument for value, in good faith, and without notice that it is defective or is overdue.

CAUTION
Only a holder *can qualify as an HDC.*

Two of the most important concepts of the law of negotiable instruments are that of "holder" and "holder in due course." A **holder** is a person in possession of an instrument that is payable to bearer or an identified person who is in possession of an instrument payable to that person [UCC 1–201(20)]. The holder of a negotiable instrument has the same rights as an assignee of an ordinary nonnegotiable contract. That is, the holder is subject to all of the claims and defenses that can be asserted against the transferor.

The concept of holder in due course is unique to the area of negotiable instruments. A **holder in due course (HDC)** is a holder who takes an instrument for value, in good faith, and without notice that it is defective or is overdue. An HDC takes a negotiable instrument free of all claims and most defenses that can be asserted against the transferor of the instrument. Only real defenses—and not personal defenses—may be asserted against an HDC. (Defenses are discussed later in this chapter.) Thus, an HDC can acquire greater rights from those of the transferor.

The difference between holders and holders in due course is illustrated in this example: John purchases an automobile from Shannen. At the time of sale, Shannen tells John that the car has had only one previous owner and has been driven only 20,000 miles. John, relying on these statements, purchases the car. He pays 10 percent down and signs a promissory note to pay the remainder of the purchase price, with interest, in 12 equal monthly installments. Shannen transfers the note to Patricia. Then John discovers the car has actually had four previous owners and had been driven 100,000 miles. If Patricia were a holder (but not an HDC) of the note, John could assert Shannen's fraudulent representations against enforcement of the note by Patricia. John could rescind the note and refuse to pay Patricia. Patricia's only recourse would be against Shannen.

If Patricia qualified as an HDC, however, the result would be different. John could not assert Shannen's fraudulent conduct against enforcement of the note by Patricia. This is because this type of fraud is a personal defense that cannot be raised against an HDC. Therefore, Patricia could enforce the note against John. John's only recourse would be against Shannen, if she could be found.

REQUIREMENTS FOR HDC STATUS

To qualify as an HDC, the transferor must meet the requirements established by the UCC: The person must be the *holder* of a negotiable instrument that was taken (1) for value (2) in good faith (3) without notice that it is overdue, dishonored, or encumbered in any way and (4) bearing no apparent evidence of forgery, alterations, or irregularity [UCC 3-302]. These requirements are discussed in the sections that follow. Exhibit 17.1 illustrates the holder in due course doctrine.

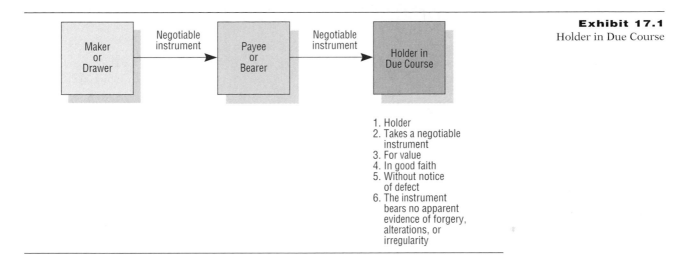

Exhibit 17.1
Holder in Due Course

Taking for Value

The holder must have *given value* for the negotiable instrument to qualify as an HDC [UCC 3-302(a)(2)(i)]. For example, suppose Ted draws a check "payable to the order to Mary Smith" and delivers the check to Mary. Mary indorses it and gives it as a gift to her daughter. Mary's daughter cannot qualify as an HDC because she has not given value for it. The purchaser of a limited interest in a negotiable instrument is an HDC only to the extent of the interest purchased.

Under the UCC, value has been given if the holder [UCC 3-303]

1. Performs the agreed-upon promise
2. Acquires a security interest or lien on the instrument
3. Takes the instrument in payment of or as security for an antecedent claim
4. Gives a negotiable instrument as payment
5. Gives an irrevocable obligation as payment

If a person promises to perform but has not yet done so, no value has been given and he or she is not an HDC. For example, Karen executes a note payable to Fred for promise to pay the note in 90 days. Before Amy pays for the note, Karen discovers that the goods she purchased from Fred are defective. Karen can raise this defect against enforcement of the note by Amy because no value has yet been given for the note. If Amy had already paid for the note, she would qualify as an HDC, and Karen could not raise the issue of defect against enforcement of the note by Amy.

Taking in Good Faith

A holder must take the instrument in **good faith** to qualify as an HDC [UCC 3-302(a)(2)(ii)]. Good faith means honesty in fact in the conduct or transaction concerned [UCC 1-201(19)]. Honesty in fact is a subjective test that examines the holder's

BUSINESS BRIEF
If a holder of a negotiable instrument qualifies as a holder in due course (HDC), *the HDC takes the instrument free of all claims and most defenses that can be asserted by other parties. In other words, the instrument is almost as good as cash.*

good faith Honesty in fact in the conduct or transaction concerned. This is a subjective test.

actual belief. A holder's subjective belief can be inferred from the circumstances. For example, if a holder acquires an instrument from a stranger under suspicious circumstances and at a deep discount, it could be inferred that the holder did not take the instrument in good faith. However, a naive person who acquired the same instrument at the same discount might be found to have acted in good faith and thereby qualify as an HDC. Each case must be reviewed separately.

Note that the good faith test applies only to the holder. It does not apply to the transferor of the instrument. For example, suppose a thief steals a negotiable instrument and transfers it to Harry. Harry does not know that the instrument is stolen. Harry meets the good faith test and qualifies as an HDC.

Taking Without Notice

Except as allowed under the shelter principle (discussed later in this chapter), a person cannot qualify as an HDC if he or she has notice that the instrument is defective in any of the following ways [UCC 3-302(a)(2)]:

- It is overdue
- It has been dishonored
- It contains an unauthorized signature or has been altered
- There is a claim to it by another person
- There is a defense against it

time instrument An instrument that specifies a definite date for payment of the instrument.

Overdue Instruments If a **time instrument** is not paid on its expressed due date, it becomes overdue the next day. The fact that an instrument has not been paid when due indicates that there is some defect to its payment.

CONSIDER THIS EXAMPLE: Suppose a promissory note is due June 15, 1998. To qualify as an HDC, a purchaser must acquire the note before midnight of June 15, 1998. A purchaser who acquires the note on June 16 or later is only a holder, but not an HDC.

Often, a debt is payable in installments or in a series of notes. If a maker misses an installment payment or fails to pay one note in a series of notes, the purchaser of the instrument is on notice that it is overdue [UCC 3-304(b)].

demand instrument An instrument payable on demand.

A **demand instrument** is payable on demand. A purchaser cannot be an HDC if the instrument is acquired either (1) after demand or (2) at an unreasonable length of time after its issue. A "reasonable time" for presenting a check for payment is presumed to be 90 days. Business practices and the circumstances of the case determine a reasonable time for the payment of other demand instruments [UCC 3-304(a)].

dishonored Occurs when an instrument has been presented for payment and payment has been refused.

Dishonored Instruments An instrument is **dishonored** when it is presented for payment and payment is refused. A holder who takes the instrument with notice of its dishonor cannot qualify as an HDC. For example, a person who takes a check that has been marked by the payor bank "payment refused—not sufficient funds" cannot qualify as an HDC.

red light doctrine A doctrine that says a holder cannot qualify as an HDC if he or she has notice of an unauthorized signature or an alteration of the instrument, or any adverse claim against or defense to its payment.

Red Light Doctrine A holder cannot qualify as an HDC if he or she has notice that the instrument contains an unauthorized signature or has been altered, or that there is any adverse claim against or defense to its payment. This is commonly referred to as the **red light doctrine**.

Notice of a defect is given when the holder has (1) actual knowledge of the defect, (2) received a notice or notification of the defect, or (3) reason to know from the facts and circumstances that the defect exists [UCC 1-201(25)]. The filing of a public notice does not of itself constitute notice unless the person actually reads the public notice [UCC 3-302(b)].

No Evidence of Forgery, Alteration, or Irregularity

A holder does not qualify as an HDC if at the time the instrument was issued or negotiated to the holder it bore apparent evidence of forgery or alteration or was otherwise so irregular or incomplete as to call into question its authenticity [UCC 3-302(a)(1)].

Clever and undetectable forgeries and alterations are not classified as obvious irregularities. Determining whether a forgery or alteration is apparent and whether the instrument is so irregular or incomplete that its authenticity should be questioned are issues of fact that must be decided on a case-by-case basis.

Payee as an HDC

Payees generally do not meet the requirements for being an HDC because they know about any claims or defenses against the instrument. However, in a few situations, a payee who does not have such knowledge would qualify as an HDC.

CONSIDER THIS EXAMPLE: Suppose Kate purchases an automobile from Jake for $5,000. Jake owes Sherry Smith $5,000 from another transaction. Jake has Kate make out the $5,000 check for the automobile "paying to the order of Sherry Smith." Jake gives the check to Sherry. The car Jake sold to Kate is defective, and she wants to rescind the purchase. Sherry (payee), who did not have notice of the defect in the car, is an HDC. As such, Sherry can enforce the check against Kate. Kate's only recourse is to recover from Jake.

"Bad money drives out good money."
Sir Thomas Gresham (1560)

BUSINESS CHECKLIST

Acquiring HDC Status Under the Shelter Principle

A holder who does qualify as a holder in due course in his or her own right becomes a holder in due course if he or she acquires the instrument through a holder in due course. This is called the **shelter principle**.

CONSIDER THIS EXAMPLE: Jason buys a used car from Debbie. He pays 10 percent down and signs a negotiable promissory note promising to pay Debbie the remainder of the purchase price with interest in 36 equal monthly installments. At the time of sale, Debbie materially misrepresented the mileage of the automobile. Later, Debbie negotiates the note to Eric, who has no notice of the misrepresentation. Eric, a holder in due course, negotiates the note to Jaime. Assume Jaime does not qualify as an HDC in her own right. However, she becomes an HDC because she acquired the note through an HDC (Eric). Jaime can enforce the note against Debbie.

To qualify as an HDC under the shelter principle, the following rules apply:

- The holder does not have to qualify as an HDC in his or her own right
- The holder must acquire the instrument from an HDC or be able to trace his or her title back to an HDC
- The holder must not have been a party to a fraud or illegality affecting the instrument
- The holder cannot have notice of a defense or claim against the payment of the instrument.

SIGNATURE LIABILITY OF PARTIES

signature liability
A person cannot be held contractually liable on a negotiable instrument unless his or her signature appears on the instrument. Also called *contract liability*.

A person cannot be held contractually liable on a negotiable instrument unless his or her signature appears on it [UCC 3-401(a)]. Therefore, this type of liability is often referred to as **signature liability** or **contract liability**. The signatures on a negotiable instrument identify those who are obligated to pay it. If it is unclear who the signer is, parol evidence can identify the signer. This liability does not attach to bearer paper because no indorsement is needed.

signer   A person signing an instrument who acts in the capacity of (1) a maker of notes and certificates of deposit, (2) a drawer of drafts and checks, (3) a drawee who certifies or accepts checks and drafts, (4) an indorser who indorses an instrument, (5) an agent who signs on behalf of others, or (6) an accommodation party.

Signers of instruments sign in many different capacities, including makers of notes and certificates of deposit, drawers of drafts and checks, drawees who certify or accept checks and drafts, indorsers who indorse an instrument, agents who sign on behalf of others, and accommodation parties. The location of the signature on the instrument generally determines the signer's capacity. For example, a signature in the lower right-hand corner of a check indicates that the signer is the drawer of the check, and a signature in the lower right-hand corner of a promissory note indicates the signer is the maker of the note. The signature of the drawee named in a draft on the face of the draft or other location on the draft indicates that the signer is an acceptor of the draft. Most indorsements appear on the back or reverse side of an instrument. Unless the instrument clearly indicates that such a signature is made in some other capacity, it is presumed to be that of the indorser.

Every party that signs a negotiable instrument (except qualified indorser and agents that properly sign the instrument) is either primarily or secondarily liable on the instrument. The following discussion outlines the particular liability of signers.

Signature Defined

signature   Any name, word, or mark used in lieu of a written signature; any symbol that is (1) handwritten, typed, printed, stamped, or made in almost any other manner and (2) executed or adopted by a party to authenticate a writing.

The **signature** on a negotiable instrument can be any name, word, or mark used in lieu of a written signature [UCC 3-401(b)]. In other words, a signature is any symbol that is (1) handwritten, typed, printed, stamped, or made in almost any other manner and (2) executed or adopted by a party to authenticate a writing [UCC 1-201(39)]. This rule permits trade names and other assumed names to be used as signatures on negotiable instruments.

The unauthorized signature of a person on an instrument is ineffective as that person's signature. It is effective as the signature of the unauthorized signer in favor of an HDC, however. For example, a person who forges a signature on a check may be held liable to an HDC. An unauthorized signature may be ratified [UCC 3-403(a)].

Agent's Signatures

agent   A person who has been authorized to sign a negotiable instrument on behalf of another person.

principal   A person who authorizes an agent to sign a negotiable instrument on his or her behalf.

A person may either sign a negotiable instrument him- or herself or authorize a representative to sign the instrument on his or her behalf [UCC 3-401(a)]. The representative is the **agent** and the represented person is the **principal**. The authority of an agent to sign an instrument is established under general agency law. No special form of appointment is necessary.

Authorized Signature   If an authorized agent signs an instrument by signing either the principal's name or the agent's own name, the principal is bound as if the signature was made on a simple contract. It does not matter whether the principal is identified in the instrument [UCC 3-402(2)].

Suppose Anderson was the agent for Puttkammer. The following signatures on a negotiable instrument would bind Puttkammer on the instrument:

1. Puttkammer, by Anderson, agents

2. Puttkammer

3. Puttkammer, Anderson

4. Anderson

An authorized agent's personal liability on an instrument he or she signs on behalf of a principal depends on the information disclosed in the signature. The agent has no liability if the signature shows unambiguously that it is made on behalf of a principal who is identified in the instrument [UCC 3-402(b)(1)]. Signature 1 ("Puttkammer, by Anderson, agent") satisfies this requirement.

If the unauthorized agent's signature does not show unambiguously that the signature was made in a representative capacity and the agent cannot prove the original parties did not intend him or her to be liable, the agent is liable (1) to an HDC who took the instrument without notice that the agent was not intended to be liable on the instrument and (2) to any other person other than an HDC [UCC 3-402(b)(2)]. Signature 2 ("Puttkammer") shows such a signature.

Signatures 3 ("Puttkammer, Anderson") and 4 ("Anderson") place the agent at risk of personal liability to an HDC that does not have notice that the agent was not intended to be liable on the instrument. To avoid liability to a non-HDC for these signatures, the agent would have to prove that the third-party non-HDC did not intend to hold the agent liable on the instrument.

There is one exception to these rules. If an agent signs his or her name as the drawer of a check without indicating the agent's representative status and the check is payable from the account of the principal who is identified on the check, the agent is not liable on the check [UCC 3-402(c)].

Unauthorized Signature

An **unauthorized signature** is a signature made by a purported agent without authority from the purported principal. Such a signature arises if (1) a person signs a negotiable instrument on behalf of a person for whom he or she is not an agent or (2) an authorized agent exceeds the scope of his or her authority. An unauthorized signature by a purported agent does not act as the signature of the purported principal. The purported agent is liable to any person who in good faith pays the instrument or takes it for value [UCC 3-403(a)].

The purported principal is liable if he or she ratifies the unauthorized signature [UCC 3-403(a)].

CONSIDER THIS EXAMPLE: A purported agent signs a contract and promissory note to purchase a building for a purported principal. Suppose that the purported principal likes the deal and accepts it. He has ratified the transaction and is liable on the note.

Primary Liability

Makers of promissory notes and certificates of deposit have **primary liability** for the instrument. Upon signing a promissory note, the maker unconditionally promises to pay the amount stipulated in the note when it is due. Makers are absolutely liable to pay the instrument, subject only to certain real defenses. The holder need not take any action to give rise to this obligation. Generally, the maker is obligated to pay the note according to its original terms. If the note was incomplete when it was issued, the maker is obligated to pay the note as completed as long as he or she authorized the terms as they were filled in [UCC 3-412].

A draft or a check is an order from a drawer to a drawee to pay the instrument to a payee (or other holder) according to its terms. No party is primarily liable when the draft or check is issued because such instruments are merely an order to pay. Thus, a drawee who refuses to pay a draft or a check is not liable to the payee or holder. If there has been a wrongful dishonor of the instrument, the drawee may be liable to the drawer for certain damages.

On occasion, a drawee is requested to accept a draft or check. Acceptance of a draft occurs when the drawee writes the word *accepted* across the face of the draft. The acceptor—that is, the drawee—is primarily liable on the instrument. A check,

CAUTION
To avoid personal liability on a negotiable instrument, the agent should properly sign the instrument to indicate his or her agency status and the identity of the principal.

unauthorized signature A signature made by a purported agent without authority from the purported principal.

CAUTION
The unauthorized signature of a person on a negotiable instrument is ineffective as that person's signature unless he or she ratifies the unauthorized signature.

primary liability Absolute liability to pay a negotiable instrument, subject to certain real defenses.

BUSINESS BRIEF
The following parties are primarily liable *on negotiable instruments:*
1. *Makers* of promissory notes and certificates of deposit and
2. *Acceptors* of drafts and checks.

which is a special form of draft, is accepted when it is certified by a bank. The bank's certification discharges the drawer and all prior indorsers from liability on the check. Note that the bank may choose to refuse to certify the check without liability. The issuer of a cashier's check also is primarily liable on the instrument [UCC 3-411].

In the following case, the court held that a comaker was primarily liable on a promissory note.

CASE 17.1

Grand Island Production Credit Assn.
v. Humphrey
388 N.W.2d 807 (1986) Supreme Court of Nebraska

Facts The Grand Island Production Credit Association (Grand Island) is a federally chartered credit union. On November 25, 1980, Carl M. and Beulah C. Humphrey, husband and wife, entered into a loan agreement with Grand Island for a $50,000 line of credit. Mr. and Mrs. Humphrey signed a line of credit promissory note that provided in part: "As long as the Borrower is not in default, the Association will lend to the Borrower, and the Borrower may borrow and repay and reborrow at any time from date of said "Line of Credit" Promissory Note in accordance with the terms thereof and prior to maturity thereof, up to an aggregate maximum amount of principal at any one time outstanding of $50,000."

Mr. Humphrey borrowed money against the line of credit to purchase cattle. In January 1981, Mrs. Humphrey went to Grand Island's office and told the loan officer that she had left Mr. Humphrey and filed for a divorce. She told the loan officer not to advance any more money to Mr. Humphrey for cattle purchases. When the Humphreys failed to pay the outstanding balance on the line of credit, Grand Island sued Mr. and Mrs. Humphrey to recover the unpaid balance of $13,936.71. A default judgment was entered against Mr. Humphrey. The district court held Mrs. Humphrey not liable for the full outstanding balance. Grand Island appealed.

Issue Was Mrs. Humphrey a co-maker of the line of credit promissory note, and therefore primarily liable for the outstanding principal balance of the note, plus interest?

Decision Yes. The state supreme court held that Mrs. Humphrey was a comaker on the line of credit

promissory note and was therefore primarily liable to Grand Island in the amount of $13,936.71, plus interest. Reversed.

Reason The court stated, "Under the provisions of the Nebraska UCC, the maker of a note engages that he or she will pay the instrument according to its tenor at the time of his or her engagement." Mrs. Humphrey admits that she signed the promissory note and the supplemental agreement. Consequently, as a comaker of the note, she is jointly and severally liable for the obligations of the note. If Mrs. Humphrey was to be relieved of this obligation, it was a matter that she needed to arrange and take up with her husband in the divorce action. No such arrangement could, however, be binding upon Grand Island, which entered into this transactions in reliance upon the promise of both Mr. Humphrey and Mrs. Humphrey that they would be liable and would pay the amounts so advanced.

CASE QUESTIONS

Critical Legal Thinking Should family problems, such as the separation and divorce action in this case, take precedent over the commercial law rules of the UCC? Why or why not?

Ethics Was it ethical for Mrs. Humphrey to deny liability on the promissory note in this case?

Business Implication What would have been the economic effects if the district court's decision had been upheld in this case?

Secondary Liability

Drawers of checks and drafts and unqualified indorsers of negotiable instruments have **secondary liability** on the instrument. This liability is similar to that of a guarantor of a simple contract. It arises when the party primarily liable on the instrument defaults and fails to pay the instrument when due.

If an unaccepted draft or check is dishonored by the drawee or acceptor, the drawer is obliged to pay it according to its terms either when it is issued or, if incomplete when issued, as properly completed [UCC 3-414(a)].

CONSIDER THIS EXAMPLE: Elliot draws a check on City Bank "payable to the order of Phyllis Jones." When Phyllis presents the check for payment, City Bank refuses to pay it. Phyllis can collect the amount of the check from Elliot. This is because Elliot—the drawer—is secondarily liable on the check when it is dishonored.

Unqualified indorsers have secondary liability on negotiable instruments. In other words, they must pay any dishonored instrument to the holder or to any subsequent indorser according to its terms, when issued or properly completed. Unless otherwise agreed, indorsers are liable to each other in the order in which they indorsed the instrument [UCC 3-415(a)].

CONSIDER THIS EXAMPLE: Dara borrows $10,000 from Todd and signs a promissory note promising to pay Todd this amount plus interest in one year. Todd indorses the note and negotiates it to Frank. Frank indorses the note and negotiates it to Linda. Dara refuses to pay the note when it is presented for payment by Linda. Because Frank became secondarily liable on the note when he indorsed it to Linda, he must pay the note to her. He can then require Todd to pay the note because Todd (as payee) became secondarily liable on the note when he indorsed it to Frank. Todd can then enforce the note against Dara. Linda could have skipped over Frank and required the payee, Todd, to pay the note. In this instance Frank would have been relieved of any further liability because he indorsed the instrument after the payee.

Qualified indorsers (i.e., indorsers who indorse instruments "without recourse" or similar language that disclaims liability) are not secondarily liable on the instrument. This is because they have expressly disclaimed liability [UCC 3-415(b)]. The drawer can disclaim all liability on a draft (but not a check) by drawing the instrument "without recourse." In this instance, the drawer becomes a qualified drawer [UCC 3-414(e)]. However, many payees will not accept a draft or check that has been drawn without recourse.

Requirements for Imposing Secondary Liability

Parties are secondarily liable on a negotiable instrument only if the following requirements are met:

1. *The instrument is properly presented for payment.* **Presentment** is a demand for acceptance or payment of an instrument made upon the maker, acceptor, drawee, or other payor by or on behalf of the holder. Presentment may be made by any commercially reasonable means, including oral, written, or electronic communication. Presentment is effective when it is received by the person to whom presentment is made [UCC 3-501].
2. *The instrument is dishonored.* An instrument is **dishonored** when acceptance or payment of the instrument is refused or cannot be obtained from the party required to accept or pay the instrument within the prescribed time after presentment is duly made [UCC 3-502].
3. *Notice of the dishonor is timely given to the person to be held secondarily liable on the instrument.* A secondarily liable party cannot be compelled to accept or pay the instrument unless proper **notice of dishonor** has been given. Notice may be given by any commercially reasonable means. The notice must reasonably identify the

---

secondary liability
Liability on a negotiable instrument that is imposed on a party only when the party primarily liable on the instrument defaults and fails to pay the instrument when due.

indorsers' liability
Unqualified indorsers are secondarily liable on negotiable instruments they indorse; *qualified indorsers* disclaim liability and are not secondarily liable on instruments they indorse.

BUSINESS BRIEF
The following parties are secondarily liable *on negotiable instruments: (1)* drawers *on unaccepted drafts and checks and (2)* unqualified indorsers.

presentment A demand for acceptance or payment of an instrument made upon the maker, acceptor, drawee, or other payor by or on behalf of the holder.

notice of dishonor The formal act of letting the party with secondary liability to pay a negotiable instrument know that the instrument has been dishonored.

instrument and indicate that it has been dishonored. Return of an instrument given to a bank for collection is sufficient notice of dishonor. Banks must give notice of dishonor before midnight of the next banking day following the day that presentment is made. Others must give notice of dishonor within 30 days of the following the day on which the person receives notice of dishonor [UCC 3-503].

In the following case, the court held that an indorser was not secondarily liable on a check because he had not received proper notice of dishonor.

CASE 17.2

Clements v. Central Bank of Georgia
29 U.C.C. Rep.Serv. 1536 (1980) Court of Appeals of Georgia

Facts On September 19, 1978, Mr. Ridley drew a check on a Tennessee bank made payable to the order of Mr. Clements. On September 25, 1978, Clements indorsed the check and negotiated it to Continental Equity Corporation (Continental). Continental indorsed the check and deposited it in the Central Bank of Georgia (Central Bank) for collection. Central Bank sent the check to the Tennessee bank for payment. On September 29, 1978, the branch manager of the Tennessee bank informed Central Bank by telephone that Ridley's check was "no good" because of insufficient funds. Central Bank authorized the Tennessee bank to hold the check. During October, Central Bank made several unsuccessful attempts to collect the check from Ridley. On October 21, 1978, Central Bank requested the Tennessee bank to return the check. On November 3, Central Bank received the check, and on that date it sent written notice to Clements that Ridley's check has been dishonored. Central Bank sued Clements (the indorser) to recover on the check. The court granted summary judgment to Central Bank. Clements appealed.

Issue Did the Central Bank of Georgia give timely notice of dishonor of the check to Clements, the indorser, in order to hold Clements secondarily liable on Ridley's check?

Decision No. The court of appeals held that Central Bank did not give timely notice to the indorser,

Clements. Therefore, he is not secondarily liable on the check he indorsed. Reversed.

Reason Every indorser engages that upon dishonor and any necessary notice of dishonor and protest he or she will pay the instrument according to its tenor at the time of his or her indorsement to the holder. Unless excused, notice of any dishonor is necessary to charge any indorser. The notice of dishonor to the indorser, Clements, on November 3 came too late as a matter of law. The delay in notice of dishonor to the indorser was not due to circumstances beyond Central Bank's control, but was due simply to the bank's failure to give it when the bank itself had notice of the dishonor and was under obligation to take action.

CASE QUESTIONS

Critical Legal Thinking Should indorsers be held secondarily liable on a negotiable instrument that is drawn or made by another party? Why or why not?

Ethics Was it ethical for Central Bank to try to hold the indorser Clements liable on the check?

Business Implication Who bore the loss of the uncollected check in this case?

Accommodation Party

accommodation party
A party who signs an instrument and lends his or her name (and credit) to another party to the instrument.

The party who signs the instrument for the purpose of lending his or her name (and credit) to another party to that instrument is the **accommodation party**. The accommodation party, who may sign the instrument as maker, drawer, acceptor, or indorser, is obliged to pay the instrument in the capacity in which he or she signs [UCC 3-419(a) and (b)]. An accommodation party who pays an instrument can recover reimbursement from the accommodated party and enforce the instrument against him or her [UCC 3-419(e)].

Guarantee of Payment The accommodation party may sign an instrument guaranteeing either payment or collection. An accommodation party who signs an instrument **guaranteeing payment** is primarily liable on the instrument. That is, the debtor can seek payment on the instrument directly from the accommodation maker without first seeking payment from the maker.

guaranteeing payment
A form of accommodation in which the accommodating party guarantees *payment* of a negotiable instrument; the accommodation party is *primarily liable* on the instrument.

CONSIDER THIS EXAMPLE: Sonny, a college student, wants to purchase an automobile on credit from ABC Motors. He does not have sufficient income or credit history to justify the extension of credit to him alone. Sonny asks his mother to cosign the note to ABC Motors, which she does. Mother is an accommodation party and is primarily liable on the note.

Guarantee of Collection An accommodation party may sign an instrument **guaranteeing collection** rather than payment of an instrument. In this situation, the accommodation party is only secondarily liable on the instrument. To reserve this type of liability, the signature of the accommodation party must be accompanied by words indicating that he or she is guaranteeing collection rather than payment of the obligation.

guaranteeing collection
A form of accommodation in which the accommodating party guarantees *collection* of a negotiable instrument; the accommodation party is *secondarily liable* on the instrument.

An accommodation party that guarantees collection is obligated to pay the instrument only if (1) execution of judgment against the other party has been returned unsatisfied, (2) the other pary is insolvent or in an insolvency proceeding, (3) the other party cannot be served with process, or (4) it is otherwise apparent that payment cannot be obtained from the other party [UCC 3-419(d)].

ETHICAL PERSPECTIVE

Why Be So Accommodating?

An accommodating party is one who signs a negotiable instrument in any capacity for the purpose of lending his or her name to it. The accommodating party does not have to receive any consideration for signing the instrument and may be bound to pay it even though the accommodating was made gratuitously [UCC 3-419(b)]. Consider the following case.

Michael and Marilu Burke were married in September 1971. Shortly after the marriage, Michael formed a partnership with his cousin to operate an automobile dealership. In 1973, Michael decided to buy his cousin out of the dealership. Michael's father agreed to loan Michael

$25,000 for this purpose. However, Michael's father refused to make the loan unless Marilu cosigned the promissory note. Michael's father prepared the promissory note for $25,000, plus interest, and took the note to the home of Michael and Marilu, where they both signed it. Michael's father paid Michael a $25,000 check. The check was payable to Michael Burke only. Marilu did not receive any of the proceeds herself. Sometime after the note was executed, Michael and Marilu separated. Michael defaulted on the note. Michael's father sued Marilu to recover the amount of the loan. Marilu tried to avoid liability by asserting that

the note was unenforceable against her because she received no consideration for signing it.

The trial and appellate courts held that Marilu was an accommodation party and was therefore liable on Michael's note to his father. Marilu was required to pay Michael's father $31,167. The appellate court held that separate consideration is not required to establish primary liability as an accommodation maker. The court stated, "As is true with suretyship in general, the accommodating party is bound by the consideration moving to the primary obligator and the obligation of the accommodation maker need not be

continued

supported by separate or additional consideration." [*Burke v. Burke*, 412 N.E.2d 204 (Ill. App. 1980)]

1. Did Michael Burke act ethically in this case? Did Michael's father act ethically in this case? Did Marilu Burke act ethically in denying liability on the note?
2. Why do you think Michael's father sued Marilu in this case?

WARRANTY LIABILITY OF PARTIES

implied warranties
The law *implies* certain warranties on transferors of negotiable instruments. There are two types of implied warranties: transfer and presentment.

In addition to signature liability, transferors can be held liable for breaching certain **implied warranties** when negotiating instruments. Warranty liability is imposed whether or not the transferor signed the instrument. Note that transferors make implied warranties; they are not made when the negotiable instrument is originally issued.

There are two types of implied warranties: transfer warranties and presentment warranties. Transfer and presentment warranties shift the risk of loss to the party who was in the best position to prevent the loss. This is usually the party who dealt face to face with the wrongdoer. Both of these implied warranties are discussed in the sections that follow.

Transfer Warranties

transfer Any passage of an instrument other than its issuance and presentment for payment.

Any passage of an instrument other than its issuance and presentment for payment is considered a **transfer**. Any person who transfers a negotiable instrument for consideration makes the following five warranties to the transferee. If the transfer is by indorsement, the transferor also makes these warranties to any subsequent transferee [UCC 3-416(a):].

transfer warranties Any of the following five implied warranties:
1. The transferor has good title to the instrument or is authorized to obtain payment or acceptance on behalf of one who does have good title
2. All signatures are genuine or authorized
3. The instrument has not been materially altered
4. No defenses of any party are good against the transferor; and
5. The transferor has no knowledge of any insolvency proceeding against the maker, or acceptor, or the drawer of an unaccepted instrument.

1. The transferor has good title to the instrument or is authorized to obtain payment or acceptance on behalf of one who does have good title
2. All signatures are genuine or authorized
3. The instrument has not been materially altered
4. No defenses of any party are good against the transferor
5. The transferor has no knowledge of any insolvency proceeding against the maker, the acceptor, or the drawer of an unaccepted instrument.

Transfer warranties cannot be disclaimed with respect to checks, but they can be disclaimed with respect to other instruments. An indorsement that states "without recourse" disclaims the transfer warranties [UCC 3-416(c)].

A transferee who took the instrument in good faith may recover damages for breach of transfer warranty from the warrantor equal to the loss suffered. The amount recovered cannot exceed the amount of the instrument plus expenses and interest [UCC 3-416(b)].

CONSIDER THIS EXAMPLE: Jill issues a $1,000 note to Adam. Adam cleverly raises the note to $10,000 and negotiates the note to Nick. Nick indorses the note and negotiates it to Matthew. When Matthew presents the note to Jill for payment, she has to pay only the original amount of the note—$1,000. Matthew can collect the remainder of the note ($9,000) from Nick based on a breach of the transfer warranty. If Nick is lucky, he can recover the $9,000 from Adam.

Presentment Warranties

Any person who presents a draft or check for payment or acceptance makes the following warranties to a drawee or acceptor who pays or accepts the instrument in good faith [UCC 3-417(a)]:

1. The presenter has good title to the instrument or is authorized to obtain payment or acceptance of the person who has good title
2. The instrument has not been materially altered
3. The presenter has no knowledge that the signature of the maker or drawer is unauthorized.

A drawee who pays an instrument may recover damages for breach of **presentment warranty** from the warrantor. The amount that can be recovered is limited to the amount paid by the drawee less the amount the drawee received or is entitled to receive from the drawer because of the payment, plus expenses and interest [UCC 3-417(b)].

CONSIDER THIS EXAMPLE: Suppose Maureen draws a $1,000 check on City Bank "payable to the order of Paul." Paul cleverly raises the check to $10,000 and indorses and negotiates the check to Neal. Neal presents the check for payment to City Bank. As the presenter of the check, Neal makes the presentment warranties of UCC 3-417(1) to City Bank. City Bank pays the check as altered ($10,000) and debits Maureen's account. When Maureen discovers the alteration, she demands that the bank recredit her account, which the bank does. City Bank can recover against the presenter (Neal) based on breach of the presentment warranty that the instrument was not altered when it was presented. Neal can recover against the wrongdoer (Paul) based on breach of the transfer warranty that the instrument was not altered.

presentment warranties Any person who presents a draft or check for payment or acceptance makes the following three warranties to a drawee or acceptor who pays or accepts the instrument in good faith:
1. The presentor has good title to the instrument or is authorized to obtain payment or acceptance of the person who has good title
2. The instrument has not been materially altered; and
3. the presenter has no knowledge that the signature of the maker or drawer is unauthorized.

DEFENSES

The creation of negotiable instruments can give rise to a defense against its payment. Many of these defenses arise from the underlying transaction. There are two general types of defenses: real defense and personal defenses. A **holder in due course** (or a holder through an HDC) takes the instrument free from personal defenses but not real defenses. Personal and real defenses can be raised against a normal holder of a negotiable instrument. Both of these types of defenses are discussed in the sections that follow.

holder in due course (HDC) A holder of a negotiable instrument who takes an instrument free of all claims and most defenses that can be asserted by other parties.

Real Defenses

Real (or universal) defenses can be raised against both holders and HDCs [UCC 3-305(b)]. If a real defense is proven, the holder or HDC cannot recover on the instrument. Real defenses are discussed in the following subsections.

real defense A defense that can be raised against both holders and HDCs.

Minority Infancy, or **minority**, is a real defense to a negotiable instrument to the extent that it is a defense to a simple contract [UCC 3-305(a)(1)(i)]. In most states, a minor who does not misrepresent his or her age can disaffirm contracts, including negotiable instruments. Usually, minors must pay the reasonable value for necessities of life.

Extreme Duress Ordinary duress is a personal defense (discussed later in this chapter). **Extreme duress** is a real defense against the enforcement of a negotiable instrument by a holder or an HDC [UCC 3-305(a)(1)(ii)]. Extreme duress usually requires some form of force or violence (e.g., a promissory note signed at gunpoint).

extreme duress Extreme duress, but not ordinary duress, is a real defense against enforcement of a negotiable instrument.

Mental Incapacity Adjudicated mental incompetence is a real defense that can be raised against holders and HDCs [UCC 3-305(a)(1)(ii)]. Such a person cannot issue a negotiable instrument; the instrument is void from its inception. Nonadjudicated mental incompetence, which usually is only a personal defense, is discussed later.

Illegality If an instrument arises out of an illegal transaction, the illegality is a real defense if the law declares the instrument void [UCC 3-305(a)(1)(ii)].

CONSIDER THIS EXAMPLE: Assume that a state's law declares gambling to be illegal and gambling contracts to be void. Gordon wins $1,000 from Jerry in an illegal poker game. He signs a promissory note promising to pay Gordon this amount plus interest in 30 days. Gordon negotiates this note to Dawn, an HDC. When Dawn presents the note to Jerry for payment, Jerry can raise the real defense of illegality against the enforcement of the note. Dawn's recourse is against Gordon.

If the law makes an illegal contract voidable instead of void, it is only a personal defense. This is discussed later in this chapter.

discharge in bankruptcy
A real defense against the enforcement of a negotiable instrument; bankruptcy law is intended to relieve debtors of burdensome debts, including negotiable instruments.

Discharge in Bankruptcy Bankruptcy law is intended to relieve debtors of burdensome debts, including obligations to pay negotiable instruments. Thus, **discharge in bankruptcy** is a real defense against the enforcement of a negotiable instrument by a holder or an HDC [UCC 3-305(a)(1)(iv)].

CONSIDER THIS EXAMPLE: Hunt borrows $10,000 from Amy and signs a note promising to pay Amy this amount plus interest in one year. Amy negotiates the note to Richard, an HDC. Before the note is due, Hunt declares bankruptcy and receives a discharge of his unpaid debts. Richard cannot thereafter enforce the note against Hunt, but he can recover against Amy.

fraud in the inception
A real defense against the enforcement of a negotiable instrument; a person has been deceived into signing a negotiable instrument thinking that it is something else.

Fraud in the Inception Fraud in the inception (also called **fraud in the factum** or **fraud in the execution**) is a real defense against the enforcement of a negotiable instrument by a holder or an HDC [UCC 3-305(a)(1)(iii)]. It occurs when a person is deceived into signing a negotiable instrument thinking that it is something else.

CONSIDER THIS EXAMPLE: Suppose Sam, a door-to-door salesman, convinces Lance, an illiterate consumer, to sign a document purported to be an agreement to use a set of books on a 90-day trial basis. In actuality, the document is a promissory note in which Lance has agreed to pay $1,000 for the books. Sam negotiates the note to Stephanie, an HDC. Lance can raise the real defense of fraud in the inception against the enforcement of the note by Stephanie. Stephanie, in turn, can recover from Sam.

CAUTION
Distinguishing between fraud in the inception *(real defense) and* fraud in the inducement *(personal defense) can be difficult.*

A person is under a duty to use reasonable efforts to ascertain what he or she is signing. The court inquires into a person's age, experience, education, and other factors before allowing fraud in the inception to be asserted as a real defense to defeat an HDC. Fraud in the inducement (discussed later) in only a personal defense.

forgery A real defense against the enforcement of a negotiable instrument; the unauthorized signature of a maker, drawer, or indorser.

Forgery Another real defense to the payment of a negotiable instrument is **forgery**. The unauthorized signature of a maker, drawer, or indorser is wholly inoperative as that of the person whose name is signed unless that person either ratifies it or is precluded from denying it. In the latter case, a person can be stopped from raising the defense of forgery if his or her negligence substantially contributes to the forgery. A forged signature operates as the signature of the forger. Thus, the forger is liable on the instrument [UCC 3-403(a)].

Material Alteration An instrument that has been fraudulently and **materially altered** cannot be enforced by an ordinary holder. Material alteration consists of adding to any part of a signed instrument, removing any part of a signed instrument, making changes in the number or relations of the parties, or the unauthorized completion of an incomplete instrument.

Under the UCC rule that words control figures, correcting the figure on a check to correspond to the written amount on the check is not a material alteration [UCC 3-118(c)]. If an alteration is not material, the instrument can be enforced by any holder in the original amount for which the drawer wrote the check [UCC 3-407(b)].

Material alteration of a negotiable instrument is only a partial defense against an HDC. Subsequent holders in due course can enforce any instrument, including an altered instrument, according to its original terms if the alteration is not apparent. An obvious change puts the holder on notice of the alteration and disqualifies him or her as an HDC [UCC 3-407(c)].

material alteration
A partial defense against enforcement of a negotiable instrument by an HDC. An HDC can enforce an altered instrument in the original amount for which the drawer wrote the check.

Personal Defenses

Although **personal defenses** cannot be raised against an HDC, they can be raised against enforcement of a negotiable instrument by an ordinary holder. Personal defenses are discussed in the subsections that follow.

personal defense
A defense that can be raised against enforcement of a negotiable instrument by an ordinary holder but not against an HDC.

CAUTION
Personal defenses cannot be raised against an HDC.

Breach of Contract Breach of contract is one of the most common defenses raised by a party to a negotiable instrument. This is a personal defense that is effective only against an ordinary holder.

CONSIDER THIS EXAMPLE: When Brian purchases a used car on credit from Karen, he signs a note promising to pay Karen the $10,000 purchase price plus interest in 36 equal monthly installments. The sales agreement warrants that the car is in perfect working condition. A month later the car's engine fails; the cost of repair is $3,000. Brian, the maker of the note, can raise breach of warranty as a defense against enforcement of the note by Karen.

The outcome would be different if Karen negotiated the promissory note to Max (an HDC) immediately after the car was sold to Brian. Max would be an HDC and Brian could not raise the breach of warranty defense against him. Max could enforce the note against Brian. Brian's only recourse would be to seek recovery for breach of warranty from Karen.

CAUTION
Breach of the underlying contract cannot be raised as a defense against enforcement of a negotiable instrument by an HDC.

Fraud in the Inducement **Fraud in the inducement** occurs when a wrongdoer makes a false statement (i.e., a misrepresentation) to another person to lead that person to enter into a contract with the wrongdoer. Negotiable instruments often arise out of such transactions. Fraud in the inducement is a personal defense that is not effective against HDCs. It is effective against ordinary holders, however.

CONSIDER THIS EXAMPLE: Morton represents to investors that he will accept funds to drill for oil and that the investors will share in the profits from the oil wells. However, he plans to use these funds himself. Relying on Morton's statements, Mimi draws a $50,000 check payable to him. Morton absconds with the funds. Because Morton is an ordinary holder, Mimi can raise the personal defense of fraud in the inducement and, if she stops payment on the check before Morton receives payment, not pay the check.

If Morton had negotiated the check to Tim, an HDC, Tim could enforce the check against Mimi. Because personal defenses are not effective against Tim (an HDC), Mimi's only recourse is to recover against the wrongdoer (Morton) if he can be found.

fraud in the inducement
A personal defense against the enforcement of a negotiable instrument; a wrongdoer makes a false statement to another person to lead that person to enter into a contract with the wrongdoer.

Other Personal Defenses The following personal defenses can be raised against enforcement of a negotiable instrument by an ordinary holder:

1. Mental illness that makes a contract voidable instead of void (usually a nonadjudicated mental illness)
2. Illegality of a contract that makes the contract voidable instead of void
3. Ordinary duress or undue influence [UCC 3-305(a)(1)(ii)]
4. Discharge of an instrument by payment or cancellation [UCC 3-602 and 3-604].

In the following case, the court had to decide whether an asserted defense was real or personal.

CASE 17.3

Kedzie & 103rd Currency Exchange, Inc. v. Hodge

601 N.E.2d 803 (1992) Appellate Court of Illinois

Facts Beula M. Hodge hired Fred Fentress to perform plumbing services and paid him a check in partial advance payment for the services to be rendered. Fentress cashed the check at Kedzie & 103rd Currency Exchange, Inc. (Exchange). Before the check was presented for payment, Hodge notified her bank to stop payment on the check because Fentress did not appear at her home to begin work, and she discovered that he was not a licensed plumber as required by law. The Exchange, as holder in due course, sued Hodge to recover the amount of the check. Hodge asserted the defense of illegality against the payment of the check. The trial court agreed with Hodge and dismissed the complaint. The Exchange appealed.

Issue Was the fact that Fentress was not a licensed plumber a real defense that could be validly asserted against the Exchange, an HDC?

Decision Yes. The appellate court held that the fact that Fentress did not have a plumber's license was an illegality and therefore a real defense to the enforcement of the check by the Exchange. Affirmed.

Reason Under the UCC, a holder in due course takes a negotiable instrument free of all defenses except real defenses. One real defense that may be asserted against an HDC is illegality. The appellate court held that the disputed contract was an illegal contract because Fentress did not have the required license to perform plumbing services as required by law. Therefore, the contract was null and void. Hodge could validly assert this real defense against the Exchange's attempt to enforce the check against her.

CASE QUESTIONS

Critical Legal Thinking Should any defenses be allowed to be asserted against an HDC? Explain.

Ethics Did Hodge act unethically in stopping payment on the check?

Business Implication Could the Exchange have done anything differently to protect itself against loss in this type of situation?

CONTEMPORARY BUSINESS ENVIRONMENT

The FTC Eliminates HDC Status with Respect to Consumer Credit Transactions

In certain situations, the HDC rule can cause a hardship for the consumer. To illustrate, Greg, a consumer, purchases a stereo on credit from Lou's Stereo. He signs a note promising to pay the purchase price plus interest to Lou's Stereo in 12 equal monthly installments. Lou's Stereo immediately negotiates the note at a discount to City Bank for cash. City Bank is an HDC. The stereo is defective.

Greg would like to stop payment on it, but the HDC rule prevents him from asserting any personal defenses against City Bank. Under the UCC, Greg's only recourse is to sue Lou's Stereo. However, this is often an unsatisfactory result because Greg has no leverage against Lou's Stereo, and bringing a court action is expensive and time-consuming.

To correct this harsh result, the Federal Trade Commission (FTC) has adopted a rule that eliminates HDC status with regard to negotiable instruments arising out of certain *consumer* credit transactions [16 C.F.R. §433.2 (1987)]. This federal law takes precedence over state UCCs.

The rule equates the HDC of a consumer credit contract with the assignee of a simple contract. Thus, sellers of goods and services are prevented from separating the consumer's duty to pay the credit and the seller's duty to perform. This subjects the HDC of a consumer credit instrument to *all* of the defenses and claims of the consumer. In the prior example, Greg can raise the defect in the stereo as a defense against enforcement of the promissory note by City Bank, an HDC.

The FTC rule applies to consumer credit transactions in which (1) the buyer signs a sales contract that includes a promissory note, (2) the buyer signs an installment sales contract that contains a waiver of defense clause, and (3) the seller arranges consumer financing with a third-party lender. Note that payment for goods and services with a check is not covered by this rule because it is not a credit transaction.

The FTC rule requires that the following clause be included in bold type in covered consumer credit sales and installment contracts:

NOTICE: ANY HOLDER OF THIS CONSUMER CREDIT CONTRACT IS SUBJECT TO ALL CLAIMS AND DEFENSES WHICH THE DEBTOR COULD ASSERT AGAINST THE SELLER OF THE GOODS OR SERVICES OBTAINED PURSUANT HERETO OR WITH THE PROCEEDS HEREOF. RECOVERY HEREUNDER BY THE DEBTOR SHALL NOT EXCEED AMOUNTS PAID BY THE DEBTOR HEREUNDER.

A consumer creditor may assert the FTC rule to prevent enforcement of a note that arose from a covered transaction. The FTC can impose a fine of $10,000 for each violation.

DISCHARGE

The UCC specifies when and how certain parties are **discharged** (relieved) from liability on negotiable instruments. Generally, all parties to a negotiable instrument are discharged from liability if (1) the party primarily liable on the instrument pays it in full to the holder of the instrument or (2) a drawee in good faith pays an unaccepted draft or check in full to the holder. When a party other than a primary obligor (e.g., an indorser) pays a negotiable instrument, that party and all subsequent parties to the instrument are discharged from liability [UCC 3-602].

The holder of a negotiable instrument can discharge the liability of any party to the instrument by *cancellation* [UCC 3-604]. Cancellation can be accomplished by (1) any manner apparent on the face of the instrument or the indorsement (e.g., writing "canceled" on the instrument) or (2) destroying or mutilating a negotiable instrument with the intent of eliminating the obligation.

Intentionally striking out the signature of an indorser cancels that party's liability on the instrument and the liability of all subsequent indorsers. Prior indorsers are not discharged from liability. The instrument is not canceled if it is destroyed or mutilated by accident or by an unauthorized third party. The holder can bring suit to enforce the destroyed or mutilated instrument.

A party to a negotiable instrument sometimes posts collateral as security for the payment of the obligation. Other parties (e.g., holders, indorsers, accommodation parties) look to the credit standing of the party primarily liable on the instrument, the collateral (if any) that is posted, and the liability of secondary parties for the payment of the instrument when it is due. A holder owes a duty not to impair the rights of others when seeking recourse against the liable parties or the collateral. Thus, a holder who either (1) releases an obligor from liability or (2) surrenders the collateral without the consent of the parties who would benefit thereby discharges those parties from their obligation on the instrument [UCC 3-605(e)]. This is called **impairment of the right of recourse**.

discharge Actions or events that relieve certain parties from liability on negotiable instruments. There are three methods of discharge: (1) payment of the instrument, (2) cancellation, and (3) impairment of the right of recourse.

impairment of right of recourse Certain parties (holders, indorsers, accommodation parties) are discharged from liability on an instrument if the holder
1. Releases an obligor from liability or
2. Surrenders collateral without the consent of the parties who would benefit by it.

WORKING THE WEB

Doing Business Guides A group of law firms called Lex Mundi has written guides to doing business in many jurisdictions. Some are even available on audio if you have the right computer equipment.

Visit at http://www.hg.org/guides.html

American Bar Association, Business Law Section Find out all about the Business Law Section of the ABA by visiting its Web site.

Visit at http://www.abanmet.org/buslaw/home.html

World Wide Legal Information Association Find out all about law in the United States, Canada, Australia, New Zealand, and the United Kingdom. There is a dictionary and other features as well.

Visit at http://www.wwlia.org/wwlia.htm

US Federal Trade Commission The U.S. Federal Trade Commission has a Web site full of trade information.

Visit at http://www.ftc.gov

United States International Trade Commission This quasi-judicial agency provides objective trade expertise to both the legislative and executive branches of government, determines the impact of imports on U.S. agencies, and directs actions against unfair trade practices.

Visit at http://www.usitc.gov/

CYBER EXERCISES:

1. Is there a Doing Business Guide for Sweden?
2. From the ABA Business Law Section Web site, navigate to the Women's Business Law Network. Find out about its mentor program.
3. Who is the Webmaster of the World Wide Legal Information Association?
4. Using the U.S. Federal Trade Commission site, find the regional office closest to you.
5. Using the U.S. International Trade Commission Web site, find U.S. trade statistics.

CHAPTER SUMMARY

HOLDER VERSUS HOLDER IN DUE COURSE, P. 388

Holder versus Holder in Due Course	1. *Holder.* A person who is in possession of a negotiable instrument that is drawn, issued, or indorsed to him or his order, or to bearer, or in blank. a. *Rights of a holder.* A holder has the same rights as the assignee of an ordinary contract. A holder is subject to all claims and defenses that can be asserted against the transferor. 2. *Holder in due course (HDC).* A holder who takes a negotiable instrument for value, in good faith, and without notice that it is defective or is overdue. a. *Rights of an HDC.* An HDC takes a negotiable instrument free of all claims and most defenses that can be asserted against the transferor. Thus, an HDC can acquire greater rights than those of the transferor.

REQUIREMENTS FOR HDC STATUS, P. 389

Requirements for HDC Status	To qualify as an HDC, the transferee must meet the following requirements: 1. Be a holder 2. Take the negotiable instrument for value 3. Take the instrument in good faith 4. Take the instrument without notice that it is overdue, dishonored, or encumbered in any way 5. In addition, the instrument must bear no apparent evidence of forgery, alteration, or irregularity

Taking for Value	Value has been given for a negotiable instrument if the holder:
	1. Performs the agreed-upon promise
	2. Acquires a security interest or lien on the instrument
	3. Takes the instrument in payment of or as security for an antecedent claim
	4. Gives a negotiable instrument as payment
	5. Gives an irrevocable obligation as payment.
Taking in Good Faith	A holder must take the instrument in good faith to qualify as an HDC. Good faith means honesty in fact in the conduct or transaction. It is the holder's subjective belief that can be inferred from the circumstances.
Taking Without Notice	A person cannot qualify as an HDC if he or she has notice that the instrument is defective in any of the following ways:
	1. It is overdue
	2. It has been dishonored
	3. It contains an unauthorized signature or has been altered
	4. There is a claim to it by another person
	5. There is a defense against it.
No Evidence of Forgery, Alteration, or Irregularity	A holder cannot become an HDC to an instrument that is apparently forged or altered or is so otherwise irregular or incomplete as to call into question its authenticity.
The Shelter Principle-Holder through an HDC	1. *Shelter principle*. A rule that says a holder who does not qualify as an HDC in his or her own right becomes an HDC if he or she acquires the instrument through an HDC.
	2. *Limitations on the shelter principle*. Persons who participated in the fraud or illegality or have notice of a defense or claim against an instrument cannot improve their position by later acquiring the instrument through an HDC.

SIGNATURE LIABILITY OF PARTIES, P. 392

Signature Liability of Parties	1. *Signature liability*. A person cannot be held contractually liable on a negotiable instrument unless his or her signature appears on the instrument. Also called *contract liability*.
	2. *Signers*. Persons can sign an instrument in the capacity of a(n)
	a. *Maker* of notes and certificates of deposit
	b. *Drawer* of drafts and checks
	c. *Drawee* who certifies or accepts checks and drafts
	d. *Indorser* who indorses an instrument
	e. *Agent* who signs on behalf of others
	f. *Accommodation* party.
	3. *Liability of signers*. Every party that signs a negotiable instrument (except qualified indorsers and agents that properly sign the instrument) is either *primarily* or *secondarily* liable on the instrument.
Signature Defined	The signature on a negotiable instrument can be any name, word, or mark used in lieu of a written signature. A signature may be (a) handwritten, typed, printed, stamped, or made in almost any other manner and (b) executed or adopted by a party to authenticate a writing.
Agent's Signatures	1. *Agent*. A person who has been authorized to sign a negotiable instrument on behalf of another person.
	2. *Principal*. A person who authorizes an agent to sign a negotiable instrument on his or her behalf.

3. *Authorized signature*. An agent's signature on a negotiable instrument that is authorized by the principal.
   a. *Principal's liability*. A principal is liable on a negotiable instrument signed on his or her behalf by an authorized agent if either the name of the principal or the name of the agent (or both) appears on the instrument.
   b. *Agent's liability:*
      i. *Unambiguous signature*. An authorized agent is not personally liable on a negotiable instrument he or she signs on behalf of a principal if the signature shows unambiguously that it is made on behalf of a principal who is identified in the instrument.
      ii. *Ambiguous signature*. An authorized agent is personally liable to the following parties on a negotiable instrument if the signature does not show unambiguously that it is made in a representative capacity or the principal is not identified in the instrument:
         a. To a holder in due course (HDC) who took the instrument without notice that the agent was not intended to be liable on the instrument
         b. To any other person other than an HDC unless the agent proves that the original parties did not intend the agent to be liable on the instrument
         c. *Special rule for checks*. An agent who signs a *check* from the account of a principal who is identified on the check without indicating the agent's representative capacity is not personally liable on the check.
4. *Unauthorized signature*. A signature made by a *purported agent* on behalf of a *purported principal* without the purported principal's authority.
   a. *Liability of the purported principal*. An unauthorized signature by a purported agent does not act as the signature of the purported principal. The purported principal is not liable on the instrument.
   b. *Liability of the purported agent*. The purported agent is liable to any person who in good faith pays the instrument or takes it for value.

Primary Liability	Liability of certain signers to pay a negotiable instrument, subject to certain real defenses.
	1. *Parties who have primary liability*. The following signers have *primary liability* to pay a negotiable instrument:
	  a. *Makers* of promissory notes and certificates of deposit
	  b. *Acceptors* of drafts and checks (e.g., a bank that certifies a check)

Secondary Liability	Liability on a negotiable instrument that is imposed on a party only when the party primarily liable on the instrument defaults and fails to pay the instrument when due.
	1. *Parties who have secondary liability*. The following signers have *secondary liability* to pay a negotiable instrument:
	  a. *Drawers* of drafts and checks if the check is dishonored by the drawee or acceptor
	  b. *Unqualified indorsers* if the primary obligor fails to pay the instrument.
	2. *Qualified indorsers*. Qualified indorsers (i.e., indorsers who indorse instruments "without recourse" or similar language that disclaims liability) are not secondarily liable on the instrument.
	3. *Requirements for imposing secondary liability*. Parties are secondarily liable on a negotiable instrument only if the following requirements are met:

	a. The instrument is properly *presented* for payment. *Presentment* is a demand for acceptance or payment of an instrument made upon the maker, acceptor, drawee, or other payor by or on behalf of the holder.
	b. The instrument is *dishonored. Dishonor* occurs when acceptance or payment of the instrument is refused or cannot be obtained from the party required to accept or pay the instrument within the prescribed time after presentment is duly made.
	c. *Notice of dishonor* is timely given to the person to be held secondarily liable on the instrument. *Notice of dishonor* may be given by any commercially reasonable means.
Accommodation Party	1. *Accommodation.* Occurs when a party signs a negotiable instrument to lend his or her name (and credit) to another party to the instrument.
	2. *Accommodation party.* The party who signs an instrument and lends his or her name (and credit) to another party to the instrument.
	3. *Accommodated party.* The party to whom an accommodation party lends his or her name and credit on a negotiable instrument.
	4. *Types of liability.* An accommodation party may sign an instrument guaranteeing either *payment* or *collection.*
	a. *Guaranteeing payment.* A form of accommodation where the accommodation party *guarantees payment* of a negotiable instrument. The accommodation party is *primarily liable* on the instrument with the accommodated party. For example, an *accommodated maker* is primarily liable on a promissory note he or she signs. The debtor can seek payment from the accommodation maker without first seeking payment from the maker.
	b. *Guaranteeing collection.* A form of accommodation in which the accommodation party *guarantees collection* of a negotiable instrument. The accommodation party is *secondarily liable* on the instrument. For example, an *accommodation indorser* is secondarily liable on a check he or she indorses. The holder cannot seek payment from the accommodation indorser unless he or she first seeks to recover payment from the primary obligor and is unsuccessful. To reserve this type of liability, the accommodation party's signature must be accompanied by words indicating that he or she is guaranteeing collection rather than payment of the obligation.

WARRANTY LIABILITY OF PARTIES, P. 398

Warranty Liability of Parties	The law *implies* certain warranties on transferors of negotiable instruments. There are two types of *implied warranties*: 1. Transfer warranties 2. Presentment warranties.
Transfer Warranties	1. *Transfer.* Any passage of an instrument other than its issuance and presentment for payment.
	2. *Transfer warranties.* Any person who transfers a negotiable instrument for consideration makes the following five warranties to the transferee:
	a. The transferor has good title to the instrument or is authorized to obtain payment or acceptance on behalf of one who does have good title
	b. All signatures are genuine or authorized
	c. The instrument has not been materially altered
	d. No defenses of any party are good against the transferor

	e. The transferor has no knowledge of any insolvency proceeding against the maker, or acceptor, or the drawer of an unaccepted instrument.
	3. *Breach of transfer warranty*. A transferee who takes an instrument in good faith may recover damages for *breach of transfer warranty* from the warrantor equal to the loss suffered. The amount cannot exceed the amount of the instrument plus expenses and interest.
Presentment Warranties	1. *Presentment*. The demand for acceptance or payment of the instrument made upon the maker, acceptor, drawee, or other party by or on behalf of the holder.
	2. *Presentment warranties*. Any person who presents a draft or check for payment or acceptance makes the following three warranties to a drawee or acceptor who in good faith pays or accepts the instrument:
	a. The presenter has good title to the instrument or is authorized to obtain payment or acceptance of the person who has good title
	b. The instrument has not been materially altered
	c. The presenter has no knowledge that the signature of the maker or drawer is unauthorized.
	3. *Breach of presentment warranty*. A drawee who pays an instrument may recover damages for breach of presentment warranty from the warrantor. The amount that can be recovered is limited to the amount paid by the drawee less the amount the drawee received or is entitled to receive from the drawer because of the payment, plus expenses and interest.

DEFENSES, P. 399

Defenses	*Types of defenses*. The creation of negotiable instruments may give rise to a defense against payment of the instrument. There are two types of defenses:
	1. *Real defenses*. Defenses that can be raised against holders and holders in due course (HDCs) and
	2. *Personal defenses*. Defenses that can be raised against holders but not against HDCs.
Real Defenses	Defenses against the enforcement of a negotiable instrument that *can be raised against both holders and HDCs*. Real defenses include the following:
	1. *Minority*. In most states, minors who do not misrepresent their age can disaffirm contracts, including negotiable instruments.
	2. *Extreme duress*. A person who has signed a negotiable instrument under *extreme duress* (e.g., because of force or violence, or threat of force or violence) may raise this duress as a defense to the enforcement of the instrument.
	3. *Mental incapacity*. An instrument that was signed by a person who has been adjudicated mentally incompetent is void.
	4. *Illegality*. If an instrument arises out of an illegal transaction, the illegality is a real defense if the law declares the instrument void.
	5. *Discharge in bankruptcy*. If an obligor's duty to pay a negotiable instrument has been discharged in bankruptcy, that person is relieved of the obligation to pay the instrument.
	6. *Fraud in the inception*. Occurs when a person is deceived into signing a negotiable instrument thinking that it is something else. Fraud in the inception, also called *fraud in the factum* or *fraud in the execution*, is a real defense against enforcement of an instrument.
	7. *Forgery*. The unauthorized signature of a maker, drawer, or indorser is wholly inoperative as that of the person whose name is signed. This is

	a real defense unless the person whose name has been signed ratifies it or is precluded from raising the defense (e.g., his or her negligence substantially contributed to the forgery). 8. *Material alteration*. Material alteration of a negotiable instrument is a partial defense against an HDC. An HDC can enforce an altered instrument according to its original tenor but not to the raised amount.

Personal Defenses	Defenses against the enforcement of a negotiable instrument that can be raised against holders but cannot be raised against HDCs. Personal defenses include the following:
	1. *Breach of contract*. The breach of contract by one of the original parties at the time of contracting can be raised against the enforcement of an instrument by a holder. This defense is not effective against an HDC, however.
	2. *Fraud in the inducement*. Occurs when a wrongdoer makes a false representation to another person to lead that person to enter into a contract with the wrongdoer. This type of fraud may be raised as a defense against a holder, but not against an HDC.
	3. *Other personal defenses*. The following additional personal defenses can be raised against enforcement of a negotiable instrument by an ordinary holder but not against an HDC:
	  a. *Mental illness* that makes the contract voidable instead of void (usually a nonadjudicated mental illness)
	  b. *Illegality* of a contract that makes the contract voidable instead of void
	  c. *Ordinary duress* or undue influence
	  d. *Discharge* of an instrument by *payment* or *cancellation*.

The FTC eliminates HDC status with respect to consumer credit transactions	1. *Consumer credit transaction*. A transaction whereby a consumer purchases goods or services on credit and signs a negotiable instrument (note) agreeing to pay the remainder of the purchase price. 2. *FTC rule*. The Federal Trade Commission (FTC) has adopted a rule that *eliminates HDC status* with regard to negotiable instruments that arise out of certain consumer credit transactions. 3. *Effect of the rule*. All defenses and claims that can be raised by the consumer purchaser against holders can also be raised against HDCs. Thus, both personal and real defenses can be raised against an HDC in this situation.

DISCHARGE, P. 403

Discharge	Actions or events that relieve certain parties from liability on negotiable instruments. The three methods of discharge follow: 1. *Payment*. Generally, all parties to an instrument are discharged from liability if (a) the party primarily liable on the instrument pays it in full to the holder or (b) the drawee pays an unaccepted draft or check in full to the holder. 2. *Cancellation*. Cancellation of the instrument discharges the liability of any party to the instrument. Cancellation can be accomplished by (a) any manner apparent on the face of the instrument or the indorsement (e.g., writing "canceled" on the instrument) or (b) destroying or mutilating the instrument with the intent of eliminating the obligation. 3. *Impairment of the right of recourse*. Certain parties (holders, indorsers, accommodation parties) are discharged from liability on an instrument if the holder (a) releases an obligor from liability or (b) surrenders collateral without the consent of the parties who would benefit by it.

CRITICAL LEGAL THINKING CASES

17.1 Holder in Due Course On May 8, 1974, Royal Insurance Company Ltd. (Royal) issued a draft in the amount of $12,000 payable through the Morgan Guaranty Trust Company (Morgan Guaranty). The draft was made payable to Gary E. Terrell in settlement of a claim on an insurance policy for fire damage to premises located at 3031 North 11th Street, Kansas City, Kansas. On May 9, the attorney for Mr. and Mrs. Louis Wexler notified Royal that Terrell's clients had an insurable interest in the damaged property. As a result, Royal immediately stopped payment on the draft. On the same day, the draft was indorsed by Gary E. Terrell and deposited in his account at the UAW-CIO Local #31 Federal Credit Union (Federal). Over the next two days, Terrell withdrew $9,000 from this account. Immediately upon receiving the draft, Federal indorsed it and forwarded it to Morgan Guaranty for payment. The draft was returned to Federal on May 14 with the notation "payment stopped." When Royal refused to pay Federal the amount of the draft, Federal sued. The basis of the suit was whether Federal was a holder in due course. Who wins? [*UAW-CIO Local #31 Federal Credit Union v. Royal Insurance Company, Ltd.*, 594 S.W.2d 276 (Mo. 1980)]

17.2 Taking for Value On September 30, 1976, Betty Ellis and her then husband W.G. Ellis executed and delivered to the Standard Finance Company (Standard) a promissory note in the amount of $2,800. After receiving the note, Standard issued a check to the couple for $2,800. The check was made payable to "W.G. Ellis and Betty Ellis." The check was cashed after both parties indorsed it. Shortly thereafter, the Ellises divorced. Mrs. Ellis claims that (1) she never saw or used the money and (2) Standard understood that all of the money went to her ex-husband. W.G. Ellis was declared bankrupt. When the note became due in 1980, Betty Ellis refused to pay it. Standard sued her, seeking payment as a holder in due course. She claimed that Standard was not a holder in due course in regard to her because she never received consideration for the note, and therefore, Standard did not take the note for value. Who wins? [*Standard Finance Company, Ltd. v. Ellis*, 657 P.2d 1056 (Hawaii App. 1983)]

17.3 Notice of Dishonored Instrument In 1974, William and Eugene Slough executed two notes payable to the order of Quality Mark, Inc. (Quality Mark). The notes were made in payment of the debts of a partnership in which the Sloughs were involved. The aggregate amount of the notes was $42,150. They were due on or before January 1, 1986. On the day the instruments were executed, Quality Mark assigned them for consideration to Philip Baer, Jr. In 1975, Baer sold the notes at discount to the Southtowne Company (Southtowne). One year later, Southtowne resold the notes to Edward Rettig. By this time, the notes had been discounted to the point that Rettig paid only $5,000 for them. However, Southtowne assured Rettig that the notes had not yet been dishonored. Shortly after Rettig's purchase, the Sloughs announced that they had already defaulted on the notes. Rettig sued all the prior indorsers. Southtowne claimed that the Sloughs had no defenses against Rettig because he was a holder in due course. The

Sloughs claim that because the notes had been discounted to less than 50 percent of their value, Rettig must have taken them with notice of this dishonor. Who wins? [*Rettig v. Slough*, No. 5-82-7, Slip Op. (Ohio App. 1984)]

17.4 Illegality In 1976, Victor Bisharat became a member of the Casanova Club, a British corporation operating a legal casino in London. That year, he purchased £6,350 worth of gambling chips, which he then lost while gambling at the casino. Bisharat paid for the chips with a series of nine bearer checks. Bisharat was the drawer of the checks, all of which were drawn on the Hartford National Bank located in Connecticut. When the Casanova Club presented the checks to the bank for payment, they all were returned to the club with the notation "unpaid for reason: insufficient funds." The Club then brought suit against Bisharat in a Connecticut state court to recover the amount owed. Bisharat defended the suit by claiming that the checks arose out of a gambling debt and were therefore part of an illegal transaction. Gambling is illegal in Connecticut, and gambling debts are not legally enforceable in that state. The Casanova Club claims to be a holder in due course of the checks. Who wins? [*Casanova Club v. Bisharat*, 35 UCC Rep Serv 1207 (Conn. 1983)]

17.5 Fraud in the Factum John Wade was employed by Mike Fazzari. Fazzari was an immigrant who was unable to speak or read English. In December 1957, Wade prepared a promissory note in the amount of $400. The instrument was payable at the Glen National Bank, Watkins Glen, New York. Wade took the note to Fazzari and told him that the document was a statement of wages earned by Wade during the course of his employment. Fazzari signed the instrument after Wade told him it was necessary for income tax purposes. Fazzari was not in debt to Wade and there was no consideration given for the note. On April 10, 1958, the note was presented to the First National Bank of Odessa by Wellington Doane, a customer of the bank and an indorsee of the payee, Wade. Doane indorsed the check in blank and accepted a $400 cashier's check in exchange of the note. Can the First National Bank of Odessa enforce payment of the note as a holder in due course? [*First National Bank of Odessa v. Fazzari*, 179 N.E.2d 493 (N.Y. App. 1961)]

17.6 Fraud in the Inducement J.H. Thompson went to the Central Motor Company (Central), an automobile dealership, to purchase a car. With the assistance of Central's sales manager, Ed Boles, Thompson selected a 1966 Imperial automobile. Boles drew up a loan agreement that stipulated 35 monthly installments of $125 and a final installment of $5,265. Under this agreement, Thompson would be charged an annual interest rate of 8 percent. Boles assured Thompson that when the $5,265 installment became due he would be allowed to sign a second note to cover that amount. Thompson was told that the interest rate on this second note would also be 8 percent. With this assurance, Thompson signed the original loan agreement and note and made all the payments except the final one. When Thompson went to Central to sign the second note he was told that the interest rate on the second installment note would be 12 percent—not 8 percent. Thompson refused to sign the second note or make the balloon payment on the original note. Instead, he returned the car. Central was able to sell the car but sued Thompson to recover a deficiency judgment. Who wins? [*Central Motor Company v. J.H. Thompson*, 465 S.W.2d 405 (Tex. App. 1971)]

17.7 Federal Trade Commission Rule Warren and Kristina Mahaffey were approached by a salesman from the Five Star Solar Screens Company (Five Star). The salesman offered to install insulation in their home at a cost of $5,289. After being told that the insulation would reduce their heating bills by 50 percent, the Mahaffeys agreed to the purchase. To pay for the work, the Mahaffeys executed a note promising to pay the purchase price with interest in installments. The note, which was secured by a deed of trust on the Mahaffeys' home, contained the following language: "Notice: Any holder of this consumer credit contract is subject to all claims and defenses which the debtor could assert against the seller of goods or services obtained pursuant hereto or with the proceeds thereof." Several days after Five Star finished working at the Mahaffeys' home, it sold the installment note to Mortgage Finance Corporation (Mortgage Finance).

There were major defects in the way the insulation was installed in the Mahaffey home. Large holes were left in the walls and heater blankets and roof fans were never delivered as called for by the purchase contract. Because of these defects, the Mahaffeys refused to make the payments due on the note. Mortgage Finance instituted foreclosure proceedings to collect the money owed. Can the Mahaffeys successfully assert the defense of breach of contract against the enforcement of the note by Mortgage Finance? [*Mahaffey v. Investor's National Security Company*, 747 P.2d 890 (Nev. 1987)]

17.8 Transfer Warranties David M. Cox was a distributor of tools manufactured and sold by Matco Tools Corporation (Matco). Cox purchased tools from Matco pursuant to a credit line that he repaid as the tools were sold. The credit line was secured by Cox's Matco tool inventory. In order to expedite payment on Cox's line of credit, Matco decided to authorize Cox to deposit any customer checks that were made payable to "Matco Tools" or "Matco" into Cox's own account. Matco's controller sent Cox's bank, Pontiac State Bank (Pontiac), a letter stating that Cox was authorized to make such deposits. Several years later, some Matco tools were stolen from Cox's inventory. The Travelers Indemnity Company (Travelers), which insured Cox against such a loss, sent Cox a settlement check in the amount of $24,960. The check was made payable to "David M. Cox and Matco Tool Co." Cox indorsed the check and deposited it in his account at Pontiac. Pontiac forwarded the check through the banking system for payment by the drawee bank. Cox never paid Matco for the destroyed tools. Matco sued Pontiac for accepting the check without the proper indorsements. Is Pontiac liable? [*Matco Tools Corporation v. Pontiac State Bank*, 41 UCC Rep Serv 883 (E.D.Mich. 1985)]

17.9 Presentment Warranties John Waddell Construction Company (Waddell) maintained a checking account at the Longview Bank & Trust Company (Longview Bank). Waddell drafted a check from this account made payable to two payees,

Engineered Metal Works (Metal Works) and E.G. Smith Construction (Smith Construction). The check was sent to Metal Works, which promptly indorsed the check and presented it to the First National Bank of Azle (Bank of Azle) for payment. The Bank of Azle accepted the check with only Metal Works' indorsement and credited Metal Works' account. The Bank of Azle subsequently presented the check to Longview Bank through the Federal Reserve System. Longview Bank accepted and paid the check. When Waddell received the check along with its monthly checking statements from Longview Bank, a company employee noticed the missing indorsement and notified Longview Bank. Longview Bank returned the check to the Bank of Azle, and the Bank of Azle's account was debited the amount of the check at the Federal Reserve. Did the Bank of Azle breach its warranty of good title? [*Longview Bank & Trust Company v. First National Bank of Azle*, 750 S.W.2d 297 (Tex. App. 1988)]

17.10 Maker's Liability In March 1977, James Wright met with Jones, the president of The Community Bank (Community Bank), to request a loan of $7,500. Because Wright was already obligated on several existing loans, he was informed that his request would have to be reviewed by the bank's loan committee. Jones suggested that this delay could be avoided if the loan were made to Mrs. Wright. Wright asked his wife to go to the bank and "indorse" a note for him. Mrs. Wright went to the bank and spoke to Jones. Although she claims that Jones told her that she was merely indorsing the note, the language of the note clearly indicated that she would be liable in the case of default. Mrs. Wright signed the instrument in its lower right-hand corner. Wright did not sign the instrument. The $7,500 was deposited directly into Wright's business account. The Wrights were subsequently separated. Following the separation, Mrs. Wright received notice that she was in default on the note. The notice indicated that she was solely obligated to repay the instrument. Is Mrs. Wright obligated to repay the note? [*The Community Bank v. Wright*, 267 S.E.2d 159 (Va. 1980)]

17.11 Drawer's Liability Carlisle Distributing Co., Inc. (Carlisle), owed William Paladino $10,000. To pay this debt, Carlisle delivered a $10,000 check drawn on an Arkansas bank made payable to Paladino. Paladino indorsed the check and delivered it to Wildman Stores, Inc. (Wildman), as security for an $8,000 loan he had received from that company. Seventeen months after receiving the check, Wildman presented it for payment at the bank upon which it had been drawn. The payor bank dishonored the check due to insufficient funds. Wildman informed Carlisle of the dishonor and demanded payment of the $10,000. Carlisle refused Wildman's demand. Wildman sued Carlisle to collect the $10,000. The statute of limitations for enforcing a negotiable instrument in Arkansas is five years. Who wins? [*Wildman Stores, Inc. v. Carlisle Distributing Co., Inc.*, 688 S.W.2d 748 (Ark. App. 1985)]

17.12 Liability of Accommodation Makers John Valenti wanted to operate an Amoco service station. He contracted with American Oil Company (Amoco), the licensor of Amoco service stations, to lease a service station and become a dealer of Amoco products. The documents that made up the lease agreement included a promissory note and guaranty. Because Valenti had no established credit history, Amoco required that his father be a cosigner. Both Valentis signed the lease and note. After about one year, the younger Valenti abandoned the operation. Amoco sued both Valentis to recover on the note and guaranty. The suit against the son was dropped when Amoco learned that he had no assets from which to satisfy a judgment. The father claimed that Amoco could not go after him because it was not suing his son. Who wins? [*American Oil Company v. Valenti*, 28 UCC Rep Serv 118 (Conn.Sup. 1979)]

17.13 Liability of an Accommodation Indorser The Georgia Farm Bureau Mutual Insurance Company (Georgia Farm Bureau) issued a check payable to the order of Willie Mincey, Jr., and MIC for $658. Without indorsing the check, MIC forwarded it to Mincey for his indorsement. Mincey indorsed the check and attempted to cash it at the First National Bank of Allentown (First National). First National would not accept the check because Mincey was not a customer of the bank. Mincey returned to the bank later that day with his uncle, Montgomery, who was a customer of the bank. First National accepted the check after Montgomery added his indorsement to Mincey's. First National forwarded the check to the drawee bank, which dishonored it because it did not bear MIC's indorsement. First National sued Montgomery for the amount of the check as an accommodation indorser. Who wins? [*First National Bank of Allentown v. Montgomery*, 27 Rep Serv 164 (Pa.Com.Pl. 1979)]

17.14 Principal's Liability John Smith was the corporate secretary for Carriage House Mobile Homes, Inc. (Carriage House). Beginning on November 9, 1973, Smith signed a series of checks totaling $13,900 made payable to Danube Carpet Mills (Danube). The checks were in payment for carpeting ordered by Carriage House. Each check was signed in the following manner: "Carriage House Mobile Homes, Inc., General Account, By: /s/ John Smith." When Danube presented the checks for payment to the drawee bank, the First State Bank of Phil Campbell, Alabama (First State Bank), payment was refused. The reason for the refusal was that the checks were drawn against uncollected funds. The holder of these checks, Southeastern Financial Corporation, sued Smith and Carriage House to recover the $13,900. Who is liable on the checks? [*Southeastern Financial Corporation v. Smith*, 397 F.Supp. 649 (N.D.Ala. 1975)]

17.15 Authorized Agent's Liability Richard G. Lee was the president of Village Homes, Inc. (Village Homes). Village Homes had several outstanding loans from Farmers & Merchants National Bank of Hattan, North Dakota (Farmers Bank) that were in default. Lee and Farmers Bank worked out an arrangement to consolidate the delinquent loans and replace them with a new loan. The new loan would be secured by a promissory note. The parties drafted a note in the amount of $85,000 with a 17 percent annual interest rate. Lee signed the note without indicating that he was signing as an agent of Village Homes. The name "Village Homes, Inc." did not appear on the note. Six months after the note was signed, Village Homes defaulted on it. Farmers Bank sued Lee, seeking to hold him personally liable for the note. Who wins? [*Farmers & Merchants National Bank of Hattan, North Dakota v. Lee*, 333 N.W.2d 792 (N.D. 1983)]

ETHICS CASES

17.16 Anthony and Dolores Angelini entered into a contract with Lustro Aluminum Products, Inc. (Lustro). Under the contract, Lustro agreed to replace exterior veneer on the Angelini home with Gold Bond Plasticrylic avocado siding. The cash price for the job was $3,600 and the installment plan price was $5,363.40. The Angelinis chose to pay on the installment plan and signed a promissory note as security. The note's language provided that it would not mature until 60 days after a certificate of completion was signed. Ten days after the note was executed Lustro assigned it for consideration to General Investment Corporation (General), an experienced home improvement lender. General was aware that Lustro (1) was nearly insolvent at the time of the assignment and (2) had engaged in questionable business practices in the past. Lustro never completed the installation of siding at the Angelini home. General demanded payment of the note from the Angelinis as a holder in due course. Did General act morally in this case? Who wins? [*General Investment Corporation v. Angelini*, 278 A.2d 193 (N.J. 1971)]

17.17 Marvin Ornstein resides in Pipersville, Pennsylvania. After submitting credit applications, he received a $10,000 line of credit from both the MGM Grand Hotel and Caesar's Palace, in Las Vegas, Nevada. In April 1977, Ornstein traveled to Las Vegas on a gambling junket and borrowed $5,000 at Caesar's

Palace. In June 1977, he went to the MGM Grand Hotel and borrowed $10,000. In each instance, the borrowed money was advanced in the form of gambling chips, in exchange for which Ornstein executed counterchecks (i.e., markers) evidencing the debt. Ornstein did not repay the borrowed money. In November 1978, the casinos assigned their claims against Ornstein to National Recovery Systems (NRS), a New York corporation that is a credit and collection agency for casinos. Did Ornstein act ethically in not repaying his gambling markers? Does the fact that the notes arose from a gambling debt make them illegal and, if so, is this illegality a real defense that can be asserted against enforcement of the notes by an HDC? [*National Recovery Systems v. Ornstein*, 541 F. Supp. 1131 (E.D.Pa. 1982)]

17.18 In 1976, Gerald Tinker purchased for investment purposes a used 1972 Jaguar from De Maria Porsche Audi, Inc. (De Maria). De Maria represented to Tinker, prior to making the sale, that the automobile was in good operating condition, was powered by its original engine, and had never been involved in a major collision. Tinker relied on these representations and executed a retail installment contract and note with De Maria. The contract and note contained the FTC-required notice. De Maria assigned the contract and note to Central Bank of Miami (Central Bank), which provided floor financing for De Maria.

Tinker had problems with the automobile immediately after its purchase. The car operated poorly and Tinker soon discovered that it was not powered by its original engine, had previously been involved in a major collision, and was determined to be a total loss by its previous owner's insurance company. The title held by the owner preceding De Maria stated that it was a "parts car." The title obtained by Tinker from De Maria did not contain this disclaimer. When De Maria failed to replace or successfully repair the automobile after it became totally inoperable, Tinker ceased making payments on the note and sued De Maria and Central Bank for fraud. Central Bank counterclaimed for the amount due on the note. Is it ethical for a third-party lender to assert its HDC status to collect on a note when the seller has engaged in fraud or other misconduct? Does the FTC rule prevent Central Bank from being a holder in due course? [*Tinker v. De Maria Porsche Audi, Inc.*, 459 So.2d 487 (Fla.App. 1984)]

CRITICAL LEGAL THINKING WRITING ASSIGNMENT

Read Case A.17 in the Case Appendix [*Kedzie & 103rd Currency Exchange, Inc. v. Hodge*]. This case is excerpted from the appellate court opinion. Review and brief the case. In your brief, be sure to answer the following questions:

1. Who was the drawer of the check? Who was the payee of the check?

2. What firm cashed the check? Did it qualify as a holder in due course (HDC)?
3. What defense did the defendant assert?
4. Was the defense effective against enforcement of the negotiable instrument?

CHAPTER 18

CHECKS, WIRE TRANSFERS,

AND THE BANKING SYSTEM

Chapter Objectives

*After studying this chapter,
you should be able to*

1. Describe the system of processing and collecting checks through the banking system
2. Describe the difference among certified, cashier's, and traveler's checks
3. Define stale and postdated checks
4. Identify when a bank engages in a wrongful dishonor of a check
5. Describe the liability of parties when a signature or indorsement on a check is forged
6. Describe the liability of parties when a check has been altered
7. Describe the requirements of the Expedited Funds Availability Act
8. Explain a bank's midnight deadline for determining whether to dishonor a check
9. Describe electronic fund transfer systems
10. Define a wire transfer and describe the main provisions of Article 4A of the Uniform Commercial Code (UCC)

Chapter Contents

- The Bank-Customer Relationship
- The Uniform Commercial Code
- Ordinary Checks
- Special Types of Checks
  Case 18.1 *New Covenant Community Church v. Federal National Bank & Trust Co. of Shawnee, Oklahoma (OK)*
- Honoring Checks
  Business Checklist New Requirements for Postdating Checks
  Case 18.2 *Buckley v. Trenton Savings Fund Society (NJ)*
  Business Checklist UCC Rule on "Full Payment" Checks
- Forged Signatures and Altered Checks
  Ethical Perspective Sinking the Banks' "Float"
- Bank's Duty to Accept Deposits
  Business Application The Federal Reserve System
  Business Application Missing the "Midnight Deadline"—A Bank Turns into a Pumpkin
- Electronic Fund Transfer Systems
  Contemporary Business Environment Consumer Rights Provided by the Electronic Fund Transfer Act
  International Perspective Commercial Wire Transfers: Article 4A of the Uniform Commercial Code
- Working the Web
- Chapter Summary
- Critical Legal Thinking Cases
- Ethics Cases
- Critical Legal Thinking Writing Assignment

> *Bankers have no right to establish a customary law among themselves, at the expense of other men.*
>
> Justice Foster
> *Hankey v. Trotman, 1 Black,*
> *W. 1 (1746)*

Checks are the most common form of negotiable instruments used in this country. More than 70 billion checks are written annually. Checks act both as a substitute for money and as a recordkeeping device, but they do not serve a credit function. In addition, billions of dollars are transferred each day by **wire transfer** between businesses and banks. This chapter discusses the various forms of checks, the procedure for paying and collecting checks through the banking system, the duties and liabilities of banks and other parties in the collection process, and electronic fund transfers.

"Money speaks sense in a language all nations understand."

Aphra Behn
(1640–1689)
The Rover

THE BANK–CUSTOMER RELATIONSHIP

When a customer makes a deposit into a bank, a **creditor–debtor relationship** is formed. The customer is the creditor and the bank is the debtor. In effect, the customer is loaning money to the bank.

A *principal–agent relationship* is created if (1) the deposit is a check that the bank must collect for the customer or (2) the customer writes a check against his or her account. The customer is the principal and the bank is the agent. The bank is obligated to follow the customer's order to collect or pay the check. The rights and duties of a bank and a checking account and wire transfer customer are contractual. The signature card and other bank documents signed by the customer form the basis of the contract.

creditor–debtor relationship Created when a customer deposits money into the bank; the customer is the creditor and the bank is the debtor.

THE UNIFORM COMMERCIAL CODE

The following articles of the Uniform Commercial Code (UCC) establish rules for creating, collecting, and enforcing checks and wire transfers:

- **Article 3 (Negotiable Instruments)** establishes the requirements for finding a negotiable instrument. Because a check is a negotiable instrument, the provisions of Article 3 apply. **Revised Article 3** was promulgated in 1990. The provisions of Revised Article 3 will serve as the basis of the discussion of Article 3 in this chapter.
- **Article 4 of the UCC (Bank Deposits and Collections)** establishes the rules and principles that regulate bank deposit and collection procedures for checking accounts offered by commercial banks, NOW accounts (negotiable orders of withdrawal), and other checklike accounts offered by savings and loan associations, savings banks, credit unions, and other financial institutions. Article 4 controls if the provisions of Article 3 and 4 conflict [UCC 4-102(a)]. Article 4 was substantially amended in 1990. The amended Article 4 will serve as the basis of the discussion of Article 4 in this chapter.
- **Article 4A (Funds Transfers)** establishes rules that regulate the creation and collection of and liability for wire transfers. Article 4A was added to the UCC in 1989.

Article 3 of the UCC Sets forth the requirements for finding a negotiable instrument, including checks.

Revised Article 3 A revision of Article 3 promulgated in 1990.

Article 4 of the UCC Establishes the rules and principles that regulate bank deposit and collection procedures.

Article 4A of the UCC Article added to the UCC in 1989 that establishes rules regulating the creation and collection of and liability for wire transfers.

ORDINARY CHECKS

Most adults and businesses have at least one checking account at a bank. A customer opens a checking account by going to the bank, completing the necessary forms (including a signature card), and making a deposit to the account. The bank issues checks to the customer. The customer then uses the checks to purchase goods and services. When the check is presented for payment, the bank verifies the drawer's signature by matching the signature on the check to the one on the signature card.

Parties to a Check

check An order by the drawer to the drawee bank to pay a specified sum of money from the drawer's checking account to the named payee (or holder).

drawer of a check The checking account holder and writer of the check.

drawee of a check The bank where the drawer has his or her account

payee of a check The party to whom the check is written.

UCC 3-104(f) defines a **check** as an order by the drawer to the drawee bank to pay a specified sum of money from the drawer's checking account to the named payee (or holder). There are three parties to an ordinary check:

1. The **drawer**—the customer who maintains the checking account and writes (draws) checks against the account
2. The **drawee** (or **payor bank**)—the bank on which the check is drawn
3. The **payee**—the party to whom the check is written.

CONSIDER THIS EXAMPLE: The Kneadery Restaurant has a checking account at Mountain Bank. The Kneadery writes a check for $1,500 from this account to Sun Valley Bakery to pay for food supplies. The Kneadery Restaurant is the drawer, Mountain Bank is the drawee, and Sun Valley Bakery is the payee.

Indorsement of a Check

indorsement of a check Occurs when a payee indorses a check to another party by signing the back of the check.

indorser The payee who indorses a check to another party.

indorsee The party to whom a check is indorsed.

The payee is a *holder* of the check. As such, the payee has the right to either (1) demand payment of the check or (2) *indorse* the check to another party by signing the back of the check. This latter action is called **indorsement of a check.** The payee is the **indorser**, and the person to whom the check is indorsed is the **indorsee**. The indorsee in turn becomes a holder who can either demand payment of the check or indorse it to yet another party. Any subsequent holder can demand payment of the check or further transfer the check [UCC 3-204(a)].

CONSIDER THIS EXAMPLE: Referring to the previous example, the Sun Valley Bakery may either present the Kneadery Restaurant's check to Mountain Bank for payment, or it can indorse the check to another party. Assume that Sun Valley Bakery indorses the check to the Flour Company in payment for flour. Sun Valley Bakery is the indorser and the Flour Company is the indorsee. The Flour Company may either present the check for payment or indorse it to another party, and so on.

SPECIAL TYPES OF CHECKS

bank check A certified check, a cashier's check, or a traveler's check, the payment for which the bank is solely or primarily liable.

If a payee fears there may be insufficient funds in the drawer's account to pay the check when it is presented for payment or that the drawer has stopped payment of the check, the payee may be unwilling to accept an ordinary check from the drawer. However, the payee might be willing to accept a **bank check**; that is, a certified check, a cashier's check, or a traveler's check. These types of checks usually are considered "as good as cash" since the bank is solely or primarily liable for payment. These forms of checks are discussed in the following paragraphs.

Certified Checks

certified check A type of check where a bank agrees in advance (*certifies*) to accept the check when it is presented for payment

process of certification The accepting bank writes or stamps the word *certified* on the ordinary check of an account holder and sets aside funds from that account to pay the check.

When a bank certifies a check, it agrees in advance to (1) accept the check when it is presented for payment and (2) pay the check out of funds set aside from the customer's account and either placed in a special certified check account or held in the customer's account. Certified checks do not become stale. Thus, they are payable at any time from the date they were issued.

The check is certified when the bank writes or stamps the word *certified* across the face of an ordinary check. The certification should also contain the date and the amount being certified and the name and title of the person at the bank who certifies the check. Note that the bank is not obligated to certify a check. The bank's refusal to do so is not a dishonor of the check [UCC 3-409(d)].

Exhibit 18.1
A Certified Check

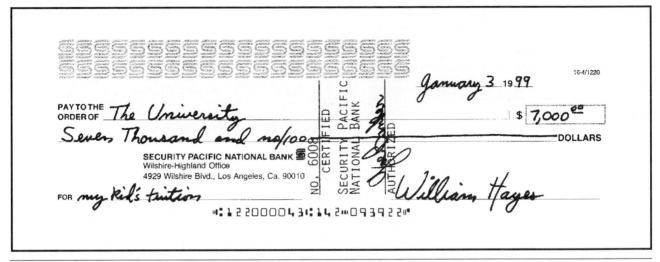

PAY TO THE ORDER OF *The University*

Seven Thousand and no/100

January 3 19 99

16-4/1220

$ 7,000.00

DOLLARS

SECURITY PACIFIC NATIONAL BANK
Wilshire-Highland Office
4929 Wilshire Blvd., Los Angeles, Ca. 90010

FOR *my kid's tuition*

William Hayes

⑈1 2 2000043⑈142⑈093922⑈

Liability on a Certified Check Either the drawer or the payee (or holder) can present the check to the drawee bank for certification. If the drawee bank certifies the check, the drawer is discharged from liability on the check, regardless of who obtained the certification [UCC 3-414(c)]. The holder must recover from the certifying bank. The obligated bank can be held liable for the amount of the check, expenses, and loss of interest resulting from nonpayment. If the bank refuses to pay after receiving notice of particular circumstances giving rise to such damages, it can also be held liable for consequential damages [UCC 3-411].

Problems may arise if a certified check was altered (e.g., the amount of the check increased). If the alteration occurred before the check was certified, the certifying bank is liable for the certified amount. If the check was altered after certification, the bank is liable for only the certified amount, not the raised amount. The drawer cannot stop payment on a certified check. Because certification constitutes acceptance of the check, the certifying bank can revoke its certification only in limited circumstances [UCC 3-413].

Cashier's Checks

A person can purchase a **cashier's check** from a bank by paying the amount of the check plus a fee for issuing the check. Usually, a specific payee is named. The purchaser does not have to have a checking account at the bank. The check is a noncancellable negotiable instrument upon issue.

A cashier's check is a two-party check for which (1) the issuing bank serves as both the drawer and the drawee and (2) the holder serves as payee [UCC 3-104(g)]. The bank, which has been paid for the check, guarantees its payment. When the check is presented for payment, the bank debits its own account [UCC 3-412].

An obligated bank that wrongfully refuses to pay a cashier's check is liable to the person asserting the right to enforce the check for expenses and loss of interest resulting from nonpayment and consequential damages [UCC 3-411].

Traveler's Checks

Traveler's checks derive their name from the fact that individuals often purchase them to use as a safe substitute for cash while on vacations or other trips. They may be issued by banks or by companies other than banks (e.g., American Express). A

CAUTION
The drawer is discharged from liability if the drawee bank certifies a check.

BUSINESS BRIEF
Many businesses require payment by certified or cashier's checks because these are "as good as cash." By doing so, businesses avoid the problem of being paid by normal checks that may "bounce."

cashier's check A check issued by a bank where the customer has paid the bank the amount of the check and a fee. The bank guarantees the payment of the check.

traveler's check A form of check sold by banks and other issuers. They are issued without a named payee. The purchaser fills in the payee's name when he or she uses the check to purchase goods or services.

Exhibit 18.2
A Cashier's Check

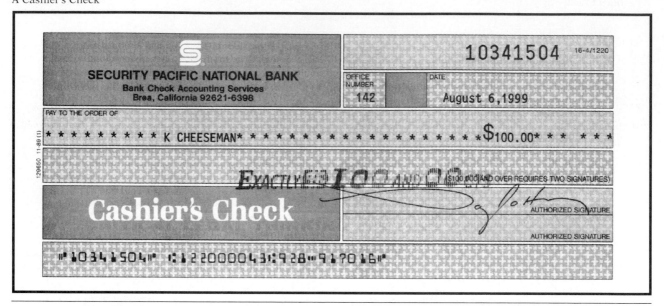

traveler's check is a two-party instrument, where the issuing bank serves as both the drawer and the drawee. It is drawn by the bank upon itself.

Traveler's checks may be purchased in many denominations, including $10, $20, $50, and $100. Unlike cashier's checks, traveler's checks are issued without a named payee. The checks have two signature blanks. The purchaser signs one blank when the traveler's checks are issued. The purchaser enters the payee's name and signs the second blank when he or she uses the check to purchase goods or services. The traveler's check is not a negotiable instrument until it is signed the second time [UCC 3-104(i)].

Purchasers of traveler's checks do not have to have a checking account at the issuing bank. The purchaser pays the bank the amount of the checks to be issued. When a traveler's check is presented for payment, the bank debits its own account. Most banks

Exhibit 18.3
A Traveler's Check

charge a fee for this service, but some banks merely earn interest on the "float" while the checks are not written. If a traveler's check is stolen or lost prior to its use, the purchaser can stop payment on the check. Payment cannot be stopped once the check has been negotiated.

In the following case, the court held that a stop–payment order on a cashier's check was not valid.

CASE 18.1

New Covenant Community Church v. Federal National Bank & Trust Co. of Shawnee, Oklahoma
734 P.2d 1318 (1990) Court of Appeals of Oklahoma

Facts On June 30, 1982, Living Way Ministries Church (Living Way) purchased a cashier's check in the amount of $325,000 from Federal National Bank & Trust Co. of Shawneee, Oklahoma (Bank). The payee on the cashier's check was the New Covenant Community Church (Church). Living Way promptly negotiated the check to Church in satisfaction of a previously incurred obligation. On July 1, 1982, with proper indorsement, Church deposited the check with the Penn Square Bank in Oklahoma City. The following day, July 2, 1982, Penn Square Bank was closed by the Federal Deposit Insurance Corporation (FDIC). Immediately upon learning of the demise of Penn Square Bank, both Church and Living Way made demand on Bank to stop payment on the cashier's check. Bank informed them it could not stop payment, and the check was paid. Due to the failure of Penn Square Bank, Church lost $215,262 of the 325,000. Church sued Bank to recover the lost money and $1 million in punitive damages. The trial court granted Bank's motion to dismiss. Church appealed.

Issue Is Bank liable for damages for not stopping payment on the cashier's check?

Decision The court of appeals held Bank was not liable for not stopping payment on the cashier's check. Affirmed.

Reason The appeals court noted that as a general rule, neither a bank nor a bank customer may order a stop payment on a cashier's check. The court held that any stop payment order from Church that came after the date of issuance of the check on June 30, 1982, came after the check was accepted and violated the provisions of Section 4-303(1)(a).

CASE QUESTIONS

Critical Legal Thinking Should the UCC permit stop payment orders on ordinary checks? On bank checks?

Ethics Did Church act ethically in trying to recover money from Bank?

Business Implication As a supplier of goods or services, when would you demand a bank check from a customer?

HONORING CHECKS

When a customer opens a checking account at a bank, the customer impliedly agrees to keep sufficient funds in the account to pay any checks written against it. Thus, when the drawee bank receives a properly drawn and payable check, the bank is under a duty to **honor** the check and charge (debit) the drawer's account the amount of the check [UCC 4-401(a)].

honor Payment of a drawer's properly drawn check by the drawee bank.

Stale Checks

Occasionally, payees or other holders in possession of a check fail to present the check immediately to the payor bank for payment. A check that has been outstanding for more than six months is considered **stale**, and the bank is under no obligation to pay it. A bank that pays a stale check in good faith may charge the drawer's account [UCC 4-404].

stale check A check that has been outstanding for more than six months.

Incomplete Checks

Drawers sometimes write checks that omit certain information, such as the amount of the check or the payee's name, either on purpose or by mistake. In such cases, the payee or any holder can complete the check, and the payor bank that in good faith makes payment on the completed check, can charge the customer's account the amount of the completed check unless it has notice that the completion was improper [UCC 3-407(c) and 4-401(d)(2)]. The UCC places the risk of loss of an incomplete item on the drawer.

CONSIDER THIS EXAMPLE: Suppose Richard, who owes Sarah $500, draws a check payable to Sarah on City Bank. Richard signs the check but leaves the amount blank. Sarah fraudulently fills in "$1,000" and presents the check to City Bank, which pays it. City Bank can charge Richard's account $1,000. Richard's only recourse is to sue Sarah. However, if Richard telephoned the bank to tell them that he owed Sarah only $500, then City Bank would be liable for paying any greater amount to Sarah.

Death or Incompetence of a Drawer

Checks may be paid against the accounts of deceased customers or customers who have been adjudicated incompetent until the bank has actual knowledge of such condition and had reasonable opportunity to act on the information. In the case of a deceased customer, the bank may pay or certify checks drawn on the deceased customer's account on or prior to the date of death for 10 days after the date of death. This rule applies unless a person claiming an interest in the account, such as an heir or a taxing authority, orders the bank to stop payment. A bank that pays such a check when it should not have is liable for the amount improperly paid [UCC 4-405].

BUSINESS CHECKLIST

New Requirements for Postdating Checks

Prior to a recent revision of Article 4 of the UCC, all a drawer had to do to **post-date** a check was to write the check and date it at a date in the future. The bank was then obligated not to pay the check until this later date, and if it did pay the check sooner it was liable for any damages caused to the drawer.

In 1990, Article 4 was amended to make it more difficult to postdate a check. Under new UCC 4-401(c), in order to require a bank to abide by a postdated check, the drawer must take the following steps:

- The drawer must postdate the check to some date in the future.
- The drawer must give *separate written notice* to the bank describing the check with reasonable certainty and notifying the bank not to pay the check until date on the check.

Stop-Payment Orders

A **stop-payment order** is an order by a drawer of a check to the payor bank not to pay or certify a check. Only the drawer can order a stop payment. If the signature of more than one person is required to draw on an account, any of these persons may stop payment on the account. The bank must be given a reasonable opportunity to act on a stop–payment order. The order is ineffectual if the bank has already accepted or certified the check.

The stop–payment order can be given orally or in writing. An **oral order** is binding on the bank for only 14 calendar days, unless confirmed in writing during this time. A

written order is effective for six months. It can be renewed in writing for additional six-month periods [UCC 4-403].

If the payor bank fails to honor a valid stop–payment order, it must recredit the customer's account. The bank is subrogated to the rights of the drawer. In addition, the bank is liable only for the actual damages suffered by the drawer. The drawer must prove the fact and amount of loss resulting from the payment of a check on which a stop–payment order was issued.

CONSIDER THIS EXAMPLE: Suppose Karen buys a car from Silvio. She pays for the car by drawing a $10,000 check on City Bank payable to the order of Silvio. Karen thinks the car is defective and stops payment on the check. If City Bank mistakenly pays Silvio over the stop–payment order, it is liable and must recredit Karen's account. However, if it is determined that the car is not defective, City Bank does not have to recredit Karen's account. This is because Karen has suffered no actual loss— she owed Silvio for the car.

Overdrafts

If the drawer does not have enough money in his or her account when a properly payable check is presented for payment, the payor bank can either (1) dishonor the check or (2) honor the check and create an overdraft in the drawer's account [UCC 4-401(a)]. The bank notifies the drawer of the dishonor and returns the check to the holder marked "insufficient funds." The holder often resubmits the check to the bank, hoping that the drawer has deposited more money into the account and the check will clear. If the check does not clear, the holder's recourse is against the drawee of the check.

If the bank chooses to pay the check even though there are insufficient funds in the drawer's account, it can later charge the drawer's account for the amount of the **overdraft** [UCC 4-401(a)]. This is because there is an implied promise that the drawer will reimburse the bank for paying checks the drawer orders the bank to pay. If the drawer does not fulfill this commitment, the bank can sue to recover payment for the overdrafts and overdraft fees. A bank cannot charge interest on the amount of the overdraft without the drawer's permission. Therefore, many banks offer optional overdraft protection to their customers.

Wrongful Dishonor

If the bank does not honor a check when there are sufficient funds in a drawer's account to pay a properly payable check, it is liable for **wrongful dishonor**. The payor bank is liable to the drawer for damages proximately caused by the wrongful dishonor as well as for consequential damages, damages caused by criminal prosecution, and such. A payee or holder cannot sue the bank for damages caused by the wrongful dishonor of a drawer's check. The only recourse for the payee or holder is to sue the drawer to recover the amount of the check [UCC 4-402].

In the following case, the court held that a customer was not entitled to recover for mental distress caused by the dishonor of checks.

written order A stop–payment order that is good for six months after the date it is written.

CAUTION
When a check is dishonored because of insufficient funds, it is said to have "bounced" (i.e., like a rubber check).

overdraft The amount of money a drawer owes a bank after it has paid a check despite insufficient funds in the drawer's account.

wrongful dishonor Occurs when there are sufficient funds in a drawer's account to pay a properly payable check, but the bank does not do so.

CASE 18.2

Buckley v. Trenton Savings Fund Society
544 A.2d 857 (1988) Supreme Court of New Jersey

Facts In 1975, Joseph E. Buckley, Jr., then on the verge of taking his bar exam, opened a checking account in his name at Trenton Savings Fund Society (Bank). From 1979 through 1982, 30 checks drawn on his account were returned to him for insufficient *continued* funds. Some of the overdrafts were attributable to checks drawn by his wife, who signed his name as the drawer. In 1981, Buckley separated from his wife. As part of their separation agreement, Buckley agreed to pay his wife $150 per week to support her and their four children. On January 14, 1984, Mrs. Buckley tried to cash one of Buckley's $150 checks at the Bank's Robbinsville branch. The Bank refused to cash the check because she did not maintain an account there and could not otherwise identify herself. Mrs. Buckley cashed the check at the Bank's Ewing branch where she was known. Two months later, the Robbinsville branch again refused to cash one of Buckley's checks for Mrs. Buckley. She again cashed the check at the Ewing branch.

Buckley sued the Bank for wrongful dishonor of his checks. He alleged intentional infliction of emotional distress and sought damages for emotional distress and punitive damages. Buckley testified at trial that after both events, his wife, with whom he was engaged "in earnest divorce negotiations," berated him, that his friends and relatives did not accept his explanation why the checks were not cashed at the Robbinsville branch, and that his mother, father, and best friend continued to refuse to talk to him. The trial court awarded Buckley $25,000 damages for emotional distress but refused to award him punitive damages. The appellate court reversed. Buckley appealed.

Issue Is the Bank liable for the wrongful dishonor of the checks?

Decision No. The state supreme court held that Buckley failed to establish a cause of wrongful dis-

honor against the Bank. The supreme court remanded the case to the trial court for entry of an order dismissing the complaint.

Reason The court held that in order for a drawer to recover damages for emotional distress for wrongful dishonor, the wrongful dishonor must be the result of intentional conduct, willful or wanton conduct, or gross negligence of the drawer bank. The court held that the Bank did not engage in a wrongful dishonor that would warrant the recovery of damages for emotional distress. The court stated, "Slight emotional distress arising from the occasional dishonor of a check is one of the regrettable aggravations of living in today's society."

The court also held that Buckley could not recover punitive damages. Punitive damages are recoverable for wrongful dishonor only if a bank dishonors a check maliciously or with wanton recklessness. Neither of these circumstances applied in this case.

CASE QUESTIONS

Critical Legal Thinking Should damages for emotional distress be awarded for wrongful dishonor? Why or why not?

Ethics Do you think the lawsuit in this case was justified?

Business Implication Are "bad checks" (checks written against insufficient funds) a very big problem for businesses? How can a business protect itself from taking bad checks?

BUSINESS CHECKLIST

UCC Rule on "Full Payment" Checks

Often, when parties dispute the amount of money owed under a contract, the person owing the money will send a check for an amount less than that demanded by the other side and mark "Full and final payment" on the check. What should the party who receives the check do? If they cash the check, are they giving up the right to sue to recover the balance believed to be still owed?

The courts have not been consistent in answering these questions. Under the common law, most courts held that a party who cashed a full payment check gave up the right to sue the sender for any additional sums. By cashing the check, the common law held that there was an accord and satisfaction of the underlying dispute.

Prior to 1990, Section 1-207 of the Uniform Commercial Code (UCC 1-207) provided an opposite rule for sales contracts. UCC 1-207 stipulated that a seller of goods who received a full payment check from a buyer could cash the check and preserve the right to sue the buyer for additional amounts by writing the words *under protest, without prejudice,* or similar language on the back of the check before indorsing it.

State courts and legislatures throughout the country adopted one of these two rules. Sometimes a state would adopt both rules, the common law rule for service contracts and the UCC rule for sales contracts. Needless to say, contracting parties were often confused as to which rule applied to their transaction.

In 1990, the National Conference of Commissioners on Uniform State Laws revised UCC 1-207 to be in accord with the common law rule. Under this revision, the cashing of a full payment check as payment of a disputed sales contract is considered an accord and satisfaction that prevents the casher from suing the sender for any more damages.

Critics argue that the common law rule and new UCC 1-207 place the recipient of a full payment check in a cruel dilemma: (1) Cash the check and forfeit the right to sue the sender for further damages, or (2) return the check to the sender and preserve the right to sue for the full amount deemed due. Proponents of the change to UCC 1-207 argue that more certainty has been placed in the law. They also assert that the sender should be the master of his or her offer and has reason to expect that the offer will either be accepted or the check returned.

In this policy dispute, the Commissioners obviously favor the senders of full payment checks. It is expected that many states that follow the old UCC rule will amend their Uniform Commercial Codes to reflect the 1990 change in UCC 1-207.

FORGED SIGNATURES AND ALTERED CHECKS

Major problems associated with checks are that (1) certain signatures are sometimes forged and (2) the check itself may have been altered prior to presentment for payment. The UCC rules that apply to these situations are discussed in the following paragraphs. These rules apply to all types of negotiable instruments but are particularly important concerning checks.

"The love of money is the root of all evil."
Bible I Timothy 6:10

Forged Signature of the Drawer

When a check is presented to the payor bank for payment, the bank is under a duty to verify the drawer's signature. This usually is done by matching the signature on the signature card on a file at the bank to the signature on the check.

A check with a forged drawer's signature is called a **forged instrument**. A forged signature is wholly inoperative as the signature of the drawer. The check is not "properly payable" because it does not contain an order of the drawer. The payor bank cannot charge the customer's account if it pays a check over the forged signature. If the bank has charged the customer's account, it must recredit the account. The forged check must be dishonored [UCC 3-401].

The bank can recover only from the party who presented the check to it for payment if that party has knowledge that the signature of the drawer on the check was unauthorized [UCC 3-417(a)(3)]. The forger is liable on the check because the forged signature acts as the forger's signature [UCC 3-403(a)]. Although the payor bank can sue the forger, the forger usually cannot be found or is judgment-proof.

forged instrument
A check with a forged drawer's signature on it.

BUSINESS BRIEF
The ultimate loss for the payment of a check over the forged signature of the drawer *usually falls on the bank that paid the check. The payor bank may recover from the forger, if he or she can be found.*

altered check   A check that has been altered without authorization that modifies the legal obligation of a party.

original tenor   The original amount for which the drawer wrote the check.

presentment warranty Each prior transferor warrants that the check has not been altered.

forged indorsement   The forged signature of the payee or other holder.

transfer warranties   Each prior transferor warrants that he has good title to the check and that all signatures on the check are authentic and authorized.

CONSIDER THIS EXAMPLE: Suppose Gregory has a checking account at Country Bank. Lana steals a check, completes it, and forges Gregory's signature. She endorses it to Mike, who knows that Gregory's signature has been forged. Mike indorses it to Barbara, who is innocent and does not know of the forgery. She presents it to Country Bank, the payor bank, which pays the check. Country Bank may recover from the original forger, Lana, and from Mike, who knew of the forger. It cannot recover from Barbara because she did not have knowledge of the forgery.

Altered Checks

Sometimes, a check is altered before it is presented for payment. This is an unauthorized change in the check that modifies the legal obligation of a party [UCC 3-407(a)]. The payor bank can dishonor an **altered check** if it discovers the alteration.

If the payor bank pays the altered check, it can charge the drawer's account for the **original tenor** (i.e., original amount) of the check but not the forged amount [UCC 3-407(c); UCC 4-401(d)(1)].

In addition, it can recover the difference between the altered amount and the original tenor from the party who presented the altered check for payment. This is because the presenter of the check for payment and each prior transferor **warrant** that the check has not been altered [UCC 3-417(a)(2)]. If there has been an alteration, each party in the chain of collection can recover from the preceding transferor based on a breach of this warranty. This is called the **presentment warranty**. The ultimate loss usually falls on the party that first paid the altered check because that party was in the best position to identify the alteration. The forger is liable for the altered amount—if he or she can be found and is not judgment–proof.

CONSIDER THIS EXAMPLE: Father draws a $100 check on City Bank made payable to his daughter. The daughter alters the check to read $1,000 and cashes the check at the liquor store. The liquor store presents the check for payment to City Bank. City Bank pays the check. Father is liable only for the original tenor of the check ($100), and City Bank can charge the father's account this amount. City Bank is liable for the $900 difference, but it can recover this amount from the liquor store for breach of the presentment warranty. The liquor store can seek to recover the $900 from the daughter.

Forged Indorsements

A payee or holder can indorse a check to another person by signing the back of the check. The forged signature of the payee or other holder is called a **forged indorsement**. The payee or holder whose signature was forged is not liable on the check. A payor bank cannot charge the drawer's account if it pays a check over a forged indorsement. If the bank previously charged the drawer's account, it must recredit the amount charged [UCC 3-401].

Each prior transferor warrants that he has good title to the check and that all signatures of the check are authentic and authorized [UCC 3-416]. This warranty is called the **transfer warranty**. It works the same way all along the collection line. A payor bank that pays a check containing a forged indorsement can recover from the prior transferor based on the breach of transfer warranties. The ultimate loss usually falls on the party that took the check from the forger, and any further recovery must be from the forger.

CONSIDER THIS EXAMPLE: Suppose Joe draws a check on City Bank payable to the order of Anne and gives it to Anne. Ted steals the check from Anne, forges Anne's indorsement, and cashes the check at the liquor store. The liquor store deposits the check at Country Bank for collection, and Country Bank presents it to City Bank for payment. City Bank pays the check. Neither Joe nor Anne is liable on the check. Based on the breach of transfer warranties, City Bank can recover from Country Bank, Country Bank can recover from the liquor store, and the liquor store can recover from Ted, the thief. Country Bank and the liquor store are liable even though they did not have knowledge of the forgery.

Drawer's Negligence

The bank is not liable for paying a check over a forged signature of the drawer or on an altered check if the **drawer's negligence** substantially contributed to the forgery or alteration [UCC 3-406]. For example, the drawer would be liable if a company fails to control a facsimile machine that is used to sign checks and someone steals it and forges checks. The drawer would also be liable if he or she drew a poorly completed check that was later altered. However, if the payor bank was negligent in paying such a check, the payor bank and the drawer would share liability in proportion to their negligence.

drawer's negligence The drawer is liable if his or her negligence led to his or her forged signature or the alteration of a check. The payor bank is not liable in such circumstances.

Failure to Examine Bank Statements in a Timely Manner

Ordinarily, banks send their checking account customers monthly statements of account. The canceled checks usually accompany the statement, although banks are not required to send them. If the canceled checks are not sent to the customer, the statement of account must provide sufficient information to allow the customer to identify the checks paid (e.g., check number, amount, date of payment) [UCC 4-406(a)]. In addition, if the checks are not returned to the customer, the bank must retain either the original checks or legible copies for seven years. A customer may request the checks or copies of them during this period [UCC 4-406(b)].

The customer owes a duty to examine the statements (and canceled checks, if received) promptly and with reasonable care to determine whether any payment was not authorized because a check was altered or a signature was forged. The customer must promptly notify the bank of unauthorized payments [UCC 4-406(c)]. The customer is liable if the payor bank suffers a loss because the customer fails to perform these duties [UCC 4-406(d)(1)].

If the same wrongdoer engages in a **series of forgeries or alterations** on the same account, the customer must report to the payor bank within a reasonable period of time, not exceeding 30 calendar days from the date that the bank statement was made available to the customer [UCC 4-406(d)(2)]. The customer's failure to do so discharges the bank from liability on all similar forged or altered checks after this date and prior to notification.

The drawer's failure to report a forged or altered check to the bank within one year of receiving the bank statement and canceled checks containing it relieves the bank of any liability for paying the instrument [UCC 4-406(e)]. After that time, the payor bank is not required to recredit the customer's account for the amount of the forged or altered check even if the customer later discovers the forgery or alteration.

BUSINESS BRIEF
Banks are no longer required to return canceled checks to customers with their monthly statements. Instead, they are required to keep the check or legible copies for seven years and to provide the check or a copy of it to customers upon request.

CAUTION
A checking account customer owes a duty to examine bank statements promptly and with reasonable care to determine if any payment was made because of alteration of a check or forged signature of the customer.

ETHICAL PERSPECTIVE

Sinking the Banks' "Float"

Prior to 1987, bank customers complained that banks took too long to credit their accounts with checks they had received from others. Banks responded that they needed the time to make sure the deposited checks "cleared." A 1986 House Banking Committee report found that banks typically earned more than $300 million per year because of the interest-free "float period" between the time a check was deposited and the time the funds were released to customers.

The **Expedited Funds Availability Act** [12 U.S.C. §§
continued

4001-4010] enacted by Congress in 1987, and **Regulation CC** [12 C.F.R. Part 229], which was adopted by the Federal Reserve Board, to implement the Act, establish maximum time limits within which the funds from checks deposited in accounts must be available to account holders, require banks to make certain disclosures, and require banks to pay interest on deposited funds.

The law requires cash and "low-risk" items to be available for withdrawal on the business day following the banking day on which they are deposited. For example, if a low-risk check is deposited on Monday, the funds must be available to the customer on Tuesday. Low-risk items include U.S. Treasury checks, checks drawn on a state or unit of general local government, cashier's and certified checks, U.S. Postal Service money order, checks drawn on a Federal Reserve bank, checks drawn on a branch of the depository bank, and wire transfers.

Local checks—that is, checks drawn on a a bank located in the same Federal Reserve check–processing region as the bank in which the check was deposited—

must be available for withdrawal by the second business day following the banking day of deposit. Nonlocal checks may be held until the fifth business day following the banking day on which they were deposited.

The law permits banks to extend the maximum time within which funds must be available in the following situations: (1) deposits made to accounts established by new customers within the preceding 30 days, (2) deposits made in any one day to all accounts of a customer that total over $5,000, (3) redeposited checks, (4) deposits to an account that has been repeatedly overdrawn in the preceding six months, (5) deposits which the depository bank has reasonable cause to believe will be uncollectible, (6) emergency conditions such as war, equipment or computer failure, or emergency conditions beyond the depository bank's control. Banks must notify their customers when they extend the hold on a deposit under one of these exceptions.

The law requires banks to pay interest on deposits to interest-bearing accounts within one day of receiving cash deposits, wire

transfers, or on us checks (i.e., when the payor bank and the drawer bank are same). Banks must begin paying interest on other deposits within two days of their deposit.

Banks must give their account holders information on when funds will be available to them. In addition, customers must be notified of the funds availability rules. The Federal Reserve Board prepared a model policy disclosure statement that banks may use for this purpose.

The law imposes civil liability on banks that violate either the Act or any regulations adopted thereunder. In an individual action, liability is between $100 and $1,000. In a class action, the total award may not exceed the lesser of $500,000 or 1 percent of the net worth of the bank. A bank is not liable for a bona fide error.

The federal law preempts any conflicting state law except in one respect: State law may mandate faster funds availability than federal law.

1. Why did banks take so long to "clear" checks in the past?
2. Are the current clearing deadlines fair to bank customers?

BANK'S DUTY TO ACCEPT DEPOSITS

Article 4 of the UCC Article 4 of the UCC that governs the process of collecting checks through the banking system.

payor bank The bank where the drawer has a checking account and on which the check is drawn.

depository bank The bank where the payee or holder has an account.

collecting bank The depository bank and other banks in the collection process (other than the payor bank).

A bank is under a duty to accept deposits into a customer's account. This includes collecting checks that are drawn on other banks and made payable or indorsed to the depositor. The collection process, which may involve several banks, is governed by Article 4 of the UCC.

The Collection Process

When a payee or holder receives a check, he or she can either go to the drawer's bank (**the payor bank**) and present the check for payment in cash or—as is more common—deposit the check into a bank account at his or her own bank. This bank is called the **depository bank**. (The depository bank may also serve as the payor bank if both parties have accounts at the same bank.)

The depository bank must present the check to the **payor bank** for collection. At this point in the process, the Federal Reserve System (discussed next) and other banks may be used in the collection of a check. The depository bank and these other banks are called **collecting banks**. Banks in the collection process that are not the depository or payor bank are called **intermediary banks**. A bank can have more than one role during the collection process [UCC 4-105]. The collection process is illustrated in Exhibit 18.4.

intermediary bank A bank in the collection process that is not the depository or payor bank.

Exhibit 18.4
The Check Collection Process

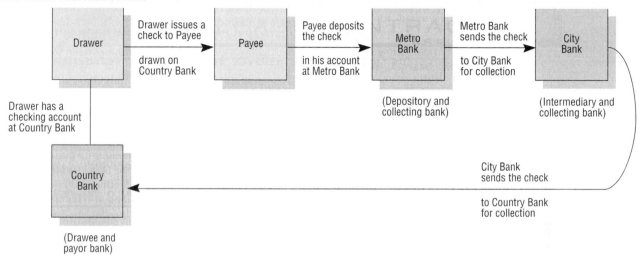

BUSINESS APPLICATION

The Federal Reserve System

The **Federal Reserve System** assists banks in the collection of checks. The Federal Reserve System consists of 12 regional Federal Reserve banks located in different geographical areas of the country. Rather than send a check directly to another bank for collection, member banks may submit paid checks to the Federal Reserve banks for collection.

Most banks in this country have accounts at the regional Federal Reserve banks. This is usually done by electronic presentment (i.e., by computer). The Federal Reserve banks debit and credit the accounts of these banks daily to reflect the collection and payment of checks. Banks pay the Federal Reserve banks a fee for this service. In large urban areas, private clearinghouses may provide a similar service [UCC 4-110; UCC 4-213(a)].

Deferred Posting

The **deferred posting rule** applies to all banks in the collection process. This rule allows banks to fix an afternoon hour of 2:00 P.M. or later as a cutoff hour for the purpose of processing checks. Any check or deposit of money received after this cutoff hour is treated as received on the next banking day [UCC 4-108]. Saturdays, Sundays, and holidays are not banking days unless the bank is open to the public for carrying on substantially all banking functions [UCC 4-104(a)(3)].

deferred posting rule A rule that allows banks to fix an afternoon hour of 2:00 P.M. or later as a cutoff hour for the purpose of processing items.

Provisional Credits

When a customer deposits a check into a checking account for collection, the depository bank does not have to pay the customer the amount of the check until the check **"clears"**—that is, until final settlement occurs (discussed below). The depository bank

provisional credit Occurs when a collecting bank gives credit to a check in the collection process prior to its final settlement. Provisional credits may be reversed if the check does not "clear."

may **provisionally credit** the customer's account. Each bank in the collection process provisionally credits the account of the prior transferor [UCC 4-201(a)]. If the check is dishonored by the payor bank (e.g., insufficient funds, a stop–payment order or closed account), the check is returned to the payee or holder, and the provisional credits are reversed. The collecting bank must either return the check to the prior transferor or notify that party within a reasonable time that provisional credit is being revoked. If the collecting bank fails to do this, it is liable for any losses caused by its delay [UCC 4-214].

Depository banks often allow their customers to withdraw the funds prior to final settlement. If the bank later learns that the check was dishonored, it can debit the customer's account for the amount withdrawn. If this is not possible (e.g., the payee or holder does not have sufficient funds in his or her account or has closed the account), the depository bank can sue the customer to recover the funds.

Final Settlement

final settlement Occurs when the payor bank either (1) pays the check in cash (2) settles for the check without having a right to revoke the settlement, or (3) fails to dishonor the check within certain statutory time periods.

A check is finally paid when the payor bank either (1) pays the check in cash (2) settles for the check without having a right to revoke the settlement or (3) fails to dishonor the check within certain statutory time periods. These time periods are discussed in the following paragraphs. When a check is finally settled, the provisional credits along the chain of collecting banks **"firm up"** and become **final settlements** [UCC 4-215(a)].

"on us" item A check that is presented for payment where the depository bank is also the payor bank. That is, the drawer and payee or holder have accounts at the *same* bank.

"On Us" Checks If the drawer and the payee or holder have accounts at the same bank, the depository bank is also the payor bank. The check is called an **"on us" item** when it is presented for payment by the payee or holder. In this case, the bank has until the opening for business on the second banking day following the receipt of the check to dishonor it. If it fails to do so, the check is considered paid. The payee or holder can withdraw the funds at this time [UCC 4-215(e)(2)].

CONSIDER THIS EXAMPLE: Christine and Jim each have checking accounts at Country Bank. On Tuesday morning, Christine deposits a $1,000 check from Jim into her account. Country Bank issues a provisional credit to Christine's account for this amount. On Thursday morning when the bank opens for business, the check is considered honored.

"on them" item A check presented for payment by the payee or holder where the depository bank and the payor bank are not the same bank.

"On Them" Checks If the drawer and the payee or holder have accounts at different banks, the payor and depository bank are not the same bank. In this case, the check is called an **"on them" item.**

midnight deadline The midnight of the next banking day following the banking day on which the bank received the "on them" check for collection.

Midnight Deadline Each bank in the collection process, including the payor bank, must take proper action on the check prior to its "midnight deadline." The **midnight deadline** is the midnight of the next banking day following the banking day on which the bank received an "on them" check for collection [UCC 4-104(a)(10)]. Collecting banks are permitted to act within a reasonably longer time, but the bank then has the burden of establishing the timeliness of its action [UCC 4-202(b)].

This deadline is of particular importance to the payor bank: If the payor bank does not dishonor a check by its midnight deadline, the bank is **accountable** (liable) for the face amount of the check. It does not matter whether the check is properly payable or not [UCC 4-302(a)]. For example, if on Wednesday morning a payor bank receives an on them check drawn on an account at the bank, it has until midnight of the next banking day, Thursday, to dishonor the check. If it does not, the check is considered paid by the bank.

This deadline does not apply to "on us" checks. As stated previously, "on us" checks clear when the bank opens on the second business day following receipt of the check (unless they are dishonored).

Presentment of an "On Them" Check Across the Counter

Instead of depositing an on them check for collection, a depositor can physically present the check for payment at the payor bank. This is called **presentment across the counter**. In this case, the payor bank has until the end of that banking day to dishonor the check. If it fails to do so, it must pay the check [UCC 4-301(a)].

presentment across the counter When a depositor physically presents the check for payment at the payor bank instead of depositing an "on them" check for collection.

Deposit of Money A deposit of money to an account becomes available for withdrawal at the opening of the next banking day following the deposit [UCC 4-215(f)].

BUSINESS APPLICATION

Missing the "Midnight Deadline"—A Bank Turns into a Pumpkin

In processing checks for collection, each bank in the collection process must take proper action on the check prior to its **"midnight deadline."** The midnight deadline is the midnight of the next banking day following the banking day in which the bank received an "on them" item—that is, a check drawn on another bank—for collection. What happens if a bank misses its midnight deadline and the check bounces? The following case answers this question.

Robert Dean Financial (RDF), a mortgage broker, and George I. Benny, one of its clients, used Chicago Title Insurance Company (Title Company) as the escrow agent to close certain real estate transactions they were engaged in. RDF and Benny wrote checks totalling $17 million drawn on their account at the San Mateo, California, branch office of Cali-

fornia Canadian Bank. The checks were payable to the Title Company as payee.

The Title Company deposited the checks from RDF and Benny at its bank, the Bank of San Francisco, for collection. This bank forwarded them to Crocker Bank, which in turn forwarded them to the San Francisco home office of California Canadian Bank for presentment. The next day, the home office of California Canadian Bank sent the checks to its San Mateo branch office for payment. The San Mateo branch dishonored the checks because there were no funds in the drawers' accounts to pay the checks. The checks left the San Mateo branch by courier for California Canadian Bank's in-house data processing and computer center prior to the midnight deadline, but the checks were not delivered back to

Crocker Bank until the next day—which was after the midnight deadline.

Unfortunately, RDF and Benny were engaged in a massive check fraud operation, and as a result either the Title Company or California Canadian Bank would end up bearing the loss. Litigation ensued between these two parties. The court held that California Canadian Bank should bear the loss because it failed to return the dishonored checks to Crocker Bank before the midnight deadline prescribed by the UCC. With interest, the judgment against California Canadian Bank totalled $25 million. This is a high price to pay for being one day late in returning bounced checks! [*Chicago Title Insurance Company v. California Canadian Bank*, 1 Cal.App.4th 798, 2 Cal.Rptr.2nd 422 (Cal.App. 1992)]

The "Four Legals" That Prevent Payment of a Check

Sometimes, the payor bank receives some form of notice that affects the payment of a check that has been presented for collection and is in the process of being posted. The following types of notice or actions—known as **the four legals**—effectively prevent payment of the check:

four legals Four notices or actions that prevent the payment of a check if they are received by the payor bank before it has finished its process of posting the check for payment.

1. Receipt of a notice affecting the account, such as a notice of the customer's death, adjudgment of incompetence, or bankruptcy.
2. Receipt of service of a court order or other legal process that "freezes" the customer's account, such as a writ of garnishment.
3. Receipt of a stop–payment order from the drawer.
4. The payor bank's exercise of its right of setoff against the customer's account.

If one of these four legals is received before the payor bank has finished its process of posting, the check cannot be paid contrary to the legal notice or action. However, the account is not affected if the check was paid or the process of posting was completed before the notice was received. The process of posting is considered completed when (1) the responsible bank officer has made a decision to pay the check, and (2) the proper book entry has been made to charge the drawer's account the amount of the check.

Liability of Collecting Banks for Their Own Negligence

duty of ordinary care Collecting banks are required to exercise ordinary care in presenting and sending checks for collection.

The collecting bank owes a **duty to use ordinary care** in presenting and sending a check for collection, sending notices of dishonor, and taking other actions in the collection process. Failure to do so constitutes *negligence*. A collecting bank that takes proper action on a check prior to its midnight deadline is deemed to have exercised ordinary care. A bank is liable only for losses caused by its own negligence [UCC 4-202].

ELECTRONIC FUND TRANSFER SYSTEMS

Computers and electronic technology have made it possible for banks to offer electronic payment and collection systems to bank customers. This technology is collectively referred to as **electronic fund transfer systems (EFTS)**. EFTS are supported by contracts among and between customers, banks, private clearinghouses, and other third parties. The most common forms of EFTS are discussed in the following paragraphs.

electronic fund transfer systems (efts) Electronic payment and collection systems that are facilitated by computers and other electronic technology.

Automated Teller Machines

automated teller machine (ATM) An EFTS at a convenient location that is connected on-line to the bank's computers; customers use ATMs to withdraw cash from bank accounts, cash checks, make deposits, and make payments owed to the bank.

An **automated teller machine (ATM)** is an electronic machine that is located either on a bank's premises or at some other convenient location, such as a shopping center or supermarket. These devices are connected on-line to the bank's computers. Bank customers are issued a secret personal identification number (PIN) to access their bank accounts through ATMs.

Although ATMs commonly are used when the bank is closed, they also are used as an alternative means of conducting bank business when the bank is open. They may be used to withdraw cash from bank accounts, cash checks, make deposits to checking or savings accounts, and make payments owed to the bank.

Point-of-Sale Terminals

Many banks issue **debit cards** to customers. Debit cards replace checks in that customers can use them to make purchases. No credit is extended. Instead, the customer's bank account is immediately debited for the amount of the purchase.

point-of-sale (pos) terminal A terminal at a merchant's checkout counter that is connected on-line to the bank's computers; a debit card or credit card can be used to make purchases at POS terminals.

Debit cards can be used only if the merchant has a **point-of-sale (POS) terminal** at the checkout counter. These terminals are connected on-line to the bank's computers. To make a purchase, the customer inserts the debit card into the terminal for the amount of the purchase. If there are sufficient funds in the customer's account, the transaction will debit the customer's account and credit the merchant's account for the amount of the purchase. If there are insufficient funds in the customer's account, the purchase is rejected unless the customer has overdraft protection.

Some POS terminals allow for the extension of credit in the transaction. Gasoline station and supermarket POS terminals are examples of this type of terminal.

Direct Deposits and Withdrawals

Many banks provide the service of paying recurring payments and crediting recurring deposits on behalf of customers. Commonly, payments are for utilities, insurance premiums, mortgage payments, and the like. Social security checks, wages, and dividend and interest checks are examples of recurring deposits. To provide this service, the customer's bank and the payee's bank must belong to the same clearinghouse.

Pay-by-Telephone and Pay-by-Computer Systems

Many banks permit customers to pay bills from their bank account by use of a telephone or a personal computer. To do so, the customer must enter his or her PIN and account number, the amount of the bill to be paid, and the account number of the payee to whom the funds are to be transferred. Such programs are increasing in popularity. Some banks are offering incentives to customers who pay by computer.

"A banker so very careful to avoid risk would soon have no risk to avoid."
Lord MacNaghten
Bank of England v. Vagliano Brothers
(1891)

CONTEMPORARY BUSINESS ENVIRONMENT

Consumer Rights Provided by the Electronic Fund Transfer Act

In 1978, Congress enacted the **Electronic Fund Transfer Act** [15 U.S.C. § 1693 et seq,] to regulate consumer fund transfers. The Federal Reserve Board, which is empowered to enforce the provisions of the Act, has adopted **Regulation E** to further interpret it. Regulation E has the force of law.

The Electronic Fund Transfer Act and Regulation E establish the following consumer rights:

1. **Unsolicited cards.** A bank can send unsolicited EFTS debit cards to a consumer only if the card is not valid for use. Unsolicited cards can be validated for use by a consumer's specific request.

2. **Correcting errors.** A customer has 60 days from the receipt of a bank statement to notify the bank of any error that appears on a bank statement. This notice can be oral or written. The bank has 10 days to investigate. In the alternative, the bank can recredit the customer's account and take an additional 45 days

to investigate. If there is no error, the bank can redebit the customer's account, plus interest.

3. **Lost or stolen debit cards.** Debit cards are sometimes lost or stolen. If a customer notifies the issuer bank within two days of learning that his or her debit card has been lost or stolen, the customer is liable for only $50 for unauthorized use. If a customer does not notify the bank within this two-day period, the customer's liability increases to $500. If the customer fails to notify the bank within 60 days after an unauthorized use appears on the customer's bank statement, the customer can be held liable for more than $500. Federal law allows states to impose a lesser liability on customers for lost or stolen debit cards.

4. **Evidence of transaction.** Other than for a telephone transaction, a bank must provide a customer with a written receipt of a transaction made

through a computer terminal. This receipt is prima facie evidence of the transaction.

5. **Bank statements.** A bank must provide a monthly statement to an EFTS customer at the end of the month that the customer conducts a transaction. Otherwise, a quarterly statement must be provided to the customer. The statement must include the date and amount of the transfer, the name of the retailer, the location or identification of the terminal, and the fees charged for the transaction. Bank statements must also contain the address and telephone number where inquiries or errors can be reported.

Banks are required to disclose the foregoing information to their customers. A bank is liable for wrongful dishonor when it fails to pay an electronic fund transfer when there are sufficient funds in the customer's account to do so.

INTERNATIONAL PERSPECTIVE

Commercial Wire Transfers: Article 4A of the Uniform Commercial Code

Commercial or **wholesale wire transfers** are often used to transfer payments between businesses

and financial institutions. Up to $5 trillion per day are transferred over the two principal wire pay-

ment systems—the **Federal Reserve wire transfer network**

continued

(Fedwire) and the **New York Clearing House Interbank Payments Systems (CHIPS)**. A wire transfer often involves a large amount of money (multimillion–dollar transactions are commonplace). The benefits of using wire transfers are their speed—most transfers are completed in the same day—and low cost. Banks sometimes require a customer to pay for a fund transfer in advance. On other occasions, however, a bank will extend credit to a customer and pay the fund transfer. The customer is liable to pay the bank for any properly paid fund transfer.

Article 4A—Fund Transfers of the UCC, which was promulgated in 1989, governs wholesale wire transfers. Most states have adopted this article. Where adopted, Article 4A governs the rights and obligations between parties to a fund transfer unless they have entered into a contrary agreement. Article 4A applies only to *commercial* electronic fund transfers; consumer electronic fund transfers subject to the Electronic Fund Transfer Act are not subject to Article 4A.

Fund transfers are often used to facilitate international commercial transactions. Consider the following example: Suppose Diebold Corporation, a corporation located in the United States, wants to pay Japanese Steel, a Japanese Corporation, for supplies it purchased. Instead of delivering a negotiable instrument such as a check to Japanese Corporation, a corporation located in Japan, Diebold instructs its bank to wire the funds to Japanese Corporation's bank with instructions to credit Japanese Corporation's account. Diebold's order is called a *payment order*. Diebold is the *originator* of the wire transfer and Japanese Corporation is the *beneficiary*. Diebold's bank is called the *originator's bank* and Japanese Corporation's bank is called the *beneficiary's bank*. In more complex transactions, there may be one or more additional banks known as *intermediary banks* between the originator's bank and the beneficiary's bank [UCC 4A-103(a)].

If a receiving bank mistakenly pays a greater amount to the beneficiary than ordered, the originator is liable for only the amount he or she instructed to be paid. The receiving bank that erred has the burden of recovering any overpayment from the beneficiary [UCC 4A-303(a)]. If a wrong beneficiary is paid, the originator is not obliged to pay his or her payment order. The bank that issued the erroneous payment order has the burden of recovering the payment from the improper beneficiary [UCC 4A-303(c)].

Banks and customers usually establish security procedures (e.g., codes, identifying numbers, or words) to prevent unauthorized electronic payment orders. To protect the bank from liability for unauthorized payment orders, the security procedure must be commercially reasonable. If the bank verifies the authenticity of a payment order by complying with such a security procedure and pays the order, the customer is bound to pay the order even if it was not authorized [UCC 4A-202]. The customer is not liable if it can prove that the unauthorized order was not initiated by an employee or other agent or by a person who obtained that information from a source controlled by the customer [UCC 4A-203].

WORKING THE WEB

Internet Banking and Financial Index Here is a site where you can find out about careers in banking, national banks, international banks, mortgage banks, bank technology, and other resources.

Visit at http://www.ddsi.com/banking/

World Bank Find out all about the World Bank Group at their Web site.

Visit at http://www.worldbank.org/

Legal Information Institute Banking Law Materials Cornell University's Legal Information Institute maintains a list of banking law materials that will link you to many banking resources.

Visit at http://www.law.cornell.edu/topics/banking.html

Organization for Economic Development The Organization for Economic Development (OECD) maintains a Web site full of useful information.

Visit at http://www.oecd.org/

Bank of Canada   Everything you ever wanted to know about the Bank of Canada is available at its Web site.

Visit at http://www.bank–banque–canada.ca/english/intro-e.htm

CYBER EXERCISES:

1. Using the Internet Banking and Financial Index, find a U.S. bank in your state.

2. Using the World Bank Web site, find the date of the next annual Conference on Development Economics.

3. From the Legal Information Institute–Banking Law Materials site, find the Federal Deposit Insurance Corporation home page.

4. From the OECD Web site, find and print the summary of a free document called *Electronic Commerce Opportunities and Challenges for Government (The Sacher Report).*

5. Is information on the Bank of Canada Web site available in English?

CHAPTER SUMMARY

THE BANK–CUSTOMER RELATIONSHIP, P. 415

| The Bank–Customer Relationship | 1. *Creditor–debtor relationship.* Occurs when a customer (the *depositor*) deposits money into his or her account at a financial institution. In effect, the customer is loaning money to the financial institution. The customer is the *creditor* and the financial institution is the *debtor*. |
| | 2. *Principal–agent relationship.* Occurs when a customer writes a check against his or her checking account or deposits a check into his or her account for collection by the financial institution. The customer is the *principal*, and the financial institution is the *agent*. |

THE UNIFORM COMMERCIAL CODE, P. 415

The Uniform Commercial Code	The following *articles* of the Uniform Commercial Code (UCC) govern the creation, collection, and enforcement of checks and wire transfers:
	1. *Article 3.* Sets forth the requirements for creating a negotiable instrument, including checks. *Revised Article 3* was promulgated in 1990
	2. *Article 4.* Establishes rules and principles that regulate the deposit and collection of *checks* by the banking system
	3. *Article 4A.* Article of the UCC promulgated in 1989 that establishes rules and principals regulating the creation and collection of and liability for *wire transfers.*

ORDINARY CHECKS, P. 415

Ordinary Checks	1. *Check.* An order by a checking account holder (the *drawer*) to the financial institution at which the account is located (the *drawee*) to pay a named person (the *payee*) the amount of the check.
	2. *Drawer.* The checking account holder and writer of the check.
	3. *Drawee.* The financial institution on which the check is drawn.
	4. *Payee.* The party to whom the check is written.

SPECIAL TYPES OF CHECKS, P. 416

| Special Types of Checks | *Bank checks.* Special types of checks for which the bank is solely or primarily liable. *Bank checks* include certified checks, cashier's checks, and traveler's checks. These bank checks are considered "as good as cash" because the issuing bank has guaranteed their payment. |

Certified Check	A type of check where a bank agrees in advance (*certifies*) to accept and pay the check when it is presented for payment. Occurs when the issuer or holder takes an ordinary check to the bank and the bank writes "certified" on the check. The bank sets aside funds from the issuer's account to pay the check when it is presented for payment.
Cashier's Check	A check issued by a bank where a person pays the bank the amount of the check and a fee, and the bank guarantees that it will pay the check when it is presented for payment. The person purchasing a cashier's check does not have to have a checking account at the bank.
Traveler's Check	A form of check sold by banks and other issuers. The purchaser of the traveler's checks signs them at the time of purchase. When the checks are used to purchase goods or services, the purchaser again signs the check and fills in the payee's name. Purchasers of traveler's checks do not have to have an account at the issuing bank.

HONORING CHECKS, P. 419

Honoring Checks	*Honor*. When a drawee bank receives a properly drawn check and there are sufficient funds in the drawer's account to pay the check, the bank must **honor** the check and pay it.
Stale Check	A check that has been outstanding for more than six months before it is presented for payment. *Payment of a stale check*. A bank is under no obligation to pay a stale check. A bank that pays a stale check in good faith may charge the drawer's account.
Incomplete Check	A check that omits certain information, such as the amount of the check or the payee's name. *Payment of an incomplete check*. A bank may pay an incomplete check **as completed** by the payee as long as it acts in good faith and without notice that the completion was improper.
Postdated Check	A check that is dated with a date in the future. *Payment of a postdated check*. A bank may pay a postdated check and charge the drawer's account, even though payment is made before the date on the check, *unless* the drawer has given the bank *separate notice* (notice in addition to the date on the check) stating not to pay the postdated check until its date and describing the check with reasonable certainty. Oral notice is good for 14 days, and written notice is good for six months, which may be renewed for additional six-month periods. A bank that pays a postdate check over such notice is liable for damages resulting there-from.
Death or Incompetence of a Drawer	1. *Death of drawer*. A bank may pay or certify checks drawn on a deceased account for 10 days after receiving actual notice of the customer's death unless a person claiming an interest in the account (e.g., heir or taxing authority) stops payment on the checks. 2. *Incompetence of drawer*. A bank may pay checks of a customer adjudicated incompetent until the bank has received actual notice of the customer's adjudication of incompetence.
Stop-Payment Orders	An order by a drawer of a check to the payor bank not to pay or certify a check. An oral stop-payment order is binding on the bank for only 14

	days; a written stop-payment order is binding for six months, and may be renewed for additional six-month periods. 1. *Payment over a stop–payment order*. If the payor bank fails to honor a stop–payment order and pays the check, it must recredit the customer's account the amount paid. The bank is subrogated to the rights of the drawer.
Overdraft	*Insufficient funds*. Occurs when a drawer does not have sufficient funds in his or her account to cover a check the drawer has written. The check is said to have "bounced." 1. *Overdraft*. When a check is presented for payment and there are insufficient funds in the drawer's account to pay the check, the payor bank may either (1) dishonor the check or (2) honor the check and create an *overdraft* in the drawer's account. The bank can later charge the drawer's account the amount of the overdraft or sue the drawer to recover this amount.
Wrongful Dishonor	Occurs when a payor bank dishonors a drawer's properly payable check when it is presented for payment even though there are sufficient funds in the account to honor the check. 1. *Liability for wrongful dishonor*. The payor bank is liable to the drawer for damages proximately caused by the wrongful dishonor of a check, plus consequential damages, and damages caused by criminal prosecution.

FORGED SIGNATURES AND ALTERED CHECKS, P. 423

Forged Signature of the Drawer	1. *Forged instrument*. A check on which the *drawer's signature* has been forged.
	2. *Liability on a forged instrument:*
	   a. *Drawer*. A forged signature is wholly inoperative as the signature of the drawer. Therefore, the drawer is not liable on a forged instrument, and the bank cannot charge the drawer's account the amount paid. If the bank has charged the drawer's account, the account must be recredited.
	   b. *Forger*. The forger is liable on the check because the forged signature acts as the forger's signature.
	   c. *Prior transfers*. Prior transferors who had *knowledge* that the signature of the drawer was forged are liable on the forged instrument.
	   d. *Payor bank*. A payor bank that has charged the drawer's account for a forged instrument must seek recovery from the forger and prior transferors who had knowledge of the forged signature. The ultimate loss for the payment of a forged check usually falls on the payor bank (unless it can recover from the forger).

Altered Check	A check that has been altered without authorization of the drawer that modifies the legal obligation of a party.
	1. *Liability on an altered check:*
	   a. *Drawer*. If a payor bank pays an altered check, it can charge the drawer's account the *original tenor* (original amount) of the check. The drawer is not liable for the altered amount.
	   b. *Forger*. The person who altered the check is liable on the check for the amount above the original tenor.
	   c. *Prior transferors*. The presenter of the check for payment and all prior transferors *warrant* that the check has not been altered. This is

	called a *presentment warranty*. Therefore, the payor bank can recover from the presenter for breach of this warranty, and each party in the chain of collection can recover from the preceding transferor based on the breach of this warranty. The ultimate loss usually falls on the party that first paid the altered check (unless that party can recover from the forger). d. *Payor bank*. Can recover from the presentor of the altered check, any prior transferor, or the forger.

Forged Indorsement	The forged signature of the *payee* or *other holder* on the instrument. For example, a forger forges the indorsement of a payee on the back of a check.
	
	1. *Liability on a forged indorsement.*
	   a. *Indorser*. The payee or holder (indorser) whose signature has been forged is not liable on the check.
	   b. *Forger*. The forger is liable on the check.
	   c. *Prior transferors*. If a payor bank pays a check containing a forged indorsement, it can recover from the prior transferor based on breach of *transfer warranty*. Each party in the chain of collection can recover from the prior transferor based on the breach of this warranty.
	   d. *Payor bank*. Can recover from the prior transferor, any prior transferor, or the forger.

Drawer's Negligence	The payor bank is not liable for paying a check over the forged signature of the drawer or on an altered check if the *drawer's negligence* substantially contributed to the forgery or alteration.
Failure to Examine Bank Statements in a Timely Manner	1. *Duty to examine bank statements*. A bank customer owes a duty to examine bank statements (and canceled checks, if received) *promptly* and with *reasonable care* to determine if any payment was not authorized because of the forged signature of the customer or alteration of a check. The customer must notify the bank of unauthorized payments. 2. *Failure to examine bank statements*. A customer who fails to examine bank statements promptly and reasonably and notify the bank of unauthorized payments is liable for any losses suffered by the bank because of this failure. 3. *Series of forgeries or alterations*. If the *same wrongdoer* engages in a series of forgeries or alterations on the same account, the customer must report that to the payor bank within a reasonable time, not exceeding 30 calendar days from the date that the bank statement was made available to the customer. The customer's failure to do so discharges the bank from liability on all similar forged or altered checks after this date and prior to notification.

BANK'S DUTY TO ACCEPT DEPOSITS, P. 426

The Collection Process	1. *Bank's duty to accept deposits*. A bank owes a duty to accept deposits into a customer's account. This includes collecting checks that are drawn on other banks and made payable or indorsed to the customer. 2. *Collection process*. If a customer deposits a check drawn on another bank into his or her account at a bank, his or her bank may send the check directly to the payor bank or through other banks until it is received by the payor bank for payment.

	3. *Banks in the collection process.* The *banks* that may be involved in the collection process are: a. *Depository bank.* The bank at which the *payee* or *holder* has an account and deposits a check into this account to be collected. b. *Payor bank.* The bank where the *drawer* has a checking account and which will pay the check if properly payable. (The payor bank and depository bank will be the same bank if both the drawer and the payee or holder have accounts at the same bank.) c. *Collecting bank.* Any bank in the collection process other than the payor bank. The depository bank is also a collecting bank. d. *Intermediary bank.* A bank in the collection process other than the depository and payor banks.
The Federal Reserve System	A series of 12 regional Federal Reserve banks that assist banks in the collection of checks. The Federal Reserve banks act as collecting banks by debiting and crediting the accounts of banks at the Federal Reserve banks daily to reflect the collection and payment of checks.
Deferred Posting	1. *Deferred posting rule.* Rule that allows banks to fix an afternoon hour of *2:00 P.M.* or *later* as a *cutoff hour* for the purpose of processing checks. Any check or deposit received after this cutoff hour is treated as received the next banking day. 2. *Banking days.* Days that a bank is open to the public for carrying on substantially all banking functions.
Provisional Credit	Occurs when a bank in the collection process credits a customer's account with the amount of a deposited check before the check has cleared by final settlement. 1. *Reversal of provisional credits.* If a deposited check does not clear (e.g., insufficient funds, stop–payment order), all provisional credits may be reversed.
Final Settlement	Occurs when the payor bank either (1) pays the check in cash, (2) settles for the check without having a right to revoke the settlement, or (3) fails to dishonor the check within certain statutory time periods. When a check is finally settled, all provisional credits "firm up" and become final settlements. 1. *Statutory deadlines.* Article 4 establishes the following *statutory deadlines* for collecting and payor banks to act on checks: a. *"On us" check.* A check that is presented for payment where the drawer and payee or holder have accounts at the *same bank.* That is, the payor bank is also the depository bank. In this case, the bank has until the opening for business on the second banking day following the receipt of the check to dishonor it. If it fails to do so, the check is considered paid. b. *"On them" check.* A check that is presented for payment where the drawer and payee or holder have accounts at *different banks.* That is, the payor bank and the depository bank are different banks. In this case, each bank in the collection process, including the payor bank, must take proper action on the check (particularly the payor bank to dishonor the check) prior to its "midnight deadline." *Midnight deadline* is the midnight of the next banking day following the banking day on which the bank received the "on them" check for collection.

	c. *Presentment across the counter.* Occurs when a payee or holder physically presents an "on them" check for payment at the payor bank rather than using the collection process. In this case, the payor bank has until the end of that banking day to dishonor the check. If it fails to do so, it must pay the check.
The "Four Legals" That Prevent Payment of a Check	*The "four legals."* Four notices or actions that prevent the payment of a check if they are received by the payor bank before it has finished its *process of posting* the check for payment. The "four legals" are: 1. Receipt of a notice affecting the account, such as a notice of the customer's death, adjudgment of incompetence, or bankruptcy 2. Receipt of service of a court order or other legal process that "freezes" the customer's account, such as a writ of garnishment 3. Receipt of a stop–payment order from the drawer 4. The payor bank's exercise of its right to *setoff* against the customer's account.
Liability of Collecting Banks for Their Own Negligence	1. *Duty of ordinary care.* Collecting banks are required to exercise *ordinary care* in presenting and sending checks for collection. 2. *Liability for negligence.* A collecting bank that fails to exercise ordinary care in the collection of checks is negligent. A collecting bank is liable for losses caused by its *negligence* in the collection process.
Expedited Funds Availability Act	A federal statute that establishes maximum time limits within which funds from checks deposited into customer's accounts must be made available to account holders. The act also requires banks to pay interest on deposited funds, thus eliminating the interest-free *"float"* banks previously earned from deposited—but not yet credited—deposits.

ELECTRONIC FUND TRANSFER SYSTEMS, P. 430

Electronic Fund Transfer Systems	Electronic payment and collection systems that are facilitated by computers and other electronic technology. Commonly referred to as *EFTS.*
Automated Teller Machines	An EFTS at a convenience location that is connected on-line to the bank's computers. Customers use ATMs to withdraw cash from bank accounts, cash checks, make deposits, make payments owed to the bank, and conduct other transactions.
Point-of-Sale Terminals	A terminal at a merchant's checkout counter that is connected on-line to the bank's computers. *Debit cards*, which replace checks, are usually used at POS terminals. The amount of the purchase is immediately debited from the customer's account. Credit cards may also be used at some POS terminals.
Direct Deposits and Withdrawals	Service provided by many banks whereby they will credit *recurring deposits* (e.g., social security checks) to customer's accounts and make *recurring payments* (e.g., mortgage payments, insurance premiums) from customers' accounts.
Pay-by-Telephone and Pay-by-Computer Systems	Many banks permit customers to pay bills from their accounts by use of a telephone or a personal computer.
Electronic Fund Transfer Act	A federal statute that regulates *consumer* electronic fund transfers. 1. *Regulation E.* A regulation adopted by the Federal Reserve Board that interprets and enforces the Electronic Fund Transfer Act.

2. *Consumer rights.* The Electronic Fund Transfer Act and Regulation E establish certain consumer rights concerning the solicitation, use, and liability for lost or stolen credit cards.

COMMERCIAL WIRE TRANSFERS, P. 431

Commercial Wire Transfers	The transfer of funds electronically by wire between businesses and financial institutions.
	1. *Wire payment systems.* The two principal wire payment systems in this country are the Federal Reserve wire transfer network (*Fedwire*) and the New York Clearing House Interbank Payments System (*CHIPS*).
	2. *Article 4A of the UCC.* Article 4A of the UCC governs the creation of, transfer, collection of and liability for commercial wire transfers.

CRITICAL LEGAL THINKING CASES

18.1 Cashier's Check In October 1978, Dr. Graham Wood purchased a cashier's check in the amount of $6,000 from Central Bank of the South (Bank). The check was made payable to Ken Walker and was delivered to him. In September 1979, the Bank's branch manager informed Wood that the cashier's check was still outstanding. Wood subsequently signed a form requesting that payment be stopped and a replacement check issued. He also agreed to indemnify the bank for any damages resulting from the issuance of the replacement check. The Bank issued a replacement check to Wood. In April 1980, Walker deposited the original cashier's check in his bank, which was paid by Bank. Bank requested that Woods repay the bank $6,000. When he refused, Bank sued Woods to recover this amount. Who wins? [*Wood v. Central Bank of the South*, 435 So.2d 1287 (Ala. App. 1982)]

18.2 Overdraft Louise Kalbe maintained a checking account at the Pulaski State Bank (Bank) in Wisconsin. In December 1981, Kalbe made out a check for $7,260.00 payable to cash. Thereafter, she misplaced it but did not report the missing check to the bank or stop payment on it. In January 1982, some unknown person presented the check to a Florida bank for payment. The Florida bank paid the check and sent it to Bank for collection. Bank paid the check even though it created a $6,542.12 overdraft in Kalbe's account. Bank requested Kalbe pay this amount. When she refused, Bank sued Kalbe to collect the overdraft. Who wins? [*Pulaski State Bank v. Kalbe*, 364 N.W.2d 162 (Wis. App. 1985)]

18.3 Wrongful Dishonor Larry J. Goodwin and his wife maintained a checking and savings account at City National Bank of Fort Smith (Bank). The Bank also had a customer named Larry K. Goodwin. In November 1985, two loans of Larry K. Goodwin were in default. The Bank mistakenly took money from Larry J. Goodwin's checking account to pay the loans. On Saturday, November 30, 1985, the Goodwins received written notice that four of their checks, which were written to merchants, had been dishonored for insufficient

funds. When the Goodwins investigated, they discovered that their checking account balance was zero and the bank had placed their savings account on hold. After being informed of the error, Bank promised to send letters of apology to the four merchants and to correct the error. However, the Bank subsequently "bounced" several other checks of the Goodwins. Eventually, the bank notified all of the parties of its error. On January 14, 1986, the Goodwins closed their accounts at the bank and were paid the correct balances due. They sued the bank for consequential and punitive damages for wrongful dishonor. Who wins? [*City National Bank of Fort Smith v. Goodwin*, 783 S.W.2d 335 (Ark. 1990)]

18.4 Stale Check On June 30, 1972, Charles Ragusa & Son (Ragusa), a partnership consisting of Charles and Michael Ragusa, issued a check in the amount of $5,000 payable to Southern Masonry, Inc. (Southern). The check was drawn on Community State Bank (Bank). Several days later, Southern informed Ragusa that the check has been lost. Ragusa issued a replacement check for the same amount and sent it to Southern, which was cashed. At the same time, Ragusa gave a verbal stop payment to Bank regarding the original check. In July 1975, the original check was deposited by Southern into its account at the Bank of New Orleans. When the check was presented to Bank, it paid it and charged $5,000 against Ragusa's account. The partnership was not made aware of this transaction until August 4, 1975, when it received its monthly bank statement. Ragusa demanded that Bank recredit its account $5,000. When the bank refused to do so, Ragusa sued. Who wins? [*Charles Ragusa & Son v. Community State Bank*, 360 So.2d 231 (La.App. 1978)]

18.5 Postdated Check David Siegel maintained a checking account with the New England Merchants National Bank (Bank). On September 14, 1973, Siegel drew and delivered a $20,000 check payable to Peter Peters. The check was dated November 14, 1973. Peters immediately deposited the check in his own bank, which forwarded it for collection. On September

17, 1973, Bank paid the check and charged it against Siegel's account, Siegel discovered that the check had been paid when another of his checks was returned for insufficient funds. Siegel informed Bank that the check to Peters was postdated November 14 and requested that the bank return the $20,000 to his account. When Bank refused, Siegel sued for wrongful debit of his account. Must Bank recredit Siegel's account? [*Siegel v. New England Merchants National Bank*, 437 N.E.2d 218 (Mass.Sup. 1982)]

18.6 Stop Payment Dynamite Enterprises, Inc. (Dynamite), a corporation doing business in Florida, maintained a checking account at Eagle National Bank of Miami (Bank). Sometime in 1985, Dynamite drew a check on this account payable to one of its business associates. Before the check had been cashed or deposited, Dynamite issued a written stop–payment order to Bank. Bank informed Dynamite that it would not place a stop–payment order on the check because there were insufficient funds in the account to pay the check. Several weeks later the check was presented to Bank for payment. By this time, sufficient funds had been deposited in the account to pay the check. Bank paid the check and charged Dynamite's account. When Dynamite learned that the check had been paid, it requested Bank to recredit its account. When Bank refused, Dynamite sued to recover the amount of the check. Who wins? [*Dynamite Enterprises, Inc. v. Eagle National Bank of Miami*, 517 So.2d 112 (Fla. App.1987)]

18.7 Examining Bank Statements Mr. Gennone maintained a checking account at People's National Bank & Trust Co. of Pennsylvania (Bank). In June 1965, Gennone noticed that he was not receiving his bank statements and canceled checks. When Gennone contacted the bank, he was informed that the statements had been mailed to him. The bank agreed to hold future statements so that he could pick them up in person. Gennone picked up the statements, but did not reconcile the balance of the account. As a result, it was not until March 1967 that he discovered that beginning in January 1966 his wife had forged his signature on 25 checks. Gennone requested the bank to reimburse him for the amount of these checks. When the bank refused, Gennone sued the bank to recover. Who wins? [*Gennone v. Peoples National Bank & Trust Co.*, 9 UCC Rep.Serv. 707 (Pa.1971)]

18.8 Deferred Posting Dr. Robert L. Pracht received a check in the amount of $6,571.25 from Northwest Feedyards in payment for three loads of corn. The check was drawn on a checking account at Oklahoma State Bank (Bank). Pracht also maintained an account at the bank. On Friday, January 17, 1975, Pracht indorsed the check and gave it to an associate to deposit to Pracht's account at the bank. When the associate arrived at the bank around 3:00 P.M., he discovered that the bank's doors were locked. After gaining the attention of a bank employee, the associate was allowed into the bank, where he gave the check and deposit slip to a teller. Because the bank's computer had shut down at 3:00 P.M., the teller put the check aside. The associate testified that several bank employees were working at their desks as he left the bank. The bank was not open on Saturday, or Sunday. On Monday, January 20, 1975, the bank dishonored the check due to insufficient funds. Pracht sued to recover the amount of the check from the bank. Who wins? [*Pracht v. Oklahoma State Bank*, 26 UCC Rep. Serv. 141 (Okla. 1979)]

18.9 Right of Setoff On November 28, 1978, States Steamship Company (States Steamship) drew a check for $35, 948 on its checking account at Crocker National Bank (Crocker). The check was made payable to Nautilus Leasing Services, Inc. (Nautilus). Nautilus deposited the check in its account at Chartered Bank of London, which forwarded the check to Crocker for collection. The check was received at Crocker's processing center at 8:00 A.M. on Friday, December 1, 1978.

At the time the check was presented for payment, States Steamship was indebted to Crocker for loans in the amount of $2 million. These loans were payable on demand. During the latter part of 1978, States Steamship was in severe financial difficulty and was conducting merger negotiations with another steamship company. On the morning of Monday, December 4, 1978, Crocker learned that these merger negotiations had broken down and demanded immediate payment of the $2 million. Crocker then seized the $1,726,032 in States Steamship's checking account at the bank. This action left States Steamship's account with a zero balance. States Steamship's check to Nautilus, as well as other checks that had been presented for payment, were returned unpaid. Nautilus sued Crocker to recover the amount of the check. Who wins? [*Nautilus Leasing Services, Inc. v. Crocker National Bank*, 195 Cal.Rptr. 478 (Cal.App. 1983)]

ETHICS CASES

18.10 Ethical Perspective In 1982, Actors Equity, a union that represents 37,000 stage actors and actresses, sought to hire a new comptroller. A man named Nicholas Scotti applied for the position and submitted an extensive resume showing that he was currently employed by Paris Maintenance Co. as its comptroller. Scotti also stated that he had held various financial positions with the Equitable Life Assurance Society and the Investors Funding Corporation. Officers of Actors Equity interviewed Scotti and offered him the job. No attempt was made to verify Scotti's background or prior employment history.

Actors Equity maintained a checking account at the Bank of New York. During the first six months as comptroller, Scotti forged the signature of the appropriate company employee on four Actors Equity checks totaling $100,000. The checks were made payable to N. Piscotti and were cashed by Scotti and paid by the Bank of New York. The forged signatures were of professional quality. After Scotti resigned as comptroller, the forgeries were discovered. Subsequent investigation revealed that Scotti's real name was Piscotti, the information on his resume was false, and he had an extensive criminal record. Actors Equity sued the drawee bank to recover the $100,000. Did

Scotti act ethically in this case? Should Actors Equity have sued the bank to recover on the forged checks? Who wins? [*Fireman's Fund Insurance Co. v. The Bank of New York*, 539 N.Y.S.2d 339 (N.Y.Sup. 1989)]

18.11 Ethical Perspective Golden Gulf, Inc. (Golden Gulf) opened a checking account at AmSouth Bank, N.A. (AmSouth). On August 27, 1988, Golden Gulf entered into a subscription agreement wherein Albert M. Rossini agreed to pay $250,000 for stock in the company. Rossini tendered a check drawn on the Mark Twain Bank in Kansas City, Missouri, to Golden Gulf for that amount. Golden Gulf deposited the check in its checking account at AmSouth on August 30, 1988. On September 2, 1988, Golden Gulf contacted AmSouth and asked if the funds were "available." AmSouth said the funds were available for use. Golden Gulf requested AmSouth to wire transfer the funds to it in New York for use in that state. AmSouth complied with the request. On September 7, 1988, AmSouth received notice from the Mark Twain Bank that Rossini's check would not be paid due to insufficient funds. On September 8, 1988, AmSouth notified Golden Gulf that the check has been dishonored. AmSouth revoked the credits it had given to Golden Gulf's account, resulting in an overdraft of $248,965.69. AmSouth sued to recover this amount. Did Golden Gulf act ethically in this case? Did AmSouth extend a provisional or final settlement to Golden Gulf's account? [*Golden Gulf, Inc. v. AmSouth Bank, N.A.*, 565 So.2d 114 (Ala. 1990)]

 CRITICAL LEGAL THINKING WRITING ASSIGNMENT

Read Case A.18 in the Case Appendix [*First American Bank and Trust v. Rishoi*]. This case is excerpted from the U.S. Supreme Court opinion. Review and brief the case. In your brief, be sure to answer the following questions:

1. Who was the plaintiff? Who was the defendant?
2. What type of negotiable instrument was at issue in this case?
3. Was the issuer's dishonor of the negotiable instrument proper or wrongful?

CHAPTER 19

CREDIT, SURETYSHIP,

AND SECURED TRANSACTIONS

Chapter Objectives

*After studying this chapter,
you should be able to*

1. Distinguish between unsecured and secured credit
2. Define a secured transaction in personal property
3. Describe the scope of Article 9 of the UCC
4. Define the floating-lien concept
5. Describe the perfection of a security interest by filing a financing statement
6. Describe the perfection of a security interest by methods other than by filing a financing statement
7. Define a purchase money security interest
8. Identify limits on self-help in repossessing collateral
9. Define and distinguish between surety and guaranty contracts
10. Define creditor's rights of attachment, execution, and garnishment

Chapter Contents

Creditors have better memories than debtors.

Benjamin Franklin
Poor Richard's Almanak
(1758)

The American economy is a credit economy. Consumers borrow money to make major purchases (e.g., homes, automobiles, appliances) and use credit cards (e.g., Visa or MasterCard) to purchase goods and services at restaurants, clothing stores, and the like. Businesses use credit to purchase equipment, supplies, and other goods and services. In a credit transaction, the borrower is the **debtor** and the lender is the **creditor**.

debtor The borrower in a credit transaction.

creditor The lender in a credit transaction.

Because lenders are reluctant to loan large sums of money simply on the borrower's promise to repay, many of them take a *security interest* either in the item purchased or some other property of the debtor. The property in which the security interest is taken is called *collateral*. If the debtor does not pay the debt, the creditor can foreclose on and recover the collateral.

A lender who is unsure whether a debtor will have sufficient income or assets to repay a loan may require another person to guarantee payment. If the borrower fails to repay the loan, that person is responsible for paying it. This is called *suretyship*.

This chapter discusses types of credit, secured transactions in personal property, and suretyship.

BUSINESS BRIEF
The United States is a credit economy. Businesses and individual persons use credit to purchase many goods and services.

TYPES OF CREDIT

Credit may be extended on either an *unsecured* or *secured* basis. The following sections discuss these types of credit.

Unsecured Credit

Unsecured credit does not require any security (collateral) to protect the payment of the debt. Instead, the creditor relies on the debtor's promise to repay the principal (plus any interest) when it is due. If the debtor fails to make the payments, the creditor may bring legal action and obtain a judgment against him or her. If the debtor is *judgment-proof* (i.e., has little or no property or no income that can be garnished), the creditor may never collect.

unsecured credit Credit that does not require any security (collateral) to protect the payment of the debt.

Secured Credit

To minimize the risk associated with extending unsecured credit, a creditor may require a security interest in the debtor's property (collateral). The collateral secures payment of the loan. This is called **secured credit**. Security interests may be taken in real, personal, intangible, and other property.

If the debtor fails to make the payments when due, the collateral may be repossessed to recover the outstanding amount. Generally, if the sale of the collateral is insufficient to repay the amount of the loan (plus any interest), the creditor may bring a lawsuit against the debtor to recover a **deficiency judgment** for the difference. Some states prohibit or limit deficiency judgments with respect to certain types of loans.

secured credit Credit that requires security (collateral) to secure payment of the loan.

deficiency judgment Judgment of a court that permits a secured lender to recover other property or income from a defaulting debtor if the collateral is insufficient to repay the unpaid loan.

BUSINESS APPLICATION

Klondike Bar's Claim Melts

Generally, a creditor would rather be a secured creditor than an unsecured creditor because of the extra protection and priority status the secured position gives the creditor. The following case shows why.

Sunstate Dairy & Food Products Co. (Sunstate) distributed dairy products in Florida. It had the following two debts among its other debts:

1. On November 19, 1990, Sunstate borrowed money from Barclays Business Credit, Inc. (Barclays), and signed a security agreement granting Barclays a continuing security interest in and lien upon substantially all of Sunstate's personal property, including all of Sunstate's inventory, equip-

ment, accounts receivable, and general intangibles then existing or thereafter acquired. Barclays perfected its security interest by filing a financing statement with the proper state government authorities.

2. On February 14, 1992, Sunstate purchased $49,512 of Klondike ice cream bars from Isaly Klondike Company (Klondike) on credit. Klondike did not take a security interest in the ice cream bars.

On February 19, 1992, Sunstate filed for bankruptcy. At that time, Sunstate owed Barclays $10,050,766, while $47,731 of unpaid-for Klondike bars remained in Sunstate's possession. Barclays and Klondike fought over the Klondike

bars. Klondike filed a motion with the court seeking to reclaim the Klondike bars. Barclays sought to enforce its security agreement and recover the Klondike bars.

The court sided with Barclays because it was a secured creditor with a perfected security interest. The court found that Klondike, as an unsecured creditor, had no legal right to reclaim the Klondike bars. Klondike was merely one of many unsecured general creditors that would receive but pennies-on-the-dollar in Sunstate's bankruptcy. Klondike learned a costly lesson: It is better to be a secured creditor than an unsecured creditor. [*In the Matter of Sunstate Dairy & Food Products Co.*, 145 Bankr. 341, 19 U.C.C. Rep.Serv.2d 113 (Bk.M.D. Fla.)]

SECURITY INTERESTS IN REAL PROPERTY

mortgage   A collateral arrangement where a property owner borrows money from a creditor who uses a deed as collateral for repayment of the loan.

mortgagor   The owner-debtor in a mortgage transaction.

mortgagee   The creditor in a mortgage transaction.

note and deed of trust   An alternative to a mortgage in some states.

A person who owns real property who borrows money from a creditor will often be required to pledge the real property as security for the repayment of the loan. Usually, an instrument called a **mortgage** is used to accomplish this. The owner-debtor is the **mortgagor**, and the creditor is the **mortgagee**.

CONSIDER THIS EXAMPLE: Suppose General Electric purchases a manufacturing plant for $10 million, pays $2 million cash as a down payment, and borrows the remaining $8 million from City Bank. To secure the loan, City Bank requires General Electric to give it a mortgage on the plant. If General Electric defaults on the loan, the bank may take action under state law to foreclose on the property.

Some state laws provide for the use of a **note and deed of trust** in place of a mortgage. The note is the instrument that evidences the borrower's debt to the lender; the deed of trust is the instrument that gives the creditor a security interest in the debtor's property that is pledged as collateral. Mortgages and deeds of trust are discussed in Chapter 29, Real Property. Most of the remainder of this chapter discusses secured transactions in personal property.

SECURITY INTERESTS IN PERSONAL PROPERTY— ARTICLE 9 OF THE UCC

Article 9 of the UCC   An article of the Uniform Commercial Code that governs secured transactions in personal property.

Article 9 of the UCC governs secured transactions in personal property. Article 9 had been adopted in one form or another by all states except Louisiana. Although there may be some variance between the states, most of the basics of Article 9 are the same.

When a creditor extends credit to a debtor and takes a security interest in some personal property of the debtor, it is called a *secured transaction*. The *secured party* is the seller, lender, or other party in whose favor there is a security interest, including a party to whom accounts or chattel paper have been sold [UCC 9-105(1)].

Secured Transactions

Exhibit 19.1 illustrates a two-party **secured transaction.** This occurs, for example, when a seller sells goods to a buyer on credit and retains a security interest in the goods.

secured transaction A transaction that is created when a creditor makes a loan to a debtor in exchange for the debtor's pledge of personal property as security.

Exhibit 19.1
Two-Party Secured Transaction

A three-party secured transaction is illustrated in Exhibit 19.2. This type of situation occurs when a seller sells goods to a buyer who has obtained financing from a third-party lender (e.g., bank) who takes a security interest in the goods sold.

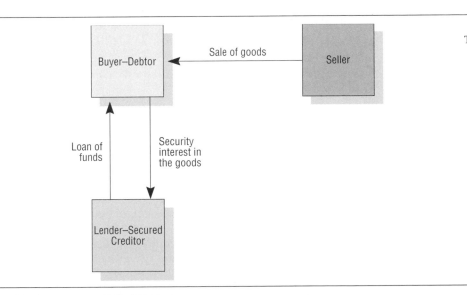

Exhibit 19.2
Three-Party Secured Transaction

CREATING A SECURITY INTEREST IN PERSONAL PROPERTY

Requirements for Creating a Security Interest

A secured party must meet the requirements discussed below to have an enforceable secured interest in collateral.

Written Security Agreement Unless the creditor has possession of the collateral, there must be a written security agreement. To be valid, a written **security agreement** must (1) clearly describe the collateral so that it can be readily identified, (2) contain the debtor's promise to repay the creditor, including terms of repayment (e.g., the interest rate, time of payment), (3) set forth the creditor's rights upon the debtor's default, and (4) be signed by the debtor [UCC 9-203(1)].

security agreement The agreement between the debtor and the secured party that creates or provides for a security interest.

CONSIDER THIS EXAMPLE: Suppose Ashley borrows $1,000 from Chris and gives Chris her gold ring as security for the loan. This agreement does not have to be in writing because the creditor is in possession of the collateral. This oral security agreement is enforceable. However, if Ashley retained possession of the ring, a written security interest describing the collateral (the ring) and signed by Ashley would be required.

Value Given to the Debtor The secured party must give value to the debtor. **Value** is defined as any consideration sufficient to support a simple contract [UCC 1-201(44)]. Normally, a creditor gives value by extending credit to the debtor to buy newly purchased goods. However, value can also be given as security for or in total or partial satisfaction of preexisting claims. There is no security agreement if the debtor does not owe a debt to the creditor.

Debtor Has Rights in Collateral The debtor must have a current or future legal right in or the right to possession of the collateral. For example, a debtor may give a creditor a security interest in goods currently owned or in the possession of the debtor, or in goods to be later acquired by the debtor. A debtor who does not have ownership or possessory rights to property cannot give a security interest in that property.

If these requirements are met, the rights of the secured party **attach** to the collateral. **Attachment** means that the creditor has an enforceable security interest against the debtor and can satisfy the debt out of the designated collateral (subject to priority rules discussed later in this chapter) [UCC 9-203(2)].

attachment The creditor has an enforceable security interest against the debtor and can satisfy the debt out of the designated collateral.

Personal Property Subject to a Security Agreement

A security interest may be given in various types of **personal property**, including the following:

personal property Property that consists of tangible property such as automobiles, furniture, and jewelry; intangible property such as securities, patents, and copyrights; and instruments, chattel paper, documents of title, and accounts.

- **Goods** including (1) consumer goods bought or used primarily for personal, family, or household purposes, (2) equipment bought or used primarily for business, (3) farm products, including crops, livestock, and supplies used or produced in farming operations, (4) inventory held for sale or lease, including work in progress and materials, and (5) fixtures that are affixed to real estate so as to become a part thereof
- **Instruments** such as checks, notes, stocks, bonds, and other investment securities
- **Chattel paper** (i.e., a writing or writings that evidence both a monetary obligation and a security interest, such as a conditional sales contract)
- **Documents of title**, including bills of lading, warehouse receipts, and such
- **General intangibles**, such as patents, copyrights, money, franchises, royalties, and the like

Article 9 does not apply to transactions involving real estate mortgages, landlord's liens, artisan's or mechanic's liens, liens on wages, judicial liens, and the like [UCC 9-104]. These types of liens are usually covered by other laws. Further, certain security interests governed by federal statutes are exempt from Article 9. For example, security interests in airplanes are subject to the provisions of the Federal Aviation Act.

The Floating-Lien Concept

floating lien A security interest in property that was not in the possession of the debtor when the security agreement was executed; this includes *after-acquired property*, *future advances*, and *sale proceeds*.

A security agreement may provide that the security interest attaches to property that was not originally in the possession of the debtor when the agreement was executed. This is usually referred to as a **floating lien**. A floating lien can attach to the types of property discussed in the following subsections.

After-Acquired Property

after-acquired property Property that the debtor acquires after the security agreement is executed.

Many security agreements contain a clause that gives the secured party a security interest in **after-acquired property** of the debtor. After-acquired property that the debtor acquires after the security agreement is executed [UCC 9-204(1)].

CONSIDER THIS EXAMPLE: Manufacturing Corp. borrows $100,000 from First Bank and gives the bank a security interest in both its current and after-acquired inventory. If Manufacturing Corp. defaults on its loan to First Bank, the bank can claim any available original inventory as well as enough after-acquired inventory to satisfy its secured claim.

Sales Proceeds Unless otherwise stated in the security agreement, if a debtor sells, exchanges, or disposes of collateral subject to such an agreement, the secured party automatically has the right to receive the **proceeds** of the sale, exchange, or disposition [UCC 9-203(3) and 9-306].

sale proceeds The resulting assets from the sale, exchange, or disposal of collateral subject to a security agreement.

CONSIDER THIS EXAMPLE: Zip, Inc., is a retail automobile dealer. To finance its inventory of new automobiles, Zip borrows money from First Bank and gives the bank a security interest in the inventory. Zip sells an automobile subject to the security agreement to Phyllis, who signs an installment sales contract agreeing to pay Zip for the car in 24 equal monthly installments. If Zip defaults on its payment to First Bank, the bank is entitled to receive the remaining payments from Phyllis.

Future Advances Often, debtors establish a continuing or revolving line of credit at a bank. Certain personal property of the debtor is designated as collateral for future loans from the line of credit. A maximum limit that the debtor may borrow is set, but the debtor can draw against the line of credit at any time. Any **future advances** made against the line of credit are subject to the security interest in the collateral. A new security agreement does not have to be executed each time a future advance is taken against the line of credit [UCC 9-204(3)].

future advances Personal property of the debtor that is designated as collateral for future loans from a line of credit.

PERFECTING A SECURITY INTEREST

The concept of **perfection of a security interest** establishes the right of a secured creditor against other creditors who claim an interest in the collateral. Perfection is a legal process. The three main methods of perfecting a security interest under the UCC are discussed in the following sections.

perfection of a security interest Establishes the right of a secured creditor against other creditors who claim an interest in the collateral.

Perfection by Filing a Financing Statement

Often, a creditor's physical possession of the collateral is impractical because it would deprive the debtor of use of the collateral (e.g., farm equipment, industrial machinery, and consumer goods). At other times, it is simply impossible (e.g., accounts receivable). Filing a **financing statement** in the appropriate government office is the most common method of perfecting a creditor's security interest in such collateral. The person who files the financing statement should request the filing officer to note the file number, date, and hour of filing on his or her copy of the document [UCC 9-402(1)]. A financing statement covering fixtures is called a *fixture filing*.

financing statement A document filed by a secured creditor with the appropriate government office that constructively notifies the world of his or her security interest in personal property.

Financing statements are available for review by the public. They serve as constructive notice to the world that the creditor claims an interest in the property. Financing statements are effective for five years from the date of filing. A *continuation statement* may be filed up to six months prior to the expiration of the financing statement's five-year term. Such statements are effective for a new five-year term. Succeeding continuation statements may be filed [UCC 9-403(2) and (3)].

To be enforceable, the financing statement must contain (1) the debtor's name and mailing address, (2) the name and address of the secured party from whom information concerning the security interest can be obtained, and (3) a statement (preferable exactly as shown in the security agreement) indicating the types, or describing the items, of collateral. The secured party can file the security agreement as a financing statement [UCC 9-402(1)].

State law specifies where the financing statement must be filed. The UCC provides that a state may choose either the secretary of state, the county clerk in the county of

BUSINESS BRIEF
It is good practice for a creditor who plans on taking a security interest in personal property to check whether any previous financing statements have been filed concerning the property and, if not, to properly file a financing statement covering its interest in the property.

the debtor's residence, or, if the debtor is not a resident of the state, then in the county where the goods are kept or other county office or both. Most states require financing statements covering farm equipment, farm products, accounts, and consumer goods to be filed with the county clerk [UCC 9-401].

In the following two cases, the courts found there was a defective filing of the financing statements.

CASE 19.1

In Re Walker
142 Bankr. 484 (1992) United States Bankruptcy Court, Middle District of Florida

Facts John Deere Company (Deere) manufactures and sells farm equipment. On August 30, 1989, Richard Walker purchased a Model 2955 Tractor and a Model 265 Loader from Deere on credit. Walker signed a security agreement covering the equipment. Prior to October 1, 1989, Florida law required that financing statements on farm equipment be filed in the official records in the county of the debtor's place of business. Effective October 1, 1989, the farm equipment portion of the state's Article 9 was removed, making the office of the secretary of state in Tallahassee, Florida, the proper place to file. On October 2, 1989, Deere recorded the financing statement covering the farm equipment sold to Walker in the official records in Nassau County, Florida. After Walker filed for bankruptcy, Deere filed a motion to recover the farm equipment from the bankruptcy estate.

Issue Did Deere have a perfected security interest in the farm equipment?

Decision No. The bankruptcy court held that Deere did not have a perfected security interest in the

farm equipment because it had filed its financing statement in the wrong place. The court denied Deere's motion.

Reason As of October 1, 1989, anyone who wanted to investigate whether a financing statement on the Deere equipment purchased by Walker had been filed would have to look at the records in the secretary of state's office. The court held that the new filing requirement must be strictly construed, and because Deere did not comply with the new law, its financing statement was ineffective. Its security interest in the farm equipment at issue was not perfected.

CASE QUESTIONS

Critical Legal Thinking Should Article 9's filing requirements be strictly construed? Why or why not?

Ethics There seem to be no ethical problems in this case. Do you agree?

Business Implication What is the risk if a creditor improperly files a financing statement?

CASE 19.2

In Re Greenbelt Cooperative, Inc.
124 Bankr. 465, 14 U.C.C.R. Serv.2d 920 (1991) United States Bankruptcy Court, Maryland

Facts Greenbelt Cooperative, Inc. (Greenbelt) was a consumer-owned cooperative engaged in the retail furniture business. It engaged in the business under the trade name SCAN, and it was well known among consumers by that name. On May 4, 1987, Greenbelt executed an Equipment Lease and Security Agreement with Raymond Leasing Corporation (Raymond) to

lease forklifts, racking, and other items. At the conclusion of the lease term, Greenbelt could purchase the equipment for $1. On July 6, 1987, Raymond filed a financing statement covering the equipment in the proper state government office. Raymond listed "SCAN Furniture" as the debtor on the financing statement. On December 4, 1988, Greenbelt filed for bankruptcy.

The bankruptcy trustee made a motion to avoid Raymond's claimed security interest in the equipment.

Issue Did Raymond properly identify the debtor on the financing statement?

Decision No. The bankruptcy court held that Raymond failed to identify the actual debtor in its financing statement. The court voided Raymond's lien on the equipment.

Reason For a financing statement to be effective, the UCC requires that it be filed under the legal name of the debtor or under a name that is substantially similar to the legal name of the debtor, so that it would not mislead a reasonably diligent creditor searching the financing records. The court held that a filing under SCAN Furniture would not be found by those looking for security interests in the assets of Greenbelt Cooperative, Inc. Consequently, Raymond's financing statement was not sufficient to perfect its security interests in Greenbelt's assets.

CASE QUESTIONS

Critical Legal Thinking Should creditors searching financing records be required to search for financing statements filed under the debtor's trade names as well as its legal name?

Ethics Did the bankruptcy trustee act ethically in avoiding the secured creditor's security interest?

Business Implication Was the filing of the financing statement under the wrong name an error that could have easily been prevented?

Perfection by Possession of Collateral

No financing statement has to be filed if the creditor has physical possession of the collateral. The rationale behind this rule is that if someone other than the debtor is in possession of the property, then a potential creditor is on notice that another may claim an interest in the debtor's property. A secured creditor who holds the debtor's property as collateral must use reasonable care in its custody and preservation [UCC 9-207].

perfection by possession of the collateral If a secured creditor has physical possession of the collateral, no financing statement has to be filed; the creditor's possession is sufficient to put other potential creditors on notice of his or her secured interest in the property.

CONSIDER THIS EXAMPLE: Suppose Karen borrows $3,000 from Alan and gives her motorcycle to him as security for the loan. Another creditor obtains a judgment against Karen. This creditor cannot recover the motorcycle from Alan. Even though Alan has not filed a financing statement, his security interest in the motorcycle is perfected because he has possession of the motorcycle.

Generally, a security interest in money and most negotiable instruments can be perfected by taking a possession of the collateral. A security interest in negotiable documents is temporarily perfected for 21 days without filing a financing statement or taking possession of the documents or instruments [UCC 9-304(4) and (5)].

Perfection by a Purchase Money Security Interest in Consumer Goods

Sellers and lenders often extend credit to consumers to purchase consumer goods. **Consumer goods** include furniture, television sets, stereos, home appliances, and other goods used primarily for personal, family, or household purposes.

A creditor who extends credit to a consumer to purchase a consumer good under a written security agreement obtains a **purchase money security interest** in the goods. This automatically perfects the creditor's security interest at the time of the sale. The creditor does not have to file a financing statement or take possession of the goods to perfect his or her security interest. This is called *perfection by attachment* or the *automatic perfection rule*.

purchase money security interest An interest a creditor automatically obtains when it extends credit to a consumer to purchase consumer goods.

Two types of consumer goods are excepted from this rule. Financing statements must be filed to perfect a security interest in motor vehicles and fixtures [UCC 9-302(1)(d)].

CONSIDER THIS EXAMPLE: Assume that Marcia buys a $3,000 large-screen television for her home on credit extended by the seller, Circuit City. Circuit City requires Marcia to sign a security agreement. Circuit City has a purchase money security interest in the television that is automatically perfected at the time of the credit sale. Now suppose Marcia borrowed the money from Country Bank to buy the television for cash from Circuit City. If the bank required Marcia to sign a security agreement, its security interest in the television is automatically perfected at the time Marcia buys the television from Circuit City.

In the following case, the court had to decide whether a purchase money security interest had been created.

CASE 19.3

In Re Phillips
55 Bankr. 663 (1985) United States Bankruptcy Court, Western District of Virginia

Facts Charlene T. Philips and her husband, Jacob, owned the Village Variety 5 & 10 Store in Bloomfield, Virginia. Charlene was also employed as a computer science teacher at the Wytheville Community College. On December 1, 1984, Charlene entered into a retail installment contract to purchase an IBM computer and other equipment from Holdren's Inc. The contract, which was also a security agreement, provided for total payment of $3,175.68 in equal monthly installments of $132.32. Charlene testified that she told the salesperson at Holdren's that she was purchasing the computer equipment for use in her teaching assignments and for use at the variety store. She received a special discount price given to teachers. Holdren's did not file a financing statement regarding the computer equipment. On December 1, 1984, Holdren's assigned the installment contract to Creditway of America (Creditway). On June 26, 1985, Mr. and Mrs. Phillips filed a petition for Chapter 7 liquidation bankruptcy. The balance due and owing on the computer was $2,597.79. Creditway filed a motion with the bankruptcy court to recover the computer and equipment.

Issue Is the computer and other equipment "consumer goods" in which the second party obtained a perfected purchase money security interest?

Decision No. The bankruptcy court held that the secured creditor did not have a perfected purchase

money security interest in the collateral because the collateral was equipment, not consumer goods. The court denied the secured creditor's motion to recover the collateral.

Reason If the computer goods were classified as "consumer goods," the secured creditor would not have to file a financing statement to have a perfected security interest in the collateral. However, in this case, the court classified the goods as "equipment" because the goods were purchased for business purposes. This required the secured creditor to file a financing statement to perfect its security interest, which it did not do. The secured creditor holds an unperfected security interest in the collateral.

CASE QUESTIONS

Critical Legal Thinking Should purchase money security interests be given priority over other security interests? Why or why not?

Ethics Was there any unethical conduct in this case?

Business Implication Are secured creditors who perfect their security interests always guaranteed of being able to be paid from the collateral upon default?

Information Requests and Certificate of Filing

The debtor may request information from the secured creditor about the status of the indebtedness at any time. The debtor is entitled to one statement every six months without charge; the secured party may charge up to $10 for each additional statement. The request must be in the form of a signed writing that indicates (1) what the debtor believes to be the aggregate indebtedness as of a specific date or (2) the identity of the collateral securing the indebtedness. The debtor may request the secured party to approve or correct the statement and return it. The secured party must send a written reply within two weeks of receipt of the request. Failure to do so makes the secured party liable for any resulting loss to the debtor [UCC 9-208].

Any person may request a filing officer to issue a **certificate of filing** showing (1) whether any presently effective financing statements naming a particular debtor are on file, (2) the date and hour of any such filing, and (3) the names and addresses of the secured parties. The filing officer may charge a fee for this service. Such requests are usually made by persons contemplating extending credit to the debtor [UCC 9-407(2)].

certificate of filing A document that shows (1) whether any presently effective financing statement naming a particular debtor is on file, (2) the date and hour of any such filing, and (3) the names and addresses of the secured parties.

Assignment, Amendment, and Release

A secured party may assign all or part of his or her rights under a financing statement. This is done when the secured party of record files a signed **statement of assignment** in the place where the original financing statement was filed. The statement of assignment must contain the name of the secured party of record, the name of the debtor, the file number, the date of the filing of the financing statement, the name of the assignee, and a description of the collateral [UCC 9-405(2)].

statement of assignment A document that is filed when a secured party assigns all or part of his other rights under a financing statement.

A financing statement may be **amended** by filing a writing signed by both the debtor and the secured party [UCC 9-402(4)]. A secured party of record may release all or any part of any collateral described in a filed financing statement. A release ends the secured party's security interest in the collateral named in the release [UCC 9-406].

Termination

When a secured consumer debt is paid, the secured party must file a **termination statement** with each filing officer with whom the financing statement was filed. The termination statement must be filed within one month after the debt is paid or 10 days after receipt of the debtor's written demand, whichever occurs first. In all other cases, the secured party must either file a termination with each filing officer with whom the financing statement has been filed or send the termination statement to the debtor within 10 days of receipt of a written demand by the debtor. If the affected secured party fails to file or send the termination statement as required, he or she is liable to the debtor for $100. In addition, the secured party is liable for any other losses caused to the debtor [UCC 9-404(1)].

termination statement A document filed by the secured party that ends a secured interest because the debt has been paid.

CONTEMPORARY BUSINESS ENVIRONMENT

Perfection of Security Interests In Automobiles

Automobiles, like many other forms of personal property are easily movable from state to state. Under the UCC, a secured party who has properly perfected a security interest has either (1) four months after the collateral is moved to another state or (2) the period of time remaining under the perfection in the original state, whichever expires first, to perfect his or her security interest in the property in the new state. Any subsequent perfected security interest in the new state prevails if the secured party does not comply with this rule [UCC 9-103(1)(d) and 9-103(3)(e)].

Most states have enacted **state vehicle licensing statutes** that require security interests in motor vehicles to be noted on **certificates of title** to motor vehicle. In most states, these statutes take precedence over the UCC. If the security interest is not noted on a vehicle's certificate of title, and the buyer does not have knowledge of the defect in title, the buyer is permitted to rely on the ownership and registration certificates without any further inquiry—that is, without having to search for UCC financing statements.

PRIORITY OF CLAIMS

Often, two or more creditors claim an interest in the same collateral or property. The priority of the claims is determined according to (1) whether the claim is unsecured or secured and (2) the time at which secured claims were attached or were perfected.

UCC Rules for Determining Priority

The UCC establishes the following set of rules for determining **priority** among *conflicting claims* of creditors [UCC 9-301(1)(a), 9-312(5), 9-315(2)]:

1. **Secured versus unsecured claims.** A creditor who has the only secured interest in the debtor's collateral has priority over unsecured interests.

2. **Competing unperfected secured claims.** If two or more secured parties claim an interest in the same collateral, but neither has a perfected claim, the first to attach has priority.

3. **Perfected versus unperfected claims.** If two or more secured parties claim an interest in the same collateral, but only one has perfected his or her security interest, the perfected security interest has priority.

4. **Competing perfected secured claims.** If two or more secured parties have perfected security interests in the same collateral, the first to perfect (e.g., by filing a financing statement or taking possession of the collateral) has priority.

5. **Perfected secured claims in fungible, commingled goods.** If a security interest in goods is perfected but the goods are later commingled with other goods in which there are perfected security interests and the goods become part of a product or mass and lose their identity, then the security interests rank equally according to the ratio that the cost of goods to which each interest originally attached bears to the cost of the total product or mass.

Exceptions to the Perfection-Priority Rule

Perfection does not always protect a secured party from third-party claims. As discussed in the sections that follow, the UCC recognizes several exceptions to the perfection-priority rule.

Purchase Money Security Interest—Inventory as Collateral Under certain circumstances, a perfected purchase money security interest prevails over perfected nonpurchase money security interests in after-acquired property. The order of perfection is irrelevant. If the collateral is inventory, the perfected purchase money security interest prevails if the purchase money secured party gives written notice of the perfection to the perfected nonpurchase money secured party before the debtor receives possession of the inventory [UCC 9-312(3)].

CONSIDER THIS EXAMPLE: Toy Shops, Inc., a retailer, borrows money from First Bank for working capital. In return, First Bank gets a security interest in all of Toy Shops' current and after-acquired inventory. First Bank perfects its security interest by filing a financing statement. Later, Toy Shops purchases new inventory on credit from Mattel, a toy manufacturer. Mattel perfects its purchase money security interest by filing a financing statement. It notifies First Bank of this fact prior to delivery of the new inventory. Toy Shops defaults on its loans. Mattel's lien has priority.

Purchase Money Security Interest—Noninventory as Collateral If the collateral is something other than inventory, the perfected purchase money security interest would prevail over a perfected nonpurchase money security interest in after-acquired property if it was perfected before or within 10 days after the debtor receives possession of the collateral [UCC 9-312(4)].

priority The order in which conflicting claims of creditors in the same collateral are solved.

"Creditor: One of a tribe of savages dwelling beyond the Financial Straits and dreaded for their desolating excursions."
Ambrose Bierce
The Devil's Dictionary
(1911)

CAUTION
Perfection does not always protect a secured party from third-party claims. Consider the following exceptions as discussed: (1) purchase money security interests involving inventory, (2) purchase money security interests involving goods other than inventory, (3) buyers in the ordinary course of business, (4) secondhand consumer goods, (5) artisan's and mechanic's liens.

"Debt is the prolific mother of folly and of crime."
Benjamin Disraeli
Henriette Temple
(1837)

"Debt: A rope to your foot, cockleburs in your hair, and a clothespin on your tongue."
Frank McKinney Hubbard
The Roycroft Dictionary (1923)

CONSIDER THIS EXAMPLE: On September 1, Matco, a manufacturer, borrows money for working capital from First Bank and gives First Bank a security interest in its current and after-acquired equipment. First Bank perfects its security interest by filing a financing statement. On September 20, Matco purchases a new piece of equipment on credit from Allegheny Industries, an equipment manufacturer. On September 30, Allegheny perfects its purchase money security interest by filing a financing statement. Matco defaults on its loans.

Here, Allegheny's perfected purchase money security interest prevails because the lien was perfected within 10 days after the debtor received the collateral. If Allegheny had waited until October 1 to perfect its purchase money security interest, First Bank would have prevailed.

Buyers in the Ordinary Course of Business A **buyer in the ordinary course of business** who purchases goods from a merchant takes the goods free of any perfected or unperfected security interest in the merchant's inventory even if the buyer knows of the existence of the security interest. This rule is necessary because buyers would be reluctant to purchase goods if the merchant's creditors could recover the goods if the merchant defaults on loans owed to secured creditors [UCC 9-307(1)].

buyer in the ordinary course of business A person who in good faith and without knowledge of another's ownership or security interest in goods buys the goods in the ordinary course of business from person in the business of selling goods of that kind [UCC 1-201(9)].

CONSIDER THIS EXAMPLE: Suppose Central Car Sales, Inc., a new car dealership, finances all of its inventory of new automobiles at First Bank. First Bank takes a security interest in Central's inventory of cars and perfects this security interest. Kim, a buyer in the ordinary course of business, purchases a car from Central for cash. The car cannot be recovered from Kim even if Central defaults on its payments to the bank.

Secondhand Consumer Goods Buyers of secondhand consumer goods take free of security interest if they do not have actual or constructive knowledge about the security interest, give value, and buy the goods for personal, family, or household purposes. The filing of a financing statement by a creditor provides constructive notice of the security interest [UCC 9-307(2)].

"If one wants to know the real value of money, he needs but to borrow some from his friends."
Confucius
Analects
(c. 500 B.C.)

CONSIDER THIS EXAMPLE: Suppose Anne purchases a microwave oven on credit from Stearns, Inc., a retailer, to be used for household purposes. Pursuant to a security agreement, Stearns, Inc., acquires an automatically perfected purchase money security interest in the oven. Suppose Stearns, Inc., does not file a financing statement. Anne sells the microwave oven to her neighbor, Jeff, for cash. Anne defaults on her loan payments to Stearns, Inc. Stearns, Inc., cannot recover the microwave oven from Jeff. Note, however, that Stearns, Inc., could recover the oven from Jeff if it had filed a financing statement prior to the sale to Jeff.

DEFAULT

Article 9 defines the rights, duties, and remedies of the secured party and the debtor in the event of default. The term *default* is not defined. Instead, the parties are free to define it in their security agreement. Failure to make scheduled payments when due, bankruptcy of the debtor, breach of the warranty of ownership as to the collateral, and other such events are commonly defined in the security agreement as default [UCC 9-501(1)].

default Failure to make scheduled payments when due, bankruptcy of the debtor, breach of the warranty of ownership as to the collateral, and other events defined by the parties to constitute default.

SECURED CREDITOR'S REMEDIES

Upon default by the debtor, the secured party may reduce his or her claim to judgment, foreclose, or otherwise enforce his or her security interest by any available judicial procedure [UCC 9-501(1)]. The UCC provides the secured party with the remedies discussed in the following sections.

"Debtors are liars."
George Herbert
Jacula Prudentum
(1651)

Taking Possession of the Collateral

repossession A right granted to a secured creditor to take possession of the collateral upon default by the debtor.

Most secured parties seek to cure a default by taking possession of the collateral. This is usually done by **repossessing** the goods from the defaulting debtor. After repossessing the goods, the secured party can either (1) retain the collateral or (2) sell or otherwise dispose of it and satisfy the debt from the proceeds of the sale or disposition. There is one caveat: The secured party must act in good faith, with commercial reasonableness, and with reasonable care to preserve the collateral in his or her possession [UCC 9-503].

CONSIDER THIS EXAMPLE: Western Drilling, Inc., purchases a piece of oil-drilling equipment on credit from Haliburton, Inc. Haliburton files a financing statement covering its security interest in the equipment. If Western Drilling fails to make the required payments, Haliburton can foreclose on its lien and repossess the equipment.

retention of collateral If a secured creditor repossesses collateral upon a debtor's default, he or she may propose to retain the collateral in satisfaction of the debtor's obligation.

"We are either debtors or creditors before we have had time to look around."
Johann Wolfgang von Goethe
Elective Affinities
Bk. II (1808)

Retention of Collateral A secured creditor who repossesses collateral may propose to retain the collateral in satisfaction of the debtor's obligation. Notice of the proposal must be sent to the debtor unless he or she has signed a written statement renouncing this right. In the case of consumer goods, no other notice need be given. Otherwise, notice of the proposal must be sent to any other secured party who has given written notice of a claim of interest in the collateral.

A secured creditor may not **retain the collateral** (and must dispose of the collateral) in the following two situations:

1. *Written objection.* The secured party receives a written objection to the proposal from a person entitled to receive notice within 21 days after the notice was sent [UCC 9-505(2)].
2. *Consumer goods.* The debt involves consumer goods and the debtor has paid 60 percent of the cash price or loan. In this case, the secured creditor must dispose of the goods within 90 days after taking possession of them. A consumer may renounce his or her rights under this section [UCC 9-505(1)].

A secured creditor may retain the collateral as satisfaction of the debtor's obligation if neither of the preceding two situations prevents this action.

disposition of collateral
If a secured creditor repossess collateral upon a debtor's default, he or she may sell, lease, or otherwise dispose of it in a commercially reasonable manner.

"Words pay no debts."
William Shakespeare
Troilus and Cressida
Act III

Disposition of Collateral A secured party who chooses not to retain the collateral may sell, lease, or otherwise dispose of it in its then condition or following any commercially reasonable preparation or processing. **Disposition of the collateral** may be by public or private proceedings. The method, manner, time, place, and terms of the disposition must be commercially reasonable.

The secured party must notify the debtor in writing about the time and place of any public and private sale or any other intended disposition of the collateral unless the debtor has signed a statement renouncing or modifying his rights to receive such notice. In the case of consumer goods, no other notification need be sent. In other cases, the secured party must send notice to any other secured party from whom the secured party has received written notice of a claim of an interest in the collateral. Notice of the sale or disposition is not required if the collateral is perishable, threatens to decline steadily in value, or is of a type customarily sold on a recognized market [UCC 9-504(3)]. Disposition discharges the security interest under which it is made as well as any subordinate security interests or liens [UCC 9-504(4)].

Proceeds from Disposition The proceeds from a sale, lease, or other disposition of the collateral must be applied in the following order:

1. Reasonable expenses of retaking, holding, and preparing the collateral for sale, lease, or other disposition are paid first. Attorney's fees and legal expenses may be paid if provided for in the security agreement and not prohibited by law.

2. Satisfaction of the balance of the indebtedness owed by the debtor to the secured party is next made.

3. Satisfaction of subordinate (junior) security interests whose written notifications of demand have been received before distribution of the proceeds is completed are paid third. The secured party may require subordinate interests to furnish reasonable proof of his or her interest [UCC 9-504(1)].

4. The debtor is entitled to receive any surplus that remains [UCC 9-504(2)].

ETHICAL PERSPECTIVE

The Repo Man

If a debtor defaults on a loan, the law permits a secured creditor to use self-help to take physical possession of the goods pledged as collateral. Self-help is allowed as long as it does not cause a *breach of the peace*. This means that the use of force, threats of force, fraud, and violence are prohibited [UCC 9-503]. Many secured parties hire repossession companies to repossess automobiles, equipment, and other secured property. Was there a breach of peace in the following case?

C. W. Rutherford (C. W.) purchased a 1974 Cadillac automobile from Big Three Motors, Inc. (Big Three Motors). Big Three Motors extended credit to C. W. In exchange, C. W. signed a security agreement giving Big Three Motors a security interest in the Cadillac to secure the loan. C. W. defaulted by failing to make several scheduled payments for the automobile.

Christine Rutherford, C. W.'s common-law wife, testified at trial as follows: While she was driving the Cadillac on Interstate 65 in Mobile County, Alabama, Fred E. Roan and another Big Three Motors employee, who were in a truck, forced Christine to pull her car off the road. They parked the truck to block Christine's access back on the Interstate. After Christine and Roan exchanged words, Roan got into the Cadillac and rode with her to the Big Three Motors dealership. After arriving at the dealership, Christine locked the car, took the keys, and went into the office. When Christine left the office, she discovered that someone had taken the Cadillac from the spot where she had parked it. An employee of Big Three Motors informed her that the car had been put "in storage" because C. W. owed payments.

C. W. and Christine Rutherford sued Big Three Motors for dam-

ages. The jury found that Big Three Motors' actions constituted a breach of the peace in violation of the UCC. Therefore, its repossession of the Cadillac automobile was a wrongful possession. The jury returned a verdict in favor of C. W. for $10,000 punitive damages and in favor of Christine Rutherford for $15,000 punitive damages. The state supreme court agreed, stating that the jury could reasonably conclude from the evidence that "Big Three Motors used force, trickery, and fraud in the repossession of the Cadillac." [*Big Three Motors, Inc. v. Rutherford*, 432 So.2d 483 (Ala. 1983)]

1. Did the employees of Big Three Motors act ethically?

2. Should secured creditors be allowed to use self-help to repossess goods from defaulting debtors?

3. Is the breach of the peace standard easy to apply?

Deficiency Judgment Unless otherwise agreed, if the proceeds from the disposition of the collateral are not sufficient to satisfy the debt to the secured party, the debtor is personally liable to the secured party for the deficiency. The secured party may bring an action to recover a **deficiency judgment** against the debtor. If the underlying transaction was a sale of accounts or chattel paper, the debtor is liable for any deficiency only if the security agreement so provides [UCC 9-504(2)].

CONSIDER THIS EXAMPLE: Sean borrows $15,000 from First Bank to purchase a new automobile. He signs a security agreement giving First Bank a purchase money security interest in the automobile. Sean defaults after making payments that reduce the debt to $13,250. First Bank repossesses the automobile and sells it at a public auction for $11,000. The selling expenses and sales commission are $1,250. This is deducted

deficiency judgment
A judgment that allows a secured creditor to successfully bring a separate legal action to recover a deficiency from the debtor. Entitles the secured creditor to recover the amount of the judgment from the debtor's other property.

from the proceeds. The remaining $9,750 is applied to the $13,250 balance of the debt. Sean remains personally liable to First Bank for the $3,500 deficiency.

right of redemption A right granted to a defaulting debtor or other secured creditor to recover the collateral from a secured creditor before he or she contracts to dispose of it or exercises his or her right to retain the collateral. Requires the redeeming party to pay the full amount of the debt and expenses caused by the debtor's default.

Redemption Rights The debtor or another secured party may *redeem* the collateral before the priority lienholder has disposed of it, entered into a contract to dispose of it, or discharged the debtor's obligation by exercising a right to retain the collateral. The right of redemption may be accomplished by payment of all obligations secured by the collateral, all expenses reasonably incurred by the secured party in retaking and holding the collateral, and any attorney's fees and legal expenses provided for in the security agreement and not prohibited by law [UCC 9-506].

Relinquishing the Security Interest and Proceeding to Judgment on the Underlying Debt

judgment on the underlying debt A right granted to a secured creditor to relinquish his or her security interest in the collateral and sue a defaulting debtor to recover the amount of the underlying debt.

Instead of repossessing the collateral, the secured creditor may relinquish his or her security interest in the collateral and proceed to judgment against the debtor to recover the underlying debt. This course of action is rarely chosen unless the value of the collateral has been reduced below the amount of the secured interest and the debtor has other assets from which to satisfy the debt [UCC 9-501(1)].

CONSIDER THIS EXAMPLE: Suppose Jack borrows $100,000 from First Bank to purchase a piece of equipment, and First Bank perfects its security interest in the equipment for this amount. Jack defaults on the loan. If the equipment has gone down in value to $60,000 at the time of default, but Jack has other personal assets to satisfy the debt, it may be in the bank's best interest to relinquish its security interest and proceed to judgment on the underlying debt.

The secured party is not required to elect one of these remedies. Instead, if one remedy is unsuccessful, the secured party can move on to the next. If the collateral is documents, the secured party may proceed either as to the documents or as to the goods covered thereby [UCC 9-501(1)].

Security Agreements Covering Real and Personal Property

If a security agreement covers both real property and personal property (i.e., fixtures), the secured party may either (1) proceed against the personal property under Article 9 or (2) proceed as to both properties in accordance with the rights and remedies provided for real property under state law. If the latter course is chosen, the provisions of Article 9 do not apply [UCC 9-501(4)].

BUSINESS CHECKLIST

Artisan's and Mechanic's Liens

If a worker in the ordinary course of business works on or provides materials to another person with respect to goods, most states have statutes that grant an **artisan's** or **mechanic's lien** on the goods until the work or materials are paid for. For example, if an owner takes his car into an automobile service department or body shop for repairs, the mechanic who repairs the car has an automatic lien on the car in the amount of the services and materials provided to repair the car. If the car owner refuses or fails to pay the bill, the mechanic can sell the car to pay off his lien.

> The following rules apply to artisan's and mechanic's liens:
>
> • The owner of an automobile or other good authorizes an artisan or mechanic to repair the good.
> • The artisan or mechanic does the work and provides the material as requested.
> • The owner does not pay for the services rendered and materials provided.
> • The artisan or mechanic gives the required notices and sells the automobile or other good pursuant to the requirements of the relevant state statute.
> • If the sale proceeds exceed the amount of the artisan's or mechanic's lien, the balance is paid to offer lienholders in the goods, and then to the owner.
> • Artisan's and mechanic's liens are given priority over any existing lien on the goods. Artisan's and mechanic's liens are therefore called **super-priority liens** (e.g., bank loans).

CONSIDER THIS EXAMPLE: Suppose Janice borrows money from First Bank to purchase an automobile. First Bank has a purchase money security interest in the car and files a financing statement. The automobile is involved in an accident. Janice takes the car to Joe's Repair Shop to be repaired. Joe's retains a mechanic's lien in the car for the amount of the repair work. When the repair work is completed, Janice refuses to pay. She also defaults on her payments to First Bank. If the car is sold to satisfy the liens, the mechanic's lien is paid in full from the proceeds before First Bank is paid anything.

SURETY AND GUARANTY ARRANGEMENTS

Sometimes a creditor refuses to extend credit to a debtor unless a third person agrees to become liable on the debt. The third person's credit becomes the security for the credit extended to the debtor. This relationship may be either a surety or guaranty arrangement. Each of these arrangements is discussed in the following paragraphs.

Surety Arrangement

In a strict **surety arrangement**, a third person—known as the *surety* or *co-debtor*—promises to be liable for the payment of another person's debt. A person who acts as a surety is commonly called an *accommodation party* or *cosigner*. Along with the principal debtor, the surety is primarily liable for paying the principal debtor's debt when it is due. The principal debtor does not have to be in default on the debt, and the creditor does not have to have exhausted all its remedies against the principal debtor before seeking payment from the surety.

Guaranty Arrangement

In a **guaranty arrangement**, a third person (the *guarantor*) agrees to pay the debt of the principal debtor if the debtor defaults and does not pay the debt when it is due. In this type of arrangement, the guarantor is secondarily liable on the debt. In other words, the guarantor is obligated to pay the debt only if the principal debtor defaults and the creditor has attempted unsuccessfully to collect the debt from the debtor.

Defenses of a Surety or Guarantor

Generally, the defenses the principal debtor has against the creditor may also be asserted by a surety or guarantor. For example, if credit has been extended for the

BUSINESS BRIEF
Many businesses will not sell goods and services to minors or persons with a bad credit history unless a competent adult cosigns or guarantees payment.

surety arrangement   An arrangement where a third party promises to be *primarily* liable with the borrower for the payment of the borrower's debt.

guaranty arrangement   An arrangement where a third party promises to be *secondarily liable* for the payment of another's debt.

purchase of a piece of machinery that proves to be defective, the debtor and surety both can assert the defect as a defense to liability. The defenses of fraudulent inducement to enter into the surety or guaranty agreement and duress may also be cited as personal defenses to liability. The surety or guarantor cannot assert the debtor's incapacity (i.e., minority or insanity) or bankruptcy as a defense against liability. However, the surety's or guarantor's own incapacity or bankruptcy may be asserted.

Right of Subrogation

right of subrogation The right that says the surety or guarantor acquires all of the creditor's rights against the debtor when a surety or guarantor pays a debt owed to a creditor by a debtor.

When a surety or guarantor pays a debt owed to a creditor by a debtor, the surety or guarantor acquires all of the creditor's rights against the debtor. This is called the **right of subrogation**. For example, suppose Taymour borrows $100,000 from City Bank, and Sabrina guarantees the payment of the debt. Taymour defaults and City Bank collects the $100,000 from Sabrina. Under her right of subrogation, Sabrina acquires City Bank's right to collect the $100,000. She may bring a legal action to recover this amount from Taymour.

In the following case, the court had to decide whether there was a surety or guaranty contract.

CASE 19.4

General Motors Acceptance Corp. v. Daniels
492 A.2d. 1306 (1985) Court of Appeals of Maryland

Facts In June 1981, John Daniels agreed to purchase a used automobile from Lindsay Cadillac Company (Lindsay Cadillac). Because John had a poor credit rating, his brother, Seymour, agreed to cosign with him. General Motors Acceptance Corp. (GMAC), a company engaged in the business of financing automobiles, agreed to finance the purchase. On June 23, 1981, Seymour accompanied John to Lindsay Cadillac. John signed the contract on the line designated "Buyer." Seymour signed the contract on the line designated "Co-Buyer." In May 1982, GMAC declared the contract in default. After attempting to locate the automobile for several months, GMAC brought this action against the Daniels brothers. Because service of process was never effected upon John, the case proceeded to trial against only Seymour. The trial court found that Seymour had entered into a guaranty contract and that Seymour was not liable because GMAC had not yet proceeded against John. GMAC appealed.

Issue Was the contract Seymour signed a guaranty or surety contract?

Decision The court of appeals held that Seymour signed a surety contract and thus agreed to be primarily liable with his brother John for the purchase

of the automobile. GMAC was therefore not required to proceed against John in the first instance. Reversed.

Reason If the contract Seymour signed was a guaranty contract, he would have been only secondarily liable on his brother's loan. This was not the situation in this case, however, because Seymour signed the contract on the line on the contract designated "Co-Buyer." The contract clearly stated that all buyers agreed to be jointly and severally liable for the purchase of the vehicle. Seymour executed the same contract as his brother, thereby making himself a party to the original contract. These facts established the existence of a surety contract upon which Seymour became primarily liable.

CASE QUESTIONS

Critical Legal Thinking What purposes do guaranty and surety contracts serve? Explain.

Ethics Did Seymour act ethically in trying to avoid liability for his brother's loan?

Business Implication As a lender, would you rather have a third party sign as a surety or guarantor?

COLLECTION REMEDIES

When a debt is past due, the creditor may bring a legal action against the debtor. If the creditor is successful, the court will award a *judgment* against the debtor. The judgment will state that the debtor owes the creditor a specific sum of money. The amount usually consists of principal and interest past due on the debt, other costs resulting from the debtor's default, and court costs. A creditor's remedies are discussed in the following sections.

Attachment

Many states allow creditors to **attach** (or seize) the debtor's property to collect on a debt while their lawsuit is pending. This is a prejudgment remedy. To obtain a writ of attachment the creditor must follow the strict procedures of state law. This generally involves posting a bond with the court. The bond, which assures the debtor of recovery if the creditor loses his or her lawsuit, must cover court costs, the debtor's costs for the loss of use of the property, and the value of the attached property.

The debtor must be given notice and a hearing prior to the seizure of the property. The creditor must file an affidavit with the court (1) stating that the debtor is in default on the payment of a debt owed the creditor, (2) naming the statutory ground under which attachment is sought, and (3) giving evidence that the debtor is attempting to transfer the property prior to trial.

When the court issues a writ of attachment, the sheriff may seize and hold the subject property pending the outcome of the creditors lawsuit. If the lawsuit is successful, the seized property is sold to satisfy the judgment and costs of sale. Any surplus is paid to the debtor.

attachment Seizure by the creditor of property in the debtor's possession in order to collect on a debt while their lawsuit is pending.

Execution

Execution is a postjudgment remedy. A writ of execution is a court order directing the sheriff to seize the debtor's property and authorizing a judicial sale of that property. The proceeds are used to pay the creditor the amount of the final judgment. Any surplus must be paid to the debtor.

Most states provide that certain real and personal property is exempt from attachment or execution. For example, many states provide a homestead exemption, which permits the debtor to retain his or her residence either in its entirety or up to a certain dollar amount. Exempt personal property usually includes furniture (up to a certain dollar amount), clothing, pets and livestock, vehicles (up to a certain dollar amount), tools of trade, and such.

execution Postjudgment seizure and sale of the debtor's property to satisfy a creditor's judgment against the debtor.

Garnishment

Garnishment is another postjudgment remedy. Garnishment is directed against property of the debtor that is in the possession of third persons. To avail oneself of this remedy, the creditor (also known as the *garnishor*) must go to court to seek a writ of garnishment. The third person is called the *garnishee*. Common garnishees are employers who possess wages due a debtor, banks in possession of funds belonging to the debtor, and other third parties in the possession of property of the debtor.

To protect debtors from abusive and excessive garnishment actions by creditors, Congress enacted Title III of the Consumer Credit Protection Act.[1] This allows debtors who are subject to a writ of garnishment to retain the greater of (1) 75 percent of their weekly disposable earnings (after taxes) or (2) an amount equal to 30 hours of work paid at federal minimum wage. State law limitations on garnishment control if they are more stringent than federal law.

garnishment A postjudgment remedy that is directed against property of the debtor that is in the possession of third persons.

Composition of Creditor's Agreements

composition agreement
An agreement that a debtor and several creditors enter into; if the debtor is overextended and owes several creditors money, the creditors agree to accept payment of a sum less than the debt as full satisfaction of the debtor's debts.

If a debtor is overextended and owes several creditors money, the creditors can enter into an agreement with the debtor whereby they agree to accept payment of a sum less than the debt as full satisfaction of the debtor's debts. This type of arrangement is called a **composition of creditors' agreements** or a **composition agreement**. Not all of the creditors must assent. Creditors who do not assent may proceed to collect or settle their claims in their own way. If the debtor fails to perform a composition agreement, the creditors may elect to enforce the composition or the original debt.

Assignment for the Benefit of Creditors

assignment for the benefit of creditors An assignment that allows debtors voluntarily to assign title to their property to a trustee or an assignee for the benefit of their creditors.

Many states provide for an **assignment for the benefit of creditors**. This assignment allows debtors voluntarily to assign title to their property to a trustee or an assignee for the benefit of their creditors. The creditors have the choice of accepting or rejecting this tender of assets. Creditors who accept the tender are paid on a pro rata basis with the proceeds from the sale of the assets. If a creditor rejects the offer, the creditor may proceed with a legal action against any of the debtor's remaining nonexempt assets.

INTERNATIONAL PERSPECTIVE

Availability of International Credit

Commercial banks offer some financing of international and export operations. National governments and international organizations also provide credit for international investments. Nevertheless, businesses often find it extremely difficult to obtain credit to finance international operations. This is because international ventures and transactions are perceived as riskier than domestic transactions. Third-world countries also have a hard time obtaining credit to develop their economies.

The **International Bank for Reconstruction and Development**, commonly called the **World Bank**, is a United Nations agency that finances development projects in member nations. The World Bank is primarily funded by developed nations. Projects include the building of dams, roads, power plants, and other infrastructure. The World Bank also engages in direct investment in private enterprises through a combination of loans and equity investments.

Nations have also created and capitalized regional development banks that extend loans and offer loan guarantees to assist the economic development in member nations. These include the African Development Bank, the Asian Development Bank, the Arab Fund for Economic and Social Development, the Caribbean Development Bank, the European Investment Bank, and the InterAmerican Development Bank (composed of Latin American countries).

National governments often extend credit to private businesses to stimulate export sales. For example, the **Export-Import Bank (Eximbank)** supports U.S. companies engaged in exporting by loaning overseas buyers funds at below-market rates of interest to purchase U.S.-made goods. The Eximbank also provides loan guarantees and insurance to foreign buyers of U.S. products. Credits have been extended for the purchase of agricultural products, heavy machinery, airplanes, and such. The Eximbank often works closely with commercial banks in structuring credit to foreign buyers.

As international trade continues to develop and become more important to the United States and other countries, credit will become more available to finance international investment and trade.

WORKING THE WEB

Lender Liability Law Page This page, presented by an attorney for a large bank, provides accurate and authoritative information about lender liability as well to links to case law and other World Wide Web legal resources.
Visit at http://www.america.net/~jerryb/index.html

Debtor Links Debtor Links is the first Web site dedicated to helping debtors. It contains accurate information on laws, specific issues, credit, international issues, and other information.
Visit at http://apocalypse.berkshire.net/~mkb/debtlink.html

Fannie Mae Fannie Mae is the world's largest source of home mortgage funds. This Web site contains links to listings of Fannie Mae-owned properties for sale.
Visit at http://www.fanniemae.com/

Restatement of Suretyship and Guaranty The American Law Institute comprehensively sets forth and analyzes the doctrines, principles, and policies of suretyship law in the Restatement of the Law Third, Suretyship and Guaranty.
Visit at http://www.ali.org/ali/Surety.htm

SalesLeadsUSA From this site, produced by American Business Information, Inc., you can find many businesses and order in-depth company profiles. You can also look up businesses and people using the American Yellow Pages and American Directory Assistance.
Visit at http://www.abii.com/

CYBER EXERCISES:

1. From the Lender Liability Law Page, find an overview of lender liability theories and print it out.
2. From Debtor Links, find and print out a Better Business Bureau document on credit repair.
3. From the Fannie Mae Web site, find out if there are any Fannie Mae-owned homes in your city that are available for sale.
4. How many tentative drafts of the Restatement of Suretyship and Guaranty are there?
5. Using SalesLeadsUSA, find a business in your city.

CHAPTER SUMMARY

TYPES OF CREDIT, P. 443

Unsecured Credit	Credit that does not require any security (collateral) to protect the payment of the loan. 1. *Recovery of unpaid loan*. If the debtor does not pay the loan, the creditor may bring a legal action and obtain a *judgment* against the debtor. The debtor is called *judgment-proof* if he or she has no money to pay the judgment.
Secured Credit	Credit that requires security (collateral) that secures the payment of the loan. 1. *Collateral*. The property that is pledged as security for the loan.

SECURITY INTERESTS IN REAL PROPERTY, P. 444

Mortgage	1. *Mortgage*. The instrument that represents a security interest in real property. 2. *Mortgagor*. The owner-debtor who pledges his or her real property as security for a loan. 3. *Mortgagee*. The creditor who holds a security interest in the owner-debtor's real property.

Note and Deed of Trust	Some states use a note and deed of trust as an alternative to a mortgage. 1. *Note.* The instrument that evidences the debt. 2. *Deed of trust.* The instrument that gives the creditor a security interest in the owner-debtor's real property.

SECURITY INTERESTS IN PERSONAL PROPERTY—ARTICLE 9 OF THE UCC, P. 444

Article 9 of the UCC	An article of the Uniform Commercial Code that governs secured transactions in personal property.
Secured Transactions	Transactions that are created when a creditor makes a loan to a debtor in exchange for the debtor's pledge of personal property as security. 1. *Two-party secured transaction.* Where a seller sells goods to a buyer on credit and retains a security interest in the goods. 2. *Three-party secured transaction.* Where a seller sells goods to a buyer who has obtained financing from a third-party lender (e.g., bank) who takes a security interest in the goods sold.

CREATING A SECURITY INTEREST IN PERSONAL PROPERTY, P. 445

Requirements for Creating a Security Interest	1. *Requirements:*
	  a. Written security agreement
	  b. Value given to the debtor
	  c. Debtor has rights in collateral
	If these requirements are met, the rights of the secured creditor *attach* to the collateral.
	2. *Attachment.* The creditor has an enforceable security interest against the debtor and can satisfy the debt out of the designated collateral.

Personal Property Subject to a Security Agreement	1. *Goods* 2. *Instruments* (i.e., checks, notes, stocks, bonds) 3. *Chattel paper* (i.e., conditional sales contracts) 4. *Documents of title* (i.e., bills of lading, warehouse receipts) 5. *Accounts* (i.e., accounts receivable) 6. *General intangibles* (i.e., patents, copyrights, royalties, franchises)
The Floating-Lien Concept	*Floating lien.* Occurs when a security agreement provides that the security interest attaches to personal property that was not originally in the possession of the debtor when the agreement was executed. This property may include: 1. *After-acquired property.* Property acquired after the security agreement is executed. 2. *Sale proceeds.* Proceeds from the sale, exchange, or disposal of collateral subject to the security agreement. 3. *Future advances.* Personal property of the debtor that is designated as collateral for future loans taken against a line of credit.

PERFECTING A SECURITY INTEREST, P. 447

Perfection of a Security Interest	Establishes the right of the secured creditor against other creditors who claim an interest in the collateral. The UCC provides the following three methods of perfecting a security interest.
Perfection by Filing a Financing Statement	The creditor files a *financing statement* with the appropriate government recording office. This puts the world on notice of the creditor's security interest in the property. This is the most common form of perfecting a security interest.

Perfection by Possession of Collateral	If the creditor has physical possession of the collateral, no financing statement has to be filed. This is the least common form of perfecting a security interest.
Perfection by a Purchase Money Security Interest in Consumer Goods	A creditor (seller or lender) who extends credit to a consumer to purchase a *consumer good* under a written security agreement obtains a *purchase money security interest* in the goods. This automatically perfects the creditor's security interest at the time of the sale. The creditor does not have to file a financing statement to perfect his security interest. This is called *perfection by attachment* or the *automatic perfection rule*.
Information Requests and Certificate of Filing	*Certificate of filing.* A document that a person can request of the government filing officer that states (1) whether any presently effective financing statement naming a particular debtor is on file, (2) the date and hour of any such filing, and (3) the names and addresses of the secured parties.
Assignment, Amendment, and Release	1. *Statement of assignment.* A document that shows that the secured party has transferred all or part of his or her rights under a financing statement to another party. 2. *Amendment.* A writing that is signed by both the debtor and the secured creditor showing that the financing statement has been amended. 3. *Release.* A document showing that the secured creditor has released all or part of any collateral described in a financing statement.
Termination	*Termination statement.* A document that must be filed by a secured creditor within a specified number of days after a secured consumer debt has been paid. This statement must be filed where the original financing statement has been filed.

PRIORITY OF CLAIMS, P. 452

UCC Rules for Determining Priority	The UCC establishes the following rules for determining *priority* among conflicting claims of creditors to the collateral: 1. *Secured versus unsecured claims.* Secured claims have priority over unsecured claims. 2. *Competing unperfected secured claims.* The first claim to attach has priority. 3. *Perfected versus unperfected claims.* The perfected claim has priority. 4. *Competing perfected secured claims.* The first to perfect has priority. 5. *Perfected secured claims in fungible, commingled goods.* The security interests rank equally according to the ratio that the cost of goods to which each interest originally attached bears to the cost of the total product or mass.
Exceptions to the Perfection-Priority Rule	Perfection does not always protect a secured creditor from third-party claims. The UCC recognizes the following *exceptions to the perfection-priority rule*. 1. *Purchase money security interest—collateral as inventory.* A perfected *purchase* money security interest in *inventory* prevails over a perfected *nonpurchase* money security interest in after-acquired property. 2. *Purchase money security interest—noninventory as collateral.* A perfected *purchase* money security interest in *noninventory* prevails over a perfected *nonpurchase* money security interest in after-acquired

	property if it was perfected before or within 10 days after the debtor receives possession of the collateral. 3. *Buyers in the ordinary course of business*. A buyer in the ordinary course of business who purchases goods from a merchant takes the goods free of any perfected or unperfected security interest in the merchant's inventory, even if the buyer knows of the existence of the security interest. 4. *Secondhand consumer goods*. Buyers of secondhand consumer goods take free of security interests if they do not have actual or constructive knowledge about the security interest, give value, and buy the goods for personal, family, or household purposes. 5. *Artisan's and mechanic's liens*. Artisan's or mechanic's liens for services or materials provided prevail over all other security interests in goods unless a statute provides otherwise.
DEFAULT, P. 453	
Default	The parties may define the actions or inactions that cause default under the agreement. This usually includes failure to make scheduled payments when due, bankruptcy of the debtor, and breach of other terms of the agreement.
SECURED CREDITOR'S REMEDIES, P. 453	
Secured Creditor's Remedies	Article 9 of the UCC provides the secured creditor with the following remedies upon the debtor's default.
Taking Possession of the Collateral	*Repossession*. The secured creditor can use self-help to take physical possession of the collateral as long as it does not cause a *breach of the peace*. 1. *Deficiency judgment*. If the proceeds from the disposition of the collateral are not sufficient to satisfy the debt, the secured party may obtain a *deficiency judgment* against the debtor holding the debtor personally liable for the difference. 2. *Redemption rights*. The debtor may *redeem* the collateral within a statutorily stipulated period of time after repossession by payment of all obligations owed on the debt and all expenses reasonably incurred by the secured creditor in repossessing and holding the collateral.
Relinquishing the Security Interest and Proceeding to Judgment on the Underlying Debt	This course of action is usually taken only when the value of the collateral has been reduced below the amount of the secured interest and the debtor has other assets from which to satisfy the debt.
SURETY AND GUARANTY ARRANGEMENTS, P. 457	
Surety and Guaranty Arrangements	Occur when a creditor refuses to extend credit to a debtor without further security, and a third person agrees to provide that security by agreeing to become liable on the debt.
Surety Agreement	A third party—called the *surety* or *co-debtor*—promises to be liable for another person's debt. The surety is *primarily liable* for payment of the debt when it is due, along with the principal debtor. The creditor does not have to attempt to collect the debt from the principal debtor before demanding payment from the surety.
Guaranty Arrangement	A third party—called the *guarantor*—agrees to pay the debt of the principal debtor if the debtor *defaults* and does not pay the debt when it

	is due. The guarantor is *secondarily liable* and has to pay the debt only if the creditor has attempted unsuccessfully to collect the debt from the debtor.
Right of Subrogation	When a surety or guarantor has been made to pay a debt owed by the principal debtor, the surety or guarantor acquires all of the creditor's rights against the debtor and may recover the amount it paid on the debtor's behalf.

COLLECTION REMEDIES, P. 459

Collection Remedies	If a creditor sues a debtor or obtains a *judgment* against a debtor, the creditor can utilize the following collection remedies to recover from the debtor.
Attachment	A *prejudgment* court order that permits the seizure of the debtor's property while the lawsuit is pending. The creditor must follow the procedures established by state law, give the debtor notice, and post a bond with the court.
Execution	A *postjudgment* court order that permits the seizure of the debtor's property that is in the *possession of the debtor*. Certain property is exempt from levy (e.g., homestead exemption).
Garnishment	A *postjudgment* court order that permits the seizure of the debtor's property in the *possession of third parties* (e.g., wages to be paid to the debtor by his or her employer). Garnishment is subject to limitations established by federal and state law.
Composition of Creditor's Agreements	An agreement that a debtor and creditors enter into whereby the creditors agree to accept payment of a sum less than the debt as full satisfaction of the debtor's debts. Creditors who do not assent to the agreement may proceed to collect or settle their claims against the debtor in their own way.
Assignment for the Benefit of Creditors	An offer by the debtor to voluntarily assign title to his or her property to a trustee or an assignee for the benefit of his or her creditors. Creditors may either accept or reject this tender of assets. Creditors who accept the offer agree not to sue the debtor and are paid on a pro rata basis from the proceeds of the sale of the assets. Creditors who reject the offer may proceed to collect or settle their claims against the debtor in their own way.

CRITICAL LEGAL THINKING CASES

19.1 Financing Statement In 1984, C&H Trucking, Inc. (C&H) borrowed $19,747.56 from S&D Petroleum Company, Inc. (S&D). S&D hired Clifton M. Tamsett to prepare a security agreement naming C&H as the debtor and giving S&D a security interest in a 1984 Mack truck. The security agreement prepared by Tamsett declared that the collateral also secured any other indebtedness or liability of the debtor to the secured party direct or indirect, absolute or contingent, due or to become due, now existing or hereafter arising, including all future advances or loans which may be made at the option of the secured party.

Tamsett failed to file a financing statement or the executed agreement with the appropriate government office. C&H subsequently paid off the original debt, and S&D continued to extend new credit to C&H. In March 1986, when C&H owed S&D over $17,000, S&D learned that (1) C&H was insolvent, (2) the Mack truck had been sold, and (3) Tamsett had failed to file the security agreement. Does S&D have a security interest in the Mack truck? Is Tamsett liable to S&D? [*S&D Petroleum Company, Inc. v. Tamsett*, 534 N.Y.S.2d 800 (N.Y.Sup.Ct.App. 1988)]

19.2 Priority of Security Agreements On July 15, 1980, World Wide Tracers, Inc. (World Wide), sold certain of its assets and properties, including equipment, furniture, uniforms, accounts receivable, and contract rights, to Metropolitan Protection, Inc. (Metropolitan). To secure payment of the purchase price, Metropolitan executed a security agreement and financing statement in favor of World Wide. The agreement, which stated that "all of the property listed on Exhibit A (equipment, furniture and fixtures) together with any property of the debtor acquired after July 15, 1980" was collateral, was filed with the Minnesota secretary of state on July 15, 1980.

In February 1982, State Bank (Bank) loaned money to Metropolitan, which executed a security agreement and financing statement with the Minnesota secretary of state's office on March 3, 1982. The financing statement contained the following language describing the collateral:

> All accounts receivable and contract rights owned or hereafter acquired. All equipment now owned and hereafter acquired, including but not limited to, office furniture and uniforms.

When Metropolitan defaulted on its agreement with World Wide in the fall of 1982, World Wide brought suit asserting its alleged security agreement in Metropolitan's accounts receivable. The bank filed a counterclaim, asserting its perfected security interest in Metropolitan's accounts receivable. Who wins? [*World Wide Tracers, Inc. v. Metropolitan Protection, Inc.*, 384 N.W.2d 442 (Minn. 1986)]

19.3 Floating Lien On March 17, 1973, Joseph H. Jones and others (debtors) borrowed money from Columbus Junction State Bank (Bank) and executed a security agreement in favor of the Bank. On March 29, 1973, the Bank perfected its security interest by filing financing statements covering "equipment, farm products, crops, livestock, supplies, contract rights, and all accounts and proceeds thereof" with the Iowa secretary of state. On January 28, 1978, the Bank filed a continuation statement with the Iowa secretary of state. On January 31, 1986, the debtors filed for Chapter 7 (liquidation) bankruptcy. The bankruptcy collected $10,073 from the sale of the debtors' 1985 crops and an undetermined amount of soybeans harvested in 1986 on farmland owned by the debtors. The bankruptcy trustee claims the funds and soybeans on behalf of the bankruptcy estate. The Bank claims the funds and soybeans as a perfected secured creditor. Who wins? [*In re Jones*, 79 B.R. 839 (Bk.N.D. Iowa 1987)]

19.4 Sale Proceeds Murphy Oldsmobile, Inc. (Murphy), operated an automobile dealership that sold new and used automobiles. General Motors Acceptance Corporation (GMAC) loaned funds to Murphy to finance the purchase of new automobiles as inventory. The loan was secured by a duly perfected security agreement in all existing and after-acquired inventory and the proceeds therefrom. Section 9-306 of the New York UCC provides that a security interest in collateral continues in "identifiable proceeds." During the first week of May 1980, Murphy received checks and drafts from the sale of the secured inventory in the amount of $97,888, which it deposited in a general business checking account at Norstar Bank (Bank). During that week, Murphy defaulted on certain loans it had received from the Bank. The Bank exercised its right of setoff and seized the funds on deposit in Murphy's checking account. GMAC sued to enforce its security claim against these funds. Who wins? [*General Motors Acceptance Corporation v. Norstar Bank, N.A.*, 532 N.Y.S.2d 685 (N.Y.Sup.Ct. 1988)]

19.5 Property Subject to a Security Agreement In March 1982, the First National Bank of Chicago (Bank) loaned more than $6 million to J. Catton Farms, Inc. (Catton), a huge farming operation. The loan was secured by "receivables, accounts, inventory, equipment, and fixtures and the proceeds and products thereof" and "all accounts, contract rights including, without limitation, all rights under installment sales contracts and lease rights with respect to rental lands, instruments, documents, chattel paper and general intangibles in which the debtor has or hereafter acquires any right." To perfect its security interest, the Bank filed the security agreement in the appropriate state or county recording office in every state in which the Catton's farms were located.

In March 1983, Catton signed a payment in kind (PIK) contract with the U.S. Department of Agriculture whereby it agreed not to plant specific crops (corn) and would receive payment in kind after the growing season. On April 30, 1983, Catton filed for Chapter 11 (reorganization) bankruptcy. Catton assigned its right to receive the payment in kind to Cargill, a large grain elevator company, in exchange for over $200,000 cash. The payment in kind was made to Cargill under the assignment. The corn received by Cargill was estimated to be worth $334,666. The Bank filed a motion with the bankruptcy court to enforce its security interest against the payment in kind. Does the Bank have a security interest in the payment in kind? [*J. Catton Farms, Inc. v. First National Bank of Chicago*, 779 F.2d 1242 (7th Cir. 1985)]

19.6 Moved Goods Valley Bank has a general security interest in "all equipment" of a debtor known as Curtis Press. Rockwell International Credit Corporation (Rockwell) has a purchase money security interest in a particular item of equipment acquired by the debtor. Both security interests were duly perfected in Idaho. Generally, the purchase money security interest held by Rockwell has priority over the general security interest held by Valley Bank. A controversy arose after the debtor moved the equipment to Wyoming and then defaulted in the obligations owed to both Rockwell and Valley Bank. UCC 9-103, which has been adopted by both Idaho and Wyoming, provides that the perfection of a security interest follows the collateral into a foreign jurisdiction for a period of four months or the expiration of the perfection period, whichever is less.

Neither Rockwell nor Valley Bank reperfected their security interest in the equipment within the time requirement. Eventually, Valley Bank located the equipment in Wyoming and reperfected its security interest by taking possession of the collateral. Rockwell then belatedly reperfected its security interest by filing a continuation statement with the Wyoming secretary of state. Rockwell brought this action to recover the equipment from Valley Bank, alleging that its purchase money security interest has priority over Valley Bank's general security interest. Who wins? [*Rockwell International Credit Corporation v. Valley Bank*, 707 P.2d 517 (Idaho App. 1985)]

19.7 Priority of Security Interests Clyde and Marlys Trees, owners of the Wine Shop, Inc. borrowed money from the American Heritage Bank & Trust Company (Bank). They personally and on behalf of the corporation executed a promissory note, security agreement, and financing statement to the Bank. The Bank properly filed a security agreement and financing statement naming the Wine Shop's inventory, stock in trade, furniture, fixtures, and equipment "now owned or hereafter to be acquired" as collateral. The Trees also borrowed money from a junior lienholder, whose promissory note was secured by the same collateral. The Wine Shop subsequently defaulted on both notes. Without informing the Bank, the junior lienholder took over the assets of the Wine Shop and transferred them to a corporation, O.&E., Inc. Fearing that its security interest would not be adequately protected, the Bank filed a motion to enforce its security interest. Can the Bank enforce its security interest even though the collateral was transferred to another party? [*American Heritage Bank & Trust Company v. O.&E., Inc.*, 576 P.2d 566 (Colo.App. 1978)]

19.8 Priority of Security Interests On October 8, 1980, Paul High purchased various items of personal property and livestock from William and Marilyn McGowens (McGowens). To secure the purchase price, High granted the McGowens a security interest in the personal property and livestock. On December 18, 1980, High borrowed $86,695 from Nebraska State Bank (Bank) and signed a promissory note granting the Bank a security interest in all his farm products, including but not limited to all of his livestock. On December 20, 1980, the Bank perfected its security agreement by filing a financing statement with the county clerk in Dakota County, Nebraska. The McGowens perfected their security interest by filing a financing statement and security agreement with the county clerk on April 28, 1981. In 1984, High defaulted on the obligations owed to the McGowens and the Bank. Whose security interest has priority? [*McGowen v. Nebraska State Bank*, 427 N.W.2d 772 (Neb. 1988)]

19.9 Purchase Money Security Interest In 1974, Prior Brothers, Inc. (PBI), began financing its farming operations through the Bank of California, N.A. (Bank). The Bank's loans were secured by PBI's equipment and after-acquired property. On March 22, 1974, the Bank filed a financing statement perfecting its security interest. On April 8, 1976, PBI contacted the International Harvester dealership in Sunnyside, Washington, about the purchase of a new tractor. A retail installment contract for a model 1066 International Harvester tractor was executed. PBI took delivery of the tractor "on approval," agreeing that if it decided to purchase the tractor it would inform the dealership of its intention and send a $6,000 down payment. On April 22, 1976, the dealership received a $6,000 check. The dealership filed a financing statement concerning the tractor on April 27, 1976. Later, when PBI went into receivership, the dealership filed a complaint asking the court to declare that its purchase money security interest in the tractor had priority

over the Bank's security interest. Did it? [*In the Matter of Prior Brothers, Inc.*, 632 P.2d 522 (Wash. App. 1981)]

19.10 Purchase Money Security Interest In 1973, Sandwich State Bank (Sandwich) made general farm loans to David Klotz and Hinckley Grain Company. The loan was secured by the assets of Klotz's farm and after-acquired property. Sandwich filed a financing statement with the Kane County Recorder to perfect its security interest. Sandwich filed the necessary continuation statements so its security interest remained in effect up to and during the time of trial. On February 3, 1984, DeKalb Bank (DeKalb) loaned Klotz funds for the particular purpose of purchasing certain cattle. DeKalb filed a financing statement on February 3, 1984 to perfect its security interest in the cattle. The cattle in question all were purchased using funds loaned to Klotz by DeKalb. When Klotz defaulted on its loan to DeKalb, DeKalb sued to enforce its security interest and to recover possession of the cattle. Does DeKalb's security interest have priority over Sandwich's security interest? [*DeKalb Bank v. Klotz*, 502 N.E.2d 1256 (Ill.App. 1987)]

19.11 Buyer in the Ordinary Course of Business Heritage Ford Lincoln Mercury, Inc. (Heritage), was in the business of selling new cars. In April 1978, Heritage entered into an agreement with Ford Motor Credit Company (Ford) whereby Ford extended a continuing line of credit to Heritage to purchase vehicles. Heritage granted Ford a purchase money security interest in all motor vehicles it owned and thereafter acquired and in all proceeds from the sale of such motor vehicles. Ford filed its financing statement with the secretary of state of Kansas on May 11, 1978. When the dealership experienced financial trouble, two Heritage officers decided to double finance certain new cars by issuing dealer papers to themselves and obtaining financing for two new cars from First National Bank & Trust Company of El Dorado (Bank). The loan proceeds were deposited in the dealership's account to help its financial difficulties. The cars were available for sale. When the dealership closed its doors and turned over the car inventory to Ford, the Bank alleged that it had priority over Ford because the Heritage officers were buyers in the ordinary course of business. Who wins? [*First National Bank and Trust Company of El Dorado v. Ford Motor Credit Company*, 646 P.2d 1057 (Kan. 1982)]

19.12 Artisan's Lien On April 25, 1985, Ozark Financial Services (Ozark) loaned money to Lonnie and Patsy Turner to purchase a tractor truck unit. The Turners signed a security agreement giving Ozark a security interest in the tractor truck. Ozark properly filed a financing statement giving public notice of its security interest. In June 1985, the Turners took the truck to Pete & Sons Garage, Inc. (Pete & Sons), for repairs. When the Turners arrived to pick up the truck, they could not pay for the repairs. Pete & Sons returned the truck to the Turners upon their verbal agreement that if they did not pay for the repairs, they would return the truck to Pete & Sons. The Turners did not pay Pete & Sons for the repair services and defaulted on the loan payments due Ozark. Ozark brought this action to recover the truck under its security agreement. Pete & Sons asserts that it has a common law artisan's lien on the truck for the unpaid repair services that it claims takes priority over Ozark's security interest. Who wins? [*Ozark Financial Services v. Turner*, 735 S.W.2d 374 (Mo.App. 1987)]

19.13 Repossession of Collateral Kent Cobado sold Gerald Hilliman and John Szata a herd of cattle. To secure payment of the purchase price, the buyers granted Cobado a security interest in 66 cows and one bull. Cobado protested when it learned that the buyers had culled a number of cattle from the herd. The buyers gave Cobado 37 replacement cows as additional security. Cobado filed a financing statement with the office of the clerk of county.

Cobado continued to be disturbed by the buyers' continuing practice of culling cattle from the herd. Suddenly, without any prior warning, Cobado, aided by two men, arrived at the buy-

ers' premises. Szata was advised of Cobado's intention to repossess the collateral. Szata replied that all of the payments had been made on time. Cobado restated his intent. The county sheriff arrived before the cattle could be loaded onto Cobado's trucks. The sheriff warned Cobado that he would be arrested if he left with the cattle. Cobado ignored the warning, loaded the cattle onto the trucks, and left with the cattle. Was Cobado's repossession of the cattle proper under Article 9 of the UCC? [*Hilliman v. Cobado*, 499 N.Y.S.2d 610 (N.Y.Sup.Ct. 1986)]

ETHICS CASES

19.14 Ethical Perspective On February 26, 1982, Jessie Lynch became seriously ill and needed medical attention. Her sister, Ethel Sales, took her to the Forsyth Memorial Hospital in North Carolina for treatment. Lynch was admitted for hospitalization. Sales signed Mrs. Lynch's admission form, which included the following section:

> The undersigned in consideration of hospital services being rendered or to be rendered by Forsyth County Memorial Hospital Authority, Inc., in Winston-Salem, N.C., to the above patient, does hereby guarantee payment to Forsyth County Hospital Authority, Inc., on demand all charges for said services and incidentals incurred on behalf of such patient.

Mrs. Lynch received the care and services rendered by the hospital until her discharge over 30 days later. The total bill during her hospitalization amounted to $7,977. When Mrs. Lynch refused to pay the bill, the hospital instituted an action against Lynch and Sales to recover the unpaid amount. Is Sales liable? Did Sales act ethically in denying liability? Did she have a choice when she signed the contract? [*Forsyth County Memorial Hospital Authority, Inc.*, 346 S.E.2d 212 (N.C.App. 1986)]

19.15 Ethical Perspective On February 25, 1975, Harder & Sons, Inc., an International Harvester dealership in Ionia, Michigan, sold a used International Harvester 1066 diesel tractor to Terry Blaser on an installment contract. Although the con-

tract listed Blaser's address as Ionia County, Blaser informed Harder at the time of purchase that he was going to work and live in Barry County. Blaser took delivery of the tractor at his Ionia County address on February 28, 1975. On the same day, Harder filed a financing statement, which was executed by Blaser with the installment contract, in Barry County. The state of Michigan UCC requires an Article 9 financing statement to be filed in the debtor's county of the residence. The contract and security agreement were immediately assigned to International Harvester Credit Corporation (International Harvester).

Blaser subsequently moved to Barry County for about three months, then to Ionia County for a few months, then to Kent County for three weeks, and then to Muskegon County, where he sold the tractor to Jay and Dale Vos. At the time of sale, Blaser informed the Vos brothers that he owned the tractor. He did not tell them that it was subject to a lien. The Vos brothers went to First Michigan Bank & Trust Company (Bank) to obtain a loan to help purchase the tractor. When the Bank checked the records of Ionia County and found that no financing statement was filed against the tractor, it made a $7,000 loan to the Vos brothers to purchase the tractor. On May 19, 1977, International Harvester filed suit to recover the tractor from the Vos brothers on the grounds that it had a prior perfected security interest. Did Blaser act ethically in this case? Who wins? [*International Harvester Credit Corporation v. Vos.*, 290 N.W.2d 401 (Mich.App. 1980)]

CRITICAL LEGAL THINKING WRITING ASSIGNMENT

Read Case A.19 in the Case Appendix [*Davenport v. Chrysler Credit Corporation*]. This case is excerpted from the court of appeals opinion. Review and brief the case. In your brief, be sure to answer the following questions:

1. Who was the plaintiff? Who was the defendant?

2. Was there a default in the repayment of the loan? What actions did the creditor take to recover the security?
3. Was there a "breach of the peace" in the repossession of the vehicle?
4. What damages did the court award? How were they calculated?

NOTE

[1]15 U.S.C. §§ 1601 et seq.

CHAPTER 20

BANKRUPTCY

AND REORGANIZATION

Chapter Objectives

*After studying this chapter,
you should be able to*

1. Describe the procedure for filing for bankruptcy
2. Define the concept of "fresh start" and the discharge of unpaid debts
3. Describe a Chapter 7 liquidation bankruptcy
4. Define an automatic stay in bankruptcy
5. Identify voidable transfers and preferential payments
6. List the order of priority for paying creditors in a Chapter 7 bankruptcy
7. Define secured and unsecured creditors' rights in bankruptcy
8. Describe how a business is reorganized in a Chapter 11 bankruptcy
9. Define an executory contract and explain how it can be avoided in bankruptcy
10. Describe a Chapter 13 consumer debt adjustment bankruptcy

Chapter Contents

- Overview of Federal Bankruptcy Law
- Chapter 7 Liquidation Bankruptcy
- Property of the Bankruptcy Estate
  Case 20.1 *In re Witwer (Bk.C.D.Cal.)*
  Contemporary Business Environment Homestead Exemptions: More Than Just a Log Cabin
- Distribution of Property and Discharge
  Case 20.2 *In re Williams (Bk.E.D.N.C.)*
  Business Checklist Whether a Debtor Should Sign a Reaffirmation Agreement
- Chapter 11 Reorganization Bankruptcy
  Case 20.3 *In re Johns-Manville Corp. (Bk.S.D.N.Y.)*
  Business Application Dow Corning Files for Bankruptcy
- Plan of Reorganization
- Chapter 13 Consumer Debt Adjustment
  International Perspective Reorganization Under British Bankruptcy Law
- Working the Web
- Chapter Summary
- Critical Legal Thinking Cases
- Ethics Cases
- Critical Legal Thinking Writing Assignment

> *A trifling debt makes a man your debtor, a large one makes him your enemy.*
>
> Seneca
> *Epistulae Morales ad Lucilium,*
> 63–65

The extension of credit from creditors to debtors in commercial and personal transactions is important to the viability of the American and world economies. However, on occasion, borrowers become overextended and are unable to meet their debt obligations.

> *"Small debts are like small shot; they are rattling on every side, and can scarcely be escaped without a wound: great debts are like cannon; of loud noise, but little danger."*
> Samuel Johnson
> *Letter to Joseph Simpson* (1759)

Years ago in Britain and Europe, persons who could not meet their debts were sentenced to debtors' prisons or indentured to their creditors until the debt was "worked off." In order to avoid such harsh results, many of these countries adopted bankruptcy laws that were intended to achieve a better balance between debtors' rights and creditors' rights.

The founders of our country thought the plight of debtors was so important that they included a provision in the U.S. Constitution giving Congress the authority to establish uniform bankruptcy laws. The goal of federal bankruptcy law is to give debtors a "fresh start" by relieving them from legal responsibility for past debts. This chapter discusses federal bankruptcy law, which is the exclusive law that governs throughout this country.

OVERVIEW OF FEDERAL BANKRUPTCY LAW

HISTORICAL NOTE
Under the old Bankruptcy Act, a debtor in bankruptcy was called a bankrupt. *Under the Bankruptcy Reform Act of 1978, a debtor in bankruptcy is called a* debtor.

Bankruptcy Code The name given to the Bankruptcy Reform Act of 1978, as amended.

Article 1, section 8, clause 4 of the U.S. Constitution provides that "The Congress shall have the power . . . to establish . . . uniform laws on the subject of bankruptcies throughout the United States."

Federal bankruptcy law establishes procedures for filing for bankruptcy, resolving creditors' claims, and protecting debtors' rights. Bankruptcy law is exclusively federal law; there are no state bankruptcy laws.

The Bankruptcy Code – Federal Law

CAUTION
Bankruptcy law is federal law. There are no state bankruptcy laws.

Congress enacted the original *Bankruptcy Act* in 1878. It was amended in 1938 by the *Chandler Act*, and that law was completely revised by the *Bankruptcy Reform Act of 1978*.[1] The 1978 Act, which became effective on October 1, 1979, substantially changed—and eased—the requirements for filing bankruptcy.

Several years later, Congress enacted the *Bankruptcy Amendments and Federal Judgeship Act of 1984*,[2] which made bankruptcy courts part of the federal district court system and attached a bankruptcy court to each district court. Bankruptcy judges are appointed by the President for 14-year terms. Other provisions of the 1984 amendments remedied abuses and misuses of bankruptcy and clarified procedures for filing bankruptcy. The Bankruptcy Reform Act of 1978, as amended, is referred to as the **Bankruptcy Code**.

core proceedings
Proceedings that bankruptcy judges decide that have to do with creditor claims, deciding preferences, confirming plans of reorganization, and so on.

Jurisdiction of the Bankruptcy Courts

Bankruptcy judges decide **core proceedings** (e.g., allowing creditor claims, deciding preferences, confirming plans of reorganization, and the like) regarding bankruptcy cases. *Noncore proceedings* concerning the debtor (e.g., decisions on personal injury, divorce, and other civil proceedings) are resolved in federal or state court. The jurisdiction of the bankruptcy courts became effective on July 10, 1984.

> *"Poor bankrupt."*
> William Shakespeare
> *Romeo and Juliet* (1595)

Types of Bankruptcy

The Bankruptcy Code is divided into chapters. Chapters 1, 3, and 5 include definitional provisions and provisions for the administration of bankruptcy proceedings.

They apply to all forms of bankruptcy. The most common forms of bankruptcy are provided by the following chapters: Chapter 7 (liquidation), Chapter 11 (reorganization), and Chapter 13 (consumer debt adjustment). The remaining chapters of the Bankruptcy Code govern the bankruptcies of municipalities, stockbrokers, and railroads.

The "Fresh Start"

The primary purpose of federal bankruptcy law is to discharge the debtor from burdensome debts. That is, the law gives debtors a **"fresh start"** by freeing them from legal responsibility for past debts by (1) protecting debtors from abusive activities by creditors in collecting debts, (2) preventing certain creditors from obtaining an unfair advantage over other creditors, (3) protecting creditors from actions of the debtor that would diminish the value of the bankruptcy estate, (4) providing for the speedy, efficient, and equitable distribution of the debtor's nonexempt property to claimholders, and (5) preserving existing business relations.

fresh start The goal of federal bankruptcy law—to discharge the debtor from burdensome debts and allow him or her to begin again.

CHAPTER 7 LIQUIDATION BANKRUPTCY

Chapter 7 liquidation bankruptcy (also called **straight bankruptcy**) is the most familiar form of bankruptcy. In this type of proceeding, the debtor's nonexempt property is sold for cash, the cash is distributed to the creditors, and any unpaid debts are *discharged*. Any person, including individuals, partnerships, and corporations, may be debtors in a Chapter 7 proceeding. Certain businesses, including banks, savings and loan associations, credit unions, insurance companies, and railroads, are prohibited from filing bankruptcy under Chapter 7.

Chapter 7 liquidation bankruptcy The most familiar form of bankruptcy; the debtor's nonexempt property is sold for cash, the cash is distributed to the creditors, and any unpaid debts are discharged.

Bankruptcy Procedure

The filing and maintenance of a Chapter 7 case must follow certain procedures. The following paragraphs outline the major steps in the liquidation process.

Filing a Petition A Chapter 7 bankruptcy is commenced when a **petition** is filed with the bankruptcy court. The petition may be filed by either the debtor (voluntary) or one or more creditors (involuntary).

Voluntary petitions only have to state that the debtor has debts; insolvency (i.e., that debts exceed assets) need not be declared. The petition must include the following schedules: (1) a list of secured and unsecured creditors, including their addresses and the amount of debt owed to each, (2) a list of all property owned by the debtor, including property claimed to be exempt by the debtor, (3) a statement of the financial affairs of the debtor, and (4) a list of the debtor's current income and expenses. The petition must be signed and sworn to under oath. Married couples may file a joint petition.

An **involuntary petition** can be filed against any debtors who can file a voluntary petition under Chapter 7 except farmers, ranchers, and nonprofit organizations. An involuntary petition must allege that the debtor is not paying his or her debts as they become due. If the debtor has more than 12 creditors, the petition must be signed by at least 3 of them. If there are 12 or fewer creditors, any creditor can sign the petition. The creditor or creditors who sign the petition must have valid unsecured claims of at least $5,000 (in the aggregate).

petition A document filed with the bankruptcy court that sets the bankruptcy proceedings into motion.

voluntary petition A petition filed by the debtor; states that the debtor has debts.

involuntary petition A petition filed by creditors of the debtor; alleges that the debtor is not paying his or her debts as they become due.

Order for Relief The filing of either a voluntary petition or an unchallenged involuntary petition constitutes an **order for relief**. If the debtor challenges an involuntary petition, a trial will be held to determine whether an order for relief should be granted. If the order is granted, the case is accepted for further bankruptcy proceedings. In the case of an involuntary petition, the debtor must file the same schedules filed by voluntary debtors.

order for relief The filing of a voluntary petition, an unchallenged involuntary petition, or a grant of an order after a trial of a challenged involuntary petition.

Meeting of the Creditors   Within a reasonable time (not less than 10 days or more than 30 days) after the court grants an order for relief, the court must call a **meeting of the creditors** (also called the **first meeting of the creditors**). The judge cannot attend this meeting. However, the debtor must appear at the meeting and submit to questioning by creditors. Creditors may ask questions regarding the debtor's financial affairs, disposition of property prior to bankruptcy, possible concealment of assets, and such. The debtor may have an attorney present at this meeting.

Appointment of a Trustee   A trustee must be appointed in a Chapter 7 proceeding. An interim trustee is appointed by the court when an order for relief is entered. A **permanent trustee** is elected at the first meeting of the creditors. Trustees, who are often lawyers or accountants, are entitled to receive reasonable compensation for their services and reimbursement for expenses. When appointed, the trustee becomes the legal representative of the bankrupt debtor's estate. Generally, the trustee must do the following:

- Take immediate possession of the debtor's property
- Separate secured and unsecured property
- Set aside exempt property
- Investigate the debtor's financial affairs
- Employ disinterested professionals (e.g., attorneys, accountants, and appraisers) to assist in the administration of the estate
- Examine proof of claims
- Defend, bring, and maintain lawsuits on behalf of the estate
- Invest the property of the estate
- Sell or otherwise dispose of property of the estate
- Distribute the proceeds of the estate
- Make reports to the court, creditors, and debtor regarding the administration of the estate

Proof of Claims   Unsecured creditors must file a **proof of claim** stating the amount of their claim against the debtor. The form for the statement is provided by the court. The proof of claim must be "timely filed." Generally, this means within six months of the first meeting of the creditors. Secured creditors are not required to file proof of claim. However, a secured creditor whose claim exceeds the value of the collateral may submit a proof of claim and become an unsecured claimant as to the difference.

The claim must be allowed by the court before a creditor is permitted to participate in the bankruptcy estate. Any part of interest may object to a claim. If an objection to a claim is raised, the court will hold a hearing to determine the validity and amount of the claim.

Automatic Stay

The filing of a voluntary or involuntary petition automatically stays—that is, suspends—certain action by creditors against the debtor or the debtor's property.[3] This is called an **automatic stay**. The stay, which applies to collection efforts of both secured and unsecured creditors, is designed to prevent a scramble for the debtor's assets in a variety of court proceedings. The following creditor actions are stayed:

1. Instituting or maintaining legal actions to collect prepetition debts
2. Enforcing judgments obtained against the debtor
3. Obtaining, perfecting, or enforcing liens against property of the debtor
4. Attempting to set off debts owed by the creditor to the debtor against the creditor's claims in bankruptcy
5. Nonjudicial collection efforts, such as self-help activities (e.g., repossession of a car).

The court also has the authority to issue injunctions preventing creditor activity not covered by the automatic stay provision. Actions to recover alimony and child support are not stayed in bankruptcy. The automatic stay does not preclude collection efforts

---

meeting of the creditors
A meeting of the creditors in a bankruptcy case that must occur not less than 10 days or more than 30 days after the court grants an order for relief.

permanent trustee   A legal representative of the bankruptcy debtor's estate, usually an accountant or a lawyer; elected at the first meeting of the creditors.

proof of claim   A document required to be filed by unsecured creditors that states the amount of their claim against the debtor.

automatic stay   The result of the filing of a voluntary or involuntary petition; the suspension of certain actions by creditors against the debtor or the debtor's property.

BUSINESS BRIEF
The importance of the automatic stay in bankruptcy should not be underestimated. For example, in Pennzoil v. Texaco, *Texaco filed a voluntary petition in bankruptcy to stay any attempt by Pennzoil to perfect its $10-billion judgment against Texaco.*

by creditors against codebtors and guarantors of the bankrupt debtor's debts, except (1) in a Chapter 13 bankruptcy (discussed later in this chapter) or (2) if the codebtor is also in bankruptcy.

Relief from Stay A secured creditor may petition the court for a **relief from stay**. This usually occurs in situations involving depreciating assets in which the secured property is not adequately protected during the bankruptcy proceeding. The court may opt to provide adequate protection rather than granting relief from stay. In such cases, the court may (1) order cash payments equal to the amount of the depreciation, (2) grant an additional or replacement lien, or (3) grant an "indubitable equivalent" (e.g., a guarantee from a solvent party).

relief from stay May be granted in situations involving depreciating assets where the secured property is not adequately protected during the bankruptcy proceeding; asked for by a secured creditor.

PROPERTY OF THE BANKRUPTCY ESTATE

The **bankruptcy estate** is created upon the commencement of a Chapter 7 proceeding. It includes all of the debtor's legal and equitable interests in real, personal, tangible, and intangible property, wherever located, that exist when the petition is filed. The debtor's separate and community property are included in the estate.

Property acquired after the petition does not become part of the bankruptcy estate. The only exceptions are gifts, inheritances, life insurance proceeds, and property from divorce settlements that the debtor is entitled to receive within 180 days after the petition is filed. Earnings from property of the estate—such as rents, dividends, and interest payments—are property of the estate.

bankruptcy estate An estate created upon the commencement of a Chapter 7 proceeding that includes all of the debtor's legal and equitable interests in real, personal, tangible, and intangible property, wherever located, that exist when the petition is filed, minus exempt property.

Exempt Property

Because the Bankruptcy Code is not designed to make the debtor a pauper, certain property is exempt from the bankruptcy estate. The debtor may retain **exempt property**.

The Bankruptcy Code establishes a *federal* exemption scheme (see Exhibit 20.1).

exempt property Property that may be retained by the debtor pursuant to federal or state law; the debtor's property that does not become part of the bankruptcy estate.

Exhibit 20.1
Federal Exemptions from the Bankruptcy Estate

1. Interest up to $7,500 in value in property used as a residence (real or personal property), and burial plots. This is called the homestead exemption.

2. Interest up to $1,000 in value in one motor vehicle.

3. Interest up to $200 per item in household goods and furnishings, wearing apparel, appliances, books, animals, crops, or musical instruments, up to an aggregate value of $4,000 for all items.

4. Interest in jewelry up to $500 that is held for personal use.

5. Interest in any property the debtor chooses (including cash) up to $400, plus up to $3,750 of any unused portion of the $7,500 homestead exemption.

6. Interest up to $750 in value in implements, tools, or professional books used in the debtor's trade.

7. Any unmatured life insurance policy owned by the debtor (other than a credit life insurance contract), and up to $4,000 of any accrued dividends, interest, or cash surrender value of any unmatured life insurance policy.

8. Professionally prescribed health aids.

9. Many government benefits regardless of value, including Social Security benefits, unemployment compensation, veteran's benefits, disability benefits, and public assistance benefits.

10. Certain rights to receive income, including alimony and support payments, pension benefits, profit sharing, and annuity payments, but only to the extent reasonably necessary to support the debtor or his dependents.

11. Interests in wrongful death benefits, life insurance proceeds, and personal injury awards (up to $7,600) to the extent reasonably necessary to support the debtor or his dependents, and crime victim compensation awards without limit.

State Law Exemptions The Bankruptcy Code also permits states to enact their own exemptions. States that do so may (1) give debtors the option of choosing between federal and state exemptions or (2) require debtors to follow state law.[4] The exemptions available under state law are often quite liberal. For example, homestead exemptions are often higher under state law than under the federal exemption scheme. Many states require the debtor to file a *Declaration of Homestead* prior to bankruptcy. This document is usually filed in the county recorder's office in the county in which the property is located.

If the debtor's equity in property (above liens and mortgages) exceeds the exemption limits, the trustee may liquidate the property to realize the excess value for the bankruptcy estate.

CONSIDER

States that provide liberal exemptions (e.g., California, Florida, Texas) are called "debtors' havens."

CONSIDER THIS EXAMPLE: Assume that the debtor owns a home worth $100,000 that is subject to a $60,000 mortgage. The trustee may sell the home, pay off the mortgage, pay the debtor $7,500 (applying the federal exemption), and use the remaining proceeds ($32,500) for distribution to the debtor's creditors.

In the following case, the court found that an asset was exempt from the debtor's bankruptcy estate.

CASE 20.1

In Re Witwer
148 Bankr. 930 (1992) United States Bankruptcy Court, Central District of California

Facts Dr. James J. Witwer is the sole stockholder, sole employee, and president of James J. Witwer, M.D., Inc., a California corporation under which he practices medicine. He is also the sole beneficiary of the corporation's retirement plan, which was established in 1970. On October 21, 1991, Witwer filed a voluntary petition for relief under Chapter 7 (liquidation). At the time, the value of the assets in his retirement plan was $1.8 million. California law exempted retirement plans from a debtor's bankruptcy estate. When Witwer claimed that his retirement plan was exempt from the bankruptcy estate, several creditors filed objections.

Issue Is Witwer's retirement plan exempt from the bankruptcy estate?

Decision Yes. The bankruptcy court held that Witwer's retirement plan is fully exempt from his bankruptcy estate.

Reason Under California law, the assets of a retirement plan are entirely exempt if the plan was designed and used for retirement purposes. The bankruptcy court found this to be the case concerning the

retirement plan established by Witwer. The court stated, "Regardless of the inequities that may result from a debtor's use of the California exemption scheme, this court is constrained by the plain meaning of the statutes in the context of this case. Allowing the debtor to retain over $1.8 million in retirement benefits in bankruptcy while being discharged from debts legitimately owed to creditors seems fundamentally unfair." The court concluded that under the Bankruptcy Code, the size of a debtor's bankruptcy estate is "subject to the vagaries of state exemption law."

CASE QUESTIONS

Critical Legal Thinking Do you think bankruptcy law was intended to reach the result in this case?

Ethics Was it ethical for the debtor to declare bankruptcy and wipe out his unsecured creditors while retaining $1.8 million in his retirement account?

Business Implication Should business men and women establish and fund retirement programs?

CONTEMPORARY BUSINESS ENVIRONMENT

Homestead Exemptions: More than Just a Log Cabin

When the term *homestead* is used, many people think of the Wild West, wide-open prairies, and a pioneer's log cabin built with sweat and tears. Long ago, many states enacted laws that protected a debtor's homestead from greedy creditors.

Today, a debtor's homestead may be a condo in a luxury apartment building or a multimillion-dollar split-level home. Depending on state law, at least a portion of the equity in a debtor's homestead may still be protected from creditors if the owner declares bankruptcy. For example, New York exempts $20,000 of equity in a married couple's home from the bankruptcy estate ($10,000 for a single debtor). California exempts $45,000 for a married couple and

$35,000 for a single debtor. These exemptions look generous compared to most states except Florida and Texas.

The Florida constitution and statutes give a homestead exemption from bankruptcy without dollar limit. The homestead is 160 acres outside a municipality and one-half acre inside a municipality.

The Texas homestead exemption is even bigger. Texas has an urban homestead of one acre and a rural homestead of up to 200 acres, without any dollar limit.

Florida and Texas are known as "debtor's havens" because of their generous homestead exemptions from bankruptcy. In fact, relocating to these states has become attractive to people in

financial difficulty, who take what money they have and place it beyond the reach of their creditors in homesteads in these states before declaring bankruptcy. How long a person must reside in the state before declaring bankruptcy is an open question. It is just one factor in deciding whether the debtor has engaged in a bankruptcy fraud that makes the debtor's debts nondischargeable. So far, few bankruptcies have been undone under such a charge.

Proponents of homestead exemptions argue that they are needed to provide a debtor with a fresh start and a roof over his or her head. Critics argue that debtors are using homestead exemptions to run roughshod over creditors.

Voidable Transfers

The Bankruptcy Code prevents debtors from making unusual payments or transfers of property on the eve of bankruptcy that would unfairly benefit the debtor or some creditors at the expense of others. The following sections discuss the transfers that may be avoided by the bankruptcy court.

Preferential Transfers within Ninety Days before Bankruptcy A **preferential transfer** occurs when (1) a debtor transfers property to a creditor within 90 days before the filing of a petition in bankruptcy, (2) the transfer is made for an antecedent (preexisting) debt, and (3) the creditor would receive more from the transfer than it would from Chapter 7 liquidation. The Bankruptcy Code presumes that the debtor is insolvent during this 90-day period.

CONSIDER THIS EXAMPLE: Assume that six months prior to filing bankruptcy the debtor purchases $10,000 of equipment on credit from a supplier. Within 90 days of filing the petition the debtor still owes the money to this creditor, which is not due for 120 days. The debtor pays the creditor the $7,000 before filing the petition. In a Chapter 7 liquidation proceeding, the creditor would have received $1,000. This payment is a voidable preference because it is made within 90 days of filing the petition, is made to pay an antecedent debt, and gives the creditor more than he would receive in liquidation.

There are exceptions to the 90-day rule. They include (1) transfers for current consideration (e.g., equipment purchased for cash within 90 days of the petition),

voidable transfer An unusual payment or transfer of property by the debtor on the eve of bankruptcy that would unfairly benefit the debtor or some creditors at the expense of other creditors. Such transfer may be avoided by the bankruptcy court.

preferential transfer Occurs when (1) a debtor transfers property to a creditor within 90 days before the filing of a petition in bankruptcy, (2) the transfer is made for a preexisting debt, and (3) the creditor would receive more from the transfer than it would from Chapter 7 liquidation.

preferential lien Occurs when (1) a debtor gives an unsecured creditor a secured interest in property within 90 days before the filing of a petition in bankruptcy, (2) the transfer is made for a preexisting debt, and (3) the creditor would receive more because of this lien than it would as an unsecured creditor.

preferential transfer to an insider A transfer of property by an insolvent debtor to an "insider" within one year before the filing of a petition in bankruptcy.

fraudulent transfer Occurs when (1) a debtor transfers property to a third person within one year before the filing of a petition in bankruptcy, and (2) the transfer is made by the debtor with an intent to hinder, delay, or defraud creditors.

CAUTION
Sometimes prior to declaring bankruptcy debtors transfer property to others as gifts or for less than fair market value, sometimes with a promise that the property will be returned to the debtor after the bankruptcy is over. This is bankruptcy fraud.

(2) credit payments made in the ordinary course of the debtor's business (e.g., supplies purchased on credit and paid for within the normal payment term of 30 days after purchase and scheduled payments on long-term debt), and (3) payment of up to $600 by a consumer-debtor to a creditor within 90 days of the petition.

Preferential Liens Debtors sometimes attempt to favor certain unsecured creditors on the eve of bankruptcy by giving them a secured interest in property. This type of interest is called a **preferential lien**. Preferential liens occur when (1) the debtor gives the creditor a secured interest in property within 90 days of the petition, (2) the secured interest is given for an antecedent debt, and (3) the creditor would receive more because of this lien than it would as an unsecured creditor in liquidation.

Preferential Transfers to Insiders The Bankruptcy Code provides that preferential transfers and liens made to "insiders" within one year of the filing of the petition in bankruptcy may be avoided by the court. **Insiders** are defined as relatives, partners, partnerships, officers and directors of a corporation, corporations, and others that have a relationship with the debtor. To avoid a transfer to an insider within the one-year period (other than the first 90 days prior to the petition), the trustee must prove that the debtor was insolvent at the time of the transfer.

Fraudulent Transfers Section 548 of the Bankruptcy Code gives the court the power to avoid **fraudulent transfers** of property that occur within one year of the filing of the petition in bankruptcy. Any transfer of property by the debtor made with actual intent to "hinder, delay, or defraud" creditors is considered a voidable fraudulent transfer. The debtor's actual intent must be proved, although it may be inferred from the circumstances. For example, a transfer of property by an insolvent debtor for substantially less than fair market value would be voidable as a fraudulent transfer. In addition, Section 544(b) of the Bankruptcy Code gives the trustee the power to avoid fraudulent transfers made in violation of state fraudulent conveyances acts. Because these acts usually contain a longer statute of limitations (e.g., six years), a court can avoid any fraudulent transfer made during this period.

If a transfer is voided, a bona fide good faith purchaser must receive the value he or she paid for the property. Thus, if an insolvent debtor sold property worth $50,000 to a bona fide purchaser for $30,000 within the one-year period and the court rescinds the transfer, the trustee must return the $30,000 to the bona fide purchaser.

DISTRIBUTION OF PROPERTY AND DISCHARGE

Priority of Distribution

distribution of property
Nonexempt property of the bankruptcy estate must be distributed to the debtor's secured and unsecured creditors pursuant to the *statutory priority* established by the Bankruptcy Code.

Under Chapter 7, the nonexempt property of the bankruptcy estate must be distributed to the debtor's secured and unsecured creditors. The statutory priority of distribution of property is discussed in the following sections.

BUSINESS BRIEF
Secured creditors are made whole in a Chapter 7 bankruptcy if the value of the collateral equals or exceeds the amount of their security interest.

Secured Creditors A secured creditor's claim to the debtor's property has priority over the claims of unsecured creditors. The secured creditor may (1) accept the collateral in full satisfaction of the debt; (2) foreclose on the collateral and use the proceeds to pay the debt; or (3) allow the trustee to retain the collateral, dispose of it at sale, and remit the proceeds of the sale to him.

If the value of the collateral exceeds the secured interest, the excess becomes available to satisfy the claims of the debtor's unsecured creditors. Before the excess funds are released, however, the secured creditor is allowed to deduct reasonable fees and costs resulting from the default. If the value of the collateral is less than the secured interest, the secured creditor becomes an unsecured creditor to the difference.

Unsecured Creditors The Bankruptcy Code stipulates that unsecured claims are to be satisfied out of the bankruptcy estate in the order of their statutory priority.[5] The statutory priority of unsecured claims is as follows:

1. Fees and expenses of administrating the estate, including court costs, trustee fees, attorneys' fees, appraisal fees, and other costs of administration.
2. Unsecured claims of "gap" creditors who sold goods or services on credit to the debtor in the ordinary course of the debtor's business between the date of the filing of the petition and the date of the appointment of the trustee or issuance of the order for relief (whichever occurred first).
3. Unsecured claims for wages, salary, or commissions earned by the debtor's employees within 90 days immediately preceding the filing of the petition, up to $2,000 per employee.
4. Unsecured claims for contributions to employee benefit plans based on services performed within 180 days immediately preceding the filing of the petition. This priority may not exceed the number of employees covered by the plan multiplied by $2,000.
5. Farm producers and fishermen against debtors who operate grain storage facilities or fish produce storage or processing facilities, up to $2,000 per claim.
6. Unsecured claims for cash deposited by a consumer with the debtor prior to the filing of the petition in connection with either the purchase, lease, or rental of property or the purchase of services that were not delivered or provided by the debtor, up to $900 per claim.
7. Certain tax obligations owed by the debtor to federal, state, and local governmental units. Taxes entitled to this priority are specifically set forth in 11 U.S.C. Section 350.
8. Claims of general unsecured creditors.
9. If there is any balance remaining after the allowed claims of the creditors are satisfied, it is returned to the debtor.

Each class must be paid in full before any lower class is paid anything. If a class cannot be paid in full, the claims of that class are paid pro rata (proportionately).

Discharge

After the property is distributed to satisfy the allowed claims, the remaining unpaid claims are **discharged** (i.e., the debtor is no longer legally responsible for them). Only individuals may be granted a discharge. Discharge is not available to partnerships and corporations. These entities must liquidate under state law before or upon completion of the Chapter 7 proceeding. A debtor can be granted a discharge in a Chapter 7 proceeding only once every six years.

CONSIDER THIS EXAMPLE: Maryjane files for Chapter 7 bankruptcy. At the time of filing, she has many unsecured creditors. Nordstrom's Department Store is one of them. She owes Nordstrom $3,000. The bankruptcy estate has only enough assets to pay unsecured creditors 10 cents on the dollar. Nordstrom's receives $300; the remaining $2,700 is discharged. Nordstrom's cannot thereafter collect this money and will write it off as a bad debt.

Nondischargeable Debts

The following debts are not dischargeable in a Chapter 7 proceeding:

- Claims for taxes accrued within three years prior to the filing of the petition in bankruptcy
- Certain fines and penalties payable to federal, state, and local governmental units
- Claims based on the debtor's liability for causing willful or malicious injury to a person or property

"I will pay you some, and, as most the debtors do, promise you infinitely."
William Shakespeare
Henry IV, Pt. II (1597)

BUSINESS BRIEF
Generally, unsecured creditors often receive little, if anything, in a Chapter 7 bankruptcy.

discharge The termination of the legal duty of a debtor to pay debts that remain unpaid upon the completion of a bankruptcy proceeding.

"It is the policy of the law that the debtor be just before he be generous."
Finch, J.
Hearn 45 St. Corp. v. Jano (1940)

CAUTION
Not all debts are dischargeable in bankruptcy.

- Claims arising from the fraud, larceny, or embezzlement by the debtor while acting in a fiduciary capacity
- Alimony, maintenance, and child support
- Unscheduled claims
- Claims based on the consumer–debtor's purchase of luxury goods of more than $500 from a single creditor within 40 days of the filing of the petition
- Cash advances in excess of $1,000 obtained by a consumer–debtor by use of a revolving line of credit or credit card within 20 days of the filing of the petition
- Judgments and consent decrees against the debtor for liability incurred as a result of the debtor's operation of a motor vehicle while legally intoxicated

consumer discharges not allowed

Creditors who have nondischargeable claims against the debtor may participate in the distribution of the bankruptcy estate. The nondischarged balance may be pursued by creditors against the debtor after bankruptcy.

In the following case, the court denied discharge of a debt.

CASE 20.2

In Re Williams

106 Bankr. 87 (1989) United States Bankruptcy Court, Eastern District of North Carolina

Facts Charles E. Williams obtained a credit card from Hudson Belk Company (Belk), a retail store. On October 22, October 27, and November 5, 1988, Williams charged purchases of $1,058 to his Belk account. The charges reflected purchases of $63 designer perfume, Gucci handbags costing $204 and $250, and stuffed animals. Williams testified that the purchases were Christmas presents for family members. On November 4, 1988, Williams filed a voluntary petition for Chapter 7 bankruptcy. Belk moved that the debts incurred by Williams not be discharged in bankruptcy.

Issue Should the debts incurred by Williams to Belk be discharged in bankruptcy?

Decision The bankruptcy court held that the debts incurred by Williams to Belk were not dischargeable in bankruptcy.

Reason The bankruptcy court held that the debts incurred by Williams on October 22 and October 27, 1988 were not dischargeable because they were

luxury goods purchased within 40 days of declaring bankruptcy. The court held that the debts incurred by Williams on November 5, 1988 were not dischargeable because these purchases were made after the debtor filed his bankruptcy petition and, as such, are not subject to this bankruptcy proceeding. The court stated, "Under the circumstances, it is beyond question that the items of these types and amounts were nonessential, indulgent, and extravagant." The court said this was illegal "loading up" on luxury goods prior to declaring bankruptcy.

CASE QUESTIONS

Critical Legal Thinking Is the "luxury goods" exception to discharge easy to apply?

Ethics Did Williams act ethically in this case? Do you think he knew what he was doing?

Business Implication How much do you think personal bankruptcies cost businesses each year?

Acts That Bar Discharge

CAUTION
Certain acts by the debtor may bar discharge.

Any party of interest may file an objection to the discharge of a debt. The court will then hold a hearing. Discharge of the unsatisfied debts will be denied if the debtor

- Made false representations about his or her financial position when he or she obtained an extension of credit
- Transferred, concealed, or removed property from the estate with the intent to hinder, delay, or defraud creditors

- Falsified, destroyed, or concealed records of his or her financial condition
- Failed to account for any assets
- Failed to submit to questioning at the meeting of the creditors (unless excused)

If the discharge is obtained through the fraud of the debtor, a party of interest may bring a motion to have the bankruptcy revoked. The bankruptcy court may revoke a discharge within one year after it was granted.

Discharge of Student Loans

Many students who borrowed a lot of money in student loans sought to avoid paying back their loans by filing a voluntary petition for bankruptcy immediately on leaving college. Section 523(a)(8)(B) of the Bankruptcy Code was enacted to prevent this by mandating that student loans can only be discharged in bankruptcy within seven years after they are due if nondischarge would cause an undue hardship to the debtor and his or her dependents. Thereafter, students' loans may be discharged like other debts. Undue hardship would include not being able to pay for food or shelter for the debtor or the debtor's family.

Cosigners (e.g., parents who guarantee their child's student loan) must also meet the heightened undue hardship test to discharge their obligation during the statutory seven-year period.

discharge of student loans
A student loan may be discharged within the first five years after it is due only if nondischarge would cause an *undue hardship* on the debtor or the debtor's family. After seven years, student loans may be discharged like other debts.

✔ BUSINESS CHECKLIST

Whether a Debtor Should Sign a Reaffirmation Agreement

Creditors often attempt to persuade a debtor to agree to pay an unsatisfied debt that is dischargeable in bankruptcy. A debtor may voluntarily choose to enter into a **reaffirmation agreement**, which is a formal agreement that sets out the terms of repayment. Before signing a reaffirmation agreement, the debtor needs to decide if there is an important reason to do so, such as the continuation of a valuable relationship with the creditor.

To prevent abuses, the Bankruptcy Code stipulates that the following requirements must be met before a reaffirmation agreement is legally enforceable:

- The reaffirmation agreement must be made before the debtor is granted a discharge
- The agreement must be filed with the court
- If the debtor is not represented by an attorney, court approval of the agreement is necessary
- The debtor may rescind the agreement at any time prior to discharge or within 60 days after filing the agreement with the court, whichever is later. This right of rescission must be conspicuously stated in the reaffirmation agreement.

CHAPTER 11 REORGANIZATION BANKRUPTCY

Chapter 11 of the Bankruptcy Code provides a method for reorganizing the debtor's financial affairs under the supervision of the Bankruptcy Court.[6] Its goal is to reorganize the debtor with a new capital structure so that it will emerge from bankruptcy as a viable concern. This option, which is referred to as **reorganization bankruptcy**, is often in the best interests of the debtor and its creditors.

Chapter 11 A bankruptcy method that allows reorganization of the debtor's financial affairs under the supervision of the Bankruptcy Court.

BUSINESS BRIEF

Chapter 11 is used primarily by businesses to reorganize their finances under the protection of the bankruptcy court. The debtor usually emerges from bankruptcy a "leaner" business, having restructured and discharged some of its debts.

Reorganization Proceeding

Chapter 11 is available to individuals, partnerships, corporations, nonincorporated associations, and railroads. It is not available to banks, savings and loan associations, credit unions, insurance companies, stockbrokers, or commodities brokers. The majority of Chapter 11 proceedings are filed by corporations.

A Chapter 11 petition may be filed voluntarily by the debtor or involuntarily by its creditors. The principles discussed earlier under Chapter 7 regarding the filing of petitions, the first meeting of creditors, the entry of the order for relief, automatic stay, and relief from stay also apply to Chapter 11 proceedings.

In the following case, the court held that a debtor qualified for reorganization under Chapter 11.

CASE 20.3

In Re Johns-Manville Corp.

36 Bankr. 727 (1984) United States Bankruptcy Court, Southern District of New York

Facts The Johns-Manville Corporation (Manville) was a major corporation that manufactured and sold a variety of products. Some of the products it produced, particularly insulation products used in buildings, contained asbestos. It has been shown that asbestos injures persons who come in contact with the dust from this substance. Exposure to asbestos can result in one of three diseases: (1) asbestosis, a chronic disease of the lungs that causes shortness of breath, (2) mesothelioma, a fatal cancer of the lining of the chest, and (3) lung and other cancers.

By 1982, more than 16,000 asbestos-related lawsuits were filed against Manville. In most cases that have reached judgment, the jury has awarded compensatory and punitive damages against Manville. It is estimated that up to 120,000 such lawsuits will eventually be filed against Manville that will result in liability that will exceed $3 billion. On August 26, 1982, after a careful and deliberate review of epidemiological and financial data, Manville filed a voluntary petition under Chapter 11 of the Bankruptcy Code. An Asbestos Committee composed of attorneys for clients who have allegedly been injured by asbestos manufactured by Manville filed a motion to have Manville's bankruptcy petition dismissed.

Issue Does Manville qualify to reorganize under Chapter 11 of the Bankruptcy Code?

Decision Yes. The bankruptcy court held that the Johns-Manville Corporation qualified to reorganize under Chapter 11 of the Bankruptcy Code. The court dismissed the Asbestos Committee's motion to dismiss Manville's bankruptcy petition. The court appointed a legal representative to represent the interests of future claimants.

Reason In reaching its decision, the bankruptcy court stated, "A principal goal of the Bankruptcy Code is to provide open access to the bankruptcy process. . . . [T]he drafters of the Bankruptcy Code envisioned that a financially beleaguered debtor with real debt and real creditors should not be required to wait until the economic situation is beyond repair in order to file a reorganization petition. This philosophy is a corollary of the key aim of Chapter 11 of the Code, that of avoidance of liquidation. . . .

"Manville must not be required to wait until its economic picture has deteriorated beyond salvation to file for reorganization. Similarly, Manville's purported motivation in filing to obtain a breathing spell from asbestos litigation should not conclusively establish its lack of intent to rehabilitate and justify the dismissal of its petition. In this case, it is undeniable that there has been no sham or hoax perpetrated on the court in that Manville is a real business with real creditors in pressing need of economic reorganization. . . .

"It is abundantly clear that the Manville reorganization will have to be accountable to future asbestos claimants whose compelling interest must be safeguarded in order to leave a residue of assets sufficient to accommodate a meaningful resolution of the Manville asbestos-related health problems. Manville expects a proliferation of claims in the next 30 years by those previously exposed who will manifest these diseases in this period. Accordingly, in order to resolve Manville's deep economic crisis, the rights of future claimants must be considered and represented at this crucial point in the reorganization case so as to avoid functional extinction of the debtor enterprise. Thus, because none of the existing committees of unsecured creditors and present asbestos claimants represents this key group, a separate and distinct representative for these parties in interest must be established so that these claimants have a role in the formulation of such a plan."

Comment On November 28, 1988, the court approved a plan of reorganization. The plan created the Manville Corporation with its primary business in forest products and construction materials. The plan also created the Manville Personal Injury Settlement Trust, which represents claimants of asbestos-related injuries. The Trust owns 50 percent of Manville's new common stock as well as convertible preferred stock and a $1.8 billion bond. In 1992, the Trust converted its preferred stock into common stock and now owns about 80 percent of Manville. Beginning in 1992, the Trust received 20 percent of Manville's net profits. Since its creation, the Trust has settled more than

25,000 personal injury claims, paying out more than $1 billion to injured victims. More than 150,000 claims remain.

CASE QUESTIONS

Critical Legal Thinking Should companies be permitted to reorganize under bankruptcy law? Or should liquidation be the only type of bankruptcy allowed?

Ethics Does a company act socially responsibly when it files bankruptcy to discharge liability for tort-related injuries?

Business Implication Why does a company declare Chapter 11 bankruptcy rather than Chapter 7 bankruptcy? Does a company have to be insolvent to declare bankruptcy voluntarily?

Debtor-in-Possession

In most Chapter 11 cases, the debtor is left in place to operate the business during the reorganization proceeding. In such cases, the debtor is called a **debtor-in-possession**. The court may appoint a trustee to operate the debtor's business only upon a showing of cause, such as fraud, dishonesty, or gross mismanagement by the debtor or its management. However, even if a trustee is not appointed, the court may appoint an examiner to investigate the debtor's financial affairs.

The debtor-in-possession (or the trustee if one is appointed) has the same powers and duties as a trustee in a Chapter 7 proceeding. In addition, the debtor-in-possession (or trustee) is empowered to operate the debtor's business during the bankruptcy proceeding. This includes authority to enter into contracts, purchase supplies, incur debts, and so on. Some suppliers will accept only cash for their goods or services during this time, while others will extend credit. Credit extended by postpetition unsecured creditors in the ordinary course of business is given automatic priority as an administrative expense in bankruptcy. Further, upon notice and hearing, the court may create a secured interest by granting a postpetition unsecured creditor a lien on the debtor-in-possession's property.

Creditors' Committees

After an order for relief is granted, the court will appoint a **creditors' committee** composed of representatives of the class of unsecured claims. Generally, the creditors holding the seven largest claims are appointed to the committee. The court may also appoint a committee of secured creditors and a committee of equity holders. Committee members owe a fiduciary duty to represent the interest of the class. Committees may appear at bankruptcy court hearings, participate in the negotiation of a plan of reorganization, assert objections to proposed plans, and the like.

Small Business Bankruptcies

Under *Section 217* of the *Bankruptcy Reform Act of 1994*, businesses with total debts of less than $2 million can elect a "fast track" for the processing of its Chapter 11 case. This new procedure makes creditors' committees optional and sets up deadlines

debtor-in-possession A debtor who is left in place to operate the business during the reorganization proceeding.

BUSINESS BRIEF
Approximately 20,000 U.S. companies file for Chapter 11 protection each year.

creditors' committee The creditors holding the seven largest unsecured claims are usually appointed to the creditors' committee. Representatives of the committee appear at Bankruptcy Court hearings, participate in the negotiation of a plan of reorganization, assert objections to proposed plans, and so on.

small business bankruptcy Section 217 of the Bankruptcy Reform Act of 1994 provides an expedited procedure for Chapter 11 bankruptcy filed by small businesses with less than $2 million of debt.

aimed at concluding the case within 160 days of the bankruptcy filing. Because the majority of Chapter 11 cases involves small businesses, this new procedure is expected to be used by many small business debtors. Large business bankruptcies will not be permitted to use the new expedited procedure.

BUSINESS APPLICATION

Dow Corning Files for Bankruptcy

In May 1995, Dow Corning Corporation, a company headquartered in Midland, Michigan, filed for Chapter 11 bankruptcy protection. It did so because it had been sued by thousands of women who had silicone-gel breast implants inserted in their bodies that had been made by Dow Corning. In the lawsuits, the women asserted that the breast implants ruptured, leaked, and caused various forms of cancer, autoimmunal diseases, lupus, scleroderma, inflammation, and other harmful effects.

After juries had rendered many multimillion dollar judgments against the company, Dow Corning agreed to place $2 billion in a fund over a 30-year period to settle most of these lawsuits. Other manufacturers of silicon-gel breast implants agreed to contribute $2.5 billion. Unexpectedly, more than 400,000 of the two million women who had had silicone gel breast implants filed claims against the fund.

When a federal judge decided that the fund was inadequately

capitalized and threatened to allow the claimants to sue Dow Corning and the other manufacturers, Dow Corning filed for Chapter 11 bankruptcy. This bankruptcy filing froze Dow Corning's agreement to contribute the $2 billion and jeopardizes the worldwide settlement of these cases. A judge has ruled that plaintiffs may pursue cases against Dow Corning and the other manufacturers.

PLAN OF REORGANIZATION

plan of reorganization
A plan that sets forth a proposed new capital structure for the debtor to have when it emerges from reorganization bankruptcy. The debtor has the exclusive right to file the first plan of reorganization; any party of interest may file a plan thereafter.

CAUTION
In a Chapter 11 proceeding, creditors have claims *and equity holders have* interests.

disclosure statement A statement that must contain adequate information about the proposed plan of reorganization, which is supplied to the creditors and equity holders after court approval.

The debtor has the exclusive right to file a **plan of reorganization** with the bankruptcy court within the first 120 days after the date of the order for relief. The debtor also has the right to obtain creditor approval of the plan within the first 180 days after the date of the order. After that, any party of interest (i.e., a trustee, a creditor, or an equity holder) may propose a plan. The court has discretion to extend the 120- and 180-day periods in complex cases.

The plan of reorganization sets forth the debtor's proposed new capital structure. In a Chapter 11 proceeding, creditors have claims and equity holders have interests. The plan must designate the different classes of claims and interests. The reorganization plan may propose altering the rights of creditors and equity holders. For example, it might require claims and interests to be reduced, the conversion of unsecured creditors to equity holders, the sale of assets, or the like.

Disclosure Statement

The debtor must supply the creditors and equity holders with a **disclosure statement** that contains adequate information about the proposed plan of reorganization. The court must approve the disclosure statement before it is distributed.

Executory Contracts

Under the Bankruptcy Code, the debtor-in-possession (or trustee) is given the authority to assume or reject **executory contracts** (i.e., contracts that are not fully performed by both sides). In general, unfavorable executory contracts will be rejected and favorable executory contracts will be assumed. For example, a debtor-in-possession may reject an unfavorable lease. Court approval is necessary to reject an executory contract. Executory contracts may also be rejected in Chapter 7 and Chapter 13 proceedings.

Rejection of Collective Bargaining Agreements Companies that file for Chapter 11 reorganization sometimes argue that agreements with labor unions that still have years to run are executory contracts that may be rejected in bankruptcy. The U.S. Supreme Court has upheld the right of companies to reject union contracts in bankruptcy.[7] The court held that rejection was permitted if necessary for the successful rehabilitation of the debtor.

Subsequently, labor unions lobbied Congress for a change in the law. Congress responded by enacting Section 1113 of the 1984 amendments to the Bankruptcy Code. Section 1113 established the following multistep process that must be followed before a collective bargaining agreement may be rejected or modified:

1. The debtor must make a proposal to the union regarding the modification of the agreement
2. The debtor must meet with the union to discuss the proposal
3. The court must hold a hearing if the union refuses to accept the proposal.

If these requirements are met, the court may order the modification or rejection of the labor agreement if (1) such rejection or modification is necessary to the reorganization, (2) the debtor acted in good faith, and (3) the balance of equities favors rejection or modification of the collective bargaining agreement.

> **executory contract** A contract that has not been fully performed. With court approval, executory contracts may be rejected by a debtor in bankruptcy.

> **BUSINESS BRIEF**
> *A collective bargaining agreement may be rejected or modified as an executory contract if (1) it is necessary to the reorganization, (2) the debtor acted in good faith, and (3) the balance of the equities favors rejection or modification of the agreement.*

CONFIRMATION OF A PLAN OF REORGANIZATION

A plan of reorganization must be **confirmed** by the court before it becomes effective. The plan may be confirmed by either (1) the acceptance method or (2) the "cram down" method. These two methods are discussed in the paragraphs that follow. If more than one plan is proposed, the court may confirm only one plan.

> **confirmation** The bankruptcy court's approval of a plan of reorganization.

Confirmation by the Acceptance Method

Classes of creditors and interests must be given the opportunity to vote to accept or reject the plan before the court considers its confirmation. Under *Section 1129(a)*—that is, the **acceptance method**—the court must confirm a plan of reorganization if the following tests are met:

1. The plan must be in the best interests of each class of claims and interests as indicated by either (a) a unanimous vote of acceptance by the members of the class or (b) the property received by the class members under the plan is worth at least as much as they would receive upon liquidation.
2. The plan must be feasible. That is, the debtor must have a good probability of surviving as a going concern. The court examines the debtor's estimated earnings and expenses as proposed by the plan before making this determination.
3. At least one class of claims must vote to accept the plan. A plan is deemed accepted by a class of claims if at least one-half the number of creditors who vote accept the plan and the accepting creditors represent two-thirds of the dollar amount of allowed creditors who vote.
4. Each class of claims and interests is nonimpaired. A class is nonimpaired if (a) its legal, equitable, and contractual rights are unaltered by the plan or (b) the class votes to accept the plan. A class of claims accepts the plan if one-half the number who vote accept the plan and they represent two-thirds of the dollar amount of allowed claims that vote accept the plan. A class of interests accepts a plan if at least two-thirds the amount of interests that vote accept the plan.

> **CONSIDER**
> *Creditors and equity holders are given the opportunity to vote on the confirmation of a plan of reorganization.*

> **acceptance method** The bankruptcy court must approve a plan of reorganization if (1) the plan is in the *best interests* of each class of claims and interests, (2) the plan is *feasible*, (3) at least one class of claims *votes* to accept the plan, and (4) each class of claims and interests is *nonimpaired*.

A plan of reorganization cannot discriminate unfairly against members of a class. For example, no member of any class can receive more than any other member of that class. No class of claims or interests may be paid more than the full amount of its claim.

Confirmation by the Cram Down Method

If a dissenting class of claims is impaired, the plan of reorganization cannot be confirmed using the acceptance method. However, the court can force an impaired class to participate in a plan of reorganization under the **cram down method** of *Section 1129(b)*. As discussed in the following subsections, to be crammed down, the plan must be fair and equitable to the impaired class.

cram down method A method of confirmation of a plan of reorganization where the court forces an impaired class to participate in the plan of reorganization.

Secured Creditors A plan is fair and equitable to an impaired class of secured creditors if the reorganization allows the class to (1) retain its lien on the collateral (whether the property is retained by the debtor or transferred to another party), (2) place a lien on the proceeds from the sale of the collateral, or (3) receive an "indubitable equivalent," such as a lien on other property.

Unsecured Creditors A reorganization plan is fair and equitable to an impaired class of unsecured creditors if (1) that class is paid cash or property that has a discounted present value equal to the allowed amount of the claim or (2) no class below it receives anything in the plan (the **absolute priority rule**).[8]

absolute priority rule A rule that says a reorganization plan is fair and equitable to an impaired class of unsecured creditors or equity holders if no class below it receives anything in the plan.

CONSIDER THIS EXAMPLE: Assume that in a Chapter 11 case there is a class of secured creditors, a class of unsecured creditors, and a class of equity holders. The secured creditors vote to accept the plan. The unsecured creditors, who are impaired because they are given only 10 percent of their claim, vote to reject the plan. Nevertheless, the plan can be crammed down on the unsecured class under the absolute priority rule if the plan does not give the equity holders anything.

HISTORICAL NOTE
The term cram down *derives from the notion that the plan of reorganization is being "crammed down the throats" of the impaired dissenting class.*

Equity Holders A plan is fair and equitable to an impaired class of equity holders if that class is paid the greater of (1) the fixed liquidation preference (if any), (2) the fixed redemption preference (if any), or (3) the discounted present value of their equity interest. Alternatively, the absolute priority rule can be applied to an impaired equity class if no class below it receives anything.

Discharge

discharge Creditors' claims that are not included in a Chapter 11 reorganization are discharged.

Upon confirmation of a plan of reorganization, the debtor is granted a **discharge** of all claims not included in the plan. The plan is binding on all parties when it is confirmed.

CHAPTER 13 CONSUMER DEBT ADJUSTMENT

Chapter 13 A rehabilitation form of bankruptcy that permits the courts to supervise the debtor's plan for the payment of unpaid debts by installments.

Chapter 13, which is called a **consumer debt adjustment**, is a rehabilitation form of bankruptcy for natural persons. Chapter 13 permits the courts to supervise the debtor's plan for the payment of unpaid debts by installments. Prior to the 1978 act, this type of adjustment was referred to as a "wage earner plan."

The debtor has several advantages under Chapter 13. They include avoidance of the stigma of Chapter 7 liquidation, retention of more property than is exempt under Chapter 7, and less expense and less complication than a Chapter 7 proceeding. The creditors have advantages, too. They may recover a greater percentage of the debts owed them than they would under a Chapter 7 proceeding.

Filing the Petition

A Chapter 13 proceeding can be initiated only by the voluntary filing of a petition by the debtor who alleges that he or she is (1) insolvent or (2) unable to pay his or her debts when they become due. The petition must state that the debtor desires to effect an extension or composition of debts, or both. An *extension* provides for a longer period of time for the debtor to pay his or her debts. A *composition* provides for a reduction of debts.

Only individuals (including sole proprietors) with regular income who owe individually (or with their spouse) noncontingent, liquidated, unsecured debts of less than $100,000 and secured debts of less than $350,000 may file such a petition. The key is the debtor's regular income, which may be from any source, including wages, salary, commissions, income from investments, social security, pension income, or public assistance. The amount of the debtor's assets is irrelevant. Most Chapter 13 petitions are filed by homeowners who want to protect nonexempt equity in their residences.

When (or shortly after) the petition is filed, the debtor must file a list of creditors, assets, and liabilities with the court. The court then schedules a meeting of creditors. The debtor must appear at this meeting. Creditors may submit proof of claims, which will be allowed or disallowed by the court. No creditor committees are appointed, but the court must appoint a trustee upon confirmation of the plan.

Automatic Stay

The filing of a Chapter 13 petition automatically stays (1) liquidation bankruptcy proceedings, (2) judicial and nonjudicial actions by creditors to collect prepetition debts from the debtor, and (3) collection activities against codebtors and guarantors of consumer debts. The automatic stay continues until the Chapter 13 plan is completed or dismissed. The stay does not apply to business debts.

The Plan of Payment

The debtor's plan of payment must be filed within 15 days of filing the petition. The debtor must file information about his or her finances, including a budget of estimated income and expenses during the period of the plan. The plan period cannot exceed three years unless the court approves a longer period (of up to five years). During the plan period, the debtor retains possession of his or her property, may acquire new property and incur debts, and so on.

The debtor must begin making the planned installment payments to the trustee within 30 days after the plan is filed. These interim payments must continue until the plan is confirmed or denied. If the plan is denied, the trustee must return the interim payments to the debtor, less any administrative costs. If the plan is confirmed, the debtor must continue making payments to the trustee. The trustee is responsible for remitting these payments to the creditors. The trustee is paid 10 percent of the debts paid under the plan.

A Chapter 13 plan may be modified if the debtor's circumstances materially change. For example, if the debtor's income subsequently decreases, the court may decrease the debtor's payments under the plan. Request for the modification of a plan may be made by the debtor, the trustee, or a creditor. If an interested party objects to the modification, the court must hold a hearing to determine whether it should be approved.

Confirmation of the Plan

The plan may modify the rights of unsecured creditors and some secured creditors. Any objections they have may be voiced at the confirmation hearing held by the court. The plan must (1) be proposed in good faith, (2) pass the feasibility test (e.g., the debtor must be able to make the proposed payments), and (3) be in the best interests of the creditors (i.e., the present value of the payments must equal or exceed the amount that the creditors would receive in a Chapter 7 liquidation proceeding).

CAUTION
A Chapter 13 proceeding can be initiated only by the voluntary filing of a petition by the debtor. Creditors cannot file an involuntary petition to place a debtor in Chapter 13 bankruptcy.

"Debt rolls a man over and over, binding him hand and foot, and letting him hang upon the fatal mesh until the long-legged interest devours him."
Henry Ward Beecher
Proverbs from Plymouth Pulpit (1887)

NOTE
Chapter 13 is a form of reorganization bankruptcy. The debtor must file a proposed plan of payment *on how the debts are to be rescheduled.*

"Beggars can never be bankrupts."
Thomas Fuller
Gnomologia
(1732)

Secured Creditors The plan must be submitted to the secured creditors for acceptance. The plan will be confirmed if the secured creditors unanimously accept it. If a secured creditor does not accept the plan, the court may still confirm the plan if (1) it permits the secured creditor to retain its lien and the value of the plan's distribution to the creditor is more than its secured interest or (2) the debtor surrenders the property securing the claim to the secured creditor.

Unsecured Creditors Although a vote of unsecured creditors is not required for confirmation of a Chapter 13 plan, their objection to the plan can delay or defeat confirmation. The court cannot confirm the plan unless (1) it proposes to pay the objecting unsecured creditor the present value of his claim or (2) the debtor agrees to commit all of his or her disposable income during the plan period to pay his or her creditors. (Disposable income is all income not necessary to maintain the debtor and her dependents.)

CONSIDER THIS EXAMPLE: Suppose a debtor earns $1,800 per month, of which $1,200 is reasonably necessary to support the debtor and his family. If the $400 per month disposable income is committed to pay prepetition debts, the court may confirm the plan even if the debts of the unsecured creditors are substantially modified or liquidated.

Discharge

discharge A discharge is granted to a debtor in a Chapter 13 consumer debt adjustment only after all of the payments under the plan are completed by the debtor.

The court will grant an order **discharging** the debtor from all unpaid debts covered by the plan after all of the payments required under the plan are completed. All debts are dischargeable under Chapter 13 except alimony and child support and priority debts such as trustee fees. Dischargeable debts include student loans, fraudulently incurred debts, and debts arising from malicious or willful injury from drunken driving. Thus, a Chapter 13 discharge may be more beneficial to a debtor than a Chapter 7 liquidation discharge. A discharge can be revoked within one year if it was obtained by fraud. There is a timebar to filing a petition for a Chapter 13 proceeding. Thus, a debtor may file successive petitions for Chapter 13 bankruptcy.

hardship discharge A discharge granted if (1) the debtor fails to complete the payments due to unforeseeable circumstances, (2) the unsecured creditors have been paid as much as they would have been paid in a Chapter 7 liquidation proceeding, and (3) it is not practical to modify the plan.

Hardship Discharge Even if the debtor does not complete the payments called for in the plan, the court may grant the debtor a **hardship discharge**. Such a discharge will be granted if (1) the debtor fails to complete the payments due to unforeseeable circumstances (e.g., the debtor loses his job through no fault of his own), (2) the unsecured creditors have been paid as much as they would have been paid in a Chapter 7 liquidation proceeding, and (3) it is not practical to modify the plan.

INTERNATIONAL PERSPECTIVE

Reorganization under British Bankruptcy Law

Many of our country's forefathers were debtors fleeing the harsh laws of Britain and European countries where debtors were often sent to debtors' prisons or were required to work off the debt owed to creditors. When this country was founded, the right to declare bankruptcy was considered just as important as the right to free speech,

and both rights were included in the U.S. Constitution.

Even today, U.S. bankruptcy law treats debtors more leniently than the bankruptcy laws of other countries. Consider the case of bankruptcy reorganization laws in Britain versus those of the United States.

In 1987, Britain enacted a new

bankruptcy law for handling the reorganization of bankrupt companies. Basically, the law banishes lawyers from the reorganization process and puts it in the hands of specially licensed accountants. When a firm files for reorganization bankruptcy in Britain, an administrative order is issued. The order permits the creditors of the troubled company to appoint a team of bankruptcy accountants to handle the company's reorganization.

British law assumes that the company's misfortune is not a result of bad luck but is based on mismanagement by the company's officers and directors. Consequently, the bankruptcy accountants are empowered to re- move the firm's existing manage- ment and take over control of its operations. The accountants then orchestrate the reorganization and sale of the company's assets.

Many U.S. bankruptcy lawyers allege that British bankruptcy law tramples too hard on debtors' rights. They argue that British law thwarts the "fresh start" theory underlying American bankruptcy law. Pro- ponents of the British system argue that it is faster, cheaper, and more efficient than a bank- ruptcy reorganization under Chapter 11 of the U.S. Bank- ruptcy Code. They assert that the British system does not cod- dle debtors nor make lawyers rich as the U.S. bankruptcy sys- tem does.

WORKING THE WEB

Bankruptcy Online Information for Bankruptcy Online comes from Federal Filings Business News, a leading provider of bankruptcy news covering major Chapter 11 bankruptcy cases in the United States.
Visit at http://www.fedfil.com/bankruptcy/

Bankruptcy Statistics Bankruptcy Statistics are compiled by the American Bankruptcy Institute.
Visit at http://www.abiworld.org/stats/statsfront.html

American Bankruptcy Institute The American Bankruptcy Institute Web site provides ac- curate and authoritative information about bankruptcy.
Visit at http://www.abiworld.org/

Legal Resources—Bankruptcy This Web site compiles materials on bankruptcy, taxes, credit repair, and other related subjects.
Visit at http://www.legalresource.com/

Bankruptcy Alternatives This Web site, compiled by an attorney, gives detailed information about alternatives to bankruptcy.
Visit at http://www.berkshire.net/~mkb/

CYBER EXERCISES:
1. Using Bankruptcy Online, find and visit the pages on Status of Major Bankruptcies.
2. Using the Bankruptcy Statistics Web site, find out how many business filings there were in 1990.
3. From the American Bankruptcy Institute Web site, check out the section called "Bankruptcy Specialists."
4. Using the Legal Resources—Bankruptcy Web site, find materials on bankruptcy in Italy.
5. Using the Bankruptcy Alternatives Web site, find and print out a document on unsecured creditors.

CHAPTER SUMMARY

OVERVIEW OF FEDERAL BANKRUPTCY LAW, P. 470

Bankruptcy	1. *Bankruptcy Reform Act of 1978, as amended*. Federal statute that establishes the requirements and procedures for filing bankruptcy. Called the *Bankruptcy Code*. 2. *Bankruptcy courts*. Have exclusive jurisdiction to hear bankruptcy cases. A bankruptcy court is attached to each federal district court. Bankruptcy judges are appointed for 14-year terms.
The "Fresh Start"	The purpose of bankruptcy is to discharge the debtor from burdensome debts.

CHAPTER 7 LIQUIDATION BANKRUPTCY, P. 471

Chapter 7 Bankruptcy	The debtor's nonexempt property is sold for cash, the cash is distributed to the creditors, and any unpaid debts are discharged. Also called *liquidation bankruptcy*.

Bankruptcy Procedure	1. *Filing a petition*. The filing of a petition commences a bankruptcy case.
	  a. *Voluntary petition*. Filed by the debtor
	  b. *Involuntary petition*. Filed by a creditor or creditors
	2. *Order for relief*. Designates that the bankruptcy court has accepted the case for further proceedings.
	3. *Meeting of the creditors*. The debtor must appear at this meeting and answer questions by the creditors. Also called the *first meeting of the creditors*.
	4. *Appointment of a trustee*. A *permanent trustee* is elected at the first meeting of the creditors in a Chapter 7 case.
	5. *Proof of claims*. Unsecured creditors must file proof of claim stating the amount of their claim against the debtor.

Automatic Stay	The filing of a bankruptcy petition *stays* (suspends) certain legal actions against the debtor or the debtor's property. 1. *Relief from stay*. A secured creditor may petition the court for a relief from stay in situations involving depreciating assets and the creditor is not adequately protected during the bankruptcy proceeding.

PROPERTY OF THE BANKRUPTCY ESTATE, P. 473

Property of the Bankruptcy Estate	1. *Bankruptcy estate*. Includes the following:
	  a. All of the debtor's legal and equitable interests in real, personal, tangible, and intangible property at the time the petition is filed
	  b. Gifts, inheritances, life insurance proceeds, and property from divorce settlements that the debtor is entitled to receive within 180 days after the petition is filed.

Exempt Property	The Bankruptcy Code permits the debtor to retain certain property that does not become part of the bankruptcy estate. Exemptions are stipulated in federal and state law.
Voidable Transfers	The following transfers and preferences are voidable by the trustee: 1. *Preferential transfer within 90 days before bankruptcy*. Transfer must be for an antecedent debt and give the creditor more than he or she would receive in bankruptcy. 2. *Preferential liens within 90 days before bankruptcy*. Transfer must be for an antecedent debt, and the creditor would receive more because of this lien than he or she would as an unsecured creditor in bankruptcy. 3. *Preferential transfer to an insider within one year before bankruptcy*. The transferee must be an "insider" (e.g., relative, business associate) and the creditor insolvent. 4. *Fraudulent transfer within one year before bankruptcy*. Transfer of property by the debtor with the actual intent to hinder, delay, or defraud creditors.

DISTRIBUTION OF PROPERTY AND DISCHARGE, P. 476

Priority of Distribution	Nonexempt property of the bankruptcy estate is distributed to the creditors in the following statutory priority: 1. *Secured creditors*. Either obtains the collateral or the collateral is sold and the secured creditor is paid. If the value of the collateral exceeds

	the secured interest, the excess becomes available to pay other creditors. If the value of the collateral is less than the secured interest, the secured creditor becomes an unsecured creditor to the difference. 2. *Unsecured creditors*. Unsecured creditors are paid in priority established by the Bankruptcy Code. Each class must be paid in full before any lower class is paid anything. If a class cannot be paid in full, the claims of that class are paid pro rata (proportionately).
Discharge	*Discharge of unpaid claims*. After the nonexempt property is distributed, the remaining unpaid claims of the debtor are *discharged*; the debtor's legal obligation to pay these unpaid debts is terminated. Discharge is available only to individuals.
Nondischargeable Debts	The Bankruptcy code stipulates that certain debts are not dischargeable.
Acts that Bar Discharge	The bankruptcy court may deny discharge of debts if the debtor has engaged in prohibited conduct.
Discharge of Student Loans	A student loan may be discharged within the first seven years after it is due only if nondischarge would cause an *undue hardship* on the debtor or his or her family: Thereafter, student loans may be discharged like other debts.
CHAPTER 11 REORGANIZATION BANKRUPTCY, P. 479	
Chapter 11 Reorganization Bankruptcy	Provides a method for reorganizing the debtor's financial affairs under the supervision of the bankruptcy court.
Reorganization Proceeding	1. Procedure. The principles discussed earlier under Chapter 7 regarding the filing of petitions, the first meeting of the creditors, the entry of the order for relief, and automatic stay also apply in Chapter 11 proceedings.
Debtor-in-Possession	In most Chapter 11 cases, the debtor is left in place to operate the business during the reorganization proceeding. In such cases, the debtor is called a *debtor-in-possession*. 1. *Trustee*. The court may appoint a trustee to operate the debtor's business only upon a showing of cause, such as fraud, dishonesty, or gross mismanagement by the debtor or its management.
Creditors' Committees	The court will appoint a committee of unsecured creditors (usually creditors holding the seven largest claims). The court may also appoint committees of secured creditors and equity holders. Committees participate in the bankruptcy proceeding and in the negotiation of a plan of reorganization.
PLAN OF REORGANIZATION, P. 482	
Plan of Reorganization	Sets forth the debtor's proposed new capital structure. The debtor has the exclusive right to file a plan within the first 120 days after the date of the order for relief.
Disclosure Statement	The debtor must supply the creditors and equity holders with a disclosure statement that contains adequate information about the proposed plan of reorganization.
Executory Contracts	The debtor-in-possession (or trustee) may assume or reject executory contracts. A special procedure has been established for rejecting union collective bargaining agreements.

CONFIRMATION OF A PLAN OF REORGANIZATION, P. 483	
Confirmation of a Plan of Reorganization	A plan of reorganization must be confirmed by the bankruptcy court before it becomes effective. Confirmation may be by either of the following methods.
Confirmation by the Acceptance Method	As established by Section 1129(a) of the Bankruptcy Code.
Confirmation by the Cram Down Method	As provided for by Section 1129(b) of the Bankruptcy Code.
Discharge	Upon confirmation of a plan of reorganization, the debtor is granted a discharge of all claims not included in the plan. The debtors' legal obligation to pay the discharged debts is terminated.
CHAPTER 13 CONSUMER DEBT ADJUSTMENT, P. 484	
Chapter 13 Consumer Debts Adjustment	A rehabilitation form of bankruptcy that permits bankruptcy courts to supervise the debtor's plan for the repayment of unpaid debts by installments. Called *consumer debt adjustment* bankruptcy or *Chapter 13 bankruptcy*.
The Plan of Payment	The debtor must file a plan of payment. The plan period cannot exceed three years unless the court approves a longer period (of up to five years). A plan may be modified if the debtor's circumstances materially change. 1. *Trustee.* A permanent trustee will be appointed by the court. The debtor makes payments to the trustee, who is responsible for remitting payments to the creditors.
Discharge	The court will grant an order discharging the debtor from all unpaid debts covered by the plan only after all of the payments required under the plan are completed. 1. *Hardship discharge.* The court can grant the debtor a hardship discharge even if the debtor can not complete the payments called for by the plan if (1) the failure to make the payments was caused by an unforeseeable circumstance, (2) the creditors have been paid as much as they would have been paid in a Chapter 7 liquidation proceeding, and (3) it is not practical to modify the plan.

CRITICAL LEGAL THINKING CASES

20.1 Petition In March 1988, Daniel E. Beren, John M. Elliot, and Edward F. Mannino formed Walnut Street Four, a general partnership, to purchase and renovate an office building in Harrisburg, Pennsylvania. They borrowed more than $200,000 from Hamilton Bank to purchase the building and begin renovation. Disagreements among the partners arose when the renovation costs exceeded their estimates. When Beren was unable to obtain assistance from Elliot and Mannino regarding obtaining additional financing, the partnership quit paying its debts. Beren filed an involuntary petition to place the partnership into Chapter 7 bankruptcy. The other partners objected to

the bankruptcy filing. At the time of the filing, the partnership owed debts of more than $380,000 and had approximately $550 in the partnership bank account. Should the petition for involuntary bankruptcy be granted? [*In re Walnut Street Four*, 106 B.R. 56 (Bk.M.D. Pa. 1989)]

20.2 Bankruptcy Estate In 1983, Bill K. and Marilyn E. Hargis, husband and wife, filed a Chapter 11 bankruptcy proceeding. In 1984, more than 120 days after the bankruptcy petition was filed, Bill died. His life was insured for $700,000. His wife was the beneficiary of the policy. The bankruptcy trustee moved to recover the $700,000 as property of the bankruptcy estate. Who gets the insurance proceeds? [*In re Matter of Hargis*, 887 F.2d 77 (5th Cir. 1989)]

20.3 Stay In 1985, James F. Kost filed a voluntary petition for relief under Chapter 11 of the Bankruptcy Code. First Interstate Bank of Greybull (First Interstate) held a first mortgage on the debtor's residence near Basin, Wyoming. Appraisals and other evidence showed that the house was worth $116,000. The debt owed to First Interstate was almost $103,000 and was increasing at the rate of $32.46 per day. The debtor had only an 11.5 percent equity cushion in the property. Further evidence showed that the (1) Greybull/Basin area was suffering from tough economic times, (2) there were more than 90 homes available for sale in the area, (3) the real estate market in the area was declining, (4) the condition of the house was seriously deteriorating and the debtor was not financially able to make the necessary improvements, and (5) the insurance on the property had lapsed. First Interstate moved for a relief from stay so that it could foreclose on the property and sell it. Should the motion be granted? [*In re James F. Kost*, 102 B.R. 829 (D.Wyo. 1989)] *yes - relief from Stay.*

20.4 A Fraudulent Transfer In November 1974, Peter and Geraldine Tabala (debtors), husband and wife, purchased a house in Clarkstown, New York. In November 1976, they purchased a Carvel ice cream business for $70,000 with a loan obtained from People's National Bank. In addition, the Carvel Corporation extended trade credit to the debtors. On October 23, 1978, the debtors conveyed their residence to their three daughters, ages 9, 19, and 20, for no consideration. Debtors continued to reside in the house and to pay maintenance expenses and real estate taxes due on the property. On the date of the transfer the debtors owed obligations in excess of $100,000. On March 28, 1980, the debtors filed a petition for Chapter 7 bankruptcy. The bankruptcy trustee moved to set aside the debtors' conveyance of their home to their daughters as a fraudulent transfer. Who wins? [*In re Tabala*, 11 B.R. 405 (Bk.S.D. N.Y. 1981)] *Bank - lacks consideration*

20.5 Preferential Payment Air Florida System, Inc. (Air Florida), an airline company, filed a voluntary petition to reorganize under Chapter 11 of the Bankruptcy Code. Within 90 days prior to the commencement of the case, Air Florida paid $13,575 to Compania Panamena de Aviacion, S.A. (COPA), in payment of an antecedent debt. This payment enabled COPA to receive more than it would have received if Air Florida were liquidated under Chapter 7. Is the payment to COPA an avoidable preferential transfer? [*In re Jet Florida System, Inc., f/k/a Air Florida System, Inc.*, 105 B.R. 137 (Bk.S.D.Fla. 1989)] *yes.*

20.6 Discharge On September 20, 1985, Jane Gnidovec, David Towell, and Robert Dawson (plaintiffs) obtained a judgment in state court against Alwan Brothers Co., Inc., and Alwan Brothers Partnership and its general partners (jointly Alwans) for $110,059 compensatory damages and $750,000 punitive damages. When the judgment was upheld on appeal, Alwans filed a voluntary petition for Chapter 11 bankruptcy. Is the judgment for compensatory damages and punitive damages dischargeable in bankruptcy? [*In re Alwan Brothers Co., Inc.*, 105 B.R. 886 (Bk.C.D.Ill. 1989)] *yes*

20.7 Executory Contract On October 15, 1980, The Record Company, Inc. entered into a purchase agreement to buy certain retail record stores from Bummbusiness, Inc. All assets and inventory were included in the deal. The Record Company agreed to pay Bummbusiness $20,000 and to pay the $380,000 of trade debt owed by the stores. In exchange, Bummbusiness agreed not to compete with the new buyer for two years within a 15-mile radius of the stores and to use its best efforts to obtain an extension of the due dates for the trade debt. The Record Company began operating the stores, but shortly thereafter filed a petition for Chapter 11 Bankruptcy. At the time of the bankruptcy filing (1) The Record Company owed Bummbusiness $10,000 and owed the trade debt of $380,000 and (2) Bummbusiness was obligated not to compete with The Record Company. Can The Record Company reject the purchase agreement? [*In re The Record Company*, 8 B.R. 57 (Bk.S.D.Ind. 1981)]

20.8 Plan of Reorganization Richard P. Friese (debtor) filed a voluntary petition for Chapter 11 bankruptcy. In May 1989, debtor filed a plan of reorganization that divided his creditors into three classes. The first class, administrative creditors, were to be paid in full. The second class, unsecured creditors, were to receive 50 percent on their claims. The IRS was the third class. It was to receive $20,000 on confirmation and the balance in future payments. No creditors voted to accept the plan. The unsecured creditors are impaired because their legal, equitable, and contractual rights are being altered. Can the bankruptcy court confirm debtor's plan of reorganization? [*In re Friese*, 103 B.R. 90 (Bk.S.D.N.Y. 1989)] *no*

20.9 Consumer Debt Adjustment Manuel Guadalupe (debtor) was a tool and die machinist who was employed at Elco Industries for more than five years. He accumulated more than $19,000 in unsecured debt, including deficiencies owed after secured creditors repossessed a van (leaving a deficiency of $1,066) and a car (leaving a deficiency of $3,130). Shortly after the second automobile was repossessed, the debtor borrowed approximately $19,000 from the Elco Credit Union to purchase a 1988 four-wheel-drive Chevrolet Blazer. The $472 monthly payment was to be taken directly from the debtor's earnings.

On February 28, 1989, the debtor filed a voluntary petition for Chapter 13 bankruptcy. The schedule listed total secured debts of $22,132, which included the debt for the Blazer, furniture, and a camcorder. Total unsecured debt was $19,575, which included $2,160 owed to General Finance Corporation (General). The debtor's budget projected that $700 per month would be left over for funding the Chapter 13 plan after his monthly expenses were deducted from his $25,000 gross income. Secured creditors were to be paid in full; unsecured creditors would receive 10 percent of their claims. General objected to the plan. Should the debtor's Chapter 13 plan be confirmed? [*In re Guadalupe*, 106 B.R. 155 (Bk.N.D.Ill. 1989)]

20.10 Student Loan Donald Wayne Doyle obtained a guaranteed student loan to enroll in a school for training truck drivers. Due to his impending divorce, the debtor never attended the program. The first monthly installment of approximately $50 to pay the student loan became due on September 1, 1988. On September 16, 1988, the debtor filed a voluntary petition for Chapter 7 bankruptcy.

The debtor is a 29-year-old man who earns approximately $1,000 per month at an hourly wage of $7.70 as a truck driver, a job that he held for 10 years. The debtor resided on a farm where he performed work in lieu of paying rent for his quarters. The debtor was paying monthly payments of $89 on a bank loan for his former wife's vehicle, $200 for his truck, $40 for health insurance, $28 for car insurance, $120 for gasoline and vehicular maintenance, $400 for groceries and meals, and $25 for telephone charges. In addition, a state court had ordered the debtor to pay $300 per month to support his children, ages four and five. The debtor's parents were assisting him by buying him $130 of groceries per month. Should the debtor's student loan be discharged in bankruptcy? [*In re Doyle*, 106 B.R. 272 (Bk.N.D.Ala. 1989)]

ETHICS CASES

20.11 Ethical Perspective Scott Greig Keebler (debtor) became indebted and his debts exceeded his assets. The Internal Revenue Service (IRS) had levied his wages for nonpayment of taxes. The debtor was healthy and capable of earning a substantial income. Evidence showed that the debtor did not try his best to pay his debts, lived an affluent lifestyle, and determined not to pay his principal creditors. The debtor voluntarily quit his job and filed a voluntary petition for Chapter 7 bankruptcy. The petition stated that he was unemployed. Shortly after filing for bankruptcy, the petitioner resumed work. Should the debtor's Chapter 7 case be dismissed because he filed the petition in bad faith? [*In re Scott Greig Keebler*, 106 B.R. 662 (Bk.D.Hawaii)]

20.12 Ethical Perspective On February 3, 1983, Douglas G. and Aleta Brantz (the debtor), husband and wife, borrowed $40,000 from Meritor Financial Services, Inc. (Meritor), and signed a promissory note evidencing the debt. The proceeds of the loan were used in a business operated by Mr. Brantz.

After a portion of the debt had been paid, the business began to fail and the Brantzes defaulted on the loan. The debtors made several attempts to cure the default but failed. On August 11, 1988, Meritor filed a collection action and obtained a judgment lien against the debtors' residence.

On August 16, 1988, a $40,000 mortgage on the debtors' home in favor of Aleta's parents, Philip and Sondra Schley, was recorded. The mortgage was dated February 1, 1988. On May 25, 1989, the debtors filed a voluntary petition for bankruptcy. The parties stipulated that the debtors' home was worth $65,000 and was subject to unvoidable mortgages of $38,000. The Schleys asserted their mortgage of $40,000 preceded Meritor's judicial lien of $28,441. The debtors also claimed an exemption of $15,800 in the premises. Who wins? Was the debtors' behavior unethical? [*In re Brantz*, 106 B.R. 62 (Bankr.E.D.Pa. 1989)]

CRITICAL LEGAL THINKING WRITING ASSIGNMENT

Read Case A.20 in the Case Appendix [*Dewsnup v. Timm*]. This case is excerpted from the U.S. Supreme Court opinion. Review and brief the case. In your brief, be sure to answer the following questions:

1. Who was the the debtor? Who was the creditor? What was the collateral for the secured loan?

2. What amount did the the debtor owe on the loan when he filed for bankruptcy? What was the value of the collateral at this time?

3. Succinctly state the issue that was presented to the U.S. Supreme Court.

4. How did the Supreme Court decide this issue? Explain.

NOTES

1 11 U.S.C. §§ 101–1330.

2 P.L. 98–353.

3 11 U.S.C. § 362(a).

4 The following states require debtors to take state law exemptions: Alabama, Alaska, Arizona, Arkansas, California, Colorado, Delaware, Florida, Georgia, Idaho, Illinois, Indiana, Iowa, Kansas, Kentucky, Louisiana, Maine, Maryland, Missouri, Montana, Nebraska, Nevada, New Hampshire, New York, North Carolina, North Dakota, Oklahoma, Oregon, South Carolina, South Dakota, Tennessee, Utah, Virginia, West Virginia, and Wyoming.

5 11 U.S.C. § 507.

6 11 U.S.C. §§ 1101–1174.

7 *National Labor Relations Board v. Bildisco and Bildisco*, 465 U.S. 513, 104 S.Ct. 1188 (1984).

8 The absolute priority rule was announced in *Consolidated Rock Products Co. v. Du Bois*, 312 U.S. 510, 61 S.Ct. 675 (1941). The doctrine was codified in the Bankruptcy Reform Act of 1978.

CHAPTER 21

AGENCY

Chapter Objectives

*After studying this chapter,
you should be able to*

1. Define an agency
2. Identify and define a principal-independent contractor relationship
3. Describe how express, implied, and apparent agencies are created
4. List and describe the agent's duties to the principal
5. List and describe the principal's duties to the agent
6. Describe the principal's and agent's liability on third-party contracts
7. Explain the doctrine of *respondent superior*
8. Identify and describe the principal's liability for the tortious conduct of an agent
9. Describe how an agency is terminated by the acts of the parties and by operation of law
10. Identify a wrongful termination of an agency

Chapter Contents

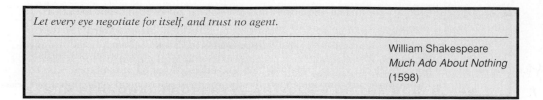

Let every eye negotiate for itself, and trust no agent.

William Shakespeare
Much Ado About Nothing
(1598)

If businesspeople had to personally conduct all of their business, the scope of their activities would be severely curtailed. Partnerships would not be able to operate; corporations could not act through managers and employees; and sole proprietorships would not be able to hire employees. The use of agents (or agency), which allows one person to act on behalf of another, solves this problem. There are many examples of agency relationships. They include a salesperson who sells goods for a store, an executive who works for a corporation, a partner who acts on behalf of a partnership, an attorney who is hired to represent a client, a real estate broker who is employed to sell a house, and so on. Agency is governed by a large body of common law, known as **agency law**. This law, which is a mixture of contract law and tort law, is discussed in this chapter.

agency law The large body of common law that governs agency; a mixture of contract law and tort law.

THE NATURE OF AGENCY

Agency relationships are formed by the mutual consent of a principal and an agent. Section 1(1) of the Restatement (Second) of Agency defines an *agency* as a *fiduciary relationship* "which results from the manifestation of consent by one person to another that the other shall act in his behalf and subject to his control, and consent by the other so to act." The Restatement (Second) of Agency is the reference source of the rules of agency. A party who employs another person to act on his or her behalf is called a **principal**. A party who agrees to act on behalf of another is called an **agent**. The principal–agent relationship is commonly referred to as an *agency*.

principal The party who employs another person to act on his or her behalf.

agent The party who agrees to act on behalf of another.

agency The principal–agent relationship; the fiduciary relationship "which results from the manifestation of consent by one person to another that the other shall act in his behalf and subjects to his control, and consent by the other so to act."

Agency Relationship Must Have Legal Purpose

An agency can be created only to accomplish a lawful purpose. Agency contracts that are created for illegal purposes or are against public policy are void and unenforceable. For example, a principal cannot hire an agent to kill another person.

Some agency relationships are prohibited by law. For example, (1) unlicensed agents cannot be hired to perform the duties of certain licensed professions (e.g., doctors and lawyers), (2) agents cannot be employed to vote in public elections or serve a criminal sentence, and (3) certain personal service contracts, such as those entered into for a professional sports personality or movie star, cannot be executed by an agent without the consent of the party with whom the principal contracted.

CAUTION
Some agency relationships are prohibited by law.

Persons Who Can Initiate an Agency Relationship

Any person who has the capacity to contract can appoint an agent to act on his or her behalf. Generally, persons who lack **contractual capacity**, such as insane persons and minors, cannot appoint an agent. However, the court can appoint a legal guardian or other representative to handle the affairs of insane persons, minors, and others who lack capacity to contract. With court approval, these representatives can enter into enforceable contracts on behalf of the persons they represent.

Almost anyone, including someone who lacks the capacity to contract, can act as an agent for another person. For example, an adult principal can employ a child to convey a contract offer to a third person. The agent's lack of contractual capacity is immaterial because the third party is entering into a contract with the identified principal, not the agent.

KINDS OF EMPLOYMENT RELATIONSHIPS

Businesses usually have three kinds of **employment relationships**: (1) employer–employee relationships, (2) principal–agent relationships, and (3) principal–independent contractor relationships. These relationships are discussed in the following sections.

Types

1.

Employer–Employee Relationship

An employer–employee relationship exists when an employer hires an employee to perform some form of physical service. For example, a welder on General Motors Corporation's assembly line is employed in an employee–employer relationship because he performs a physical task. These relationships used to be referred to as *master–servant* relationships. However, the term *master–servant* is anachronistic and usually is not used today.

The welder in the previous example is not an agent because he cannot enter into contracts on behalf of General Motors Company. If the company empowered him to enter into contracts, he would become an agent.

It is important to note that the term *employee* has no separate legal significance in the law of agency. An employee is not an agent unless he or she is specifically empowered to enter into contracts on the principal employer's behalf.

2.

Principal–Agent Relationship

A **principal–agent relationship** is formed when an employer hires an employee and gives that employee authority to act and enter into contracts on his or her behalf. The extent of this authority is governed by any express agreement between the parties and implied from the circumstances of the agency.

Employees may enter into contracts that are within the scope of their employment. For example, the president of a corporation usually has the authority to enter into major contracts on the corporation's behalf, but a supervisor on the corporation's assembly line may have the authority only to purchase the supplies necessary to keep the line running.

3.

Principal–Independent Contractor Relationship

Principals often employ outsiders—that is, persons and businesses who are not employees—to perform certain tasks on their behalf. These persons and businesses are called **independent contractors**. Doctors, dentists, consultants, stockbrokers, architects, certified public accountants, real estate brokers, and plumbers are examples of other types of professions and trades that commonly act as independent contractors. An independent contractor who is a professional, such as a lawyer, is called a *professional agent*.

A principal can authorize an independent contractor to enter into contracts. Principals are bound by the authorized contracts of their independent contractors. For example, if a client authorizes an attorney to settle a case within a certain dollar amount and the attorney does so, the settlement agreement is binding. Generally, a principal is not liable for the torts of an independent contractor. There are several exceptions to this rule that are discussed in this chapter.

Independent Contractor Defined Section 2 of the Restatement (Second) of Agency defines an **independent contractor** as "a person who contracts with another to do something for him who is not controlled by the other nor subject to the other's right to control with respect to his physical conduct in the performance of the undertaking."

Independent contractors usually work for a number of clients, have their own offices, hire employees, and control the performance of their work. Merely labeling

employment relationships
(1) Employer–employee
(2) principal–agent and
(3) principal–independent contractor.

employer–employee relationship A relationship that results when an employer hires an employee to perform some form of physical service.

principal–agent relationship An employer hires an employee and gives that employee authority to act and enter into contracts on his or her behalf.

independent contractor A person or business who is not an employee who is employed by a principal to perform a certain task on his behalf.

definition of *independent contractor* "A person who contracts with another to do something for him who is not controlled by the other nor subject to the other's right to control with respect to his physical conduct in the performance of the undertaking" [Restatement (Second) of Agency].

someone an "independent contractor" is not enough. The crucial factor in determining whether someone is an employee or an independent contractor is the *degree of control* that the employer has over the agent. Critical factors in determining independent contractor status include the following:

- Whether the worker is engaged in a distinct occupation or an independently established business
- The length of time the agent has been employed by the principal
- The amount of time that agent works for the principal
- Whether the principal supplies the tools and equipment used in the work
- The method of payment, whether by time or by the job
- The degree of skill necessary to complete the task
- Whether the worker hires employees to assist him
- Whether the employer has the right to control the manner and means of accomplishing the desired result

If an examination of these factors shows that the principal asserts little control, the person is an independent contractor. Substantial control indicates an employer–employee relationship.

In the following case, the court applied these factors in order to determine whether an injured worker was an employee or an independent contractor.

> **CAUTION**
> *The crucial factor in determining whether a person is an employee or an independent contractor is the* degree of control *that the principal has over that person.*

CASE 21.1

Torres v. Reardon

3 Cal.App. 4th 831, 5 Cal.Rptr. 2d 52 (1992) California Court of Appeal

Facts Jose Torres was a self-employed gardener, doing business under the name Jose Torres Gardening Service. From 1984 until June 1988, Torres performed weekly general gardening services at several homes in Torrance, California, including the home of Michael and Ona Reardon (Reardons). In June 1988, the Reardons employed Torres to trim a 70-foot-tall tree located in their front yard. At 11:00 A.M., on the morning of June 20, 1988, Torres arrived at the Reardons' home with one helper. The Reardons were not at home. David Boice, Reardons' next-door neighbor, cautioned Torres to take care in cutting a large branch 25 feet from the ground that overhung the roof of Boice's house.

When Torres was ready to cut the branch, Boice came outside to hold a rope that was tied to the branch, with the intention of pulling the branch away from his house as it fell. Torres positioned himself on the branch next to the trunk and began to cut at a point just beyond where he was standing. According to Torres, Boice pulled on the rope when Torres was not expecting a pull. As a result, Torres's chain saw "kicked back," and Torres fell from the tree, landing on his back. Torres was rendered a paraplegic as a result of his fall.

Torres sued the Reardons to recover for his injuries, alleging that he was their employee and therefore could recover from them for failing to provide him with workers' compensation insurance. The Reardons countered this argument by saying that Torres was an independent contractor to whom they were not liable. The trial court agreed with the Reardons and granted their motion for summary judgment. Torres appealed.

Issue Was Torres an employee or an independent contractor?

Decision The court of appeals held that Torres was an independent contractor and that the Reardons were not liable to him. Affirmed.

Reason Uncontradicted evidence showed that (1) Torres was engaged in a distinct occupation and an independently established business, (2) Torres supplied his own tools and equipment used in the work, (3) Torres hired his own employees, (4) Torres was not hired by the day or hour but contracted with the Reardons to produce the specific result of trimming the tree for an agreed-upon price of $350, (5) the Reardons did not control the manner or means of accomplishing the desired result, and (6) the work that Torres contracted to perform was not work ordinarily done in the course of the Reardons' business but was maintenance work done on their home. Therefore, Torres was an independent contractor, not an employee of the Reardons.

CASE QUESTIONS

Critical Legal Thinking Suppose that Torres had negligently cut the branch and it had fallen on

Boice and injured him. Could Boice have recovered damages from the Reardons? Explain.

Ethics Did Torres act ethically in suing the Reardons? Why do you think he did so?

Business Implication Can businesses reduce their liability exposure by hiring more independent contractors and fewer employees to do jobs?

FORMATION OF THE AGENCY RELATIONSHIP

An agency and the resulting authority of an agent can arise in any of these four ways: (1) express agency, (2) implied agency, (3) apparent agency, and (4) agency by ratification. Each of these types of agencies are discussed in the sections that follow.

Express Agency

Express agency is the most common form of agency. In an express agency, the agent has the authority to contract or otherwise act on the principal's behalf as expressly stated in the agency agreement. In addition, the agent may also possess certain implied or apparent authority to act on the principal's behalf (as discussed later in this chapter).

Express agency occurs when a principal and an agent expressly agree to enter into an agency agreement with each other. Express agency contracts can be either oral or written unless the Statute of Frauds stipulates that they must be written. For example, in most states a real estate broker's contract to sell real estate must be in writing.

If the principal and agent enter into an **exclusive agency contract**, the principal cannot employ any agent other than the exclusive agent. If the principal does so, the exclusive agent can recover damages from the principal. If an agency is not an exclusive agency, the principal can employ more than one agent to try to accomplish a stated purpose. When multiple agents are employed, the agencies with all of the agents terminate when any one of the agents accomplishes the stated purpose.

Power of Attorney A **power of attorney** is one of the most formal types of express agency agreements. It is often used to give an agent the power to sign legal documents, such as deeds to real estate, on behalf of the principal. There are two kinds of powers of attorney: *general*, which confers broad powers on the agent to act in any matters on the principal's behalf; and **special**, which limits the agent to those acts specifically enumerated in an agreement. The agent is called an **attorney-in-fact** even though he does not have to be a lawyer. Powers of attorney must be written. Usually, they also must be notarized. A general power of attorney is shown in Exhibit 21.1.

Implied Agency

In many situations, a principal and an agent do not expressly create an agency. Instead, the agency is implied from the conduct of the parties. This type of agency is referred to as **implied agency**. The extent of the agent's authority is determined from the particular facts and circumstances of the situation. Implied authority can be conferred by either industry custom, prior to dealing between the parties, the agent's position, the acts deemed necessary to carry out the agent's duties, and other factors the court deems relevant. Implied authority cannot conflict with express authority or with stated limitations on express authority.

express agency An agency that occurs when a principal and an agent expressly agree to enter into an agency agreement with each other.

exclusive agency contract A contract a principal and agent enter into that says the principal cannot employ any agent other than the exclusive agent.

power of attorney An express agency agreement that is often used to give an agent the power to sign legal documents on behalf of the principal.

attorney-in-fact The agent in a power of attorney situation.

implied agency An agency that occurs when a principal and an agent do not expressly create an agency, but it is inferred from the conduct of the parties.

Exhibit 21.1
A Sample General Power
of Attorney

Power of Attorney

Know All Men by These Presents: That _____

_____

the undersigned (jointly and severally, if more than one) hereby make, constitute and appoint _____

_____

My true and lawful Attorney for me and in my name, place and stead and for my use and benefit:

(a) To ask, demand, sue for, recover, collect and receive each and every sum of money, debt, account, legacy, bequest, interest, dividend, annuity and demand (which now is or hereafter shall become due, owing or payable) belonging to or claimed by me, and to use and take any lawful means for the recovery thereof by legal process or otherwise, and to execute and deliver a satisfaction or release therefor, together with the right and power to compromise or compound any claim or demand;

(b) To exercise any or all of the following powers as to real property, any interest therein and/or any building thereon: To contract for, purchase, receive and take possession thereof and of evidence of title thereto; to lease the same for any term or purpose, including leases for business, residence and oil and/or mineral development; to sell, exchange, grant or convey the same with or without warranty; and to mortgage, transfer in trust, or otherwise encumber or hypothecate the same to secure payment of a negotiable or non-negotiable note or performance of any obligation or agreement;

(c) To exercise any or all of the following powers as to all kinds of personal property and goods, wares and merchandise, chosen in action and other property in possession or in action: To contract for, buy, sell, exchange, transfer and in any legal manner deal in and with the same; and to mortgage, transfer in trust, or otherwise encumber or hypothecate the same to secure payment of a negotiable or non-negotiable note or performance of any obligation or agreement.

(d) To borrow money and to execute an deliver negotiable or non-negotiable notes therefor with or without security; and to loan money and receive negotiable or non-negotiable notes therefor with such security as said Attorney shall deem proper;

(e) To create, amend, supplement and terminate any trust and to instruct and advise the trustee of any trust wherein I am or may be trustor or beneficiary; to represent and vote stock, exercise stock rights, accept and deal with any dividend, distribution or bonus, join in any corporate financing, reorganization, merger, liquidation, consolidation or other action and the extension, compromise, conversion, adjustment, enforcement or foreclosure, singly or in conjunction with others of any corporate stock, bond, note, debenture or other security; to compound, compromise, adjust, settle and satisfy any obligation, secured or unsecured, owing by or to me and to give or accept any property and/or money whether or not equal to or less in value than the amount owning in payment, settlement or satisfaction thereof;

(f) To transact business of any kind or class and as my act and deed to sign, execute, acknowledge and deliver any deed, lease, assignment of lease, covenant, indenture, indemnity, agreement, mortgage, deed of trust, assignment of mortgage or of the beneficial interest under deed of trust, extension or renewal of any obligation, subordination or waiver or priority, hypothecation, bottomry, charter-party, bill of lading, bill of sale, bill, bond, note, whether negotiable or non-negotiable, receipt, evidence of debt, full or partial release or satisfaction of mortgage, judgment and other debt, request for partial or full reconveyance of deed of trust and such other instruments in writing of any kind or class as may be necessary or proper in the premises.

Giving and Granting unto my said Attorney full power and authority to do and perform all and every act and thing whatsoever, requiste, necessary or appropriate to be done in and about the premises as fully to all intents and purposes as I might or could do if personally present, hereby ratifying all that my said Attorney shall lawfully do or cause to be done by virtue of these presents. The powers and authority hereby conferred upon my said Attorney shall be applicable to all real and personal property or interests therein now owned or hereafter required by me and wherever situate.

My said Attorney is empowered hereby to determine in said Attorney's sole discretion the time when, purpose for and manner in which any power herein conferred upon said Attorney shall be exercised, and the conditions, provisions and covenants of any instrument or document which may be executed by said Attorney pursuant hereto; and in the acquisition or disposition of real or personal property, my said Attorney shall have exclusive power to fix the terms thereof for cash, credit and/or property, and if on credit with or without security.

The undersigned, if a married person, hereby further authorizes and empowers my said Attorney, as my duly authorized agent, to join in my behalf, in the execution of any instrument by which any community real property or any interest therein, now owned or hereafter acquired by my spouse and myself, or either of us, is sold, leased, encumbered, or conveyed.

When the context to requires, the masculine gender includes the feminine and/or neuter, and the singular number includes the plural.

Witness my hand this _____ day of _____, 19 _____.

STATE OF CALIFORNIA
COUNTY OF   } SS

On _____ before me, the undersigned, a
Notary Public in and for said State personally
appeared. _____

_____ personally known
to me (or proved to me on the basis of
satisfactory evidence) to be the person_____
whose name _____ subscribed to the within
instrument and acknowledged that_____
executed the same.
WITNESS my hand and official seal.

Signature _____

_____
Name (Typed or Printed)   (This area for official seal)

Incidental Authority

Often, even an express agency agreement does not provide enough detail to cover all contingencies that may arise in the future regarding the performance of the agency. In this case, the agent possesses certain implied authority to act. This implied authority is sometimes referred to as **incidental authority**.

Emergency Powers

Certain emergency situations may arise in the course of an agency. If the agent cannot contact the principal for instructions, the agent has implied **emergency powers** to take all actions reasonably necessary to protect the principal's property and rights.

Apparent Agency

Apparent agency (or **agency by estoppel**) arises when a principal creates the appearance of an agency that in actuality does not exist. Where an apparent agency is established, the principal is estopped from denying the agency relationship and is bound to contracts entered into by the apparent agent while acting within the scope of the ap-

incidental authority
Implied power that an agent has where the terms of the express agency agreement do not cover the contingency that has arisen.

apparent agency Agency that arises when a principal creates the appearance of an agency that in actuality does not exist.

parent agency. Note that it is the principal's actions—not the agent's—that create an apparent agency.

CAUTION

Where an apparent agency is established, the principal is estopped from denying the agency relationship.

CONSIDER THIS EXAMPLE: Suppose Georgia Pacific Inc. interviews Albert Iorio for a sales representative position. Mr. Iorio, accompanied by Jane Franklin, the national sales manager, visits retail stores located in the open sales territory. While visiting one store, Jane tells the store manager, "I wish I had more sales reps like Albert." Nevertheless, Albert is not hired. If Albert later enters into contracts with the store on behalf of Georgia Pacific and Jane has not controverted the impression of Albert she left with the store manager, the company will be bound to the contract.

Agency by Ratification

agency by ratification An agency that occurs when (1) a person misrepresents him or herself as another's agent when in fact he or she is not and (2) the purported principal ratifies the unauthorized act.

Agency by ratification occurs when (1) a person misrepresents him- or herself as another's agent when in fact he or she is not and (2) the purported principal ratifies (accepts the unauthorized act). In such cases, the principal is bound to perform, and the agent is relieved of any liability for misrepresentation.

CONSIDER THIS EXAMPLE: Bill Levine sees a house for sale and thinks his friend Sherry Maxwell would want it. Bill Levine enters into a contract to purchase the house from the seller and signs the contract "Bill Levine, agent for Sherry Maxwell." Because Bill is not Sherry Maxwell's agent, she is not bound to the contract. However, if Sherry agrees to purchase the house, there is an agency by ratification. The ratification "relates back" to the moment Bill Levine entered into the contract. Upon ratification of the contract, Sherry Maxwell is obligated to purchase the house.

CONTEMPORARY BUSINESS ENVIRONMENT

Apparent Agency in Franchising

Franchising has become a major form of conducting business in the United States. In a franchise agreement, one company (called the **franchisor**) licenses another company (called the **franchisee**) to use its trade name, trademarks and service marks, and trade secrets. Many fast-food restaurants, gasoline stations, motels and hotels, and other businesses are operated in this fashion.

The franchisor and franchisee are independently owned businesses. A principal–agent relationship usually is not created by the franchise. If no express or implied agency is created, the franchisor would not normally be civilly liable for the tortious conduct (e.g., negligence) of the franchisee. Liability could be imposed on the

franchisor, however, if an apparent agency is shown. Consider the following case.

The Howard Johnson Company (HJ) operates a chain of hotels, motels, and restaurants across the United States. Approximately 75 percent of the HJ motor lodges are owned and operated by franchisees who are licensed by HJ to do business under the "Howard Johnson" trade name and trademarks. The rest are company-owned.

Orlando Executive park, Inc. (OEP) is a corporate franchisee that owns and operates a Howard Johnson motor lodge franchise in Orlando, Florida. The motor lodge is a part of a large complex known as "Howard Johnson's Plaza" located off Interstate 4. The motor

lodge contains approximately 300 guest rooms in six separate buildings.

P.D.R. (name withheld by the court), a 35-year-old married woman and mother of a small child, worked as a supervisor for a restaurant chain. Her work occasionally required her to travel and stay overnight in Orlando. On October 22, 1975, P.D.R. stopped to stay at the Howard Johnson motor lodge in Orlando. At approximately 9:30 P.M., P.D.R. registered for her previously reserved room at the lodge. The registration form did not inform her that the hotel was an HJ franchisee. P.D.R. parked her car in the motor lodge parking lot and proceeded with her suitcase to her ground-floor room in Building A, which was located directly behind the registration office. P.D.R. then went back to her car to get some papers. After obtaining the papers from her car, P.D.R. returned to Building A. As she proceeded down an interior hallway of the building toward her room, she was accosted by a man she had previously seen standing behind the registration office. The man struck her in the throat and neck and choked her until she became semi-conscious. When P.D.R. fell to the floor, her assailant sat on top of her and stripped her of her jewelry. He then dragged her down the hallway to beneath a secluded stairway and brutally beat her. The assailant then disappeared into the night and has never been identified.

P.D.R. suffered serious physical and psychological injury, including memory loss, mental confusion, and an inability to tolerate and communicate with people. She lost her job within one year of the assault. P.D.R. suffers perma-nent injury that requires expensive, long-term medical and psychiatric treatment. P.D.R. brought a tort action against OEP and HJ and sought actual and punitive damages against both of them.

The jury had little trouble finding that OEP had breached its duty of care and was liable. Evidence showed that other criminal activity had occurred previously on the premises but that OEP failed to warn guests, including P.D.R., of the danger. In fact, OEP management actively discouraged criminal investigations by sheriff's deputies, thus minimizing any deterrent effect they may have had. Further evidence showed that the dark and secluded stairwell area where P.D.R. was dragged was a security hazard that should have been boarded up or better lit.

The jury also found HJ liable to P.D.R. under the doctrine of apparent agency. The appellate court stated "While OEP might not be HJ's agent for all purposes, the signs, national advertising, uniformity of building design and color schemes allow the public to assume that this and other similar motor lodges are under the same ownership. An HJ official testified that it was the HJ marketing strategy to appear as a 'chain that sells a product across the nation.'" The court continued, "There was sufficient evidence for the jury to reasonably conclude that HJ represented to the traveling public that it could expect a particular level of service at a Howard Johnson Motor Lodge. The uniformity of signs, design, and color schemes easily leads the public to believe that each motor lodge is under common ownership or conforms to common standards, and the jury could find they are intended to do so." The appellate court upheld an award of $750,000 compensatory damages against OEP and HJ jointly. [*Orlando Executive Park, Inc. v. P.D.R.*, 402 So.2d 442 (Fla.App. 1981)]

AGENT'S DUTIES

An agent owes certain duties to the principal. These duties may be either set forth in the agency agreement or implied by law. Generally, agents owe the principal the duties of (1) performance, (2) notification, (3) loyalty, (4) obedience, and (5) accountability. Each of these duties is discussed in the sections that follow.

Duty of Performance

An agent who enters into a contract with a principal has two distinct obligations: (1) performing the lawful duties expressed in the contract and (2) meeting the standards of reasonable care, skill, and diligence implicit in all contracts. Collectively, these duties are referred to as the agent's **duty of performance**.

Normally, an agent is required to render the same standard of care, skill, and diligence that a fictitious reasonable agent in the same occupation would render in the same locality and under the same circumstances. For instance, a general medical practitioner in a rural area would be held to the standard of a reasonable general practitioner in rural areas. The standard might be different than the standard for a general medical practitioner in a big city. In some professions, such as accounting, a national standard of performance (called "generally accepted accounting standards"), is imposed. If an agent holds himself or herself as possessing higher-than-customary skills, the agent will be held to this higher standard of performance. For example, a lawyer who claims to be a specialist in securities law will be held to a reasonable specialist-in-securities-law standard.

duty of performance An agent's duty to a principal that includes (1) performing the lawful duties expressed in the contract and (2) meeting the standards of reasonable care, skill, and diligence implicit in all contracts.

An agent who does not perform his or her express duties or fails to use the standard degree of care, skill, or diligence is liable to the principal for breach of contract. An agent who has negligently (or intentionally) failed to perform properly is also liable in tort.

Duty of Notification

duty of notification An agent's duty to notify the principal of information he or she learns from a third party or other source that is important to the principal.

In the course of an agency, the agent usually learns information that is important to the principal. This information may come from third parties or other sources. The agent's duty to notify the principal of such information is called the **duty of notification**. The agent is liable to the principal for any injuries resulting from a breach of this duty.

imputed knowledge Information that is learned by the agent that is attributed to the principal.

Imputed Knowledge Most information learned by an agent in the course of the agency is **imputed** to the principal. This means that the principal is assumed to know what the agent knows. This is so even if the agent does not tell the principal certain relevant information.

Duty of Loyalty

duty of loyalty A duty an agent owes the principal not to act adversely to the interests of the principal.

Because the agency relationship is based on trust and confidence, an agent owes the principal a **duty of loyalty** in all agency-related matters. Thus, an agent owes a fiduciary duty not to act adversely to the interests of the principal. If this duty is breached, the agent is liable to the principal. The most common types of loyalty by an agent are discussed in the following subsections.

dual agency A situation that occurs when an agent acts for two or more different principals in the same transaction.

Dual Agency An agent cannot meet a duty of loyalty to two parties with conflicting interests. Dual agency occurs when an agent acts for two or more different principals in the same transaction. This practice generally is prohibited unless all of the parties involved in the transaction agree to it. If an agent acts as an undisclosed dual agent, he or she must forfeit all compensation received in the transaction.

Some agents, such as intermediaries and finders, are not considered dual agents. This is because they only bring interested parties together; they do not take part in any negotiations.

usurp an opportunity When an agent appropriates an opportunity for him- or herself by failing to let the principal know about it.

Usurping an Opportunity An agent cannot usurp an opportunity that belongs to the principal. For example, a third-party offer to an agent must be conveyed to the principal. The agent cannot appropriate the opportunity for himself or herself unless the principal rejects it after due consideration. Opportunities to purchase real estate, businesses, products, ideas, and other property are subject to this rule.

self-dealing When an agent deals with the principal (e.g., selling property to or buying property from the principal).

Self-Dealing Agents generally are prohibited from undisclosed self-dealing with the principal. For example, a real estate agent who is employed to purchase real estate for a principal cannot secretly sell his own property in the transaction. However, the deal is lawful if the principal agrees to buy the property after the agent discloses his ownership.

misuse of confidential information An agent cannot disclose or misuse confidential information about the principal's affairs obtained during an agency.

Misuse of Confidential Information In the course of an agency, the agent often acquires confidential information about the principal's affairs (e.g., business plans, technological innovations, customer lists, trade secrets, and such). The agent is under a legal duty not to disclose or misuse such information either during or after the course of the agency. There is no prohibition against using general information, knowledge, or experience acquired during the course of the agency.

Competing with the Principal Agents are prohibited from competing with the principal during the course of an agency unless the principal agrees. The reason for this rule is that an agent cannot meet his or her duty of loyalty when his or her personal interests conflict with the principal's interests. If the parties have not entered into an enforceable covenant not to compete, an agent is free to compete with the principal when the agency has ended.

competing with the principal An agent cannot compete with the principal during the course of an agency unless the principal agrees.

ETHICAL PERSPECTIVE

Double Agent

Wartime "double agents" have been the subject of numerous novels and movies. Most of these stories end with one side or the other (or both) finding out a secret, and the double agent suffering the consequences of his or her double-dealing. The law of agency treats dual agents with the same disdain. Instead of bloodshed, though, agency law hits the double agent in the pocketbook. Consider the following case.

Del Rayo Properties (Del Rayo) hired L. Byron Culver & Associates (Culver), a real estate brokerage firm, to find suitable real estate for acquisition by Del Rayo. Culver became aware of approximately 33.5 acres of land owned by Jaoudi Industrial & Trading Corporation (Jaoudi) located in Rancho Santa Fe, California. Culver obtained approval from Del Rayo to enter into negotiations on Del Rayo's behalf to acquire Jaoudi's property.

On February 8, 1985, Culver telephoned Joseph Jaoudi, president of the company, and inquired

if the 33.5 acres in Rancho Santa Fe were for sale. Jaoudi indicated that they were. Culver asked whether it could list the property, and Jaoudi agreed to give Culver a one-time listing for that particular property. Jaoudi and Culver agreed on a 3 percent commission.

On February 13, 1985, Culver presented Jaoudi with a written offer from Del Rayo to purchase the property for $1,750,000. When Jaoudi inquired whether Culver and Del Rayo were associated in any way, Culver denied any association. Jaoudi agreed to the deal.

Prior to the closing of escrow on March 13, 1985, Jaoudi instructed the escrow not to pay the commission to Culver. Escrow closed and Culver did not receive the commission. Culver sued Jaoudi to recover the commission. Jaoudi defended by arguing that Culver was an undisclosed dual agent who did not deserve to collect the commission because of his double-dealing.

The court held that a real estate agent must refrain from dual

representation in a sale transaction unless he obtains the consent of both principals after full disclosure. This Culver did not do. The trial and appellate courts denied Culver recovery of the $52,500 commission. The appellate court stated, "The fact that Jaoudi Industrial received a financial benefit from Culver's efforts is of no consequence on the issue of no recovery for failure to disclose a dual agency. A bar to recovery is a matter of public policy." [*L. Byron Culver & Associates v. Jaoudi Industrial & Trading Corporation*, 1 Cal.App.4th 300, 1 Cal.Rptr.2d 680 (Cal.App. 1991)]

1. Did Culver act ethically in this case?
2. What policy underlies the rule against undisclosed dual agents?
3. Did Jaoudi act ethically in refusing to pay the commission? Should Jaoudi benefit financially from Culver's secret conduct?

Duty of Obedience

Both gratuitous agents and agents for hire have a duty to obey the lawful instructions of the principal during the performance of the agency. This is called the **duty of obedience**.

If the principal's instructions are unclear or confusing, the agent is required to inquire and seek clearer directions from the principal. If this is not possible, the agent owes a duty to act in good faith and in a reasonable manner based on the circumstances. In emergency situations in which the principal cannot be consulted, the agent

duty of obedience A duty that agents have to obey the lawful instructions of the principal during the performance of the agency.

can deviate from the principal's property. In effect the agent may use his or her own best judgment in acting on the principal's behalf.

The agent owes no duty to obey the principal's instructions to engage in crimes, torts, or unethical conduct. If the agent does so, he or she will be personally liable (as is the principal). For example, a sales representative can ignore the principal's instructions to misrepresent the quality of the principal's goods.

Duty of Accountability

duty of accountability
A duty that an agent owes to maintain an accurate accounting of all transactions undertaken on the principal's behalf.

Unless otherwise agreed, an agent owes a duty to maintain an accurate accounting of all transactions undertaken on the principal's behalf. This **duty of accountability** includes keeping records of all property and money received and expended during the course of the agency. A principal has a right to demand an accounting from the agent at any time, and the agent owes a legal duty to make the accounting. This duty also requires the agent to (1) maintain a separate account for the principal and (2) use the principal's property in an authorized manner.

CAUTION
A "constructive trust" is created by law, rather than agreement, to impose a duty to transfer property to another.

Any property, money, or other benefit received by the agent in the course of the agency belongs to the principal. For example, all secret profits received by the agent are the property of the principal. If an agent breaches the agency contract, the principal can sue the agent to recover damages caused by breach. The court can impose a **constructive trust** on any secret profits on property purchased with secret profits for the benefit of the principal.

PRINCIPAL'S DUTIES

The principal owes certain duties to the agent. These duties, which can be expressed in the agency contract or implied by law, include (1) the duty of compensation, (2) the duty of reimbursement and indemnification, (3) the duty of cooperation, and (4) the duty to provide safe working conditions.

Duty of Compensation

duty of compensation
A duty that a principal owes to pay an agreed-upon amount to the agent either upon the completion of the agency or at some other mutually agreeable time.

A principal owes a **duty to compensate** an agent for services provided. Usually, the agency contract (whether written or oral) specifies the compensation to be paid. The principal must pay this amount either upon the completion of the agency or at some other mutually agreeable time.

If there is no agreement as to the amount of compensation, the law implies a promise that the principal will pay the agent the customary fee paid in the industry. If the compensation cannot be established by custom, the principal owes a duty to pay the reasonable value of the agent's services.

There is no duty to compensate a gratuitous agent. However, gratuitous agents who agree to provide their services free of charge may be paid voluntarily.

Certain types of agents traditionally perform their services on a **contingency fee** basis. Under this type of arrangement, the principal owes a duty to pay the agent the agreed-upon contingency fee only if the agency is completed. Real estate brokers, finders, lawyers, and salespersons often work on this basis.

Duties of Reimbursement and Indemnification

duty of reimbursement
A duty that a principal owes to repay money to the agent if the agent spent his or her own money during the agency on the principal's behalf.

In carrying out the agency, an agent may spend his or her own money on the principal's behalf. Unless otherwise agreed, the principal owes a **duty to reimburse** the agent for all such expenses if they were (1) authorized by the principal, (2) within the scope of the agency, and (3) necessary to discharge the agent's duties in carrying out the agency. For example, a principal must reimburse an agent for authorized business trips taken on the principal's behalf.

A principal also owes a **duty to indemnify** the agent for any losses the agent suffers because of the principal. This duty usually arises when an agent is held liable for the principal's misconduct. For example, suppose an agent enters into an authorized contract with a third party on the principal's behalf, the principal fails to perform on the contract, and the third party recovers a judgment against the agent. The agent can recover indemnification of this amount from the principal.

duty to indemnify A duty that a principal owes to protect the agent for losses the agent suffered during the agency because of the principal's misconduct.

Duty of Cooperation

Unless otherwise agreed, the principal owes a **duty to cooperate** with and assist the agent in the performance of the agent's duties and the accomplishment of the agency. For example, unless otherwise agreed, a principal who employs a real estate agent to sell her house owes a duty to allow the agent to show the house to prospective purchasers during reasonable hours.

duty to cooperate A duty that a principal owes to cooperate with and assist the agent in the performance of the agent's duties and the accomplishment of the agency.

Duty to Provide Safe Working Conditions

The principal owes a **duty to provide safe working conditions** to its agents. This includes safe premises, equipment, and other working conditions. The principal also owes a duty to inspect for unsafe working conditions, to warn agents of dangerous conditions, and to repair and remedy unsafe conditions. Agents can sue principals for violating these duties. Federal and state statutes establish many safety standards for the workplace.

duty to provide safe working conditions A duty that a principal owes to provide safe premises, equipment, and other working conditions; also includes inspection by the principal to ensure safety.

CONTRACT LIABILITY TO THIRD PARTIES

A principal who authorizes an agent to enter into a contract with a third party is liable on the contract. Thus, the third party can enforce the contract and recover damages if the principal fails to perform it (see Exhibit 21.2).

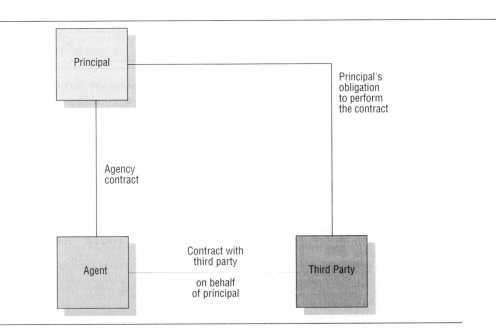

Exhibit 21.2
The Principal–Agent Relationship

Principal

Principal's obligation to perform the contract

Agency contract

Agent

Contract with third party on behalf of principal

Third Party

The agent can also be held liable on the contract in certain circumstances. Imposition of such liability depends on whether the agency is classified as (1) fully disclosed, (2) partially disclosed, or (3) undisclosed.

Fully Disclosed Agency

A **fully disclosed agency** results if the third party entering into the contract knows (1) that the agent is acting as an agent for a principal and (2) the actual identity of the principal.[1] The third party has the requisite knowledge if the principal's identity is disclosed to the third party by either the agent or some other source.

In a fully disclosed agency, the contract is between the principal and the third party. Thus, the principal, who is called a **fully disclosed principal**, is liable on the contract. The agent, however, is not liable on the contract because the third party relied on the principal's credit and reputation when the contract was made. An agent is liable on the contract if he or she guarantees that the principal will perform the contract.

Defective Signature The agent's signature on a contract entered into on the principal's behalf is important because it can establish the agent's status and liability. For instance, in a fully disclosed agency the agency's signature must clearly indicate that he or she is acting as an agent for a specifically identified principal. Example of proper signatures include "Allison Adams, agent for Peter Perceival," "Peter Perceival, by Allison Adams, agent," and "Peter Perceival, by Allison Adams."

An agent who is authorized to sign a contract for a fully disclosed principal but fails to properly do so can be held personally liable on the contract. For example, in the prior example a partially disclosed agency would be created if the contract was signed "Allison Adams, agent." If Adams merely signed the contract "Allison Adams," the agency would be an undisclosed agency.

BUSINESS APPLICATION

The New York Times Recycled by the Court

If a person or business is acting as another's agent, it is best for the agent to disclose the existence of the agency and the identity of the principal to the third party. The reason for doing so is for the agent to avoid liability. Consider the following case.

Glynn-Palmer Associates, Inc. (Glynn-Palmer) is an advertising agency located in New York City. One of the duties of an advertising agency is to place advertisements for clients on radio, television, billboards, and in print media. Glynn-Palmer prepared an advertisement for one of its clients—Worldwide S.O.S.—and contacted *The New York Times* to run the advertisement in its daily newspaper. The *Times* provided an application form to Glynn-Palmer. Glynn-Palmer completed the form, which disclosed the name of the client, the space required, the date the advertisement was to run, and the price. The *Times* ran the advertisement and billed Glynn-Palmer for the services. Glynn-Palmer sent the bill on to Worldwide S.O.S. When the bill was not paid, the *Times* brought suit against Glynn-Palmer to recover the unpaid balance. Was there a fully disclosed agency?

The court found that there was a fully disclosed agency and that Glynn-Palmer (the agent) was not liable for Worldwide S.O.S.'s (the principal) debt to *The New York Times*. The court found that the *Times* was aware that the advertisement in question was not for Glynn-Palmer, because the name of the client—Worldwide S.O.S.—was disclosed on the application form and appeared on the *Times* bill. [*The New York Times Co. v. Glynn-Palmer Associates, Inc.*, 525 N.Y.S.2d 565 (N.Y. 1988)]

Partially Disclosed Agency

A **partially disclosed agency** occurs if the agent discloses his or her agency status but does not reveal the principal's identity and the third party does not know the principal's identity from another source. The nondisclosure may be because (1) the principal instructs the agent not to disclose his or her identity to the third party or (2) the agent forgets to tell the third party the principal's identity. In this kind of agency, the principal is called a **partially disclosed principal**.

In a partially disclosed agency, both the principal and the agent are liable on third-party contracts.[2] This is because the third party must rely on the agent's reputation, integrity, and credit because the principal is unidentified. If the agent is made to pay the contract, the agent can sue the principal for indemnification. The third party and the agent can agree to relieve the agent's liability.

Undisclosed Agency

An **undisclosed agency** occurs when the third party is unaware of either the existence of an agency or the principal's identity. The principal is called an **undisclosed principal**. Undisclosed agencies are lawful. They are often used when the principal feels that the terms of the contract would be changed if his or her identity were known. For example, a wealthy person may use an undisclosed agency to purchase property if the person thinks that the seller would raise the price of the property if their identity was revealed.

In an undisclosed agency, both the principal and the agent are liable on the contract with the third party. This is because the agent, by not divulging that he or she is acting as an agent, becomes a principal to the contract. The third party relies on the reputation and credit of the agent in entering into the contract. If the principal fails to perform the contract, the third party can recover against the principal or the agent. If the agent is made to pay the contract, he or she can recover indemnification from the principal.

In the following case, the court was presented with the issue of whether an agent was liable on a contract.

> **CAUTION**
> *In a partially disclosed agency, both the principal and the agent are liable to the third party if the principal fails to perform the contract.*

> **undisclosed agency** An agency that occurs when the third party is unaware of either (1) the existence of an agency or (2) the principal's identity.

> **CAUTION**
> *In an undisclosed agency, both the principal and the agent are liable to the third party if the principal fails to perform the contract.*

CASE 21.2

You'll See Seafoods, Inc. v. Gravois

520 So.2d 461 (1988) Court of Appeals of Louisiana

Facts In 1978, James Gravois purchased a restaurant and named it "The Captain's Raft." The restaurant was actually owned by Computer Tax Services of La., Inc., a corporation owned by Gravois. Gravois did not inform the managers, employees, or suppliers that the restaurant was owned by a corporation. Further, the menus were printed with the name "The Captain's Raft" with no indication it was a corporate entity. Supplies purchased by the restaurant were paid for by checks signed by Gravois with no indication of his agency capacity. You'll See Seafoods, Inc. (You'll See) supplied fresh seafood to the restaurant and was paid for the merchandise by checks signed by Gravois. On February 28, 1984, You'll See filed suit against Gravois dba The Captain's Raft to recover unpaid invoices. Gravois responded by saying that he was merely acting as an agent for a corporate principal. The corporation was in bankruptcy.

Issue Was Gravois liable on the debt owed You'll See?

Decision Yes. The appellate court held that Gravois was an agent for an undisclosed corporate principal and, therefore, was liable for the debts owed to You'll See.

Reason An agent has the burden of proving he disclosed his capacity and the identity of his principal if he wishes to escape personal liability for a contract he entered into with a third party on behalf of his principal. Gravois failed to do this.

CASE QUESTIONS

Critical Legal Thinking Should agents for undisclosed principals be held personally liable on contracts? Why or why not?

Ethics Did Gravois act ethically in arguing that the debts owed to You'll See belonged to the corporation and not himself individually?

Business Implication Why do you think Gravois wanted the debts to be placed in the corporation? Why do you think You'll See did not want the debts placed in the corporation?

implied warranty of authority   An agent who enters into a contract on behalf of another party impliedly warrants that he or she has the authority to do so.

ratification   When a principal accepts an agent's unauthorized contract.

Agent Exceeding the Scope of Authority

An agent who enters into a contract on behalf of another party impliedly warrants that he or she has the authority to do so. This is called the agent's **implied warranty of authority**. If the agent exceeds the scope of his or her authority, the principal is not liable on the contract unless the principal **ratifies** it. The agent, however, is liable to the third party for breaching the implied warranty of authority. To recover, the third party must show (1) reliance on the agent's representation and (2) ignorance of the agent's lack of status.

TORT LIABILITY TO THIRD PARTIES

The principal and the agent are each personally liable for their own tortious conduct. The principal is liable for the tortious conduct of an agent who is acting within the scope of his or her authority. The agent, however, only is liable for the tortious conduct of the principal if he or she directly or indirectly participates in or aids and abets the principal's conduct.

The courts have applied a broad and flexible standard in interpreting scope of authority in the context of employment. Although other factors may also be considered, the courts rely on the following factors to determine whether an agent's conduct occurred within the scope of his or her employment:

- Was the act specifically requested or authorized by the principal?
- Was it the kind of act that the agent was employed to perform?
- Did the act occur substantially within the time period of employment authorized by the principal?
- Did the act occur substantially within the location of employment authorized by the employer?
- Was the agent advancing the principal's purpose when the act occurred?

Where liability is found, tort remedies are available to the injured party. These remedies include recovery for medical expenses, lost wages, pain and suffering, emotional distress, and in some cases, punitive damages. As discussed in the following sections, the three main sources of tort liability for principals and agents are misrepresentation, negligence, and intentional torts.

Misrepresentation

misrepresentation   An assertion that is made that is not in accord with the facts.

Intentional misrepresentations are also known as **fraud** or **deceit**. They occur when an agent makes statements that he or she knows are not true. An **innocent misrepresentation** occurs when an agent negligently makes a misrepresentation to a third party.

A principal is liable for the intentional and innocent misrepresentations made by an agent acting within the scope of employment. The third party can either (1) rescind the contract with the principal and recover any considerations paid or (2) affirm the contract and recover damages.

CONSIDER THIS EXAMPLE: Assume that (1) a car salesman is employed to sell the principal's car and (2) the principal tells the agent that the car was repaired after it was involved in a major accident. If the agent intentionally tells the buyer that the car was never involved in an accident, the agent has made an intentional misrepresentation. Both the principal and the agent are liable for this misrepresentation.

respondeat superior
A rule that says an employer is liable for the tortious conduct of its employees or agents while they are acting within the scope of its authority.

Negligence

Principals are liable for the negligent conduct of agents acting within the scope of their employment. This liability is based on the common law doctrine of **respondeat**

superior ("let the master answer"), which, in turn, is based on the legal theory of **vicarious liability** (liability without fault). In other words, the principal is liable because of his or her employment contract with the negligent agent, not because the principal was personally at fault.

In the following case, the court applied these elements in deciding whether an employer was liable for the negligent conduct of its employee.

CASE 21.3

Edgewater Motels, Inc. v. Gatzke and Walgreen Co.
277 N.W.2d 11 (1979) Supreme Court of Minnesota

Facts Arlen Gatzke (Gatzke) was a district manager for the Walgreen Company (Walgreen). In August 1979, Gatzke was sent to Duluth, Minnesota to supervise the opening of a new Walgreen restaurant. In Duluth, Gatzke stayed at the Edgewater Motel (Edgewater). While in Duluth, Gatzke was "on call" 24 hours a day to other Walgreen stores located in his territory. About midnight of the evening of August 23, 1979, Gatzke, after working 17 hours that day, went with several other Walgreen employees to a restaurant and bar to drink. Within one hour's time, Gatzke had consumed three "doubles" and one single brandy Manhattan. About 1:30 A.M., he went back to the Edgewater Motel and filled out his expense report. Soon thereafter a fire broke out in Gatzke's motel room. Gatzke escaped, but the fire spread and caused extensive damage to the motel. Evidence showed that Gatzke smoked two packs of cigarettes a day. An expert fire reconstruction witnesses testified that the fire started from a lit cigarette in or next to the wastepaper basket in Gatzke's room. Edgewater Motels, Inc., sued Gatzke and Walgreen. The parties stipulated that the damage to the Edgewater Motel was $330,360. The jury returned a verdict against defendants Gatzke and Walgreen. The court granted Walgreen's post-trial motion for judgment notwithstanding the verdict. Plaintiff Edgewater and defendant Gatzke appealed.

Issue Was Gatzke's act of smoking within his "scope of employment" making his principal, the Walgreen Company, vicariously liable for his negligence?

Decision Yes. The supreme court held that Gatzke's negligent act of smoking was within the scope of his employment while acting as an employee of the Walgreen Company. The supreme court reinstated the jury's verdict awarding damages to plaintiff Edgewater Motels, Inc.

Reason In reaching its decision, the supreme court stated, "After careful consideration of the issue we are persuaded that smoking can be an act within an employee's scope of employment. It seems only logical to conclude that an employee does not abandon his employment as a matter of law while temporarily acting for his personal comfort when such activities involve only slight deviations from work that are reasonable under the circumstances, such as eating, drinking, or smoking.... The record indicates that Gatzke was an executive type of employee who had no set working hours. His room at the Edgewater Motel was his office away from home."

CASE QUESTIONS

Critical Legal Thinking Should smoking cigarettes be held to be within an employee's "scope of employment"? Why or why not?

Ethics Do employers owe a duty to police the personal habits of their employees?

Business Implication Because of the dangers of smoking, would employers be justified in hiring only nonsmokers as employees?

Frolic and Detour Agents sometimes do things during the course of their employment to further their own interests rather than the principal's. For example, an agent might take a detour to run a personal errand while on assignment for the principal. This is commonly referred to as a *frolic and detour*. Negligence actions stemming from frolic and detour are examined on a case-by-case basis. Agents always are personally liable for their tortious conduct in such situations. Principals generally are relieved of liability if the agent's frolic and detour is substantial. However, if the deviation is minor, the principal is liable for the injuries caused by the agent's tortious conduct.

CONSIDER THIS EXAMPLE: A salesperson stops home for lunch while on an assignment for his principal. While leaving his home, the agent hits and injures a pedestrian with his automobile. The principal is liable if the agent's home was not too far out of the way from the agent's assignment. However, the principal would not be liable if an agent who is supposed to be on assignment to Los Angeles flies to San Francisco to meet a friend and is involved in an accident. The facts and circumstances of each case will determine its outcome.

The "Coming and Going" Rule Under the common law, a principal generally is not liable for injuries caused by its agents and employees while they are on their way to or from work. This so-called **coming and going rule** applies even if the principal supplies the agent's automobile or other transportation or pays for its gasoline, repairs, and other automobile operating expenses. This rule is quite logical. Because principals do not control where their agents and employees live, they should not be held liable for tortious conduct of agents on their way to and from work.

Dual-Purpose Mission Sometimes, principals request that agents run errands or conduct other acts on their behalf while the agent or employee is on personal business. In this case, the agent is on a **dual-purpose mission**. That is, he or she is acting partly for himself or herself and partly for the principal. Most jurisdictions hold both the principal and the agent liable if the agent injures someone while on such a mission.

CONSIDER THIS EXAMPLE: Suppose a principal asks an employee to drop a package off at a client's office on the employee's way home. If the employee negligently injures a pedestrian while on this dual-purpose mission, the principal is liable to the pedestrian.

In the following case, the court found that an employee was not acting within the scope of her employment when negligence caused injuries to a third person.

---

coming and going rule
A rule that says a principal is generally not liable for injuries caused by its agents and employees while they are on their way to or from work.

dual-purpose mission
An errand or other act that a principal requests of an agent while the agent is on his or her own personal business.

CASE 21.4

Sussman v. Florida East Coast Properties, Inc.
557 So.2d 74 (1990) District Court of Appeal of Florida

Facts Elizabeth Paraiso, a fitness instructor at a health spa owned by Florida East Coast Properties, Inc. (Properties), received a telephone call from a fellow employee asking her to stop off at a supermarket on the way to work and pick up a birthday cake for another employee's birthday party. Paraiso departed for work earlier than usual and deviated five blocks from her normal route in order to purchase the cake. Paraiso lost control of the car when she reached over to prevent the cake from falling off the seat. The car left the road and struck William Sussman as he sat on a bench waiting for a bus. Sussman sued Properties to recover damages for his injuries. The trial

court granted summary judgment to Properties. Sussman appealed.

Issue Was Paraiso acting within the scope of her employment when she struck Sussman with her car?

Decision No. The court held that Properties was not liable to Sussman. Affirmed.

Reason In order for an employer to be liable for an employee's tortious act, the employee must be found to be acting within the scope of her employment. Here, the court applied the coming and going rule and found that Paraiso was not acting within the scope of her employment when she purchased the cake for a fellow employee and negligently injured Sussman.

CASE QUESTIONS

Critical Legal Thinking What is the policy underlying the coming and going rule? Do you agree with this rule?

Ethics Do you think the employer should have been held liable in this case?

Business Implication Should an employer be concerned about how "accident prone" a person is before the employer hires that person as an employee?

Intentional Torts

Intentional torts include such acts as assault, battery, false imprisonment, and other intentional conduct that causes injury to another person. A principal is not liable for the intentional torts of agents and employees that are committed outside the principal's scope of business. For example, if an employee attends a sporting event after working hours and gets into a fight with another spectator at the event, the employer is not liable.

However, a principal is liable under the doctrine of vicarious liability for intentional torts of agents and employees committed within the agent's scope of employment. The courts generally apply one of the tests discussed below in determining whether an agent's intentional torts were committed within the agent's scope of employment.

intentional tort Occurs when a person has intentionally committed a wrong against (1) another person or his or her character, or (2) another person's property.

The Motivation Test
Under the **motivation test**, if the agent's motivation in committing the intentional tort is to promote the principal's business, the principal is liable for any injury caused by the tort. However, if the agent's motivation in committing the intentional tort was personal, the principal is not liable even if the tort took place during business hours or on business premises. For example, a principal is not liable if his agent was motivated by jealousy to beat up someone on the job who dated her boyfriend.

motivation test A test to determine the liability of the principal; if the agent's motivation is committing the intentional tort to promote the principal's business, then the principal is liable for any injury caused by the tort.

The Work-Related Test
Some jurisdictions have rejected the motivation test as too narrow. These jurisdictions apply the **work-related test** instead. Under this test, if an agent commits an intentional tort within a work-related time or space—for example, during working hours or on the principal's premises—the principal is liable for any injuries caused by the agent's intentional torts. Under this test, the agent's motivation is immaterial.

In the following case, the court applied the work-related test in determining whether an employer was liable for its agent's intentional tort.

work-related test A test to determine the liability of a principal; if an agent commits an intentional tort within a work-related time or space, the principal is liable for any injury caused by the agent's intentional tort.

CASE 21.5

Desert Cab Inc. v. Marino
823 P.2d 898 (1992) Supreme Court of Nevada

Facts On October 6, 1986, Maria Marino, a cab driver with Yellow-Checkered Cab Company (Yellow Cab), and James Edwards, a cab driver with Desert Cab Company (Desert Cab), parked their cabs at the taxicab stand at the Sundance Hotel and Casino in Las Vegas to await fares. Marino's cab occupied the first position in the line and Edwards occupied the third. As Marino stood alongside her cab conversing with the driver of another taxi, Edwards began *continued* verbally harassing her from inside his cab. When Marino approached Edwards to inquire as to the reason for the harassment, a verbal argument ensued. Edwards jumped from his cab, grabbed Marino by her neck and shoulders, began choking her, and threw her in front of his taxicab. A bystander pulled Edwards off of Marino and escorted her back to her cab. Marino sustained injuries that rendered her unable to work for a time. Edwards was convicted of misdemeanor assault and battery. Marino brought a personal injury action against Desert Cab. The jury found Desert Cab liable and awarded Marino $65,000. Desert Cab appealed.

Issue Is Desert Cab liable for the intentional tort of its employee?

Decision Yes. The appellate court held that Desert Cab was liable for the intentional tort committed by its employee.

Reason Under the doctrine of respondent superior, an employer is liable for the intentional torts committed by its employees within the scope of their employment. For liability to be imposed on the employer, the intentional tort must be work-related. The court held that Edwards' intentional conduct of assault and battery against Marino was work related and Desert Cab was therefore liable to Marino.

CASE QUESTIONS

Critical Legal Thinking Should employers be held liable for the intentional torts of their employees?

Ethics Did Desert Cab act ethically in denying liability?

Business Implication Should employers give prospective employees psychological examinations to determine if they have any dangerous propensities?

LIABILITY FOR INDEPENDENT CONTRACTORS' TORTS

BUSINESS BRIEF

A principal is generally not liable for the tortious conduct of independent contractors it hires. However, a principal is liable for the tortious conduct of an independent contractor involving (1) a nondelegable duty, (2) a special risk, or (3) the negligent selection of the independent contractor.

A principal generally is not liable for the torts of its independent contractors. Independent contractors are personally liable for their own torts. The rationale behind this rule is that principals do not control the means by which the results are accomplished. Nevertheless, there are several exceptions to this rule:

- **Nondelegable duties.** Certain duties may not be delegated. For example, railroads owe a duty to maintain safe railroad crossings. They cannot escape this liability by assigning the task to an independent contractor.
- **Special risks.** Principals cannot avoid strict liability for dangerous activities assigned to independent contractors. For example, the use of explosives, clearing land by fire, crop dusting, and such involve special risks that are shared by the principal.
- **Negligence in the selection of an independent contractor.** A principal who hires an unqualified or knowingly dangerous person as an independent contractor is liable if that person injures someone while on the job.

In the following case, the court had to decide whether a duty was nondelegable.

CASE 21.6

MBank El Paso, N.A. v. Sanchez
836 S.W.2d 151 (1992) Supreme Court of Texas

Facts Yvonne Sanchez borrowed money from MBank El Paso (MBank) to purchase an automobile. She gave MBank a security interest in the vehicle to secure the loan. When Sanchez defaulted on the loan MBank hired El Paso Recovery Service, an independent contractor, to repossess the automobile. The

two men who were dispatched to Sanchez's house found the car parked in the driveway, and hooked it to a tow truck. Sanchez demanded that they cease their efforts and leave the premises, but the men nonetheless continued with the repossession. Before the men could tow the automobile into the street,

Sanchez jumped into the car, locked the doors, and refused to leave. The men towed the car at a high rate of speed to the repossession yard. They parked the car in the fenced repossession yard, with Sanchez inside, and padlocked the gate. Sanchez was left in the repossession lot with a Doberman Pinscher guard dog loose in the yard. Later, she was rescued by the police. The law prohibits the repossession of a vehicle if a breach of peace would occur. Sanchez filed suit against MBank, alleging that it was liable for the tortious conduct of El Paso Recovery Service. The trial court granted summary judgment to MBank, but the court of appeals reversed. MBank appealed.

Issue Is the repossession of a vehicle an inherently dangerous activity in which a secured creditor remains liable for the physical harm resulting from the repossessor's tortious conduct?

Decision Yes. The supreme court of Texas held that MBank, the principal, was liable for the tortious conduct of El Paso Recovery Service, an independent contractor.

Reason The court held that the act of repossessing an automobile from a defaulting debtor is an inherently dangerous activity and a nondelegable duty. The court concluded that El Paso Recovery Service had breached the peace in repossessing the car from Sanchez and caused her physical and emotional harm. The court held that MBank, the principal, could not escape liability by hiring an independent contractor to do this task. The court found MBank liable to Sanchez.

CASE QUESTIONS

Critical Legal Thinking Should a principal remain liable for certain "nondelegable" duties even though these duties are assigned to independent contractors to perform? Why or why not?

Ethics Did MBank act ethically in trying to escape liability in this case? Explain.

Business Implication What are the benefits of assigning tasks to independent contractors to perform rather than to employees to perform? Are there detriments in doing so?

CRIMINAL LIABILITY OF PRINCIPALS AND AGENTS

Principals and agents are personally liable for their own criminal conduct. However, a principal generally is not criminally liable for the common law crimes (murder, rape, and such) committed by its agents because the requisite criminal intent (mens rea) is not present. In other words, a principal who is unaware of the crimes committed by its agents cannot be found criminally liable because he could not have intended the crimes to be committed.

There are several exceptions to this rule. Principals are criminally liable for the crimes of their agents if they (1) direct or approve of the crime, (2) participate or assist in the commission of the crime, or (3) violate a regulatory statute (e.g., antitrust law). Because corporations and businesses cannot be put in jail, criminal penalties against corporate or business principals usually consist of sanctions such as fines or the loss or suspension of necessary licenses.

BUSINESS BRIEF
An employer may try to characterize an employment relationship as that of a principal–independent contractor to avoid tort liability of the contractor. The injured plaintiff, on the other hand, may try to characterize it as a principal–agent relationship so the employer will be held liable for the agent's torts.

TERMINATION OF AN AGENCY

An agency contract is similar to other contracts in that it can be terminated either by an act of the parties or by operation of law. These different methods of terminations are discussed next. Note that when an agency relationship is terminated, the agent can no longer represent the principal or bind the principal to contracts.

Termination by Acts of the Parties

The parties to an agency contract can terminate an agency contract by agreement or by their actions. The four methods of termination of an agency relationship by **acts of the parties** are explained in the following subsections.

termination by acts of the parties An agency may be terminated by the following acts of the parties: (1) mutual agreement, (2) lapse of time, (3) purpose achieved, and (4) occurrence of a specified event.

Mutual Agreement As with any contract, the parties to an agency contract can mutually agree to terminate their agreement. By doing so, the parties relieve each other of any further rights, duties, obligations, or powers provided for in the agency contract. Either party can propose the termination of an agency contract.

Lapse of Time Agency contracts are often written for a specific period of time. The agency terminates when the specified time period elapses. Suppose, for example, that the principal and agent enter into an agency contract "beginning January 1, 1998 and ending December 31, 2000." The agency automatically terminates on December 31, 2000. If the agency contract does not set forth a specific termination date, the agency terminates after a reasonable time has elapsed. The courts often look to the custom of an industry in determining the reasonable time for the termination of the agency.

Purpose Achieved A principal can employ an agent for the time it takes to accomplish a certain task, purpose, or result. Such agencies automatically terminate when they are completed. For example, suppose a principal employs a licensed real estate broker to sell his house. The agency terminates when the house is sold and the principal pays the broker the agreed-upon compensation.

Occurrence of a Specified Event An agency contract can specify that the agency exists until a specified event occurs. The agency terminates when the specified event happens. For example, if a principal employs an agent to take care of her dog until she returns from a trip, the agency terminates when the principal returns from the trip.

BUSINESS CHECKLIST

Required Notification of the Termination of an Agency

If the agency is terminated by agreement between the parties, the principal is under a duty to give certain third parties notification of the termination. Unless otherwise required, the notice can be from the principal or some other source (e.g., the agent). If an agency terminates by operation of law, there is no duty to notify third parties about the termination, however.

The termination of an agency extinguishes an agent's actual authority to act on the principal's behalf. However, if the principal fails to give the proper notice of termination to a third party, the agent still has apparent authority to bind the principal to contracts with these third parties. If this happens, the contract is enforceable against the principal. The principal's only recourse is against the agent to recover damages caused by these unauthorized contracts.

The following notification requirements must be met:

* **Parties who dealt with the agent.** Direct notice of termination must be given to all persons with whom the agent dealt. Although the notice may be either written or oral, it is better practice to give written notice.
* **Parties who have knowledge of the agency.** The principal must give direct or constructive notice to any third party who has knowledge of the agency but with whom the agent has not dealt. **Direct notice** often is in the form of a letter. **Constructive notice** usually consists of placing a notice of the termina-

> tion of the agency in a newspaper serving the relevant community. This notice is effective even against persons who do not see it.
> - **Parties who have no knowledge of the agency.** Generally, a principal is not obligated to give notice of termination to strangers who have no knowledge of the agency. However, a principal who has given the agent written authority to act but fails to recover the writing upon termination of the agency may be liable to strangers who later rely on this writing and deal with the agent. The laws of most states provide that this liability can be avoided by giving constructive notice (e.g., newspaper announcement) of the termination of the agency.

Termination by Operation of Law

Agency contracts can be terminated by **operation of law** as well as by agreement. The six methods of termination an agency relationship by operation of law are discussed in the following subsections.

Death The death of either the principal or the agent terminates the agency relationship. This rule is based on the old legal principle that because a dead person cannot act, no one can act for him or her. Note that the agency terminates even if one party is unaware of the other party's death. An agent's actions that take place after the principal's death do not bind the principal's estate.

Insanity The insanity of either the principal or the agent generally terminates the agency relationship. A few states have modified this rule to provide that a contract entered into by agent on behalf of an insane principal is enforceable if (1) the insane person has not been adjudged insane, (2) the third party does not have knowledge of the principal's insanity at the time of contracting, and (3) the enforcement of the contract will prevent injustice.

Bankruptcy The agency relationship is terminated if the principal is declared bankrupt. Bankruptcy requires the filing of a petition for bankruptcy under federal bankruptcy law. With few exceptions, neither the appointment of a state court receiver nor the principal's financial difficulties or insolvency terminates the agency relationship. The agent's bankruptcy usually does not terminate an agency unless the agency's credit standing is important to the agency relationship.

Impossibility The agency relationship terminates if a situation arises that makes its fulfillment impossible. The following circumstances can lead to termination on this ground:

- **The loss or destruction of the subject matter of the agency.** For example, assume that a principal employs an agent to sell his horse, but the horse dies before it is sold. The agency relationship terminates at the moment the horse dies.
- **The loss of a required qualification.** For example, suppose a principal employs a licensed real estate agent to sell her house and the real estate agent's license is revoked. The agency terminates at the moment the license is revoked.
- **A change in the law.** For example, suppose that a principal employs an agent to trap alligators. If a law is passed that makes trapping alligators illegal, the agency contract terminates when the law becomes effective.

Changed Circumstances An agency terminates when there is an unusual change in circumstances that would lead the agent to believe that the principal's original instructions should no longer be valid. For example, a principal employs a licensed

termination by operation of law An agency is terminated by operation of law, including: (1) death of the principal or agent, (2) insanity of the principal or agent, (3) bankruptcy of the principal, (4) impossibility of performance, (5) changed circumstances, and (6) war between the principal's and agent's countries.

real estate agent to sell a farm for $100,000. The agent thereafter learns that oil has been discovered on the property that makes it worth $1 million. The agency terminates because of this change in circumstances.

War The outbreak of a war between the principal's country and the agent's country terminates the agency relationship between the parties. Such an occurrence usually makes the performance of the agency contract impossible.

Wrongful Termination of an Agency Contract

Generally, agency contracts that do not specify a definite time for their termination can be terminated at will by either the principal or the agent without liability to the other party. When a principal terminates an agency contract, it is called a **revocation of authority**. When an agent terminates an agency, it is called a **renunciation of authority**.

Unless an agency is irrevocable, both the principal and the agent have an individual power to terminate any agency contract unilaterally. Note that having the power to terminate an agency agreement is not the same as having the right to terminate it. The **unilateral termination** of an agency contract may be wrongful. If the principal's or agent's termination of an agency contract breaches the contract, the other party can sue for damages for **wrongful termination**.

CONSIDER THIS EXAMPLE: A principal employs a licensed real estate agent to sell his house. The agency contract gives the agent an exclusive listing for three months. After one month, the principal unilaterally terminates the agency. The principal has the power to do so, and the agent can no longer act on behalf of the principal. However, because the principal did not have the right to terminate the contract, the agent can sue him and recover damages (i.e., lost commission) for wrongful termination.

Irrevocable Agency

An **agency coupled with an interest** is a special type of agency relationship that is created for the agent's benefit. This type of agency is **irrevocable** by the principal (e.g., the principal cannot terminate it). An agency coupled with an interest is commonly used in security agreements to secure loans.

CONSIDER THIS EXAMPLE: Heidi Norville owns a piece of real estate. She goes to Wells Fargo Bank to obtain a loan on the property. The bank makes the loan but requires her to sign a security agreement (e.g., a mortgage) pledging the property as collateral for the loan. The security agreement contains a clause that appoints that bank as Ms. Norville's agent and permits the bank to sell the property and recover the amount of the loan from the sale proceeds if she defaults on her payments. This agency is irrevocable by Ms. Norville, the principal.

An agency coupled with an interest is not terminated by the death or incapacity of either the principal or the agent. It terminates only when the agent's obligations are performed. However, the parties can expressly agree that an agency coupled with an interest is terminated.

---

revocation of authority
When a principal terminates an agency contract.

renunciation of authority
When an agent terminates an agency.

wrongful termination
The termination of an agency contract in violation of the terms of the agency contract. The nonbreaching party may recover damages from the breaching party.

CAUTION
The distinction between the power *and the* right *to terminate an agency is critical. Be certain it is clear.*

agency coupled with an interest A special type of agency relationship that is created for the agent's benefit; irrevocable by the principal.

INTERNATIONAL PERSPECTIVE

Foreign Agents and Distributors

Before a business can sell internationally, it must decide what form the international aspects of its business should operate under. The simplest way of conducting international business is to engage in direct export or import sales. For example, if Flour Corporation wishes to sell equipment overseas, it can merely enter into a contract with a company in a foreign country that wishes to buy the equipment. Flour Corporation is the **exporter** and the firm in the foreign country is the **importer**. If a U.S. company buys goods from a firm in a foreign country, the roles are reversed: The U.S. company is the importer and the foreign country is the exporter. The benefits of conducting international business this way are that it is inexpensive and usually just involves contracts and possible documents of exchange. Such sales might be subject to import or export restrictions, however.

Often, the business in a foreign country will appoint a local agent or sales representative to represent it in the foreign country. A **sales representative** may solicit and take orders for his or her foreign employer but does not have the authority to bind the company contractually. A **sales agent**, on the other hand, may enter into contracts on his or her foreign employer's behalf. The scope of a sales agent's or representative's authority should be explicitly stated in the employment agreement. Sales agents and representatives do not take title to the goods. They are usually paid commissions for business that they generate. Companies may use foreign sales agents or representatives because it is required by law in the other country or it is the most commercially feasible way to conduct business in that country.

Another commonly used form for engaging in international sales is through a **foreign distributor**. The distributor is usually a local firm and is separate and independent from the exporter. Distributors take title to the goods. They are usually given an exclusive territory (e.g., a country or portion of a country). Distributors make a profit on reselling the goods in the foreign country. A foreign distributor is usually used when a company wants a greater presence in a foreign market than is possible through a sales agent or representative.

The benefits to the exporter of using a distributor are that it (1) saves the investment of having to establish a branch or subsidiary in the foreign country, (2) places most of the risk of loss on the distributor, (3) avoids laws against foreign investment, and (4) insulates the exporter against tort and contract liability because the foreign distributor is an independent contractor and not an employee.

WORKING THE WEB

U.S. Small Business Administration This site is a one stop shop for information about Small Business Administration programs and services.

Visit at http://www.sbaonline.sba.gov/

Restatement of the Law of Agency The Restatement of the Law Second Agency deals with the relations between principal and agent, principal and third person, and agent and third person. It was developed by the American Law Institute.

Visit at http://www.ali.org/ali/Agency.htm

FLSA Home Page This Web site contains lots of valuable information dealing with the federal Fair Labor Standards Act.

Visit at http://www.albany.net/~chk/chk.htm

U.S. Department of Labor The U.S. Department of Labor has a Web site full of employment-related information.

Visit at http://www.dol.gov/

Employment Standards Administration The Employment Standards Administration Web site contains information and links to information about labor standards.

Visit at http://www.dol.gov/dol/esa/

CYBER EXERCISES:
1. Check out the Internet Business Cards on the Small Business Administration site.
2. Is a third Restatement of the Law of Agency currently under development?
3. Using the FLSA Web site, find information about exempt and nonexempt employees.
4. Find information about Welfare to Work on the U.S. Department of Labor Web site.
5. Find the Family and Medical Leave Act on the Employment Standards Administration Web site.

CHAPTER SUMMARY

THE NATURE OF AGENCY, P. 494

The Nature of Agency	1. *Agency.* A fiduciary relationship which results from the manifestation of consent by one person to act on behalf of another person with that person's consent.
	2. *Parties:*
	   a. *Principal.* Party who employs another person to act on his or her behalf.
	   b. *Agent.* Party who agrees to act on behalf of another person.

KINDS OF EMPLOYMENT RELATIONSHIPS, P. 495

Employer–Employee Relationship	An employer (master) hires an employee (servant) to perform some form of physical service. An employee is not an agent unless the principal authorizes him or her to enter into contracts on the principal's behalf.
Principal–Agent Relationship	An employer hires an employee and authorizes the employee to enter into contracts on the employer's behalf.
Principal-Independent Contractor Relationship	Principal employs a person who is not an employee of the principal. The independent contractor has authority only to enter into contracts authorized by the principal.

FORMATION OF THE AGENCY RELATIONSHIP, P. 497

Express Agency	Principal and agent expressly agree in words to enter into an agency agreement. The agency contract may be oral or written unless the Statute of Frauds requires it to be in writing.
Implied Agency	An agency is implied (inferred) from the conduct of the parties.
Apparent Agency	Arises when a principal creates an appearance of an agency that in actuality does not exist. Also called *agency by estoppel* or *ostensible agency*.
Agency by Ratification	Occurs when a person misrepresents him- or herself as another's agent when he or she is not and the purported principal ratifies (accepts) the unauthorized act.

AGENT'S DUTIES, P. 501

Duty of Performance	Performance of the lawful duties expressed in the agency contract with reasonable care, skill, and diligence.
Duty of Notification	Agent owes duty to notify principal of any information he learns that is important to the agency. Information learned by the agent in the course of the agency is *imputed* to the principal.
Duty of Loyalty	Agent's duty not to act adversely to the interests of the principal. The most common breaches of loyalty are: 1. *Dual agency.* Agency cannot act on behalf of two different principals in same transaction unless the principals agree. 2. *Usurping an opportunity.* Agent cannot usurp (take) an opportunity belonging to the principal as his or her own. 3. *Self-dealing.* Agent cannot deal with the principal unless his or her position is disclosed, and the principal agrees to deal with the agent. 4. *Misuse of confidential information.* Agent is under a legal duty not to disclose or misuse confidential information learned within the course of an agency.

	5. *Competing with the principal.* Agents are prohibited from competing with the principal during the course of an agency unless the principal agrees.
Duty of Obedience	Agent must obey the lawful instructions of the principal during the performance of the agency.
Duty of Accountability	Agent must maintain an accurate accounting of all transactions undertaken on the principal's behalf. A principal may demand an accounting from the agent at any time.

PRINCIPAL'S DUTIES, P. 504

Duty of Compensation	Principal must pay the agent agreed-upon compensation. If there is not agreement, the principal must pay what is customary in the industry or, if there is no custom, then the reasonable value of the services.
Duties of Reimbursement and Indemnification	Principal must *reimburse* an agent for all expenses paid that were authorized by the principal, within the scope of the agency, and necessary to discharge the agent's duties. The principal must *indemnify* the agent for any losses suffered because of the principal's acts.
Duty of Cooperation	The principal must cooperate with and assist the agent in the performance of the agent's duties and the accomplishment of the agency.
Duty to Provide Safe Working Conditions	Principal must provide safe working conditions, warn agents of dangerous conditions, and repair and remedy unsafe conditions.

CONTRACT LIABILITY TO THIRD PARTIES, P. 505

Fully Disclosed Agency	The third party into the contract knows that the agent is acting for a principal and knows the identity of the principal. The principal is liable on the contract; the agent is not liable on the contract.
Partially Disclosed Agency	The third party knows that the agent is acting for a principal but does not know the identity of the principal. Both the principal and the agent are liable on the contract.
Undisclosed Agency	The third party does not know that the agent is acting for a principal. Both the principal and the agent are liable on the contract.

TORT LIABILITY TO THIRD PARTIES, P. 508

Tort Liability	Principals are liable for the *tortious conduct* of an agent who is acting within the *scope of his or her authority.* Liability is imposed for misrepresentation, negligence, and intentional torts.
Misrepresentation	Principals are liable for intentional and innocent misrepresentations made by an agent acting within the scope of his of her employment.
Negligence	Principals are liable for the negligent conduct of agents acting within the scope of their employment. Special negligence doctrines include: 1. *Frolic and detour.* Principals are generally relieved of liability if the agent's negligent act occurred on a substantial frolic and detour from the scope of employment. 2. *Coming and going* rule. Principals are not liable if the agent's tortious conduct occurred while on the way to or from work. 3. *Dual-purpose mission.* If the agent is acting on his or her own behalf and on behalf of the principal, the principal is generally liable for the agent's tortious conduct.

Intentional Torts	States apply one of the following rules: 1. *Motivation test.* The principal is liable if the agent's intentional tort was committed to promote the principal's business. 2. *Work-related test.* The principal is liable if the agent's intentional tort was committed within a work-related time or space. Agents are personally liable for their own tortious conduct.

LIABILITY FOR INDEPENDENT CONTRACTOR'S TORTS, P. 512

Liability for Independent Contractor's Torts	Generally, principals are not liable for the tortious conduct of independent contractors. Exceptions to the rule are for: 1. *Nondelegable duties* 2. *Special risks* 3. *Negligence in selecting an independent contractor.* Independent contractors are personally liable for their own torts.

CRIMINAL LIABILITY OF PRINCIPALS AND AGENTS, P. 513

Criminal Liability of Principals and Agents	Principals generally are not liable for the common law crimes of their agents unless the principal (1) directed or approved of the crime, (2) participated or assisted in the commission of the crime, or (3) the crime violated a regulatory statute. Agents are personally liable for their own criminal conduct.

TERMINATION OF AN AGENCY, P. 513

Termination by Acts of the Parties	The following *acts of the parties* terminate agency contracts: 1. *Mutual agreement.* Parties mutually agree to terminate an agency contract. 2. *Lapse of time.* The stipulated time period of the agency expires. 3. *Purpose achieved.* The stipulated purpose of the agency is achieved. 4. *Occurrence of a specified event.* The occurrence of a stipulated event happens.
Termination by Operation of Law	Agency contracts can be terminated by *operation of law*. This includes the following methods: 1. *Death.* Death of either the principal or the agent. 2. *Insanity.* Insanity of either the principal or the agent. 3. *Bankruptcy.* Bankruptcy of the principal. 4. *Impossibility.* A situation arises that makes the performance of the agency contract impossible. 5. *Changed circumstances.* An unusual circumstance would lead the agent to believe that the principal's original instructions are no longer valid. 6. *War.* Outbreak of war between the principal's country and the agent's country.
Notification of Termination	If an agency is terminated by agreement between the parties, the principal must notify third parties as follows: 1. *Parties who deal with the agent.* Direct notice must be given to these parties. 2. *Parties who have knowledge of the agency.* Direct or constructive (e.g., public notice in newspapers) notice must be given to these parties. 3. *Parties who have no knowledge of the agency.* No notice need be given to these parties.

	If the proper notice of the termination of the agency is not given, the agent has *apparent authority* to bind the principal to contracts. The principal and agent each have the *power* to terminate an agency at any time. After termination, the agent can no longer act on behalf of the principal. The terminating party may not, however, have had the *right* to terminate the agency, and may be held liable for damages caused by *wrongful termination* of the agency.
Wrongful Termination of an Agency Contract	If an agency is for an agreed-upon term or purpose, the *unilateral termination* of the agency contract by either the principal or the agent constitutes the *wrongful termination* of the agency. The breaching party is liable to the other party for damages caused by the breach.
Irrevocable Agency	An *agency with an interest* is a special type of agency that is irrevocable by the principal. Commonly used in security interests to secure loans.

CRITICAL LEGAL THINKING CASES

21.1 Creation of an Agency Renaldo, Inc., dba Baker Street, owns and operates a nightclub in Georgia. On the evening in question plaintiff Ginn became "silly drunk" at the nightclub and was asked by several patrons and the manager to leave the premises. The police were called and Ginn left the premises. When Ginn realized that his jacket was still in the night club, he attempted to reenter the premises. He was met at the door by the manager, who refused him admittance. When Ginn persisted, an unidentified patron, without the approval of the manager, pushed Ginn, who lost his balance and fell backward. To break his fall, Ginn put his hand against the door jamb. The unidentified patron slammed the door on Ginn's hand and held it shut for several minutes. Ginn, who suffered severe injuries to his right hand, sued the nightclub for damages. Was the unidentified patron an agent of the nightclub? [*Ginn v. Renaldo, Inc.*, 359 S.E.2d 390 (Ga. App. 1987)]

21.2 Independent Contractor The Butler Telephone Company, Inc. (Butler) contracted with the Sandidge Construction Company (Sandidge) to lay 18 miles of telephone cable in a rural area. In the contract, Butler reserved the right to inspect the work for compliance with the terms of the contract. Butler did not control how Sandidge performed the work. Johnnie Carl Pugh, an employee of Sandidge, was killed on the job when the sides to an excavation in which he was working caved in on top of him. Evidence disclosed that the excavation was not properly shored or sloped and that it violated general safety standards. Pugh's parents and estate brought a wrongful death action against Butler. Is Butler liable? [*Pugh v. Butler Telephone Company, Inc.*, 512 So.2d 1317 (Ala. 1987)]

21.3 Independent Contractor Mercedes Connolly and her husband purchased airline tickets and a tour package for a tour to South Africa from Judy Samuelson, a travel agent doing business as International Tours of Manhattan. Samuelson sold tickets for a variety of airline companies and tour operators, including African Adventurers, that was the tour operator for Connolly's tour. Connolly injured her left ankle and foot on September 27, 1984, while the tour group was on a walking tour to see hippopotami in a river at the Sabi Sabi Game Reserve. Connolly fell while trying to cross a six-inch-deep stream. She sued Samuelson for damages. Is Samuelson liable? [*Connolly v. Samuelson*, 671 F.Supp. 1312 (D.Kan. 1987)]

21.4 Implied Agency Tom and Judith Sullivan owned real property on which they obtained a loan from the Federal Land Bank of Omaha (FLB). The property secured the loan. The Sullivans defaulted on the loan, and the FLB brought an action to foreclose on the mortgage. The FLB's lawyer wrote a letter to the Sullivans outlining a settlement offer. A copy of the letter was sent to the FLB's regional office located in Yankton, South Dakota. The regional office did not notify the attorney that he did not have authority to offer the settlement without its permission. When the Sullivans accepted the settlement offer, the FLB regional office refused to approve the deal. The Sullivans sued to enforce it. Did the attorney for the FLB have authority to settle the case? [*Federal Land Bank of Omaha v. Sullivan*, 430 N.W.2d 700 (S.D. 1988)] *yes - this is actual authority*

21.5 Apparent Agency Gene Mohr and James Loyd each own 50 percent of Tri-County Farm Equipment Company (Tri-County). Tri-County has its depository bank account at First National Bank of Olathe, Kansas. Loyd also personally owns an oil business known as Earthworm Energy (Earthworm), which has its bank account at the State Bank of Stanley. Neither Mohr nor Tri-County have any ownership interest in Earthworm. Mohr did not indicate to the State Bank of Stanley that Loyd had any authority to sign checks personally on behalf of Tri-County. In 1982, Loyd took eight checks that were payable to Tri-County and endorsed and deposited them into Earthworm's account at the State Bank of Stanley. Mohr brought an action for conversion against the State Bank of Stanley to recover the amount of the checks. The bank argued in defense that Loyd had apparent authority to deposit the checks in his personal business account. Did Loyd possess apparent authority? [*Mohr v. State Bank of Stanley*, 734 P.2d 1071 (Kan. 1987)]

no

21.6 Ratification After Francis Pusateri retired, he met with Gilbert J. Johnson, a stockbroker with E. F. Hutton & Co., Inc., and informed Johnson that he wished to invest in tax-free bonds and money market accounts. Pusateri opened an investment account with E. F. Hutton and checked the box stating his objective was "tax-free income and moderate growth." During the course of a year, Johnson churned Pusateri's funds in volatile securities and options. Johnson kept telling Pusateri that his account was making money, and the monthly statement from E. F. Hutton did not indicate otherwise. The manager at E. F. Hutton was aware of Johnson's activities but did nothing to prevent them. When Johnson left E. F. Hutton, Pusateri's account—which had been called the "laughingstock" of the office—had shrunk from $196,000 to $96,880. Pusateri sued E. F. Hutton for damages. Is E. F. Hutton liable? [*Pusateri v. E. F. Hutton & Co., Inc.*, 225 C.R. 526 (Cal. App. 1986)]

21.7 Reasonable Care and Skill Norman R. Barton and his wife decided to vacation in Florida in November 1984. In March 1984, they contacted Wonderful World of Travel, Inc., a travel agency licensed by the state of Ohio, to make the arrangements. They requested a room with a view of the ocean, a kitchenette so they would be saved the expense of dining out, free parking, and a free spa. In August, with the Barton's approval, the travel agency made reservations at the Beau Rivage motel in Bal Harbour, Florida. The travel agency did not confirm the reservations prior to the Bartons' departure in November. When the Bartons arrived at the motel, they found it closed, chained, and guarded. The only other hotel or motel in the area was a Sheraton, which was almost triple the room cost of the Beau Rivage. The Sheraton overlooked the ocean, but it did not have a kitchenette, free parking, or free spa privileges. The Bartons stayed at the Sheraton. They sued the travel agent upon their return. Is the travel agent liable for the increased costs incurred by the Bartons? [*Barton v. Wonderful World of Travel, Inc.*, 502 N.E.2d 715 (Ohio Mun. 1986)]

21.8 Imputed Knowledge On March 31, 1981, Iota Management Corporation (Iota) entered into a contract to purchase the Bel Air West Motor Hotel in the City of St. Louis from Boulevard Investment Company (Boulevard). The agreement contained the following warranty: "Seller has no actual notice of any substantial defect in the structure of the Hotel or in any of its plumbing, heating, air-conditioning, electrical, or utility systems."

When the buyer inspected the premises, no leaks in the pipes were visible. Iota purchased the hotel for $2 million. When Iota removed some of the walls and ceilings during remodeling, it found evidence of prior repairs to leaking pipes and ducts, as well as devices for catching water (e.g., milk cartons, cookie sheets, and buckets). The estimate to repair these leaks was $500,000. Evidence at trial showed that Cecil Lillib-

ridge, who was Boulevard's maintenance supervisor from 1975 until the sale of the hotel in 1981, had actual knowledge of these problems and had repaired some of the pipes. Iota sued Boulevard to rescind the contract. Is Boulevard liable? [*Iota Management Corporation v. Boulevard Investment Company*, 731 S.W.2d 399 (Mo. App. 1987)]

21.9 Dual Agency Chemical Bank is the primary bank for Washington Steel Corporation (Washington Steel). As an agent for Washington Steel, Chemical Bank expressly and impliedly promised that it would advance the best interests and welfare of Washington Steel. During the course of the agency, Washington Steel provided the bank with comprehensive and confidential financial information, other data, and future business plans.

At some point during the agency, TW Corporation (TW) and others approached Chemical Bank to request a loan of $7 million to make a hostile tender offer for the stock of Washington Steel. Chemical Bank agreed and became an agent for TW. Management at Chemical Bank did not disclose its adverse relationship with TW to Washington Steel, did not request Washington Steel's permission to act as an agent for TW, and directed employees of the bank to conceal the bank's involvement with TW from Washington Steel. After TW commenced its public tender offer, Washington Steel filed suit seeking to obtain an injunction against Chemical Bank and TW. Who wins? [*Washington Steel Corporation v. TW Corporation*, 465 F.Supp. 1100 (W.D.Pa. 1979)]

21.10 Duty of Loyalty Peter Shields was the president and member of the board of directors of Production Finishing Corporation (Production Finishing) from 1974 through August 1981. The company provided steel polishing services. It did most, if not all, of the polishing work in the Detroit area except for that of the Ford Motor Company (Ford). (Ford did its own polishing.) Shields discussed this matter with Ford on behalf of Production Finishing on several occasions. When Shields learned that Ford was discontinuing its polishing operation, he incorporated Flat Rock Metal and submitted a confidential proposal to Ford that provided that he would buy Ford's equipment and provide polishing services to Ford. It was not until he resigned from Production Finishing that he informed the board of directors that he was pursuing the Ford business himself. Production Finishing sued Shields. Did Shields breach his fiduciary duty of loyalty to Production Finishing? [*Production Finishing Corporation v. Shields*, 405 N.W.2d 171 (Mich. App. 1987)] *yes*

21.11 Personal Guaranty In May 1978, Sebastian International, Inc. (Sebastian) entered into a five-year lease for a building in Chadsworth, California. In September 1980, with the consent of the master lessors, Sebastian sublet the building to West Valley Grinding, Inc. (West Valley). In conjunction with the execution of the sublease, the corporate officers of West Valley, including Kenneth E. Peck, each signed a guaranty of lease personally assuring the payment of West Valley's rental obligations. The guaranty contract referred to Peck in his individual capacity; however, on the signature line he was identified as "Kenneth Peck, Vice President." In May 1981, West Valley went out of business, leaving 24 months remaining on the sublease. After unsuccessful attempts to secure another subleasee, Sebastian surrendered the leasehold back to the master lessors and brought suit against Peck to recover the unpaid rent. Peck argued he was not personally liable because his signature was that of an agent for a disclosed principal and not that of a principal himself. Who wins? [*Sebastian International, Inc. v. Peck*, 195 C.A.3d 803, 240 C.R. 911 (Cal. App. 1987)]

21.12 Contract Liability G. Elvin Grinder of Marbury, Maryland, was a building contractor who, prior to May 1, 1973, did business as an individual and traded as "Grinder Construction." Grinder maintained an open account, on his individual credit, with Bryans Road Building & Supply Co., Inc. (Bryans). Grinder would purchase materials and supplies from Bryans on credit and later pay the invoices. On May 1, 1973, G. Elvin Grinder Construction, Inc., a Maryland corporation, was formed with Grinder personally owning 52 percent of the stock of the corporation. Grinder did not inform Bryans that he had incorporated and continued to purchase supplies on credit from Bryans under the name "Grinder Construction." In May 1978, after certain invoices were not paid by Grinder, Bryans sued Grinder personally to recover. Grinder asserted that the debts were owed by the corporation. Bryans amended its complaint to include the corporation as a defendant. Who is liable to Bryans? [*Grinder v. Bryans Road Building & Supply Co., Inc.*, 432 A.2d 453 (Md. App. 1981)]

21.13 Contract Liability In the spring of 1974, certain residents of Harrisville, Utah, organized the Golden Spike Little League for the youngsters of the town. This was an unincorporated association. David Anderson and several other organizers contracted with Smith & Edwards, a sporting goods store, that agreed to give them favorable prices on merchandise. During the course of the summer, parents went into Smith & Edwards and picked up uniforms and equipment for their children and other Little Leaguers. At the end of the summer, Smith and Edwards sent them a bill for $3,900. Fund-raising activities produced only $149, and the organizers refused to pay the difference. Smith & Edwards sued Anderson and the other organizers for the unpaid balance. Are the organizers personally liable for the debt? [*Smith & Edwards v. Anderson*, 557 P.2d 132 (Utah 1978)]

21.14 Tort Liability Intrastate Radiotelephone, Inc. (Intrastate) is a public utility that supplies radiotelephone utility service to the general public for radiotelephones, pocket pagers, and beepers. Robert Kranhold, an employee of Intrastate, was authorized to use his personal vehicle on company business. On the morning of March 9, 1976, when Kranhold was driving his vehicle to Intrastate's main office, he negligently struck a motorcycle being driven by Michael S. Largey, causing severe and permanent injuries to Largey. The accident occurred at the intersection where Intrastate's main office is located. Evidence showed that Kranhold acted as a consultant to Intrastate, worked both in and out of Intrastate's offices, and had no set hours of work, often attended meetings at Intrastate's offices, and went to Intrastate's offices to pick things up or drop things off. Largey sued Intrastate for damages. Is Intrastate liable? [*Largey v. Radiotelephone, Inc.*, 136 C.A.3d 660, 186 C.R. 520 (Cal. App. 1982)] Yes, they are

Vicariously liable

ETHICS CASES

21.15 The Hagues, husband and wife, owned a 160-acre tract that they decided to sell. On March 19, 1976, they entered into a listing agreement with Harvey C. Hilgendorf, a licensed real estate broker, which gave Hilgendorf the exclusive right to sell the property for a period of 12 months. Hague agreed to pay Hilgendorf a commission of 6 percent of the accepted sale price if a bona fide buyer was found during the listing period.

By letter of August 13, 1976, Hague terminated the listing agreement with Hilgendorf. Hilgendorf did not acquiesce to Hague's termination, however. On September 30, 1976, Hilgendorf presented an offer to the Hagues from a buyer willing to purchase the property at the full listing price. The Hagues ignored the offer and sold the property to another buyer. Hilgendorf sued the Hagues for breach of the agency agreement. Did the Hagues act ethically in this case? Who wins the lawsuit? [*Hilgendorf v. Hague*, 293 N.W.2d 272 (Iowa 1980)]

21.16 The National Biscuit Company (Nabisco) is a corporation that produces and distributes cookies and other food products to grocery stores and other outlets across the nation. In October 1968, Nabisco hired Ronnell Lynch as a cookie salesman–trainee. On March 1, 1969, Lynch was assigned his own sales territory. Lynch's duties involved making sales calls, taking orders, and making sure that shelves of stores in his territory were stocked with Nabisco products. During the period March 1 to May 1, 1969, Nabisco received numerous complaints from store owners in Lynch's territory that Lynch was overly aggressive and was taking shelf space for Nabisco products that was reserved for competing brands.

On May 1, 1969, Lynch visited a grocery store that was managed by Jerome Lange. Lynch was there to place previously delivered merchandise on the store's shelves. An argument developed between Lynch and Lange. Lynch became very angry and started swearing. Lange, the store manager, told Lynch to stop swearing or leave the store, because children were present. Lynch became uncontrollably angry and went behind the counter and dared Lange to a fight. When Lange refused to fight, Lynch proceeded to viciously assault and batter Lange, causing severe injuries. Lange sued Nabisco. Was it ethical for Nabisco to deny liability in this case? Do you think the prior complaints against Lynch had any effect on the decision reached in this case? Is Nabisco liable for the intentional tort (assault and battery) of its employee, Ronnell Lynch? [*Lange v. National Biscuit Company*, 211 N.W.2d 783 (Minn. 1983)]

CRITICAL LEGAL THINKING WRITING ASSIGNMENT

Read Case A.21 in the Case Appendix [*District of Columbia v. Howell*]. This case is excerpted from the court of appeals opinion. Review and brief the case. In your brief, be sure to answer the following questions:

1. Was A. Louis Jagoe hired by the District of Columbia as an employee or as an independent contractor?

2. Describe the accident that occurred. Who was injured?
3. Normally, an employer is not liable for the tortious conduct of an independent contractor it has hired. Describe the "special risks" exception to this rule.
4. What damages were awarded to the plaintiff?

NOTES
[1] Restatement (Second) of Agency, § 4.
[2] Restatement (Second) of Agency, § 321.

CHAPTER 22

SOLE PROPRIETORSHIPS

AND FRANCHISES

Chapter Objectives

*After studying this chapter,
you should be able to*

1. Define a sole proprietorship and describe how it is created
2. Describe the liability of sole proprietors
3. Define a franchise and the parties to a franchise arrangement
4. List and describe the various forms of franchises
5. Describe the disclosures required by state and federal disclosure rules
6. Describe the rights and duties of the parties to a franchise agreement
7. Explain how a franchisor licenses its trademarks, service marks, and trade secrets to franchisees
8. Identify the contract and tort liability of franchisors and franchisees
9. Define tying arrangements and identify when they are illegal in a franchise arrangement
10. Describe the remedies available for the wrongful termination of a franchise

Chapter Contents

- Sole Proprietorships
- Franchises
- Disclosure Protection
  Contemporary Business Environment Federal Trade Commission Rule
  Business Checklist Required Disclosures of Earnings and Sales Projections by Franchisors
- The Franchise Agreement
  Ethical Perspective Häagen-Dazs Ice Cream Franchise Melts
- Trademark Law, Trade Secrets, and Franchising
  Case 22.1 *Baskin-Robbins Ice Cream Co. v. D&L Ice Cream Co., Inc. (E.D.N.Y.)*
- Contract and Tort Liability of Franchisors and Franchisees
  Case 22.2 *Martin v. McDonald's Corp. (IL)*
  Case 22.3 *Cislaw v. Southland Corp. (CA)*
  Case 22.4 *Holiday Inn, Inc. v. Shelburne (FL)*
- Antitrust Law and Franchising
  Business Application Sports Franchises: I'll Take My Ball and Go Home
- Termination of Franchises
  International Perspective International Franchising
- Working the Web
- Chapter Summary
- Critical Legal Thinking Cases
- Ethics Cases
- Critical Legal Thinking Writing Assignment

> *It has been uniformly laid down in this Court, as far back as we can remember, that good faith is the basis of all mercantile transactions.*
>
> Buller, J.
> *Salomons v. Nissen* (1788)

A person who wants to start a business must decide whether the business should operate as one of the five major forms of business organization—*sole proprietorship, general partnership, limited partnership, corporation*—or some other available legal business form (limited liability company). The selection depends on many factors including the ease and cost of formation, the capital requirements of the business, the flexibility of management decisions, the extent of personal liability, tax considerations, and the like.

Franchising is an important method for distributing goods and services to the public. Originally pioneered by the automobile and soft drink industries, franchising today is used in many other forms of business. The 700,000-plus franchise outlets in the United States account for more than 25 percent of retail sales and about 15 percent of the gross national product (GNP).

This chapter discusses sole proprietorships and franchises in detail. General partnerships, limited partnerships, limited liability companies, and corporations are discussed in chapters 23–27.

SOLE PROPRIETORSHIPS

sole proprietorship
A form of business where the owner is actually the business; the business is not a separate legal entity.

In a **sole proprietorship**, the owner is the business. There is no separate legal entity. Sole proprietorships are the most common form of business organization in the United States. Many small businesses—and a few large ones—operate in this way.

There are several major advantages to operating a business as a sole proprietorship. They include the following:

1. Formation is easy and cost is low
2. The owner has the right to make all management decisions concerning the business, including those involving hiring and firing employees
3. The sole proprietor owns all of the business and has the right to receive all of the business's profits
4. A sole proprietorship can be easily transferred to sold if and when the owner desires to do so; no other approval (such as from partners or shareholders) is necessary

There are important disadvantages to this business form, too. They are (1) the sole proprietor's access to capital is limited to personal funds plus any loans he or she can obtain, and (2) the sole proprietor is legally responsible for the business's contracts, and the torts committed by the proprietor and his or her employees in the course of employment.

Creation of a Sole Proprietorship

It is simple to create a sole proprietorship. There are no formalities, and no federal or state government approval is required. Some local governments require all businesses, including sole proprietorships, to obtain a license to do business within the city. If no other form of business organization is chosen, the business is by default a sole proprietorship.

BUSINESS BRIEF
A sole proprietorship is easy to form and requires no formal filing with state or federal government authorities.

Business Name

A sole proprietorship can operate under the name of the sole proprietor or a **trade name**. For example, the author of this book can operate a sole proprietorship under the name "Henry R. Cheeseman" or under a trade name such as "The Big Cheese." Operating under a trade name is commonly designated as a **dba (doing business as)** (e.g., Henry R. Cheeseman, doing business as "The Big Cheese").

Most states require all businesses that operate under a trade name to file a fictitious business name statement (or certificate of trade name) with the appropriate government agency. The statement must contain the name and address of the applicant, the trade name, and the address of the business. Most states also require notice of the trade name to be published in a newspaper of general circulation serving the area in which the applicant does business.

These requirements are intended to disclose the real owner's name to the public. Noncompliance can result in a fine. Some states prohibit violators from maintaining lawsuits in the state's courts. A sample fictitious business name statement is shown in Exhibit 22.1.

dba Abbreviation: doing business as fictitious business name statement. An official document that must be filed with the appropriate government agency in order for the sole proprietorship to be able to use the name.

fictitious business name statement An official document that must be filed with the appropriate government agency in order for the sole proprietorship to be able to use the name.

Exhibit 22.1

Sample Fictitious Business Name Statement

Return To:

Name: Richard S. Roe
Address: 9000 Wilshire Boulevard
City: Beverly Hills, CA 90210
Telephone # (213) 273-5000
Cust. Ref. # 53247

☒ First Filing ☐ Renewal Filing
Current Registration No.

PUBLISH IN:

COUNTY CLERK'S FILING STAMP

FICTITIOUS BUSINESS NAME STATEMENT

THE FOLLOWING PERSON(S) IS (ARE) DOING BUSINESS AS:

1 Fictitious Business Name(s)
Mountain and Shore Mortgage Company

2 Street Address & City of Principal place of Business in California — Zip Code
9000 Wilshire Boulevard Beverly Hills California 90210

3 Full name of Registrant — (if corporation - incorporated in what state)
Richard S. Roe
Residence Address — City — State — Zip Code
100 Palm Drive Beverly Hills California 90212
Full Name of Registrant — (if corporation - incorporated in what state)
Residence Address — City — State — Zip Code
Full name of Registrant — (if corporation - incorporated in what state)
Residence Address — City — State — Zip Code
Full name of Registrant — (if corporation - incorporated in what state)
Residence Address — City — State — Zip Code

4 This Business is conducted by: (check one only)
(X) an individual ( ) a general partnership ( ) joint venture ( ) a business trust
( ) co-partners ( ) husband and wife ( ) a corporation ( ) a limited partnership
( ) an unincorporated association other than a partnership ( ) other—*please specify*)

5 The registrant commenced to transact business under the fictitious business name or names listed above on

6 **a.** Signed:
SIGNATURE — Richard S. Roe TYPE OR PRINT NAME
SIGNATURE — TYPE OR PRINT NAME
SIGNATURE — TYPE OR PRINT NAME

b. If Registrant a corporation sign below:
CORPORATION NAME
SIGNATURE & TITLE
TYPE OR PRINT NAME

This statement was filed with the County Clerk of Los Angeles County on date indicated by file stamp above.

NOTICE THIS FICTITIOUS NAME STATEMENT EXPIRES FIVE YEARS FROM THE DATE IT WAS FILED IN THE OFFICE OF THE COUNTY CLERK. A NEW FICTITIOUS BUSINESS NAME STATEMENT MUST BE FILED BEFORE THAT TIME. THE FILING OF THIS STATEMENT DOES NOT OF ITSELF AUTHORIZE THE USE IN THIS STATE OF A FICTITIOUS BUSINESS NAME IN VIOLATION OF THE RIGHTS OF ANOTHER UNDER FEDERAL, STATE, OR COMMON LAW (SEE SECTION 14400 ET SEQ., BUSINESS AND PROFESSIONS CODE).

I HEREBY CERTIFY THAT THIS COPY IS A CORRECT COPY OF THE ORIGINAL STATEMENT ON FILE IN MY OFFICE.

COUNTY CLERK

BY — DEPUTY

File No.

Personal Liability of Sole Proprietors

BUSINESS BRIEF
A major detriment of operating a business as a sole proprietorship is that the owner is personally liable for the debts of the business.

The sole proprietor bears the entire risk of loss of the business; that is, the owner will lose his or her entire capital contribution if the business fails. In addition, the sole proprietor has **unlimited personal liability**. Therefore, creditors may recover claims against the business from the sole proprietor's personal assets (e.g., home, automobile, and bank accounts).

franchise Established when one party licenses another party to use the franchisor's trade name, trademarks, commercial symbols, patents, copyrights, and other property in the distribution and selling of goods and services.

CONSIDER THIS EXAMPLE: Suppose Ken Smith opens a clothing store called The Rap Shop and operates it as a sole proprietorship. Mr. Smith files the proper statement and publishes the necessary notice of the use of the trade name. He contributes $25,000 of his personal funds to the business and borrows $100,000 in the name of the business from a bank. Assume that after several months Mr. Smith closes the business because it was unsuccessful. At the time it is closed, the business has no assets, owes the bank $100,000, and owes rent, trade credit, and other debts of $25,000. Here, Mr. Smith is personally liable to pay these debts from his personal assets.

FRANCHISES

franchisor The party who does the licensing in a franchise situation.

franchisee The party who is licensed by the franchisor in a franchise situation.

A **franchise** is established when one party (the **franchisor** or **licensor**) licenses another party (the **franchisee** or **licensee**) to use the franchisor's trade name, trademarks, commercial symbols, patents, copyrights, and other property in the distribution and selling of goods and services. Generally, the franchisor and the franchisee are established as separate corporations. The term *franchise* refers to both the agreement between the parties and the franchise outlet.

Franchising has several advantages, including: (1) allowing the franchisor to reach lucrative new markets, (2) giving the franchisee access to the franchisor's knowledge and resources while running an independent business, and (3) assuring consumers of uniform product quality.

A typical franchise arrangement is illustrated in Exhibit 22.2.

Exhibit 22.2
Parties to a Typical Franchise Arrangement

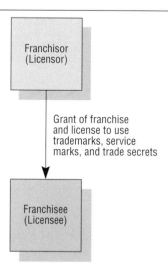

Franchisor (Licensor)

Grant of franchise and license to use trademarks, service marks, and trade secrets

Franchisee (Licensee)

distributorship franchise The franchisor manufactures a product and licenses a retail franchisee to distribute the product to the public.

Types of Franchises

Distributorship Franchises The franchisor manufacturers a product and licenses a retail dealer to distribute the product to the public. For example, the Ford Motor Company manufactures automobile and franchises independently owned automobile dealers (franchisees) to sell them to the public.

Processing Plant Franchise The franchisor provides a secret formula or the like to the franchisee. The franchisee then manufactures the product at its own location and distributes it to retail dealers. For example, the Coca-Cola Corporation, which owns the secret formulas for making Coca-Cola and other soft drinks, licenses regional bottling companies to manufacture and distribute soft drinks under the "Coca-Cola" and other brand names.

processing plant franchise The franchisor provides a secret formula or process to the franchisee, and the franchisee manufactures the product and distributes it to retail dealers.

Chain-Style Franchises The franchisor licenses the franchisee to make and sell its product or services to the public from a retail outlet serving an exclusive geographical territory. Most fast-food franchises use this form. For example, the Pizza Hut Corporation franchises independently owned restaurant franchises to make and sell pizzas to the public under the "Pizza Hut" name.

chain-style franchise The franchisor licenses the franchisee to make and sell its products or distribute services to the public from a retail outlet serving an exclusive territory.

Area Franchises The franchisor authorizes the franchisee to negotiate and sell franchises on behalf of the franchisor. The area franchisee is called a *subfranchisor* (see Exhibit 22.3). An area franchise is granted for a certain designated geographical area, such as a state, a region, or another agreed-upon area.

area franchise The franchisor authorizes the franchisee to negotiate and sell franchises on behalf of the franchisor.

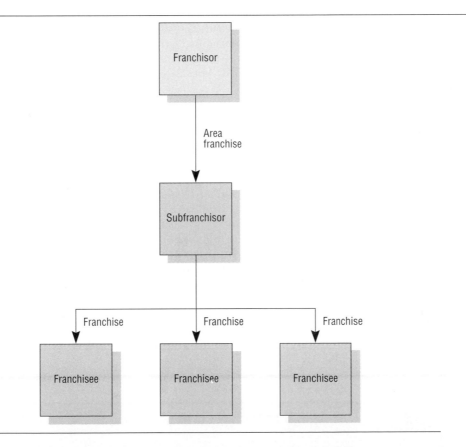

Exhibit 22.3
Example of an Area Franchise

DISCLOSURE PROTECTION

In the past, certain franchisors made material misrepresentations and omissions to facts to potential franchisees concerning the financial future of its franchises. Since then, the **Federal Trade Commission (FTC)** and many states have enacted laws that promote full disclosure to prospective franchisees.

Federal Trade Commission (FTC) Federal government agency empowered to enforce federal franchising rules.

State Disclosure Laws

Prior to the 1970s, franchising was not highly regulated to either state or federal governments. In 1971, California enacted its *Franchise Investment Law*.[1] It requires franchisors to register and deliver disclosure documents to prospective franchisees. Since then, many other states have enacted franchise disclosure statutes. For a while, franchisors struggled to comply with the various state statutes. Finally, in the mid-1970s, the state franchise administrators developed a uniform disclosure document called the **Uniform Franchise Offering Circular (UFOC)**.

The UFOC and state laws require the franchisor to make specific presale disclosures to prospective franchisees. Information that must be disclosed includes a description of the franchisor's business, balance sheets and income statements of the franchisor for the preceding three years, material terms of the franchise agreement, any restrictions on the franchisee's territory, grounds for termination of the franchise, and other relevant information.

Uniform Franchise Offering Circular (UFOC)
A uniform disclosure document that requires the franchisor to make specific presale disclosures to prospective franchisees.

FTC's Franchise Rule

FTC Franchise Rule
A rule set out by the FTC that requires franchisors to make full presale disclosures to prospective franchisees.

In 1979, the **FTC's Franchise Rule** became law. The FTC Rule requires franchisors to make full presale disclosure nationwide to prospective franchisees.[2] The FTC does not require the registration of the disclosure document prior to its use. The UFOC satisfies both state regulators and the FTC. If a franchisor violates FTC disclosure rules, the wrongdoer is subject to an injunction against further franchise sales, civil fines of up to $10,000 per violation, and an FTC civil action on behalf of injured franchisees to recover damages from the franchisor that were caused by the violation.

CONTEMPORARY BUSINESS ENVIRONMENT

Federal Trade Commission Rule

The FTC requires that the following statement appear in at least 12-point boldface type on the cover of a franchisor's required disclosure statement to prospective franchisees.

To protect you, we've required your franchisor to give you this information.

We haven't checked it, and don't know if it's correct. It should help you make up your mind. Study it carefully. While it includes some information about your contract, don't rely on it alone to understand
your contract. Read all of your contract carefully. Buying a franchise is a complicated investment. Take your time to decide. If possible, show your contract and this information to an adviser, like a lawyer or an accountant. If you find anything you think may be wrong or anything important that's been left out, you should let us know about it. It may be against the law. There may also be laws on franchising in your state. Ask your state agencies about them.

BUSINESS CHECKLIST

Required Disclosures of Earnings and Sales Projections by Franchisors

Franchisors often make sales and earnings projections to try to entice prospective franchisees to invest in their franchise. In order to prevent fraud, the Federal Trade Commission (FTC) had adopted rules that require certain disclosures to be made to prospective franchisees if the franchisor makes sales or earnings projections based on actual or hypothetical figures.

If the franchisor uses the *actual* sales, income, and profit figures of an existing franchise to base such projection on, the franchisor must disclose the following:

- The number and percentage of its actual franchises that have obtained such results; and
- A cautionary statement in at least 12-point boldface type that reads, "Caution: Some outlets have sold (or earned) this amount. There is no assurance you'll do as well. If you rely upon our figures, you must accept the risk of not doing so well."

If the franchisor uses *hypothetical examples*, the franchisor must disclose:

- The assumptions underlying the estimates
- The number and percentage of actual franchises that have obtained such results
- A cautionary statement in at least 12-point boldface print that reads, "Caution: These figures are only estimates of what we think you may earn. There is no assurance you'll do as well. If you rely upon our figures, you must accept the risk of not doing so well."

THE FRANCHISE AGREEMENT

A prospective franchisee must apply to the franchisor for a franchise. The application often includes detailed information about the applicant's previous employment, financial, and educational history, credit status, and so on. If an applicant is approved, the parties enter into a **franchise agreement** that sets forth the terms and conditions of the franchise. Although some states permit oral franchise agreements, most have enacted a Statute of Frauds that requires franchise agreements to be in writing. To prevent unjust enrichment, the courts will occasionally enforce oral franchise agreements that violate the Statute of Frauds.

franchise agreement
An agreement that the franchisor and the franchisee enter into that sets forth the terms and conditions of the franchise.

Common Terms of a Franchise Agreement

Franchise agreements usually do not have much room for negotiation. Generally, the agreement is a standard form contract prepared by the franchisor. Franchise agreements cover the following topics:

1. **Quality control standards.** The franchisor's most important assets are its name and reputation. The **quality control standards** set out in the franchise agreement—such as the franchisor's right to make periodic inspections of the franchisee's premises and operations—are intended to protect these assets. Failure to meet the proper standards can result in loss of the franchise.
2. **Training requirements.** Franchises and their personnel usually are required to attend training programs either on-site or at the franchisor's training facilities.
3. **Covenant-not-to-compete.** Covenants-not-to-compete prohibit franchisee from competing with the franchisor during a specific time and in a specified area after the termination of the franchise. Unreasonable (overextensive) covenants-not-to-compete are void.
4. **Arbitration clause.** Most franchise agreements contain an **arbitration clause** that provides that any claim or controversy arising from the franchise agreement or an alleged breach thereof is subject to arbitration. The U.S. Supreme Court has held such clauses to be enforceable.[3]

BUSINESS BRIEF
The public expects each franchisee of a franchisor to sell products or services of a similar quality. If one franchisee sells products or services of a lesser quality, it reflects on the entire franchise. Therefore, a franchisor should set exacting quality control standards in the franchise agreement.

5. Other terms and conditions. Capital requirements; restrictions on the use of the franchisor's trade name, trademarks, and logo; standards of operation; duration of the franchise; record-keeping requirements; sign requirements; hours of operation; prohibition as to the sale or assignment of the franchise; conditions for the termination of the franchise; and other specific terms pertinent to the operation of the franchise and the protection of the parties' rights are included in the agreement.

Franchise Fees Franchise fees payable by the franchisee are usually stipulated in the franchise agreement. The franchisor may require the franchisee to pay any or all of the following fees:

1. **Initial license fee.** A lump-sum payment for the privilege of being granted a franchise
2. **Royalty fee.** A fee for the continued use of the franchisor's trade name, property, and assistance that is often computed as a percentage of the franchisee's gross sales
3. **Assessment fee.** A fee for such things as advertising and promotional campaigns, administrative costs, and the like, billed as either a flat monthly or annual fee or as a percentage of gross sales
4. **Lease fees.** Payment for any land or equipment leased from the franchisor, billed as either a flat monthly or annual fee or as a percentage of gross sales or other agreed-upon amount
5. **Cost of supplies.** Payment for supplies purchased from the franchisor

Sample provisions from a franchise agreement are set forth in Exhibit 22.4.

Exhibit 22.4
Sample Provisions from a
Franchise Agreement

FRANCHISE AGREEMENT

Agreement, this 2nd day of January, 1996, between ALASKA PANCAKE HOUSE, INC., an Alaska corporation located in Anchorage, Alaska (hereinafter called the Company) and PANCAKE SYRUP COMPANY, INC., a Michigan corporation located in Detroit, Michigan (hereinafter called the Franchisee), for one KLONDIKE PANCAKE HOUSE restaurant to be located in the City of Mackinac Island, Michigan.

RECITALS

A. The Company is the owner of proprietary and other rights and interests in various service marks, trademarks, and trade names used in its business including the trade name and service mark "KLONDIKE PANCAKE HOUSE."

B. The Company operates and enfranchises others to operate restaurants under the trade name and service mark "KLONDIKE PANCAKE HOUSE" using certain recipes, formulas, food preparation procedures, business methods, business forms, and business policies it has developed. The Company has also developed a body of knowledge pertaining to the establishment and operation of restaurants. The Franchisee acknowledges that he does not presently know these recipes, formulas, food preparation procedures, business methods, or business policies, nor does the Franchisee have these business forms or access to the Company's body of knowledge.

C. The Franchisee intends to enter the restaurant business and desires access to the Company's recipes, formulas, food preparation procedures, business methods, business forms, business policies, and body of knowledge pertaining to the operation of a restaurant. In addition, the Franchisee desires access to information pertaining to new developments and techniques in the Company's restaurant business.

D. The Franchisee desires to participate in the use of the Company's rights in its service marks and trademarks in connection with the operation of one restaurant to be located at a site approved by the Company and the Franchisee.

E. The Franchisee understands that information received from the Company or from any of its officers, employees, agents, or franchisees is confidential and has been developed with a great deal of effort and expense. The Franchisee acknowledges that the information is being made available to him so that he may more effectively establish and operate a restaurant.

F. The Company has granted and will continue to grant others, access to its recipes, formulas, food preparation procedures, business methods, business forms, business policies, and body of knowledge pertaining to the operation of restaurants and information pertaining to new developments and techniques in its business.

G. The Company has and will continue to license others to use its service marks and trademarks in connection with the operation of restaurants at Company-approved locations.

H. The Franchise Fee and Royalty constitute the sole consideration to the Company for the use by the Franchisee of its body of knowledge, systems, and trademarks rights.

I. The Franchisee acknowledges that he received the Company's franchise offering prospectus at or prior to the first personal meeting with a Company representative and at least ten (10) business days prior to the signing of this Agreement and that he has been given the opportunity to clarify provisions he did not understand and to consult with an attorney or other professional advisor. Franchisee represents he understands and agrees to be bound by the terms, conditions, and obligations of this Agreement.

J. The Franchisee acknowledges that he understands that the success of the business to be operated by him under this Agreement depends primarily upon his efforts and that neither the Company nor any of its agents or representatives have made any oral, written, or visual representations or projections of actual or potential sales, earnings, or net or gross profits. Franchisee understands that the restaurant operated under this Agreement may lose money or fail.

AGREEMENT

Acknowledging the above recitals, the parties hereto agree as follows:

1. Upon execution of this Agreement, the Franchisee shall pay to the Company a Franchise Fee of $30,000 that shall not be refunded in any event.

2. The Franchisee shall also pay to the Company, weekly, a Royalty equal to eight (8%) percent of the gross sales from each restaurant that he operates throughout the term of this Agreement. "Gross sales" means all sales or revenues derived from the Franchisee's location exclusive of sales taxes.

3. The Company hereby grants to the Franchisee:

a. Access to the Company's recipes, formulas, food preparation procedures, business methods, business forms, business policies, and body of knowledge pertaining to the operation of a restaurant.

b. Access to information pertaining to new developments and techniques in the Company's restaurant business.

c. License to use of the Company's rights in and to its service marks and trademarks in connection with the operation of one restaurant to be located at a site approved by the Company and the Franchisee.

4. The Company agrees to:

a. Provide a training program for the operation of restaurants using the Company's recipes, formulas, food preparation procedures, business methods, business forms, and business policies. The Franchisee shall pay all transportation, lodging, and other expenses incurred in attending the program. The Franchisee must attend the training program before opening his restaurant.

b. Provide a Company Representative that the Franchisee may call upon for consultation concerning the operation of his business.

c. Provide the Franchisee with a program of assistance that shall include periodic consultations with a Company Representative, publish a periodical advising of new developments and techniques in the Company's restaurant business, and grant access to Company personnel for consultations concerning the operation of his business.

5. The Franchisee agrees to:

a. Begin operation of a restaurant within 365 days. The restaurant will be at a location found by the Franchisee and approved by the Company. The Company or one of its designees will lease the premises and sublet them to the Franchisee at cost. The Franchisee will then construct and equip his unit in accordance with Company specifications contained in the Operating Manual. Upon written request from the Franchisee, the Company will grant a 180-day extension that is effective immediately upon receipt of the request. Under certain circumstances, and at the sole discretion of the Company, the Company may grant additional time in which to open the business. In all instances, the location of each unit must be approved by the Company and the Franchisee. If the restaurant is not operating within 365 days, or within any approved extensions, this Agreement will automatically expire.

b. Operate his business in compliance with applicable laws and governmental regulations. The Franchisee will obtain at his expense, and keep in force, any permits, licenses, or other consents required for the leasing, construction, or operation of his business. In addition, the Franchisee shall operate his restaurant in accordance with the Company's Operating Manual, which may be amended from time to time as a result of experience, changes in the law, or changes in the marketplace. The Franchisee shall refrain from conducting any business or selling any products other than those approved by the Company at the approved location.

c. Be responsible for all costs of operating his unit, including but not limited to, advertising, taxes, insurance, food products, labor, and utilities. Insurance shall include, but not be limited to, comprehensive liability insurance including products liability coverage in the minimum amount of $1,000,000. The Franchisee shall keep these policies in force for the mutual benefit of the parties. In addition, the Franchisee shall save the Company harmless from any claim of any type that arises in connection with the operation of his business.

BUSINESS BRIEF

*If the franchise agreement
is breached, the aggrieved
party can sue the breaching
party for rescission of the
agreement, restitution, and
damages.*

Breach of the Franchise Agreement

A lawful franchise agreement is an enforceable contract. Each party owes a duty to adhere to and perform under the terms of the franchise agreement. If the agreement is breached, the aggrieved party can sue the breaching party for rescission of the agreement, restitution, and damages.

ETHICAL PERSPECTIVE

Häagen-Dazs Ice Cream Franchise Melts

Franchise agreements are detailed documents that are carefully drafted to spell out the rights and duties of the parties. A franchisee must be careful to read and understand the terms of the agreement, as the following case demonstrates.

In the late 1950s, Reuben Mattus developed a "super premium" ice cream and named it "Häagen-Dazs" to give the product a Scandinavian flair. Mattus began selling Häagen-Dazs ice cream in prepackaged pints to small stores and delicatessens in the New York metropolitan area. During the 1970s, sales of the product were expanded into some grocery stores and other retail outlets.

In 1976, Reuben's daughter, Doris Mattus-Hurley, opened the first "Häagen-Dazs Shoppe" in Brooklyn Heights, New York. After this shop prospered, Mattus-Hurley began franchising other shops to independent franchisees throughout the country. Häagen-Dazs ice cream is manufactured, distributed, and franchised through a variety of corporate entities (collectively referred to as Häagen-Dazs). The franchise agreement, which has been the same since 1978, grants a limited license to the franchisee to operate a single shop under the

Häagen-Dazs trademark at a specific location for a specified term ranging from 5 to 12 years. The franchisee agrees to purchase all its ice cream from the franchisor at prices set by Häagen-Dazs.

In 1983, the Pillsbury Company (Pillsbury), a diversified international food and restaurant company headquartered in Minneapolis, Minnesota, purchased the Häagen-Dazs company, including its franchise operations. The franchise agreements were assigned to Pillsbury as part of the sale. Pillsbury decided that it could maximize sales of Häagen-Dazs ice cream by expanding sales through methods of distribution that did not involve franchisees. Pillsbury substantially increased sales of Häagen-Dazs products to national grocery store chains, convenience stores like 7-Eleven, and other retail outlets.

This change severely harmed sales at existing franchises. Franchisees located in many states sued Pillsbury, alleging breach of the franchise agreement. Plaintiffs claimed that the defendant breached the franchise agreement by distributing Häagen-Dazs ice cream through nonfranchised outlets that were not "upscale" and by mass distribution of prepack-

aged pints that competed with franchise outlet sales.

The district court held that the express terms of the franchise agreement had not been violated. The franchise agreement expressly reserved the right of the franchisor to distribute Häagen-Dazs products "through not only Häagen-Dazs Shoppes, but through any other distribution method, which may from time to time be established." The court held that this language gave Pillsbury the right to aggressively distribute prepackaged pints of Häagen-Dazs ice cream through nonfranchise outlets, even though that distribution adversely affected retail sales by franchisees. The district court granted Pillsbury's motion for summary judgment. [*Carlock v. Pillsbury Company*, 719 F.Supp. 791 (D.Minn. 1989)]

1. Even though the express terms of the franchise agreement allowed Pillsbury to distribute Häagen-Dazs ice cream through nonfranchise outlets, do you think Pillsbury acted ethically in doing so?
2. Should a covenant of good faith and fair dealing be implied in franchise agreements? Why or why not?

TRADEMARK LAW, TRADE SECRETS, AND FRANCHISING

A franchisor's ability to maintain the public's perception of the quality of the goods and services associated with its trade name, **trademarks**, and **service marks** is the essence of its success. The size of the advertising budgets of many franchisors support this view.

Trademarks

The **Lanham Trademark Act**, which was enacted in 1946, provides for the registration of trademarks and service marks with the *Federal Patent and Trademark Office* in Washington, D.C. Most franchisors license the use of their trade names, trademarks, and service marks and prohibit their franchisees from misusing these marks.

Trademark Infringement

Anyone who uses a mark without authorization may be sued for **trademark infringement**. The trademark holder can seek to recover damages and obtain an injunction prohibiting further unauthorized use of the mark.

In the following case, the court found that the defendant franchisee had infringed a franchisor's trademark.

trademarks and service marks A distinctive mark, symbol, name, word, motto, or device that identifies the goods or services of a particular franchisor.

Lanham Trademark Act An act enacted in 1946 that provides for the registration of trademarks and service marks with the Federal Patent and Trademark Office in Washington, D.C.

CASE 22.1

Baskin-Robbins Ice Cream Co. v. D&L Ice Cream Co., Inc.

576 F.Supp. 1055 (1983) United States District Court Eastern District, New York

Facts The Baskin-Robbins Ice Cream Company (Baskin-Robbins) is a franchisor that has established a system of more than 2,700 franchise ice cream retail stores nationwide. The franchisees agree to purchase ice cream in bulk only from Baskin-Robbins or an authorized Baskin-Robbins source, to sell only Baskin-Robbins ice cream under the "Baskin-Robbins" marks, and to keep specific business hours. Franchisees agree to pay ice cream invoices to Baskin-Robbins when due. If ice cream invoices are not paid within seven days of delivery of the ice cream, payment by certified check is required. If such check is not received, prepayment in cash is then required. If Baskin-Robbins must institute a lawsuit for a breach of the franchise agreement, the franchisee is required to pay all costs incurred by Baskin-Robbins if it is successful in the lawsuit.

In 1978, Baskin-Robbins entered into a standard Franchise Agreement with D&L Ice Cream Co., Inc., granting it a franchise to operate a retail ice cream store in Brooklyn, New York. During the course of the franchise, D&L consistently failed to maintain proper business hours and failed to satisfy ice cream invoices when due. Baskin-Robbins properly invoked its right to require payment by certified check. When such payment was not received, Baskin-Robbins required prepayment for ice cream deliveries. D&L then purchased bulk ice cream from other manufacturers and sold it in its store, bearing the Baskin-Robbins trademarks. Upon discovering this fact, Baskin-Robbins sent a Notice of Termination to D&L. D&L ignored the notice and continued to operate the Baskin-Robbins store and sell other brands of ice cream in cups and containers bearing the Baskin-Robbins trademarks. Baskin-Robbins sued D&L for trademark infringement.

Issue Did D&L infringe Baskin-Robbins trademarks?

Decision Yes. The district court held that D&L had engaged in trademark infringement. The court held that Baskin-Robbins was entitled to a permanent injunction, to recover outstanding monies owed by D&L, to all profits made by D&L as a result of the trademark infringement, and to full costs and attorney's fees incurred in connection with this litigation.

Reason The court held that the sale by a franchised licensee of unauthorized products, that is, products outside the scope of the license, is likely to confuse the public into believing that such products are in fact manufactured or authorized by the trademark owner, when in fact they are not. D&L's activities during the course of its franchise agreement constituted an infringement of Baskin-Robbins' federally registered trademarks.

CASE QUESTIONS

Critical Legal Thinking Should a franchisor's trademarks and service marks be protected by law? Why or why not?

Ethics Did the franchisee act ethically in this case?

Business Implication Why was Baskin-Robbins so concerned about D&L's activities? Explain.

Misappropriation of Trade Secrets

trade secrets Ideas that make a franchise successful but do not qualify for trademark, patent, or copyright protection.

Trade secrets are ideas that make a franchise successful but do not qualify for trademark, patent, or copyright protection. Most state laws protect trade secrets.

The misappropriation of a trade secret is called **unfair competition**. The holder of the trade secret can sue the offending party for damages and an injunction to prohibit further unauthorized use of the trade secret.

CONTRACT AND TORT LIABILITY OF FRANCHISORS AND FRANCHISEES

Direct Liability

BUSINESS BRIEF
Franchisors and franchisees are liable for their own contracts and torts.

Franchisors and franchisees are liable for their own contracts. The same is true of tort liability. For example, if a person is injured by a franchisee's negligence, the franchisee is liable.

In the following case, the court held that a franchisor was directly liable to the plaintiffs.

CASE 22.2

Martin v. McDonald's Corp.
572 N.E.2d. 1073 (1991) Appellate Court of Illinois

Facts McDonald's Corporation (McDonald's) is a franchisor that licenses franchisees to operate fast food restaurants and to use McDonald's trademarks and service marks. One such franchise was located in Oak Forest, Illinois.

Recognizing the threat of armed robbery at its franchises, especially in the time period immediately after closing, McDonald's established an entire corporate division to deal with security problems at franchises. McDonald's prepared a manual for restaurant security operations and required its franchisees to adhere to these procedures.

Jim Carlson was McDonald's regional security manager for the area in which the Oak Forest franchise was located. Carlson visited the Oak Forest franchise on October 31, 1979, to inform the manager of security procedures. He specifically mentioned these rules: (1) No one should throw garbage out the back door after dark, and (2) trash and grease were to be taken out the side glass door at least one hour prior to closing. During his inspection, Carlson noted that the locks had to be changed at the restaurant and an alarm system needed to be installed for the back door. Carlson never followed up to determine whether these security measures had been taken.

On the evening of November 29, 1979, a six-woman crew, all teenagers, was working to clean up and close the Oak Forest restaurant. Laura Martin, Therese Dudek, and Maureen Kincaid were members of that crew. A person later identified as Peter Logan

appeared at the back of the restaurant with a gun. He ordered the crew to open the safe and get him the money, and then ordered them into the refrigerator. In the course of moving the crew into the refrigerator, Logan shot and killed Martin and assaulted Dudek and Kincaid. Dudek and Kincaid suffered severe emotional distress from the assault.

Evidence showed that Logan had entered the restaurant through the back door. Trial testimony proved that the work crew used the back door exclusively, both before and after dark, and emptied garbage and grease through the back door all day and night. There was evidence that the latch on the back door did not work properly. Evidence also showed that the crew had not been instructed about the use of the back door after dark, had never received copies of McDonald's security manual, and the required warning about not using the back door after dark had not been posted at the restaurant.

The parents of Laura Martin, Therese Dudek, and Maureen Kincaid sued McDonald's to recover damages for negligence. The trial court awarded damages of $1,003,445 to the Martins for the wrongful death of their daughter and awarded $125,000 each to Dudek and Kincaid. McDonald's appealed.

Issue Is McDonald's Corporation liable for negligence?

Decision Yes. The appellate court held that McDonald's was negligent for not following up and making sure that the security deficiencies it had found at the Oak Forest franchise had been corrected. Affirmed.

Reason The appellate court held that McDonald's had voluntarily assumed a duty to the crew at the Oak Forest franchise by establishing and requiring the franchisee to implement certain security measures, and by obligating itself to inspect the restaurant to see that the required security measures were implemented. The court held that McDonald's was liable for its own negligence due to the failure of security measures and the failure of its employee, Carlson, to follow up to determine that the security deficiencies at the Oak Forest franchise had been corrected. The appellate court held that there was ample evidence

for the jury to determine that McDonald's had breached its assumed duty to the plaintiffs.

CASE QUESTIONS

Critical Legal Thinking Should businesses be held liable for criminal actions of others? Why or why not?

Ethics Should McDonald's have denied liability in this case?

Business Implication What is the benefit to a franchisor to establish and require its franchisees to adhere to security rules? Is there any potential detriment? Explain.

Independent Contractor Status

If properly organized and operated, the franchisor and franchisee are separate legal entities. Therefore, the franchisor deals with the franchisee as an **independent contractor**. Because there is no agency relationship, neither party is liable for the contracts or torts of the other.

In the following case, the court applied the independent contractor rule and held that the franchisor was not liable for the tortious conduct of a franchisee.

BUSINESS BRIEF

If properly organized and operated as a separate business, a franchisee is not the agent of the franchisor, and the franchisor is not liable for the franchisee's contracts or torts.

CASE 22.3

Cislaw v. Southland Corp.

4 Cal.App.4th 1284, 6 Cal.Rptr.2d 386 (1992) Court of Appeal of California

Facts The Southland Corporation (Southland) owns the "7-Eleven" trademark and licenses franchisees to operate convenience stores using this trademark. Each franchise is independently owned and operated. The franchise agreement stipulates that the franchisee is an independent contractor who is authorized to make all inventory, employment, and operational decisions for the franchise.

Timothy Cislaw, 17 years old, died of respiratory failure on May 10, 1984. His parents filed a wrongful death action against the franchisee and Southland, alleging that Timothy's death resulted from his consumption of Djarum Specials clove cigarettes sold at a Costa Mesa, California, 7-Eleven franchise store. After answering the complaint, Southland moved for summary judgment, arguing that it is not liable for the alleged tortious conduct of its franchisee because the franchisee was an independent contractor. The plaintiffs alleged that the franchisee was Southland's agent, and therefore Southland was liable for its agent's alleged negligence of selling the clove ciga-

rettes to their son. The trial court granted Southland's motion. The Cislaws appealed.

Issue Was the Costa Mesa franchisee an agent of the Southland Corporation?

Decision No. The court of appeals held that the Costa Mesa 7-Eleven franchisee was not an agent of the Southland Corporation but was an independent contractor. Affirmed.

Reason The franchisor–franchisee arrangement does not create a principal–agent relationship unless the franchisor has the right to exercise substantial control over the operations of the franchisee. Although the franchise agreement gave Southland the right to establish the hours of operation of its franchises, to protect its "7-Eleven" trademark from misuse by the franchisee, and to set cleanliness and quality control standards at its franchises, the agreement did not give Southland the right to control the

continued

day-to-day operations of its Costa Mesa franchise. The court found that because the franchisee made all inventory, employment, and day-to-day operational decisions, it was an independent contractor.

CASE QUESTIONS

Critical Legal Thinking Should franchisors be automatically held liable for the tortious conduct of their franchisees? Why or why not?

Ethics Did the Cislaws act ethically in suing Southland?

Business Implication How careful must a franchisor be to retain enough control to protect the quality of the goods and service sold by its franchisees but not to retain too much control so as to become liable for the actions of its franchisees?

Agency Status

apparent agency Agency that arises when a franchisor creates the appearance that a franchisee is its agent when in fact an actual agency does not exist.

If the franchisee is the **actual** or **apparent agent** of the franchisor, the franchisor is responsible for the torts and contracts of the franchisee committed or entered into within the scope of the agency. **Apparent agency** is created when a franchisor leads a third person into believing that the franchisee is its agent. For example, a franchisor and franchisee who use the same trade name and trademarks and make no effort to inform the public of their separate legal status may find themselves in such a situation. Mere use of the same name does not automatically make the franchisor liable for the franchisee's actions.

In the following case, the court found that a franchisee was the apparent agent of the franchisor, thereby making the franchisor liable for the tortious conduct of the franchisee.

CASE 22.4

Holiday Inn, Inc. v. Shelburne
576 So.2d 322 (1991) District Court of Appeal of Florida

Facts Holiday Inn, Inc. (Holiday Inn) is a franchisor that licenses franchisees to operate hotels using its trademarks and service marks. Holiday Inn licensed Hospitality Venture to operate a franchised hotel in Fort Pierce, Florida. The Rodeo Bar, which had a reputation as the "hottest bar in town," was located in the hotel.

The Holiday Inn and Rodeo Bar did not have sufficient parking, so security guards posted in the Holiday Inn parking lot required Rodeo Bar patrons to park in vacant lots that surrounded the hotel but were not owned by the hotel. The main duty of the guards was to keep the parking lot open for hotel guests. Two unarmed security guards were on duty on the night in question. One guard drank on the job, and the other was an untrained temporary fill-in.

The record disclosed that although the Rodeo Bar had a capacity of 240 people, the bar regularly admitted 270 to 300 people, with 50 to 75 people waiting outside. Fights occurred all the time in the bar and

the parking lots, and often there were three or four fights a night. Police reports involving 58 offenses, including several weapons charges, as well as battery and assault charges, had been filed during the previous 18 months.

On the night in question, the two groups involved in the altercation did not leave the Rodeo Bar until closing time. According to the record, these individuals exchanged remarks as they moved toward their respective vehicles in the vacant parking lots adjacent to the Holiday Inn. Ultimately, a fight erupted. The evidence shows that during the course of physical combat, Mr. Carter shot David Rice, Scott Turner, and Robert Shelburne. Rice died from his injuries.

Rice's heirs, Turner, and Shelburne sued the franchisee, Hospitality Venture, and the franchisor, Holiday Inn, for damages. The trial court found Hospitality Venture negligent for not providing sufficient security to prevent the foreseeable incident that took the life of Rice and injured Turner and Shelburne. The court also found that Hospitality Venture was the apparent agent of Holiday Inn, and therefore Holiday Inn was vicariously liable for its franchisee's tortious conduct. Turner was awarded $3,825,000 for his injuries. Shelburne received $1 million, and Rice's interests were awarded $1 million. Hospitality Venture and Holiday Inn appealed.

Issue Are the franchisee and the franchisor liable?

Decision Yes. The court of appeals held that the franchisee was negligent and that the franchisee was the apparent agent of the franchisor. Affirmed.

Reason A franchisee is always liable for its own tortious conduct. A franchisor may be held liable for the tortious conduct of a franchisee if the franchisee is the "apparent agent" of the franchisor. This occurs when the franchisor misleads the public into believing that the franchise is really owned and operated by the franchisor, even though it is not. Here, the court held that Holiday Inn led the public into believing that its franchisees were part of Holiday Inn's system, and not independently owned businesses. The court held that Holiday Inn's reservation system, as well as the signs at the Fort Pierce franchise hotel, gave this appearance to the public. Therefore, Holiday Inns is vicariously liable for the tortious conduct of its franchisee.

CASE QUESTIONS

Critical Legal Thinking What does the doctrine of apparent agency provide? How does it differ from actual agency? Explain.

Ethics Did Hospitality Venture act ethically in denying liability? Did Holiday Inn act ethically in denying liability?

Business Implication Why do you think that plaintiffs included Holiday Inn as a defendant in their lawsuit? Do you think the damages that were awarded were warranted?

ANTITRUST LAW AND FRANCHISING

Tying Arrangements

A **tying arrangement** is a restraint of trade where a seller refuses to sell one product (the tying product) to a customer unless the customer agrees to purchase a second product (the tied product) from the seller. Most tying arrangement in goods violate *Section 3 of the Clayton Antitrust Act*. Tying arrangements involving goods or services are unreasonable restraints of trade in violation of *Section 1 of the Sherman Antitrust Act*.

These laws are intended to prevent sellers from using their market power in a product to force sales of another product. A party injured by an unlawful tying arrangement can sue the wrongdoer for treble (triple) damages if he or she can prove that:

1. The wrongdoer tied the sales of two separate products or services
2. More than a de minimus (small) amount of commerce was affected
3. Sufficient market power existed to enforce the arrangement
4. The arrangement caused an unreasonable restraint of trade or a substantial lessening of competition

tying arrangement A restraint of trade where a seller refuses to sell one product or service to a customer unless the customer agrees to purchase a second product or service from the seller.

BUSINESS APPLICATION

Sports Franchises: I'll Take My Ball and Go Home

Brooklyn lost the Dodgers, Minneapolis lost the Lakers, and Baltimore lost the Colts. Despite the adage that time heals all wounds, these and other American cities that have lost their home team franchises have never been quite the same. In addition to the emotional toll on fans, the economic cost of team relocation on the ex-hometown can be staggering.

continued

The leagues that grant professional sports franchises frown upon team relocation and many incorporate clauses into teams' contracts that prohibit teams from relocating. When teams have packed their bags in defiance of these provisions—and many have—the leagues have gone to court. In response, teams have charged that the anti-relocation provisions guarantee an existing home team a monopoly over a city's sports market. As such, they argue, these rules violate antitrust laws because they prevent teams from entering the markets of their choice and freely competing with other teams.

The leading case in this area involved the infamous decision of Al Davis, an owner of the Oakland Raiders, to move his professional football team from Oakland to Los Angeles in 1980. At the time, the NFL's relocation rule required approval of a request to move by 75 percent of the owners. The vote on the Oakland deal was not even close—22 teams voted against the move and another 5 teams abstained. The Raiders sued the NFL, claiming that the league's relocation rules violated the Sherman Antitrust Act. The court held that the relocation rule was adopted especially to prevent competition among teams in each

city in violation of the Sherman Act. The NFL rule was struck down.

While the court decision in this case clearly strikes a blow for free competition, it also virtually ensures that there will be more team relocations—and more heartbroken home team fans—in the future. Note: In 1995, Al Davis fled Los Angeles and moved the Raiders back to Oakland. This time, no other owner voted against the move. [*Los Angeles Memorial Coliseum Commission v. National Football League*, 726 F.2d 1381 (9th Cir. 1984), cert. denied, 469 U.S. 990 (1984)]

TERMINATION OF FRANCHISES

BUSINESS BRIEF

A franchisor can terminate a franchise agreement for "just cause" (e.g., nonpayment of franchise fees by the franchisee, continued failure to meet quality control standards).

The franchise agreement usually contains provisions that permit the franchisor to terminate the franchise if certain events occur. The franchisor's right to terminate a franchise has been the source of a lot of litigation.

Termination "For Cause"

Most franchise agreements permit franchisors to terminate the franchise "for cause." For example, the continued failure of a franchisee to meet legitimate quality control standards is just cause.

Unreasonably strict application of a just cause termination clause constitutes wrongful termination. For example, a single failure to meet a quality control standard is not cause for termination.

Wrongful Termination

Termination-at-will clauses in franchise agreements are generally held to be void on the grounds that they are unconscionable. The rationale for this position is that the franchisee has spent time, money, and effort developing the franchise.

wrongful termination
Termination of a franchise without just cause.

If a franchise is terminated without just cause, the franchisee can sue the franchisor for **wrongful termination**. The franchisee can recover damages caused by the unlawful termination and recover the franchise.

Petroleum Marketing Practices Act

"It is the privilege of a trader in a free country, in all matters not contrary to law, to regulate his own mode of carrying it on according to his own discretion and choice."
B. Alderson
Hilton v. Eckersley
(1855)

Gasoline stations are among the oldest franchises in the United States. The *Petroleum Marketing Practices Act*, enacted in 1979, prohibits oil company franchisors from terminating gasoline station franchises without just cause.[4]

Automobile Dealers Day in Court Act

Automobile company franchisors are prohibited from terminating automobile dealer franchises without just cause. The *Automobile Dealers Day in Court Act* was enacted to ensure that this does not happen.[5]

INTERNATIONAL PERSPECTIVE

International Franchising

Franchising as a form of business is well established in the United States. Sometimes, it seems that certain types of franchises (e.g., gasoline stations) have saturated the market. The international market presently offers the greatest opportunity for U.S. franchisors to expand their businesses. Many U.S. franchisors view international expansion as their number one priority. However, in addition to providing lucrative new markets, international franchising also poses greater difficulties and more risks.

The expansion into other countries through franchising means that U.S. franchisors can expand internationally without the huge capital investments that would be required if they tried to penetrate these markets with company-owned stores or branches. In addition, a foreign franchisee will know things about the cultural and business traditions of the foreign country that the franchisor will not. Consequently, the fran-

chisee will be better able to serve the consumers and customers in a particular market.

Utilizing this foreign expertise probably means that U.S. franchisors will grant area franchises in many foreign countries. The U.S. franchisor will rely on the area franchisee to locate, investigate, and approve individual franchisees.

Foreign franchising is not without its difficulties, however. For example, the host country's laws may differ from U.S. laws. This will have to be taken into consideration in drafting the franchise agreement and operating the franchise. Foreign cultures may also require different advertising, marketing, and promotional approaches. In addition, the franchisor may be subjecting itself to government regulation in the host country. A regional group like the European Community (EC) may possibly become involved. Finally, different dispute settlement procedures may be in place that will

have to be used if there is a dispute between the U.S. franchisor and the foreign franchisee.

To aid the development of U.S. franchising abroad, the federal **Agency for International Development (USAID)** guarantees loans to U.S. franchisor's area licensees and franchisees in developing countries. The foreign franchisee would seek financing from its own bank, but the USAID would back 50 percent of the loan through a guarantee. Franchisors must apply and be approved to participate in the program.

In addition to U.S. franchisors expanding to other countries, foreign franchisors also view the United States as a potential market. This will provide an opportunity for U.S. entrepreneurs to become franchisees for foreign franchisors. In the future, U.S. consumers will be able to purchase foreign goods and services from franchises located in this country.

WORKING THE WEB

The Franchise Handbook: On-Line This Web site contains articles on franchising, lists of worldwide franchise associations, and a directory of business opportunities.

Visit at http://www.franchise1.com/

FranNet FranNet is the world's largest network of franchise consultants. It contains a large research library.

Visit at http://www.frannet.com/

International Franchise Association At the International Franchise Association site, you can search by company name, category, investment range, and location. It serves as a resource center for current and prospective franchisees and franchisors.

Visit at http://www.franchise.org/

International Business Resources on the World Wide Web This site is produced by
continued

Michigan State University Center for International Business Education and Research. It contains a lot of valuable international trade information.

Visit at http://ciber.bus.msu.edu/busres.htm

The Trade Zone   The Trade Zone is provided by the reference section of the Global Trade Center.

Visit at http://www.tradezone.com/trdzone.htm

CYBER EXERCISES:

1. Using the *Franchise Handbook: On-Line*, find the article "Franchising Health Care." Who is the author?

2. Using FranNet, find and read an article in the research library called "Retail Franchises: Opportunity Window."

3. Find a franchise opportunity in your area using the International Franchise Association site.

4. Using International Business Resources on the World Wide Web, find the Export Process Assistant.

5. Check out Global Roulette in the Trade Zone.

CHAPTER SUMMARY

SOLE PROPRIETORSHIPS, P. 526

Sole Proprietorships	A form of business where the owner and the business are one. The business is not a separate legal entity.
Business Name	A sole proprietorship can operate under the name of the sole proprietor or a *trade name*. Operating under a trade name is commonly designated as a *dba (doing business as)*. If a trade name is used, a *fictitious business name statement* must be filed with the appropriate state government office.
Personal Liability of Sole Proprietors	The sole proprietor is personally liable for the debts and obligations of the sole proprietorship.

FRANCHISES, P. 528

Franchises	Established when one party licenses another party to use the franchisor's trade name, trademarks, commercial symbols, patents, copyrights, and other property in the distribution and selling of goods and services. 1. *Franchisor*. The party who does the licensing in a franchise arrangement. Also called the *licensor*. 2. *Franchisee*. The party who is licensed by the franchisor in a franchise arrangement. Also called the *licensee*.
Types of Franchises	1. *Distributorship franchise*. The franchisor manufactures a product and licenses a retail franchisee to distribute the product to the public. 2. *Processing plant franchise*. The franchisor provides a secret formula or process to the franchisee, and the franchisee manufactures the product and distributes it to retail dealers. 3. *Chain-style franchise*. The franchisor licenses the franchisee to make and sell its products or distribute its services to the public from a retail outlet serving an exclusive territory. 4. *Area franchise*. The franchise authorizes the franchisee to negotiate and sell franchises on behalf of the franchisor in designated areas. The area franchisee is called a *subfranchisor*.

DISCLOSURE PROTECTION, P. 529

State Disclosure Laws	Many states have enacted statutes that require franchisors to make specific presale disclosures to prospective franchisees. Some states use a uniform disclosure document called the *Uniform Franchise Offering Circular (UFOC)*.
FTC's Franchise Rule	The *Federal Trade Commission (FTC)* requires franchisors to make presale disclosures to prospective franchisees. If the franchisor uses actual or hypothetical sales or income data in its sales materials, the franchisor must disclose assumptions underlying any estimates, how many franchises have obtained such results, and it must provide a mandated precautionary statement.

THE FRANCHISE AGREEMENT, P. 531

The Franchise Agreement	An agreement that the franchisor and franchisee enter into that sets for the terms and conditions of the franchise (e.g., quality control standards, covenants not to compete).
Franchise Fees	*Franchise fees.* A franchisee may be required to pay any or all of the following franchise fees to the franchisor. 1. *Initial license fee.* A lump-sum payment for the privilege of being granted a franchise. 2. *Royalty fee.* A fee for the continued use of the franchisor's trade name, property, and assistance, that is often computed as a percentage of the franchisee's gross sales. 3. *Assessment fee.* A fee for such things as advertising and promotional campaigns, administrative costs, and the like, billed either as a flat monthly fee or annual fee or as a percentage of gross sales. 4. *Lease fees.* Payment for any land or equipment leased from the franchisor, billed either as a flat monthly or annual fee or as a percentage of gross sales or other agreed-upon amount. 5. *Cost of supplies.* Payment for supplies purchased from the franchisor.
Breach of the Franchise Agreement	1. *Performance of the franchise agreement.* Each party to a franchise agreement owes a duty to adhere to and perform under the terms of the agreement. 2. *Breach of the franchise agreement.* A lawful franchise agreement is an enforceable contract. If a franchise agreement is breached, the aggrieved party can sue the breaching party for rescission of the agreement, restitution, and damages.

TRADEMARK LAW, TRADE SECRETS, AND FRANCHISING, P. 534

Trademarks	1. *Trademarks and service marks.* A distinctive mark, symbol, name, word, motto, or device that identifies the goods or services of a particular franchisor. 2. *Licensing of marks.* A franchisor *licenses* the use of its trademarks and service marks to its franchisees in the franchise agreement.
Trademark Infringement	Anyone who uses a mark without authorization from the franchisor may be sued for *trademark infringement*. The franchisor can recover damages and obtain an injunction prohibiting further unauthorized use of the mark.

Misappropriation of Trade Secrets	1. *Trade secrets*. Ideas, formulas, and methods of doing business that make a franchise successful but do not qualify for trademark, patent, or copyright protection. 2. *Misappropriation of trade secrets*. Anyone who steals and uses a franchisor's trade secret is liable for misappropriation of a trade secret. The franchisor can recover damages and obtain an injunction prohibiting further unauthorized use of the trade secret.
CONTRACT AND TORT LIABILITY OF FRANCHISORS AND FRANCHISEES, P. 536	
Direct Liability	Franchisors and franchisees are liable for their own contracts and torts.
Independent Contractor Status	A separately organized and operated business that is not the agent of another party with whom it does business. This is the typical franchisor–franchisee arrangement. There is no agency relationship, so neither party is liable for the other's contracts or torts.
Agency Status	1. *Actual agency*. An arrangement that occurs where a franchisor expressly or impliedly by its conduct makes a franchisee its agent. The franchisor is liable for the contracts entered into and torts committed by the franchisee while acting within the scope of the agency. 2. *Apparent agency*. Agency that arises when a franchisor creates the appearance that a franchisee is its agent when in fact an actual agency does not exist. The franchisor is liable for the contracts entered into and torts committed by the franchisee acting as an apparent agent.
ANTITRUST LAW AND FRANCHISING, P. 539	
Antitrust Law	*Tying arrangement*. A restraint of trade where a seller refuses to sell one product or service to a customer unless the customer agrees to purchase a second product or service from the seller. Tying arrangements by franchisors violate federal antitrust law.
TERMINATION OF FRANCHISES, P. 540	
Termination of Franchises	*Termination "for cause."* Most franchise agreements and state and federal laws, permit a franchisor to terminate the franchise "for cause" (e.g., nonpayment of franchise fees by the franchisee, continued failure of the franchisee to meet quality control standards).
Wrongful Termination	1. *Termination at will*. Most state and federal laws regulating franchising prohibit franchisors from terminating franchises at will. This is to prevent a franchisor from taking advantage of the goodwill developed at the franchise location by the franchisee. 2. *Wrongful termination*. If a franchisor terminates a franchise agreement without just cause, the franchisee can sue the franchisor for *wrongful termination*. The franchisee can recover damages caused by the wrongful termination and recover the franchise.
Special Federal Statutes	1. *Petroleum Marketing Practices Act*. A federal statute that prohibits oil company franchisors from terminating gasoline station franchises without just cause. 2. *Automobile Dealers Day in Court Act*. A federal statute that prohibits automobile company franchisors from terminating automobile dealer franchisees without just cause.

CRITICAL LEGAL THINKING CASES

22.1 Franchise Agreement H&R Block, Inc. (Block), is a franchisor that licenses franchises to provide tax preparation services to customers under the "H&R Block" service mark. In 1975, June McCart was granted an H&R Block franchise at 900 Main Street, Rochester, New York. From 1972 to 1979, her husband, Robert, was involved in the operation of an H&R Block franchise in Rensselaer, New York. After that, he assisted June in the operation of her H&R franchise. All of the McCarts' income during the time in question came from the H&R Block franchises.

The H&R Block franchise agreement that June signed contained a provision whereby she agreed not to compete (1) in the business of tax preparation (2) within 250 miles of the franchise (3) for a period of two years after the termination of the franchise. Robert did not sign the Rochester franchise agreement. On December 31, 1981, June wrote a letter to H&R Block giving notice she was terminating the franchise. Shortly thereafter, the McCarts sent a letter to people who had been clients of the Rochester H&R Block office informing them that June was leaving H&R Block and that Robert was opening a tax preparation service in which June would assist him. H&R Block granted a new franchise in Rochester to another franchisee. It sued the McCarts to enforce the covenant not to compete against them. Who wins? [*McCart v. H&R Block, Inc.*, 470 N.E.2d 756 (Ind.App. 1984)]

22.2 Franchise Agreement Libby-Broadway Drive-In, Inc. (Libby), is a corporation licensed to operate a "McDonald's" fast food franchise restaurant by the McDonald's System, Inc. (McDonald's). Libby was granted a license to operate a McDonald's store in Cleveland, Ohio, and was granted an exclusive territory in which McDonald's could not grant another franchise. The area was described as "bound on the north by the south side of Miles Avenue, on the west and south side by Turney Road, on the east by Warrensville Center Road." In December 1976, McDonald's granted a franchise to another franchisee to operate a McDonald's restaurant on the west side of Turney Road. Libby sued McDonald's, alleging a breach of the franchise agreement. Is McDonald's liable? [*Libby-Broadway Drive-In, Inc. v. McDonald's System, Inc.*, 391 N.E.2d (Ill.App. 1979)]

22.3 Disclosure My Pie International, Inc. (My Pie), an Illinois corporation, is a franchisor that licenses franchisees to open pie shops under its trademark name. My Pie has licensed 13 restaurants throughout the country, including one owned by Dowmont, Inc. (Dowmont) in Glen Ellyn, Illinois. The Illinois Franchise Disclosure Act requires a franchisor that desires to issue franchises in the state to register with the state or qualify for an exemption from registration and to make certain disclosures to prospective franchisees. My Pie granted the license to Dowmont without registering with the state of Illinois or qualifying for an exemption from registration and without making the required disclosures to Dowmont. Dowmont operated its restaurant as a "My Pie" franchise between July 1976 and May 1980, and since then has operated it under the name "Arnold's." Dowmont paid franchise royalty fees to My Pie prior to May 1980. My Pie sued Dowmont for breach of the franchise agreement and recover royalties it claimed was due from Dowmont. Dowmont filed a counterclaim seeking to rescind the franchise agreement and recover the royalties it had paid to My Pie. Who wins? [*My Pie International, Inc. v. Dowmont, Inc.*, 687 F.2d 919 (7th Cir. 1982)]

22.4 Tort Liability Georgia Girl Fashions, Inc. (Georgia Girl) is a franchisor that licenses franchisees to operate women's retail clothing stores under the "Georgia Girl" trademark. Georgia Girl granted a franchise to a franchisee to operate a store on South Cobb Drive in Smyrna, Georgia. Georgia Girl did not supervise or control the day-to-day operations of the franchisee. Melanie McMullan entered the store to exchange a blouse that she had previously purchased at the store. When she found nothing that she wished to exchange the blouse for, she began to leave the store. At that time, she was physically restrained and accused of shoplifting the blouse. McMullan was taken to the local jail, where she was held until her claim of prior purchase could be verified. The store then dropped the charges against her and she was released from jail. McMullan filed an action against the store owner and Georgia Girl to recover damages for false imprisonment. Is Georgia Girl liable? [*McMullan v. Georgia Girl Fashions, Inc.*, 348 S.E.2d 748 (Ga.App. 1988)]

22.5 Tort Liability The Seven-Up Company (Seven-Up) is a franchisor that licenses local bottling companies to manufacture, bottle, and distribute soft drinks using the "7-Up" trademark. The Brooks Bottling Company (Brooks) is a Seven-Up franchisee that bottles and sells 7-Up soft drinks to stores in Michigan. Under the franchise agreement, the franchisee is required to purchase the 7-Up syrup from Seven-Up, but it can purchase its bottles, cartons, and other supplies from independent suppliers if Seven-Up approves the design of these articles.

Brooks used cartons designed and manufactured by Olinkraft, Inc., using a design that Seven-Up had approved. Sharon Proos Kosters, a customer at Meijers Thrifty Acre Store in Holland, Michigan, removed a cardboard carton containing six bottles of 7-Up from a grocery store shelf, put it under her arm, and walked toward the check-out counter. As she did so, a bottle slipped out of the carton and fell on the floor and exploded, causing a piece of glass to strike Kosters in her eye as she looked down; she was blinded in that eye. Evidence showed that the 7-Up carton was designed to be held from the top and was made without a strip on the side of the carton that would prevent a bottle from slipping out if held underneath. Kosters sued Seven-Up to recover damages for her injuries. Is Seven-Up liable? [*Kosters v. Seven-Up Company*, 595 F.2d 347 (6th Cir. 1979)]

22.6 Antitrust Chicken Delight, Inc. (Chicken Delight), is a franchisor that has licensed hundreds of franchisees to operate takeout and home delivery retail stores for the sale of fried chicken and other products under the "Chicken Delight" trademark. Chicken Delight franchisees do not have to pay an initial franchise fee or any royalty fees. Instead, the franchise agreement requires franchisees to purchase their necessary supplies—including cookers, fryers, other equipment, packaging supplies, seasoning mixes, and other products—from Chicken Delight. The prices charged by Chicken Delight for these products is higher than the price of comparable products sold by independent suppliers. Most of these products are not considered trade secrets and are not too complicated for other suppliers to provide. Several franchisees sued Chicken Delight, alleging that Chicken Delight had engaged in an illegal tying arrangement in violation of Section 1 of the Sherman Act. Who wins? [*Siegel v. Chicken Delight, Inc.*, 448 F.2d 43 (9th Cir. 1971)]

22.7 Antitrust Baskin-Robbins Ice Cream Company (Baskin-Robbins), is a national franchisor that licenses franchisees to operate retail ice cream stores using "Baskin-Robbins" trademarks and service marks. Baskin-Robbins develops flavors and types of ice cream that are unique to Baskin-Robbins. The formulations of these ice creams are trade secrets. Baskin-Robbins licenses third parties to manufacture the ice cream pursuant to Baskin-Robbins' specifications. The third-party manufacturers have signed secrecy contracts agreeing to keep Baskin-Robbins' trade secrets confidential. The franchise agreements with the retail franchisees require them to purchase their ice cream from only the third-party manufacturers licensed by Baskin-Robbins. Is this an illegal tying arrangement? [*Krehl v. Baskin-Robbins Ice Cream Company*, 664 F.2d 1348 (9th Cir. 1982)]

22.8 Trademark The Kentucky Fried Chicken Corporation (KFC) is the franchisor of "Kentucky Fried Chicken" restaurants. Franchisees must purchase equipment and supplies from manufacturers approved in writing by KFC. Equipment includes cookers, fryers, ovens, and the like; supplies include carry-out boxes, napkins, towelettes, and plastic eating utensils known as "sporks." These products are not trade secrets. KFC may not "unreasonably withhold" approval of any suppliers who apply and whose goods are tested and found to meet KFC's quality control standards. The 10 manufacturers who went through KFC's approval process were approved. KFC also sells supplies to franchisees in competition with these independent suppliers. All supplies, whether produced by KFC or the independent suppliers, must contain "Kentucky Fried Chicken" trademarks.

Upon formation in 1972, Diversified Container Corporation (Diversified) began manufacturing and selling supplies to Kentucky Fried Chicken franchisees without applying for or receiving KFC's approval. All of the items sold by Diversified contained Kentucky Fried Chicken trademarks. Diversified represented to franchisees that its products met "all standards" of KFC and that it sold "approved supplies." Diversified even affixed Kentucky Fried Chicken trademarks to the shipping boxes in which it delivered supplies to franchisees. Evidence showed that Diversified's products did not meet the quality control standards set by KFC. KFC sued Diversified for trademark infringement. Who wins? [*Kentucky Fried Chicken Corporation v. Diversified Container Corporation*, 549 F.2d 368 (5th Cir. 1977)]

22.9 Trademark Ramada Inns, Inc. (Ramada Inns), is a franchisor that licenses franchisees to operate motor hotels using the "Ramada Inns" trademarks and service marks. In August 1977, the Gadsden Motor Company (Gadsden), a partnership, purchased a motel in Attalla, Alabama, and entered into a franchise agreement with Ramada Inns to operate it as a Ramada Inns motor hotel. In 1982, the motel began receiving poor ratings from Ramada Inns inspectors, and Gadsden fell behind on its monthly franchise fee payments. Despite proddings from Ramada Inns, the motel never met Ramada Inns' operational standards again. On November 17, 1983, Ramada Inns properly terminated the franchise agreement, citing quality deficiencies and Gadsden's failure to pay past due franchise fees. The termination notice directed Gadsden to remove any materials or signs identifying the motel as a Ramada Inns. Gadsden continued using Ramada Inns' signage, trademarks, and service marks inside and outside the motel. In September 1984, Ramada Inns sued Gadsden for trademark infringement. Who wins? [*Ramada Inns, Inc. v. Gadsden Motel Company*, 804 F.2d 1562 (11th Cir.)]

22.10 Termination of a Franchise In 1976, Amoco Oil Company (Amoco) purchased the land in question and constructed a two-bay gasoline station at a total cost of $125,000. The property was then leased to Robert F. Burns, who operated an Amoco franchise gasoline station. The franchise was maintained through a series of written one-year leases. The leases provided for automatic renewal unless either party gave written notice of cancellation prior to the end of the current term. On June 8, 1977, Amoco gave Burns written notice of nonrenewal and directed Burns to vacate the premises effective September 10, 1977. Evidence showed that the gasoline station had been suffering a steadily decreasing sales volume and that the station was an unprofitable location for Amoco. Evidence further showed that no reasonable steps could be taken to increase the sales volume at the site to make it profitable. Amoco planned on discontinuing the sale of gasoline at the site and selling the property. Burns sued Amoco for wrongful termination. Who wins? [*Amoco Oil Company v. Burns*, 437 A.2d 381 (Pa. 1981)]

22.11 Termination of a Franchise Kawasaki Motors Corporation (Kawasaki), a Japanese corporation, manufactures motorcycles that it distributes in the United States through its subsidiary, Kawasaki Motors Corporation, U.S.A. (Kawasaki USA). Kawasaki USA is a franchisor that grants franchises to dealerships to sell Kawasaki motorcycles. In 1971, Kawasaki USA granted the Kawasaki Shop of Aurora, Inc. (Dealer), a franchise to sell Kawasaki motorcycles in Aurora, Illinois. The franchise changed locations twice. Both moves were within the five-mile exclusive territory granted the Dealer in the franchise agreement.

The Dealer did not obtain Kawasaki USA's written approval for either move as required by the franchise agreement. Kawasaki USA acquiesced to the first move, but not the second. At the second new location, the Dealer also operated Honda and Suzuki motorcycle franchises and was negotiating to operate a Yamaha franchise. The Kawasaki franchise agreement expressly permitted multiline dealerships. Kawasaki USA objected to the second move, asserting that the dealer had not received written approval for the move as required by the franchise agreement. However, evidence showed that the real reason Kawasaki objected to the move was because it did not want its motorcycles to be sold at the same location as other manufacturers' motorcycles. Kawasaki terminated the dealer's franchise. The dealer sued Kawasaki USA for wrongful termination. Who wins? [*Kawasaki Shop of Aurora, Inc. v. Kawasaki Motors Corporation, U.S.A.*, 544 N.E.2d 457 (Ill.App. 1989)]

ETHICS CASES

22.12 Ethical Perspective The Southland Corporation (Southland) owned the "7-Eleven" trademark and licensed franchisees throughout the country to operate 7-Eleven stores. The franchise agreement provides for fees to be paid to Southland by each franchisee based on a percentage of gross profits. In return, franchisees receive a lease of premises, a license to use the 7-Eleven trademark and trade secrets, advertising merchandise, and bookkeeping assistance. Vallerie Campbell purchased an existing 7-Eleven store in Fontana, California, and became a Southland franchisee. The franchise was designated #13974 by Southland. As part of the purchase, she applied to the state of California for transfer of her beer and wine license from the prior owner. Southland also executed the application. California approved the transfer and issued the license to "Campbell Vallerie Southland #13974."

On September 9, 1978, an employee of Campbell's store sold beer to Jesse Lewis Cope, a minor who was allegedly intoxicated at the time. After drinking the beer, Cope drove his vehicle and struck another vehicle. Two occupants of the other vehicle, Denise Wickham and Tyrone Crosby, were severely injured, and a third occupant, Cedrick Johnson, was killed. Johnson (through his parents), Wickham and Crosby sued Southland—but not Campbell—to recover damages. Is Southland Corporation legally liable for the tortious acts of its franchisee? Is it morally responsible? [*Wickham v. The Southland Corporation*, 168 Cal.App.3d 49, 213 Cal.Rptr. 825 (Cal.App. 1985)]

22.13 Ethical Perspective KFC Corporation (KFC), with its principal place of business in Louisville, Kentucky, is the franchisor of "Kentucky Fried Chicken" restaurants. KFC's registered trademarks and service marks include "Kentucky Fried Chicken," "It's Finger Lickin' Good," the portrait of Colonel Harlan Sanders, and others. KFC grants a license to its franchisees to use these marks in connection with the preparation and sale of "Original Recipe Kentucky Fried Chicken." Original

Recipe Kentucky Fried Chicken, which is sold only by KFC franchisees, is prepared by a special cooking process featuring the use of a secret recipe seasoning known as "KFC Seasonings." This blend of seasoning was developed by KFC's founder, Colonel Harlan Sanders. As a condition of each franchise agreement, KFC requires that its franchisees use only KFC Seasoning in connection with the preparation and sale of Kentucky Fried Chicken.

KFC Seasoning is a trade secret. To make the seasoning, KFC has entered into contracts with two spice blenders, the John W. Sexton Co., Inc. (Sexton), and Strange Co. (Strange). Each of these companies blends approximately one half of the spices of KFC Seasoning: neither has knowledge of the complete formulation of KFC Seasoning, and both entered into secrecy agreements to maintain the confidentiality of their formulation. After the seasoning is blended by Sexton and Strange, it is mixed together and sold directly to all KFC franchisees. KFC does not receive a royalty or other economic benefit from the sale of KFC Seasoning. KFC's relationship with Sexton and Strange has existed for more than 25 years; no other companies are licensed to blend KFC Seasoning.

Marion-Kay Company, Inc. (Marion-Kay), is a spice blender engaged in the manufacture of chicken seasoning known as "Marion-Kay Seasoning." in 1973, Marion-Kay requested permission from KFC to sell its seasoning products to KFC franchisees. KFC refused the request. In 1977, KFC learned that Marion-Kay was supplying some KFC franchisees with Marion-Kay seasoning and demanded it cease this practice. When Marion-Kay refused, KFC sued it for interference with contractual relations. Marion-Kay filed a counterclaim, alleging violation of antitrust law. Who wins? Was KFC justified in preventing Marion-Kay from blending its seasonings? Did Marion-Kay act morally in selling seasoning to KFC franchisees? [*KFC Corporation v. Marion-Kay Company, Inc.*, 620 F.Supp. 1160 (S.D.Ind. 1985)]

CRITICAL LEGAL THINKING WRITING ASSIGNMENT

Read Case A.22 in the Case Appendix [*Little v. Howard Johnson Company*]. This case is excerpted from the court of appeals opinion. Review and brief the case. In your brief, be sure to answer the following questions:

1. Describe how the plaintiff was injured. Whom did she sue?

2. Was Howard Johnson Company directly liable for the plaintiff's injuries? Explain.

3. Was the franchisee an actual agent of Howard Johnson Company?

4. Did Howard Johnson's actions create an apparent agency between it and the franchisee?

NOTES

[1] Cal.Corp. Code §§ 31000–31019.
[2] 16 CFR Part 436.
[3] *Southland Corporation v. Keating*, 465 U.S. 1, 104 S.Ct. 852, 79 L.Ed.2d 1 (1985).
[4] 15 # U.S.C. §§ 1221 et seq.
[5] 15 # U.S.C. §§ 2801 et seq.

CHAPTER 23

PARTNERSHIPS AND LIMITED

LIABILITY COMPANIES

Chapter Objectives

*After studying this chapter,
you should be able to*

1. Define a general and limited partnership
2. Describe how general partnerships are formed and what provisions should appear in a partnership agreement
3. List and explain the rights among partners
4. Define the duties of loyalty and care among partners and identify violations of these duties
5. Describe the property rights of the partnership and partners
6. Explain the liability of partners for contracts of the partnership
7. Explain the tort liability of partners
8. Describe the process for dissolving and winding up a partnership
9. Define a limited liability company
10. Identify and describe the liability of members of a limited liability company

Chapter Contents

- General Partnerships
- Formation of General Partnerships
  Case 23.1 *Vohland v. Sweet (IN)*
- Rights Among Partners
- Duties Among Partners
- Property Rights of the Partnership and Partners
  Case 23.2 *Murgoitio v. Murgoitio (ID)*
- Liability of Partners to Third Parties
  Case 23.3 *Zuckerman v. Antenucci (NY)*
- Termination of Partnerships
  Case 23.4 *Lemay Bank & Trust Co. v. Lawrence (MO)*
- Limited Partnerships
  Contemporary Business Environment Master Limited Partnerships
- Limited Liability Partnerships
- Limited Liability Companies
  Business Checklist Why Operate a Business on LLC?
  Business Application Dream Works SKG: The Ultimate LLC
  International Perspective Partnerships Outside the United States
- Working the Web
- Chapter Summary
- Critical Legal Thinking Cases
- Ethics Cases
- Critical Legal Thinking Writing Assignment

> *One of the most fruitful sources of ruin to men of the world is the recklessness or want of principle of partners, and it is one of the perils to which every man exposes himself who enters into partnership with another.*
>
> V.C. Malins
> *Mackay v. Douglas,*
> 14 Eq. 106 at 118 (1872)

Many businesses are owned by multiple owners. Such businesses cannot operate as sole proprietorships, but the owners can choose to operate as a corporation or as one of several noncorporate forms of legal entity. These include general partnerships, limited partnerships, or limited liability companies. The formation of each of these noncorporate types of businesses, the attributes of each, and the rights and duties of the owners of each of these forms of business are discussed in this chapter. Corporations are discussed in the next chapter.

GENERAL PARTNERSHIPS

General, or ordinary, partnerships have been recognized since ancient times. The English common law of partnerships governed early U.S. partnerships. The individual states expanded the body of partnership law.

A **general partnership**, or partnership, is a voluntary association of two or more persons for carrying on a business as co-owners for profit. The formation of a partnership creates certain rights and duties among partners and with third parties. These rights and duties are established in the partnership agreement and by law. **General partners**, or partners, are personally liable for the debts and obligations of the partnership.

general partnership A voluntary association of two or more persons for carrying on a business as co-owners for profit. Also called a *partnership*.

Uniform Partnership Act (UPA)

In 1914, the National Conference of Commissioners on Uniform State Laws (a group of lawyers, judges, and legal scholars) promulgated the **Uniform Partnership Act (UPA)**. The UPA codifies partnership law. Its goal was to establish consistent partnership law that was uniform throughout the United States. The UPA has been adopted in whole or in part by 48 states,[1] the District of Columbia, Guam, and the Virgin Islands. Because it is so important, the UPA will form the basis of the study of general partnerships in this chapter.

Uniform Partnership Act (UPA) Model act that codifies partnership law. Most states have adopted the UPA in whole or part.

The UPA covers most problems that arise in the formation, operation, and dissolution of ordinary partnerships. Other rules of law or equity govern if there is no applicable provision of the UPA.[2]

Entity Theory of Partnerships

The UPA adopted the **entity theory** of partnership, which considers partnerships as separate legal entities. As such, partnerships can hold title to personal and real property, transact business in the partnership name, and the like.

entity theory A theory that holds that partnerships are separate legal entities that can hold title to personal and real property, transact business in the partnership name, and the like.

FORMATION OF GENERAL PARTNERSHIPS

A general partnership may be formed with little or no formality. The following paragraphs discuss the formation of general partnerships.

general partnership An association of two or more persons to carry on, as co-owners, a business for profit [UPA § 6(1)].

Definition of a Partnership

A business must meet four criteria to qualify as a partnership under the UPA.[3] It must be (1) an association of two or more persons (2) carrying on a business (3) as co-owners (4) for profit. Each of these elements is discussed in the following paragraphs.

Association of Two or More Persons

Partnerships are voluntary associations of two or more persons.[4] All partners must agree to the participation of each copartner. A person cannot be forced to be a partner or to accept another person as a partner. The UPA definition of person includes natural persons, partnerships (including limited partnerships), corporations, limited liability companies, and other associations.[5]

Carrying on a Business

The mere co-ownership of property by joint tenancy, tenancy in common, tenancy by the entireties, joint property, community property, or part ownership does not itself establish a partnership.[6] A business—trade, occupation, or profession—must be carried on.[7] Generally, this means a series of transactions carried on over a period of time. Single or isolated transactions usually do not qualify as a partnership.

"The partner of my partner is not my partner."
Legal Maxim

Co-ownership of a Business

Co-ownership of a business is essential to create a partnership. The most important factors in determining co-ownership is whether the parties share the business's profits and management responsibility.

Receipt of a share of business profits is prima facie evidence of a partnership because nonpartners usually are not given the right to share in the business's profits. No inference of the existence of a partnership is drawn if profits are received in payment of (1) a debt owed to a creditor in installments or otherwise, (2) wages owed to an employee, (3) rent owed to a landlord, (4) an annuity owed to a widow, widower, or representative of a deceased partner, (5) interest owed on a loan, or (6) consideration for the sale of goodwill of a business.[8] An agreement to share losses of a business is strong evidence of a partnership.

The right to participate in the management of a business is important evidence for determining the existence of a partnership, but it is not conclusive evidence because the right to participate in management is sometimes given to employees, creditors, and others. It is compelling evidence of the existence of a partnership if a person is given the right to share in profits, losses, and management of a business.

Profit Motive

The organization or venture must have a profit motive in order to qualify as a partnership, even though the business does not actually have to make a profit. Nonprofit organizations, such as charitable or fraternal organizations, cannot be organized as partnerships because they do not meet this requirement.

In the following case, the court had to decide whether a partnership had been created.

CASE 23.1

Vohland v. Sweet

435 N.E.2d 860 (1982) Court of Appeals of Indiana

Facts Norman E. Sweet began working for Charles Vohland as an hourly employee at a garden nursery owned by Vohland in 1956, when he was a youngster. Upon completion of military service (from 1958 to 1960), Sweet resumed his former employment. In 1963, Charles Vohland retired and his son Paul Vohland (Vohland) commenced what became known as Vohland's Nursery, the business of which was landscape gardening. Vohland purchased the in-

terests of his brothers and sisters in the nursery. At that time, Sweet's status changed. He was to receive a 20-percent share of the net profit of the business after all expenses were paid, including labor, supplies, plants, and other expenses. Sweet contributed no capital to the enterprise. The compensation was paid on an irregular basis—every several weeks Vohland and Sweet would sit down, compute the income received and expenses paid, and Sweet would be issued a check for 20 percent of the balance. No Social Security or income taxes were withheld from Sweet's checks.

Vohland and Sweet did not enter into a written agreement. No partnership income tax returns were filed by the business. Sweet's tax returns declared that he was a self-employed salesman. He paid self-employment Social Security taxes. Vohland handled all of the finances and books of the nursery and borrowed money from the bank solely in his own name for business purposes. Vohland made most of the sales for the business. Sweet managed the physical aspects of the nursery, supervised the care of the nursing stock, and oversaw the performance of the contracts for customers. Sweet testified that in the early 1970s Vohland told him:

> He was going to take me in and that I wouldn't have to punch a time clock anymore, that I would be on a commission basis and that I would be—have more of an interest in the business if I had an interest in the business. He referred to it as a "piece of the action."

Vohland denied making this statement. Sweet brought this action for dissolution of the alleged partnership and for an accounting. He sought payment for 20 percent of the business's inventory. The trial court held in favor of Sweet and awarded him $58,733. Vohland appealed.

Issue Did Vohland and Sweet enter into a partnership?

Decision Yes. The court of appeals held that a partnership had been created between Vohland and Sweet. Affirmed.

Reason Receipt by a person of a share of the profits is prima facie evidence that he or she is a partner in a business. Here, Sweet shared in the profits of the nursery. Although the parties called Sweet's sharing in the profits a "commission," the court stated that the term "when used by landscape gardeners and not lawyers, should not be restricted to its technical definition." The court found that the absence of a capital contribution by Sweet was not controlling and that his contribution of labor and skill would suffice.

CASE QUESTIONS

Critical Legal Thinking Do you think a partnership was formed in this case? Should all partnership agreements be required to be in writing?

Ethics Do you think either party acted unethically in this case?

Business Implication What are the economic consequences of finding a partnership?

Partnership Name

An ordinary partnership can operate under the names of any one or more of the partners or under a fictitious business name. If the partnership operates under a fictitious name, it must file a fictitious business name statement with the appropriate government agency and publish a notice of the name in a newspaper of general circulation where the partnership does business. The name selected by a partnership cannot indicate that it is a corporation (e.g., it cannot contain the term *Inc.*) and cannot be similar to the name used by any existing business entity.

BUSINESS BRIEF
Partnerships often operate under a fictitious business name. Those that do must file a fictitious business name statement with the appropriate government agency.

Partnership Capital

Money and property contributed by partners for the permanent use of the partnership is called **partnership capital**. Such property cannot be withdrawn from the partnership prior to dissolution unless all of the partners consent to the withdrawal.

The partners can make loans of property or money to the partnership. Partners who do so become creditors of the partnership. Loans and the value of services provided to a partnership are not included in the partnership capital.

partnership capital
Money and property contributed by partners for the permanent use of the partnership.

Duration of Partnership

The duration of a partnership can be for a fixed term (e.g., five years) or until a particular undertaking is accomplished (e.g., until a real estate development is completed) or it can be for an unspecified term. A partnership with a fixed duration is called a **partnership for a term**. A partnership with no fixed duration is called a **partnership at will**.

partnership for a term
A partnership with a fixed duration.

partnership at will
A partnership with no fixed duration.

The Partnership Agreement

The agreement to form a partnership may be oral, written, or implied from the conduct of the parties. It may even be created inadvertently. No formalities are necessary, although a few states require general partnerships to file **certificates of partnership** with an appropriate government agency. Partnership agreements of partnerships that exist for more than one year or are authorized to deal in real estate must be in writing under the Statute of Frauds.

certificate of partnership
A document that a partnership must file with the appropriate state government agency in some states to acknowledge that the partnership exists.

It is good practice for partners to put their partnership agreement in writing. A written document is important evidence of the terms of the agreement, particularly if a dispute arises among the partners.

partnership agreement
A written partnership agreement that the partners sign.

Written Partnership Agreement A written partnership agreement is called a **partnership agreement** or **articles of partnership**. The partners can agree to almost any term in their partnership agreement, except terms that are illegal. The articles of partnership can be short and simple or long and complex. In all events, however, the partnership agreement should contain the following information:

- The firm name
- The names and addresses of the partners
- The principal office of the partnership
- The nature and scope of the partnership business
- The duration of the partnership
- The capital contributions of each partner
- The division of profits and losses among the partners
- The salaries, if any, to be paid to partners
- The duties of the partners regarding the management of the partnership
- Limitations, if any, on the authority of partners to bind the partnership
- Provisions for the admission and withdrawal of partners from the firm, and the terms, conditions, and notices required for withdrawal
- Provisions for continuing the partnership upon the withdrawal of a partner, death of a partner, or other dissolution of the partnership and
- Any other provisions deemed relevant by the partners

BUSINESS BRIEF
Although oral partnership agreements are enforceable, it is better practice for the partners to have a written partnership agreement. This will prevent many misunderstandings that could lead to lawsuits among partners.

If the agreement fails to provide for an essential term or contingency, the provisions of the UPA control. Thus, the UPA acts as a gap-filling device to the partners' agreement. A sample partnership agreement is shown in Exhibit 23.1.

Exhibit 23.1
Sample Partnership Agreement

PARTNERSHIP AGREEMENT

The parties to this agreement, Sarah Smith, Jeffrey Gold, and Min-Wer Chen, hereby agree to form a partnership on the terms and conditions set forth below.

1. The name of the partnership is Smith, Gold, and Chen.
2. The purpose of the partnership is to practice the profession of law and to do all other acts incidental thereto pursuant to the laws of the state of Florida and the rules and regulations of the State Bar of Florida.
3. The office of the partnership shall be located in Dade County, Florida.
4. The partnership shall commence on January 1, 1999 and shall continue until dissolved by mutual agreement of the parties.
5. The initial capital of the partnership shall consist of One Hundred Thousand Dollars ($100,000). All capital of the partnership shall be contributed equally by the partners.
6. The net income and/or profits or net losses from the partnership business shall be divided equally between the partners.
7. The partners shall devote their entire time, attention, and influence to the affairs of the partnership.
8. No partner, during the continuance of the partnership, shall pursue, or become directly or indirectly interested in, any business or occupation that is in conflict with either the business of

the partnership or with the rights, duties, and responsibilities of such partners to the partnership.

9.   Each partner shall have an interest in the conduct of the affairs of the partnership and, except as otherwise provided in this partnership agreement, all decisions shall be by the majority vote of the partners.

10.   All funds of the partnership shall be deposited in the First National Bank of Florida, and all withdrawals therefrom may be made upon checks signed by at least two partners.

11.   The partnership books, records, and accounts shall be kept at the principal place of business. All books, records, and accounts of the partnership shall be open to inspection by any partner.

12.   The fiscal year of the partnership shall commence on January 1st of each year and end on December 31st of that year.

13.   The admission of a new partner shall require the unanimous approval of all existing partners. The capital contributions to be made by, and the participation percentage in profits and losses, of the new partner shall be determined by vote of a majority in interest of the existing partners. Each new partner must, before being admitted, agree in writing to be bound by the provisions of this partnership agreement.

14.   Upon the dissolution of the partnership by reason of the death, permanent incapacity, or withdrawal of any partner, the remaining partners may, if they so desire, continue the business, and they shall have the right to purchase the interest of the other partner by paying to such partner or his or her personal representative or the person legally entitled to payment, the value of his or her interest, consisting of (1) the balance of the partner's capital account as of the last day of the month of death, incapacity, or withdrawal and (2) the partner's share of profits for the current calendar year not yet reflected in his or her capital account as of the last day of the month of death, incapacity, or withdrawal. Such payments shall be made within 120 days after the last day of the month of the death, incapacity, or withdrawal. The preceding payments shall be reduced by the amount of the partner's share of any losses for the current calendar year.

The value of the partnership interest shall be determined as follows: (a) by mutual agreement, or, if that proves impossible, (b) the partners desiring to continue the business shall select one individual as an appraiser and the retiring partner or his or her representative shall select one individual as an appraiser, who shall mutually determine such value. In the event said appraisers are unable to mutually agree as to such value, within 30 days after their appointment, they shall select and designate one additional appraiser for this purpose whose appraisement shall be binding on all parties.

15.   This partnership agreement may be amended at any time, but any amendment must be in writing and signed by each person who is then a partner.

16.   This partnership agreement shall be binding on and issue to the benefit of the respective successors, assigns, and personal representatives of the partners, except to the extent of any contrary provision in the partnership agreement.

17.   If any term, provision, or condition of this partnership agreement is held by a court of competent jurisdiction to be invalid, void, or unenforceable, the rest of the agreement shall remain in full force and effect and shall in no way be affected, impaired, or invalidated.

18.   This partnership agreement contains the entire understanding of the partners regarding their rights and duties in the partnership. Any alleged oral representations or modifications concerning this agreement shall be of no force or effect unless contained in a subsequent written amendment signed by the partner to be charged.

19.   This partnership agreement has been made and entered into in accordance with the laws of the state of Florida, and said agreement shall be construed and applied in all respects in accordance with the laws of that state.

20.   In the event of serious disagreement or dispute between any of the partners regarding any aspect of the partnership business, that disagreement or dispute shall be resolved by submitting the matter to arbitration. The arbitrators of any disagreement or dispute shall be the American Arbitration Association. The decision of the arbitrators shall be final and binding.

IN WITNESS WHEREOF, the parties have executed this partnership agreement at Miami, Florida, on January 1, 1999.

_____   _____

Sarah Smith   Jeffrey Gold

                                         _____

                                         Min-Wer Chen

Partnership by Estoppel

A **partnership by estoppel** arises when a person who is not a partner either makes a representation or consents to a partner's representation that he or she is a partner. The nonpartner (or **ostensible partner**) is liable to any person who reasonably relied on the representation when deciding to extend credit to the partnership. The nonpartner has the same liability as an actual partner. Both the nonpartner and the partner who consents to the representation are *estopped*—forbidden—from denying liability.[9] If all of the partners of a partnership consent to the representation, the credit contract becomes an obligation of the partnership.

Agency Law as the Basis of Partnership Relations

Many of the rights, duties, and liabilities of partners are governed by the principles of agency law.[10] Every partner is an agent of the partnership for purposes of its business[11] and an agent of every other partner concerning his or her own acts. Each partner is also a principal of every other partner concerning their acts. Thus, the law of partnership is governed by the principles of agency law.

RIGHTS AMONG PARTNERS

BUSINESS BRIEF
The formation of a general partnership creates certain rights and duties among partners and with third parties.

When partners enter into a general partnership, the law provides that the partners have certain rights. The extent of these rights is discussed in the following paragraphs.

Right to Participate in Management

management Unless otherwise agreed, each partner has a right to participate in the management of the partnership and has an equal vote on partnership matters.

In the absence of an agreement to the contrary, all partners have equal rights in the **management** and conduct of the partnership business.[12] In other words, each partner has one vote regardless of the proportional size of his or her capital contribution or share in the partnership's profits. Under the UPA, a simple majority decides most ordinary partnership matters.[13] If the vote is tied, the action being voted on is considered to be defeated. The following issues require the unanimous consent of the partners:

1. Assignment of partnership property for the benefit of creditors
2. Disposal of the goodwill of the business
3. Actions that would make it impossible to carry on the ordinary business of the partnership
4. Submission of a partnership claim or liability to arbitration[14]
5. Admission of a new partner to the partnership[15]
6. Actions in contravention of the partnership agreement[16]
7. Actions that are not apparently for the carrying on of the business of the partnership in the usual way or that change the nature of the business[17]

The partners may agree to modify the majority and unanimous consent rules just discussed. The partners may delegate management responsibility to a committee of partners or to a managing partner. The partnership agreement can also create classes of partners with unequal voting powers.

Right to Share in Profits and Losses

BUSINESS BRIEF
Unless otherwise agreed, partners have a right to an equal share in the partnership's profits (and losses). Therefore, partners should agree in writing how profits and losses from the partnership will be divided. This will avoid disputes in the future.

Unless otherwise agreed, the UPA mandates that a partner has the right to an equal share in the partnership's profits and losses.[18] Partnership agreements often provide that profits and losses are to be allocated in proportion to the partners' capital contributions. The right to share in the profits of the partnership is considered to be the right to share in the earnings from the investment of capital.

CONSIDER THIS EXAMPLE: Suppose LeAnn Pearson and Mark Butler form a partnership. Ms. Pearson contributes $75,000 capital and Mr. Butler contributes $25,000 capital. They do not have an agreement as to how profits or losses are to be shared.

Assume the partnership makes $100,000 in profits. Under the UPA, Ms. Pearson and Mr. Butler share the profits equally—$50,000 each. If the partnership lost $100,000, Ms. Pearson and Mr. Butler would share the loss equally—$50,000 each.

Where a partnership agreement provides for the sharing of profits but is silent as to how losses are to be shared, losses are shared in the same proportion as profits. The reverse is not true. If a partnership agreement provides for the sharing of losses but is silent as to how profits are to be shared, profits are shared equally.

Expressly providing how profits and losses are to be shared by partners can increase the benefits to partners. For example, partners with high incomes from other sources can benefit most from the losses by a partnership.

Right to Compensation

Unless otherwise agreed, the UPA provides that no partner is entitled to remuneration for his or her performance in the partnership's business.[19] Under this rule, partners are not entitled to receive either a salary for providing services to the partnership, even if the services provided are disproportionate to the services provided by other partners, or rents for personal property used by the partnership. However, the agreement may specifically state that a particular partner is to receive such remuneration.

Under the UPA, it is implied that partners will devote full time and service to the partnership. Thus, unless otherwise agreed, income earned by partners from providing services elsewhere belongs to the partnership.[20]

> **CAUTION**
> *A partner is not entitled to compensation for services provided to the partnership unless the partnership agreement so provides.*

Right of Indemnification

Partners sometimes incur personal travel, business, and other expenses on behalf of the partnership. A partner is entitled to **indemnification** (i.e., reimbursement) for such expenditures if they are reasonably incurred in the ordinary and proper conduct of the business and for the preservation of partnership property.[21]

> **indemnification** Right of a partner to be reimbursed for expenditures incurred on behalf of the partnership.

Right to Return of Advances

A partner who makes an **advance** (loan) to the partnership becomes a creditor of the partnership. The partner is entitled to repayment of the loan, but this right is subordinated to the claims of creditors who are not partners.[22] The partner is entitled to receive interest from the date of the advance.[23]

Right to Return of Capital

Upon termination of a partnership, the partners are entitled to have their capital contributions returned to them.[24] However, this right is subordinated to the rights of creditors, who must be paid their claims first.[25] Unless otherwise agreed, no interest is paid on a partner's capital contribution.[26]

Right to Information

Every partner has the right to demand true and full information from any partner of all things affecting the partnership.[27] The corollary to this rule is that each partner has a duty to provide such information upon the receipt of a reasonable demand. The personal representative (lawyer or accountant) of a partner or deceased partner has the same rights and duties in this regard as the party represented.

The partnership books (financial records, tax records, and such) must be kept at the partnership's principal place of business unless all of the partners consent to their removal.[28] The partners have an absolute right to inspect and copy these records.

> **CAUTION**
> *The partners of a general partnership have an absolute right to inspect and copy the partnership's books and records.*

> **action for an accounting** A formal judicial proceeding in which the court is authorized to (1) review the partnership and the partners' transactions and (2) award each partner his or her share of the partnership assets.

Right to an Accounting

Partners are not permitted to sue the partnership or other partners at law. Instead, they are given the right to bring an **action for an accounting** against other partners.

An accounting is a formal judicial proceeding in which the court is authorized to (1) review the partnership and the partners' transactions and (2) award each partner his or her share of the partnership assets.[29] It results in a money judgment for or against partners according to the balance struck.

DUTIES AMONG PARTNERS

Partners owe certain duties to the partnership and the other partners. These duties include (1) a duty of loyalty, (2) a duty of obedience, (3) a duty of care, and (4) a duty to inform. Each of these is discussed in the sections that follow.

Duty of Loyalty

duty of loyalty A duty that a partner owes not to act adversely to the interests of the partnership.

Partners are in a fiduciary relationship with one another. As such, they owe each other a **duty of loyalty**. This duty is imposed by law and cannot be waived. If there is a conflict between partnership interests and personal interests, the partner must choose the interest of the partnership.

BUSINESS BRIEF

Partners breach their duty of loyalty if they

1. Self-deal with the partnership without permission;

2. Usurp a partnership opportunity;

3. Compete with the partnership without permission;

4. Make secret profits from partnership business;

5. Disclose confidential partnership information;

6. Misuse partnership property, or

7. Other breaches of their fiduciary duty.

Examples of the Breach of the Duty of Loyalty Some basic forms of breach of loyalty involve the following:

1. **Self-dealing.** Self-dealing occurs when a partner deals personally with the partnership, such as buying or selling goods or property to the partnership. Such actions are permitted only if full disclosure is made and consent of the other partners is obtained. For example, suppose a partnership in which Dan is a partner is looking for a piece of property on which to build a new store. Dan owns a desirable piece of property. In order to sell the property to the partnership, Dan must first disclose his ownership interest and receive his partners' consent.

2. **Usurping a partnership opportunity.** A partner who is offered an opportunity on behalf of the partnership cannot take the opportunity for him- or herself. In other words, if a third party offers an opportunity to a partner in his or her partnership status (e.g., the opportunity to purchase a business), the partner cannot take the opportunity for him- or herself before offering it to the partnership. If the partnership rejects the opportunity, the partner is free to pursue it if it does not violate any other duty he or she owes to the partnership.

3. **Competing with the partnership.** A partner may not compete with the partnership without the permission of the other partners. For example, a partner in a partnership that operates an automobile dealership cannot open a competing automobile dealership without her co-partners' permission.

4. **Secret profits.** Partners may not make secret profits from partnership business. For example, a partner may not keep a kickback from a supplier.

5. **Breach of confidentiality.** Partners owe a duty to keep partnership information (e.g., trade secrets, customer lists, and the like) confidential.

6. **Misuse of property.** Partners owe a duty not to use partnership property for personal use.

A partner who breaches the duty of loyalty must disgorge any profits made from the breach to the partnership. In addition, the partner is liable for any damages caused by the breach.

Duty of Obedience

duty of obedience A duty that partners must adhere to the provisions of the partnership agreement and the decisions of the partnership.

The **duty of obedience** requires the partners to adhere to the provisions of the partnership agreement and the decisions of the partnership. A partner who breaches this duty is liable to the partnership for any damages caused by the breach.

CONSIDER THIS EXAMPLE: Jodie, Bart, and Denise form a partnership to develop real property. Their partnership agreement specifies that acts of the partners are limited to those necessary to accomplish the partnership's purpose. Suppose Bart, acting alone, loses $100,000 of partnership funds in commodities trading. Bart is personally liable to the partnership for the lost funds because he breached the partnership agreement.

Duty of Care

A partner must use reasonable care and skill in transacting partnership business. The **duty of care** calls for the partners to use the same level of care and skill that a reasonable business manager in the same position would use in the same circumstances. Breach of the duty of care is **negligence**. A partner is liable to the partnership for any damages caused by his or her negligence. The partners are not liable for honest errors in judgment.

CONSIDER THIS EXAMPLE: Suppose Tina, Eric, and Brian form a partnership to sell automobiles. Tina, who is responsible for ordering inventory, orders large expensive cars. Assume that a war breaks out in the Middle East which interrupts the supply of oil to the United States. The demand for large cars drops substantially, and the partnership cannot sell its inventory. Tina is not liable because the duty of care was not breached. The situation might have been different if the war had broken out before the order was placed.

Duty to Inform

Partners owe a **duty to inform** their copartners of all information they possess that is relevant to the affairs of the partnership.[30] Even if a partner fails to do so, the other partners are imputed with knowledge of all notices concerning any matters relating to partnership affairs. Knowledge is also imputed regarding information acquired in the role of partner that affects the partnership and should have been communicated to the other partners.[31]

CONSIDER THIS EXAMPLE: Suppose Ted and Diane are partners. Ted knows that a piece of property owned by the partnership contains dangerous toxic wastes but fails to tell Diane of this fact. Even though Diane does not have actual knowledge of this fact, it is imputed to her.

duty of care The obligation partners owe to use the same level of care and skill that a reasonable person in the same position would use in the same circumstances. A breach of the duty of care is *negligence*.

duty to inform A duty a partner owes to inform his or her co-partners of all information he or she possesses that is relevant to the affairs of the partnership.

CAUTION
Knowledge acquired by a partner concerning matters relating to partnership affairs is imputed to the other partners even if they are not informed of the information.

PROPERTY RIGHTS OF THE PARTNERSHIP AND PARTNERS

There is an important distinction between property owned by the partnership and individual partners' property rights in the partnership.

Partnership Property

All property originally brought into the partnership on account of the partnership is **partnership property**. Unless otherwise stated in the partnership agreement, property that is subsequently acquired by purchase or otherwise on account of the partnership or with partnership funds is also partnership property. This is true even if title is retained by the individual partners.[32]

The partnership agreement should indicate which property originally contributed by partners is partnership property. It is good practice to keep a written record of all partnership property that is subsequently contributed, used, or acquired by the partnership.

Title to real property owned in the partnership name can be conveyed only in that name.[33] Any partner can execute the conveyance of title in the partnership name.[34] If title to partnership property is held in the name of one or more partners rather than in

partnership property Property that is originally brought into the partnership on account of the partnership and property that is subsequently acquired by purchase or otherwise on account of the partnership or with partnership funds.

the partnership name, title to the property can be transferred only by a conveyance signed by these partners.

Specific partnership property is subject to attachment or execution by creditors of the partnership.

The question of whether property belonged to the partnership was raised in the following case.

CASE 23.2

Murgoitio v. Murgoitio
726 P.2d 685 (1986) Supreme Court of Idaho

Facts In the early 1900s, J.H. Murgoitio (James) immigrated to the United States from Spain and began a small dairy operation on a 40-acre tract of land in Ada County, Idaho (the Home 40). James had three sons, R.J. (Ray), L.L. (Lou), and J.C. (Joe). At a young age, Ray was seriously injured in a fire, which hampered his activities in future years. As the sons grew up, they gradually accepted more responsibility for dairy operations, and ultimately a partnership arrangement in which each of the four men had a 25 percent interest. Over the years, the size of the partnership operation increased. In 1942, James purchased two parcels of land, the Kellogg 80, which he deeded to Lou, and the Kellogg 40, which he deeded to Ray. In 1947, James purchased another parcel of land, the Boyce 40, and deeded it to his three sons. All of these properties were used for partnership business.

In 1952, the three sons purchased their father's interest in the partnership. The Home 40 was deeded to the sons in connection with the purchase. The sons then formed a new partnership in which Lou and Joe each held a 40 percent interest and Ray a 20 percent interest. No written partnership agreement was ever drafted. Throughout the 1950s and 1960s, the partnership continued to grow and acquire additional parcels of land. Each of the new parcels of land was deeded to an individual partner rather than the partnership. The land was paid for from partnership funds, the income from the land went into the partnership, and the expenses and improvements on the land were paid for with partnership funds. Evidence showed that the partnership was the only source of income for all of the partners.

The partnership continued to grow in the 1970s, when Joe's and Lou's sons began to assist in the partnership. In 1978, Lou declared to his brothers that he was dissolving the partnership effective December 31, 1978. On August 14, 1979, he initiated this action seeking the court's assistance in winding up the partnership. Ray died on December 11, 1979, survived by two brothers and two sisters. One sister, Ana, was appointed a personal representative of his estate. The trial court concluded that the approximately 875 acres of property at issue exceeded $6 million in value. Lou asserted that the real property belonged to the individual partners according to record title. Joe and Ana took the position that the partnership owned all of the real property. The trial court held in favor of Joe and Ana and appointed a receiver to sell the property. Lou appealed.

Issue Is the real property whose title is held in the names of individual partners partnership property?

Decision Yes. The supreme court of Idaho held that the real property was partnership property. Affirmed.

Reason Unless a contrary intent is shown, property acquired with partnership funds is presumed to belong to the partnership. The court held that the title to the property in question was taken in individual names only as a matter of convenience. The record revealed the following evidence in support of the trial court's finding that the property was owned by the partnership: All the property was purchased with partnership funds. The partnership paid the taxes, insurance, and maintenance on the property. All improvements to the property were made with partnership funds, and the property was occupied, managed, and used as an integral part of the partnership business.

CASE QUESTIONS

Critical Legal Thinking Should how title is held determine whether property is partnership property? Or should other facts be considered? Explain.

Ethics Do you think any party acted unethically in this case?

Business Implication Why do you think this suit developed?

Partners' Rights in Partnership Property

A partner is a co-owner with the other partners of the specific partnership property as a **tenant in partnership**.[35] This is a special legal status that exists only in a partnership. Upon the death of a partner, the deceased partner's right in specific partnership property vests in the remaining partner or partners—it does not pass to his or her heirs or next of kin. This is called the **right of survivorship**. Upon the death of the last surviving partner, the rights in specific partnership property vest in the deceased partner's legal representative.[36] The value of the deceased partner's interest in the partnership passes to his or her beneficiaries or heirs upon his or her death, however.

right of survivorship Rule that states that a deceased partner's right in specific partnership property vests with the remaining partners upon his or her death.

Assignment of a Partnership Interest A **partner's interest** in a partnership is his or her share of the profits and surplus of the partnership. This is the partner's personal property.[37] A partner may voluntarily **assign** his or her partnership interest to a third party. The assignment can be full or partial. The assignee does not become a partner of the partnership or acquire any management or information rights. The assigning partner remains a partner with all rights and duties of a partner.

The assignment of a partnership interest merely entitles the assignee to receive the profits to which the assigning partner is entitled. When the partnership is dissolved, the assignee is entitled to receive the rights on liquidation to which the assigning partner is entitled.[38]

partner's interest A partner's share of profits and surplus of the partnership.

Judgment Creditors If the creditor of an individual partner obtains a judgment against the partner, the creditor becomes a **judgment creditor**. To satisfy the debt, a judgment creditor can ask the court to issue a **charging order** against the debtor–partner's partnership interest. A charging order, which is a form of judicial lien, entitles the judgment creditor to be paid from the debtor–partner's partnership profits. The partnership or any other partner can redeem the interest charged by paying the judgment creditor the amount due on the judgment.[39]

Judgment creditors do not become partners and are not entitled to participate in the management of the partnership. The debtor–partner against whom the charging order is issued remains a partner with all of the rights and duties of a partner.

charging order A document that the court issues against the debtor–partner's partnership interest in order to satisfy a debt.

CAUTION
A judgment creditor does not become a partner in the partnership.

LIABILITY OF PARTNERS TO THIRD PARTIES

Partners must deal with third parties in conducting partnership business. This often includes entering into contracts with third parties on behalf of the partnership. It also includes the risk of injury to a third person. Contract and tort liability of partnerships and their partners are discussed in the following paragraphs.

Contract Liability

As a legal entity, a partnership must act through its agents, that is, its partners. Contracts entered into with suppliers, customers, lenders, or others on the partnership's behalf are binding on the partnership if the partner who enters into the contract had express,[40] implied,[41] emergency,[42] or apparent authority[43] to enter into the contract. In some instances, the partners may decide to ratify an unauthorized contract. If they do, the ratification binds the partnership to the contract from the time of its execution.

Joint Liability for Partnership Contracts Under the UPA, partners are **jointly liable** for the contracts and debts of the partnership.[44] This means that a third party who sues to recover on a partnership contract or debt must name all of the partners in the lawsuit. If such a lawsuit is successful, the plaintiff can collect the entire amount of the judgment against any or all of the partners. If the third party's suit does not name all of the partners, the judgment cannot be collected against any of the partners or the partnership assets. Similarly, releasing any partner from the lawsuit releases them all.

joint liability Partners are *jointly liable* for contracts and debts of the partnership. This means that a plaintiff must name the partnership and all of the partners as defendants. If successful, the plaintiff can recover the entire amount of the judgment from any or all of the partners.

A partner who is made to pay more than his or her proportionate share of contract liability may seek **indemnification** from the partnership and from those partners who have not paid their share of the loss.

Tort Liability

While acting on partnership business, a partner or an employee of the partnership may commit a tort that causes injury to a third person. This tort could be caused by a negligent act, a breach of trust (such as embezzlement from a customer's account), a breach of fiduciary duty, defamation, fraud, or other intentional tort. The partnership is liable if the act is committed while the person is acting within the ordinary course of partnership business or with the authority of his or her co-partners.[45]

joint and several liability
Partners are *joint and severally liable* for tort liability of the partnership. This means that the plaintiff can sue one or more of the partners separately. If successful, the plaintiff can recover the entire amount of the judgment from any or all of the defendant-partners.

Joint and Several Liability for Torts Under the UPA, partners are **jointly and severally liable** for torts and breaches of trust.[46] This is so even if a partner did not participate in the commission of the act. This type of liability permits a third party to sue one or more of the partners separately. Judgment can be collected only against the partners who are sued. The partnership and partners who are made to pay tort liability may seek indemnification from the partner who committed the wrongful act. A release of one partner does not discharge the liability of other partners.

CONSIDER THIS EXAMPLE: Suppose Nicole, Jim, and Maureen form a partnership. Assume that Jim, while on partnership business, causes an automobile accident that injures Kurt, a pedestrian. Kurt suffers $100,000 in injuries. Kurt, at his option, can sue Nicole, Jim, or Maureen separately, or any two of them, or all of them.

A judgment against one partner does not extinguish the liability of the other partners. For example, if Kurt could recover only $25,000 from Nicole, he can later sue Jim or Maureen to recover the remaining $75,000. The injured party can collect only once for his injuries. The decision of the first action is usually conclusive as to liability. Thus, if in the first action against one partner the court found the partnership not liable, the third party cannot bring another action against other partners.

The court applied the doctrine of joint and several liability in the following case.

CASE 23.3

Zuckerman v. Antenucci
478 N.Y.S.2d 578 (1984) Supreme Court, Queens County, New York

Facts Jose Pena and Joseph Antenucci were both medical doctors who were partners in a medical practice. Both doctors treated Elaine Zuckerman during her pregnancy. Her son, Daniel Zuckerman, was born with severe physical problems. Elaine, as Daniel's mother and natural guardian, brought this medical malpractice suit against both doctors. The jury found that Dr. Pena was guilty of medical malpractice but that Dr. Antenucci was not. The amount of the verdict totaled $4 million. The trial court entered judgment against Dr. Pena but not against Dr. Antenucci. The plaintiffs have made a posttrial motion for judgment against both defendants.

Issue Is Dr. Antenucci jointly and severally liable for the medical malpractice of his partner, Dr. Pena?

Decision Yes. The court held that both partners were jointly and severally liable for the judgment.

Reason A partnership is liable for the tortious act of a partner, and a partner is jointly and severally liable for tortious acts chargeable to the partnership. When a tort is committed by the partnership, the wrong is imputable to all of the partners jointly and severally, and an action may be brought against all or any of them in their individual capacities or against the partnership as an entity. Therefore, even though the jury found that defendant, Antenucci was not guilty of any malpractice in his treatment of the patient, but that defendant Pena, his partner, was guilty of malpractice in his treatment of the patient, they were then both jointly and severally liable for the malpractice committed by defendant Pena by operation of law.

CASE QUESTIONS

Critical Legal Thinking What is joint and several liability? How does it differ from joint liability?

Ethics Is it ethical for a partner to deny liability for torts of other partners?

Business Implication What types of insurance should a partnership purchase? Why?

Liability of Incoming Partners

A new partner who is admitted to the partnership is liable for the existing debts and obligations (*antecedent debts*) of the partnership only to the extent of his or her capital contributions.[47] The new partner is personally liable for debts and obligations incurred by the partnership after becoming a partner.

CAUTION
A new partner is liable for antecedent debts only up to his or her capital contribution.

TERMINATION OF PARTNERSHIPS

General partnerships are dissolved and terminated in three stages: (1) dissolution, (2) winding up, and (3) termination. The **dissolution** of a partnership is "the change in the relation of the partners caused by any partner ceasing to be associated in the carrying on of the business."[48]

dissolution "The change in the relation of the partners caused by any partner ceasing to be associated in the carrying on of the business" [UPA Section 29].

Dissolution by Act of the Partners

A partnership is dissolved by the following acts of the partners[49]:

1. **Termination of a stated time or purpose.** A partnership that is formed for a specific time (e.g., 10 years) or purpose (e.g., the completion of a real estate development) dissolves automatically upon the expiration of the time or the accomplishment of the objective.

2. **Withdrawal of a partner.** Any partner of a **partnership at will** (i.e., one without a stated time or purpose) may rightfully withdraw and dissolve the partnership at any time.

3. **Expulsion of a partner.** If the partnership agreement provides that partners can be expelled upon the happening of certain events, then expulsion of a partner in accordance with the provision dissolves the partnership.

4. **Admission of a partner.** The admission of a new partner to an existing partnership dissolves the partnership. The new partnership is comprised of the continuing partners and the newly admitted partners.

5. **Mutual agreement of the partners.** All of the partners of an ordinary partnership may at any time mutually agree to dissolve the partnership.

BUSINESS BRIEF
It is often stated that the question is not whether a partnership will be dissolved, but only when.

Wrongful Dissolution A partner has the power to withdraw and dissolve the partnership at any time, but he or she may not have the right to do so. For example, a partner who withdraws from a partnership before the expiration of the term stated in the partnership agreement does not have the right to do so. The partner's action causes a **wrongful dissolution** of the partnership. The partner is liable for damages caused by the wrongful dissolution of the partnership.

wrongful dissolution When a partner withdraws from a partnership without having the right to do so at that time.

Dissolution by Operation of Law

A partnership is dissolved by operation of law upon the happening of any of the following events:

1. **Death of any partner.** A partnership dissolves automatically when a partner dies.[50] This is because the liability of the other partners is affected by the partner's death. Even if the partnership agreement allows the remaining partners to continue the partnership, a new partnership is created.

2. **Bankruptcy of any partner or the partnership.** The liquidation bankruptcy of either a partner or the partnership dissolves the partnership.[51] The bankruptcy of a partner affects that partner's ability to meet his or her obligations and liabilities, including partnership liabilities. The partnership does not dissolve if a partner becomes insolvent.

3. **Illegality.** Any event that makes it unlawful for the business of the partnership to be carried on, or for the partners to carry it on, dissolves the partnership.[52]

Dissolution by Judicial Decree

judicial decree of dissolution   Order of the court that dissolves a partnership. An application or petition must be filed by a partner or an assignee of a partnership interest with the appropriate state court; the court will issue a judicial decree of dissolution if warranted by the circumstances.

A partnership may be dissolved by a **judicial decree of dissolution**. To obtain such a decree, an application or petition must be filed by either a partner or an assignee of a partnership interest with the appropriate state court. The circumstances must indicate that dissolution is an equitable solution. Some of the more common reasons that result in the issuances of a judicial decree of dissolution are:[53]

1. A partner is adjudicated insane or is shown to be of unsound mind.

2. A partner becomes incapable of performing his or her partnership duties. For example, a partner is involved in an accident or becomes ill.

3. A partner is guilty of improper conduct that either prejudices his or her ability to perform partnership business (e.g., a partner commits fraud on the other partners) or willfully and persistently breaches the partnership agreement (e.g., enters into unauthorized contracts).

4. The partnership can be carried on only at a loss.

Notice of Dissolution

CAUTION

If a partnership is dissolved other than by operation of law, notice of the dissolution must be given to certain third parties. Partners may be liable for debts and obligations incurred on behalf of the partnership after the dissolution if the required notice is not given.

actual notice   Verbal or written notice to a third party that states clearly how the partnership ended.

constructive notice Usually written notice to a third party that is put into general circulation, such as in a newspaper.

The dissolution of a partnership terminates the partners' actual authority to enter into contracts or otherwise act on behalf of the partnership.[54] Notice of dissolution must be given to all partners. If a partner who has not received notice of dissolution enters into a contract on behalf of the partnership in the course of partnership business, the contract is binding on all of the partners.

Notice of dissolution must be given to certain third parties if the partnership is dissolved other than by operation of law. The degree of notice depends on the relationship of the third person with the partnership.[55]

1. Third parties who have actually dealt with the partnership must be given **actual notice** (verbal or written) of dissolution or have acquired knowledge of the dissolution from another source.

2. Third parties who have not dealt with the partnership but have knowledge of it must be given either actual or **constructive notice** of dissolution. Constructive notice consists of publishing a notice of dissolution in a newspaper of general circulation serving the area where the business of the partnership was regularly conducted.

3. Third parties who have not dealt with the partnership and do not have knowledge of it do not have to be given notice.

If proper notice is not given to a required third party after the dissolution of a partnership, and a partner enters into a contract with the third party, liability may arise on the grounds of apparent authority.

Notification of the dissolution of a partnership was not given to a creditor in the following case.

CASE 23.4

Lemay Bank & Trust Co. v. Lawrence
710 S.W.2d 318 (1986) Missouri Court of Appeals

Facts In 1974, Emil Heimos, Jr., and Milton D. Lawrence were engaged in a general partnership known as H&G Equipment Co. (H&G). H&G borrowed money from the Lemay Bank & Trust Co. (Lemay Bank) for partnership purposes. On July 26, 1974, Heimos and his wife executed a personal guaranty whereby they guaranteed payment of any existing or future debts of the partnership to Lemay Bank. At some point in 1975, Heimos and Lawrence dissolved their partnership by mutual agreement. However, neither of them notified Lemay Bank of this fact. On May 17, 1977, Lawrence executed a demand note for $21,800, purportedly on behalf of H&G to Lemay Bank. Three more notes were subsequently executed by Lawrence on behalf of H&G to Lemay Bank, the last one on December 2, 1979. When the last note became due and was not paid, Lemay Bank sued Heimos to recover the debt. The trial court held in favor of Heimos. Lemay Bank appealed.

Issue Is Heimos liable to Lemay Bank on the notes?

Decision Yes. The court of appeals held that Heimos was still liable on the notes because Lemay

Bank had not been given notice of the dissolution of the partnership. Reversed.

Reason The court stated, "Defendants seemingly suggest that Lemay Bank should have inferred from the circumstances or discovered through its own investigation that the partnership had been dissolved. The law, however, places no such duty upon a partnership creditor; rather, it is the duty of the partners to 'bring home' the notice of dissolution to the creditors. This Heimos and Lawrence failed to do."

CASE QUESTIONS

Critical Legal Thinking Should creditors be required to investigate whether partnerships they deal with have been dissolved?

Ethics Do you think Heimos intentionally failed to notify Lemay Bank of the dissolution of the partnership?

Business Implication What is the moral of this case?

Continuation of the Partnership after Dissolution

The surviving or remaining partners are given the right to continue the partnership after dissolution. It is good practice for the partners of a partnership to enter into a **continuation agreement** that expressly sets forth the events that allow for continuation of the partnership, the amount to be paid to outgoing partners, and other details.

When a partnership is continued, the old partnership is dissolved and a new partnership is created. The new partnership is composed of the remaining partners and any new partners admitted to the partnership. The creditors of the old partnership become creditors of the new partnership and have equal status with the creditors of the new partnership.[56]

Liability of Outgoing Partners The dissolution of a partnership does not of itself discharge the liability of outgoing partners for existing partnership debts and obligations. An outgoing partner can be relieved of liability if the outgoing partner, the continuing partners, and the creditor enter into a **novation agreement** that expressly relieves the outgoing partner from liability.[57]

continuation agreement
A document that expressly sets forth the events that allow for continuation of the partnership, the amount to be paid outgoing partners, and other details.

novation agreement
Agreement between a continuing partnership, a creditor of the partnership, and an outgoing partner expressly relieving the outgoing partner of liability to the creditor.

Winding Up and Distribution of Assets

winding up Process of liquidating the partnership's assets and distributing the proceeds to satisfy claims against the partnership.

Unless the partnership is continued, the **winding up** of the partnership follows its dissolution. The process of winding up consists of the liquidation (sale) of partnership assets and the distribution of the proceeds to satisfy claims against the partnership.

Usually, the surviving or remaining partners have the right to wind up the partnership. A bankrupt partner cannot participate in the winding up of a partnership. If a surviving partner performs the winding up, he or she is entitled to reasonable compensation for his or her services.[58] If a partner proves fraud, embezzlement, gross mismanagement, or some other breach of fiduciary duty by other partners, that partner can ask the court to wind up the affairs of the partnership. If the court grants the request, a receiver will be appointed to wind up the partnership's affairs.

distribution of assets
Upon the winding up of a dissolved partnership, the assets of the partnership are distributed in the following order [UPA § 40(b)]:
1. Creditors (except partners who are creditors)
2. Creditor–partners
3. Capital contributions
4. Profits

After the partnership assets have been liquidated and reduced to cash, the proceeds are distributed to satisfy claims against the partnership. The debts are satisfied in the following order: (1) creditors (except partners who are creditors) (2) creditor–partners (3) capital contributions and (4) profits.[59] The partners can agree to change the priority of distribution among themselves. In certain circumstances, they can also choose to take a distribution in kind rather than cash. If the partnership cannot satisfy its creditors' claims, the partners are personally liable for the partnership's debts and obligations.[60]

termination Occurs automatically when the process of winding up is completed. It ends the legal existence of the partnership.

Termination

After the proceeds are distributed, the partnership automatically terminates. **Termination** ends the legal existence of the partnership.[61]

LIMITED PARTNERSHIPS

limited partnership
A special form of partnership that is formed only if certain formalities are followed. It has both general and limited partners.

Limited partnerships are statutory creations that have been used since the Middle Ages. They include both general (manager) and limited (investor) partners. **General partners** are given the right to manage the partnership. **Limited partners** cannot participate in management in their limited partnership status. The general partners have unlimited personal liability for the debts and obligations of the limited partnership. Limited partners are liable only to the extent of their capital contribution, unless they have lost their limited liability status for some reason. Today, all states have enacted statutes that provide for the creation of limited partnerships. Limited partnerships are used for such business ventures as investing in real estate, drilling oil and gas wells, investing in movie productions, and the like. Certain formalities must be followed to establish a limited partnership.

NOTE
Louisiana, which follows the civil law, calls limited partnerships partnerships in commendam.

The Revised Uniform Limited Partnership Act

Revised Uniform Limited Partnership Act (RULPA)
A 1976 revision of the ULPA that provides a more modern comprehensive law for the formation, operation, and dissolution of limited partnerships.

In 1916 the National Conference of Commissioners on Uniform State Laws, a group composed of lawyers, judges, and legal scholars, promulgated the **Uniform Limited Partnership Act (ULPA)**. The ULPA contains a uniform set of provisions for the formation, operation, and dissolution of limited partnerships. Most states originally enacted this law.

In 1976, the National Conference on Uniform State Laws promulgated the **Revised Uniform Limited Partnership Act (RULPA)**, which provides a more modern comprehensive law for the formation, operation, and dissolution of limited partnerships. This law supersedes the ULPA in the states that have adopted it. The RULPA provides the basic foundation for the discussion of limited partnership law in the following materials.

general partners Partners in a limited partnership who invest capital, manage the business, and are personally liable for partnership debts.

General and Limited Partners

limited partners Partners in a limited partnership who invest capital but do not participate in management and are not personally liable for partnership debts beyond their capital contribution.

Limited partnerships have two types of partners: (1) **general partners** who invest capital, manage the business, and are personally liable for partnership debts and (2) **limited partners**, who invest capital but do not participate in management and are not personally liable for partnership debts beyond their capital contribution.

A limited partnership must have at least one or more general partners and one or more limited partners.[62] There are no restrictions on the number of general or limited partners allowed in a limited partnership. Any person may be a general or limited partner. This includes natural persons, partnerships, limited partnerships, trusts, estates, associations, and corporations.[63] A person may be both a general and a limited partner in the same limited partnership.[64]

A Corporation as the Sole General Partner The RULPA permits a corporation to be the sole general partner of a limited partnership.[65] Where this is permissible, it affects the liability of the limited partnership. This is because the limited partners are liable only to the extent of their capital contributions and the corporation acting as general partner is liable only to the extent of its assets.

Admission of New Partners When a limited partnership has been formed, a new limited partner can be added only upon the written consent of all partners unless the limited partnership agreement provides otherwise. New general partners can be admitted only with the specific consent of each partner.[66] The limited partnership agreement cannot waive the right of partners to approve the admission of new general partners.

CAUTION
A corporation may be the sole general partner of a limited partnership. Shareholders of corporations are liable only up to their capital contributions.

Formation of Limited Partnerships

The creation of a limited partnership is formal and requires public disclosure. The entity must comply with the statutory requirements of the RULPA, or other state statute.

Certificate of Limited Partnership Under the RULPA, two or more persons must execute and sign a **certificate of limited partnership**.[67] The certificate must contain the following information:[68]

1. Name of the limited partnership
2. General character of the business
3. Address of the principal place of business, and the name and address of the agent to receive service of legal process
4. Name and business address of each general and limited partner
5. The latest date upon which the limited partnership is to dissolve
6. Amount of cash, property, or services (and description of property or services) contributed by each partner, and any contributions of cash, property, or services promised to be made in the future
7. Any other matters that the general partners determine to include

certificate of limited partnership A document that two or more persons must execute and sign that makes the limited partnership legal and binding.

The certificate of limited partnership must be filed with the secretary of state of the appropriate state and, if required by state law, with the county recorder in the county or counties in which the limited partnership carries on business. The limited partnership is formed when the certificate of limited partnership is filed.[69]

Limited Partnership Agreement Although not required by law, the partners of a limited partnership often draft and execute a **limited partnership agreement** (also called the **articles of limited partnership**) that sets forth the rights and duties of the general and limited partner, the terms and conditions regarding the operation, termination, and dissolution of the partnership, and so on. Where there is no such agreement, the certificate of limited partnership serves as the articles of limited partnership.

limited partnership agreement A document that sets forth the rights and duties of the general and limited partners, the terms and conditions regarding the operation, termination and dissolution of the partnership, and so on.

Offering Circular Limited partnership interests in a limited partnership are often sold to investors. These investors must be given an **offering circular** that describes the issuer, its business, the terms of the partnership agreement, and other relevant information.

defective formation
Occurs when (1) a certificate
of limited partnership is not
properly filed, (2) there are
defects in a certificate that
is filed, or (3) some other
statutory requirement for
the creation of a limited
partnership is not met.

CAUTION
*A limited partner may be
held liable as a general
partner if the limited
partnership is defectively
formed.*

BUSINESS BRIEF
*It is a good practice to
have a written limited
partnership agreement
that sets forth in detail the
rights and duties of both
general and limited
partners. This will reduce
later disputes and
lawsuits.*

Defective Formation Defective formation occurs when (1) a certificate of limited partnership is not properly filed, (2) there are defects in a certificate that is filed, or (3) some other statutory requirement for the creation of a limited partnership is not met. If there is a substantial defect in the creation of a limited partnership, persons who thought they were limited partners can find themselves liable as general partners. Such persons who erroneously but in good faith believe they have become limited partners can escape liability as general partners by either (1) causing the appropriate certificate of limited partnership (or certificate of amendment) to be filed or (2) withdrawing from any future equity participation in the enterprise and causing a certificate showing this withdrawal to be filed. Nevertheless, the limited partner remains liable to any third party who transacts business with the enterprise before either certificate is filed if the third person believed in good faith that the partner was a general partner at the time of the transaction.[70]

Rights and Duties of General and Limited Partners

The rights, powers, duties, and responsibilities of the partners in a limited partnership are specified in the articles of limited partnership or the certificate of limited partnership, the state's limited partnership statute, and the common law. The general partners of a limited partnership have the same rights, duties, and powers as partners in a general partnership.[71]

Limited partners have virtually the same rights as general partners. They have a right to inspect the partnership's books and records and a right to an accounting. They can also assign their partnership interest unless they have agreed otherwise.

Voting Rights It is good practice to establish voting rights in the limited partnership agreement or certificate of limited partnership. The limited partnership agreement can provide which transactions must be approved by which partners (i.e., general, limited, or both).[72] General and limited partners may be given unequal voting rights.

Share of Profits and Losses The limited partnership agreement may specify how profits and losses from the limited partnership are to be allocated among the general and limited partners. If there is no such agreement, the RULPA provides that profits and losses from a limited partnership are shared on the basis of the value of the partner's capital contribution.[73] A limited partner is not liable for losses beyond his or her capital contribution.

CONTEMPORARY BUSINESS ENVIRONMENT

Master Limited Partnerships

One of the major drawbacks for investors who are limited partners in a limited partnership is that their investment usually is not liquid because there is no readily available market for buying and selling limited partnership interests. The introduction of **master limited partnerships (MLPs)** is changing this situation.

An MLP is a limited partnership whose limited partnership interests are traded on organized securities exchanges such as the New York Stock Exchange. Often, MLPs are created by corporations who transfer certain corporate assets (such as real estate) to an MLP and then sell limited partnership interests to the public. The corporation usually remains as the general partner. Some MLPs are formed to make original investments.

There are tax benefits to owning a limited partnership interest in an MLP rather than corporate stock. MLPs pay no income tax—partnership income and losses flow directly onto the individual partner's income tax return. Profit and other distributions of MLPs also avoid the double taxation of corporate dividends.

Liability of General and Limited Partners

The **general partners** of a limited partnership have unlimited liability for the debts and obligations of the limited partnership. This liability extends to debts that cannot be satisfied with the existing capital of the limited partnership. Generally **limited partners** are liable only for the debts and obligations of the limited partnership up to their capital contributions.

Limited Partners and Management As a trade-off for limited liability, limited partners give up their right to participate in the control and management of the limited partnership. This means, in part, that limited partners have no right to bind the partnership to contracts or other obligations. Under the RULPA, a limited partner is liable as a general partner if his or her participation in the control of the business is substantially the same as that of a general partner, but the limited partner is liable only to persons who reasonably believed him or her to be a general partner.[74]

Fiduciary Duties of Partners

The general partners owe the **fiduciary duties** of care and loyalty to the limited partnership and limited partners. Limited partners generally do not owe a fiduciary duty to the limited partnership or its partners because of the limited nature of their interest in business.

Dissolution of Limited Partnerships

A limited partnership may be dissolved and its affairs wound up just like an ordinary partnership. The RULPA establishes rules for the dissolution and winding up of limited partnerships.

After the partnership assets have been liquidated, the debts are satisfied in the following order: (1) creditors (including partners who are creditors) (2) unpaid distributions (3) capital contributions (4) the remainder of the proceeds.[75]

LIMITED LIABILITY PARTNERSHIPS

Many states have enacted legislation to permit the creation of **limited liability partnerships (LLPs)**. In an LLP, there does not have to be a general partner who is personally liable for the debts and obligations of the partnership. Instead, *all* partners are limited partnership who stand to lose only their capital contribution should the partnership fail. None of the partners is personally liable for the debts and obligations of the partnership. Many states restrict the use of this new form of business to certain types of professionals, such as lawyers, accountants, and other licensed professionals.

LLPs must be created formally by filing articles of partnership with the secretary of state of the state in which the LLP is organized. LLPs enjoy the "flow through" tax benefit of other types of partnerships, that is, there is no tax paid at the partnership level and all profits and losses are reported on the individual partners' income tax returns.

Many law firms and most of the major accounting firms have converted to LLP status.

LIMITED LIABILITY COMPANIES

In recent years, a majority of states have approved a new form of business entity called a **limited liability company (LLC)**. An LLC is an unincorporated business entity that combines the most favorable attributes of both partnerships and corporations. Because of this fact, many existing businesses will switch to this type of entity, and many new businesses will organize as LLCs.

BUSINESS BRIEF
General partners of a limited partnership have unlimited liability for debts and obligations of the partnership. Limited partners are liable only up to their capital contribution.

CAUTION
As a trade-off for limited liability, limited partners give up their right to participate in the control and management of the limited partnership. If a limited partner participates in forbidden activities, he can become liable as a general partner.

limited liability partnership A limited liability partnership (LLP) is a special form of partnership that may be formed by professionals such as accountants, lawyers, and doctors.

BUSINESS BRIEF
In a limited liability partnership, the partners are not personally liable for the partnership debts and obligations beyond their capital contribution.

limited liability company A limited liability company (LLC) is an unincorporated form of business.

members The owners of an LLC.

Special Attributes of an LLC

The owners of LLCs are usually called **members**. LLCs have several special attributes. Like shareholders of corporations, members are not personally liable for the obligations of an LLC beyond their capital contributions.

CONSIDER THIS EXAMPLE: Jasmin, Annie, and Lucille form an LLC, and each contributes $20,000 in capital. If the LLC fails with $200,000 in debt, each of the members will lose her capital contribution but will not be personally liable for the rest of the unpaid debts.

Another major feature of an LLC is the ability to be taxed as a partnership. In order to be taxed as a partnership instead of a corporation, an LLC can possess only four of the following six corporate attributes: (1) associates, (2) an objective to carry on business and divide gains, (3) limited liability, (4) centralized management, (5) continuity of life, and (6) free transferability of interests [Treas. Reg. §301.7701–2(a)(1)]. The easiest of these to give up are continuity of life (by choosing a limited duration) and free transferability of interests (by placing restrictions on the transferability of interests). If two of the six corporate attributes are missing, an LLC enjoys the same pass-through tax status of a partnership.

BUSINESS CHECKLIST

Why Operate a Business as an LLC?

Why should an LLC be used instead of an S Corporation or a partnership? S Corporations and partnerships are subject to many restrictions and adverse consequences which do not exist with an LLC, including the following:

- S Corporations cannot have shareholders other than estates, certain trusts, and individuals (who cannot be nonresident aliens). S Corporations can have no more than 35 shareholders, one class of stock, and may not own more than 80 percent of another corporation. LLCs have no such restrictions.
- In a general partnership, the partners are personally liable for the obligations of the partnership. Members of LLCs have limited liability.
- Limited partnerships must have at least one general partner who is personally liable for the obligations of the partnership (although this can be a corporation). Limited partners are precluded from participating in the management of the business. An LLC provides limited liability to all members, even though they participate in management of the business.

Formation of an LLC

articles of organization
The formal document that must be filed with the secretary of state to form an LLC.

Forming an LLC is very similar to organizing a corporation. Two or more persons (which includes individuals, partnerships, corporations, and associations) may form an LLC for any lawful purpose. To form an LLC, **articles of organization** must be filed with the appropriate state office, usually the secretary of state's office. The articles of organization must state the LLC's name, duration, and other information required by statute or that the organizers deem important to include. The name of an LLC must contain the words *Limited Liability Company* or the abbreviation *L.L.C.* or *L.C.*

LLCs will provide new opportunities and alternatives for doing business, particularly to small- and medium-sized businesses and professionals. However, because two or more persons are necessary to form an LLC, sole proprietorships cannot use an LLC as a business entity.

BUSINESS APPLICATION

Dream Works SKG: The Ultimate LLC

In 1995, Steven Spielberg, Jeffrey Katzenberg, and David Geffen formed **Dream Works SKG**, which is designed to be a major movie and recording production company. Spielberg's fame and money came from directing such films as *E.T.;* Katzenberg was a leading executive at Disney; and Geffen built and sold Geffen Records. These multimillionaire, multimedia giants are combining their talents to form a formidable entertainment company to challenge existing movie studios and recording companies.

Interestingly, Dream Works was hatched as a Delaware LLC. The organizers chose an LLC because it is taxed as a partnership and the profits (or losses) will flow directly to the owners, but like a corporation the owners are protected from personal liability beyond their capital contributions.

Dream Works plans to issue several classes of stock, or interests. The three principals will put up $100 million ($33.3 million each) for **"SKG" stock**. The SKG stock grants the principals 100 percent voting control and 67 percent of the firm's profits. In addition, each principal will have a seven-year employment contract that pays them $1 million annually, plus other fringe benefits and perquisites on terms that are customary for similarly situated executives in the entertainment industry.

Dream Works will raise the other $900 million of its planned $1 billion capital from other investors, who will receive a third of future profits. The other investors will be issued the following classes of stock:

Class	Investment
A	**Outside investors.** Class A stock will be sold to big investors with more than $20 million to invest. Microsoft's co-founder, Paul Allen, has purchased $500 million of Class A stock. Class A investors will get seats on the board of directors.
S	**Outside investors.** Class S stock will be issued for smallish, "strategic" investments with other companies for cross-marketing purposes.
E	**Employees.** Employees will be granted the right to participate in an employee stock purchase plan.

Proponents of Dream Works argue that it is the greatest collection of talent ever assembled in the entertainment business. Critics argue that an investment in Dream Works might just be a not-so-dreamy deal.

INTERNATIONAL PERSPECTIVE

Partnerships Outside the United States

The British forms of business organizations are essentially the same as those in the United States. Partnership law, in particular, is virtually identical. Thus, in both countries (and in countries following the British model) a partnership is an association of two or more persons carrying on a business with the intent to make a profit.

In civil law countries, including France and Germany, every form of business organization, including a partnership, is a "company" (*société* in French, *Gesellschaft* in German). A French partnership, because it is a company, is considered as having separate legal or juridical personality independent from its partners and thus can own property, sue, or be sued in its own name. At the election of the partners, it can also opt to be treated as a separate tax entity and pay taxes as if it were a corporation. In Germany, by comparison, a partnership does not have a separate juridical personality. So, even though a German partnership is a company, it is the partners who own the property, and the partners must sue or be sued.

Although partnerships are categorized as companies in both France and Germany, they remain associations of persons who have *continued* full individual liability for the actions of their company. Similarly, because they are associations, they must have two or more partners.

Partnerships are supposed to generate profits for the partners. In Germany, however, the partnership agreement may include a "Leonine clause." Such clauses can exclude a particular partner from sharing in either the profits or losses of the company. In France a Leonine clause is void.

A specialized form of partnership, the limited partnership, is recognized in civil law countries. At least one partner must be a general partner (with personal unlimited liability) and one must be a limited partner. Limited partners have limited liability of the kind that investors in stock companies have. They may invest only cash or property in France, but in Germany services may be fixed and recognized as a contribution. In both countries persons can be either general or limited partners, but they can't be both. Limited partners can participate in the internal administration of the partnership, and in Germany they can be given broad powers to deal with third parties on behalf of the partnership.

Germany recognizes another type of partnership—the silent partnership. This is a secret relationship between partners that is unknown to third parties. The active partner conducts the business in his or her name alone, never mentioning the silent partner. So long as the silent partner's participation is not disclosed, his risk is limited to the amount he invested. Silent partnerships are useful business forms for investment in Germany because the interest paid to the silent partner is treated as interest on a loan and is therefore tax deductible as a business expense from the earnings of the active partner. In France, where partnerships are regarded as separate legal entities, a silent partnership is not recognized as a separate entity and, therefore, is not governed by partnership law.

WORKING THE WEB

'Lectric Law Library This site is hard to describe. Developed by the University of Nevada and highly acclaimed as a "wonder of the Web," this site is a must visit for legal researchers. Take a tour of this virtual law library, and you will wish all Web sites were this much fun.
Visit at http://www.lectlaw.com/

llc-USA This Web site is a good resource for people interested in limited liability companies.
Visit at http://www.llc-usa.com/

US Business Advisor This site is a one stop electronic link to government information, services, and transactions for business.
Visit at http://www.business.gov/

Idea Café—The Small Business Channel This site provides a fun approach to serious business. Here is a place to find out about financing a business, creating good relationships with customers, and more.
Visit at http://www.ideacafe.com/

International Small Business Consortium This site is a good source of knowledge, products, and services for those interested in small business.
Visit at http://www.isbc.com/

CYBER EXERCISES:
1. Visit the Business Law Lounge of the 'Lectric Law Library. Find and print out a document called "Limited Liability Companies: A Summary."
2. Visit the Reference Room of the 'Lectric Law Library. Find and read an article called "Limited Liability Partnerships and Limited Liability Limited Partnerships." Who is the author?
3. Find the Resources page of the llc-USA site. Print out and read the materials on "Limited Liability Company History."
4. Using the U.S. Small Business Advisor, find out how to address and package your mail.
5. Using the ISBC site, find and print out tips on how to "Market Successfully on the WWW/Internet."

CHAPTER SUMMARY

GENERAL PARTNERSHIPS, P. 549

General Partnerships	1. *Uniform Partnership Act (UPA).* Model act that codifies partnership law. Most states have adopted all or part of the UPA. 2. *Entity theory of partnerships.* A theory that holds that partnerships are *separate legal entities* that can hold title to personal and real property, transact business in the partnership name, and the like. 3. *Taxation of partnerships.* Partnerships do not pay federal income taxes. The income and losses of partnership flow onto individual partners' federal income tax returns.

FORMATION OF GENERAL PARTNERSHIPS, P. 549

Formation of General Partnerships	1. *General partnership.* An association of two or more persons to carry on as co-owners of a business for profit [UPA § 6(1)].
	2. *Partnership name.* A general partnership can operate under the names of any one or more of the partners or under a fictitious business name.
	3. *Partnership capital.* Money and property contributed by partners for the permanent use of the partnership.
	4. *Duration of partnership.*
	  a. *Partnership for a term.* A partnership with a fixed duration
	  b. *Partnership at will.* A partnership with no fixed duration

The Partnership Agreement	Agreement establishing a general partnership. It sets forth the terms of the partnership. It is good practice to have a written partnership agreement that the partners sign. 1. *Certificate of partnership.* A document that general partnerships must file with the appropriate state government agency in some states.
Partnership by Estoppel	Arises when a person who is not a partner either makes a representation or consents to a partner's representation that he or she is a partner. 1. *Ostensible partner.* The nonpartner in a partnership by estoppel. This person is liable to any person who relied on the representation that he or she was a partner when deciding to extend credit to the partnership.
Agency Law as the Basis of Partnership Relations	Every partner is an *agent* of the partnership for purposes of its business and an agent of every other partner.

RIGHTS AMONG PARTNERS, P. 554

Rights among Partners	1. *Right to participate in management.* Unless otherwise agreed, each partner of a general partnership has a right to participate in the management of the partnership and has an equal vote on partnership business. 2. *Right to share in profits.* Unless otherwise agreed, partners have the right to an equal share in the partnership's profits and losses. Partnership agreements often provide that profits and losses are to be allocated in proportion to the partners' capital contributions. 3. *Right to compensation.* A partner is not entitled to compensation for services provided to the partnership unless the partnership agreement so provides. 4. *Right to indemnification.* Right of a partner to be reimbursed for expenditures incurred on behalf of the partnership. 5. *Right to return of advances.* An *advance* is money loaned by a partner to the partnership. The partner is entitled to repayment of the loan only after other creditors have been paid.

6. *Right to return of capital.* Upon termination of the partnership, the partners are entitled to have their capital contributions returned to them. This right is subordinated to the rights of creditors, who must be paid their claims first.

7. *Right to information.* Partners have an absolute right to inspect and copy the partnership's books and records. Every partner has the right to demand true and full information from any partner of all things affecting the partnership.

8. *Right to an accounting.* Partners have the right to bring an *action for an accounting* against other partners. This is a formal judicial proceeding in which the court is authorized to (1) review the partnership and the partners' transactions and (2) award each partner his or her share of the partnership assets.

DUTIES AMONG PARTNERS, P. 556

Duty of Loyalty	A duty that a partner owes not to act adversely to the interests of the partnership.
	1. *Examples.* Examples of the breach of the duty of loyalty include:
	  a. *Self-dealing* with the partnership without permission
	  b. *Usurping* a partnership opportunity
	  c. *Competing* with the partnership without permission
	  d. Making *secret profits* from the partnership
	  e. Disclosing *confidential* partnership information
	  f. *Misusing partnership property*
	  g. Other breaches of partner's *fiduciary duties*

Duty of Obedience	A duty that partners must adhere to the provisions of the partnership agreement and the decisions of the partnership.
Duty of Care	The obligation partners owe to use the same level of care and skill that a reasonable person in the same position would use in the same circumstances. 1. *Negligence.* A breach of the duty of care is negligence. A partner is liable to the partnership for any damages caused by his or her negligence.
Duty to Inform	A duty a partner owes to inform his or her co-partners of all information he or she possesses that is relevant to the affairs of the partnership. 1. *Imputed knowledge.* Knowledge acquired by a partner concerning matters relating to partnership affairs is *imputed* to the other partners even if they are not informed of the information.

PROPERTY RIGHTS OF THE PARTNERSHIP AND PARTNERS, P. 557

Partnership Property	Property that is originally brought into the partnership on account of the partnership and property that is subsequently acquired by purchase or otherwise on account of the partnership or with partnership funds.
Partners' Rights in Partnership Property	1. *Attachment and execution of partnership property.* Specific partnership property is subject to attachment or execution by creditors of the partnership. 2. *Tenant in partnership.* A partner is a co-owner with the other partners of the specific partnership property as a *tenant in partnership.* 3. *Right of survivorship.* Rule that states that a deceased partner's right in specific partnership property vests with the remaining partners upon his or her death.

Partners' Interest in Partnership	1. *Partner's interest.* A partner's interest in a partnership is his or her right to share in the profits and surplus of the partnership. This is the partner's personal property.
	2. *Right of inheritance.* The value of a deceased partner's interest in a partnership transfers to his or her beneficiaries or heirs upon his or her death. The beneficiary or heir does not become a partner of the partnership.
	3. *Assignment.* A partner may *assign* (transfer) his or her interest in a partnership. The assignee acquires the assignor–partner's right to the profits and surplus of the partnership. The assignee does not become a partner of the partnership.
	4. *Judgment creditor.* A creditor of an individual partner who obtains a judgment against the partner. A judgment creditor can obtain a *charging order* against the debtor–partner's partnership interest in order to satisfy the debt. A judgment creditor does not become a partner in the partnership.

LIABILITY OF PARTNERS TO THIRD PARTIES, P. 559

Contract Liability	1. *Partners' contract liability.* A contract entered into by a partner with a third party on behalf of a partnership is binding on the partnership if the partner had the following authority:
	a. *Express authority.* Authority of a partner to enter into a contract that is expressly granted either orally or in writing.
	b. *Implied authority.* Authority of a partner to enter into a contract that is implied from the partnership's business, the express power of the partners, the customs of the industry, and the like.
	c. *Apparent authority.* Authority of a partner that arises when a partner's implied authority has been restricted, but a third party who deals with this partner has not been informed of this fact and enters into a contract with the partnership.
	2. *Ratification.* The partners can decide to *ratify* an unauthorized contract. The ratification binds the partnership to the contract from the time of execution.
	3. *Partnership liability.* A partnership is liable for the contracts entered into on its behalf by partners acting with express, implied, or apparent authority, or where unauthorized contracts have been ratified by the partners.
	4. *Joint liability of partners.* Partners are *personally liable* for contracts and debts of the partnership. This is *joint liability*, meaning that a plaintiff must name the partnership and *all* of the partners as defendants. If successful, the plaintiff can recover the entire amount of the judgment from any or all of the partners.

Tort Liability	1. *Tort.* Occurs when a partner causes injury to a third party by his or her negligent act, breach of trust, breach of fiduciary duty, or intentional tort.
	2. *Partnership liability.* The partnership is liable to third persons who are injured by torts committed by a partner while he or she is acting within the ordinary course of partnership business.
	3. *Joint and several liability of partners.* Partners are *personally liable* for torts committed by partners acting on partnership business. This liability is *joint and several*. This means that the plaintiff can sue *one or more* of the partners separately. If successful, the plaintiff can recover the entire amount of the judgment from any or all of the defendant-partners.

Liability of Incoming Partners	A new partner who is admitted to the partnership is liable for the existing debts and obligations (*antecedent debts*) of the partnership only to the extent of his or her capital contribution. The new partner is personally liable for debts and obligations incurred by the partnership after becoming a partner.

TERMINATION OF PARTNERSHIPS, P. 561

Dissolution of Partnerships	The change in the relation of the partners caused by any partner ceasing to be associated in the carrying on of the business [UPA § 29].
Types of Dissolution	1. *Dissolution by act of the partners*. 　a. Termination of a stated time or purpose 　b. Withdrawal of a partner 　c. Expulsion of a partner 　d. Admission of a partner 　e. Mutual agreement of the partners. 2. *Dissolution by operation of law*. 　a. Death of any partner 　b. Bankruptcy of any partner or the partnership 　c. Illegality of the partnership's business. 3. *Dissolution by judicial decree*. A partner or assignee may file a petition with the court seeking the *judicial dissolution* of a partnership. The petitioner must show that there is cause to dissolve the partnership (e.g., mismanagement, improper conduct by a partner, partnership can be carried on only at a loss), and the court must find that dissolution is an equitable solution.
Wrongful Dissolution	Occurs when a partner withdraws from a partnership without having the *right* to do so at the time. The partner is liable for damages caused by the wrongful dissolution of the partnership.
Notice of Dissolution	1. *Notice of dissolution to partners*. Notice of dissolution must be given to all partners. If a partner who has not received notice of dissolution enters into a contract on behalf of the partnership in the course of partnership business, the contract is binding on all of the partners. 2. *Notice of dissolution to third parties*. The following notice must be given to third parties when a partnership has been dissolved other than by operation of law: 　a. *Actual notice*. Must be given to third parties who have actually dealt with the partnership. 　b. *Constructive notice*. Must be given to third parties who have not dealt with the partnership but have knowledge of it. Constructive notice is given by publishing a notice of dissolution in a newspaper of general circulation serving the area where the business of the partnership is conducted. 　c. *No notice*. Parties who have not dealt with the partnership and do not have knowledge of it do not have to be given notice.
Continuation of the Partnership After Dissolution	The surviving or remaining partners are given the right to continue the partnership after dissolution. When a partnership is continued, the old partnership is dissolved and a new partnership is created. 1. *Continuation agreement*. A document that expressly sets forth the events that allow for continuation of the partnership, the amount to be paid to outgoing partners, and other details.

	2. *Creditors' status.* The creditors of the old partnership become creditors of the new partnership and have equal status with the creditors of the new partnership. 3. *Liability of outgoing partners.* An outgoing partner is liable for existing partnership debts unless the creditor, other partners, and the outgoing partner enter into a *novation agreement* that expressly relieves the outgoing partner of liability to the creditor.

Winding Up and Distribution of Assets	1. *Winding up.* Process of liquidating the partnership's assets and distributing the proceeds to satisfy claims against the partnership.
	2. *Priority of distribution of assets.* Upon the winding up of a dissolved partnership, the assets of the partnership are distributed in the following order [UPA § 40(b)]:
	  a. Creditors (except partners who are creditors)
	  b. Creditor–partners
	  c. Capital contributions
	  d. Profits

Termination	Occurs automatically when the process of winding up is completed. It ends the legal existence of the partnership.

LIMITED PARTNERSHIPS, P. 564

Uniform Limited Partnership Act	1. *Uniform Limited Partnership Act (ULPA).* A 1916 model act that contains a uniform set of provisions for the formation, operation, and dissolution of limited partnerships. 2. *Revised Uniform Limited Partnership Act (RULPA).* A 1976 revision of the ULPA that provides a more modern comprehensive law for the formation, operation, and dissolution of limited partnerships.

Limited Partnerships	1. *Limited partnerships.* A special form of partnership that has both limited and general partners.
	  a. *General partners.* Partners in a partners partnership who invest capital, manage the business, and are personally liable for partnership debts.
	  b. *Limited partners.* Partners in a limited partnership who invest capital but do not participate in management and are not personally liable for partnership debts beyond their capital contributions.
	2. *Corporation as sole general partner.* A corporation may be the sole general partner of a limited partnership. Shareholders of corporations are liable only up to their capital contributions.

Formation of Limited Partnerships	1. *Certificate of limited partnership.* A document that two or more persons must execute and sign that establishes a limited partnership. The certificate of limited partnership must be filed with the secretary of state of the appropriate state. 2. *Limited partnership agreement.* A document that sets forth the rights and duties of general and limited partners, the terms and conditions regarding the operation, termination, and dissolution of the partnership, and so on. 3. *Offering circular.* Document that is provided to investors of limited partnership interests that describes the issuer, its business, the terms of the partnership agreement, and other relevant information. 4. *Defective formation.* Occurs when (a) a certificate of limited partnership is not properly filed, (b) there are defects in a certificate

	that is filed, or (c) some other statutory requirement for the creation of a partnership is not met. A limited partner may be held liable as a general partner if the limited partnership is defectively formed.
Share of Profits and Losses	1. *Share of profits and losses*. Unless otherwise agreed, profits and losses from a limited partnership are shared on the basis of the value of the partner's capital contributions. A limited partner is not liable for losses beyond his or her capital contribution. The limited partnership agreement may specify how profits and losses are to be allocated among the general and limited partners.
Liability of General and Limited Partners	1. *General partners*. General partners of a limited partnership have *unlimited personal liability* for the debts and obligations of the limited partnership. 2. *Limited partners*. Limited partners of a limited partnership are liable only for the debts and obligations of the limited partnership up to their capital contributions. 3. *Limited partners and management*. Limited partners have no right to participate in the management of the partnership. A limited partner is *liable as a general partner* if his or her participation in the control of the business is substantially the same as that of a general partner, but the limited partner is liable only to persons who reasonably believed him or her to be a general partner.
Fiduciary Duties of Partners	The general partners of a limited partnership owe the fiduciary duties of care and loyalty to the limited partnership and limited partners. Limited partners do not owe a fiduciary duty to the limited partnership or its partners because of the limited nature of their interest in the business.

Dissolution of Limited Partnerships	A limited partnership may be dissolved and its affairs wound up just like an ordinary partnership.
	1. *Priority of distribution of assets*. Upon the winding up of a dissolved limited partnership, the assets of the partnership are distributed in the following order [RULPA § 804]:
	  a. Creditors (including partners who are creditors)
	  b. Unpaid distributions
	  c. Capital contributions
	  d. Remainder of the proceeds

LIMITED LIABILITY COMPANIES, P. 567	

Limited Liability Companies	1. *Limited liability company (LLC)*. A special form of unincorporated business entity that combines the tax benefits of a partnership with the limited personal liability attribute of a corporation.
	2. *Members*. Owners of an LLC.
	3. *Articles of organization*. A document that owners of an LLC must execute, sign, and file with the secretary of state of the appropriate state to form an LLC.
	4. *Taxation*. An LLC can be taxed as a partnership if it possesses four or fewer of the following attributes:
	  a. Associates
	  b. Objective to carry on business and divide gains
	  c. Limited liability
	  d. Centralized management
	  e. Continuity of life
	  f. Free transferability of interests

CRITICAL LEGAL THINKING CASES

23.1 Partnership or Sole Proprietorship? D. W. Jessen and William A. Gamble were college classmates who graduated from Louisiana State University (L.S.U.) in 1940 with degrees in civil engineering. After World War II, Gamble returned to L.S.U. for further study, while Jessen established a civil engineering practice in Lake Charles, Louisiana. On June 22, 1949, Gamble joined Jessen in Jessen's already established practice. Gamble was initially paid a flat salary. In two or three years, the arrangement changed to where Gamble received 40 percent of the net income of the practice. This agreement was never reduced to writing. The matter of a partnership was never discussed thereafter.

From the beginning, Jessen had the final say in the hiring and firing of employees, what work would be done, and what equipment would be purchased. Jessen owned all of the equipment, signed all contracts, the bank account was in the name of "C. W. Jessen, CE," and only he could sign checks. Applications for civil engineering licenses for the firm listed Jessen as the "owner" and Gamble as an "associate" or "chief engineer." Income tax was never withheld from Gamble's paycheck, and a W-2 form was issued to him at the end of the year. Firm letters and correspondence did not include Gamble as a partner. From 1949 to 1981, other engineers associated with the firm were paid a salary calculated as a percentage of net profits.

In 1981, Gamble retired from the practice and sued Jessen for dissolution of their alleged partnership and for an accounting. Gamble sought payment for his share of the accounts receivable, his percentage of work completed but unbilled, and payment for his share of the partnership assets. Was the business a sole proprietorship or a partnership? [*Gamble v. Jessen*, 491 So.2d 483 (La. App. 1986)]

23.2 Partnership In early 1986, Thomas Smithson, a house builder and small-scale property developer, decided that a certain tract of undeveloped land in Franklin, Tennessee, would be extremely attractive for development into a subdivision. Smithson contacted the owner of the property, Monsanto Chemical Company (Monsanto), and was told that the company would sell the property at the "right price."

Smithson did not have the funds with which to embark unassisted in the endeavor, so he contacted Frank White, a co-owner of the Andrews Realty Company, and two agents of the firm, Dennis Devrow and Temple Ennis. Smithson showed them a sketch map with the proposed layout of the lots, roads, and so forth. Smithson testified that they all orally agreed to develop the property together, and in lieu of a financial investment, Smithson would oversee the engineering of the property. Subsequently, H. R. Morgan was brought into the deal to provide additional financing.

Smithson later discovered that White had contacted Monsanto directly. When challenged about this, White assured Smithson that he was still "part of the deal" but refused to put the agreement in writing. White, Devrow, Ennis, and Morgan purchased the property from Monsanto. They then sold it to H.A.H. Associates, a corporation, for a $184,000 profit. When they refused to pay Smithson, he sued to recover an equal share of the profits. Was a partnership formed between Smith-

son and the defendants? [*Smithson v. White*, 1988 W.L. 42645 (Tenn. App. 1988)]

23.3 Partnership Richard Filip owned Trans Texas Properties (Trans Texas). Tracy Peoples was an employee of the company. In order to obtain credit to advertise in the *Austin American-Statesman* newspaper, which was owned by Cox Enterprises, Inc. (Cox), Peoples completed a credit application that listed Jack Elliot as a partner in Trans Texas. Evidence showed that Elliot did not own an interest in Trans Texas and did not consent to or authorize Peoples to make this representation to Cox. Cox made no effort to verify the accuracy of the representation and extended credit to Trans Texas. When Trans Texas defaulted on payments owed Cox, Cox sued both Filip and Elliot to recover the debt. Is Elliot liable? [*Cox Enterprises, Inc. v. Filip and Elliot*, 538 S.W.2d 836 (Tex. App. 1976)]

23.4 Partnership by Estoppel Virgil Welch leased the feed concession at the Ruidoso, New Mexico, race track. Sam Dunn guaranteed the $65,000 note securing the lease. While Welch operated the business, Dunn had the sole right to maintain records, inventory controls, and accounts receivable. They opened a joint checking account in the name of "Ruidoso Downs Feed Concession."

Welch entered into a contract with Anderson Hay and Grain Co. (Anderson) to purchase feed for the concession. Anderson extended credit to the business on the strength of Dunn's financial responsibility. Someone stated in the presence of an Anderson representative and Dunn that Welch and Dunn were partners; Dunn did not state otherwise. When payments to Anderson became past due, it would call Dunn on the telephone and Dunn would send a check. When the account became substantially overdue, Anderson sued Welch and Dunn to recover the debt. Dunn answered, claiming that he was not a partner in Ruidoso Downs Feed Concession. Is Dunn liable on the debt owed Anderson? [*Anderson Hay and Grain Co. v. Dunn*, 467 P.2d 5 (N.M. 1970)]

23.5 Compensation In 1976, a partnership was formed to own and manage a medical office building. The partnership agreement did not provide that the general partners would be paid compensation for services provided in the furtherance of partnership business. One partner, Sidney Newman, devoted substantial time to managing the building, including leasing space, collecting rents, designing and drawing plans for medical suites as they were leased, dealing with tenants' complaints and requests, and performing other management duties. Over the objection of another partner, Penny Broffman, the partnership paid Newman $100,000 for his services during a one-year period. Broffman sued to recover this compensation. Who wins? [*Broffman v. Newman*, 213 Cal.App.3d 252, 261 Cal.Rptr. 532 (Cal. App. 1989)]

23.6 Fiduciary Duty In January 1977, Charles Fial and Roger J. Steeby entered into a partnership called "Audit Consultants" to perform auditing services. Pursuant to the agreement, they shared equally the equity, income, and profits of the partnership. Originally, they performed the auditing services themselves, but as business increased, they engaged independent contractors to do some of the audit work. Fial's activities generated approximately 80 percent of the partnership's revenues. Unhappy with their agreement to divide the profits equally, Fial wrote a letter to Steeby on July 11, 1984, dissolving the partnership.

Fial asserted that the clients should be assigned based on who brought them into the business. Fial formed a new business called "Audit Consultants of Colorado, Inc." He then terminated the partnership's contracts with many clients and put them under contract with his new firm. Fial also terminated the partnership's contracts with the independent contractor auditors and signed many of these auditors with his new firm. The partnership terminated on May 24, 1985. Steeby brought an action against Fial, alleging breach of fiduciary duty and seeking a final accounting. Who wins? [*Steeby v. Fial*, 765 P.2d 1081 (Colo. App. 1988)]

23.7 Tort Liability Edgar and Selwyn Husted, attorneys, formed Husted and Husted, a law partnership. Herman McCloud, who was the executor of his mother's estate, hired them as attorneys for the estate. When taxes were due on the estate, Edgar told McCloud to make a check for $18,000 payable to the Husted and Husted Trust Account and that he would pay the Internal Revenue Service from this account. There was no Husted and Husted trust account. Instead, Edgar deposited the check into his own personal account and converted the funds to his own personal use. When Edgar's misconduct was uncovered, McCloud sued the law firm for conversion of estate funds. Is the partnership liable for Edgar's actions? [*Husted v. McCloud*, 436 N.E.2d 341 (Ind. App. 1982)]

23.8 Tort Liability Thomas McGrath was a partner in the law firm of Torbenson, Thatcher, Treadwell & Schoonmaker. At approximately 4:30 P.M. on February 11, 1980, McGrath went to a restaurant-cocktail establishment in Kirkland, Washington. From that time until about 11:00 P.M. he imbibed considerable alcohol while socializing and discussing personal and firm-related business. After 11:00 P.M., McGrath did not discuss firm business but continued to socialize and drink until approximately 1:45 A.M., when he and Frederick Hayes, another bar patron, exchanged words. Shortly thereafter, the two encountered each other outside, and after another exchange, McGrath shot Hayes. Hayes sued McGrath and the law firm for damages. Who is liable? [*Hayes v. Torbenson, Thatcher, McGrath, Treadwell & Schoonmaker*, 749 P.2d 178 (Wash. App. 1988)]

23.9 Notice of Dissolution In 1976, Leonard Sumter, Sr., entered into a partnership agreement with his son, Michael T. Sumter, to conduct a plumbing business in Shreveport, Louisiana, under the name "Sumter Plumbing Company." On June 18, 1976, the father, on behalf of the partnership, executed a credit application with Thermal Supply of Louisiana, Inc. (Thermal) for an open account to purchase supplies on credit. From that date until the spring of 1988, the Sumters purchased plumbing supplies from Thermal on credit and paid their bills without fail. Both partners and one employee signed for supplies at Thermal. In May 1980, the partnership was dissolved, and all outstanding debts to Thermal were paid in full.

The Sumters did not, however, notify Thermal that the partnership had been dissolved.

A year later, the son decided to reenter the plumbing business. He used the name previously used by the former partnership, listed the same post office address for billing purposes, and hired the employee of the former partnership who signed for supplies at Thermal. The father decided not to become involved in this venture. The son began purchasing supplies on credit from Thermal on the open credit account of the former partnership. Thermal was not informed that he was operating a new business. When the son defaulted on payments to Thermal, it sued the original partnership to recover the debt. Is the father liable for these debts? [*Thermal Supply of Louisiana, Inc. v. Sumter*, 452 So.2d 312 (La. App. 1984)]

23.10 Liability of Withdrawing Partner In 1982, Ralph Neitzert entered into a partnership agreement with his brother to operate Jolly Jug Liquors, a retail liquor store. The brother was the managing partner and was responsible for the store's day-to-day operation. During May 1983, the partners met with a representative of Colo-Tex Leasing, Inc. (Colo-Tex) to discuss leasing refrigeration equipment for the store. The partners provided their individual financial statements to Colo-Tex, and on June 9, 1983, the partnership entered into a lease with Colo-Tex. The refrigeration equipment, which was custom fabricated for the Neitzerts' liquor store, was installed in July 1983. The lease specified a 60-month term at $1,188 per month. In July 1983, Neitzert conveyed his interest in the partnership to his sister. Monthly payments were made by the partnership to Colo-Tex for approximately 13 months. Colo-Tex sued the partnership when the payments ceased. Is Ralph liable to Colo-Tex? [*Colo-Tex Leasing, Inc. v. Neitzert*, 746 P.2d 972 (Colo. App. 1987)]

23.11 Liability of General Partners Pat McGowan, Val Somers, and Brent Robertson were general partners of Vermont Place, a limited partnership formed on January 20, 1984, for the purpose of constructing duplexes on an undeveloped tract of land in Fort Smith, Arkansas. The general partners appointed McGowan and his company, Advance Development Corporation (Advance), to develop the project, including contracting with materialmen, mechanics, and other suppliers. None of the limited partners took part in the management or control of the partnership.

On September 3, 1984, Somers and Robertson discovered that McGowan had not been paying the suppliers. They removed McGowan from the partnership and took over the project. The suppliers sued the partnership to recover the money owed them. The partnership assets were not sufficient to pay all of their claims. Who is liable to the suppliers? [*National Lumber Company v. Advance Development Corporation*, 732 S.W.2d 840 (Ark. 1987)]

23.12 Liability of Limited Partners Union Station Associates of New London (USANL) is a limited partnership formed under the laws of Connecticut. Allen M. Schultz, Anderson Notter Associates, and the Lepton Trust were limited partners. The limited partners did not take part in the management of the partnership. The National Railroad Passenger Association (NRPA) entered into an agreement to lease part of a railroad facility from USANL. The NRPA sued the USANL for allegedly breaching the lease and also named the limited partners as defendants. Are the limited partners liable? [*National Railroad Passenger Association v. Union Station Associates of New London*, 643 F.Sup. 192 (D.D.C. 1986)]

23.13 Formation of a Limited Partnership Robert K. Powers and Lee M. Solomon were among other limited partners of the Cosmopolitan Chinook Hotel (Cosmopolitan), a limited partnership. On October 25, 1972, Cosmopolitan entered into a contract to lease and purchase neon signs from Dwinell's Central Neon. The contract identified Cosmopolitan as a "partnership" and was signed on behalf of the partnership, "R. Powers, President." At the time the contract was entered into, Cosmopolitan had taken no steps to file its certificate of limited partnership with the state as required by limited partnership law. The certificate was not filed with the state until several months after the contract was signed. When Cosmopolitan defaulted on payments due under the contract, Dwinell's sued Cosmopolitan and its general and limited partners. Are the limited partners liable? [*Dwinell's Central Neon v. Cosmopolitan Chinook Hotel*, 587 P.2d 191 (Wash. App. 1978)]

ETHICS CASES

23.14 Ethical Perspective Harriet Hankin, Samuel Hankin, Moe Henry Hankin, Perch P. Hankin, and Pauline Hankin, and their spouses, for many years operated a family partnership composed of vast real estate holdings. Some of the properties included restaurants, industrial buildings, shopping centers, golf courses, a motel chain, and hundreds of acres of developable ground, estimated to be worth $72 million in 1977. In that year, because of family disagreement and discontent, the Hankin family agreed to dissolve the partnership. When they could not agree on how to liquidate the partnership assets, in August 1977, Harriet and Samuel (collectively called Harriet) initiated this equity action.

Based on assurances from Moe and Perch that they would sell the partnership assets as quickly as possible and at the highest possible price, the court appointed them as liquidators of the partnership during the winding-up period. Based on similar assurances, the court again appointed them liquidators for the partnership in 1979. But by 1981, only enough property had been sold to retire the debt of the partnership. Evidence showed that Moe and Perch had not aggressively marketed the remaining properties and that Moe wished to purchase some of the properties for himself at a substantial discount from their estimated value. Six years and three appeals to the Superior Court later, Harriet brought this action seeking the appointment of a receiver to liquidate the remaining partnership assets.

Did the winding-up partners breach their fiduciary duties? Should the court appoint a receiver to liquidate the remaining partnership assets? Did Moe Henry Hankin act ethically in this case? [*Hankin v. Hankin*, 493 A.2d 675 (Pa. 1985)]

23.15 Ethical Perspective John Gilroy, an established commercial photographer in Kalamazoo, Michigan, had a small contractual clientele of schools for which he provided student portrait photographs. In 1974, Robert Conway joined Gilroy's established business and they formed a partnership called "Skylight Studios." Both partners solicited schools with success, and gross sales, which were $40,000 in 1974, increased every year and amounted to more than $200,000 in 1980.

On June 1, 1981, Conway notified Gilroy that the partnership was dissolved. Gilroy discovered that Conway had closed up the partnership's place of business and opened up his own business, had purchased equipment and supplies in preparation of opening his own business and charged them to the partnership, had taken with him the partnership's employees and most of its equipment, had personally taken over business of some customers by telling them that the partnership was being dissolved, and withdrew partnership funds for personal use. Gilroy sued Conway for an accounting, alleging that Conway had converted partnership assets. Did Conway act ethically in this case? Who wins? [*Gilroy v. Conway*, 391 N.W.2d 419 (Mich.App. 1986)]

CRITICAL LEGAL THINKING WRITING ASSIGNMENT

Read Case A.23 in the Case Appendix [*Catalina Mortgage Company, Inc. v. Monier*]. This case is excerpted from the supreme court of Arizona's opinion. Review and brief the case. In your brief, be sure to answer the following questions:

1. Who was the plaintiff? Who were the defendants?
2. What business arrangement were the defendants engaged in? How did this lead to the lawsuit?
3. What is joint and several liability?
4. Did the court impose joint and several liability in this case?

NOTES

[1] Georgia and Louisiana have not adopted the UPA. These states enacted their own partnership statutes.
[2] UPA § 5.
[3] UPA § 6(1).

[4] UPA § 18(g).
[5] UPA § 2.
[6] UPA § 7(2).
[7] UPA § 2.

[8] UPA § 7.
[9] UPA § 16.
[10] UPA § 4(3).
[11] UPA § 9(1).
[12] UPA § 18(e).
[13] UPA § 18(h).
[14] UPA § 9(3).
[15] UPA § 18(g).
[16] UPA § 18(h).
[17] UPA § 9(2).
[18] UPA § 18(a).
[19] UPA § 18(f).
[20] UPA § 21.
[21] UPA § 18(b).
[22] UPA § 40(b).
[23] UPA § 18(c).
[24] UPA § 18(a).
[25] UPA § 40(b).
[26] UPA § 18(d).
[27] UPA § 20.
[28] UPA § 19.
[29] UPA § 24.
[30] UPA § 20.
[31] UPA § 12.
[32] UPA § 8.
[33] UPA § 8(3).
[34] UPA § 10(1).
[35] UPA § 25(1).
[36] UPA § 25(2)C.
[37] UPA § 26.
[38] UPA § 27.
[39] UPA § 28.
[40] UPA § 18(h).
[41] UPA § 9(1).

[42] UPA § 11.
[43] UPA §§ 9(1) and 9(4).
[44] UPA § 15(b).
[45] UPA §§ 13 and 14.
[46] UPA § 15(a).
[47] UPA § 17.
[48] UPA § 29.
[49] UPA § 31(1).
[50] UPA § 31(4).
[51] UPA § 31(5).
[52] UPA § 31(3).
[53] UPA § 32(1).
[54] UPA § 33.
[55] UPA § 35.
[56] UPA § 41.
[57] UPA § 36.
[58] UPA § 18(f).
[59] UPA § 40(b).
[60] UPA §§ 40(d) and (f).
[61] UPA § 30.
[62] RULPA § 101(7).
[63] RULPA § 101(11).
[64] RULPA § 404.
[65] RULPA § 101(11).
[66] RULPA § 401.
[67] RULPA §§ 201 and 206.
[68] RULPA § 201(a).
[69] RULPA § 210(b).
[70] RULPA § 304.
[71] RULPA § 403.
[72] RULPA §§ 302 and 405.
[73] RULPA § 503.
[74] RULPA § 303(a).
[75] RULPA § 804.

CHAPTER 24

THE NATURE, FORMATION,

AND FINANCING

OF CORPORATIONS

Chapter Objectives

*After studying this chapter,
you should be able to*

1. Define a corporation
2. List and describe the major characteristics of a corporation
3. Describe the process for forming a corporation
4. Define an **S** Corporation and describe its tax benefits
5. Distinguish between publicly held and closely held corporations
6. Identify when promoters are liable on preincorporation contracts
7. Define common stock and distinguish between authorized, issued, treasury, and outstanding shares
8. Describe the preferences associated with preferred stock
9. Distinguish between debentures, bonds, and notes
10. Describe the express and implied powers of a corporation

Chapter Contents

- Nature of the Corporation
  Case 24.1 *Joslyn Manufacturing Co. v. T.L. James & Co., Inc. (5th Cir.)*
  Contemporary Business Environment
  S Corporations
- Classifications of Corporations
  Ethical Perspective Professionals Dodge Corporate Liability
- Promoters' Activities
  Case 24.2 *Coopers & Lybrand v. Fox (CO)*
- Incorporation Procedures
  Business Checklist Selecting a Corporate Name
  International Perspective The Organization and Operation of the Multinational Corporation
- Financing the Corporation
  Case 24.3 *Pittelman v. Pearce (CA)*
- Corporate Powers
  International Perspective *Conducting Business in a Foreign Country*
- Working the Web
- Chapter Summary
- Critical Legal Thinking Cases
- Ethics Cases
- Critical Legal Thinking Writing Assignment

> *A corporation is an artificial being, invisible, intangible, and existing only in the contemplation of law. Being the mere creature of the law, it possesses only those properties which the charter of its creation confers upon it, either expressly, or as incidental to its very existence. These are such as are supposed best calculated to effect the object for which it was created. Among the most important are immortality, and, if the expression may be allowed, individuality; properties by which a perpetual succession of many persons are considered as the same, and may act as a single individual.*
>
> John Marshall, Chief Justice,
> U.S. Supreme Court
> *Dartmouth College v. Woodward,*
> 4 Wheaton 518, 636 (1819)

corporation A fictitious legal entity that is created according to statutory requirements.

Corporations are the most dominant form of business organization in the United States. They generate more than 80 percent of the country's gross business receipts. Corporations may have one owner or thousands of owners. Owners of corporations are called **shareholders**.

shareholders The owners of corporations whose ownership interests are evidenced by stock certificates.

Corporations were first formed in medieval Europe. Great Britain granted charters to certain trading companies from the 1500s to the 1700s. The English law of corporations applied in most of the colonies until 1776. After the War of Independence, each state in the United States developed its own corporation law.

Originally, corporate charters were individually granted by state legislatures. In the late 1700s, however, the states began enacting **general corporation statutes** that permitted corporations to be formed without the separate approval of the legislature. Today, most corporations are formed pursuant to general corporation laws of the states.

The nature, formation, and financing of corporations are discussed in this chapter.

NATURE OF THE CORPORATION

corporation codes State statutes that regulate the formation, operation, and dissolution of corporations.

Corporations can only be created pursuant to the laws of the state in which the business is being incorporated. These statutes—commonly referred to as **corporation codes**—regulate the formation, corporation, and dissolution of corporations. The state legislature may amend its corporate statute at any time. Such changes may require the corporation's articles of incorporation to be amended.

The courts interpret state corporation statutes to decide individual corporate and shareholder disputes. As a result, a body of common law has evolved concerning corporate and shareholder rights and obligations.

Public and Private Corporations

public corporation A corporation formed to meet a specific governmental or political purpose.

Government-owned (or **public**) **corporations** are formed to meet a specific governmental or political purpose. For example, most cities and towns are formed as corporations, as are most water, school, sewage, and park districts. Local government corporations are often called **municipal corporations**.

private corporation A corporation formed to conduct privately owned business.

Private corporations are formed to conduct privately owned business. They are owned by private parties, not the government. Most corporations fall into this category. This chapter discusses private corporations.

The Corporation as a Legal "Person"

legal entity A corporation is a separate legal entity—an *artificial person*—that can own property, sue and be sued, enter into contracts, and such.

A corporation is a separate **legal entity** (or **legal person**) for most purposes. Corporations are treated, in effect, as artificial persons created by the state who can sue or be sued in their own names, enter into and enforce contracts, hold title to and transfer property, and be found civilly and criminally liable for violations of law. Because corporations cannot be put in prison, the normal criminal penalty is the assessment of a fine, loss of a license, or other sanction. The characteristics of partnerships and corporations are compared in Exhibit 24.1.

ITEM	PARTNERSHIP	CORPORATION
Liability of owners	General partners have unlimited personal liability for partnership debts and obligations. Limited partners' liability for partnership debts and obligations is limited to their investment.	Shareholders' liability for corporate debts and obligations is limited to their investment.
Transferability of ownership	Partners cannot transfer their ownership interests without the consent of all partners. Limited partners' interests are usually freely transferable.	Shares, which represent ownership interest, are freely transferable.
Management	Every general partner has a right to participate equally in the management of the partnership. Limited partners have no right to participate in the management of the partnership.	Shareholders elect the directors, who appoint the managers of the corporation. Shareholders have no right to participate in the management of the corporation.
Duration	A partnership cannot have perpetual existence. A partnership is terminable at will unless a definite term is provided. The death, incapacity, or withdrawal of a partner dissolves the partnership.	A corporation may have perpetual existence.
Taxation	Partnerships are not taxed as separate entities. Partnership losses and income flow directly to the partners' tax returns.	C corporations are taxed as separate legal entities. Shareholders are taxed on dividends paid by the corporation. S corporations are not taxed as separate legal entities. Corporation losses and income flow directly to the shareholders' tax returns.

Exhibit 24.1
Comparison of Characteristics of Partnerships and Corporations

Characteristics of Corporations

Corporations have the following unique characteristics:

- **Limited liability of shareholders.** As separate legal entities, corporations are liable for their own contracts and debts. Generally, the shareholders have only limited liability. That is, they are liable only to the extent of their capital contributions.
- **Free transferability of shares.** Corporate shares are freely transferable by the shareholder by sale, assignment, pledge, or gift unless they are issued pursuant to certain exemptions from securities registration. Shareholders may agree among themselves on restrictions on the transfer of shares. National securities markets, such as the New York Stock Exchange, the American Stock Exchange, and NASDAQ, have been developed for the organized sale of securities.

"The corporation is, and must be, the creature of the state, into its nostrils the state must breathe the breath of a fictitious life for otherwise it would be no animated body but individualistic dust."
Frederic Wm. Maitlind
Introduction to Glerke, Political Theories of the Middle Ages

- **Perpetual existence.** Corporations exist in perpetuity (i.e., forever) unless a specific duration is stated in the corporation's articles of incorporation. The existence of a corporation can be voluntarily terminated by the shareholders. Corporations may be involuntarily terminated by the corporation's creditors if an involuntary petition for bankruptcy against the corporation is granted. The death, insanity, or bankruptcy of a shareholder, director, or officer of the corporation does not affect its existence.
- **Centralized management.** The board of directors makes policy decisions concerning the operation of the corporation. The members of the board of directors are elected by the shareholders. The directors, in turn, appoint corporate officers to run the corporation's day-to-day operations. Together, the directors and the officers form the corporate "management."

The doctrine of limited liability of shareholders was imposed by the court in the following case.

CASE 24.1

Joslyn Manufacturing Co. v. T.L. James & Co., Inc.

893 F.2d 80 (1990) United States Court of Appeals, Fifth Circuit

Facts The Lincoln Creosoting Company, Inc. (Lincoln) was a Louisiana corporation that was incorporated in 1935. The company operated a wood-treating creosoting plant on its property. Although the company had a treatment plant, creosoting chemicals dripped into an open pit and were washed away by rain to surrounding land areas and waterways. From 1935 to 1950, Lincoln was 60 percent owned by T.L. James & Company, Inc. (James & Co.). Lincoln maintained separate books and records; held regularly scheduled shareholders and directors meetings; owned its own property and equipment; maintained its own employees, payroll, insurance, pension plan, and worker's compensation program; and filed its own tax returns. Thus, Lincoln, the subsidiary corporation, was run separately from its parent corporation, James & Co.

In 1950, Lincoln was sold to Joslyn Manufacturing Company (Joslyn), who in turn sold the plant in 1969. Since that time, the property passed through six separate owners, the last of which subdivided the property. The current owners of the property and adjacent property owners brought suit under federal and state environmental statutes to recover damages from Joslyn and Lincoln's other prior owners for environmental cleanup costs. Joslyn, which was ordered to clean up the contaminated site, sued James & Co. to recover costs of the cleanup. James & Co. asserted in defense that it was merely a shareholder of Lincoln and was protected by the limited liability doctrine. The district court granted James & Co.'s motion for summary judgment. Joslyn appealed.

Issue Is James & Co. liable for the environmental pollution caused by Lincoln?

Decision No. The court of appeals held that the corporate doctrine of limited liability shielded James & Co. from liability for the environmental pollution caused by Lincoln.

Reason Under corporate law, a shareholder's liability for the debts and obligations of a corporation is limited to his or her capital contribution. In this case, Lincoln was operated as a separate corporation with adequate capital and observed all corporate formalities. Therefore, James & Co., a shareholder of Lincoln, is not liable for environmental pollution caused by Lincoln. The court of appeals noted that Congress is capable of creating statutes that hold shareholders liable for the acts of corporations but held that Congress had not done so in this case.

CASE QUESTIONS

Critical Legal Thinking Should parent corporations be held liable for the acts of subsidiary corporations? Or should they be accorded limited liability like other shareholders?

Ethics Is it ethical for a shareholder to hide behind the shield of limited liability?

Business Implication Should Congress eliminate the concept of limited liability for shareholders of corporations that have caused environmental pollution?

The Revised Model Business Corporation Act

The Committee on Corporate Laws of the American Bar Association (the Committee) first drafted the *Model Business Corporation Act (MBCA)* in 1950. The model act was intended to provide a uniform law regulating the formation, operation, and termination of corporations.

In 1984, the committee completely revised the MBCA and issued the **Revised Model Business Corporation Act (RMBCA)**. Certain provisions of the RMBCA have been amended since 1984. The RMBCA arranged the provisions of the act more logically, revised the language of the act to be more consistent, and made substantial changes in the provisions of the model act. Many states have adopted all or part of the RMBCA. The RMBCA will serve as the basis for the discussion of corporations law in this book.

Federal Laws Affecting Corporations

There is no general federal corporation law governing the formation and operation of private corporations. Many federal laws regulate the operation of private corporations. These include federal securities laws, labor laws, antitrust laws, consumer protection laws, environmental protection laws, bankruptcy laws, and the like. These federal statutes are discussed in separate chapters later in this book.

Model Business Corporation Act (MBCA) A model act drafted in 1950 that was intended to provide a uniform law for regulation of corporations.

Revised Model Business Corporation Act (RMBCA) A revision of the MBCA in 1984 that arranged the provisions of the act more logically, revised the language to be more consistent, and made substantial changes in the provisions.

CONTEMPORARY BUSINESS ENVIRONMENT

S Corporations

Corporations are separate legal entities. As such, they generally must pay corporate income taxes to federal and state governments. If a corporation distributes its profits to shareholders in the form of dividends, shareholders must pay personal income tax on the dividends. This double taxation of corporations is one of the major disadvantages of doing business in the corporate form. Some corporations and their shareholders can avoid **double taxation** by electing to be an S Corporation.

In 1982, Congress enacted the **Subchapter S Revision Act**. The act divided all corporations into two groups: **S Corporations**, which are those that elect to be taxed under Subchapter S (formerly **Subchapter S Corporations**); and **C Corporations**, which are all other corporations [26 U.S.C. § 6242 et seq.].

If a corporation elects to be taxed as an S Corporation, it pays no federal income tax at the

corporate level. As in a partnership, the corporation's income or loss flows to the shareholders' individual income tax returns. Thus, this election is particularly advantageous if (1) the corporation is expected to have losses that can be offset against other income of the shareholder or (2) the corporation is expected to make profits and the shareholder's income tax bracket is lower than the corporation's. Profits are taxed to the shareholders even if the income is not distributed. The shares retain other attributes of the corporate form, including limited liability.

Corporations that meet the following criteria can elect to be taxed as S Corporations:

1. The corporation must be a domestic corporation
2. The corporation cannot be a member of an affiliated group
3. The corporation can have no more than 75 shareholders

4. Shareholders must be individuals, estates, or certain trusts. Corporations and partnerships cannot be shareholders
5. Shareholders must be citizens or residents of the United States. Nonresident aliens cannot be shareholders
6. The corporation cannot have more than one class of stock. Shareholders do not have to have equal voting rights
7. No more than 20 percent of the corporation's income can be from passive investment income.

An S Corporation election is made by filing Form 2553 with the Internal Revenue Service (IRS). The election can be rescinded by shareholders who collectively own at least a majority of the shares of the corporation. However, if the election is rescinded, another S Corporation election cannot be made for five years.

CLASSIFICATIONS OF CORPORATIONS

Corporations are classified based on their locations, purpose, or owners. The various classifications or corporations are discussed in the following sections.

Domestic, Foreign, and Alien Corporations

domestic corporation A corporation in the state in which it was formed.

foreign corporation A corporation in any state or jurisdiction other than the one in which it was formed.

alien corporation A corporation that is incorporated in another country.

A corporation is a **domestic corporation** in the state in which it is incorporated. It is a **foreign corporation** in all other states and jurisdictions. For example, suppose a corporation incorporates in Texas and does business in Montana. The corporation is a domestic corporation in Texas and a foreign corporation in Montana. An **alien corporation** is a corporation that is incorporated in another country. In most instances, alien corporations are treated as foreign corporations.

A state can require a foreign corporation to qualify to conduct intrastate commerce within the state. Where a foreign corporation is required to qualify to do intrastate commerce in a state, it must obtain a *certificate of authority* from the state.[1] This requires the foreign corporation to file certain information with the secretary of state, pay the required fees, and appoint a registered agent for service of process.

Conduct that usually constitutes "doing business" includes maintaining an office to conduct intrastate business, selling personal property in intrastate business, entering into contracts involving intrastate commerce, using real estate for general corporate purposes, and the like. Activities that generally are not considered doing business within the state include maintaining, defending, or settling a lawsuit or administrative proceeding; maintaining bank accounts; effectuating sales through independent contractors; soliciting orders through the mail; securing or collecting debts; transacting any business in interstate commerce; and the like.[2]

Conducting intrastate business in a state in which it is not qualified subjects the corporation to fines. In addition, the corporation cannot bring a lawsuit in the state, although it can defend itself against lawsuits and administrative proceedings brought by others.[3]

BUSINESS BRIEF

Although Ford Motor Company's headquarters office and major automobile plants are located in the state of Michigan, it is incorporated in the state of Delaware. Therefore, it is a domestic corporation in Delaware and a foreign corporation in the other 49 states.

Profit and Nonprofit Corporations

profit corporation A corporation created to conduct a business for profit that can distribute profits to shareholders in the form of dividends.

nonprofit corporation A corporation that is formed to operate charitable institutions, colleges, universities, and other not-for-profit entities.

Private corporations may be further classified as either for profit or nonprofit. **Profit corporations** are created to conduct a business for profit and can distribute profits to shareholders in the form of dividends. Most private corporations fit this definition.

Nonprofit corporations are formed for charitable, educational, religious, or scientific purposes. Although nonprofit corporations may make a profit, they are prohibited by law from distributing this profit to their members, directors, or officers. About a dozen states have enacted the *Model Nonprofit Corporations Act* that governs the formation, operation, and termination of nonprofit corporations. All other states have their own individual statutes that govern the formation, operation, and dissolution of such corporations.

Publicly Held and Closely Held Corporations

publicly held corporation A corporation that has many shareholders and whose securities are often traded on national stock exchanges.

Publicly held corporations have many shareholders. Often, they are large corporations with hundreds or thousands of shareholders whose shares are traded on organized securities markets. IBM Corporation and General Motors Corporation are examples of publicly held corporations. The shareholders rarely participate in the management of such corporations.

A *closely held* (or *close*) *corporation* is one whose shares are owned by few shareholders who are often family members, relatives, or friends. Frequently, the shareholders are involved in the management of the corporation. The shareholders sometimes enter into buy-and-sell agreements that prevent outsiders from becoming shareholders.

Professional Corporations

Professional corporations are formed by professionals such as lawyers, accountants, physicians, dentists, and the like. The abbreviations *P.C.* (professional corporation), *P.A.* (professional association), or *S.C.* (service corporation) often identify professional corporations. Shareholders of professional corporations are often called *members.* Generally, only licensed professionals may become members.

All states permit the incorporation of professional corporations, although some states allow only designated types of professionals to incorporate. Professional corporations have normal corporate attributes and are formed like other corporations.

Members of the corporation are not usually liable for the torts committed by its agents or employees. Some states impose liability on members for the malpractice of other members of the corporation.

professional corporation
A corporation formed by lawyers, doctors, or other professionals.

ETHICAL PERSPECTIVE

Professionals Dodge Corporate Liability

Professionals may form corporations to limit their liability. Consider the following case.

Three lawyers, Howard R. Cohen, Richard L. Stracher, and Paul J. Bloom, formed a professional corporation to engage in the practice of law. The three men were the sole shareholders, directors, and officers of the corporation. The corporation entered into an agreement to lease office space from We're Associates Company (We're Associates) in a building in Lake Success, New York. The lease was executed on behalf of the corporation "by Paul J. Bloom, Vice President." We're Associates sued the corporation and its three shareholders to recover $9,000 allegedly due and owing under the lease.

The trial court dismissed the plaintiff's case, and the appellate court affirmed. The appellate court noted that prior to 1970, attorneys, physicians, and other professionals in New York were barred from joining with other members of their respective professions in organizing corporations for the purpose of rendering professional services. In that year, however, with the enactment of Article 15 of the Business Corporation Law, New York joined other states in affording the privilege of incorporation to professionals.

In holding that the three lawyers who formed the professional corporation were not personally liable to We're Associates on the corporation's lease, the appellate court stated, "It is well established that in the absence of some constitutional, statutory, or charter provision, the shareholders of a corporation are not liable for its contractual obligations and that parties having business dealings with a corporation must look to the corporation itself and not the shareholders for payment of their claims. Indeed, this insulation from individual liability for corporate obligations is one of the fundamental purposes of operating through corporate form . . . The members of professional corporations are to enjoy the same benefits of limited liability afforded to shareholders of any other form of corporation."

The court concluded, "Any analysis of the possible ethical considerations or moral obligations of attorneys in this situation is a separate matter and does not bear upon the substantive legal issue of the scope of liability under the statute." [*We're Associates Company v. Cohen, Stracher & Bloom, P.C.*, 478 N.Y.S.2d 670 (N.Y.App. 1984)]

1. Did the attorneys act morally in not paying the lease payments themselves?
2. How could We're Associates have protected itself in this case?

PROMOTERS' ACTIVITIES

The **promoter** is the person or persons who organize and start the corporation, negotiate and enter into contracts in advance of its formation, find the initial investors to finance the corporation, and so on. As discussed shortly, these activities may subject the promoter to personal liability.

promoter A person or persons who organize and start the corporation, negotiate and enter into contracts in advance of its formation, find the initial investors to finance the corporation, and so forth.

promoters' contracts A collective term for such things as leases, sales contracts, contracts to purchase property, and employment contracts entered into by promoters on behalf of the proposed corporation prior to its actual incorporation.

Promoters' Liability

Promoters often enter into contracts on behalf of the corporation prior to the actual incorporation of the corporation. **Promoters' contracts** include leases, sales contracts, contracts to purchase property, employment contracts, and the like. If the corporation never comes into existence, the promoters have joint personal liability on the contract unless the third party specifically exempts them from such liability.

If the corporation is formed, it becomes liable on a promoter's contract only if it agrees to become bound to the contract. This requires a resolution of the board of directors to be bound by the promoter's contract.

The promoter remains liable on the contract unless the parties enter into a novation.[4] A *novation* is a three-party agreement whereby the corporation agrees to assume the contract liability of the promoter with the consent of the third party. After a novation, the corporation is solely liable on the promoter's contract.

In the following case, the court found a promoter liable on a promoter's contract.

CASE 24.2

Coopers & Lybrand v. Fox
758 P.2d 683 (1988) Colorado Court of Appeals

Facts On November 3, 1981, Garry J. Fox met with a representative of Coopers & Lybrand (Coopers), a national accounting firm. Fox informed Coopers that he was acting on behalf of a corporation he was in the process of forming, G. Fox and Partners, Inc., and requested a tax opinion and other accounting service for the corporation. Coopers accepted the engagement with the knowledge that the corporation was not yet in existence. The corporation was incorporated on December 4, 1981, Coopers completed its work by mid-December and billed the corporation and Fox $10,827 for services rendered. When neither Fox nor the corporation paid the bill, Coopers sued Fox as a promoter to recover the debt. The trial court held in favor of Fox. Coopers appealed.

Issue Is Fox liable on the Coopers & Lybrand contract as a promoter?

Decision Yes. The court of appeals held that Fox was liable, as a matter of law, under the doctrine of promoter liability. Reversed.

Reason The uncontroverted facts place Fox squarely within the definition of a promoter. As a

general rule, promoters are personally liable for the contracts they make, though made on behalf of a corporation to be formed. The well-recognized exception to the general rule of promoter liability is that if the contracting party agrees to look solely to the corporation and not to the promoter for payment, then the promoter incurs no personal liability. As the proponent of an alleged agreement to release the promoter from liability, the promoter has the burden of proving the release agreement. Here, Fox did not prove that such an agreement existed.

CASE QUESTIONS

Critical Legal Thinking Should promoters be held liable on their contracts even if the corporation is subsequently formed and accepts the contract as its own?

Ethics Did Fox act ethically in this case?

Business Implication To avoid promoters liability, when should contracts on behalf of a proposed corporation be executed?

Subscription for Shares

subscription agreement An agreement by a person to purchase shares of a corporation once it is incorporated.

Prior to incorporation, a person can enter into a **subscription agreement** agreeing to purchase shares of the corporation once it is incorporated. Unless otherwise provided, a subscription agreement is irrevocable for six months. If a **subscriber** defaults in payment of money or property under a subscription agreement, the corporation may either (1) collect the amount owed as any other debt or (2) rescind the agreement and sell the shares to another party.[5]

INCORPORATION PROCEDURES

Corporations are creatures of statute. Thus, the organizers of the corporation must comply with the state's **incorporation** statute to form a corporation. Although relatively similar, the procedure for incorporating a corporation varies somewhat from state to state. The procedure for incorporating a corporation is discussed in the following paragraphs.

Purpose

A corporation can be formed for "any lawful purpose." Many corporations include a **general purpose clause** in their articles of incorporations (see Exhibit 24.2). Such a

incorporation The process of forming a corporation.

general purpose clause A clause that is often included in the articles of incorporation that authorizes the corporation to engage in any activity permitted corporations by law.

**ARTICLES OF INCORPORATION
OF THE BIG CHEESE CORPORATION**

ONE: The name of this corporation is:

THE BIG CHEESE CORPORATION

TWO: The purpose of this corporation is to engage in any lawful act or activity for which a corporation may be organized under the General Corporation Law of California other than the banking business, the trust company business, or the practice of a profession permitted to be incorporated by the California Corporations Code.

THREE: The name and address in this state of the corporation's initial agent for service of process is:

Nikki Nguyen, Esq.
1000 Main Street
Suite 800
Los Angeles, California 90010

FOUR: This corporation is authorized to issue only one class of shares which shall be designated common stock. The total number of shares it is authorized to issue is 1,000,000 shares.

FIVE: The names and address of the persons who are appointed to act as the initial directors of this corporation are:

Min-Wer Chen	100 Maple Street
	Los Angeles, California 90005
Fred Richards	200 Spruce Road
	Los Angeles, California 90006
Thomas Blanford	300 Palm Drive
	Los Angeles, California 90007
Teadora Valdez	400 Willow Lane
	Los Angeles, California 90008

SIX: The liability of the directors of the corporation from monetary damages shall be eliminated to the fullest extent possible under California law.

SEVEN: The corporation is authorized to provide indemnification of agents (as defined in Section 317 of the Corporation Code) for breach of duty to the corporation and its stockholders through bylaw provisions or through agreements with the agents, or both, in excess of the indemnification otherwise permitted by Section 317 of the Corporations Code, subject to the limits on such excess indemnification set forth in Section 204 of the Corporations Code.

IN WITNESS WHEREOF, the undersigned, being all the persons named above as the initial directors, have executed these Articles of Incorporation.

Dated: _____   _____

_____

_____

_____

Exhibit 24.2
Sample Provisions from
Corporate Bylaws

clause allows the corporation to engage in any activity permitted corporations by law. Corporations may choose to limit the purpose or purposes of the corporation by including a **limited purpose clause** in the articles of incorporation.[6] For example, a corporation may be organized "to engage in the business of real estate development."

limited purpose clause
A clause that limits the purpose or purposes of the corporation.

CAUTION
Care must be taken to select a corporate name that is distinguishable from existing corporate names.

Corporate Name

A corporate name selected for a new corporation must be distinguishable from existing corporate names.[7] This rule is intended to avoid confusion among consumers of corporate goods and services. A corporation may sue another corporation or business for using a name similar or identical to its own name. In addition, the name must contain the words *corporation, company, incorporated,* or *limited* or an abbreviation of one of these words (i.e., *Corp., Co., Inc.,* or *Ltd.*).[8]

Corporate names cannot contain any word or phrase that indicates or implies that it is organized for any purpose other than those stated in the articles of incorporation. In other words, a corporate name cannot contain the word *Bank* if the corporation is not authorized to conduct the business of banking.

BUSINESS CHECKLIST

Selecting a Corporate Name

When starting a new corporation, the organizers must choose a name for the entity. To ensure that the name selected is not already being used by another business, the organizers should take the following steps [RMBCA § 4.01]:

- Choose a name (and alternative names) for the corporation. The name must contain the words *corporation, company, incorporated,* or *limited* or an abbreviation of one of these words (i.e., *Corp., Co., Inc.,* or *Ltd.*).
- Make sure that the name chosen does not contain any word or phrase that indicates or implies that the corporation is organized for any purpose other than those stated in the articles of incorporation. For example, a corporate name cannot contain the word *Bank* if it is not authorized to conduct the business of banking.
- Determine whether the name selected is federally trademarked by another company and is therefore unavailable for use. Trademark lawyers and specialized firms will conduct trademark searches for a fee.
- Determine whether the chosen name is similar to other nontrademarked names and is therefore unavailable for use. Lawyers and specialized firms will conduct such searches for a fee.
- When the corporate name selected is determined to be available, reserve the name by filing an application with and paying the required fee to the Secretary of State of the state of incorporation. The name may be reserved for a nonrenewable period (e.g., 120 days). During this time the organizers should complete the process of incorporation.

BUSINESS BRIEF
Corporations are creatures of statute; they can be formed only if certain statutory formalities are followed.

Selecting a State for Incorporation

A corporation can be incorporated in only one state even though it can do business in all other states in which it qualifies to do business. In choosing a state for incorporation, the incorporators, directors, and/or shareholders must consider the corporations' codes of the states under consideration.

For the sake of convenience, most corporations (particularly small ones) choose the state in which the corporation will be doing most of its business as the state for incorporation. Large corporations generally opt to incorporate in the state with the laws that are most favorable to the corporation's internal operations (e.g., Delaware).

Incorporators

One or more persons, partnerships, domestic or foreign corporations, or other associations may act as an **incorporator** of a corporation.[9] The incorporator's primary duty is to sign the articles of incorporation. Incorporators often become shareholders, directors, or officers of the corporation.

Articles of Incorporation

The **articles of incorporation** (or **corporate charter**) is the basic governing document of the corporation. It must be drafted and filed with, and approved by, the state before the corporation can be officially incorporated. Under the RMBCA, the articles of incorporation must include the following:[10]

1. The name of the corporation
2. The number of shares the corporation is authorized to issue
3. The address of the corporation's initial registered office and the name of the initial registered agent
4. The name and address of each incorporator

The articles of incorporation may also include provisions concerning (1) the period of duration, which may be perpetual, (2) the purpose or purposes for which the corporation is organized, (3) limitation or regulation of the powers of the corporation, (4) regulation of the affairs of the corporation, and (5) any provisions that would otherwise be contained in the corporation's bylaws.

Exhibit 24.2 illustrates a sample articles of incorporation.

Amending the Articles of Incorporation The articles of incorporation can be amended to contain any provision that could have been lawfully included in the original document.[11] Such an amendment must show that (1) the board of directors adopted a resolution recommending the amendment and (2) the shareholders voted to approve the amendment.[12] The board of directors of a corporation may approve an amendment to the articles of incorporation without shareholder approval if the amendment does not affect rights attached to shares.[13] After the amendment is approved by the shareholders, the corporation must file *articles of amendment* with the secretary of state.[14]

Prior to incorporation, the incorporators can reserve a proposed corporate name (if available) by filing an application with the secretary of state. Under the RMBCA, the name can be reserved for a nonrenewable 120-day period.[15]

Registered Agent

The articles of incorporation must identify a **registered office** with a designated **registered agent** (either an individual or a corporation) in the state of incorporation.[16] The registered office does not have to be the same as the corporation's place of business. A statement of change must be filed with the secretary of state of the state of incorporation if either the registered office or the registered agent is changed.

The registered agency is empowered to accept service of process on behalf of the corporation. For example, if someone were suing the corporation, the complaint and summons would be served on the registered agent. If no registered agent is named or the registered agent cannot be found at the registered office with reasonable diligence, service may be made by mail or alternative means.[17]

NOTE
More than half of the corporations listed on the New York Stock Exchange are incorporated in Delaware because of its favorable laws.

incorporator The person or persons, partnerships, or corporations who are responsible for incorporation of a corporation.

articles of incorporation The basic governing document of the corporation. This document must be filed with the secretary of state of the state of incorporation.

CAUTION
The Corporation Code of each state sets out the information that must be included in the articles of incorporation.

"Corporation: An ingenious device for obtaining individual profit without individual responsibility."
Ambrose Bierce
The Devil's Dictionary (1911)

registered agent A person or corporation that is empowered to accept service of process on behalf of the corporation.

Corporate Bylaws

bylaws A detailed set of rules that are adopted by the board of directors after the corporation is incorporated that contains provisions for managing the business and the affairs of the corporation.

In addition to the articles of incorporation, corporations are governed by their **bylaws**. Either the incorporators or initial directors can adopt the bylaws of the corporation. The bylaws, which govern the internal management structure of the corporation, are much more detailed than are the articles of incorporation. Bylaws may contain any provision for managing the business and affairs of the corporation that are not inconsistent with law or the articles of incorporation.[18] They do not have to be filed with any government official. The bylaws are binding on the directors, officers, and shareholders of the corporation.

Typically, the bylaws specify the time and place of the annual shareholders' meeting, how special meetings of shareholders are called, the time and place of annual and monthly board of directors' meetings, how special meetings of the board of directors are called, the notice required for meetings, the quorum necessary to hold a shareholders' or board of directors' meeting, the required vote necessary to enact a corporate matter, the corporate officers and their duties, the committees that are to be kept, directors' and shareholders' inspection rights of corporate records, the procedure for transferring shares of the corporation, and such. Sample provisions of corporate bylaws are set forth in Exhibit 24.3.

Exhibit 24.3
Sample Provisions from
Corporate Bylaws

BYLAWS
OF THE BIG CHEESE CORPORATION

ARTICLE I   Offices

Section 1. Principal Executive Office.   The corporation's principal executive office shall be fixed and located at such place as the Board of Directors (herein called the "Board") shall determine. The Board is granted full power and authority to change said principal executive office from one location to another.

Section 2. Other Offices. Branch or subordinate offices may be established at any time by the Board at any place or places.

ARTICLE II   Shareholders

Section 1. Annual Meetings. The annual meetings of shareholders shall be held on such date and at such time as may be fixed by the Board. At such meetings, directors shall be elected and any other proper business may be transacted.

Section 2. Special Meetings. Special meetings of the shareholders may be called at any time by the Board, the Chairman of the Board, the President, or by the holders of shares entitled to cast not less than ten percent of the votes at such meeting. Upon request in writing to the Chairman of the board, the President, any Vice President or the Secretary by any person (other than the Board) entitled to call a special meeting of shareholders, the officer forthwith shall cause notice to be given to the shareholders entitled to vote that a meeting will be held at a time requested by the person or persons calling the meeting, not less than thirty-five nor more than sixty days after the receipt of the request. If the notice is not given within twenty days after receipt of the request, the persons entitled to call the meeting may give the notice.

Section 3. Quorum. A majority of the shares entitled to vote, represented in person or by proxy, shall constitute a quorum at any meeting of shareholders. If a quorum is present, the affirmative vote of a majority of the shares represented and voting at the meeting (which shares voting affirmatively also constitute at least a majority of the required quorum) shall be he act of the shareholders, unless the vote of a greater number or voting by classes is required by law or by the Articles, except as provided in the following sentence. The shareholders present at a duly called or held meeting at which a quorum is present may continue to do business until adjournment, notwithstanding the withdrawal of enough shareholders to leave less than a quorum, if any action taken (other than adjournment) is approved by at least a majority of the shares required to constitute a quorum.

ARTICLE III   Directors

Section 1. Election and Term of Office. The directors shall be elected at each annual meeting of the shareholders, but if any such annual meeting is not held or the directors are not elected thereat, the directors may be elected at any special meeting of shareholders held for that purpose. Each director shall hold office until the next annual meeting and until a successor has been elected and qualified.

Section 2. Quorum. A majority of the authorized number of directors constitutes a quorum of the Board for the transaction of business. Every act or decision done or made by a majority of the directors present at a meeting duly held at which a quorum is present shall be regarded as the act of the Board, unless a greater number be required by law or by the Articles. A meeting at which a quorum is initially present may continue to transact business notwithstanding the withdrawal of directors, if any action taken is approved by at least a majority of the required quorum for such meeting.

Section 3. Participation in Meetings by Conference Telephone. Members of the Board may participate in a meeting through use of conference telephone or similar communications equipment, so long as all members participating in such meeting can hear one another.

Section 4. Action Without Meeting. Any action required or permitted to be taken by the Board may be taken without a meeting if all members of the board shall individually or collectively consent in writing to such action. Such consent or consents shall have the same effect as a unanimous vote of the Board and shall be filed with the minutes of the proceedings of the Board.

The board of directors has the authority to amend the bylaws unless the articles of incorporation reserve that right for the shareholders. The shareholders of the corporation have the absolute right to amend the bylaws even though the bylaws may also be amended by the board of directors.[19]

Organizational Meeting

An **organizational meeting** of the initial directors of the corporation must be held after the articles of incorporation are filed. At this meeting, the directors must adopt the bylaws, elect corporate officers, and transact such other business as may come before the meeting.[20] The latter category includes such matters as accepting share subscriptions, approving the form of the stock certificate, authorizing the reimbursement of promoters' expenses, selecting a bank, choosing an auditor, forming committees of the board of directors, fixing the salaries of officers, hiring employees, authorizing the filing of applications for government licenses to transact the business of the corporation, and empowering corporate officers to enter into contracts on behalf of the corporation. Exhibit 24.4 contains a sample corporate resolutions from an organizational meeting of a corporation.

BUSINESS BRIEF

The bylaws, which are much more detailed than the articles of incorporation, regulate the internal management structure of the corporation.

organizational meeting A meeting that must be held by the initial directors of the corporation after the articles of incorporation are filed.

Exhibit 24.4

Sample Corporate Resolutions from an Organizational Meeting

MINUTES OF FIRST MEETING
OF BOARD OF DIRECTORS
OF THE BIG CHEESE CORPORATION
JANUARY 3, 1999
10:00 A.M.

The Directors of said corporation held their first meeting on the above date and at the above time pursuant to required notice.

The following Directors, constituting a quorum of the Board of Directors, were present at such meeting:

continued

Exhibit 24.4
Sample Corporate
Resolutions from an
Organizational Meeting
(continued)

Min-Wer Chen
Fred Richards
Thomas Blanford
Teadora Valdez

Upon motion duly made and seconded, Kathleen Cheeseman was unanimously elected Chairman of the meeting and Peter Ney was unanimously elected Secretary of the meeting.

1. Articles of Incorporation and Agent for Service of Process

The Chairman stated that the Articles of Incorporation of the Corporation were filed in the office of the California Secretary of State. The Chairman presented to the meeting a certified copy of the Articles of Incorporation. The Secretary was directed to insert the copy in the Minute Book. Upon motion duly made and seconded, the following resolution was unanimously adopted:

RESOLVED, that the agent named as the initial agent for service of process in the Articles of Incorporation of this corporation is hereby confirmed as this corporation's agent for the purpose of service of process.

2. Bylaws

The matter of adopting Bylaws for the regulation of the affairs of the corporation was next considered. The Secretary presented to the meeting a form of Bylaws, which was considered and discussed. Upon motion duly made and seconded, the following recitals and resolutions were unanimously adopted:

WHEREAS, there has been presented to the directors a form of Bylaws for the regulation of the affairs of this corporation; and

WHEREAS, it is deemed to be in the best interests of this corporation that said Bylaws be adopted by this Board of Directors as the Bylaws of this corporation;

NOW, THEREFORE, BE IT RESOLVED, that Bylaws in the form presented to this meeting are adopted and approved as the Bylaws of this corporation until amended or repealed in accordance with applicable law.

RESOLVED FURTHER, that the Secretary of this corporation is authorized and directed to execute a certificate of the adoption of said Bylaws and to enter said Bylaws as so certified in the Minute book of this corporation, and to see that a copy of said Bylaws is kept at the principal executive or business office of this corporation in California.

3. Corporate Seal

The secretary presented for approval a proposed seal of the corporation. Upon motion duly made and seconded, the following resolution was unanimously adopted:

RESOLVED, that a corporate seal is adopted as the seal of this corporation in the form of two concentric circles, with the name of this corporation between the two circles and the state and date of incorporation within the inner circle.

4. Stock Certificate

The Secretary presented a proposed form of stock certificate for use by the corporation. Upon motion duly made and seconded, the following resolution was unanimously adopted:

RESOLVED, that the form of stock certificate presented to this meeting is approved and adopted as the stock certificate of this corporation.

The secretary was instructed to insert a sample copy of the stock certificate in the Minute Book immediately following these minutes.

5. Election of officers

The Chairman announced that it would be in order to elect officers of the corporation. After discussion and upon motion duly made and seconded, the following resolution was unanimously adopted:

RESOLVED, that the following persons are unanimously elected to the offices indicated opposite their names

Title	Name
Chief Executive Officer	Min-Wer Chen
President	Fred Richards
Secretary and Vice President	Thomas Blanford
Treasurer	Teadora Valdez

There being no further business to come before the meeting, on motion duly made, seconded and unanimously carried, the meeting was adjourned.

Corporate Seal

Most corporations adopt a **corporate seal**.[21] Generally, the seal is a design that contains the name of the corporation and the date of incorporation. It is imprinted by the corporate secretary on certain legal documents (e.g., real estate deeds and the like) that are signed by corporate officers or directors. The seal is usually affixed by a metal stamp.

Corporate Status

The RMBCA provides that corporate existence begins when the articles of incorporation are filed. The secretary of state's filing of the articles of incorporation is conclusive proof that the incorporators satisfied all conditions to incorporation. After that, only the state can bring a proceeding to cancel or revoke the incorporation or involuntarily dissolve the corporation. Third parties cannot thereafter challenge the existence of the corporation or raise it as a defense against the corporation.[22] The corollary to this rule is: Failure to file articles of incorporation is conclusive proof of the nonexistence of the corporation.

corporate seal A design that contains the name of the corporation and the date of incorporation. It is imprinted by the corporate secretary on certain legal documents using a metal stamp containing the design.

BUSINESS BRIEF
Under the "bright line" test of RMBCA Section 2.03 the filing of the articles of incorporations is conclusive proof *that a corporation exists. After that, only the state can challenge the status of the corporation; third parties cannot.*

INTERNATIONAL PERSPECTIVE

The Organization and Operation of the Multinational Corporation

In the past the size, power, and range of activities of corporations were limited. This changed at the beginning of the 20th century, when corporations won the right to own stock in each other. National corporate networks soon followed. Eventually, parent corporations, mostly American, expanded these networks overseas by setting up subsidiary corporations under the laws of other countries. These international networks (or multinational enterprises) are made up of companies of different nationalities that constitute a single economic unit connected by shareholding, managerial control, or contractual agreement. The simplest international operating structure is one that subcontracts with independent firms in the host country to carry out sales or purchases. "National multinational" firms that establish wholly owned branches and subsidiaries overseas are somewhat more complex. "International multinational" firms are even more complicated. They are made up of two or more parents from different countries that co-own operating businesses in two or more countries.

The Ford Motor Company is an example of a national multinational firm. Organized in the United States at the beginning of this century, Ford has always viewed the entire world as its market. The company's policy is for the American parent to own and control all of its overseas subsidiaries. Ford's 10 European sub-
continued

sidiaries are all owned entirely by the American parent. The Mitsubishi Group is another example of this organizational format. It is actually made up of several Japanese companies that use joint directors' meetings to coordinate their activities in Japan and overseas.

The Royal Dutch/Shell Group is an example of an international multinational corporation. In 1907, the Dutch and British parents each formed a wholly owned holding company in their respective countries. Each then transferred the ownership of the operating subsidiary to the holding company and exchanged shares in the holding companies. The Dutch parent held 60 percent of each holding company, and the British parent held 40 percent. In addition, the management and operation of the two companies was organized to function as a single economic unit. Unilever, Dunlop Pirelli, and VFW/Fokker also operate under an international multinational umbrella.

There is a special type of international multinational: a publicly owned transnational enterprise. One example is Air Afrique, which was created by several West African countries through the use of a treaty granting each government a voice in the company's operation.

FINANCING THE CORPORATION

equity securities
Representation of ownership rights to the corporation. Also called *stocks*.

A corporation needs to finance the operation of its business. The most common way to do this is by selling equity securities and debt securities. **Equity securities** (or **stocks**) represent ownership rights in the corporation. Debt securities do not. They in fact represent debts owed to creditors of the corporation. Funds may also be obtained by borrowing money from banks, receiving an extension of credit from suppliers, or selling commercial paper to investors.

Common Stock

common stock A type of equity security that represents the *residual* value of the corporation.

common stockholder
A person who owns common stock.

common stock certificate
A document that represents the common shareholder's investment in the corporation.

Common stock is an equity security that represents the residual value of the corporation. Persons who own common stock are called **common stockholders**. A common stockholder's investment in the corporation is represented by a **common stock certificate**. Common shareholders have the right to elect directors and to vote on mergers and other important matters. In return for their investment, common shareholders receive *dividends* declared by the board of directors. However, common stock has no preferences. That is, creditors and preferred shareholders receive their required interest and dividend payments before common shareholders.

Common stock does not have a fixed maturity date. If the corporation is liquidated, the creditors and preferred shareholders are paid the value of their interests first, and the common shareholders are paid the value of their interest (if any) last. Corporations may issue different classes of common stock.[23]

A sample share of common stock is shown in Exhibit 24.5.

par value A value assigned to common shares by the corporation that sets the lowest price at which the shares may be issued by the corporation.

Par Value and No Par Shares Common shares are sometimes categorized as either par or no par. **Par value** is a value assigned to common shares by the corporation, usually in the articles of incorporation, which sets the lowest price at which the shares may be issued by the corporation. It does not affect the market value of the shares. Most shares that are issued by corporations are *no par shares*. No par shares are not assigned a par value. The RMBCA has eliminated the concept of par value.

Preferred Stock

preferred stock A type of equity security that is given certain preferences and rights over common stock.

preferred stockholder
A person who owns preferred stock.

Preferred stock is an equity security that is given certain preferences and rights over common stock.[24] The owners of preferred stock are called **preferred stockholders**. Preferred stockholders are issued a *preferred stock certificate* to evidence their ownership interest in the corporation.

Exhibit 24.5
Sample Stock Certificate

Preferred stock can be issued in classes or series. One class of preferred stock can be given preferences over another class of preferred stock. Like common shareholders, preferred shareholders have limited liability. Preferred shareholders generally are not given the right to vote for the election of directors or such. However, they are often given the right to vote on mergers or if the corporation has not made the required dividend payments for a certain period of time (e.g., three years).

Preferences Preferences of preferred stock must be set forth in the articles of incorporation. Preferred stock may have any or all of the following preferences or rights:

- **Dividend preference.** The right to receive **a fixed dividend** at set periods during the year (e.g., quarterly). The dividend rate is usually a set percentage of the initial offering price.

    CONSIDER THIS EXAMPLE: Suppose a stockholder purchased $10,000 or a preferred stock that pays an 8 percent dividend annually. The stockholder has the right to receive $800 each year as a dividend on the preferred stock.

- **Liquidation preference.** The right to be paid before common stockholders if the corporation is dissolved and liquidated. A liquidation preference is normally a stated dollar amount.

BUSINESS BRIEF
Preferred stock is given certain preferences *and its value is based on these preferences; common stock has no preferences and represents the* residual *value of the corporation.*

dividend preference
The right to receive a fixed dividend at stipulated periods during the year (e.g., quarterly).

liquidation preference
The right to be paid a stated dollar amount if the corporation is dissolved and liquidated.

CONSIDER THIS EXAMPLE: A corporation issues a preferred stock that has a liquidation preference of $200. This means that if the corporation is dissolved and liquidated, the holder of each preferred share will receive at least $200 before the common shareholders receive anything. Note that since the corporation must pay its creditors first, there may be insufficient funds to pay this preference.

- **Cumulative dividend right.** Corporations must pay a preferred dividend if they have the earnings to do so. **Cumulative preferred stock** provides that any missed dividend payments must be paid in the future to the preferred shareholders before the common shareholders can receive any dividends. The amount of unpaid cumulative dividends is called **dividend arrearages**. Usually, arrearages can be accumulated for only a limited period of time (such as three years). If the preferred stock is **noncumulative**, there is no right of accumulation. In other words, the corporation does not have to pay any missed dividends.

- **Right to participate in profits. Participating preferred stock** allows the stockholder to participate in the profits of the corporation along with the common stockholders. Participation is in addition to the fixed dividend paid on preferred stock. The terms of participation vary widely. Usually, the common stockholders must be paid a certain amount of dividends before participation is allowed. **Nonparticipating preferred stock** does not have a right to participate in the profits of the corporation beyond its fixed dividend rate. Most preferred stock falls into this category.

- **Conversion right. Convertible preferred stock** permits the stockholders to convert their shares into common stock. The terms and exchange rate of the conversion are established when the shares are issued. The holders of the convertible preferred stock usually exercise this option if the corporation's common stock increases significantly in value. Preferred stock without a conversion feature is called **nonconvertible preferred stock**. Nonconvertible stock is more common.

The preceding list of preferences and rights is not exhaustive.[25] Corporations may establish other preferences and rights for preferred stock.

Redeemable Stock Redeemable preferred stock (or **callable preferred stock**) permits the corporation to redeem (i.e., buy back) the preferred stock at some future date. The terms of the redemption are established when the shares are issued. Corporations usually redeem the shares when the current interest rate falls below the dividend rate of the preferred shares. Preferred stock that is not redeemable is called nonredeemable preferred stock. Nonredeemable stock is more common.

Consideration to be Paid for Shares

The RMBCA allows shares to be issued in exchange for any benefit to the corporation, including cash, tangible property, intangible property, promissory notes, services performed, contracts for services to be performed, or other securities of the corporation. In the absence of fraud, the judgment of the board of directors or shareholders as to the value of consideration received for shares is conclusive.[26]

Authorized, Issued, and Outstanding Shares

The number of shares provided for in the articles of incorporation are called **authorized shares**.[27] The shareholders may vote to amend the articles of incorporation to increase this amount. Authorized shares that have been sold by the corporation are called **issued shares**. Not all authorized shares have to be issued at the same time. Authorized shares that have not been issued are called **unissued shares**. The board of directors can vote to issue unissued shares at any time without shareholder approval.

---

cumulative preferred stock Stock that provides that any missed dividend payments must be paid in the future to the preferred shareholders before the common shareholders can receive any dividends.

participating preferred stock Stock that allows the stockholder to participate in the profits of the corporation along with the common stockholders.

convertible preferred stock Stock that permits the stockholders to convert their shares into common stock.

redeemable preferred stock Stock that permits the corporation to buy back the preferred stock at some future date.

BUSINESS BRIEF
Shares of a corporation may be sold in exchange for any property or benefit to the corporation as determined by the board of directors.

authorized shares The number of shares provided for in the articles of incorporation.

issued shares Shares that have been sold by the corporation.

A corporation is permitted to repurchase its own shares.[28] Repurchased shares are commonly called **treasury shares**. Treasury shares cannot be voted by the corporation, and dividends are not paid on these shares. Treasury shares can be reissued by the corporation. The shares that are in shareholder hands, whether originally issued or reissued treasury shares, are called **outstanding shares**. Only outstanding shares have the right to vote.[29]

> **treasury shares** Shares of stock repurchased by the company itself.
>
> **outstanding shares** Shares of stock that are in shareholder hands.

Stock Options and Stock Warrants

A corporation can grant stock options (options) and stock warrants (warrants) that permit parties to purchase common or preferred shares at a certain price for a set time.[30]

Corporations commonly grant **stock options** to top-level managers. They are nontransferable. A stock option gives the recipient the right to purchase shares of the corporation from the corporation at a stated price (called the *striking price*) for a specified period of time (called the *option period*). If the profitability of the corporation and the market value of its securities increase during the option period, the holder of the option is likely to *exercise the option*, that is, purchase the shares subject to the option.

A **stock warrant** is a stock option that is evidenced by a certificate. Warrants are commonly issued in conjunction with other securities. A warrant holder can exercise the warrant and purchase the common stock at the strike price any time during the warrant period. Warrants can be transferable or nontransferable.

> **stock option** A nontransferable right to purchase shares of the corporation from the corporation at a stated price for a specified period of time.
>
> **stock warrant** A stock option that is evidenced by a certificate. Warrants can be transferable or nontransferable.

Debt Securities

A corporation often raises funds by issuing debt securities.[31] **Debt securities** (also called **fixed income securities**) establish a debtor–creditor relationship in which the corporation borrows money from the investor to whom the debt security is issued. The corporation promises to pay interest on the amount borrowed and to repay the principal at some stated maturity date in the future. The corporation is the debtor and the holder is the creditor. There are three classifications of debt securities: debentures, bonds, and notes.

A **debenture** is a long-term (often 30 years or more), unsecured debt instrument that is based on the corporation's general credit standing. If the corporation encounters financial difficulty, unsecured debenture holders are treated as general creditors of the corporation (i.e., they are paid only after the secured creditors' claims are met).

A **bond** is a long-term debt security that is secured by some form of *collateral* (e.g., real estate, personal property, and such). Thus, bonds are the same as debentures except that they are secured. Secured bondholders can foreclose on the collateral in the event of nonpayment of interest, principal, or other specified events.

A **note** is a debt security with a maturity of five years or less. Notes can be either unsecured or secured. They usually do not contain a conversion feature. They are sometimes made redeemable.

> **debt securities** Securities that establish a debtor–creditor relationship in which the corporation borrows money from the investor to whom the debt security is issued.
>
> **debenture** A long-term unsecured debt instrument that is based on the corporation's general credit standing.
>
> **bond** A long-term security that is secured by some form of collateral.
>
> **note** A debt security with a maturity of five years or less.

Indenture Agreement The terms of a debt security are commonly contained in a contract between the corporation and the holder known as an **indenture agreement** (or simply an **indenture**). The indenture generally contains the maturity date of the debt security, the required interest payments, the collateral (if any), conversion rights into common or preferred stock, call provisions, any restrictions on the corporation's right to incur other indebtedness, the rights of holders upon default, and such. It also establishes the rights and duties of the indenture trustee. Generally, a trustee is appointed to represent the interest of the debt security holders. Bank trust departments often serve in this capacity.

In the following case, the court held that directors of a corporation do not owe a fiduciary duty to debenture holders.

> **indenture agreement** A contract between the corporation and the holder that contains the terms of a debt security.

CASE 24.3

Pittelman v. Pearce
6 Cal.App.4th 1436, 8 Cal.Rptr.2d 359 (1992) Court of Appeal of California

Facts In 1986, Steven Pittelman purchased a 25-year, 8¼-percent convertible subordinated debenture issued by American Medical International, Inc. (AMI) for $1,000. In 1989, AMI was acquired in a leveraged buyout by IMA Acquisition Corporation (IMA). To complete the purchase of 86 percent of the stock of AMI, IMA borrowed $2.4 billion from banks and through the issue of high-yield junk bonds. IMA paid interest rates from 16.75 percent to 24 percent on this debt.

Following the leveraged buyout, IMA caused the merger of AMI and IMA. After the merger, IMA's $2.4 billion debt became AMI's obligation. The merged company had to sell off important assets to help pay some of the bank loans. Pittelman's low-interest-yielding debenture became a "junk bond," and it sank in value. Pittelman sued the directors of AMI to recover this lost value as damages. He alleged in a class action that the directors had breached a fiduciary duty of honesty and loyalty that they owed to him and the other 8¼-percent debenture holders. The trial court granted the defendant's motion for summary judgment. Pittelman appealed.

Issue Do directors of a corporation owe a fiduciary duty to debenture holders?

Decision No. The court of appeal held that directors of a corporation do not owe a fiduciary duty to debenture holders. Affirmed.

Reason The court of appeal held that neither a corporation nor its directors owe any fiduciary duty to the corporation's debenture holders. The court held that the relationship between a corporation and the holders of its debt securities is contractual in nature. In this case, the indenture agreement with the 8¼-percent debenture holders did not prohibit AMI from taking on additional debt. Therefore, there was no breach of contract. The court noted that a corporation and its directors cannot owe a fiduciary duty to both debenture holders and shareholders because these parties often have opposing interests and because they already owe a fiduciary duty to shareholders. The board of directors would be hard pressed to make decisions that could meet this duty to both shareholders and debenture holders.

CASE QUESTIONS

Critical Legal Thinking Should directors be held to owe a fiduciary duty to debenture holders? Why or why not?

Ethics Even though the directors did not act illegally, did they act unethically toward the 8¼-percent debenture holders?

Business Implication Is investing in debentures of a corporation always a "safe" investment? Explain.

CORPORATE POWERS

A corporation has the same basic rights to perform acts and enter into contracts as a physical person.[32] The express and implied powers of a corporation are discussed in the following paragraphs.

Express Powers

express powers Powers given to a corporation by (1) the U.S. Constitution, (2) state constitutions, (3) federal statutes, (4) state statutes, (5) articles of incorporation, (6) bylaws, and (7) resolutions of the board of directors.

A corporation's **express powers** are found in (1) the U.S. Constitution, (2) state constitutions, (3) federal statutes, (4) state statutes, (5) articles of incorporation, (6) bylaws, and (7) resolutions of the board of directors. Corporation statutes normally state the express powers granted to the corporation.

Generally, a corporation has the power to purchase, own, lease, sell, mortgage, or otherwise deal in real and personal property; make contracts; lend money; borrow money; incur liabilities; issue notes, bonds, and other obligations; invest and reinvest funds; sue and be sued in its corporate name; make donations for the public welfare or for charitable, scientific, or educational purposes; and the like. RMBCA Section 3.02 provides a list of express corporate powers.

Corporations formed under general incorporation laws cannot engage in certain businesses, such as banking, insurance, or operating public utilities. Corporations must obtain a corporate charter under special incorporation statutes and receive approval of special government administrative agencies before engaging in these businesses.

Implied Powers

Neither the governing laws nor the corporate documents can anticipate every act necessary for a corporation to carry on its business. **Implied powers** allow the corporation to exceed its express powers in order to accomplish its corporate purpose. For instance, a corporation has the implied power to open a bank account, reimburse its employees for expenses, engage in advertising, purchase insurance, and the like.

implied powers   Powers beyond express powers that allow a corporation to accomplish its corporate purpose.

Ultra Vires Acts

An act by a corporation that is beyond its express or implied powers is called an **ultra vires act**. The following remedies are available if an ultra vires act is committed:

1. Shareholders can sue for an injunction to prevent the corporation from engaging in the act
2. The corporation (or the shareholders on behalf of the corporation) can sue the officers or directors who caused the act for damages
3. The attorney general of the state of incorporation can bring an action to enjoin the act or to dissolve the corporation.[33]

ultra vires act   An act by a corporation that is beyond its express or implied powers.

INTERNATIONAL PERSPECTIVE

Conducting Business in a Foreign Country

A corporation organized in one country may wish to conduct business in other countries. To do so, it has a variety of choices available to it depending upon the extent of involvement and market penetration desired, the amount of capital to be invested, the legal and cultural restrictions of the foreign country, and so on. The major forms of conducting business in a foreign country are discussed in the following paragraphs. Each fact pattern must be analyzed to determine which form best suits the situation.

Direct Export and Import Sales
The simplest form of conducting international business is to engage in **direct export** or **import** sale. For example, if Haliburton Corporation wishes to

sell equipment overseas, it can merely enter into a contract with a company in a foreign country that wishes to buy the equipment. Haliburton Corporation is the **exporter** and the firm in the foreign country is the **importer**. If a U.S. company buys goods from a firm in a foreign country, the roles are reversed. The main benefits of conducting international business this way are: (1) It is inexpensive and (2) it usually involves just entering into contracts.

Sales Agents, Representatives, and Distributorships Companies wishing to do business in a foreign country often appoint a local agent or representative to represent them in that country. A **sales representative** may solicit

and take orders for his or her foreign employer but does not have the authority to bind the company contractually. A **sales agent**, on the other hand, may enter into contracts on his or her foreign employer's behalf. The scope of a sales agent's or representative's authority should be explicitly stated in the employment agreement. Sales agents and representatives do not take title to the goods. They are usually paid commissions for business that they generate.

Another commonly used form for engaging in international sales is through a **foreign distributor**. Often, the distributor is a local firm that is separate and independent from the exporter. Distributors are usually given an exclusive
continued

territory (e.g., a country or portion of a country). A distributor takes title to the goods and makes a profit on the resale of the goods in the foreign country. A foreign distributor generally is used when a company wants a greater presence in a foreign market than is possible through a sales agent or representative.

Branch Office A company can enter a foreign market by establishing a **branch** in the foreign country. Branches are often used where a corporation wants to enter a foreign market in a substantial way but wants to retain exclusive control over the operation. For example, an American manufacturing company can establish a presence in a foreign country by building a plant there. A branch is not a separate corporation. It is merely an extension of the corporate owner and is wholly owned by the home corporation.

There are detriments to this form of operation. For instance, it is expensive (because the owner must build or lease plant or office premises), and it exposes the owner to tort and contract liability in the foreign country and to foreign laws.

Subsidiary Corporation A business can enter a foreign market by establishing a separate corporation to conduct business in a foreign country. Such a corporation, which is called a **subsidiary**, must be formed pursuant to the laws of the country in which it is to be located. The **parent corporation** usually owns all or a majority of the subsidiary corporation. The parent corporation and the subsidiary corporation are separate legal entities that are individually capitalized.

A foreign subsidiary is usually used where the parent corporation wants to establish a substantial presence in a foreign country. The benefit of using a subsidiary corporation over a branch is that it isolates the parent corporation from the tort and contract liability of the subsidiary corporation (and vice verse), unless the foreign country's laws provide otherwise. On the other hand, establishing and operating a subsidiary corporation in a foreign country is often expensive and complicated. Also, it exposes the subsidiary corporation to the laws of the foreign country.

Other Forms of Conducting International Business In addition to the previously discussed forms of conducting business in foreign countries, corporations may enter into **joint ventures** with foreign corporations; grant **franchises** to foreign franchisees; and/or **license** trade names, trademarks, patents, and other intellectual property rights to foreign companies.

WORKING THE WEB

Many large corporations have well developed Web sites. Here are some good examples.

Information corporation: Microsoft.
   Visit at http://www.microsoft.com

Manufacturing   corporation: Hewlett Packard.
   Visit at http://www.hp.com

Service corporation: Federal Express.
   Visit at http://www.fedex.com

International   corporation: Daimler-Benz.
   Visit at http://www.daimler-benz.com/

Publishing corporation: Prentice Hall (business law site).
   Visit at http://www.prenhall.com/phblaw

CYBER EXERCISES:
1–5. Visit all of these large corporations. Notice the different techniques used in developing the Web sites. See what kind of information each site has.

CHAPTER SUMMARY

NATURE OF THE CORPORATION, P. 582

Nature of the Corporation	1. *Corporation.* A legal entity created pursuant to the laws of the state of incorporation. 2. *Corporations Codes.* State statutes that govern the formation, operation, and dissolution of corporations.
The Corporation as a "Legal Person"	A corporation is a separate legal entity—an *artificial person*—that can own property, sue and be sued, enter into contracts, and such.
Characteristics of Corporations	1. *Limited liability of shareholders.* Shareholders are liable for the debts and obligations of the corporation only to the extent of their capital contributions. 2. *Free transferability of shares.* Shares of a corporation are freely transferable by shareholders unless they are expressly restricted. 3. *Perpetual existence.* Corporations exist in perpetuity unless a specific duration is stated in the corporation's articles of incorporation. 4. *Centralized management.* The *board of directors* of the corporation makes policy decisions of the corporation. Corporate *officers* appointed by the board of directors run the corporation's day-to-day operations. Together, the directors and officers form the corporation's "management."
The Revised Model Business Corporation Act	1. *Model Business Corporation Act (MBCA).* A model act drafted in 1950 that was intended to provide a uniform law for the regulation of corporations. 2. *Revised Model Business Corporation Act (RMBCA).* A revision of the MBCA promulgated in 1984 that arranged the provision of the model act more logically, revised the language to be more consistent, and made substantial changes that modernized the provisions of the act.

CLASSIFICATIONS OF CORPORATIONS, P. 586

Domestic, Foreign, and Alien Corporations	1. *Domestic corporation.* A corporation in the state in which it is incorporated. 2. *Foreign corporation.* A corporation in any state other than the one in which it is incorporated. A domestic corporation often transacts business in states other than its state of incorporation; hence it is a foreign corporation in these other states. A foreign corporation must obtain a *certificate of authority* from these other states to transact intrastate business in those states. 3. *Alien corporation.* A corporation that is incorporated in another country. Alien corporations are treated as foreign corporations for most purposes.
Profit and Nonprofit Corporations	1. *Profit corporation.* A corporation created to conduct a business for profit that can distribute profits to shareholders in the form of dividends. 2. *Nonprofit corporation.* A corporation that is formed to operate charitable institutions, colleges, universities, and other not-for-profit entities. There are no shareholders of these corporations.
Public and Private Corporations	1. *Public corporation.* A corporation formed to meet a specific governmental or political purpose. Also called a *government-owned* corporation. *Municipal corporations* (i.e., cities) are an example. 2. *Private corporation.* A corporation formed to conduct privately owned businesses. It may be large or small.

Publicly Held and Closely Held Corporations	1. *Publicly held corporation.* A corporation that has many shareholders and whose securities are often traded on national stock exchanges. General Motors Corporation is an example. 2. *Closely held corporation.* A corporation that is owned by one or a few shareholders. Examples are family-owned corporations. They are also called close corporations.
Professional Corporations	Corporations formed by lawyers, doctors, and other professionals. Shareholders of professional corporations are usually called *members*. Members must be licensed to practice the profession for which the corporation is formed.

PROMOTERS' ACTIVITIES, P. 587

Promoters' Liability	1. *Promoter.* A person or persons who organize and start the corporation, negotiate and enter into contracts in advance of formation, find the initial investors to finance the corporation, and so forth. 2. *Promoter's contract.* A contract entered into by a promoter on behalf of a proposed corporation prior to its actual incorporation. These often include leases, sales contracts, contracts to purchase property, and so forth. 3. *Liability of promoters for promoters' contracts.* Promoters are personally liable for promoters' contracts unless (a) the corporation ratifies the contract as its own when it is formed; and (b) the corporation, the promoter, and the third party with whom the contract is with enter into a *novation* agreement that expressly releases the promoter from liability.
Subscription for Shares	1. *Subscription agreement.* An agreement by a person to purchase shares of a corporation once the corporation is incorporated. 2. *Subscriber.* Person who subscribes to purchase shares of a corporation once it is incorporated. Subscription agreements are enforceable against subscribers.

INCORPORATION PROCEDURES, P. 589

Incorporation Procedures	1. *Incorporation.* The process of incorporating (forming) a new corporation. 2. *Corporation Code.* Corporations are creatures of statute; they can be formed only if certain statutory formalities contained in the state's Corporation Code are followed.
Selecting a State of Incorporation	A corporation can be incorporated in only one state, although it can conduct business in other states.
Incorporators	The person or persons, partnerships, or corporations who are responsible for incorporating a new corporation.
Articles of Incorporation	The basic governing document of a corporation. This document must be filed with the secretary of state of the state of incorporation. It is a public document. It is also called the *corporate charter*. 1. *Information to be set forth in the articles of incorporation.* The Corporation Code of each state sets out the information that must be included in the articles of incorporation. Additional information may be included in the articles of incorporation as deemed necessary or desirable by the incorporators. 2. *Amending the articles of incorporation.* The articles of incorporation can be amended to contain any provision that could have been lawfully

	included in the original articles of incorporation. After an amendment is approved by the shareholders, the corporation must file *articles of amendment* with the secretary of state.
Other Issues Concerning Incorporation	1. *Corporate name.* A corporate name selected for a new corporation must be distinguishable from existing corporate names. A corporate name may be reserved for a limited period of time while the corporation is being formed.
	2. *Purpose.* A corporation can be formed for "any lawful purpose." Corporations can limit the purposes of the corporation by including a *limited-purpose clause* in the articles of incorporation that stipulates the purposes and activities the corporation can engage in.
	3. *Registered agent.* A new corporation must designate a person or corporation that is empowered to accept *service of process* on behalf of the corporation. A new designation must be made annually.
Corporate Bylaws	*Bylaws.* A detailed set of rules that are adopted by the board of directors after the corporation is formed that contain provisions for managing the business and affairs of the corporation. This document does not have to be filed with the secretary of state.
Organizational Meeting	A meeting that must be held by the initial directors of the corporation after the articles of incorporation are filed. At this meeting, the directors adopt the bylaws, elect corporate officers, ratify promoters' contracts, adopt a corporate seal, and transact such other business as may come before the meeting.
	1. *Minutes.* The written recording of the actions taken by the directors at the organizational and other directors' meetings.
Corporate Seal	A design that contains the name of the corporation and the date of incorporation. It is imprinted by the corporate secretary on certain legal documents using a metal stamp containing the design.
Corporate Status	1. *RMBCA rule.* The filing of the articles of incorporation is *conclusive proof* that a corporation exists. After that, only the state can challenge the status of the corporation; third parties cannot. Failure to file articles of incorporation is conclusive proof that the corporation does not exist. The state and third parties may challenge the existence of the corporation.
	2. *Common law doctrines.* Prior to the RMBCA, the courts developed the following rules regarding corporate status:
	a. *De jure corporation.* A corporation that was in complete or substantial compliance with the requirements of incorporation. Neither the state nor third parties could challenge its existence.
	b. *De facto corporation.* A corporation that substantially failed to comply with the requirements of incorporation. If the incorporators made a good faith attempt to comply with the statute and the enterprise conducted business as a corporation, only the state, and not third parties, could challenge its existence as a corporation. If these elements were not met, third parties could also challenge the status of the purported corporation.
	c. *Corporation by estoppel.* Even if a corporation did not qualify as a de facto corporation, a third party who dealt with the business believing it to be a corporation was *estopped* (prevented) from raising the issue of defective incorporation against the business.

FINANCING THE CORPORATION, P. 596

Financing the Corporation	*Equity securities.* Securities that represent the ownership rights to the corporation. They are also called *stocks.* Equity securities consist of *common stock* and *preferred stock.*
Common Stock	A type of equity security that represents the *residual value* of the corporation. Common stock has no preferences, and its shareholders are paid dividends and assets upon liquidation only after creditors and preferred shareholders have been paid. 1. *Common stockholder.* A person who owns common stock. 2. *Common stock certificate.* A document that represents the common shareholder's investment in the corporation. 3. *Par value.* A value assigned by the corporation to common shares that sets the lowest price at which the shares may be issued by the corporation. *No par shares* are not assigned a par value. The RMBCA has eliminated the concept of par value.

Preferred Stock	A type of equity security that is given certain preferences and rights over common stock.
	1. *Preferred stockholder.* A person who owns preferred stock.
	2. *Preferred stock certificate.* A document that represents the preferred stockholder's investment in the corporation.
	3. *Preferences and rights.* Preferred stock may have any or all of the following preferences or rights:
	  a. *Dividend preference.* The right to receive a fixed dividend at stipulated periods during the year (e.g., quarterly).
	  b. *Liquidation preference.* The right to be paid a stated dollar amount if the corporation is dissolved and liquidated. The corporation must pay its creditors first, however.
	  c. *Cumulative dividend right. Cumulative preferred stock* is stock that provides that any missed dividend payments must be paid in the future to the preferred shareholders before the common shareholders can receive any dividends.
	  d. *Right to participate in profits. Participating preferred stock* is preferred stock that allows the stockholder to participate in the profits of the corporation along with the common stockholders on an expressly stated basis.
	  e. *Conversion right. Convertible preferred stock* is preferred stock that permits stockholders to convert their shares into common stock at a stipulated conversion price.
	4. *Redeemable preferred stock.* Preferred stock that may be bought back by the corporation at a specified price at some future date. This is also called a *callable preferred stock.*

Consideration to Be Paid for Shares	Shares may be issued in exchange for any benefit to the corporation, including cash, tangible property, intangible property, promissory notes, services performed, contracts for services to be performed, or other securities of the corporation.
Authorized, Issued, and Outstanding Shares	1. *Authorized shares.* The number of shares provided for in the articles of incorporation. The shareholders may amend the articles of incorporation to increase this amount. 2. *Issued shares.* Authorized shares that have been sold by the corporation.

	3. *Unissued shares.* Authorized shares that have not been sold by the corporation. 4. *Treasury shares.* Issued shares that have been repurchased by the corporation. They may be resold by the corporation. 5. *Outstanding shares.* Shares that are in shareholder hands, whether originally issued or reissued treasury shares. Only outstanding shares have the right to vote.

Stock Options and Stock Warrants	1. *Stock option.* A nontransferable right to purchase shares of the corporation from the corporation at a stated price for a specified period of time.
	  a. *Striking price.* The stated price at which the stock may be bought at a future date.
	  b. *Option period.* The specified period of time for exercising a stock option.
	  c. *Exercising the option.* The act of purchasing the shares subject to the option by the holder of the option.
	Stock options are usually granted to the management of a corporation.
	2. *Stock warrant.* A stock option that is represented by a certificate. They are commonly issued in conjunction with another security. Warrants may be transferable or nontransferable.

Debt Securities	Securities that establish a *debtor–creditor* relationship in which the corporation borrows money from the investor to whom the debt security is issued. 1. *Debenture.* A *long-term unsecured* debt instrument that is based on the corporation's general credit rating. 2. *Bond.* A *long-term* debt security that is *secured* by some form of property. The property securing the bond is called *collateral*. In the event of nonpayment of interest, principal, or other specified events, bondholders can foreclose on and obtain the collateral. 3. *Note.* A *short-term* debt instrument with a maturity of five years or less. They can be either unsecured or secured. 4. *Indenture agreement.* The contract between the corporation and debt security holders that contains the terms of the agreement between the corporations and the holders.

CORPORATE POWERS, P. 600

Corporate Powers	1. *Express powers.* A corporation has the express powers granted to it by the U.S. Constitution, state constitutions, federal statutes, state statutes (particularly the state's Corporation Code), articles of incorporation, bylaws, and resolution of the board of directors. 2. *Implied powers.* Powers that are implied that allow a corporation to accomplish its corporate purpose.

Ultra Vires Acts	Acts by a corporation that are beyond its express or implied powers.
	1. *Remedies.* The following remedies are available if an *ultra vires* act is committed:
	  a. Shareholders can sue for an *injunction* to prevent the corporation from engaging in the act.
	  b. The corporation (or shareholders on behalf of the corporation) can sue the officers and directors who caused the act for *damages*.
	  c. The attorney general of the state of incorporation can bring an action to enjoin the act or to dissolve the corporation.

CRITICAL LEGAL THINKING CASES

24.1 Legal Entity Jeffrey Sammak was the owner of a contracting business known as Senaco. In the early part of 1980, Sammak decided to enter the coal reprocessing business. In April 1980, Sammak attended the "Coal Show" in Chicago, Illinois, at which he met representatives of the Deister Concentrator Co., Inc. (Deister). Deister was incorporated under the laws of Pennsylvania. Sammak began negotiating with Deister to purchase equipment to be used in his coal reprocessing business. Deister sent Sammak literature guaranteeing a certain level of performance for the equipment. On April 3, 1981, Sammak purchased the equipment. After the equipment was installed, Sammak became dissatisfied with its performance. Sammak believes that Deister breached an express warranty and wants to sue. Can a suit be brought against a corporation such as Deister? [*Blackwood Coal v. Deister Co., Inc.*, 626 F.Supp. 727 (E.D.Pa. 1985)]

24.2 Limited Liability of Shareholders Joseph M. Billy was an employee of the USM Corporation (USM). USM is a publicly held corporation. On October 21, 1976, Billy was at work when a 4,600-pound ram from a vertical boring mill broke loose and crushed him to death. Billy's widow brought suit against USM alleging that the accident was caused by certain defects in the manufacture and design of the vertical boring mill and in the two moving parts directly involved in the accident, a metal lifting arm and the 4,600-pound ram. If Mrs. Billy's suit is successful, can the shareholders of USM Corporation be held personally liable for any judgment against USM? [*Billy v. Consolidated Mach. Tool Corp.*, 412 N.E.2d 934, 51 N.Y.2d 152 (N.Y.App. 1980)]

24.3 Type of Corporation William O'Donnel and Vincent Marino worked together as executives of a shipping container repair company known as Marine Trailers. Marine Trailers' largest customer was American Export Lines (American Export). When American Export became unhappy with the owners of Marine Trailers, it let O'Donnel and Marino know that if they formed their own company, American Exports would give them their business. O'Donnel and Marino decided to take American Export's suggestion and bought the majority of shares of a publicly traded corporation known as Marine Repair Services, Inc. (Repair Services). O'Donnel and Marino operated Repair Services as a container repair company at the Port of New York. The company prospered, expanding to five other states and overseas. Marino and O'Donnel's initial $12,000 investment paid off. Ten years after buying the company, both men were earning more than $150,000 a year in salary alone. What type of corporation is Marine Repair Services? [*O'Donnel v. Marine Repair Services, Inc.*, 530 F.Supp. 1199 (S.D.N.Y. 1982)]

24.4 Type of Corporation Hutchinson Baseball Enterprises, Inc. (Hutchinson, Inc.), was incorporated under the laws of Kansas on August 31, 1980. Among the purposes of the corporation according to its bylaws is to "promote, advance, and sponsor baseball, which shall include Little League and Amateur baseball, in the Hutchinson, Kansas area." The corporation is involved in a number of activities, including the leasing of a field for American Legion teams, furnishing instructors as coaches for Little League teams, conducting a Little League Camp, and the leasing of a baseball field to a local junior college for a nominal fee. Hutchinson, Inc. raises money through ticket sales to amateur baseball games, concessions, and contributions. Any profits are used to improve the playing fields. Profits are never distributed to the corporation's directors or members. What type of corporation is Hutchinson, Inc.? [*Hutchinson Baseball Enterprises, Inc. v. Commissioner of Internal Revenue*, 696 F.2d 757 (10th Cir. 1982)]

24.5 Type of Corporation In November 1979, Elmer Balvik and Thomas Sylvester formed a partnership, named Weldon Electric, for the purpose of engaging in the electrical contracting business. Balvik contributed $8,000 and a vehicle worth $2,000, and Sylvester contributed $25,000 to the partnership's assets. The parties operated the business as a partnership until 1984, when they decided to incorporate. Stock was issued to Balvik and Sylvester in proportion to their partnership ownership interests, with Sylvester receiving 70 percent and Balvik 30 percent of the stock. Balvik and his wife and Sylvester and his wife were the four directors of the corporation. Sylvester was elected president of the corporation. Balvik was vice president. The corporation's bylaws stated that "sales of shares of stock by any shareholder shall be as set forth in a 'Buy Sell Agreement' entered into by the shareholder." What type of corporation is Weldon Electric? [*Balvik v. Sylvester*, 411 N.W.2d 383 (N.D. 1987)]

24.6 Type of Corporation Leo V. Mysels was the president of Florida Fashions of Interior Design, Inc. (Florida Fashions). Florida Fashions, which was a Pennsylvania corporation, had never registered to do business in the state of Florida. In 1973, while acting in the capacity of a salesman for the corporation, Mysels took an order for goods from Francis E. Barry. The transaction took place in Florida. Barry paid Florida Fashions for the goods ordered. When Florida Fashions failed to perform its obligations under the sales agreement, Barry brought suit in Florida. What type of corporation was Florida Fashions in regard to the state of Pennsylvania and to the state of Florida? Can Florida Fashions defend itself in a lawsuit? [*Mysels v. Barry*, 332 So.2d 38 (Fla.App. 1976)]

24.7 Corporate Name Lippman, Inc., a wholly owned subsidiary of Litton, Inc., was incorporated on September 11, 1973, under the laws of the state of Wisconsin. As a subsidiary, Lippman, Inc. seldom transacted business under its own name. On October 4, 1976, organizers filed articles of incorporation with the secretary of state of Wisconsin to form a corporation called Lippman-Milwaukee, Inc. Lippman, Inc. and the proposed Lippman-Milwaukee, Inc., were two separate entities with different businesses and different owners. After the secretary of state granted a certificate of incorporation to Lippman-Milwaukee, Inc., Lippman, Inc. sued to prevent Lippman-Milwaukee, Inc. from using the name. Lippman, Inc. claimed that the name of the new corporation was too similar and could cause confusion. Who wins? [*Litton Systems, Inc. v. Lippman-Milwaukee, Inc.*, 481 F.Supp. 788 (E.D.Wis. 1979)]

24.8 Promoter's Liability On December 27, 1972, the Homes Corporation, a closely held corporation whose sole stockholders were Jerry and Beverly Ann Allen, purchased 10 acres of real estate near Kahaluu on the island of Oahu, Hawaii. The Homes Corporation made a down payment of $50,000. It was the Allens' intention to obtain approval for a planned unit development (PUD) from the city and county of Honolulu and then develop the property with some 60 condominium townhouses. To further this project, the Allens sought an outside investor. Herbert Handley, a real estate developer from Texas, decided to join the Allens' project. The two parties entered an agreement whereby a new Hawaiian corporation would be formed to build the condominiums, with Handley owning 51 percent of the corporation's stock and the Allens the remaining 49 percent. The two parties began extensive planning and design of the project. They also took out a $69,500 loan from the Bank of Hawaii. After a year had gone by, Handley informed the Allens that he was no longer able to advance funds to the project. Soon thereafter, the city and county denied their PUD zoning application. The new corporation was never formed. Who is liable for the failed condominium project's contractual obligations? [*Handley v. Ching*, 627 P.2d 1132 (Hawaii App. 1981)]

24.9 Promoter's Contracts Martin Stern, Jr., was an architect who worked in Nevada. In January 1969, Nathan Jacobson asked Stern to draw plans for Jacobson's new hotel/casino, the Kings Castle at Lake Tahoe. Stern agreed to take on the project and immediately began preliminary work. At this time, Stern dealt directly with Jacobson, who referred to the project as "my hotel." In February 1969, Stern wrote to Jacobson detailing, among other things, the architect's services and fee. Stern's plans were subsequently discussed by the two men and Stern's fee was set at $250,000. On May 9, 1969, Jacobson formed Lake Enterprises, Inc., a Nevada corporation of which Jacobson was the sole shareholder and president. Lake Enterprises was formed for the purpose of owning the new casino. During this period, Stern was paid monthly by checks drawn on an account belonging to another corporation controlled by Jacobson. Stern never agreed to a contract with any of these corporations and always dealt exclusively with Jacobson. When Stern was not paid the full amount of his architectural fee, he sued Jacobson to recover. Jacobson claims that he is not personally liable for any of Stern's fee because a novation has taken place. Who wins? [*Jacobson v. Stern*, 605 P.2d 198 (Nev. 1980)]

24.10 Preferred Stock On June 24, 1970, Commonwealth Edison Co., Inc. (Commonwealth Edison) through its underwriters, sold 1 million shares of preferred stock at an offering price of $100 per share. Commonwealth Edison wanted to issue the stock with a dividend rate of 9.26 percent, but its

major underwriter, First Boston Corporation, advised that a rate of 9.44 percent should be paid. According to First Boston, a shortage of investment funds existed and a higher dividend rate was necessary for a successful stock issue. Commonwealth Edison's management was never happy with the high dividend rate being paid on this preferred stock. On April 2, 1971, Commonwealth Edison's vice chairman was quoted in the report of the annual meeting of the corporation as saying that "we were disappointed in the 9.44 percent dividend rate on the preferred stock we sold last August, but we expect to refinance it when market conditions make it feasible." On March 20, 1972, Commonwealth Edison, pursuant to the terms under which the stock was sold, bought back the 1 million shares of preferred stock at a price of $110 per share. What type of preferred stock is this? [*The Franklin Life Insurance Company v. Commonwealth Edison Company*, 451 F.Supp. 602 (S.D.Ill. 1978)]

24.11 Debt Securities United Financial Corporation of California (United Financial) was incorporated in the state of Delaware on May 8, 1959. United Financial owned the majority of a California savings and loan association as well as three insurance agencies. In 1960, the original investors in United Financial decided to capitalize on an increase in investor interest in savings and loans. In June 1960, the first public offering of United Financial stock was made. The stock was sold as a unit, with 60,000 units being offered. Each unit consisted of two shares of United Financial stock and one $100, 5-percent interest bearing debenture bond. This initial offering was a success. It provided $7.2 million to the corporation, of which $6.2 million was distributed as a return of capital to the original investors. What is the difference between the stock offered for sale by United Financial and the debenture bonds? [*Jones v. H. F. Ahmanson & Company*, 1 Cal.3d 93, 81 Cal.Rptr. 592 (Cal. 1969)]

24.12 Ultra Vires Doctrine Beau Monde, Inc. (Beau Monde) was a corporation formed to act as a condominium association. The association collected maintenance fees and cared for the common grounds of the Beau Monde Condominium Complex. These grounds included recreation and garage space. The common areas were originally held under a 99-year lease. The association's bylaws stated that the corporation did not have the power to take any action without first holding a meeting and obtaining the approval of the association's members. In the early 1980s, Beau Monde's board of directors decided to purchase the land it had been leasing. The board took the action without holding a meeting and obtaining the approval of the association's members. Some of the members sued for an injunction to prevent the corporation from buying the land. Who wins? [*Beau Monde, Inc. v. Bramson*, 446 So.2d 164 (Fla.App. 1984)]

ETHICS CASES

24.13 Ethical Perspective John A. Goodman was a real estate salesman in the state of Washington. In 1979, Goodman sold an apartment building that needed extensive renovation to Darden, Dorman, & Stafford Associates (DDS), a general

partnership. Goodman represented that he personally had experience in renovation work. During the course of the negotiations on a renovation contract, Goodman informed the managing partner of DDS that he would be forming a corporation to do the work. A contract was executed in August 1979 between DDS and "Building Design and Development (In Formation), John A. Goodman, President." The contract required the renovation work to be completed by October 15. Goodman immediately subcontracted the work, but the renovation was not completed on time. DDS also found that the work that was completed was of poor quality. Goodman did not file the articles of incorporation for his new corporation until November 1. The partners of DDS sued Goodman to hold him liable for the renovation contracts. Goodman denied personal liability. Was it morally correct for Goodman to deny liability? Is Goodman personally liable? [*Goodman v. Darden, Dorman, & Stafford Associates*, 670 P.2s 648 (Wash. 1983)]

24.14 Ethical Perspective The Houston Astros Sports Association (HSA) is a Texas corporation that owns and operates the Astrodome and Houston Astros Baseball Club. John M. McMullen controlled 34 percent of the stock and was chairman of the board of directors. Don A. Sanders owned 2 percent of the stock. In 1984, minority shareholders tried to enter a voting agreement with 51 percent of the stock to remove McMullen from management. Sanders's 2 percent was included in the 51 percent, but he decided to withdraw from the agreement, leaving the shareholders with only 49 percent. Sanders claimed he agreed to withdraw because of oral promises made by McMullen to him, particularly that McMullen would vote his shares to have Sanders on the board of directors. Because of Sanders's decision, McMullen was able to regain control of HSA. He purchased more shares until he controlled 63 percent of the stock. Sanders spent $13 million to purchase shares and increased his ownership to 13 percent. In November 1986, Sanders was not reelected to the board of directors because McMullen did not vote for him. Sanders sued McMullen for breaching their alleged voting agreement. If there was an oral agreement, would it have been ethical not to honor it? Was the shareholder voting agreement between Sanders and McMullen enforceable? [*Sanders v. McMullen*, 868 F.2d 1465 (5th Cir. 1989)]

CRITICAL LEGAL THINKING WRITING ASSIGNMENT

Read Case A.24 in the Case Appendix [*Johnson v. Dodgen*]. This case is excerpted from the state supreme court's opinion. Review and brief the case. In your brief, be sure to answer the following questions:

1. Who were the plaintiffs? Who were the defendants?

2. Describe the contract alleged to have been breached in this case.
3. Was the contract signed by a corporation?
4. Did the court find the individual defendant liable on the contract?

NOTES

1 RMBCA § 15.01(a).
2 RMBCA § 15.01(b),(c).
3 RMBCA § 15.02.
4 RMBCA § 2.04.
5 RMBCA § 6.20
6 RMBCA § 3.01.
7 RMBCA § 4.01(b).
8 RMBCA § 4.01(a).
9 RMBCA § 2.01.
10 RMBCA § 2.02(a).
11 RMBCA § 10.01.
12 RMBCA § 10.03.
13 RMBCA § 10.02.
14 RMBCA § 10.06.
15 RMBCA § 4.02
16 RMBCA § 5.01.
17 RMBCA § 5.04.
18 RMBCA § 2.06.
19 RMBCA § 10.20
20 RMBCA § 2.05.
21 RMBCA § 3.02(2).
22 RMBCA § 2.03.
23 RMBCA § 6.01(a),(b).
24 RMBCA § 6.01(c).
25 RMBCA § 6.01(d)
26 RMBCA § 6.21(b),(c).
27 RMBCA § 6.01.
28 RMBCA § 6.31.
29 RMBCA § 6.03.
30 RMBCA § 6.24.
31 RMBCA § 3.02(7).
32 RMBCA § 3.02.
33 RMBCA § 3.04.

CHAPTER 25

RIGHTS, DUTIES, AND LIABILITY

OF CORPORATE DIRECTORS,

OFFICERS, AND SHAREHOLDERS

Chapter Objectives

*After studying this chapter,
you should be able to*

1. Describe the function of shareholders, directors, and officers in managing the affairs of a corporation
2. Describe how shareholders' and directors' meetings are called and conducted
3. Distinguish between straight and cumulative voting for directors
4. Explain the director's authority to pay dividends
5. Describe the agency authority of officers to enter into contracts on behalf of a corporation
6. Distinguish how the management of close corporations differs from that of publicly held corporations
7. Describe a director's and officer's duty of care and the business judgment rule
8. Describe a director's and officer's duty of loyalty and how this duty is breached
9. Describe directors' and officers' liability insurance and corporate indemnification
10. Define the piercing the corporate veil or alter ego doctrine

Chapter Contents

> *The law does not permit the stockholders to create a sterilized board of directors.*
>
> Collins, J.
> *Manson v. Curtis* (1918)

"To supervise wisely the great corporations is well; but to look backward to the days when business was polite pillage and regard our great business concerns as piratical institutions carrying letters of marque and reprisal is a grave error born in the minds of little men. When these little men legislate they set the brakes going uphill."
Elbert Hubbard
(1856–1915)
Notebook

Shareholders, directors, and officers have different rights in managing the corporation. The shareholders elect the directors and vote on other important issues affecting the corporation. The directors are responsible for making policy decisions and employing officers. The officers are responsible for the corporation's day-to-day operations.

As a legal entity, a corporation can be held liable for the acts of its directors and officers and for authorized contracts entered into on its behalf. The directors and officers of a corporation have certain rights and owe certain duties to the corporation and its shareholders. A director or officer who breaches any of these duties can be held personally liable to the corporation, to its shareholders, or to third parties. A corporation can purchase insurance against certain of these losses. Except in a few circumstances, shareholders do not owe a fiduciary duty to other shareholders or the corporation.

This chapter discusses the rights, duties, and liability of corporate shareholders, directors, and officers.

RIGHTS OF SHAREHOLDERS

CAUTION
Shareholders are not agents of the corporation. They cannot bind the corporation to contracts.

A corporation's shareholders own the corporation. Nevertheless, they are not agents of the corporation (i.e., they cannot bind the corporation to any contracts), and the only management duties they have is the right to vote on matters such as the election of directors and the approval of fundamental changes in the corporation.

Shareholder Meetings

annual shareholders' meeting   Meeting of the shareholders of a corporation that must be held annually by the corporation to elect directors and to vote on other matters.

Annual shareholders' meetings are held to elect directors, choose an independent auditor, or to take other actions. The meeting must be held at the time fixed in the bylaws.[1] If the meeting is not held within either 15 months or the last annual meeting or 6 months after the end of the corporation's fiscal year, whichever is earlier, a shareholder may petition the court to order the meeting held.[2]

special shareholders' meetings   Meetings of shareholders that may be called to consider and vote on important or emergency issues, such as a proposed merger, amending the articles of incorporation, and such.

Special shareholders' meetings may be called by the board of directors, the holders of at least 10 percent of the voting shares of the corporation, or any other person authorized to do so by the articles of incorporation or bylaws (e.g., the president).[3] Special meetings may be held to consider important or emergency issues, such as a merger or consolidation of the corporation with one or more other corporations, the removal of directors, amending the articles of incorporation, or dissolution of the corporation.

Any act that can be taken at a shareholders' meeting can be taken without a meeting if all of the corporate shareholders sign a written consent approving the action.[4]

Notice of Meetings   The corporation is required to give the shareholders written *notice* of the place, day, and time of annual and special meetings. If the meeting is a special meeting, the purpose of the meeting must also be stated. Only matters stated in the notice of a special meeting can be considered at the meeting. The notice, which must be given not less than 10 days or more than 50 days before the date of the meeting, may be given in person or by mail.[5] If the required notice is not given or is defective, any action taken at the meeting is void.

Proxies

Shareholders do not have to attend the shareholders' meeting to vote. Shareholders may vote by *proxy*; that is, they can appoint another person (the proxy) as their agent to vote at the shareholders' meeting. The proxy may be directed exactly how to vote the shares or may be authorized to vote the shares at his or her discretion. Proxies must be in writing. The written document itself is called the **proxy** (or **proxy card**). Unless otherwise stated, a proxy is valid for 11 months.[6]

Voting Requirements

At least one class of shares of the corporation must have voting rights. The RMBCA permits corporations to grant more than one vote per share to some classes of stock and less than one vote per share to others.[7]

Only those shareholders who own stock as of a set date may vote at a shareholders' meeting. This date, which is called the **record date**, is set forth in the corporate by-laws. The record date may not be more than 70 days before the shareholders' meeting.[8]

The corporation must prepare a **shareholders' list** that contains the names and addresses of the shareholders as of the record date and the class and number of shares owned by each shareholder. This list must be available for inspection at the corporation's main office.[9]

Quorum Unless otherwise provided in the articles of incorporation, if a majority of shares entitled to vote are represented at the meeting in person or by proxy, there is a **quorum** to hold the meeting. Once quorum is present, the withdrawal of shares does not affect the quorum of the meeting.[10]

Vote Required for Elections Other than for Directors The affirmative vote of the majority of the voting shares represented at a shareholders' meeting constitutes an act of the shareholders for actions other than for the election of directors.[11]

CONSIDER THIS EXAMPLE: Suppose there are 20,000 shares outstanding of a corporation. Assume that a shareholders' meeting is duly called to amend the articles of incorporation and that 10,001 shares are represented at the meeting. A quorum is present because a majority of the shares entitled to vote are represented at the meeting. Suppose that 5,001 shares are voted in favor of the amendment. The amendment passes. In this example, just over 25 percent of the shares of the corporation bound the other shareholders to the action taken at the shareholders' meeting.

Voting Methods for Electing Directors The election of directors by shareholders may be by one of the following two methods:

1. **Straight (noncumulative) voting.** Unless otherwise stated in the corporation's articles of incorporation, voting for the election of directors is by the **straight voting method**. This voting method is quite simple. Each shareholder votes the number of shares he or she owns on candidates for each of the positions open for election. Thus, a majority shareholder can elect the entire board of directors.

   CONSIDER THIS EXAMPLE: Assume that a corporation has 10,000 outstanding shares. Erin Caldwell owns 5,100 shares (or 51 percent) and Michael Rhodes owns 4,900 shares (49 percent). Suppose that three directors of the corporation are to be elected. Ms. Caldwell casts 5,100 votes each for her chosen candidates. Mr. Rhodes votes 4,900 shares for each of his chosen candidates, who are different from those favored by Ms. Caldwell. Each of the three candidates whom Ms. Caldwell voted for wins with 5,100 votes.

2. **Cumulative voting.** The articles of incorporation may provide for cumulative voting for the election of directors. Under this method, a shareholder can accumulate all of his or her votes and vote them all for one candidate or split them among several candidates. This means that each shareholder is entitled to multiply the num-

proxy card The written document that a shareholder signs authorizing another person to vote his or her shares at the shareholders' meeting in the event of the shareholder's absence.

record date A date specified in the corporate bylaws that determines whether a shareholder may vote at a shareholders' meeting.

shareholders' list A list that contains the names and addresses of the shareholders as of the record date and the class and number of shares owned by each shareholder.

quorum The required number of shares that must be represented in person or by proxy to hold a shareholders' meeting. The RMBCA establishes a majority of outstanding shares as a quorum.

straight voting method Each shareholder votes the number of shares he or she owns on candidates for each of the positions open for election.

cumulative voting A shareholder can accumulate all of his or her votes and vote them all for one candidate or split them among several candidates.

BUSINESS BRIEF
*Corporations must hold
annual shareholders'
meetings for the election
of directors and voting
on other matters.
Shareholders can appear
at the meeting and ask
questions of corporate
management.*

ber of shares he or she owns by the number of directors to be elected and cast the product for a single candidate or distribute the product among two or more candidates.[12] Cumulative voting gives a minority shareholder a better opportunity to elect someone to the board of directors.

CONSIDER THIS EXAMPLE: Suppose Lisa Monroe owns 1,000 shares. Assume that four directors are to be elected to the board. Under cumulative voting, Ms. Monroe can multiply the number of shares she owns by the number of directors to be elected. She can take the resulting number of votes (4,000) and cast them all for one candidate or split them. Examples of cumulative voting are set forth in Exhibit 25.1.

Exhibit 25.1
Examples of Cumulative
Voting

Formula for Cumulative Voting   A shareholder can use the following formula to determine whether or not he owns a sufficient number of shares to elect a director to the board of directors using cumulative voting:

$$\frac{S \times T}{D + 1} + 1 = X$$

where: X is the number of shares needed by a shareholder to elect a director to the board, S is the number of shares that actually vote at the shareholders' meeting; T is the number of directors the shareholder wants to elect; and D is the number of directors to be elected at the shareholders' meeting.

Example 1   Suppose there are 9,000 outstanding shares of a corporation. Shareholder 1 owns 1,000 shares, shareholder 2 owns 4,000 shares, and shareholder 3 owns 4,000 shares. Assume nine directors are to be elected to the board of directors. All the shares are voted. Under cumulative voting, does shareholder 1 have enough votes to elect a director to the board? the answer is yes:

$$\frac{9{,}000 \times 1}{9 + 1} + 1 = 901$$

Example 2   If a board of directors is divided into classes and are elected by staggered elections, the ability of a minority shareholder to elect a director to the board is diminished. Suppose in Example 1 that the corporation staggered the election of the board of directors so that three directors are elected each year to serve three-year terms. How many shares would a shareholder have to own to elect a director to the board?

$$\frac{9{,}000 \times 1}{3 + 1} + 1 = 2{,}251$$

Because of the staggered election of the board of directors, shareholder 1 (who owns 1,000 shares) would not be able to elect a director to the board without the assistance of another shareholder.

**supramajority voting
requirement**   A
requirement that a greater
than majority of shares
constitutes quorum or the
vote of the shareholders.

Supramajority Voting Requirement   The articles of incorporation or the bylaws of a corporation can require a greater than majority of shares to constitute quorum or the vote of the shareholders.[13] This is called a **supramajority (or supermajority) voting requirement**. Such votes are often required to approve mergers, consolidations, the sale of substantially all of the assets of the corporation, and such. To add a supramajority voting requirement, the amendment must be adopted by the number of shares of the proposed increase. For example, to increase a majority voting requirement to an 80-percent supramajority voting requirement would require an 80-percent affirmative vote.

Voting Agreements

Sometimes shareholders agree in advance how their shares will be voted. There are two major forms of shareholder agreements:

1. **Voting trusts.** A voting trust is an arrangement whereby shareholders transfer their stock certificates to a trustee. Legal title to these shares is held in the name of the trustee. In exchange, **voting trust certificates** are issued to the shareholders. The trustee of the voting trust is empowered to vote the shares held by the trust. The trust may either specify how the trustee is to vote the shares or authorize the trustee to vote the shares at his or her discretion. The members of the trust retain all other incidents of ownership of the stock.

A voting trust agreement must be in writing and cannot exceed 10 years. It must be filed with the corporation and is open to inspection by shareholders of the corporation.[14]

2. **Voting agreements.** Two or more shareholders may enter into an agreement that stipulates how they will vote their shares for the election of directors or other matters that require shareholder vote. These agreements are not limited in duration and do not have to be filed with the corporation. They are specifically enforceable.[15] Shareholders voting agreements can be either revocable or irrevocable.[16]

Right to Transfer Shares

Subject to certain restrictions, shareholders have the right to transfer their shares. The transfer of securities is governed by **Article 8 of the Uniform Commercial Code (UCC)**. Most states have adopted all or part of Article 8. Usually, shares are transferred by indorsement and delivery of the shares to the new owner.

If a stock certificate has been lost, stolen, or destroyed, the corporation is required to issue a **replacement certificate** if the shareholder posts an indemnity bond to protect the corporation from loss for issuing the replacement certificate. If a lost or stolen certificate reappears in the hands of a bona fide purchase, that certificate must be registered by the corporation. The corporation can recover on the indemnity bond.

Transfer Restrictions

Shareholders may enter into agreements with one another to prevent unwanted persons from becoming owners of the corporation.[17] The following are the most common form of agreements:

- **Right of first refusal.** An agreement entered into by shareholders whereby they grant each other the right of first refusal to purchase shares they are going to sell. A selling shareholder must offer his or her shares for sale to the other parties to the agreement before selling them to anyone else. If the shareholders do not exercise their right of first refusal, the selling shareholder is free to sell his or her shares to another party. A right of first refusal may be granted to the corporation as well.
- **Buy-and-sell agreement.** An agreement entered into by shareholders that requires selling shareholders to sell their shares to the other shareholders or to the corporation at the price specified in the agreement. The price of the shares is normally determined by a formula that considers, among other factors, the profitability of the corporation. The purchase of shares of a deceased shareholder pursuant to a buy-and-sell agreement is often funded by the purchase of life insurance.

voting trust The shareholders transfer their stock certificates to a trustee who is empowered to vote the shares.

shareholder voting agreements Agreement between two or more shareholders agreeing on how they will vote their shares.

Article 8 of the UCC The article of the UCC that governs transfer of securities.

NOTE
A large percentage of stock owned by individuals are held in "street name" by their brokerage houses. The brokerage house is called the nominal holder, *and the client is called the* beneficial owner.

right of first refusal agreement An agreement that requires the selling shareholder to offer his or her shares for sale to the other parties to the agreement before selling them to anyone else.

buy-and-sell agreement An agreement that requires selling shareholders to sell their shares to the other shareholders or to the corporation at the price specified in the agreement.

Preemptive Rights

preemptive rights
Rights that give existing shareholders the option of subscribing to new shares being issued in proportion to their current ownership interest.

The articles of incorporation can grant shareholders preemptive rights. **Preemptive rights** give existing shareholders the option of subscribing to new shares being issued by the corporation in proportion to their current ownership interest in the corporation.[18] Such a purchase can prevent a shareholder's interest in the corporation from being *diluted*. Shareholders are given a reasonable period of time (such as 30 days) to exercise their preemptive rights. If the shareholders do not exercise their preemptive rights during this time, the shares can then be sold to anyone.

CONSIDER THIS EXAMPLE: Suppose that the ABC Corporation has 10,000 outstanding shares and that Lina Norton owns 1,000 shares (10 percent). Assume that the corporation plans to raise more capital by issuing another 10,000 shares of stock. With preemptive rights, Ms. Norton must be offered the option to purchase 1,000 of the 10,000 new shares before they are offered to the public. If she does not purchase them, her ownership in the corporation will be diluted from 10 percent to 5 percent.

Right to Receive Information and Inspect Books and Records

annual financial statement
A statement provided to the shareholders that contains a balance sheet, an income statement, and a statement of changes in shareholder equity.

right of inspection A right that shareholders have to inspect the books and records of the corporation.

Shareholders have the right to be informed about the affairs of the corporation. A corporation must furnish its shareholders with an **annual financial statement** containing a balance sheet, an income statement, and a statement of changes in shareholder equity.[19]

Shareholders have an absolute **right to inspect** the shareholders' list, the articles of incorporation, the bylaws, and the minutes of shareholders' meetings held within the past three years. To inspect accounting and tax records, minutes of board of directors' and committee meetings, and minutes of shareholders' meetings held more than three years in the past, a shareholder must demonstrate a "proper purpose."[20] Proper purposes include deciding how to vote in a shareholder election, identifying fellow shareholders to communicate with them regarding corporate matters, investigating the existence of corporate mismanagement or improper action, and the like. A shareholder can employ an agent, such as a lawyer, an accountant, or a business manager, to inspect the books and records of the corporation on behalf of the shareholders.[21]

Derivative Lawsuits

derivative lawsuit
A lawsuit a shareholder brings against an offending party on behalf of the corporation when the corporation fails to bring the lawsuit.

"It appears to me that the atmosphere of the temple of Justice is polluted by the presence of such things as companies."
L. J. James
Wilson v. Church
(1879)

If a corporation is harmed by someone, the directors of the corporation have the authority to bring an action on behalf of the corporation against the offending party to recover damages or other relief. If the corporation fails to bring the lawsuit, shareholders have the right to bring the lawsuit on behalf of the corporation. This is called a **derivative action** or **derivative lawsuit**.[22]

A shareholder can bring a derivative action if he or she (1) was a shareholder of the corporation at the time of the act complained of; (2) fairly and adequately represents the interests of the corporation;[23] and (3) made a written demand upon the corporation to take suitable actions, and the corporation either rejected the demand or 90 days have expired from the date of the demand.[24]

A derivative lawsuit will be dismissed by the court if either a majority of independent directors or a panel of independent persons appointed by the court determine that the lawsuit is not in the best interests of the corporation. This decision must be reached in good faith and only after conducting a reasonable inquiry.[25]

If a shareholder derivative action is successful, any award goes into the corporate treasury. The plaintiff–shareholder is entitled to recover payment for reasonable expenses, including attorney's fees, incurred in bringing and maintaining the derivative action.[26] Any settlement of a derivative action requires court approval.[27]

The right to bring a derivative lawsuit was the issue in the following case.

CASE 25.1

Kamen v. Kemper Financial Services, Inc.

111 S.Ct. 1711, 114 L.Ed.2d 152 (1991) United States Supreme Court

Facts Jill S. Kamen is a shareholder of Cash Equivalent Fund, Inc. (Fund), a mutual fund that employs Kemper Financial Services, Inc. (Kemper), as its investment adviser. Kamen brought a derivative lawsuit on behalf of the Fund against Kemper, alleging that Kemper violated fiduciary duties owed to the Fund as imposed by the Investment Company Act of 1940 (Act), a federal statute. Kamen did not make a demand on the Fund's board of directors to sue Kemper any earlier. She alleged that it would have been futile to do so because the directors were acting in a conspiracy with Kemper. The Act was silent as to the rule concerning derivative actions under the Act. The trial court granted Kemper's motion to dismiss the lawsuit. The court of appeals adopted a "universal demand rule" as part of the federal common law and affirmed. This rule requires a shareholder always to make a demand on the directors of a corporation before bringing a derivative lawsuit. Kamen appealed to the U.S. Supreme Court.

Issue Should federal law adopt the universal demand rule for bringing derivative actions?

Decision No. The U.S. Supreme Court refused to adopt the universal demand rule as federal common law but instead held that federal law should follow the appropriate state law concerning demands in de-

rivative lawsuits if a federal statute is silent as to this issue. Reversed.

Reason The Supreme Court held that where a federal statute is silent as to the demand rule, the appropriate state law concerning demand should be followed. Therefore, the universal demand rule cannot become part of the federal common law. Thus, this exception should be applied in states that recognize a "futility" exception to the demand rule. This exception provides that a shareholder is excused from making a demand on the directors of a corporation to sue a third party if the directors are involved in the alleged wrongdoing or are otherwise not disinterested parties.

CASE QUESTIONS

Critical Legal Thinking Which do you think is the better rule: (1) the universal demand rule or (2) the futility exception rule?

Ethics Should Kamen have given the directors of the Fund the opportunity to have sued Kemper before she did?

Business Implication Do derivative lawsuits serve any legitimate purposes? Explain.

RIGHTS OF DIRECTORS

The **board of directors** of a corporation is responsible for formulating the policy decisions affecting the management, supervision, and control of the operation of the corporation.[28] Consequently, the board has certain rights and duties. The board's rights are discussed subsequently; its duties are discussed later in this chapter.

Policy decisions that are made by the board of directors include deciding the business or businesses in which the corporation should be engaged, selecting and removing the top officers of the corporation, determining the capital structure of the corporation, declaring dividends, and the like.

The board may initiate certain actions that require shareholders' approval. These actions are initiated when the board of directors adopt a **resolution** that approves a transaction and recommends that it be submitted to the shareholders for a vote. Examples of such transactions include mergers, sale of substantially all of the corporation's assets outside the course of ordinary business operations, amending the articles of incorporation, and the voluntary dissolution of the corporation.

Selecting Directors

Boards of directors are typically composed of inside directors and outside directors. An **inside director** is a person who is also an officer of the corporation. For example, the president of a corporation often sits as a director of the corporation.

board of directors A panel of decision makers, the members of which are elected by the shareholders.

BUSINESS BRIEF

The directors of a corporation are responsible for formulating the policy decisions affecting the corporation.

resolution A decision adopted by the board of directors that approves a transaction.

inside director A member of the board of directors who is also an officer of the corporation.

An **outside director** is a person who sits on the board of directors of a corporation but is not an officer of that corporation. Outside directors are often officers and directors of other corporations, bankers, lawyers, professors, and others. Outside directors are often selected for their business knowledge and expertise.

There are no special qualifications that a person must meet to be elected a director of a corporation. A director need not be a resident of the state of incorporation or a shareholder of the corporation. The articles of incorporation or bylaws may prescribe qualifications for directors, however.[29]

Number of Directors

Number of Directors A board of directors can consist of one or more individuals. The number of initial directors is fixed by the articles of incorporation. This number can be amended in the articles of incorporation or the bylaws. The articles of incorporation or bylaws can establish a variable range for the size of the board of directors. The exact number of directors within the range may be changed from time to time by the board of directors or the shareholders.[30]

Term of Office

The term of a director's office expires at the next annual shareholders' meeting following his or her election, unless terms are staggered.[31] The RMBCA allows boards of directors that consist of nine or more members to be divided into two or three classes (each class to be as nearly equal in number as possible) that are elected to serve *staggered terms* of two or three years.[32] The specifics of such an arrangement must be outlined in the articles of incorporation.

CONSIDER THIS EXAMPLE: Suppose a board of directors consists of nine directors. The board can be divided into three classes of three directors each, each class to be elected to serve a three-year term. Only three directors of the nine-member board would come up for election each year. This nine-member board could have also been divided into two classes of five and four directors, each class to be elected to two-year terms.

Vacancies and Removal of Directors

Vacancies and Removal of Directors Vacancies on the board of directors can occur because of death, illness, the resignation of a director before the expiration of his or her term, or an increase in the number of positions on the board. Such vacancies can be filled by the shareholders or the remaining directors.[33]

Any director—or the entire board of directors—can be removed from office by a vote of the holders of a majority of the shares entitled to vote at the election. The articles of incorporation provide that directors can be removed only for cause, however.[34] This could be for defalcation, breach of the duty of loyalty, gross mismanagement, and such.

Meetings of the Board of Directors

The directors can act only as a board. They cannot act individually on the corporation's behalf. Every director has the right to participate in any meeting of the board of directors. Each director has one vote. Directors cannot vote by proxy.

Regular meetings of the board of directors are held at the times and places established in the bylaws. Such meetings can be held without notice. The board can call special meetings as provided in the bylaws.[35] **Special meetings** usually are convened for such reasons as issuing new shares, considering proposals to merge with other corporations, adopting maneuvers to defend against hostile takeover attempts, and the like. Unless a notice requirement is waived, the directors must be given at least two days' notice of special meetings.[36]

The board of directors may act without a meeting if all of the directors sign written consents that set forth the actions taken. Such consent has the effect of a unanimous vote.[37] The RMBCA permits meetings of the board to be held via conference calls.[38]

Quorum and Voting Requirement A simple majority of the number of directors established in the articles of incorporation or bylaws usually constitutes a **quorum** for transacting business. However, the articles of incorporation and bylaws may increase this number. If a quorum is present, the approval or disapproval of a majority of the quorum binds the entire board. The articles of incorporation or bylaws can require a greater than majority of directors to constitute quorum or the vote of the board.[39]

quorum The number of directors necessary to hold a board of directors' meeting or transact business of the board.

CONTEMPORARY BUSINESS ENVIRONMENT

Committees of the Board of Directors

In the current complex business world, the demands on directors have increased. To help handle this increased work load, boards of directors have turned to creating committees of their members to handle specific duties. Board members with special expertise or interests are appointed to the various committees.

Unless the articles of incorporation or bylaws provide otherwise, the board of directors may create committees of the board and delegate certain powers to those committees [RMBCA § 8.25]. All members of board committees must be directors. An act of a committee pursuant to delegated authority is the act of the board of directors.

Committees commonly appointed by the board of directors include the following:

- **Executive committee.** This committee is usually granted authority to (1) act on certain matters on behalf of the board during the interim period between board meetings and (2) conduct preliminary investigations of proposals on behalf of the full board. Most members of the committee are inside directors because it is easier for them to meet to address corporate matters.
- **Audit committee.** Recommends independent public accountants and supervises the audit of the financial records of the corporation by the accountants.
- **Nominating committee.** Nominates the management slate of directors to be submitted for shareholder vote.
- **Compensation committee.** Approves management compensation, including salaries,

bonuses, stock options, fringe benefits, and such.
- **Investment committee.** Responsible for investing and reinvesting the funds of the corporation.
- **Litigation committee.** Reviews and decides whether to pursue requests by shareholders for the corporation to sue persons who have allegedly harmed the corporation.

The following powers cannot be delegated to committees but must be exercised by the board itself: (1) declaring dividends, (2) initiating actions that require shareholders' approval, (3) appointing members to fill vacancies on the board, (4) amending the bylaws, (5) approving a plan of merger that does not require shareholder approval (short-form merger), and (6) authorizing the issuance of shares.

Compensation of Directors

Originally, it was considered an honor to serve as a director. No payment was involved. Today, directors often are paid an annual retainer and an attendance fee for each meeting attended. Unless otherwise provided in the articles of incorporation, the directors are permitted to fix their own compensation.[40]

Right of Inspection

Corporate directors are required to have access to the corporation's books and records, facilities and premises, as well as any other information affecting the operation of the corporation. This right of inspection is absolute. It cannot be limited by the articles of incorporation, the bylaws, or board resolution.

BUSINESS BRIEF
To reflect modern technology, the RMBCA permits board of directors' meetings to be held via conference call.

Directors' Authority to Pay Dividends

For-profit corporations operate to make a profit. The objective of the shareholders is to share in those profits, either through capital appreciation, the receipt of dividends, or both. **Dividends** are paid at the discretion of the board of directors.[41] The directors are responsible for determining when, where, how, and how much will be paid in dividends. This authority cannot be delegated to a committee of the board of directors or to officers of the corporation.

When a corporation declares a dividend, it sets a date usually a few weeks prior to the actual payment that is called the **record date**. Persons who are shareholders on that date are entitled to receive the dividend even if they sell their shares before the payment date. When declared, a cash or property dividend cannot be revoked. Shareholders can sue at law to recover declared but unpaid dividends.

The board of directors may opt to retain the profits in the corporation to be used for corporate purposes rather than pay them as dividends. Profits retained by the corporation are called **retained earnings**.

Legal Restrictions on the Payment of Dividends   The law imposes certain restrictions on the payment of dividends to common shareholders. Under the RMBCA, a dividend cannot be paid if (1) the corporation would not be able to pay its debts as they became due in the usual course of business, or (2) the corporation's total assets would be less than its total liabilities, and these would be insufficient funds to pay liquidation preferences to preferred shareholders if the corporation were terminated.[42]

Directors who vote for or assent to an illegal dividend or distribution are jointly and severally liable to the corporation for that amount.[43]

Stock Dividends   Corporations may use additional shares of stock as a dividend. **Stock dividends** are not a distribution of corporate assets. They are paid in proportion to the existing ownership interests of shareholders, so they do not increase a shareholder's proportionate ownership interest.

CONSIDER THIS EXAMPLE: Suppose Betty owns 1,000 shares (or 10 percent) of the 10,000 outstanding shares of the ABC Corporation. If the ABC Corporation declares a stock dividend of 20 percent, Betty will receive a stock dividend of 200 shares. She now owns 1,200 shares—or 10 percent—of a total of 12,000 outstanding shares.

---

dividend   Distribution of profits of the corporation to shareholders.

CAUTION
Dividends are not automatically paid to shareholders; they are paid at the discretion of the board of directors.

record date   A date that determines whether a shareholder receives payment of a declared dividend.

retained earnings   Profits retained by the corporation and not paid out as dividends.

CAUTION
There are certain legal restrictions on the payment of dividends if the corporation is experiencing financial difficulties.

stock dividend   Additional shares of stock paid as a dividend.

BUSINESS CHECKLIST

Indemnification and D & O Insurance Protection for Corporate Directors and Officers

Directors and officers of corporations are sometimes personally named in lawsuits that involve actions they have taken on behalf of the corporation. Such lawsuits often are brought by disgruntled shareholders or third parties who claim they have suffered damages because of the director's or officer's negligence or other conduct.

Directors and officers can protect themselves against personal liability by making sure the corporation does the following:

- Purchases **directors and officers liability insurance (D & O Insurance)**— Corporations can purchase D & O insurance from private insurance companies by paying an annual premium for the insurance. The insurance company is required to defend a corporate director or officer who has been sued in his or her corporate capacity. The insurance company is also required, subject to the terms of the insurance coverage, to pay the litigation costs incurred in defending the lawsuit (e.g., attorney's fees and court costs) and any judgments or settlement costs. Most D & O policies contain deductible clauses and maximum coverage limits. [RMBCA § 8.57]

- Provide **indemnification**—Corporations may provide that directors and officers who are sued in their corporate capacities will be **indemnified** by the corporation for the costs of the litigation as well as any judgments or settlements stemming from the lawsuit. Indemnification means that the corporation—and not the director or officer personally—pays these costs. The RMBCA provides that a court may order indemnification if a director or officer is found to be fairly and reasonably entitled to such indemnification. [RMBCA § 8.54 and 8.56(1)]

RIGHTS OF OFFICERS

The board of directors has the authority to appoint the **officers** of the corporation. The officers are elected by the board of directors at such time and by such manner as prescribed in the corporation's bylaws. The directors can delegate certain management authority to the officers of the corporation. The officer's duties to the corporation are discussed in the next section of this chapter.

At minimum, most corporations have the following officers: (1) a president, (2) one or more vice presidents, (3) a secretary, and (4) a treasurer. The bylaws or the board of directors can authorize duly appointed officers the power to appoint assistant officers. The same individual may simultaneously hold more than one office in the corporation.[44] The duties of each officer are specified in the bylaws of the corporation.

officers Employees of the corporation who are appointed by the board of directors to manage the day-to-day operations of the corporation.

CAUTION
Although theoretically shareholders own the corporation and directors make the policy decisions, officers are often more powerful than the shareholders and the directors. Officers are often criticized for operating corporations for their own self-interest.

Agency Authority of Officers

Officers and agents of the corporation have such authority as may be provided in the bylaws of the corporation or as determined by resolution of the board of directors.[45] As agents, the authority of officers to bind a corporation to contracts is derived from express authority, implied authority, and apparent authority.

Corporate officers are not personally liable for authorized contracts entered into on behalf of the corporation as long as the officer signs the contract in an agency capacity and discloses the identity of the principal (the corporation).

Ratification of Unauthorized Actions A corporation can **ratify** an unauthorized act of a corporate officer or agent. For example, suppose an officer acts outside the scope of his or her employment and enters into a contract with a third person. If the corporation accepts the benefits of the contract, it has ratified the contract and is bound by it. The ratification relates back to the moment the unauthorized act was performed. Officers are liable on an unauthorized contract if the corporation does not ratify it.

ratification The acceptance by a corporation of an unauthorized act of a corporate officer or agent.

Removal of Officers

Unless an employment contract provides otherwise, any officer of a corporation may be removed by the board of directors. The board only has to determine that the best interests of the corporation will be served by such removal.[46] Officers who are removed in violation of an employment contract can sue the corporation for damages.

CONTEMPORARY BUSINESS ENVIRONMENT

Managing Close Corporations

Many of the formal rules in state corporation statutes are designed to govern the management of large publicly held corporations. These rules may not be relevant for regulating the management of **close corporations**; that is, corporations with few shareholders who often work for the corporation and manage its day-to-day operations.

To correct this problem, a **Model Statutory Close Corporation Supplement (Supplement)** has been added to the RMBCA. Only corporations with 50 or fewer shareholders may elect statutory close corporation (SCC) status. To choose this status, the following requirements must be met:

1. Two-thirds of the shares of each class of shares of the corporation must approve the election [Supp. § 3(b)]
2. The articles of incorporation must contain a statement that the corporation is a statutory close corporation [Supp. § 3(a)]
3. The share certificates must conspicuously state that the shares have been issued by a statutory close corporation [Supp. § 10].

The Supplement permits SCCs to dispense with some of the formalities of operating a corporation. For example, if all of the shareholders approve, an SCC may operate without a board of directors, and the articles of incorporation contain a statement to that effect [Supp. § 21]. The powers and affairs of the corporation are then managed by the shareholders. An SCC need not adopt bylaws if the provisions required by law to be contained in the articles of incorporation or a shareholders' agreement [Supp. § 22]. An SCC need not hold annual shareholders' meetings unless one or more shareholders demand in writing that such meetings be held [Supp. § 23]. The shareholders may enter into a shareholders' agreement about how the corporation will be managed [Supp. § 20(a)]. In effect, the shareholders can treat the corporation as a partnership for governance purposes [Supp. § 20(b) (3)]. Selecting statutory close corporation status does not affect the limited liability of shareholders [Supp. § 25].

The Supplement contains a mandatory right of first refusal. A

shareholder of an SCC who desires to transfer his or her shares must first offer them to the corporation on the same terms that a third party is willing to pay for them [Supp. § 12]. If the corporation does not purchase the shares, other holders of the same class of shares may purchase them on the offered terms [Supp. § 11]. Only after the shares have been rejected by the corporation and other shareholders can they be sold to nonshareholders. The articles of incorporation of an SCC may include a provision requiring the corporation to purchase a deceased shareholder's shares [Supp. § 14].

The articles of incorporation of an SCC may authorize one or more shareholders to dissolve the corporation at will or upon the occurrence of a specified event or contingency [Supp. § 33]. Judicial dissolution may be ordered by a court if there is an unbreakable deadlock in the management of the corporation; the directors have acted in an illegal, oppressive, or fraudulent manner; or other such statutory grounds [Supp. § 40].

LIABILITY OF CORPORATE DIRECTORS AND OFFICERS

fiduciary duty Duty of loyalty, honesty, integrity, trust, and confidence owed by directors and officers to their corporate employers.

A corporation's directors and officers owe the **fiduciary duties** of trust and confidence to the corporation and its shareholders. More specifically, they owe the (1) duty of obedience, (2) duty of care, and (3) duty of loyalty. Each of these is discussed in detail in the paragraphs that follow.

duty of obedience A duty that directors and officers of a corporation have to act within the authority conferred upon them by the state corporation statute, the articles of incorporation, the corporate bylaws, and the resolutions adopted by the board of directors.

Duty of Obedience

The directors and officers of a corporation must act within the authority conferred upon them by the state corporation statute, the articles of incorporation, the corporate bylaws, and the resolutions adopted by the board of directors. This duty is called the **duty of obedience**. Directors and officers who either intentionally or negligently act outside their authority are personally liable for any resultant damages caused to the corporation or its shareholders.

CONSIDER THIS EXAMPLE: Suppose the articles of incorporation authorize the corporation to invest in real estate only. If a corporate officer invests corporate funds in the commodities markets, the officer is liable to the corporation for any losses suffered.

Duty of Care

The **duty of care** requires corporate directors and officers to use care and diligence when acting on behalf of the corporation. To meet this duty, the directors and officers must discharge their duties (1) in good faith, (2) with the care that an ordinary prudent person in a like position would use under similar circumstances, and (3) in a manner he or she reasonably believes to be in the best interests of the corporation.[47]

A director or officer who breaches this duty of care is personally liable to the corporation and its shareholders for any damages caused by the breach. Such breaches, which are normally caused by **negligence**, often involve a director's or officer's failure to (1) make a reasonable investigation of a corporate matter, (2) attend board meetings on a regular basis, (3) properly supervise a subordinate who causes a loss to the corporation through embezzlement and such, or (4) keep adequately informed about corporate affairs. Breaches are examined by the courts on a case-by-case basis.

Business Judgment Rule The determination of whether a corporate director or officer has met his or her duty of care is measured as of the time the decision is made—the benefit of hindsight is not a factor. Therefore, the directors and officers are not liable to the corporation or its shareholders for honest mistakes of judgment. This is called the **business judgment rule**.

CONSIDER THIS EXAMPLE: Suppose after conducting considerable research and investigation, the directors of a major automobile company decide to produce a large and expensive automobile. When the car is introduced to the public for sale, few of the automobiles are sold because of the public's interest in buying smaller, less expensive automobiles. Because this was an honest mistake of judgment on the part of corporate management, their judgment is shielded by the business judgment rule.

The court had to decide whether directors were protected by the business judgment rule in the following case.

duty of care A duty that corporate directors and officers have to use care and diligence when acting on behalf of the corporation.

negligence Failure of a corporate director or officer to exercise this duty of care while conducting the corporation's business.

business judgment rule A rule that says directors and officers are not liable to the corporation or its shareholders for honest mistakes of judgment.

BUSINESS BRIEF

Were it not for the protection afforded by the business judgment rule, many high-risk but socially desirable endeavors might not be undertaken.

CASE 25.2

Smith v. Van Gorkom
488 A.2d 858 (1985) Supreme Court of Delaware

Facts Trans Union Corporation (Trans Union) was a publicly traded, diversified holding company that was incorporated in Delaware. Its principal earnings were generated by its railcar leasing business. Jerome W. Van Gorkom was a Trans Union officer for more than 24 years, its chief executive officer for more than 17 years, and the chairman of the board of directors for 2 years. Van Gorkom, a lawyer and certified public accountant, owned 75,000 shares of Trans Union. He was approaching 65 years of age and mandatory retirement. Trans Union's board of directors was composed of 10 members—five inside directors and five outside directors.

In September 1980, Van Gorkom decided to meet with Jay A. Pritzker, a well-known corporate takeover specialist and a social acquaintance of Van Gorkom's, to discuss the possible sale of Trans Union to Pritzker. Van Gorkom met Pritzker at Pritzker's home on Saturday, September 13, 1980. He did so without consulting Trans Union's board of directors. At this meeting, Van Gorkom proposed a sale of Trans Union to Pritzker at a price of $55 per share. The stock was trading at about $38 in the market. On Monday, September 15, Pritzker notified Van Gorkom that he was interested in the $55 cash-out *continued* merger proposal. Van Gorkom, along with two inside directors, privately met with Pritzker on September 16 and 17. After meeting with Van Gorkom on Thursday, September 18, Pritzker notified his attorney to begin drafting the merger documents.

On Friday, September 19, Van Gorkom called a special meeting of Trans Union's board of directors for the following day. The board members were not told the purpose of the meeting. At the meeting, Van Gorkom disclosed the Pritzker offer and described its terms in a 20-minute presentation. Neither the merger agreement nor a written summary of the terms of the agreement was furnished to the directors. No valuation study as to the value of Trans Union was prepared for the meeting. After two hours, the board voted in favor of the cash-out merger with Pritzker's company at $55 per share for Trans Union's stock. The board also voted not to solicit other offers. The merger agreement was executed by Van Gorkom during the evening of September 20 at a formal social event he hosted for the opening of the Chicago Lyric Opera's season. Neither he nor any other director read the agreement prior to its signing and delivery to Pritzker.

Trans Union's board of directors recommended the merger be approved by its shareholders and distributed proxy materials to the shareholders, stating that the $55 per share price for their stock was fair. In the meantime, Trans Union's board of directors took steps to dissuade two other possible suitors who showed an interest in purchasing Trans Union. On February 10, 1981, 69.9 percent of the shares of Trans Union stock was voted in favor of the merger. The merger was consummated. Alden Smith and other Trans Union shareholders sued Van Gorkom and the other directors for damages. The plaintiffs alleged that the defendants were negligent in their conduct in selling Trans Union to Pritzker. The Delaware Court of Chancery held in favor of the defendants. The plaintiffs appealed.

Issue Did Trans Union's directors breach their duty of care?

Decision Yes. The supreme court of Delaware held that the defendant directors had breached their duty of care. The supreme court remanded the case to the court of chancery to conduct an evidentiary hearing to determine the fair value of the shares represented by the plaintiff's class. If that value is higher than $55 per share, the difference shall be awarded to the plaintiffs as damages. Reversed and remanded.

Reason The business judgment rule exists to protect and promote the full and free exercise of the managerial power granted to Delaware directors. The rule itself is a presumption that in making a business decision, the directors of a corporation acted (1) on an informed basis, (2) in good faith, and (3) in the honest belief that the action taken was in the best interests of the company. Thus, the party attacking a board decision as uninformed must rebut the presumption that its business judgment was an informed one. The determination of whether a business judgment is an informed one turns on whether the directors have informed themselves prior to making a business decision, of all material information available to them. Under the business judgment rule, there is no protection for directors who have made an unintelligent or unadvised judgment. The supreme court held that the business judgment rule did not protect the directors' actions in this case. The court stated, "The directors (1) did not adequately inform themselves as to Van Gorkom's role in forcing the sale of the company and in establishing the per share purchase price; (2) they were uninformed as to the intrinsic value of the company; and (3) given these circumstances, at a minimum, they were grossly negligent in approving the sale of the company upon two hours' consideration, without prior notice, and without the exigency of a crisis or emergency."

CASE QUESTIONS

Critical Legal Thinking What does the business judgment rule provide? Is this a good rule? Explain.

Ethics Do you think that Van Gorkom and the other directors had the shareholders' best interests in mind? Were the plaintiff–shareholders being greedy?

Business Implication Is there any liability exposure for sitting on a board of directors?

Reliance on Others Corporate directors and officers usually are unable to investigate personally every corporate matter brought to their attention. Under the RMBCA, directors and officers are entitled to rely on information, opinions, reports, or statements, including financial statements and other financial data, prepared or presented by the following:[48]

- Officers and employees of the corporation whom the director believes are reliable and competent in the matter presented

- Lawyers, public accountants, and other professionals as to any matters that the director reasonably believes to be within the person's professional or expert competence
- A committee of the board of directors upon which the director does not serve as to matters within the committee's designated authority and which committee the director reasonably believes to merit confidence.

A director is not liable if such information is false, misleading, or otherwise unreliable unless he or she has knowledge that would cause such reliance to be unwarranted.[49] The degree of an officer's reliance on such sources is more limited than that given to directors because they are more familiar with corporate operations.

Dissent to Directors' Action On some occasions, individual directors may oppose the action taken by the majority of the board of directors. To avoid liability for such action, the dissenting director must either resign from the board or register his or her **dissent**. Dissent may be registered by (1) entering it in the minutes of the meeting, (2) filing a written dissent with the secretary before the adjournment of the meeting, or (3) forwarding a written dissent by registered mail to the secretary immediately following the adjournment of the meeting.[50] A dissenting director who has not attended the meeting must follow the latter course of action to register his or her dissent.

dissension When an individual director opposes the action taken by the majority of the board of directors.

ETHICAL PERSPECTIVE

Should Directors Be Left Off the Hook?

In the past, being made a member of a board of directors of a corporation was considered to be an honor. Many persons outside the company, such as lawyers, doctors, businesspeople, professors, and others, were asked to sit on boards because of their knowledge, expertise, or contacts. Meetings were held once a month and usually did not take a lot of time, and votes were often just a formality to "rubber stamp" management's preordained decisions.

In the 1980s all this changed. The primary cause was the explosion of lawsuits against boards of directors by disgruntled shareholders, bondholders, and others. Under the law, directors are personally liable for their intentional or negligent conduct that causes harm to others. Most of these lawsuits alleged that directors were negligent in one regard or another, and juries often agreed.

Large and mid-sized corporations usually purchased directors' and officers' liability insurance—

D&O insurance—that paid any judgments. Many small corporations could not afford to carry such insurance. When D&O carriers were hit with increasing payouts, they did what any good businessperson would do—raised the premiums, increased the deductibles, and reduced the activities covered by the insurance. This created a so-called "insurance crisis," as many corporations' coverage was severely reduced or they were forced to go "bare" and not carry D&O insurance because of the high expense.

Inside directors, that is, directors who are also executives of the corporation, remained on boards because of their vested interests, and their liability as officers would remain anyhow. But "outside directors," that is, the directors from outside the company, began fleeing from corporations and refusing to accept nominations to boards of directors. The honor of sitting on a board of directors became a liability, and all

their personal assets—house, investments, and bank accounts—were at risk.

In response to this situation, in 1985 the Delaware legislature enacted a statute that provided that an outside director of a Delaware corporation could not be held liable for ordinary negligence. Thus, this statute overrode the common law of negligence as it applied to outside directors. The law was hailed as a landmark, and many major corporations that were not already incorporated in Delaware abandoned their current states of incorporation and reincorporated there.

Within the years since, many other states have enacted similar statutes. The Revised Model Business Corporation Act contains a similar provision [RMBCA § 2.02(b)(4)]. The main features of these statutes are that they

- Apply to outside directors but not to inside directors

continued

- Relieve liability for ordinary negligence but not for intentional conduct, recklessness, or gross negligence
- Do not apply to violations of federal and state securities laws.

Proponents of these laws assert that they are necessary to attract the most qualified individuals to sit on corporate boards of directors. Critics argue that the laws are merely a scam whereby fat-cat directors are favorably treated and relieved of liability for their negligent conduct when no one else in society (e.g., motorists, entrepreneurs) is given the same privilege.

1. Should "outside" directors be relieved of ordinary negligence liability? Why or why not?
2. Do you think outside directors will act more or less carefully because of RMBCA § 2.02(b)(4)?

Duty of Loyalty

duty of loyalty A duty that directors and officers have not to act adversely to the interests of the corporation and to subordinate their personal interests to those of the corporation and its shareholders.

The **duty of loyalty** requires directors and officers to subordinate their personal interests to those of the corporation and its shareholders. Justice Benjamin Cardozo defined the duty of loyalty as follows:

> [A corporate director or officer] owes loyalty and allegiance to the corporation—a loyalty that is undivided and an allegiance that is influenced by no consideration other than the welfare of the corporation. Any adverse interest of a director [or officer] will be subjected to a scrutiny rigid and uncompromising. He may not profit at the expense of his corporation and in conflict with its rights; he may not for personal gain divert unto himself the opportunities that in equity and fairness belong to the corporation.
>
> Many forms of conduct permissible in a workaday world for those acting at arm's length are forbidden to those bound by fiduciary ties. Not honesty alone, but the punctilio of an honor the most sensitive, is then the standard of behavior. As to this there has developed a tradition that is unbending and inveterate.[51]

If a director or officer breaches his or her duty of loyalty and makes a secret profit on a transaction, the corporation can sue the director or officer to recover the secret profit. Some of the most common breaches of the duty of loyalty are discussed in the following paragraphs.

usurping a corporate opportunity A director or officer steals a corporate opportunity for himself or herself.

Usurping a Corporate Opportunity Directors and officers may not personally usurp (steal) a corporate opportunity for themselves. **Usurping a corporate opportunity** constitutes a violation of a director's or officer's duty of loyalty. If usurping is proven, the corporation can (1) acquire the opportunity from the director or officer and (2) recover any profits made by the director or officer. However, the director or officer is free personally to take advantage of a corporate opportunity if it was fully disclosed and presented to the corporation and the corporation rejected it.

In the following case, the court held that a corporate officer usurped a corporate opportunity.

CASE 25.3

Hill v. Southeastern Floor Covering Co., Inc.

596 So.2d 874 (1992) Supreme Court of Mississippi

Facts Danny Hill was an officer and the general manager of Southeastern Floor Covering Company, Inc. (Southeastern). Southeastern did jobs in floor covering and ceilings for general contractors. Southeastern did much of its own work, and it subcontracted out the work it could not do. Southeastern often subcontracted asbestos removal work to Southern Interiors (Interiors). In 1983, Southeastern bid on a job with Chata Construction Company for various work. Hill made a deal with the owner of Interiors to bid on the asbestos work on the Chata project without Southeastern being involved. Chata awarded the asbestos work to Interiors, and Hill made $90,000 on the transaction. When Southeastern discovered this fact, it sued Hill to recover his secret profits. The trial court held that Hill had breached his duty of loyalty to Southeastern by usurping a corporate opportunity, and it awarded Southeastern $90,000. Hill appealed.

Issue Did Hill violate his duty of loyalty to his corporate employer?

Decision Yes. The supreme court of Mississippi held that Hill violated his duty of loyalty by usurping a corporate opportunity. Affirmed.

Reason The doctrine of corporate opportunity prohibits directors and officers from appropriating to themselves business opportunities which in fair-

ness should belong to the corporation. The supreme court held that Hill diverted an opportunity that could have been Southeastern's, and thereby violated his duty of loyalty.

CASE QUESTIONS

Critical Legal Thinking When can a corporate director or officer take an opportunity for him- or herself? Explain.

Ethics Did Hill act ethically in this case? Do you think he usurped a corporate opportunity?

Business Implication Do you think the award in this case is sufficient to deter breaches of loyalty by corporate directors and officers?

Self-dealing Under the RMBCA, a contract or transaction with a corporate director or officer is voidable by the corporation if it is unfair to the corporation.[52] Contracts of a corporation to purchase property from, sell property to, or make loans to corporate directors or officers where the director or officer has not disclosed his or her interest in the transaction are often voided under this standard. Contracts or transactions with corporate directors or officers are enforceable if their interest in the transaction has been disclosed to the corporation and the disinterested directors or the shareholders have approved the transaction.

Competing with the Corporation Directors and officers cannot engage in activities that *compete* with the corporation unless full disclosure is made and a majority of the disinterested or shareholders approve the activity. The corporation can recover any profits made by the nonapproved competition and any other damages caused to the corporation.

Liability for Crimes

Corporate directors, officers, employees, and agents are personally liable for the crimes they commit while acting on behalf of the corporation. Criminal law sanctions include fines and imprisonment.

Under the law of agency, corporations are liable for the crimes committed by its directors, officers, employees, or agents while acting within the scope of their employment. Because a corporation cannot be placed in prison, the criminal penalty imposed on a corporation usually is the assessment of a monetary fine or the loss of some legal privilege (such as a license).

self-dealing If the directors or officers engage in purchasing, selling, or leasing of property with the corporation, the contract must be fair to the corporation; otherwise, it is voidable by the corporation. The contract or transaction is enforceable if it has been fully disclosed and approved.

CAUTION
Directors and officers may not compete with their corporation unless the competitive activity has been fully disclosed and approved.

BUSINESS APPLICATION

States Enact Constituency Statutes

Under the traditional *business judgment rule*, directors of a corporation owe a *fiduciary duty* to

act on an informed basis, with reasonable care, and in good faith. Historically, this duty has

been rigidly and exclusively owed to the corporation and its share-
continued

holders and to no others. Under this classical theory of the corporation, the rights of other constituents—such as employees, bondholders and creditors, suppliers and customers—exist by contract, period.

This view prevailed during the 1980s, when leveraged buyouts and the greed of corporate raiders caused the demise of many venerable companies, dislodged workers, destroyed pension rights, and ruined many local economies. In response, more than 30 states have enacted constituency statutes that allow directors to consider constituents other than

shareholders when making decisions.

For example, Minnesota adopted the following statute:

In discharging the duties of the position of director, a director may, in considering the best interests of the corporation, consider the interests of the corporation's employees, customers, suppliers, and creditors, the economy of the state and nation, community and societal considerations, and the long-term as well as short-term interests of the corporation and its shareholders, including the possibility that these interests may be best served by the continued inde-

pendence of the corporation. [Minn. Stat. § 302A.251(5)]

Most constituency statutes are permissive, not mandatory. That is, directors may take into account nonstockholder interests but are not required to do so.

Constituency statutes recognize the complex nature of the modern corporation and the modern view that shareholders are not the only "owners" of corporations. These statutes acknowledge the rights of a variety of participants, including lenders, employees, managers, suppliers, distributors, customers, and the local communities in which corporations are located.

LIABILITY OF SHAREHOLDERS

limited liability Liability that shareholders have only to the extent of their capital contribution. Shareholders are generally not personally liable for debts and obligations of the corporation.

Shareholders of a corporation generally have **limited liability** (i.e., they are liable for the debts and obligations of the corporation only to the extent of their capital contribution). However, shareholders can be found personally liable if (1) the corporate entity is disregarded or (2) a controlling shareholder breaches a fiduciary duty to minority shareholders.

Disregard of the Corporate Entity

If a shareholder or shareholders dominate a corporation and misuse it for improper purposes, a court of equity can disregard the corporate entity and hold the shareholders of a corporation personally liable for the corporation's debts and obligations. This doctrine is commonly referred to as **piercing the corporate veil**. It is often resorted to by unpaid creditors who are trying to collect from shareholders a debt owed by the corporation.

piercing the corporate veil A doctrine that says if a shareholder dominates a corporation and misuses it for improper purposes, a court of equity can disregard the corporate entity and hold the shareholder personally liable for the corporation's debts and obligations.

Courts will pierce the corporate veil if (1) the corporation has been formed without sufficient capital (i.e., thin capitalization) or (2) separateness has not been maintained between the corporation and its shareholders (e.g., commingling of personal and corporate assets, failure to hold required shareholders' meetings, failure to maintain corporate records and books). The courts examine this doctrine on a case-by-case basis.

The piercing the corporate veil doctrine was raised in the following case.

CASE 25.4

Kinney Shoe Corp. v. Polan
939 F.2d 209 (1991) United States Court of Appeals, Fourth Circuit

Facts In 1984, Lincoln M. Polan formed Industrial Realty Company (Industrial), a West Virginia corporation. Polan was the sole shareholder of Industrial.

Although a certificate of incorporation was issued, no organizational meeting was held and no officers were elected. Industrial issued no stock certificates because nothing was ever paid into the corporation. Other corporate formalities were not observed. Polan, on behalf of Industrial, signed a lease to sublease commercial space in a building controlled by Kinney Shoe Corporation (Kinney). The first rental payment to Kinney was made out of Polan's personal funds, and no further payments were made on the lease. Kinney filed suit against Industrial and obtained a judgment of $66,400 for unpaid rent. When the amount was unpaid by Industrial, Kinney sued Polan individually and sought to pierce the corporate veil to collect from Polan. The district court held for Polan. Kinney appealed.

Issue Is Polan personally liable for Industrial's debts?

Decision Yes. The court of appeals pierced the corporate veil and held Polan personally liable on Industrial's debt to Kinney. Reversed.

Reason The court of appeals found that Industrial's corporate veil should be pierced because the corporation was undercapitalized, corporate formalities were not observed, and Polan commingled his funds with those of the corporation. The court stated that Polan tried to limit his liability by "setting up a paper curtain constructed of nothing more than Industrial's certificate of incorporation." The court allowed Kinney to pierce the corporate veil to reach the responsible party and produce an equitable result.

CASE QUESTIONS

Critical Legal Thinking Is the doctrine of piercing the corporate veil needed? Should parties like Kinney bear the risk of dealing with corporations like Industrial?

Ethics Is it ethical for persons to form corporations to avoid personal liability? Should this be allowed?

Business Implication What is the risk if corporate formalities are not observed? Explain.

Controlling Shareholders' Breach of Fiduciary Duty

Shareholders usually do not owe a fiduciary duty to their fellow shareholders. However, many courts have held that a **controlling shareholder** does owe a fiduciary duty to minority shareholders. A controlling shareholder is one who owns a sufficient number of shares to control the corporation effectively. This may or may not be majority ownership.

The courts have held the controlling shareholders breach their fiduciary duty to minority shareholders if they:

controlling shareholder
A shareholder that owns a sufficient number of shares to control the corporation effectively.

- Sell assets of the corporation that cause an unusual loss to the minority shareholders
- Sell corporate assets to themselves at less than fair market value
- Sell controlling interest in the corporation to someone whom they know intends to loot the corporation, and does
- Take other action that oppresses the minority shareholders

This is a developing area of the law. The courts examine each case on its particular facts.

INTERNATIONAL PERSPECTIVE

Nationalization of Privately Owned Property by Foreign Nations

When a company invests capital in a foreign country in plant, equipment, bank accounts and such, it runs the risk that that country may **nationalize** (seize) its assets. International law recognizes the right of nations to nationalize private property owned by foreigners if done for a public purpose. Nationalization of assets occurs more often in undeveloped *continued* or developing countries than in developed countries. Nationalization can be classified as

- **Expropriation**—The owner of the property is paid just compensation by the government that seized the property
- **Confiscation**—The owner receives no payment or inadequate payment from the government that has seized the property.

When a foreign government confiscates property of U.S. firms, there are few legal remedies available to the owners. Many lawsuits in U.S. courts to recover damages from the foreign government are barred by the act of state doctrine and the doctrine of sovereign immunity. The U.S. government may try to recover payment for the firms through diplomatic means, but this is often not successful.

The United States has created the **Overseas Private Investment Corporation (OPIC)**, a government agency, which insures U.S. citizens and businesses against losses incurred as a result of the confiscation of their assets by foreign governments. This is often called **political risk insurance**. Low-cost premiums are charged for the insurance. Any insured that receives a payment under this insurance program must assign its claim against the foreign government to OPIC. The **United States Export-Import Bank (Eximbank)** also offers insurance protection against confiscation to U.S. firms engaged in exporting. Political risk insurance is also available through several private insurance companies.

WORKING THE WEB

One of the easiest ways to start surfing the Internet is to subscribe to an Internet service provider. Internet service providers (ISPs) will enable you to have an e-mail address and access via modem to the Internet. Some ISPs also maintain databases of information that are included with a subscription. Most ISPs charge between $15 and $25 per month for this service. Most large ISPs will give you some free hours to try their services. Some Internet service providers include the following:

America Online
Visit at http://www.aol.com

Compuserve
Visit at http://www.compuserve.com

Microsoft Internet Explorer (Microsoft Network)
Visit at http://www.microsoft.com/default.htm

Prodigy
Visit at http://www.prodigy.com

Local Internet providers
Many areas have a number of local ISPs.

CYBER EXERCISES:
1–4. Visit all of the major ISPs. How many free hours can you get from each to try out their services?
5. Check out local ISPs. Find out if they are cheaper than the big services. Find out what services they provide.

CHAPTER SUMMARY

RIGHTS OF SHAREHOLDERS, P. 612

Rights of Shareholders	*Ownership rights.* Shareholders of the corporation own the corporation.
Shareholder Meetings	1. *Annual shareholders' meeting.* Meeting of the shareholders of a corporation that must be held annually by the corporation to elect directors and to vote on other matters.
	2. *Special shareholders' meeting.* Meetings of shareholders that may be called to consider and vote on important or emergency matters, such

	as a proposed merger, amending the articles of incorporation, and so forth. 3. *Notice of shareholders' meetings.* The corporation must notify shareholders of the place, day, and time of annual and special shareholder meetings. If the required notice is not given or is defective, any action taken at the meeting is void.
Proxies	1. *Proxy.* Shareholders may appoint another person (the *proxy*) as their agent to vote their shares at shareholders' meetings. 2. *Proxy card.* Written document that a shareholder signs which authorizes another person to vote his or her shares at a shareholders' meeting.

Voting Requirements	1. *Record date.* A date specified in the corporate bylaws that determines whether a shareholder may vote at a shareholders' meeting. Only persons who are shareholders on the record date are permitted to vote at the meeting.
	 2. *Shareholders' list.* A list that contains the names and addresses of the shareholders as of the record date and the class and number of shares owned by each shareholder. This list must be made available to all shareholders.
	 3. *Quorum.* The required number of shares that must be represented in person or by proxy in order to hold a shareholders' meeting. The RMBCA establishes a majority of outstanding shares as a quorum.
	 4. *Vote required for elections other than for directors.* The affirmative vote of the *majority* of the voting shares represented at a shareholders' meeting constitutes an act of the shareholders for actions other than for the election of directors.
	 5. *Voting methods for electing directors:*
	   a. *Straight (noncumulative) voting.* Unless otherwise stated, each shareholder votes the number of shares he or she owns on candidates for each of the positions open for election. The candidate or candidates with the most votes win the open position or positions.
	   b. *Cumulative voting.* The articles of incorporation may provide for cumulative voting. Under this method, a shareholder is entitled to multiply the number of shares he or she owns by the number of directors to be elected and cast the product for a single candidate or distribute the product among two or more candidates.
	 6. *Supramajority voting requirement.* The articles of incorporation or bylaws can require a greater than majority of shares to constitute quorum or the vote of the shareholders (e.g., 80 percent). Also called *supermajority voting requirement*.

Voting Agreements	1. *Voting trust.* An arrangement whereby participating shareholders transfer their shares to a trustee who is then empowered to vote the shares held by the trust. Shareholders are issued *voting trust certificates* that evidence their interest in the trust. 2. *Voting agreements.* An agreement between two or more shareholders agreeing on how they will vote their shares. Voting agreements are enforceable.
Right to Transfer Shares	1. *Article 8 of the Uniform Commercial Code (UCC).* Shareholders have the right to transfer their nonrestrictive shares. Article 8 of the Uniform Commercial Code governs the transfer of securities.

	2. *Lost or stolen stock certificates.* If a stock certificate is lost, stolen, or destroyed, the corporation is required to issue a *replacement certificate* if the shareholder posts an indemnity bond to protect the corporation from loss for issuing the replacement certificate.
Transfer Restrictions	1. *Right of first refusal.* An agreement that requires the selling shareholder to offer his or her shares for sale to the other parties to the agreement before selling them to anyone else. 2. *Buy-and-sell agreement.* An agreement that requires selling shareholders to sell their shares to the other shareholders or to the corporation at the price specified in the agreement.
Preemptive Rights	Rights that give existing shareholders the option of subscribing to new shares being issued by the corporation in proportion to their current ownership interest.
Right to Receive Information and Inspect Books and Records	1. *Annual financial statement.* A corporation must furnish its shareholders with an *annual financial statement* containing a balance sheet, an income statement, and a statement of changes in shareholder equity. 2. *Inspection rights.* Shareholders have the *absolute right* to inspect the shareholders' list, the articles of incorporation, the bylaws, and the minutes of shareholders' meetings held within the past three years. They have the right to inspect accounting and tax records, minutes of board of directors' and committee meetings, and minutes of shareholders' meetings held more than three years in the past if they demonstrate a *proper purpose*.
Derivative Lawsuits	A lawsuit a shareholder brings on behalf of the corporation against an offending party who has injured the corporation when the directors of the corporation fail to bring the suit. The shareholder must make a written *demand* upon the corporation to bring the lawsuit, and the corporation either rejects it or 90 days expire without the corporation bringing the requested lawsuit.
RIGHTS OF DIRECTORS, P. 617	
Rights of Directors	1. *Board of directors.* A panel of decision makers for the corporation, the members of which are elected by the shareholders. 2. *Policy decisions.* The directors of a corporation are responsible for formulating the *policy* decisions affecting the corporation, such as deciding what businesses to engage in, determining the capital structure of the corporation, selecting and removing top officers of the corporation, and the like. 3. *Resolutions.* The board of directors can adopt a resolution that approves a transaction that requires shareholder vote and recommends it to shareholders.
Selecting Directors	1. *Inside director.* A member of the board of directors who is also an officer of the corporation. 2. *Outside director.* A member of the board of directors who is not an officer of the corporation. 3. *Qualifications.* There are no qualifications to serve as a director unless the articles of incorporation or bylaws prescribe qualifications. 4. *Number of directors.* A board of directors can consist of one or more individuals. The articles of incorporation fix the number of initial directors. This number can be amended by the articles of incorporation or bylaws.

	5. *Variable range.* The articles of incorporation or bylaws can establish a *variable range* for the size of the board of directors. The exact number of directors within the range may be changed from time to time by the board of directors or the shareholders.
Term of Office	1. *Annual term.* The term of a director's office expires at the next annual shareholders' meeting following his or her election unless terms are staggered.
	2. *Staggered terms.* If a board of directors consists of nine or more members, it may be divided into two or three *classes* (each class to be as nearly equal in number as possible), and classes can be elected to serve *staggered terms* of two or three years.
	3. *Vacancies.* Vacancies on the board of directors can be filled by the shareholders or the remaining directors.
	4. *Removal of directors.* Any director, or the entire board of directors, can be removed from office by the shareholders. The articles of incorporation provide that directors can be removed only for cause.
Meetings of the Board of Directors	1. *Regular meeting.* A meeting of the board of directors held at the time and place scheduled in the bylaws.
	2. *Special meeting.* A meeting of the board of directors convened to discuss an important or emergency matter, such as a proposed merger, a hostile attempt, and such.
	3. *Written consents.* The board of directors may act without a meeting if all of the directors sign written consents that set forth the action taken.
	4. *Conference call.* Board of directors may meet via conference call if all of the directors can hear and participate in the call.
	5. *Quorum.* A simple *majority* of a number of directors established in the articles of incorporation or bylaws constitutes a quorum for transacting business.
	6. *Vote.* The approval or disapproval of a *majority* of the quorum binds the entire board.
	7. *Supramajority vote.* The articles of incorporation or bylaws may require a greater than majority of directors to constitute quorum or the vote of the board.
Committees of the Board of Directors	*Committees of the board of directors.* Unless the articles of incorporation or bylaws provide otherwise, the board of directors may create committees of its members and delegate certain powers to those committees. The most common committees are:
	1. *Executive committee.* Has authority to (1) act on certain matters during the interim period between board meetings and (2) conduct preliminary investigations of proposals on behalf of the board.
	2. *Audit committee.* Recommends independent public accountants and supervises the audit of the financial records of the corporation by the accountants.
	3. *Nominating committee.* Nominates the management slate of directors to be submitted for shareholder vote.
	4. *Compensation committee.* Approves management compensation, including salaries, bonuses, stock option plans, fringe benefits, and such.
	5. *Investment committee.* Responsible for investing and reinvesting the funds of the corporation.
	6. *Litigation committee.* Reviews and decides whether to pursue requests by shareholders for the corporation to sue persons who have allegedly harmed the corporation.

Compensation of Directors	Directors are usually paid an annual retainer and an attendance fee for each meeting attended.
Right of Inspection	Corporate directors have an *absolute right* to have access to the corporation's books and records, facilities and premises, as well as any other information affecting the operation of the corporation.
Directors' Authority to Pay Dividends	1. *Directors' authority to pay dividends.* The board of directors has the *discretion* to pay *dividends* to shareholders or *retain earnings* for use by the corporation. 2. *Record date.* When a corporation declares a dividend, it sets a date usually a few weeks prior to the actual payment which establishes the *record date* for payment of the dividend. Shareholders as of that date will be paid the dividend. 3. *Legal restrictions on the payment of dividends.* A dividend cannot be paid if (a) the corporation would not be able to pay its debts as they became due in the usual course of business, or (b) the corporation's total assets would be less than its total liabilities, and there would be insufficient funds to pay liquidation preferences to preferred shareholders if the corporation were terminated. 4. *Stock dividends.* The issuance of additional shares of stock to the shareholders as a dividend. They are paid in proportion to the existing ownership interests of shareholders, so they do not increase a shareholder's proportionate ownership interest.

RIGHTS OF OFFICERS, P. 621

Rights of Officers	*Officers.* Employees of the corporation who are appointed by the board of directors to manage the *day-to-day operations* of the corporation.
Agency Authority of Officers	Officers and agents of the corporation have the following authority to bind the corporation to contracts with third parties: 1. *Express authority.* Authority derived from corporation statutes, articles of incorporation, bylaws, and resolutions of the board of directors. 2. *Implied authority.* Authority implied from the officer's position and the facts and circumstances of the situation. 3. *Apparent authority.* Authority that arises when a third person is reasonably led to believe that an officer has authority to act when in fact the officer does not have express authority. 4. *Ratification.* A corporation can ratify an unauthorized act of a corporate officer. The ratification relates back to the moment the unauthorized act was performed.
Removal of Officers	Unless an employment contract provides otherwise, any officer of a corporation may be removed by the board of directors.

LIABILITY OF CORPORATE DIRECTORS AND OFFICERS, P. 622

Liability of Corporate Directors and Officers	*Fiduciary duties.* Corporate directors and officers owe the fiduciary duties of trust and confidence to the corporation and its shareholders. These include the duties of *obedience, care,* and *loyalty.*
Duty of Obedience	A duty that directors and officers of a corporation have to act within the authority conferred upon them by the state corporation statute, the articles of incorporation, the corporate bylaws, and the resolutions adopted by the board of directors.

Duty of Care	A duty that corporate directors and officers have to use care and diligence when acting on behalf of the corporation. This duty is discharged if they perform their duties (a) in good faith, (b) with the care that an *ordinary prudent person* in a like position would use under similar circumstances, and (c) in a manner he or she reasonably believes to be in the best interests of the corporation. 1. *Negligence.* Failure of a corporate director or officer to exercise this duty of care when conducting the corporation's business. 2. *Business judgment rule.* A rule that says directors and officers are not liable to the corporation or its shareholders for honest mistakes of judgment. 3. *Reliance on others.* Directors and officers may rely on information and reports prepared by competent and reliable officers and employees, lawyers, public accountants, and other professionals, as well as committees of the board of directors as long as such reliance is warranted. 4. *Dissent to directors' action.* When an individual director opposes the action taken by the majority of the board of directors, he or she would register his or her dissent by (a) entering it in the minutes of the meeting, (b) filing a written dissent with the secretary before the adjournment of the meeting, or (c) forwarding a written dissent by registered mail to the secretary immediately following the adjournment of the meeting if the director has not attended the meeting.

Duty of Loyalty	A duty that directors and officers have to act adversely to the interest of the corporation and to subordinate their personal interests to those of the corporation and its shareholders.
	1. *Common examples of breaches of the duty of loyalty:*
	  a. *Self-dealing.* The corporation may void any transaction with a director or officer if it is *unfair to the corporation*. This usually involves undisclosed self-dealing by a director or officer with the corporation.
	  b. *Usurping a corporate opportunity.* A director or officer may not personally *usurp (steal)* an opportunity that belongs to the corporation. The corporation can acquire the opportunity from the director or officer and recover any profits made by the director or officer.
	  c. *Competing with the corporation.* Directors and officers may not compete with their corporation unless the competitive activity has been fully disclosed to the corporation and approved by a majority of disinterested directors or shareholders.

Insurance	Corporations can purchase *directors' and officers' liability insurance (D & O insurance)* that pays the cost to defend litigation against directors and officers and pays any judgment or settlement of the lawsuit.
Indemnification	The corporation must *indemnify (pay back)* any director or officer of litigation expenses incurred in a lawsuit won by the director or officer. The corporation may indemnify a director or officer who loses a lawsuit as long as the director or officer was not adjudged liable to the corporation or did not improperly obtain personal benefit for him- or herself in the challenged transaction. Directors and officers may not be paid insurance or indemnification for intentional conduct that harmed third parties.

Liability for Crimes	1. *Liability of directors and officers.* Corporate directors and officers are *personally liable* for the crimes they commit while acting on behalf of the corporation. Criminal sanctions include fines and imprisonment.
	2. *Liability of the corporation.* Under the law of *agency*, corporations are liable for the crimes committed by its directors and officers while acting within the scope of their authority. Criminal sanctions include monetary fines and loss of legal privileges (e.g., loss of a license).

LIABILITY OF SHAREHOLDERS, P. 628

Liability of Shareholders	*Limited liability.* Shareholders of corporations generally have *limited liability:* That is, they are liable for the debts and obligations of the corporation only to the *extent of their capital contribution* to the corporation.
Disregard of the Corporate Entity	Shareholders may be found *personally liable* for the debts and obligations of the corporation under the following two doctrines:
	1. *Piercing the corporate veil.* Courts can *disregard the corporate entity* and hold shareholders personally liable for the debts and obligations of the corporation if (a) the corporation has been formed without sufficient capital (*thin capitalization*) or (b) separateness has not been maintained between the corporation and its shareholders (e.g., commingling of personal and corporate assets, failure to hold required shareholders' meetings, and such). Also called the *alter ego doctrine*.
	2. *Controlling shareholders' breach of fiduciary duty.* As a general rule, shareholders do not owe a fiduciary duty to fellow shareholders or the corporation. Some courts hold that a *controlling shareholder* owes a fiduciary duty to minority shareholders. Controlling shareholders are personally liable to minority shareholders if their actions breach this fiduciary duty and cause injury to the minority shareholders.

CRITICAL LEGAL THINKING CASES

25.1 Shareholder Meeting Ocilla Industries, Inc. (Ocilla) owned 40 percent of the stock of Direct Action Marketing, Inc. (Direct Action). Direct Action was a New York corporation that specialized in the marketing of products through billing inserts. In 1985 Ocilla helped place Howard Katz and Joseph Esposito on Direct Action's five-member board of directors. A dispute between Ocilla and the two directors caused Ocilla to claim that Katz and Esposito wanted excess remuneration in exchange for leaving the board at the end of their terms. As a result of this, no shareholders' meeting was held between September 19, 1986 and January 27, 1988. Under the Model Business Corporations Act, can Ocilla compel Direct Action to hold the meeting earlier? [*Ocilla Industries, Inc. v. Katz*, 677 F.Supp. 1291 (E.D.N.Y. 1987)]

25.2 Special Meeting Jack C. Schoenholtz was a shareholder and member of the board of directors of Rye Psychiatric Hospital Center, Inc. (Rye Hospital). The hospital was incorporated in 1973. By 1977, a split had developed among the board of directors concerning the operation of the facility. Three directors stood on one side of the dispute, and three directors on the other.

In an attempt to break the deadlock, Schoenholtz, who owned more than 10 percent of the corporation's voting stock, asked the corporation's secretary to call a special meeting of the shareholders. In response, the secretary sent a notice to the shareholders stating that a special meeting of the shareholders would be held on November 12, 1982, "for the purpose of electing directors." The meeting was held as scheduled. Some stockholders brought suit claiming that the special shareholders' meeting was not called properly. Who wins? [*Rye Psychiatric Hospital Center, Inc. v. Schoenholtz*, 476 N.Y.S.2d 339 (A.D. 2 Dept. 1984)]

25.3 Irrevocable Proxy George Biggons, William Smith, and Gerald Zollar were all shareholders in GRG Operating, Inc. (GRG). On May 13, 1983, Zollar contributed $1,000 of his own funds so that the corporation could begin to do business. In exchange for this contribution, Gibbons and Smith both granted Zollar the right to vote their shares of GRG stock. They gave Zollar a signed form that stated that "Gibbons and Smith, for a period of 10 years from the date hereof, appoint Zollar as their proxy. This proxy is solely intended to be an irrevocable proxy." A year after the agreement was signed, Gibbons and

Smith wanted to revoke their proxies. Can they? [*Zollar v. Smith*, 710 S.W.2d 155 (Tex. App. 1986)]

25.4 Shareholder Voting Agreement Bookstop, Inc. (Bookstop) was founded in 1982 by Gary Hoover. The corporation met with early and marked success. By 1985, it was one of the largest retail booksellers in the state of Texas and had expanded into California. In order to finance this rapid growth, Hoover sought outside investors. In 1985, Hoover agreed to sell 18 percent of Bookstop's common stock to H.E. Butt Grocery Co. (HEB). As part of the sale of the stock, the parties agreed that each had the right to place two nominees on Bookstop's board of directors. For several years, the parties abided by the terms of the agreement. A dispute then arose between Bookstop's shareholders. Can the shareholders' agreement be enforced? [*Crown Books Corporation v. Bookstop, Inc.*, 1990 WL 26166 (Del.Ch. 1990)]

25.5 Transfer Restrictions Stater Brothers Markets (Stater Brothers), a chain of supermarkets located throughout southern California, was a wholly owned subsidiary of Petrolane, Inc. (Petrolane). The company's top executives and an outside investor named Lisa Garrett purchased the chain in a leveraged buyout in March 1983. The executives, known collectively as the La Cadena group, bought 51 percent of Stater Brother's stock; Garrett owned the other 49 percent. In an effort to preserve the continuity of harmonious management, Garrett and the La Cadena group entered into a stockholders' agreement effective March 22, 1983. The agreement prohibited the sale of any Stater Brothers stock without the consent of the other stockholders. Absent such consent, the nonselling stockholders were given the right of first refusal to meet the terms of the proposed sale and be substituted for the outside investor. Is this agreement valid? [*Garrett v. Brown*, 511 A.2d 1044 (Del.Supreme 1986)]

25.6 Right to Inspect Records On July 20, 1983, Helmsman Management Services, Inc. (Helmsman) became a 25 percent stockholder of A&S Consultants, Inc. (A&S), a Delaware corporation. Helmsman paid $50,000 for its interest in A&S. At the time of the stock purchase, Helmsman was also a customer of A&S, paying the company for the use of a computer software program. Since 1983, Helmsman verified A&S's billings by a periodic review of certain of A&S's books and records. In January 1986, Helmsman conducted a review of A&S's records over a six-day period. The review showed that A&S had never paid any dividends on the stock held by Helmsman and that Helmsman had never received notice of A&S's stockholder meetings. Suspecting that A&S was being mismanaged, Helmsman sent a letter to A&S asking to inspect all of A&S's records. The letter stated several purposes for the inspection, including to (1) determine the reasons for nonpayment of dividends and (2) gain information to be used in determining how to vote in stockholders' elections. Under the Model Business Corporations Act, should Helmsman's request be honored? [*Helmsman Management Services, Inc. v. A&S Consultants, Inc.*, 525 A.2d 160 (Del.Ch. 1987)]

25.7 Board of Directors Meeting Dick Gregory was the chairman of the board of directors of Correction Connection, Inc. (CCI). CCI's bylaws permit special meetings of the board of directors if each board member is given notice of the meeting and informed of the business to be conducted at the meeting. On September 27, 1988, a notice of a special meeting of the board of directors was sent to each director, including Gregory. The notice specified the meeting date of September 30, 1988, and the agenda for the meeting, which included a plan to acquire additional capital. The meeting began as planned on September 30, and reconvened on October 4, October 6, and October 7. Gregory did not attend any of the meetings. In Gregory's absence, the board voted to issue certain authorized but unissued shares of the corporation's stock. Gregory objected to this decision and brought an action to prevent the stock from being issued. Who wins? [*Gregory v. Depte*, 1989 WL 67329 (E.D.Pa. 1989)]

25.8 Dividends Gay's Super Markets, Inc. (Super Markets) was a corporation formed under the laws of the state of Maine. Hannaford Bros. Co. held 51 percent of the corporation's common stock. Lawrence F. Gay and his brother Carrol were both minority shareholders in Super Markets. Lawrence Gay was also the manager of the corporation's store at Machias, Maine. On July 5, 1971, he was dismissed from his job. At the January 1972 meeting of Super Market's board of directors, a decision was made not to declare a stock dividend for 1971. The directors cited expected losses from increased competition and the expense of opening a new store as reasons for not paying a dividend. Lawrence Gay claims that the reason for not paying a dividend was to force him to sell his shares in Super Markets. Lawrence sued to force the corporation to declare a dividend. Who wins? [*Gay v. Gay's Super Markets, Inc.*, 343 A.2d 577 (Maine Sup. 1975)]

25.9 Duty of Loyalty Edward Hellenbrand ran a comedy club known as the Comedy Cottage in Rosemont, Illinois. The business was incorporated, with Hellenbrand and his wife as the corporation's sole shareholders. The corporation leased the premises in which the club was located. In 1978, Hellenbrand hired Jay Berk as general manager of the club. In 1980, Berk was made vice president of the corporation and given 10 percent of its stock. Hellenbrand experienced health problems and moved to Nevada, leaving Berk to manage the daily affairs of the business. In June 1984, the ownership of the building where the Comedy Cottage was located changed hands. Shortly thereafter the club's lease on the premises expired. Hellenbrand instructed Berk to negotiate a new lease. Berk arranged a month-to-month lease but had the lease agreement drawn up in his name instead of that of the corporation. When Hellenbrand learned of this, he fired Berk. Berk continued to lease the building in his own name and opened his own club there, known as the Comedy Company, Inc. Hellenbrand sued Berk for an injunction to prevent Berk from leasing the building. Who wins? [*Comedy Cottage, Inc. v. Berk*, 495 N.E.2d 1006 (Ill. App. 1986)]

25.10 Duty of Loyalty Lawrence Gaffney was the president and general manager of Ideal Tape Co. (Ideal). Ideal, which was a subsidiary of Chelsea Industries, Inc. (Chelsea) was engaged in the business of manufacturing pressure-sensitive tape. In 1975, Gaffney recruited three other Ideal executives to join him in starting a tape manufacturing business. The four men remained at Ideal for the two years it took them to plan the new enterprise. During this time, they used their positions at Ideal to travel around the country to gather business ideas, recruit potential customers, and purchase equipment for their business. At no time did they reveal to Chelsea their intention to open a competing business. In November 1977, the new business was incorporated as Action Manufacturing Co. (Action). When executives at Chelsea discovered the existence of the new venture, Gaffney and the others resigned from Chelsea. Chelsea sued them for damages. Who wins? [*Chelsea Industries, Inc. v. Gaffney*, 449 N.E.2d 320 (Mass.Sup. 1983)]

25.11 Indemnification William G. Young was a director of Pool Builders Supply, Inc. (Pool Builders). Pool Builders experienced financial difficulties and was forced to file for bankruptcy. Eddie Lawson was appointed the receiver for the creditors of the corporation. Lawson believed that Young had mismanaged the corporation. Lawson filed a suit against Young and Pool Builders, alleging that Young had used Pool Builders personally to obtain money, goods, and property from creditors on the credit of the corporation. Lawson's suit also alleged that Young attempted to convert corporate assets for his own use. Young defended the suit for himself and the corporation. At trial, the judge found insufficient evidence to support Lawson's charges, and the suit was dismissed. Young now seeks to have Pool Builders pay the legal fees he incurred while defending the suit. Can Young recover this money from the corporation? [*Lawson v. Young*, 486 N.E.2d 1177 (Ohio App. 1984)]

25.12 Derivative Lawsuit In 1948, four brothers—Monnie, Mechel, Merko, and Sam Dotlich—formed a partnership to run a heavy equipment rental business. By 1957, the company had been incorporated as Dotlich Brothers, Inc. Each of the brothers owned 25 percent of the corporation's stock, and each served on the board of directors. In 1951, the business acquired a 56-acre tract of land in Speedway, Indiana. This land was held in the name of Monnie Dotlich. Each of the brothers was aware of this arrangement. By 1976, the corporation had purchased six other pieces of property, which were all held in Monnie's name. Sam Dotlich was not informed that Monnie was the record owner of these other properties. In 1976, Sam

discovered this irregularity and requested that the board of directors take action to remedy the situation. When the board refused to do so, Sam initiated a lawsuit on behalf of the corporation. Can Sam bring this lawsuit? [*Dotlich v. Dotlich*, 475 N.E.2d 331 (Ind. App. 1985)]

25.13 Piercing the Corporate Veil M. R. Watters was the majority shareholder of several closely held corporations, including Wildhorn Ranch, Inc. (Wildhorn). All these businesses were run out of Watter's home in Rocky Ford, Colorado. Wildhorn operated a resort called the Wildhorn Ranch Resort in Teller County, Colorado. Although Watters claimed that the ranch was owned by the corporation, the deed for the property listed Watters as the owner. Watters paid little attention to corporate formalities, holding corporate meetings at his house, never taking minutes of these meetings, and paying the debts of one corporation with the assets of another. During August 1986, two guests of Wildhorn Ranch Resort drowned while operating a paddleboat at the ranch. The family of the deceased guests sued for damages. Can Watters be held personally liable? [*Geringer v. Wildhorn Ranch, Inc.*, 760 F.Supp. 1442 (D.Colo. 1988)]

25.14 Shareholder Liability Robert Orchard and Arthur Covelli owned seven McDonald's franchises in Erie, Pennsylvania. Each individual franchise was owned by a separate corporation. Orchard owned a 27-percent interest in each of these corporations, and Covelli owned 73 percent. Although Orchard and Covelli worked together harmoniously for many years, they eventually became dissatisfied with the relationship. In 1977, they unsuccessfully attempted to have Covelli buy out Orchard's stock. Covelli became angry with Orchard and had him terminated from his position as vice president of the corporations. Six months later, Covelli removed Orchard from the corporations' boards of directors and replaced him with his own son. Covelli also allowed three of the corporations' franchise agreements with McDonald's to lapse and then resigned them in his own name. Throughout this period, Orchard received no dividends or other compensations from the corporations. Orchard sued Covelli for damages. Who wins? [*Orchard v. Covelli*, 590 F.Supp. 1548 (W.D.Pa. 1984)]

ETHICS CASES

25.15 Ethical Perspective Alfred S. Johnson, Incorporated (Corporation) was incorporated in 1955 by Alfred S. Johnson, who owned 70 shares of the corporation. Two employees of the corporation, James DeBaun and Walter Stephens, owned 20 and 10 shares, respectively. When Johnson died in 1965, his will created a testamentary trust in which his 70 shares were placed. Johnson's will named First Western Bank and Trust Company (Bank) trustee for the trust. Several years later Bank decided to sell the 70 shares but did not tell anyone associated with Corporation of its decision. An appraising was obtained that valued the corporation at $326,000 as a going concern.

On May 27, 1968, Raymond J. Mattison submitted an offer to purchase the 70 shares for $250,000, payable in $50,000 in

securities of companies Mattison owned and the $200,000 balance over a five-year period. Bank obtained a Dun & Bradstreet report that showed several outstanding tax liens against Mattison. The bank accepted Mattison's explanation that they were not his fault. At the time, Mattison owed Bank a judgment for fraud. Bank was also aware that Mattison owed unpaid debts and that several entities in which he was involved were insolvent. Bank did not investigate these matters. If it had, the public records of Los Angeles County would have revealed 38 unsatisfied judgments against Mattison and his entities totaling $330,886, 54 pending lawsuits claiming damages of $373,588, and 18 tax liens aggregating $20,327. Bank agreed to sell the 70 shares to Mattison and accepted the assets of Corporation as security for the repayment of the $200,000 balance. As part of the transaction, Bank required Mattison to agree to have Corporation give its banking business to Bank.

At the time of sale, Corporation was a successful going business with a bright future: It had cash of $76,000 and other liquid assets of over $120,000. Its net worth was about $220,000. Corporation was profitable, and its trend of earnings indicated a pattern of growth. Mattison immediately implemented a systematic scheme to loot Corporation. He (1) diverted $73,000 in corporate cash to himself and a shell company he owned, (2) caused Corporation to assign all of its assets, including accounts receivable, to the shell company, (3) diverted all corporate mail to a post office box and extracted incoming checks to Corporation, (4) refused to pay corporate creditors on time or at all, (5) issued payroll checks without sufficient corporate funds, and (6) removed Corporation's books and records. On June 20, 1969, hopelessly insolvent, Corporation shut down operations and was placed in receivership. At that time, its debts exceeded its assets by over $200,000. DeBaun's and Stephens' shares were worthless. They sued Bank for damages, alleging that Bank, as the majority shareholder of the Corporation, breached its fiduciary duty to the minority shareholders.

Did the bank have knowledge of the dangerous situation in which it placed the Corporation? Did Bank, as the controlling shareholder of Corporation, breach its fiduciary duty to the minority shareholders? [*DeBaun v. First Western Bank and Trust Co.*, 46 Cal.App.3d 791, 120 Cal. Rptr. 354 (Cal. App. 1975)]

25.16 Ethical Perspective Jon-T Chemicals, Inc. (Chemicals) was an Oklahoma corporation engaged in the fertilizer and chemicals business. John H. Thomas was its majority shareholder and its president and board chairman. In April 1971, Chemicals incorporated Jon-T Farms, Inc. (Farms) as a wholly owned subsidiary to engage in the farming and land-leasing business. Chemicals invested $10,000 to establish Farms. All the directors and officers of Farms were directors and officers of Chemicals, and Thomas was its president and board chairman. In addition, Farms used offices, computers, and accountants of Chemicals without paying a fee and Chemicals paid the salary of Farms' only employee. Chemicals made regular informal advances to pay Farms' expenses. This reached $7.5 million by January 1975.

Thomas and Farms engaged in a scheme whereby they submitted fraudulent applications for agricultural subsidies from the federal government under the Uplands Cotton Program. As a result of these applications, the Commodity Credit Corporation, a government agency, paid more than $2.5 million in subsidies to Thomas and Farms. After discovering the fraud, the federal government obtained criminal convictions against Thomas and Farms. In a separate civil action, the federal government obtained a $4.7 million judgment against Thomas and Farms, finding them jointly and severally liable for the tort of fraud. Farms declared bankruptcy, and Thomas was unable to pay the judgment. Because Thomas and Farms were insolvent, the federal government sued Chemicals to recover the judgment. Was Farms the alter ego of Chemicals, permitting the United States to pierce the corporate veil and recover the judgment from Chemicals? Did Thomas act ethically in this case? [*United States of America v. Jon-T Chemicals, Inc.*, 768 F.2d 868 (5th Cir. 1985)]

CRITICAL LEGAL THINKING WRITING ASSIGNMENT

Read Case A.25 in the Case Appendix [*United States v. WRW Corporation*]. This case is excerpted from the court of appeals opinion. Review and brief the case. In your brief, be sure to answer the following questions:

1. Who was the plaintiff? What was it suing for?
2. Who were the defendants?
3. Explain the doctrine of piercing the corporate veil.
4. Did the court find the defendants personally liable?

NOTES

[1] Revised Model Business Corporation Act (RMBCA) § 7.01

[2] RMBCA § 7.03.

[3] RMBCA § 7.02.

[4] RMBCA § 7.04.

[5] RMBCA § 7.05.

[6] RMBCA § 7.22.

[7] RMBCA § 6.01.

[8] RMBCA § 7.07.

[9] RMBCA § 7.20.

[10] RMBCA § 7.25(a), (b).

[11] RMBCA § 7.25(c).

[12] RMBCA § 7.28.

[13] RMBCA § 7.27.

[14] RMBCA § 7.30.

[15] RMBCA § 7.31.

[16] RMBCA § 7.22(d).

[17] RMBCA § 6.27.

[18] RMBCA § 6.30.

[19] RMBCA § 16.20.

[20] RMBCA § 16.02.

[21] RMBCA § 16.03.

[22] RMBCA § 7.40.

[23] RMBCA § 7.41.

[24] RMBCA § 7.42.

[25] RMBCA § 7.44.

[26] RMBCA § 7.46.

[27] RMBCA § 7.45.

[28] RMBCA § 8.01.

[29] RMBCA § 8.02.

[30] RMBCA § 8.03.

[31] RMBCA § 8.05.

[32] RMBCA § 8.06.

[33] RMBCA § 8.10.

[34] RMBCA § 8.08(a).

[35] RMBCA § 8.20(a).

[36] RMBCA § 8.22, 8.23.

[37] RMBCA § 8.21.

[38] RMBCA § 8.20(b).

[39] RMBCA § 8.24.

[40] RMBCA § 8.11.

[41] RMBCA § 6.40.

[42] RMBCA § 6.40(c).

[43] RMBCA § 8.33.

[44] RMBCA § 8.40.

[45] RMBCA § 8.41.

[46] RMBCA § 8.43(b).

[47] RMBCA § 8.30(a) and § 8.42(a).

[48] RMBCA § 8.30(b) and § 8.42(b).

[49] RMBCA § 8.30(c) and § 8.42(c).

[50] RMBCA § 8.24(d).

[51] *Meinhard v. Salmon*, 164 N.E.2d 545, 546 (N.Y.App. 1928).

[52] RMBCA § 8.31.

CHAPTER 26

MERGERS, ACQUISITIONS, AND TERMINATION OF CORPORATIONS

Chapter Objectives

*After studying this chapter,
you should be able to*

1. Describe the process for soliciting proxies from shareholders
2. Define proxy contests
3. Identify when a shareholder can include a proposal in proxy materials
4. Distinguish between a merger and a consolidation
5. Describe the process for approving a merger or consolidation
6. Describe dissenting shareholder appraisal rights
7. Define a tender offer
8. Describe poison pills, white knight mergers, greenmail, and other defensive maneuvers to prevent a hostile takeover
9. Analyze the lawfulness of state antitakeover statutes
10. Describe the process of winding up, liquidating, and terminating a corporation

Chapter Contents

- Solicitation of Proxies
  Contemporary Business Environment The SEC's Proxy Rules
- Shareholder Proposals
  Ethical Perspective Shareholder Resolutions: Do They Promote Social Responsibility of Business?
- Mergers and Acquisitions
- Dissenting Shareholder Appraisal Rights
  Case 26.1 *In the Matter of the Appraisal of Shell Oil Company (DE)*
- Tender Offers
  Contemporary Business Environment Leveraged Buyouts
  Ethical Perspective Golden Parachutes: When Is the Landing Too "Cushy"?
- Fighting a Tender Offer
  Contemporary Business Environment Time-Warner-Paramount: Just Say No!
  Business Application The Saga of Paramount-Viacom-QVC
- State Antitakeover Statutes
  Case 26.2 *CTS Corp. v. Dynamica Corp. (U.S.)*
- Dissolution and Termination of Corporations
  Business Checklist When Shareholders Can Request Judicial Dissolution of a Corporation
  International Perspective The Exon-Florio Law: Regulating Foreign Acquisitions of U.S. Businesses
- Working the Web
- Chapter Summary
- Critical Legal Thinking Cases
- Ethics Cases
- Critical Legal Thinking Writing Assignment

> *The biggest corporation, like the humblest private citizen, must be held to strict compliance with the will of the people.*
>
> Theodore Roosevelt
> Speech, 1902

fundamental changes
Major events in a corporation's life. These include proxy contests, mergers, consolidations, hostile tender offers, and dissolution and termination.

"The usual trade and commerce is cheating all round by consent."
Thomas Fuller
Gnomologia (1732)

During the course of its existence, a corporation can go through certain **fundamental changes**. A corporation must seek shareholder approval for many changes. This requires the solicitation of votes or proxies from shareholders. Persons who want to take over the management of a corporation often conduct proxy contests to try to win over shareholder votes.

Corporations often engage in acquisitions of other corporations or businesses. This can occur by friendly merger or consolidation or by hostile tender offer. A corporation can erect certain barriers or impediments to a hostile takeover. Takeovers obviously affect bondholders of a corporation, as well as its stockholders.

Eventually, a corporation can be dissolved and terminated, either by voluntary agreement of the shareholders or, in some circumstances, by judicial order. Certain formalities must be followed in terminating a corporation.

This chapter discusses fundamental changes to a corporation, including the solicitation of proxies, mergers and consolidations, hostile tender offers, and the dissolution and termination of corporations.

SOLICITATION OF PROXIES

proxy card A written document signed by a shareholder that authorizes another person to vote the shareholder's shares.

Corporate shareholders have the right to vote on the election of directors, mergers, charter amendments, and the like. They can exercise their power to vote either in person or by proxy.[1] Voting by proxy is common in large corporations with thousands of shareholders located across the country and the world.

A **proxy** is a written document (often called a **proxy card**) completed and signed by the shareholder and sent to the corporation (see Exhibit 26.1). The proxy authorizes another

Exhibit 26.1
Proxy Card

KMART CORPORATION
ANNUAL MEETING OF SHAREHOLDERS
TO BE HELD ON MAY 27, 1992

Directors Recommend: A vote for election of directors and a vote for proposal(s) 2,3,4

Election of Directors 1- 1-Lilyan H. Affinito '95,2-Willie D. Davis '95,3-Joseph P. Flannery '95,4-Richard S. Miller '95,5-Enrique C. Falla '94

☐ For all nominees
☐ Withhold all nominees

Instructions: to withhold authority to vote for any individual nominee, place an 'X' in this box ☐ and strike a line through the nominee's name listed above.

FOR	AGAINST	ABSTAIN	
☐	☐	☐	2—Proposal to amend restated articles of incorporation to increase authorized common stock
☐	☐	☐	3—Proposal to approve director's stock plan
☐	☐	☐	4—Proposal to approve 1992 stock option plan
			Note Such other business as may properly come before the meeting or any adjournment thereof

person—the proxy holder—to vote the shares at the shareholders' meeting as directed by the shareholder. The proxy holder is often a director or officer of the corporation.

Federal Proxy Rules

Section 14(a) of the Securities Exchange Act of 1934 gives the Securities and Exchange Commission (SEC) the authority to regulate the solicitation of proxies.[2] The federal proxy rules promote full disclosure. In other words, management or any other party soliciting proxies from shareholders must prepare a **proxy statement** that fully describes (1) the matter for which the proxy is being solicited, (2) who is soliciting the proxy, and (3) any other pertinent information.

A copy of the proxy, the proxy statement, and all other solicitation material must be filed with the SEC at least 10 days before the materials are sent to the shareholders. If the SEC requires additional disclosures, the solicitation can be held up until these disclosures are made.

Exhibit 26.2 contains the cover page from a proxy statement.

Section 14(a) Provision of the Securities Exchange Act of 1934 that gives the SEC the authority to regulate the solicitation of proxies.

proxy statement A document that fully describes (1) the matter for which the proxy is being solicited, (2) who is soliciting the proxy, and (3) any other pertinent information.

Exhibit 26.2
Cover Page from a Proxy Statement

PROXY STATEMENT

SPECIAL MEETING OF SHAREHOLDERS OF NCR CORPORATION
MARCH 28, 1991

ANNUAL MEETING OF SHAREHOLDERS OF NCR CORPORATION
MARCH 28, 1991

This Proxy Statement is furnished by the Board of Directors (the "Board") of NCR Corporation ("NCR", or the "Company") to shareholders of the Company in connection with the solicitation of proxies by the Board for use at the Special Meeting of Shareholders (the "Special Meeting") to be held on Thursday, March 28, 1991, at 11:00 a.m. EST, and at the Annual Meeting of Shareholders (the "Annual Meeting") to be held on Thursday, March 28, 1991, at 11:30 a.m. EST, and at any adjournment or adjournments thereof. The Special Meeting is being called pursuant to the request of holders of more than 25 percent of the outstanding shares of Common Stock, par value $5.00 per share, of the Company ("Common Stock") in accordance with the Maryland General Corporation Law following solicitation by American Telephone and Telegraph Company ("AT&T"). The Board has fixed the close of business on March 1, 1991 as the record date for determining shareholders entitled to notice of, and to vote at, the Special Meeting and the Annual Meeting. This Proxy Statement and the enclosed BLUE proxy cards are first being mailed to shareholders on or about February 26, 1991. **The Company will furnish its Annual Report to Shareholders for the 1990 fiscal year at least 20 calendar days before the date of the Special Meeting and the Annual Meeting of Shareholders.**

At the Special Meeting, shareholders will consider, and vote upon, the proposals made by AT&T and opposed by the Board (the "AT&T Proposals") to remove all of the current members of the Board, to replace such members of the Board with AT&T's own nominees and to adopt a non-binding, precatory resolution relating to AT&T's effort to take over the Company. The AT&T Proposals were made by AT&T in furtherance of its attempt to take over the Company by means of an unsolicited tender offer by Subsidiary Corporation, a wholly owned subsidiary of AT&T, for all outstanding shares of Common Stock at a net cash price of $90 per share (the "Offer").

At the Annual Meeting, shareholders will consider, and vote upon, the election of four Class B Directors to hold office for three years, the appointment of Price Waterhouse as the Company's independent accountants for 1991 and three shareholder proposals (the "Shareholder Proposals"). AT&T has commenced its proxy solicitation to replace the

continued

Exhibit 26.2
(continued)

current Class B Directors with AT&T's nominees in furtherance of its attempt to acquire the Company.

Your Board has opposed the Offer and AT&T's efforts to acquire the Company because it unanimously determined that (i) the Offer is not in the best interests of the Company, its shareholders and other stakeholders, (ii) the consideration of $90 per share of Common Stock to be paid to shareholders pursuant to the Offer is grossly inadequate and unfair to the Company's shareholders and (iii) in light of the Company's future prospects, the Company's remaining independent would be a superior alternative to the Offer.

THE BOARD UNANIMOUSLY AND VIGOROUSLY OPPOSES AT&T'S SOLICITATION OF PROXIES AND URGES YOU NOT TO SIGN ANY PROXY CARD SENT TO YOU BY AT&T. WHETHER OR NOT YOU HAVE PREVIOUSLY EXECUTED A PROXY CARD SOLICITED BY AT&T, THE BOARD URGES YOU TO REJECT AT&T'S SOLICITATION AND SUPPORT YOUR BOARD BY PROMPTLY SIGNING, DATING, AND MAILING THE ENCLOSED BLUE SPECIAL MEETING AND BLUE ANNUAL MEETING PROXY CARDS.

Antifraud Provision

Section 14(a) of the Securities Exchange Act of 1934 prohibits material misrepresentations or omissions of a material fact in the proxy materials. Known-false statements of facts, reasons, opinions, or beliefs in proxy solicitation materials are actionable. Violations of this rule can result in civil and criminal actions by the SEC and the Justice Department, respectively. The courts have implied a private cause of action under this provision. Thus, shareholders who are injured by a material misrepresentation or omission in proxy materials can sue the wrongdoer and recover damages. The court can also order a new election if a violation is found.

Proxy Contests

Shareholders sometimes oppose the actions taken by the incumbent directors and management. These shareholders can challenge the incumbent management in a **proxy contest** in which both sides solicit proxies from the other shareholders. The side that receives the greatest number of votes wins the proxy contest. Such contests are usually held with regard to the election of directors.

Management must either (1) provide a list of shareholders to the dissenting group or (2) mail the proxy solicitation materials of the challenging group to the shareholders.

Reimbursement of Expenses In a proxy contest, both sides usually spend considerable amounts of money on legal expenses, media campaigns, mailers, telephone solicitations, and the like. If a proxy contest involves an issue of policy, the corporation must reimburse the incumbent management for their expenses whether they win or lose the proxy contest. The expenses of the dissenting group are reimbursed only if they win the proxy contest. If the proxy contest involves a personal matter, neither side may recover its expenses from the corporation.

---

proxy contest When opposing factions of shareholders and managers solicit proxies from other shareholders, the side that receives the greatest number of votes wins the proxy contest.

CAUTION
Section 14(a) of the 1934 act prohibits misrepresentations or omissions of a material fact in proxy materials. The SEC, U.S. Justice Department, or shareholders who are injured by the misrepresentation or omission may sue the wrongdoer.

CONTEMPORARY BUSINESS ENVIRONMENT

The SEC's Proxy Rules

Critics argued for a long time that the SEC's proxy rules did not require sufficient or clear enough disclosures for shareholders to make informed decisions. Finally, in 1992, after three years of study, the SEC adopted new proxy rules. The new rules are designed to allow shareholders to communicate more easily with each other and to give them additional information about management and its compensation.

Prior to the adoption of the 1992 rules, any shareholder who wished to communicate with 10 or more fellow shareholders faced the daunting and expensive task of filing proxy solicitation materials with the SEC. This tended to thwart shareholder communication and insulate management from shareholder criticism. The 1992 rules exempt oral and written communications to shareholders from any shareholder who is not seeking proxy voting authority from these requirements. For instance, shareholders can now ask each other how the corporation should be run or suggest changes. They have to register with the SEC only if they decide to solicit proxies.

Shareholders who own more than $5 million of a company's securities are not covered by this rule. They must still register any written communication to shareholders with the SEC.

Another 1992 rule change requires companies seeking proxies to "unbundle" the propositions set for shareholder vote so that the shareholders can vote on each separate issue. The old proxy rules allowed companies to bundle the propositions and present them as one package for a single shareholder vote. This tactic prevented shareholders from considering the merits of individual propositions.

The 1992 rules also require all companies to include performance charts in their annual reports. These charts must compare the company's stock performance with that of a general index of companies, such as the Standard and Poor's 500, and companies in its peer group index (e.g., retailers).

Finally, the 1992 rules broadened the disclosure requirements concerning executive compensation. The 1992 rules mandate that companies provide tables in their annual reports that succinctly summarize executive compensation for the chief executive officer and its four other most highly compensated executives for the past three years. The tables must disclose salary, stock options, stock appreciation rights, and long-term incentive plans of these executives, including the value of each item. This is the change that generated the most attention.

Proponents of these rule changes assert that shareholders will now get the information they need to make informed decisions. Some argue for disclosure of even more information to shareholders. Some company management members, particularly the most highly compensated executives, dislike the new rules.

SHAREHOLDER PROPOSALS

At times, shareholders might wish to present issues for a vote to other shareholders. The Securities Exchange Act of 1934 and SEC rules adopted thereunder permit a shareholder to submit a proposal to be considered by other shareholders if (1) the shareholder owned at least $1,000 of the corporation's stock for at least two years and (2) the proposal does not exceed 550 words. Such **shareholder proposals** are usually made when the corporation is soliciting proxies from its shareholders.

If management does not oppose the proposal, it may be included in the proxy materials issued by the corporation. Even if management is not in favor of the proposal, the shareholder has the right to include it in the proxy materials if it (1) does not violate federal or state law, (2) relates to the corporation's business, (3) concerns a policy issue (and not the day-to-day operations of the corporation), and (4) does not involve the payment of dividends. The (SEC) rules on what resolutions can be submitted to shareholders. A resolution needs 10 percent support the year it is introduced to be included on the ballot the next year.

shareholder proposal
A proposal submitted by a shareholder to other shareholders, provided he or she meets certain requirements set out in the Securities Exchange Act of 1934 and SEC rules adopted thereunder. The SEC determines if a shareholder proposal qualifies to be submitted to other shareholders for vote.

ETHICAL PERSPECTIVE

Shareholder Resolutions: Do They Promote Social Responsibility of Business?

In recent years, shareholders have become more active in corporate governance. This is evidenced by the hundreds of shareholder resolutions that are filed each year for vote at annual shareholder meetings.

During the 1980s, apartheid in South Africa was the primary *continued* issue of shareholder issues. Prompted by such proposals and the publicity they generated, many U.S. companies left South Africa. The number of shareholder proposals concerning South Africa have decreased in recent years as the government there has taken steps to give the black majority more power.

In the 1990s, the fastest growth is in shareholder resolutions urging more corporate sensitivity to the environment. The biggest corporate target in this area has been Exxon Corporation, whose March 1989 *Valdez* oil spill fouled the Alaska coastline. Other environmental issues that have appeared as shareholder resolutions address global warming of the ozone layer, overcutting of the rain forests in Brazil, and saving the spotted owl in the Northwest. Shareholder resolutions promoting environmental concerns are expected to continue to increase in the future.

Several new themes have emerged as well. Ever since the SEC, which oversees what resolutions can be included in proxy statements, reversed an earlier position and has now held that cigarette smoking is an area in which shareholders are entitled to vote, resolutions opposing tobacco products are appearing in proxy statements. These resolutions urge cigarette manufacturers, such as Philip Morris Co. and American Brands, to quit producing cigarettes and media companies to quit advertising them. Such resolutions are expected to increase in the future.

Other recent shareholder resolutions deal with proposals to prohibit animal testing by companies, place a moratorium on nuclear weapons and a ban on the use of nuclear power, force U.S. companies to pull out of British-ruled Northern Ireland, and dismantle antitakeover devices.

Most shareholder resolutions have a slim chance of being enacted because large-scale investors usually support management. They can, however, cause a corporation to change the way it does business. For example, to avoid the adverse publicity such issues can create, some corporations voluntarily adopt the changes contained in shareholder proposals. Others negotiate settlements with the sponsors of resolutions to get the measures off the agenda before the annual shareholder meetings.

Furthermore, shareholder resolutions are no longer just the bailiwick of individual or eccentric shareholders. Many state, municipal, and private pension funds now advocate socially responsible investing. These funds, which own billions of dollars of stock in American companies, are flexing their muscles and sponsoring shareholder resolutions to protect the environment, to promote ethics, and to curtail the greed of corporate managers.

1. Do you think shareholder proposals cause companies to act more socially responsible? Explain.
2. Should investors be socially conscious when making investments? Why or why not?

MERGERS AND ACQUISITIONS

BUSINESS BRIEF
Mergers, consolidations, share exchanges, and sale of assets are friendly in nature. That is, both corporations have agreed to the combination of corporations or acquisition of assets.

merger Occurs when one corporation is absorbed into another corporation and ceases to exist.

Corporations can agree to friendly acquisitions or combinations of one another. This can be by merger, consolidation, share exchange, or sale of assets. Each of these types of combinations is discussed in the following paragraphs.

Mergers

A **merger** occurs when one corporation is absorbed into another corporation and ceases to exist. The corporation that continues to exist is called the *surviving corporation*. The other is called the *merged corporation*.[3] The surviving corporation gains all the rights, privileges, powers, duties, obligations, and liabilities of the merged corporation. Title to property owned by the merged corporation transfers to the surviving corporation without formality or deeds. The shareholders of the merged corporation receive stock or securities of the surviving corporation or other consideration as provided in the plan of merger.

Suppose, for example, that Corporation A and Corporation B merge, and it is agreed that Corporation A will absorb Corporation B. Corporation A is the surviving corporation. Corporation B is the merged corporation. A symbolic representation of this merger is A + B = A (see Exhibit 26.3).

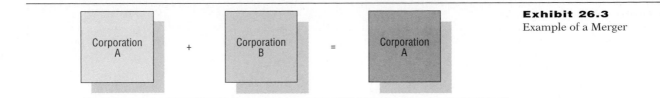

Exhibit 26.3
Example of a Merger

Consolidations

A **consolidation** occurs when two or more corporations combine to form an entirely new corporation (i.e., there is no surviving corporation). The new corporation is called the *consolidated corporation*, and the articles of incorporation of the new corporation replace the articles of incorporation of the component corporations.

consolidation Occurs when two or more corporations combine to form an entirely new corporation.

CONSIDER THIS EXAMPLE: Corporation A and Corporation B consolidate to form a new organization called Corporation C. A symbolic representation of this combination is A + **B** = **C** (see Exhibit 26.4).

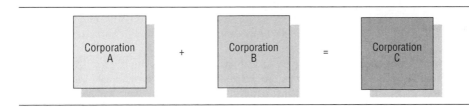

Exhibit 26.4
Example of a Consolidation

The new corporation accedes to all the rights, privileges, powers, duties, obligations, and liabilities of the constituent corporations. Title to property owned by the component corporations transfers to the new corporation without any formality. The shareholders receive stock or other securities in the consolidated corporation or other agreed-upon consideration.

Today, consolidations are not used very often because it is generally advantageous for one of the corporations to survive. The Revised Model Business Corporation Act (RMBCA) has deleted all reference to consolidations.

Share Exchanges

One corporation can acquire all the shares of another corporation through a **share exchange**. In a share exchange, both corporations retain their separate legal existence. After the exchange, one corporation (**parent corporation**) owns all of the shares of the other corporation (**subsidiary corporation**)[4] (see Exhibit 26.5.) Such exchanges are often used to create holding company arrangements (e.g., bank or insurance holding companies).

share exchange When one corporation acquires all the shares of another corporation while both corporations retain their separate legal existence.

parent corporation A corporation that owns the shares of another corporation.

CONSIDER THIS EXAMPLE: Suppose Corporation H is a bank holding company that wishes to acquire First Bank. Assume that Corporation H offers to exchange its shares for those of First Bank and that First Bank's shareholders approve of the transaction. After the share exchange, Corporation H is the parent corporation, and the First Bank is the wholly owned subsidiary of Corporation H.

Required Approvals

An ordinary merger or share exchange requires (1) the recommendation of the board of directors of each corporation and (2) an affirmative vote of the majority of shares of each corporation that are entitled to vote.[5] The articles of incorporation or corporate

Exhibit 26.5
Example of a
Share Exchange

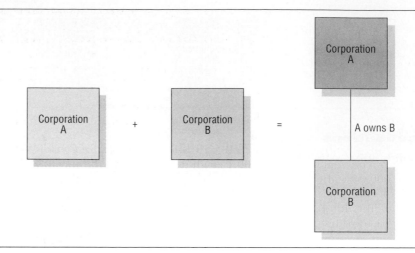

An ordinary merger or share exchange requires (1) the recommendation of the board of directors of each corporation and (2) an affirmative vote of the majority of shares of each corporation that are entitled to vote.

bylaws can require the approval of a **supramajority**, such as 80 percent of the voting shares.

The approval of the surviving corporation's shareholders is not required if the merger or share exchange increases the number of voting shares of the surviving corporation by 20 percent or less.[6]

The approved **articles of merger or share exchange** must be filed with the secretary of state. The state normally issues a **certificate of merger or share exchange** to the surviving corporation after all the formalities are met and the requisite fees are paid.[7]

Short-Form Mergers

short-form merger   A merger between a parent corporation and a subsidiary corporation that does not require the vote of the shareholders of either corporation or the board of directors of the subsidiary corporation.

If one corporation (called the *parent corporation*) owns 90 percent or more of the outstanding stock of another corporation (known as the *subsidiary corporation*), a **short-form merger** procedure may be followed to merge the two corporations. The short-form merger procedure is simpler than an ordinary merger because neither the approval of the shareholders of either corporation nor of the board of directors of the subsidiary corporation is needed. All that is required is the approval of the board of directors of the parent corporation.[8]

Sale or Lease of Assets

sale or lease of assets
When one corporation sells, leases, or otherwise disposes of all, or substantially all, of its property in other than the usual and regular course of business.

A corporation may sell, lease, or otherwise dispose of all, or substantially all, of its property in other than the usual and regular course of business. Such a sale or lease transaction requires (1) the recommendation of the board of directors and (2) an affirmative vote of the majority of the shares of the selling or leasing corporation that is entitled to vote (unless a greater vote is required).[9] This rule prevents the board of directors from selling all or most of the assets of the corporation without shareholder approval.

DISSENTING SHAREHOLDER APPRAISAL RIGHTS

The court must determine the "fair value" of the shares of dissenting shareholders. Courts usually use appraisers to assist in determining this value.

Specific shareholders sometimes object to a proposed ordinary or short-form merger, share exchange, or sale or lease of all or substantially all of the property of the corporation, even though the transaction received the required approvals. Objecting shareholders are provided a statutory right to dissent and obtain payment of the fair value of their shares.[10] This is referred to as a **dissenting shareholder appraisal right** (or appraisal right). Shareholders have no other recourse unless the transaction is unlawful or fraudulent.

The corporation must notify shareholders of the existence of their appraisal rights before the transaction can be voted on.[11] To obtain appraisal rights, a dissenting shareholder must (1) deliver written notice of his or her intent to demand payment of his or her shares to the corporation before the vote is taken and (2) not vote his or her shares in favor of the proposed action.[12] The shareholder must deposit his or her share certificates with the corporation.[13] Shareholders who fail to comply with these statutory procedures lose their appraisal rights.

As soon as the proposed action is taken, the corporation must pay each dissenting shareholder the amount the corporation estimates to be the fair value of his or her shares, plus accrued interest.[14] If the dissenter is dissatisfied, the corporation must petition the court to determine the fair value of the shares.[15]

After a hearing, the court will issue an order declaring the fair value of the shares. Appraisers may be appointed to help in determining this value. Court costs and appraisal fees usually are paid by the corporation. However, the court can assess these costs against the dissenters if they acted arbitrarily, vexatiously, or not in good faith.[16]

The court had to determine the appraisal value of a company's shares in the following case.

dissenting shareholder appraisal rights
Shareholders who object to a proposed merger, share exchange, or sale or lease of all or substantially all of the property of a corporation have a right to have their shares valued by the court and receive cash payment of this value from the corporation.

CASE 26.1

In the Matter of the Appraisal of Shell Oil Company
607 A.2d 1213 (1992) Supreme Court of Delaware

Facts Royal Dutch Petroleum Company (Royal Dutch), a large natural resource conglomerate, owned 94.6 percent of the stock of Shell Oil Company (Shell). The remaining shares of Shell were held by minority public shareholders. On June 7, 1985, Royal Dutch effectuated a short-form merger with Shell and offered $60 cash per share for the outstanding shares of Shell it did not own. After the merger was complete, 1,005,001 shares had not accepted the offer and qualified for appraisal rights. The Delaware Chancery Court conducted an appraisal hearing. The parties offered extensive evidence through expert witnesses. These experts gave the following estimated per share value for Shell's shares:

Valuation Method	Shell's Expert	Shareholders' Expert
Liquidation value	$57	$100
Comparative value	$60	$106
Market value	$43–$45	$92–$143

Liquidation value was the estimated value if Shell were dissolved and its assets sold. Comparative value was an estimate based on a price reflected by prices in similar transactions in the oil and gas industry. Market value was an estimated price that Shell shares would sell for without the effect of merger speculation.

Issue What price should Shell be required to pay its minority shareholders who demanded appraisal rights?

Decision The chancery court determined that the fair value was $71.20 per share. It further held that the shareholders were entitled to 10 percent interest on that amount from the date of the merger to the date of payment. The Supreme Court of Delaware affirmed this award.

Reason The chancery court assigned little or no weight to the valuations reached by the experts because it found that they lacked objectivity. The court stated, "In this case, each party's valuation evidence was replete with deficiencies and so susceptible to bias that indiscriminate endorsement of either would have been indefensible. The opinions expressed by the expert witnesses significantly reflected the desires of their clients." The chancery court reviewed the evidence and used its broad discretion to arrive at a valuation of $71.20 per share.

CASE QUESTIONS

Critical Legal Thinking Should the law provide dissenting shareholder appraisal rights? Why or why not?

Ethics Do you think expert witnesses act objectively?

Business Implication Is there a temptation for a company to "low-ball" the cash-out price offered to shareholders in a merger? Explain.

TENDER OFFERS

tender offer An offer that an acquirer makes directly to a target corporation's shareholders in an effort to acquire the target corporation.

target corporation The corporation that is proposed to be acquired in a tender offer situation.

tender offeror The party that makes a tender offer.

Recall that a merger, a consolidation, a share exchange, or a sale of assets all require the approval of the board of directors of the corporation whose assets or shares are to be acquired. If the board of directors of the target corporation does not agree to the merger or acquisition, the acquiring corporation can make a **tender offer** for the shares directly to the shareholders of the **target corporation**. The shareholders each make an individual decision about whether to sell their shares to the **tender offeror** (see Exhibit 26.6). Such offers are often referred to as *hostile tender offers*.

The tender offeror's board of directors must approve the offer, although the shareholders do not have to approve. The offer can be made for all or a portion of the shares of the target corporation.

In a tender offer, the tendering corporation and the target corporation retain their separate legal status. A successful tender offer is sometimes, however, followed by a merger of the two corporations.

Exhibit 26.6
Illustration of a Tender Offer

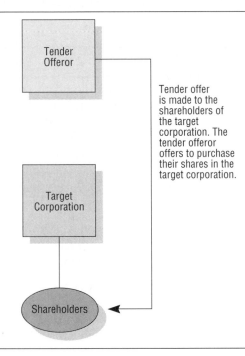

Tender offer is made to the shareholders of the target corporation. The tender offeror offers to purchase their shares in the target corporation.

The Williams Act

Prior to 1968, tender offers were not federally regulated. However, securities that were issued in conjunction with such offers had to be registered with the SEC or qualify for an exemption from registration. Tender offers made with cash were not subject to any federal disclosure requirements.

Williams Act An amendment to the Securities Exchange Act of 1934 made in 1968 that specifically regulates all tender offers.

In 1968, Congress enacted the **Williams Act** as an amendment to the Securities Exchange Act of 1934.[17] This act specifically regulates all tender offers, whether they are made with securities, cash, or other consideration. The act establishes certain disclosure requirements and antifraud provisions.

Tender Offer Rules

The Williams Act does not require the tender offeror to notify either the management of the target company or the SEC until the offer is made.[18] Detailed information regarding the terms, conditions, and other information concerning the tender offer must be disclosed at that time.

CONTEMPORARY BUSINESS ENVIRONMENT

Leveraged Buyouts

A raider or other party making a tender offer usually does not have the hundreds of millions or billions of dollars necessary to purchase the stock from the shareholders of the target corporation. Instead, a raider relies heavily on the fact that the money can be raised from creditors (e.g., banks). Many tender offers are not possible without such loans. Because of the use of borrowed money, these acquisitions are called **leveraged buyouts (LBOs)**.

A typical LBO works as follows. The raider identifies a potential target and then contacts a large commercial bank and an investment banker. The commercial bank, for a large fee, agrees to supply some of the funds necessary to make the initial acquisition. The bank will be paid off at a later date, after the acquisition is successful. The funds to pay back the bank usually come from the raider selling off some of

the assets of the target corporation. These bank loans are often referred to as **bridge loans**.

Most of the rest of the purchase price comes from money raised by the investment banker by selling **junk bonds** of the acquiring firm to investors. Junk bonds are nothing more than risky bonds that pay a higher rate of interest than normal corporate bonds. Generally, the buyers are banks, savings and loan associations, pension funds, investment pools, and wealthy individuals. The investment banker is paid a huge fee by the raider for raising this money.

With the money in hand—or at least the pledge that the money will be there when it is needed—the raider commences its hostile tender offer for the shares of the target corporation. When the desired number of shares are tendered, the tender offer is closed using the money borrowed from

the bank and raised through the sale of junk bonds. The raider's investment in the tender offer usually amounts to 5 percent or 10 percent of the total.

After the tender offer is completed, the tender offeror—which is usually a shell corporation that is saddled with huge debts (i.e., the bank loans and junk bonds)—merges with the target corporation. The target corporation has all of the assets (e.g., brand names) and income. The resulting entity is a highly leveraged corporation. Its capital structure consists of a low amount of equity and huge amounts of debt.

The raider usually has to sell off some of the assets to pay the bank loans, fees, and other expenses of the takeover. Some LBOs are successful, but others run into problems because the income from the remaining assets is not sufficient to pay the interest on the junk bonds.

Tender offers are governed by the following rules:

1. The offer cannot be closed before 20 business days after the commencement of the tender offer.
2. The offer must be extended for 10 business days if the tender offeror increases the number of shares that it will take or the price that it will pay for the shares.
3. The **fair price rule** stipulates that any increase in price paid for shares tendered must be offered to all shareholders, even those who have previously tendered their shares.
4. The **pro rata rule** holds that the shares must be purchased on a pro rata basis if too many shares are tendered.

A shareholder who tenders his or her shares has the absolute right to withdraw them at any time prior to the closing of the tender offer. The dissenting shareholder appraisal rights are not available.

Antifraud Provision

Section 14(e) of the Williams Act prohibits fraudulent, deceptive, and manipulative practices in connection with a tender offer.[19] Violations of this section can result in civil charges brought by the SEC or criminal charges brought by the Justice Department. The courts have implied a private civil cause of action under Section 14(e). Therefore, a shareholder who has been injured by a violation of Section 14(e) can sue the wrongdoer for damages.

fair price rule A rule that says any increase in price paid for shares tendered must be offered to all shareholders, even those who have previously tendered their shares.

pro rata rule A rule that says shares must be purchased on a pro rata basis if too many shares are tendered.

Section 14(e) A provision of the Williams Act that prohibits fraudulent, deceptive, and manipulative practices in connection with a tender offer.

ETHICAL PERSPECTIVE

Golden Parachutes: When Is the Landing Too "Cushy"?

The term *golden parachute* has been coined to describe the large severance payments received by top executives when they leave their employ at a corporation. They are called "golden" because of their lucrative nature. They are called "parachutes" because they are "pulled" when an executive leaves or is fired from a company that has been taken over.

Golden parachutes—formally called change-in-control severance agreement plans—are long-term employment contracts. They usually provide that all cash payments and stock options due under the contract become due and payable immediately upon the occurrence of the trigger—the takeover of the company.

CONSIDER THIS EXAMPLE: A company enters into a three year employment contract with its president and agrees to pay a $1 million salary annually and grants options to purchase 10,000 shares of the company stock at $10 per share. The contract includes a golden parachute clause in the event of a takeover. Suppose the company is taken over in a $15-per-share tender offer. The president can "pull" his parachute and demand $3 million in salary as well as making $1.5 million profit by exercising her stock options.

Two benefits of golden parachutes are often cited. First, they are necessary to lure talented executives and keep them from looking for other positions when a takeover of the company is pending. Second, they act as an anti-takeover device, thus protecting the company from hostile takeovers. Both of these reasons have been challenged as a cover-up for the real reason for golden parachutes: top executives' greed.

Golden parachutes are often criticized by lower-level managers and rank-and-file workers who complain that management can walk away in comfort after a takeover, whereas they are left hanging out to dry. To address these concerns, some companies have added "silver parachutes" to protect lower-level managers and "tin parachutes" to protect wage-earning workers in case of a takeover. As the names indicate, the compensation paid under these plans is much lower than that paid under golden parachutes.

In the past, the SEC has held that golden parachutes need only be approved by a company's outside directors, rather than by a vote of the shareholders. In a recent decision involving a proposed golden parachute to be installed by Transamerica Corporation, the SEC changed its position and ruled that the company must submit the plan for shareholder vote. This decision sends a signal that golden parachutes will receive closer scrutiny in the future than they have in the past.

1. Do you think top executives' compensation is too high? Explain.
2. Are golden parachutes a legitimate compensation scheme? Or are they an egregious example of management greed?

FIGHTING A TENDER OFFER

BUSINESS BRIEF

Target corporations initiate and implement a variety of defensive maneuvers and tactics to defend against unwanted hostile tender offers.

The incumbent management of many targets of hostile tender offers do not want the corporation taken over by the tender offeror. Therefore, they engage in varied activities to impede and defeat the tender offer.

Defensive Strategies and Tactics

Some of the strategies and tactics used by incumbent management in defending against hostile tender offers follow:

crown jewel A valuable asset of the target corporation that the tender offeror particularly wants to acquire in the tender offer.

1. *Persuasion of shareholders.* Media campaigns are organized to convince shareholders that the tender offer is not in their best interests.
2. *Delaying lawsuits.* Lawsuits are filed alleging that the tender offer violates securities laws, antitrust laws, or other laws. The time gained by this tactic gives management the opportunity to erect or implement other defensive maneuvers.
3. *Selling a crown jewel.* Such assets as profitable divisions or real estate that are particularly attractive to outside interests are sold. This tactic makes the target corporation less attractive to the tender offeror.

4. *Adopting a poison pill.* **Poison pills** are defensive strategies that are built into the target corporation's articles of incorporation, corporate bylaws, or contracts and leases. For example, contracts and leases may provide that they will expire if the ownership of the corporation changes hands. These tactics make the target corporation more expensive to the tender offeror.

5. *White knight merger.* White knight mergers are mergers with friendly parties, that is, parties that promise to leave the target corporation and/or its management intact.

6. *Pac-man (or reverse) tender offer.* The target corporation makes a tender offer on the tender offeror. Thus, the target corporation tries to purchase the tender offeror.

7. *Issuing additional stock.* Placing additional stock on the market increases the number of outstanding shares that the tender offeror must purchase in order to gain control of the target corporation.

8. *Creating an employee stock ownership plan (ESOP).* A company creates an ESOP and places a certain percentage of the corporation's securities (e.g., 15 percent) in it. The ESOP is then expected to vote the shares it owns against the potential acquirer in a proxy contest or tender offer because the beneficiaries (i.e., the employees) have a vested interest in keeping the company intact.

9. *Flip-over and flip-in rights plans.* These plans provide that existing shareholders of the target corporation may convert their shares for a greater amount (e.g., twice the value) of shares of the acquiring corporation (**flip-over rights plan**) or debt securities of the target company (**flip-in rights plan**). Rights plans are triggered if the acquiring firm acquires a certain percentage (e.g., 20 percent) of the shares of the target corporation. They make it more expensive for the acquiring firm to take over the target corporation.

10. *Greenmail and standstill agreements.* Most tender offerors purchase a block of stock in the target corporation before making an offer. Occasionally, the tender offeror will agree to give up its tender offer and agree not to purchase any further shares if the target corporation agrees to buy back the stock at a premium over fair market value. This payment is called **greenmail**. The agreement of the tender offeror to abandon its tender offer and not purchase any additional stock is called a *standstill agreement*.

There are many other strategies and tactics that target companies initiate and implement in defending against a tender offer.

poison pill An item that appears in the target corporation's articles of incorporation, bylaws, or other documents that triggers an event that makes the target corporation unattractive to potential tender offerors.

greenmail The purchase by a target corporation of its stock from an actual or perceived tender offeror at a premium.

CONTEMPORARY BUSINESS ENVIRONMENT

Time-Warner-Paramount: Just Say No!

Time, Inc. (Time) is a publishing company that publishes *People, Money, Sports Illustrated,* and other magazines and newspapers and owns cable television and pay television channels. Warner Communications, Inc. (Warner) is a communications company that produces and sells movies, television programs, and records, and owns cable stations. In 1989, after years of negotiations, Time and

Warner agreed to a merger. Based on the agreed-upon ratio of exchange, Time shareholders were to receive $120 in stock of the new Time/Warner for each share of Time stock they owned. The shareholder meetings to vote on the merger were set.

Paramount Communications, Inc. (Paramount) is a film production and distribution company. For years it had been looking for

an acquisition in the publishing and communications industry. Two weeks before the Time shareholders were to vote on the planned merger with Warner, Paramount announced a hostile tender offer for Time's shares at $175 per share.

Time, which was obviously going to lose the shareholder vote, canceled the proposed merger

continued

with Warner and made a friendly tender offer to acquire 50 percent of Warner's stock for $70 per share. This acquisition would make Time too big for Paramount to take over. In addition, the vote of Time shareholders would not be required.

Time had other defensive maneuvers in place as well. These consisted of flip-over and flip-in rights plans that would permit Time shareholders to exchange their Time shares for approximately twice the value of the tender offerors' securities if the poison pills were removed by Time's management before the tender offer was completed.

Paramount sued Time, alleging that Time management's refusal to dismantle the poison pills and put Time on the block violated their fiduciary duty. In defense, Time argued that the merger of Time and Warner was in the best interests of Time shareholders over the long run. In other words, the long-term benefits of the combination of Time and Warner and their cultures would create synergism that would pay off in the future; Paramount's tender offer offered only one-time short-term profits.

The Delaware court, applying the business judgment rule, sided with Time. The court held that

the projected long-term benefits to Time shareholders justified Time management's refusal to dismantle the poison pills. The court stated, "The corporation law does not operate on the theory that directors are obligated to follow the wishes of a majority of shares. In fact, directors, not shareholders, are charged with the duty to manage the firm." Thus, incumbent management of a target corporation can "just say no" to a tender offer as long as it can show that it is acting in the long-term interests of the shareholders. [*Paramount Communications, Inc. v. Time, Inc.* 571 A.2d 1140 (Del. 1990)]

Business Judgment Rule

fiduciary duty The duty the directors of a corporation owe to act carefully and honestly when acting on behalf of the corporation.

The board of directors of a corporation owes a **fiduciary duty** to the corporation and its shareholders. This duty, which requires the board to act carefully and honestly, is truly tested when a tender offer is made for the stock of the company. That is because shareholders and others then ask whether the board's initiation and implementation of defensive measures were taken in the best interests of the shareholders or to protect the board's own interests and jobs.

business judgment rule A rule that protects decisions of the board of directors that acts on an informed basis, in good faith, and in the belief that the decision was in the best interests of the corporation and its shareholders.

The legality of defensive strategies is examined using the **business judgment rule**. This rule protects the decisions of a board of directors that acts on an informed basis, in good faith, and in the honest belief that the action taken was in the best interests of the corporation and its shareholders.[20] In the context of a tender offer, the defensive measures chosen by the board must be reasonable in relation to the threat posed.[21]

BUSINESS APPLICATION

The Saga of Paramount-Viacom-QVC

In the past, the Delaware courts generally sided with the management of target companies in suits involving hostile raids. In most of these cases, the Delaware courts upheld defensive maneuvers taken by target companies to fend off unwanted suitors. This long line of cases ended with a recent Delaware court decision concerning the takeover of Paramount Communications, Inc.

It all started on September 12, 1993, when Viacom, Inc. (Viacom) and Paramount Communications, Inc. (Paramount) announced a friendly merger agreement. Basically, Viacom and its chairman and largest shareholder, billionaire Sumner Redstone, were taking over Paramount. Viacom controlled national cable networks, including Showtime and The Movie Channel. Paramount's hold-

ings included Paramount Pictures, the Simon & Schuster publishing house, Madison Square Garden, the New York Knicks basketball team, and the New York Rangers hockey team. Both sides touted the synergism of the marriage of these two companies into a media colossus.

There was only one hitch to this merger: Five days later QVC Network, Inc. (QVC), a rival cable operator led by Barry Diller, made a $90-per-share hostile bid for Paramount that topped Viacom's offer. QVC owned the Home Shopping Channel. Paramount's board of directors, which was dominated by its chairman, Martin Davis, did not want to be taken over by QVC. Paramount's board adopted the following anti-takeover strategies:

1. A **"no-shop" provision** whereby the Paramount board guaranteed Viacom that it would not investigate QVC's offer or meet with QVC.
2. A **lockup option** that granted Viacom (but not QVC) the right to buy 23.7 million shares of Paramount at $69.14 each if a bidder other than Viacom bought Paramount. (This would cost a competing bidder almost $400 million.)

3. An agreement to drop certain **poison pill** defenses as to Viacom, but not as to QVC. (Thus, Viacom could pursue its acquisition of Paramount, but QVC could not.)

QVC sued Paramount in Delaware Chancery Court, alleging that these tactics violated the Paramount board of directors' fiduciary duties to the corporation and its shareholders. To many observers' surprise, the Delaware court agreed with QVC. The court ruled that the no-shop provision was unlawful, stating that Paramount directors "had a duty to continue their search for the best value available to shareholders." The court also invalidated the "lockup option" stock purchase plan as being an illegal transfer of corporate wealth to Viacom at the expense of Paramount shareholders.

The chancery court held that the poison pills Paramount had erected must be dismantled for QVC (and any other bidder) as they had been for Viacom. The court also ordered that Paramount be put on the block and auctioned to the highest bidder. The Delaware Supreme Court affirmed this decision.

Both sides lined up their lawyers, investment banks, and commercial banks, as well as enlisting other companies, to assist them in the bidding process. Most significantly, Viacom merged with Blockbuster Entertainment, a national video rental chain, in making its bid. On February 15, 1994, after escalating bids by both sides, the five-month saga ended when Viacom won the right to buy Paramount with a $10-billion-plus bid.

STATE ANTITAKEOVER STATUTES

Many states have enacted statutes that are aimed at protecting corporations that are either incorporated in or do business within the state from hostile takeovers. Many of these state statutes have been challenged as being unconstitutional because they violate the Williams Act and the Commerce and Supremacy Clauses of the U.S. Constitution.

In the following case, the U.S. Supreme Court held that a state antitakeover law was constitutional.

state antitakeover statutes Statutes enacted by state legislatures that protect corporations incorporated in or doing business in the state from hostile takeovers.

CASE 26.2

CTS Corp. v. Dynamics Corp.
481 U.S. 69, 107 S.Ct. 1637, 95 L.Ed.2d 67 (1987) United States Supreme Court

Facts On March 4, 1986, Indiana enacted the Control Share Acquisitions Chapter (Act). The act covers corporations that (1) are incorporated in Indiana and have at least 100 shareholders, (2) have their primary place of business or substantial assets in Indiana, and (3) have either 10 percent of their shareholders in Indiana or 10 percent of their shares owned by Indiana residents. The act provides that if an entity acquires 20 percent or more of the voting shares of a covered corporation, the acquirer loses voting rights to these shares unless a majority of the disinterested shareholders of the acquired corporation vote to restore such voting rights. The acquirer can request that such vote be held within 50 days after its acquisition. If the shareholders do not restore the voting rights, the target corporation may redeem the shares from the acquirer at fair market value, but it is not required to do so.

continued

On March 10, 1986, Dynamics Corporation of America (Dynamics), a Delaware corporation, announced a tender offer for one million shares of CTS Corporation (CTS), an Indiana corporation covered by the act. The purchase of these shares would have brought Dynamics' voting interest in CTS to 27.5 percent. Dynamics sued in federal court, alleging that Indiana's Control Share Acquisition Chapter was unconstitutional. The federal district court held for Dynamics. The court of appeals affirmed. CTS appealed.

Issue Does the Indiana Control Share Acquisitions Chapter conflict with the Williams Act or violate the Commerce Clause of the U.S. Constitution by unduly burdening interstate commerce?

Decision The U.S. Supreme Court held that the Indiana Control Share Acquisitions Chapter neither conflicted with the Williams Act nor violated the Commerce Clause of the U.S. Constitution. Reversed.

Reason In finding that the state law did not conflict with the Williams Act, the Supreme Court stated: "By allowing such shareholders to vote as a group, the act protects them from the coercive aspects of some tender offers. If, for example, shareholders believe that a successful tender offer will be followed by a purchase of nontendering shares at a depressed price [in a second-tier merger], individual shareholders may tender their shares—even if they doubt the tender offer is in the corporation's best interest—to protect themselves from being forced to sell their shares at a depressed price. In such a situation under the Indiana Act, the shareholders as a group, acting in the corporation's best interest, could reject the offer although individual shareholders might be inclined to accept it. The desire of the Indi-

ana legislature to protect shareholders of Indiana corporations from this type of coercive offer does not conflict with the Williams Act. Rather, it furthers the federal policy of investor protection."

In holding that the state antitakeover statute did not unduly burden interstate commerce, the Court stated: "Every state in this country has enacted laws regulating corporate governance. By prohibiting certain transactions and regulating others, such laws necessarily affect certain aspects of interstate commerce. This necessarily is true with respect to corporations with shareholders in states other than the state of incorporation. Large corporations that are listed on national exchanges, or even regional exchanges, will have shareholders in many states and shares that are traded frequently. This beneficial free market system depends at its core upon the fact that a corporation is organized under, and governed by, the law of a single jurisdiction, traditionally the corporate law of the state of its incorporation. It thus is an accepted part of the business landscape in this country for states to create corporations, to prescribe their powers, and to define the rights that are acquired by purchasing their shares."

CASE QUESTIONS

Critical Legal Thinking Should states be permitted to adopt antitakeover statutes? Why or why not? Whom do you think these statutes actually protect?

Ethics Is it ethical for a target corporation's management to assert a state antitakeover statute?

Business Implication What are the economic effects of a state antitakeover statute?

DISSOLUTION AND TERMINATION OF CORPORATIONS

The life of a corporation may be terminated voluntarily or involuntarily. The methods for dissolving and terminating corporations are discussed in the following paragraphs.

Voluntary Dissolution

voluntary dissolution A corporation that has begun business or issued shares can be dissolved upon recommendation of the board of directors and a majority vote of the shares entitled to vote.

A corporation can be **voluntarily dissolved**. If the corporation has not commenced business or issued any shares, it may be dissolved by a vote of the majority of the incorporators or initial directors.[22] After that, the corporation can be voluntarily dissolved if the board of directors recommends dissolution and a majority of shares entitled to vote (or a greater number if required by the articles of incorporation or bylaws) votes for dissolution.[23]

For a voluntary dissolution to be effective, **articles of dissolution** must be filed with the secretary of state of the state of incorporation. A corporation is dissolved upon the effective date of the articles of dissolution.[24]

Administrative Dissolution

The secretary of state can obtain **administrative dissolution** of a corporation if the corporation (1) failed to file an annual report, (2) failed for 60 days to maintain a registered agent in the state, (3) failed for 60 days after a change of its registered agent to file a statement of such change with the secretary of state, (4) did not pay its franchise fee or (5) the period of duration stated in the corporation's articles of incorporation has expired.[25]

Administrative dissolution is simple. If the corporation does not cure the default within 60 days of being notified of it, the secretary of state issues a **certificate of dissolution** that dissolves the corporation.[26]

> **administrative dissolution** Involuntary dissolution of a corporation that is ordered by the secretary of state if the corporation has failed to comply with certain procedures required by law.

Judicial Dissolution

A corporation can be involuntarily dissolved by a judicial proceeding. **Judicial dissolution** can be instituted by shareholders, creditors, or the state for any reason listed in the following paragraphs. If a court judicially dissolves a corporation, it enters a **decree of dissolution** that specifies the date of dissolution.[27] The courts are often reluctant to dissolve a corporation by judicial decree.

> **judicial dissolution** Occurs when a corporation is dissolved by a court proceeding instituted by shareholders, creditors or the state. Permitted only for certain reasons.

Dissolution by the State The attorney general of the state of incorporation can obtain judicial dissolution of a corporation if the corporation (1) procured its articles of incorporation through fraud or (2) exceeded or abused the authority conferred upon it by law.[28]

Dissolution by Creditors Corporate creditors can obtain a judicial dissolution of an insolvent corporation if (1) the creditor's claim was reduced to judgment and the execution of the judgment has been returned unsatisfied or (2) the corporation admitted in writing that the creditor's claim is due and owing.[29]

✔ **BUSINESS CHECKLIST**

When Shareholders Can Request Judicial Dissolution of a Corporation

Shareholders and directors of smaller, closely held corporations sometimes disagree about management and policy decisions concerning the operation of the business. What happens if there is a deadlock as to the direction the corporation should take, or if damage is being caused to corporate assets? Most corporation statutes solve this problem by providing that a shareholder can go to court and seek judicial dissolution of a corporation in the following situations:

- The directors are deadlocked in the management of corporate affairs, the shareholders are unable to break the deadlock, and irreparable injury is being suffered by or threatened to the corporation;
- The shareholders are deadlocked in voting power and have failed for at least two consecutive annual meetings to elect directors whose terms have expired;
- The acts of the directors or those in control of the corporation are illegal, oppressive, or fraudulent; or
- The corporate assets are being misapplied or wasted. [RMBCA § 14.30(2)]

Winding Up, Liquidation, and Termination

A dissolved corporation continues its corporate existence but may not carry on any business, except as required to **wind up and liquidate** its business and affairs.[30]

> **winding up and liquidation** The process by which a dissolved corporation's assets are collected, liquidated, and distributed to creditors, shareholders, and other claimants.

In a voluntary dissolution, the liquidation is usually carried out by the board of directors. If (1) the dissolution is involuntary or (2) the dissolution is voluntary but the directors refuse to carry out the liquidation, a court-appointed receiver carries out the winding up and liquidation of the corporation.[31]

termination The ending of a corporation that occurs only after the winding up of the corporation's affairs, liquidation of its assets, and distribution of the proceeds to the claimants.

Termination occurs only after the winding up of the corporation's affairs, the liquidation of its assets, and the distribution of the proceeds to the claimants. The liquidation of its assets are paid to claimants according to the following priority: (1) expenses of liquidation and creditors according to their respective lien and contract rights, (2) preferred shareholders according to their liquidation preferences and contract rights, and (3) common shareholders.

The dissolution of a corporation does not impair any rights or remedies available against the corporation, or its directors, officers, or shareholders for any right or claim existing or incurred prior to dissolution.

INTERNATIONAL PERSPECTIVE

The Exon-Florio Law: Regulating Foreign Acquisitions of U.S. Businesses

Until 1988, foreign investors had virtually the same rights to acquire businesses located in the United States as domestic investors. However, the **Exon-Florio Law** of 1988 [50 U.S.C. 2170], as amended by the **Byrd-Exon Amendment** of 1992 [Pub. L. No. 102–484, Sec. 837], mandates the President of the United States to suspend, prohibit, or dismantle the acquisition of U.S. businesses by foreign investors if there is credible evidence that the foreign investor might take action that threatens to impair the "national security."

Exon-Florio is administered through the **Committee on Foreign Investment in the United States (CFIUS)**, an interagency committee that is chaired by the U.S. Treasury Department. The provisions apply to mergers, acquisitions, takeovers, stock purchases, asset purchases, joint ventures, and proxy contests that would result in foreign control of U.S. businesses engaged in interstate commerce in the United States. The U.S. business could be a corporation, partnership, sole proprietorship, or some other business. The size of the U.S. operation is irrelevant.

Exon-Florio and the regulations adopted thereunder do not define the term *national security*. The Treasury Department has interpreted the term broadly to include not only defense contractors but also other businesses. The following factors must be considered in conducting a national security analysis of a proposed foreign U.S. investment:

1. The domestic production needed for defense requirements for national security.
2. The potential effect of a transaction on the international technological leadership of the United States in areas affecting national security.
3. The potential effect of a transaction on sales of military goods to any country that is identified as supporting terrorism.

The term *control* includes any investment exceeding 10 percent ownership in a U.S. business by a foreign investor. The Exon-Florio provision does not apply to "greenfield" investments by foreigners—that is, startups of new businesses.

When a foreign investor proposes to acquire an interest in a U.S. business, it may voluntarily notify CFIUS of its intention. CFIUS must commence its investigation within 30 days after receipt of written notification of the transaction. The investigation must be completed within 45 days after receipt of such notice, and the President must announce a decision to take no action no later than 15 days after completion of the investigation. If the President finds a threat to the national security, the acquisition may be prohibited. If the foreign investor chooses not to notify CFIUS and completes the acquisition, it remains indefinitely subject to divestment if the President subsequently determines that the acquisition threatens the national security. The President's decision is not subject to judicial review.

Proponents of Exon-Florio argue that the law is needed to protect U.S. interests in vital industries. Critics allege that the law could discourage foreign investments in the United States.

WORKING THE WEB

Law firm Web sites vary in form and content. Some are a simple page listing the specialties of the firm and a link to the firm's e-mail address. Others are more well developed and elaborate. Some contain general legal information and links to other sources of information. Here are some law firm Web sites that have won numerous awards:

Brobeck, Phleger & Harrison This site directs new visitors to a virtual "receptionist" where they will find general information about the firm and a breakdown of what is available through the site.

    Visit at http://www.brobeck.com

Satterlie, Stephens, Burke & Burke This site has pages devoted to immigration and cyberlaw. It contains attractive graphics and is easy to use.

    Visit at http://www.ssbb.com

Procopio, Cory, Hargreaves & Savitch This Web site looks like a law firm's physical office space with content organized in different rooms.

    Visit at http://www.procopio.com

KuesterLaw This is one of the most comprehensive collections of technology resources on the Web, with original materials as well as links to other sites, all in an easy to navigate format.

    Visit at http://www.kuesterlaw.com

The Tax Prophet This site combines snappy graphics with an abundance of content and a bit of humor to create one of the most popular legal sites on the Internet.

    Visit at http://www.taxprophet.com

CYBER EXERCISES:

1. On the Brobeck, Phleger & Harrison site, visit the Business Litigation Practice Area. Where does Albert R. Karel practice?
2. Where is the principal office of Satterlee, Stephens, Burke & Burke?
3. From the Procopio Web site, go to the law library. Under Starting a Business, find and print out a document called *How to Collect and Pay Sales Tax*.
4. What is the specialty of Jeffrey Kuester's firm?
5. In what newspaper does the Tax Prophet's columns appear?

CHAPTER SUMMARY

SOLICITATION OF PROXIES, P. 642

Solicitation of Proxies	1. *Proxy*. Shareholders can exercise their right to vote on the election of directors, mergers, charter amendments, and the like, either in person or by *proxy*. 2. *Proxy card*. A written document signed by a shareholder that authorizes another person to vote the shareholder's shares.
Federal Proxy Rules	*Section 14(a)*. Provision of the Securities Exchange Act of 1934 that authorizes the *Securities and Exchange Commission (SEC)* to regulate the solicitation of proxies. 1. *Solicitation of proxies*. Occurs when management or others seek to obtain proxies from a corporation's shareholders. 2. *Proxy statement*. Written document that must be given to shareholders by management and others who are soliciting shareholder proxies. The statement must fully describe (a) the matter for which the proxy is being solicited, (b) who is soliciting the proxy, and (c) any other pertinent information. 3. *Filing with the SEC*. Proxy statements must be filed with the SEC at least 10 days before the materials are sent to shareholders.

1992 SEC Proxy Rules	In 1992, the SEC adopted proxy rules that provide the following: 1. *Shareholder communication.* Shareholders may communicate orally or in writing with other shareholders without filing a proxy statement with the SEC if the shareholder is not seeking proxy voting authority. This rule does not apply to shareholders who own more than $5 million of the company's voting shares, who must register any written communication to shareholders with the SEC. 2. *Unbundled proposals.* Companies seeking proxies may not bundle proposition for a single shareholder vote. Propositions must be presented separately to shareholders for vote. 3. *Company performance.* Companies must include performance charts in their annual reports comparing the company's stock performance to a general stock index (e.g., Standard and Poor's 500) and that company's per group index (e.g., retailers). 4. *Executive compensation disclosure.* Companies must provide tables in their annual reports summarizing the compensation for the chief executive officer and their four other most highly compensated executives for the past three years. This includes salary, stock options, stock appreciation rights, and long-term incentive plans.
Antifraud Provision	Section 14(a) of the 1934 act prohibits misrepresentation or omissions of a material fact in proxy materials. The SEC, U.S. Justice Department, shareholders, and others may sue the wrongdoer. This requires a showing of *scienter* (i.e., intent or recklessness).

Proxy Contests	Occurs when opposing factions of shareholders and managers solicit proxies from other shareholders; the side that receives the greatest number of votes wins the proxy contest.
	1. *Opposing groups:*
	  a. *Incumbent group.* Management-sponsored slate of proposed directors.
	  b. *Insurgent group.* Slate of proposed directors sponsored by the group that is challenging the incumbent group.
	2. *Reimbursement of expenses.* In a proxy contest that involves a *policy issue*, the corporation pays the incumbent management's expenses whether they win or lose the proxy contest. If the insurgent group wins the proxy contest, the corporation must reimburse them their expenses, too. If the proxy contest concerned a *personal matter*, neither side may recover its expenses from the corporation.

SHAREHOLDER PROPOSALS, P. 645

Shareholder Proposals	Proposal submitted by a shareholder or group of shareholders to be considered and voted by the corporation's shareholders. Most shareholder proposals concern social issues (e.g., protection of the environment, discontinuation of the manufacture and sale of dangerous products). 1. *Inclusion in proxy materials.* If management does not oppose the proposal, it may be included in the proxy materials issued by the corporation. If management opposes the shareholder proposal, the SEC rules on whether the proposal must be submitted to the shareholders in the corporation's proxy materials. 2. *Requirements.* To be included in the corporation's proxy materials, the shareholder proposal must (a) not violate federal or state law, (b) relate to the corporation's business, (c) concern policy issues (and not the day-to-day operations of the corporation), and (d) not concern the payment of dividends.

MERGERS AND ACQUISITIONS, P. 646	
Mergers and Acquisitions	Mergers, consolidations, and share exchanges are *friendly* combinations of corporations. 1. *Merger*. Occurs when one corporation is absorbed into another corporation and ceases to exist. The corporation that continues to exist after a merger is called the *surviving corporation*. The corporation that is absorbed in the merger and ceases to exist as a separate entity is called the *merged corporation*. 2. *Consolidation*. Occurs when two or more corporations combine to form an entirely new corporation. The new corporation is called the *consolidated corporation*. 3. *Share exchange*. Occurs when one corporation acquires all the shares of another corporation while both corporations retain their separate legal existence. The corporation that owns the shares of the other corporation is called the *parent corporation*. The corporation that is owned by the other corporation is called the *subsidiary corporation*.
Required Approvals	1. *Required approvals*. An ordinary merger or share exchange requires (a) the recommendation of the board of directors of each corporation and (b) an affirmative vote of the majority of shares of each corporation that is entitled to vote (unless a greater vote is required). 2. *No shareholder vote required*. The approval of the surviving corporation's shareholders is not required if the merger or share exchange increases the number of voting shares of the surviving corporation by 20 percent or less. 3. *Articles of merger or share exchange*. Document that must be filed with the secretary of state once the merger or share exchange is completed.
Short-Form Mergers	A merger between a *parent corporation* and a *subsidiary corporation* in which the parent corporation owns 90 percent or more of the subsidiary corporation. 1. *Required approval*. Only the approval of the board of directors of the parent corporation is required to effectuate a short-form merger. The vote of the shareholders of either corporation and the board of directors of the subsidiary corporation are not required.
Sale or Lease of Assets	1. *Sale or lease of assets not in the usual and regular course of business*. Sale, lease, or disposition by a corporation of all or substantially all of its assets not in the usual and regular course of business. 2. *Required approval*. Requires (a) the recommendation of the board of directors and (b) an affirmative vote of the majority of the shares of the selling or leasing corporation that is entitled to vote (unless a greater vote is required).
DISSENTING SHAREHOLDER APPRAISAL RIGHTS, P. 648	
Dissenting Shareholder Appraisal Rights	Statutory right of shareholders who object to a proposed merger, share exchange, or sale or lease of all or substantially all of the property of the corporation to have their shares valued by the court and receive cash payment of this value from the corporation. 1. *Procedures*. The corporation must notify shareholders of their appraisal rights. To obtain appraisal rights, the shareholder must (a) deliver written notice to the corporation of his or her intent to demand payment of his or her shares before the vote is taken and (b) not vote his or her shares in favor of the proposed action.

	2. *Fair value.* If the shareholder does not accept the value offered by the corporation, the court will determine the *fair value* of the shares. The court may hire appraisers to assist in making this determination. Costs of this proceeding are usually borne by the corporations.

TENDER OFFERS, P. 650

Tender Offers	An offer that an acquirer makes directly to a *target corporation's shareholders* in an effort to acquire the target corporation or control of the target corporation. 1. *Tender offeror.* The party that makes a tender offer. 2. *Target corporation.* The corporation that is proposed to be acquired in a tender offer situation.
The Williams Act	Federal statute that regulates all tender offers. The Securities and Exchange Commission (SEC) is empowered to administer the Williams Act.
Tender Offer Rules	1. *Notification.* The tender offeror does not have to notify the SEC or the target corporation's management until the tender offer is made. 2. *Completion.* The tender offer cannot be closed before 15 business days after the commencement of the offer. 3. *Extension.* The offer must be extended for 10 business days if the tender offeror increases the number of shares it will take or the price it will pay for the shares. 4. *Fair price rule.* Stipulates that any increase in price paid for shares tendered must be offered to all shareholders, even those who have previously tendered their shares. 5. *Pro rata rule.* Provides that shares must be purchased on a *pro rata basis* if too many shares are tendered. 6. *Withdrawal rights.* Shareholders who tender their shares have an absolute right to withdraw them at any time prior to the closing of the tender offer.
Antifraud Provision	*Section 14(e).* A provision of the Williams Act that prohibits fraudulent, deceptive, and manipulative practices in connection with a tender offer.

FIGHTING A TENDER OFFER, P. 652

Fighting a Tender Offer	The management of the target corporation often takes one or more of the following steps to try to defeat a hostile tender offer: 1. Persuade the shareholders not to tender their shares. 2. File delaying lawsuits (e.g., antitrust lawsuits). 3. Sell the *crown jewels* (e.g., a valuable asset that the tender offeror is particularly interested in acquiring). 4. Adopt *poison pills* (e.g., contract provisions that make contracts and leases expire). 5. Find a *white knight* to purchase the corporation in a friendly acquisition. 6. Conduct a *pac-man tender offer* (i.e., a reverse tender offer to acquire the tender offeror). 7. Issue additional stock to friendly parties. 8. Create an *employee stock ownership plan (ESOP)* and issue stock to the ESOP. 9. Adopt *flip-over* and *flip-in rights plans* that make it more expensive for the tender offeror to acquire shares. 10. Pay *greenmail* by purchasing the shares held by the tender offeror at a premium. Obtain a *standstill agreement* whereby the offeror agrees not to purchase shares of the target corporation for a stipulated period of time.

	11. Engage in other strategies and tactics that make it more difficult for a tender offeror to complete its tender offer.
Business Judgment Rule	A rule that protects the decisions of the board of directors that acts on an *informed basis*, in *good faith*, and in the *honest belief that the action taken was in the best interests of the corporation and its shareholders*. 1. *Tender offers*. The actions of the management of a target corporation in fighting a tender offer are judged by the business judgment rule. The defensive measure must be reasonable in relation to the threat posed.

STATE ANTITAKEOVER STATUTES, P. 655

State Antitakeover Statutes	Statutes enacted by state legislatures that are aimed at protecting corporations that are either incorporated in or doing business within the state from hostile takeovers. 1. *Lawfulness*. State antitakeover statutes are lawful if they do not conflict with the federal *Williams Act* or unduly burden interstate commerce in violation of the *Commerce Clause* of the U.S. Constitution.

DISSOLUTION AND TERMINATION OF CORPORATIONS, P. 656

Voluntary Dissolution	Dissolution of a corporation by the incorporators or initial directors if the corporation has not begun business or issued shares, and by the majority vote of shareholders if the corporation has begun business or issued shares. 1. *Articles of dissolution*. Document that is filed with the secretary of state of the state of incorporation when a corporation has been voluntarily dissolved.
Administrative Dissolution	Involuntary dissolution of a corporation that is ordered by the secretary of state if the corporation has failed to comply with certain procedures required by law (e.g., failure to pay franchise tax). 1. *Certificate of dissolution*. Document that is filed by the secretary of state when a corporation is administratively dissolved.
Judicial Dissolution	Dissolution of a corporation by a court proceeding instituted by the following: 1. *The state*. If the corporation (a) procured its articles of incorporation through fraud or (b) exceeded or abused the authority conferred upon it by law. 2. *Creditors*. If the corporation is insolvent and if (a) the creditor's claim is reduced to judgment and the judgment is unsatisfied, or (b) the corporation admits in writing that the creditor's claim is due and owing. 3. *Shareholders*. If (a) the directors are *deadlocked* concerning the management of the corporation and the shareholders cannot break the deadlock; (b) the shareholders have been deadlocked in voting for directors for at least two years; (c) the persons in control of the corporation are acting illegally, oppressively, or fraudulently; or (d) the corporate assets are being misapplied or wasted. 4. *Decree of dissolution*. Order issued by the court when a corporation has been judicially dissolved.
Winding Up, Liquidation, and Termination	1. *Winding up and liquidation*. The process by which a dissolved corporation's assets are collected, liquidated, and distributed to creditors, shareholders, and other claimants. 2. *Termination*. The ending of a corporation that occurs only after the winding up of the corporation's affairs, the liquidation of its assets, and the distribution of the proceeds and property to the claimants.

CRITICAL LEGAL THINKING CASES

26.1 Proxy Disclosure Western Maryland Company (Western) was a timbering and mining concern. A substantial portion of its stock was owned by CSX Minerals (CSX), its parent corporation. The remaining shares were owned by several minority shareholders, including Sanford E. Lockspeiser. Western's stock was not publicly traded. In 1983, the board of directors of Western voted to merge the company with CSX. Western distributed a proxy statement to the minority shareholders that stated that CSX would vote for the merger and recommended approval of the merger by the other shareholders. The proxy materials disclosed Western's natural resource holdings in terms of acreage of minerals and timber. It also stated real property values as carried on the company's books, that is, a book value of $17.04 per share. It included an opinion of the First Boston Corporation, an investment banking firm, that the merger was fair to shareholders; First Boston did not undertake an independent evaluation of Western's physical assets. Lockspeiser sued, alleging that the proxy materials were misleading because they did not state the tonnage of Western's coal reserves, timber holdings in board feet, and actual value of Western's assets. Did Lockspeiser state a claim for relief? [*Lockspeiser v. Western Maryland Company*, 768 F.2d 558 (4th Cir. 1985)]

26.2 Proxy Contest The Medfield Corporation (Medfield) is a publicly held corporation engaged in operating hospitals and other health-care facilities. Medfield established March 1, 1974, as the date for its annual shareholders meeting, at which time the board of directors would be elected. In its proxy statement, management proposed the incumbent slate of directors. A group known as the Medfield Shareholders Committee (Committee) nominated a rival slate of candidates and also solicited proxies. Medfield sent proxy solicitation to shareholders that

1. Failed to disclose that Medfield had been overpaid more than $1.8 million by Blue Cross and that this amount was due and owing Blue Cross.
2. Failed to disclose that Medicare funds were being withheld because of Medfield's nonpayment.
3. Failed to disclose adequately self-dealing by one of the directors with Medfield who owned part of a laboratory used by Medfield.
4. Failed to disclose that Medfield was attempting to sell two nursing homes.
5. Impugned the character, integrity, and personal reputation of one of the rival candidates by stating that he had previously been found liable for patent infringement when, in fact, the case had been reversed on appeal.

At the annual meeting, the incumbent slate of directors received 50 percent of the votes cast against 44 percent of the insurgent slate of directors. The Gladwins, who own voting stock, sued to have the election overturned. Who wins? [*Gladwin v. Medfield Corporation*, 540 F.2d 1266 (5th Cir. 1976)]

26.3 Reimbursement for Expenses Incurred in a Proxy The Fairchild Engine and Airplane Corporation (Fairchild) is a privately held corporation. Its management proposed the incumbent slate of directors for election at its annual shareholders meeting. An insurgent slate of directors challenged the incumbents for election to the board. After the solicitation of proxies and a hard-fought proxy contest, the insurgent slate of directors was elected. Evidence showed the proxy contest was waged over matters of corporate policy and for personal reasons. The old board of directors had spent $135,000 out of corporate funds to wage the proxy contest. The insurgents had spent $127,000 of their personal funds in their successful proxy contest and sought reimbursement from Fairchild for this amount. The payment of these expenses was ratified by a 16-to-1 majority vote of the stockholders. Mr. Rosenfeld, an attorney who owned 25 of the 2,300,000 outstanding shares of the corporation, filed an action to recover the amounts already paid by the corporation and to prevent any further payments of these expenses. Who wins? [*Rosenfeld v. Fairchild Engine and Airplane Corporation*, 128 N.E.2d 291 (N.Y.App. 1955)]

26.4 Shareholder Proposal The National Medical Committee for Human Rights (Committee) is a nonprofit corporation that is organized to advance concerns for human life. The Committee received a gift of shares of Dow Chemical (Dow) stock. Dow manufactured napalm, a chemical defoliant that was used during the Vietnam conflict. The Committee objected to the sale of napalm by Dow primarily because of its concerns for human life. The Committee owned sufficient shares for a long enough time to propose a shareholder's resolution as long as it met the other requirements to propose such a resolution. The Committee proposed that the following resolution be included in the proxy materials circulated by management for the 1969 annual shareholders meeting:

> RESOLVED, that the shareholders of the Dow Chemical Company request that the Board of Directors, in accordance with the law, consider the advisability of adopting a resolution setting forth an amendment to the composite certificate of incorporation of the Dow Chemical Company that the company shall not make napalm.

Dow's management refused to include the requested resolution in its proxy materials. The Committee sued, alleging that its resolution met the requirements to be included in the proxy materials. Who wins? [*Medical Community for Human Rights v. Securities and Exchange Commission*, 432 F.2d 659 (D.C. Cir. 1970)]

26.5 Merger During the last six months of 1980, the board of directors of Plant Industries, Inc. (Plant), under the guidance of Robert B. Bregman, the chief executive officer of the corporation, embarked on a course of action that resulted in the sale of several unprofitable subsidiaries. Mr. Bregman then engaged in a course of action to sell Plant National (Quebec) Ltd., a subsidiary that constituted Plant's entire Canadian operations. This was a profitable subsidiary that constituted more than 50 percent of Plant's assets, sales, and profits. Do Plant's shareholders have to be accorded voting and appraisal rights regarding the sale of this subsidiary? [*Katz v. Bregman*, 431 A.2d 1274 (Del. Ch. 1981)]

26.6 Dissenting Shareholder Appraisal Rights Over a period of several years, the Curtiss-Wright Corporation (Curtiss-Wright) purchased 65 percent of the stock of Dorr-Oliver Incorporated (Dorr-Oliver). In early 1979, Curtiss-Wright's board of directors decided that a merger with Dorr-Oliver would be beneficial to Curtiss-Wright. The board voted to approve a merger of the two companies and to pay $23 per share to the stockholders of Dorr-Oliver. The Dorr-Oliver board and 80 percent of Dorr-Oliver's shareholders approved the merger. The merger became effective on May 31, 1979. John Bershad, a minority shareholder of Dorr-Oliver, voted against the merger, but thereafter tendered his 100 shares and received payment of $2,300. Bershad subsequently sued, alleging that the $23 per share paid to Dorr-Oliver shareholders was grossly inadequate. Can Bershad obtain minority shareholder appraisal rights? [*Bershad v. Curtiss-Wright Corporation*, 535 A.2d 840 (Del. 1987)]

26.7 Fighting a Tender Offer On October 30, 1981, Mobil Corporation (Mobil) made a tender offer to purchase up to 40 million outstanding common shares of stock in Marathon Oil Company (Marathon) for $85 per share in cash. It further stated its intentions to follow the purchase with a merger of the two companies. Mobil was primarily interested in acquiring Marathon's oil and mineral interests in certain properties, including the Yates Field. The Marathon directors immediately held a board meeting and determined to find a white knight. Negotiations developed between Marathon and United States Steel Corporations (U.S. Steel). On November 18, 1981, Marathon and U.S. Steel entered into an agreement whereby U.S. Steel would make a tender offer for 30 million common shares of Marathon stock at $125 per share, to be followed by a merger of the two companies.

The Marathon–U.S. Steel agreement was subject to the following two conditions: (1) U.S. Steel was given an irrevocable option to purchase 10 million authorized but unissued shares of Marathon common stock for $90 per share (or 17 percent of Marathon's outstanding shares), and (2) U.S. Steel was given an option to purchase Marathon's interest in oil and mineral rights in Yates Field for $2.8 billion (Yates Field option). The latter option could be exercised only if U.S. Steel's offer did not succeed and if a third party gained control of Marathon. Evidence showed that Marathon's interest in the Yates Field was worth up to $3.6 billion. Marathon did not give Mobil either of these two options. Mobil sued, alleging that these two options violated Section 14(e) of the Williams Act. Who wins? [*Mobil Corporation v. Marathon Oil Company*, 669 F.2d 366 (6th Cir. 1981)]

26.8 Fighting a Tender Offer The Fruehauf Corporation (Fruehauf) is engaged in the manufacture of large trucks and industrial vehicles. The Edelman group made a cash tender offer for the shares of Fruehauf for $48.50 per share. The stock sold in the low $20-per-share range a few months earlier. Fruehauf's management decided to make a competing management-led leveraged buyout (MBO) tender offer for the company in conjunction with Merrill Lynch. The MBO would be funded using $375 million borrowed from Merrill Lynch, $375 million borrowed from Manufacturers Hanover Bank, and $100 million contributed by Fruehauf Corporation. Total equity contribution to the new company under the MBO would be only $25 million: $10 million to $15 million from management and the rest from Merrill Lynch. In return for their equity contributions, management would receive between 40 percent and 60 percent of the new company.

Fruehauf's management agreed to pay $30 million to Merrill Lynch for brokerage fees that Merrill Lynch could keep even if the deal did not go through. Management also agreed to a no-shop clause, whereby they agreed not to seek a better deal with another bidder. Incumbent management received better information about the goings-on. They also gave themselves golden parachutes that would raise the money for management's equity position in the new company.

The Edelman group informed Fruehauf's management that it could top their bid, but Fruehauf's management did not give them the opportunity to present their offer. Management's offer was accepted. The Edelman group sued, seeking an injunction. Did Fruehauf's management violate the business judgment rule? [*Edelman v. Fruehauf Corporation*, 798 F.2d 882 (6th Cir. 1986)]

26.9 Poison Pill Defense Household International, Inc. (Household) is a diversified holding company with its principal subsidiaries engaged in financial services, transportation, and merchandising. On August 14, 1984, the board of directors of Household adopted a 48-page "Rights Plan" by a 14-to-2 vote. Basically, the plan provides that Household common stockholders are entitled to the issuance of one irrevocable right per common share if any party acquires 20 percent of Household's shares. The right permits Household shareholders to purchase $200 of the common stock of the tender offeror for $100. In essence, this forces any party interested in taking over Household to negotiate with Household's directors. Dyson-Kissner-Moran Corporation (DKM), which was interested in taking over Household, filed suit alleging that this flip-over rights plan violated the business judgment rule. Who wins? [*Moran v. Household International, Inc.*, 500 Ad.2d 1346 (Del. 1985)]

26.10 State Antitakeover Statute The state of Illinois enacted a statute that protects certain defined "target companies" from unwanted takeovers. The protection extends to (1) corporations of which shareholders located in Illinois own 10 percent of a class of equity securities and (2) corporations that are incorporated in Illinois or have their principal place of business in state. Tender offers for protected companies must be registered with the Illinois secretary of state 20 days before the proposed tender offer is made. The secretary may call a hearing at any time during the 20-day waiting period. The statute does not provide a deadline for when the hearing must be completed. The secretary may deny the tender offer if he finds that it is inequitable.

Chicago Rivet and Machine Co. (Chicago Rivet) is a publicly held Illinois corporation that is covered by the Illinois antitakeover statute. On July 19, 1979, MITE Corporation (MITE), a Delaware corporation, made a cash tender offer for all of the outstanding shares of Chicago Rivet. MITE did not comply with the Illinois Act and brought suit challenging the lawfulness of the state law. Is the Illinois antitakeover statute lawful? [*Edgar, Secretary of State of Illinois v. MITE Corporation*, 457 U.S. 624, 102 S.Ct. 2629 (1982)]

26.11 State Antitakeover Statute The state of Wisconsin enacted an antitakeover statute that protects corporations that are incorporated in Wisconsin and have their headquarters, substantial operations, or 10 percent of their shares or shareholders in the state. The statute prevents any party that acquires a 10 percent interest in a covered corporation from engaging in a business combination (e.g., merger) with the covered corporation for three years unless approval of the management is obtained in advance of the combination. Wisconsin firms cannot opt out of the law. This statute effectively eliminates hostile leveraged buyouts, because buyers must rely on the assets and income of the target company to help pay off the debt incurred in effectuating the takeover.

The Universal Foods Corporation (Universal) is a Wisconsin corporation covered by the statute. On December 1, 1988, Amanda Acquisition Corporation (Amanda) commenced a cash tender offer for up to 75 percent of the stock of Universal. Universal asserted the Wisconsin law. Is Wisconsin's antitakeover statute lawful? [*Amanda Acquisition Corporation v. Universal Foods*, 877 F.2d 496 (7th Cir. 1989), cert. denied 110 S.Ct. 367, 107 L.Ed.2d 353 (1989)]

26.12 Deadlock In 1955, William Davis and James L. Sheerin incorporated a business that was initially started by Davis. Davis owned 55 percent of the corporation's stock. Sheerin owned 45 percent. Davis and his wife, Catherine, served as directors, officers, and employees of the corporation. Davis served as president and ran the day-to-day operations of the business. Sheerin was a director and officer of the corporation but was not an employee. Over the years, the business acquired six parcels of real estate.

In 1985, the Davises denied Sheerin the right to inspect the corporate books unless Sheerin produced his stock certificate. Davis denied that Sheerin owned a 45-percent interest in the real estate acquired by the business. The Davises also claimed that Sheerin had made a gift to them, in the late 1960s, of his interest in the corporation. The corporate records, however, clearly showed that Sheerin owned a 45-percent interest in the corporation. At the time of suit, this interest was valued at $550,000. Prior to suit, the Davises tried to purchase Sheerin's interest for substantially less. Sheerin sued. Was there a shareholder deadlock? What remedy should be granted? [*Davis v. Sheerin*, 754 S.W.2d 375 (Tex.App. 1988)]

ETHICS CASES

26.13 Ethical Perspective MCA, Inc. (MCA), a corporate holding company, owned 92 percent of the stock of Universal Pictures Company (Universal) and 100-percent of the stock of Universal City Studios, Inc. (Universal City). On March 25, 1966, these two subsidiaries merged pursuant to Delaware's short-form merger statute. The minority shareholders of Universal were offered $75 per share for their shares. Francis I. Du Pont & Company and other minority shareholders (plaintiffs) rejected the offer and then perfected their dissenting shareholder appraisal rights. On March 29, 1973, the appraiser filed a final report in which he found the value of the Universal stock to be $91.47 per share. Both parties filed exceptions to this report.

The parties' ultimate disagreement is, of course, over the value of the stock. Plaintiffs submit that the true value is $131.89 per share; defendant says it is $52.36. The computations are as follows:

Plaintiffs

Value Factor	Value	Weight	Result
Earnings	$129.12	70%	$ 90.38
Market	144.36	20	28.87
Assets	126.46	10	12.64
Value per share			$131.89

Defendants

Value Factor	Value	Weight	Result
Earnings	$51.93	70%	$36.35
Dividends	41.66	20	8.33
Assets	76.77	10	7.68
Value per share			$52.36

Appraiser

Value Factor	Value	Weight	Result
Earnings	$92.89	80%	$74.31
Assets	85.82	20	17.16
Value per share			$91.47

Defendant takes exception to the appraiser's failure to find that in the years prior to merger the industry was declining and that Universal was ranked near its bottom. The defendant argues that Universal was in the business of producing and distributing feature motion pictures for theatrical exhibition. It contends that such business, generally, was in a severe decline at the time of merger and that Universal, in particular, was in a vulnerable position because it had failed to diversify, its feature films were of low commercial quality, and, unlike other motion picture companies, substantially all of its film library had already been committed to distributors for television exhibition. In short, defendant pictures Universal as a weak "wasting asset" corporation in a sick industry with poor prospects for revival.

The stockholders see a different company. They say that Universal's business was indeed the production and distribution of feature films, but not merely for theatrical exhibition. They argue that there was a dramatic increase in the television market for such feature films at the time of the merger. This new market, they contend, gave great new value to a fully amortized film library and significantly enhanced the value of Universal's current and future productions. They equate the television market to the acquisition of a new and highly profitable business whose earnings potential was just beginning to be realized at the time of the merger. Finally, say the plaintiffs, the theatrical market itself was recovering in 1966. Thus, they paint the portrait of a well-suited corporation in a rejuvenated industry.

Did the parties act ethically in arriving at their proposed value of the company? What is the value of the minority shareholder's shares of Universal Pictures Company? [*Francis I. Du Pont & Company v. Universal City Studios, Inc.*, 312 A.2d 344 (Del. Ch. 1973)]

26.14 Ethical Perspective Realist, Inc. (Realist) is a Delaware corporation that has its principal place of business in Wisconsin. In March 1988, Royal Business Group, Inc. (Royal), a New Hampshire corporation, acquired 8 percent of the outstanding voting stock of Realist. Royal sent a series of letters to Realist, declaring its intention to acquire all of Realist's outstanding shares at an above-market premium. Realist repulsed Royal's overtures. Unbeknownst to Royal, Realist began negotiations to acquire Ammann Laser Technik AG (Ammann), a Switzerland-based company.

Royal instituted a proxy contest and nominated two candidates for the two Realist directorships to be filed at Real-

ist's June 6, 1989 annual shareholders meeting. Realist and Royal both submitted proxy statements to Realist's shareholders.

The insurgent Royal nominees prevailed. On June 30, 1989, Realist announced that it had acquired Ammann. This acquisition made Realist much less attractive as a takeover target. Royal immediately withdrew its offer to acquire Realist and sued Realist to recover the $350,000 it had spent in connection with the proxy contest. Royal alleged that Realist had engaged in fraud in violation of Section 14(a) of the Securities Exchange Act of 1934 by failing to disclose its secret negotiations with Ammann in its proxy materials. The basis of Royal's complaint was that if Realist had disclosed that it intended to acquire Ammann, Royal would not have engaged in the costly proxy contest. Is Realist liable to Royal? Did Realist act unethically in seeking to acquire Ammann to thwart Royal's takeover attempt? [*Royal Business Group, Inc. v. Realist, Inc.*, 933 F.2d 1056 (1st Cir. 1991)]

CRITICAL LEGAL THINKING WRITING ASSIGNMENT

Read Case A.26 in the Case Appendix [*Neal v. Alabama By-Products Corporation*]. Review and brief the case. In your brief, be sure to answer the following questions:

1. What are dissenting shareholder appraisal rights?
2. What type of transaction occurred that triggered these rights in this case?

3. What value were the dissenting shareholders offered in the original transaction? What value is being offered by the corporation in the court proceeding? What value are the dissenting shareholders seeking in the court proceeding?
4. What amount did the court determine to be the fair value of the shares?

NOTES

[1] RMBCA § 7.22.
[2] 15 U.S.C. 78N(A).
[3] RMBCA § 11.01.
[4] RMBCA § 11.02.
[5] RMBCA § 11.03.
[6] RMBCA § 11.03(G).
[7] RMBCA § 11.05.
[8] RMBCA § 11.04.
[9] RMBCA § 12.02.
[10] RMBCA § 13.02.
[11] RMBCA § 13.20.
[12] RMBCA § 13.21.
[13] RMBCA § 13.23.
[14] RMBCA § 13.25.
[15] RMBCA § 13.30.
[16] RMBCA § 13.31.
[17] 15 U.S.C. 78N(d)–(e).
[18] Section 13(d) of the Securities Exchange Act of 1934 requires that any party who acquires 5 percent or more of

any equity security of a company registered with the SEC must report the acquisition to the SEC and disclose its intentions regarding the acquisition. This is public information.
[19] 15 U.S.C. 78N(e).
[20] *Smith v. Van Gorkum*, 488 A.2d 858 (Del. 1985).
[21] *Unocal Corporation v. Mesa Petroleum Company*, 493 A.2d 946 (Del. 1985).
[22] RMBCA § 14.01.
[23] RMBCA § 14.02.
[24] RMBCA § 14.03.
[25] RMBCA § 14.20.
[26] RMBCA § 14.21.
[27] RMBCA § 14.33.
[28] RMBCA § 14.30(1).
[29] RMBCA § 14.30(3).
[30] RMBCA § 14.05.
[31] RMBCA § 14.32.

CHAPTER 27

SECURITIES REGULATION

AND INVESTOR PROTECTION

Chapter Objectives

After studying this chapter,
you should be able to

1. Define a security for purposes of federal and state securities laws
2. Describe how securities are registered with the Securities and Exchange Commission
3. Describe the requirements for qualifying for intrastate and small offering exemptions from registration
4. Describe the requirements for qualifying for a private placement exemption from registration
5. Define insider trading that violates Section 10(b) of the Securities Exchange Act of 1934
6. Describe the liability of tippers and tippees for insider trading
7. Describe short-swing profits that violate Section 16(b) of the Securities Exchange Act of 1934
8. Describe the criminal liability and penalties for violating federal securities laws
9. Describe how the Racketeer Influenced and Corrupt Organizations Act (RICO) applies to securities, law, and cases
10. Describe commodities trading and apply the antifraud provision of the Commodity Exchange Act

Chapter Contents

- The Securities and Exchange Commission (SEC)
- Definition of a Security
  Case 27.1 *Hocking v. Dubois (9th Cir.)*
- The Securities Act of 1933—Registration of Securities
- Securities Exempt from Registration
- Transactions Exempt from Registration
- Liability Provisions of the Securities Act of 1933
  Case 27.2 *Escott v. BarChris Construction Corp. (S.D.N.Y.)*
- The Securities Exchange Act of 1934—Trading in Securities
- Insider Trading
  Case 27.3 *Securities and Exchange Commission v. Texas Gulf Sulphur Co. (2d Cir.)*
  Case 27.4 *United States v. O'Hagan* (U.S.)
- Liability Provisions of the Securities Exchange Act of 1934
  Business Application Michael Milken: The Rise and Fall of the Junk Bond King
- Short-Swing Profits
  Business Checklist Securities Investors' Accounts Insured by the Securities Investor Protection Corporation (SIPC)
- Other Federal Securities Laws
- State Securities Laws
- Commodities Regulation
  Ethical Perspective Commodity "Boiler Rooms"
  International Perspective Enforcement of International Securities Laws
- Working the Web
- Chapter Summary
- Critical Legal Thinking Cases
- Ethics Cases
- Critical Legal Thinking Writing Assignment

> *The fraud on the market theory is based on the hypothesis that, in an open and developed securities market, the price of a company's stock is determined by the available material information regarding the company and its business. Misleading statements will therefore defraud purchasers of stock even if the purchasers do not directly rely on the misstatements.*
>
> *Basic, Inc. v. Levinson*
> 438 U.S. 224, 108 S.Ct. 978,
> 99 L.Ed.2d 194 (1988)

The federal government did not regulate the securities and commodities markets in this country until after the stock market crash of 1929. Investors bought securities and commodities with little, if any, disclosure. Fraud in these transactions was common.

After the crash, Congress enacted a series of statutes designed to regulate securities and commodities markets. The **Securities Act of 1933** requires disclosure by companies and others who wish to issue securities to the public. The **Securities Exchange Act of 1934** was enacted to prevent fraud in the subsequent trading of securities, including insider trading. The **Commodity Exchange Act** was enacted in 1936 to regulate the trading of commodities. Other securities and commodities statutes and amendments have been passed by Congress. Many states have enacted their own securities laws as well.

This chapter discusses federal and state securities laws and regulations that provide investor protection.

BUSINESS BRIEF
Federal law did not regulate the securities markets until after the Stock Market Crash of 1929. Securities laws are designed to help prevent a similar crash today.

THE SECURITIES AND EXCHANGE COMMISSION (SEC)

The Securities Exchange Act of 1934 created the **Securities and Exchange Commission (SEC)** and empowered it to administer federal securities laws. The SEC is an administrative agency composed of five members who are appointed by the president. The major responsibilities of the SEC follow:

1. Adopting rules (also called regulations) that further the purpose of the federal securities statutes. These rules have the force of law.
2. Investigating alleged securities violations and bringing enforcement actions against suspected violators. This may include a recommendation of criminal prosecution. Criminal prosecutions of violations of federal securities laws are brought by the U.S. Department of Justice.
3. Regulating the activities of securities brokers and advisors. This includes registering brokers and advisors and taking enforcement action against those who violate securities laws.

Securities and Exchange Commission (SEC)
Federal administrative agency that is empowered to administer federal securities laws. The SEC can adopt rules and regulations to interpret and implement federal securities laws.

DEFINITION OF A SECURITY

A **security** must exist before securities laws apply. Securities are defined as follows:

1. Interests or instruments that are commonly known as securities (e.g., common stock, preferred stock, bonds, debentures, and warrants)
2. Interests or instruments that are expressly mentioned in securities acts (e.g., pre-organization subscription agreements; interests in oil, gas, and mineral rights; and deposit receipts for foreign securities)
3. **Investment contracts**, that is, any contract whereby an investor invests money or other consideration in a common enterprise and expects to make a profit off the significant efforts of others. Limited partnership interests, pyramid sales schemes, and investments in farm animals accompanied by care agreements have been found to be securities under this test, which is known as the **Howey test**.[1]

security (1) An interest or instrument that is common stock, preferred stock, a bond, a debenture, or a warrant, (2) an interest or instrument that is expressly mentioned in securities acts, and (3) an investment contract.

In the following case, the court found an investment to be a security subject to federal securities laws.

CASE 27.1

Hocking v. Dubois
839 F.2d 560 (1988) United States Court of Appeals, Ninth Circuit

Facts Gerald Hocking visited Hawaii and became interested in buying a condominium there as an investment. Maylee Dubois, who was a licensed real estate broker in Hawaii, agreed to help Hocking find a suitable unit. Dubois found a condominium unit owned by Tovik and Yaacov Liberman that was for sale. The unit was located in a resort complex developed by Aetna Life Insurance Company (Aetna) and managed by the Hotel Corporation of the Pacific (HCP). Aetna and HCP offered purchasers of condominium units in the project to participate in a rental pool agreement. The Libermans had not participated in the pool. Hocking purchased the unit from the Libermans and entered into a rental pool agreement with HCP. Hocking subsequently filed suit against Dubois, alleging violations of federal securities laws. The trial court granted summary judgment in favor of the defendants. Hocking appealed.

Issue Was the offer of a condominium unit with an option to participate in a rental pool agreement a "security" under federal securities laws?

Decision Yes. The court of appeals held that the transaction constituted an offer of a security, and that Hocking could sue Dubois for alleged violations of federal securities laws. Reversed and remanded.

Reason Generally, simple transactions in real estate, without more, do not satisfy the *Howey* criteria. When a purchaser is motivated exclusively by a desire to occupy or develop the land personally, no security is involved. Real estate transactions may involve an offer of securities when an investor is offered both an interest in real estate *and* a collateral expectation of profits. The court held that under the

three *Howey* criteria an offer of a condominium with a rental pool agreement constitutes an offer of an investment contract.

1. *Investment of money.* Hocking invested money in the condominium.
2. *Common enterprise.* Each investor buys one share—a condominium—in a common venture that pools the rents from all of the units. The success of each participant's individual investment clearly depends on the entire rental pool agreement's success.
3. *Expectation of profits produced by others' efforts.* Where a rental pool is made available in the course of the offering, what is really being sold to the purchaser is an investment contract whereby profits are expected to be produced, if at all, through the efforts of a party other than the purchaser–owner.

The court stated that the definition of an *investment contract* "embodies a flexible principle capable of adaptation to meet the countless and variable schemes devised by those who seek the use of the money of others on the promise of profits."

CASE QUESTIONS

Critical Legal Thinking What is an investment contract? Why did Congress leave the definition of a *security* flexible?

Ethics Did Dubois act unethically in denying liability under federal securities laws?

Business Implication Why did the plaintiff allege the transaction involved a security? Explain.

THE SECURITIES ACT OF 1933—REGISTRATION OF SECURITIES

Securities Act of 1933
A federal statute that primarily regulates the issuance of securities by corporations, partnerships, associations, and individuals.

The **Securities Act of 1933** primarily regulates the issuance of securities by a corporation, a general or limited partnership, an unincorporated association, or an individual. Unless a security or transaction qualifies for an exemption (discussed later in this chapter), **Section 5** of the Securities Act of 1933 requires securities offered to the public through the use of the mails or any facility of interstate commerce to be registered with the SEC by means of a registration statement and an accompanying prospectus.

Registration Statement

A covered issuer must file a written **registration statement** with the SEC. The issuer's lawyer normally prepares the statement with the help of the issuer's management, accountants, and underwriters.

A registration statement must contain descriptions of (1) the securities being offered for sale, (2) the registrant's business, (3) the management of the registrant, including compensation, stock options and benefits, and material transactions with the registrant, (4) pending litigation, (5) how the proceeds from the offering will be used, (6) government regulation, (7) the degree of competition in the industry, and (8) any special risk factors. In addition, the registration statement must be accompanied by financial statements as certified by certified public accountants.

Registration statements usually become effective 20 business days after they are filed unless the SEC requires additional information to be disclosed. A new 20-day period begins each time the registration statement is amended. At the registrant's request, the SEC may "accelerate" the **effective date** (i.e., not require the registrant to wait 20 days after the last amendment is filed).

The SEC does not pass upon the merits of the securities offered. It decides only whether the issuer has met the disclosure requirements.

Prospectus

The **prospectus** is a written disclosure document that must be submitted to the SEC along with the registration statement. The prospectus, which contains much of the same information as the registration statement, is used as a selling tool by the issuer. It is provided to prospective investors to enable them to evaluate the financial risk of the investment.

A prospectus must contain the following language in capital letters and boldface (usually red) type:

> THESE SECURITIES HAVE NOT BEEN APPROVED OR DISAPPROVED BY THE SECURITIES AND EXCHANGE COMMISSION OR ANY STATE SECURITIES COMMISSION NOR HAS THE SECURITIES AND EXCHANGE COMMISSION OR ANY STATE SECURITIES COMMISSION PASSED UPON THE ACCURACY OR ADEQUACY OF THIS PROSPECTUS. ANY REPRESENTATION TO THE CONTRARY IS A CRIMINAL OFFENSE.

A copy of the cover of a prospectus is set forth in Exhibit 27.1.

Limitations on Activities during the Registration Process

Section 5 of the Securities Act of 1933 limits the types of activities that an issuer, an underwriter, and a dealer may engage in during the registration process. These limitations are divided into three time periods: (1) the prefiling period (2) the waiting period and (3) the posteffective period.

The Prefiling Period The **prefiling period** begins when the issuer first contemplates issuing the securities and ends when the registration statement is filed. During this time, the issuer cannot either sell or offer to sell the securities. The issuer also cannot **condition the market** for the upcoming securities offering. This rule effectively makes it illegal for an issuer to engage in a public relations campaign (e.g., newspaper and magazine articles and advertisements) that touts the prospects of the company and the planned securities issue. However, sending annual reports to shareholders and making public announcements of factual matters (such as the settlement of a strike) are permissible because they are considered normal corporate disclosures.

The Waiting Period The **waiting period** begins when the registration statement is filed with the SEC and continues until the registration statement is declared effective. The issuer is encouraged to condition the market during this time. Thus, the

NOTE
Section 5 of the Securities Act of 1933 requires an issuer to register securities with the SEC before they can be sold to the public.

registration statement Document that an issuer of securities files with the SEC that contains required information about the issuer, the securities to be issued, and other relevant information.

CAUTION
The SEC does not pass upon the merits of the registered securities.

prospectus A written disclosure document that must be submitted to the SEC along with the registration statement and given to prospective purchasers of the securities.

BUSINESS BRIEF
In 1995, Netscape, Inc. went "public" by issuing shares of stock to investors after registering the securities with the Securities and Exchange Commission. Netscape's stock price went from $28 to $75 on its first day of trading as a public company.

prefiling period A period of time that begins when the issuer first contemplates issuing the securities and ends when the registration statement is filed.

waiting period A period of time that begins when the registration statement is filed with the SEC and continues until the registration statement is declared effective. Only certain activities are permissible during the waiting period.

PROSPECTUS

4,200,000 Shares

MARVEL ENTERTAINMENT GROUP, INC.

Common Stock

All of the 4,200,000 shares of Common Stock of Marvel Entertainment Group, Inc. ("Marvel" or the "Company") offered hereby are being offered by Marvel. Prior to this offering there has been no public market for any securities of Marvel. For a discussion of the factors that were considered in determining the initial public offering price, see "Underwriting."

The Common Stock has been approved for listing on the New York Stock Exchange ("NYSE") subject to official notice of issuance.

See "Investment Considerations" for a discussion of certain factors which should be considered by prospective purchasers of the securities offered hereby.

THESE SECURITIES HAVE NOT BEEN APPROVED OR DISAPPROVED BY THE SECURITIES AND EXCHANGE COMMISSION OR ANY STATE SECURITIES COMMISSION, NOR HAS THE SECURITIES AND EXCHANGE COMMISSION OR ANY STATE SECURITIES COMMISSION PASSED UPON THE ACCURACY OR ADEQUACY OF THIS PROSPECTUS. ANY REPRESENTATION TO THE CONTRARY IS A CRIMINAL OFFENSE.

	Price to Public	Underwriting Discount(1)	Proceeds to Company(2)
Per Share	$16.50	$1.06	$15.44
Total (3)	$69,300,000	$4,452,000	$64,848,000

(1) The Company has agreed to indemnify the several Underwriters against certain liabilities under the Securities Act of 1933. See "Underwriting."

(2) Before deducting expenses payable by the Company estimated at $1,100,000.

(3) The Company's current sole stockholder has granted the several Underwriters an option to purchase up to an additional 600,000 shares of Common Stock solely to cover over-allotments. If such option is exercised in full, proceeds to the Company's current sole stockholder will be $9,264,000, which amount is net of underwriting discount of $636,000. See "Underwriting."

The shares of Common Stock are offered by the several Underwriters, subject to prior sale, when, as and if issued to and accepted by them, subject to approval of certain legal matters by counsel for the Underwriters. The Underwriters reserve the right to withdraw, cancel or modify such offer and to reject orders in whole or in part. It is expected that delivery of the shares of Common Stock will be made in New York, New York on or about July 22, 1991.

Merrill Lynch & Co.   The First Boston Corporation

The date of this Prospectus is July 15, 1991.

---

issuer may (1) make oral offers to sell (including face-to-face and telephone conversations), (2) distribute a **preliminary prospectus** (usually called a red herring) which contains most of the information to be contained in the final prospectus except for price, (3) distribute a **summary prospectus**, which is a summary of the important terms contained in the prospectus, and (4) publish **tombstone ads** in newspapers and other publications. (An example of a tombstone ad is depicted in Exhibit 27.2.) Unapproved writings, such as brochures, as well as actual sales are prohibited during the waiting period.

Exhibit 27.2
An Example of a
Tombstone Ad

The Posteffective Period The **posteffective period** begins when the registration statement becomes effective and runs until the issuer either sells all of the offered securities or withdraws them from sale. Thus, the issuer and its underwriter and dealers may close the offers received prior to the effective date and solicit new offers and sales.

Prior to or at the time of confirming a sale or sending a security to a purchaser, the issuer (or its representative) must deliver a **final prospectus** (also called a **statutory prospectus**) to the investor. Failure to do so is a violation of Section 5.

posteffective period The period of time that begins when the registration statement becomes effective and runs until the issuer either sells all of the offered securities or withdraws them from sale.

final prospectus A final version of the prospectus that must be delivered by the issuer to the investor prior to or at the time of confirming a sale or sending a security to a purchaser.

The investor may rescind his or her purchase if the issuer violates any of the prohibitions on activities during these periods. If an underwriter or dealer violates any of these prohibitions, the SEC may issue sanctions, including the suspension of securities licenses.

Regulation A Offerings

Regulation A A regulation that permits the issuer to sell securities pursuant to a simplified registration process.

Regulation A permits an issuer to sell up to $5 million of securities during a 12-month period pursuant to a simplified registration process. Such offerings may have an unlimited number of purchasers who do not have to be sophisticated investors.

This regulation also stipulates that offerings exceeding $100,000 must file an **offering statement** with the SEC. The offering statement requires less disclosure than a registration statement and is less costly to prepare. Investors must be provided with an offering circular prior to the purchase of securities. There are no resale restrictions on the securities.

SECURITIES EXEMPT FROM REGISTRATION

BUSINESS BRIEF
Certain securities do not have to be registered with the SEC.

Certain *securities* are exempt from registration. Once a security is granted an exemption, the exemption lasts forever. It does not matter how many times the security is transferred. Exempt securities include the following:

1. Securities issued by any government in the United States (e.g., municipal bonds issued by city governments)
2. Short-term notes and drafts that have a maturity date that does not exceed nine months (e.g., commercial paper issued by corporations)
3. Securities issued by nonprofit issuers, such as religious institutions, charitable institutions, and colleges and universities
4. Securities of financial institutions (e.g., banks and savings associations) that are regulated by the appropriate banking authorities
5. Securities issued by common carriers (e.g., railroads and trucking companies) that are regulated by the Interstate Commerce Commission (ICC)
6. Insurance and annuity contracts issued by insurance companies
7. Stock dividends and stock splits
8. Securities issued in a corporate reorganization in which one security is exchanged for another security.

TRANSACTIONS EXEMPT FROM REGISTRATION

CAUTION
If a business plans to issue nonexempt securities, it must either (1) register the securities with the SEC or (2) qualify for an exemption from registration.

Certain *transactions* in securities are exempt from registration. Exempt transactions are subject to the antifraud provisions of the federal securities laws. Therefore, the issuer must provide investors with adequate information—including annual reports, quarterly reports, proxy statements, financial statements, and so on—even though a registration statement is not required. The exempt transactions are discussed in the paragraphs that follow.

Nonissuer Exemption

Nonissuers, such as average investors, do not have to file a registration statement prior to reselling securities they have purchased. This is because the Securities Act of 1933 exempts securities transactions not made by an issuer, an underwriter, or a dealer from registration.[2] For example, an investor who owns shares of IBM can resell these shares to another at any time without having to register with the SEC.

Intrastate Offerings

intrastate offering exemption An exemption from registration that permits local businesses to raise capital from local investors to be used in the local economy without the need to register with the SEC.

The **intrastate offerings exemption** permits local businesses to raise capital from local investors to be used in the local economy without the need to register with the

SEC.[3] An issuer can qualify for this exemption in only one state. There is no limit on the dollar amount of capital that can be raised pursuant to an intrastate offering exemption.

Issuers must meet three requirements to qualify for this exemption[4]:

1. The issuer must be a resident of the state for which the exemption is claimed. A corporation is a resident of the state in which it is incorporated
2. The issuer must be doing business in that state. This requires that 80 percent of the issuer's assets are located in the state, 80 percent of its gross revenues are derived from the state, its principal office is located in the state, and 80 percent of the proceeds of the offering will be used in the state
3. The purchasers of the securities all must be residents of that state.

Private Placements

An issue of securities that does not involve a public offering is exempt from the registration requirement.[5] This exemption—known as the **private placement exemption**—allows issuers to raise capital from an unlimited number of accredited investors without having to register the offering with the SEC.[6] There is no dollar limit on the amount of securities that can be sold pursuant to this exemption.

An **accredited investor** may be any of the following:[7]

1. Any natural person (including spouse) who has a net worth of at least $1 million
2. Any natural person who has had an annual income of at least $200,000 for the previous two years and reasonably expects to make $200,000 income in the current year
3. Any corporation, partnership, or business trust with total assets in excess of $5 million
4. Insiders of the issuers, such as executive officers and directors of corporate issuers and general partners of partnership issuers
5. Certain institutional investors, such as registered investment companies, pension plans, colleges and universities, and the like.

No more than 35 **nonaccredited investors** may purchase securities pursuant to a private placement exemption. Nonaccredited investors must be sophisticated investors, however, either through their own experience and education or through representatives (such as accountants, lawyers, and business managers). General selling efforts, such as advertising to the public, are not permitted.

Small Offerings

Rule 504 exempts the sale of securities not exceeding $1 million during a 12-month period from registration.[8] The securities may be sold to an unlimited number of accredited and unaccredited investors, but general selling efforts to the public are not permitted.

Resale Restrictions

Restricted Securities *Securities* sold pursuant to the intrastate, private placement, or small offering exemptions are called **restricted securities** because they cannot be resold for a limited period of time after their initial issue. The following restrictions apply.

- **Rule 147** stipulates that securities sold pursuant to an *intrastate offering exemption* cannot be sold to nonresidents for a period of nine months.
- **Rule 144** provides that securities sold pursuant to the **private placement** or **small offering exemption** must be held for two years from the date when the securities are last sold by the issuer. After that time, investors may sell the greater of (1) 1 percent of the outstanding securities of the issuer or (2) the average weekly volume of trading in the securities (i.e., the four-week moving average) in any three-month pe-

private placement exemption An exemption from registration that permits issuers to raise capital from an unlimited number of accredited investors and no more than 35 nonaccredited investors without having to register the offering with the SEC.

CAUTION
Up to 35 nonaccredited investors may purchase securities pursuant to a private placement exemption. They must be sophisticated investors through their own experience and education or through representatives.

small offering exemption An exemption from registration for the sale of securities not exceeding $1 million during a 12-month period.

restricted securities Securities that were issued for investment purposes pursuant to the intrastate, private placement, or small offering exemption.

riod. Information about the issuer must be available to the public. Generally, all restrictions are lifted after three years.

Preventing Transfer of Restricted Securities

To protect the nontransferability of **restricted shares**, the issuer must

1. Require the investors to sign an affidavit stating that they are buying the securities for investment, acknowledging that they are purchasing restricted securities, and promising not to transfer the shares in violation of the restriction
2. Place a legend on the stock certificate describing the restriction
3. Notify the transfer agent not to record a transfer of the securities that would violate the restriction.

CAUTION
The issuer must take certain actions to ensure that restricted securities are not sold in violation of the restrictions imposed by Rules 144 and 147.

If the issuer has taken these precautions, it will not lose its exemption from registration even if isolated transfers of stock occur in violation of the restricted periods. Otherwise, the issuer may lose its exemption from registration on the ground that it has sold unregistered securities in violation of Section 5. In such instances, all purchasers are permitted to rescind their purchases of the securities.

Rule 144A

To establish a more liquid and efficient secondary market in unregistered securities, the SEC adopted **Rule 144A** in 1990. This rule permits "qualified institutional investors"—defined as institutions that own and invest at least $100 million in securities—to buy unregistered securities without being subject to the holding periods of Rule 144. This rule is designed to create an institutional market in unregistered securities as well as to permit foreign issuers to raise capital in this country from sophisticated investors without making registration process disclosures.

BUSINESS BRIEF
To increase the liquidity of unregistered securities, the SEC adopted Rule 144A in 1990 that permits "qualified institutional investors" to buy unregistered securities without being subject to the holding periods of Rule 144.

Integration of Exempt Offerings

Separate offerings that qualify for individual exemptions from registration will be **integrated** if they are really part of one large offering. This larger offering must then be examined to see if it qualifies for an exemption from registration. In deciding whether to integrate offerings, the SEC and the courts examine whether the offerings (1) are part of a single plan of financing, (2) involve the issuance of the same class of securities, (3) are made about the same time, (4) receive the same consideration, and (5) are made for the same general purpose.

integration of offerings
When separate offerings that might otherwise qualify for individual exemptions are combined if they are really part of one large offering.

Safe harbor rules protect securities offerings made more than six months before or after the current offering from being integrated with the present offering.[9] This creates a 12-month period outside of which none of the securities offering will be integrated with the current offering.

CAUTION
If offerings are integrated and the combined offering does not qualify for an exemption, the issuer has illegally sold unregistered securities. This subjects the issuer to certain civil fines and criminal penalties. In addition, purchasers may rescind their purchases and recover the price they paid.

CONSIDER THIS EXAMPLE: On January 1, the ABC Corporation issued $4 million of common stock for cash to 25 accredited and 15 sophisticated but nonaccredited investors, some of whom are located out of state. The proceeds are to be used for working capital. This offering qualifies for the private placement exemption.

On April 1 of the same year ABC Corporation issued another $4 million of common stock for cash to 25 accredited and 25 sophisticated but nonaccredited investors, some of whom are located out of state. The proceeds are to be used for working capital. Again, this individual offering qualifies for the private placement exemption.

These offerings must be integrated because they occur within six months of each other, are the same security and for the same consideration, and the proceeds are used for the same purpose. The integrated offering does not qualify for an exemption from registration. There are 40 nonaccredited investors, too many to qualify for the private placement exemption. The integrated offering does not qualify for the intrastate exemption (there are out-of-state investors) or for the Rule 504 small offering exemption (the securities issued exceed $1 million). As a remedy, the investors can rescind their purchases because there has been a violation of Section 5 of the 1933 Act.

LIABILITY PROVISIONS OF THE SECURITIES ACT OF 1933

Violations of the Securities Act of 1933 may result in various penalties and remedies against the perpetrator. These penalties and remedies are discussed in the following paragraphs.

Criminal Liability

Section 24 of the 1933 act imposes criminal liability on any person who willfully violates either the act or the rules and regulations adopted thereunder.[10] The maximum penalty is five years of imprisonment. Criminal actions are brought by the U.S. Justice Department.

> **Section 24** A provision of the Securities Act of 1933 that imposes criminal liability on any person who willfully violates the 1933 Act or the rules or regulations adopted thereunder.

SEC Actions

The SEC may (1) issue a **consent order** whereby a defendant agrees not to violate securities laws in the future but does not admit to violating securities laws in the past, (2) bring an action in federal district court to obtain an **injunction**, or (3) request the court to grant ancillary relief, such as **disgorgement of profits** by the defendant.

Private Actions

Private parties who have been injured by violations of the 1933 act have recourse against the violator, as discussed in the following paragraphs.

Section 12 **Section 12** of the 1933 act imposes civil liability on any person who violates the provisions of Section 5 of the Act. Violations include selling securities pursuant to an unwarranted exemption, making misrepresentations concerning the offer or sale of securities, and other violations. The purchaser's remedy for a violation of Section 12 is either to rescind the purchase or to sue for damages.

> **Section 12** A provision of the Securities Act of 1933 that imposes civil liability on any person who violates the provisions of Section 5 of the Act.

Section 11 **Section 11** of the 1933 act provides for civil liability for damages when a registration statement on its effective date misstates or omits a material fact. Liability under Section 11 is imposed on those who (1) intentionally defraud investors or (2) are negligent in not discovering the fraud. Thus, the issuer, certain corporate officers (chief executive officer, chief financial officer, chief accounting officer), directors, signers of the registration statement, underwriters, and experts (accountants who certify financial statements and lawyers who issue legal opinions that are included in a registration statement) may be liable.

All defendants except the issuer may assert a **due diligence defense** against the imposition of Section 11 liability. If this defense is proven, the defendant is not liable. To establish a due diligence defense, the defendant must prove that after reasonable investigation, he or she had reasonable grounds to believe and did believe that at the time the registration statement became effective, the statements contained therein were true and that there was no omission of material facts.

The following is a classic case where the court imposed civil liability on defendants who failed to prove their due diligence defense.

> **Section 11** A provision of the Securities Act of 1933 that imposes civil liability on persons who intentionally defraud investors by making misrepresentations or omissions of material facts in the registration statement or who are negligent for not discovering the fraud.
>
> **due diligence defense** A defense to a Section 11 action that, if proven, makes the defendant not liable.

CASE 27.2

Escott v. BarChris Construction Corp.

283 F.Supp. 643 (1968) United States District Court, Southern District of New York

Facts In 1961, BarChris Construction Corp. (BarChris), a company primarily engaged in the construction and sale of bowling alleys, was in need of additional financing. To raise working capital, BarChris decided to issue debentures to investors. A
continued

registration statement, including a prospectus, was filed with the SEC on March 30, 1961. After two amendments, the registration statement became effective May 16, 1961. Peat, Marwick, Mitchell & Co. (Peat, Marwick) audited the financial statements of the company that were included in the registration statement and prospectus. The debentures were sold by May 24, 1961. Investors were provided a final prospectus concerning the debentures. Unbeknown to the investors, however, the registration statement and prospectus contained the following material misrepresentations and omissions of material fact:

1. Current assets on the 1960 balance sheet were overstated $609,689 (15 percent)
2. Contingent liabilities of April 30, 1961, were understated $618,853 (42 percent)
3. Sales for the quarter ending March 31, 1961, were overstated $519,810 (32 percent)
4. Gross profits for the quarter ending March 31, 1961, were overstated $230,755 (92 percent)
5. Backlog of orders as of March 31, 1961, was overstated $4,490,000 (186 percent)
6. Loans to officers of BarChris of $386,615 were not disclosed
7. Customer delinquencies and BarChris's potential liability thereto of $1,350,000 were not disclosed
8. The use of the proceeds of the debentures to pay old debts was not disclosed. In 1962, BarChris was failing financially, and on October 29, 1962, it filed a petition for protection to be reorganized under federal bankruptcy law. On November 1, 1962, BarChris defaulted on interest payments due to be paid on the debentures to investors. Barry Escott and other purchasers of the debentures brought this civil action against executive officers, directors, and the outside accountants of BarChris. The plaintiffs alleged that the defendants had violated Section 11 of the Securities Act of 1933 by submitting misrepresentations and omissions of material facts in the registration statement filed with the SEC.

Issue Are the defendants liable for violating Section 11?

Decision Yes. The district court held that the defendants had failed to prove their due diligence defenses.

Reason The district court addressed the liability of the individual defendants and the accounting firm.

Russo. Russo was, to all intents and purposes, the chief executive officer of BarChris. He was a member of the executive committee. He was familiar with all aspects of the business. He was thoroughly aware of BarChris's stringent financial condition in May 1961. In short, Russo knew all the relevant facts. He could not have believed that there were no untrue statements or material omissions in the prospectus. Russo has no due diligence defenses.

Vitolo and Pugliese. They were the founders of the business. Vitolo was president and Pugliese was vice president. Vitolo and Pugliese each are men of limited education. It is not hard to believe that for them the prospectus was difficult reading, if indeed they read it at all. But whether it was or not is irrelevant. The liability of a director who signs a registration statement does not depend upon whether or not he read it or, if he did, whether or not he understood what he was reading. And in any case, there is nothing to show that they made any investigation of anything that they may not have known about or understood. They have not proved their due diligence defenses.

Trilling. Trilling was BarChris's controller. He signed the registration statement in that capacity, although he was not a director. He was a comparatively minor figure in BarChris. He was not considered an executive officer. Trilling may well have been unaware of several of the inaccuracies in the prospectus. But he must have known of some of them. As a financial officer, he was familiar with BarChris's finances and with its books of account. Trilling did not sustain the burden of proving his due diligence defenses.

Auslander. Auslander was an "outside" director, that is, one who was not an officer of BarChris. He was chairman of the board of Valley Stream National Bank in Valley Stream, Long Island. In February 1961 Vitolo asked him to become a director of BarChris. Vitolo gave him an enthusiastic account of BarChris's progress and prospects. As an inducement, Vitolo said that when BarChris received the proceeds of a forthcoming issue of securities, it would deposit $1 million in Auslander's bank. Auslander was elected a director on April 17, 1961. The registration statement in its original form had already been filed, of course, without his signature. On May 10, 1961, he signed a signature page for the first amendment to the registration statement that was filed with the SEC on May 11, 1961. This was a separate sheet without any document attached. Auslander did not know that it was a signature page for a registration statement. He vaguely understood that it was something "for the SEC. " Auslander never saw a copy of the registration statement in its final form. Section 11 imposes liability upon a director no matter how new he is. Auslander has not established his due diligence defenses.

Peat, Marwick. Peat, Marwick's work was in general charge of a member of the firm, Cummings, and more immediately in charge of Peat, Marwick's manager, Logan. Most of the actual work was performed by a senior accountant, Berardi, who had junior assistants, one of whom was Kennedy. Berardi was then about 30 years old. He was not yet a CPA. He had had no previous experience with the bowling industry. This was his first job as a senior accountant. He could hardly have been given a more difficult assignment.

First and foremost is Berardi's failure to discover that Capital Lanes had not been sold. This error affected both the sales figure and the liability side of the balance sheet. Berardi erred in computing the contingent liabilities. Berardi did not make a reasonable investigation in this instance. The purpose of reviewing events subsequent to the date of a certified balance sheet (referred to as an S-1 review when made with reference to a registration statement) is to ascertain whether any material change has occurred in the company's financial position that should be disclosed in order to prevent the balance sheet figures from being misleading. The scope of such a review, under generally accepted auditing standards, is limited. It does not amount to a complete audit. Berardi made the S-1 review in May 1961. He devoted a little over two days to it, a total of 20½ hours. He did not discover any of the errors or omissions pertaining to the state of affairs in 1961, all of which were material. Apparently the only BarChris officer with whom Berardi communicated was Trilling. He could not recall making any inquiries of Russo, Vitolo, or Pugliese. In conducting the S-1 review, Berardi did not examine any important financial records other than the trial balance. As to minutes, he read only the board of directors' minutes of BarChris. He did not read such minutes as there were of the executive committee. He did not know that there was an executive committee. He did not read the minutes of any subsidiary. He asked questions, he got answers that

he considered satisfactory, and he did nothing to verify them.

Berardi had no conception of how tight the cash position was. He did not discover that BarChris was holding up checks in substantial amounts because there was no money in the bank to cover them. He did not know of the officers' loans. He never read the prospectus, so he was not even aware that there had ever been any problem about loans. There had been a material change for the worse in BarChris's financial position. That change was sufficiently serious so that the failure to disclose it made the 1960 figures misleading. Berardi did not discover it. As far as results were concerned, his S-1 review was useless.

Accountants should not be held to a standard higher than that recognized in their profession. Berardi's review did not come up to that standard. He did not take some of the steps that Peat, Marwick's written program prescribed. He did not spend an adequate amount of time on a task of this magnitude. Most important of all, he was too easily satisfied with glib answers to his inquiries. There were enough danger signals to require some further investigation on his part. Generally accepted accounting standards required such further investigation under these circumstances. It is not always sufficient merely to ask questions. Here, again, the burden of proof is on Peat, Marwick. That burden has not been satisfied. Peat, Marwick has not established its due diligence defense.

CASE QUESTIONS

Critical Legal Thinking Should defendants in a Section 11 lawsuit be permitted to prove a due diligence defense to the imposition of liability? Or should liability be strictly imposed?

Ethics Who do you think committed the fraud in this case? Did any of the other defendants act unethically?

Business Implication Who do you think bore the burden of paying the judgment in this case?

THE SECURITIES EXCHANGE ACT OF 1934—TRADING IN SECURITIES

Unlike the Securities Act of 1933, which regulates the original issuance of securities, the **Securities Exchange Act of 1934** primarily regulates subsequent trading. It provides for the registration of certain companies with the SEC, the continuous filing of periodic reports by these companies to the SEC, and the regulation of securities exchanges, brokers, and dealers, and contains provisions that assess civil and criminal liability on violators of the 1934 act and rules and regulations adopted thereunder.

Securities Exchange Act of 1934 A federal statute that primarily regulates the trading in securities.

Continuous Reporting Requirements

The Securities Exchange Act of 1934 requires issuers (1) with assets of more than $5 million and at least 500 shareholders, (2) whose equity securities are traded on a national securities exchange, or (3) who have made a registered offering under the Securities Act of 1933, to file periodic reports with the SEC. These issuers, called **reporting companies**, must file an annual report **(Form 10-K)**, quarterly reports **(Form 10-Q)**, and monthly reports within 10 days of the end of the month in which a material event (such as a merger) occurs **(Form 8-K)**. These reports may be sent to the SEC on computer tapes or disks.

Section 10(b) and Rule 10b-5

Section 10(b) A provision of the Securities Exchange Act of 1934 that prohibits the use of manipulative and deceptive devices in the purchase or sale of securities in contravention of the rules and regulations prescribed by the SEC.

Section 10(b) is one of the most important sections in the entire 1934 act. It prohibits the use of manipulative and deceptive devices in contravention of the rules and regulations prescribed by the SEC.

Pursuant to its rule-making authority, the SEC has adopted **Rule 10b-5**, which provides that:

> It shall be unlawful for any person, directly or indirectly, by use of any means or instrumentality of interstate commerce or of the mails, or of any facility of any national securities exchange,
> a. to employ any device, scheme, or artifice to defraud,
> b. to make any untrue statement of a material fact or to omit to state a material fact necessary in order to make the statements made, in light of the circumstances under which they were made, not misleading, or
> c. to engage in any act, practice, or course of business that operates or would operate as a fraud or deceit upon any person, in connection with the purchase or sale of any security.

Rule 10b-5 A rule adopted by the SEC to clarify the reach of Section 10(b) against deceptive and fraudulent activities in the purchase and sale of securities.

Rule 10b-5 is not restricted to purchases and sales of securities of reporting companies.[11] All transfers of securities, whether made on a stock exchange, in the over-the-counter market, in a private sale, or in connection with a merger, are subject to this rule.[12] The U.S. Supreme Court has held that only conduct involving **scienter** (intentional conduct) violates Section 10(b) and Rule 10b-5. Negligent conduct is not a violation.[13]

scienter Means intentional conduct. Scienter is required for there to be a violation of Section 10(b) and Rule 10b-5.

Section 10(b) and Rule 10b-5 require reliance by the injured party on the misstatement. However, many sales and purchases of securities occur in open market transactions (e.g., over stock exchanges) where there is no direct communication between the buyer and the seller.

INSIDER TRADING

insider trading When an insider makes a profit by personally purchasing shares of the corporation prior to public release of favorable information or by selling shares of the corporation prior to the public disclosure of unfavorable information.

One of the most important purposes of Section 10(b) and Rule 10b-5 is to prevent **insider trading**. Insider trading occurs when a company employee or company advisor uses material nonpublic information to make a profit by trading in the securities of the company. This practice is considered illegal because it allows insiders to take advantage of the investing public.

In the *Matter of Cady, Roberts & Co.*,[14] the SEC announced that the duty of an insider who possesses material nonpublic information has a duty to either (1) abstain from trading in the securities of the company or (2) disclose the information to the person on the other side of the transaction.

Insiders

For purposes of Section 10(b) and Rule 10b-5, **insiders** are defined as (1) officers, directors, and employees at all levels of the company, (2) lawyers, accountants, consultants, and other agents and representatives who are hired by the company on a temporary and nonemployee status to provide services or work to the company, and (3) others who owe a fiduciary duty to the company.

Following are classical and nonclassical cases of insider trading.

CASE 27.3

Securities and Exchange Commission v. Texas Gulf Sulphur Co.

401 F.2d 833 (1968) United States Court of Appeals, Second Circuit

Facts Texas Gulf Sulphur Co. (TGS) had for several years conducted aerial geophysical surveys in eastern Canada. On November 12, 1963, TGS drilled an exploratory hole—Kidd 55—near Timmins, Ontario. Assay reports showed that the core from this drilling proved to be remarkably high in copper, zinc, and silver. Because TGS did not own the mineral rights to properties surrounding the drill site, TGS kept the discovery secret, camouflaged the drill site, and diverted drilling efforts to another site. This allowed TGS to engage in extensive land acquisition around Kidd 55.

Eventually, rumors of a rich mineral strike began circulating. On Saturday, April 11, 1964, *The New York Times* and the *New York Herald-Tribune* published unauthorized reports of TGS drilling efforts in Canada and its rich mineral strike. On Sunday, April 12, officers of TGS met with a public relations consultant and drafted a press release that was issued that afternoon. The press release appeared in morning newspapers of general circulation on Monday, April 13. It read in pertinent part:

> The work done to date has not been sufficient to reach definite conclusions and any statement as to size and grade of ore would be premature and possibly misleading. When we have progressed to the point where reasonable and logical conclusions can be made, TGS will issue a definite statement to its stockholders and to the public in order to clarify the Timmins project.

The rumors persisted. On April 16, 1964, at 10:00 A.M., TGS held a press conference for the financial media. At this conference, which lasted about 10 minutes, TGS disclosed the richness of the Timmins' mineral strike and that the strike would run to at least 25 million tons of ore. In early November 1963, TGS stock was trading at $17⅜ per share. On April 15, 1964, the stock closed at $29⅜. Several officers, directors, and other employees of TGS who had knowledge of the mineral strike at Timmins traded in the stock of TGS during the period November 12, 1963, to April 16, 1964. By May 15, 1964, the stock was selling at $58¼.

The Securities and Exchange Commission (SEC) brought this action against David M. Crawford and Francis G. Coates, two TGS executives who possessed the nonpublic information about the ore strike and who traded in TGS securities. The SEC sought to rescind their stock purchases. The district court found Crawford liable for insider trading but dismissed the complaint against Coates. Appeals were taken from this judgment.

Issue Are Crawford and Coates liable for trading on material inside information in violation of Section 10(b) and Rule 10b-5?

Decision Yes. The court of appeals held that both executives, Crawford and Coates, had engaged in illegal insider trading.

Reason The insiders here were not trading on an equal footing with the outside investors. They alone were in a position to evaluate the probability and magnitude of what seemed from the outset to be a major ore strike.

Crawford. Crawford telephoned his orders to his Chicago broker about midnight on April 15 and again at 8:30 A.M. on April 16 with instructions to buy at the opening of the Midwest Stock Exchange that morning. The trial court's finding that "he sought to, and did, 'beat the news,'" is well documented by the record. Before insiders may act upon material information, such information must have been effectively disclosed in a manner sufficient to ensure its availability to the investing public. Particularly here, where a formal announcement to the entire financial news media had been promised in a prior official release known to the media, all insider activity must await dissemination of the promised official announcement.

Coates. Coates was absolved by the court below because his telephone order was placed shortly before 10:20 A.M. on April 16, which was after the announcement had been made even though the news could not be considered already a matter of public information. This result seems to have been predicated upon a misinterpretation of dicta in *Cady, Roberts,* where the SEC instructed insiders to "keep out of the market until the established procedures for public release of the information are carried out instead of hastening to execute transactions in advance of, and in frustration of, the objectives of the release." The reading of a news release, which prompted Coates into action, is merely the first step

continued

in the process of dissemination required for compliance with the regulatory objective of providing all investors with an equal opportunity to make informed investment judgments. Assuming that the contents of the official release could instantaneously be acted upon, at the minimum Coates should have waited until the news could reasonably have been expected to appear over the media of widest circulation, the Dow Jones broad tape, rather than hastening to ensure an advantage to himself and his broker son-in-law.

CASE QUESTIONS

Critical Legal Thinking Should insider trading be illegal? Why or why not?

Ethics Did Crawford and Coates act ethically in this case?

Business Implication How can businesses protect against their employees engaging in insider trading? Explain.

CASE 27.4

United States v. O'Hagan
1997 WI. 345229 (1997) United States Supreme Court

Facts James O'Hagan was a partner in the law firm of Dorsey & Whitney in Minneapolis, Minnesota. In July 1988, Grand Metropolitan PLC (Grand Met), a company based in London, England, hired Dorsey & Whitney to represent it in a secret tender offer for the stock of the Pillsbury Company (Pillsbury), headquartered in Minneapolis. On August 18, 1988, O'Hagan began purchasing call options for Pillsbury stock. Each call option gave O'Hagan the right to purchase 100 shares of Pillsbury stock at a specified price. O'Hagan continued to purchase call options in August and September, and became the largest holder of call options for Pillsbury stock. In September, O'Hagan also purchased 5,000 shares of Pillsbury common stock at $39 per share. These purchases were all made while Grand Met's proposed tender offer for Pillsbury remained secret to the public. When Grand Met publicly announced its tender offer in October, 1988, Pillsbury stock increased to nearly $60 per share. O'Hagan sold his Pillsbury call options and common stock, making a profit of more than $4.3 million.

The Securities and Exchange Commission (SEC) investigated, and the Justice Department charged O'Hagan with criminally violating Section 10(b) and Rule 10b-5. Because this was not a case of classical insider trading because O'Hagan did not trade in the stock of his law firm's client, Grand Met, the government alleged that O'Hagan was liable under the "misappropriation theory" for trading in Pillsbury stock by engaging in deceptive conduct by misappropriating the secret information about Grand Met's tender offer from his employer, Dorsey & Whitney, and from its client, Grand Met. The district court found

O'Hagan guilty, and sentenced him to 41 months in prison. The Eighth Circuit Court of Appeals reversed, finding that liability under Section 10(b) and Rule 10b-5 cannot be based on the misappropriation theory. The government appealed to the U.S. Supreme Court.

Issue Can a defendant be criminally convicted of violating Section 10(b) and Rule 10b-5 based on the misappropriation theory?

Decision Yes. The Supreme Court held that a defendant can be criminally convicted of violating Section 10(b) and Rule 10b-5 under the misappropriation theory.

Reason Under the "traditional" or "classical theory" of insider trading liability, Section 10(b) and Rule 10b-5 are violated when a corporate *insider* trades in the securities of *their* corporation on the basis of material, nonpublic information. Trading on such information qualifies as a "deceptive device" under Section 10(b) because a relationship of trust and confidence exists between the shareholders of a corporation and those insiders who have obtained confidential information by reason of their position with that corporation.

The "misappropriation theory" holds that a person commits fraud "in connection with" a securities transaction, and thereby violates Section 10(b) and Rule 10b-5, when they misappropriate confidential information for securities trading purposes, in breach of a duty owed to the source of the information. Under this theory, a fiduciary's undisclosed, self-serving use of a principal's information to purchase or sell securities, in breach of a duty of loyalty and confidentiality, defrauds the principal of the exclusive use of that information.

The two theories are complementary, each addressing efforts to capitalize on nonpublic information through the purchase or sale of securities. The classical theory targets a corporate insider's breach of duty to shareholders with whom the insider transacts; the misappropriation theory outlaws trading on the basis of nonpublic information by a corporate "outsider" in breach of a duty owed not to a trading party, but to the source of the information.

The misappropriation theory comports with Section 10(b)'s language, which requires deception "in connection with the purchase or sale of any security," not deception of an identifiable purchaser or seller. In sum, considering the inhibiting impact on market participation of trading on misappropriated information, and the congressional purposes underlying Section 10(b), it makes scant sense to hold a lawyer like O'Hagan a Section 10(b) violator if he works for a law firm representing the target of a ten-

der offer, but not if he works for a law firm representing the bidder. The text of the statute requires no such result. The misappropriation at issue here was probably made the subject of a Section 10(b) charge because it meets the statutory requirement that there be "deceptive" conduct "in connection with" securities transactions.

CASE QUESTIONS

Critical Legal Thinking Should the misappropriation theory be recognized as a basis for criminal liability under Section 10(b) and Rule 10b-5? Do you agree with the Supreme Court's decision?

Ethics If the Supreme Court had upheld the Eighth Circuit's decision, would ethics alone be enough to prevent persons like O'Hagan from trading on secret information?

Business Implication Will the securities markets be more or less honest because of the Supreme Court's ruling?

Tipper–Tippee Liability

A person who discloses material nonpublic information to another person is called a **tipper**. The person who receives such information is known as the **tippee**. The tippee is liable for acting on material information that he or she knew or should have known was not public. The tipper is liable for the profits made by the tippee. If the tippee tips other persons, both the tippee (who is now a tipper) and the original tipper are liable for the profits made by these remote tippees. The remote tippees are liable for their own trades if they knew or should have known that they possessed material inside information.

tipper A person who discloses material nonpublic information to another person.

tippee The person who receives material nonpublic information from a tipper.

LIABILITY PROVISIONS OF THE SECURITIES EXCHANGE ACT OF 1934

The civil and criminal penalties that may be assessed for violations of the Securities Exchange Act of 1934 are discussed in the following paragraphs.

Criminal Liability

Section 32 of the Securities Exchange Act of 1934 makes it a criminal offense to willfully violate the provisions of the act or the rules and regulations adopted thereunder.[15] Upon conviction, a natural person may be fined up to $1 million, imprisoned for up to 10 years, or both. A person cannot be imprisoned unless he or she had knowledge of the rule or regulation violated, however, a corporation or other entity may be fined up to $2.5 million for violating Section 32.

Section 32 A provision of the Securities Exchange Act of 1934 that imposes criminal liability on any person who willfully violates the 1933 Act or the rules or regulations adopted thereunder.

SEC Actions

The SEC may investigate suspected violations of the Securities Exchange Act of 1934 and the rules and regulations adopted thereunder. The SEC may enter into **consent orders** with defendants, seek **injunctions** in federal district court, or seek court orders requiring defendants to **disgorge** illegally gained profits.

Insider Trading Sanctions Act of 1984 A federal statute that permits the SEC to obtain a civil penalty of up to three times the illegal benefits received from insider trading.

In 1984, Congress enacted the **Insider Trading Sanctions Act**,[16] which permits the SEC to obtain a civil penalty of up to three times the illegal profits gained or losses avoided on insider trading. The fine is payable to the U.S. Treasury.

Private Actions

private action A private plaintiff has an *implied* right under Section 10(b) and Rule 10b-5 to sue to rescind the securities contract or recover damages.

Although Section 10(b) and Rule 10b-5 do not expressly provide for a private right of action, courts have implied such a right. Generally, a private plaintiff may seek rescission of the securities contract or recover damages (e.g., disgorgements of the illegal profits by the defendants).

BUSINESS APPLICATION

Michael Milken: The Rise and Fall of the Junk Bond King

When Michael Milken was a student at the Wharton School of Business at the University of Pennsylvania, he studied and fell in love with junk bonds. To him, these bonds were not junk, but a road to riches. Junk bonds are nothing more than bonds that pay a high rate of interest because the company that issues them is highly leveraged with debt—ergo, the high interest rate reflects the greater risk to the investor.

Milken arrived in Beverly Hills, where he headed up the junk bond division of Drexel Burnham Lambert, Inc., a Wall Street investment house. He became the architect of junk bond trading, which fueled the get-rich scheme of the 1980s—the leveraged buyout.

On one side of the transaction, Milken found companies and takeover artists who wanted to sell junk bonds to raise cash to buy companies. On the other side

of the transaction, he found investors—savings and loans, insurance companies, and wealthy investors—who were willing to buy the bonds because their high yield would make the "bottom line" look profitable. And Milken and Drexel earned fees—lots and lots of fees. By the time he was 40, Milken was a billionaire.

In September 1988, the SEC charged Milken, Drexel, and others with numerous violations of securities laws. Several months later, Drexel made a deal with federal prosecutors to plead guilty to six felonies and to pay $650 million in fines and restitution. As part of its deal, Drexel also agreed to settle with the SEC and to cooperate with the ongoing investigation.

Six months later, Milken was indicted on 98 counts of racketeering and securities fraud. Determined to vindicate himself, Milken entered a plea of not guilty.

For the next year, Milken's lawyers and federal prosecutors tried to negotiate a settlement of the charges. Finally, in April 1990, Milken agreed to plead guilty to charges of filing false documents with the SEC, mail fraud, and filing false tax returns. He also agreed to pay $600 million in fines. In March 1992, Milken agreed to pay an additional $500 million to settle private civil lawsuits against him.

U.S. District Court Judge Kimba Wood sentenced Milken to a maximum of 10 years in prison. He was released after 22 months for good behavior and for cooperating with federal authorities in several other insider trading cases. Judge Wood then assigned him to work full-time for three years with D.A.R.E., a program to help keep young people off drugs.

Estimates are that Milken and his family have between $500 million and $1 billion left.

SHORT-SWING PROFITS

Section 16(a) A section of the Securities Exchange Act of 1934 that defines a *statutory insider* for Section 16 purposes.

Section 16(a) of the 1934 act defines any person who is an executive officer, a director, or a 10-percent shareholder of an equity security of a reporting company as a **statutory insider** for Section 16 purposes. Statutory insiders must file reports with the SEC disclosing their ownership and trading in the company's securities.[17] These reports must be filed within 10 days after the end of the month in which the trade occurs.

Section 16(b)

Section 16(b) requires that any profits made by a statutory insider on transactions involving so-called **short-swing profits**—that is, trades involving equity securities occurring within six months of each other—belong to the corporation.[18] The corporation may bring a legal action to recover these profits. Involuntary transactions, such as forced redemption of securities by the corporation or an exchange of securities in a bankruptcy proceeding, are exempt. Section 16(b) is a strict liability provision. Generally, no defenses are recognized. Neither intent nor the possession of inside information need be shown. (See Exhibit 27.3 for a comparison of Section 10(b) and Section 16(b).)

Section 16(b) A section of the Securities Exchange Act of 1934 that requires that any profits made by a statutory insider on transactions involving short-swing profits belong to the corporation.

short-swing profits Profits made by statutory insiders on trades involving equity securities occurring within six months of each other.

Exhibit 27.3
Section 10(b) and Section 16(b) Compared

Element	Section 10(b) and Rule 10b-5	Section 16(b)
Covered securities	All securities	Securities required to be registered with the SEC under the 1934 Act
Inside information	Defendant made a misrepresentation or traded on inside (or perhaps misappropriated) information	Short-swing profits recoverable whether or not they are attributable to misrepresentation, inside information, or misappropriation
Recovery	Belongs to the injured purchaser or seller	Belongs to the corporation

CONSIDER THIS EXAMPLE: Rosanne is the president of a corporation and a statutory insider who does not possess any inside information. On February 1, she purchases 1,000 shares of her employer's stock at $10 per share. On June 1, she sells the stock for $14 per share. The corporation can recover the $4,000 profit because the trades occurred within six months of each other. Rosanne would have to wait until after August 1 to sell the securities.

SEC Rules

In 1991, the SEC adopted new rules concerning Section 16.[19] This was the first major change in the rules in 57 years. These rules:

- Clarify the definition of *officer* to include only executive officers who perform policy-making functions. This would include the president, the chief executive officer, the vice presidents in charge of business units or divisions, the principal financial officer, the principal accounting officer, and the like. Officers who run day-to-day operations but are not responsible for policy decisions are not included.
- Create a new *Form 5* report that must be filed by all insiders within 45 days of the end of the company's calendar year.
- Relieve insiders of liability for transactions that occur within six months before becoming an insider. For example, if a noninsider buys shares of his or her company January 15, becomes an insider March 15, and sells the shares May 15, the January 15 purchase is not matched against the May 15 sale.
- Continue the rule that insiders are liable for transactions that occur within six months of the last transaction engaged in while an insider. For example, if an insider buys shares in his company April 30 and leaves the company May 15, this purchase must be matched against any sale of the company's shares that occurs on or before October 30.

"Fraud is infinite in variety; sometimes it is audacious and unblushing; sometimes it pays a sort of homage to virtue, and then it is modest and retiring; it would be honesty itself, if it could only afford it."
Lord Macnaghten
Reddaway v. Banham
(1896)

- Treat derivative securities (e.g., stock options, warrants) as follows: The acquisition or disposition of a derivative security is a Section 16 event; the exercise of the derivative security is a nonevent for Section 16 purposes. For example, suppose a company issues a stock option to its president May 15, who exercises the option June 15 and sells the shares on December 1. There is no violation of Section 16.
- Require companies to disclose delinquent filings of Section 16 forms in their proxy statements.

BUSINESS CHECKLIST

Securities Investors' Accounts Insured by the Securities Investor Protection Corporation (SIPC)

Millions of investors use securities brokerage firms to buy, sell, and hold their securities in "street name." What happens if a securities firm that holds these securities fails? The securities are insured by the **Securities Investor Protection Corporation (SIPC)**, a private insurance company that is funded by annual assessments paid by securities firms.

Some vital statistics and information that investors should know about the SIPC insurance are:

- The SIPC provides insurance coverage of up to $500,000 per customer
- Of the $500,000 coverage, only $100,000 of cash is covered per customer
- Unlike deposit insurance for savings and checking accounts at banks, the SIPC is not backed by the full faith and credit of the U.S. government
- The SIPC currently has under $1 billion in its coffers and an additional $500 million line of credit with banks it can draw on. This is sufficient to cover the failure of many small brokerage firms, but is inadequate to cover the failure of large brokerage firms.

OTHER FEDERAL SECURITIES LAWS

Securities Enforcement Remedies and Penny Stock Reform Act of 1990

Securities Enforcement Remedies and Penny Stock Reform Act of 1990
A federal statute that gives the SEC greater enforcement powers and increases and expands the remedies available for securities violations.

The **Securities Enforcement Remedies and Penny Stock Reform Act of 1990**[20] added new weapons to the SEC's enforcement powers. Namely, it authorizes

- **Cease-and-desist orders.** After holding an appropriate administrative proceeding, the SEC may order a *cease-and-desist order* against any person who is violating, has violated, or is about to violate any provision of federal securities laws to cease and desist from committing such violation. The act authorizes the SEC to issue a *temporary cease-and-desist order* prior to completion of the proceeding if it determines that the alleged violation is likely to result in substantial dissipation or conversion of assets, significant harm to investors or the public interest, or losses to the **Securities Investor Protection Corporation (SIPC)**.
- **Civil money penalties.** The SEC may bring an action in federal court seeking *civil money penalties* against any person or entity for violating federal securities laws, SEC rules or regulations, and SEC cease-and-desist orders. The court may assess penalties as the greater of (1) the defendant's pecuniary gain obtained as a result of the violation or (2) any one of the following three tiers of fines, as the circumstances warrant:

Tier 1: $5,000 for a natural person or $50,000 for any other person
Tier 2: $50,000 for a natural person or $250,000 for any other person
Tier 3: $100,000 for a natural person or $500,000 for any other person

• **Penny stock reform.** In the past, there has been significant fraud in the sale of penny stocks. **Penny stocks** are low-priced stocks (e.g., stocks that are sold for a few cents to a few dollars). The act requires the SEC to adopt rules to require securities brokers and dealers to provide specific information to investors concerning stock prices and the inherent risk of the penny stock market. This enhanced disclosure should help prevent some penny stock fraud.

Market Reform Act of 1990

The **Market Reform Act of 1990**[21] establishes a number of measures to enhance financial market stability. It authorizes the SEC to promulgate rules to proscribe manipulative practices related to market price levels and trading practices during periods of extraordinary market volatility. Under this authority, the SEC sets limits on program trading (i.e., computer-driven trading strategies). The act also authorizes the SEC to take emergency action (e.g., suspend trading) to ensure fair and orderly markets during periods of market stress.

Market Reform Act of 1990
A federal statute that authorizes the SEC to regulate trading practices during periods of extraordinary market volatility.

Racketeer Influenced and Corrupt Organizations Act

The **Racketeer Influenced and Corrupt Organizations Act (RICO)** makes it a federal crime to engage in a pattern of racketeering activity.[22] Because securities fraud falls under the definition of racketeering activity, the government often brings a RICO allegation in conjunction with a securities fraud allegation.

In addition, persons injured by a RICO violation can bring a private civil action against the violator and recover treble (triple) damages, but only if the defendant has been criminally convicted in connection with the securities fraud.[23] A third-party independent contractor (e.g., an outside accountant) must have participated in the operation or management of the enterprise to be liable for civil RICO.[24]

Racketeer Influenced and Corrupt Organizations Act (RICO) A federal statute that provides for both criminal and civil penalties.

Private Securities Litigation Reform Act of 1995

Sometimes companies include forward-looking statements about future economic plans and projections of financial data in prospectuses and other documents filed with the SEC and provided to investors. The **Private Securities Litigation Reform Act of 1995** provides a *safe harbor* from liability for companies that make such statements if they are accompanied by meaningful cautionary statements that identify risk factors that could cause actual results to differ from those in the statement.

Private Securities Litigation Reform Act of 1995
Provides a safe harbor from liability for companies that make forward-looking statements that are accompanied by meaningful cautionary statements of risk factors.

STATE SECURITIES LAWS

Most states have enacted securities laws. These laws, which are often called **blue-sky laws**, generally require the registration of certain securities and provide exemptions from registration. They also contain broad antifraud provisions.

The **Uniform Securities Act** has been adopted by many states. This act is drafted to coordinate state securities laws with federal securities laws.

NOTE
State securities laws presumably originated to protect investors from foolishly buying a piece of the blue sky.

COMMODITIES REGULATION

Commodities include grains (e.g., wheat, soybeans, oats), animals (e.g., cattle, hogs), animal products (e.g., pork bellies), foods (e.g., sugar, coffee), metals (e.g., gold, silver), and oil. Sellers and buyers of these products can enter into **cash contracts** for their sale. In the 19th century, cash markets developed at major transportation centers, such as Chicago and St. Louis, where food processors and others purchased needed products from farmers, ranchers, and other commodity producers.

commodities Grains, animals, animal products, foods, metals, and oil.

In an attempt to avoid the chaos of many cash sales occurring at once (e.g., after harvest), farmers and ranchers began entering into **forward contracts** for the sale of commodities. For example, at planting time, a farmer can enter into a contract to sell his barley to Miller Brewing Company after it is harvested. Such contracts are individually negotiated.

Eventually, a futures market in commodities developed. The remainder of this section discusses commodity futures markets.

Commodity Futures Contracts

commodity futures contract An agreement to buy or sell a specific amount and type of a commodity at some future date under standardized terms established by the CFTC.

A **commodity futures contract** is an agreement to buy or sell a specific amount and type of a commodity at some future date at a price established at the time of contracting. For example, a futures contract may be to sell 5,000 bushels of oats on July 31 at $2.87 per bushel.

The Commodity Futures Trading Commission (CFTC), a federal administrative agency, establishes standardized terms for futures contracts (e.g., quantity and quality of the commodity, time and place of delivery). Thus, each similar contract is *fungible*. This makes the contracts liquid, that is, they can be bought and sold on the commodities exchanges just as stocks and bonds are bought and sold on securities exchanges. Farmers, ranchers, food processors, milling companies, mineral producers, oil companies, and investors often use futures contracts to **hedge** against volatile prices in cash markets.

hedging To try to avoid or lessen loss by making a counterbalancing investment.

Option contracts on futures contracts are traded on commodities exchanges. For the payment of a fee a purchaser can buy the right to buy and sell a futures contract within a set period of time.

Commodity Exchange Act

Commodity Exchange Act A federal statute that regulates the trading of commodity futures contracts.

Commodity Futures Trading Commission (CFTC) A federal administrative agency that administers and enforces the Commodity Exchange Act, as amended.

The **Commodity Exchange Act (CEA)** was enacted by Congress in 1936 to regulate the trading of commodity futures contracts. The **Commodity Futures Trading Commission Act**, which was enacted in 1974, significantly amended the prior act.[25] The 1974 amendments created the **Commodity Futures Trading Commission (CFTC)** to administer and enforce the CEA. The CFTC is a federal administrative agency consisting of five members appointed by the President.

The CFTC has the authority to regulate trading and options in commodities futures contracts. It has the power to adopt regulations, conduct investigations, bring administrative proceedings against suspected violators, issue cease-and-desist orders and injunctions, and impose civil fines. Suspected criminal violations can be referred to the Justice Department for criminal action.

Designation of Contract Markets

commodity exchange An exchange over which commodity futures contracts are bought and sold on an impersonal basis.

Commodities exchanges have been established at different locations across the country where commodity futures contracts can be bought and sold by food producers, farmers, and speculators. The major commodity exchanges follow:

- The Chicago Board of Trade (CBOT)
- The Chicago Mercantile Exchange (CME)
- The Commodity Exchange New York (COMEX)
- Kansas City Board of Trade (KBOT)
- New York Coffee, Sugar, & Cocoa Exchange (NYCSCE)
- New York Cotton Exchange (NYCTN)
- New York Mercantile Exchange (NYME)
- New York Futures Exchange (NYF).

▐ **BUSINESS BRIEF** ▐
Commodities are traded over the Chicago Board of Trade and other commodities exchanges located throughout the United States.

The CFTC has the authority to designate a commodities exchange as a **contract market** to trade in a particular commodities futures contract (e.g., pork bellies). An exchange can be designated a contract market for a number of commodities. To be designated a contract market, the exchange must agree to adhere to the CEA and regulations adopted by the CFTC and to engage in substantial self-regulation.

Antifraud Provision

Section 4b of the CEA prohibits fraudulent conduct in connection with any order or contract of sale of any commodity for future delivery.[26] The CFTC has adopted **Rule 32.9**, which makes it unlawful to cheat, deceive a person, or make false reports or statements concerning commodity futures and option contracts.[27] Both of these laws require *scienter*, that is, intentional, willful, or reckless conduct. Negligent conduct is not actionable under these laws.

Section 4b A provision of the Commodity Exchange Act that prohibits fraudulent conduct in connection with any order or contract of sale of any commodity for future delivery.

Rule 32.9 A rule adopted by the CFTC to clarify the reach of Section 4b against fraudulent conduct in the purchase and sale of commodity futures contracts.

ETHICAL PERSPECTIVE

Commodity "Boiler Rooms"

Investing in commodity futures contracts is a very risky venture. An investor can make, or lose, a fortune quickly. But investment risk is not the only risk involved. An investor must be careful not to get burned by a commodities "boiler room" fraud. Consider the following case.

Crown Colony Commodity Options, Ltd. (Crown Colony) is a New York corporation that maintains an office in Miami, Florida. Since February 1976, Crown Colony has been engaged primarily in the business of offering and selling London commodity options to investors throughout the United States. The Miami office is a "boiler room" operation consisting of 50 telephone cubicles with WATS lines that are used by another company to sell wigs by telephone during the day, and by Crown Colony to sell options at night. Crown Colony made no attempt to hire sales representatives with any knowledge of the commodity markets. The training given sales representatives was geared to produce sales and overcome customer resistance, and they were told the less they knew about commodities, the better sales representatives they would be. Evidence showed that intense

pressure was brought to bear on sales representatives to produce sales. They received a 10 percent commission of the purchase price paid by a customer for an option.

Crown Colony employed a highly standardized system for contacting customers in the effort to persuade them to invest in commodity options. The initial contact with a customer consisted of the presentation of a script or canned sale pitch called a "front." These fronts were calculated to "stimulate greed" of potential customers by emphasizing the opportunity for unlimited profits in commodity options. The fronts were misleading and inaccurate, and the predictions contained therein were made without a reasonable belief of their accuracy. Moreover, Crown Colony frequently informed investors that a commodity was trading at less than its actual market price in order to be able to report a sharp price "rise" at a later date and thus pressure customers to "get in while the getting was good."

After being qualified during the front, an investor was ordinarily "papered," or sent various brochures purporting to describe the mechanics of option trading, the nature of Crown Colony's

business, and the advantages of investing in whatever option was being promoted at the time. This literature abounds with misleading, incomplete, and deceptive statements. After being papered, an investor was again telephoned by a Crown Colony representative, who presented a second canned sales pitch called a "drive." Like the fronts used by Crown Colony, the drives contained many misleading and deceptive statements intended to pressure customers into investing in options.

It was also the regular practice of Crown Colony to "load" and "roll" customers who made an initial option purchase. "Loading" refers to the policy of attempting to sell additional options to a customer who has once purchased, without respect to the investor's realistic ability to afford further investment. "Rolling" consists of exercising a customer's option that has turned out to be profitable and reinvesting all or a portion of the proceeds in another option on a different commodity for the purpose of generating extra commissions.

The Commodity Futures Trading Commission (CFTC) sued the owners, managers, and certain *continued* sales representatives of Crown Colony. The district court found that the defendants had engaged in a plethora of grave, willful violations of the Commodity Exchange Act. The court noted, "Not a single defendant has expressed regret for his past conduct or indicated a recognition of its gravity.

Their past actions speak louder than their present words." The court issued an injunction against further violations of the Commodity Exchange Act. *[Commodity Futures Trading Commission v. Crown Colony Commodity Options, Ltd.*, 434 F.Supp. 911 (S.D.N.Y. 1977)]

1. Do you think many commodity futures "boiler rooms" operate in this country?
2. Why do investors get "taken" by commodities frauds? Do they get what they deserve?
3. Was the penalty sufficient in this case? What good does an injunction do?

INTERNATIONAL PERSPECTIVE

Enforcement of International Securities Laws

The United States is not the only country in the world that outlaws insider trading and securities fraud. For example, Britain has outlawed insider dealing in securities for years. In 1993, the British government even implemented new legislation to strengthen its insider trading laws. The French insider trading law makes it illegal for a person to trade on nonpublic information received by reason of his or her position or profession. The European Community (EC) has directed all member countries to adopt laws against insider trading.

Although other countries have enacted securities laws that prohibit forms of insider trading, no country enforces securities laws as strictly as the United States. For instance, Japan has an insider trading law that is rarely enforced.

Many persons who engage in illegal insider trading in the United States often do so using businesses or "fronts" located in other countries. In addition, these traders often deposit their ill-gotten gains in secret bank accounts located in off-shore bank havens. Can U.S. authorities obtain documents and evidence, as well as information about the location of bank accounts, from other countries? The answer is yes, in many situations.

In 1990, Congress enacted the **International Securities Enforcement Cooperation Act** [P.L. 101-550, 104 Stat. 2713]. The act authorizes the SEC to cooperate with foreign securities authorities, to provide records to foreign securities authorities, and to sanction securities professionals in this country who violate foreign securities laws.

The U.S. Securities and Exchange Commission (SEC) has entered in **memoranda of understanding**, or **MOUs**, with several foreign governments or authorities. As a general rule, the MOUs provide that the SEC and its foreign counterparts will cooperate in the enforcement of each country's securities laws. Thus, the SEC can obtain evidence about the location of bank accounts and other information concerning persons suspected of violating U.S. securities laws from foreign authorities. Currently, the SEC has entered into MOUs with Argentina, Brazil, Canada, France, Great Britain, Italy, Japan, the Netherlands, and Switzerland.

As securities trading becomes more international and global markets are developed, it is going to become easier for investors and others to engage in insider trading and securities fraud across national boundaries. The United States and other countries will have to enact laws that will reach global securities fraud and cooperate in finding, prosecuting, and penalizing perpetrators of securities frauds.

WORKING THE WEB

U.S. Securities and Exchange Commission This large government Web site links you to many securities materials.
  Visit at http://www.sec.gov/

Securities Act of 1933 This searchable copy of the Act is maintained by the University of Cincinnatti.
  Visit at http://www.law.uc.edu/CCL/33Act/

Securities Act of 1934 This searchable copy of the Act is maintained by the University of Cincinnatti.
  Visit at http://www.law.uc.edu/CCL/34Act/

Securities Law Home Page This site is an on-line guide to securities law.
  Visit at http://www.seclaw.com/

Wall Street Research Net Want to find out information about a company or get a com-

pany's current stock quote? Then this is the site for you.
  Visit at http://www.wsrn.com/home/company Research.html

CYBER EXERCISES:

1. If you have a complaint or question about your investments, you might want to contact the U.S. Securities and Exchange Commission, Office of Investor Education and Assistance. What is its e-mail address?
2. What subject does Section 4 of the Securities Act of 1933 cover?
3. What commission does the Securities Act of 1934 establish?
4. Using the Securities Law Home Page, read the current issue of Securities Law Letter.
5. Using Wall Street Research Net, find a current stock quote for your favorite company.

CHAPTER SUMMARY

THE SECURITIES AND EXCHANGE COMMISSION (SEC), P. 669

The Securities and Exchange Commission (SEC)	Created in 1934, it is a federal administrative agency empowered to administer federal securities laws. The SEC can adopt rules and regulations to interpret and implement federal securities statutes.

DEFINITION OF A SECURITY, P. 669

Definition of a Security	*Security.* A security must be found before federal securities laws apply. A *security* is defined as: 1. *Common securities.* Interests or instruments that are commonly known as securities, such as common stock, preferred stock, debentures, and warrants. 2. *Statutorily defined securities.* Interests and instruments that are expressly mentioned in securities acts as being securities, such as interests in oil, gas, and mineral rights. 3. *Investment contracts.* A flexible standard for defining a security. Under the *Howey* test, a security exists if (1) an investor invests money (2) in a common enterprise and (3) expects to make a profit off the significant efforts of others.

THE SECURITIES ACT OF 1933—REGISTRATION OF SECURITIES, P. 670

The Securities Act of 1933	A federal statute that primarily regulates the *issuance* of securities by corporations, partnerships, associations, and individuals.

Registration Statement	1. *Section 5.* A provision of the 1933 Act that requires an issuer to register its securities with the SEC prior to selling them to the public if the securities or transaction do not qualify for an exemption from registration. 2. *Registration statement.* Document that an issuer of securities files with the SEC to register its securities. It must contain information about the issuer, the securities to be issued, and other relevant information.
Prospectus	A written disclosure document that is submitted to the SEC with the registration statement. It is distributed to prospective investors to enable them to evaluate the financial risk of the investment.
Limitations on Activities during the Registration Process	1. *Prefiling period.* Begins when the issuer first contemplates issuing securities and ends when the registration statement is filed with the SEC. During this period, the issuer cannot (1) offer to sell securities, (2) sell securities, or (3) *condition the market.* 2. *Waiting period.* Begins when the registration statement is filed with the SEC and ends when the registration statement becomes effective. During this time, the issuer cannot (1) sell securities or (2) use unapproved writing to offer to sell the securities. The issuer may make oral offers, distribute *preliminary* and *summary prospectuses,* and publish *tombstone ads.* 3. *Posteffective period.* Begins when the registration statement becomes effective and runs until the issuer either sells all of the offered securities or withdraws them from sale. The issuer may offer to sell the securities during this period. The issuer must deliver a *final prospectus* (*statutory prospectus*) to a purchaser prior to or at the time of confirming the sale or sending the security to the purchaser.
Regulation A Offerings	*Regulation A.* A regulation that permits an issuer to sell securities pursuant to a simplified registration process.

SECURITIES EXEMPT FROM REGISTRATION, P. 674

Securities Exempt from Registration	The following *securities* are exempt from the SEC registration process: 1. Securities issued by any government in the United States (e.g., municipal bonds issued by city governments) 2. Short-term notes and drafts that have a maturity date that does not exceed nine months (e.g., commercial paper issued by corporations) 3. Securities issued by nonprofit issuers, such as religious institutions, charitable institutions, and colleges and universities 4. Securities of financial institutions (e.g., banks and savings associations) that are regulated by the appropriate banking authorities 5. Securities issued by common carriers (e.g., railroads and trucking companies) that are regulated by the Interstate Commerce Commission (ICC) 6. Insurance and annuity contracts issued by insurance companies 7. Stock dividends and stock splits 8. Securities issued in a corporate reorganization where one security is exchanged for another security

TRANSACTIONS EXEMPT FROM REGISTRATION, P. 674

Transactions Exempt from Registration	The following *transactions* are exempt from the SEC registration process: (1) nonissuer transactions, (2) intrastate offerings, (3) private placements, and (4) small offerings.

Nonissuer Exemption	Securities transactions *not* by an issuer, an underwriter, or a dealer are exempt from SEC registration. This covers normal purchases of securities by investors.

Intrastate Offerings	A local business can issue securities without dollar limit without registering with the SEC if the following requirements are met:
	1. The issuer is a resident of the state (e.g., the corporation is incorporated in the state).
	2. The issuer is *doing business* in the state. This requires that:
	  a. 80 percent of the issuer's assets are located in the state.
	  b. 80 percent of the issuer's gross revenues are derived from the state.
	  c. The issuer's principal office is located in the state.
	  d. 80 percent of the proceeds of the offering will be used in the state.
	3. The purchasers of the securities all are residents of the state.

Private Placements	An issue of securities that does not involve a public offering is exempt from SEC registration. There is no dollar limit on the amount of securities that can be issued pursuant to this exemption. Securities can be sold to any number of *accredited investors*, but to no more than 35 *nonaccredited investors*.
	1. *Accredited investors.* These include:
	  a. Any natural person (including spouse) who has a net worth of at least $1 million
	  b. Any natural person who has had an annual income of at least $200,000 for the previous two years and reasonably expects to make $200,000 income in the current year
	  c. Any corporation, partnership, or business trust with total assets in excess of $25 million
	  d. Insiders of the issuers, such as executive officers and directors of corporate issuers and general partners of partnership issuers
	  e. Certain institutional investors, such as registered investment companies, pension plans, colleges and universities, and the like.

Small Offerings	An offering of securities that does not exceed $1 million during a 12-month period is exempt from SEC registration. The securities may be sold to any number of purchasers.
	1. *Restricted securities.* Securities sold pursuant to the intrastate, private placement, or small offering exemptions are called *restricted securities*.
	2. *Rule 147.* An SEC rule stipulating that securities sold pursuant to an *intrastate offering exemption* cannot be sold to nonresidents for a period of nine months.
	3. *Rule 144.* An SEC rule stipulating that securities sold pursuant to the *private placement* or *small offering exemption* must be held for two years; limited sales may be made between years two and three; then unlimited sales are permitted.
	4. *Preventing transfer of restricted securities.* To prevent the illegal transfer of restricted securities, the issuer must take the following precautions:
	  a. *Affidavit.* Require investors to sign an affidavit stating that they are buying the securities for investment, and promising not to transfer the restricted securities until the restrictions no longer apply.
	  b. *Legend.* Place a legend on the stock certificate describing the restriction.
	  c. *Transfer agent.* Appoint and notify the transfer agent not to record a transfer of the securities that would violate the restriction.

	5. *Rule 144A*. An SEC rule that permits *qualified institutional investors*—defined as institutions that own and invest at least $100 million in securities—to buy unregistered securities without being subject to the holding periods of Rule 144.
Integration of Exempt Offerings	Separate exempt offerings of securities will be *integrated* (added together) if they occur within six months of each other and they are found to be similar and part of the same offering. 1. *Safe harbor rule*. Exempt securities offerings made more than six months before or after the current offering are not integrated with the current offering. 2. *Integrated offering*. If two or more exempt offerings are integrated, they are considered one offering. This *integrated offering* must be examined to determine whether it qualifies for any exemption from SEC registration.

LIABILITY PROVISIONS OF THE SECURITIES ACT OF 1933, P. 677

Criminal Liability	*Section 24* of the 1933 Act imposes criminal liability on any person who willfully violates either the act or the rules and regulations adopted thereunder. Criminal actions are brought by the U.S. Justice Department.
SEC Actions	The SEC may seek the following remedies: 1. *Consent order*. The SEC may issue a consent order whereby a defendant agrees not to violate securities laws in the future but does not admit to violating securities laws in the past. 2. *Injunction*. The SEC may bring an action in federal district court to obtain an injunction. 3. *Disgorgement of profits*. The SEC may request the court to order the defendant to disgorge illegally gained profits.
Private Actions	Private parties who have been injured by a violation of the 1933 Act may sue the violator to rescind the securities contract to recover damages. The plaintiff may sue under: 1. *Section 12*. A provision of the 1933 Act that imposes civil liability on any person who violates the provisions of Section 5 of the act (e.g., sells unregistered securities). 2. *Section 11*. A provision of the 1933 Act that imposes civil liability on persons who intentionally defraud investors by making misrepresentations or omissions of material facts in the registration statement, or are negligent in not discovering the fraud. a. *Due diligence defense*. A defense to a Section 11 action that, if proven, makes the defendant not liable. This requires the defendant to have made a reasonable investigation and had reasonable grounds to believe and did believe that the statements made in the registration statement were true.

THE SECURITIES EXCHANGE ACT OF 1934—TRADING IN SECURITIES, P. 679

The Securities Exchange Act of 1934	A federal statute that primarily regulates the *trading* of securities.
Continuous Reporting Requirements	1. *Reporting companies*. Issuers (1) with assets of more than $5 million and at least 500 shareholders, (2) whose equity securities are traded on a national securities exchange, or (3) who have made a registered offering under the Securities Act of 1933.

	2. *Reporting requirements.* Reporting companies must file the following reports with the SEC: (1) annual reports (*Form 10-K*), (2) quarterly reports (*From 10-Q*), and (3) monthly reports (*Form 8-K*) within 10 days of the end of the month in which a material event (e.g., merger) occurs.
Section 10(b) and Rule 10b-5	1. *Section 10(b).* A provision of the 1934 Act that prohibits the use of manipulative and deceptive devices in the purchase or sale of securities in contravention of the rules and regulations prescribed by the SEC. 2. *Rule 10b-5.* A rule adopted by the SEC to clarify the reach of Section 10(b) against defective and fraudulent activities in the purchase and sale of securities. 3. *Scienter.* Only conduct involving *scienter* (intentional conduct) violates Section 10(b) and Rule 10b-5. Negligent conduct is not a violation.

INSIDER TRADING, P. 680

Insider Trading	Occurs when an insider makes a profit by purchasing shares of the corporation prior to public release of favorable information or selling shares of the corporation prior to public disclosure of unfavorable information. Insider trading violates Section 10(b) and Rule 10b-5. 1. *Cady, Roberts rule.* An insider who possesses material nonpublic information must either (1) abstain from trading in the securities of the company or (2) disclose the information to the person from whom he or she purchases or to whom he or she sells the securities.
Insiders	Insiders for Section 10(b) and Rule 10b-5 purposes include all employees of the company, independent contractors hired by the company on a temporary basis to provide services or work to the company, and others who owe a fiduciary duty to the company.
Tipper–Tippee Liability	1. *Tipper.* A person who discloses material nonpublic information to another person. 2. *Tippee.* A person who receives material nonpublic information from a tipper. 3. *Tippee's liability.* The tippee is liable for acting on material information received from a tipper if he or she knew or should have known that the information was not public. The tippee must disgorge profits made on the tip. 4. *Tipper's liability.* The tipper is liable for his own profits and the profits made by the tippee.

LIABILITY PROVISIONS OF THE SECURITIES EXCHANGE ACT OF 1934, P. 683

Criminal Liability	*Section 32* of the 1934 Act imposes criminal liability on any person who willfully violates the 1934 Act or the rules and regulations adopted thereunder. Criminal actions are brought by the U.S. Justice Department.
SEC Actions	The SEC may enter into *consent orders* with defendants, seek *injunctions* in federal district court, or seek orders requiring defendants to *disgorge* illegally gained profits. 1. *Treble damages.* The *Insider Trading Securities Act of 1984* permits the SEC to obtain a civil penalty of up to three times the illegal benefits received from insider trading.

Private Actions	*Section 10(b).* A private plaintiff has an *implied right* under Section 10(b) and Rule 10b-5 to sue to rescind the securities contract or recover damages from a defendant who has engaged in manipulative and deceptive practices that have caused the plaintiff injury.

SHORT-SWING PROFITS, P. 684

Short-Swing Profits	1. *Statutory insiders. Section 16(a)* of the Securities Exchange Act of 1934 defines a *statutory insider* for Section 16 purposes as any person who is an executive officer, a director, or a 10-percent shareholder of an equity security of a reporting company.
Section 16(b)	1. *Short-swing profits.* Profits made by statutory insiders on trades involving equity securities that occur within six months of each other. 2. *Section 16(b).* A provision of the 1934 Act that requires that any profits made by a statutory insider on transactions involving short-swing profits belong to the corporation.
1991 SEC Rules	Rules issued by the SEC that clarify the persons and transactions subject to Section 16 short-swing profit rules.

OTHER FEDERAL SECURITIES LAWS, P. 686

Securities Enforcement Remedies and Penny Stock Reform Act of 1990	A federal statute that gives the SEC greater enforcement powers in the following ways: 1. *Cease-and-desist orders.* After holding an appropriate administrative proceeding, the SEC may order a *cease-and-desist order* that orders a party not to violate securities statutes, regulations, or orders. 2. *Civil money penalties.* The SEC may bring an action in federal district court seeking *civil money penalties* against any person or entity for violating federal securities laws, SEC rules and regulations, and SEC cease-and-desist orders. 3. *Penny stock reform.* The SEC has adopted rules that require securities brokers and dealers to provide specific information to investors concerning the inherent risk of the penny stock market.
Market Reform Act of 1990	Federal statute that authorizes the SEC to regulate trading practices during periods of extraordinary market volatility, including regulating computer-driven *program trading.* The act also authorizes the SEC to take emergency action (e.g., suspend trading) when warranted.
Racketeer Influenced and Corrupt Organization Act (RICO)	Federal statute that provides for both criminal and civil penalties for engaging in a *pattern or practice of racketeering activities.* Sometimes securities fraud qualifies as a RICO violation. *Treble damages* are available in a civil RICO action.

STATE SECURITIES LAWS, P. 687

State Securities Laws	Most states have enacted securities laws that regulate the issuance and trading of securities. These acts are often patterned after, and are designed to coordinate with, federal securities laws. The *Uniform Securities Act,* which is a model state securities act, has been adopted by many states.

COMMODITIES REGULATION, P. 687

Commodities Regulation	*Commodity.* Includes grains, animals, animal products, foods, metals, and oil.

	1. *Cash contract.* A contract entered into by a seller and a buyer for the sale of a commodity. The sale is *negotiated* between the parties and occurs *immediately*.
	2. *Forward contract.* A contract entered into by a seller and a buyer for the sale of a commodity sometime in the future. The sale is *negotiated* between the parties, but will be completed at a specified *future date*.
Commodity Futures Contracts	A contract to buy or sell a specific amount and type of a commodity at some future date under *standardized terms* established by the Commodity Futures Trading Commission (CFTC). The sale is not negotiated between the parties but occurs over an impersonal *commodities exchange*. The terms of similar contracts are the same.
	1. *Option contract.* A contract on a futures contract whereby a purchaser pays a fee for the right to buy or sell a specified commodity futures contract within a set period of time.
Commodity Exchange Act (CEA)	A federal statute that, as amended, regulates the trading of commodity futures contracts.
	1. *Commodities Futures Trading Commission (CFTC).* Federal administrative agency that administers and enforces the Commodity Exchange Act, as amended.
Designations of Contract Markets	1. *Commodity exchange.* An impersonal market over which commodity futures are traded. Major commodity exchanges are located in various places in the United States.
	2. *Contract market.* A designated commodity exchange that trades in a particular commodity futures contract. An exchange can be designated a contract market for a number of commodities.
Antifraud Provision	1. *Section 4b.* A provision of the Commodity Exchange Act that prohibits fraudulent conduct in connection with any order or contract of sale of any commodity for future delivery.
	2. *Rule 32.9.* A rule adopted by the CFTC to clarify the reach of Section 4b against fraudulent conduct in the purchase and sale of commodity futures contracts.

CRITICAL LEGAL THINKING CASES

27.1 Definition of a Security Dare To Be Great, Inc. (Dare) is a Florida corporation wholly owned by Glenn W. Turner Enterprises, Inc. (Turner). Dare offered self-improvement courses aimed at improving self-motivation and sales ability. In return for an investment of money, the purchaser received certain tapes, records, and written materials. In addition, depending on the level of involvement, the purchaser had the opportunity to help sell the Dare courses to others and to receive part of the purchase price as a commission. There were four different levels of involvement.

The task of salespersons was to bring prospective purchasers to "Adventure Meetings." The meetings, which were conducted by Dare people and not the salespersons, were conducted in a preordained format that included great enthusiasm, cheering and chanting, exuberant handshaking, standing on chairs, and shouting. Dare people and the salespersons dressed in modern, expensive clothes, displayed large sums of cash, drove new and expensive automobiles, and engaged in "hard-sell" tactics to induce prospects to sign their name and part with their money. In actuality, few Dare purchasers ever attained the wealth promised. The tape recordings and materials distributed by Dare were worthless. Is this sales scheme a "security" that should have been registered with the SEC? [*Securities and Exchange Commission v. Glenn W. Turner Enterprises, Inc.*, 474 F.2d 476 (9th Cir. 1973)]

27.2 Definition of a Security The Farmers' Cooperative of Arkansas and Oklahoma (Co-Op) was an agricultural cooperative that had approximately 23,000 members. To raise money to support its general business operations, Co-Op sold promissory notes (notes) to investors that were payable upon demand. The Co-Op offered the notes to both members and nonmembers, advertised the notes as an "investment program," and offered an interest rate higher than that available on savings accounts at financial institutions. More than 1,600 people purchased notes worth a total of $10 million. Subsequently, the Co-Op filed for bankruptcy. A class of holders of the notes filed suit against Ernst & Young, a national firm of certified public accountants that had audited Co-Op's financial statements, alleging that Ernst & Young had violated Section 10(b) of the Securities Exchange Act of 1934. Are the notes issued by Co-Op "securities"? [*Reves v. Ernst & Young*, 495 U.S. 56, 110 S.Ct. 945, 108 L.Ed.2d 47 (1990)]

27.3 Intrastate Offering Exemption The McDonald Investment Company (McDonald) was a corporation organized and incorporated in the state of Minnesota. The principal and only place of business from which the company conducted operations was located in Rush City, Minnesota. More than 80 percent of the company's assets were located in, and more than 80 percent of its income was derived from, Minnesota. On January 18, 1972, McDonald sold securities to Minnesota residents only. The proceeds from the sale were used entirely to make loans and other investments in real estate and other assets located outside the state of Minnesota. The company did not file a registration statement with the SEC. Does this offering qualify for an intrastate offering exemption from registration? [*Securities and Exchange Commission v. McDonald Investment Company*, 343 F.Supp. 343 (D.Minn. 1972)]

27.4 Transaction Exemption Continental Enterprises, Inc. (Continental) had 2,510,000 shares of stock issued and outstanding. Louis E. Wolfson and members of his immediate family and associates owned in excess of 40 percent of those shares. The balance was in the hands of approximately 5,000 outside shareholders. Wolfson was Continental's largest shareholder and the guiding spirit of the corporation who gave direction to and controlled the company's officers. Between August 1, 1960, and January 31, 1962, without public disclosure, Wolfson and his family and associates sold 55 percent of their stock through six brokerage houses. Wolfson and his family and associates did not file a registration statement with the SEC with respect to these sales. Do the securities sales by Wolfson and his family and associates qualify for an exemption for registration as a sale "not by an issuer, underwriter, or dealer"? [*United States v. Wolfson*, 405 F.2d 779 (2d Cir. 1968)]

27.5 Insider Trading Chiarella worked as a "markup man" in the New York composing room of Pandick Press, a financial printer. Among the documents that Chiarella handled were five secret announcements of corporate takeovers. The tender offerors had hired Pandick Press to print the offers, which would later be made public when the tender offers were made to the shareholders of the target corporations. When the documents were delivered to Pandick Press, the identities of the acquiring and target corporations were concealed by blank spaces or false names. The true names would not be sent to Pandick Press until the night of the final printing.

Chiarella was able to deduce the names of the target companies before the final printing. Without disclosing this knowledge, he purchased stock in the target companies and sold the

shares immediately after the takeover attempts were made public. Chiarella realized a gain of $30,000 in the course of 14 months. The federal government indicted Chiarella for criminal violations of Section 10(b) of the Securities Exchange Act of 1934. Is Chiarella guilty? [*Chiarella v. United States*, 445 U.S. 222, 100 S.Ct. 1108, 63 L.Ed.2d 348 (1980)]

27.6 Section 10(b) Leslie Neadeau was the president of T.O.N.M. Oil & Gas Exploration Corporation (TONM). Charles Lazzaro was a registered securities broker employed by Bateman Eichler, Hill Richards, Inc. (Bateman Eichler). The stock of TONM was traded in the over-the-counter market. Lazzaro made statements to potential investors that he had "inside information" about TONM, including that (1) vast amounts of gold had been discovered in Surinam and that TONM had options on thousands of acres in the gold-producing regions of Surinam, (2) the discovery was "not publicly known but would be subsequently announced", and (3) when this information was made public, TONM stock, which was then selling from $1.50 to $3.00 per share, would increase to $10.00 to $15.00 within a short period of time and might increase to $100.00 per share within a year.

The potential investors contacted Neadeau at TONM, who confirmed that the information was not public knowledge. In reliance on Lazzaro's and Neadeau's statements, the investors purchased TONM stock. The so-called "inside information" turned out to be false, and the shares declined substantially below the purchase price. The investors sued Lazzaro, Bateman Eichler, Neadeau, and TONM, alleging violations of Section 10(b) of the Securities Exchange Act of 1934. The defendants asserted that the plaintiffs' complaint should be dismissed because they participated in the fraud. Who wins? [*Bateman Eichler, Hill Richards, Inc. v. Berner*, 472 U.S. 299, 105 S.Ct. 2622, 86 L.Ed.2d 215 (1985)]

27.7 Insider Trading Donald C. Hoodes was the chief executive officer of the Sullair Corporation (Sullair). As an officer of the corporation, he was regularly granted stock options to purchase stock of the company at a discount. On July 20, 1982, Hoodes sold 6,000 shares of Sullair common stock for $38,350. On July 31, 1982, Sullair terminated Hoodes as an officer of the corporation. On August 20, 1982, Hoodes exercised options to purchase 6,000 shares of Sullair stock that cost him $3.01 per share ($18,060) at the time they were trading at $4.50 per share ($27,000). Hoodes did not possess material nonpublic information about Sullair when he sold or purchased the securities of the company. The corporation brought suit against Hoodes to recover the profits Hoodes made on these trades. Who wins? [*Sullair Corporation v. Hoodes*, 672 F.Supp. 337 (N.D.Ill. 1987)]

27.8 Insider Trading In January and February 1986, Mrs. Weill was a patient of Dr. Robert Howard Willis, a psychiatrist. During the course of their sessions, Mrs. Weill disclosed that her husband, Sanford I. Weill, a wealthy businessman, had developed an interest in becoming the chief executive officer of BankAmerica Corporation. She also disclosed that Mr. Weill was secretly negotiating with representatives of BankAmerica and that he had secured a commitment from Shearson Loeb Rhodes, an investment banking firm, to invest $1 billion in BankAmerica if he was successful in his negotiations. None of this information was public knowledge.

From approximately January 14, 1986, until February 6, 1986, Dr. Willis purchased 13,000 shares of BankAmerica common stock for himself and his children at prices ranging from $12 1/8 to $14 3/4 per share. On February 20, 1986, BankAmerica disclosed Mr. Weill's proposal. The price of BankAmerica's stock went up on the news. On February 21, 1986, Dr. Willis sold all of the BankAmerica shares at $15 3/8 per share, making a total profit of $27,475. The United States brought criminal charges against Dr. Willis for insider trading in violation of § 10(b). Who wins? Did Willis act ethically? [*United States v. Willis*, 737 F.Supp. 269 (S.D.N.Y. 1990)]

27.9 Commodities Regulation Dr. Thomas Puckett is a retired pathologist who successfully ran his own pathology lab. He and his wife met a representative of Rufenacht, Bromagen & Hertz (RB&H) at a dinner party in 1984. Puckett, who had actively traded in stocks since 1955 and had twice traded in commodity futures with other brokerage firms, opened a commodities trading account at RB&H. He signed a risk disclosure statement that stated that the risk of loss in trading commodity futures contracts was substantial and that he could incur a total loss of funds invested.

Dr. Puckett began trading in commodity futures contracts ranging from pork bellies to index futures. His account was nondiscretionary; that is, he made all trading decisions. Evidence showed that RB&H never tried to influence Dr. Puckett's choice of trades. Dr. Puckett spent several days each week at RB&H's offices, where he used a quote machine and a news service provided on a screen. During a 38-month period, Dr. Puckett lost over $2 million. He generally knew his losses on the day they were incurred and covered the losses with a check that afternoon or the next morning. To pay the losses, he sold his stock portfolio and began liquidating his pension plan. Dr. Puckett quit trading in September 1987 on the advice of his son. He then sued RB&H to recover his losses, alleging commodities fraud in violation of Section 4b of the Commodity Futures Act. Who wins? [*Puckett v. Rufenacht, Bromagen & Hertz*, 903 F.2d 1014 (5th Cir. 1990)]

27.10 Commodities Regulation Sol Kotz owned Kolar, Inc., an Arizona business engaged in aircraft scrap and salvage. In early 1976, Kotz opened a commodities trading account with Bache Halsey Stuart, Inc. (Bache), a commodities brokerage firm. At the urging of account executives at Bache, Kotz invested heavily in silver futures, although he had no experience in this area. Most of his purchases were made "on margin"; that is, he borrowed part of the purchase price from Bache. Kotz relied on the account executives' representations that (1) the price of silver would climb rapidly, (2) Bache handled the accounts for the Hunt family of Texas and the Hunts had been investing heavily in silver futures, and (3) Bache was buying silver for its own account. These were misrepresentations. In fact, Bache was recommending to other clients not to purchase silver futures.

Silver prices dropped, and Kotz had to borrow large sums of money to meet margin calls. Bache failed to carry out some of Kotz's sell orders that would have reduced his losses. A short time later, Kotz noticed an article in *The Wall Street Journal* about impending legislation authorizing the federal government to release large quantities of silver bullion from the national stockpile. Bache had known of the legislation but had not disclosed this information to its clients. In September 1981, Kotz closed his account at Bache, having incurred $750,000 in trading losses. In order to meet margin calls, Kotz had to sell most of the inventory of his aircraft business and distress sales, incurring substantial additional losses. Kotz sued Bache for commodities fraud under Section 4b of the Commodity Futures Act. Who wins? [*Kotz v. Bache Halsey Stuart, Inc.*, 685 F.2d 1204 (9th Cir. 1982)]

27.11 Commodities Regulations Michael Wasnick opened a trading account at Refco, Inc., a commodities brokerage firm. For 30 of the 79 months between 1979 and 1986, Wasnick traded commodity futures contracts through Refco. Wasnick personally directed Refco to make specific trades. Wasnick generally lost substantially. His trading followed a pattern: He would start to get behind and then react with a large number of very active trades. He frequently made day trades in many different commodities. He lost more than $1.4 million between 1979 and 1986. After Wasnick's account at Refco was closed, he sued Refco to recover all his losses, alleging a violation of Section 4b of the Commodity Exchange Act. Who wins? [*Wasnick v. Refco, Inc.*, 911 F.2d 345 (9th Cir. 1990)]

ETHICS CASES

27.12 Ethical Perspective Stephen Murphy owned Intertie, a California company that was involved in financing and managing cable television stations. Murphy was both an officer of the corporation and chairman of the board of directors. Intertie would buy a cable television station, make a small cash down payment, and finance the remainder of the purchase price. It would then create a limited partnership and sell the cable station to the partnership for a cash down payment and a promissory note in favor of Intertie. Finally, Intertie would lease the station back from the partnership. Intertie purchased more than 30 stations and created an equal number of limited partnerships, from which it received more than $7.5 million from approximately 400 investors.

Evidence showed that most of the limited partnerships were not self-supporting but that this fact was not disclosed to investors. Intertie commingled partnership funds, taking funds generated from the sale of new partnership offerings to meet debt service obligations of previously sold cable systems; Intertie also used funds from limited partnerships that were formed but that never acquired cable systems. Intertie did not keep any records regarding the qualifications of investors to purchase the securities and also refused to make its financial statements available to investors.

Intertie suffered severe financial difficulties and eventually filed for bankruptcy. The limited partners suffered substantial losses. Did each of the limited partnership offerings alone qualify for the private placement exemption from registration? Should the 30 limited partnership offerings be integrated? [*Securities and Exchange Commission v. Murphy*, 626 F.2d 633 (9th Cir. 1980)].

27.13 Ethical Perspective R. Foster Winans, a reporter for *The Wall Street Journal*, was one of the writers of the "Heard on the Street" column, a widely read and influential column in the *Journal*. This column frequently included articles that discussed the prospects of companies listed on national and regional stock exchanges and the over-the-counter market. David Carpenter worked as a news clerk at the *Journal*. The *Journal* had a conflict of interest policy that prohibited employees from using nonpublic information learned on the job for their personal benefit. Winans and Carpenter were aware of this policy.

Kenneth P. Felis and Peter Brant were stockholders at the brokerage house of Kidder Peabody. Winans agreed to provide Fells and Brant with information that was to appear in the "Heard" column in advance of its publication in the *Journal*. Carpenter served as a messenger between the parties. Based on

this advance information, the brokers bought and sold securities of companies discussed in the "Heard" column. During 1983 and 1984, prepublication trades of approximately 27 "Heard" columns netted profits of almost $690,000. The parties used telephones to transfer information. *The Wall Street Journal* is distributed by mail to many of its subscribers.

Eventually, Kidder Peabody noticed a correlation between the "Heard" column and trading by the brokers. After an SEC investigation, criminal charges were brought against defendants Winans, Carpenter, and Fells in United States District Court. Brant became the government's key witness. Winans and Fells were convicted of conspiracy to commit securities, mail, and wire fraud. Carpenter was convicted of aiding and abetting the commission of securities, mail, and wire fraud. The defendants appealed their convictions. Can the defendants be held criminally liable for conspiring to violate, and aiding and abetting the violation of, Section 10(b) and Rule 10b-5 of securities law? Did Winans act ethically in this case? Did Brant act ethically by turning government's witness? [*United States v. Carpenter*, 484 U.S. 19, 108 S.Ct. 316, 98 L.Ed.2d 275 (1987)]

CRITICAL LEGAL THINKING WRITING ASSIGNMENT

Read Case A.27 in the Case Appendix [*Lampf, Pleva, Lipkind, Prupis & Petigrow v. Gilbertson*]. This case is excerpted from the U.S. Supreme Court opinion. Review and brief the case. In your brief, be sure to answer the following questions:

1. Were the limited partnership interests "securities"?

2. What statute did the plaintiffs allege that the defendants had violated?
3. Succinctly state the issue presented to the U.S. Supreme Court.
4. How did the U.S. Supreme Court decide this issue?

NOTES

[1] *Securities and Exchange Commission v. W. J. Howey Co.*, 328 U.S. 293, 66 S.Ct. 1100 (1946).
[2] Securities Act of 1933, § 4(1).
[3] Securities Act of 1933, § 3(a)(11).
[4] SEC Rule 147.
[5] Securities Act of 1933, § 4(2).
[6] SEC Rule 506.
[7] SEC Rule 501.
[8] Securities Act of 1933, § 3(b).
[9] SEC Rules 502(a) and 147(b)(2).
[10] 15 U.S.C. § 77x.
[11] Litigation instituted pursuant to § 10(b) and Rule 10b-5 must be commenced within one year after the discovery of the violation and within three years after such violation [*Lampf, Pleva, Lipkind, Prupis & Petigrow v. Gilbertson*, 111 S.Ct. 2773 (1991)].
[12] The U.S. Supreme Court has held that the sale of a business is a sale of securities that is subject to Section 10(b). See *Gould v. Ruefenacht*, 471 U.S. 701, 105 S.Ct. 2308 (1985) (where 50 percent of a business was sold) and *Landreth*

Timber Co. v. Landreth, 471 U.S. 681, 105 S.Ct. 2297 (1985) (where 100 percent of a business was sold).
[13] *Ernst & Ernst v. Hochfelder*, 425 U.S. 185, 96 S.Ct. 1375 (1976).
[14] 40 SEC 907 (1961).
[15] 15 U.S.C. § 78 ff.
[16] P.L. 98–376.
[17] 15 U.S.C. § 78l.
[18] 15 U.S.C. § 78p(b).
[19] Ownership Reports and Trading by Officers, Directors and Principal Security Holders, Exchange Act Release No. 28869.
[20] P.L. 101–429, 104 Stat. 931 (1990).
[21] P.L. 101–432, 104 Stat. 963 (1990).
[22] 18 U.S.C. §§ 1961–1968.
[23] Private Securities Litigation Reform Act of 1995.
[24] *Reves v. Ernst & Young*, 113 S.Ct. 1163 (1993).
[25] 7 U.S.C. §§ 1–17a.
[26] 7 U.S.C. § 6b.
[27] 17 C.F.R. § 32.9.

CHAPTER 28

PERSONAL PROPERTY

AND BAILMENTS

Chapter Objectives

*After studying this chapter,
you should be able to*

1. Define personal property
2. Describe the methods for acquiring ownership in personal property
3. Explain how ownership rights are transferred by gift *inter vivos* and gift *causa mortis*
4. Describe how title to personal property is acquired by purchase, production, accession, and confusion
5. Describe and apply rules regarding ownership rights in mislaid, lost, and abandoned property
6. Define ordinary bailments
7. List and describe the elements for creating a bailment
8. List and describe the rights and duties of bailors and bailees
9. Explain the liability of bailees for lost, damaged, or destroyed goods in ordinary bailment situations
10. Explain the liability of bailees in special bailment situations

Chapter Contents

> *Property and law are born and must die together.*
>
> Jeremy Bentham
> *Principles of the Civil Code*,
> 1 Works 309

"Property is the most ambiguous of categories. It covers a multitude of rights which have nothing in common except that they are exercised by persons and enforced by the state."
R. H. Tawney
The Acquisitive Society
(1921), Ch. V

Private ownership of property forms the foundation of our economic system. As such, a comprehensive body of law has been developed to protect property rights. The law protects the rights of property owners to use, sell, dispose, control, and prevent others from trespassing on their rights.

In this country, property is expressly provided protection in the U.S. Constitution. The Fifth Amendment provides, "No person shall be . . . deprived of life, liberty, or property, without due process of law; nor shall private property be taken for public use, without just compensation." The Fourteenth Amendment provides, "No State shall . . . deprive any person of life, liberty, or property, without due process of law." These rights are not absolute. The government can acquire private property for public use (e.g., for highways, parks, and the like) as long as it pays just compensation for the property.

The first part of this chapter discusses the kinds of personal property, methods of acquiring ownership in personal property, and property rights in mislaid, lost, and abandoned property. The second part of this chapter discusses bailments—situations where possession (but not title to) personal property is delivered to another party for transfer, safekeeping, or other purpose.

THE NATURE OF PERSONAL PROPERTY

real property The land itself as well as buildings, trees, soil, minerals, timber, plants, and other things permanently affixed to the land.

personal property Property that consists of tangible property, such as automobiles, furniture, and jewelry, and intangible property, such as securities, patents, and copyrights.

tangible property All real property and physically defined personal property such as goods, animals, and minerals.

intangible property Rights that cannot be reduced to physical form such as stock certificates, CDs, bonds, copyrights, and such.

There are two kinds of property: real property and personal property. **Real property** includes land and property that is permanently attached to it. For example, minerals, crops, timber, and buildings that are attached to land are generally considered real property. **Personal property** (sometimes referred to as goods or chattels) consists of everything that is not real property. Real property can become personal property if it is removed from the land. For example, a tree that is part of a forest is real property; a tree that is cut down is personal property.

Personal property that is permanently affixed to land or buildings is called a *fixture*. Such property, which includes things like heating systems and storm windows, is categorized as real property. Unless otherwise agreed, fixtures remain with a building when it is sold. Personal property (e.g., furniture, pictures, and other easily portable household items) may be removed by the seller prior to sale.

Personal property can be either tangible or intangible. **Tangible property** includes physically defined property such as goods, animals, minerals, and such. **Intangible property** represents rights that cannot be reduced to physical form, such as stock certificates, certificates of deposit, bonds, and copyrights.

Real and personal property may be owned by one person or by more than one person. If property is owned concurrently by two or more persons, there is *concurrent ownership*.

ACQUIRING OWNERSHIP IN PERSONAL PROPERTY

"Personal property has no locality."
C. J. Lord
Loughborough
Sill v. Worswick (1791)

Personal property may be acquired or transferred with a minimum of formality. Commerce would be severely curtailed if the transfers of such items were difficult. The methods for acquiring ownership in personal property are discussed below.

By Possession

A person can acquire ownership in unowned personal property by **taking possession** of it or **capturing** it. The most notable unowned objects are things in their natural state. For example, people who obtain the proper fishing license acquire ownership of all the fish they catch. This type of property acquisition was important when this country was being developed. In today's urbanized society, however, there are few unowned objects, and this method of acquiring ownership in personal property has become less important.

taking possession
A method of acquiring ownership of unowned personal property.

By Purchase or Production

The most common method of acquiring title to personal property is by **purchasing** the property from its owner. For example, Urban Concrete Corp. owns a large piece of equipment. City Builders, Inc. (City Builders) purchases the equipment from Urban Concrete for $50,000. Urban Concrete signs over the title to the equipment to City Builders. City Builders is now the owner of the equipment.

Production is another common method of acquiring ownership in personal property. Thus, a manufacturer who purchases raw materials and produces a finished product owns that product.

purchasing property The most common method of acquiring title to personal property.

By Gift

A **gift** is a voluntary transfer of property without consideration. The lack of consideration is what distinguishes a gift from a purchase. The person making a gift is called the **donor**. The person who receives the gift is called the **donee**. There are three elements of a valid gift:

1. **Donative intent.** For a gift to be effective, the donor must have intended to make a gift. Donative intent can be inferred from the circumstances or language used by the donor. The courts also consider such factors as the relationship of the parties, the size of the gift, the mental capacity of the donor, and so on.
2. **Delivery.** Delivery must occur for there to be a valid gift. Although *physical delivery* is the usual method of transferring personal property, it is sometimes impracticable. In such circumstances, *constructive delivery* (or *symbolic delivery*) is sufficient. For example, if the property being gifted is kept in a safe-deposit box, physically giving the key to the donee is enough to signal the gift. Most intangible property is transferred by writing conveyance (e.g., conveying a stock certificate represents a transfer of ownership in a corporation).
3. **Acceptance.** *Acceptance* usually is not a problem because most donees readily accept gifts. In fact, the courts presume acceptance unless there is proof that the gift was refused. Nevertheless, a person cannot be forced to accept an unwanted gift.

gift A voluntary transfer of title to property without payment of consideration by the donee. To be a valid gift, the following three elements must be shown: (1) *donative intent* (2) *delivery* and (3) *acceptance*.

donor A person who gives a gift.

donee A person who receives a gift.

CAUTION
The donee must accept the gift for the gift to be effective.

Gifts *Inter Vivos* and Gifts *Causa Mortis* A gift made during a person's lifetime which is an irrevocable present transfer of ownership is an ***inter vivos* gift**. A **gift *causa mortis*** is a gift that is made in contemplation of death. A gift *causa mortis* is established when (1) the donor makes a gift in anticipation of approaching death from some existing sickness or peril, and (2) the donor dies from such sickness or peril without having revoked the gift. Gifts *causa mortis* can be revoked by the donor up until the time he or she dies. A gift *causa mortis* takes precedent over a prior conflicting will.

***inter vivos* gift** A gift made during a person's lifetime that is an irrevocable present transfer of ownership.

gift *causa mortis* A gift that is made in contemplation of death.

CONSIDER THIS EXAMPLE: Suppose Sandy is a patient in the hospital. She is to have a major operation from which she may not recover. Prior to going into surgery, Sandy removes her diamond ring and gives it to her friend Pamela, stating, "In the event of my death, I want you to have this." This is a gift *causa mortis*. If Sandy dies as a result of the operation, the gift is effective; Pamela owns the ring. If Sandy lives, the requisite condition for the gift (her death) has not occurred. Therefore, the gift is not effective and Sandy can recover the ring from Pamela.

In the following case, the court had to determine whether a gift of a valuable painting had been made.

CASE 28.1

Gruen v. Gruen
505 N.Y.S.2d 849 (1986) Court of Appeals of New York

Facts Victor Gruen was a successful architect. In 1959, Victor purchased a painting titled *Schloss Kammer am Attersee II* by a noted Austrian modernist, Gustav Klimt, and paid $8,000 for the painting. In 1963, Victor wrote a letter to his son Michael, then an undergraduate student at Harvard University, giving the painting to Michael but reserving a life estate in the painting. The letter stated:

> Dear Michael:
> The 21st birthday, being an important event in life, should be celebrated accordingly. I therefore wish to give you as a present the oil painting by Gustav Klimt of Schloss Kammer which now hangs in the New York living room.
> Happy birthday again.
> Love,
> s/ Victor

As Victor retained a life interest in the painting, Michael never took possession of the painting. Victor died on February 14, 1980. The painting was appraised at $2.5 million. When Michael requested the painting from his stepmother, Kemija Gruen, she refused to turn it over to him. Michael sued to recover the painting. The trial court held in favor of the stepmother. The appellate division reversed. The stepmother appealed.

Issue Did Victor Gruen make a valid *inter vivos* gift of the Klimt painting to his son Michael?

Decision Yes. The appellate court held that Victor Gruen had made a valid *inter vivos* gift of the Klimt painting to his son Michael. The court affirmed the judgment of the appellate division in favor of Michael Gruen.

Reason The appellate court held that the elements necessary to create a valid *inter vivos* gift had been met. First, the court held that the evidence was conclusive that Victor had the requisite *donative intent* to transfer ownership of the painting to Michael in 1963. Second, the court stated that physical *delivery* of the painting was not required in this case because Victor intended to retain a life estate in the painting. The court held that Victor's letter constituted constructive delivery of the painting. Third, the court found that Michael *accepted* the gift. Evidence showed that Michael had told several of his friends and classmates about the gift when it was made in 1963 and that he had retained the letter for more than 17 years to verify the gift after his father died.

CASE QUESTIONS

Critical Legal Thinking Should donors who make *inter vivos* gifts be required to relinquish physical possession of the property to the donee?

Ethics Did the stepmother act ethically in refusing to turn the painting over to Michael?

Uniform Gift to Minors Act and **Revised Uniform Gift to Minors Act** Acts that establish procedures for adults to make gifts of money and securities to minors.

Uniform Gifts to Minors Acts All states have adopted in whole or in part the **Uniform Gift to Minors Act** or the **Revised Uniform Gift to Minors Act**. These laws establish procedures for adults to make irrevocable gifts of money and securities to minors. Gifts of money can be made by depositing the money in an account with a financial institution with the donor or another trustee (such as another adult or the bank) as custodian for the minor. Gifts of securities can be made by registering the securities in the name of a trustee as custodian for the minor. The laws give custodians broad discretionary powers to invest the money or securities for the benefit of the minor.

By Will or Inheritance

Title to personal property frequently is acquired by **will** or **inheritance**. If the person who dies has a valid will, the property is distributed to the *beneficiaries*, pursuant to the provisions of that will. Otherwise, the property is distributed to the *heirs* as provided in the relevant state's inheritance statute.

will or **inheritance** A way to acquire title to property that is a result of another's death.

By Accession

Accession occurs when the value of personal property increases because it is added to or improved by natural or manufactured means. Accession that occurs naturally belongs to the owner (e.g., a colt that is born to a mare belongs to the mare's owner). If accession occurs by manufactured means and the owner consents to the improvement, the owner acquires title to the improvement but must pay the improver for labor and services. For example, a business owner who contracts to have an addition built onto his or her factory owns the new structure but must pay the contract price to the improver.

accession Occurs when the value of personal property increases because it is added to or improved by natural or manufactured means.

Wrongful Improvement If the improvement was made wrongfully, the owner acquires title to the improved property and does not have to pay the improver for the value of the improvements. For instance, suppose a thief steals a car and puts a new engine in it. The owner is entitled to recover the car as improved without having to pay the thief for the improvements.

Mistaken Improvement If the improvement was mistakenly made by the improver, the courts generally follow these rules:

1. If the improvements can be easily separated from the original article, the improver must remove the improvements and pay any damages caused by such removal. For example, a builder who puts the wrong door on a house must replace that door with the correct door at his own cost.
2. If the improvements cannot be removed, the owner owns title to the improved property and does not have to pay the improver for the improvements. For example, if a builder misreads blueprints and extends an addition to a building too far, the building owner is entitled to keep the improvement at no extra cost. In some cases, if the improvements are substantial and cannot be removed, the court can permit the improver to acquire title to the personal property by paying the owner the value of the original article.

"The right of property enables an industrious man to reap where he has sown."
Anonymous

By Confusion

Confusion occurs if two or more persons commingle fungible goods (i.e., goods that are exactly alike, such as the same grade of oil, grains, cattle, or the like). Title to goods can be acquired by confusion.

The owners share ownership in the commingled goods in proportion to the amount of goods contributed. It does not matter whether the goods were commingled by agreement or by accident. For example, if three farmers agree to store the same amount of grade B winter wheat in a silo, each of them owns one-third. When the grain is sold, the profits are divided into three parts; if the silo burns to the ground, each suffers one-third of the loss. If goods are wrongfully or intentionally commingled without permission, the innocent party acquires title to them.

confusion Occurs if two or more persons commingle fungible goods; title is then acquired by confusion.

By Divorce

When a marriage is dissolved by a divorce, the parties obtain certain rights in the property of the marital estate. Often, a settlement of property rights is reached. If not, the court must decide the property rights of the spouses.

In the following case, the court decided the spouses' ownership rights to personal property upon divorce.

CASE 28.2

Giha v. Giha
609 A.2d 945 (1992) Supreme Court of Rhode Island

Facts On October 7, 1987, Nagib Giha (husband) filed a complaint for divorce from Nelly Giha (wife) on the grounds of irreconcilable differences. On May 20, 1988, the parties reached an agreement for the disposition of their property that provided they would divide equally the net proceeds from the sale of their marital assets. They had to wait a statutory waiting period before the divorce was final. On December 25, 1988, the husband learned that he had won $2.4 million in the Massachusetts MEGABUCKS state lottery. The husband kept this fact secret. After the waiting period was over, the family court entered its final judgment severing the parties' marriage on April 27, 1989. The husband claimed his lottery prize on October 6, 1989. In December 1990, after learning of the lottery winnings, the wife sued to recover the lottery prize. She alleged that the lottery prize was a marital asset because her husband had won it before their divorce was final. The trial court dismissed her complaint. The wife appealed.

Issue Was the $2.4 million lottery prize personal property of the marital estate?

Decision Yes. The appellate court held that the parties remained as husband and wife until the entry of final judgment of divorce in April 1989. Therefore, the lottery prize was a marital asset. Reversed and remanded.

Reason The court held that the marital agreement did not sever either the matrimonial or economic ties between the husband and the wife. Because the parties' marriage remained in effect during the statutory waiting period so did the property rights each spouse had in the property acquired by the other spouse during that period. The court concluded that the lottery prize was a marital asset.

CASE QUESTIONS

Critical Legal Thinking Should a spouse's lottery winnings be considered separate property? Why or why not?

Ethics Did the husband act ethically in this case?

MISLAID, LOST, AND ABANDONED PROPERTY

Often, people find another person's personal property. Ownership rights to the property differ depending on whether the property is mislaid, lost, or abandoned. The following sections discuss these legal rules.

Mislaid Property

mislaid property When an owner voluntarily places property somewhere and then inadvertently forgets it.

Property is **mislaid** when its owner voluntarily places the property somewhere and then inadvertently forgets it. It is likely that the owner will return for the property upon realizing that it was misplaced.

The owner of the premises where the property is mislaid is entitled to take possession of the property against all except the rightful owner. This right is superior to the rights of the person who finds it. Such possession does not involve a change of title. Instead, the owner of the premises becomes an involuntary bailee of the property (bailments are discussed later in this chapter) and owes a duty to take reasonable care of the property until it is reclaimed by the owner.

CAUTION

The owner of the premises where personal property is mislaid is entitled to take possession of the property against all except the rightful owner.

Lost Property

lost property When a property owner leaves property somewhere because of negligence, carelessness, or inadvertence.

Property is considered **lost** when its owner negligently, carelessly, or inadvertently leaves it somewhere. The finder obtains title to such property against the whole world except the true owner. The lost property must be returned to its rightful owner whether the finder discovers the loser's identity or the loser finds him. A finder who refuses to return the property is liable for the tort of conversion and the crime of larceny. Many states require the finder to conduct a reasonable search (e.g., place advertisements in newspapers) to find the rightful owner.

CONSIDER THIS EXAMPLE: If a commuter finds a diamond ring on the floor of a subway station in New York City, the ring is considered lost property. The finder can claim title to the ring against the whole world except the true owner. If the true owner discovers that the commuter has her ring, she may recover it from the finder.

Estray Statutes

Most states have enacted **estray statutes** that permit a finder of mislaid or lost property to clear title to the property if

1. The finder reports the found property to the appropriate government agency and then turns over possession of the property to this agency

2. Either the finder or the government agency posts notices and publishes advertisements describing the lost property

3. A specified time (usually a year or a number of years) has passed.

Many state estray statutes provide that the government receive a portion of the value of the property. Some statutes provide that title cannot be acquired in found property that is the result of illegal activity. For example, title has been denied to finders of property and money deemed to have been used for illegal drug purchases.

The court applied an estray statute in the following case.

CAUTION

The finder of lost property obtains title to the found property against everyone except the true owner.

estray statutes Statutes that permit a finder of mislaid or lost property to clear title to the property if (1) the finder reports the found property to the appropriate government agency and turns over possession of the property to this agency, (2) either the finder or the government agency posts notices and publishes advertisements describing the lost property, and (3) a specified amount of time has passed without the rightful owner's reclaiming the property.

CASE 28.3

Willsmore v. Township of Oceola, Michigan
308 N.W.2d 796 (1981) Court of Appeals of Michigan

Facts While hunting on unposted and unoccupied property in Oceola Township, Michigan, Duane Willsmore noticed an area with branches arranged in a crisscross pattern. When he kicked aside the branches and sod, he found a watertight suitcase in a freshly dug hole. Willsmore informed the Michigan State Police of his find. A state trooper and Willsmore together pried open the suitcase and discovered $383,840 in cash. The state police took custody of the money, which was deposited in an interest-bearing account. Michigan's "Lost Goods Act" provides that the finder and the township in which the property was found must share the value of the property if the finder publishes required notices and the true owner does not claim the property within one year.

Willsmore published the required notices and brought a declaratory judgment action seeking a determination of the ownership of the money. Thomas Powell, the owner of the land on which the suitcase was found, claimed he was the owner of the suitcase. After Powell incorrectly named the amount of money in the suitcase, he asserted his Fifth Amendment

right not to testify at his deposition and at trial. The trial court awarded the money equally to Willsmore and the Township of Oceola. Powell appealed.

Issue Who is the owner of the lost suitcase and its contents?

Decision The appellate court held that Willsmore and the Township of Oceola were the owners of the briefcase and its contents. The appellate court affirmed the judgment of the trial court and ordered that Willsmore and the township each receive one-half the proceeds of the find after Willsmore's costs were deducted.

Reason First, the court held that Powell had not met his burden of proving that he was the true owner of the suitcase of money. Then, the court held that the requirements of Michigan's estray law had been met. The money was awarded to the finder, Willsmore, and the township. The court stated: "The Lost Goods Act encourages the goals that this court
continued

considers important. It provides certainty of title to property by eventually vesting clear title after a set period of time. It encourages honesty in finders by providing incentives for compliance. The Act provides notice to potential true owners and publication to seek them out. The public obtains a portion of the benefit of a find through receipt of one-half of the value by the township."

CASE QUESTIONS

Critical Legal Thinking Do estray statutes serve a useful social purpose? Should the government get half of the find?

Ethics If you had found the suitcase, would you have turned it in to the government?

Abandoned Property

CAUTION

The finder of abandoned property *obtains title to the found property against everyone including the original owner.*

Property is classified as **abandoned** if (1) an owner discards the property with the intent to relinquish his or her rights in it or (2) an owner of mislaid or lost property gives up any further attempts to locate it. Anyone who finds abandoned property acquires title to it. The title is good against the whole world, including the original owner. For example, property left at a garbage dump is **abandoned property**. It belongs to the first person who claims it.

BUSINESS APPLICATION

Who Owns the Treasure Trove on the *SS Central America*?

On Saturday, September 12, 1857, the *SS Central America*, a luxurious steamship that made frequent trips between New York and Panama, lost a desperate three-day battle to keep itself afloat. It sank 169 miles off the coast of South Carolina. The ship carried 587 passengers, many of whom were returning from California, where they had recovered gold from newly discovered mines. Only 166 passengers survived. Insurance companies paid claims for the $1.2 million (1857 value) of gold bullion that sank with the ship.

For nearly 130 years, the *SS Central America* lay peacefully in the cold waters off the East Coast. In 1981, the Columbus-America Discovery Group found the sunken ship with its estimated $1 billion of gold (current value). Several of the insurance companies that paid the claims in 1857 sued, claiming some of the loot belonged to them.

The court of appeals, which applied the maritime Law of Salvage to the case, agreed. Under this doctrine, the original owners retain ownership to treasure trove, and the salvor is entitled to a very liberal award for finding it. The court ordered the treasure trove from the *SS Central America* to be divided between the insurance companies and the salvor. [*Columbus-America Discovery Group v. Atlantic Mutual Insurance Company*, 974 F.2d 450 (4th Cir. 1992)]

BAILMENTS

bailment A transaction where an owner transfers his or her personal property to another to be held, stored, delivered, or for some other purpose. Title to the property does not transfer.

bailor The owner of property in a bailment.

bailee A holder of goods who is not a seller or a buyer (e.g., a warehouse or common carrier).

A **bailment** occurs when the owner of personal property delivers his or her property to another person to be held, stored, or delivered, or for some other purpose. In a bailment, the owner of the property is the **bailor**. The party to whom the property is delivered for safekeeping, storage, or delivery (e.g., warehouse or common carrier, or such) is the **bailee** (see Exhibit 28.1). Almost everyone has been involved in a bailment transaction.

A bailment is different than a sale or a gift because title to the goods does not transfer to the bailee. Instead, the bailee must follow the bailor's directions concerning the goods. For example, suppose Hudson Corp. is relocating offices and hires American Van Lines to move its office furniture and equipment to the new location. American

Van Lines (the bailee) must follow Hudson's (the bailor) instructions regarding delivery. The law of bailments establishes the rights, duties, and liabilities of parties to a bailment.

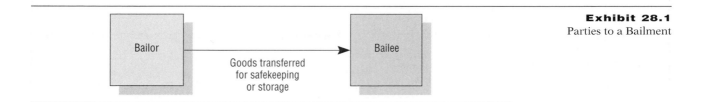

Exhibit 28.1
Parties to a Bailment

Elements Necessary to Create a Bailment

Three elements are necessary to create a bailment: personal property, delivery of possession, and a bailment agreement.

1. **Personal property.** Only *personal property* can be bailed. The property can be *tangible* (e.g., automobiles, jewelry, and animals) or *intangible* (e.g., stocks, bonds, and promissory notes).

2. **Delivery of possession.** Delivery of possession involves two elements: (1) The bailee has exclusive control over the personal property, and (2) the bailee must knowingly accept the personal property.

   CONSIDER THIS EXAMPLE: No bailment is created if a patron goes into a restaurant and hangs her coat on an unattended coat rack. This is because other patrons have access to the coat. However, bailment is created if the patron checked her coat with a checkroom attendant because the restaurant has assumed exclusive control over the coat. If valuable property was left in the pocket of the coat, there would be no bailment of that property because the checkroom attendant did not knowingly accept it.

   Most bailments are created by *physical delivery*. For example, Great Lakes Shipping, Inc. delivers a vessel to Marina Repairs, Inc. for repairs. *Constructive delivery* can create a bailment, too. For example, there has been constructive delivery of an automobile if the owner gives someone the keys and registration to his car.

3. **Bailment agreement.** The creation of a bailment does not require any formality. A bailment may be either express or implied. Most *express bailments* can be either written or oral. However, under the Statute of Frauds, a bailment must be in writing if it is for more than one year. An example of an *implied bailment* is the finding and safeguarding of lost property.

Bailments generally expire at a specified time or when a certain purpose is accomplished. A **bailment for a fixed term** terminates at the end of the term, or sooner by mutual consent of the parties. A party who terminates a bailment in breach of the bailment agreement is liable to the innocent party for damages resulting from the breach. Bailments without a fixed term are called **bailments at will**. A bailment at will can be terminated at any time by either party. Gratuitous bailees or bailors can generally be permitted to terminate a fixed-term bailment prior to expiration of the term.

Upon termination of the bailment, the bailee is legally obligated to do as the bailor directs with the property. Unless otherwise agreed, the bailee is obligated to return the identical goods bailed. Where commingled *fungible goods* are involved (e.g., grain), identically equivalent goods may be returned by the bailee.

In the following case, the court had to determine whether or not a bailment had been created.

elements of a bailment
The following three elements are necessary to create a bailment: (1) personal property (2) delivery of possession and (3) a bailment agreement.

"Laws are always useful to persons of property, and hurtful to those who have none."

Jean-Jacques Rousseau
Du Contrat Social
(1761)

bailment for a fixed term
A bailment that terminates at the end of the term or sooner by mutual consent of the parties.

bailment at will A bailment without a fixed term; can be terminated at any time by either party.

CASE 28.4

Magliocco v. American Locker Co., Inc.
239 Cal.Rptr. 497 (1987) Court of Appeals of California

Facts Richard George Whitehurst told Salvatore Magliocco that he could buy gold that had been smuggled out of Vietnam by American soldiers who now sought to sell it. Magliocco agreed to purchase the gold for $409,000. To pay for it, Magliocco placed $409,000 in cash in a locked briefcase, which was then placed in a suitcase provided by Whitehurst that had a combination lock. Both men knew the combination. They then went to the Richmond, California, Greyhound bus station, where Magliocco placed the suitcase in a coin-operated locker owned and operated by American Locker Company, Inc. Magliocco kept the key.

Shortly thereafter, a Whitehurst accomplice told an employee of the Greyhound station that he had lost the key to his locker. The employee opened the locker with a master key. When the man opened the combination lock to the briefcase, the employee released the suitcase to him. When Whitehurst did not contact Magliocco as planned to permit him to inspect the gold, Magliocco discovered the locker was empty. Magliocco sued Greyhound Lines, Inc., and American Locker Company, Inc., for damages. The jury found a bailment and held in favor of Magliocco. The defendants appealed.

Issue Was a bailment created between Magliocco and Greyhound and American Locker?

Decision No, a bailment was not created when Magliocco used the coin-operated locker at the Richmond Greyhound bus station. The appellate court reversed the trial court's judgment and ordered Magliocco to pay all costs of the appeal.

Reason The appellate court held that a necessary element of bailment—that possession of the stored goods is given to the bailee—cannot be established in a case involving use of a coin-operated locker. The court reasoned that no bailment existed because the user who retains a key to the locker never relinquishes primary physical control of the items stored, even if the person making the lockers available has a master key. Thus, one who stores items in a coin-operated locker does not create a bailment.

CASE QUESTIONS

Critical Legal Thinking Do you think the assessment of the loss fell on the proper party? Why or why not?

Ethics Did Magliocco act ethically in suing Greyhound and American Locker? Whose fault was it that the money was stolen?

Business Implication What would be the impact on coin-operated locker businesses if the jury's verdict were allowed to stand?

Ordinary Bailments

ordinary bailments
(1) Bailments for the sole benefit of the bailor, (2) bailments for the sole benefit of the bailee, and (3) bailments for the mutual benefit of the bailor and bailee.

bailment for the sole benefit of the bailor
A gratuitous bailment that benefits only the bailor. The bailee owes only a *duty of slight care* to protect the bailed property.

duty of slight care A duty not to be grossly negligent in caring for something in one's possession.

There are three classifications of **ordinary bailments**. The difference among these categories is the degree of care owed by the bailee in protecting the bailed property. The three types of ordinary bailments follow:

- **Bailments for the sole benefit of the bailor** are *gratuitous bailments* that benefit only the bailor. They arise when the bailee is requested to care for the bailor's property as a favor. The bailee owes only a **duty of slight care** to protect the bailed property—that is, he or she owes a duty not to be grossly negligent in caring for the bailed goods.

  CONSIDER THIS EXAMPLE: The Watkins are going on vacation and ask their neighbors, the Smiths, to feed their dog, which is allowed to run free. The Smiths diligently feed the dog, but the dog runs away and does not return. The Smiths are not liable for the loss of the dog.

An **involuntary bailment** arises when someone finds lost or misplaced property. An involuntary bailee owes a duty of slight care to protect the bailed property.

- **Bailments for the sole benefit of the bailee** are gratuitous bailments that solely benefit the bailee. They generally arise when a bailee requests to use the bailor's property for personal reasons. In this situation, the bailee owes a **duty of great care** (or **utmost care**) to protect the bailed property—that is, he or she owes a duty not to be slightly negligent in caring for the bailed goods.

  CONSIDER THIS EXAMPLE: Suppose Mitch borrows Courtney's lawn mower (free of charge) to mow his own lawn. Mitch is the bailee. Courtney is the bailor. This bailment is for the sole benefit of the bailee. Suppose Mitch, while mowing his lawn, leaves the lawn mower in his front yard while he goes into his house to answer the telephone. While he is gone, the lawn mower is stolen. Here, Mitch will be held liable to Courtney for the loss of the lawn mower. This is because Mitch breached his duty of great care to protect the lawn mower.

- **Mutual benefit bailments** are bailments that benefit both parties. The bailee owes a **duty of reasonable care** (or **ordinary care**) to protect the bailed goods. This means that the bailee is liable for any goods that are lost, damaged, or destroyed because of his or her negligence. The law presumes that if bailed property is lost, damaged, destroyed, or stolen while in the possession of the bailee, it is because of lack of proper care by the bailee; the bailee may rebut this presumption by the introduction of appropriate evidence. Commercial bailments, where the bailor pays the bailee compensation to store, hold, or transport bailed goods, fall into this category.

  CONSIDER THIS EXAMPLE: Suppose ABC Garment Co. delivers goods to Lowell, Inc., a commercial warehouseman, for storage. A fee is charged for this service. ABC Garment Co. receives the benefit of having its goods stored, and Lowell, Inc., receives the benefit of being paid compensation for storing the goods. In this example, Lowell, Inc. (the bailee) owes a duty of ordinary care to protect the goods.

Some states have eliminated these categories of ordinary bailments, ruling that all bailees owe a duty of reasonable care regardless of whether or not they benefit from the bailment.

Bailee's Rights During the term of a bailment, the bailee has the right to exclusive possession of the bailed property. This right is temporary, however, since the property must be returned when the bailment is terminated. If a fixed-term mutual benefit bailment is terminated by the bailor prior to the expiration of its term, the bailee can recover damages for the breach of the bailment contract. Generally, a bailor or bailee can terminate a gratuitous bailment at any time without liability.

In some bailments, the bailee has the right to use the bailed property. This right is determined from the terms of the bailment contract and the facts and circumstances surrounding the bailment. For example, suppose a farmer leases a farm tractor for the summer months. During the course of the bailment, the farmer may use the tractor to plow his fields.

In a mutual benefit bailment, the bailee has a right to be compensated for work done or services provided to the bailor. The amount of compensation is usually stated in the bailment contract. If no specific amount is stated, reasonable compensation is presumed. Bailees usually obtain a **possessory lien** (also called an **artisan's lien**) on the bailed property for compensation owed by the bailor. If the bailor refuses to or cannot fulfill this commitment, most states permit the bailee to foreclose on the lien, sell the bailed property at a judicial sale, and recover the amount of compensation due from the sale proceeds. Any excess proceeds must be returned to the bailor.

Gratuitous bailees are not entitled to compensation for services provided. However, they are entitled to reimbursement for all costs and expenses rendered in protecting the bailed property.

---

bailment for sole benefit of the bailee A gratuitous bailment that benefits only the bailee. The bailee owes a *duty of great care* to protect the bailed property.

duty of utmost care A duty of care that goes beyond ordinary care.

mutual benefit bailment A bailment for the mutual benefit of the bailor and bailee. The bailee owes a *duty of reasonable care* to protect the bailed property.

duty of reasonable care The duty that a reasonable bailee in like circumstances would owe to protect the bailed property.

bailee's rights Depending on the type of bailment, bailees may have the right to (1) exclusive possession of the bailed property, (2) use of the bailed property, or (3) compensation for work done or services provided.

possessory lien Lien obtained by a bailee on bailed property for the compensation owed by the bailor to the bailee.

Bailor's Duties   Many of the bailor's duties complement the bailee's rights. The bailor owes the duty to pay the agreed-upon compensation to the bailee and to not interfere with the bailee's possessory interest during the term of the bailment.

One of the bailor's primary duties is to notify the bailee of any defects in the bailed property that could cause injury to the bailee or others. The extent of this duty depends on the type of bailment. In a bailment for the sole benefit of the bailee, the bailor must notify the bailee of any known defects in the bailed property. In a bailment for the mutual benefit of both parties, the bailor must notify the bailee of any known defects or defects that could have been discovered through reasonable inspection.

A bailor who fails to fulfill these duties is liable for damages caused by the defects. In addition, bailors can be held liable for breach of any express or implied warranties they make about the bailed property.

BUSINESS CHECKLIST

Parking Lots: Who Is Liable if Your Car Is Stolen?

Who is liable when a car is stolen while parked in a commercial lot or garage? The answer to this question depends on whether the parking lot is considered to be a bailee of an automobile or merely a lessor of parking space.

It is clear that parking lots and garages are bailees of automobiles once they assume control and possession of the automobile. Thus, if a valet parking attendant parks the car and keeps the keys, it is relatively certain that a court will recognize the existence of a bailment and hold the garage liable if the vehicle is stolen. Disclaimers to the contrary (either on the ticket or posted at the parking lot) are usually held to be ineffective.

On the other hand, if the owner of a car parks his or her own car in a parking lot and takes the keys, this is considered a lease. The general rule in this case is that the "landlord"—the parking lot—is not responsible for the safety of the car.

Article 7 of the UCC
An article of the Uniform Commercial Code that provides a detailed statutory scheme for the creation, perfection, and foreclosure on common carriers' and warehouse operators' liens.

SPECIAL BAILMENTS

consignor The person shipping the goods. The bailor.

common carrier A firm (the bailee) that offers transportation services to the general public. Owes a *duty of strict liability* to the bailor.

consignee The person to whom the bailed goods are to be delivered.

duty of strict liability A duty that common carriers owe that says if the goods are lost, damaged, destroyed, or stolen, the common carrier is liable even if it was not at fault for the loss.

Special Bailees

Special (or *extraordinary*) *bailees* include common carriers, innkeepers, and warehouse companies. Special bailees must follow most of the rules applicable to ordinary bailees. In addition, they are subject to special liability rules contained in **Article 7 of the Uniform Commercial Code (UCC)**.

Common Carriers

Common carriers offer transportation services to the general public. Commercial airlines, railroads, public trucking companies, public pipeline companies, and such are common carriers. Many common carriers are regulated by the government.

The delivery of goods to a common carrier creates a mutual benefit bailment. The person shipping the goods is the **shipper** or **consignor** (the bailor). The transportation company is called the **common carrier** (the bailee). The person to whom the goods are to be delivered is called the **consignee**.

Common carriers are held to a **duty of strict liability**.[1] This means that if the goods are lost, damaged, destroyed, or stolen, the common carrier is liable even if it was not at fault for the loss. Common carriers are not liable for the loss, damage, or destruction of goods caused by (1) an act of God (e.g., a tornado), (2) an act of a public enemy (e.g., terrorist activity), (3) an order of the government (e.g., statutes, court decisions, and government regulations), (4) an act of the shipper (e.g., improper packaging), or (5) the inherent nature of the goods (e.g., perishability).

Common carriers can limit their liability to a stated dollar amount by expressly stating that in the bailment agreement. Federal law requires common carriers that take advantage of such limitation to offer shippers the opportunity to pay a premium and declare a higher value for the goods.[2]

Warehouse Companies

A **warehouseman** (or **warehouse company**) is a bailee engaged in the business of storing property for compensation.[3] Warehousemen are subject to the rights, duties, and liabilities of an ordinary bailee. As such, they owe a *duty of reasonable care* to protect the bailed property in its possession from harm or loss.[4] Warehousemen are liable only for loss or damage to the bailed property caused by their own negligence. They are not liable for loss or damage caused to bailed goods by another person's negligence or conduct.

Warehousemen can limit the dollar amount of their liability if they offer the bailor the opportunity to increase the liability limit for the payment of an additional charge.[5] Warehouse companies are subject to a comprehensive set of federal and state statutes that govern the operation of warehouse facilities.

> **warehouse company**
> A bailee engaged in the business of storing property for compensation. Owes a *duty of reasonable care* to protect the bailed property.

Innkeepers

An **innkeeper** is the owner of a facility that provides lodging to the public for compensation (e.g., a hotel or motel). Under the common law, innkeepers are held to a *strict liability standard* regarding loss caused to the personal property of transient guests. Permanent lodgers are not subject to this rule.

Almost all states have enacted statutes that limit the liability of innkeepers. Most of these statutes allow innkeepers to avoid liability for loss caused to guests' property if (1) a safe is provided in which the guests' valuable property may be kept and (2) the guests are aware of the safe's availability. Most state laws also allow innkeepers to limit the dollar amount of their liability by notifying their guests of this limit (e.g., by posting a notice on each guest room door). This limitation on liability does not apply if the loss is caused by an innkeeper's negligence.

> **innkeepers statutes**
> State statutes that limit an innkeeper's common law liability. An innkeeper can avoid liability for loss caused to a guest's property if (1) a safe is provided in which the guest's valuable property may be kept and (2) the guest is notified of this fact.

BUSINESS APPLICATION

Loss of Property Lawsuit Lodged Against Innkeeper

Marvin J. Frockt, a traveling jewelry salesman, checked into a Comfort Inn (Inn) in North Carolina owned by Max H. Goodloe and others. Frockt had in his possession a jewelry sample case that contained approximately $150,000 worth of gems and jewels. Frockt requested that the desk clerk place the case in the safe provided by Inn, stating that the case was "very valuable." The clerk did not give Frockt a receipt for the case.

North Carolina law states that innkeepers have a duty to safely keep up to $500 worth of money, jewelry, or other valuables for any guest who requests such a service. The innkeeper is required to give the guest a receipt that plainly states this limitation on liability. Innkeepers have no liability for valuables that are not given to them for safekeeping. In addition, the statute requires the following:

Every innkeeper shall keep posted in every room of his house occupied by guests, and in the office, a printed copy of this Article and of all regulations relating to the conduct of guests. This Chapter shall not apply to innkeepers, or their guests, where the innkeeper fails to keep such notices posted. [N.C.Gen.Stat. § 72]

Inn had not posted the required notice. When Frockt called
continued

for his case the next day, it could not be located and was never recovered. Frockt sued the owners of Inn for damages. Is Inn's liability limited to $500?

The defendants urged that N.C.Gen.Stat. Section 72 held Inn harmless for loss or damage to plaintiff above the statutory amount of $500. The court noted that the defendants' argument would be persuasive absent two facts: (1) the receipt given by plaintiff by Inn—actually, given the Inn by plaintiff—did not have plainly printed upon it a copy of Section 72 and (2) the evidence is uncontradicted that Inn did not display in the office copies of Section 72.

In holding that Inn's liability for the lost case was not limited to $500, the court stated: "The consequences of failing to post notice as required by Section 72-6 are clear: rather than benefiting from the protection afforded by the statute, the innkeeper must look to the common law to define its duties and liabilities. The common law rule in North Carolina is that the innkeeper is strictly liable for the loss of a guest's property, except in a few rare instances, such as where such loss is occasioned by the guest's own negligence. Had the Inn wished to alleviate the draconian effect of the common law rule, it had only to follow the dictates of the statute by posting the notice required therein. This it did not do; consequently, it will not be heard to complain that the rule is untenable."

INTERNATIONAL PERSPECTIVE

When Airlines Lose Luggage

Every day airlines are bailors for hundreds of thousands of pieces of luggage that are checked by domestic and international travelers. As bailors, the common law would impose liability on airlines for the full value of any luggage lost or damaged by their negligence.

However, two statutes protect the airlines from the harsh results of the common law of bailments. Under the first statute, the *Civil Aeronautics Act of 1938*, [49 U.S.C. § 646], which applies to domestic flights, airlines can limit their liability for passengers' lost or damaged property to a specific dollar amount per pound or per item by filing tariffs with the Civil Aeronautics Board (CAB). The current tariff is $1,250 per piece of luggage.

The only way for passengers to beat the limitations of liability is to declare that the value of their property exceeds the tariffs and then pay a fee for additional coverage.

The second statute is the *Warsaw Convention*, [49 U.S.C. § 1502], which was concluded in 1929. This statute limits recovery for luggage that is lost or damaged on international flights. Passengers can purchase additional coverage upon check-in.

Undoubtedly, passengers who fail to declare the excess value of their luggage will lose money if their luggage is lost. However, the limitations of liability contained in both the Civil Aeronautics Act and the Warsaw Convention are widely viewed as necessary protection for airlines.

WORKING THE WEB

There are many kinds of personal property. Listed here are some Web sites that will help you protect your personal property.

Internet commerce:

World Wide Web Multimedia Law Page
This page contains all sorts of links to multimedia property issues.

Visit at http://www.batnet.com/oikoumone/index. html

National Telecommunications and Information Administration This Department of Commerce agency is responsible for domestic and international telecommunications and information policy issues as well as being the President's principle advisor on these issues.

Visit at http://www.ntia.doc.gov/

Internet Legal Issues All sorts of Internet legal issues, including property rights, are discussed on this site.

Visit at http://www.faegre.com/internet/net.html

Keeping your property in divorce:

Divorce Survival Guide Find out how you will fare in a divorce.

Visit at http://www.webwise.com/divorce

Your dog:

Nolo Press Nolo Press is a self-help law center that publishes a lot of books about law for lay people.

It is a great source of lawyer jokes, too.

Visit at http://www.nolo.com

(And to find out all about dogs, check out the American Kennel Club Web page at http://www.akc.org)

CYBER EXERCISES:

1. Find an article called "Introduction to Hot Issues in Electronic Commerce" on the World Wide Web Multimedia Law Page. What proposed UCC article does it discuss?
2. Where is the laboratory of the National Telecommunications and Information Administration, the Institute for Telecommunications Sciences, located?
3. From the Internet Legal Issues site, find and print an article called "Who Owns Your WWW Home Page"?
4. From the Divorce Survival Guide site, find the divorce survival tools.
5. From the Nolo Press Web page, find and print out an article called "When a Dog is a Lemon."

CHAPTER SUMMARY

THE NATURE OF PERSONAL PROPERTY, P. 702

Personal Property	*Personal property.* Consists of everything that is not real property. Sometimes referred to as goods or *chattels*.
	 1. Types of personal property:
	   a. *Tangible property.* Physically defined property such as goods, animals, and minerals.
	   b. *Intangible property.* Rights that cannot be reduced to physical form, such as stock certificates, bonds, and copyrights.

ACQUIRING OWNERSHIP IN PERSONAL PROPERTY, P. 702

Methods of Acquiring Ownership in Personal Property	1. *Possession or capture.* Taking possession of or capturing unowned property, such as wild animals.
	 2. *Purchase.* Purchasing the property from its rightful owner.
	 3. *Production.* Producing a finished product from raw materials and supplies.
	 4. *Gift.* Voluntary transfer of property by its owner to a donee without consideration.
	   a. Three elements necessary to create a valid gift:
	     i. *Donative intent.* The donor must have intended to make a gift. This intent can be inferred from the circumstances.
	     ii. *Delivery.* Delivery of the personal property must be made to the donee. This may be by *physical delivery*, or where impracticable, by *constructive* (or *symbolic*) *delivery*.

   iii. *Acceptance*. The donee must accept the gift. Donees are free to reject gifts that they do not want.
  b. Types of gifts:
   i. Gifts *inter vivos*. Gifts made during a donor's lifetime that are irrevocable present transfers of ownership.
   ii. Gifts *causa mortis*. Gifts that are made in anticipation of death. A gift *causa mortis* is established if
    (a) The donor makes a gift in anticipation of approaching death from an existing illness or peril, and
    (b) The donor dies from such illness or peril without having revoked the gift.
 5. *Will*. Gift to beneficiaries named in a will.
 6. *Inheritance*. Heirs stipulated in an inheritance statute.
 7. *Accession*. Occurs when the value of personal property increases because it is added to or improved by natural or manufactured means.
 8. *Confusion*. Where fungible goods are commingled, the owners share title to the commingled goods in proportion to the amount of goods contributed.
 9. *Divorce*. When a marriage is dissolved by a divorce, the parties obtain certain rights in the property of the marital estate.

MISLAID, LOST, AND ABANDONED PROPERTY, P. 706

Mislaid, Lost, and Abandoned Property

1. *Mislaid property*. Personal property that an owner voluntarily places somewhere and then inadvertently forgets. The owner of the premises where the property is mislaid does not acquire title to the property but has the right of possession against all except the rightful owner. The rightful owner can reclaim the property.
2. *Lost property*. Personal property that an owner leaves somewhere because of negligence or carelessness. The finder obtains title to the property against the whole world except the true owner. The rightful owner can reclaim the property.
 a. *Estray statutes*. State statutes that permit a finder of mislaid or lost property to obtain title to the property. To obtain clear title, the finder must:
  i. Report the find to the appropriate government agency and turn over possession of the property to the agency,
  ii. Post and publish required notices, and
  iii. Wait the statutorily required time (e.g., one year) without the rightful owner claiming the property.
3. *Abandoned property*. Personal property that an owner has discarded, or mislaid or lost property that the owner gives up any further attempt to locate. The finder acquires title to the property. The prior owner cannot reclaim the property.

BAILMENTS, P. 708

Bailment

Bailment. Occurs when the owner of personal property delivers the property to another person to be held, stored, or delivered, or for some other purpose.
1. Parties to a bailment:
 a. *Bailor*. Owner of the property.
 b. *Bailee*. Party to whom the property is delivered.
2. Three elements necessary to create a bailment:
 a. *Personal property*. Only personal property can be bailed.

	b. *Delivery of possession.* The bailee must knowingly accept the property and have exclusive control over it. c. *Bailment agreement.* There must be a bailment agreement. *Express bailments* may be oral or written unless required to be in writing by the Statute of Frauds. A bailment may be *implied* from the circumstances.
Types of Bailments	1. *Bailment for a fixed term.* Bailment that terminates at the end of a stipulated term. May be terminated prior to the end of the term by mutual assent of the bailor and bailee. 2. *Bailments at will.* Bailments without a fixed term. May be terminated at any time by either party.

Ordinary Bailments	1. *Bailments for the sole benefit of the bailor:*
	  a. *Gratuitous bailment.* Arises when the bailee is requested to care for the bailor's property as a favor.
	  b. *Involuntary bailment.* Arises when the bailee finds lost or misplaced property and decides to protect it.
	  c. *Duty of care.* The bailee owes a duty of *slight care;* that is, the bailee is liable for *gross negligence.*
	2. *Bailments for the sole benefit of the bailee:*
	  a. *Gratuitous bailment.* A gratuitous bailment that arises when the bailee uses the bailor's property for personal reasons without paying compensation.
	  b. *Duty of care.* The bailee owes a duty of *great care* (or *utmost care*) and is liable for *slight negligence.*
	3. *Bailments for the mutual benefit of the bailor and the bailee:*
	  a. *Mutual benefit bailment.* Arises when both parties benefit from the bailment. This includes commercial bailments.
	  b. *Duty of care.* The bailee owes a duty of *reasonable care* (or *ordinary care*) and is liable for *ordinary negligence.*

SPECIAL BAILMENTS, P. 712

Special Bailees	1. *Common carriers.* Companies that offer transportation services to the public, such as airlines, railroads, trucking firms, and such. The parties are:
	  a. *Consignor or shipper.* The person shipping the goods. The bailor.
	  b. *Common carrier.* The transportation company. The bailee.
	  c. *Consignee.* Party to whom the goods are to be delivered.
	  d. *Duty of care.* Common carriers owe a duty of *strict liability;* that is, if the goods are lost, damaged, destroyed, or stolen, the common carrier is liable even if it was not its fault.
	2. *Warehouse companies.* Companies that engage in the business of storing property for compensation.
	  a. *Duty of care.* Warehouse companies owe a duty of *reasonable care* (or *ordinary care*) to protect the bailed goods from loss or damage.
	3. *Innkeepers.* The owner of a facility that provides lodging to the public for compensation (e.g., a hotel or motel).
	  a. *Duty of care.* Under the common law, innkeepers owe a duty of *strict liability* regarding loss caused to guests' property.
	  b. *Innkeepers' statutes.* Laws that have been enacted to limit the liability of innkeepers for loss or damage to guests' property. The innkeeper must post required notices to be covered by the law.

CRITICAL LEGAL THINKING CASES

28.1 Personal Property or Fixture NYT Cable TV is a division of The New York Times Company (NYT) that operates a cable television station in Camden County, New Jersey. NYT has erected a 250-foot-high cable antenna tower on real property to distribute its broadcast signals. The structure is attached to a large concrete foundation in the ground and consists of a large vertical triangular steel superstructure connected by steel crossbars and circular metal ties. The Camden County Board of Taxation assessed a real property tax on the property, including the cable television tower. NYT opposed the tax, alleging that the cable television tower was personal property—not real property—which was exempt from the real property tax. Who wins? [*NYT Cable TV v. Borough of Audubon, New Jersey*, 553 A.2d 1368 (N.J. Sup. 1989)]

28.2 Accession On June 6, 1983, Mack's Used Cars & Parts, Inc. (Mack's) sold a 1975 model GMC one-ton truck with a 1979 Atlas wrecker assembly attached thereto to Jack W. Weaver on credit. At the time of the purchase, the wrecker assembly was bolted to the frame of the truck, and its hydraulic boom operated off the transmission of the truck. To protect its credit extension to Weaver, Mack's took a security interest in the vehicle and perfected its interest by a notation on the truck's title. Mack's filed a financing statement with the Tennessee secretary of state covering the vehicle. Weaver subsequently sold the vehicle to McCall, who removed the wrecker assembly from the truck and sold the wrecker assembly to the Tennessee Truck & Equipment Co. (Tennessee Truck). When the original extension of credit was not paid, Mack's brought this action to repossess the vehicle and also to repossess the wrecker assembly from Tennessee Truck. Who wins? [*Mack's Used Cars & Parts, Inc. v. Tennessee Truck & Equipment Co.*, 694 S.W.2d 323 (Tenn. App. 1985)]

28.3 Gift *Causa Mortis* Olga V. Watson lived in an apartment building that was managed by Edward P. McCarton. During 1980, Watson's health started to deteriorate, and she eventually began to call on McCarton for assistance in her daily affairs. By 1982, Watson's health had deteriorated to the point where she could no longer take care of herself. McCarton arranged for her to move into his apartment. Except for a brief stay in a nursing home, Watson lived in McCarton's apartment until her death. During her stay, she met many of McCarton's relatives. On July 26, 1981, two days before her death, Watson stated that she realized she was dying and asked McCarton to write down her wishes for the disposition of her assets. She directed that McCarton receive her stocks and bonds worth $235,000 and that McCarton's relatives receive her bank accounts worth $354,000. The stock certificates, bonds, and bank statements were located in a dresser in the McCarton apartment. Later, it was discovered that Watson had prepared a will several years earlier in which she left one-half of her estate to her sister and the other half to a nephew. Evidence showed that once, when Watson received a letter from the nephew demanding his inheritance, she stated, "He won't get a dime from me." The will was admitted to probate. Which prevails, Watson's gift letter or the old will? [*McCarton v. Estate of Watson*, 693 P.2d 192 (Wash. App. 1984)]

28.4 Uniform Gift to Minors Act Between 1972 and 1984, Theodore Alexander Buder's father made substantial cash gifts to his minor grandchildren. The Buders divorced during this period. The cash gifts, typically in the form of checks made directly payable to the children, were given to Buder with the understanding that he would safeguard the money and invest it on behalf of the children. Buder invested various amounts of the children's money in blue chip stocks traded over the New York and American stock exchanges. In 1974, he began investing substantial sums of the children's money in speculative penny stocks. The stocks were purchased in Buder's name as custodian for the children as required by the Uniform Gift to Minors Act (UGMA). At one point, almost half of the children's money was invested in penny stocks. All of the penny stocks except one suffered substantial losses. Buder's ex-wife, Sartore, sued him, alleging he breached his fiduciary duty owed to the children under the UGMA. She sought to recover the funds lost by Buder's investment of the children's fund in penny stocks. Who wins? [*Buder v. Sartore*, 774 P.2d 1383 (Colo. 1989)]

28.5 Lost Property In June 1983, Danny Lee Smith and his brother, Jeffrey Allen Smith, found a 16-foot fiberglass boat lying beside the roadway in Mobile County, Alabama. Seeing two sheriff's deputies, they stopped them to discuss the boat. Over the Smiths' objections, the deputies impounded the boat. The Smiths made it clear that, if the true owner of the boat was not found, they wanted the boat. The true owner did not claim the boat. Mobile County claimed the boat and wanted to auction it off to raise money for county recreational programs. The Smiths claimed the boat as finders. Alabama did not have an estray statute that applied to the situation. Who gets the boat? [*Smith v. Sheriff Purvis*, 474 So.2d 1131 (Ala. App. 1985)]

28.6 Abandoned Property Late in 1975, police officers of the city of Miami, Florida responded to reports of a shooting at the apartment of Carlos Fuentes. Fuentes had been shot in the neck and shoulder and, shortly after police arrived, was moved to a hospital. In an ensuing search of the apartment, the police found assorted drug paraphernalia, a gun, and cash in the amount of $58,591. The property was seized, taken to the police station, and placed in custody. About nine days later, the police learned that Fuentes had been discharged from the hospital. All efforts by police to locate Fuentes and his girlfriend, a co-occupant of Fuentes' apartment, were unsuccessful. Neither Fuentes nor his girlfriend ever came forward to claim any of the items taken by the police from their apartment. About four years later, in 1979, James W. Green and Walter J. Vogel, the owners of the apartment building in which Fuentes was a tenant, sued the city of Miami to recover the cash found in Fuentes' apartment. The state of Florida intervened in the case, also claiming an interest in the money. Who wins? [*State of Florida v. Green*, 456 So.2d 1309 (Fla. App. 1984)]

28.7 Bailment On February 4, 1976, James D. Merritt leased a storage locker from Nationwide Warehouse Co., Ltd. (Nationwide) and agreed to pay $16 per month lease for the locker. Merritt placed various items in the leased premises but never informed Nationwide as to the nature or quantity of articles stored therein. Merritt was free to store or remove whatever he wished without consultation with, permission from, or notice to, Nationwide. Merritt locked the leased premises with his own lock and key. Nationwide was not furnished with a key. Subsequently, certain personal property belonging to Merritt disappeared from the storage space. Merritt sued Nationwide to recover damages of $5,275. Was a bailment created between Merritt and Nationwide? [*Merritt v. Nationwide Warehouse Co., Ltd.*, 605 S.W.2d 250 (Tenn. App. 1980)]

28.8 Liability for Lost Goods On May 14, 1980, Clarence Williams brought his wife's fur coat to Debonair Cleaners for cleaning and storage. The clerk told him that Debonair was experienced in such matters and that the charge would be 3 percent of the stated value of the coat. Williams stated that the coat was worth $13,000 and the clerk gave Williams a claim check and informed Williams that the total fee for storage would be $390, to be paid when the coat was retrieved. That evening, Williams related the substance of his conversation with the clerk to his wife, Armicia, and gave her the claim check. Approximately eight months later, Armicia went to Debonair to retrieve her coat. She presented the claim check to the clerk who, after searching the premises for the coat, told her that it could not be located. Williams was informed that the coat had probably been stolen during a break-in and burglary. Williams sued Debonair to recover the value of the coat. Who wins? [*Mahallati v. Williams*, 479 A.2d 300 (D.C. App. 1984)]

28.9 Gratuitous Bailment Marsha Hamilton and Andrea Morris were guests at a dinner party attended by approximately 25 people. The party began about 7:00 P.M. and ended at approximately 1:00 A.M. Alcoholic beverages were served throughout the evening. At approximately 11:30 P.M., while working in the kitchen, Hamilton removed her watch and placed it on the counter. About midnight, Hamilton left the kitchen and went outside. After about 15 minutes, she became ill and fled to the bathroom. Shortly after Hamilton left the kitchen, Morris saw the watch on the counter and, fearing for its safety, picked it up and carried it in her hand as she looked for Hamilton. When Hamilton came out of the bathroom, she and her fiancé left the party. Morris was unable to find Hamilton and cannot recall precisely what she did with the watch. She testified that she either gave it to Hamilton's fiancé or put it somewhere in the host's house for safekeeping. Hamilton's fiancé testified that Morris did not give him the watch. The next day, Hamilton discovered that she did not have her watch but, in a search of the host's home, the watch was not recovered. Hamilton sued Morris for damages. Who wins? [*Morris v. Hamilton*, 302 S.E.2d 51 (Va. 1983)]

28.10 Parking Lot's Liability Allright, Inc. is a parking lot operator in Houston, Texas. On January 18, 1980, Kirkland

Strauder drove his 1978 Buick Regal automobile to a Houston Allright parking lot, placed it in a row of cars to be parked by the attendant, handed the attendant his keys, and was given a receipt by the attendant. When Strauder returned two hours later to reclaim his car, it could not be found. Strauder reported the car stolen. Allright could not explain the loss of the car, which was found one and one-half weeks later, wrecked and stripped. Strauder sued Allright for damages. Who wins? [*Allright, Inc. v. Strauder*, 679 S.W.2d 31 (Tex. App. 1984)]

28.11 Conversion of Bailed Property Alan Brotman and Prem Sahai were the owners and managers of the Brotman Investment Corporation, which was engaged in the business of selling rare coins. In August 1980, Leonard Fazio purchased silver coins worth $4,998 from Corporation. The coins were to be put into Corporation's vault for safekeeping. It was understood that Fazio could demand the return of the coins at any time. In November 1980, Fazio unsuccessfully demanded that his coins are returned. Evidence showed that the coins never made it into the vault and that the coins had been converted for one of the cobailee's own use. Fazio sued Brotman and Sahai for damages. Who wins? [*Fazio v. Brotman and Sahai*, 371 N.W.2d 842 (Iowa App. 1985)]

28.12 Warehouse Company Vernon Pittman Van Lines (Pittman) is a warehouse company which stores goods for a fee. On May 31, 1977, Trudy Royster hired Pittman to store some of her furniture and household goods. Royster paid Pittman a monthly fee for such services. When Royster decided to remove a few items from storage on September 9, 1979, she found her furniture and cartons in a state of disarray. Several pieces of furniture were substantially damaged, including broken legs, scratches, and so on. Pittman did not produce any evidence showing how the furniture was damaged. Royster sued Pittman to recover damages. Who wins? [*Royster v. Pittman*, 691 S.W.2d 305 (Mo. App. 1985)]

28.13 Disclaimer of Liability On January 23, 1982, Joseph Conboy, his wife, and a group of friends convened in Manhattan, New York, for a party at Studio 54, a discotheque where patrons dance to recorded music played on high-fidelity sound equipment. The Conboy party checked their coats, 14 in all, with the coatroom attendant. After paying a $0.75 charge per coat, they received seven check stubs. A small sign in the coatroom stated, "Liability for lost property in this coat/check room is limited to $100 per loss of misplaced article." Conboy testified that he did not notice it when he checked his coat, and that the coatroom attendant did not call his attention to the sign. At the end of the evening, Conboy and the other guests of the party attempted to reclaim their coats. Conboy's one-month-old $1,350 leather coat was missing. Conboy sued Studio 54 for damages. Is the disclaimer of liability enforceable? [*Conboy v. Studio 54, Inc.*, 449 N.Y.S.2d 391 (N.Y. 1982)]

ETHICS CASES

28.14 Ethical Perspective When Dr. Arthur M. Edwards died, leaving a will disposing of his property, he left the villa-type condominium in which he lived, its "contents," and

$10,000 to his stepson, Ronald W. Souders. Dr. Edwards left the residual of his estate to other named legatees. In administrating the estate, certain stock certificates, passbook savings accounts, and other bank statements were found in Dr. Edwards's condominium. Souders claimed that these items belonged to him because they were "contents" of the condominium. The other legatees opposed Souders's claim, alleging that the disputed property was intangible property and not part of the contents of the condominium. The value of the property was as follows: condominium, $138,000; furniture in condominium, $4,000; stocks, $377,000; and passbook and other bank accounts, $124,000. Who is entitled to the stocks and bank accounts? Do you think Souders acted ethically in this case? [*Souders v. Johnson*, 501 So.2d 745 (Fla. App. 1987)]

28.15 Ethical Perspective Darryl Kulwin was employed by Nova Stylings, Inc. (Nova) as a jewelry salesman. In that capacity, he traveled throughout the country carrying with him jewelry owned and manufactured by Nova to show to prospective buyers. Kulwin was visiting Panoria Ruston, who was a guest registered with the Red Roof Inn in Overland Park, Kansas. Ruston and Kulwin met at the Inn and later made plans to leave to go to dinner. Kulwin asked Ruston to make arrangements with the desk clerk to leave his sample case in the office of the Inn while they went out to dinner. Ruston asked the clerk if she could leave the bag in the manager's office of the Inn and the clerk agreed. Ruston advised the clerk that the contents of the case were valuable, but did not describe the contents of the bag.

Kansas Statute Section 36-402(b) provides:

No hotel or motel keeper in this state shall be liable for the loss of, or damage to, merchandise for sale or samples belonging to a guest, lodger or boarder unless the guest, lodger or boarder upon entering the hotel or motel, shall give notice of having merchandise for sale or samples in his possession, together with an itemized list of such property, to the hotel or motel keeper, or his authorized agent or clerk in the registration office of the hotel or motel office.

No hotel or motel keeper shall be liable for any loss of such property designated in this subsection (b), after notice an itemized statement having been given and delivered as aforesaid, in an amount in excess of two hundred fifty dollars ($250), unless such hotel or motel keeper, by specific agreement in writing, individually, or by an authorized agent or clerk in charge of the registration office of the hotel or motel, shall voluntarily assume liability for a larger amount with reference to such property. The hotel or motel keeper shall not be compelled to receive such guests, lodgers or boarders with merchandise for sale or samples.

The Inn posted the proper notice of the provisions of this act in all of the guests' rooms, including that of Ms. Ruston. An unidentified person obtained access to the manager's office and removed the case from the office. Nova sued Red Roof Inns for the alleged value of the jewelry—$650,000. Is Red Roof Inns liable? Did either party act unethically in this case? [*Nova Stylings v. Red Roof Inns, Inc.*, 747 P.2d 107 (Kan. 1987)]

CRITICAL LEGAL THINKING WRITING ASSIGNMENT

Read Case A.28 in the Case Appendix [*The Wackenhut Corporation and Delta Airlines, Inc. v. Lippert*]. This case is excerpted from the appellate court's opinion. Review and brief the case. In your brief, be sure to answer the following questions:

1. What type of bailment was created in this case?
2. What standard of care did The Wackenhut Corporation and Delta Airlines owe to Mrs. Lippert? Was this standard of care breached?

3. What did the limitation on liability tariff and clause in Delta's ticket provide? What was the dollar amount of Mrs. Lippert's loss?
4. Who did the trial court hold in favor of?
5. Did the appellate court find that the limitation on liability clause was enforceable? What reasons did the court cite to support its decision on this issue?

NOTES

[1] UCC § 7-301(1).
[2] UCC § 7-309(2).
[3] UCC § 7-102(h).

[4] UCC § 7-204(1) and 7-403(1).
[5] UCC § 7-204(2).

CHAPTER 29

REAL PROPERTY

AND LANDLORD–TENANT

RELATIONSHIP

Chapter Objectives

*After studying this chapter,
you should be able to*

1. List and describe the different types of real property
2. Describe the different types of freehold estates in land
3. Describe the different types of future interests in land
4. List and describe concurrent ownership interests in land
5. Explain how ownership interests in real property can be transferred
6. Describe the different nonpossessory interests in land
7. Explain how a landlord–tenant relationship is created
8. Identify and describe the various types of tenancy
9. List and describe the landlords' and tenants' rights and duties
10. Describe the various forms of private and public land use regulation

Chapter Contents

- Nature of Real Property
  Business Application Air Rights: Value in the Heavens
- Estates in Land
- Freehold Estates
- Future Interests
- Concurrent Ownership
  Case 29.1 *Cunningham v. Hastings (IN)*
- Transfer of Ownership of Real Property
  Ethical Perspective Modern-Day Squatters
  Business Checklist What a Person Should Do When Buying Real Estate
- Nonpossessory Interests
  Case 29.2 *Walker v. Ayres (DE)*
- Landlord–Tenant Relationship
- Types of Tenancy
  Ethical Perspective Laws Prohibit Discrimination in the Sale and Rental of Real Property
- Landlord's Duties
  Case 29.3 *Solow v. Wellner (NY)*
- Tenant's Duties
  Contemporary Business Environment Title III of the Americans with Disabilities Act
- Tort Liability of Landlords and Tenants
  Case 29.4 *Feld v. Merriam (PA)*
- Transferring Rights to Leased Property
  Contemporary Business Environment Regulatory Taking
- Land Use Control
  Case 29.5 *Guinnane v. San Francisco City Planning Commission (CA)*
  Business Checklist Rent Control
  International Perspective Sorting Out Real Property Ownership Rights in the Former East Germany
- Working the Web
- Chapter Summary
- Critical Legal Thinking Cases
- Ethics Cases
- Critical Legal Thinking Writing Assignment

> *Without that sense of security which property gives, the land would still be uncultivated.*
>
> Francois Quesnay
> (1694–1774)
> *Maximes, IV*

"Property is an instrument of humanity, Humanity is not an instrument of property."
Woodrow Wilson
Speech (1912)

Property and ownership rights in **real property** play an important part in this country's society and economy. Note that the concept of real property is concerned with the legal rights to the property rather than the physical attributes of the tangible land. That is why real property includes some items of personal property which are affixed to real property (e.g., fixtures) and other rights (e.g., minerals, air rights).

The area covered by laws concerning real property is very broad. It includes **landlord–tenant relationships** and **land use control**, among other things.

Individuals and families own or rent houses, farmers and ranchers own farmland and ranches, and businesses own or lease commercial and office buildings. In addition, (1) over half of the population rent their homes and (2) many businesses lease office space, stores, manufacturing facilities, and other commercial property. The parties to a **landlord–tenant** relationship have certain legal rights and duties which are governed by a mixture of real estate and contract law.

Although the United States has the most advanced private property system in the world, the ownership and possession of real estate is not free from government regulation. Pursuant to constitutional authority, federal, state, and local governments have enacted a myriad of laws that regulate the ownership, possession, and use of real property. These laws, which are collectively referred to as **land use control**, include zoning laws, building codes, anti-discrimination laws, and the like.

This chapter covers the law concerning the ownership and transfer of real property, landlord–tenant relationships, and land use control.

NATURE OF REAL PROPERTY

real property   The land itself as well as buildings, trees, soil, minerals, timber, plants, and other things permanently affixed to the land.

Property is usually classified as either real or personal property. **Real property** is immovable or attached to immovable land or buildings, while personal property is movable. The various types of real property are discussed in the following paragraphs.

Land and Buildings

land   The most common form of real property. Includes the land and buildings and other structures permanently attached to the land.

Land is the most common form of real property. A landowner usually purchases the **surface rights** to the land—that is, the right to occupy the land. The owner may use, enjoy, and develop the property as he or she sees fit, subject to any applicable government regulation.

surface right   The right of a landowner to use, enjoy, develop, or otherwise occupy the land as he or she sees fit, subject to any applicable government regulation.

Buildings constructed on land are real property. For example, houses, apartment buildings, manufacturing plants, and office buildings constructed on land are real property. Such things as radio towers, bridges, and the like are usually considered real property as well.

Subsurface Rights

subsurface rights   Rights to the earth located beneath the surface of the land.

The owner of land possesses **subsurface rights** (or **mineral rights**) to the earth located beneath the surface of the land. These rights can be very valuable. For example, gold, uranium, oil, or natural gas may lie beneath the surface of land. Theoretically, mineral rights extend to the center of the earth. In reality, mines and oil wells usually extend only several miles into the earth. Subsurface rights may be sold separately from surface rights.

Plant Life and Vegetation

Plant life and vegetation growing on the surface of land is considered real property. This includes both natural plant life (e.g., trees) and cultivated plant life (e.g., crops). When land is sold, any plant life growing on the land is included unless the parties agree otherwise. Plant life that is severed from the land is considered personal property.

> **plant life and vegetation** Real property that is growing in or on the surface of the land.

Fixtures

Certain personal property is so closely associated with real property that it becomes part of the realty. Such items are called **fixtures**. For example, kitchen cabinets, carpeting, and doorknobs are fixtures, but throw rugs and furniture are personal property.

Unless otherwise provided, if a building is sold, the fixtures are included in the sale. If the sale agreement is silent as to whether an item is a fixture, the courts make their determination on the basis of whether the item can be removed without causing substantial damage to the realty.

> **fixtures** Goods that are affixed to real estate so as to become a part thereof.

BUSINESS APPLICATION

Air Rights: Value in the Heavens

Common law provided that the owners of real property owned that property from the center of the earth to the heavens. This rule has been eroded by modern legal restrictions such as land use control laws, environmental protection laws, and air navigation requirements. Even today, however, the owners of land may sell or lease air space parcels above their land.

An **air space parcel** is a three-dimensional cube of air above the surface of the earth. Air space parcels are valuable property rights, particularly in densely populated metropolitan areas where building property is scarce. For example, many developments have been built in air space parcels in New York City. The most notable are Madison Square Garden and Two Penn Plaza which were built in air space parcels above Penn Station. More developments are expected to be built in air space parcels in the future.

ESTATES IN LAND

A person's ownership rights in real property is called an **estate in land** (or **estate**). An estate is defined as the bundle of **legal rights** that the owner has to possess, use, and enjoy the property. The type of estate that an owner possesses is determined from the deed, will, lease, or other document that transferred the ownership rights to him or her.

> **estate** Ownership rights in real property; the bundle of legal rights that the owner has to possess, use, and enjoy the property.

FREEHOLD ESTATES

A **freehold estate** is one where the owner has a present possessory interest in the real property; that is, the owner may use and enjoy the property as he or she sees fit, subject to any applicable government regulation or private restraint. The two types of freehold estates are estates in fee and life estates.

> **freehold estate** An estate where the owner has a present possessory interest in the real property.

Estates in Fee

A **fee simple absolute** (or **fee simple**) is the highest form of ownership of real property because it grants the owner the fullest bundle of legal rights that a person can hold in real property. It is the type of ownership most people connect with "owning"

> **fee simple absolute** A type of ownership of real property that grants the owner the fullest bundle of legal rights that a person can hold in real property.

real property. It is also the most common form of real estate ownership in the United States. A fee simple owner has the right to exclusively possess and use his or her property to the extent that the owner has not transferred any interest in the property (e.g., by lease). If a person owns real property in fee simple, his or her ownership

- Is infinite in duration (fee)
- Has no limitation on inheritability (simple)
- Does not end upon the happening of any event (absolute).

fee simple defeasible
A type of ownership of real property that grants the owner all the incidents of a fee simple absolute except that it may be taken away if a specified condition occurs or does not occur.

A **fee simple defeasible** (or **qualified fee**) grants the owner all the incidents of a fee simple absolute except that it may be taken away if a specified condition occurs or does not occur. For example, a conveyance of property to a church "as long as the land is used as a church or for church purposes" creates a qualified fee. The church has all of the rights of a fee simple absolute owner except that its ownership rights are terminated if the property is no longer used for church purposes.

Life Estates

life estate   An interest in the land for a person's lifetime; upon that person's death, the interest will be transferred to another party.

estate pour autre vie   A life estate measured in the life of a third party.

A **life estate** is an interest in real property that lasts for the life of a specified person, usually the grantee. For example, a conveyance of real property "to Anna for her life" creates a life estate. A life estate may also be measured by the life of a third party (e.g., "to Anna for the life of Benjamin"). This is called an ***estate pour autre vie***. A life estate may be defeasible (e.g., "to John for his life but only if he continues to occupy this residence"). Upon the death of named person, the life estate terminates and the property reverts back to the grantor or the grantor's estate or other designated person.

A life tenant is treated as the owner of the property during the duration of the life estate. He or she has the right to possess and use the property except to the extent that it would cause permanent **waste** of the property. A life tenant may sell, transfer, or mortgage his or her estate in the land. The mortgage, however, cannot exceed the duration of the life estate. A life tenant is obligated to keep the property in repair and to pay property taxes.

FUTURE INTERESTS

future interest   The interest that the grantor retains for him- or herself or a third party.

A person may be given the right to possess property in the future rather than currently. This right is called a **future interest**. The two forms of future interests are **reversion** and **remainder**.

Reversion

reversion   A right of possession that returns to the grantor after the expiration of a limited or contingent estate.

A **reversion** is a right of possession that returns to the grantor after the expiration of a limited or contingent estate. Reversions do not have to be expressly stated because they arise automatically by law. For example, if a grantor conveys property "to M. R. Harrington for life," the grantor has retained a reversion in the property. That is, when Harrington dies, the property reverts to the grantor or, if he is not living then, to his estate.

Remainder

remainder   If the right of possession returns to a third party upon the expiration of a limited or contingent estate.

If the right of possession returns to a third party upon the expiration of a limited or contingent estate, it is called a **remainder**. The person who is entitled to the future interest is called a **remainderman**. For example, a conveyance of property "to Joe for life, remainder to Meredith" is a vested remainder—the only contingency to Meredith's possessory interest is Joe's death.

CONCURRENT OWNERSHIP

Two or more persons may own a piece of real property. This is called **co-ownership** or **concurrent ownership**. The following forms of co-ownership are recognized: joint tenancy, tenancy in common, tenancy by the entirety, community property, condominium, and cooperative.

co-ownership When two or more persons own a piece of real property. Also called *concurrent ownership*.

Joint Tenancy

The most distinguishing feature of a **joint tenancy** is the co-owners' **right of survivorship**. This means that upon the death of one of the co-owners (or **joint tenants**) the deceased person's interest in the property automatically passes to the surviving joint tenants. Any contrary provision in the deceased's will is ineffective.

joint tenancy A form of co-ownership that includes the right of survivorship.

joint tenant Co-owner in a joint tenancy.

CONSIDER THIS EXAMPLE: Jones, one of four people who own a piece of property in joint tenancy, executes a will leaving all of his property to a university. Jones dies. The surviving joint tenants—not the university—acquire his interest in the piece of property.

To create a joint tenancy, words that clearly show a person's intent to create a joint tenancy must be used. Language such as "Marsha Leest and James Leest, as joint tenants" are usually sufficient. Some states specify that particular language must be used. Each joint tenant has a right to sell or transfer his or her interest in the property, but such conveyance terminates the joint tenancy. The parties then become tenants in common.

CAUTION
Upon the death of a joint tenant, the deceased's interest in the property automatically passes to the surviving joint tenants, not to the deceased's heirs or beneficiaries.

Tenancy in Common

In a **tenancy in common**, the interests of a surviving **tenant in common** passes to the deceased tenant's estate and not to the co-tenants.

tenancy in common A form of co-ownership in which the interest of a surviving tenant-in-common passes to the deceased tenant's estate and not to the co-tenants.

CONSIDER THIS EXAMPLE: Lopez, who is one of four tenants in common who own a piece of property, has a will that leaves all of his property to his granddaughter. When Lopez dies, the granddaughter receives his interest in the tenancy in common, and the granddaughter becomes a tenant in common with three other owners.

A tenancy in common may be created by express words, such as "Jasmin Huang and Karen Ma, as tenants in common." There is a presumption that co-ownership of real property is a tenancy in common unless another intent is clearly indicated. For example, the words "to Annie Tsui and Min-Wer Chen, as co-owners" creates a tenancy in common and not a joint tenancy. Unless otherwise agreed, a tenant in common can sell, give, devise, or otherwise transfer his or her interest in the property without the consent of the other co-owners.

Tenancy by the Entirety

Tenancy by the entirety is a form of co-ownership of real property that can be used only by married couples. This type of tenancy must be created by express words such as, "Harold Jones and Maude Jones, husband and wife, as tenants by the entireties." A surviving spouse has the right of survivorship.

tenancy by the entirety A form of co-ownership of real property that can be used only by married couples.

Tenancy by the entirety is distinguished from a joint tenancy because neither spouse may sell or transfer his or her interest in the property without the other spouse's consent. A divorce terminates the tenancy because the marriage has ceased. The tenancy is then transformed into a tenancy in common. Only about half of the states recognize a tenancy by the entirety.

In the following case, the court had to decide how to split the proceeds from the sale of real property owned by co-owners.

CASE 29.1

Cunningham v. Hastings
556 N.E.2d 12 (1990) Court of Appeals of Indiana

Facts On August 30, 1984, Warren R. Hastings and Joan L. Cunningham, who were unmarried, purchased a house together. Hastings paid $45,000 down payment toward the purchase price out of his own funds. The deed referred to Hastings and Cunningham as "joint tenants with the right of survivorship." Hastings and Cunningham occupied the property jointly. After their relationship ended, Hastings took sole possession of the property. Cunningham filed a complaint seeking partition of the real estate. Based on its determination that the property could not be split, the trial court ordered it to be sold. The trial court further ordered that $45,000 of the sale proceeds be paid to Hastings to reimburse him for his down payment, and the remainder of the proceeds be divided equally between Hastings and Cunningham. Cunningham appealed, alleging that Hastings should not have been given credit for the down payment.

Issue Is Cunningham entitled to an equal share of the proceeds of the sale of the real estate?

Decision Yes. Cunningham is entitled to an equal share of the proceeds of the sale because she and Hastings owned the property as joint tenants. The appellate court reversed the trial court's judgment and remanded the case to the trial court with instructions to order the entire proceeds of the sale to be divided equally between Cunningham and Hastings.

Reason The court stated: "The determination of the parties' interests in the present case is simple. There are only two parties involved in the joint tenancy. Once a joint tenancy relationship is found to exist between two people in a partition action, it is axiomatic that each person owns a one-half interest . . . Regardless of who provided the money to purchase the land, the creation of a joint tenancy relationship entitles each party to an equal share of the proceeds of the sale upon partition."

CASE QUESTIONS

Critical Legal Thinking Should the law recognize so many different forms of ownership of real property? Do you think most people understand the legal consequences of taking title in the various forms?

Ethics Did Cunningham act ethically in demanding one-half the value of the down payment even though she did not contribute to it?

Business Implication Could Hastings have protected the $45,000 he paid for the down payment? If so, how could he have done it?

Community Property

community property
A form of ownership in which each spouse owns an equal one-half share of the income of both spouses and the assets acquired during the marriage.

separate property In states that recognizes community property, this is property that has been acquired prior to marriage or property received by gift or inheritance during the marriage that belongs to one spouse alone.

Nine states—Arizona, California, Idaho, Louisiana, Nevada, New Mexico, Texas, Washington, and Wisconsin—recognize a form of co-ownership known as **community property**. This method of co-ownership applies only to married couples. It is based on the notion that a husband and wife should share equally in the fruits of the marital partnership. Under these laws, each spouse owns an equal one-half share of the income of both spouses and the assets acquired during the marriage. This is so regardless of who earns the income. Property that is acquired through gift or inheritance either before or during marriage remains **separate property**.

When a spouse dies, the surviving spouse automatically receives one-half the community property. The other half passes to the heirs of the deceased spouse as directed by will or by state intestate statute if there is no will.

CONSIDER THIS EXAMPLE: Suppose a husband and wife have community property assets of $1.5 million and the wife dies with a will. The husband automatically has a right to receive $750,000 of the community property. The remaining $750,000 passes as directed by the wife's will. Any separate property owned by the wife, such as jewelry she inherited, also passes in accordance with her will. Her husband has no vested interest in that property.

During the marriage, neither spouse can sell, transfer, or gift community property without the consent of the other spouse. Upon a divorce, each spouse has a right to one-half of the community property.

The location of the real property determines whether community property law applies. For example, if a married couple who lives in a noncommunity property state purchases real property located in a community property state, community property laws apply to that property.

"The right of property has not made poverty, but it has powerfully contributed to make wealth."

J. R. McCulloch (1789–1864)
Principles of Political Economy

Cooperative

A **cooperative** is a form of co-ownership of a multiple-dwelling building where a corporation owns the building and the residents own shares in the corporation. Each cooperative owner then leases a unit in the building from the corporation under a renewable long-term, proprietary lease. Individual residents may not secure loans with the units they occupy. The corporation may borrow money on a blanket mortgage, and each shareholder is jointly and severally liable on the loan. Usually, cooperative owners may not sell their shares or sublease their units without the approval of the other owners.

cooperative   A form of co-ownership of a multiple-dwelling building in which a corporation owns the building and the residents own shares in the corporation.

Condominium

Condominiums are a common form of ownership in multiple-dwelling buildings. Purchasers of a condominium (1) have title to their individual units and (2) own the common areas (e.g., hallways, elevators, parking areas, and recreational facilities) as tenants in common with the other owners. Owners may sell or mortgage their units without the permission of the other owners. Owners are assessed monthly fees for the maintenance of common areas. In addition to dwelling units, the condominium form of ownership is offered for office buildings, boat docks, and such.

condominium   A common form of ownership in a multiple-dwelling building in which the purchaser has title to the individual unit and owns the common areas as a tenant in common with the other condominium owners.

TRANSFER OF OWNERSHIP OF REAL PROPERTY

Ownership of real property may be transferred from one person to another. Title to real property may be transferred by sale; tax sale; gift, will, or inheritance; and adverse possession. The different methods of transfer provide different degrees of protection to the transferee.

Sale of Real Estate

A **sale** or **conveyance** is the most common method for transferring ownership rights in real property. An owner may offer his or her real estate for sale either by him- or herself or by using a real estate broker. When a buyer has been located and the parties have negotiated the terms of the sale, the **real estate sales contract** is executed by the parties. The Statute of Frauds in most states requires this contract to be in writing.

The seller delivers a deed to the buyer and the buyer pays the purchase price at the **closing** or **settlement**. Unless otherwise agreed, it is implied that the seller is conveying fee simple absolute title to the buyer. If either party fails to perform, the other party may sue for breach of contract and obtain either monetary damages or specific performance.

sale   The passing of title from a seller to a buyer for a price. Also called a *conveyance*.

closing   The finalization of a real estate sales transaction that passes title to the property from the seller to the buyer.

Tax Sale

If an owner of real property fails to pay property taxes, the government may obtain a lien on the property for the amount of the taxes. If the taxes remain unpaid for a statutory period of time, the government may sell the property at a **tax sale** to satisfy the **lien**. Any excess proceeds are paid to the taxpayer. The buyer receives title to the property.

Many states provide a **period of redemption** after a tax sale during which the taxpayer may redeem the property by paying the unpaid taxes and penalties. In these states, the buyer at a tax sale does not receive title to the property until the period of redemption has passed.

tax sale   A method of transferring property ownership that involves a lien on property for unpaid property taxes. If the lien remains unpaid after a certain amount of time, a tax sale is held to satisfy the lien.

Gift, Will, or Inheritance

gift A transfer of property from one person to another without exchange of money.

Ownership of real property may be transferred by **gift**. The gift is made when the deed to the property is delivered by the donor to the donee or to a third party to hold for the donee. No consideration is necessary. For example, suppose a grandfather wants to give his farm to his granddaughter. To do so, he only has to execute a deed and give the deed to her or to someone to hold for her, such as her parents.

Real property may also be transferred by **will**. For example, a person may leave a piece of real estate to his best friend by will when he dies. This does not require the transfer of a deed during the testator's lifetime. A deed will be issued to the beneficiary when the will is probated. If a person dies without a valid will, his or her property is distributed to the heirs pursuant to the applicable state intestate statute.

will or **inheritance** If a person dies with a will, his or her property is distributed to the beneficiaries as designated in the will. If a person dies without a will, his or her property is distributed to the heirs as stipulated in the state's intestate statute.

Adverse Possession

adverse possession When a person who wrongfully possesses someone else's real property obtains title to that property if certain statutory requirements are met.

In most states, a person who wrongfully possesses someone else's real property obtains title to that property if certain statutory requirements are met. This is called **adverse possession**. Property owned by federal and state governments are not subject to adverse possession.

Under this doctrine, the transfer of the property is involuntary and does not require the delivery of a deed. To obtain title under adverse possession, the wrongful possession must be

 CAUTION

Owners of property should check their property every so many years to determine if anyone is attempting to acquire title by adverse possession. If anyone is found to be doing so, the owner should take appropriate action to prevent the adverse possession.

- **For a statutorily prescribed period of time.** In most states this period is between 10 and 20 years.
- **Open, visible, and notorious.** The adverse possessor must occupy the property so as to put the owner on notice of the possession.
- **Actual and exclusive.** The adverse possessor must physically occupy the premises. The planting of crops, grazing of animals, or building of a structure on the land constitutes physical occupancy.
- **Continuous and peaceful.** The occupancy must be continuous and uninterrupted for the required statutory period. Any break in normal occupancy terminates the adverse possession. This means that the adverse possessor may leave the property to go to work, to the store, to take vacations, and such. The adverse possessor cannot take the property by force from an owner.
- **Hostile and adverse.** The possessor must occupy the property without the express or implied permission of the owner. Thus, a lessee cannot claim title to the property under adverse possession.

If the elements of adverse possession are met, the adverse possessor acquires clear title to the land. However, title is acquired only as to the property actually possessed and occupied during the statutory period, and not the entire tract. For example, an adverse possessor who occupies one acre of a 200,000-acre ranch for the statutory period of time acquires title only to that acre.

? ETHICAL PERSPECTIVE

Modern-Day Squatters

Many parts of this country, particularly the West, were settled by "squatters" who came, staked a claim to open property, farmed or ranched the property, and ac-

quired title to it from the government. The federal government encouraged such activity by holding "land rushes" that awarded title to the first person who

staked a claim to the designated lands.

Although the days of the Wild West are past, many states today recognize modern-day squatters' rights under the doctrine of adverse possession. Consider the following case.

Edward and Mary Shaughnessey purchased a 16-acre tract in St. Louis County in 1954. Subsequently, they subdivided 12 acres into 18 lots offered for sale; they retained possession of the remaining 4-acre tract. In 1967, Charles and Elaine Witt purchased lot 12, which is adjacent to the 4-acre tract. The Witts constructed and moved into a house on their lot. In 1968, they cleared an area of land that ran the length of their property and extended 40 feet onto the 4-acre tract. The Witts constructed a pool and deck, planted a garden, made a playground for their children and a dog run, and built a fence along the edge of the property line, which included the now disputed property. Neither the Witts nor the Shaughnesseys realized that the Witts had encroached on the Shaughnesseys' property.

In February 1988, the Shaughnesseys sold the 4-acre tract to Thomas and Rosanne Miller. When a survey showed the encroachment, the Millers demanded that the Witts remove the pool and cease using the property. When the Witts refused to do so, the Millers sued to quiet title. The Witts defended, arguing that they had obtained title to the disputed property by adverse possession.

The court of appeals agreed with the Witts. The court held that the Witts had proven the necessary elements for adverse possession under state law. The Witts' occupation of the land was open and notorious, actual and exclusive, hostile and adverse, continuous and peaceful, and had been in effect for over the statutory period of 10 years. The court issued an order quieting title to the disputed property in the Witts. [*Witt v. Miller*, 845 S.W.2d 665 (Mo.App. 1993)]

1. Did the Millers act ethically in trying to eject people who had occupied the land for 20 years?
2. Did the Witts act ethically in claiming title to someone else's land? Should they be allowed to benefit from their own mistake?
3. What should owners of property do to protect themselves from adverse possession claims? Explain.

Deeds

Deeds are used to convey real property by sale or gift. The seller or donor is called the **grantor**. The buyer or recipient is called the **grantee**. A deed may be used to transfer a fee simple absolute interest in real property or any lesser estate (e.g., life estate).

State laws recognize different types of deeds that provide differing degrees of protection to grantees. A **warranty deed** (deed in which the grantor warrants that he or she has sold title to the real property) contains the greatest number of warranties and provides the most protection to grantees. A **quitclaim deed** (deed in which the grantor transfers only whatever interest he or she has in the real property) provides the least amount of protection because only the grantor's interest is conveyed.

Recording Statutes

Every state has a **recording statute** that provides that copies of deeds and other documents concerning interests in real property (e.g., mortgages, liens, easements) may be filed in a government office where they become public records open to viewing by the public. Recording statutes are intended to prevent fraud and to establish certainty in the ownership and transfer of property. Instruments are usually filed in the **county recorder's office** of the county in which the property is located. A fee is charged to record an instrument.

Persons interested in purchasing the property or lending on the property should check these records to determine whether the grantor or borrower actually owns the property and whether any other parties (e.g., lienholders, mortgagees, easement holders) have an interest in the property. The recordation of a deed is not required to pass title from the grantor to the grantee. Recording the deed gives **constructive notice** to the world of the owner's interest in the property.

A party who is concerned about his or her ownership rights in a parcel of real property can bring a **quiet title action** to have a court determine the extent of those rights. Public notice of the hearing must be given so that anyone claiming an interest in the

deed A writing that describes a person's ownership interest in a piece of real property.

grantor The party who transfers an ownership interest in real property.

grantee The party to whom an interest in real property is transferred.

recording statute A state statute that requires the mortgage or deed of trust to be recorded in the county recorder's office of the county in which the real property is located.

BUSINESS BRIEF

Anyone interested in purchasing property or lending on the property should check the county recorder's records of the county in which the real property is located to determine if the grantor or borrower actually owns the property and whether any other parties have an interest in the property.

property may appear and be heard. After the hearing, the judge declares who has title to the property—that is, the court "quiets title" by its decision.

Marketable Title

good title Title that is free from any encumbrances or other defects that are not disclosed but would affect the value of the property.

A grantor has the obligation to transfer **marketable title** or **good title** to the grantee. Marketable title means that the title is free from any encumbrances, defects in title, or other defects which are not disclosed but would affect the value of the property. The three most common ways of assuring marketable title are:

Attorney's Opinion An attorney examines an **abstract of title** (i.e., a chronological history of the chain of title and encumbrances affecting the property) and renders an opinion concerning the status of the title. The attorney may be sued for any losses caused by his or her negligence in rendering the opinion.

Torrens System The Torrens system is a method of determining title to real property in a judicial proceeding at which everyone claiming an interest in the property may appear and be heard. After the evidence is heard, the court issues a **certificate of title** to the person who is determined to be the rightful owner.

Title Insurance The best way for a grantee to be sure that he or she has obtained marketable title is to purchase **title insurance** from an insurance company. The title insurer must reimburse the insured for any losses caused by undiscovered defects in the title. Each time a property is transferred a new title insurance policy must be obtained.

BUSINESS CHECKLIST

What a Person Should Do When Buying Real Estate

The most important purchase most people make in their lives is when they buy a place to live or other real estate. A potential homebuyer should spend sufficient time to investigate and analyze this decision. When purchasing a home, a person should take the following steps:

- Employ a reputable real estate broker who will represent the buyer's interests in the transaction. This broker should be someone other than the listing broker hired by the seller. The buyer's broker usually splits the real estate commission with the listing broker. The commission is usually paid by the seller from the sales proceeds from the house.
- Request that the seller fully disclose all defects in the property. If the seller refuses to do so, it would probably be wise not to purchase the property. Some states require by law that such disclosure be made by the seller to potential buyers.
- If the potential buyer decides to make an offer to purchase the house, have the offer agreement prepared by an attorney or the real estate broker. Review the offer to make sure it is correct before signing it.
- The potential buyer should make sure the offer contains any necessary contingencies. For example, if the buyer needs bank financing, he or she should make the offer contingent on being approved on finding such financing at reasonable terms.

- Make the offer contingent on a full inspection and approval of the house. The potential buyer should hire the necessary professionals, such as a general contractor, to examine the house. It is better to spend money in advance to locate any problems than to purchase the house and discover the defects at a later date.
- The potential buyer should hire a surveyor to conduct a survey to determine the true location of the lot lines and size of the property. Surveys sometimes reveal that a neighboring property owner may be encroaching on the seller's property (e.g., fence line). These problems have to be dealt with on a case-by-case basis.
- The buyer should either (1) purchase title insurance if available or (2) hire a lawyer to conduct a title search of the property. The purchase of title insurance is recommended because it warrants that the buyer has "clear title" to the property, and if this is not true the insurance company will pay the buyer any damages suffered by the buyer.
- If there is any concern that there may be environmental pollution on the property, the buyer should make his offer contingent on an environmental report. The buyer should employ a reputable and licensed environmental engineer to conduct the proper inspection of the property and prepare the report. If any environmental problems are discovered, it may be best not to purchase the property because some federal and state environmental laws place cleaning costs on the owner of the property even if that owner did not cause the pollution.
- Depending on the law of the state, the buyer should either (1) hire a lawyer to represent him or her at the closing of the transaction or (2) hire an independent escrow service to handle the closing of the transaction.

NONPOSSESSORY INTERESTS

A person may own a **nonpossessory interest** in another's real estate. The three nonpossessory interests—easements, licenses, and profits—are discussed in the following sections.

nonpossessory interest When a person holds an interest in another person's property without actually owning any part of the property.

Easements

An **easement** is an interest in land that gives the holder rights to make limited use of another's property without taking anything from it.

Easements may be expressly created by **grant** (where an owner gives another party an easement across his or her property) or **reservation** (where an owner sells land that he or she owns but reserves an easement on the land). They also may be implied by (1) **implication**, where an owner subdivides a piece of property with a well, path, road, or other beneficial appurtenant that serves the entire parcel; or by (2) **necessity**, for example, "landlocked" property has an implied easement across surrounding property to enter and exit the landlocked property. Easements can also be created by **prescription**, that is, adverse possession.

Typical easements include common driveways, party walls, rights-of-ways, and such. There are two types of easements: easements appurtenant and easements in gross.

easement A given or required right to make limited use of someone else's land without owning or leasing it.

Easements Appurtenant An **easement appurtenant** is created when the owner of one piece of land is given an easement over an adjacent piece of land. The land over which the easement is granted is called the *servient estate*. The land that benefits from the easement is called the *dominant estate*. Adjacent land is defined as two

easement appurtenant A situation created when the owner of one piece of land is given an easement over an adjacent piece of land.

estates that are in proximity to each other, but do not necessarily abut each other. An easement appurtenant runs with the land. For example, if an owner sells the servient estate, the new owner acquires the benefit of the easement. If an owner sells the dominant estate, the buyer purchases the property subject to the easement.

easement in gross An easement that authorizes a person who does not own adjacent land the right to sue another's land.

Easement in Gross An **easement in gross** authorizes a person who does not own adjacent land the right to use another's land. An easement in gross is a personal right because it does not depend on the easement holder owning adjacent land. Thus, there is no dominant estate. Examples of easements in gross include those granted to run power, telephone, and cable television lines across an owner's property. Commercial easements in gross are transferable, but ordinary, noncommercial easements in gross are not. For example, the fact that a farmer grants a hunter the right to hunt pheasant on his farm does not mean that other hunters are permitted to hunt on the farmer's property.

Responsibility for Maintenance and Repair The easement holder owes a duty to maintain and repair the easement. The owner of the estate can use the property as long as it does not interfere with the easement. For example, if a piece of property is subject to an easement for an underground pipeline, the owner of the property could graze cattle or plant crops on the land above the easement, subject to the easement holder's right to repair the pipeline.

In the following case, the court had to decide whether an easement had been created.

CASE 29.2

Walker v. Ayres
1993 Lexis 105 (1993) Supreme Court of Delaware

Facts Elizabeth Star Ayres and Clara Louise Quillen own in fee simple absolute a tract of land in Sussex County known as "Bluff Point." The tract is surrounded on three sides by Rehoboth Bay and is landlocked on the fourth side by land owned by Irvin C. Walker. At one time, the two tracts were held by a common owner. In 1878, Bluff Point was sold in fee simple absolute apart from the other holdings, thereby landlocking the parcel. A narrow dirt road, which traverses Walker's land, connects Bluff Point to a public road and is its only means of access. Ayres and Quillen sought an easement to use this road, and Walker objected. This lawsuit ensued. The trial court granted an easement. Walker appealed.

Issue Should Ayres' and Quillen's estate be granted an easement against Walker's estate?

Decision Yes. The supreme court held that an easement had been created. Affirmed.

Reason The supreme court held that an easement appurtenant had been created between two adjacent parcels of property. The court held that the easement was created by implication in 1878 when Bluff Point was separated from the rest of the holdings and landlocked at that time. The court also held that an easement was created by necessity because Bluff Point was landlocked and its only access was over Walker's property. The court found that water access, even if a reasonable substitute for land access, was not feasible because of the shallowness of the water surrounding Bluff Point.

CASE QUESTIONS

Critical Legal Thinking Should easements be recognized by the law? Why or why not?

Ethics Did Walker act ethically in denying the easement? Did Ayres and Quillen act ethically in seeking to use Walker's property?

Business Implication Does an easement increase or decrease the value of the servient estate? Of the dominant estate?

Licenses

A **license** grants a person the right to enter upon another's property for a specified and usually short period of time. The person granting the license is called the licensor; the person receiving the license is called the **licensee**. For example, a common license is a ticket to a movie theater or sporting event that grants the holder the right to enter the premises for the performance. A license does not transfer any interest in the property. A license is a personal privilege that may be revoked by the licensor at any time.

license Grants a person the right to enter upon another's property for a specified and usually short period of time.

Profits

A **profit a'pendre** (or **profit**) gives the holder the right to remove something from another's real property. Profits usually involve the right to remove gravel, minerals, grain, or timber from another's property. A **profit appurtenant** grants the owner of one piece of land the right to go onto another's adjacent land and remove things from it. A **profit in gross** authorizes someone who does not own adjacent land the right to go onto another's property and remove things from it.

profit Grants a person the right to remove something from another's real property.

LANDLORD–TENANT RELATIONSHIP

A **landlord–tenant relationship** is created when the owner of a freehold estate (i.e., an estate in fee or a life estate) transfers a right to exclusively and temporarily possess the owner's property. The tenant receives a *nonfreehold estate* in the property—that is, the tenant has a right to possession of the property but not to title to the property.

The tenant's interest in the property is called a **leasehold estate**, or **leasehold**. The owner who transfers the leasehold estate is called the **landlord**, or **lessor**. The party to whom the leasehold estate is transferred is called the **tenant**, or **lessee**.

landlord–tenant relationship A relationship created when the owner of a freehold estate (landlord) transfers a right to exclusively and temporarily possess the owner's property to another (tenant).

leasehold A tenant's interest in the property.

landlord The owner who transfers the leasehold.

tenant The party to whom the leasehold is transferred.

The Lease

The rental agreement between the landlord and the tenant is called the *lease*. Leases can generally be either oral or written except that most Statutes of Frauds require written leases for periods of time longer than one year. The lease must contain the essential terms of the parties' agreement. The lease is often a form contract which is prepared by the landlord and presented to the tenant. This is particularly true of residential leases. Other leases are negotiated between the parties. For example, Bank of America's lease of a branch office would be negotiated with the owner of the building.

TYPES OF TENANCY

There are four types of **tenancies**: (1) tenancy for years (2) periodic tenancy (3) tenancy at will and (4) tenancy at sufferance. Each is described in the following sections.

Tenancy for Years

A **tenancy for years** is created when the landlord and the tenant agree on a specific duration for the lease. Any lease for a stated period—no matter how long or short—is called a tenancy for years. Examples of such arrangements include office space leased in a highrise office building on a 30-year lease and a cabin leased for the summer.

A tenancy for years terminates automatically, without notice, upon the expiration of the stated term. Sometimes, such leases contain renewal or extension clauses. If a tenant dies during the lease term, the lease is personal property which transfers to his or her heirs.

tenancy for years A tenancy created when the landlord and tenant agree on a specific duration for the lease.

Periodic Tenancy

periodic tenancy
A tenancy created when a lease specifies intervals at which payments are due but does not specify how long the lease is for.

A **periodic tenancy** is created when a lease specifies intervals at which payments are due but which does not specify how long the lease is for. A lease that states, "Rent is due on the first day of the month" establishes a periodic tenancy. Many such leases are created by implication.

A periodic tenancy may be terminated by either party at the end of any payment interval, but adequate notice of the termination must be given. At common law, the notice period equaled the length of the payment period. That is, a month-to-month tenancy requires a one-month prior notice of termination. Most states have enacted statutes that set forth the required notice periods for termination of periodic tenancies. If a tenant dies during a periodic tenancy, the lease transfers to his or her heirs for the remainder of the current payment interval.

Tenancy at Will

tenancy at will   A lease that may be terminated at any time by either party.

A lease that may be terminated at any time by either party is a **tenancy at will**. A tenancy at will may be created expressly (e.g., "to tenant as long as landlord wishes") but is more likely to be created by implication.

At common law, a tenancy at will could be terminated by either party without advance notice—that is, notice of termination ended the lease the moment it was given. Most states have enacted statutes requiring minimum advance notice for the termination of a tenancy at will. The death of either party terminates a tenancy at will.

Tenancy at Sufferance

tenancy at sufferance
A tenancy created when a tenant retains possession of property after the expiration of another tenancy or a life estate without the owner's consent.

A **tenancy at sufferance** is created when a tenant retains possession of property after the expiration of another tenancy or a life estate without the owner's consent. That is, the owner suffers the *wrongful possession* of his or her property by the holdover tenant. This is not really a true tenancy but merely the possession of property without right. Technically, a tenant at sufferance is a trespasser.

A tenant at sufferance is liable for the payment of rent during the period of sufferance. Most states require an owner to go through certain legal proceedings, called **eviction proceedings** or **unlawful detainer actions**, to evict a holdover tenant. A few states allow owners to use self-help to evict a holdover tenant if force is not used.

ETHICAL PERSPECTIVE

Laws Prohibit Discrimination in the Sale and Rental of Real Property

Federal and state governments have enacted statutes that prohibit discrimination in the sale and rental of real property. The **Civil Rights Act** prohibits racial discrimination in all transfer of real property, including housing and commercial and industrial property [42 U.S.C. §§ 1971 et seq.]. The act prohibits private and public discrimination and

permits lawsuits to recover damages and obtain injunctions.

The **Fair Housing Act** makes it unlawful for a party to refuse to rent or sell a dwelling to any person because of his or her race, color, national origin, sex, or religion [42 U.S.C. §§ 360 et seq.]. The act also prohibits discrimination by real estate brokers, mortgage lenders, and advertisers con-

cerning the sale or rental of real property. The law does not apply to the following leases: (1) a person who owns a building of four or fewer units and occupies one of the units and leases the others and (2) a person who leases a single-family dwelling and does not own more than three single-family dwellings. To qualify for either exemption, the lessor cannot use a real estate broker or advertise in a discriminating manner.

Many states and local communities have also enacted statutes and ordinances that prohibit discrimination in the sale or lease of real property. These laws usually prohibit discrimination based on race, color, national origin, sex, or religion, but also often prohibit discrimination based on other protected classes such as age, sexual preference, and persons receiving government assistance.

1. Do you think laws prohibiting discrimination in the sale and rental of real property are necessary? Explain.
2. What public purposes are served by these laws?

LANDLORD'S DUTIES

The duties a landlord owes a tenant are either expressly provided in the lease, set forth in statute, or implied by law. The landlord's duties are discussed in the following sections.

Duty to Deliver Possession

A lease grants the tenant **exclusive possession** of the leased premises until (1) the term of the lease expires or (2) the tenant defaults on the obligations under the lease. The landlord is obligated to deliver possession of the leased premises to the tenant on the date the lease term begins. A landlord may not enter leased premises unless the right is specifically reserved in the lease.

exclusive possession A lease grants the tenant *exclusive possession* of the leased premises for the term of the lease or until the tenant defaults on the obligations under the lease.

Duty Not to Interfere with the Tenant's Right to Quiet Enjoyment

The law implies a **covenant of quiet enjoyment** in all leases. Under this covenant, the landlord may not interfere with the tenant's quiet and peaceful possession, use, and enjoyment of the leased premises. The covenant is breached if the landlord, or anyone acting with the landlord's consent, interferes with the tenant's use and enjoyment of the property. This is called **wrongful** or **unlawful eviction**. It may occur if the landlord actually evicts the tenant by physically preventing him or her from possessing or using the leased premises or if the landlord **constructively evicts** the tenant by causing the leased premises to become unfit for their intended use (e.g., by failing to provide electricity). If the landlord refuses to cure the defect after a reasonable time, a tenant who has been constructively evicted may (1) sue for damages and possession of the premises or (2) treat the lease as terminated, vacate the premises, and cease paying rent. The landlord is not responsible for wrongful acts of third persons that were done without his or her authorization.

covenant of quiet enjoyment A covenant that says a landlord may not interfere with the tenant's quiet and peaceful possession, use, and enjoyment of the leased premises.

wrongful eviction A violation of the covenant of quiet enjoyment.

"Property has its duties as well as its rights."
Benjamin Disraeli
Sybil, 1845, Bk. II, Ch. XI

Duty to Maintain the Leased Premises

At common law, the doctrine of *caveat lessee*—"lessee beware"—applied to leases. The landlord made no warranties about the quality of leased property and had no duty to repair it. The tenant took the property "as is." Modern real estate law, however, imposes certain statutory and judicially implied duties on landlords to repair and maintain leased premises.

Building Codes States and local municipalities have enacted statutes called **building** or **housing codes**. These statutes impose specific standards on property owners to maintain and repair leased premises. They often provide certain minimum standards regarding heat, water, light, and other services. Depending on the statute, violators may be subject to fines by the government, loss of their claim for rent, and imprisonment for serious violations.

building codes State and local statutes that impose specific standards on property owners to maintain and repair leased premises.

implied warranty of habitability A warranty that provides that the leased premises must be fit, safe, and suitable for ordinary residential use.

"Good fences make good neighbors."
Robert Frost
Mending Wall (1914)

Implied Warranty of Habitability The courts of many jurisdictions hold that an **implied warranty of habitability** applies to residential leases for their duration. This warranty provides that the leased premises must be fit, safe, and suitable for ordinary residential use. For example, unchecked rodent infestation, leaking roofs, unworkable bathroom facilities, and the like have been held to breach the implied warranty of habitability. On the other hand, a small crack in the wall or some paint peeling from a door does not breach this warranty.

If the landlord's failure to maintain or repair the leased premises affects the tenant's use or enjoyment of the premises, state statutes and judicial decisions provide various remedies. Generally, the tenant may (1) withhold from his or her rent the amount by which the defect reduced the value of the premises to him or her, (2) repair the defect and deduct the cost of repairs from the rent due for the leased premises, (3) cancel the lease if the failure to repair constitutes constructive eviction, or (4) sue for damages, in the amount the landlord's failure to repair the defect reduced the value of the leasehold.

In the following case, the court found a breach of the implied warranty of habitability.

CASE 29.3

Solow v. Wellner
569 N.Y. Supp. 2d 882 (1991) Civil Court of the City of New York

Facts The defendants are approximately 80 tenants of a 300-unit luxury apartment building on the upper East Side of Manhattan. The rents in the all-glass enclosed building, which won several architectural awards, ranged from $1,064 to $5,379. The landlord brought a summary proceeding against the tenants to recover rent when they engaged in a rent strike in protest against what they viewed as deteriorating conditions and services. Among other things, the evidence showed that during the period in question (May 1982–May 1988) the elevator system made tenants and their guests wait interminable lengths of time, the elevators skipped floors and opened on the wrong floors, a stench emanated from garbage stored near the garage and mice appeared in that area, fixtures were missing in public areas, water seeped into mailboxes, the air conditioning in the lobby was inoperative, and air conditioners in individual units leaked. The defendant–tenants sought abatement of rent for breach of the implied warrant of habitability.

Issue Did the landlord breach the implied warranty of habitability?

Decision Yes. The court held that the landlord had breached the implied warranty of habitability. The court abated the rent of each of the tenants individually, in total allowing the landlord to recover only 22 percent of the amount he sued for. The court

ordered the landlord to pay the tenants' attorney's fees.

Reason New York recognizes the implied warranty of habitability in residential housing. The court held that this warranty requires a landlord not only to maintain premises free of conditions that threaten the lives, safety, and welfare of the tenants but also to meet the "reasonable expectations" of tenants. The court stated, "Certain amenities not necessarily life threatening, but consistent with the nature of the bargain, fall under the protection of this warranty." The court held that the obvious expectations of the tenants of this uniquely designed apartment building on Manhattan's fashionable upper East Side had not been met.

CASE QUESTIONS

Critical Legal Thinking Should the law recognize the implied warranty of habitability? Why or why not?

Ethics Did the landlord act ethically in not correcting the defects in the building? Did the tenants act ethically in engaging in a rent strike?

Business Implication Was the remedy the court ordered appropriate in this case?

TENANT'S DUTIES

A tenant owes the landlord the duties agreed to in the lease and any duties imposed by law. The tenant's duties are discussed in the following sections.

Duty to Pay Rent

A tenant owes a duty to pay the agreed-upon amount of **rent** for the leased premises to the landlord at the agreed-upon time and terms. Generally, rent is payable in advance (e.g., on the first day of the month for use that month) although the lease may provide for other times and methods for payment. Reasonable late charges may be assessed on rent that is overdue. Several of the most common rental arrangements follow:

rent The amount that the tenant has agreed to pay the landlord for the leased premises.

- **Gross lease.** The tenant pays a gross sum to the landlord. The landlord is responsible for paying the property taxes and assessments on the property.
- **Net lease.** The tenant is responsible for paying rent and property taxes.
- **Double net lease.** The tenant is responsible for paying rent, property taxes, and utilities.
- **Net, net, net lease** (or **triple net lease**). The tenant is responsible for paying rent, property taxes, utilities, and insurance.

Landlord's Remedies for Nonpayment of Rent Upon nonpayment of rent, the landlord is entitled to recover possession of the leased premises from the tenant. This may require the landlord to evict the tenant. Most states provide a summary procedure called **unlawful detainer action** which a landlord can institute to evict a tenant. The landlord may sue to recover the unpaid rent from the tenant. The more modern rule requires the landlord to make reasonable efforts to mitigate damages (i.e., to make reasonable efforts to release the premises).

unlawful detainer action Legal process that a landlord must complete to evict a holdover tenant.

Tenants often are required to pay a **security deposit** to the landlord. In residential leases, the amount generally is equivalent to one month's rent. The landlord may apply the security deposit against unpaid rent or use it to cover the cost of repairing damages caused by the tenant to the leased premises. Any remaining security must be repaid to the tenant within 14 days after the lease is terminated. Some states require landlords to hold the security deposits in a separate trust account and to pay interest on the deposits.

security deposit An amount of money that is often used against unpaid rent or for use in covering the cost of repairing damages caused by the tenant to the leased premises.

Duty Not to Use Leased Premises for Illegal or Nonstipulated Purposes A tenant may use the leased property for any lawful purposes permitted by the lease. Leases often stipulate that the leased premises can be used only for specific purposes. If the tenant uses the leased premises for unlawful purposes (e.g., operating an illegal gambling casino) or nonstipulated purposes (e.g., operating a restaurant in a residence), the landlord may terminate the lease, evict the tenant, and sue for damages.

Duty Not to Commit Waste A tenant is under a duty not to commit **waste** to the leasehold. Waste occurs when the tenant causes substantial and permanent damage to the leased premises which decreases the value of the property and the landlord's reversionary interest in it. Waste does not include ordinary wear and tear. For example, it would be waste if the floor of the premises buckled because a tenant permitted heavy equipment to be placed on the premises. It would not be waste if the paint chipped from the walls because of the passage of time. The landlord can recover damages from the tenant for waste.

waste Occurs when a tenant causes substantial and permanent damage to the leased premises that decreases the value of the property and the landlord's reversionary interest in it.

Duty Not to Disturb Other Tenants A tenant owes a duty not to disturb the use and enjoyment of the leased premises by other tenants in the same building. For example, a tenant in an apartment building breaches this duty if he disturbs the sleep of other tenants by playing loud music throughout the night. A landlord may evict the tenant who interferes with the quiet enjoyment of other tenants.

CONTEMPORARY BUSINESS ENVIRONMENT

Title III of the Americans with Disabilities Act

On July 26, 1990, the **Americans with Disabilities Act (ADA)** was signed into law [42 U.S.C. 1201 et seq.]. Most of the provisions of the ADA became effective on January 26, 1992. The ADA is a broad civil rights statute that prohibits discrimination against disabled individuals in employment, public services, public accommodations and services, and telecommunications. **Title III** of the ADA prohibits discrimination on the basis of disability in places of public accommodation operated by private entities. The attorney general of the United States is empowered to issue regulations that interpret and enforce the ADA.

Title III of the ADA applies to public accommodations and commercial facilities such as motels, hotels, restaurants, theaters, recreation facilities, colleges and universities, department stores, retail stores, office buildings, and the like. It does not generally apply to residential facilities (single- and multifamily housing).

Title III requires facilities that are covered by the law to be designed, constructed, and altered in compliance with specific ac-

cessibility requirements established by regulations issued pursuant to the ADA. In 1991, the attorney general issued final regulations that contain minimum guidelines to make covered facilities accessible to disabled individuals. This includes constructing ramps to accommodate wheelchairs, installing railings next to steps, placing signs written in Braille in elevators and at elevator call buttons, and so on. If both the ADA and state law apply, the more stringent rule must be followed.

New construction must be built in such a manner as to be readily accessible to and usable by disabled individuals. Any alterations made to existing buildings must be made so that the altered portions of the building are readily accessible to disabled individuals to the maximum extent feasible. With respect to existing buildings, architectural barriers must be removed if such removal is readily achievable. In determining when an action is readily achievable, the factors to be considered include the nature and cost of the action, the financial resources of the facil-

ity, and the type of operations of the facility.

The ADA provides for both private right of action and enforcement by the attorney general. Individuals may seek injunctive relief and monetary damages. The attorney general may seek equitable relief and civil fines up to $50,000 for the first violation and $100,000 for any subsequent violation.

Proponents of Title III of the ADA argue that it is necessary to make public accommodations and commercial facilities accommodate the needs of the disabled. They point out that voluntary efforts to make these accommodations were too little and too late. Critics argue that the ADA creates a quagmire of regulations that are difficult to understand and that will cost landowners billions of dollars to comply with.

Building owners, managers, architects, and others involved in the design, construction, ownership, and management of public accommodation and commercial buildings must be knowledgeable about, and comply with, the provisions of Title III of the ADA.

TORT LIABILITY OF LANDLORDS AND TENANTS

Under the common law, a landlord was not liable for injuries caused on leased premises. This rule was based on the notion that the landlord had relinquished control and possession of the property to the tenant. Court decisions and statutes have eroded this no-liability rule. Now, landlords owe a **duty of reasonable care** to tenants and third parties not to negligently cause them injury. This duty is based on the foreseeability standard of ordinary negligence actions.

A tenant owes a duty of reasonable care to persons who enter upon the leased premises. If a tenant's negligence causes injury to a third person, the tenant is liable in tort for any damages sustained by the injured person. For example, a tenant who leaves a skateboard on the steps is liable for the injuries caused to a visitor who trips on it.

premises liability   Name given to liability of landlords and tenants to persons injured on their premises.

The liability of landlords and tenants to persons injured on their premises is called **premises liability**.

The following case illustrates premises liability.

CASE 29.4

Feld v. Merriam
461 A.2d 225 (1983) Superior Court of Pennsylvania

Facts Cedarbrook is a complex of approximately 1,000 apartment units located on a 36-acre tract of land in Cheltenham, Pennsylvania. It is owned by John W. Merriam. Vehicles can enter the grounds through two entrances, each of which is staffed by security guards. Automobiles park in garages located beneath each apartment building. The parking facility under Building No. 1 had spaces for 160 cars. Access to the garages could be gained through two open entrances. Additionally, garages were not well-lit. Between 1970 and 1975, the crime rate in the Cheltenham area had risen. During the three-month period preceding the criminal incident at issue in this case, 21 separate incidents of criminal activity, including robberies, burglaries at apartments, car thefts, and an assault on a tenant were reported.

On June 27, 1975, at approximately 9:00 P.M., Samuel and Peggy Feld, tenants in Building 1, drove into the Cedarbrook complex and parked their car in the garage. After getting out of their car, they walked toward the pedestrian exit. Suddenly, three armed men emerged from behind a parked car, accosted them, and robbed them at gunpoint. They then raped Mrs. Feld. Following the incident, Mrs. Feld began psychotherapy to help alleviate her severe emotional distress. Her psychiatrist testified that she would never recover from the emotional trauma of the event. Following the incident, Mr. Feld was constantly in a fearful, nervous, and agitated state. At the time of trial, he was still unable to discuss the details of the criminal episode with anyone. Although the Felds' marriage deteriorated, they remained together out of compassion for each other.

Mr. and Mrs. Feld sued Cedarbrook for damages. The jury returned a verdict that awarded $2 million compensatory damages to Mrs. Feld, $1 million compensatory damages to Mr. Feld, and $1.5 million punitive damages to each of them. Cedarbrook appealed.

Issue Is Cedarbrook liable for the criminal attack on the Felds?

Decision Yes. The appellate court affirmed the judgment except for reducing the punitive damages awarded to Mr. Feld from $1.5 million to $750,000.

Reason The appellate court stated: "A landlord is under a duty to exercise reasonable care to protect his tenants from the foreseeable criminal actions of third persons. The primary reason for imposing this duty on the landlord is the recent recognition by the courts that, in modern times, a residential lease should not be viewed as a conveyance of land, but rather, as a contract between landlord and tenant, imposing certain rights and duties upon each of them. This court believes that imposing a duty on the landlord to provide adequate security for his tenants is in keeping with the current trends in landlord–tenant law in this commonwealth."

In order to establish a prima facie case of negligence against a landlord for his failure to provide adequate security, a plaintiff must present evidence showing that the landlord had notice of criminal activity which posed risk of harm to his tenants, that he had the means to take precautions to protect the tenant against this risk of harm, and that his failure to do so was the proximate cause of the tenant's injuries. The court found that the Felds met this burden.

CASE QUESTIONS

Critical Legal Thinking Should a landlord be held liable for the criminal activities of third parties? Why or why not?

Ethics Did the landlord act ethically in not providing better security? Did the tenants act ethically by suing the landlord for criminal actions of third parties?

Business Implication Do you think the damage awards were excessive in this case? Were punitive damages warranted?

TRANSFERRING RIGHTS TO LEASED PROPERTY

Landlords may sell, gift, devise, or otherwise transfer their interests in the leased property. For example, a landlord can sell either the right to receive rents, his or her reversionary interest, or both. If complete title is transferred, the property is subject to the existing lease. The new landlord cannot alter the terms of the lease (e.g., raise the rent) during the term of the lease unless the lease so provides.

The tenant's right to transfer possession of the leased premises to another depends on the terms of the lease. Many leases permit the lessee to *assign* or *sublease* his or her rights in the property.

Assignment of the Lease

assignment A transfer by a tenant of his or her rights under a lease to another.

assignor The party who transfers the right.

assignee The party to whom the right has been transferred.

If a tenant transfers all of his or her interests under a lease, it is an **assignment**. The original tenant is the **assignor** and the new tenant is the **assignee**. Under an assignment, the assignee acquires all of the rights that the assignor had under the lease. The assignee is obligated to perform the duties that the assignor had under the lease. That is, the assignee must pay the rent and perform other covenants contained in the original lease. The assignor remains responsible for his or her obligations under the lease unless specifically released to do so by the landlord. If the landlord recovers from the assignor, the assignor has a course of action to recover from the assignee.

Sublease

sublease When a tenant transfers only some of his or her rights under the lease.

sublessor The original tenant in a sublease situation.

sublessee The new tenant in a sublease situation.

If a tenant transfers only some of his or her rights under the lease, it is a **sublease**. The original tenant is the **sublessor** and the new tenant is the **sublessee**. The sublessor is not released from his or her obligations under the lease unless specifically released by the landlord. Subleases differ from assignments in important ways. In a sublease, no legal relationship is formed between the landlord and the sublessee. Therefore, the sublessee does not acquire rights under the original lease. For example, a sublessee would not acquire the sublessor's option to renew a lease. Further, the landlord cannot sue the sublessee to recover rent payments or enforce duties under the original lease.

In most cases, tenants cannot assign or sublease their leases without the landlord's consent. This right protects the landlord from the transfer of the leasehold to someone who might damage the property or not have the financial resources to pay the rent. Most states, either by statute or judicial decision, hold that the owner's consent cannot be unreasonably withheld.

CONTEMPORARY BUSINESS ENVIRONMENT

Regulatory Taking

Federal, state, and local governments may take private property for public use. Under the Fifth Amendment of the U.S. Constitution, the government must pay "just compensation" to the owner of the land taken. For example, if the government is building a highway, it can use its power of **eminent domain** (also called **condemnation**) to forcibly buy the property upon which to build the highway. **Physical taking** of land usually generates few legal problems (except what value to place on the land, and this can be decided in a court).

Suppose a person owns land upon which he intends to build four-story apartment buildings. If the local zoning board adopts a zoning ordinance that restricts buildings in the area to two stories, the property decreases in value. Has there been a "taking"? The answer is no. The regulation serves a legitimate social function (e.g., reduces congestion, preserves views), and still leaves the landlord with a viable option—to build two-story apartment buildings.

But what if the **regulatory taking** is total. Is there a compensable taking? Consider the following situation. In 1986, David H. Lucas paid $975,000 for two residential lots on the Isle of Palms in Charleston County, South Carolina, on which he intended to build single-family homes. Single-family houses had already been built on adjacent lots. In 1988, the South Carolina legislature enacted the Beachfront Management Act. This Act encompassed Lucas's property. The Act flatly prohibited any construction of occupable improvements on "coastal land," which included Lucas's two lots.

Lucas promptly filed suit in South Carolina court, contending that the act's construction bar effected a taking of his property without payment of just compensation in violation of the Fifth Amendment. The trial court agreed, finding that the regulation rendered Lucas's lots valueless. The court ordered South Carolina to pay Lucas $1,232,387 as just compensation for the lots. The supreme court of the state reversed, and the U.S. Supreme Court agreed to hear Lucas's appeal.

In a majority opinion, the U.S. Supreme Court held that the South Carolina law constituted a compensable "regulatory taking" of Lucas's property in violation of the U.S. Constitution. The Supreme Court stated, "The Fifth Amendment is violated when land use regulation does not substantially advance legitimate state interest or denies an owner economically viable use of his land." The Supreme Court found that there was a "total taking" of Lucas's property in this case. It reversed the judgment of the state supreme court and remanded the case for proceedings consistent with its opinion.

The *Lucas* decision affords some comfort to landowners because it implies that the government cannot strip them of *all* economically viable uses of their property without paying compensation for doing so. It does not, however, protect landowners from government regulation that causes only a partial loss of the value of their land. [*Lucas v. South Carolina Coastal Council*, 112 S.Ct. 2886, 120 L.Ed.2d 798 (1992)]

LAND USE CONTROL

Generally, the ownership of property entitles the owner to use his or her property as the owner wishes. However, such use is subject to limitations imposed by either private agreement or government regulation. These limitations are collectively referred to as **land use control** or **land use regulation**.

Restrictive Covenants

A **restrictive covenant** is a private agreement between landowners that restricts the use of their land. Restrictive covenants are commonly called **building restrictions** or **CC&Rs (covenants, conditions,** and **restrictions)**. They are often used by residential developments and condominium buildings to establish uniform rules for all occupants. A sample set of restrictive covenants is set forth in Exhibit 29.1.

land use control   The collective term for the laws that regulate the possession, ownership, and use of real property.

restrictive covenant A private agreement between landowners that restricts the use of their land.

Exhibit 29.1
Sample Restrictive Covenants

DECLARATION OF COVENANTS, CONDITIONS AND RESTRICTIONS
PINE SHORES COUNTRY CLUB ASSOCIATION, INC.

Declarant, The Great Lakes Development Company, a Michigan corporation, is the owner of certain real property located in the City of Evergreen Shores, County of Mackinac, State of Michigan. The Real Property consists of residential condominium units, clubhouse, together with private streets, entryways, landscaped common areas, lakes, maintenance facilities, swimming pools and certain other recreational facilities, including a golf course consisting of eighteen holes, driving range, ten tennis courts, and a tennis clubhouse.

Together with the purchase of a condominium, each condominium purchaser, in addition to receiving a separate interest in a "Unit," will receive an undivided interest in the "Common Area," a non-exclusive easement appurtenant for ingress, egress, use and enjoyment over, upon and in The Pine Shores Country Club, subject to certain conditions more fully set forth hereinafter; and a proprietary club membership which will entitle such Owner to use the facilities of the Pine Shores Country Club subject to all of the terms and conditions hereof.

USE RESTRICTIONS
The use of the Project and each Condominium therein shall be restricted in accordance with the following provisions:

continued

Exhibit 29.1
(continued)

1. Residential Use.   None of the Units shall be used except for residential purposes.

2. Commercial Use.   No industry, business, trade, occupation or profession of any kind, whether commercial, religious, educational or otherwise, shall be conducted, maintained or permitted on any part of the Project.

3. Signs.   No sign or other advertising device of any character (including but not limited to "For Rent" or "For Lease" signs) shall be erected, maintained or displayed to the public view on any portion of the project except one sign for each Condominium, of not more than eighteen inches by twenty-four inches, advertising such Condominium for sale or lease.

4. Lawful Use.   No noxious, offensive, or unlawful activity shall be carried on, in or upon any Condominium or any part of the Project, nor shall anything be done thereon, which may be, or may become, an annoyance or offensive to the neighborhood, or which shall in any way interfere with the quiet enjoyment of each Owner of his respective Condominium.

5. Temporary Structures.   No structure of a temporary character, trailer, basement, tent, shack, garage, barn, or other out-building shall be erected, maintained or used within the Project. No trailer, camper, recreational vehicle, boat or similar equipment shall be permitted to remain within the Project unless placed or maintained within an enclosed garage.

6. Motorcycles and Mopeds.   No motorcycles, mopeds or other motorized vehicles having less than four wheels may be kept, operated or permitted on or in any part of the Project.

7. Animals.   No animals, fowl, reptiles, livestock or poultry of any kind shall be raised, bred, or kept on or in any part of the Project, except that dogs, cats or other household pets may be kept on or within the Condominiums, provided they are not kept, bred or maintained for any commercial purpose.

LANDMARK DECISION
In Shelley v. Kramer, *334 U.S. 1 (1948), the U.S. Supreme Court struck down restrictive covenants in deeds that prohibited minorities from owning residential property in certain neighborhoods.*

police power
Constitutional authority of state and local governments to enact laws to protect the public health, safety, morals, and welfare.

zoning ordinance   Local laws that are adopted by municipalities and local governments to regulate land use within their boundaries. Zoning ordinances are adopted and enforced to protect the health, safety, morals, and general welfare of the community.

Lawful restrictive covenants may be enforced in private lawsuits. For example, if several lot owners have agreed not to build houses over one story high to preserve views, any lot holder can sue another lot owner to enforce this covenant against the building of a two-story house. Restrictive covenants that discriminate based on race, national origin, sex, age, religion, or other protected class are illegal and void.

Public Regulation of Land Use

Pursuant to their constitutional "**police power**," state and local governments may enact laws to protect the public health, safety, morals, and general welfare of the community. Pursuant to this power, most counties and municipalities have enacted **zoning ordinances** to regulate land use. For example, zoning ordinances prohibiting the location of adult bookstores near residential areas have been held to be valid to protect public morals. Zoning is the primary form of land use regulation in this country.

Zoning ordinances generally (1) establish use districts within the municipality (i.e., areas are generally designated residential, commercial, or industrial), (2) restrict the height, size, and location of buildings on a building site, and (3) establish aesthetic requirements or limitations for the exterior of buildings.

A **zoning commission** usually formulates zoning ordinances, conducts public hearings, and makes recommendations to the city council, who must vote to enact an ordinance. When enacted, the zoning ordinance commission enforces the zoning ordinance. If a landowner believes that a zoning ordinance is illegal or that it has been applied unlawfully to him or his property, he may institute a court proceeding seeking judicial review of the ordinance or its application.

The following case is concerned with the lawfulness of a zoning ordinance.

CASE 29.5

Guinnane v. San Francisco City Planning Commission

209 Cal.App.3d 732, 257 Cal.Rptr. 742 (1989) California Court of Appeal

Facts In 1979, Roy Guinnane purchased four vacant lots located on Edgehill Way in San Francisco. In July 1980, the city of San Francisco designated an area as "Edgehill Woods." Guinnane's property was located in that area. In 1982, the city adopted a resolution to exercise its discretionary review power over proposed development in the Edgehill Woods area. Guinnane filed an application for a building permit to construct a four-story, 6,000-square-foot house with five bedrooms, five baths, and parking for two cars on one of his lots. Although the proposed building met the specifications of other zoning laws and building codes, the San Francisco Planning Commission disapproved the application because the proposed structure was "not in character" with other homes in the neighborhood. The board of permit appeals agreed. Guinnane appealed.

Issue Is the aesthetic zoning by the city of San Francisco lawful?

Decision Yes. The appellate court held that San Francisco's aesthetic zoning ordinance was lawful. The court found that the ordinance was enacted pursuant to the city's "police power" to protect its residents' health, safety, and welfare. The appellate court affirmed the trial court's judgment.

Reason The appellate court held that the planning commission acted within its discretion in finding that Guinnane's proposed building was "not in character" with other homes in the area. In affirming the planning commission's decision, the court stated: "The basic standard guiding the Planning Commission in discharging its function is the promotion of the public health, safety, peace, morals, comfort, convenience, and general welfare. In particular, the Commission is directed to 'protect the character and stability of residential areas.' Under the Municipal Code, any city department may exercise its discretion in deciding whether to approve any application; and in doing so, it may consider the effect of the proposed project upon the surrounding properties. We conclude that the Planning Commission is authorized to exercise independent discretionary review of a building permit application. . . ."

CASE QUESTIONS

Critical Legal Thinking Should a city be given zoning authority over the aesthetics of an area? Why or why not?

Ethics Is it ethical for a property owner to build a structure that does not comport with the character of the area?

Business Implication Are businesses helped or harmed by zoning ordinances?

Variances An owner who wishes to use his or her property for a use different from that permitted under a current zoning ordinance may seek relief from the ordinance by obtaining a **variance**. To obtain a variance, the landowner must prove that the ordinance causes an undue hardship by preventing him or her from making a reasonable return on the land as zoned. Variances are usually difficult to obtain.

variance An exception that permits a type of building or use in an area that would not otherwise be allowed by a zoning ordinance.

Nonconforming Uses Zoning laws act prospectively; that is, uses and buildings that already exist in the zoned area are permitted to continue even though they do not fit within new zoning ordinances. Such uses are called **nonconforming uses**. For example, if a new zoning ordinance is enacted making an area a residential zone, an existing funeral parlor is a nonconforming use.

nonconforming uses Uses and buildings that already exist in the zoned area that are permitted to continue even though they do not fit within new zoning ordinances.

BUSINESS CHECKLIST

Rent Control

Many local communities across the country have enacted **rent control ordinances** that stipulate the amount of rent a landlord can charge for residential housing. Most of these ordinances fix the rent at a specific amount and provide for minor annual increases. Although many communities, such as Santa Monica, California, have adopted rent control ordinances, New York City has the most famous rent control ordinance.

Landlords, of course, oppose rent control, arguing that the government, by enacting rent control, takes property from them (i.e., the higher rents they could charge absent rent control laws). The Fifth Amendment's "taking" clause generally requires just compensation to be paid to an owner whose property is taken by the government. Landlords have challenged rent control ordinances as violating the "taking" clause. The U.S. Supreme Court visited this issue in *Yee v. City of Escondido, California*, 112 S.Ct. 1522 (1992).

In that case, the city of Escondido adopted a rent control ordinance that rolled back the rent of "pads" in mobile home parks to 1986 levels. The ordinance prohibits rent increases without the approval of the city council. The owners of many mobile home parks affected by the ordinance sued the city, alleging that the law constituted an uncompensated "taking" in violation of the U.S. Constitution. The trial court, the court of appeals, the U.S. Supreme Court held otherwise and upheld the rent control ordinance.

Critics argued that rent control ordinances are merely a "regulatory tax" that transfers wealth from landowners to tenants. They also point out that tenants of Manhattan's posh upper East Side, or of Santa Monica, California, hardly deserve to be protected by rent controls. Proponents of rent control say that it is necessary to create affordable housing, particularly in high-rent urban areas. They assert that rent control serves a legitimate government purpose. Whatever the arguments, the Supreme Court has given a green light to local communities to adopt rent control ordinances.

INTERNATIONAL PERSPECTIVE

Sorting Out Real Property Ownership Rights in the Former East Germany

When the Berlin Wall tumbled in 1989, it allowed for the reunification of East and West Germany into one country. The event was heralded as a triumph for democracy because it meant the return of capitalism and private property rights to East Germany. Only one major question remained: Who owns the real property in the former East Germany?

Germany was under the influence and rule of the Nazi Party from 1933 until May 1945, when Germany surrendered to the Allies after World War II. During that time, the Nazis appropriated private property from owners. After the war, Germany was divided into West Germany, which was allied with Europe and the United States, and East Germany, which

was under the Soviet Union's control. The city of Berlin, which was located in East Germany, was also divided in half. The Berlin Wall was erected to prevent East Berliners from defecting to the West through West Berlin. From 1945 to 1949, the Soviets appropriated private property in East Germany. In 1949, the East German government was created.

Until 1989, East Germany was a communist state that owned the property of the country.

In 1990, after the reunification of Germany, the German government enacted the **Vermogensgesetz** (the **Statute for the Regulation of Open Property Questions**) and the **Anmeldeverordnung** (the **Regulation on the Filing of Claims**). Together, the statute and the regulations created a procedure for filing and proving claims to property expropriated by the Nazis before and during World War II, by the Soviets between 1945 and 1949, and by the East German government from 1949 to 1989.

The German property claims law set December 31, 1992 as the final date for the filing of claims for the return of real property. Claimants had to file an application that specified the location, kind, extent of the property, original ownership, and chain of inheritance. After examining the claims, the German authorities make decisions and award ownership rights. This process will take many years.

In the meantime, the German government enacted a new law that requires a permit for the sale or transfer of real property situated in the former East Germany. The permit will not be issued if a claim for the return of the property has been filed. A claimant can also apply for an injunction in the civil court to prevent the transfer of property until the merits of the claim have been decided.

One provision in the German claims law favors Jewish claimants. There is a presumption in the law that any property sold between January 1933 and May 1945 is to be considered to be sold under duress, unless the buyer can prove otherwise. This is because during that time period Nazi officials forced Jews to transfer their property for little or no consideration under threat of harm or death.

Resolving the property claims in the former East Germany will not be an easy task. Any other governments in other socialist or communist countries that change to a democratic, capitalist system will face similar problems. For example, real property rights in the former Union of Soviet Socialist Republics (USSR) and many East European countries probably will be determined using a procedure similar to that used in Germany.

WORKING THE WEB

U.S. Department of Housing and Urban Development HUD has a Web site full of information about housing.
Visit at http://www.hud.gov/

American Bar Association Section of Real Property, Probate, and Trust Law This section of the ABA publishes its own magazines as well as linking to other real property sites.
Visit at http://www.abanet.org/rppt/home.html

Federal Fair Housing Act A searchable copy of this Act is maintained by Cornell University.
Visit at http://www.law.cornell.edu/uscode/42/ch45.html

Legal Online Legal Online is the first Internet periodical for lawyers. It contains many useful articles about real property.
Visit at http://www.legalonline.com

TenantNews This site contains lots of information about tenants.
Visit at http://tenant.net/tenantnews/

CYBER EXERCISES:
1. From the HUD Web site, find the Ginnie Mae guides.
2. From the ABA Section of Real Property, Probate, and Trust Law site, find out about Probate and Property Magazine.
3. In what title of the U.S. Code will you find the Federal Fair Housing Act?
4. Using Legal Online, find out who wrote an article called "A Real Estate Lawyer's Guide to the Internet."
5. Use TenantNews to find the current rent guidelines for New York.

CHAPTER SUMMARY

NATURE OF REAL PROPERTY, P. 722

Nature of Real Property	*Real property* is immovable. It includes land, buildings, subsurface rights, air rights, plant life, and fixtures.

FREEHOLD ESTATES, P. 723

Freehold Estates	Estates where the owner has a present possessory interest in the real property.
Estates in Fee	1. *Fee simple absolute* (or *fee simple*). Highest form of ownership. 2. *Fee simple defeasible* (or *qualified fee*). Estate that ends if a specified condition occurs.
Life Estates	An interest in real property that lasts for the life of a specified person. Called an *estate pour autre vie* if the time is measured by the life of a third person.

FUTURE INTERESTS, P. 724

Future Interests	Right to possess real property in the future rather than currently.
Reversion	Right to possession that returns to the grantor after the expiration of a limited or contingent estate.
Remainder	Right to possession that goes to a third person after the expiration of a limited or contingent estate. The third person is called a *remainderman*.

CONCURRENT OWNERSHIP, P. 725

Concurrent Ownership	Where two or more persons jointly own real property.
Joint Tenancy	Owners may transfer their interests without the consent of co-owners. Transfer severs the joint tenancy. Under the *right of survivorship*, the interest of a deceased owner passes to his or her co-owners.
Tenancy in Common	Owners may transfer their interests without the consent of co-owners. Transfer does not sever the tenancy in common. Interest of a deceased owner passes to his or her estate.
Tenancy by the Entirety	Form of co-ownership that can be used only by a married couple. Neither spouse may transfer his or her interest without the other spouse's consent. A surviving spouse has the right of survivorship.
Community Property	Form of co-ownership that applies only to a married couple. Neither spouse may transfer his or her interest without the other spouse's consent. When a spouse dies, the surviving spouse automatically receives one-half of the community property.
Condominium	Condominium owners have title to their individual units and own the common areas as tenants in common. Owners may transfer their interest without the consent of other owners.
Cooperative	A corporation owns the building and the residents own shares of the corporation. Usually, owners may not transfer their shares without the approval of the other owners.

TRANSFER OF OWNERSHIP OF REAL PROPERTY, P. 727

Sale of Real Estate	An owner sells his or her property to another for consideration. Government obtains a lien on property for nonpayment of taxes and sells the property at a tax sale to a buyer. The buyer takes the title subject to the taxpayer's right of redemption.
Gift, Will, or Inheritance	Owners may give their property to another during their lifetime or leave their property by will to a beneficiary when they die. If a person dies without a will, his or her property is distributed to the heirs pursuant to state intestacy statutes.
Adverse Possession	A person who occupies another's property for a statutory period of time (many statutes provide 10 years) acquires title to the property if the occupation has been: 1. Open, visible, and notorious 2. Actual and exclusive 3. Continuous and peaceful 4. Hostile and adverse.
Deeds	Instrument used to convey real property by sale or gift. 1. *Warranty deed*. Provides the most protection to the grantee because the grantor makes warranties against defect in title. 2. *Quitclaim deed*. Provides least amount of protection to the grantee because the grantor transfers only the interest he or she has in the property.
Recording Statutes	Permits copies of deeds and other documents concerning interests in real property (e.g., mortgages, liens) to be filed in a government office where they become public record. Puts third parties on notice of recorded interests.
Marketable Title	Title is free from any undisclosed encumbrances, defects in title, or other defects. Methods of assuring marketable title: 1. *Attorney's opinion*. Attorney renders opinion concerning status of the title. 2. *Torrens system*. Court issues *certificate of title* to the rightful owner of the property. 3. *Title insurance*. Title insurer agrees to reimburse for losses caused by undiscovered defects in title.

NONPOSSESSORY INTERESTS, P. 731

Easements	An interest in land that gives the holder the right to make limited use of another's property without taking anything from it (e.g., driveways, party walls). 1. *Easement appurtenant*. Owner of land is given an easement over an adjacent piece of land. 2. *Easement in gross*. Authorizes a person who does not own adjacent land the right to use another's land.
Licenses	Right to enter upon another' property for a specified and usually short period of time (e.g., tickct to a sporting event).
Profits	Right of the holder to remove something from another's property (e.g., gravel, minerals).

LANDLORD–TENANT RELATIONSHIP, P. 733

Landlord–Tenant Relationship	Created when an owner of a freehold estate transfers a right to another to exclusively and temporarily possess the owner's property.
The Lease	The rental agreement between the landlord and the tenant that contains the essential terms of the parties' agreement.

TYPES OF TENANCY, P. 733

Tenancy for Years	Tenancy for a specified period of time.
Periodic Tenancy	Tenancy for a period of time determined by the payment interval.
Tenancy at Will	Tenancy that may be terminated at any time by either party.
Tenancy at Sufferance	Tenancy created by the wrongful possession of property.

LANDLORD'S DUTIES, P. 735

Duty to Deliver Possession	Landlord is obligated to deliver possession of the leased premises to the tenant on the date the lease term begins.
Duty Not to Interfere with the Tenant's Right to Quiet Enjoyment	Landlord may not interfere with the tenant's quiet and peaceful possession, use, and enjoyment of the leased premises.
Duty to Maintain the Leased Premises	Landlord owes contractual and statutory duties to repair and maintain the leased premises. The *implied warranty of habitability* requires leased premises to be fit, safe, and suitable for ordinary residential use.

TENANT'S DUTIES, P. 737

Duty to Pay Rent	Tenant owes a duty to pay the agreed-upon rent to the landlord. Reasonable late charges may be assessed on overdue rent. Common rental agreements are: 1. *Gross lease*. Requires tenants to pay a stated sum to landlord. Landlord responsible for paying property taxes and assessments on the property. 2. *Net lease*. Tenant responsible for paying rent and property taxes. 3. *Double net lease*. Tenant responsible for paying rent, property taxes, and utilities. 4. *Triple net lease*. Tenant responsible for paying rent, property taxes, utilities, and insurance.
Duty Not to Use Leased Premises for Illegal or Nonstipulated Purposes	Tenant may not use leased premises for any illegal or nonstipulated use.
Duty Not to Commit Waste	Tenant may not commit waste to the leased premises.
Duty Not to Disturb Other Tenants	Tenant may not disturb the use and enjoyment of the premises by other tenants.

TORT LIABILITY OF LANDLORDS AND TENANTS, P. 738

Tort Liability	1. *Landlord*. Owes a duty of reasonable care to tenants and third parties not to negligently cause them injury. 2. *Tenant*. Owes a duty of reasonable care to persons who enter upon the leased premises.

	3. *Premises liability*. Landlords and tenants owe a duty to protect third persons from foreseeable criminal conduct.
TRANSFERRING RIGHTS TO LEASED PROPERTY, P. 739	
Assignment of the Lease	Landlords may transfer their ownership interest in leased property. The tenant becomes a tenant of the new owner.
Sublease	Subject to the terms of the lease, tenants may assign or sublease the leased premises to a third party. The original tenant is not relieved of obligations under the lease.
LAND USE CONTROL, P. 741	
Restrictive Covenants	Agreement between landowners that restricts the use of their land. These restrictions are called *building restrictions* or *CC&Rs* (*covenants*, *conditions*, and *restrictions*). Restrictive covenants may not cause unlawful discrimination.
Public Regulation of Land Use	*Zoning ordinances*. Laws adopted by local governments that restrict the use of property, set building standards, and establish architectural requirements. 1. *Variance*. Permits an owner to make a nonzoned use of his or her property. This requires permission from a zoning board. 2. *Nonconforming use*. A nonzoned use that is permitted (grandfathered in) when an area is rezoned.

CRITICAL LEGAL THINKING CASES

29.1 Subsurface Rights In 1883, Isaac McIlwee owned one hundred acres of land in Valley Township, Guernsey County, Ohio. In that year, he sold the property to Akron & Cambridge Coal Co. in fee simple but reserved in fee simple "the surface of all said lands" to himself. Over the years, the interests in the land were transferred to many different parties. As of 1981, the Mid-Ohio Coal Company owned the rights originally transferred to Akron & Cambridge, and Peter and Irene Minnich owned the rights reserved by Isaac McIlwee in 1883. The Minniches claim they possess subsurface rights to the property except for coal rights. Who wins? [*Minnich v. Guernsey Savings and Loan Company*, 521 N.E.2d 489 (Ohio App. 1987)]

29.2 Life Estate and Remainder Baudilio Bowles died testate. His will devised to his sister, Julianita B. Vigil, "one-half of any income, rents, or profits from any real property located in Bull Creek or Colonias, New Mexico." The will contained another clause that left to his children "My interest in any real property owned by me at the time of my death, located in Bull Creek and/or Colonias, San Miguel County." The property referred to in both devises is the same property. Julianita died before the will was probated. Her heirs claim a one-half ownership interest in the real property. Bowles's children assert that they own all of his property. Who wins? [*In the Matter of the Estate of Bowles*, 764 P.2d 510 (N.M. App. 1988)]

29.3 Reversion In 1941, W.E. and Jennie Hutton conveyed land they owned to the Trustees of Schools of District Number One of the Town of Allison, Illinois, by warranty deed "to be used for school purpose only; otherwise to revert to Grantor." The School District built a school on the site, commonly known as Hutton School. The Huttons conveyed the adjoining farmland and their reversionary interest in the school site to the Jacqmains, who in turn conveyed their interest to Herbert and Betty Mahrenholz in 1959. The 1.5-acre site sits in the middle of Mahrenholz's farmland. In May 1973, the School District discontinued holding regular classes at Hutton School. Instead, it used the school building to warehouse and store miscellaneous school equipment, supplies, unused desks, and the like. In 1974, Mahrenholz filed suit to quiet title to the school property in themselves. Who wins? [*Mahrenholz v. County Board of School Trustees of Lawrence County*, 544 N.E.2d 128 (Ill. App. 1989)]

29.4 Community Property Daniel T. Yu and his wife, Bernice, owned a house and two lots as community property. On January 15, 1985, Yu entered into an agreement with Arch, Ltd. (Arch), whereby he agreed to exchange these properties for two office buildings owned by Arch. Yu signed the agreement but his wife did not. At the date set for closing, Arch performed its obligations under the agreement, executed all documents, and was prepared to transfer title to its properties to Yu. Yu, however, refused to perform his obligations under the agreement. Evidence showed that the office buildings had decreased in value from $800,000 to $700,000 from the date of the agreement to the date set for closing. Arch sued Yu to recover damages for breach of contract. Who wins? [*Arch, Ltd. v. Yu*, 766 P.2d 911 (N.M. 1988)]

29.5 Easement in Gross John L. Yutterman died in 1953 and left one piece of property, located in Fort Smith, Arkansas, to his two sons and two daughters. Each child received approximately one-fourth of the property in fee simple. A 40-foot driveway divided the property. Concerning the driveway, Yutterman's will provided as follows: "Further, a specific condition of this will and of these devises is that the forty (40) foot driveway from Free Ferry Road, three hundred (300) feet Northward, shall be kept open for the common use of the devises in this will." In 1982, one of the daughters wanted to sell her property to a third party. If the third party purchases the property, will he have an easement to use the driveway? [*Merriman v. Yutterman*, 723 S.W.2d 823 (Ark. 1987)]

29.6 Adverse Possession In 1973, Joseph and Helen Naab purchased a tract of land in a subdivision of Williamstown, West Virginia. At the time of purchase there was both a house and a small concrete garage on the property. Evidence showed that the garage had been erected sometime prior to 1952 by one of the Naab's predecessors in title. In 1975, Roger and Cynthia Nolan purchased a lot contiguous to that owned by the Naabs. The following year, the Nolans had their property surveyed. The survey indicated that one corner of the Naabs' garage encroached 1.22 feet onto the Nolans' property while the other corner encroached 0.91 feet over the property line. The Nolans requested that the Naabs remove the garage from their property. When the Naabs refused, this lawsuit ensued. Who wins? [*Naab v. Nolan*, 327 S.E.2d 151 (W.Va. 1985)]

29.7 Recording Statute On October 13, 1972, Johnnie H. Hill and his wife, Clara Mae, entered into an installment sales contract with Pinelawn Memorial Park (Pinelawn) to purchase a mausoleum crypt. They made it clear they wanted to buy crypt "D" that faced eastward toward Kinston. The Hills paid $1,035 down payment and continued to make $33.02 monthly payments. On February 13, 1974, William C. Shackelford and his wife, Jennie L., entered into an agreement with Pinelawn to purchase crypt D. They paid $1,406 down payment and two annual installments of $912. The Hills were first put on notice of the second contract when they visited Pinelawn in February 1977 and saw the Shackelford name on crypt D. The Hills then tendered full payment to Pinelawn for crypt D. On April 25, 1977, the Hills sued Pinelawn and the Shackelfords. They demanded specific performance of the contract and the deed to crypt D. Upon being served with summons, the Shackelfords discovered that they had no deed to the crypt and demanded one from Pinelawn. Pinelawn delivered them a deed dated August 18, 1977, which the Shackelfords recorded in the County Register on September 9, 1977. Who owns crypt D? [*Hill v. Pinelawn Memorial Park, Inc.*, 282 S.E.2d 779 (N.C. 1981)]

29.8 Security Deposit Community Management Corporation (landlord) entered into a rental agreement with Bowman (tenant) to lease an apartment to the tenant on a month-to-month tenancy commencing on October 1, 1981. The agreement required the tenant to give 30 days' notice before vacating the premises. The agreement also required a security deposit of $215, which would be forfeited if the tenant vacated the apartment prior to the end of a month. On September 21, 1982, the tenant informed the landlord that he was vacating the apartment as of September 30, 1982. Because the landlord had only a 9-day notice, it was unable to relet the apartment for the month of October 1982. The landlord retained the security deposit to cover rent for October. The tenant sued to recover the security deposit. Who wins? [*Bowman v. Community Management Corp.*, 469 N.E.2d 1038 (Ohio App. 1984)]

29.9 Implied Warranty of Habitability Sharon Love entered into a written lease agreement with Monarch Apartments for apartment #4 at 441 Winfield in Topeka, Kansas. Shortly after moving in, she experienced serious problems with termites. Her walls swelled, clouds of dirt came out, and when she checked on her children one night, she saw termites flying around the room. She complained to Monarch, who arranged for the apartment to be fumigated. When the termite problem persisted, Monarch moved Love and her children to apartment #2. Upon moving in, Love noticed that roaches crawled over the walls, ceilings, and floors of the apartment. She complained, and Monarch called an exterminator, who sprayed the apartment. When the roach problem persisted, Love vacated the premises. Did Love lawfully terminate the lease? [*Love v. Monarch Apartment*, 771 P.2d 79 (Kan. App. 1989)]

29.10 Tenant's Breach of Lease Susan Nylen, Elizabeth Lewis, and Julie Reed, students at Indiana University, signed a rental agreement as cosigners to lease an apartment from Park Doral Apartments. The rental term was from August 26, 1986, until August 19, 1987, at a monthly rental of $420. The tenants paid a security deposit of $420, constituting prepayment of rent for the last month of the lease term. At the end of the fall semester, Reed moved out of the apartment, and in February 1987, she refused to pay any further rent. Nylen and Lewis remained in possession of the apartment, paying only two thirds of the total rent due for the month of February. Nylen and Lewis made a payment of $280 for the rent due in March. They vacated the apartment on March 13, 1987. The landlord, who was unable to re-lease the apartment during the term, sued Reed, Nylen, and Lewis for the unpaid rent. Who wins? [*Nylen v. Park Doral Apartments*, 535 N.E.2d 178 (Ind. App. 1989)]

29.11 Landlord's Tort Liability William Long, dba Hoosier Homes, owned an apartment building in Indianapolis, Indiana. He rented a second-story apartment to Marvin Tardy. On August 20, 1984, Almedia McLayea visited Tardy with her one-month-old nephew, Garfield Dawson. As McLayea was leaving the apartment, she walked down the stairway carrying Dawson in an infant seat. As she came down four steps to a landing, which led to a flight of ten stairs, she caught her heel on a stair, slipped, and fell forward. There was no handrail along the stairway (as required by law) by which she could break her fall. Instead, her shoulder struck a window at the landing, the window broke, the rotted screen behind it collapsed, and Dawson fell through the opening to the ground below. He sustained permanent injuries, including brain damage. Dawson (through his mother) sued the landlord to recover damages for negligence. Who wins? [*Dawson v. Long*, 546 N.E.2d 1265 (Ind. App. 1989)]

29.12 Tort Liability In October 1986, Luis and Barbara Chavez leased a house they owned in Arizona to Michael and Terry Diaz. The lease provided that no pets were to be kept on the premises without prior written approval of the landlords. The Diazes, without the landlords' consent or knowledge, kept a pit bull and another dog, which was half pit bull and half Rottweiler, at the leased premises. On October 17, 1986, the Diazes' two dogs escaped from the back yard and attacked and injured Josephine Gibbons. Gibbons sued the landlords for damages. Are the landlords liable? Would the tenants be liable? [*Gibbons v. Chavez*, 770 P.2d 377 (Ariz. App. 1988)]

29.13 Restrictive Covenants The Middleton Tract consists of approximately 560 acres of land which is located in the Santa Cruz Mountains in San Mateo County, California. The land, once owned by William H. Middleton, has been subdivided into 80 parcels of various shapes and sizes that are owned by various parties. The original deeds of conveyance from Middleton to purchasers contained certain restrictive covenants. One covenant limits use of the land exclusively for "residential purposes." Most of the land consists of thickly wooded forest with redwood and Douglas fir trees. The Holmeses, who own three parcels totaling 144 acres, propose to engage in commercial logging activities on their land. The plaintiffs, who own other parcels in the track, sued the Holmeses, seeking an injunction against such commercial activities. Who wins? [*Greater Middleton Assn. v. Holmes Lumber Co.*, 222 Cal.App.3d 980, 271 Cal.Rptr. 917 (Cal.App. 1990)]

29.14 Zoning The city of Ladue is one of the finer suburban residential areas of metropolitan St. Louis. The homes in the city are considerably more expensive than surrounding areas and consist of homes of traditional design such as colonial, French provincial, and English. The city set up an architectural board to approve plans for buildings that "conform to certain minimum architectural standards of appearance and conformity with surrounding structures, and that unsightly, grotesque, and unsuitable structures, detrimental to the stability of value and the welfare of surrounding property, structures, and residents, and to the general welfare and happiness of the community, be avoided." The owner of a lot in the city submitted a plan to build a house of ultra-modern design. It was pyramid-shaped, with a flat top and triangular-shaped windows and doors. Although the house plans met other city zoning ordinances and building codes, the architectural board rejected the owner's petition for a building permit based on aesthetic reasons. The owner sued the city. Who wins? [*State of Missouri v. Berkeley*, 458 S.W.2d 305 (Mo. 1970)]

29.15 Variance The town of Hempstead, New Hampshire, enacted a zoning ordinance "in order to retain the beauty and countrified atmosphere of the town, and to promote health, safety, morals, order, convenience, peace, prosperity, and general welfare of its inhabitants." To preserve abutting property owners' views and light, the ordinance limits the homes in the town to one and one-half stories. In violation of the ordinance, John M. Alexander built a shell of a second story and a new roof on his house. After the town ordered him to halt construction and denied him permission to occupy the second floor, he applied for a variance. Should the variance be granted? [*Alexander v. Town of Hempstead*, 525 A.2d 276 (N.H. 1987)]

ETHICS CASES

29.16 Ethical Perspective On March 19, 1971, Victor and Phyllis Garber (Garber) acquired a piece of real property by warranty deed. The deed was recorded on December 30, 1971. The property consisted of 80 acres that was enclosed by a fence that had been in place for over 50 years. The enclosed area was used to graze cattle and produce hay. Subsequently, William and Herbert Doenz (Doenz) acquired a piece of real property adjacent to the Garbers'. In March 1981, Doenz employed a surveyor to locate his land's boundaries. As a result of the survey, it was discovered that the shared fence was 20 to 30 feet inside the deed line on Doenz's property. The amount of property between the old fence and the deed line was 3.01 acres. In September 1981, Doenz removed the old fence and constructed a new fence along the deed line. Garber brought suit to quiet title. Did Doenz act ethically in removing the fence? Did the Garbers act ethically in claiming title to property that originally belonged with the adjacent property? Did Garber acquire title to property between the fence and the deed line through adverse possession? [*Doenz v. Garber*, 665 P.2d 932 (Wy. 1983)]

29.17 Ethical Perspective Moe and Joe Rappaport (tenants) leased space in a shopping mall owned by Bermuda Avenue Shopping Center Associates, L.P. (landlord), to use as an indoor golf arcade. The lease was signed in May 1987, and the tenants were given possession of the leased premises on July 23, 1987. The tenants were not told by the landlord of the extensive renovations planned for the mall. From July 23 until August 18, the renovation of the mall began in front of the arcade. According to the tenants, their store sign was taken down, there was debris and dust in front of the store, the sidewalks and parking spaces in front of the store were taken away, and their business "died." The tenants closed their arcade on September 30 and sued the landlord for damages. The landlord counterclaimed, seeking to recover lost rental income. Did the landlord act ethically in not explaining the extent of the planned renovations to the tenants? Did the tenants act ethically in terminating the lease? Were the tenants constructively evicted from the leased premises? [*Bermuda Avenue Shopping Center Associates v. Rappaport*, 565 So.2d 805 (Fla.App. 1990)]

CRITICAL LEGAL THINKING WRITING ASSIGNMENT

Read Case A.29 in the Case Appendix [*Nollan v. California Coastal Commission*]. This case is excerpted from the U.S. Supreme Court opinion. Review and brief the case. In your brief, be sure to answer the following questions:

1. What did the California Coastal Commission do to try to obtain the easement across Nollans' property?
2. In whose favor did the following courts rule?
   a. Superior court
   b. Court of appeal
   c. U.S. Supreme Court
3. What is a *taking*? If a taking is found, what must the government do?
4. Succinctly state the issue that was presented to the U.S. Supreme Court in this case.
5. Could the state of California have acquired the easement across Nollans' property under its power of eminent domain?

CHAPTER 30

INSURANCE, WILLS,

AND TRUSTS

Chapter Objectives

*After studying this chapter,
you should be able to*

1. Describe the parties to an insurance contract
2. Define an insurable interest
3. List and describe the various types of life, health and disability, fire and homeowners, and automobile insurance
4. List and describe special forms of business insurance
5. Describe an insurance company's duty to defend its insured
6. Describe the requirements for making a valid will
7. List and describe special forms of wills
8. Identify how property is distributed under intestate statutes if a person dies without a will
9. Define a trust
10. Identify the parties to a trust

Chapter Contents

> *When you have told someone you have left him a legacy, the only decent thing to do is to die at once.*
>
> Samuel Butler
> (1835–1902)

insurance A means for persons and businesses to protect themselves against the risk of loss.

Insurance is a means for persons and businesses to protect themselves against the risk of loss. For example, a business may purchase fire insurance to cover its buildings. If there is a fire and the property is damaged, the insurance company will pay for all or part of the loss, depending on the policy. Similarly, an individual who purchases automobile insurance may be reimbursed by his insurer if his car is stolen. Insurance is crucial to personal, business, and estate planning.

will A way to acquire property as a result of a death.

Wills and trusts are means of transferring property. **Wills** transfer property upon a person's death. They permit people to state exactly where they want their property to go when they die. If a person dies *intestate*—that is, without a will—the deceased's property is distributed to relatives according to state statute. The property escheats (goes) to the state if there are no relatives.

Trusts are used to transfer property that is to be held and managed for the benefit of another person or persons. Although trusts are created during one's lifetime, they may be worded to become effective only upon the trustor's (or grantor's) death.

After discussing how insurance is used to protect against risk of loss, this chapter turns to the use of wills and trusts to transfer property.

INSURANCE

insured The party who pays a premium to a particular insurance company for insurance coverage.

insurer The insurance company.

Insurance is defined as a contract whereby one party undertakes to indemnify another against loss, damage, or liability arising from a contingent or unknown event. It is a means of transferring and distributing risk of loss. The risk of loss is *pooled* (i.e., spread) among all of the parties (or **insureds**) who pay premiums to a particular insurance company. The insurance company—also called the **insurer** or **underwriter**—is then obligated to pay insurance proceeds to those members of the pool who experience a loss. (For the various kinds of insurance, see Exhibit 30.1).

Exhibit 30.1
Types of Insurance

Life Insurance	
Whole life	Provides coverage during the life of the insured. It involves an element of savings. The premium is set to cover both the death benefit and an amount for investment. The value of savings grows at a fixed interest rate.
Term	Covers a limited period of time (e.g., five years). It involves no savings feature.
Universal life	Combines features of both term and whole life insurance. The value of savings grows at a variable interest rate.
Double indemnity	Provision in many life insurance policies that provides for payment of double the amount of the policy if death is caused by accident.
Key person	Life insurance taken out by business which insures the life of key executives. Also taken out by partners to insure the lives of other partners.
Annuity	Payments made to insured before death. For the payment of premiums, an insurance company agrees to make periodic payments (e.g., monthly) to the insured once he or she reaches a certain age.

Health and Disability Insurance

Health	Covers the cost of medical treatment, surgery, and hospital care.
Disability	Provides monthly income to an insured who is disabled and cannot work. Benefits are based on degree of disability.
Dental	Covers the costs of dental care.

Fire and Homeowners Insurance

Standard fire insurance policy	Protects real and personal property against loss resulting from fire, lightning, smoke, water damage, and related perils. Most policies limit recovery to damage caused by **hostile fires** (i.e., fire caused by family electrical wiring) and not **friendly fires** (e.g., damage caused by a fire contained in a fireplace). No personal liability coverage is provided.
Homeowners policy	A comprehensive insurance policy that includes coverage for the risks covered by a standard fire insurance policy as well as personal liability insurance. Includes coverage for property damage, personal injury, and medical expenses of persons injured on the insured's property.
Personal articles	Covers specific valuable items (e.g., jewelry, works of art, furs, and the like) that are usually excluded from standard fire and homeowners policies.
Renters insurance	Covers loss and damage to renter's possessions and provides personal liability coverage. Insures against the same perils as a homeowners policy.

Automobile Insurance

Collision	Property insurance that covers the insured's vehicle against risk of loss or damage when it is struck by another vehicle.
Comprehensive	Property insurance that covers the insured's vehicle against risk of loss or damage from causes other than collision; namely, fire, theft, explosion, hail, windstorm, falling objects, earthquakes, floods, hurricanes, vandalism, and riots.
Liability	Covers damage and loss that the insured causes to third parties. This includes both bodily injury and property damage. States often require drivers to carry minimum liability insurance specified by statute. The following additional coverage may be purchased:
	Other driver coverage. Liability coverage that protects the owner of a vehicle when someone else drives his or her vehicle with his or her permission.
	Drive-other coverage. Liability coverage that protects the insured while driving other vehicles.
Medical payment	Covers medical expenses incurred by the owner, passengers, and other authorized drivers of his car who are injured in an automobile accident.
Uninsured motorist	Provides coverage to the driver and passengers of a vehicle who are injured by an uninsured motorist or a hit-and-run driver.

Business Insurance

Business interruption	Reimburses a business for any lost revenues suffered during the period of time it takes to repair or reconstruct property damaged by fire or other insured peril.
Workers' compensation	Pays employees for injuries incurred while working within the scope of their employment. Most states require businesses to carry this form of insurance.
Directors' and officers' liability	Protects directors and officers of businesses from liability for actions they take on behalf of the business.
Professional practice	Covers professionals—such as attorneys, accountants, physicians, dentists, engineers, and architects—from liability for injuries resulting from their negligence in practicing their professions.
Fidelity	Protects employers against loss caused by the dishonesty and defalcation of employees.

continued

Exhibit 30.1
(continued)

Other Types of Insurance	
Credit	Pays debtors' debts if they are unable to pay because of some insured peril (e.g., death or disability). Debtors and creditors may purchase this insurance.
Title	Insures that a property owner has clear title to real property. May be purchased by the owner, or mortgages or lienholders of the property.
Marine	Covers loss or damage to the vessel and its cargo caused by perils at sea. Marine insurance is often comprehensive, covering property damage and liability for personal injury.

Special Forms of Insurance	
Umbrella policy	Liability insurance that increases coverage beyond normal policy limits. An umbrella policy pays only if the basic policy limits have been exceeded. An insurer will issue an umbrella policy only if stipulated minimum amounts of automobile and homeowners liability coverage has been purchased.
Group	Insurance that is made available to the members of a specified group (e.g., the employees of an employer). Group rates are usually less expensive than individual insurance premiums.
Self-insurance	The insured handles its own insurance risk by either (1) purchasing no insurance (*going bare*), (2) forming a *captive insurance company* from which to buy insurance, or (3) joining with others to form an *insurance pool* to spread the losses among the pool's members.

policy The insurance contract.

premium The money paid to the insurance company for insurance coverage.

"An insurance policy is like old underwear. The gaps in its cover are only shown by accident."

David Yates
(1984)

The insurance contract is called a **policy**. The money paid to the insurance company is called a **premium**. Premiums are based upon an estimate of the number of parties within the pool who will suffer the risks insured against. The estimate is based on past experience.

Sometimes an insurer will spread the risk of loss through **reinsurance**. That is, it will sell a portion of the policy's risk and right to receive premiums to other insurance companies called **reinsurers**.

Insurance policies are often sold by insurance agents or brokers. An **insurance agent** usually works exclusively for one insurance company and is an agent of that company. An **insurance broker** is an independent contractor who represents a number of insurance companies. The broker is the agent of the insured. Some insurance is sold directly by the insurer to the insured (e.g., by direct mail).

Regulation of the Insurance Industry

The **McCarran-Ferguson Act**, which was enacted by the federal government in 1945, gave the regulation of insurance to the states and exempted insurance companies from the federal antitrust laws.[1] Accordingly, each state has enacted statutes that regulate domestic and out-of-state insurance companies operating within its borders. State regulations cover the incorporation, licensing, supervision, and liquidation of insurance companies, and the licensing and supervision of insurance agents and brokers.

Insurable Interest

insurable interest A person who purchases insurance must have a personal interest in the insured item or person.

Anyone who would suffer a pecuniary (monetary) loss from the destruction of real personal property has an **insurable interest** in that property. If the insured does not have an **insurable interest** in the property being insured, the contract is treated as a wager and cannot be enforced.

Ownership creates an insurable interest. In addition, mortgagees, lienholders, and tenants have an insurable interest in property. The insurable interest in property must exist at the time of loss.

In the case of life insurance, a person must have a close family relationship or an economic benefit from the continued life of another to have an insurable interest in that person's life. Thus, spouses, parents, children, and sisters and brothers may insure each others' lives. Other more remote relationships (e.g., aunts, uncles, cousins, and so forth) require additional proof of an economic interest (e.g., proof of support). The insurable interest must exist when the life insurance policy is issued but need not exist at the time of death.

A person may insure his own life and name anyone as the **beneficiary**. The beneficiary does not have to have an insurable interest in the insured's life.

beneficiary A person or organization who will receive money from the insurer at the time of the insured's death.

BUSINESS CHECKLIST

Business Owners Purchase Key-Person Life Insurance

Small businesses, such as partnerships, limited liability companies, and close corporations often purchase key-person life insurance on the owners of the business. The company pays the premiums for the life insurance policies. The life insurance is usually used to fund buy–sell agreements among the owners of the business. Thus, if an insured owner dies, the insurance proceeds are paid to the deceased's beneficiaries. The deceased's interest in the company then reverts to either the other owners or the business, according to the terms of the buy–sell agreement.

The following steps should be followed when purchasing key-person life insurance:

- The owners must agree upon the dollar value of their ownership interests in the business.
- The owners must execute a buy–sell agreement among themselves and the company specifying how a deceased owner's interest will be purchased by the other owners or the company upon his or her death.
- The company should purchase key-person life insurance from a reputable insurance company in an amount necessary to fund the buy–sell agreement.
- The company must pay the premiums for the key-person life insurance policies when due.
- When an owner-insured dies, the other owners and the company must file the claim with the insurance company and take all other steps necessary to ensure that the deceased's beneficiaries are paid the amount specified in the buy–sell agreement in a timely fashion.

THE INSURANCE CONTRACT

Insurance contracts (**policies**) are governed by the law of contracts. Most policies are prepared on standardized forms. Some states even make that a requirement. Often, state statutes mandate that specific language be included in different types of insurance contracts. These statutes concern coverage for certain losses, how limitations on coverage must be stated in the contract, and the like. The insurance coverage is in place once the insurance policy is issued. Insurance policies often contain the clauses discussed in the following paragraphs.

CAUTION
Insureds should be careful to read insurance contracts carefully so that they fully understand what risks are covered and what risks are not covered.

Deductible Clause

deductible clause
A clause that stipulates that insurance proceeds are payable only after the insured has paid a certain amount of the damage or loss.

Deductible clauses provide that insurance proceeds are payable only after the insured has paid a certain amount of the damage or loss. Typical deductibles for automotive collision insurance are $100, $250, or $500.

Coinsurance Clause

coinsurance clause
A clause that permits an owner who insures his or her property to a certain percent of its value to recover up to the face value of the property.

The **coinsurance clause** permits an owner who insures his or her property to a certain percent of its value (e.g., 80 percent) to recover up to the face value of the policy. An owner who insures the property for less than the stated percentage must bear a proportionate share of the loss. Most fire insurance policies contain coinsurance clauses.

Exclusions from Coverage Clause

CAUTION

Insurance contracts cover only certain specified risks. They often contain exclusions *that identify risks not covered by the policy.*

Exclusion clauses stipulate certain exclusions from insurance coverage. For example, standard fire insurance policies often exclude coverage for damage caused by the storage of explosives or flammable liquids unless a special premium is paid for this coverage. Insurance policies should be read carefully to determine the extent of coverage.

In the case that follows, the court had to decide whether an exclusion clause was enforceable.

CASE 30.1

Malcom v. Farmers New World Life Insurance Co.

4 Cal.App.4th 296, 5 Cal.Rptr.2d 584 (1992) California Court of Appeal

Facts In 1982, Farmers New World Life Insurance Company (Farmers) issued two $100,000 life insurance policies on Lawrence Malcom's life. His wife, Pamela Malcom, and Medmetric Corporation, were the beneficiaries. Each policy contained a suicide provision that stated, "Suicide, whether sane or insane, will not be a risk assumed during the first two policy years. In such a case we will refund the premiums paid." In May 1984, within two years after the policies were issued, Lawrence committed suicide. The beneficiaries filed claims with Farmers seeking each policy's $100,000 benefit. When Farmers refused to pay the benefits and refunded the premiums, the beneficiaries sued Farmers for breach of the insurance contract. They argued that the suicide provision should not be enforced because it was not plain and clear and conspicuous. The trial court granted Farmers' motion for summary judgment. The beneficiaries appealed.

Issue Is Farmers liable on the two life insurance policies?

Decision No. The court of appeals held that the policies' suicide provision was conspicuous, bold,

clear, and unambiguous and was therefore enforceable. Affirmed.

Reason The suicide provision clearly and conspicuously conveyed its message in understandable language. The court based its decision on these facts: The provision contained only 27 words, none of which was beyond the working vocabulary of lay persons. Also, the suicide provision was located on the policy's third page—the first operative page after the cover page and index—and preceded by the boldface capitalized word *SUICIDE*. Finally, the suicide provision was clearly separated from its neighboring provisions by several blank lines.

CASE QUESTIONS

Critical Legal Thinking Do you think insurance contracts meet the reasonable expectations of insureds? Explain.

Ethics Did the beneficiaries act ethically in bringing this lawsuit?

Business Implication Why do life insurance contracts include suicide exclusions?

Modification of Insurance

If both the insurer and insured agree, an insurance contract may be modified. This is usually done either by adding an **endorsement** to the policy or by the execution of a document called a **rider**.

> **endorsement** An addition to an insurance policy that modifies it.
>
> **rider** A separate document that will modify an existing insurance policy.

Cancellation of Insurance

In most instances, an insured can cancel the insurance policy at any time. An insurer may cancel an insurance policy for nonpayment of premiums. Many insurance policies provide a **grace period** during which an insured may pay an overdue premium. The insurance usually remains in effect during the grace period.

> **grace period** A period of time after the actual expiration date of a payment but during which the insured can still pay an overdue premium without penalty.

Duties of Insured and Insurer

The parties to an insurance contract are obligated to perform the duties imposed by the contract. The insured owes the following duties: (1) to pay the premiums stipulated by the policy, (2) to notify the insurer after the occurrence of an insured event within the time period stated in the policy or within a reasonable time, and (3) to cooperate with the insurer in investigating claims made against the insurer.

The insurer owes two primary duties. First, the insurer owes a **duty to defend** against any suit brought against the insured must provide and pay for the lawyers and court costs necessary to defend the lawsuit. Second, the insurer owes the duty to pay legitimate claims up to policy limit. Insurers who wrongfully refuse to perform these duties are liable for damages.

> **duty to defend** An insurer owes a duty to defend an insured against a lawsuit involving a risk covered by the policy. This includes providing a lawyer and paying court costs, deposition fees, and so forth.

Subrogation

If an insurance company pays a claim to an insured for liability or property damage caused by a third party, the insurer succeeds to the right of the insured to recover from the third party. This right is called **subrogation**. For example, if a third party negligently injures an insured who had hospital and disability insurance, the insurer can sue to recover the insurance proceeds it paid from the party who caused the injury. Subrogation does not apply to life insurance policies. An insurer has no right of subrogation against his or her own insured.

> **subrogation** If an insurance company pays a claim to an insured for liability or property damage caused by a third party, the insurer succeeds to the right of the insured to recover from the third party.

BUSINESS APPLICATION

No-Fault Automobile Insurance

Until fairly recently, most automobile insurance coverage in this country was based on the principle of "fault." That is, a party injured in an accident relied on the insurance of the at-fault party to pay for his or her injuries. This system led to substantial litigation, but many accident victims were unable to recover because the at-fault party had either inadequate insurance or no insurance at all.

To remedy this problem, more than half of the states have en-acted legislation which mandates **no-fault insurance** for automobile accidents. Under this system, a driver's insurance company pays for any injuries he or she suffered in an accident, no matter who caused the accident.

Most no-fault statutes stipulate that claimants may not sue to recover damages from the party who caused the accident unless the injured party suffered serious injury (e.g., dismemberment or disfigurement) or death.

If the insured recovers the total amount from the at-fault party, he or she must reimburse his or her own insurer for insurance proceeds paid pursuant to the no-fault policy.

No-fault insurance policies provide coverage for medical expenses and lost wages. Pain and suffering are not always covered. No-fault insurance usually covers the insured, members of the insured's immediate family,
continued

authorized drivers of the automobile, and passengers.

No-fault insurance reduces litigation costs, lessens the time for an injured person to be compensated for his or her injuries, and assures the insureds that coverage is available if they are injured in an automobile accident. There is also evidence that no-fault insurance reduces the overall cost of automobile insurance. The trend of the law is to replace at-fault systems of automobile insurance with no-fault insurance.

DEFENSES OF THE INSURER

"The underwriter knows nothing and the man who comes to him to ask him to insure knows everything."

L. Scrutton
Rozanes v. Bowen
(1928)

An insurer may be liable to raise certain defenses to the imposition of liability. The most common defenses are discussed in the following paragraphs.

Misrepresentation and Concealment

Insurance companies may require applicants to disclose certain information to help them determine whether they will insure the risk and to calculate the premium. The insurer may avoid liability on the policy (1) if its decision is based on a material misrepresentation on the part of the applicant or (2) if the applicant concealed material information from the insurer. This rule applies whether the misrepresentation was intentional or non-intentional.

Many states have enacted **incontestability clauses** that prevent insurers from contesting statements made by insureds in applications for insurance after the passage of a stipulated number of years (the typical length of time is two to five years).

incontestability clause
A clause that prevents insurers from contesting statements made by insureds in applications for insurance after the passage of a stipulated number of years.

Breach of Warranty

A **warranty** is a representation of the insured that is expressly incorporated in the insurance contract:

affirmative warranty
A statement asserting that certain facts are true.

promissory warranty
Stipulates that the facts will continue to be true throughout the duration of the policy.

- An **affirmative warranty** is a statement asserting that certain facts are true (e.g., there are no environmental problems currently existing as to the property the insured is insuring).
- A **promissory warranty** stipulates that facts will continue to be true throughout the duration of the policy (e.g., the insured will not store flammable products in the insured building). An insurer may avoid liability caused by a breach of warranty.

In the following case, the court had to decide whether the insured made a misrepresentation on his application for insurance.

CASE 30.2

Peckman v. Mutual Life Insurance Company of New York

509 N.Y.S.2d 336 (1986) New York Supreme Court, Appellate Division

Facts Alan L. Peckman filed an application with the Mutual Life Insurance Company of New York (MONY) for life insurance in the face amount of $100,000 with double indemnity coverage for accidental death. On the application, Peckman indicated that for the previous six years he had been self-employed in the occupation of "marketing." MONY issued the policy, which named Alan's mother as beneficiary.

On August 5, 1981, within the contestability period of the policy, Alan's body was found in a steamer trunk with a gunshot wound to the head. Alan's mother filed a claim with MONY for the insurance proceeds from Alan's life insurance policy.

MONY denied the claim, asserting that Alan falsely misrepresented his occupation and fraudulently concealed that he was a drug dealer. The company introduced police evidence showing that Alan had been involved in the distribution of drugs for several years. Articles in newspapers stated that Alan ran a million-dollar marijuana distribution ring.

Alan's mother sued MONY to recover the insurance proceeds. The trial court granted summary judgment in favor of Alan's mother and awarded her the double indemnity insurance benefits. MONY appealed.

Issue Did the decedent misrepresent his employment on the life insurance application?

Decision No. The appellate court held that the insured had not misrepresented his employment on the life insurance application. The appellate court affirmed the trial court's judgment and award of double indemnity life insurance proceeds to the plaintiff–beneficiary.

Reason In reaching its decision, the appellate court stated: "In the instant case the applicant did not misrepresent his occupation. Webster's Dictionary defines *marketing* as 'the act or business of buying or selling in the market.' This definition clearly encompasses the applicant's alleged pursuit of drug dealing."

CASE QUESTIONS

Critical Legal Thinking Should insurance companies be permitted to group persons into "risk categories" and charge higher premiums to members of higher risk categories (e.g., smokers, teen-age drivers)?

Ethics Do you think the insured acted ethically in disclosing his occupation as marketing?

Business Implication Do you think an insurance company would issue a life insurance policy if it knew the applicant was a drug dealer?

WILLS

A **will** is a declaration of how a person wants his or her property to be distributed upon his or her death. It is a testamentary deposition of property. The person who makes the will is called the **testator** or testatrix.[2] The persons designated in the will to receive the testator's property are called **beneficiaries**.

Requirements for Making a Will

Every state has a **Statute of Wills** that establishes the requirements for making a valid will in that state. These requirements are:

- **Testamentary capacity.** The testator must have been of legal age and "sound mind" when the will was made. The courts determine testamentary capacity on a case-by-case basis. The legal age for executing a will is set by state statute.
- **Writing.** Wills must be in writing to be valid (except for dying declarations that are discussed later in this chapter). The writing may be formal or informal. Although most wills are typewritten, they can be handwritten (see the late discussion of holographic wills). The writing may be on legal paper, other paper, scratch paper, envelopes, napkins, or the like. A will may incorporate other documents by reference.
- **Testator's signature.** Wills must be signed.

Most jurisdictions require the testator's signature to appear at the end of the will. This is to prevent fraud that could occur if someone added provisions to the will below the testator's signature. Generally, courts have held that initials ("R.K.H."), a nickname ("Buffy"), title ("mother"), and even an "X" is a valid signature on a will if it can be proven that the testator intended it to be his or her signature.

- **Attestation by witnesses.** Wills must be attested to by mentally competent witnesses. Although state law varies, most states require two or three witnesses. The witnesses do not have to reside in the jurisdiction in which the testator is domiciled. Most jurisdictions stipulate that interested parties (e.g., a beneficiary under the will or the testator's

will A declaration of how a person wants his or her property distributed upon death.

testator The person who makes a will.

beneficiary A person or organization designated in the will who receives all or a portion of the testator's property at the time of the testator's death.

Statute of Wills A state statute that establishes the requirements for making a valid will.

attestation The action of a will being witnessed by two or three objective and competent people.

attorney) cannot be witnesses. If an interested party has attested to a will, state law either voids any clauses that benefit such person or voids the entire will.

Witnesses usually sign the will following the signature of the testator. This is called the **attestation clause**. Most jurisdictions require that each witness attest to the will in the presence of the other witnesses.

A will that meets the requirements of the Statute of Wills is called a **formal will**. A sample will is shown in Exhibit 30.2.

formal will A will that meets the requirements of the Statute of Wills.

Changing a Will

A will cannot be amended by merely striking out existing provisions and adding new ones. **Codicils** are the legal way to change an existing will. A codicil is a separate document that must be executed with the same formalities as a will. In addition, it must incorporate by reference the will it is amending. The codicil and the will are then read as one instrument.

CAUTION

A will cannot be amended or changed by striking out existing provisions and adding new ones on to the will itself.

codicil A separate document that must be executed to amend a will. It must be executed with the same formalities as a will.

revocation Termination of a will.

Revoking a Will

A will may be **revoked** by acts of the testator. A will is revoked if the testator intentionally burns, tears, obliterates, or otherwise destroys it. A properly executed **subsequent will** revokes a prior will if it specifically states that it is the testator's intention to do so. If the second will does not expressly revoke the prior will, the wills are read together. If any will provisions are inconsistent, the provision in the second will controls.

Wills can also be revoked by operation of law. For example, divorce or annulment revokes disposition of property to the former spouse under the will. The remainder of the will is valid. The birth of a child after a will has been executed does not revoke the will but does entitle the child to receive his or her share of the parents' estate as determined by state statute.

Uniform Simultaneous Death Act An act that provides that if people who would inherit property from each other die simultaneously, each person's property is distributed as though he or she survived.

Simultaneous Deaths

Sometimes people who would inherit property from each other die simultaneously. If it is impossible to determine who died first, the question becomes one of inheritance. The **Uniform Simultaneous Death Act** provides that each deceased person's property is distributed as though he or she survived.

CONSIDER THIS EXAMPLE: Suppose a husband and wife make wills that leave their entire estate to each other. Assume that the husband and wife are killed simultaneously in an airplane crash. Here, the husband's property would go to his relatives and the wife's property would go to her relatives.

"The power of making a will is an instrument placed in the hands of individuals for the prevention of private calamity."

Jeremy Bentham
Principles of the Civil Code
(1748)

undue influence Occurs where one person takes advantage of another person's mental, emotional, or physical weakness and unduly persuades that person to make a will; the persuasion by the wrongdoer must overcome the free will of the testator.

Undue Influence

A will may be found to be invalid if it was made as a result of **undue influence** on the testator. Undue influence can be inferred from the facts and circumstances surrounding the making of the will. For example, if an 85-year-old woman leaves all of her property to the lawyer who drafted her will and ignores her blood relatives, the court is likely to presume undue influence.

Undue influence is difficult to prove by direct evidence, but it may be proved by circumstantial evidence. The elements that courts examine to find the presence of undue influence include:

- The benefactor and beneficiary are involved in a relationship of confidence and trust
- The will contains substantial benefit to the beneficiary
- The beneficiary caused or assisted in effecting execution of the will
- There was an opportunity to exert influence

Exhibit 30.2
A Sample Will

Last Will and Testament of Florence Winthorpe Blueblood

I, FLORENCE WINTHORPE BLUEBLOOD, presently residing at Boston, County of Suffolk, Massachusetts, being of sound and disposing mind and memory, hereby make, publish, and declare this to be my Last Will and Testament.

FIRST. I hereby revoke any and all Wills and Codicils previously made by me.

SECOND. I direct that my just debts and funeral expenses be paid out of my Estate as soon as practicable after my death.

THIRD. I am presently married to Theodore Hannah Blueblood III.

FOURTH. I hereby nominate and appoint my husband as the Personal Representative of this my Last Will and Testament. If he is unable to serve as Personal Representative, then I nominate and appoint Mildred Yardly Winthorpe as Personal Representative of this my Last Will and Testament. I direct that no bond or other security be required to be posted by my Personal Representative.

FIFTH. I hereby nominate and appoint my husband as Guardian of the person and property of my minor children. In the event that he is unable to serve as Guardian, then I nominate and appoint Mildred Yardly Winthorpe Guardian of the person and property of my minor children. I direct that no bond or other security be required to be posted by any Guardian herein.

SIXTH. I give my Personal Representative authority to exercise all the powers, rights, duties, and immunities conferred upon fiduciaries under law with full power to sell, mortgage, lease, invest, or reinvest all or any part of my Estate on such terms as he or she deems best.

SEVENTH. I hereby give, devise, and bequeath my entire estate to my husband, except for the following specific bequests:

I give my wedding ring to my daughter, Hillary Smythe Blueblood.
I give my baseball card collection to my son, Theodore Hannah Blueblood IV.
In the event that either my above-named daughter or son predeceases me, then and in that event, I give, devise, and bequeath my deceased daughter's or son's bequest to my husband.

EIGHTH. In the event that my husband shall predecease me, then and in that event, I give, devise, and bequeath my entire estate, with the exception of the bequests in paragraph SEVENTH, to my beloved children or grandchildren surviving me, per stirpes.

NINTH. In the event I am not survived by my husband or any children or grandchildren, then and in that event, I give, devise, and bequeath my entire estate to Harvard University.

IN WITNESS WHEREOF, I, Florence Winthorpe Blueblood, the Testatrix, sign my name to this Last Will and Testament this 3rd day of January, 1999.

Florence Winthorpe Blueblood
(Signature)

Signed, sealed, published, and declared by the above-named Testatrix, as and for her Last Will and Testament, in the presence of us, who at her request, in her presence, and in the presence of one another, have hereunto subscribed our names as attesting witnesses, the day and year last written above.

Witness	Address
Norm Peterson	100 Beacon Hill Rd Boston, Massachuset
Clifford Claven	200 Minute Man Drive Boston, Massachusetts
Rebecca Howe	300 Charles River Place Boston, Massachusetts

- The will contains an unnatural disposition of the testator's property
- The bequests constitute a change from a former will
- The testator was highly susceptible to the undue influence

ETHICAL PERSPECTIVE

Murder She Wrote

Most states, by statute or court decision, provide that a person who murders another person cannot inherit the victim's property. This rule, often called the **murder disqualification doctrine**, is based on the public policy that a person should not benefit from his or her wrongdoing. Consider the following case.

Walter A. Gibbs resided with his mother until 1963, when he hired Delores Christenson to help care for her. He married Delores in 1964. The couple were divorced in 1973. Gibbs married Delores' twin sister, Darlene Wahl. That marriage ended in divorce in 1980.

During the winter of 1988–1989, Delores, Darlene, and Darlene's new husband, Jerry Phillips, who all were living together, experienced difficult times due to lack of money. Delores contacted Gibbs, who was over 80 years old at the time, at the nursing home where he resided and offered to move back into his house and care for him. In February 1989, Delores, Darlene, and Jerry moved Gibbs to his house and moved in with him. The group lived together as a "family" for about one year.

Gibbs had a will that named his first cousin, Bernice Boettner, as sole beneficiary. In January 1990, Delores located an attorney who drafted a new will for Gibbs, and she procured two witnesses for the will's execution. The will disinherited Gibbs' relations and left his entire estate, worth about $175,000, to Delores. Gibbs executed the will on January 3, 1990.

On January 8, 1990, Darlene and Jerry discussed killing Gibbs to "activate the will." On the morning of April 1, 1990, Darlene got a pillow from her bedroom and gave it to Jerry. Delores sat at the kitchen table approximately 17 feet from Gibbs' bed. Darlene held Gibbs' arms while Jerry smothered him. After Jerry removed the pillow, Delores went over and embraced Jerry.

In January 1991, Delores, Darlene, and Jerry were indicted on charges of murder, conspiracy to commit murder, and aiding and abetting murder. Jerry pleaded guilty to conspiracy to commit second-degree murder. Darlene was convicted of murder and sentenced to life in prison. Delores was acquitted of all charges.

Delores offered Gibbs' will for probate. Boettner filed a petition to revoke the probate of Gibbs' will and an application to disqualify Delores as the beneficiary as a willful slayer of Gibbs. Delores argued in defense that she should be allowed to inherit Gibbs' estate because she had not been criminally convicted.

The trial court held that Delores qualified as a willful slayer under the murder disqualification statute, even though she had not been convicted at her criminal trial. The state supreme court affirmed. The supreme court stated, "We are not dealing with criminal responsibility, but with a civil statute which disqualifies a person who procures the death of a testator from reaping the benefits of that death." Gibbs' prior will, which left his estate to Boettner, is subject to probate. [*In the Matter of the Estate of Walter A. Gibbs*, 490 N.W.2d 504 (S.D. 1992)]

1. Is it ethical for a beneficiary to recover life insurance proceeds if he or she has killed the insured?
2. Does the murder disqualification doctrine serve any social purpose?

TYPES OF TESTAMENTARY GIFTS

devise A gift of real estate by will.

bequest A gift of personal property by will.

In a will, a gift of real estate by will is called a **devise**. A gift of personal property by will is called a **bequest** or **legacy**. Gifts in wills can be specific, general, or residuary.

- **Specific gifts.** Gifts of specifically named pieces of property, such as a ring, a boat, or a piece of real estate.

- **General gifts.** Gifts that do not identify the specific property from which the gift is to be made, such as a cash amount that can come from any source in the decedent's estate.
- **Residuary gifts.** Gifts that are established by a residuary clause in the will. Such a clause might state that "I give my daughter the rest, remainder, and residual of my estate." This means that any portion of the estate left after the debts, taxes, and specific and general gifts have been paid belongs to the decedent's daughter.

A person who inherits property under a will or intestacy statute takes the property subject to all of the outstanding claims against it (e.g., liens, mortgages, and the like). A person can **renounce** an inheritance and often does where the liens or mortgages against the property exceed the value of the property.

Ademption and Abatement

If a testator leaves a specific gift of property to a beneficiary, but the property is no longer in the estate of the testator when he or she dies, the beneficiary receives nothing. This is called the doctrine of **ademption**.

If the testator's estate is not large enough to pay all of the devises and bequests, the doctrine of **abatement** applies. The doctrine works as follows:

- If a will provides for both general and residuary gifts, the residuary gifts are abated first. For example, suppose a testator executes a will when he owns $500,000 of property that leaves (1) $100,000 to the Red Cross, (2) $100,000 to a university, and (3) the residue to his niece. Suppose that when the testator dies his estate is worth only $225,000. Here, the Red Cross and the university each receives $100,000 and the niece receives $25,000.
- If a will provides only for general gifts, the reductions are proportionate. For example, suppose a testator's will leaves $75,000 to two beneficiaries, but the estate is only $100,000. Each beneficiary would receive $50,000.

Per Stirpes and Per Capita Distribution

A testator's will may state that property is to be left to his or her **lineal descendants** (children, grandchildren, great-grandchildren, etc.) either *per stirpes* or *per capita*. The difference between these two methods is as follows:

- **Per stirpes.** The lineal descendants inherit by representation of their parent; that is, they split what their deceased parent would have received. If their parent is not deceased, they receive nothing.
- **Per capita.** The lineal descendants equally share the property of the estate without regard to degree of relationship to the testator. That is, children of the testator share equally with grandchildren, great-grandchildren, and so forth.

CONSIDER THIS EXAMPLE: Suppose Anne dies without a surviving spouse, and she had three children—Bart, Beth, and Bruce. Bart, who survives his mother, has no children. Beth has one child, Carla, and they both survive Anne. Bruce, who predeceased his mother, had two children, Clayton and Cathy; and Cathy, who predeceased Anne, had two children, Deborah and Dominic, both of whom survive Anne.

If Anne leaves her estate to her lineal descendants *per stirpes*, Bart and Beth each get one third, Carla receives nothing because Beth is alive, Clayton gets one sixth, and Deborah and Dominic each get one twelfth. See Exhibit 30.3.

On the other hand, if Anne leaves her estate to her lineal descendants *per capita*, all of the surviving issue—Bart, Beth, Carla, Clayton, Deborah, and Dominic—share equally in the estate. That is, they each get one-sixth of Anne's estate (see Exhibit 30.4).

specific gift Gift of a specifically named piece of property.

general gift Gift that does not identify the specific property from which the gift is to be made.

residuary gift Gift of the estate left after the debts, taxes, and specific and general gifts have been paid.

ademption A principle that says if a testator leaves a specific devise of property to a beneficiary but the property is no longer in the estate when the testator dies, the beneficiary receives nothing.

abatement If the property the testator leaves is not sufficient to satisfy all the beneficiaries named in a will and there are both general and residuary bequests, the residuary bequest is abated first; if a will provides for general bequests, they are reduced proportionately if the residuary bequests are fully abated or there are none.

lineal descendants Children, grandchildren, great grandchildren, and so on of the testator.

per stirpes A distribution of the estate that makes grandchildren and great-grandchildren of the deceased inherit by representation of their parent.

per capita A distribution of the estate that makes each grandchild and great-grandchild of the deceased inherit equally with the children of the deceased.

Disinherit: the prankish action of the ghosts in cutting the pockets out of trousers.
Frank McKinney Hubbard
The Roycroft Dictionary (1923)

Exhibit 30.3
Per Stirpes Distribution

1ST DEGREE

Bart $\left(\dfrac{1}{3}\right)$

2ND DEGREE

Anne
(deceased)

Beth $\left(\dfrac{1}{3}\right)$

Carla (0)

Clayton $\left(\dfrac{1}{6}\right)$

3RD DEGREE

Bruce
(deceased)

Cathy
(deceased)

Deborah $\left(\dfrac{1}{12}\right)$

Dominic $\left(\dfrac{1}{12}\right)$

CONTEMPORARY BUSINESS ENVIRONMENT

Videotaped Wills

Many acrimonious will contests involve written wills. The contestors allege such things as mental incapacity of the testator at the time the will was made, undue influence, fraud, or duress. Although the written will speaks for itself, the mental capacity of the testator and the voluntariness of his or her actions cannot be determined from the writing alone.

If a challenge to the validity of a will has merit, it should be resolved, however, some will contests are based on unfounded allegations. After all, the testator is not there to defend his or her testamentary wishes.

To prevent unwarranted will contests, a testator can use a videotaped will to supplement a written will. Videotaping a will that can withstand challenges by disgruntled relatives and alleged heirs involves a certain amount of planning.

Exhibit 30.4
Per Capita Distribution

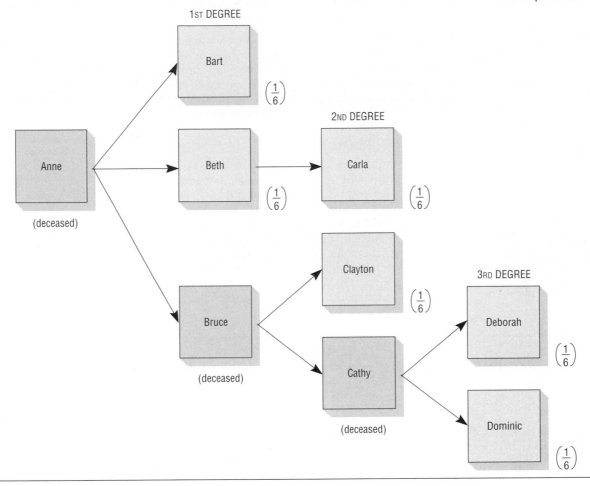

The following procedures should be followed. A written will should be prepared to comply with the state's Statute of Wills. The video session should not begin until after the testator has become familiar with the document. The video should begin with the testator reciting the will verbatim. Next, the lawyer should ask the testator questions to demonstrate the testator's sound mind and understanding of the implications of his actions. The execution ceremony—the signing of the will by the testator and the attestation by the witnesses—should be the last segment on the film. The videotape should then be stored in a safe place.

With the testator's actions crystallized on videotape, a judge or jury will be able to determine the testator's mental capacity at the time of making the will and the voluntariness of his or her testamentary gifts. In addition, fraudulent competing wills will crumble in the face of such proof.

In the future, it is likely that videotaped wills will become invaluable evidential tools. Whether such wills alone without a writing will be recognized as testamentary instruments will depend on the development of state laws.

1. Will video wills prevent fraud? Explain.

SPECIAL TYPES OF WILLS

The law recognizes several types of wills that do not meet all of the requirements previously discussed. The special types of wills admitted by the courts include:

holographic will   Will that is entirely handwritten and signed by the testator.

nuncupative will   Oral will that is made before a witness during the testator's last illness. Also called a *dying declaration* or *deathbed will*.

joint will   A will that is executed by two or more testators.

mutual wills   Occurs where two or more testators execute separate wills that leave their property to each other on the condition that the survivor leave the remaining property on his or her death as agreed by the testators.

- **Holographic wills.** Wills that are entirely handwritten and signed by the testator. The writing may be in ink, pencil, crayon, or some other writing instrument. Many states recognize the validity of such wills even though they are not witnessed.
- **Nuncupative wills.** Oral wills that are made before witnesses. Such wills are usually valid only if they are made during the testator's last illness. They are sometimes called **deathbed wills** or **dying declarations**.

Joint and Mutual Wills

If two or more testators execute the same instrument as their will, the document is called a **joint will**. A joint will may be held invalid as to one testator but not the others.

Mutual or **reciprocal wills** arise where two or more testators execute separate wills that make testamentary dispositions of their property to each other on the condition that the survivor leave the remaining property on his or her death as agreed by the testators. The wills are usually separate instruments with reciprocal terms. Because of their contractual nature, mutual wills cannot be unilaterally revoked after one of the parties has died.

The enforcement of a mutual will was at issue in the following case.

CASE 30.3

Robison v. Graham
799 P.2d 610 (1990) Supreme Court of Oklahoma

Facts Mary Kay Graham (Mary) and William Clyde Graham (Clyde) were married in 1942. On March 3, 1973, Mary and Clyde executed a mutual and cojoint will. In the will, they left all of each other's property to the survivor, with the survivor agreeing to leave half of the remaining property to Kathryn Robison and the other half in trust to William Lee Robison. Mary and Clyde agreed not to revoke, alter, or amend the will, except by mutual written consent.

The will was not revoked prior to Mary's death on April 16, 1979. In May 1981, Clyde married Stella E. Berry (Stella). He placed his property in joint tenancy with Stella and executed a new will. The new will revoked his prior one and, other than a specific devise, designated Stella as the beneficiary of the remainder of his estate. The marriage lasted until Clyde's death in 1985. Stella introduced the new will to probate. The beneficiaries of the mutual will sued, alleging breach of the mutual will. The trial court held in favor of the original beneficiaries. The court of appeals reversed. The original beneficiaries appealed.

Issue Is the mutual will enforceable?

Decision Yes. The state supreme court held that Clyde breached the mutual will that he had made with Mary. The supreme court vacated the judgment of the court of appeals and imposed a constructive trust on Clyde's estate in favor of the beneficiaries of the mutual will.

Reason A written contract to make a will may be enforced. This is especially true where the joint will is probated and the survivor accepts the benefits. The language of the will clearly expressed Clyde's and Mary's intent to make a binding and irrevocable contract concerning the disposition of their property. Clyde breached this contractual will by revoking it and executing a subsequent will.

CASE QUESTIONS

Critical Legal Thinking Should mutual wills be enforced? Why or why not?

Ethics Did Clyde act ethically in what he did?

Business Implication Why do people make mutual wills?

INTESTATE SUCCESSION

If a person dies without a will, or his will fails for some legal reason, his property is distributed to his relatives pursuant to the state's **intestacy statute**. Although these statutes differ from state to state, the general rule is that the deceased's real property is distributed according to the intestacy statute of the state where the real property is located, and the deceased's personal property is distributed according to the intestacy statute of the state where the deceased had his or her permanent residence.

Relatives who receive property under these statutes are called **heirs**. Intestacy statutes usually leave the deceased's property to his or her heirs in this order: spouse, children, lineal heirs (e.g., grandchildren, parents, brothers and sisters), collateral heirs (e.g., aunts, uncles, nieces, nephews), and other next of kin (e.g., cousins). If the deceased has no surviving relatives, the deceased's property **escheats** (goes) to the state.

In-laws do not inherit under most intestacy statutes. If a child dies before his or her parents, the child's spouse does not receive the inheritance.

intestate The state of having died without leaving a will.

intestacy statute A state statute that specifies how a deceased's property will be distributed if he or she dies without a will or if the last will is declared void and there is no prior valid will.

heir The receiver of property under intestacy statutes.

PROBATE

When a person dies, his or her property must be collected, debts and taxes paid, and the remainder of the estate distributed to the beneficiaries of the will or the heirs under the state intestacy statute. This process is called **settlement of the estate** or **probate**. The process and procedures for settling an estate are governed by state statute. A specialized state court, called the **probate court**, usually supervises the administration and settlement of an estate.

A **personal representative** must be appointed to administer the estate during its settlement phase. If the testator's will names the personal representative, that person is called an *executor* or *executrix*.[3] If no one is named or if the decedent died intestate, the court will appoint an *administrator* or *administratrix*.[4] Usually, this party is a relative of the deceased or a bank. An attorney is usually appointed to help administer the estate and to complete the probate.

settlement of the estate The process of a deceased's property being collected, debts and taxes being paid, and the remainder of the estate being distributed.

The Uniform Probate Code

The **Uniform Probate Code (UPC)** was promulgated to establish uniform rules for the creation of wills, the administration of estates, and the resolution of conflicts in settling estates. These rules provide a speedy, efficient, and less expensive method for settling estates than many existing state laws. Only about one-third of the states have adopted all or part of the UPC.

Uniform Probate Code (UPC) A model law promulgated to establish uniform rules for the creation of wills, the administration of estates, and the resolution of conflicts in settling estates.

ETHICAL PERSPECTIVE

The Right to Die and Living Wills

Technological breakthroughs have greatly increased the life span of human beings. This same technology, however, permits life to be sustained long after a person is "brain dead." Some people say they have a right to refuse such treatment. Others argue that

human life must be preserved at all costs. The U.S. Supreme Court was called upon to decide the **"right to die"** issue in the case of Nancy Cruzan.

In 1983, an automobile accident left Ms. Cruzan, a 25-year-old Missouri woman, in an irre-

versible coma. Four years later, Nancy's parents petitioned a state court judge to permit the hospital to withdraw the artificial feeding tube that had been keeping Nancy alive. The judge agreed. However, Missouri's attorney general

continued

intervened and asked an appellate court to reverse the lower court's decision. The appellate court sided with the attorney general. The appellate court held that the family had not proven with certainty that Nancy herself would have wanted the treatment stopped.

In reviewing the Missouri court's decision, eight of the nine justices of the U.S. Supreme Court acknowledged that the right to refuse medical treatment is a personal liberty protected by the U.S. Constitution. However, the Court also recognized that the states have an interest in preserving life. This interest can be expressed through a requirement for clear and convincing proof that the patient did not want to be sustained by artificial means. The Missouri attorney general then withdrew from the case, and a Missouri judge finally permitted the family to have Nancy's tubes withdrawn. She died shortly after.

The clear message of the Supreme Court's opinion is that people who do not want their lives prolonged indefinitely by artificial means had better sign **a living will** that stipulates their wishes before catastrophe strikes and they become unable to express themselves because of an illness or an accident. The living will could state which lifesaving measures they do and do not want. Alternatively, they could state that they want any such treatments withdrawn if doctors determine that there is no hope of a meaningful recovery. The living will provides clear and convincing proof of a patient's wishes with respect to medical treatment.

Although the Supreme Court's opinion seems to sanction the general use of living wills, there is widespread disparity among states on this issue. For example, several states have yet to enact legislation authorizing the use of living wills. Additionally, there is no consistency among the states

that have passed living-will laws. For example, some states permit living wills to be activated only when death is at hand. Other state statutes complicate the issue by specifying types of treatment, such as artificial feeding tubes, that cannot be withdrawn, no matter what the patient's living will says.

People realize that what happened to the Cruzans could happen to them—at any age, in any place, without warning. For the more than 80 percent of the American adult population who support the right to die, the *Cruzan* case gives the ability, through the use of a living will, to control such decisions. [*Cruzan v. Director, Missouri Department of Health*, 497 U.S. 261, 110 S.Ct. 2841, 111 L.Ed.2d 224 (1990)]

1. Should persons be granted the "right to die"? If so, under what conditions?
2. Would you sign a living will? Why or why not?

TRUSTS

trust A legal arrangement established when one person transfers title to property to another person to be held and used for the benefit of a third person.

settlor or trustor Person who creates a trust.

trustee Person who holds legal title to the trust corpus and manages the trust for the benefit of the beneficiary or beneficiaries.

beneficiary Person for whose benefit a trust is created.

trust corpus The property held in trust.

A **trust** is a legal arrangement under which one person (the **settlor**, **trustor**, or **transferor**) delivers and transfers legal title to property to another person (the **trustee**) to be held and used for the benefit of a third person (the **beneficiary**). The property held in trust is called the **trust corpus** or **trust res**. The trustee has legal title to the trust corpus, and the beneficiary has equitable title. Unlike wills, trusts are not public documents, so property can be transferred in privacy. Exhibit 30.5 shows the parties to a trust.

Trusts often provide that any trust income is to be paid to a person called the *income beneficiary*. The person to receive the trust corpus upon the termination of the trust is called the *remainderman*. The income beneficiary and the remainderman can be the same person or different persons. The designated beneficiary can be any identifiable person, animal (such as a pet), charitable organization, or other institution or cause that the settlor chooses. An entire class of persons—for example, "my grandchildren"—can be named.

A trust can allow the trustee to invade (use) the trust corpus for certain purposes. These purposes can be named (e.g., "for the beneficiary's college education"). The trust agreement usually specifies how the receipts and expenses of the trust are to be divided between the income beneficiary and the remainderman.

Generally, the trustee has broad management powers over the trust property. This means that the trustee can invest the trust property to preserve its capital and make it productive. The trustee must follow any restrictions on investments contained in the trust agreement or state statute.

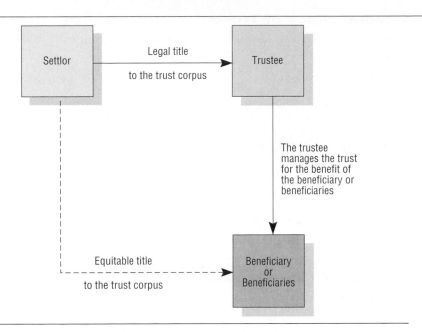

Exhibit 30.5
Parties to a Trust

TYPES OF TRUSTS

Express Trusts

Express trusts are voluntarily created by the settlor. They usually are written. The written agreement is called a **trust instrument** or **trust agreement**.

Express trusts fall into two categories. The first, *inter vivos* **trusts**, or **living trusts**, are created while the settlor is alive. The settlor transfers legal title of property to a named trustee to hold, administer, and manage for the benefit of named beneficiaries. The second, **testamentary trusts**, are created by will. In other words, the trust comes into existence when the settlor dies. If the will that establishes the trust is found to be invalid, the trust is also invalid.

Implied Trusts

Implied trusts are trusts that are imposed by law. Such trusts are divided into two categories: constructive trusts and resulting trusts.

A **constructive trust** is an equitable trust that is implied by law to avoid fraud, unjust enrichment, and injustice. In constructive trust arrangements, the holder of the actual title to property (i.e., the trustee) holds the property in trust for its rightful owner.

CONSIDER THIS EXAMPLE: Suppose Thad and Kaye are partners. Assume Kaye embezzles partnership funds and uses the stolen funds to purchase a piece of real estate. In this case, the court can impose a constructive trust under which Kaye (who holds actual title to the land) is considered a trustee who is holding the property in trust for Thad, its rightful owner.

A **resulting trust** is created by the conduct of the parties.

CONSIDER THIS EXAMPLE: Henry is purchasing a piece of real estate but cannot attend the closing. He asks his brother, Gregory, to attend the closing and take title to the property until he can return. In this case, Gregory holds the title to the property as trustee for Henry until he returns.

express trust A trust created voluntarily by the settlor.

***inter vivos* trust** A trust that is created while the settlor is alive.

testamentary trust A trust created by will; the trust comes into existence when the settlor dies.

implied trust A trust that is implied by law or from the conduct of the parties.

constructive trust An equitable trust that is imposed by law to avoid fraud, unjust enrichment, and injustice.

resulting trust A trust that is created by the conduct of the parties.

Special Types of Trusts

Trusts may be created for special purposes. Three common types of special trusts follow:

> *"A constructive trust is the formula through which the conscience of equity finds expression."*
> J. Cardozo
> *Beatty v. Guggenheim Exploration Co.* (1919)

1. **Charitable trusts**, which are created for the benefit of a segment of society or society in general. A trust that is created for the construction and maintenance of a public park is an example of a charitable trust.
2. **Spendthrift trusts**, which are designed to prevent a beneficiary's personal creditors from reaching his or her trust interest. All control over the trust is removed from the beneficiary. Personal creditors still can go after trust income that is paid to the beneficiary, however.
3. **Totten trusts**, which are created when a person deposits money in a bank account in his or her own name and holds it as a trustee for the benefit of another person. A totten trust is a tentative trust because (a) the trustee can add or withdraw funds from the account and (b) the trust can be revoked at any time prior to his death or completing delivery of the funds to the beneficiary.

TERMINATION OF A TRUST

A trust is irrevocable unless the settlor reserves the right to revoke it. Most trusts fall into the first category.

Usually, a trust either contains a specific termination date or provides that it will terminate upon the happening of an event (e.g., when the remainderman reaches a certain age). Upon termination, the trust corpus is distributed as provided in the trust agreement.

WORKING THE WEB

Business Insurance This magazine has a Web site with all kinds of information about business insurance.

Visit at http://www.businessinsurance.com/

Federal Deposit Insurance Corporation Everything you ever wanted to know about the Federal Deposit Insurance Corporation is available through its Web site.

Visit at www.fdic.gov/

Uniform Probate Code Cornell University maintains the Uniform Probate Code Web site.

Visit at http://www.law.cornell.edu/uniform/probate.html

Social Security Online The Social Security System has a Web site that gives you lots of information about retirement and other social security benefits.

Visit at http://www.ssa.gov/SSA_Home.html/

Free Advice This Web site has lots of general information on legal issues. It is not a substitute for consulting an attorney if you need one.

Visit at http://freeadvice.com/

CYBER EXERCISES:

1. Check out *Cyberbeat*, articles on insurance related technical applications and industry issues, on the Business Insurance Web site.
2. Find the directory of the Federal Deposit Insurance Corporation.
3. Has your state adopted the Uniform Probate Code? If so, has it adopted it in its entirety or in part?
4. Using Social Security Online, find out how to request your Personal Earnings and Benefit Estimate Statement.
5. Can you find Free Advice about gift tax law?

CHAPTER SUMMARY

INSURANCE, P. 754

Insurance	1. A contract whereby one party (insurer) undertakes to indemnify another party (insured) against loss, damage, or liability arising from a contingent or unknown event.
	2. Insurance is based on the concept of *risk pooling*—that is, transferring and distributing the risk of loss among a large number of persons (insureds).
	3. Parties:
	a. *Insured*. Person who purchases insurance to cover a risk.
	b. *Insurer*. The insurance company (or underwriter) that is obligated to pay insurance proceeds if an insured risk occurs.
	c. *Reinsurer*. An insurance company that purchases insurance contracts from other insurance companies and is obligated to pay insurance proceeds if an insured risk occurs.
	d. *Agent*. Party who sells insurance exclusively for one insurance company.
	e. *Broker*. Party who is an independent contractor and sells insurance for a number of insurance companies.
	f. *Policy*. The insurance contract between the insured and the insurer.
	g. *Premium*. The money the insured is obligated to pay the insurer for insurance coverage.
Insurable Interest	A person must have an insurable interest in anything he or she insures. That is, the person must benefit from the preservation of the life, health, property, or other interest insured.
Regulation of the Insurance Industry	The federal McCarran-Ferguson Act gave the regulation of insurance to the states. States have enacted laws that require the licensing of insurance agents and brokers and regulate insurance companies.

THE INSURANCE CONTRACT, P. 757

The Insurance Contract	Insurance contracts are governed by the law of contracts and statutes enacted to regulate the insurance contract.
Deductible Clause	Requires insureds to pay a certain amount of the loss before the insurer is obligated to pay.
Coinsurance Clause	Requires an owner to insure his or her property to a certain percent of its value to recover the face value of the property.
Exclusions from Coverage Clause	Stipulates exclusions from insurance coverage (e.g., preexisting conditions).
Modification of Insurance	The insurer and insured may modify an insurance contract by adding an *endorsement* to the policy or executing a document called a *rider*.
Incontestability Statutes	Prohibit insurers from contesting statements made by insureds after the passage of a stipulated number of years.
Cancellation of Insurance	*Grace period*. Time period which an insured may pay an overdue premium and during which the insurance remains in effect.
Duties of Insured and Insurer	Duties of the insured:
	1. Pay premium stipulated in the policy.
	2. Notify the insurer after the occurrence of an insured event.
	3. Cooperate with the insurer in the investigation of claims.

Duties of the insurer:	1. Defend against suits brought against the insured that involve a claim within the coverage of the policy. 2. Pay legitimate claims up to the policy limit.
Subrogation	If an insurer pays a claim to an insured for liability or property damage caused by a third party, the insurer succeeds to the right of the insured to recover from the third party.

DEFENSES OF THE INSURER, P. 760

Misrepresentation and Concealment	Misrepresentation or concealment of material information by the insured prior to the running of the incontestability period.
Breach of Warranty	An *affirmative warranty* is a statement asserting facts to be true. A *promissory warrant* stipulates that facts will continue to be true.

WILLS, P. 761

Wills	A declaration of how a person wants his or her property to be distributed upon his or her death.
Changing a Will	*Codicil.* A legal way to change an existing will. It must be executed with the same formalities as a will.
Joint and Mutual Wills	1. *Joint will.* Two or more testators execute the same instrument as their will. 2. *Mutual or reciprocal wills.* Two or more testators execute separate wills that leave property in favor of the other on condition that the survivor leave the remaining property on his or her death as agreed by the testators.
Probate	Legal process of settling a deceased person's estate.

Requirements for Making a Will	1. *Statute of Wills.* A state statute that establishes the requirements for making a valid will.
	2. The normal requirements for making a will are:
	  a. *Testamentary capacity.* The testator must have been of legal age and "sound mind" when the will was made.
	  b. *Writing.* A will must be in writing except for certain special wills.
	  c. *Testator's signature.* A will must be signed by the testator.
	  d. *Attestation by witnesses.* Wills must be attested to by the stipulated number of mentally competent and uninterested witnesses.

Parties to a Will	Parties to a will: 1. *Testator or testatrix.* Person who makes a will. 2. *Beneficiary.* Person designated in the will to receive the testator's property. There may be multiple beneficiaries. 3. *Executor or executrix.* Person named in a will to administer the testator's estate during the settlement of the estate.

TYPES OF TESTAMENTARY GIFTS, P. 764

	1. *Specific gift.* Gift of a specifically mentioned piece of property (e.g., a ring). 2. *General gift.* Gift that does not identify the specific property from which the gift is to be made (e.g., gift of cash). 3. *Residuary gift.* Gift of the remainder of the testator's estate after the debts, taxes, and specific and general gifts have been paid.
Ademption and Abatement	1. *Ademption.* If a testator leaves a specific gift but the property is no longer in the estate when the testator dies, the beneficiary of that gift receives nothing.

	2. *Abatement*. If the testator's estate is insufficient to pay the stated gifts, the gifts are abated (reduced) in the following order: (1) residuary gifts, then (2) general gifts proportionately.
Per Stirpes and Per Capita Distribution	1. *Per stirpes*. Lineal descendants inherit by representation of their parent; that is, they split what their deceased parent would have received. 2. *Per capita*. Lineal descendants equally share the property of the estate without regard to degree.

SPECIAL TYPES OF WILLS, P. 768

Special Types of Wills	1. *Holographic will*. Will that is entirely handwritten and signed by the testator. Most states recognize the validity of these wills even though they are not witnessed. 2. *Nuncupative will*. Oral wills that are made by dying persons before witnesses. Many states recognize these oral wills. Also called a *deathbed will* or a *dying declaration*.

INTESTATE SUCCESSION, P. 769

Intestate Succession	1. *Intestacy statute*. State statute that stipulates how a deceased's property will be distributed if he or she dies without leaving a will or if the will fails for some legal reason. 2. *Heirs*. Relatives who receive property under an intestacy statute. 3. *Escheat*. Intestacy statutes provide that if there are no heirs, the deceased's property goes to the state.

PROBATE, P. 769

Administrator	*Administrator or administratrix*. Person named to administer the estate of a deceased person who dies intestate. An administrator is also named where an executor is not named in a will or the executor cannot or does not serve.
Simultaneous Deaths	The Uniform Simultaneous Death Act provides that if people who would inherit property from each other die simultaneously, each deceased person's property is distributed as though he or she had survived.
Undue Influence	A will may be found to be invalid if it was made under undue influence, where one person takes advantage of another person's mental, emotional, or physical weakness and unduly persuades that person to make a will. 1. *Murder disqualification*. A person who murders another person cannot inherit the victim's property.

TRUSTS, P. 770

Trusts	A legal arrangement whereby one person delivers and transfers legal title to property to another person to be held and used for the benefit of a third person.
	1. *Trust corpus*. The property that is held in trust. Also called *trust res*.
	2. *Parties:*
	  a. *Settlor*. Person who establishes a trust. Also called a *trustor* or *transferor*.
	  b. *Trustee*. Person to whom *legal title* of the trust assets are transferred. Responsible for managing the trust assets as established by the trust and law.
	  c. *Beneficiary*. Person for whose benefit a trust is created. Holds *equitable title* to the trust assets. There can be multiple beneficiaries, including:

i. *Income beneficiary*. Person to whom trust income is to be paid.

ii. *Remainderman*. Person who is entitled to receive the trust corpus upon the termination of the trust.

TYPES OF TRUSTS, P. 771	
Express Trusts	Voluntarily created by the settlor. There are two types: 1. *Inter vivos trust*. Created while the settlor is alive. Also called a *living trust*. 2. *Testamentary trust*. Created by will and comes into existence when the settlor dies.
Implied Trusts	Imposed by law or from the conduct of the parties. There are two types: 1. *Constructive trust*. Equitable trust that is imposed by law to avoid fraud, unjust enrichment, and injustice. 2. *Resulting trust*. Trust created from the conduct of the parties.
Special Types of Trusts	1. *Charitable trust*. Created for the benefit of a segment of society or society in general. 2. *Spendthrift trust*. A trust whereby the creditors of the beneficiary cannot recover the trust's assets to satisfy debts owed to them by the beneficiary. 3. *Totten trust*. Created when a person deposits money in a bank account in his or her own name and holds it as a trust for the benefit of another person.

CRITICAL LEGAL THINKING CASES

30.1 Exclusion Richard Usher's home was protected by a homeowners policy issued by National American Insurance Company of California. The policy included personal liability insurance. A provision in the policy read: "Personal liability and coverage do not apply to bodily injury or property damage arising out the ownership, maintenance, use, loading, or unloading of a motor vehicle owned or operated by, or rented or loaned to any insured." On August 24, 1984, Usher parked a Chevrolet van he owned in his driveway. He left the van's side door open while he loaded the van in preparation for a camping trip. While Usher was inside his house, several children, including two-year-old Graham Coburn, began playing near the van. One of the children climbed into the driver's seat and moved the shift lever from "park" to "reverse." The van rolled backward, crushing Coburn and killing him. Coburn's parents sued Usher for negligence. Is the accident covered by Usher's homeowners policy? [*National American Insurance Company of California v. Coburn*, 209 Cal.App.3d 914, 257 Cal.Rptr. 591 (Cal.App. 1989)]

30.2 Uninsured Motorist Coverage Antonio Munoz and Jacinto Segura won some money from two unidentified men in a craps game in a Los Angeles park. When Munoz and Segura left the park in Segura's care, the two men followed them in another car. After chasing Segura's car for several miles on a freeway, the men in the other car fired several gunshots at Segura's car, killing Munoz. At the time of the shooting Segura

had an automobile insurance policy issued by Nationwide Mutual Insurance Company (Nationwide). Munoz was an additional insured on the policy. A provision in the policy covered damages from "an accident arising out of the use of an uninsured vehicle." Munoz's widow and child filed a claim with Nationwide to recover for Munoz's death. Nationwide rejected the claim. Who wins? [*Nationwide Mutual Insurance Company v. Munoz*, 245 Cal.Rptr. 324 (Cal.App. 1988)]

30.3 Duty to Pay Premiums The Mutual Life Insurance Company of New York (Mutual Life) issued a $100,000 life insurance policy on the life of 65-year-old Alex Brecher, effective December 22, 1977. In consideration for the policy, Brecher agreed to pay an annual insurance premium of $7,830 in 12 monthly installments. On July 14, 1983, Brecher made a written request and authorization to have the insurance company withdraw the premiums directly from his checking account at Citibank. The insurance company's first attempt to do so, on July 15, 1983, was returned unpaid. Mutual Life and Brecher were informed that one of Brecher's creditors had placed a restraining order on the bank account. On July 29, 1983, Mutual Life sent Brecher a returned check notice, advising him that the July withdrawal had been dishonored by his bank and that in order to keep the policy in force both the July and August premiums would have to be paid before August 28. Mutual Life received Brecher's check for the outstanding amounts on August 26. When Mutual Life tried to cash the check, which was drawn on the Citibank account, the bank returned it unpaid, marked "refer to maker." Brecher made no further attempts to pay the insurance premiums. He died on September 18, 1983. His widow, the beneficiary of life insurance policy, filed a claim to recover $100,000 from Mutual Life. When Mutual Life refused to pay, the widow sued. Who wins? [*Brecher v. Mutual Life Insurance Company of New York*, 501 N.Y.S.2d 879 (N.Y.A pp. 1986)]

30.4 Duty to Defend In February 1983, Judith Isenhart purchased a 1983 Dodge station wagon. She then contacted Ed Carpenter, an agent of the National Automobile and Casualty Insurance Company (National) and told him she was interested in obtaining "full coverage" for the car. The policy that Carpenter provided to Judith provided coverage for bodily injury, property damage, medical costs, and collision damage. The policy specifically exempted coverage for accidents involving "non-owned automobiles." In July 1984, Judith's 16-year-old son Matt purchased a 1969 Volkswagen. Insurance for this car was obtained from Allstate Insurance Company (Allstate). Two months after buying the car, Matt had an accident in which a passenger in the Volkswagen, Thea Stewart, was severely injured. Stewart sued Matt and Judith. Allstate agreed to defend the suit up to the limits of its policy. When National was contacted regarding the accident, the company refused to defend Judith in the suit and denied coverage based on the policy's exclusion. Must National defend Judith? [*National Automobile and Casualty Insurance Company v. Stewart*, 223 Cal.App.3d 452, 272 Cal.Rptr. 625 (Cal.App. 1990)]

30.5 Misrepresentation M&M Restaurant Inc. (M&M) operated a restaurant in the state of New York. M&M purchased fire insurance for the restaurant from St. Paul Surplus Lines Insurance Company (St. Paul). On July 10, 1984, a fire caused major damage to the restaurant. M&M submitted a claim against St. Paul for losses sustained by the restaurant in the fire. An investigation of the fire by the local police department led to the filing of criminal charges against the owners of M&M. Among the findings of the investigation was that M&M had willfully concealed factual information and misled St. Paul in obtaining the insurance. On May 25, 1989, the owners of M&M were convicted of insurance fraud, grand larceny, and falsifying business records. St. Paul refused to pay M&M's insurance claim. Who wins? [*M&M Restaurant Inc. v. St. Paul Surplus Lines Insurance Company*, N.Y. Law Journal, June 18, 1990, p. 29 (N.Y.Sup. 1990)]

30.6 Concealment A federal regulation to the Resource Conservation and Discovery Act required certain manufacturers to insure against pollution hazards. The regulation was adopted on January 12, 1981. Early in September 1981, Advanced Micro Devices, Inc. (AMD), a company covered by the regulation, purchased the required insurance from Great American Surplus Lines Insurance Company (Great American). Before issuing the policy, Great American asked AMD to disclose any preexisting conditions which could give rise to a claim retroactive to August 27, 1981. AMD warranted that there were none. AMD made this statement despite the existence of a corporation memorandum written by AMD's environmental supervisor on July 21, 1981. The memo warned that toxic waste was escaping from an underground steel tank in AMD's acid neutral-

ization system "C" and that AMD was "far from being in compliance" with environmental laws. Great American issued the insurance policy. In 1982, the government ordered AMD to undertake a $1.5 million cleanup of the toxic contaminants surrounding the steel tank in system "C." AMD filed a claim for this amount with Great American, which refused to pay. AMD sued. Who wins? [*Advanced Micro Devices, Inc. v. Great American Surplus Lines Insurance Company*, 199 Cal.App.3d 791, 245 Cal.Rptr. 44 (Cal.App. 1988)]

30.7 Subrogation In 1977, Home Indemnity Company (Home Indemnity) agreed to insure the Liberty Savings Association (Liberty), a savings and loan association, for losses that Liberty might incur through the dishonest or fraudulent acts of its employees. In August 1983, Liberty filed a proof of loss with Home Indemnity alleging losses of $579,922. The claim was based on the conversion of $98,372 by Richard Doty, the former president and managing officer of Liberty, and loan losses resulting from four unsecured loans Doty made to friends and relatives. None of the borrowers filed financial statements to qualify for the loans. Home Indemnity paid Liberty for the losses and received a general assignment of Liberty's right to recover against Doty and the borrowers. Home Indemnity then sued Liberty's board of directors, claiming they were negligent in their supervision of Doty. Who wins? [*Home Indemnity Company v. Shaffer*, 860 F.2d 186 (6th Cir. 1988)]

30.8 Formalities of a Will On or about June 10, 1959, Martha Jansa executed a will naming her two sons as executors and leaving all of her property to them. The will was properly signed and attested to by witnesses. Thereafter, Martha died. When Martha's safe-deposit box at a bank was opened, the original of this will was discovered along with two other instruments that were dated after the will. One was a handwritten document that left her home to her grandson, with the remainder of her estate to her two sons; this document was not signed. The second document was a typed version of the handwritten one; this document was signed by Martha but was not attested to by witnesses. Which of the three documents should be admitted to probate? [*In re Estate of Jansa*, 670 S.W.2d 767 (Tex.App. 1984)]

30.9 Mental Capacity On March 18, 1987, Everett Clark met with William Wham, an attorney, to discuss the preparation of a will. Clark, who had never married and lived with his sister, was to return the following day to execute his will. Clark was hospitalized that evening with a perforated ulcer. He underwent surgery on March 19. Subsequent to the surgery, and until the time of his death, he was in intensive care and unable to communicate verbally. On March 23, Clark's cousin John Bailey retrieved the will prepared by Wham and took it to attorney Frank Walker to have him finalize it. Walker testified that he took the will to the hospital on March 25. Immediately prior to the execution of the will, Walker asked Clark a few questions. Walker testified that Clark knew what he was doing. Dorothy Smith, an attesting witness, testified that Clark could not talk, but answered her questions by nodding yes or no. She asked Clark "if he knew me and if he knew we were all there and he shook his head yes." She testified that he also shook his head yes to the question "Is this your will and testament?" "Is John Bailey your cousin?" and "Do you want to leave everything to

John Bailey?" Clark signed the will with an "X." On March 26, Clark passed into a coma and died. Bailey introduced the will into probate, but another relative of Clark's challenged it. Is the will valid? [*Bailey v. Bailey*, 561 N.E.2d 367 (Ill.App. 1990)]

30.10 Inheritance In October 1973, Mr. and Mrs. Pate executed separate wills that followed a common plan in disposing of their respective estates. Each will provided for the establishment of trusts with a life estate to their son Billy, and upon his death the estate was to be distributed "in equal shares per stirpes to my natural born grandchildren." Mr. and Mrs. Pate had two sons, Billy and Wallace. Billy's first marriage ended in divorce without children. Billy's second marriage also ended in

divorce without children, although his second wife had a daughter by her previous marriage. Billy married again, and to date no children have been born to his 32-year-old wife. Wallace first married in 1952. Of that marriage five children were born, each before the time that the Pates made their wills. After that marriage ended in divorce, Wallace married his present wife. There are no children of the second marriage, but there are stepchildren by Wallace's second wife. One of Wallace's daughters has two children by her marriage. Mr. Pate died on November 9, 1979, leaving an estate of $1.6 million. Mrs. Pate died on October 21, 1983, leaving an estate of $6.7 million. Who inherits the estate? [*Pate v. Ford*, 360 S.E.2d 145 (S.C.App. 1987)]

ETHICS CASES

30.11 Ethical Perspective In 1983, Lewis Coe bought a $500,000 life insurance policy from Farmers New World Life Insurance Company (Farmers) from its authorized agent, Hannify. The policy, which was payable in monthly installments, contained a clause allowing for the insurance to remain in effect for a 31-day grace period if the insured failed to pay a premium by the due date. In February 1984, Lewis informed Hannify that he wanted to cancel the policy. Farmers sent Lewis a cancellation form that he signed and returned on or about March 1, 1984. At the time Farmer received the written cancellation notice, Lewis had paid the monthly premium for February, covering the period ending March 10, 1984. Lewis died on April 8, 1984. His widow sued Farmers for the policy proceeds claiming that Lewis died during the 31-day grace period provided by the policy. Farmers claimed the policy had been canceled and the grace period did not apply. Who wins? Did either party act unethically in this case? [*Coe v. Farmers New World Life Insurance Company*, 209 Cal.App.3d 600, 257 Cal.Rptr. 411 (Cal.App. 1989)]

30.12 Ethical Perspective In 1967, Homer and Edna Jones, husband and wife, executed a joint will that provided "We will and give to our survivor, whether it be Homer Jones or Edna Jones, all property and estate of which the first of us that dies may be seized and possessed. If we should both die in a common catastrophe, or upon the death of our survivor, we will and give all property and estate then remaining to our children, Leonida Jones Eschman, daughter, Sylvia Marie Jones, daughter, and Grady V. Jones, son, share and share alike."

Homer died in 1975, and Edna Jones received his entire estate under the 1967 will. In 1977, Edna executed a new will that left a substantially larger portion of the estate to her daughter, Sylvia Marie Jones, than to the other two children. Edna Jones died in 1982. Edna's daughter introduced the 1977 will for probate. The other two children introduced the 1967 will for probate. Did Edna act ethically in this case? Who wins? [*Jones v. Jones*, 718 S.W.2d 416 (Tex.App. 1986)]

CRITICAL LEGAL THINKING WRITING ASSIGNMENT

Read Case A.30 in the Case Appendix [*Saritejdiam, Inc. v. Excess Insurance Company, Ltd.*]. This case is excerpted from the court of appeals opinion. Review and brief the case. In your brief, be sure to answer the following questions:

1. Was the "close personal custody and control" provision in the insurance policy plain and clear?

2. Summarize the factual details of the case.
3. What public policy is served by the exclusion of coverage in this case?
4. Do you think that the insurance policy met the reasonable expectations of the insured?

NOTES

[1] 15 U.S.C. § 1011–1015.
[2] Some states use the term *testator* regardless of the gender of the person making the will.

[3] Some states use the term *executor* regardless of the gender of the named person.
[4] Some states use the term *administrator* regardless of the gender of the appointee.

CASE A.1

LEE V. WEISMAN, 120 L.ED. 2D 467, 112 S.CT. 2649 (1992)
UNITED STATES SUPREME COURT

Kennedy, Justice (joined by Blackmun, Stevens, O'Conner, and Souter).

Deborah Weisman graduated from Nathan Bishop Middle School, a public school in Providence, at a formal ceremony in June 1989. She was about 14 years old. For many years it has been the policy of the Providence School committee and the Superintendent of Schools to permit principals to invite members of the clergy to give invocations and benedictions at middle school and high school graduations. Many, but not all, of the principals elected to include prayers as part of the graduation ceremonies. Acting for himself and his daughter, Deborah's father, Daniel Weisman, objected to any prayers at Deborah's middle school graduation, but to no avail. The school principal, petitioner Robert E. Lee, invited a rabbi to deliver prayers at the graduation exercises for Deborah's class. Rabbi Leslie Gutterman, of the Temple Beth El in Providence, accepted.

It has been the custom of Providence school officials to provide invited clergy with a pamphlet entitled "Guidelines for Civic Occasions," prepared by the National Conference of Christians and Jews. The Guidelines recommended that public prayers at nonsectarian civic ceremonies be composed with "inclusiveness and sensitivity," though they acknowledge that "prayer of any kind may be inappropriate on some civic occasions." The principal gave Rabbi Gutterman the pamphlet before the graduation and advised him the invocation and benediction should be nonsectarian.

Deborah's graduation was held on the premises of Nathan Bishop Middle School on June 29, 1989. Four days before the ceremony, Daniel Weisman, in his individual capacity as a Providence taxpayer and as next friend of Deborah, sought a temporary restraining order in the United States District Court for the District of Rhode Island to prohibit school officials from including an invocation or benediction in the graduation ceremony. The court denied the motion for lack of adequate time to consider it. Deborah and her family attended the graduation, where the prayers were recited. In July 1989, Daniel Weisman filed an amended complaint seeking a permanent injunction barring petitioners, various officials of the Providence public schools, from inviting the clergy to deliver invocations and benedictions at future graduations.

The case was submitted on stipulated facts. The district court held that petitioners' practice of including invocations and benedictions in public school graduations violated the Establishment Clause of the First Amendment, and it enjoined petitioners from continuing the practice. The court applied the three-part Establishment Clause test. Under that test, to satisfy the Establishment Clause a governmental practice must (1) reflect a clearly secular purpose, (2) have a primary effect that neither advances nor inhibits religion, and (3) avoid excessive government entanglement with religion. On appeal, the United States Court of Appeals for the First Circuit affirmed.

These dominant facts mark and control the confines of our decision: State officials direct the performance of a formal religious exercise at promotional and graduation ceremonies for secondary schools. Even for those students who object to the religious exercise, their attendance and participation in the state-sponsored religious activity are in a fair and real sense obligatory, though the school district does not require attendance as a condition for receipt of the diploma.

The controlling precedents as they relate to prayer and religious exercise in primary and secondary public schools compel the holding here that the policy of the city of Providence is an unconstitutional one. It is beyond dispute that, at a minimum, the Constitution guarantees that government may not coerce anyone to support or participate in religion or its exercise, or otherwise act in a way which "establishes a state religion or religious faith, or tends to do so."

We are asked to recognize the existence of a practice of nonsectarian prayer within the embrace of what is known as the Judeo-Christian tradition, prayer which is more acceptable than one which, for example, makes explicit references to the God of Israel, or to Jesus Christ, or to a patron saint. If common ground can be defined which permits once conflicting faiths to express the shared conviction that there is an ethic and a morality which transcend human invention, the sense of community and purpose sought by all decent societies might be advanced. But though the First Amendment does not allow the government to stifle prayers which aspire to these ends, neither does it permit the government to undertake that task for itself.

The sole question presented is whether a religious exercise may be conducted at a graduation ceremony in circumstances where, as we have found, young graduates who object are induced to conform. No holding by this Court suggests that a school can persuade or compel a student to participate in a religious exercise. That is being done here, and it is forbidden by the Establishment Clause of the First Amendment.

For the reasons we have stated, the judgment of the Court of Appeals is affirmed.

Scalia, Justice (joined by Rehnquist, White, and Thomas) dissenting, expressed the view that (1) the establishment of religion clause should not have been interpreted so as to invalidate a longstanding American tradition of nonsectarian prayer at public school graduations, (2) graduation invocations and benedictions involve no psychological coercion of students to participate in religious exercises, (3) the only coercion that is forbidden by the establishment of religion clause is that which is backed by a threat of penalty, and (4) the middle school principal did not direct or control the content of the prayers in question, and thus there was no pervasive government involvement with religious activity.

CASE A.2

RAMIREZ V. PLOUGH, INC. 15 CAL. APP. 4TH 1110, 12 CAL. RPTR. 2D 423 (1992) COURT OF APPEALS OF CALIFORNIA
Thaxter, Judge.

Jorge Ramirez, a minor, by his guardian ad litem Rosa Rivera, appeals from a summary judgment in favor of Plough, Inc. Appellant sued Plough alleging negligence, product liability, and fraud. The action sought damages for injuries sustained in March of 1986 when Jorge, who was then four months old, contracted Reye's Syndrome after ingesting St. Joseph Aspirin for Children (SJAC). Plough marketed and distributed SJAC.

Reye's Syndrome is a serious disease of unknown cause characterized by severe vomiting, lethargy, or irritability, which may progress to delirium or coma. The disease generally strikes children or teenagers who are recovering from a mild respiratory tract infection, influenza, chicken pox, or other viral illnesses. The mortality rate of the disease is high, and permanent brain damage occurs in many cases. As a result of contracting Reye's Syndrome, appellant suffered catastrophic injuries including quadriplegia, blindness, and profound mental retardation.

In the early 1980's, there was significant scientific debate concerning the cause of Reye's syndrome. Several state studies suggested a statistical association between the ingestion of aspirin and the disease. In December 1982, the federal government acknowledged the debate. After considering the state studies and their critics, the federal government rejected a proposal which would require a warning label and instead, undertook an independent study. Apparently, Plough participated in efforts to influence government officials and agencies to reject the label proposal which Plough considered premature.

In December 1985, the Food and Drug Administration (FDA) requested that aspirin manufacturers voluntarily place a label on aspirin products warning consumers of the possible association between aspirin and Reye's Syndrome. Plough voluntarily complied and began including a warning and insert in SJAC packaging. On June 5, 1986, the Reye's Syndrome warning became mandatory.

In March 1986, SJAC labeling bore the following warning: "Warning: Reye's Syndrome is a rare but serious disease which can follow flu or chicken pox in children and teenagers. While the cause of Reye's Syndrome is unknown, some reports claim aspirin may increase the risk of developing this disease. Consult a doctor before use in children or teenagers with flu or chicken pox." In addition, the SJAC package insert included the following statement: "The symptoms of Reye's Syndrome can include persistent vomiting, sleepiness and lethargy, violent headaches, unusual behavior, including disorientation, combativeness, and delirium. If any of these symptoms occur, especially following chicken pox or flu, call your doctor immediately, even if your child has not taken any medication. Reye's Syndrome is serious, so early detection and treatment are vital."

Rosa Rivera purchased SJAC on March 12, 1986, and administered it to appellant who was suffering from what appeared to be a cold or upper respiratory infection. She gave appellant the aspirin without reading the directions or warnings appearing on the SJAC packaging. The packaging was in English and Ms. Rivera can speak and understand only Spanish. She did not seek to have the directions or warnings translated from English to Spanish, even though members of her household spoke English.

The trial court granted Plough's motion for summary judgment on the grounds that "there is no duty to warn in a foreign language and there is no causal relationship between plaintiff's injury and defendant's activities."

It is undisputed SJAC was marketed and intended for the treatment of minor aches and pains associated with colds, flu, and minor viral illnesses. The SJAC box promised "fast, effective relief of fever and minor aches and pains of colds." Both parties accept the premise that Plough had a duty to warn consumers that the intended use of SJAC after a viral infection or chicken pox could lead to Reye's Syndrome, an illness with serious, possibly fatal, consequences. In March 1986, federal regulations requiring a Reye's Syndrome warning had been promulgated and were final, although not yet effective. The FDA had previously solicited voluntary labeling. In response to the request for voluntary labeling, Plough started packaging SJAC with explicit warnings of the risks of Reye's Syndrome. The scientific community had already confirmed and documented the relationship between Reye's Syndrome and the use of aspirin after a viral illness. There is no doubt Plough had a duty to warn of the Reye's Syndrome risk.

The question thus is whether the warning given only in English was adequate under the circumstances. Respondent argues that as a matter of law it has no duty to place foreign-language warnings on products manufactured to be sold in the United States and that holding manufacturers liable for failing to do so would violate public policy.

While the constitutional, statutory, regulatory, and judicial authorities relied on by respondent may reflect a public policy recognizing the status of English as an official language, nothing compels the conclusion that a manufacturer of a dangerous or defective product is immunized from liability when an English-only warning does not adequately inform non-English literate persons likely to use the product.

Plough's evidence showed that over 148 foreign languages are spoken in the United States and over 23 million Americans speak a language other than English in their homes. That evidence plainly does not prove that Plough used reasonable care in giving an English-only warning. Plough, then, resorts to arguing that the burden on manufacturers and society of requiring additional warnings is so "staggering" that the courts should preclude liability as a matter of law. We are not persuaded.

Certainly the burden and costs of giving foreign-language warnings is one factor for consideration in determining whether a manufacturer acted reasonably in using only English. The importance of that factor may vary from case to case depending upon other circumstances, such as the nature of the product, marketing efforts directed to segments of the population unlikely to be English-literate, and the actual and relative size of the consumer market which could reasonably be expected to speak or read only a certain foreign language. Plough presented no evidence from which we can gauge the extent of the burden under the facts of this case.

Ramirez submitted evidence that Plough knew Hispanics were an important part of the market for SJAC and that Hispanics often maintain their first language rather than learn English. SJAC was advertised in the Spanish media, both radio and television. That evidence raises material questions of fact concerning the foreseeability of purchase by a Hispanic not literate in English and the reasonableness of not giving a Spanish-language warning. If Plough has evidence conclusively showing that it would have been unreasonable to give its label warning in Spanish because of the burden, it did not present that evidence below.

Given the triable issues of material fact, if we accepted Plough's arguments in this case in effect we would be holding that failure to warn in a foreign language is not negligence, regardless of the circumstances. Such a sweeping grant of immunity should come from the legislative branch of government, not the judicial. In deciding that Plough did not establish its right to judgment as a matter of law, we do not hold that manufacturers are required to warn in languages other than English simply because it may be foreseeable that non-English literate persons are likely to use their products. Our decision merely recognizes that under some circumstances the standard of due care may require such warning.

Because the evidence shows triable issues of material fact and because Plough did not establish its immunity from liability as a matter of law, its motion for summary judgment should have been denied.

CASE A.3

GNAZZO V. SEARLE & CO., 973 F.2D 136 (1992)
U.S. COURT OF APPEALS FOR THE SECOND CIRCUIT

Pierce, Circuit Judge.

On November 11, 1974, Gnazzo had a CU-7 intrauterine device (IUD) inserted in her uterus for contraceptive purposes. The IUD was developed, marketed, and sold by G.D. Searle & Co. (Searle). When Gnazzo's deposition was taken, she stated that her doctor had informed her that "the insertion would hurt, but not for long," and that she "would have uncomfortable and probably painful periods for the first three to four months." On October 11, 1975, Gnazzo found it necessary to return to her physician due to excessive pain and cramping. During this visit she was informed by her doctor that he thought she had Pelvic Inflammatory Disease (PID). She recalled that he stated that the infection was possibly caused by venereal disease or the use of the IUD. The PID was treated with antibiotics and cleared up shortly thereafter. Less than one year later, Gnazzo was again treated for an IUD-associated infection. This infection was also treated with antibiotics. Gnazzo continued using the IUD until it was finally removed in December of 1977.

Following a laparoscopy in March of 1989, Gnazzo was informed by a fertility specialist that she was infertile because of PID-induced adhesions resulting from her prior IUD use. Subsequent to this determination, and at the request of her then-attorneys, Gnazzo completed a questionnaire dated May 11, 1989. In response to the following question, "when and why did you first suspect that your IUD had caused you any harm?" Gnazzo responded "sometime in 1981" and explained: "I was married in April 1981 so I stopped using birth control so I could get pregnant—nothing ever happened (of course) then I started hearing and reading about how damaging IUD's could be. I figured that was the problem, however, my marriage started to crumble, so I never persued the issue."

On May 4, 1990, Gnazzo initiated the underlying action against Searle. In an amended complaint, she alleged that she had suffered injuries as a result of her use of the IUD developed by Searle. Searle moved for summary judgment on the ground that Gnazzo's claim was time-barred by Connecticut's three-year statute of limitations for product liability actions. Searle argued, inter alia, that Gnazzo knew in 1981 that she had suffered harm caused by her IUD. Gnazzo contended that her cause of action against Searle accrued only when she learned from the fertility specialist that the IUD had caused her PID and subsequent infertility.

In a ruling dated September 18, 1991, the district court granted Searle's motion for summary judgment on the ground that Gnazzo's claim was time-barred by the applicable statute of limitations. In reaching this result, the court determined that Connecticut law provided no support for Gnazzo's contention that she should not have been expected to file her action until she was told of her infertility and the IUD's causal connection. This appeal followed.

On appeal, Gnazzo contends that the district court improperly granted Searle's motion for summary judgment because a genuine issue of material fact exists as to when she discovered, or reasonably should have discovered, her injuries and their causal connection to the defendant's alleged wrongful conduct. Summary judgment is appropriate when there is no genuine issue as to any material fact and the moving party is entitled to judgment as a matter of law. We consider the record in the light most favorable to the non-movant. However, the non-movant "may not rest upon the mere allegations of denials of her pleading, but must set forth specific facts showing that there is a genuine issue for trial."

Under Connecticut law, a product liability claim must be brought within "three years from the date when the injury is first sustained or discovered or in the exercise of reasonable care should have been discovered." In Connecticut, a cause of action accrues when a plaintiff suffers actionable harm. Actionable harm occurs when the plaintiff discovers or should discover, through the exercise of reasonable care, that he or she has been injured and that the defendant's conduct caused such injury.

Gnazzo contends that "the mere occurrence of a pelvic infection or difficulty in becoming pregnant does not necessarily result in notice to the plaintiff of a cause of action." Thus, she maintains that her cause of action did not accrue until 1989 when the fertility specialist informed her both that she was infertile and that this condition resulted from her previous use of the IUD.

Under Connecticut law, however, "the statute of limitations begins to run when the plaintiff discovers some form of actionable harm, not the fullest manifestation thereof. Therefore, as Gnazzo's responses to the questionnaire indicate, she suspected "sometime in 1981" that the IUD had caused her harm because she had been experiencing trouble becoming pregnant and had "started hearing and reading about how damaging IUD's could be and had figured that was the problem." Thus, by her own admission, Gnazzo had recognized, or should have recognized, the critical link between her injury and the defendant's causal connection to it. In other words she had "discovered or should have discovered through the exercise of reasonable care, that she had been injured and that Searle's conduct caused such injury." However, as Gnazzo acknowledged in the questionnaire, she did not pursue the "issue" at the time because of her marital problems. Thus, even when viewed in the light most favorable to Gnazzo, the non-moving party, we are constrained to find that she knew by 1981 that she had "some form of actionable harm." Consequently, by the time she commenced her action in 1990, Gnazzo was time-barred by the Connecticut statute of limitations.

Since we have determined that Gnazzo's cause of action commenced in 1981, we need not address Searle's additional contention that Gnazzo's awareness in 1975 of her PID and her purported knowledge of its causal connection to the IUD commenced the running of the Connecticut statute of limitations at that time.

We are sympathetic to Gnazzo's situation and mindful that the unavoidable result we reach in this case is harsh. Nevertheless, we are equally aware that "it is within the Connecticut General Assembly's constitutional authority to decide when claims for injury are to be brought. Where a plaintiff has failed to comply with this requirement, a court may not entertain the suit.

The judgment of the district court is affirmed.

CASE A.4

BRAUN V. SOLDIER OF FORTUNE MAGAZINE, INC., 968 F.2D 1110 (1992) UNITED STATES COURT OF APPEALS FOR THE ELEVENTH CIRCUIT.

Anderson, Circuit Judge.

In January 1985, Michael Savage submitted a personal service advertisement to *Soldier of Fortune* (*SOF*). After several conversations between Savage and *SOF*'s advertising manager, Joan Steel, the following advertisement ran in the June 1985 through March 1986 issues of *SOF*:

> GUN FOR HIRE: 37-year-old professional mercenary desires jobs. Vietnam Veteran. Discrete [sic] and very private. Body guard, courier, and other special skills. All jobs considered. Phone (615) 436–9785 (days) or (615) 436–4335 (nights), or write: Rt. 2, Box 682 Village Loop Road, Gatlinburg, TN 37738.

Savage testified that, when he placed the ad, he had no intention of obtaining anything but legitimate jobs. Nonetheless, Savage stated that the overwhelming majority of the 30 to 40 phone calls a week he received in response to his ad sought his participation in criminal activity such as murder, assault, and kidnapping. The ad also generated at least one legitimate job as a bodyguard, which Savage accepted.

In late 1984 or early 1985, Bruce Gastwirth began seeking to murder his business partner, Richard Braun. Gastwirth enlisted the aid of another business associate, John Horton Moore, and together they arranged for at least three attempts on Braun's life, all of which were unsuccessful. Responding to Savage's *SOF* ad, Gastwirth and Moore contacted him in August 1985 to discuss plans to murder Braun.

On August 26, 1985, Savage, Moore, and another individual, Sean Trevor Doutre, went to Braun's suburban Atlanta home. As Braun and his sixteen-year-old son Michael were driving down the driveway, Doutre stepped in front of Braun's car and fired several shots into the car with a MAC 11 automatic pistol. The shots hit Michael in the thigh and wounded Braun as well. Braun managed to roll out of the car, but Doutre walked over to Braun and killed him by firing two more shots into the back of his head as Braun lay on the ground.

On March 31, 1988, appellees Michael and Ian Braun filed this diversity action against appellants in the United States District Court for the Middle District of Alabama, seeking damages for the wrongful death of their father. Michael Braun also filed a separate action seeking recovery for the personal injuries he received at the time of his father's death. The district court consolidated these related matters.

Trial began on December 3, 1990. Appellees contended that, under Georgia law, *SOF* was liable for their injuries because *SOF* negligently published a personal service advertisement that created an unreasonable risk of the solicitation and commission of violent criminal activity, including murder. To show that *SOF* knew of the likelihood that criminal activity would result from placing an ad like Savage's, appellees introduced evidence of newspaper and magazine articles published prior to Braun's murder which described links between *SOF* and personal service ads and a number of criminal convictions including murder, kidnapping, assault, extortion, and attempts thereof. Appellees also presented evidence that, prior to *SOF*'s acceptance of Savage's ad, law enforcement officials had contacted *SOF* staffers on two separate occasions in connection with investigations of crimes.

In his trial testimony, *SOF* president Robert K. Brown denied having any knowledge of criminal activity associated with *SOF*'s personal service ads at any time prior to Braun's murder in August 1985. Both Jim Graves, a former managing editor of *SOF*, and Joan Steel, the advertising manager who accepted Savage's advertisement, similarly testified that they were not aware of other crimes connected with *SOF* ads prior to running Savage's ad. Steel further testified that she had understood the term "Gun for Hire" in Savage's ad to refer to a "bodyguard or protection service-type thing," rather than to any illegal activity.

The jury returned a verdict in favor of appellees and awarded compensatory damages on the wrongful death claim in the amount of $2 million. The jury also awarded appellee Michael Braun $375,000 in compensatory damages and $10 million in punitive damages for his personal injury claim.

To prevail in an action for negligence in Georgia, a party must establish the following elements:

(1) A legal duty to conform to a standard of conduct raised by the law for the protection of others against unreasonable risks of harm, (2) a breach of this standard, (3) a legally attributable causal connection between the conduct and the resulting injury, and (4) some loss of damage flowing to the plaintiff's legally protected interest as a result of the alleged breach of the legal duty. To the extent that *SOF* denies that a publisher owes any duty to the public when it pub-

lishes personal service ads, its position is clearly inconsistent with Georgia law. We believe, however, that the crux of *SOF*'s argument is not that it had no duty to the public, but that, as a matter of law, there is a risk to the public when a publisher prints an "unreasonable" advertisement only if the ad openly solicits criminal activity.

SOF further argues that imposing liability on publishers for the advertisements they print indirectly threatens core, non-commercial speech to which the Constitution accords its full protection. Supreme Court cases discussing the limitations the First Amendment places on state defamation law indicate that there is no constitutional infirmity in Georgia law holding publishers liable under a negligence standard with respect to the commercial advertisements they print. Past Supreme Court decisions indicate, however, that the negligence standard that the First Amendment permits is a "modified" negligence standard. The Court's decisions suggest that Georgia law may impose tort liability on publishers for injury caused by the advertisements they print only if the ad on its face, without the need to investigate, makes it apparent that there is a substantial danger of harm to the public.

We conclude that the First Amendment permits a state to impose upon a publisher liability for compensatory damages for negligently publishing a commercial advertisement where the ad on its face, and without the need for investigation, makes it apparent that there is a substantial danger of harm to the public. The absence of a duty requiring publishers to investigate the advertisements they print and the requirement that the substance of the ad itself must warn the publisher of a substantial danger of harm to the public guarantee that the burden placed on publishers will not impermissibly chill protected commercial speech.

Our review of the language of Savage's ad persuades us that *SOF* had a legal duty to refrain from publishing it. Savage's advertisement (1) emphasized the term "Gun for Hire," (2) described Savage as a "professional mercenary," (3) stressed Savage's willingness to keep his assignments confidential and "very private," (4) listed legitimate jobs involving the use of a gun—bodyguard and courier—followed by a reference to Savage's "other special skills," and (5) concluded by stating that Savage would consider "all jobs." The ad's combination of sinister terms makes it apparent that there was a substantial danger of harm to the public. The ad expressly solicits all jobs requiring the use of a gun. When the list of legitimate jobs (i.e., bodyguard and courier) is followed by "other special skills" and "all jobs considered," the implication is clear that the advertiser would consider illegal jobs. We agree with the district court that "the language of this advertisement is such that, even though couched in terms not explicitly offering criminal services, the publisher could recognize the offer of criminal activity as readily as its readers obviously did."

We find that the jury had ample grounds for finding that *SOF*'s publication of Savage's ad was the proximate cause of Braun's injuries.

For the foregoing reasons, we AFFIRM the district court's judgment.

CASE A.5

FEIST PUBLICATIONS, INC. V. RURAL TELEPHONE SERVICE CO., INC. 499 U.S. 340, 111 S.CT. 1282, 113 L.ED.2D 358 (1991)
UNITED STATES SUPREME COURT
O'Conner, Justice.

Rural Telephone Service Company (Rural) is a certified public utility that provides telephone service to several communities in northwest Kansas. It is subject to a state regulation that requires all telephone companies operating in Kansas to issue annually an updated telephone directory. Accordingly, as a condition of its monopoly franchise, Rural publishes a typical telephone directory, consisting of white pages and yellow pages. The white pages list in alphabetical order the names of Rural's subscribers, together with their towns and telephone numbers. The yellow pages list Rural's business subscribers alphabetically by category and feature classified advertisements of various sizes. Rural distributes its directory free of charge to its subscribers, but earns revenue by selling yellow pages advertisements.

Feist Publications, Inc. is a publishing company that specializes in area-wide telephone directories. Unlike a typical directory, which covers only a particular calling area, Feist's area-wide directories cover a much larger geographical range, reducing the need to call directory assistance or consult multiple directories. The Feist directory that is the subject of this litigation covers 11 different telephone service areas in 15 counties and contains 46,878 white pages listings—compared to Rural's approximately 7,700 listings.

Of the 11 telephone companies, only Rural refused to license its listings to Feist. Rural's refusal created a problem for Feist, as omitting these listings would have left a gaping hole in its area-wide directory, rendering it less attractive to potential yellow pages advertisers. Unable to license Rural's white pages listings, Feist used them without Rural's consent.

Rural sued for copyright infringement in the District Court for the District of Kansas taking the position that Feist, in compiling its own directory, could not use the information contained in Rural's white pages. The district court granted summary judgment to Rural, explaining that "courts have consistently held that telephone directories are copyrightable" and citing a string of lower court decisions. In an unpublished opinion, the Court of Appeals for the Tenth Circuit affirmed "for substantially the reasons given by the district court."

This case concerns the interaction of two well-established propositions. The first is that facts are not copyrightable; the other, that compilations of facts generally are. The key to resolving the tension lies in understanding why facts are not copyrightable. The *sine qua non* of copyright is originality. To qualify for copyright protection, a work must be original to the author. Original, as the term is used in copyright, means only that the work was independently created by the author (as opposed to copied from other works), and that it possesses at least some minimal degree of creativity.

Originality is a constitutional requirement. The source of Congress' power to enact copyright laws is Article I, §8, C1. 8, of the Constitution, which authorizes Congress to "secure for limited Times to Authors . . . the exclusive Right to their respective Writings." It is this bedrock principle of copyright that mandates the law's seemingly disparate treatment of facts and factual compilations. No one may claim originality as to facts. This is because facts do not owe their origin to an act of authorship. The distinction is one between creation and discovery: the first person to find and report a particular fact has not created the fact; he or she has merely discovered its existence.

If the selection and arrangement of facts are original, these elements of the work are eligible for copyright protection. No matter how original the format, however, the facts themselves do not become original through association.

There is no doubt that Feist took from the white pages of Rural's directory a substantial amount of factual information. At a minimum, Feist copied the names, towns, and telephone numbers of 1,309 of Rural's subscribers. Not all copying, however, is copyright infringement, two elements must be proven: (1) ownership of a valid copyright and (2) copying of constituent elements of the work that are original. The first element is not at issue here; Feist appears to concede that Rural's directory, considered as a whole, is subject to a valid copyright because it contains some foreword text, as well as original material in its yellow pages advertisements.

The question is whether Rural has proved the second element. In other words, did Feist, by taking 1,309 names, towns, and telephone numbers from Rural's white pages, copy anything that was "original" to Rural? Certainly, the raw data does not satisfy the originality requirement. Rural may have been the first to discover and report the names, towns, and telephone numbers of its subscribers, but this data does not "owe its origin" to Rural. The question that remains is whether Rural selected, coordinated, or arranged these copyrightable facts in an original way. The selection, coordination, and arrangement of Rural's white pages do not satisfy the minimum constitutional standards for copyright protection. Rural's selection of listings could not be more obvious: it publishes the most basic information—name, town, and telephone number—about each person who applies to it for telephone service. This is "selection" of a sort, but it lacks the modicum of creativity necessary to transform mere selection into copyrightable expression. Rural expended sufficient effort to make the white pages directory useful, but insufficient creativity to make it original.

The judgment of the court of appeals is *Reversed*.

CASE A.6

SCHALK V. TEXAS, 823 S.W.2D 633 (1991)
COURT OF CRIMINAL APPEALS OF TEXAS
Miller, Judge.

Appellants Schalk and Leonard are former employees of Texas Instruments (TI). Both men have doctoral degrees and specialized in the area of speech research at TI. Schalk resigned his position with TI in April 1983 to join a newly developed company, Voice Control Systems (VCS). In February 1985, Leonard resigned from TI and joined VCS. Several TI employees eventually joined the ranks of VCS. Speech research was the main thrust of the research and development performed by VCS. In fact, VCS was a competitor of TI in this field. In April 1985 Sam Kuzbary, then employed with VCS and a former TI employee, noticed some information which he believed to be proprietary to TI stored in the memory of the computer he was using at VCS. Kuzbary contacted TI and agreed to serve as an "informant" for them. He then searched the premises of VCS and photographed materials which he recognized from his employment with TI. A TI internal investigation revealed that a few hours prior to Schalk's and Leonard's departures from TI, each appellant, utilizing TI computers, copied the entire contents of the directories respectively assigned to them. This information included computer programs which TI claimed to be its trade secrets. Officials of TI then contacted the Dallas District Attorney's office. A search of the premises of VCS resulted in the seizure of computer tapes containing the alleged TI trade secret programs from appellants' offices. Appellants were arrested.

We granted review to consider, first, whether the evidence was sufficient to establish that the computer programs named in the indictments were trade secrets, and second, to determine whether the items listed in the search warrant were sufficiently described so as to preclude a general exploratory search.

Having determined that computer programs are proper subjects for trade secret litigation under Texas civil and criminal law, we now look to the case *sub judice* to determine whether the programs which appellants copied and took with them to VCS are trade secrets as defined by §31.05 of the Penal Code.

§31.05 Theft of trade secrets:

(a) For the purposes of this section:

(4) "Trade secret" means the whole or any part of any scientific or technical information, design, process, procedure, formula, or improvement that has value and that the owner has taken measures to prevent from becoming available to persons other than those selected by the owner to have access for limited purposes.

Appellants claimed on appeal that the programs did not meet the statutory trade secrets criteria because they alleged their former employer TI failed to take "measures to prevent [the information] from becoming available to persons other than those selected by the owner." We note, as did the court of appeals, that the statute sets no standards for degree of sufficiency of the "measures" taken. Specifically, appellants pointed to considerable disclosure of speech research information, citing the "academic environment" of the laboratory in which they worked as encouraging the sharing of information, rather than maintaining secrecy. Appellants also claimed that TI policy favored protection of its research and development efforts through the patent process, as opposed to trade secret designation. Further, appellants allege that the programs that are the subject of the instant case were not listed in the TI register of trade secrets and that TI was lax in implementing its standard procedures with regard to notifying employees of trade secrets within the company. The precise issue before us in the case *sub judice* is one of the first impression in Texas, to wit: what constitutes requisite "measures" to protect trade secret status?

We now determine whether the information disclosed with TI's permission or encouragement, such as published articles, seminar papers, speeches given at public meetings, information provided to government agencies, etc., was so extensive as to destroy any trade secret status that may have existed regarding the computer software which is the subject of the instant indictments. It is axiomatic that the core element of a trade secret must be that it remain a secret, however, absolute secrecy is not required.

A trade secret can exist in a combination of characteristics and components, each of which, by itself, is in the public domain, but the unified process and operation of which, in unique combination, affords a competitive advantage and is a protestable secret. We find based on the record in this case, that the limited disclosure made by TI in regard to the speech research lab activities merely described the application and configuration of the certain elements of the software but did not reveal the actual composition of the programs. The measures used by TI to secure its premises to prevent unauthorized personnel from admission to or exposure to its proprietary research data were reasonable under the circumstances.

We need not decide today whether any one of the preventive measures listed, standing alone, is factually sufficient to support trade secret status. We do find that the combination of employment agreements, strict plant security, restricted computer access, the non-authorization of disclosure of the subject programs and the general non-disclosure of those programs by TI and its employees served to support trade secret status of the computer programs that are the subject of the instant indictments. Appellants neither requested nor received permission to copy the files containing these programs. The unauthorized copying of the article representing a trade secret constitutes an offense under V.T.C.A. Penal Code §31.05(b)(2).

Therefore we affirm the court of appeals' ruling that the subject programs are trade secrets.

CASE A.7

MARK REALTY, INC. V. ROGNESS
418 SO.2D 373 (1982)
DISTRICT COURT OF APPEALS OF FLORIDA
Cowart, Judge.

Tilman A. Rogness, owner, entered into four separate agreements with Mark Realty, Inc., a real estate broker. They were entitled "exclusive right of sale" and gave the broker, for a stated period of time, the exclusive right to sell the property for a certain stated price and on certain terms. The broker sued on the four agreements for brokerage commissions, alleging that during the time provided in the agreements the owner had conveyed the four properties. The owner's answer alleged affirmative defenses to the effect that the owner had "canceled, revoked, and terminated" the brokerage agreements before the properties were sold and that the broker had never performed under the agreements.

The trial judge construed the brokerage agreements to constitute mere offers to enter into unilateral contracts under which the broker would be entitled to a commission only if he performed by "finding a purchaser of the above property." If the documents in question are merely offers limited to acceptance by performance only, the trial judge's analysis and conclusion would be correct.

We cannot agree that the documents were only offers for a unilateral contract. The documents illustrate what has been termed "the usual practice" in the making of bargains. One party indicates what he will do and what he requires in exchange and the other then agrees. These documents, when first executed by the owner and tendered to the broker, constituted offers which, when accepted by the broker by his execution, constituted contracts. The contract is bilateral because it contains mutual promises made in exchange for each other by each of the two contracting parties.

The most common recurring brokerage transaction is one in which the owner employs a broker to find a purchaser able and willing to buy, on terms stated in advance by the owner, and in which the owner promises to pay a specific commission for the service. Such a transaction as this is an offer by the owner of a unilateral contract, an offered promise to pay by the owner, creating in the broker a power of accepting the offer by actual rendition of the requested services. The only contemplated contract between the owner and broker is a unilateral contract—a promise to pay a commission for services rendered. Such an offer of a promise to pay a commission for services rendered is revocable by the owner by notice before the broker has rendered any part of the requested service.

On the other hand, the transaction between the owner and the broker can be a bilateral contract. An owner who puts his land in the hands of a broker for sale usually clearly promises to pay a commission, but the broker rarely promises in return that he will produce a purchaser although he often promises, expressly or impliedly, that he will make certain efforts to do so. If the parties have thus made mutual promises, the transaction no longer has the status of an unaccepted offer—there is an existing bilateral contract and neither party has a power of revocation. During the term of such a contract the owner may withdraw any power the owner has given the broker to contract with a third party in the owner's name, but this is not a revocation of the contract between the owner and the broker and normally such action constitutes a breach of the brokerage contract.

In this case, the broker promised to inspect the property, to list the property with a multiple listing service, to advertise the property in the local newspaper or other media, to furnish information to inquiring cooperating brokers and prospective purchasers, to show the property, to make efforts to find a purchaser, to "make an earnest and continued effort to sell," and to direct the concentrated efforts of his organization in bringing about a sale.

In the instant case, the contract clearly provided that the brokerage commission would be paid "whether the purchaser be secured by you or me, or by any other person." Thus the contract granted the broker an exclusive right of sale and the trial court erred in construing the agreement as an offer of a unilateral contract revocable at will at any time prior to performance.

The final judgment is reversed.

CASE A.8

TRACO, INC. V. ARROW GLASS CO., INC.,
814 S.W. 2D 186 (1991)
COURT OF APPEALS OF TEXAS
Chapa, Justice.

This is a construction dispute stemming from a quotation given by Traco, Inc., a Three Rivers Aluminum Company, a material supplier of pre-engineered aluminum and glass sliding doors and windows, to Arrow Glass Company, Inc. (Arrow) a subcontractor, in connection with the USAA Towers project in San Antonio, Texas. Arrow initially brought suit against Traco on the theories of promissory estoppel and negligence for Traco's failure to supply aluminum and glass sliding doors at the quoted price. After a bench trial, the trial court held for Arrow solely under the theory of promissory estoppel and awarded Arrow judgment against Traco for damages in the amount of $75,843.38, plus attorneys' fees and prejudgment interest.

The facts of this case reflect that on or about October 9, 1986, construction bids were due for the USAA Towers, a $49 million retirement housing project located near Fort Sam Houston, Texas. There were numerous suppliers, subcontractors, and general contractors bidding to obtain work on this project, including the appellant, Traco, and the appellee, Arrow.

On bid day, a representative for Arrow received a telephone call from Dale Ferrar of Traco. Mr. Ferrar told Bill Morris, the general manager of Arrow, that Traco was a very large window and sliding glass aluminum door manufacturer in Pennsylvania. Mr. Ferrar offered its A-2 aluminum and glass sliding doors, as an alternate product substitution, to Arrow, which was bidding that portion of the project. However, after some discussion of the required specifications, the parties realized that Traco's doors would have to be modified in order to comply with the project specifications. Arrow declined to use Traco's bid and, instead, submitted its original bid, using a different supplier of doors.

At approximately noon on bid day, Mr. Ferrar phoned Mr. Morris, quoting a new price for the doors which included a modification of the frame depth which, supposedly, enabled the doors to comply with the specifications. At this time, Mr. Morris informed Mr. Ferrar that his bid was low and asked him to recheck his figures. Mr. Ferrar explained that because of Traco's size and the fact that it could manufacture its products under one roof, Traco could sell the project for that amount. Mr. Ferrar also indicated that Traco was seeking a high profile project to represent Traco in the San Antonio area.

After receiving these assurances, Mr. Morris told Mr. Ferrar that he was going to use Traco's bid. Mr. Morris then phoned the contractors to whom he had originally submitted his bid, and deducted $100,000 in reliance upon Traco's bid. Mr. Morris later told Mr. Ferrar that he had received favorable responses from three or four general contractors, and that it appeared Arrow would get the project. Mr. Morris advised Mr. Ferrar that if Arrow obtained the project, then Traco would be awarded the contract on the doors.

The oral quote by Traco was followed with a written bid confirmation on the next day, which reflected the product that would be supplied and the price agreed upon by the parties. The confirmation also included the 1¼" frame extender at a cost of $27,860, which, allegedly, brought the doors into compliance with the project specifications.

Sometime in November, long after Mr. Morris had relied upon Mr. Ferrar's representations in submitting his bid, Mr. Morris began hearing rumors that there was a problem with the door. Mr. Morris contacted Mr. Ferrar, who admitted that there was a problem with the doors meeting the architect's wind load deflection requirement in the specifications. Shortly after learning of this problem, Mr. Morris received a second quote from Traco, wherein Traco offered its A-3 doors, which were a more expensive, heavy grade commercial door that met the deflection requirement, for a price of $304,300. After receiving this bid, Morris objected to the price and demanded that Traco deliver doors meeting the project specifications at the original price quoted. Traco refused and when it became obvious that Arrow would not be able to use Traco's product, Mr. Morris contracted with another supplier who had bid on the project.

The record clearly reflects the following: that it was Traco that initially contacted Arrow and offered to do a certain specific act (supply the sliding doors required); that Mr. Ferrar phoned Mr. Morris on several occasions and discussed, among other things, the fact that the doors which Traco wished to bid would not comply with the specifications without some modification; and, that Mr. Ferrar assured Mr. Morris that the doors could be modified to comply with the specifications. Thus, under the present facts, Traco's bid gave Arrow "a right to expect or claim the performance of some particular thing"; specifically, Traco's bid constituted a promise to supply sliding doors meeting the project specifications at a specified price.

Appellant initially argues that the trial court erred in rendering judgment for Arrow because Traco's bid was revocable and properly withdrawn thirty days after it was made. Appellant primarily relies upon the argument that its sliding doors are goods as defined by the Texas Business and Commerce Code. Nevertheless, appellant's arguments ignore the appellee's basic contention and legal theory under which this suit was brought. Appellee sought relief under the equitable doctrine of promissory estoppel, on the premise that appellant's promises, by way of its *oral* bid, caused appellee to substantially rely to its detriment. The appellee relied to its detriment when it reduced its bid based on a telephone conversation with the appellant, prior to the time appellant's confirmation letter was sent or received.

We must now resolve whether the equitable theory of promissory estoppel applies to bid construction cases and, if so, whether this doctrine applies under the specific facts of this case. While no Texas case has previously applied the theory of promissory estoppel in a bid construction case, other jurisdictions have consistently applied this doctrine under similar facts, recognizing the necessity for equity in view of the lack of other remedies.

The Texas Supreme Court, in emphasizing that the underlying function of the theory of promissory estoppel is to promote equity, has stated that: "The vital principle is that he who by his language or conduct leads another to do what he would not otherwise have done, shall not subject such person to loss or injury by disappointing the expectations, upon which he acted. This remedy is always so applied as to promote the ends of justice." Clearly promissory estoppel is "a rule of equity" applied to prevent injustice. As is true in most, if not all, bid construction cases, the present situation does not involve a contract. Therefore, were we to hold that promissory estoppel does not exist in bid construction cases, this would necessarily mean that, notwithstanding any language or conduct by the subcontractor which leads the general contractor to do that which he would not otherwise have done and, thereby, incur loss or injury, the general contractor would be denied all relief. This proposition is untenable and conflicts with the underlying premise of promissory estoppel.

Section 90 of the Restatement (Second) of Contracts (1981) states the principle of promissory estoppel as follows: "A promise which the promisor should reasonably expect to induce action or forbearance on the part of the promisee or a third person and which does induce such action or forbearance is binding if injustice can be avoided only by enforcement of the promise." Accordingly, the requirements of promissory estoppel are: "(1) a promise, (2) foreseeability of reliance thereon by the promisor, and (3) substantial reliance by the promisee to his detriment." In order to invoke the doctrine of estoppel, all the necessary elements of estoppel must be present and the failure to establish even one of these elements is fatal to the claimant's cause of action.

Appellant insists, however, that because Traco was not an approved manufacturer and bid its doors as an alternate, that by its nature, Traco's bid was conditional and, therefore, promissory estoppel cannot lie. We fail to see how a bid for a specific door at a specific price, which was submitted in response to solicitations that detailed project specifications, is contingent, or somehow not final, merely because the wrong door was bid upon. The appellant's failure to receive the architect's approval was not due to new specifications but was caused by the appellant's failure to regard those specifications originally required when the appellant offered its doors. Appellant's point is rejected.

Notwithstanding the existence of this promise, the appellant argues that appellee could not have justifiably and reasonably relied upon appellant's bid because: Traco was not an approved manufacturer and bid its A-2 doors as an alternate and, further, Traco's bid was lower than the other suppliers who bid upon the contract.

Because of the withdrawal of Traco's bid, Arrow was compelled to seek another supplier of doors at a much greater cost; clearly, this constituted an injustice to the appellee. Additionally, appellee's reliance upon appellant's bid was reasonable in view of the appellant's attempts to modify its doors, and Mr. Ferrar's assurances that the doors, as modified, would meet the project specifications.

We hold that the controlling findings of fact support the promissory estoppel theory.

The judgment is affirmed.

CASE A.9

CARNIVAL LEISURE INDUSTRIES, LTD. V. AUBIN
938 F.2D 624 (1991)
UNITED STATES COURT OF APPEALS, FIFTH CIRCUIT

Garwood, Circuit Judge.

During a January 1987 visit to the Bahamas, George J. Aubin (Aubin), a Texas resident, visited Cable Beach Hotel and Casino (Casino), which was owned and operated by Carnival Leisure Industries, Ltd. (Carnival Leisure). While gambling at the Casino, Aubin received markers or chips from the Casino and the Casino received drafts drawn on Aubin's bank accounts in Texas. Aubin spent all of the markers provided on gambling, although he could also have spent them on food, beverages, souvenirs, or lodging at the Casino. Aubin ultimately gambled and lost $25,000, leaving the Casino with the same amount in bank drafts.

Carnival Leisure was unable to cash the bank drafts because Aubin had subsequently directed his bank to stop payment. Carnival Leisure sued Aubin in the United States District Court for the Southern District of Texas to enforce the debt. The district court granted Carnival Leisure's motion for summary judgment against Aubin in the amount of $25,000 and attorney's fees and costs. Carnival Leisure claimed that the debt was enforceable under Texas law because public policy had changed and now favored enforcement of gambling debts. The district court agreed. Aubin raises on appeal only the issue of whether public policy in Texas continues to prevent the enforcement of gambling debts.

Carnival Leisure claims, however, that since 1973 the public policy of Texas toward gambling and the legality of gambling debts has changed. Although gambling is generally proscribed in Texas, there has been an exception for the "social" gambler since 1973. The Texas legislature enacted the Bingo Enabling Act in 1981, the Texas Racing Act in 1986, and the Charitable Raffle Enabling Act in 1989. Provisions were added to the Texas Penal Code excepting these three activities from its general proscription against gambling.

The enactment of statutes legalizing some forms of gambling admittedly evidences some dissipation or narrowing of public disapproval of gambling, however, such statutes hardly introduce a judicially cognizable change in public policy with respect to gambling generally. The social gambling permitted is confined to private places where no one receives any benefit other than his personal winnings and all participants are subject to the same risks, a categorically vastly different kind of activity from the sort involved here. The racing, bingo, and raffling exceptions are narrow, strictly regulated exceptions to a broad public policy in Texas against most forms of gambling. Further, the kind of gambling engaged in here is not of the sort permitted by any of these exceptions.

Even if gambling legislation in Texas were evidence sufficient to warrant judicial notice of a shift in public policy with respect to legalized gambling, such a shift would not be inconsistent with a continued public policy disfavoring gambling on credit. Although Aubin could have used the loaned markers for non-gambling purposes at the Casino, it is undisputed that they were in fact used exclusively for gambling. Aubin's gambling debt therefore fits squarely within the terms of the public policy of Texas prohibiting enforcement of gambling debts owed to gambling participants incurred for the purpose of gambling.

We hold that the public policy in Texas against gambling on credit prevents enforcement of a debt incurred for the purpose of gambling and provided by a participant in the gambling activity. The district court's grant of summary judgment in favor of Carnival Leisure is accordingly reversed and this case is remanded to the district court for further proceedings consistent with this opinion.

CASE A.10

CONTINENTAL AIRLINES, INC. V. MCDONNELL DOUGLAS CORPORATION
216 CAL.APP.3D 388, 264 CAL.RPTR. 779 (1990)
COURT OF APPEALS OF CALIFORNIA

Hoffman, Associate Justice.

This action was commenced by plaintiff and respondent Continental Airlines (Continental) in Los Angeles Superior Court on December 3, 1979, and alleged, against defendant and appellant McDonnell Douglas Corporation (Douglas), causes of action for deceit. On January 30, 1986, the jury returned verdicts in favor of Continental for $17 million on its claims for fraud by misrepresentation and fraud by nondisclosure of known facts. The judgment was granted. This appeal is from that judgment. We affirm the judgment as modified.

On March 1, 1978, a Continental DC-10 aircraft, which had been delivered to Continental by Douglas in 1972, was in its takeoff roll at Los Angeles International Airport when two tires burst on the left landing gear. The captain elected to try to stop the plane, but it ran off the end of the runway at 85 miles per hour. The landing gear broke through the tarmac, burrowed into the ground, and was ripped from the wing, making a 3.7 foot hole which allowed fuel to pour from the wing fuel tanks. The plane was severely damaged by the resulting fire and rendered unrepairable.

Douglas had approached Continental in 1968 to sell Continental DC-10 aircraft. Douglas used a series of briefings and sales brochures in its sales campaign. The sales brochures given to Continental consisted of hundreds of pages of technical information drafted by Douglas' engineers, and reviewed by its top management, for the express purpose of explaining the DC-10 design and a "Detail Type Specification" to potential aircraft purchasers. That Specification, as its name implies, described the technical details of the DC-10. The Douglas briefings covered the landing gear and wing design, as did many of its brochures. Continental personnel used the brochures to write portions of Continental's "Tri-Jet Evaluation," a comparison between the DC-10 and Lockheed's L-1011, which became a basis for Continental's decision to purchase the DC-10. When Continental decided to purchase the DC-10, instead of the L-1011 aircraft, it finalized a Purchase Agreement with Douglas which incorporated by reference the Detail Specification for the DC-10.

The brochures contained statements that "the fuel tank will not rupture under crash load conditions"; that the landing gear "are designed for wipe-off without rupturing the wing fuel tank"; that "the support structure is designed to a higher strength than the gear to prevent fuel tank rupture due to an accidental landing gear overload"; that the DC-10 "is designed and tested for crashworthiness"; that the "landing gear will be tested" to demonstrate the fail-safe integrity and wipe-off characteristics of the gear design; and that "good reliability" for the DC-10 landing gear could be predicted with an "unusually high degree of confidence" because of its close similarity to the successful design on the DC-8 and DC-9 aircraft.

Douglas argues that the Uniform Commercial Code and cases interpreting it have recognized that general promotional observations of this type are merely expressions of opinion that are not actionable as fraudulent statements. The alleged false representations in the subject brochures were not statements of "opinion or mere puffing." They were, in essence, representations that the DC-10 was a safe aircraft. Promises of safety are not statements of opinion—they are representations of fact.

Douglas contends in its opening brief that there was no substantial evidence that its pre-contract representations were *material* or that Continental reasonably *relied* on them in deciding to purchase the DC-10. The materiality of the representations can hardly be questioned. Any airline shopping for aircraft to service its customers naturally searches for planes that are safe. Where representations have been made in regard to a material matter and action has been taken, in the absence of evidence showing the contrary, reliance on the representations will be presumed. Here, both materiality and reliance are demonstrated by the fact that Continental evaluated the DC-10 breakaway design in its "Tri-Jet Evaluation," which compared the DC-10 with the L-1011 for the purpose of deciding which aircraft to purchase. Douglas was the only possible source for the information; there was no way Continental could independently investigate or analyze the adequacy of that design. The foregoing provides more that substantial evidence that Continental *relied* on Douglas' representations regarding landing gear breakaway in choosing to purchase the DC-10 and that those representations were *material*.

False representations made recklessly and without regard for their truth in order to induce action by another are the equivalent of misrepresentations knowingly and intentionally uttered. Therefore, there is substantial evidence of the requisite intent for intentional fraud. For the forgoing reasons we conclude the evidence supports the jury's findings of liability for fraud. The judgment is modified to reflect an award of prejudgment interest in the amount of $9,549,750. As so modified, the judgment is affirmed.

CASE A.11

CHASE PRECAST CORPORATION V. JOHN J. PAONESSA CO. INC., 409 MASS. 371, 566 N.E. 2D 603 (1991) SUPREME JUDICIAL COURT OF MASSACHUSETTS

Lynch, Justice.

This appeal raises the question whether the doctrine of frustration of purpose may be a defense in a breach of contract action in Massachusetts, and, if so, whether it excuses the defendant John J. Paonessa Company, Inc. (Paonessa) from performance.

The claim of the plaintiff, Chase Precast Corporation (Chase), arises from the cancellation of its contracts with Paonessa to supply median barriers in a highway construction project of the Commonwealth. Chase brought an action to recover its anticipated profit on the amount of the median barriers called for by its supply contracts with Paonessa but not produced. Paonessa brought a cross action against the Commonwealth for indemnification in the event it should be held liable to Chase. After a jury-waived trial, a superior court judge ruled for Paonessa on the basis of impossibility of performance. Chase and Paonessa cross appealed. The appeals court affirmed, noting that the doctrine of frustration of purpose more accurately described the basis of the trial judge's decision than the doctrine of impossibility. We agree. We allowed Chase's application for further appellate review and we now affirm.

The pertinent facts are as follows. In 1982, the Commonwealth, through the Department of Public Works (department), entered into two contracts with Paonessa for resurfacing and improvements to two stretches of Route 128. Part of each contract called for replacing a grass median strip between the north and southbound lanes with concrete resurfacing and precast concrete median barriers. Paonessa entered into two contracts with Chase under which Chase was to supply, in the aggregate, 25,800 linear feet of concrete median barriers according to the specifications of the department for highway construction. The quantity and type of barriers to be supplied were specified in two purchase orders prepared by Chase.

The highway reconstruction began in the Spring of 1983. By late May, the department was receiving protests from angry residents who objected to use of the concrete barriers and removal of the grass median strip. Paonessa and Chase became aware of the protest around June 1. On June 6, a group of about 100 citizens filed an action in the superior court to stop installation of the concrete barriers and other aspects of the work. On June 7, anticipating modification by the department, Paonessa notified Chase by letter to stop producing concrete barriers for the projects. Chase did so upon receipt of letter the following day. On June 17, the department and the citizen's group entered into a settlement which provided, in part, that no additional concrete median barriers would be installed. On June 23, the department deleted the permanent concrete median barriers item from its contracts with Paonessa.

Before stopping production on June 8, Chase had produced approximately one-half of the concrete median barriers called for by its contracts with Paonessa, and had delivered most of them to the construction sites. Paonessa paid Chase for all that it had produced, at the contract price. Chase suffered no out-of-pocket expense as a result of cancellation of the remaining portion of barriers.

This court has long recognized and applied the doctrine of impossibility as a defense to an action of breach of contract. Under that doctrine, "where from the nature of the contract it appears that the parties must from the beginning have contemplated the continued existence of some particular specified thing as the foundation of what was to be done, then, in the absence of any warranty that the thing shall exist . . . the parties shall be excused . . . when performance becomes impossible from the accidental perishing of the thing without the fault of either party."

On the other hand, although we have referred to the doctrine of frustration of purpose in a few decisions, we have never clearly defined it. Other jurisdictions have explained the doctrine as follows: when an event neither anticipated nor caused by either party, the risk of which was not allocated by the contract, destroys the object or purpose of the contract, thus destroying the value of performance, the parties are excused from further performance.

In *Mishara Construction Co.*, we called frustration of purpose a "companion rule" to the doctrine of impossibility. Both doctrines concern the effect of supervening circumstances upon the rights and duties of the parties. The difference lies in the effect of the supervening event.

Another definition of frustration of purpose is found in the Restatement (Second) of Contracts §265 (1981). "Where, after a contract is made, a party's principal purpose is substantially frustrated without his fault by the occurrence of an event the nonoccurrence of which was a basic assumption on which the contract was made, his remaining duties to render performance are discharged, unless the language or the circumstances indicate the contrary."

Paonessa bore no responsibility for the department's elimination of the median barriers from the projects, therefore, whether it can rely on the defense of frustration turns on whether elimination of the barriers was a risk allocated by the contracts to Paonessa. The question is, given the commercial circumstances in which the parties dealt: "Was the contingency which developed one which the parties could reasonably be thought to have foreseen as a real possibility which could affect performance? Was it one of that variety of risks which the parties were tacitly assigning to the promisor by their failure to provide for it explicitly? If it was, performance will be required. If it could not be considered, performance is excused."

The record supports the conclusion that Chase was aware of the department's power to decrease quantities of contract items. The judge found that Chase had been a supplier of median barriers to the department in the past. The provision giving the department the power to eliminate items or portions thereof was standard in its contracts. The judge's finding that all parties were well aware that lost profits were not an element of damage in either of the public works projects in issue further supports the conclusion that Chase was aware of the department's power to decrease quantities, since the term prohibiting claims for anticipated profit is part of the same sentence in the standard provision as that allowing the engineer to eliminate items or portions of work. In this case, even if the parties were aware generally of the department's power to eliminate contract items, the judge could reasonably have concluded that they did not contemplate the cancellation for a major portion of the project of such a widely used item as concrete median barriers and did not allocate the risk of such cancellations.

Judgment affirmed.

CASE A.12

E.B. HARVEY & COMPANY, INC. V. PROTECTIVE SYSTEMS, INC. 1989 TENN. APP. LEXIS 105 (1989) COURT OF APPEALS OF TENNESSEE

Sanders, Presiding Judge.

The plaintiff-appellant, E.B. Harvey & Company, Inc. (Harvey) is engaged in the manufacture and wholesale of fine jewelry in Chattanooga. It has been engaged in this business for about 10 years. It maintains an inventory in excess of $1 million of gold, silver, precious stones, pearls, and other such materials related to the manufacture of jewelry. A considerable amount of its jewelry is on consignment and, by the very nature of its business, it requires a great deal of insurance. However, the insurance companies will not write the insurance unless it maintains an Underwriters Laboratories (U.L.)-approved AA burglary protection alarm system. The defendant-appellee, Protective Systems, Inc. (Protective) is one of two companies in Hamilton County which furnishes and maintains a U.L.-approved AA burglar protection system. In June, 1981, Harvey entered into a three year contract with Protective to install and maintain a burglar protection system. The contract provided:

It is agreed that Protective is not an insurer and that the payments hereinbefore named are based solely upon the value of the services herein described and it is not the intention of the parties that Protective assume responsibility for any losses occasioned by malfeasance or misfeasance in the performance of the services under this contract or for any loss or damage sustained through burglary, theft, robbery, fire, or other cause or any liability on the part of Protective by virtue of this Agreement or because of the relation hereby established.

If there shall at any time be or arise any liability on the part of Protective, by virtue of this Agreement or because of the relation hereby established, whether due to the negligence of Protective or otherwise, such liability is and shall be limited to a sum total in amount to the rental service charge hereunder for a period of service not to exceed six months, which sum shall be paid and received as liquidated damages.

The burglary and hold-up system provided to Harvey operated by means of Grade AA telephone lines between the central monitoring station of Protective and Harvey's premises. Said telephone lines were at all times owned and maintained by the South Central Bell Telephone Company. On July 22, 1984, at 11:14 P.M., an outage condition was indicated on the E.B. Harvey & Company account. For a period of two weeks prior to this date, Protective's computer had been registering an inordinate number of outage signals which had all been traced back to problems in telephone company equipment. For this reason, on July 22, 1984, Protective's president, Pendell Meyers, notified the telephone company of this condition and reported a potential problem to the police department but did not contact a representative of Harvey to notify them of the outage condition.

The phone company was unable to locate the exact nature of the problem despite several telephone conversations with Meyers. The Chattanooga Police Department patrolled the premises surrounding the Harvey's place of business twice that evening but did not note any unusual activity. The following morning when an employee of Harvey reported to work, it was discovered that a burglary had in fact taken place. Some $200,000 worth of jewelry and inventory was stolen. Harvey sued Protective for damages resulting from the burglary. It alleged that Protective was guilty of negligence for its failure to notify Harvey or its employees of the outage which appeared on the burglary monitoring equipment.

Protective, for answer, denied the allegations of Harvey's complaint and, as an affirmative defense, alleged the contract between the parties with its exculpatory and limitation of liability provisions was enforceable and binding upon Harvey. After hearing testimony, the trial court held the extent of Harvey's recovery against Protective would be 650 percent as liquidated damages. A final judgment was entered and Harvey has appealed.

There is nothing in public policy to render inoperative or nugatory the contractual limitations contained in the agreement. Limitations against liability for negligence or breach of contract have generally been upheld in this state in the absence of fraud or overreaching. Limitations such as those contained in the present contract have generally been deemed reasonable and have been sustained in actions against the providers of burglary and fire alarm systems. Such clauses do not ordinarily protect against liability for fraud or intentional misrepresentation.

We concur with the trial court. The issues are found in favor of the appellees. The judgment of the trial court is affirmed. The cost of this appeal is taxed to the appellant and the case is remanded to the trial court for collection of cost.

CASE A.13

BURNETT V. PURTELL, 1992 OHIO APP. LEXIS 3467 (1992)
COURT OF APPEALS OF OHIO
Ford, Presiding Judge.

Appellees agreed to purchase a mobile home with shed from appellant. On Saturday, March 3, 1990, appellees paid appellant $6,500 and in return were given the certificate of title to the mobile home as well as a key to the mobile home, but no keys to the shed. At the same time the certificate of title was transferred, the following items remained in the mobile home: the washer and dryer, mattress and box springs, two chairs, items in the refrigerator, and the entire contents of the shed. These items were to be retained by appellant and removed by appellant. To facilitate removal, the estate retained one key to the mobile home and the only keys to the shed.

On Sunday, March 4, 1990, the mobile home was destroyed by fire through the fault of neither party. At the time of the fire, appellant still had a key to the mobile home as well as the keys to the shed and she had not removed the contents of the mobile home nor the shed. The contents of the shed were not destroyed and have now been removed by appellant. The referee determined that the risk of loss remained with appellant because there was no tender of delivery. Appellant objected to the conclusion of law, but the trial court overruled the objection and entered judgment in favor of appellee.

First, the appellant argues that because the certificate of title was transferred, appellees were given a key to the mobile home and the full purchase price was paid by appellees, that the risk of loss had shifted from appellant to appellees. The risk of loss passes to the buyer on his receipt of the goods if the seller is a merchant; otherwise the risk passes to the buyer on tender of delivery.

Analyzing the foregoing elements it is clear that, as the trial court stated, appellant did not tender delivery. The parties agreed that appellees would purchase the mobile home and shed from appellant. The contents of both the shed and the mobile home were to be retained by appellant and removed by appellant. At the time of the fire, appellant had not removed the items that she was required to remove from either the mobile home or the shed. Additionally, all keys to the mobile home were not surrendered and none of the keys to the shed were relinquished. Under this scenario, appellant did not tender conforming goods free of items belonging to her which remained in the trailer, nor did she put the mobile home at appellee's disposition without being fettered with the items previously enumerated. Accordingly, the trial court was correct in determining that appellant did not tender delivery within the meaning of the statute, and consequently the risk of loss remained with her.

The trial court was correct in determining that appellant did not tender delivery in a manner sufficient to shift the risk of loss to appellees. Therefore, when it ordered appellant to return appellee's purchase money, it effectually mandated that the contract was "avoided."

Based on the foregoing, the judgment of the trial court is affirmed.

CASE A.14

LNS INVESTMENT COMPANY, INC. V. PHILLIPS 66 CO., 731 F. SUPP. 1484 (1990)
UNITED STATES DISTRICT COURT
O'Connor, Chief Judge.

Plaintiff is the successor to a company known as Compu-Blend Corporation (CBC) which blended, labeled, and packaged quart plastic bottles of motor oil for, among others, defendant Phillips 66 Company. On July 29, 1986, W. Peter Buhlinger, defendant's manager of lubricants (Buhlinger) wrote a letter to Dan Tutcher, plaintiff's vice president of operations (Tutcher) which read as follows:

> This will confirm our verbal agreement wherein Phillips will purchase additional quantities of plastic bottles from CBC during 1986. CBC, in an effort to increase their packaging capacity has committed to purchase several additional molds to blow the Phillips plastic one-quart container. In order to amortize the cost of the additional equipment Phillips has agreed to take delivery of a maximum of 4 million bottles to be made available by December 31, 1986. This agreement includes the production available now and to be supplemented by the additional equipment. Should CBC not be able to produce the full 4 million quarts by December 31, 1986, this agreement shall be considered satisfied. Phillips' desire is to receive as many bottles packaged with Phillips motor oil in 1986 from CBC as possible.

Plaintiff experienced numerous problems in maintaining even its pre-contract capacity. Moreover, the quality of goods plaintiff was able to deliver was frequently unacceptable to defendant. Laughlin reiterated defendant's dissatisfaction with plaintiff's products by letter dated October 15, 1986. Discussing bottles tendered by plaintiff, Laughlin stated that, "we definitely do not want bottles on the shelf of the quality submitted." On December 16, 1986, Buhlinger wrote that defendant would not renew any commitments to purchase goods from plaintiff after March 31, 1987, due to plaintiff's poor performance under the July 29 agreement. Plaintiff filed this suit on May 12, 1987, alleging, inter alia, that defendant breached the July 29 agreement by failing to purchase plaintiff's full output of plastic bottles through December 31, 1986.

Plaintiff's failure to provide either the quantity or quality of goods contemplated by the July 29 agreement entitled defendant to suspend its performance. Section 84-2-609 of the Code states as follows:

> Right to adequate assurance of performance. (1) A contract for sale imposes an obligation on each party that the other's expectation of receiving due performance will not be impaired. When reasonable grounds for insecurity arise with respect to the performance of either party the other may in writing demand adequate assurance of due performance and until he receives such assurance may if commercially reasonable suspend any performance for which he has not already received the agreed return.

It was incumbent upon plaintiff to provide adequate assurance of its future performance to defendant. Plaintiff failed to provide defendant with adequate assurance of its future performance. Official UCC Comment 4 states that what constitutes "adequate" assurance of due performance is subject to the same test of factual conditions as what constitutes "reasonable grounds for insecurity." For example, where the buyer can make use of a defective delivery, a mere promise by a seller of good repute that he is giving the matter his attention and that the defect will not be repeated, is normally sufficient. Under the same circumstances, however, a similar statement by a known corner-cutter might well be considered insufficient without the posting of a guaranty or, if so demanded by the buyer, a speedy replacement of the delivery involved. By the same token where a delivery has defects, even though easily curable, which interfere with easy use by the buyer, no verbal assurance can be deemed adequate which is not accomplished by replacement, repair, money-allowance, or other commercially reasonable cure.

Plaintiff's continual excuses for failing to perform, unaccompanied by corresonding remedial action, cannot be deemed adequate assurance under the Code. Accordingly, defendant was entitled to suspend its own performance of the contract by refusing to place orders with plaintiff and/or cancelling unfilled orders already placed, thirty days after either or both the September 18, 1986, and October 15, 1986, letters. In view of this conclusion, defendant did not breach the contract by suspending performance in December, 1986, and judgment will be entered in its favor.

Judgment for defendant.

CASE A.15

JOHNSON V. CHICAGO PNEUMATIC TOOL CO., 607 SO. 2D 615 (1992) COURT OF APPEALS OF LOUISIANA

Crain, Judge.

This is a products liability action in which William H. Johnson (Johnson) was injured in the course of his employment when a pipejack was accidently propelled toward Johnson striking him in the back pinning him between the edge of a large diameter pipe which he was grinding and the pipejack. A pipejack is a large mechanical device which is inserted into large pipes which are in the process of being joined together. The pipejack applies pressure forcing the joints into an evenly rounded shape which can then be welded together. The movement of the pipejack was controlled by an air winch manufactured by Chicago Pneumatic Tool Company (Chicago Pneumatic) which had been utilized and incorporated by McDermott, Inc. (McDermott), Johnson's employer, into a system dedicated to the fitting or joining of large diameter pipe. The accident occurred at the McDermott shipyard when a co-employee either tossed or laid a fifty gallon drum on the ground near the winch in the area where Johnson was working. The drum rolled and toppled over onto the winch throttle pushing the throttle downward which in turn activated the winch and caused the pipejack to move toward Johnson.

Johnson instituted this action against Chicago Pneumatic as manufacturer of the winch, alleging that the winch as designed and manufactured was unreasonably dangerous to normal use. McDermott intervened in this action. After trial on the merits, the jury rendered a special verdict in favor of defendant.

It is uncontroverted that at the time of the accident Johnson was working with his back to the pipejack and the winch; the winch was not being manually operated; and no one was standing at or adjacent to the winch controls. The clutch lever had previously been welded down by McDermott and as a result the clutch remained permanently engaged. Of the other winch controls, the throttle was set in the neutral position and neither the brake nor the safety lock was engaged.

In order to prevail in a products liability action a plaintiff must prove that his damage was a result of a condition of the product which made the product unreasonably dangerous to normal use. The "normal use" of a product encompasses all intended or foreseeable uses and misuses of the product. A manufacturer is obliged to adequately warn the user of any danger inherent in the normal use of the product which is not within the knowledge of or obvious to the normal user. The manufacturer is also required to anticipate the environment in which the product will be used and to notify the user of the potential risks arising from foreseeable use or misuse in the foreseeable environment.

The finding of the jury that the winch was not employed in normal use at the time of the accident is a factual determination which should not be set aside unless clearly wrong. A review of the record reveals that McDermott modified the winch by permanently engaging the clutch; that this modification permanently removed one of the safety and control features designed for its safe and proper operation; the disengagement of the clutch without the engagement of the additional safety features would have prevented the accident; the basic safety mechanisms of the winch were not utilized; the winch was installed backwards thereby requiring the operator to stand away from the controls; and the employees/operators were uninformed regarding familiarity with the controls and proper operation of the winch. After careful review of the record we conclude that the jury's determination in this matter is not manifestly erroneous.

Affirmed.

CASE A.16

FEDERAL DEPOSIT INSURANCE CORPORATION V. WOODSIDE CONSTRUCTION, INC., 979 F.2D 172 (1992) UNITED STATES COURT OF APPEALS FOR THE NINTH CIRCUIT

Hug, Circuit Judge.

This case arose when Donald Galt (Galt) signed a deed of trust note twice and signed a contract of guaranty twice. The FDIC claims that Galt is liable for $912,000, first because he signed the note as an indorser or, alternatively, because he signed the contract of guaranty as a guarantor. Galt claims that all of his signatures were in a representative capacity and that he did not sign individually as an indorser or as a guarantor. The FDIC maintains that one of the signatures on the note and one of the signatures on the contract of guaranty were signed in Galt's individual capacity, making him liable as an indorser on the note or, alternatively, as a guarantor on the contract of guaranty. The district court granted summary judgment for Galt on both the indorsement issue and the guaranty issue.

Galt obtained a loan from Alaska Mutual Bank for $912,000 on behalf of Woodside Construction of which he was an officer. The loan was evidenced by a promissory note, a deed of trust, a loan agreement, and a contract of guaranty. The signatures appeared on the note as follows:

(signature of Galt)
Woodside Construction, Inc.

signature(s)
(signature of Galt)
Donald A. Galt, President

The contract of guaranty appears on the form as follows:

Woodside Construction, Inc.
(signature of Galt)
by Donald A. Galt
Title Vice President
by (signature of Galt)
Title
Guarantors:
    Guarantor
    Donald A. Galt

As can be seen, the note bore Galt's signature below the name of the corporation, on the line designating his representative capacity as president. It also bore Galt's signature above the name of the corporation with no representative capacity designated.

The contract of guaranty bore Galt's signature below the name of the corporation, on the line designating his representative capacity, and then bore his signature on a line where no representative capacity was indicated. He did not sign on the line designated for his signature as guarantor.

Alaska National Bank merged with two other banks and became Alliance Bank, which retained this Woodside obligation. The loan was declared to be in default, and Alliance Bank instituted this action in state court. Alliance Bank was closed by the Alaska Department of Commerce and Economic Development, and the FDIC was appointed receiver. This Woodside obligation was sold by FDIC, as receiver, to FDIC in its corporate capacity. The FDIC then removed this case to federal court. The district court entered summary judgment for the FDIC against Woodside Construction on the note but entered summary judgment for Galt against the FDIC. The FDIC appeals the judgment rendered for Galt.

The manner in which Galt signed the promissory note bound him as an indorser in his individual capacity. He signed the note under the corporate name with the designation of his representative capacity. He also signed the note above the corporate name with no designation of any representative capacity. It is this latter signature that creates Galt's liability.

UCC Sec. 3-403(2) provides:

An authorized representative who signs his own name to an instrument:

(a) is personally obligated if the instrument neither names the person represented nor shows that the representative signed in a representative capacity;

(b) except as otherwise established between the immediate parties, is personally obligated if the instrument names the person represented but does not show that the representative signed in a representative capacity, or if the instrument does not name the person represented but does show that the representative signed in a representative capacity.

Here, the first signature above the principal designation fails to indicate the representative capacity, and the second signature above the representative capacity fails to indicate the principal. Because the FDIC is the holder of the note here, parol evidence of intent is inadmissible, and Galt is personally liable.

The FDIC argues that Galt is liable for attorneys' fees. The note makes the indorser liable for the costs of collection, including attorneys' fees. Because we hold that Galt is the indorser, he is liable for attorneys' fees.

The judgment is Reversed.

CASE A.17

KEDZIE & 103RD CURRENCY EXCHANGE, INC. V. HODGE, 601 N.E.2D 803 (ILL. APP. 1 DIST. (1992)

APPELLATE COURT OF ILLINOIS

Linn, Justice.

Plaintiff, Kedzie & 103rd Street Currency Exchange, Inc., cashed a check for defendant Fred Fentress (who is not a party to this appeal). Defendant Beula M. Hodge, drawer of the check, notified her bank to stop payment on the check when Fentress, engaged to perform plumbing services, did not appear at her home to begin work. As a holder in due course, plaintiff sought damages from Hodge. The trial court, however, granted Hodge's motion to dismiss based on the defense of illegality.

Plaintiff states the issue as whether a holder in due course of a check takes the check free from the defense of illegality where the drawer of the check issued it as a partial advance payment for plumbing services to be rendered, but the payee was not licensed as a plumber.

Background

Plaintiff, an Illinois corporation doing business as a currency exchange, filed suit after the $500 check it had cashed for Fentress was returned marked "payment stopped." Hodge had made out the check to "Fred Fentress—A-OK Plumbing" as partial payment, in advance, for plumbing services at her residence. When he failed to appear on the date work was to begin, Hodge directed her bank to stop payment on the check. Fentress, in the meantime, cashed the check at plaintiff currency exchange, indorsing the back as "Fred Fentress A-OK Plumbing Sole Owner." Plaintiff obtained a default judgment against Fentress.

Hodge filed a motion to dismiss the action as to her, asserting the defense of illegality. She had discovered that Fentress was not a licensed plumber listed with either the State or Chicago. Under An Act in Relation to the Licensing and Regulation of Plumbers (Plumber's Licensing Act), plumbers must obtain a license before practicing their trade. A vio-

lation of the Act is a Class B misdemeanor for the first offense. According to Hodge, the plumbing contract was illegal and void, therefore, plaintiff took the check subject to the illegality defense. The trial court agreed and entered judgment in favor of Hodge.

Opinion

Under the UCC, commercial instruments including checks are meant to be freely negotiable, and to that end a holder in due course will take the instrument free from "all defenses of any party to the instrument with whom the holder has not dealt except such incapacity, or duress, or illegality of the transaction, as renders the obligation of the party a nullity."

Comment 6 to UCC Section 3-305 explains that the question of illegality is a matter of state law and if under the law governing the contract the effect of the illegality is to make the obligation entirely null and void, the defense is good.

The dispositive issue before us, therefore, is whether under Illinois law the contract between Hodge and the plumber was null and void. If so, the defense of illegality was properly asserted and applied in this case. If the underlying obligation was merely voidable, however, the defense fails.

The Illinois legislature, by adopting Section 3-305 of the UCC, has expressly declared that illegality *is* an available defense against a holder in due course, as long as the effect of the illegality is to render the obligation sued upon null and void.

Illinois courts should not apply the illegality defense against holders in due course unless the illegal transaction is of the type that wholly nullifies the contract and thereby renders the instrument subject to the illegality defense.

In this state, the legislature has passed extensive legislation relating to the licensing of many trades and professions, recognizing that the regulation of these professions is essential to the public health, safety, and welfare. In furtherance of the legislative goals of providing standards and protecting the public health, the Plumber's Licensing Act provides that one who attempts to practice plumbing without a license may suffer substantial penalties, including criminal prosecution and fines. By judicial construction, the unlicensed plumber also forfeits his right to compensation for illegal services rendered. The contract in question is not void unless the Plumber's Licensing Act or other legislation expressly declares it to be.

As a matter of policy, plaintiff argues that it is unfair to expect a currency exchange to police the negotiable instruments it receives to ferret out possible illegalities in the underlying contracts. While the argument is reasonable enough, the same could be made for all of the defenses which defeat the rights of holders in due course. The currency exchange does not have a way to ascertain if a check has been drafted under duress, if it represents a gambling debt, or if it is the check of one without legal capacity to be bound. The so-called "real" defenses are nonetheless valid and cut off the rights of the innocent holder of the instrument to obtain recourse against makers or endorsers of the instrument in question. Currency exchanges are in the business of cashing checks and undertake the attendant risks.

We conclude that the illegality defense asserted in this case is of the type to render the obligation a nullity under Section 3-305 of the Code. Therefore, we affirm the trial court's dismissal of the action against Hodge, as maker of the check.

Affirmed.

CASE A.18

FIRST AMERICAN BANK AND TRUST V. RISHOI, 553 SO.2D 1387 (FLA. APP. 5 DIST. 1990)
DISTRICT COURT OF APPEALS OF FLORIDA
Daniel, Chief Judge.

First American Bank and Trust appeals a summary judgment in favor of William M. Rishoi as receiver for Clara Lamstein and the business she operated under the name of Interamerican Business Consultants and Associates, Inc.

In *Crosby v. Lewis*, the Crosbys had purchased $180,000 in cashier's checks, payable to Lamstein, from various banks and financial institutions. The checks were all delivered to Lamstein as investments. Lamstein's business was later closed down by the State on the ground that it was an illegal "ponzi" or pyramiding scheme. The assets of the business were placed in the control of Rishoi as receiver. Eighty thousand dollars of the cashier's checks from the Crosbys had been cashed and deposited by Lamstein prior to the receivership. However, $100,000 in cashier's checks remained uncashed in Lamstein's possession. The Crosbys requested that the banks not pay the cashier's checks. The banks issued stop payment orders on the outstanding cashier's checks and subsequently dishonored the checks when presented by the receiver for payment.

Although the issuing banks were not parties to that action, this court stated:

> The banks which issued the cashier's checks are primarily liable to the receiver, and by refusing to honor the checks, they have prima facie violated the duties imposed on them.

Rishoi thereafter instituted suit against First American Bank and Trust claiming that the bank had improperly refused to honor the cashier's checks. The court below concluded that the bank had no right to stop payment on the cashier's checks and entered summary judgment in favor of Rishoi.

On appeal, the bank argues that Rishoi is not a holder in due course and therefore it was justified in refusing to honor the cashier's checks. The bank acknowledges that a cashier's check presented by a holder in due course may not be countermanded after issue. It also acknowledges that cashier's checks are treated as the next best thing to cash in the business community. On public policy grounds, however, the bank urges that it should be able to assist its customers by stopping payment on a cashier's check which has been obtained from a customer by a criminal act.

In *Warren Finance, Inc. v. Barnett Bank of Jacksonville, N.A.*, 552 So.2d 194 (Fla. 1989), the Florida Supreme Court recently held that, in accordance with common commercial practice and the use of a cashier's check as a cash substitute, any defenses which a bank may assert to avoid payment must be narrowly limited. The court concluded that, upon presentment for payment by a holder, a bank may only assert its real and personal defenses in order to refuse payment on a cashier's check issued by the bank. The bank may not, however, rely on a third party's defenses to refuse payment. The only inquiry a bank may make on presentment of a cashier's check is whether the payee or indorsee is in fact a legitimate holder, that is, whether the cashier's check is being presented by a thief or one who simply found a lost check, or whether the check has been materially altered. The court concluded that this approach maintains the validity and use of cashier's checks yet acknowledges the valid concerns of banks.

In the present case, the receiver was a legitimate holder and the bank had no real or personal defenses to assert against his claim for payment. Thus, the bank wrongfully dishonored its own obligation and is liable for payment. Accordingly, the trial court properly entered summary judgment in favor of the receiver.

Affirmed.

CASE A.19

DAVENPORT V. CHRYSLER CREDIT CORPORATION, 818 S.W. 2D 23 (1991)
COURT OF APPEALS OF TENNESSEE
Koch, Judge.

Larry and Debbie Davenport purchased a new 1987 Chrysler LeBaron from Gary Mathews Motors on October 28, 1987. They obtained financing through Chrysler Credit Corporation (Chrysler Credit) and signed a retail installment contract requiring them to make the first of 60 monthly payments on or before December 8, 1987.

The automobile developed mechanical problems before the Davenports could drive it off the dealer's lot. Even before their first payment was due, the Davenports had returned the automobile to the dealer seven times for repair. They were extremely dissatisfied and, after consulting a lawyer, decided to withhold their monthly payments until the matter was resolved.

Chrysler Credit sent the Davenports a standard delinquency notice when their first payment was 10 days late. The Davenports did not respond to the notice, and on December 23, 1987, Chrysler Credit telephoned the Davenports to request payment. Mrs. Davenport recounted the problems with the automobile and told Chrysler Credit that she would consult her lawyer and "would let them know about the payment." After consulting the dealer, Chrysler Credit informed Mrs. Davenport that it would repossess the automobile if she did not make the payment.

Employees of American Lender Service arrived at the Davenports' home on the evening of January 14, 1988. They informed the Davenports that they were "two payments in default" and requested the automobile. The Davenports insisted that they were not in default and, after a telephone call to their lawyer, refused to turn over the automobile until Chrysler Credit obtained the "proper paperwork." The American Lender Service employees left without the car.

Before leaving for work the next morning, Mr. Davenport parked the automobile in their enclosed garage and chained its rear end to a post using a logging chain and two padlocks. He also closed the canvas flaps covering the entrance to the garage and secured the flaps with cinder blocks. When the Davenports returned from work, they discovered that someone had entered the garage, cut one of the padlocks, and removed the automobile.

American Lender Service informed Chrysler Credit on January 18, 1988 that it had repossessed the automobile. On the same day, Chrysler Credit notified the Davenports that they could redeem the car before it was offered for sale. The Davenports never responded to the notice. Instead of selling the automobile immediately, Chrysler Credit held it for more than a year because of the Davenports' allegations that the automobile was defective. In July, 1989, Chrysler Credit informed the Davenports that the automobile had been sold and requested payment of the $6,774 deficiency. The proof supports the trial court's conclusion that Chrysler Credit had a legal right to initiate repossession procedures.

The Davenports' dissatisfaction with their automobile did not provide them with a basis to unilaterally refuse to honor their payment obligations in the retail installment contract. At the time the repossession took place, the Davenports had not requested rescission of the contract, attempted to revoke their acceptance of the automobile, pursued their remedies under the "lemon law," or taken any other formal steps to resolve their dispute with the dealer concerning the automobile. The Davenports' conduct gave Chrysler Credit an adequate basis to consider the loan to be in default and to decide to protect its collateral by repossessing the automobile.

The Tennessee General Assembly preserved the secured parties' self-help remedies when it enacted the Uniform Commercial Code in 1963. It also preserved the requirement that repossessions must be accomplished without a breach of the peace. The term "breach of the peace" is a generic term that includes all violations or potential violations of the public peace and order. We can find no support for limiting "breach of the peace" to criminal context.

Secured parties may repossess their collateral at a reasonable time and in a reasonable manner. Self-help procedures such as repossession are the product of a careful balancing of the interests of secured parties and debtors. Chrysler Credit and American Lender Service do not dispute that they obtained the automobile by entering a closed garage and by cutting a lock on a chain that would have prevented them from removing the automobile. The Davenports are only entitled to recover their damages stemming directly from the manner in which American Lender Service repossessed their automobile.

We reverse the trial court's judgment dismissing the Davenports' complaint.

CASE A.20

DEWSNUP V. TIMM, 116 L.ED. 2D 903, 112 S.CT. 773 (1992)
SUPREME COURT OF THE UNITED STATES
Blackmun, Justice.

We are confronted in this case with an issue concerning §506(d) of the Bankruptcy Code. May a debtor "strip down" a creditor's lien on real property to the value of the collateral, as judicially determined, when that value is less than the amount of the claim secured by the lien?

On June 1, 1978, respondents loaned $119,000 to petitioner Aletha Dewsnup and her husband, T. LaMar Dewsnup, since deceased. The loan was accompanied by a Deed of Trust granting a lien on two parcels of Utah farmland owned by the Dewsnups. Petitioner defaulted the following year. Under the terms of the Deed of Trust, respondents at that point could have proceeded against the real property collateral by accelerating the maturity of the loan, issuing a notice of default, and selling the land at a public foreclosure sale to satisfy the debt.

Respondents did issue a notice of default in 1981. Before the foreclosure sale took place, however, petitioner sought reorganization under Chapter 11 of the Bankruptcy Code. That bankruptcy petition was dismissed, as was a subsequent Chapter 11 petition. In June 1984, petitioner filed a petition seeking liquidation under Chapter 7 of the Code. Because of the pendency of these bankruptcy proceedings, respondents were not able to proceed to the foreclosure sale.

Petitioner-debtor takes the petition that §506(a) and §506(d) are complementary and to be read together. Because, under §506(a), a claim is secured only to the extent of the judicially determined value of the real property on which the lien is fixed, a debtor can void a lien on the property pursuant to §506(d) to the extent the claim is no longer secured and thus is not "an allowed secured claim." In other words §506(a) bifurcates classes of claims allowed under §502 into secured claims and unsecured claims; any portion of an allowed claim deemed to be unsecured under §506(a) is not an "allowed secured claim" within the lien-voiding scope of §506(d). Petitioner argues that there is no exception for unsecured property abandoned by the trustee.

We conclude that respondents' alternative position, espoused also by the United States, although not without its difficulty, generally is the best of the several approaches. Therefore, we hold that §506(d) does not allow petitioner to "strip down" respondents' lien, because respondents' claim is secured by a lien and has been fully allowed pursuant to §502.

The practical effect of petitioner's argument is to freeze the creditor's secured interest at the judicially determined valuation. By this approach, the creditor would lose the benefit of any increase in the value of the property by the time of the foreclosure sale. The increase would accrue to the benefit of the debtor, a result some of the parties describe as a "windfall."

We think, however, that the creditor's lien stays with the real property until the foreclosure. That is what was bargained for by the mortgagor and the mortgagee. Any increase over the judicially determined valuation during bankruptcy rightly accrues to the benefit of the creditor, not to the benefit of the debtor and not to the benefit of other unsecured creditors whose claims have been allowed and who had nothing to do with the mortgagor-mortgagee bargain.

No provision of the pre-Code statute permitted involuntary reduction of the amount of a creditor's lien for any reason other than payment on the debt.

The judgment of the court of appeals is affirmed.

CASE A.21

DISTRICT OF COLUMBIA V. HOWELL, 607 A.2D 501 (D.C. APP. 1992) DISTRICT OF COLUMBIA COURT OF APPEALS

Farrell, Associate Judge.

The Murch School Summer Discovery Program was designed to provide hands-on education for gifted and talented eight- and nine-year-old children. The program originated in 1985 when Mrs. Gill, the Murch School principal, attended a reception at Mount Vernon College arranged by Greg Butta, a Ph.D. candidate at The American University, to advertise the success of a summer program he had conducted at Mount Vernon. The program interested Mrs. Gill, and after several discussions, Butta sent her a formal proposal for conducting a similar program at the Murch School. Gill proposed changes to the proposal, then solicited and received approval for the program from the Assis-

tant Superintendent for the District of Columbia Public Schools.

Butta hired the staff for the summer program, including some of the instructors who had taught in the Mount Vernon program. Mrs. Gill, however, reviewed all of the instructors' resumes, had veto authority over their hiring, and interviewed most of the staff, including A. Louis Jagoe, before the hiring was made final. Jagoe, who was hired to teach chemistry to the eight- and nine-year-olds in the program, held a master's degree in chemistry and was a Ph.D. candidate at The American University. Before the first general staff meeting, he told Butta that as part of the class he would do a luminescence experiment and a "cold-pack" experiment and wanted to make sparklers with the children. Jagoe and Butta discussed the safety of the sparkler experiment only in regard to the location where the children would be allowed to light the sparklers.

On August 1, 1985, a staff meeting was held at which Gill, Butta, and all instructors and counselors were present. Each instructor gave a brief talk about what he or she intended to do in class. Several instructors testified that Jagoe told the group, including Mrs. Gill, that he planned to make sparklers as one of the chemistry experiments. Gill, who was in and out of the meeting, did not remember hearing Jagoe discuss the experiment, although notes she took at the meeting reflect that she heard him discuss the luminescence and cold pack experiments and asked him questions about these. Gill spoke and emphasized the "hands-on" nature of the program and her hopes for its success.

One child attending the program was nine-year-old Dedrick Howell, whose parents enrolled him after receiving the school brochure in the mail. The accident occurred on August 12, 1985. At the beginning of the chemistry class, Jagoe distributed his "recipe" for sparklers to the children and also wrote it on the black board. Along with other chemical ingredients, the recipe called for the use of potassium perchlorate as the oxidizing agent. Potassium perchlorate was described at trial as an extremely unstable and highly volatile chemical often used to make rocket fuel. Commercially made sparklers are not made with potassium perchlorate.

The children scooped the chemicals, including the potassium perchlorate, out of jars and, using pestles, ground up the mixture in mortars. While they were combining the chemicals, Jagoe ignited three different chemical mixtures at the front of the room with a butane lighter. Butta was present for one of the ignitions when he entered the room to drop off metal hangers for use in the experiment. Mrs. Gill also entered the room at one point, and saw the children working at tables wearing goggles or glasses. She also saw Jagoe at the front of the room lighting the chemicals with a fire extinguisher on the table next to him.

The children continued to grind the material while a counselor, Rebecca Seashore, distributed pieces of metal hangers to be dipped into the mixture at a later time. Dedrick Howell was specifically told not to dip the hanger into the material until instructed to do so.

Moments later the chemicals exploded in front of Dedrick. The chemicals burned at 5,000 degrees fahrenheit, and Dedrick was burned over 25 percent of his body including his hands, arms, chest, and face.

An employer generally is not liable for injuries to third parties caused by an independent contractor over whom (or over whose work) the employer has reserved no control. There are exceptions to the rule, however, one of which is that one who employs an independent contractor to do work involving a special danger to others which the employer knows or has reason to know to be inherent in or normal to the work, or which he contemplates or has reason to contemplate when making the contract, is subject to liability for physical harm caused to such others by the contractor's failure to take reasonable precautions against such danger.

It is sufficient that work of any kind involves a risk, recognizable in advance, of physical harm to others which is inherent in the work itself, or normally to be expected in the ordinary course of the usual or prescribed way of doing it, or that the employer has special reason to contemplate such a risk *under the particular circumstances under which the work is to be done*.

The sparkler experiment combined flammable, combustible chemicals, open flame, and children; for that very reason, presumably, the children had been equipped with goggles. Though sparklers are explosives of a lesser order, conducting controlled explosions is a textbook example of an inherently dangerous activity. It was not unreasonable for the jury to concude that the manufacture of sparklers by nine-year-old children was an inherently dangerous activity.

Therefore, the jury was well within its authority in finding that Jagoe was an independent contractor performing inherently dangerous work of which the district had actual or constructive knowledge.

The judgment is affirmed as to liability and as to the award of $8 million in damages both for pain and suffering and for past medical expenses.

CASE A.22

LITTLE V. HOWARD JOHNSON CO., 183 MICH. APP. 675, 455 N.W. 2D 390 (1990) COURT OF APPEALS OF MICHIGAN

MacKenzie, Judge.

Plaintiff Joy Little was injured on January 23, 1982 when she slipped on a walkway which allegedly had not been adequately cleared of ice and snow. The walkway was located on property on which a restaurant business was being operated as a franchise of defendant, Howard Johnson Company. Plaintiff filed suit alleging liability for her injuries. In district court, Howard Johnson moved for summary disposition. The circuit court denied defendant's subsequent motion for summary disposition and the case proceeded to mediation. When it mediated at less than $10,000, the case was removed to district court for lack of circuit

court jurisdiction. The district court found no factual dispute and ruled as a matter of law that defendant was neither directly nor vicariously liable for plaintiff's injuries and, accordingly, granted the motion. The circuit court reversed without elaboration.

Little posited three theories under which she claimed Howard Johnson as a franchisor may be held liable for the injuries she sustained at the franchisee's restaurant: (1) direct liability as a possessor of the land, (2) vicarious liability based on agency principles, and (3) liability based on an apparent agency theory.

1. Direct Liability. The general rule in Michigan is that invitors are liable for known dangerous conditions of property and for dangerous conditions which might be discovered with reasonable care, however, an invitor's direct liability requires the presence of both possession and control over the land.

Little contends that defendant should be deemed a "possessor" of the land as a result of the rights of control it retained in its franchise agreement with the restaurant's franchisee. We disagree. The franchise agreement merely provides that the franchisee "at all times will maintain the interior and exterior of the buildings and surrounding premises in a clean, orderly, and sanitary condition satisfactory to Howard Johnson." In short, there is no issue of fact that defendant was a possessor of the premises who could be held directly liable for plaintiff's injuries.

2. Vicarious Liability. Generally, a principal is responsible for the negligence of its agent. In Michigan, the test for a principal-agent relationship is whether the principal has the right to control the agent. The threshold question here is what constitutes "control" sufficient to deem a franchisee to be an agent of a franchisor. Howard Johnson argues that a franchisor must have the right to control the day-to-day operations of a franchisee in order to establish an agency relationship. Little, on the other hand, maintains that an agency relationship is created where the franchisor retains the right to set standards regarding the products and services offered by the franchisee, the right to regulate such items as the furnishings and advertising used by the franchisee, and the right to inspect for conformance with the agreement. We agree with defendant.

This court has repeatedly held that in order to establish vicarious liability in such actions, the landowner must have retained some control and direction over the actual day-to-day work. It is not enough that the owner retained mere contractual control, the right to make safety inspections, or general oversight. The franchise agreement in this case primarily insured the uniformity and standardization of products and services offered by a Howard Johnson restaurant. These obligations do not affect the control of daily operations.

3. Apparent Agency. Howard Johnson argues that the district court properly concluded that no genuine issue of fact existed regarding its liability under an agency theory. We agree.

Here, Little has failed to offer any documentary evidence that she was harmed as a result of relying on the perceived fact that the franchise was an agent of Howard Johnson. No evidence was presented which indicated that plaintiff justifiably expected that the walkway would be free of ice and snow because she believed that Howard Johnson operated the restaurant.

Reversed.

CASE A.23

CATALINA MORTGAGE CO., INC. V. MONIER, 166 ARIZ. 71, 800 P.2D 574 (1990) SUPREME COURT OF ARIZONA

Feldman, Vice Chief Judge.

In 1984, Michael Monier and Talon Financial Corporation (Talon) formed the Coronado Industrial Investors Limited Partnership (Coronado). Monier and Talon were general partners; other individuals and entities were limited partners in the venture.

Shortly after its formation, Coronado purchased an office and warehouse complex in Tucson. In 1986, the partnership refinanced this property with a loan from Catalina Mortgage Company (Catalina). Talon's president, Roger Howard, executed a promissory note in the amount of $675,000 on behalf of Coronado. In mid-1987, Talon withdrew as a general partner, leaving Monier as the sole general partner in Coronado. The promissory note matured and $687,935.39 plus interest is now due and owing. Coronado filed for protection pursuant to Chapter 11 of the Bankruptcy Code.

In January 1989, Catalina filed a complaint against Monier in United States District Court, seeking judgment for the amount due on the promissory note plus interest, costs, and attorney's fees. Catalina alleged that Monier was jointly and severally liable with the partnership entity for the debt. Monier answered, contending, among other things, that because the note was an obligation of the partnership, the partnership assets had to be exhausted before the creditor sought recovery from an individual general partner.

Discussion

If a partnership's debt is contractual in nature, common law requires creditors to resort to and exhaust partnership assets before reaching the partners' individual assets. At common law, a partner is only jointly liable for the partnership's contractual debts, though partners are jointly and severally liable for tort obligations.

As adopted in most states, the Uniform Partnership Act (UPA) preserves this common law rule. The Arizona version of the UPA, however, provides that all partners are liable jointly and severally for everything chargeable to the partnership, and for all other debts and obligations of the partnership; but any partner may enter into a separate obligation to perform a partnership contract.

Catalina maintains that because the statute imposes joint and several liability on all partners, it may proceed against Monier without exhausting partnership assets. Catalina distinguishes cases from other jurisdictions that have considered the issue on the grounds that the applicable law imposed only joint liability as opposed to joint and several liability, that some states specifically provide by statute that partnership assets must be exhausted prior to imposing liability on individual partners for contractual obligations, and that the bankruptcy courts in some instances have misconstrued the state law involved.

Several liability is separate and distinct from liability of another to the extent that an independent action may be brought without joinder of others. The individual liability associated with partners that are jointly liable is not separate and distinct from the liability of all the partners jointly. Rather, that individual liability arises only after it has been shown that the partnership assets are inadequate. No direct cause of action may be maintained against the individual partners until the above condition is met. Several liability, on the other hand, imposes no such conditions precedent before one can be held individually liable.

Conclusion

We hold, therefore, that the scheme imposed by Arizona statutes is simply that a general partner is jointly and severally liable for partnership debts. The partner may be sued severally and his assets reached even though the partnership or other partners are not sued and their assets not applied to the debt. Under Arizona law a creditor may obtain a judgment against an individual general partner on a partnership debt and may reach the partner's assets prior to exhausting partnership assets.

CASE A.24

JOHNSON V. DODGEN, 451 N.W. 2D. 168 (1990) SUPREME COURT OF IOWA

Lavorato, Justice.

This breach of contract action is the aftermath of a bank failure caused by the embezzlement of $16.7 million by Des Moines stockbroker Gary Lewellyn. In 1967 Joe W. Dodgen agreed to buy controlling interest in the First National Bank of Humboldt under a stock purchase agreement (agreement) calling for monthly payments. Ben P. and Adeline G. St. John, the sellers, died shortly thereafter. Two trusts were then established to receive payments under the agreement.

Dodgen assigned the agreement to his company, Humboldt Realty Insurance Co., Inc. (Humboldt Realty), which was not in existence at the time the agreement was executed, underwent several name changes until it became known as Iowa Growthland Financial Corporation. After the bank was closed in 1982, Iowa Growthland continued to make payments under the agreement until 1984.

The trusts then sued Dodgen and Iowa Growthland for the payments that were in arrears. Dodgen and Iowa Growthland filed an answer in which they raised failure of consideration as an affirmative defense. Simply put, they were claiming that the consideration for the agreement failed when the bank went out of existence. In addition, Dodgen asserted that he was not personally liable because he signed the agreement as an agent for Humboldt Realty. In its counterclaim, Iowa Growthland sought damages on the theory of unjust enrichment for payments it made after the bank was closed.

The case was tried to a jury. By way of answers to special verdict forms, the jury found that the trustees were not entitled to recover for breach of contract, that Dodgen was indeed acting as an agent when he signed the agreement, and that Iowa Growthland was not entitled to damages for its claim of unjust enrichment.

The district court granted a new trial on all the issues. Dodgen and Iowa Growthland appealed; the trustees cross-appealed.

We reverse and remand with directions to enter judgment in favor of the trustees pursuant to Iowa Rule of Appellate Procedure 26.

I. Failure of Consideration.

Dodgen and Iowa Growthland contend that the continued existence of the bank was the essence or root of the agreement—the thing Dodgen really bargained for. They argue that when the bank was closed the consideration for Dodgen's promise to pay failed. This failure of consideration, they assert, excused any future performance on their part.

There is a difference between lack of consideration and failure of consideration. A lack of consideration means no contract is ever formed. In contrast, a failure of consideration means the contract is valid when formed but becomes unenforceable because the performance bargained for has not been rendered.

In our view the potential failure of any business that is being sold is always a risk in the contemplation of the parties. If the buyer wants protection against the risk, the simple solution is to hedge against it in the agreement. That was not done here. Consequently, Dodgen assumed that risk.

What Dodgen bargained for was control of the bank through the stock he purchased; he got it and had it for fifteen years. The fact that his investment later turned out worthless does not, in our view, constitute failure of consideration.

A. Essence of the agreement.

Under the agreement here, Dodgen agreed to purchase from St. John 506 shares of capital stock of the bank. The 506 shares represented 50.6% of the issued and outstanding stock of the bank. By this purchase, Dodgen was acquiring controlling interest in the bank.

B. The executory nature of the agreement.

This issue is inextricably intertwined with the essence of the agreement issue. Dodgen and Iowa Growthland contend that the agreement was still executory when the bank was closed because the trustees had physical possession of the stock. While the trustees are still able to turn over the stock, Dodgen and Iowa Growthland argue such a gesture would be meaningless because the asset that the stock represents is nonexistent. So, they argue, there was a failure of consideration when the bank was closed.

Here we think the parties intended title to the stock to pass to Dodgen once the stock was registered in his name. At this point several things had occurred. Dodgen had made the down payment called for in the agreement and began exercising control of the bank. Likewise, St. John had substantially performed his part of the agreement. Only two promises remained unperformed: Dodgen's full payment of the purchase price and St. John's delivery of physical possession of the stock.

In these circumstances, we think there was a constructive delivery of the stock to Dodgen. Although the collateral provision of the agreement denied Dodgen physical possession of the stock, it did give him the right to such possession upon full payment. The provision also gave him rights of ownership in all other respects. Risk of loss passed with this constructive delivery. The decline in the stock's value gave Dodgen no greater right to avoid his obligation to pay than an enhanced value would have given St. John an excuse for not delivering the stock.

C. Inability to pledge the stock as security.

It is true that under the agreement Dodgen could not borrow against the stock. Dodgen and Iowa Growthland assert this constraint as further evidence that consideration for the agreement failed. The short answer to this argument is that Dodgen should not be allowed to take advantage of a provision he agreed to.

II. Unjust Enrichment.

We have already determined that there was not, as a matter of law, a failure of consideration. In view of our holding on the failure of consideration issue, we think the district court should have sustained the trustees' motion for directed verdict on the unjust enrichment counterclaim.

III. Agency.

The trustees moved for a directed verdict against Dodgen personally because the record showed he signed the agreement. Dodgen resisted the motion, contending there was enough evidence in the record to generate a jury question on his agency defense. The only evidence on this point was Dodgen's testimony. Dodgen testified that when he signed the agreement St. John agreed that Humboldt Realty—Iowa Growthland's predecessor—would be the responsible party. The district court overruled the motion. The jury then determined that Dodgen was acting as an agent for Humboldt Realty when he signed the agreement. For reasons that follow we think the district court should have sustained the motion for directed verdict.

At the time Dodgen and St. John signed the agreement, Humboldt Realty was not in existence. Ordinarily in these circumstances Dodgen would be personally liable. The law is clear that an agent who purports to act on behalf of a nonexistent principal is liable as a party to the agreement. The rationale for the rule is simply that in such circumstances there is no agency. This situation frequently happens when a corporate promoter enters into contracts before the corporation is actually incorporated.

There is, however, an exception to this rule. If the other contracting party knows that the principal does not exist and looks to the principal alone for responsibility, the promoter is relieved of personal liability.

Here the pivotal question is whether St. John agreed to look to Humboldt Realty alone for payment. We think reasonable minds would conclude from this record that he did not.

We have substantial evidence that establishes Dodgen was acting in his personal capacity. First, as the district court ruled, the language of the agreement is unequivocal on this point. For example, the opening paragraph states that "This agreement made and entered into by and between B. P. St. John and Joe W. Dodgen said B. P. St. John being hereafter referred to as the seller and the said Joe W. Dodgen being hereafter referred to as the buyer." Moreover, Dodgen ostensibly signed the agreement in his individual capacity.

Second, St. John and Dodgen were, at the time of the agreement, very knowledgeable in financial and legal matters. It is inconceivable to us that St. John would turn over valuable assets and look solely to a nonexistent corporation for payment. It is also equally inconceivable to us that Dodgen would fail to insist on express language in the agreement that would relieve him of personal liability. Simply put, we think reasonable minds would conclude that the absence of such language meant that St. John was looking to Dodgen for payment, and Dodgen knew it.

Last, in 1982 Dodgen acknowledged his personal liability. In a letter to one of the trustees—a letter we previously mentioned—Dodgen said:

> You are also correct in that the contract between me and Ben and Adeline St. John is a personal obligation even though it was later assigned to First Investors Services, Inc.

This damaging admission coupled with the other evidence leads us to conclude that the district court should have sustained the motion for directed verdict on the agency issue.

IV. Disposition.

We reverse the post-trial ruling of the district court. We remand the case to the district court with directions to enter judgment in favor of the trustees for $160,976.26—the delinquent amount at the time of trial—together with interest and costs.

CASE A.25

UNITED STATES V. WRW CORPORATION, 986 F.2D 138 (1993)
UNITED STATES COURT OF APPEALS FOR THE SIXTH CIRCUIT
Peck, Judge.

In 1985, civil penalties totaling $90,350 were assessed against WRW Corporation (WRW), a Kentucky corporation, for serious violations of safety standards under the Federal Mine Safety and Health Act (the Act) which resulted in the deaths of two miners. Following the imposition of civil penalties, WRW liquidated its assets and went out of business.

Three individual defendants, who were the sole shareholders, officers, and directors of WRW, were later indicted and convicted for willful violations of mandatory health and safety standards under the Act. Roger Richardson, Noah Woolum, and William Woolum each served prison sentences and paid criminal fines. After his release from prison, Roger Richardson filed for bankruptcy under Chapter 7 of the Bankruptcy Code.

The United States (Government) brought this action in May of 1988 against WRW and Roger Richardson, Noah Woolum, and William Woolum to recover the civil penalties previously imposed against WRW. The district court denied the individual defendants' motion to dismiss and granted summary judgment to the Government piercing the corporate veil under state law and holding the individual defendants liable for the civil penalties assessed against WRW. For the reasons discussed herein, we affirm.

Piercing the Corporate Veil.

Having determined that the imposition of a $90,350 sanction upon the defendants does not violate principles of double jeopardy, we turn to the defendants' argument that the district court erred in holding the individual defendants liable for the penalty by piercing the corporate veil of WRW under Kentucky law.

The district court held that it was appropriate to pierce WRW's corporate veil under either an equity theory or an alter ego theory, both of which are recognized under Kentucky law. Under either theory, the following factors must be considered when determining whether to pierce the corporate veil: (1) undercapitalization, (2) a failure to observe the formalities of corporate existence, (3) non-payment or overpayment of dividends, (4) a siphoning off of funds by dominant shareholders, and (5) the majority shareholders having guaranteed corporate liabilities in their individual capacities.

The court first found that WRW was undercapitalized because it was incorporated with only $3,000 of capital, which the record indicates was insufficient to pay normal expenses associated with the operation of a coal mine. The district court next found that WRW failed to observe corporate formalities, noting that no bylaws were produced by the defendants, and all corporate actions taken by the individual defendants were without corporation authorization. Finally, although WRW never distributed any dividends to the individual defendants, and there was no evidence that the individual defendants siphoned off corporate funds, these factors alone do not mitigate against piercing the corporate veil in this case because WRW was never sufficiently capitalized and operated at a loss during its two years of active existence.

In addition to holding that the equities of this case support piercing the corporate veil, the district court held that the corporate veil should be pierced under the "alter ego" theory, because WRW and the defendants did not have separate personalities. In light of the lack of observance of corporate formalities or distinction between the individual defendants and the corporation, we agree with the district court's conclusion that "there was a complete merger of ownership and control of WRW with the individual Defendants."

The specific factual findings made by the district court amply support piercing the corporate veil of WRW and holding the individual defendants liable for the penalty assessed against the corporate entity. For all of the foregoing reasons, the judgment of the district court is Affirmed.

CASE A.26

NEAL V. ALABAMA BY-PRODUCTS CORPORATION, NO. 8282, 1990 DEL. CH. LEXIS 127 (1990) COURT OF CHANCERY OF DELAWARE

Chandler, Vice Chancellor.

Alabama By-Products Corporation (ABC) is a Delaware corporation engaged during the 1970s and 1980s (and for many years before that) primarily in three lines of business. It mined coal on a cost plus basis for Alabama Power Company (a major utility in Alabama); it mined coal for its own account from surface and underground mines that it owned; and it manufactured and sold foundry coke from a plant in Birmingham called the Tarrant plant. To a certain extent ABC was also engaged in the development and sale of timber and forestry products on lands it owned.

ABC's two classes of stock traded in the over-the-counter market and were not listed on an exchange. Trading history in the stock was sporadic, but shows that the average bid price between 1977 and 1984 ranged from $47 to $75 per share. Class A stock had voting rights, while class B stock did not. At all times relevant to this lawsuit, there were about 757,300 class A shares and 1,000,000 class B shares authorized, issued, and outstanding.

Drummond, an Alabama corporation, is also engaged in the mining and sale of coal in the state of Alabama. In 1977 it became interested in acquiring ABC. Between September 1977 and February 1978 Drummond acquired, in privately negotiated transactions,

about 75,800 class A shares of ABC stock and 188,167 class B shares. Drummond also obtained a controlling interest in Alabama Chemical Products Company (ACPC), a holding company which at the time held 476,420 class A shares of ABC stock (about 63 percent of those outstanding). Drummond paid the equivalent of $110 per share of ABC stock in these transactions. The book value of ABC's common stock on December 31, 1977, was $55.47 per share. Drummond eventually caused the liquidation of ACPC, with the resulting distribution of the ABC class A stock to Drummond and other ACPC stockholders.

Drummond reconstituted ABC's board of directors in December 1977, replacing five of the nine ABC directors with Drummond designees. At all relevant times for purposes of this litigation, a majority of ABC's directors were also directors or executive officers of Drummond. Around the time that it gained control of ABC's board, Drummond created an executive committee consisting of Gary Neal Drummond, E. A. Drummond, and the then current president of ABC. The executive committee had authority to act on behalf of ABC's board of directors. From its controlling position, Drummond caused ABC to lease some of its coal reserves to Drummond. Drummond also purchased ABC mined coal and resold it in certain markets.

In late December 1977 Drummond presented a merger proposal to ABC's board, proposing the acquisition of all outstanding shares not owned by Drummond. This proposal was later withdrawn. Three years later, in 1981, Drummond discussed with Goldman, Sachs, and Company (Goldman Sachs), its investment banker, the possibility of acquiring the remaining equity in ABC. Goldman Sachs recommended at the time that Drummond propose a cash merger at a minimum price of $85 per share. Nevertheless, Drummond decided not to pursue the acquisition at that time.

On March 17, 1983, Drummond again proposed a merger to ABC's board of directors, a proposal by which each share of ABC not owned by Drummond would have been converted into the right to receive $65 in cash and ABC would have become a wholly-owned subsidiary of Drummond. A special committee of ABC's board of directors (consisting of three ABC directors who were not directors or executive officers of Drummond) recommended the retention of the firm of Kidder, Peabody, and Company, Inc. (Kidder Peabody), to evaluate the 1983 merger proposal and to determine whether it was fair from a financial point of view to unaffiliated ABC shareholders. Kidder Peabody's report, submitted in September 1983, concluded that Drummond's $65 cash merger offer was not fair from a financial point of view to unaffiliated ABC shareholders. Drummond's 1983 proposal was later withdrawn.

Drummond acquired additional shares of ABC class A and class B stock in 1984 for $54.40 and $55 per share respectively. Although it was provided, in connection with the 1984 acquisitions, that additional payments would be made by Drummond if its board of directors formally approved a tender offer for shares or a merger with ABC within stipulated time limits, no tender offer or merger proposal was made during the time limits.

In December 1984 Drummond made a tender offer for any and all outstanding shares of class A and class B common stock of ABC at $75 per share. Neither Drummond nor ABC sought a fairness opinion from an independent investment banker or financial adviser with respect to the tender offer. Nor was a committee of outside ABC directors appointed to review or comment upon the fairness of the proposed transaction. ABC's board decided it would take no position with respect to the fairness of the tender offer price, leaving the ultimate determination to the judgment of the individual shareholder.

As a result of the tender offer, Drummond became the holder of more than 90 percent of ABC's outstanding and issued shares. Then, on August 13, 1985, Drummond effected a short-form merger under Delaware law, pursuant to which the minority shareholders were cashed out at $75.60 per share. This amount was determined by adopting the 1984 tender offer price ($75) and adding a $0.60 quarterly dividend that had been missed in 1985.

Following the August 13, 1985 merger, certain minority shareholders perfected their appraisal rights pursuant to §262 of Title 8 of the Delaware Code. These minority shareholders own approximately 50,000 class A shares and 75,000 class B shares. Neal characterizes this proceeding as a two-pronged action in which separate claims for appraisal and for unfair dealing have been joined. Drummond, as successor to ABC, is the only necessary and appropriate defendant, say petitioners, as to both the unfair dealing claim and the appraisal claim.

Neal argues they have avoided the risk of double recovery by limiting the relief requested for the unfair dealing claim to (1) costs of the proceeding, (2) reasonable attorneys' fees and disbursements, and (3) expert witness fees incurred by petitioners as part of the appraisals action.

Neal also accuses Drummond of post-merger unfair dealing, complaining that Drummond's defense of the $75.60 merger price is based on contrived liabilities and transparent efforts to ascribe negative values to certain ABC assets, all of which were not disclosed to shareholders at the time of the merger. These allegedly manipulative tactics, added to the unfair dealing associated with the notice of merger and merger price, form the basis for petitioners' unfair dealing claim and, they insist, warrant an award of litigation costs.

Neal challenges the fairness of the merger price, noting that it was fixed unilaterally by Drummond without the benefit of independent expert opinion as to its fairness. They also point out that no committee, special or otherwise, was appointed to review the fairness of the merger proposal, that the merger notice to stockholders failed to disclose certain allegedly material financial information, causing stockholders to make decisions with regard to accepting the merger price or seeking appraisal on the basis of very limited information about the assets and prospects of ABC.

Neal contends that ABC's fair value was $193.40 per share on August 13, 1985. That conclusion rests upon the testimony of their valuation expert, Mr. Kenneth McGraw, based on an analysis performed by Benchmark Valuation Consultants, a division of the accounting firm Peat Marwick Maine & Co. (Benchmark) which in turn was based in part on an analysis and valuation of ABC's coal reserves and coal mining operations by Dames & Moore, a firm with expertise in geologic, mining, and natural resource engineering.

McGraw testified that Benchmark valued ABC using three alternative methods: historical earnings, net asset value, and discounted cash flow. By the historical earnings approach, Benchmark arrived at a value of $166 per share of ABC stock. The net asset methodology resulted in a value of $205 per share. The discounted cash flow approach resulted in a valuation of $225 per share. Benchmark then applied a weighted average, assigning the greatest weight (40 percent) to the historical earnings and net asset value approaches and the lowest weight (20 percent) to the discounted cash flow methodology, to arrive at a valuation based on all three valuation methodologies, of $193.40 per share.

Respondents assert that the merger price was fair. The merger price, in fact, was extremely generous, because respondents contend that ABC's statutory fair value is only $64 per share, more than $11 less than Drummond paid in the merger. Respondents' valuation is based upon the testimony of their expert trial witnesses, Arnold Spangler, a general partner at Lazard Freres & Co. (Lazard) and Robert Wilken of Paul Weir Company (Weir) who estimated the company's coal reserves.

Lazard's valuation appears to have been based on a hybrid discounted cash flow and net asset methodology. The analysis was designed to predict the value of future cash flows from ABC's continuing operations, including ABC owned mines, power company mines, and the Tarrant coke plant over a 13 year period from 1985 through 1997. This period corresponded to either the life of a variety of ABC's long-term contracts or to the exhaustion of its coal reserves, leaving only its Tarrant coke operation viable in 1997. Lazard arrived at a net after tax cash flow that ABC's continuing operations were expected to generate from 1985 to 1997, to which Lazard applied a multiple of five against the 1997 projected net cash flow (the terminal value) arriving at a value for ABC's activities following the terminal year.

The contrasting opinions regarding ABC's value in August 1985 demonstrate how differently petitioners and respondents view the business prospects and asset valuations of ABC. These starkly contrasting views have been presented to the Court through expert witnesses who have relied on complex business valuation methodologies. Although Benchmark relied on three different methodologies, there has been remarkably little disagreement over the legitimacy of the valuation techniques used by the parties in this case. Dispute has been over the assumptions on which the methodologies have been based as well as the underlying information supplied to the experts. With expert opinions arrayed on each side of widely divergent arguments about the worth of certain assets, or the scope of certain liabilities, the Court is forced to pick and choose among the competing contentions, in search of a reasonable, and fair, value. That is this Court's mandate: determine the fair value of the stock of ABC on August 13, 1985.

Both sides have relied on a discounted future returns model and a net asset model, with petitioners' expert also using a historical earnings analysis. Other valuation approaches, with equivalent theoretical legitimacy, could have been used. But I am satisfied that respondents discounted future cash flow methodology is the appropriate valuation model in this case, especially since it was also used by petitioners' expert.

The more difficult task is to move beyond the analytical framework in order to test the underlying assumptions about ABC that the experts poured into the valuation models. This is the heart of the matter, for, as one commentator has noted, methods of valuation, including a discounted cash flow analysis, are only as good as the inputs to the model. A valuation methodology can produce a correct answer for any type of input. So the relevant question is not how correct the resulting answer is, but how correct was the input or datum that produced the answer? Accordingly this court must view the assumptions and underlying factual premises for the valuation methodology actually used by both respondents and petitioners. Not every assumption need be scrutinized, however, for the parties have managed to agree, despite their best efforts, on certain assumptions and facts. Serious disputes exist in about eight different areas. The four principal areas of disagreement concern the value of ABC's coal reserves, the value of ABC's investment in the VP-5 mine in Virginia, the amount of ABC's excess working capital and, finally, the EME report on the purported environmental liability at ABC's Tarrant coke plant. The Court is satisfied that respondents discounted future cash flow methodology is the appropriate valuation model in this case, especially since it was also used by petitioner's expert.

The fair value of the petitioners' shares subject to the court's appraisal was $180.67 per share on August 13, 1985. Petitioners shall be entitled to simple interest upon that amount at a rate of 12½ percent, payable from the date of the merger to the date of payment. The costs of this proceeding, other than expert witness costs and attorneys' fees, shall be assessed against the surviving corporation.

An Order consistent with this Memorandum Opinion has been entered.

CASE A.27

LAMPF, PLEVA, LIPKIND, PRUPIS & PETIGROW V. GILBERTSON, 111 S.CT. 2773, 115 L.ED.2D 321 (1991) UNITED STATES SUPREME COURT

Blackmun, Justice.

The controversy arises from the sale of seven Connecticut limited partnerships formed for the purpose of purchasing and leasing computer hardware and software. Petitioner Lampf, Pleva, Lipkind, Prupis & Petigrow is a West Orange, New Jersey, law firm that aided in organizing the partnerships and that provided additional legal services, including the preparation of opinion letters addressing the tax consequences of investing in the partnerships. The several plaintiff-respondents purchased units in one or more of the partnerships during the years 1979 through 1981 with the expectation of realizing federal income tax benefits therefrom.

The partnerships failed, due in part to the technological obsolescence of their wares. In late 1982 and early 1983, Gilbertson, et al., received notice that the United States Internal Revenue Service was investigating the partnerships. The IRS subsequently disallowed the claimed tax benefits because of overvaluation of partnership assets and lack of profit motive.

On November 3, 1986, and June 4, 1987, Gilbertson, et al., filed their respective complaints in the United States District Court for the District of Oregon, naming as defendant's petitioner and others involved in the preparation of offering memoranda for the partnerships. The complaints alleged that plaintiff-respondents were induced to invest in the partnerships by misrepresentations in the offering memoranda, in violation of, among other things, §10(b) of the 1934 Securities Exchange Act and Rule 10b-5. The claimed misrepresentations were said to include assurances that the investments would entitle the purchasers to substantial tax benefits; that the leasing of the hardware and software packages would generate a profit; that the software was readily marketable; and that certain equipment appraisals were accurate and reasonable. Gilbertson, et al., asserted that they became aware of the alleged misrepresentations only in 1985 following the disallowance by the IRS of the tax benefits claimed.

After consolidating the actions for discovery and pretrial proceedings, the District Court granted summary judgment for the defendants on the ground that the complaints were not timely filed. The Court of Appeals for the Ninth Circuit reversed and remanded the cases. In view of the divergence of opinion among the Circuits regarding the proper limitations period for Rule 10b-5 claims, we granted certiorari to address this important issue.

It is the usual rule that when Congress has failed to provide a statute of limitations for a federal cause of action, a court "borrows" or "absorbs" the local time limitation most analogous to the case at hand. This practice, derived from the Rules of Decision Act, has enjoyed sufficient longevity that we may assume that, in enacting remedial legislation, Congress ordinarily "intends by its silence that we borrow state law." The rule, however, is not without exception.

First, the court must determine whether a uniform statute of limitations is to be selected. Where a federal cause of action tends in practice to "encompass numerous and diverse topics and subtopics," such that a single state limitations period may not be consistently applied within a jurisdiction, we have concluded that the federal interests in predictability and judicial economy counsel the adoption of one source, or class of sources, for borrowing purposes.

Second, assuming a uniform limitations period is appropriate, the court must decide whether this period should be derived from a state or federal source. In making this judgment, the court should accord particular weight to the geographic character of the claim.

Finally, even where geographic considerations counsel federal borrowing, the aforementioned presumption of state borrowing that requires that a court determine that an analogous federal source truly affords a "closer fit" with the cause of action at issue than does any available state-law source. Although considerations pertinent to this determination will necessarily vary depending upon the federal cause of action and the available state and federal analogues, such factors as commonality of purpose and similarity of elements will be relevant.

We conclude that where, as here, the claim asserted is one implied under a statute that also contains an express cause of action with its own time limitation, a court should look first to the statute of origin to ascertain the proper limitations period. In the present litigation, there can be no doubt that the contemporaneously enacted express remedial provisions represent "a federal statute of limitations actually designed to accommodate a balance of interests very similar to that at stake here—a statute that is, in fact, an analogy to the present lawsuit more apt than any of the suggested state-law parallels." The 1934 Act contained a number of express causes of action, each with an explicit limitations period. With only one more restrictive exception, each of these includes some variation of a one-year period after discovery combined with a three-year period of repose. In adopting the 1934 Act, the 73rd Congress also amended the limitations provision of the 1933 Act, adopting the one-and-three-year structure for each cause of action contained therein. We therefore conclude that we must reject the Commission's contention that the five-year period contained in § 20A, added to the 1934 Act in 1988, is more appropriate for § 10(b) actions than is the one-and-three-year structure in the Act's original remedial provisions.

Litigation instituted pursuant to § 10(b) and Rule 10b-5 therefore must be commenced within one year after the discovery of the facts constituting the violation and within three years after such violation. As there is no dispute that the earliest of plaintiff-respondents' complaints was filed more than three years after petitioner's alleged misrepresentations, Gilbertson et al., claims were untimely.

The judgment of the court of appeals is reversed.

CASE A.28

THE WACKENHUT CORPORATION AND DELTA AIRLINES, INC. V. LIPPERT, 609 SO. 2D 1304 (1992) SUPREME COURT OF FLORIDA
Grimes, Judge.

While on her way to board a Delta Airlines flight from West Palm Beach to New York, Felice Lippert took a handbag containing approximately $431,000 worth of jewelry through a security checkpoint at Palm Beach International Airport. The security checkpoint was operated by The Wackenhut Corporation. The checkpoint consisted of a magnetometer scan of baggage and other carry-on items as well as a scan of the person which occurs as the person walks through a specially designed archway. Mrs. Lippert placed her bag on the conveyor belt as required and she walked through the archway. The archway magnetometer alarm sounded and Mrs. Lippert was briefly inspected by Wackenhut personnel. After being cleared by Wackenhut, Mrs. Lippert discovered her handbag with the jewelry was missing.

Mrs. Lippert sued Delta and Wackenhut for the value of her jewelry on a theory of negligence. Delta and Wackenhut asserted Delta's limitations of liability as their affirmative defense. The limitations of liability are expressed by reference on the back of Delta's ticket and in full in a governmentally required tariff which is posted according to federal regulations. The limitation contained in the tariff provides that:

DL shall be liable for the loss of, damage to, or delay in the delivery of a fare paying passenger's baggage, or other property (including carry on baggage, if tendered to DL's in flight personnel for storage during flight or otherwise delivered into the custody of DL). Such liability, if any, for the loss, damage, or delay in the delivery of a fare paying passenger's baggage or other property (whether checked or otherwise delivered into the custody of DL), shall be limited to an amount equal to the value of the property, plus consequential damages, if any, and shall not exceed the maximum limitation of USD $1,250 for all liability for each fare paying passenger (unless the passenger elects to pay for higher liability).

DL is not responsible for jewelry, cash, camera equipment, or other similar valuable items contained in checked or unchecked baggage, unless excess valuation has been purchased. These items should be carried by the passenger.

The trial court initially entered partial summary judgment for Delta and Wackenhut, upholding the limitation on liability to the maximum amount of $1,250. A new judge was assigned to the case by the time of trial. The jury returned a verdict for the plaintiff in the amount of $431,609, apportioning damages with Delta 65 percent liable and Wackenhut 35 percent liable. The trial court vacated the earlier partial summary judgment and entered final judgment for the plaintiff in the amount of $431,609. Delta and Wackenhut appealed the final judgment arguing that the partial summary judgment should have been given its natural effect in limiting liability to $1,250.

The district court of appeal held that the limitation on liability contained in the ticket and the tariff did not apply under the facts of the case. The court also found that a bailment for the mutual benefit of both the passenger and the airline had been created when Mrs. Lippert relinquished possession of her valuables to go through the x-ray machine. Therefore, the trial court was correct in applying the ordinary negligence standard. However, the court felt that the defendants had been unduly prejudiced by the judge's assurances throughout the pretrial proceedings and the trial that the potential judgment could not exceed $1,250. Thus, the case was remanded for a new trial with the proviso that the limitation of liability would not apply.

On petition for review in this court, Delta and Wackenhut argue for the $1,250 limitation. In addition, they contend that, because the airport security check was mandated by law, they were gratuitous bailees, who could only be held liable if grossly negligent. Mrs. Lippert cross-petitions to review the granting of a new trial.

Mrs. Lippert seems to argue that under the emphasized portion of section 1 of her ticket, quoted above, an article only becomes baggage, and therefore triggers the limitation on liability, when it reaches the cargo compartment or the cabin of the aircraft. However, this interpretation would lead to the dubious conclusion that passengers' property in transit to the airplane after being delivered to the airline at the check-in point where tickets are purchased should not be considered baggage. The phrase in the ticket's definition of baggage—"whether checked in the cargo compartment or carried in the cabin"—is more realistically construed as emphasizing that, for purposes of Delta's contract with its passengers, there is no difference between "carry-on" and "checked" baggage. Thus, the ticket's references to the cargo compartment and the cabin are merely descriptive of the words "checked" or "carried," and there can be no doubt that Mrs. Lippert's handbag was a passenger's "article or other property acceptable for transportation whether checked or carried." We believe that a ticketed passenger's property, destined for an airplane and in transit between the airport's security checkpoint and the actual airplane, constitutes "baggage" as defined by the ticket.

We hold that the $1,250 baggage limitation of liability was applicable to the loss of Mrs. Lippert's handbag while it was in the possession of Delta's agent at the airport security checkpoint. While we find the $1,250 liability limitation applicable in this case, we decline to answer the certified question because it does not precisely track the language of the tariff. We agree with the district court of appeal that the bailment created when Mrs. Lippert surrendered her handbag for inspection was for the mutual benefit of the passenger and the airline, and we adopt the court's reasoning in this respect. Our disposition of the baggage liability limitation issue renders the cross-petition moot. Because the case was tried under the proper standard of care, there is no need for a retrial. We quash the decision below to the extent that it is inconsistent with our opinion and remand the case for entry of a judgment in favor of Mrs. Lippert for $1,250.

CASE A.29

NOLLAN V. CALIFORNIA COASTAL COMMISSION
483 U.S. 825, 107 S.CT. 3141, 97 L.ED.2D 677 (1987)
UNITED STATES SUPREME COURT
Scalia, Justice.

James and Marilyn Nollan own a beachfront lot in Ventura County, California. A quarter-mile north of their property is Faria County Park, an oceanside public park with a public beach and recreation area. Another public beach area, known locally as "the Cove," lies 1,800 feet south of their lot. The Nollans originally leased their property with an option to buy. The building on the lot was a small bungalow, totaling 504 square feet, which for a time they rented to summer vacationers. After years of rental use, however, the building had fallen into disrepair, and could no longer be rented out.

The Nollans' option to purchase was conditioned on their promise to demolish the bungalow and replace it. In order to do so, they were required to obtain a coastal development permit from the California Coastal Commission. On February 25, 1982, they submitted a permit application to the Commission in which they proposed to demolish the existing structure and replace it with a three-bedroom house in keeping with the rest of the neighborhood.

The Nollans were informed that the Commission staff had recommended that the permit be granted subject to the condition that they allow the public an easement to pass across a portion of their property. This would make it easier for the public to get to Faria County Park and the Cove. The Nollans protested imposition of the condition, but the Commission overruled their objections and granted the permit subject to their recordation of a deed restriction granting the easement.

The Nollans filed a petition for a writ of administrative mandamus with the superior court. The superior court granted the writ of mandamus and directed that the permit condition be struck. The Commission appealed to the California court of appeal. While that appeal was pending, the Nollans satisfied the condition on their option to purchase by tearing down the bungalow and building the new house, and bought the property. They did not notify the Commission that they were taking that action. The court of appeal reversed the superior court. It ruled that the Nollans' "taking" claim failed because, although the condition diminished the value of the Nollans' lot, it did not deprive them of all reasonable use of their property. The Nollans appealed to this Court, raising only the constitutional "taking" question.

Had California simply required the Nollans to make an easement across their beachfront available to the public on a permanent basis in order to increase public access to the beach, rather than conditioning their permit to rebuild their house on their agreeing to do so, we have no doubt there would have been a taking. To say that the appropriation of a public easement across a landowner's premises does not constitute the taking of a property interest but rather (as Justice Brennan contends) "a mere restriction on its use," is to use words in a manner that deprives them of all their ordinary meaning. Indeed, one of the principal uses of the eminent domain power is to assure that the government be able to require conveyance of just such interests, so long as it pays for them. We have repeatedly held that, as to property reserved by its owner for private use, "the right to exclude others is one of the most essential sticks in the bundle of rights that are commonly characterized as property."

We have long recognized that land-use regulation does not effect a taking if it "substantially advances legitimate state interests" and does not "deny an owner economically viable use of his land." Whatever may be the outer limits of legitimate state interests in the takings and land-use context, this is not one of them. The building restriction is not a valid regulation of land use, but an out-and-out plan of extortion. We therefore find that the Commission's imposition of the permit condition cannot be treated as an exercise of its land-use power. To obtain easements of access private property the State must proceed through its eminent domain power.

The permit condition is simply an expression of the Commission's belief that the public interest will be served by a continuous strip of publicly accessible beach along the coast. The Commission may well be right that it is a good idea, but that does not establish that the Nollans (and other coastal residents) alone can be compelled to contribute to its realization. Rather, California is free to advance its comprehensive program if it wishes, by using its power of eminent domain for this "public purpose," but if it wants an easement across the Nollans' property, it must pay for it. Reversed.

CASE A.30

SARITEJDIAM, INC. V. EXCESS INSURANCE CO., 971 F.2D 910 (1992) UNITED STATES COURT OF APPEALS FOR THE SECOND CIRCUIT

Oakes, Chief Judge.

Saritejdiam, Inc. (Saritejdiam) is a New York corporation involved in the wholesaling of diamonds and other precious and semi-precious stones and jewelry. In June 1988, Excess Insurance Company, Ltd., et al. (the Underwriters), a group of London-based insurance companies, issued an insurance policy to Saritejdiam. The policy is called a Jeweler's Block Policy and it insures against all risks of physical loss or damage to insured interests, unless specifically excluded by the policy. This appeal requires us to analyze whether Saritejdiam satisfied a clause in the policy requiring that insured interests remain in the "close personal custody and control" of the insured or its agent while in transit.

On May 13, 1989, Mr. Robert Danilin, an independent contractor/salesman for Saritejdiam, lost a package of loose diamonds valued by Saritejdiam at $267,514.30. On that day, Danilin, his wife, and stepson were in Tuxedo, New York, visiting a townhouse they had just purchased there. At approximately 5:50 P.M., the Danilins arrived at the Orange Top Diner on Route 17 in Tuxedo for dinner. Danilin brought a camera bag into the diner containing two stiff, black diamond wallets (one of which held Saritejdiam's diamonds), his checkbook, and credit cards. The three were seated at a table. Robert placed the camera bag on top of an empty chair to his left. During dinner, he touched the camera bag to make sure it was still on the chair. When they finished eating, Danilin paid the check with cash out of his pants pocket. The three then left the diner, got into their car, and headed for a golf driving range. When the Danilins reached their destination, they discovered that the camera bag containing the diamond wallets was not in the car. They sped back to the diner. The camera bag, however, was no longer on the chair where it had been previously placed.

Connie Grievas, the daughter of the proprietors of the Orange Top Diner, apparently witnessed the events that transpired after Danilin paid his bill. Grievas was eleven years old at the time. She told Danilin's stepson and, later on, investigators for the Underwriters, that she went to clear Danilin's table after he paid his check. She noticed that a bag with a handle was left behind. Grievas then went to tell her mother that a customer had left a bag behind. Before she reached her mother, she saw two other customers, a man and a woman, take the bag and walk out. She described the man who picked up the bag as white, approximately forty years old, with shoulder-length black curly hair, standing 5'7", and wearing dark sunglasses. She described the woman as having blonde, waist-length hair.

On the same day, Saritejdiam reported the loss to the Underwriters. On June 23, 1989, after investigating the claim, the Underwriters refused to cover the lost diamonds. The Underwriters claimed that Saritejdiam had not complied with the Personal Conveyance Clause of the insurance policy. The clause provides:

> This policy only covers the insured interest in transit when in the close personal custody and control of the Assured and/or Assured's representative and/or agent at all times whilst in transit subject to hotel/motel clause, excluding all losses due to infidelity.

The denial letter states that "the results of our investigation have revealed that there is no evidence that the theft took place whilst your property was in the close personal custody and control of your salesman, Robert Danilin."

We must decide whether the loss of the diamonds at the Orange Top Diner occurred while they were in the "close personal custody and control" of Danilin, Saritejdiam's salesman/independent contractor. If so, Saritejdiam satisfied the requirements of the Personal Conveyance Clause in the policy, and the Underwriters must cover the loss. The issue traditionally arises in disputes over the rights of the finder against those of the owner of the real property on which the disputed personal property was found. The common law generally distinguished between "lost" and "mislaid" property. Property is mislaid when the owner purposely parts with possession of the property, but then unintentionally leaves it behind. We believe that under New York common law the camera bag containing Saritejdiam's diamond wallets would be classified as mislaid property. Saritejdiam's salesman purposely placed the camera bag on the adjacent chair at his table in the Orange Top Diner. He then walked away from the table and forgot to pick up the camera bag. This is a paradigmatic example of mislaid property under New York's common law definition of the term. Accordingly, we believe a New York court would hold that a person simply cannot maintain "close personal custody and control" over mislaid property.

For the foregoing reasons, we reverse the order of the district court granting summary judgment for Saritejdiam and enter summary judgment for the Underwriters.

Abatement If the property the testator leaves is not sufficient to satisfy all the beneficiaries named in a will and there are both general and residuary bequests, the residuary bequest is abated first; if a will provides for general bequests, they are reduced proportionately if the residuary bequests are fully abated or there are none. (765)

Absolute priority rule A rule that says a reorganization plan is fair and equitable to an impaired class of unsecured creditors or equity holders if no class below it receives anything in the plan. (484)

Acceptance A manifestation of assent by the offeree to the terms of the offer in a manner invited or required by the offer as measured by the objective theory of contracts. (173) Occurs when a buyer or lessee takes any of the following actions after a reasonable opportunity to inspect the goods: (1) signifies to the seller or lessor in words or by conduct that the goods are conforming or that the buyer or lessee will take or retain the goods in spite of their nonconformity; or (2) fails to effectively reject the goods within a reasonable time after their delivery or tender by the seller or lessor. Acceptance also occurs if a buyer acts inconsistently with the seller's ownership rights in the goods. (305)

Acceptance method The bankruptcy court must approve a plan of reorganization if (1) the plan is in the best interests of each class of claims and interests, (2) the plan is feasible, (3) at least one class of claims votes to accept the plan, and (4) each class of claims and interests is nonimpaired. (483)

Accession Occurs when the value of personal property increases because it is added to or improved by natural or manufactured means. (705)

Accommodation A shipment offered to the buyer as a replacement for the original shipment when the original shipment cannot be filled. (278)

Accommodation party A party who signs an instrument and lends his or her name (and credit) to another party to the instrument. (396)

Accord An agreement whereby the parties agree to accept something different in satisfaction of the original contract. (179)

Accord and satisfaction The settlement of a contract dispute. (243)

Act of state doctrine States that judges of one country cannot question the validity of an act committed by another country within that other country's own borders. It is based on the principle that a country has absolute authority over what transpires within its own territory. (66)

Action for an accounting A formal judicial proceeding in which the court is authorized to (1) review the partnership and the partners' transactions and (2) award each partner his or her share of the partnership assets. (555)

Actual notice Verbal or written notice to a third party that states clearly how the partnership ended. (562)

Actus reus "Guilty act"—the actual performance of the criminal act. (131)

Ademption A principle that says if a testator leaves a specific devise of property to a beneficiary, but the property is not longer in the estate when the testator dies, the beneficiary receives nothing. (763)

Adequate assurance of performance A party to a sales or lease contract may demand an adequate assurance of performance from the other party if there is an indication that the contract will be breached by that party. (307)

Adjudged insane A person who has been adjudged insane by a proper court or administrative agency. A contract entered into by such person is void. (192)

Administrative dissolution Involuntary dissolution of a corporation that is ordered by the secretary of state if the corporation has failed to comply with certain procedures required by law. (657)

Adverse possession When a person who wrongfully possesses someone else's real property obtains title to that property if certain statutory requirements are met. (728)

Advertisement A general advertisement is an invitation to make an offer. A specific advertisement is an offer. (168)

Affirmative warranty A statement asserting that certain facts are true. (760)

After-acquired property Property that the debtor acquires after the security agreement is executed. (446)

Agency The principal-agent relationship; the fiduciary relationship "which results from the manifestation of consent by one person to another that the other shall act in his behalf and subjects to his control, and consent by the other so to act." (494)

Agency by ratification An agency that occurs when (1) a person misrepresents him or herself as another's agent when in fact he or she is not and (2) the purported principal ratifies the unauthorized act. (500)

Agency coupled with an interest A special type of agency relationship that is created for the agent's benefit; irrevocable by the principal. (516)

Agency law The large body of common law that governs agency; a mixture of contract law and tort law. (494)

Agent A person who has been authorized to sign a negotiable instrument on behalf of another person. (392) (494)

Agreement The manifestation by two or more persons of the substance of a contract. (167)

Aiding and abetting the commission of a crime Rendering support, assistance, or encouragement to the commission of a crime; harboring a criminal after he or she has committed a crime. (144)

Alien corporation A corporation that is incorporated in another country. (586)

Allonge A separate piece of paper attached to the instrument on which the indorsement is written. (369)

Altered check A check that has been altered without authorization that modifies the legal obligation of a party. (424)

Alternative dispute resolution (ADR) Methods of resolving disputes other than litigation. (68)

Annual financial statement A statement provided to the shareholders that contains a balance sheet, an income statement, and a statement of changes in shareholder equity. (616)

Annual shareholders' meeting Meeting of the shareholders of a corporation that must be held annually by the corporation to elect directors and to vote on other matters. (612)

Answer The defendant's written response to the plaintiff's complaint that is filed with the court and served on the plaintiff. (60)

Anti-assignment clause A clause that prohibits the assignment of rights under the contract. (235)

Anti-delegation clause A clause that prohibits the delegation of duties under the contract. (236)

Anticipatory breach A breach that occurs when one contracting party informs the other that he or she will not perform his or her contractual duties when due. (256)

Anticipatory repudiation The repudiation of a sales or lease contract by one of the parties prior to the date set for performance. (307)

Apparent agency Agency that arises when a principal creates the appearance of an agency that in actuality does not exist. (499) (538)

Appellant The appealing party in an appeal. Also known as petitioner. (65)

Appellee The responding party in an appeal. Also known as respondent. (65)

Approval clause A clause that permits the assignment of the contract only upon receipt of an obligor's approval. (235)

Arbitration A form of ADR in which the parties choose an impartial third party to hear and decide the dispute. (68)

Arbitration clause A clause in contracts that requires disputes arising out of the contract to be submitted to arbitration. (68)

Area franchise The franchisor authorizes the franchisee to negotiate and sell franchises on behalf of the franchisor. (529)

Arraignment A hearing during which the accused is brought before a court and is (1) informed of the charges against him or her and (2) asked to enter a plea. (133)

Arrest warrant A document for a person's detainment based upon a showing of probable cause that the person committed the crime. (132)

Arson Willfully or maliciously burning another's building. (135)

Article 2a (leases) Article of the UCC that governs lease of goods. (275)

Article 3 of the UCC A code promulgated in 1952 that established rules for the creation of, transfer of, enforcement of, and liability on negotiable instruments. (356) (415)

Article 4 of the UCC Establishes the rules and principles that regulate bank deposit and collection procedures. (415) (426)

Article 4a of the UCC Article added to the UCC in 1989 that establishes rules regulating the creation and collection of and liability for wire transfers. (415)

Article 7 of the UCC An article of the Uniform Commercial Code that provides a detailed statutory scheme for the creation, perfection, and foreclosure on common carriers' and warehouse operators' liens. (712)

Article 8 of the UCC The article of the UCC that governs transfer of securities. (615)

Article 9 of the UCC An article of the Uniform Commercial Code the governs secured transactions in personal property. (444)

Articles of incorporation The basic governing document of the corporation. This document must be filed with the secretary of state of the state of incorporation. (591)

Articles of organization The formal document that must be filed with the secretary of state to form an LLC. (568)

Assault (1) The threat of immediate harm or offensive contact or (2) any action that arouses reasonable apprehension of imminent harm. Actual physical contact is unnecessary. (81)

Assignee The party to whom the right has been transferred. (232) (740)

Assignment The transfer of contractual rights by the obligee to another party. (232) A transfer by a tenant of his or her rights under a lease to another. (740)

Assignment and delegation Transfer of both rights and duties under the contract. (236)

Assignment for the benefit of creditors An assignment that allows debtors voluntarily to assign title to their property to a trustee or an assignee for the benefit of their creditors. (460)

Assignor The obligee who transfers the right. (232) (740)

Assumption of duties When a delegation of duties contains the term assumption or I assume the duties or other similar language, the delegatee is legally liable to the obligee for nonperformance. (236)

Assumption of the risk A defense a defendant can use against a plaintiff who knowingly and voluntarily enters into or participates in a risky activity that results in injury. (93)

Attachment The creditor has an enforceable security interest against the debtor and can satisfy the debt out of the designated collateral. (446)

Attempt to commit a crime When a crime is attempted but not completed. (144)

Attestation The action of a will being witnessed by two or three objective and competent people. (761)

Attorney-client privilege A rule that says a client can tell his or her lawyer anything about the case without fear that the attorney will be called as a witness against the client. (146)

Attorney-in-fact The agent in a power of attorney situation. (497)

Auction with reserve Unless expressly stated otherwise, an auction is an auction with reserve; that is, the seller retains the right to refuse the highest bid and withdraw the goods from sale. (170)

Auction without reserve An auction in which the seller expressly gives up his or her right to withdraw the goods from sale and must accept the highest bid. (170)

Authorized shares The number of shares provided for in the articles of incorporation. (598)

Automated teller machine (ATM) An EFTS at a convenient location that is connected on-line to the bank's computers; customers use ATMs to withdraw cash from bank accounts, cash checks, make deposits, and make payments owed to the bank. (430)

Automatic stay The result of the filing of a voluntary or involuntary petition; the suspension of certain actions by creditors against the debtor or the debtor's property. (472)

Bailee A holder of goods who is not a seller or a buyer (e.g., a warehouse or common carrier). (285) (300) (708)

Bailee's rights Depending on the type of bailment, bailees may have the right to (1) exclusive possession of the bailed property, (2) use of the bailed property, or (3) compensation for work done or services provided. (711)

Bailment A transaction where an owner transfers his or her personal property to another to be held, stored, delivered, or for some other purpose. Title to the property does not transfer. (708)

Bailment at will A bailment without a fixed term; can be terminated at any time by either party. (709)

Bailment for a fixed term A bailment that terminates at the end of the term or sooner by mutual consent of the parties. (709)

Bailment for sole benefit of the bailee A gratuitous bailment that benefits only the bailee. The bailee owes a duty of great care to protect the bailed property. (711)

Bailment for the sole benefit of the bailor A gratuitous bailment that benefits only the bailor. The bailee owes only a duty of slight care to protect the bailed property. (710)

Bailor The owner of property in a bailment. (708)

Bank check A certified check, a cashier's check, or a traveler's check, the payment for which the bank is solely or primarily liable. (416)

Bankruptcy Code The name given to the Bankruptcy Reform Act of 1978, as amended. (470)

Bankruptcy estate An estate created upon the commencement of a Chapter 7 proceeding that includes all of the debtor's legal and equitable interests in real, personal, tangible, and intangible property, wherever located, that exist when the petition is filed, minus exempt property. (473)

Bargained-for exchange Exchange that parties engage in that leads to an enforceable contract. (176)

Battery Unauthorized and harmful or offensive physical contact with another person. Direct physical contact is not necessary. (81)

Bearer paper Bearer paper is negotiated by delivery; indorsement is not necessary. (367)

Beneficiary A person or organization designated in the will who receives all or a portion of the testator's property at the time of the testator's or insured's death. (757) (761) Person for whose benefit a trust is created. (770)

Bequest A gift of personal property by will. (764)

Berne Convention An international copyright treaty. The United States and many other nations are signatories to this treaty. (114)

Bilateral contract A contract entered into by way of exchange of promises of the parties; a "promise for a promise." (157)

Blank indorsement An indorsement that does not specify a particular indorsee. It creates *bearer paper*. (369)

Board of directors A panel of decision makers, the members of which are elected by the shareholders. (617)

Bond A long-term security that is secured by some form of collateral. (599)

Breach Failure of a party to perform an obligation in a sales or lease contract. (300)

Breach of contract If a contracting party fails to perform an absolute duty owed under a contract. (254)

Breach of the duty of care A failure to exercise care or to act as a reasonable person would act. (85)

Bribery When one person gives another person money, property, favors, or anything else of value for a favor in return. Often referred to as a paying "kickback." (138)

Building codes State and local statutes that impose specific standards on property owners to maintain and repair leased premises. (735)

Burden of proof The plaintiff bears the burden of proving the allegations made in his complaint. (63)

Burglary Taking personal property from another's home, office, commercial, or other type of building. (134)

Business judgment rule A rule that protects decisions of the board of directors that acts on an informed basis, in good faith, and in the belief that the decision was in the best interests of the corporation and its shareholders. (623) (654)

Business tort A tort based on common law and on statutory law that affects business. (105)

Buy-and-sell agreement An agreement that requires selling shareholders to sell their shares to the other shareholders or to the corporation at the price specified in the agreement. (615)

Buyer in the ordinary course of business A person who in good faith and without knowledge that the sale violates the ownership or security interests of a third party buys the goods in the ordinary course of business from a person in the business of selling goods of that kind [UCC 1-201(9)]. A buyer in the ordinary course of business takes the goods free of any third-party security interest in the goods. (288) (453)

Bylaws A detailed set of rules that are adopted by the board of directors after the corporation is incorporated that contains provisions for managing the business and the affairs of the corporation. (592)

Cancellation A buyer or lessee may cancel a sales or lease contract if the seller or lessor fails to deliver conforming goods or repudiates the contract, or the buyer or lessee rightfully rejects the goods or justifiably revokes acceptance of the goods. (310) A seller or lessor may cancel a sales or lease contract if the buyer or lessee rejects or revokes acceptance of the goods, fails to pay for the goods, or repudiates the contract in part or in whole. (313)

Case brief A summary of each of the following items of a case: (1) Case name and citation (2) Key facts (3) Issue presented (4) Holding of the court (5) Court's reasoning. (18)

Cashier's check A check issued by a bank where the customer has paid the bank the amount of the check and a fee. The bank guarantees the payment of the check. (417)

Causation in fact or actual cause The actual cause of negligence. A person who commits a negligent act is not liable unless causation in fact can be proven. (87)

Certificate of deposit (CD) A two-party negotiable instrument that is a special form of note created when a depositor deposits money at a financial institution in exchange for the institution's promise to pay back the amount of the deposit plus an agreed-upon rate of interest upon the expiration of a set time period agreed upon by the parties. (360)

Certificate of filing A document that shows (1) whether any presently effective financing statement naming a particular debtor is on file, (2) the date and hour of any such filing, and (3) the names and addresses of the secured parties. (451)

Certificate of limited partnership A document that two or more persons must execute and sign that makes the limited partnership legal and binding. (565)

Certificate of partnership A document that a partnership must file with the appropriate state government agency in some states to acknowledge that the partnership exists. (552)

Certified check A type of check where a bank agrees in advance (certifies) to accept the check when it is presented for payment. (416)

Chain of distribution All manufacturers, distributors, wholesalers, retailers, lessors, and subcomponent manufacturers involved in a transaction. (337)

Chain-style franchise The franchisor licenses the franchisee to make and sell its products or distribute services to the public from a retail outlet serving an exclusive territory. (529)

Chapter 11 A bankruptcy method that allows reorganization of the debtor's financial affairs under the supervision of the Bankruptcy Court. (479)

Chapter 13 A rehabilitation form of bankruptcy that permits the courts to supervise the debtor's plan for the payment of unpaid debts by installments. (484)

Chapter 7 liquidation bankruptcy The most familiar form of bankruptcy; the debtor's nonexempt property is sold for cash, the cash is distributed to the creditors, and any unpaid debts are discharged. (471)

Charging order A document that the court issues against the debtor-partner's partnership interest in order to satisfy a debt. (559)

Check A distinct form of draft drawn on a financial institution and payable on demand. (358) An order by the drawer to the drawee bank to pay a specified sum of money from the drawer's checking account to the named payee (or holder). (416)

Closing The finalization of a real estate sales transaction that passes title to the property from the seller to the buyer. (727)

Closing arguments Statements made by the attorneys to the jury at the end of the trial to try to convince the jury to render a verdict for their client. (64)

C.O.D. shipment A type of shipment contract where the buyer agrees to pay the shipper cash upon the delivery of the goods. (304)

Codicil A separate document that must be executed to amend a will. It must be executed with the same formalities as a will. (762)

Coinsurance clause A clause that permits an owner who insures his or her property to a certain percent of its value to recover up to the face value of the property. (758)

Collateral Security against repayment of the note that lenders sometimes require; can be a car, a house, or other property. (359)

Collateral contract A promise in which one person agrees to answer for the debts or duties of another person. (218)

Collecting bank The depository bank and other banks in the collection process (other than the payor bank). (426)

Coming and going rule A rule that says a principal is generally not liable for injuries caused by its agents and employees while they are on their way to or from work. (510)

Commerce Clause A clause of the U.S. Constitution that grants Congress the power "to regulate commerce with foreign nations, and among the several states, and with Indian tribes." (12)

Commercial impracticability Nonperformance that is excused if an extreme or unexpected development or expense makes it impractical for the promisor to perform. (244)

Commercial speech Speech used by businesses, such as advertising. It is subject to time, place, and manner restrictions. (16)

Commodities Grains, animals, animal products, foods, metals, and oil. (687)

Commodity exchange An exchange over which commodity futures contracts are bought and sold on an impersonal basis. (688)

Commodity Exchange Act A federal statute that regulates the trading of commodity futures contracts. (688)

Commodity futures contract An agreement to buy or sell a specific amount and type of a commodity at some future date under standardized terms established by the CFTC. (688)

Commodity Futures Trading Commission (CFTC) A federal administrative agency that administers and enforces the Commodity Exchange Act, as amended. (688)

Common carrier A firm (the bailee) that offers transportation services to the general public. Owes a *duty of strict liability* to the bailor. (712)

Common law Developed by judges who issued their opinions when deciding a case. The principles announced in these cases became precedent for later judges deciding similar cases. (6)

Common law of contracts Contract law developed primarily by state courts. (156)

Common stock A type of equity security that represents the residual value of the corporation. (596)

Common stock certificate A document that represents the common shareholder's investment in the corporation. (596)

Common stockholder A person who owns common stock. (596)

Community property A form of ownership in which each spouse owns an equal one-half share of the income of both spouses and the assets acquired during the marriage. (726)

Comparative negligence A doctrine that applies to strict liability actions that says a plaintiff who is contributorily negligent for his or her injuries is responsible for a proportional share of the damages. (94) (346)

Compensatory damages A remedy intended to compensate a nonbreaching party for the loss of the bargain; they place the nonbreaching party in the same position as if the contract had been fully performed by restoring the "benefit of the bargain." (256) Damages that are generally equal to the difference between the value of the goods as warranted and the actual value of the goods accepted at the time and place of acceptance. (332)

Competent party's duty of restitution If a minor has transferred money, property, or other valuables to the competent party before disaffirming the contract, that party must place the minor back into status quo. (189)

Competing with the principal An agent cannot compete with the principal during the course of an agency unless the principal agrees. (503)

Complaint The document the plaintiff files with the court and serves on the defendant to initiate a lawsuit. (59)

Complete performance Occurs when a party to a contract renders performance exactly as required by the contract; discharges that party's obligations under the contract. (254)

Composition agreement An agreement that a debtor and several creditors enter into; if the debtor is overextended and owes several creditors money, the creditors agree to accept payment of a sum less than the debt as full satisfaction of the debtor's debts. (460)

Conciliation A form of mediation in which the parties choose an interested third party to act as the mediator. (70)

Concurrent condition A condition that exists when the parties to a contract must render performance simultaneously; each party's absolute duty to perform is conditioned on the other party's absolute duty to perform. (242)

Condition A qualification of a promise. There are three types of con-

ditions: conditions precedent, conditions subsequent, and concurrent conditions. (240)

Condition based on satisfaction Clause in a contract that reserves the right of a party to pay for the item or services contracted for only if they meet his or her satisfaction. (240)

Condition precedent A condition that requires the occurrence of an event before a party is obligated to perform a duty under a contract. (241)

Conditions subsequent A condition, if it occurs, that automatically excuses the performance of an existing contractual duty to perform. (241)

Condominium A common form of ownership in a multiple-dwelling building in which the purchaser has title to the individual unit and owns the common areas as a tenant in common with the other condominium owners. (727)

Confirmation The bankruptcy court's approval of a plan of reorganization. (483)

Confusion Occurs if two or more persons commingle fungible goods; title is then acquired by confusion. (705)

Consequential damages Foreseeable damages that arise from circumstances outside the contract. In order to be liable for these damages, the breaching party must know or have reason to know that the breach will cause special damages to the other party. (257) (333)

Consideration Something of legal value given in exchange for a promise. (175)

Consignee The person to whom the bailed goods are to be delivered. (712)

Consignment An arrangement in which a seller (the consignor) delivers goods to a buyer (the consignee) for sale. (286)

Consignor The person shipping the goods. The bailor. (712)

Consolidation Occurs when two or more corporations combine to form an entirely new corporation. (61) The act of a court to combine two or more separate lawsuits into one lawsuit. (647)

Conspicuous A requirement that warranty disclaimers be noticeable to the average person. (332)

Constitution of the United States of America The supreme law of the United States. (7)

Constructive notice Usually written notice to a third party that is put into general circulation, such as in a newspaper. (562)

Constructive trust An equitable trust that is imposed by law to avoid fraud, unjust enrichment, and injustice. (771)

Consumer lease A lease with a value of $25,000 or less between a lessor regularly engaged in the business of leasing or selling and a lessee who leases the goods primarily for a personal, family, or household purpose. (275)

Continuation agreement A document that expressly sets forth the events that allow for continuation of the partnership, the amount to be paid outgoing partners, and other details. (563)

Contract in restraint of trade A contract that unreasonably restrains trade. (197)

Contracts contrary to public policy Contracts that have a negative impact on society or interfere with the public's safety and welfare. (196)

Contributory negligence A doctrine that says a plaintiff who is partially at fault for his or her own injury cannot recover against the negligent defendant. (94) (346)

Controlling shareholder A shareholder that owns a sufficient number of shares to control the corporation effectively. (629)

Conversion of personal property A tort that deprives a true owner of the use and enjoyment of his or her personal property by taking over such property and exercising ownership rights over it. (83)

Convertible preferred stock Stock that permits the stockholders to convert their shares into common stock. (598)

Cooperative A form of co-ownership of a multiple-dwelling building in which a corporation owns the building and the residents own shares in the corporation. (727)

Co-ownership When two or more persons own a piece of real property. Also called concurrent ownership. (725)

Copyright infringement When a party copies a substantial and material part of the plaintiff's copyrighted work without permission. A copyright holder may recover damages and other remedies against the infringer. (115)

Copyright Revision Act of 1976 Federal statute that (1) establishes the requirements for obtaining a copyright and (2) protects copyrighted works from infringement. (114)

Core proceedings Proceedings that bankruptcy judges decide that have to do with creditor claims, deciding preferences, confirming plans of reorganization, and so on. (470)

Corporate citizenship A theory of social responsibility that says a business has a responsibility to do good. (40)

Corporate seal A design that contains the name of the corporation and the date of incorporation. It is imprinted by the corporate secretary on certain legal documents using a metal stamp containing the design. (595)

Corporation A fictitious legal entity that is created according to statutory requirements. (582)

Corporation codes State statutes that regulate the formation, operation, and dissolution of corporations. (582)

Correction of a defect A defense that permits a seller of a defective product to recall and repair the defect. The seller is not liable to purchasers who fail to have the defect corrected. (344)

Counterfeit Access Device and Computer Fraud and Abuse Act of 1984 Makes it a federal crime to access a computer knowingly to obtain (1) restricted federal government information, (2) financial records of financial institutions, and (3) consumer reports of consumer reporting agencies. (141)

Counteroffer A response by an offeree that contains terms and conditions different from or in addition to those of the offer. A counteroffer terminates an offer. (171)

Court of Appeals for the Federal Circuit A court of appeals in Washington, D.C., that has special appellate jurisdiction to review the decisions of the Claims Court, the Patent and Trademark Office, and the Court of International Trade. (53)

Court of Chancery Court that granted relief based on fairness. Also called equity court. (6)

Covenant An unconditional promise to perform. (240)

Covenant of good faith and fair dealing Under this implied covenant, the parties to a contract not only are held to the express terms of the contract but also are required to act in "good faith" and deal fairly in all respects in obtaining the objective of the contract. (264)

Covenant of quiet enjoyment A covenant that says a landlord may not interfere with the tenant's quiet and peaceful possession, use, and enjoyment of the leased premises. (735)

Cover Right of a buyer or lessee to purchase or lease substitute goods if a seller or lessor fails to make delivery of the goods or repudiates the contract, or if the buyer or lessee rightfully rejects the goods or justifiably revokes their acceptance. (312)

Cram down method A method of confirmation of a plan of reorganization where the court forces an impaired class to participate in the plan of reorganization. (484)

Crashworthiness doctrine A doctrine that says automobile manufacturers are under a duty to design automobiles so they take into account the possibility of harm from a person's body striking something inside the automobile in the case of a car accident. (341)

Creditor beneficiary Original creditor who becomes a beneficiary under the debtor's new contract with another party. (239)

Creditor beneficiary contract A contract that arises in the following situation: (1) A debtor borrows money, (2) the debtor signs an agreement to pay back the money plus interest, (3) the debtor sells the item to a third party before the loan is paid off, and (4) the third party promises the debtor that he or she will pay the remainder of the loan to the creditor. (238)

Creditor The lender in a credit transaction. (443)

Creditor-debtor relationship Created when a customer deposits money into the bank; the customer is the creditor and the bank is the debtor. (415)

Creditors' committee The creditors holding the seven largest unsecured claims are usually appointed to the creditors' committee. Representatives of the committee appear at Bankruptcy Court hearings, participate in the negotiation of a plan of reorganization, assert objections to proposed plans, and so on. (481)

Crime An act done by an individual in violation of those duties that he or she owes to society and for the breach of which the law provides that the wrongdoer shall make amends to the public. (130)

Criminal conspiracy When two or more persons enter into an agreement to commit a crime and an overt act is taken to further the crime. (143)

Criminal fraud Obtaining title to property through deception or trickery. (136)

Criminal law A crime is a violation of a statute for which the government imposes a punishment. (130)

Critical legal thinking The process of specifying the issue presented by a case, identifying the key facts in the case and applicable law, and then applying the law to the facts to come to a conclusion that answers the issue presented. (17)

Cross-complaint Filed by the defendant against the plaintiff to seek damages or some other remedy. (61)

Crown jewel A valuable asset of the target corporation that the tender offeror particularly wants to acquire in the tender offer. (652)

Cumulative preferred stock Stock that provides that any missed dividend payments must be paid in the future to the preferred shareholders before the common shareholders can receive any dividends. (598)

Cumulative voting A shareholder can accumulate all of his or her votes and vote them all for one candidate or split them among several candidates. (613)

Cure An opportunity to repair or replace defective or nonconforming goods. (302)

Damages A buyer or lessee may recover damages from a seller or lessor who fails to deliver the goods or repudiates the contract; damages are measured as the difference between the contract price (or original rent) and the market price (or rent) at the time the buyer or lessee learned of the breach. (313)

Damages for accepted nonconforming goods A buyer or lessee may accept the damages caused by the breach from the seller or lessor or deduct the damages from any part of the purchase price or rent still due under the contract. (314)

DBA (doing business as fictitious business name statement) An official document that must be filed with the appropriate government agency in order for the sole proprietorship to be able to use the name. (527)

Debenture A long-term unsecured debt instrument that is based on the corporation's general credit standing. (599)

Debt securities Securities that establish a debtor-creditor relationship in which the corporation borrows money from the investor to whom the debt security is issued. (599)

Debtor The borrower in a credit transaction. (443)

Debtor-in-possession A debtor who is left in place to operate the business during the reorganization proceeding. (481)

Declaration of duties If the delegatee has not assumed the duties under a contract, the delegatee is not legally liable to the obligee for nonperformance. (236)

Deductible clause A clause that stipulates that insurance proceeds are payable only after the insured has paid a certain amount of the damage or loss. (758)

Deed A writing that describes a person's ownership interest in a piece of real property. (729)

Defamation of character False statement(s) made by one person about another. In court, the plaintiff must prove that (1) the defendant made an untrue statement of fact about the plaintiff and (2) the statement was intentionally or accidentally published to a third party. (107)

Default Failure to make scheduled payments when due, bankruptcy of the debtor, breach of the warranty of ownership as to the collateral, and other events defined by the parties to constitute default. (453)

Defect Something wrong, inadequate, or improper in manufacture, design, packaging, warning, or safety measures of a product. (340)

Defect in design A defect that occurs when a product is improperly designed. (341)

Defect in manufacture A defect that occurs when the manufacturer fails to (1) properly assemble a product, (2) properly test a product, or (3) adequately check the quality of the product. (340)

Defect in packaging A defect that occurs when a product has been placed in packaging that is insufficiently tamper-proof. (342)

Defective formation Occurs when (1) a certificate of limited partnership is not properly filed, (2) there are defects in a certificate that is filed, or (3) some other statutory requirement for the creation of a limited partnership is not met. (566)

Defendant's case Process by which the defendant (1) rebuts the plaintiff's evidence, (2) proves affirmative defenses, and (3) proves allegations made in a cross-complaint. (64)

Deferred posting rule A rule that allows banks to fix an afternoon hour of 2:00 P.M. or later as a cutoff hour for the purpose of processing items. (427)

Deficiency judgment Judgment of a court that permits a secured lender to recover other property or income from a defaulting debtor if the collateral is insufficient to repay the unpaid loan. (443) A judgment that allows a secured creditor to successfully bring a separate legal action to recover a deficiency from the debtor. Entitles the secured creditor to recover the amount of the judgment from the debtor's other property. (455)

Delegatee The party to whom the duty has been transferred. (235)

Delegation of duties A transfer of contractual duties by the obligor to another party for performance. (235)

Delegator The obligor who transferred his or her duty. (235)

Demand instrument An instrument payable on demand. (365) (390)

Demand note A note payable on demand. (359)

Deponent Party who gives his or her deposition. (61)

Deposition Oral testimony given by a party or witness prior to trial. The testimony is given under oath and is transcribed. (61)

Depository bank The bank where the payee or holder has an account. (426)

Derivative lawsuit A lawsuit a shareholder brings against an offending party on behalf of the corporation when the corporation fails to bring the lawsuit. (616)

Destination contract A contract that requires the seller to deliver the goods either to the buyer's place of business or to another destination specified in the sales contract. (282) The seller bears the risk of loss during transportation. (284) (301)

Devise A gift of real estate by will. (764)

Disaffirmance The act of a minor to rescind a contract under the infancy doctrine. Disaffirmance may be done orally, in writing, or by the minor's conduct. (188)

Discharge Actions or events that relieve certain parties from liability on negotiable instruments. There are three methods of discharge: (1) payment of the instrument, (2) cancellation, and (3) impairment of the right of recourse. (403) The termination of the legal duty of a debtor to pay debts that remain unpaid upon the completion of a bankruptcy proceeding. (477) Creditors' claims that are not included in a Chapter 11 reorganization are discharged. (484) A discharge is granted to a debtor in a Chapter 13 consumer debt adjustment only after all of the payments under the plan are completed by the debtor. (486)

Discharge in bankruptcy A real defense against the enforcement of a negotiable instrument; bankruptcy law is intended to relieve debtors of burdensome debts, including negotiable instruments. (400)

Discharge of student loans A student loan may be discharged within the first five years after it is due only if nondischarge would cause an undue hardship on the debtor or the debtor's family. After seven years, student loans may be discharged like other debts. (479)

Disclosure statement A statement that must contain adequate information about the proposed plan of reorganization, which is supplied to the creditors and equity holders after court approval. (482)

Discovery A legal process during which parties engage in various activities to discover facts of the case from the other party and witnesses prior to trial. (61)

Dishonored Occurs when an instrument has been presented for payment and payment has been refused. (390)

Disposition of collateral If a secured creditor repossess collateral upon a debtor's default, he or she may sell, lease, or otherwise dispose of it in a commercially reasonable manner. (454)

Disposition of goods A seller or lessor that is in possession of goods at the time the buyer or lessee breaches or repudiate the contract may in good faith resell, release, or otherwise dispose of the goods in a commercially reasonable manner and recover damages, including incidental damages, from the buyer or lessee. (309)

Dissension When an individual director opposes the action taken by the majority of the board of directors. (625)

Dissenting shareholder appraisal rights Shareholders who object to a proposed merger, share exchange, or sale or lease of all or substantially all of the property of a corporation have a right to have their shares valued by the court and receive cash payment of this value from the corporation. (649)

Dissolution "The change in the relation of the partners caused by any partner ceasing to be associated in the carrying on of the business" [UPA Section 29]. (561)

Distinctive A brand name that is unique and fabricated. (118)

Distribution of assets Upon the winding up of a dissolved partnership, the assets of the partnership are distributed in the following order [UPA § 40(b)]: (1) Creditors (except partners who are creditors) (2) creditor-partners (3) capital contributions and (4) profits. (564)

Distribution of property Nonexempt property of the bankruptcy estate must be distributed to the debtor's secured and unsecured creditors pursuant to the statutory priority established by the Bankruptcy Code. (476)

Distributorship franchise The franchisor manufactures a product and licenses a retail franchisee to distribute the product to the public. (528)

Diversity of citizenship A case between (1) citizens of different states, (2) a citizen of a state and a citizen or subject of a foreign country, and (3) a citizen of a state and a foreign country where a foreign country is the plaintiff. (56)

Dividend Distribution of profits of the corporation to shareholders. (620)

Dividend preference The right to receive a fixed dividend at stipulated periods during the year (e.g., quarterly). (597)

Doctrine of sovereign immunity States that countries are granted immunity from suits in courts of other countries (subject to certain exceptions). (66)

Doctrine of strict liability in tort A tort doctrine that makes manufacturers, distributors, wholesalers, retailers, and others in the chain of distribution of a defective product liable for the damages caused by the defect irrespective of fault. (336)

Document of title An actual piece of paper, such as a warehouse receipt or bill of lading, that is required in some transactions of pick up and delivery. (282)

Domestic corporation A corporation in the state in which it was formed. (586)

Donee A person who receives a gift. (703)

Donee beneficiary contract A contract entered into with the intent to confer a benefit or gift on an intended third party. (238)

Donee beneficiary The third party on whom the benefit is to be conferred. (238)

Donor A person who gives a gift. (703)

Double jeopardy clause A clause of the Fifth Amendment that protects persons from being tried twice for the same crime. (147)

Draft A three-party instrument that is an unconditional written order by one party that orders the second party to pay money to a third party. (357)

Dram shop act Statute that makes taverns and bartenders liable for in-

juries caused to or by patrons who are served too much alcohol. (91)

Drawee of a check The financial institution where the drawer has his or her account. (359) (416)

Drawee of a draft The party who must pay the money stated in the draft. (357) Also called the acceptor of a draft. (357)

Drawer of a check The checking account holder and writer of the check. (359) (416)

Drawer of a draft The party who writes the order for a draft. (357)

Drawer's negligence The drawer is liable if his or her negligence led to his or her forged signature or the alteration of a check. The payor bank is not liable in such circumstances. (425)

Dual agency A situation that occurs when an agent acts for two or more different principals in the same transaction. (502)

Dual-purpose mission An errand or other act that a principal requests of an agent while the agent is on his or her own personal business. (510)

Due diligence defense A defense to a Section 11 action that, if proven, makes the defendant not liable. (677)

Duress Occurs when one party threatens to do a wrongful act unless the other party enters into a contract. (215)

Duty not to willfully or wantonly injure The duty an owner owes a trespasser to prevent intentional injury or harm to the trespasser when the trespasser is on his or her premises. (92)

Duty of accountability A duty that an agent owes to maintain an accurate accounting of all transactions undertaken on the principal's behalf. (504)

Duty of care The obligation partners owe to use the same level of care and skill that a reasonable person in the same position would use in the same circumstances. A breach of the duty of care is negligence. (85) (557) A duty that corporate directors and officers have to use care and diligence when acting on behalf of the corporation. (623)

Duty of compensation A duty that a principal owes to pay an agreed-upon amount to the agent either upon the completion of the agency or at some other mutually agreeable time. (504)

Duty of loyalty A duty an agent owes the principal not to act adversely to the interests of the principal. (502) A duty that a partner owes not to act adversely to the interests of the partnership. (556) A duty that directors and officers have not to act adversely to the interests of the corporation and to subordinate their personal interests to those of the corporation and its shareholders. (626)

Duty of notification An agent's duty to notify the principal of information he or she learns from a third party or other source that is important to the principal. (502)

Duty of obedience A duty that partners must adhere to the provisions of the partnership agreement and the decisions of the partnership. (503) (556) A duty that directors and officers of a corporation have to act within the authority conferred upon them by the state corporation statute, the articles of incorporation, the corporate bylaws, and the resolutions adopted by the board of directors. (622)

Duty of ordinary care The duty an owner owes an invitee or a licensee to prevent injury or harm when the invitee or licensee steps on the owner's premises. (92) Collecting banks are required to exercise ordinary care in presenting and sending checks for collection. (430)

Duty of performance An agent's duty to a principal that includes (1) performing the lawful duties expressed in the contract and (2) meeting the standards of reasonable care, skill, and diligence implicit in all contracts. (501)

Duty of reasonable care The duty that a reasonable bailee in like circumstances would owe to protect the bailed property. (711)

Duty of reimbursement A duty that a principal owes to repay money to the agent if the agent spent his or her own money during the agency on the principal's behalf. (504)

Duty of slight care A duty not to be grossly negligent in caring for something in one's possession. (710)

Duty of strict liability A duty that common carriers owe that says if the goods are lost, damaged, destroyed, or stolen, the common carrier is liable even if it was not at fault for the loss. (712)

Duty of utmost care A duty of care that goes beyond ordinary care that says common carriers and innkeepers have a responsibility to provide security to their passengers or guests. (92) (711)

Duty to cooperate A duty that a principal owes to cooperate with and assist the agent in the performance of the agent's duties and the accomplishment of the agency. (505)

Duty to defend An insurer owes a duty to defend an insured against a lawsuit involving a risk covered by the policy. This includes providing a lawyer and paying court costs, deposition fees, and so forth. (759)

Duty to indemnify A duty that a principal owes to protect the agent for losses the agent suffered during the agency because of the principal's misconduct. (505)

Duty to inform A duty a partner owes to inform his or her co-partners of all information he or she possesses that is relevant to the affairs of the partnership. (557)

Duty to provide safe working conditions A duty that a principal owes to provide safe premises, equipment, and other working conditions; also includes inspection by the principal to ensure safety. (505)

Easement A given or required right to make limited use of someone else's land without owning or leasing it. (731)

Easement appurtenant A situation created when the owner of one piece of land is given an easement over an adjacent piece of land. (731)

Easement in gross An easement that authorizes a person who does not own adjacent land the right to sue another's land. (732)

Economic duress Occurs when one party to a contract refuses to perform his or her contractual duties unless the other party pays an increased price, enters into a second contract with the threatening party, or undertakes a similar action. (215)

Electronic fund transfer systems (EFTS) Electronic payment and collection systems that are facilitated by computers and other electronic technology. (430)

Electronic Funds Transfer Act Makes it a federal crime to use, furnish, sell, or transport a counterfeit, stolen, lost, or fraudulently obtained ATM card, code number, or other device used to conduct electronic funds transfers. (141)

Elements of a bailment The following three elements are necessary to create a bailment: (1) personal property (2) delivery of possession and (3) a bailment agreement. (709)

Emancipation When a minor voluntarily leaves home and lives apart from his or her parents. (191)

Embezzlement The fraudulent conversion of property by a person to whom that property was entrusted. (138)

Employer-employee relationship A relationship that results when an employer hires an employee to perform some form of physical service. (495)

Employment relationships (1) Employer-employee (2) principal-agent and (3) principal-independent contractor. (495)

Endorsement An addition to an insurance policy that modifies it. (759)

Entity theory A theory that holds that partnerships are separate legal entities that can hold title to personal and real property, transact business in the partnership name, and the like. (349)

Enumerated powers Certain powers delegated to the federal government by the states. (11)

Equal dignity rule A rule that says that agent's contracts to sell property covered by the Statute of Frauds must be in writing to be enforceable. (219)

Equity A doctrine that permits judges to make decisions based on fairness, equality, moral rights, and natural law. (162)

Equity securities Representation of ownership rights to the corporation. Also called stocks. (596)

Estate Ownership rights in real property; the bundle of legal rights that the owner has to possess, use, and enjoy the property. (723)

Estate pour autre vie A life estate measured in the life of a third party. (724)

Estray statutes Statutes that permit a finder of mislaid or lost property to clear title to the property if (1) the finder reports the found property to the appropriate government agency and turns over possession of the property to this agency, (2) either the finder or the government agency posts notices and publishes advertisements describing the lost property, and (3) a specified amount of time has passed without the rightful owner's reclaiming the property. (707)

Ethical fundamentalism When a person looks to an outside source for ethical rules or commands. (31)

Ethical relativism A moral theory that holds that individuals must decide what is ethical based on their own feelings as to what is right or wrong. (34)

Ethics A set of moral principles or values that governs the conduct of an individual or a group. (30)

Exceptions to the writing requirements of the Statute of Frauds (1) Specially manufactured goods, (2) admissions in pleadings or court, and (3) part acceptance. (280)

Exclusionary rule A rule that says evidence obtained from an unreasonable search and seizure can generally be prohibited from introduction at a trial or administrative proceeding against the person searched. (144)

Exclusive agency contract A contract a principal and agent enter into that says the principal cannot employ any agent other than the exclusive agent. (497)

Exclusive possession A lease grants the tenant *exclusive possession* of the leased premises for the term of the lease or until the tenant defaults on the obligations under the lease. (735)

Exculpatory clause A contractual provision that relieves one (or both) parties to the contract from tort liability for ordinary negligence. (198)

Executed contract A contract that has been fully performed on both sides; a completed contract. (160)

Execution Postjudgment seizure and sale of the debtor's property to satisfy a creditor's judgment against the debtor.

Executive branch The part of the government that consists of the President and Vice President. (11)

Executive order An order issued by a member of the executive branch of the government. (8)

Executory contract A contract that has not been fully performed by either or both sides. (160) With court approval, executory contracts may be rejected by a debtor in bankruptcy. (483)

Exempt property Property that may be retained by the debtor pursuant to federal or state law; the debtor's property that does not become part of the bankruptcy estate. (473)

Express agency An agency that occurs when a principal and an agent expressly agree to enter into an agency agreement with each other. (497)

Express contract An agreement that is expressed in written or oral words. (159)

Express powers Powers given to a corporation by (1) the U.S. Constitution, (2) state constitutions, (3) federal statutes, (4) state statutes, (5) articles of incorporation, (6) bylaws, and (7) resolutions of the board of directors. (600)

Express trust A trust created voluntarily by the settlor. (771)

Express warranty A warranty that is created when a seller or lessor makes an affirmation that the goods he or she is selling or leasing meet certain standards of quality, description, performance, or condition. (326)

Extortion Threat to expose something about another person unless that other person gives money or property. Often referred to as "blackmail." (135)

Extreme duress Extreme duress, but not ordinary duress, is a real defense against enforcement of a negotiable instrument. (399)

Failure to provide adequate instruction A defect that occurs when a manufacturer does not provide detailed directions for safe assembly and use of a product. (344)

Failure to warn A defect that occurs when a manufacturer does not place a warning on the packaging of products that could cause injury if the danger is unknown. (343)

Fair price rule A rule that says any increase in price paid for shares tendered must be offered to all shareholders, even those who have previously tendered their shares. (651)

Fair use doctrine A doctrine that permits certain limited use of a copyright by someone other than the copyright holder without the permission of the copyright holder. (115)

False imprisonment The intentional confinement or restraint of another person without authority or justification and without that person's consent. (81)

Federal Patent Statute of 1952 Federal statute that establishes the requirements for obtaining a patent and protects patented inventions from infringement. (111)

Federal question A case arising under the U.S. Constitution, treaties, and federal statutes and regulations. (56)

Federal Trade Commission (FTC) Federal government agency empowered to enforce federal franchising rules. (529)

Federalism The United States form of government; the federal government and the 50 state governments share powers. (11)

Fee simple absolute A type of ownership of real property that grants the owner the fullest bundle of legal rights that a person can hold in real property. (723)

Fee simple defeasible A type of ownership of real property that grants the owner all the incidents of a fee simple absolute except that it may be taken away if a specified condition occurs or does not occur. (724)

Felony The most serious type of crime; inherently evil crime. Most crimes against the person and some business-related crimes are felonies. (131)

Fictitious business name statement An official document that must be filed with the appropriate government agency in order for the sole proprietorship to be able to use the name. (527)

Fictitious payee rule A rule that says a drawer or maker is liable on a forged or unauthorized indorsement of a fictitious payee. (376)

Fiduciary duty The duty the directors of a corporation owe to act carefully and honestly when acting on behalf of the corporation. (622) (654)

Final prospectus A final version of the prospectus that must be delivered by the issuer to the investor prior to or at the time of confirming a sale or sending a security to a purchaser. (673)

Final settlement Occurs when the payor bank either (1) pays the check in cash (2) settles for the check without having a right to revoke the settlement, or (3) fails to dishonor the check within certain statutory time periods. (428)

Finance lease A three-party transaction consisting of the lessor, the lessee, and the supplier. (275)

Financing statement A document filed by a secured creditor with the appropriate government office that constructively notifies the world of his or her security interest in personal property. (447)

Fireman's rule Rule that provides that firefighters, police officers, and other government workers who are injured while providing the services they are trained and paid to perform cannot sue the person who negligently caused the emergency situation to which they responded. (92)

Fixed amount A requirement of a negotiable instrument that ensures that the value of the instrument can be determined with certainty. (363)

Fixed amount of money A negotiable instrument must contain a promise or order to pay a fixed amount of money. (363)

Fixtures Personal property that is permanently affixed to the real property, such as built-in cabinets in a house. (216) Goods that are affixed to real estate so as to become a part thereof. (723)

Floating lien A security interest in property that was not in the possession of the debtor when the security agreement was executed; this includes *after-acquired property*, *future advances*, and *sale proceeds*. (446)

Foreign corporation A corporation in any state or jurisdiction other than the one in which it was formed. (586)

Forged document The forged signature of a payee or holder on a negotiable instrument. (374)

Forged indorsement The forged signature of the payee or other holder. (424)

Forged instrument A check with a forged drawer's signature on it. (423)

Forgery Fraudulently making or altering a written document that affects the legal liability of another person. (135) A real defense against the enforcement of a negotiable instrument; the unauthorized signature of a maker, drawer, or indorser. (400)

Formal contract A contract that requires a special form or method of creation. (159)

Formal will A will that meets the requirements of the Statute of Wills. (762)

Forum-selection clause Contract provision that designates a certain court to hear any dispute concerning nonperformance of the contract. (57)

Four legals Four notices or actions that prevent the payment of a check if they are received by the payor bank before it has finished its process of posting the check for payment. (429)

Franchise Established when one party licenses another party to use the franchisor's trade name, trademarks, commercial symbols, patents, copyrights, and other property in the distribution and selling of goods and services. (528)

Franchise agreement An agreement that the franchisor and the franchisee enter into that sets forth the terms and conditions of the franchise. (531)

Franchisee The party who is licensed by the franchisor in a franchise situation. (528)

Franchisor The party who does the licensing in a franchise situation. (528)

Fraud by concealment Occurs when one party takes specific action to conceal a material fact from another party. (212)

Fraud in the inception A real defense against the enforcement of a negotiable instrument; a person has been deceived into signing a negotiable instrument thinking that it is something else. (400)

Fraud in the inception Occurs if a person is deceived as to the nature of his or her act and does not know what he or she is signing. (211)

Fraud in the inducement Occurs when the party knows what he or she is signing but has been fraudulently induced to enter into the contract. (212) A personal defense against the enforcement of a negotiable instrument; a wrongdoer makes a false state-ment to another person to lead that person to enter into a contract with the wrongdoer. (401)

Fraudulent transfer Occurs when (1) a debtor transfers property to a third person within one year before the filing of a petition in bankruptcy and (2) the transfer is made by the debtor with an intent to hinder, delay, or defraud creditors. (476)

Freedom of speech The right to oral, written, and symbolic speech protected by the First Amendment. (15)

Freehold estate An estate where the owner has a present possessory interest in the real property. (723)

Fresh start The goal of federal bankruptcy law—to discharge the debtor from burdensome debts and allow him or her to begin again. (471)

Frustration of purpose A doctrine that excuses the performance of contractual obligations if (1) the object or benefit of a contract is made worthless to a promisor, (2) both parties knew what the purpose was, and (3) the act that frustrated the purpose was unforeseeable. (245)

FTC Franchise Rule A rule set out by the FTC that requires franchisors to make full presale disclosures to prospective franchisees. (530)

Fully disclosed agency An agency that results if the third party entering into the contract knows (1) that the agent is acting as an agent for a principal and (2) the actual identity of the principal. (506)

Fully protected speech Speech that the government cannot prohibit or regulate. (15)

Fundamental changes Major events in a corporation's life. These include proxy contests, mergers, consolidations, hostile tender offers, and dissolution and termination. (642)

Future advances Personal property of the debtor that is designated as collateral for future loans from a line of credit. (447)

Future goods Goods not yet in existence (ungrown crops, unborn stock animals). (282)

Future interest The interest that the grantor retains for him- or herself or a third party. (724)

Gambling statutes Statutes that make certain forms of gambling illegal. (195)

Gap-filling rule A rule that says an open term can be "read into" a contract. (276)

Garnishment A postjudgment remedy that is directed against property of the debtor that is in the position of third persons. (266)

General gift Gift that does not identify the specific property from which the gift is to be made. (765)

General partners Partners in a limited partnership who invest capital, manage the business, and are personally liable for partnership debts. (564)

General partnership A voluntary association of two or more persons for carrying on a business as co-owners for profit [UPA § 6(1)]. Also called a partnership. (549)

General purpose clause A clause that is often included in the articles of incorporation that authorizes the corporation to engage in any activity permitted corporations by law. (589)

General-jurisdiction trial court A court that hears cases of a general nature that are not within the jurisdiction of limited-jurisdiction trial courts. Testimony and evidence at trial are recorded and stored for future reference. (50)

Generally known dangers A defense that acknowledges that certain products are inherently dangerous and are known to the general population to be so. (344)

Generic name A term for a mark that has become a common term for a product line or type of service and therefore has lost its trademark protection. (120)

Genuineness of assent The requirement that a party's assent to a contract be genuine. (209)

Gift A voluntary transfer of title to property without payment of consideration by the donee. To be a valid gift, the following three elements must be shown: (1) donative intent (2) delivery and (3) acceptance. (703) (728)

Gift *causa mortis* A gift that is made in contemplation of death. (703)

Gift promise An unenforceable promise because it lacks consideration. (176)

Good faith Honesty in fact in the conduct or transaction concerned. This is a subjective test. (389)

Good faith purchaser for value A person to whom good title can be transferred from a person with voidable title. The real owner cannot reclaim goods from a good faith purchaser for value. (287)

Good faith subsequent lease A person to whom a lease interest can be transferred from a person with voidable title. The real owner cannot reclaim the goods from the subsequent lessee until the lease expires. (288)

Good Samaritan laws Statutes that relieve medical professionals from liability for ordinary negligence when they stop and render aid to victims in emergency situations. (91)

Good title Title that is free from any encumbrances or other defects that are not disclosed but would affect the value of the property. (730)

Goods Tangible things that are movable at the time of their identification to the contract. (273)

Government contractor defense A defense that says a contractor who was provided specifications by the government is not liable for any defect in the product that occurs as a result of those specifications. (345)

Grace period A period of time after the actual expiration date of a payment but during which the insured can still pay an overdue premium without penalty. (759)

Grantee The party to whom an interest in real property is transferred. (729)

Grantor The party who transfers an ownership interest in real property. (729)

Greenmail The purchase by a target corporation of its stock from an actual or perceived tender offeror at a premium. (653)

Guaranteeing collection A form of accommodation in which the accommodating party guarantees collection of a negotiable instrument; the accommodation party is secondarily liable on the instrument. (397)

Guaranteeing payment A form of accommodation in which the accommodating party guarantees payment of a negotiable instrument; the accommodation party is primarily liable on the instrument. (397)

Guarantor The person who agrees to pay the debt if the primary debtor does not. (218)

Guaranty arrangement An arrangement where a third party promises to be secondarily liable for the payment of another's debt. (457)

Guaranty contract The contract between the guarantor and the original creditor. (218)

Guest statutes Statute that provides that if a driver of a vehicle voluntarily and without compensation gives a ride to another person, the driver is not liable to the passenger for injuries caused by the driver's ordinary negligence. (91)

Hardship discharge A discharge granted if (1) the debtor fails to complete the payments due to unforeseeable circumstances, (2) the unsecured creditors have been paid as much as they would have been paid in a Chapter 7 liquidation proceeding, and (3) it is not practical to modify the plan. (486)

Hedging To try to avoid or lessen loss by making a counterbalancing investment. (688)

Heir The receiver of property under intestacy statutes. (769)

Holder A person who is in possession of a negotiable instrument that is drawn, issued, or indorsed to him or her or his or her order, or to bearer, or in blank. (388) What the transferee becomes if a negotiable instrument has been transferred by negotiation. (367)

Holder in due course (HDC) A holder who takes a negotiable instrument for value, in good faith, and without notice that it is defective or is overdue. (388) (399)

Holographic will Will that is entirely handwritten and signed by the testator. (768)

Honor Payment of a drawer's properly drawn check by the drawee bank. (419)

Hung jury A jury that cannot come to a unanimous decision about the defendant's guilt. The government may choose to retry the case. (133)

Identification of goods Distinguishing the goods named in the contract from the seller's or lessor's other goods. (281)

Illegal consideration A promise to refrain from doing an illegal act. Such a promise will not support a contract. (178)

Illusory promise A contract into which parties enter, but one or both of the parties can choose not to perform their contractual obligations. Thus, the contract lacks consideration. (177)

Immoral contract A contract whose objective is the commission of an act that is considered immoral by society. (197)

Immunity from prosecution The government agrees not to use any evidence given by a person granted immunity against that person. (146)

Impairment of right of recourse Certain parties (holders, indorsers, accommodation parties) are discharged from liability on an instrument if the holder (1) Releases an obligor from liability or (2) surrenders collateral without the consent of the parties who would benefit by it. (403)

Implied agency An agency that occurs when a principal and an agent do not expressly create an agency, but it is inferred from the conduct of the parties. (497)

Implied powers Powers beyond express powers that allow a corporation to accomplish its corporate purpose. (601)

Implied term A term in a contract which can reasonably be supplied by the courts. (168)

Implied trust A trust that is implied by law or from the conduct of the parties. (771)

Implied warranties The law implies certain warranties on transferors of negotiable instruments. There are two types of implied warranties: transfer and presentment. (398)

Implied warranty arising from a course of dealing A warranty that is implied from a previous course of dealing between the parties. (331)

Implied warranty arising from usage of trade A warranty that is implied from customs of the industry or market. (331)

Implied warranty of authority An agent who enters into a contract on behalf of another party impliedly warrants that he or she has the authority to do so. (508)

Implied warranty of fitness for a particular purpose A warranty that

arises where a seller or lessor warrants that the goods will meet the buyer's or lessee's expressed needs. (330)

Implied warranty of fitness for human consumption A warranty that applies to food or drink consumed on or off the premises of restaurants, grocery stores, fast food outlets, and vending machines. (329)

Implied warranty of habitability A warranty that provides that the leased premises must be fit, safe, and suitable for ordinary residential use. (736)

Implied warranty of merchantability Unless properly disclosed, a warranty that is implied that sold or leased goods are fit for the ordinary purpose for which they are sold or leased. (328)

Implied-in-fact condition A condition that can be implied from the circumstances surrounding a contract and the parties' conduct. (242)

Implied-in-fact contract A contract in which agreement between parties has been inferred from their conduct. (159)

Impossibility of performance Nonperformance that is excused if the contract becomes impossible to perform; must be objective impossibility, not subjective. (243)

Imposter A person who impersonates a payee and induces a maker or drawer to issue an instrument in the payee's name and to give it to the imposter. (375)

Imposter rule A rule that says if an imposter forges the indorsement of the named payee, the drawer or maker is liable on the instrument and bears the loss. (375)

Imputed knowledge Information that is learned by the agent that is attributed to the principal. (502)

In pari delicto When both parties are equally at fault in an illegal contract. (200)

In personam jurisdiction Jurisdiction over the parties to a lawsuit. (56)

In rem jurisdiction Jurisdiction to hear a case because of jurisdiction over the property of the lawsuit. (57)

In transit A state in which goods are in the possession of a bailee or carrier and not in the hands of the buyer, seller, lessee, or lessor. (308)

Incidental authority Implied power that an agent has where the terms of the express agency agreement do not cover the contingency that has arisen. (499)

Incidental beneficiary A party who is unintentionally benefited by other people's contracts. (239)

Incidental damages When goods are resold or released, incidental damages are reasonable expenses incurred in stopping delivery, transportation charges, storage charges, sales commissions, and so on. (309)

Incontestability clause A clause that prevents insurers from contesting statements made by insureds in applications for insurance after the passage of a stipulated number of years. (760)

Incorporation The process of forming a corporation. (589)

Incorporation by reference When integration is made by express reference in one document that refers to and incorporates another document within it. (221)

Incorporator The person or persons, partnerships, or corporations who are responsible for incorporation of a corporation. (591)

Indemnificaiton Right of a partner to be reimbursed for expenditures incurred on behalf of the partnership. (555)

Indenture agreement A contract between the corporation and the holder that contains the terms of a debt security. (599)

Independent contractor A person or business who is not an employee who is employed by a principal to perform a certain task on his behalf. "A person who contracts with another to do something for him who is not controlled by the other nor subject to the other's right to control with respect to his physical conduct in the performance of the undertaking" [Restatement (Second) of Agency]. (495)

Indictment The charge of having committed a crime (usually a felony), based on the judgment of a grand jury. (133)

Indorsee The party to whom a negotiable instrument is indorsed. (368) (416)

Indorsement The signature (and other directions) written by or on behalf of the holder somewhere on the instrument. (368)

Indorsement for deposit or collection An indorsement that makes the indorsee the indorser's collecting agent (e.g., "for deposit only"). (373)

Indorsement of a check Occurs when a payee indorses a check to another party by signing the back of the check. (416)

Indorser The payee who indorses a negotiable instrument to another party. (368) (416)

Indorsers' liability Unqualified indorsers are secondarily liable on negotiable instruments they indorse; qualified indorsers disclaim liability and are not secondarily liable on instruments they indorse. (395)

Infancy doctrine A doctrine that allows minors to disaffirm (cancel) most contracts they have entered into with adults. (188)

Inferior performance Occurs when a party fails to perform express or implied contractual obligations that impair or destroy the essence of the contract. (256)

Informal contract A contract that is not formal. Valid informal contracts are fully enforceable and may be sued upon if breached. (160)

Information The charge of having committed a crime (usually a misdemeanor), based on the judgment of a judge (magistrate). (133)

Injunction A court order that prohibits a person from doing a certain act. (263)

Injury The plaintiff must suffer personal injury or damage to his or her property in order to recover monetary damages for the defendant's negligence. (86)

Innkeepers statutes State statutes that limit an innkeeper's common law liability. An innkeeper can avoid liability for loss caused to a guest's property if (1) a safe is provided in which the guest's valuable property may be kept and (2) the guest is notified of this fact. (713)

Innocent misrepresentation Occurs when a person makes a statement of fact that he or she honestly and reasonably believes to be true, even though it is not. (212)

Insane, but not adjudged insane A person who is insane but has not been adjudged insane by a court or administrative agency. A contract entered into by such person is generally voidable. Some states hold that such a contract is void. (193)

Inside director A member of the board of directors who is also an officer of the corporation. (617)

Insider trading When an insider makes a profit by personally purchasing shares of the corporation prior to public release of favorable information or by selling shares of the corporation prior to the public disclosure of unfavorable information. (680)

Insider Trading Sanctions Act of 1984 A federal statute that permits the SEC to obtain a civil penalty of up to three times the illegal benefits received from insider trading. (684)

Installment contract A contract that requires or authorizes the goods to be delivered and accepted in separate lots. (303)

Instrument Term that means negotiable instrument. (357)

Insurable interest A person who purchases insurance must have a personal interest in the insured item or person. (756)

Insurance A means for persons and businesses to protect themselves against the risk of loss. (754)

Insured The party who pays a premium to a particular insurance company for insurance coverage. (754)

Insurer The insurance company. (754)

Intangible property Rights that cannot be reduced to physical form such as stock certificates, CDs, bonds, copyrights, and such. (702)

Integration The combination of several writings to form a single contract. (221)

Integration of offerings When separate offerings that might otherwise qualify for individual exemptions are combined if they are really part of one large offering. (676)

Intellectual property Objects such as inventions, writings, trademarks, and so on, which are often a business's most valuable asset. (111)

Intended beneficiary A third party who is not in privity of contract but who has rights under the contract and can enforce the contract against the obligor. (237)

Intentional infliction of emotional distress A tort that says a person whose extreme and outrageous conduct intentionally or recklessly causes severe emotional distress to another person is liable for that emotional distress. Also known as the *tort of outrage*. (83)

Intentional interference with contractual relations A tort that arises when a third party induces a contracting party to breach the contract with another party. (264)

Intentional misrepresentation Intentionally defrauding another person out of money, property, or something else of value. (94) Also called *fraud*. (211) When a seller or lessor fraudulently misrepresents the quality of a product and a buyer is injured thereby. (334)

Intentional tort A category of torts that requires that the defendant possessed the intent to commit a wrong against (1) another person or his or her character, or (2) another person's property. (511) that caused the plaintiff's injuries. (81)

***Inter vivos* gift** A gift made during a person's lifetime that is an irrevocable present transfer of ownership. (703)

***Inter vivos* trust** A trust that is created while the settlor is alive. (771)

Intermediary bank A bank in the collection process that is not the depository or payor bank. (427)

Intermediate appellate court An intermediate court that hears appeals from trial courts. (50)

Interrogatories Written questions submitted by one party to another party. The questions must be answered in writing within a stipulated time. (61)

Interstate commerce Commerce that moves between states or that affects commerce between states. (13)

Intervention The act of others to join as parties to an existing lawsuit. (61)

Intestacy statute A state statute that specifies how a deceased's property will be distributed if he or she dies without a will or if the last will is declared void and there is no prior valid will. (769)

Intestate The state of having died without leaving a will. (769)

Intoxicated person A person who is under contractual incapacity because of ingestion of alcohol or drugs to the point of incompetence. (193)

Intrastate offering exemption An exemption from registration that permits local businesses to raise capital from local investors to be used in the local economy without the need to register with the SEC. (674)

Invasion of the right to privacy A tort that constitutes the violation of a person's right to live his or her life without being subjected to unwarranted and undesired publicity. (108)

Involuntary petition A petition filed by creditors of the debtor; alleges that the debtor is not paying his or her debts as they become due. (471)

Issued shares Shares that have been sold by the corporation. (598)

Joint and several liability Partners are *joint and severally liable* for tort liability of the partnership. This means that the plaintiff can sue one or more of the partners separately. If successful, the plaintiff can recover the entire amount of the judgment from any or all of the defendant-partners. (560)

Joint liability Partners are *jointly liable* for contracts and debts of the partnership. This means that a plaintiff must name the partnership and all of the partners as defendants. If successful, the plaintiff can recover the entire amount of the judgment from any or all of the partners. (559)

Joint tenancy A form of co-ownership that includes the right of survivorship. (725)

Joint tenant Co-owner in a joint tenancy. (725)

Joint will A will that is executed by two or more testators. (768)

Judgment The official decision of the court. (65)

Judgment notwithstanding the verdict In a civil case, the judge may overturn the jury's verdict if he or she finds bias or jury misconduct. (64)

Judgment on the underlying debt A right granted to a secured creditor to relinquish his or her security interest in the collateral and sue a defaulting debtor to recover the amount of the underlying debt. (456)

Judicial branch The part of the government that consists of the Supreme Court and other federal courts. (11)

Judicial decision A decision about an individual lawsuit issued by federal and state courts. (8)

Judicial decree of dissolution Order of the court that dissolves a partnership. An application or petition must be filed by a partner or an assignee of a partnership interest with the appropriate state court; the court will issue a judicial decree of dissolution if warranted by the circumstances. (562)

Judicial dissolution Occurs when a corporation is dissolved by a court proceeding instituted by shareholders, creditors or the state. Permitted only for certain reasons. (657)

Jurisprudence The philosophy or science of law. (4)

Jury instruction Instructions given by the judge to the jury that inform them of the law to be applied in the case. (64)

Kantian or duty ethics A moral theory that says that people owe moral duties that are based on universal rules such as the categorical imperative "Do unto others as you would have them do unto you." (32)

Land The most common form of real property. Includes the land and buildings and other structures permanently attached to the land. (722)

Land use control The collective term for the laws that regulate the possession, ownership, and use of real property. (741)

Landlord The owner who transfers the leasehold. (733)

Landlord-tenant relationship A relationship created when the owner of a freehold estate (landlord) transfers a right to exclusively and temporarily possess the owner's property to another (tenant). (733)

Lanham Trademark Act An act enacted in 1946 that provides for the registration of trademarks and service marks with the Federal Patent Office in Washington, D.C. (117) (535)

Lapse of time An offer terminates when a stated time period expires. If no time is stated, an offer terminates after a reasonable time. (172)

Larceny Taking another's personal property other than from his or her person or building. (134)

Law "That which must be obeyed and followed by citizens subject to sanctions or legal consequences; a body of rules of action or conduct prescribed by controlling authority, and having binding legal force." (*Black's Law Dictionary*) (2)

Law court A court that developed and administered a uniform set of laws decreed by the kings and queens after William the Conqueror; legal procedure was emphasized over merits at this time. (6)

Lease A transfer of the right to the possession and use of the named goods for a set term in return for certain consideration. (275)

Leasehold A tenant's interest in the property. (733)

Legal entity A corporation is a separate legal entity—an *artificial person*—that can own property, sue and be sued, enter into contracts, and such. (582)

Legal insanity A state of contractual incapacity as determined by law. (192)

Legally enforceable contract If one party fails to perform as promised, the other party can use the court system to enforce the contract and recover damages or other remedy. (155)

Legislative branch The part of the government that consists of Congress (the Senate and the House of Representatives). (11)

Lessee The person who acquires the right to possession and use of goods under a lease. (275)

Lessor The person who transfers the right of possession and use of goods under the lease. (275)

Libel A false statement that appears in a letter, newspaper, magazine, book, photograph, movie, video, and so on. (107)

License Grants a person the right to enter upon another's property for a specified and usually short period of time. (733)

Licensing statute Statute that requires a person or business to obtain a license from the government prior to engaging in a specified occupation or activity. (195)

Life estate An interest in the land for a person's lifetime; upon that person's death, the interest will be transferred to another party. (724)

Limited liability Liability that shareholders have only to the extent of their capital contribution. Shareholders are generally not personally liable for debts and obligations of the corporation. (628)

Limited liability company A limited liability company (LLC) is an unincorporated form of business. (567)

Limited liability partnership A limited liability partnership (LLP) is a special form of partnership that may be formed by professionals such as accountants, lawyers, and doctors. (567)

Limited partners Partners in a limited partnership who invest capital but do not participate in management and are not personally liable for partnership debts beyond their capital contribution. (564)

Limited partnership A special form of partnership that is formed only if certain formalities are followed. It has both general and limited partners. (564)

Limited partnership agreement A document that sets forth the rights and duties of the general and limited partners, the terms and conditions regarding the operation, termination and dissolution of the partnership, and so on. (565)

Limited protected speech Speech that cannot be forbidden by the government, but that is subject to *time, place, and manner restrictions*. (15)

Limited purpose clause A clause that limits the purpose or purposes of the corporation. (390)

Limited-jurisdiction trial court A court that hears civil cases involving small dollar amounts. (50)

Lineal descendants Children, grandchildren, great grandchildren, and so on of the testator. (765)

Liquidated damages Damages that will be paid upon a breach of contract and that are established in advance. (258)

Liquidation preference The right to be paid a stated dollar amount if the corporation is dissolved and liquidated. (597)

Litigation The process of bringing, maintaining, and defending a lawsuit. (59)

Long-arm statute A statute that extends a state's jurisdiction to nonresidents who were not served a summons within the state. (57)

Lost property When a property owner leaves property somewhere because of negligence, carelessness, or inadvertence. (706)

Mail fraud The use of mail to defraud another person. (137)

Mailbox rule A rule that states that an acceptance is effective when it is dispatched, even if it is lost in transmission. (174)

Main purpose or leading object exception If the main purpose of a transaction and an oral collateral contract is to provide pecuniary benefit to the guarantor, the collateral contract does not have to be in writing to be enforced. (219)

Maker of a CD The bank (borrower). (360)

Maker of a note The party who makes the promise to pay (borrower). (359)

Management Unless otherwise agreed, each partner has a right to participate in the management of the partnership and has an equal vote on partnership matters. (554)

Mark The collective name for trademarks, service marks, certification marks, and collective marks that all can be trademarked. (118)

Market Reform Act of 1990 A federal statute that authorizes the SEC to regulate trading practices during periods of extraordinary market volatility. (687)

Material alteration A partial defense against enforcement of a negotiable instrument by an HDC. An HDC can enforce an altered instrument in the original amount for which the drawer wrote the check. (401)

Material breach A breach that occurs when a party renders inferior performance of his or her contractual duties. (256)

Maximize profits A theory of social responsibility that says a corporation owes a duty to take actions that maximize profits for shareholders. (36)

Mediation A form of ADR in which the parties choose a neutral third party to act as the mediator of the dispute. (70)

Meeting of the creditors A meeting of the creditors in a bankruptcy case that must occur not less than 10 days or more than 30 days after the court grants an order for relief. (472)

Members The owners of an LLC. (568)

Mens rea "Evil intent"—the possession of the requisite state of mind to commit a prohibited act. (131)

Merchant A person who (1) deals in the goods of the kind involved in the transaction, or (2) by his or her occupation holds him or herself out as having knowledge or skill peculiar to the goods involved in the transaction. (274)

Merchant protection statutes A statute that allows merchants to stop, detain, and investigate suspected shoplifters without being held liable for false imprisonment if (1) there are reasonable grounds for the suspicion, (2) suspects are detained for only a reasonable time, and (3) investigations are conducted in a reasonable manner. (82)

Merger Occurs when one corporation is absorbed into another corporation and ceases to exist. (646)

Merger clause A clause in a contract that stipulates that it is a complete integration and the exclusive expression of the parties' agreement. Parol evidence may not be introduced to explain, alter, contradict, or add to the terms of the contract. (221)

Midnight deadline The midnight of the next banking day following the banking day on which the bank received the "on them" check for collection. (428)

Minor A person who has not reached the age of majority. (188)

Minor breach A breach that occurs when a party renders substantial performance of his or her contractual duties. (254)

Minor's duty of restoration As a general rule a minor is obligated only to return the goods or property he or she has received from the adult in the condition it is in at the time of disaffirmance. (189)

Mirror image rule States that in order for there to be an acceptance, the offeree must accept the terms as stated in the offer. (173)

Misdemeanor A less serious crime; not inherently evil but prohibited by society. Many crimes against property are misdemeanors. (131)

Mislaid property When an owner voluntarily places property somewhere and then inadvertently forgets it. (706)

Misrepresentation An assertion that is made that is not in accord with the facts. (211) (508)

Misuse A defense that relieves a seller of product liability if the user abnormally misused the product. Products must be designed to protect against foreseeable misuse. (345)

Misuse of confidential information An agent cannot disclose or misuse confidential information about the principal's affairs obtained during an agency. (502)

Mitigation A nonbreaching party is under a legal duty to avoid or reduce damages caused by a breach of contract. (260)

Mixed sale A sale that involves the provision of a service and a good in the same transaction. (274)

Model business corporation act (MBCA) A model act drafted in 1950 that was intended to provide a uniform law for regulation of corporations. (585)

Money A "medium of exchange authorized or adopted by a domestic or foreign government" [UCC 1–201(24)]. (364)

Moral minimum A theory of social responsibility that says a corporation's duty is to make a profit while avoiding harm to others. (37)

Mortgage A collateral arrangement where a property owner borrows money from a creditor who uses a deed as collateral for repayment of the loan. (216) (444)

Mortgagee The creditor in a mortgage transaction. (444)

Mortgagor The owner-debtor in a mortgage transaction. (444)

Motion for judgment on the pleadings Motion that alleges that if all the facts presented in the pleadings are taken as true, the moving party would win the lawsuit when the proper law is applied to these asserted facts. (62)

Motion for summary judgment Motion that asserts that there are no factual disputes to be decided by the jury; if so, the judge can apply the proper

law to the undisputed facts and decide the case without a jury. These motions are supported by affidavits, documents, and deposition testimony. (63)

Motivation test A test to determine the liability of the principal; if the agent's motivation is committing the intentional tort to promote the principal's business, then the principal is liable for any injury caused by the tort. (511)

Mutual benefit bailment A bailment for the mutual benefit of the bailor and bailee. The bailee owes a duty of reasonable care to protect the bailed property. (711)

Mutual mistake of fact A mistake made by both parties concerning a material fact that is important to the subject matter of the contract. (210)

Mutual mistake of value A mistake that occurs if both parties know the object of the contract but are mistaken as to its value. (210)

Mutual wills Occurs where two or more testators execute separate wills that leave their property to each other on the condition that the survivor leave the remaining property on his or her death as agreed by the testators. (768)

National courts The courts of individual nations. (65)

Necessaries of life A minor must pay the reasonable value of food, clothing, shelter, medical care, and other items considered necessary to the maintenance of life. (190)

Negligence A tort related to defective products in which the defendant has breached a duty of due care and caused harm to the plaintiff. (335) Failure of a corporate director or officer to exercise this duty of care while conducting the corporation's business. (623)

Negligence per se Tort where the violation of a statute or ordinance constitutes the breach of the duty of care. (90)

Negligent infliction of emotional distress A tort that permits a person to recover for emotional distress caused by the defendant's negligent conduct. (89)

Negotiable instrument A special form of contract that satisfies the requirements established by Article 3 of

the UCC. Also called commercial paper. (356) It must meet these requirements: (1) be in writing, (2) be signed by the maker or drawer, (3) be an unconditional promise or order to pay, (4) state a fixed amount of money, (5) not require any undertaking in addition to the payment of money, (6) be payable on demand or at a definite time, and (7) be payable to order or to bearer. (361)

Negotiation Transfer of a negotiable instrument by a person other than the issuer to a person who thereby becomes a *holder*. (367)

Nominal damages Damages awarded when the nonbreaching party sues the breaching party even though no financial loss has resulted from the breach; usually consists of $1 or some other small amount. (258)

Noncompete clause An agreement whereby a person agrees not to engage in a specified business or occupation within a designated geographical area for a specified period of time following the sale. (198)

Nonconforming uses Uses and buildings that already exist in the zoned area that are permitted to continue even though they do not fit within new zoning ordinances. (743)

Nonnegotiable contract Fails to meet the requirements of a negotiable instrument and, therefore, is not subject to the provisions of UCC Article 3. (366)

Nonpossessory interest When a person holds an interest in another person's property without actually owning any part of the property. (731)

Nonprofit corporation A corporation that is formed to operate charitable institutions, colleges, universities, and other not-for-profit entities. (586)

Nonrestrictive indorsement An indorsement that has no instructions or conditions attached to the payment of the funds. (373)

Note A debt security with a maturity of five years or less. (599)

Note and deed of trust An alternative to a mortgage in some states. (444)

Notice of dishonor The formal act of letting the party with secondary liability to pay a negotiable instrument know that the instrument has been dishonored. (395)

Novation An agreement that substitutes a new party for one of the original contracting parties and relieves the exiting party of liability on the contract. (243)

Novation agreement Agreement between a continuing partnership, a creditor of the partnership, and an outgoing partner expressly relieving the outgoing partner of liability to the creditor. (563)

Nuncupative will Oral will that is made before a witness during the testator's last illness. Also called a dying declaration or deathbed will. (768)

Objective theory of contracts A theory that says the intent to contract is judged by the reasonable person standard and not by the subjective intent of the parties. (167)

Obligation An action a party to a sales or lease contract is required by law to carry out. (300)

Offer "The manifestation of willingness to enter into a bargain, so made as to justify another person in understanding that his assent to that bargain is invited and will conclude it." (Section 24 of Restatement (Second) of Contracts) (167)

Offeree The party to whom an offer to enter into a contract is made. (155) (167)

Offeror The party who makes an offer to enter into a contract. (155) (167)

Officers Employees of the corporation who are appointed by the board of directors to manage the day-to-day operations of the corporation. (621)

One-year rule An executory contract that cannot be performed by its own terms within one year of its formation must be in writing. (217)

"On them" item A check presented for payment by the payee or holder where the depository bank and the payor bank are not the same bank. (428)

"On us" item A check presented for payment by the payee or holder where the depository bank and the payor bank are not the same bank. (428)

Opening statements Statements made by the attorneys to the jury in which they summarize the factual and legal issues of the case. (63)

Order for relief The filing of a voluntary petition, an unchallenged involuntary petition, or a grant of an order after a trial of a challenged involuntary petition. (471)

Order paper Order paper is negotiated by (1) *delivery* and (2) *indorsement*. (367)

Order to pay A drawer's unconditional order for a drawee to pay a payee. (362)

Ordinances Laws enacted by local government bodies such as cities and municipalities, counties, school districts, and water districts. (8)

Ordinary bailments (1) Bailments for the sole benefit of the bailor, (2) bailments for the sole benefit of the bailee, and (3) bailments for the mutual benefit of the bailor and bailee. (710)

Organizational meeting A meeting that must be held by the initial directors of the corporation after the articles of incorporation are filed. (593)

Original tenor The original amount for which the drawer wrote the check. (424)

Outside director A member of the board of directors who is not an officer of the corporation. (618)

Outstanding shares Shares of stock that are in shareholder hands. (599)

Overdraft The amount of money a drawer owes a bank after it has paid a check despite insufficient funds in the drawer's account. (421)

palming off Unfair competition that occurs when a company tries to pass off one of its products as that of a rival. (105)

par value A value assigned to common shares by the corporation that sets the lowest price at which the shares may be issued by the corporation. (596)

parent corporation A corporation that owns the shares of another corporation. (647)

parol evidence rule A rule that says if a written contract is a complete and final statement of the parties' agreement, any prior or contemporaneous oral or written statements that alter, contradict, or are in addition to the terms of the written contract are inadmissible in court regarding a dispute over the contract. (221) (281)

part performance A doctrine that allows the court to order an oral contract for the sale of land or transfer of another interest in real property to be specifically performed if it has been partially performed and performance is necessary to avoid injustice. (217)

partially disclosed agency An agency that occurs if the agent discloses his or her agency status but does not reveal the principal's identity and the third party does not know the principal's identity from another source. (506)

participating preferred stock Stock that allows the stockholder to participate in the profits of the corporation along with the common stockholders. (598)

partner's interest A partner's share of profits and surplus of the partnership. (559)

partnership agreement A written partnership agreement that the partners sign. (552)

partnership at will A partnership with no fixed duration. (551)

partnership by estoppel When a person who is not a partner either makes a representation or consents to a partner's representation that he or she is a partner. (554)

partnership capital Money and property contributed by partners for the permanent use of the partnership. (551)

partnership for a term A partnership with a fixed duration. (551)

partnership property Property that is originally brought into the partnership on account of the partnership and property that is subsequently acquired by purchase or otherwise on account of the partnership or with partnership funds. (557)

past consideration A prior act or performance. Past consideration (e.g., prior acts) will not support a new contract. New consideration must be given. (178)

patent infringement Unauthorized use of another's patent. A patent holder may recover damages and other remedies against a patent infringer. (112)

payable on demand or at a definite time requirement A negotiable instrument must be payable either on demand or at a definite time. (365)

payee of a CD The depositor (lender). (360)

payee of a check The party to whom the check is written. (359) (416)

payee of a draft The party who receives the money from a draft. (357)

payee of a note The party to whom the promise to pay is made (lender). (359)

payor bank The bank where the drawer has a checking account and on which the check is drawn. (426)

penal codes A collection of criminal statutes. (130)

per capita A distribution of the estate that makes each grandchild and great-grandchild of the deceased inherit equally with the children of the deceased. (763)

perfect tender rule A rule that says if the goods or tender of a delivery fails in any respect to conform to the contract, the buyer may opt either (1) to reject the whole shipment, (2) to accept the whole shipment, or (3) to reject part and accept part of the shipment. (301)

perfection by possession of the collateral If a secured creditor has physical possession of the collateral, no financing statement has to be filed; the creditor's possession is sufficient to put other potential creditors on notice of his or her secured interest in the property. (449)

perfection of a security interest Establishes the right of a secured creditor against other creditors who claim an interest in the collateral. (447)

periodic tenancy A tenancy created when a lease specifies intervals at which payments are due but does not specify how long the lease is for. (734)

permanency requirement A requirement of negotiable instruments that says they must be in a permanent state, such as written on ordinary paper. (361)

permanent trustee A legal representative of the bankruptcy debtor's estate, usually an accountant or a lawyer; elected at the first meeting of the creditors. (472)

personal defense A defense that can be raised against enforcement of a negotiable instrument by an ordinary holder but not against an HDC. (401)

personal property Property that consists of tangible property such as automobiles, furniture, and jewelry; intangible property such as securities, patents, and copyrights; and instruments, chattel paper, documents of title, and accounts. (446) (702)

personal satisfaction test Subjective test that applies to contracts involving personal taste and comfort. (241)

per stirpes A distribution of the estate that makes grandchildren and great-grandchildren of the deceased inherit by representation of their parent. (763)

petition A document filed with the bankruptcy court that sets the bankruptcy proceedings into motion. (471)

petition for certiorari A petition asking the Supreme Court to hear one's case. (54)

physical or mental examination Upon request of a party, the court may order another party to submit to a physical or mental examination prior to trial. (62)

piercing the corporate veil A doctrine that says if a shareholder dominates a corporation and misuses it for improper purposes, a court of equity can disregard the corporate entity and hold the shareholder personally liable for the corporation's debts and obligations. (628)

plaintiff The party who files the lawsuit. (59)

plaintiff's case Process by which the plaintiff introduces evidence to prove the allegations contained in the complaint. (63)

plan of reorganization A plan that sets forth a proposed new capital structure for the debtor to have when it emerges from reorganization bankruptcy. The debtor has the exclusive right to file the first plan of reorganization; any party of interest may file a plan thereafter. (482)

plant life and vegetation Real property that is growing in or on the surface of the land. (723)

plea A statement the accused makes about the crime he or she has or has not committed. The accused may plead (1) guilty, (2) not guilty, or (3) nolo contendere. (133)

pleadings The paperwork that is filed with the court to initiate and respond to a lawsuit. (59)

point-of-sale (POS) terminal A terminal at a merchant's checkout counter that is connected on-line to the bank's computers; a debit card or credit card can be used to make purchases at POS terminals. (430)

poison pill An item that appears in the target corporation's articles of incorporation, bylaws, or other documents that triggers an event that makes the target corporation unattractive to potential tender offerors. (653)

police power Constitutional authority of state and local governments to enact laws to protect the public health, safety, morals, and welfare. (742) within their borders. (14)

policy The insurance contract. (756)

portability requirement A requirement of negotiable instruments that says they must be able to be easily transported between areas. (361)

possessory lien Lien obtained by a bailee on bailed property for the compensation owed by the bailor to the bailee. (711)

posteffective period The period of time that begins when the registration statement becomes effective and runs until the issuer either sells all of the offered securities or withdraws them from sale. (673)

power of attorney An express agency agreement that is often used to give an agent the power to sign legal documents on behalf of the principal. (497)

precedent A rule of law established in a court decision. Lower courts must follow the precedent established by higher courts. (8)

preemption doctrine The concept that federal law takes precedent over state or local law. (12)

preemptive rights Rights that give existing shareholders the option of subscribing to new shares being issued in proportion to their current ownership interest. (616)

preexisting duty A promise lacks consideration if a person promises to perform an act or do something he or she is already under an obligation to do. (177)

preferential lien Occurs when (1) a debtor gives an unsecured creditor a secured interest in property within 90 days before the filing of a petition in bankruptcy, (2) the transfer is made for a preexisting debt, and (3) the creditor would receive more because of this lien than it would as an unsecured creditor. (476)

preferential transfer Occurs when (1) a debtor transfers property to a creditor within 90 days before the filing of a petition in bankruptcy, (2) the transfer is made for a preexisting debt, and (3) the creditor would receive more from the transfer than it would from Chapter 7 liquidation. (475)

preferential transfer to an insider A transfer of property by an insolvent debtor to an "insider" within one year before the filing of a petition in bankruptcy. (476)

preferred stock A type of equity security that is given certain preferences and rights over common stock. (596)

preferred stockholder A person who owns preferred stock. (596)

prefiling period A period of time that begins when the issuer first contemplates issuing the securities and ends when the registration statement is filed. (671)

premises liability Name given to liability of landlords and tenants to persons injured on their premises. (738)

premium The money paid to the insurance company for insurance coverage. (756)

prenuptial agreement A contract entered into by parties prior to marriage that defines their ownership rights in each other's property; must be in writing. (219)

presentment A demand for acceptance or payment of an instrument made upon the maker, acceptor, drawee, or other payor by or on behalf of the holder. (395)

presentment across the counter When a depositor physically presents the check for payment at the payor bank instead of depositing an "on them" check for collection. (429)

presentment warranties Any person who presents a draft or check for payment or acceptance makes the following three warranties to a drawee or acceptor who pays or accepts the instrument in good faith: (1) The presentor has good title to the instrument or is authorized to obtain payment or acceptance of the person who has good title, (2) the instrument has not been materially altered, and (3) the presenter has no knowledge that the

signature of the maker or drawer is unauthorized. (399)

presentment warranty Each prior transferor warrants that the check has not been altered. (424)

pretrial hearing A hearing before the trial in order to facilitate the settlement of a case. Also called a settlement conference. (62)

primary liability Absolute liability to pay a negotiable instrument, subject to certain real defenses. (393)

principal A person who authorizes an agent to sign a negotiable instrument on his or her behalf. (392) (494)

principal-agent relationship An employer hires an employee and gives that employee authority to act and enter into contracts on his or her behalf. (495)

priority The order in which conflicting claims of creditors in the same collateral are solved. (452)

private action A private plaintiff has an implied right under Section 10(b) and Rule 10b-5 to sue to rescind the securities contract or recover damages. (684)

private corporation A corporation formed to conduct privately owned business. (582)

private placement exemption An exemption from registration that permits issuers to raise capital from an unlimited number of accredited investors and no more than 35 nonaccredited investors without having to register the offering with the SEC. (675)

Private Securities Litigation Reform Act of 1995 Provides a safe harbor from liability for companies that make forward-looking statements that are accompanied by meaningful cautionary statements of risk factors. (687)

privity of contract The state of two specified parties being in a contract. (232) (333)

pro rata rule A rule that says shares must be purchased on a pro rata basis if too many shares are tendered. (651)

process of certification The accepting bank writes or stamps the word certified on the ordinary check of an account holder and sets aside funds from that account to pay the check. (416)

processing plant franchise The franchisor provides a secret formula or

process to the franchisee, and the franchisee manufactures the product and distributes it to retail dealers. (529)

product disparagement False statements about a competitor's products, services, property, or business reputation. (107)

production of documents Request by one party to another party to produce all documents relevant to the case prior to trial. (61)

products liability The liability of manufacturers, sellers, and others for the injuries caused by defective products. (325)

professional corporation A corporation formed by lawyers, doctors, or other professionals. (587)

professional malpractice The liability of a professional who breaches his or her duty of ordinary care. (88)

profit Grants a person the right to remove something from another's real property. (733)

profit corporation A corporation created to conduct a business for profit that can distribute profits to shareholders in the form of dividends. (586)

promise to pay A maker's (borrower's) unconditional and affirmative undertaking to repay a debt to a payee (lender). (362)

promissory estoppel An equitable doctrine that permits enforcement of oral contracts that should have been in writing. It is applied to avoid injustice. (180) An equitable doctrine that prevents the withdrawal of a promise by a promisor if it will adversely affect a promisee who has adjusted his or her position in justifiable reliance on the promise. (219)

promissory note A two-party negotiable instrument that is an unconditional written promise by one party to pay money to another party. (359)

promissory warranty Stipulates that the facts will continue to be true throughout the duration of the policy. (760)

promoter A person or persons who organize and start the corporation, negotiate and enter into contracts in advance of its formation, find the initial investors to finance the corporation, and so forth. (587)

promoters' contracts A collective term for such things as leases, sales contracts, contracts to purchase property, and employment contracts entered into by promoters on behalf of the proposed corporation prior to its actual incorporation. (588)

proof of claim A document required to be filed by unsecured creditors that states the amount of their claim against the debtor. (472)

proper dispatch An acceptance must be properly addressed, packaged, and posted to fall within the mailbox rule. (173)

prospectus A written disclosure document that must be submitted to the SEC along with the registration statement and given to prospective purchasers of the securities. (671)

provisional credit Occurs when a collecting bank gives credit to a check in the collection process prior to its final settlement. Provisional credits may be reversed if the check does not "clear." (428)

proximate cause or legal cause A point along a chain of events caused by a negligent party after which this party is no longer legally responsible for the consequences of his or her actions. (87)

proxy card The written document that a shareholder signs authorizing another person to vote his or her shares at the shareholders' meeting in the event of the shareholder's absence. (613) (642)

proxy contest When opposing factions of shareholders and managers solicit proxies from other shareholders, the side that receives the greatest number of votes wins the proxy contest. (644)

proxy statement A document that fully describes (1) the matter for which the proxy is being solicited, (2) who is soliciting the proxy, and (3) any other pertinent information. (643)

public corporation A corporation formed to meet a specific governmental or political purpose. (582)

public use doctrine A doctrine that says a patent may not be granted if the invention was used by the public for more than one year prior to the filing of the patent application. (112)

publicly held corporation A corporation that has many shareholders and whose securities are often traded on national stock exchanges. (586)

punitive damages Damages that are awarded to punish the defendant, to deter the defendant from similar conduct in the future, and to set an example for others. (264)

purchase money security interest An interest a creditor automatically obtains when it extends credit to a consumer to purchase consumer goods. (449)

purchasing property The most common method of acquiring title to personal property. (703)

Qualified indorsement An indorsement that includes the notation "without recourse" or similar language that disclaims liability of the indorser. (371)

Qualified indorser An indorser who signs a qualified indorsement to an instrument. (371)

Quasi in rem jurisdiction Jurisdiction allowed a plaintiff who obtains a judgment in one state to try to collect the judgment by attaching property of the defendant located in another state. (57)

Quasi or implied-in-law contract An equitable doctrine whereby a court may award monetary damages to a plaintiff for providing work or services to a defendant even though no actual contract existed. The doctrine is intended to prevent unjust enrichment and unjust detriment. (161)

Quasi-contract An equitable doctrine that permits the recovery of compensation even though no enforceable contract exists between the parties. (262)

Quorum The required number of shares that must be represented in person or by proxy to hold a shareholders' meeting. The RMBCA establishes a majority of outstanding shares as a quorum. (613) (619)

Racketeer Influenced and Corrupt Organizations Act (RICO) Federal statute that authorizes civil and criminal penalties for engaging in a pattern of racketeering activities. (95) (139) (687)

Ratification The act of a minor after the minor has reached the age of majority by which he or she accepts a contract entered into when he or she was a minor. (189) When a principal accepts an agent's unauthorized con-

tract. (508) The acceptance by a corporation of an unauthorized act of a corporate officer or agent. (621)

Rawls's social contract A moral theory that says each person is presumed to have entered into a social contract with all others in society to obey moral rules that are necessary for people to live in peace and harmony. (33)

Real defense A defense that can be raised against both holders and HDCs. (399)

Real property The land itself as well as buildings, trees, soil, minerals, timber, plants, crops, and other things permanently affixed to the land. (216) (702) (722)

Reasonable person test Objective test that applies to commercial contracts and contracts involving mechanical fitness. (241)

Receiving stolen property A person (1) knowingly receives stolen property and (2) intends to deprive the rightful owner of that property. (135)

Reclamation The right of a seller or lessor to demand the return of goods from the buyer or lessee under specified situations. (309)

Record date A date that determines whether a shareholder receives payment of a declared dividend and whether a shareholder may vote at a shareholders' meeting. (613) (620)

Recording statute A state statute that requires the mortgage or deed of trust to be recorded in the county recorder's office of the county in which the real property is located. (729)

Recovery of damages A seller or lessor may recover damages measured as the difference between the contract price (or rent) and the market price (or rent) at the time and place the goods were to be delivered, plus incidental damages, from a buyer or lessee who repudiates the contract or wrongfully rejects tendered goods. (310)

Recovery of goods from an insolvent seller or lessor A buyer or lessee who has wholly or partially paid for goods before they are received may recover the goods from a seller or lessor who becomes insolvent within 10 days after receiving the first payment; the buyer or lessee must tender the remaining purchase price or rent due under the contract. (311)

Recovery of lost profits If the recovery of damages would be inadequate to put the seller or lessor in as good a position as if the contract had been fully performed by the buyer or lessee, the seller or lessor may recover lost profits, plus an allowance for overhead and incidental damages, from the buyer or lessee. (310)

Recovery of the purchase price or rent A seller or lessor may recover the contracted-for purchase price or rent from the buyer or lessee if the buyer or lessee (1) fails to pay for accepted goods, (2) breaches the contract and the seller or lessor cannot dispose of the goods, or if (3) the goods are damaged or lost after the risk of loss passes to the buyer or lessee. (310)

Red light doctrine A doctrine that says a holder cannot qualify as an HDC if he or she has notice of an unauthorized signature or an alteration of the instrument, or any adverse claim against or defense to its payment. (390)

Redeemable preferred stock Stock that permits the corporation to buy back the preferred stock at some future date. (598)

Reformation An equitable doctrine that permits the court to rewrite a contract to express the parties' true intentions. (262)

Registered agent A person or corporation that is empowered to accept service of process on behalf of the corporation. (591)

Registration statement Document that an issuer of securities files with the SEC that contains required information about the issuer, the securities to be issued, and other relevant information. (671)

Regular meeting A meeting held by the board of directors at the time and place established in the bylaws. (618)

Regulation A A regulation that permits the issuer to sell securities pursuant to a simplified registration process. (674)

Regulatory statute A licensing statute enacted to protect the public. (195)

Rejection Express words or conduct by the offeree that rejects an offer. Rejection terminates the offer. (170)

Rejection of nonconforming goods If the goods or the seller's or lessor's tender of delivery fails to conform to the contract, the buyer or lessee may (1) reject the whole, (2) accept the whole, or (3) accept any commercial unit and reject the rest. (311)

Relief from stay May be granted in situations involving depreciating assets where the secured property is not adequately protected during the bankruptcy proceeding; asked for by a secured creditor. (473)

Remainder If the right of possession returns to a third party upon the expiration of a limited or contingent estate. (724)

Rent The amount that the tenant has agreed to pay the landlord for the leased premises. (737)

Renunciation of authority When an agent terminates an agency. (516)

Replevin An action by a buyer or lessor to recover scarce goods wrongfully withheld by a seller or lessor. (313)

Reply Filed by the original plaintiff to answer the defendant's cross-complaint. (61)

Repossession A right granted to a secured creditor to take possession of the collateral upon default by the debtor. (454)

Res ipsa loquitur Tort where the presumption of negligence arises because (1) the defendant was in exclusive control of the situation and (2) the plaintiff would not have suffered injury but for someone's negligence. The burden switches to the defendant(s) to prove they were not negligent. (91) An action to rescind the contract. (209) Rescission is available if there has been a material breach of contract, fraud, duress, undue influence, or mistake. (261)

Residuary gift Gift of the estate left after the debts, taxes, and specific and general gifts have been paid. (765)

Resolution A decision adopted by the board of directors that approves a transaction. (617)

Respondent superior A rule that says an employer is liable for the tortious conduct of its employees or agents while they are acting within the scope of its authority. (508)

Restatement of the Law of Contracts A compilation of model contract law

principles drafted by legal scholars. The Restatement is not law. (157)

Restitution Returning of goods or property received from the other party in order to rescind a contract; if the actual goods or property is not available, a cash equivalent must be made. (261)

Restricted securities Securities that were issued for investment purposes pursuant to the intrastate, private placement, or small offering exemption. (675)

Restrictive covenant A private agreement between landowners that restricts the use of their land. (741)

Restrictive indorsement An indorsement that contains some sort of instruction from the indorser. (373)

Resulting trust A trust that is created by the conduct of the parties. (771)

Retained earnings Profits retained by the corporation and not paid out as dividends. (620)

Retention of collateral If a secured creditor repossesses collateral upon a debtor's default, he or she may propose to retain the collateral in satisfaction of the debtor's obligation. (454)

Revenue-raising statute A licensing statute with the primary purpose of raising revenue for the government. (196)

Reversion A right of possession that returns to the grantor after the expiration of a limited or contingent estate. (724)

Revised Article 3 A comprehensive revising of the UCC law of negotiable instruments, which was released in 1990, that reflects modern commercial practices. (356) (415)

Revised Model Business Corporation Act (RMBCA) A revision of the MBCA in 1984 that arranged the provisions of the act more logically, revised the language to be more consistent, and made substantial changes in the provisions. (585)

Revised Uniform Limited Partnership Act (RULPA) A 1976 revision of the ULPA that provides a more modern comprehensive law for the formation, operation, and dissolution of limited partnerships. (564)

Revocation Withdrawal of an offer by the offeror terminates the offer. (170) (305) Termination of a will. (762)

Revocation of authority When a principal terminates an agency contract. (516)

Reward To collect a reward, the offeree must (1) have knowledge of the reward offer prior to completing the requested act and (2) perform the requested act. (170)

Rider A separate document that will modify an existing insurance policy. (759)

Right of first refusal agreement An agreement that requires the selling shareholder to offer his or her shares for sale to the other parties to the agreement before selling them to anyone else. (615)

Right of inspection A right that shareholders have to inspect the books and records of the corporation. (616)

Right of redemption A right granted to a defaulting debtor or other secured creditor to recover the collateral from a secured creditor before he or she contracts to dispose of it or exercises his or her right to retain the collateral. Requires the redeeming party to pay the full amount of the debt and expenses caused by the debtor's default. (456)

Right of subrogation The right that says the surety or guarantor acquires all of the creditor's rights against the debtor when a surety or guarantor pays a debt owed to a creditor by a debtor. (458)

Right of survivorship Rule that states that a deceased partner's right in specific partnership property vests with the remaining partners upon his or her death. (559)

Robbery Taking personal property from another person by use of fear or force. (134)

Rule 10b-5 A rule adopted by the SEC to clarify the reach of Section 10(b) against deceptive and fraudulent activities in the purchase and sale of securities. (680)

Rule 32.9 A rule adopted by the CFTC to clarify the reach of Section 4b against fraudulent conduct in the purchase and sale of commodity futures contracts. (689)

Sabbath law A law that prohibits or limits the carrying on of certain secular activities on Sundays. (195)

Sale The passing of title from a seller to a buyer for a price. Also called a conveyance. (727)

Sale on approval A type of sale in which there is no actual sale unless and until the buyer accepts the goods. (285)

Sale or lease of assets When one corporation sells, leases, or otherwise disposes of all, or substantially all, of its property in other than the usual and regular course of business. (648)

Sale or return A contract that says the seller delivers goods to a buyer with the understanding that the buyer may return them if they are not used or resold within a stated or reasonable period of time. (285)

Sale proceeds The resulting assets from the sale, exchange, or disposal of collateral subject to a security agreement. (447)

Satisfaction The performance of an accord. (179)

Scienter Means intentional conduct. Scienter is required for there to be a violation of Section 10(b) and Rule 10b-5. (680)

Search warrant A warrant issued by a court that authorizes the police to search a designated place for specified contraband, articles, items, or documents. The search warrant must be based on probable cause. (144)

Secondary liability Liability on a negotiable instrument that is imposed on a party only when the party primarily liable on the instrument defaults and fails to pay the instrument when due. (395)

Secondary meaning When an ordinary term has become a brand name. (118)

Section 4b A provision of the Commodity Exchange Act that prohibits fraudulent conduct in connection with any order or contract of sale of any commodity for future delivery. (689)

Section 10(b) A provision of the Securities Exchange Act of 1934 that prohibits the use of manipulative and deceptive devices in the purchase or sale of securities in contravention of the rules and regulations prescribed by the SEC. (680)

Section 11 A provision of the Securities Act of 1933 that imposes civil liability on persons who intentionally defraud investors by making misrepresentations or omissions of material facts in the registration statement or who are negligent for not discovering the fraud. (677)

Section 12 A provision of the Securities Act of 1933 that imposes civil liability on any person who violates the provisions of Section 5 of the Act. (677)

Section 14(a) Provision of the Securities Exchange Act of 1934 that gives the SEC the authority to regulate the solicitation of proxies. (643)

Section 14(e) A provision of the Williams Act that prohibits fraudulent, deceptive, and manipulative practices in connection with a tender offer. (651)

Section 16(a) A section of the Securities Exchange Act of 1934 that defines any person who is an executive officer, a director, or a 10 percent shareholder of an equity security of a reporting company as a statutory insider for Section 16 purposes. (684)

Section 16(b) A section of the Securities Exchange Act of 1934 that requires that any profits made by a statutory insider on transactions involving short-swing profits belong to the corporation. (685)

Section 24 A provision of the Securities Act of 1933 that imposes criminal liability on any person who willfully violates the 1933 Act or the rules or regulations adopted thereunder. (677)

Section 32 A provision of the Securities Exchange Act of 1934 that imposes criminal liability on any person who willfully violates the 1933 Act or the rules or regulations adopted thereunder. (683)

Secured credit Credit that requires security (collateral) to secure payment of the loan. (443)

Secured transaction A transaction that is created when a creditor makes a loan to a debtor in exchange for the debtor's pledge of personal property as security. (445)

Securities Act of 1933 A federal statute that primarily regulates the issuance of securities by corporations, partnerships, associations, and individuals. (670)

Securities and Exchange Commission (SEC) Federal administrative agency that is empowered to administer federal securities laws. The SEC can adopt rules and regulations to interpret and implement federal securities laws. (669)

Securities Enforcement Remedies and Penny Stock Reform Act of 1990 A federal statute that gives the SEC greater enforcement powers and increases and expands the remedies available for securities violations. (686)

Securities Exchange Act of 1934 A federal statute that primarily regulates the trading in securities. (679)

Security (1) An interest or instrument that is common stock, preferred stock, a bond, a debenture, or a warrant, (2) an interest or instrument that is expressly mentioned in securities acts, and (3) an investment contract. (669)

Security agreement The agreement between the debtor and the secured party that creates or provides for a security interest. (445)

Security deposit An amount of money that is often used against unpaid rent or for use in covering the cost of repairing damages caused by the tenant to the leased premises. (737)

Self-dealing If the directors or officers engage in purchasing, selling, or leasing of property with the corporation, the contract must be fair to the corporation; otherwise, it is voidable by the corporation. The contract or transaction is enforceable if it has been fully disclosed and approved. (502) (627)

Self-incrimination The Fifth Amendment states that no person shall be compelled in any criminal case to be a witness against him- or herself. (145)

Separate property In states that recognizes community property, this is property that has been acquired prior to marriage or property received by gift or inheritance during the marriage that belongs to one spouse alone. (726)

Service mark A mark that distinguishes the services of the holder from those of its competitors. (118)

Service of process A summons is served on the defendant to obtain personal jurisdiction over him or her. (56)

Settlement of the estate The process of a deceased's property being collected, debts and taxes being paid, and the remainder of the estate being distributed. (769)

Settlor or trustor Person who creates a trust. (770)

Share exchange When one corporation acquires all the shares of another corporation while both corporations retain their separate legal existence. (647)

Shareholder proposal A proposal submitted by a shareholder to other shareholders, provided he or she meets certain requirements set out in the Securities Exchange Act of 1934 and SEC rules adopted thereunder. The SEC determines if a shareholder proposal qualifies to be submitted to other shareholders for vote. (645)

Shareholder voting agreements Agreement between two or more shareholders agreeing on how they will vote their shares. (615)

Shareholders The owners of corporations whose ownership interests are evidenced by stock certificates. (582)

Shareholders' list A list that contains the names and addresses of the shareholders as of the record date and the class and number of shares owned by each shareholder. (613)

Shipment contract A contract that requires the seller to ship the goods to the buyer but not to a specifically named destination (301) via a common carrier. (282) The buyer bears the risk of loss during transportation. (283)

Short-form merger A merger between a parent corporation and a subsidiary corporation that does not require the vote of the shareholders of either corporation or the board of directors of the subsidiary corporation. (648)

Short-swing profits Profits made by statutory insiders on trades involving equity securities occurring within six months of each other. (685)

Sight draft A draft payable on sight. Also called a demand draft. (357)

Signature Any name, word, or mark used in lieu of a written signature; any symbol that is (1) handwritten, typed, printed, stamped, or made in almost any other manner and (2) executed or adopted by a party to authenticate a writing. (392)

Signature liability A person cannot be held contractually liable on a negotiable instrument unless his or her signature appears on the instrument. Also called contract liability. (392)

Signature requirement A negotiable instrument must be signed by the drawer or maker. Any symbol executed or adopted by a party with a present intent to authenticate a writing qualifies as his or her signature. (361)

Signer A person signing an instrument who acts in the capacity of (1) a maker of notes and certificates of deposit, (2) a drawer of drafts and checks, (3) a drawee who certifies or accepts checks and drafts, (4) an indorser who indorses an instrument, (5) an agent who signs on behalf of others, or (6) an accommodation party. (392)

Slander Oral defamation of character. (107)

Small business bankruptcy Section 217 of the Bankruptcy Reform Act of 1994 provides an expedited procedure for Chapter 11 bankruptcy filed by small businesses with less than $2 million of debt. (481)

Small claims court A court that hears civil cases involving small dollar amounts. (50)

Small offering exemption An exemption from registration for the sale of securities not exceeding $1 million during a 12-month period. (675)

Social host liability Rule that provides that social hosts are liable for injuries caused by guests who become intoxicated at a social function. States vary as to whether they have this rule in effect. (91)

Social responsibility Duty owed by businesses to act socially responsible in producing and selling goods and services. (36)

Sole proprietorship A form of business where the owner is actually the business; the business is not a separate legal entity. (526)

Special federal courts Federal courts that hear matters of specialized or limited jurisdiction. (52)

Special indorsement An indorsement that contains the signature of the indorser and specifies the person (indorsee) to whom the indorser intends the instrument to be payable. Creates *order paper*. (370)

Special meeting A meeting convened by the board of directors to discuss new shares, merger proposals, hostile takeover attempts, and so forth. (618)

Special shareholders' meetings Meetings of shareholders that may be called to consider and vote on important or emergency issues, such as a proposed merger, amending the articles of incorporation, and such. (612)

Specific gift Gift of a specifically named piece of property. (765)

Specific performance A remedy that orders the breaching party to perform the acts promised in the contract; usually awarded in cases where the subject matter is unique, such as in contracts involving land, heirlooms, paintings, and the like. (261) (312)

Stakeholder interest A theory of social responsibility that says a corporation must consider the effects its actions have on persons other than its stockholders. (40)

Stale check A check that has been outstanding for more than six months. (419)

Standing to sue The plaintiff must have some stake in the outcome of the lawsuit. (56)

Stare decisis Latin: "to stand by the decision." Adherence to precedent. (8)

State antitakeover statutes Statutes enacted by state legislatures that protect corporations incorporated in or doing business in the state from hostile takeovers. (655)

State supreme court The highest court in a state court system; it hears appeals from intermediate state courts and certain trial courts. (51)

Statement of assignment A document that is filed when a secured party assigns all or part of his other rights under a financing statement. (451)

Statement of opinion A remark that is the seller's or lessor's own commendation about the goods; such opinions usually do not create an express warranty. (327)

Statute Written law enacted by the legislative branch of the federal and state governments that establishes certain courses of conduct that must be adhered to by covered parties. (8)

Statute of Frauds State statute that requires certain types of contracts to be in writing. (216)

Statute of limitation Statute that establishes the time period during which a lawsuit must be brought; if the lawsuit is not brought within this period, the injured party loses the right to sue. (246) (306)

Statute of repose A statute that limits the seller's liability to a certain number of years from the date when the product was first sold. (346)

Statute of Wills A state statute that establishes the requirements for making a valid will. (761)

Stock dividend Additional shares of stock paid as a dividend. (620)

Stock option A nontransferable right to purchase shares of the corporation from the corporation at a stated price for a specified period of time. (599)

Stock warrant A stock option that is evidenced by a certificate. Warrants can be transferable or nontransferable. (599)

Stop-payment order An order by a drawer of a check to the payor bank not to pay or certify a check. (420)

Stopping delivery of goods in transit A seller or lessor may stop delivery of goods in transit if he or she learns of the buyer's or lessee's insolvency or the buyer or lessee repudiates the contract, fails to make payment when due, or gives the seller or lessor some other right to withhold the goods. (309)

Straight voting method Each shareholder votes the number of shares he or she owns on candidates for each of the positions open for election. (613)

Strict liability Liability without fault. (95)

Strict or absolute liability Standard for imposing criminal liability without a finding of mens rea (intent). (131)

Subject matter jurisdiction Jurisdiction over the subject matter of a lawsuit. (56)

Sublease When a tenant transfers only some of his or her rights under the lease. (740)

Sublessee The new tenant in a sublease situation. (740)

Sublessor The original tenant in a sublease situation. (740)

Subrogation If an insurance company pays a claim to an insured for liability or property damage caused by a third party, the insurer succeeds to the right of the insured to recover from the third party. (759)

Subscription agreement An agreement by a person to purchase shares of a corporation once it is incorporated. (588)

Substantial performance Performance by a contracting party that deviates only slightly from complete performance. (254)

Subsurface rights Rights to the earth located beneath the surface of the land. (722)

Summons A court order directing the defendant to appear in court and answer the complaint. (60)

Superseding event A defendant is not liable for injuries caused by a superseding or intervening event for which he or she is not responsible. (93)

Supervening event An alteration or modification of a product by a party in the chain of distribution that absolves all prior sellers from strict liability. (344)

Supervening illegality The enactment of a statute or regulation or court decision that makes the object of an offer illegal. This terminates the offer. (172)

Supramajority voting requirement A requirement that a greater than majority of shares constitutes quorum or the vote of the shareholders. (614)

Supremacy Clause A clause of the U.S. Constitution that establishes that the federal Constitution, treaties, federal laws, and federal regulations are the supreme law of the land. (11)

Surety arrangement An arrangement where a third party promises to be primarily liable with the borrower for the payment of the borrower's debt. (457)

Surface right The right of a landowner to use, enjoy, develop, or otherwise occupy the land as he or she sees fit, subject to any applicable government regulation. (722)

Taking possession A method of acquiring ownership of unowned personal property. (703)

Tangible property All real property and physically defined personal property such as goods, animals, and minerals. (702)

Target corporation The corporation that is proposed to be acquired in a tender offer situation. (650)

Tax sale A method of transferring property ownership that involves a lien on property for unpaid property taxes. If the lien remains unpaid after a certain amount of time, a tax sale is held to satisfy the lien. (727)

Tenancy at sufferance A tenancy created when a tenant retains possession of property after the expiration of another tenancy or a life estate without the owner's consent. (734)

Tenancy at will A lease that may be terminated at any time by either party. (734)

Tenancy by the entirety A form of co-ownership of real property that can be used only by married couples. (725)

Tenancy for years A tenancy created when the landlord and tenant agree on a specific duration for the lease. (733)

Tenancy in common A form of co-ownership in which the interest of a surviving tenant-in-common passes to the deceased tenant's estate and not to the co-tenants. (725)

Tenant The party to whom the leasehold is transferred. (733)

Tender of delivery The obligation of the seller to transfer and deliver goods to the buyer in accordance with the sales contract. (300)

Tender of performance Tender is an unconditional and absolute offer by a contracting party to perform his or her obligations under the contract. (254)

Tender offer An offer that an acquirer makes directly to a target corporation's shareholders in an effort to acquire the target corporation. (650)

Tender offeror The party that makes a tender offer. (650)

Termination Occurs automatically when the process of winding up of the corporation's affairs, liquidation of its assets, and distribution of the proceeds to the claimants. (658) is completed. It ends the legal existence of the partnership. (564)

Termination by acts of the parties An agency may be terminated by the

following acts of the parties: (1) mutual agreement, (2) lapse of time, (3) purpose achieved, and (4) occurrence of a specified event. (513)

Termination by operation of law An agency is terminated by operation of law, including: (1) death of the principal or agent, (2) insanity of the principal or agent, (3) bankruptcy of the principal, (4) impossibility of performance, (5) changed circumstances, and (6) war between the principal's and agent's countries. (515)

Termination statement A document filed by the secured party that ends a secured interest because the debt has been paid. (451)

Testamentary trust A trust created by will; the trust comes into existence when the settlor dies. (771)

Testator The person who makes a will. (761)

Time draft A draft payable at a designated future date. (357)

Time instrument An instrument payable (1) at a fixed date, (2) on or before a stated date, (3) at a fixed period after sight, or (4) at a time readily ascertainable when the promise or order is issued. (357) (365) (390)

Time note A note payable at a specific time. (359)

Tippee The person who receives material nonpublic information from a tipper. (683)

Tipper A person who discloses material nonpublic information to another person. (683)

Title Legal, tangible evidence of ownership of goods. (282)

Tort A wrong. There are three categories: (1) intentional torts, (2) unintentional torts (negligence), and (3) strict liability. (81)

Tort of misappropriation of the right to publicity An attempt by another person to appropriate a living person's name or identity for commercial purposes. (109)

Trade acceptance A sight draft that arises when credit is extended (by a seller to a buyer) with the sale of goods. The seller is both the drawer and the payee, and the buyer is the drawee. (357)

Trade secrets A product formula, pattern, design, compilation of data, cus-

tomer list, or other business secrets. Ideas that make a franchise successful but do not qualify for trademark, patent, or copyright protection. (106) (536)

Trademark A distinctive mark, symbol, name, word, motto, or device that identifies the goods of a particular business. (118)

Trademark infringement Unauthorized use of another's mark. The holder may recover damages and other remedies from the infringer. (119)

Trademarks and service marks A distinctive mark, symbol, name, word, motto, or device that identifies the goods or services of a particular franchisor. (535)

Transfer Any passage of an instrument other than its issuance and presentment for payment. (398)

Transfer warranties Any of the following five implied warranties: (1) The transferor has good title to the instrument or is authorized to obtain payment or acceptance on behalf of one who does have good title (2) All signatures are genuine or authorized (3) The instrument has not been materially altered (4) No defenses of any party are good against the transferor, and (5) The transferor has no knowledge of any insolvency proceeding against the maker, or acceptor, or the drawer of an unaccepted instrument. (398) (424)

Traveler's check A form of check sold by banks and other issuers. They are issued without a named payee. The purchaser fills in the payee's name when he or she uses the check to purchase goods or services. (417)

Treasury shares Shares of stock repurchased by the company itself. (599)

Treaty A compact made between two or more nations. (7)

Treble damages Civil damages three times actual damages may be awarded to persons whose business or property is injured by a RICO violation. (95)

Trespass to land A tort that interferes with an owner's right to exclusive possession of land. (84)

Trespass to personal property A tort that occurs whenever one person injures another person's personal property or interferes with that person's enjoyment of his or her personal property. (84)

Trial briefs Documents submitted by the parties' attorneys to the judge that contain legal support for their side of the case. (63)

Trier of fact The jury in a jury trial; the judge where there is not a jury trial. (63)

Trust A legal arrangement established when one person transfers title to property to another person to be held and used for the benefit of a third person. (770)

Trust corpus The property held in trust. (770)

Trustee Person who holds legal title to the trust corpus and manages the trust for the benefit of the beneficiary or beneficiaries. (770)

Tying arrangement A restraint of trade where a seller refuses to sell one product or service to a customer unless the customer agrees to purchase a second product or service from the seller. (539)

U.S. Constitution The fundamental law of the United States of America. It was ratified by the states in 1788. (11)

U.S. courts of appeals The federal court system's intermediate appellate courts. (52)

U.S. District Courts The federal court system's trial courts of general jurisdiction. (52)

U.S. Supreme Court The highest court in the land. It is located in Washington, D.C. (53)

UCC Statute of Frauds A rule that requires all contracts for the sale of goods costing $500 or more and lease contracts involving payments of $1,000 or more to be in writing. (219) (279)

UCC statute of limitations A rule that provides that an action for breach of any written or oral sales or lease contract must commence within four years after the cause of action accrues. The parties may agree to reduce the limitations period to one year. (314) (333)

Ultra vires act An act by a corporation that is beyond its express or implied powers. (601)

Unauthorized signature A signature made by a purported agent without authority from the purported principal. (393)

Unconditional Promises to pay and orders to pay must be unconditional in order for them to be negotiable. (363)

Unconditional promise or order to pay requirement A negotiable instrument must contain either an unconditional promise to pay (note or CD) or an unconditional order to pay (draft or check). (362)

Unconscionability A doctrine under which courts may deny enforcement of unfair or oppressive contracts. (201)

Unconscionable disclaimer A disclaimer that is so oppressive or manifestly unfair that it will not be enforced by the court. (332)

Undisclosed agency An agency that occurs when the third party is unaware of either (1) the existence of an agency or (2) the principal's identity. (507)

Undue influence Occurs where one person takes advantage of another person's mental, emotional, or physical weakness and unduly persuades that person to enter into a contract; the persuasion by the wrongdoer must overcome the free will of the innocent party or testator. (213) (762)

Unenforceable contract A contract in which the essential elements to create a valid contract are met, but there is some legal defense to the enforcement of the contract. (160)

Unfair competition Competition that violates the law. (105)

Uniform Commercial Code (UCC) Comprehensive statutory scheme that includes laws that cover aspects of commercial transactions. (156) (273)

Uniform Franchise Offering Circular (UFOC) A uniform disclosure document that requires the franchisor to make specific presale disclosures to prospective franchisees. (530)

Uniform Gift to Minors Act and Revised Uniform Gift to Minors Act Acts that establish procedures for adults to make gifts of money and securities to minors. (704)

Uniform Negotiable Instruments Law (NIL) The predecessor of the UCC developed by the National Conference of Commissioners of Uniform Laws; used from 1886 until 1952. (356)

Uniform Partnership Act (UPA) Model act that codifies partnership law. Most states have adopted the UPA in whole or part. (549)

Uniform Probate Code (UPC) A model law promulgated to establish uniform rules for the creation of wills, the administration of estates, and the resolution of conflicts in settling estates. (769)

Uniform Simultaneous Death Act An act that provides that if people who would inherit property from each other die simultaneously, each person's property is distributed as though he or she survived. (762)

Unilateral contract A contract in which the offeror's offer can be accepted only by the performance of an act by the offeree; a "promise for an act." (157)

Unilateral mistake When only one party is mistaken about a material fact regarding the subject matter of the contract. (209)

Unintentional tort or negligence A doctrine that says a person is liable for harm that is the foreseeable consequence of his or her actions. (84)

Unlawful detainer action Legal process that a landlord must complete to evict a holdover tenant. (737)

Unprotected speech Speech that is not protected by the First Amendment and may be forbidden by the government. (16)

Unqualified indorsement An indorsement whereby the indorser promises to pay the holder or any subsequent indorser the amount of the instrument if the maker, drawer, or acceptor defaults on it. (371)

Unqualified indorser An indorser who signs an *unqualified indorsement* to an instrument. (371)

Unreasonable search and seizure Any search and seizure by the government that violates the Fourth Amendment. (144)

Unsecured credit Credit that does not require any security (collateral) to protect the payment of the debt. (443)

Usurp an opportunity When an agent appropriates an opportunity for him- or herself by failing to let the principal know about it. (502)

Usurping a corporate opportunity A director or officer steals a corporate opportunity for himself or herself. (626)

Usury law A law that sets an upper limit on the interest rate that can be charged on certain types of loans. (194)

Utilitarianism A moral theory that dictates that people must choose the action or follow the rule that provides the greatest good to society. (31)

Valdez Principles Recently, a group called the Coalition for Environmentally Responsible Economies (CERES)—which takes its acronym from the Roman goddess of agriculture—released a set of 10 commitments it calls the *Valdez Principles* to guide corporations regarding their social responsibility to protect the environment. (39)

Valid contract A contract that meets all of the essential elements to establish a contract; a contract that is enforceable by at least one of the parties. (160)

Variance An exception that permits a type of building or use in an area that would not otherwise be allowed by a zoning ordinance. (743)

Venue A concept that requires lawsuits to be heard by the court with jurisdiction that is nearest the location in which the incident occurred or where the parties reside. (58)

Verdict Decision reached by the jury. (64)

Violation A crime that is neither a felony nor a misdemeanor that is usually punishable by a fine. (131)

Void contract A contract that has no legal effect; a nullity. (160)

Void title A thief acquires no title to the goods he or she steals. (287)

Voidable contract A contract in which one or both parties have the option to avoid their contractual obligations. If a contract is avoided, both parties are released from their contractual obligations. (160)

Voidable title Title that a purchaser has if the goods were obtained by (1) fraud, (2) a check that is later dishonored, or (3) impersonating another person. (287)

Voidable transfer An unusual payment or transfer of property by the debtor on the eve of bankruptcy that

would unfairly benefit the debtor or some creditors at the expense of other creditors. Such transfer may be avoided by the bankruptcy court. (475)

Voir dire Process whereby prospective jurors are asked questions by the judge and attorneys to determine if they would be biased in their decision. (63)

Voluntary dissolution A corporation that has begun business or issued shares can be dissolved upon recommendation of the board of directors and a majority vote of the shares entitled to vote. (656)

Voluntary petition A petition filed by the debtor; states that the debtor has debts. (471)

Voting trust The shareholders transfer their stock certificates to a trustee who is empowered to vote the shares. (615)

Waiting period A period of time that begins when the registration statement is filed with the SEC and continues until the registration statement is declared effective. Only certain activities are permissible during the waiting period. (671)

Warehouse company A bailee engaged in the business of storing property for compensation. Owes a duty of reasonable care to protect the bailed property. (713)

Warranties of quality Seller's or lessor's assurance to buyer or lessee that the goods meet certain standards of quality. Warranties may be expressed or implied. (326)

Warranty A buyer's or lessee's assurance that the goods meet certain standards. (325)

Warranty against infringements A seller or lessor who is a merchant who regularly deals in goods of the kind sold or leased automatically warrants that the goods are delivered free of any third-party patent, trademark, or copyright claim. (326)

Warranty against interference The lessor warrants that no person holds claim or interest in the goods that arose from an act or omission of the lessor that will interfere with the lessee's enjoyment of its leasehold interest. (326)

Warranty disclaimer Statements that negate express and implied warranties. (332)

Warranty of good title Sellers warrant that they have valid title to the goods they are selling and that the transfer of title is rightful. (325)

Warranty of no security interests Sellers of goods warrant that the goods they sell are delivered free from any third-party security interests, liens, or encumbrances that are not known to the buyer. (325)

Waste Occurs when a tenant causes substantial and permanent damage to the leased premises that decreases the value of the property and the landlord's reversionary interest in it. (737)

White-collar crimes Crimes usually involving cunning and deceit rather than physical force. (136)

Will or inheritance A way to acquire title to property that is a result of another's death. (705) (754) If a person dies with a will, his or her property is distributed to the beneficiaries as designated in the will. If a person dies without a will, his or her property is distributed to the heirs as stipulated in the state's intestate statute. (728) (761)

Williams Act An amendment to the Securities Exchange Act of 1934 made in 1968 that specifically regulates all tender offers. (650)

Winding up Process of liquidating the partnership's assets and distributing the proceeds to satisfy claims against the partnership. (564)

Winding up and liquidation The process by which a dissolved corporation's assets are collected, liquidated, and distributed to creditors, shareholders, and other claimants. (657)

Wire fraud The use of telephone or telegraph to defraud another person. (137)

Withholding delivery The act of the seller or lessor purposefully refusing to deliver goods to the buyer or lessee upon breach of the sales or lease contract by the buyer or lessee or the insolvency of the buyer or lessee. (308)

Work-related test A test to determine the liability of a principal; if an agent commits an intentional tort within a work-related time or space, the principal is liable for any injury caused by the agent's intentional tort. (511)

Writ of certiorari An official notice that the Supreme Court will review one's case. (54)

Written order A stop-payment order that is good for six months after the date it is written. (421)

Wrongful dishonor Occurs when there are sufficient funds in a drawer's account to pay a properly payable check, but the bank does not do so. (421)

Wrongful dissolution When a partner withdraws from a partnership without having the right to do so at that time. (561)

Wrongful eviction A violation of the covenant of quiet enjoyment. (735)

Wrongful termination Termination of a franchise without just cause. The termination of an agency contract in violation of the terms of the agency contract. The nonbreaching party may recover damages from the breaching party. (516) (540)

Zoning ordinance Local laws that are adopted by municipalities and local governments to regulate land use within their boundaries. Zoning ordinances are adopted and enforced to protect the health, safety, morals, and general welfare of the community. (742)